Take a closer look at key ecological concepts an[d]
Ecology in Depth and *Environmental Applicatio[ns]*

ECOLOGY IN DEPTH

ENVIRONMENTAL APPLICATIONS

ECOLOGY

A Canadian Context

Bill Freedman
Department of Biology, Dalhousie University

Jeffrey A. Hutchings
Department of Biology, Dalhousie University

Darryl T. Gwynne
University of Toronto in Mississauga

John P. Smol
Department of Biology, Queen's University

Roger Suffling
Faculty of Environment, University of Waterloo

Roy Turkington
Department of Botany, and Biodiversity Research Centre, University of British Columbia

Richard L. Walker
Department of Biological Sciences, University of Calgary

NELSON EDUCATION

NELSON EDUCATION

Ecology: A Canadian Context

by Bill Freedman, Jeffrey A. Hutchings, Darryl T. Gwynne, John P. Smol, Roger Suffling, Roy Turkington, and Richard L. Walker

Vice President, Editorial Director:
Evelyn Veitch

Editor-in-Chief, Higher Education:
Anne Williams

Publisher:
Paul Fam

Senior Marketing Manager:
Sean Chamberland

Managing Developmental Editor:
Lesley Mann

Photo Researcher and Permissions Coordinator:
Julie Pratt

Senior Content Production Manager:
Natalia Denesiuk Harris

Production Service:
S4Carlisle Publishing Services

Copy Editor:
Cat Haggert

Proofreader:
Deb DeBord

Indexer:
Nancy Kopper

Production Coordinator:
Ferial Suleman

Design Director:
Ken Phipps

Managing Designer:
Franca Amore

Interior Design:
Dianna Little

Box Icon Photos:
A Canadian Ecologist:
© iStockphoto.com/Bart Coenders;
Ecology in Depth: © iStockphoto
.com/Andrejs Zemdega;
Environmental Applications:
© iStockphoto.com/Doxa

Cover Design:
Jennifer Leung

Cover Image:
Doug Morris

Compositor:
S4Carlisle Publishing Services

Printer:
RR Donnelley

Printed and bound in the United States of America
1 2 3 4 5 6 7 13 12 11 10

For more information contact Nelson Education Ltd., 1120 Birchmount Road, Toronto, Ontario, M1K 5G4. Or you can visit our Internet site at http://www.nelson.com

Library and Archives Canada Cataloguing in Publication

Ecology : a Canadian context / Bill Freedman ... [et al.].

Includes bibliographical references and index.
ISBN: 978-0-17-650114-3

1. Ecology—Textbooks.
I. Freedman, Bill

QH541.E3192 2010 577
C2010-901630-0

ISBN-13: 978-0-17-650114-3
ISBN-10: 0-17-650114-2

To the natural world—may it ever be sustained and complete.

–BF and DG

To my dear little girl, Alexandra.

–JH

To my students, who have inspired me far more than I could ever have inspired them.

–JPS

To Petra.

–RS

To my dear wife, Evelyn, who encouraged me to participate in this project and then willingly relinquished endless hours of together-time to allow me to complete it.

–RT

To Drexel, who taught me about perseverance in the face of difficulty.

–RLW

BRIEF CONTENTS

TABLE OF CONTENTS

CHAPTER 5

Population Ecology

CHAPTER 6

Behavioural Ecology

CHAPTER 7

Physiological Ecology

CHAPTER 8

Life Histories

CHAPTER 9

Community Ecology

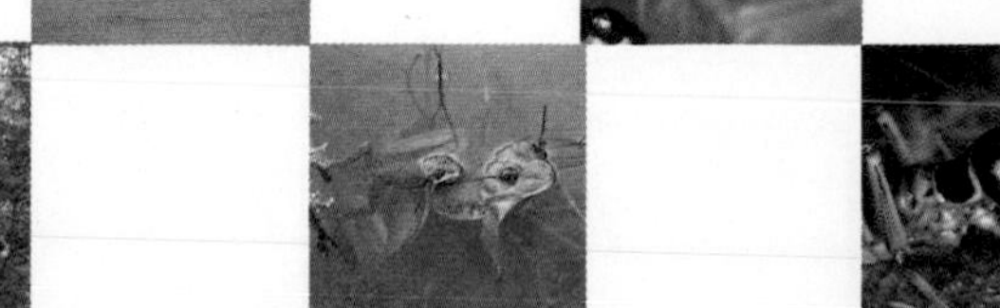

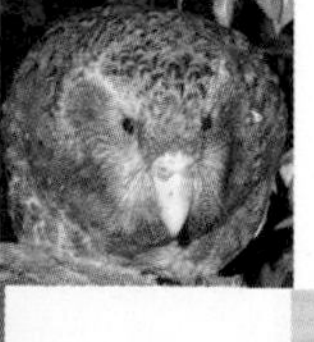

CHAPTER 10

Disturbance and Succession

CHAPTER 11

Biomes and Ecozones

CHAPTER 12

Biodiversity

CHAPTER 13

Landscape Ecology

CHAPTER 14

Conservation of the Natural World

CHAPTER 15

Resource Ecology

CHAPTER 16

Paleoecology: Lessons from the Past

CHAPTER 17

Ecology and Society

PREFACE

The Context of Ecology

Ecology is a vital way of knowing. This is because its knowledge and predictions help us to understand the functioning of the natural world, the station of humans within that domain, and how our use of its resources can be undertaken on a sustainable basis. For these reasons, the wisdom of ecology can beneficially inform key aspects of our society and economy.

Ecology has a global base of data and understanding and a universal set of principles, which are relevant anywhere on Earth. A goal of any introductory textbook in ecology is to facilitate the understanding of that core of its knowledge. However, ecology also involves the study of wild species and their higher-level aggregations, such as populations, communities, and landscapes. In that sense, ecology has a profound spatial context, which extends from relatively local situations, to much larger regional scales, and ultimately to the entire biosphere. The boundaries of countries are not ecoregional in their layout, meaning they were not designed according to natural ecological precincts. Nevertheless, national borders do specify particular expanses of land and sea. That spatial fact provides an important context for the ways that ecology is taught and learned in any country.

In this sense, Canada supports particular arrangements and dynamics of ecosystems and species, which are affected by the human economy in specific ways. The natural ecosystems of our country range from temperate Carolinian forest in extreme southern Ontario, to true desert in the southern Okanagan Valley of British Columbia, to high-arctic tundra on the islands of Nunavut and the Northwest Territories. On the Pacific coast there are humid temperate rainforests, while in the centre of Canada there are expansive montane and boreal forests and prairie grasslands, and on the Atlantic coast a mixture of temperate and boreal forests. The marine realms range from frigid and ice-covered waters north of Ellesmere Island, to boreal and temperate ecosystems in more southerly reaches of the marine estate of Canada. The ecological communities that occur in these far-flung ecoregions of Canada, and the species they sustain, comprise the essence of the biodiversity of our country.

The peoples of Canada have always esteemed the natural values of their lands. The First Nations venerated animals and plants that were exploited as food, medicine, and materials, as well as the habitats that they all shared. An attitude of respect and awe of the natural world was also held by many early European and other immigrants to Canada, although those feelings were tempered by trepidation felt because of their often precarious circumstances of living in or at the edge of wilderness. Today Canada supports an astonishing cosmopolitan and multicultural society, but we still appreciate the natural world, as witnessed by its prominence in our literature, art, video, stamps, coinage, and other cultural expressions. Many of our students are newcomers to this country, and great numbers have been raised exclusively in urban environments. It is vitally important that they mature with a solid understanding of the ecological life support system, whether of the vast tundra and forest of the North or the more familiar parks and backyards of Canada's cities.

Notwithstanding the apparent high regard with which the peoples of Canada have always viewed the natural world, many of our native species and natural ecosystems are at great risk of disappearing. This damage has been caused by extensive conversions of natural habitats into human-dominated land uses, and by additional degradation caused by alien species and diseases, excessive resource harvesting, pollution, and other anthropogenic stressors. These are exceedingly important environmental damages, and also socioeconomic ones because they pose a grave threat to the longer-term sustainability of the Canadian economy. In large part those damages are ecological in character, as are their mitigations.

A Canadian Approach

Clearly, there is an essential Canadian context to learning about ecology. This obvious deduction is the reason why we have chosen to develop this textbook—*Ecology: A Canadian Context*—which you are now beginning to read. It is our belief that this new book will be helpful to Canadian students as they seek to learn about ecology, but in the context of our country. We also believe that this textbook will assist instructors of ecology in colleges and universities in Canada, in ways that books developed in other countries cannot do as well. We sincerely hope that you will appreciate, and benefit from, our efforts to achieve these goals.

It is important to recognize that this textbook has emerged from a process that is different from the more common process of "Canadianizing" versions of textbooks that were originally developed for use by students and instructors in a different country, usually the United States. Instead of taking the relatively easy path of modifying an existing textbook by inserting some Canadian content, we have created a totally new one, from the ground up. This book was specifically designed and written for Canadian students and their instructors in Canada, by Canadians.

In essence, the approach we took was to identify the core subject areas of ecology, which are relevant in all countries, and to develop clear explanations of the basic principles. Wherever it was suitable, however, we illustrated those basics using data and case material relevant to Canada, and usually derived from studies by Canadian ecologists. This is not to say that our book does not also contain abundant international material, because it certainly does. The key point is that the essential context of our treatment of introductory ecology is a balanced integration of global and Canadian contexts.

Ecology, Evolution, and Sustainability

This textbook is about the fundamentals of ecology within a Canadian context. However, evolution and sustainability also provide essential perspectives for the study of ecology, and we have striven to integrate these themes into the book wherever they are relevant. The vitally important subjects of evolution and evolutionary relationships are examined across the curriculum, whenever they are helpful in understanding concepts and case material. We have also used this approach to explore the vital intersection of ecology and sustainability and to integrate those links whenever subjects such as resource depletion, pollution, and the conservation of biodiversity are examined. In addition, however, there are two chapters that explore these imperative themes more comprehensively—one about resource ecology, and the other about the conservation of the natural world.

Organization

The field of ecology is wide and interdisciplinary, so much so that it cannot all be covered in an introductory-level class or in a textbook of a sensible length. When this book was being planned, we consulted with colleagues and anonymous reviewers, who advised us that they wanted to see a textbook of modest length (and price) that covered the key themes of ecology, but not necessarily the entirety of its subject matter. To achieve that goal, we divided the field into 17 chapters, which are interconnected where relevant, but are still organized in ways that make them suitable for teaching and learning as independent units.

We have organized *Ecology: A Canadian Context* into the following 17 chapters:

Chapter 1: Introduction to Ecology

This chapter establishes the foundations of ecology, and examines its methodology within the context of the principles and practices of scientific investigation. A further section examines evolution as an overarching theme of ecology, and another explains how ecological considerations are vital to framing the sustainability of the human economy.

Chapter 2: Environmental Factors

Here we examine the environmental factors that influence species and ecosystems. While noting that ecosystems are always subjected to pervasive change, we examine considerations that might result in change being viewed as ecological or economic damage.

Chapter 3: Ecological Energetics

This chapter explains the forms in which energy may exist and the laws of thermodynamics that govern their transformations. The energy budget of Earth is described, including the vital greenhouse effect that helps to maintain the planet within a range of temperature appropriate for life and ecosystems. We then examine ecological energetics, beginning with the fixation of solar energy by primary producers, moving through the passage of fixed energy along food webs, and ending with decomposition as a process that oxidizes dead organic matter to return degraded energy and simple inorganic molecules back to the environment.

Chapter 4: Nutrients and Their Cycling

Nutrients are explained as substances needed for the healthy physiology and growth of organisms. The cycling of the following nutrients is examined: carbon, nitrogen, phosphorus, and sulphur, and the bases calcium, magnesium, potassium, and sodium. We also investigate soil as an ecosystem, including influences on the formation of dominant kinds of soils.

Chapter 5: Population Ecology

This chapter describes the ways that populations may vary over time, including exponential and logistical changes and their explanatory models. The influences of age structure, competition, and trophic interactions on population change are explored, including their evolutionary contexts.

Chapter 6: Behavioural Ecology

In this chapter we examine interactions occurring among behaviour, ecological relationships, and adaptive evolutionary change. The principal topic areas are foraging, defence against predators, sexual selection, and the evolution of social behaviour.

Chapter 7: Physiological Ecology

This field is examined through the adaptive physiological traits of animals in relation to their environmental conditions. Particular attention is paid to thermo-biology, water and ionic balances, gas exchange and transport, and acid–base balances.

Chapter 8: Life Histories

This chapter distills the diverse life histories of species into sets of responses that are results of the dynamic interplay of biological variation and natural selection. The principal subject areas examined are the costs of reproduction, life histories and fitness, trade-offs between the numbers of offspring and their sizes, alternative life histories, and influences of anthropogenic harvesting.

Chapter 9: Community Ecology

Ecological communities are examined as groups of species that live together and interact, directly or indirectly, through competition for scarce resources, herbivory, predation, disease, and facilitation. Environmental and biological influences on the structure and dynamics of communities are examined, including adaptive responses.

Chapter 10: Disturbance and Succession

The causes and consequences of disturbances are explained, including those caused by natural and anthropogenic influences. This is followed by consideration of the mechanisms and patterns of successional recovery, including case studies of both primary and secondary succession.

Chapter 11: Biomes and Ecozones

The major biomes of the world are described, in both the terrestrial and marine realms, as are key habitats such as types of wetlands and anthropogenic ecosystems. The terrestrial and marine ecozones of both Canada and North America are examined.

Chapter 12: Biodiversity

The hierarchical levels of biodiversity are explained, beginning with genetic variation, then species richness, and extending to the community-scale patches on landscapes and seascapes. The ways of measuring biodiversity at these various scales are also examined. The reasons why biodiversity is important are explained, including its intrinsic value and the vital goods and services that are provided to humans and their economy.

Chapter 13: Landscape Ecology

This chapter describes spatial approaches to the structure and dynamics of landscapes, including both natural and anthropogenic effects. The major ways of measuring the attributes of landscapes are explored, including the use of geographical information systems.

Chapter 14: Conservation of the Natural World

The modern extinction crisis is examined and is put into the context of previous mass extinctions caused by natural forces. The basic tenets of conservation biology are explained, including the design and stewardship of protected areas. The biodiversity-at-risk of Canada is described, as are the conservation roles and responsibilities of governments and other organizations. The chapter ends with success stories involving cases of endangered species that have been rescued from the brink of extinction.

Chapter 15: Resource Ecology

Ecological economics are explained as a foundation for understanding the concept of economic sustainability and its fundamental reliance on renewable resources rather than non-renewable ones. Systems of harvesting and managing bio-resources are explained, and international and Canadian case material is presented to illustrate the phenomenon of over-harvesting. Improved management systems that would allow sustainable use are described, including integrated ones that can accommodate both the economic values of resources as well as ecological considerations such as biodiversity and environmental services.

Chapter 16: Paleoecology: Lessons from the Past

Longer-term ecological changes are described, as are the paleoecological methods that have allowed their causes and consequences to be examined. The importance of paleoecological studies to understanding environmental issues is also examined.

Chapter 17: Ecology and Society

This final chapter examines the concept of ecological integrity and the processes of ecological monitoring and research and environmental impact assessment. Ecological sustainability is also explained, as is the importance of the knowledge and wisdom of ecology, and the work of ecologists in guiding progress to that goal.

Features of the Text

In-Chapter Features and Learning Aids

The defining attributes of this textbook are the ways that it presents the fundamentals of ecology within a Canadian context, while integrating the concepts of evolution and sustainability wherever they are relevant. The book contains a number of features that help to further these goals:

- **Boxed Features.** All chapters have stand-alone boxed elements that present detailed examinations of selected important concepts or helpful case material. The three types of boxes are (1) **Ecology in Depth**, which is intended to provide a detailed investigation of important concepts; (2) **Environmental Applications**, an in-depth look at real-world applications of content discussed in the chapter; and (3) **A Canadian Ecologist**, which highlights prominent studies done by ecologists who have worked in Canada.

- **Tables, Figures, and Photos.** We have gone to great lengths to present easily digestible and abundant information in tables and figures, as well as plentiful and attractive photos that illustrate species, habitats, and concepts that are well communicated in a visual medium.
- **Key Terms.** Whenever we mention a word or phrase that is a core part of the lexicon of ecology, it is highlighted and defined. All of these terms are reproduced at the end of the chapter and aggregated into a comprehensive **glossary** at the end of the book.

End-of-Chapter Learning and Review

Each chapter ends with a number of features that help to cultivate learning of the subject matter. These are:

- **Vocabulary of Ecology.** This is a list of all key terms that were presented in the chapter, supplemented by page references to the chapter. Full definitions are included in the end-of-book glossary.
- **Questions for Review and Discussion.** A number of questions are presented for students to answer. These are intended to assist in review of the subject matter, while aiding comprehension and facilitating in-class discussion of certain topics. The *Instructor's Manual* for the book provides suggested answers for all of these questions.
- **Helpful Websites.** At the end of most chapters is a list of open-access websites that provide additional information and analysis relevant to the subject matter. These websites are selected from those of governments, non-governmental organizations, professional associations, and academia.

End-of-Book Features

Readers will find the following resources at the end of the book:

- **References and Additional Readings.** All references cited in the chapter are listed in a comprehensive bibliography at the back of the book. The References section also includes important articles and books that are essential to an understanding of the topic or recommended for further reading.
- **Glossary.** Definitions for all chapter key terms are provided in this essential resource. Page references are included to help students review these key terms in the context of the original discussion. In addition to key terms, the Glossary includes definitions for other important terms or concepts that students may find challenging or unfamiliar.
- **Indexes.** Three types of index are included for readers' ease of reference. They consist of Name, Species, and Subject indexes.

Nelson Education Teaching Advantage

The **Nelson Education Teaching Advantage (NETA)** program is designed to deliver research-based resources that promote student engagement and higher-order thinking and enable the success of Canadian students and educators.

The primary NETA components are the *Guide to Classroom Engagement* and our *Testing Advantage* resources.

The Guide to Classroom Engagement

The foundational principles underlying the NETA *Guide to Classroom Engagement for Ecology* are student-centred learning, deep learning, active learning, and creating positive classroom environments. Each NETA *Guide* includes a section outlining the research underlying these principles, which will help you create engaging classrooms. The structure of the *Guide* was created by Dr. Roger Fisher, and validated by an interdisciplinary board of scholars of teaching and learning.

The customized lesson plan component of the *Guide to Classroom Engagement for Ecology* was written by the book's lead author, Professor Bill Freedman of Dalhousie University, in consultation with the author team. In addition, the *Ecology* authors have created a traditional Instructor's Manual (see "Ancillaries for Instructors" below). Select the "NETA Engagement" button on the *Ecology* Instructor's Resource CD for the NETA *Guide* with customized lesson plans and the Instructor's Manual.

Testing Advantage Resources

Nelson Education Ltd. understands that the highest quality multiple-choice test bank provides the means to measure ***higher-level thinking*** skills as well as recall. In response to instructor concerns, and recognizing the importance of multiple-choice testing in today's classroom, we have created the assessment component of the Nelson Education Teaching Advantage (NETA) program to ensure the value of our test banks.

The assessment component of our NETA program was created in partnership with David DiBattista, a 3M National Teaching Fellow, professor of psychology at Brock University, and researcher in the area of multiple-choice testing. All test bank authors have received training by Prof. DiBattista in constructing effective multiple choice questions and creating questions that assess higher-level thinking. Prof DiBattista also reviewed selected chapters of the *Ecology* Test Bank to ensure these best practices were followed.

All NETA test banks are accompanied by David DiBattista's guide for instructors, *Multiple Choice Tests: Getting Beyond Remembering*. This guide has been designed to assist you in using Nelson test banks to achieve the desired outcomes in your course. Select the "NETA Assessment" button on the Instructor's Resource CD for a digital copy of this valuable resource, as well as the *Ecology* Test Bank and computerized test bank (see "Ancillaries for Instructors" below for more information).

Ancillaries for Instructors

Key instructor ancillaries are provided on the *Instructor's Resource CD* (ISBN 978-0-17-647223-8), giving instructors the ultimate tool for customizing lectures and presentations. The IRCD includes

- *NETA Engagement*: *Instructor's Manual* and *Guide to Classroom Engagement for Ecology*. The Instructor's Manual for *Ecology: A Canadian Context* includes group activities, answers to all the end-of-chapter Questions for Review and Discussion, and more. It was created by the authors of *Ecology:* Bill Freedman, Jeff Hutchings, Darryl Gwynne, John Smol, Roger Suffling, Roy Turkington, and Richard Walker. A copy of the *Guide to Classroom Engagement for Ecology*, with lesson plans customized for *Ecology* by its authors, accompanies the Instructor's Manual.
- *NETA Assessment: Test Bank, ExamView® Computerized Test Bank,* and *Multiple Choice Tests: Getting Beyond Remembering*. Test bank files are provided in rich text format for easy editing and printing with all common word-processing formats. All test bank questions are also provided in the ExamView® computerized version. This easy-to-use software is compatible with Microsoft® Windows and Mac. Create tests by selecting questions from the question bank, modifying these questions as desired, and adding new questions you write yourself. You can administer quizzes online and export tests to WebCT, Blackboard, and other formats. The test bank was created for *Ecology: A Canadian Context* by Monika Havelka of the University of Toronto. A copy of David DiBattista's *Multiple Choice Tests: Getting Beyond Remembering* accompanies the testing materials for *Ecology*.
- *Microsoft® PowerPoint®*. Key concepts from *Ecology: A Canadian Context* are presented in PowerPoint® format, with generous use of figures, photographs, and short tables from the text. The PowerPoint® presentation for *Ecology: A Canadian Context* was created by Peter Ryser of Laurentian University.
- *Image Library*. Customize your own Microsoft® PowerPoint® presentations using figures, tables, illustrations, and photographs from the book. These items are provided in jpeg format for your use. (Note: a small number of items may not be available due to copyright restrictions.)

Another valuable resource for instructors is JoinIn™ on TurningPoint® classroom response software, customized for *Ecology: A Canadian Context* by Peter Ryser of Laurentian University. Now you can author, deliver, show, access, and grade, all in PowerPoint® ... with no toggling back and forth between screens! JoinIn™ on Turning Point® is the only classroom response software tool that gives you true PowerPoint® integration. With JoinIn™ you are no longer tied to your computer. You can walk about your classroom as you lecture, showing slides and collecting and displaying responses with ease. There is simply no easier or more effective way to turn your lecture hall into a personal, fully interactive experience for your students. If you can use PowerPoint®, you can use JoinIn™ on TurningPoint®! (Contact your Nelson Education publishing representative for details.)

Ancillaries for Students

- **Companion Website**. Visit **www.ecology.nelson.com** for additional resources, including self-testing review quizzes. Other resources planned for the website include material related to careers in ecology, ranging from academia to jobs in governmental agencies, environmental NGOs, and the private sector, as well as weblinks to other helpful ecology resources.

- **CL E-book.** Take your ecology experience to the next level with our Cengage Learning E-book! The CL E-book gives students access to an integrated, interactive learning environment with advanced learning tools and a user interface that lets students control their learning experience. An innovative offering will be online growth models that allow students to interact with content to show computer-simulated cause-and-effect models of ecological systems using varying parameters.

Acknowledgements

A number of our colleagues and friends generously provided their time and effort to review drafts of the material in various chapters. These ecologists and other scientists pointed out informative case material of which we were unaware, corrected inadvertent errors in our work, improved our writing and presentation, or helped us in other important ways. We are exceedingly grateful to the following people for their kind help with this book:

Maydianne Andrade, University of Toronto, ON
James Basinger, University of Saskatchewan, Saskatoon, SK
Stephen Beauchamp, Environment Canada, Dartmouth, NS
Paul Bentzen, Dalhousie University, Halifax, NS
Paul Catling, Biosystematics Research Institute, Agriculture Canada, Ottawa, ON
Brian Cumming, Queen's University, Kingston, ON
Terry Curran of Dryden, ON
Les Cwynar, University of New Brunswick, Fredericton, NB
Eva Dodsworth, University of Waterloo, ON
Angelo Gioviazzo of Guelph, ON
Richard Harington, Canadian Museum of Nature, Ottawa, ON
Greg Henry, University of British Columbia, Vancouver, BC
Tom Hutchinson, Trent University, Peterborough, ON
Dan Krause, Nature Conservancy of Canada, Guelph, ON
John Lewis, University of Waterloo, ON
Ian McLaren, Dalhousie University, Halifax, NS
Matt Meston, University of Waterloo, ON
Curt Meine, Aldo Leopold Foundation, Baraboo, WI
Neal Michelutti, Queen's University, Kingston, ON
Ron O'Dor, Dalhousie University, Halifax, NS
Michael Paterson, Department of Fisheries and Oceans, Winnipeg, MB
David Patriquin, Dalhousie University, Halifax, NS
Michael Pisaric, Carleton University, Ottawa, ON
Helen Rodd, University of Toronto, ON
Alexandra Rouillard, Queen's University, Kingston, ON
Kathleen Rühland, Queen's University, Kingston, ON
Daniel Ruzzante, Dalhousie University, Halifax, NS
James Savelle, McGill University, Montreal, QC
Janet Silbernagel, University of Wisconsin, Madison
Graham Stinson, Natural Resources Canada, Victoria, BC
Josef Svoboda, Erindale Campus, University of Toronto, Mississauga, ON
John Theberge, University of Waterloo, and Wolf Ecosystem Research, Oliver, BC
Mary Theberge, Wolf Ecosystem Research, Oliver, BC
Stephen Woodley, Parks Canada, Hull, PQ
Boris Worm, Dalhousie University, Halifax, NS
Steve Xu, University of Waterloo, ON

In addition, the publisher commissioned a number of reviews from instructors of ecology classes at several universities and colleges in Canada. These people also provided invaluable commentary on the structure of the textbook, on the book proposal plan, and on draft chapters. These people were

Dawn Bazely, York University, ON
Christine Beauchamp, Dalhousie University, NS
Hugh Broders, Saint Mary's University, NS
Nancy Flood, Thompson Rivers University, BC
Gail Fraser, York University, ON
Leland J. Jackson, University of Calgary, AB
Dennis Lehmkuhl, University of Saskatchewan, SK
John Markham, University of Manitoba, MB
Trevor Pitcher, University of Windsor, ON
William Tonn, University of Alberta, AB
Nigel Waltho, Carleton University, ON
Scott Wilson, University of Regina, SK

Roger Suffling would like to thank class members of ENVS469, 2008 and 2009, University of Waterloo, Ontario.

Roy Turkington would like to thank "those BIOL302 undergraduate students who provided some brutally honest feedback on my writing—Ashley Wingerak, Bartosz Sienkiewicz, Ching Maggie Lam, Deirdre O'Brien, Gladys Oka, Jacques Flores, Keshika Nanda, Lauren MacLeod, Min Je Woo, and Theraesa Coyle. And to Bill Neill, Tony Sinclair, Gary Bradfield and Wayne Goodey, my co-teachers in ecology over the past 33 years—you will never know how much I learned from you, and your imprint is probably seen throughout Chapter 9."

Thanks are also due to the many people who worked on the production of *Ecology: A Canadian Context*, including Cat Haggert, copyeditor; Carolyn Jongeward for her substantive edit of several early chapters; Julie Pratt, permissions, photograph, and art researcher; Dianna Little, designer; Vanavan Jayaraman, Project Manager at S4Carlisle Publishing Services; and staff at Nelson Education, including Paul Fam, Publisher; Lesley Mann, Managing Developmental Editor; Natalia Denesiuk Harris, Senior Content Production Manager; Ferial Suleman, Production Coordinator; Franca Amore, Managing Designer; and Sean Chamberland, Senior Marketing Manager.

Finally, a word about the chapter-opening photographs. Bill Caulfeild-Browne has been taking pictures for 50 years. From his base in Tobermory, Ontario, Bill travels across Canada and the world to explore and capture the beauty of nature. His photographs have been featured in one-man exhibitions in Mississauga and Toronto and in books, calendars, websites, fine art prints, and the *Toronto Star*. We are pleased to present Bill's work at the start of each chapter of *Ecology: A Canadian* Context and invite you to view his galleries at http://www.billcaulfeild-browne.com/index.html.

We would be most grateful if any readers of this book could send us any suggestions they might have for improvements.

We sincerely hope that this book will be helpful as you learn about ecology.

Bill Freedman, Dalhousie University

Jeffrey A. Hutchings, Dalhousie University

Darryl T. Gwynne, University of Toronto

John P. Smol, Queen's University

Roger Suffling, University of Waterloo

Roy Turkington, University of British Columbia

Richard L. Walker, University of Calgary

April 2010

YOUR TOUR OF *ECOLOGY*

Each chapter of *Ecology: A Canadian Context* engages students from beginning to end.

CHAPTER 5

Population Ecology

Each chapter begins with a list of ***Learning Objectives*** for the chapter. Use these objectives to guide your study and test your understanding of important topics. The ***Chapter Outline*** shows the main topics and boxes—a useful tool for reviewing the chapter.

A Canadian Ecologist profiles Canadian ecologists, from historical role-models like John Macoun to the work of R. L. Jefferies, David Schindler, Charles Krebs, and others. Learn about the exciting research being done in Canada!

A CANADIAN ECOLOGIST 1.1

Chris Pielou: Mathematical Ecology and More

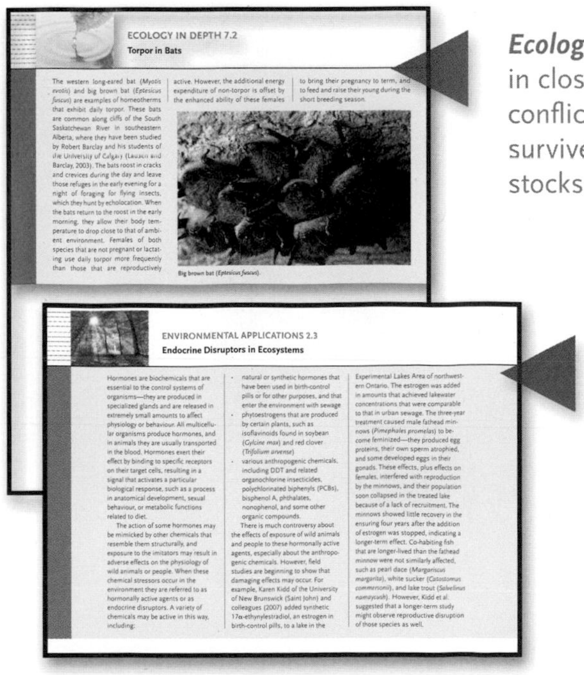
ECOLOGY IN DEPTH 7.2

Torpor in Bats

ENVIRONMENTAL APPLICATIONS 2.3

Endocrine Disruptors in Ecosystems

Ecology in Depth boxes examine important concepts in close detail. Explore topics like genes and individuals in conflict, how mountain pine beetles produce antifreeze to survive winters in central B.C., and conservation of carbon stocks of natural ecosystems.

What can forestry learn from wildfires? How does eutrophication—pollution by nutrients—happen? You'll find the answers to these and other questions in the ***Environmental Applications*** boxes throughout the text.

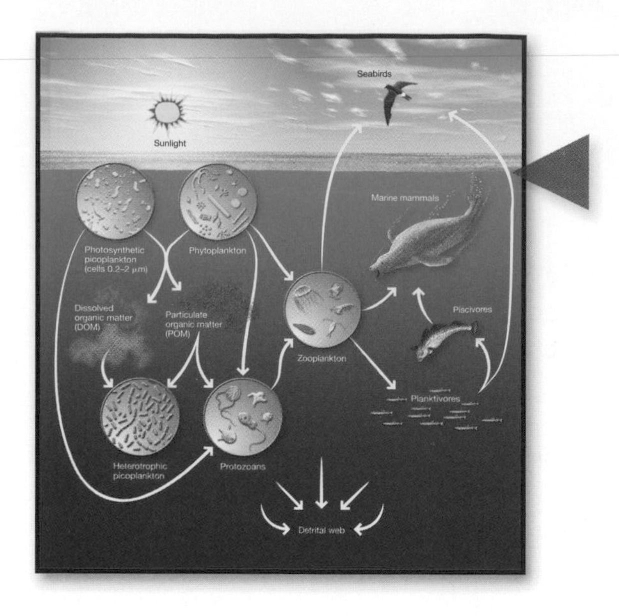

Many concepts in ecology tend to be abstract and theoretical. ***Stunning, full-colour visuals*** throughout the book will consolidate key points and indicate their relationships so that you better understand these concepts.

Vocabulary of Ecology is an end-of-chapter feature that lists the key terms of each chapter with page references so you can locate the original context. Use this list to review important terms. Definitions are provided in the ***Glossary*** at the end of the book.

Questions for Review and Discussion help you check your understanding of the key issues and think beyond basic concepts.

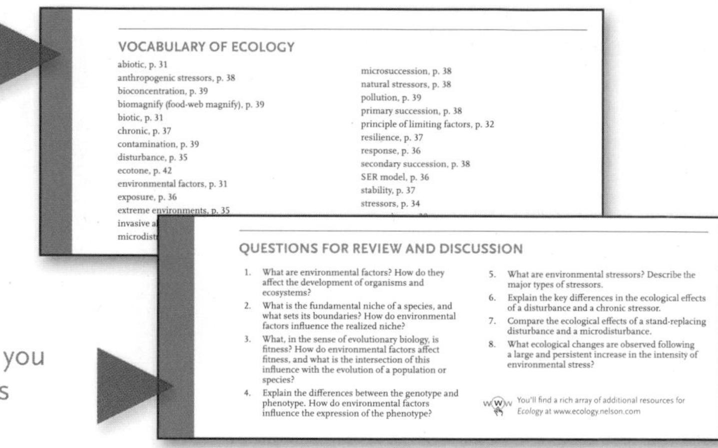

VOCABULARY OF ECOLOGY

abiotic, p. 31
anthropogenic stressors, p. 38
bioconcentration, p. 39
biomagnify (food-web magnify), p. 39
biotic, p. 31
chronic, p. 37
contamination, p. 39
disturbance, p. 35
ecotone, p. 42
environmental factors, p. 31
exposure, p. 36
extreme environments, p. 35
invasive a
microdist
microsuccession, p. 38
natural stressors, p. 38
pollution, p. 39
primary succession, p. 38
principle of limiting factors, p. 32
resilience, p. 37
response, p. 36
secondary succession, p. 38
SER model, p. 36
stability, p. 37
stressors, p. 34

QUESTIONS FOR REVIEW AND DISCUSSION

1. What are environmental factors? How do they affect the development of organisms and ecosystems?
2. What is the fundamental niche of a species, and what sets its boundaries? How do environmental factors influence the realized niche?
3. What, in the sense of evolutionary biology, is fitness? How do environmental factors affect fitness, and what is the intersection of this influence with the evolution of a population or species?
4. Explain the differences between the genotype and phenotype. How do environmental factors influence the expression of the phenotype?
5. What are environmental stressors? Describe the major types of stressors.
6. Explain the key differences in the ecological effects of a disturbance and a chronic stressor.
7. Compare the ecological effects of a stand-replacing disturbance and a microdisturbance.
8. What ecological changes are observed following a large and persistent increase in the intensity of environmental stress?

You'll find a rich array of additional resources for *Ecology* at www.ecology.nelson.com

HELPFUL WEBSITES

BRITISH ECOLOGICAL SOCIETY (BES)
http://www.britishecologicalsociety.org/
The BES is the professional organization for ecologists in the United Kingdom. Excellent educational resources are posted on its website.

CANADIAN SOCIETY FOR ECOLOGY AND EVOLUTION (CSEE)
http://www.ecoevo.ca/
The CSEE is the Canadian professional organization for ecologists. It exists to promote the study of ecology and evolution, to raise awareness with the public and decision makers, and to foster interactions among ecologists.

ECOLOGICAL SOCIETY OF AMERICA (ESA)
http://esa.org/
The ESA is a leading organization for ecologists in North America. It is a professional organization, and also posts excellent educational resources on its website. The ESA has a Canada Chapter (http://www.esa.org/canada/) devoted to the ecology of Canadian ecoregions.

ECOLOGY GLOBAL NETWORK
http://www.ecology.com/index.php
This website has information about ecology and environmental issues.

NATIONAL CENTER FOR SCIENCE EDUCATION
http://www.natcenscied.org/article.asp
The National Center for Science Education is an interest group whose mandate involves promoting the teaching of science and evolution.

PROJECT 2061, AMERICAN ASSOCIATION FOR THE ADVANCEMENT OF SCIENCE (AAAS)
http://www.project2061.org/default_flash.htm
The American Association for the Advancement of Science provides an overview of issues related to science literacy. Project 2061 is a long-term AAAS initiative to advance literacy in science, mathematics, and technology.

You'll find a rich array of additional resources for *Ecology* at www.ecology.nelson.com.

There is a wealth of interesting materials to be found online. Use ***Helpful Websites*** to explore key topics in ecology in more depth.

Three indexes have been developed to aid your navigation of the text: a Name Index, a Species Index, and a Subject Index.

Instructor's Resources

The *Instructor's Resource* CD saves time on lecture preparation—robust supplements are all a click away.

The *Instructor's Resource CD* for ***Ecology: A Canadian Context*** integrates all relevant resources: PowerPoint® slides, NETA Test Bank in ExamView® (electronic) and Word-compatible formats, NETA Instructor's Guide to Classroom Engagement, Image Library, and more.

Each chapter's ***Microsoft® PowerPoint® lecture slides*** offer the following features:

- **Selected figures, photographs**, and **brief tables** from the book
- **Slides** with book-specific questions
- **Bulleted points** listing key concepts
- **Ability** for you to edit the slides to fit your needs, including the addition of figures and text art from the **Image Library**

The ***Image Library*** (above right) includes figures, photographs, and short tables from the book in JPEG format, ready for you to add to PowerPoint® slides, overheads, tests, or course web-sites. (Some images may not be available due to copyright restrictions.)

The *Nelson Education Teaching Advantage (NETA)* program has been developed to provide you with the best ancillaries—test banks that challenge students and instructional activities that will engage them in the classroom. Manuals explaining how to use NETA ancillaries to their fullest are provided on the *Instructor's Resource* CD.

- The **NETA Test Bank** delivers quality multiple-choice questions that go beyond testing for recall and actually measure higher-level thinking. The ExamView® Test Generator format lets you select and modify questions and add new items. You can administer quizzes online and export tests to WebCT, Blackboard, and other formats such as Angel. Test bank files are also provided in rich text format for easy editing and printing with all common word-processing formats. A guide to creating effective tests—*Multiple Choice Tests: Getting Beyond Remembering*—accompanies the test materials.
- The **NETA *Instructor's Manual*** provides lesson plans for each chapter that set out opportunities to engage students through questions, activities, and group work. Answers to the chapter-ending *Questions for Review and Discussion* are provided. Principles for ensuring classroom engagement, plus customized lesson plans, are included in the accompanying *Guide to Classroom Engagement.*

Our companion website, CL E-book™, and JoinIn™ on TurningPoint® make learning interactive.

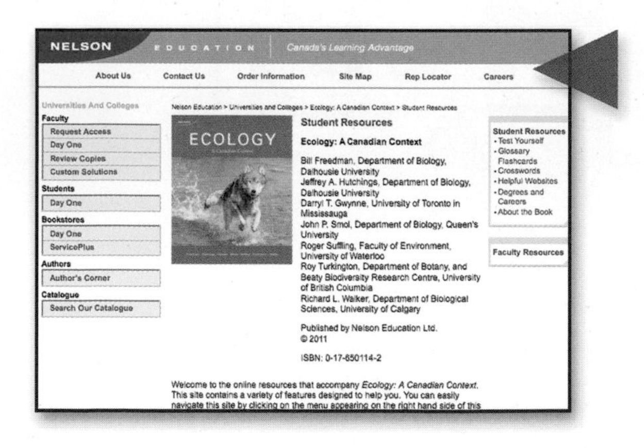

Our ***Companion Website*** includes resources for students and instructors. Students will find self-assessment quizzes to help them review chapter contents, plus information about careers in ecology—ranging from academia to jobs in governmental agencies, environmental NGOs, and the private sector. Instructors will be able to access downloadable ancillaries, including the NETA *Instructor's Manual,* NETA Test Bank, ExamView® Computerized Test Bank, and PowerPoint® slides. Go to **www.ecology.nelson.com** for these and other resources!

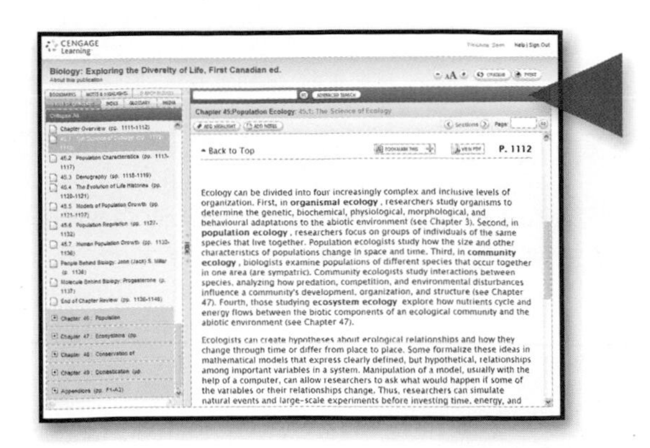

Take your ecology experience to the next level with our ***Cengage Learning E-book***! The CL E-book gives students access to an integrated, interactive learning environment with advanced learning tools and a user interface that lets students control their learning experience. (See sample CL E-book format at left.)

A tool for instant in-class quizzes and polls

Here's an easy way to increase students' participation in class! Nelson Education Ltd. is pleased to offer you **JoinIn™ on TurningPoint®** content for classroom response systems tailored to *Ecology: A Canadian Context*. Our agreement to offer TurningPoint® software lets you pose book-specific questions and display students' answers seamlessly within the Microsoft® PowerPoint® slides of your own lecture, in conjunction with the "clicker" hardware of your choice. It's a great tool for motivating students to come to class and pay attention. We provide the software and questions for each chapter of the text on ready-to-use Microsoft® PowerPoint® slides.

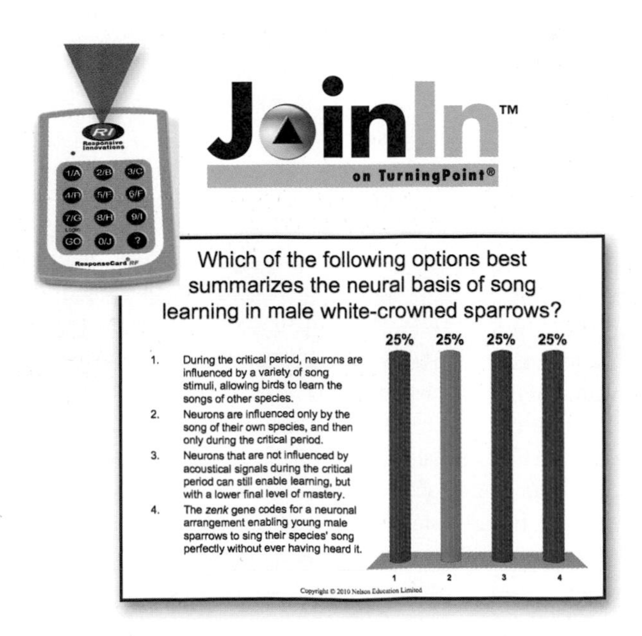

ABOUT THE AUTHORS

Bill Freedman

Bill Freedman is an ecologist and environmental scientist. He received his M.Sc. and Ph.D. degrees from the University of Toronto, where he studied in the Department of Botany. He has taught in the Department of Biology at Dalhousie University, Halifax, Nova Scotia, since 1979.

The conceptual framework of Bill's research is the influence of environmental stressors on biodiversity and other structural and functional attributes of ecosystems. Understanding the influence of stressor regimes is of theoretical interest, and it also helps guide the management of ecological damage caused by disturbance and pollution. Bill's research has examined the environmental effects of a wide range of industrial activities (particularly forestry practices), as well as the environmental effects of acidification, eutrophication, metals, pesticides, and sulphur dioxide. Other interests include carbon storage in ecosystems, urban ecology, arctic ecology, the biodiversity of Sable Island, the design of environmental monitoring programs, and ecologically sustainable systems of resource harvesting. More than 100 refereed publications in journals have resulted from this work, plus several hundred book and encyclopedia chapters, research reports, and other documents. Bill is engaged in developing curriculum materials in support of higher education, and as part of that work he has written several textbooks, including *Environmental Ecology* (2nd edition, 1995), and *Environmental Science: A Canadian Perspective* (5th edition, 2009). Bill has served on the board of directors of the Nature Conservancy of Canada since 1992 and was the chair of that board from 2007 to 2009. He has also participated in several environmental impact assessments of proposed and operating industrial facilities, and has served on advisory panels to government. In 2006, Bill received a Canadian Environment Award, Gold Medal Level, in the category of Community Awards for Conservation, from the Canadian Geographic Society. In 2007, he received a Career Achievement Award from the Canadian Council of University Biology Chairs. Bill is an enthusiastic naturalist and traveller and loves to spend time in wild places.

Jeffrey A. Hutchings

Jeffrey A. Hutchings is professor of Biology and Canada Research Chair in Marine Conservation and Biodiversity at Dalhousie University. He received his B.Sc. from the University of Toronto and his M.Sc. and Ph.D. from Memorial University of Newfoundland; and he undertook postdoctoral research at the University of Edinburgh and Fisheries and Oceans Canada in St. John's, Newfoundland. In addition to Jeff's teaching and research responsibilities, he is chair (2006–2010; member from 2001–2012) of the Committee on the Status of Endangered Wildlife in Canada (COSEWIC), the national independent body responsible for advising the federal Minister of the Environment on the status of species at risk in Canada. He is chair of the Royal Society of Canada Expert Panel on Ocean Health and Marine Biodiversity (2009–2011), and vice president (2010–2011) and incoming president (2012–2013) of the Canadian Society for Ecology and Evolution. Additional professional responsibilities have included editor of the *Canadian Journal of Fisheries and Aquatic Sciences* (2002–2007); member (2003–2005) and co-chair (2005–2006) of the Evolution and Ecology Grant Selection Committee of NSERC (Natural Sciences and Engineering Research Council:); chair (2008–2009) of NSERC's Vanier Canada Graduate Scholarships Selection Committee; editorial board member for *Proceedings of the Royal Society B* (2009–2011), *Evolutionary Applications* (2007–present), and *Environmental Reviews* (2008–present); and member of the Royal Society of Canada's Expert Panel on the Future of Food Biotechnology (2000–2001) and Committee on Expert Panels (2008–present).

Born in Orillia, Ontario, Jeff made his initial environmental forays into the landscapes of nearby Shield lakes and outports of Newfoundland. His maturing interests in ecology ultimately stemmed from field experiences ranging from mountainous terrain near Kispiox (British Columbia) to lakes and rivers adjoining Georgian Bay (Ontario), and from interior and coastal Newfoundland and Labrador to high-latitude lakes on Baffin and Ellesmere Islands (Nunavut). His current research centres on questions related to life history evolution, behavioural ecology, phenotypic plasticity, population dynamics, and conservation biology of marine and anadromous fishes, particularly Atlantic cod (*Gadus morhua*), Atlantic salmon (*Salmo salar*), and brook trout (*Salvelinus fontinalis*). From an applied perspective, this work has bearing on questions pertaining to the depletion, recovery, and sustainable exploitation of marine fishes; interactions between wild and farmed Atlantic salmon; the biodiversity of Canadian fishes; and the communication of science to decision makers and to society.

Darryl T. Gwynne

Darryl T. Gwynne was born in Bristol, England, and moved to Canada in 1966. He is a professor of biology at the University of Toronto in Mississauga. He received a B.Sc. in Biology at the University of Toronto in 1974 and a Ph.D. in Zoology and Entomology from Colorado State University in 1979. After conducting postdoctoral research at the University of New Mexico, in 1981 he took up a Queen Elizabeth II Research Fellowship at the University of Western Australia. Since 1987 he has been at the University of Toronto, where he currently teaches animal behaviour and a fourth year "Topics in Ecology and Evolution" course.

Darryl's research seeks to understand the factors that control sexual selection and the "typical" sexual differences in behaviour and structure, such as ornaments and weapons. His studies and those of his students have investigated the consequences of mating systems as diverse as those with extreme sexual selection on males (harem defence and male weaponry in New Zealand weta, a group of cricket relatives) to the key study species, those that are rare examples of female competition for mates. The common element in the life histories of most of the study species are important goods and services offered by the males, such as prey used by dance flies, and specialized glandular secretions in other insects. The value of these gifts has led—for some species—to role reversals in behaviour, with females competing for access to gift-bearing males and occasionally the evolution of male-like ornamentation in females.

Darryl is author of over 100 scientific papers, several popular articles, and a book (*Katydids and Bush-Crickets: Reproductive Behavior and Evolution of the Tettigoniidae*, Cornell University Press, 2001). He is several chapters into a new book, a popular tome on sexual selection that focuses on the life histories of insects found in the area of his home in the Credit River Valley.

B. Clark.

John P. Smol

John P. Smol is a professor in the Department of Biology at Queen's University, with a cross-appointment to the School of Environmental Studies, where he also holds the Canada Research Chair in Environmental Change. He received a B.Sc. from McGill University, an M.Sc. from Brock University, and a Ph.D. from Queen's University. Following postdoctoral work in the High Arctic with the Geological Survey of Canada, he became a faculty member at Queen's University. He has also held adjunct appointments at several universities in Canada and the United States.

John founded the Paleoecological Environmental Assessment and Research Lab (PEARL) in 1991—a group of about 30 researchers dedicated to the study of global environmental change, focusing primarily on lake ecology. An ISI Highly Cited Researcher, he has authored about 400 journal publications and book chapters, and completed 19 books, including his textbook *Pollution of Lakes and Rivers: A Paleoenvironmental Perspective*, now in its second edition. He has lectured on all seven continents, including as the 2008 Rutherford Lecturer at the Royal Society (London). He was the founding editor of the international *Journal of Paleolimnology* (1987–2007), is the current editor of the journal *Environmental Reviews*, is editor of the *Developments in Paleoenvironmental Research* book series, and is on the editorial boards of several additional journals. Since 1990, he has received over 25 national and international research and teaching awards, including an NSERC Steacie Fellowship, the 1992 Steacie Prize (awarded to Canada's top young scientist or engineer), a Canada Council Killam Fellowship, the Geological Association of Canada Past-Presidents' Medal, the Botanical Society of America Darbaker Prize, the Rigler Prize from the Society of Canadian Limnologists, the Royal Society of Canada Miroslaw Romanowski Medal for advances in the environmental sciences, an NSERC Award of Excellence, and the American Society of Limnology and Oceanography Hutchinson Award. The Royal Canadian Geographical Society named him as the 2008 Environmental Scientist of the Year (an honour shared with his brother, Jules Blais, of the University of Ottawa). In 2009, he was presented with the Killam Prize for the Natural Sciences from the Canada Council, as well as the Premier's Discovery Award for Life Sciences and Medicine. He has received two honorary doctorates: a Doctor of Laws from St. Francis Xavier University and an honorary Doctor of Philosophy from the University of Helsinki. In December 2004, John was awarded the NSERC Herzberg Gold Medal as Canada's top scientist or engineer.

John has also received six teaching awards, including the W. T. Barnes Teaching Excellence Award, the Chancellor A. Charles Baillie Teaching Award, and the inaugural Queen's University Award for Excellence in Graduate Supervision. In 2007, he was presented with the T. Geoffrey Flynn Advancement Champion Award for his work on scientific communication and outreach activities, and in 2009 he was presented with a 3M National Teaching Fellowship, considered by many to be Canada's top teaching honour.

Roger Suffling

Roger Suffling came to the School of Planning at the University of Waterloo following the obtaining of degrees in botany and ecology and weed science and employment in environmental consulting. He teaches ecology, park planning, ecological policy making, environmental impact assessment, landscape ecology, and ecological restoration.

Suffling's research interests centre on the landscape ecology and management of boreal forests, the role of forest fires, and global warming effects on the ecology and economy of Canada's mid-north. Equally, he and his students research the ecology and management of urban ecosystems. Suffling has published numerous papers on these topics and has been a consultant for companies; First Nations; local, provincial, and national governments and a royal commission. He chairs an Ontario government scientific advisory committee on woodland caribou conservation, and for over 30 years has participated in numerous environmental assessments and conservation issues in northern Ontario. Many of these activities focus on applying ecological principles to management of incremental landscape change, whether this is caused by urban growth, forest fires, recreation, or forest harvest. Roger has travelled to over 20 countries in his study of ecology but has a special passion for the people and ecosystems of northern Ontario. For a decade, through the Quetico Foundation, he co-organized a youth program for northern Ontario students to conduct landscape scale research in Quetico Provincial Park, a large wilderness reserve in northwestern Ontario. Roger's hobbies include a garden that manages to manage itself, family history, cross-country skiing, and wilderness canoeing. As an immigrant to Canada, Roger is profoundly grateful for the gifts that this vast and magnificent country has afforded him in friendships and beautiful landscapes. He is concerned that the next generation of Canadians must build a more sustainable society.

Roy and Evelyn Turkington

Roy Turkington was born in Northern Ireland. After earning his B.Sc. (Hons) degree in Biological and Environmental Studies from the New University of Ulster in Northern Ireland and his doctorate from the University College of North Wales, Roy immigrated with his wife to Canada where he did postdoctoral research at the University of Western Ontario. Roy is a professor in the Department of Botany and the Beaty Biodiversity Research Centre at the University of British Columbia in Vancouver. He teaches two undergraduate courses in ecology, and an undergraduate and graduate course in plant ecology. He is primarily an experimental field ecologist investigating population-level processes, such as competition and herbivory as influences on community structure, specifically species diversity and ecosystem function.

Roy's research, and that of his students, is supported primarily by the Natural Sciences and Engineering Research Council (NSERC Canada) and has been conducted in a wide range of community types such as the boreal forest in northern Canada, grasslands in western Canada and the United Kingdom, Garry oak ecosystems, the Negev desert in Israel, riverine forests in the Serengeti National Park in Tanzania, and the subtropical forests of southern China.

Roy has published more than 130 papers and book chapters and has served on the editorial boards of *Agro-Ecosystems*, the *Canadian Journal of Botany*, and the *Israeli Journal of Ecology and Evolution*. He has been on the editorial board of the *Journal of Ecology* for almost 20 years. In pursuit of his academic career, Roy and his wife have spent sabbaticals in Wales, Turkey, Northern Ireland, Israel, and China.

In his spare time, Roy has a keen amateur interest in Middle Eastern and Biblical archaeology. He and his wife Evelyn are avid travellers and enjoy the outdoors. Together they have trekked the Annapurna circuit, the Mount Everest base camp, the High Atlas, and the Inca trail. For many years they have been involved in the AWANA children's ministry. Roy and Evelyn have two married children, Alistair and Andrea—and by the time this book is published, they will be very proud grandparents!

Richard L. Walker

Richard Walker completed his Ph.D. in Animal Physiology at Michigan State University in 1975 and immediately accepted a faculty position at the University of Calgary in the Department of Biological Sciences, where he remains an active faculty member. While in graduate school, Richard developed a keen interest in environmental physiology and the effects of pollutants on aquatic animals. He has had the privilege of working with some of Canada's leading environmental physiologists and has published journal articles on aluminum toxicity in brook trout.

His interest in fish and crustacean physiology has most recently resulted in publications on hormonal modulation of intestinal amino acid transporters in fish, and cardiovascular and ventilatory responses to stress in lobsters.

Richard loves to teach and has received several teaching excellence awards from the Students' Union and from the Faculty of Science. He lectures in courses in Introductory Animal Biology, Comparative Animal Physiology, and Human Physiology and is in charge of the laboratory teaching in physiology.

As an avid hiker, backpacker, and skier, Richard considers himself very fortunate to live in the foothills of the Canadian Rockies. He also makes forays to the west coast where he enjoys sailing with family and friends.

ECOLOGY

A Canadian Context

CHAPTER 1

Introduction to Ecology

BILL FREEDMAN, Department of Biology, Dalhousie University

LEARNING OBJECTIVES

After studying this chapter you should be able to

1. Define ecology and explain its interdisciplinary nature and where its subject areas fit within the hierarchical organization of the universe.
2. Explain the various subject areas of ecology, including their varying scales of interest in space, time, and levels of organization within the biosphere.
3. Explain the geological structure and dynamics of planet Earth.
4. Describe the nature of scientific investigation, its core methodologies, and explain and why it is vital to understanding the structure and function of the natural world.
5. Discuss the theory of evolution, including the essential role of natural selection, and explain why it provides a pervasive context for knowledge and research in ecology.
6. Understand why the knowledge of ecology is vital to guiding the process of sustainable development.

Autumn landscape at Abraham Lake, AB. Photo by Bill Caulfeild-Browne

CHAPTER OUTLINE

1.1 Foundations of Ecology

Ecology and the Natural World

Arguably, the greatest questions that any scientist could ask are about how the natural world is organized. What are the connections among the components of nature, both living and non-living, and how are they changing? What sources of energy drive the processes by which matter is moved about and reorganized into different forms, including the biochemicals of organisms? What physical laws govern these relationships? Clearly, the physical sciences, especially physics and chemistry, are fundamental to answering these big questions. This is because, in essence, matter and energetics are physical attributes, even when they occur in organisms. Moreover, virtually all the universe is inanimate, meaning it is devoid of life.

There is, however, one tiny bit of the universe (relatively speaking) where life and ecosystems are known to exist—it is the biosphere of Earth. Within that context, the sciences of biology and ecology are also central to understanding the natural world. Knowledge of biology is essential to understanding the genesis of life, its functioning, and its evolution. Ecology is specifically relevant to ecosystems—spaces in which groups of organisms are interacting and evolving under the influence of myriad environmental factors, including other organisms.

Because of its context within the realm of the greatest questions of science, the knowledge of ecology has intrinsic worth—it allows us to better understand the functional organization of the natural world. In fact, most ecologists took up their profession because of their fascination with fundamental questions about life, ecosystems, the universe, and everything.

But ecological knowledge is also important for practical, day-to-day reasons that are related to the inherent need of people for the necessities and amenities of life; for resources—food, materials, energy, and shelter—and for the aesthetics of pleasure and satisfaction. In this sense, the wisdom of ecology can be applied to solving vital

The pale blue dot is an image of Earth taken in 1990 by the spacecraft *Voyager 1* from a vast distance of about 5.9 billion km. This furthest-ever image of Earth shows the planet against the astonishing vastness of space, and reminds us of the lonely and precarious existence of the only place in the universe that is definitely known to sustain life and ecosystems. Earth is the tiny light spot at the centre-right, within the vertical light-purple band. The phrase "pale blue dot" was coined by Carl Sagan (1934–1996), an astronomer and author who also wrote a book with that title.

problems related to the supply and quality of resources and the sustainability of their use. Moreover, applied ecological knowledge is crucial to conserving the biodiversity of Earth, which must be done even while our economy harvests necessary resources from extensive areas.

Applied research in ecology also involves big questions, particularly those that are related to natural resources and the damages that human activities might be causing to ecosystems and biodiversity—these are important considerations with respect to the sustainable limits of the human economy. Ecologists and other environmental specialists have useful professional advice to offer to society with respect to these aspects of sustainable development. That counsel is received by decision makers in government and private-sector businesses, and also by ordinary citizens, who consider it when making choices about actions that carry a risk of causing environmental damage. We examine these subjects in more detail in Chapter 17.

For our immediate purposes in this book about ecology, it is sufficient to acknowledge that it is vitally important that the economy of Canada and all countries be undertaken in ways that are truly sustainable. This means that the economy does not degrade its essential resource base, or cause wanton ecological damage, even while enabling large numbers of people to have healthy and productive lives. Sustainable development is among the most important of national and global issues, and its only alternative, which is not acceptable, is non-sustainability. By many measures we are presently on that latter pathway, and if it is followed much longer the economy could collapse because of the inexorable effects of insufficient resources and environmental deterioration. That catastrophe would result in misery for a shocking number of people, and it would be awful for other species and natural ecosystems. Such a terrible outcome can yet be avoided, and one of the keys to that happening is for society to consider the advice offered by ecologists and other environmental specialists about prudent use of the natural capital of Earth. At the same time, we must do all that is necessary to conserve the planet's natural heritage of biodiversity. These are big challenges, but they can and must be met.

Organisms and Environment

A simple working definition of **ecology** is "the study of the relationships of organisms and their environment." The word was first used (as *oekologie*) in 1869 by Ernst Haeckel (1834–1919), a German biologist and philosopher, to mean "the study of the natural environment including the relations of organisms to one another and to their surroundings" (Odum and Barrett, 2005). The etymology of the word is from the Greek words *oikos* or "house" and *logos* or "the study of."

However, as a means of systematic investigation of the natural world, the roots of ecology are much older than the word itself, extending to early inquiries by ancient philosophers, such as the Greeks, Hippocrates (*ca.* 460–377 B.C.E.) and Aristotle (384–322 B.C.E.). Today, the kinds of studies that those philosophers undertook would be labelled as **natural history**—the investigation of organisms in their wild habitats that also extends to an interest in all natural phenomena, including physical ones, even astronomy. Investigations in natural history are relatively simple—usually, few or no quantitative (measured) data are collected and a rigorous scientific methodology is not used (see section 1.2). The study of natural history is still popular—it is undertaken by many people who are fascinated by wild plants, birds, invertebrates, and other marvels of nature, often with a view to collecting unique observations or specimens.

Bill Freedman

The knowledge of ecology can be applied to the management of natural resources, such as in forestry. This timber-harvesting machine is used to clear-cut and de-limb trees. This image is from a site near Truro in Nova Scotia.

Ecology, however, is a scientific branch of learning—it is a systematic and quantitative enterprise. Ecologists work by proposing testable hypotheses that are related to some aspect of the organization or functioning of the natural world. They design and undertake methodical research to investigate those questions, usually by studying patterns that have been observed in nature and by using experimental techniques. Ecologists also apply statistical approaches to analyzing the significance of differences they have observed along natural gradients in nature or among experimental treatments—these can involve variations in the abundance of organisms or in the strength and influence of environmental factors. Once ecologists have gained a quantitative understanding of apparent controls of the system being studied, they may develop conceptual or mathematical models that predict the likely results of manipulations of key variables, or of the consequences of other kinds of environmental change.

Ecologists may use extremely sophisticated tools in their research, such as high-capacity computing systems, advanced instrumentation for chemical analysis, remote-sensing technology, and tracking devices suitable for animals as large as whales or as small as butterflies. This is not, however, always the case—much ecological research involves less-sophisticated measurements of the natural world, such as estimates of the abundance of trees or birds in a woodlot, or measurements of temperature using a thermometer. Even simple methodologies can be useful in ecological research, so long as they yield data that are reasonably accurate and repeatable, and are gained in the context of a properly designed investigation.

Fundamentals

A higher goal of ecology is to understand how variations in the distribution and abundance of species are affected by **environmental factors** (or **influences**; **Figure 1.1**). The factors may be **inorganic** (**abiotic** or **non-living**), such as temperature, moisture, nutrients, and wildfire, or they may be **organic** (**biotic**) and associated with the influences of other organisms. The biotic influences can involve such interactions as

- **competition**, in which organisms interfere with one another as they vie for access to resources whose supply is less than the biological demand; *intraspecific competition* occurs among individuals of the same species, and *interspecific* is between species;
- **herbivory**, which involves animals feeding on the tissues of plants, thereby affecting the biomass and productivity of their food species;
- **predation**, in which one species of animal kills and eats another kind; and
- **parasitism** and **disease**, which are also feeding relationships but do not necessarily result in the host being killed.

With so much of the planetary surface covered with water, we might wonder why Earth was not in fact named "Water." This image was taken by a weather satellite on 25 August 1992, as Hurricane Andrew was making landfall on the coast of Louisiana.

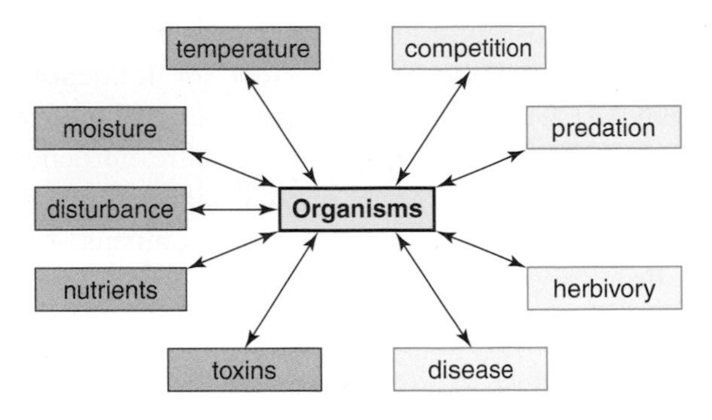

FIGURE 1.1

Organisms and Environment. Ecology is the study of the relationships of organisms and their environment. Environmental influences can be biotic (green) or abiotic (orange), and the relationships are reciprocal, meaning that organisms also exert an influence on environmental factors.

The word **ecosystem (ecological system)** is often used in the context of ecological research and writing. It is, however, a generalized term that cannot be precisely defined—rather, an ecosystem is a space in which organisms are interacting with one another and with environmental factors, and it is delimited for the purposes of studying it. In this sense, a tiny ecosystem might be identified as existing within a container formed by a pitcher plant (such as *Sarracenia purpurea*, the provincial flower of Newfoundland and Labrador), which includes retained rainwater, algae, and a few specialized invertebrates. The largest ecosystem we know of is the biosphere, which is bounded by the presence of all organisms on Earth and includes the environmental factors with which they interact, such as sunlight.

Ecosystems are said to have **structural attributes**, which are commonly reported in units of quantity per area, such as the following:

- biomass, or the weight of organic matter, often stated in kilograms per square metre (kg/m^2) or tonnes/ha (t/ha), usually on a dry-weight basis to avoid the vagaries of water content
- density—the number of individuals per m^2 or per ha
- species richness—the number of species per unit area

When studying a large area, as is often done, ecologists use sub-sampling procedures to estimate the average values of these sorts of structural measures. However, close attention is paid to estimates of their spatial variation, which is itself considered an important structural feature.

The **functional attributes** of ecosystems are rates of change of the structural ones, and they are typically measured as change of the amount per unit area and time, such as the following:

- productivity, or the rate of increase of biomass, often measured as $g/m^2 \cdot year$ or $t/ha \cdot yr$
- nutrient fluxes, or the rate of movement of vital chemicals, such as the fixation of atmospheric nitrogen in $kg/ha \cdot yr$
- water flow, for example in a stream, as $m^3/ha \cdot yr$

Ecologists are often interested in knowing about changes in the structural and functional attributes of ecosystems—their past conditions, which provide a historical context for the present circumstances, as well as the likely future values. Sometimes the change is rapid, as occurs after a disturbance, such as a wildfire or a clear-cut of a forest. Disturbances are followed by a period of ecological recovery, known as succession, which has its own longer-term dynamics. These subjects are examined in more detail in the sections that follow.

Ecology within the Hierarchy of Organization

The natural world comprises the universe and all things in it. Within that inestimable space, the astonishing complexity of nature may be rendered more easily understandable if we first organize it in a hierarchical manner (**Figure 1.2**).

The universe is the biggest entity within that layered system. It includes billions of stars (one estimate is 10^{21} or 1000 billion billion) and likely an even larger number of planets. Earth is one particular world. It orbits the Sun, a medium-sized star, as do seven additional planets along with various comets, asteroids, and other objects that together compose a seemingly ordinary solar system. Earth is the third-closest planet to the Sun, orbiting it every 365 days at an average distance of 149 million km, and rotating on its own axis every 24 hours. Earth is a spherical body, with a solid diameter of 12 700 km. About 70 percent of its surface is covered by liquid water and the rest by terrestrial rocks, sand, ice, and vegetation. With so much of the planetary surface covered with water, we might wonder why Earth was not in fact named "Water."

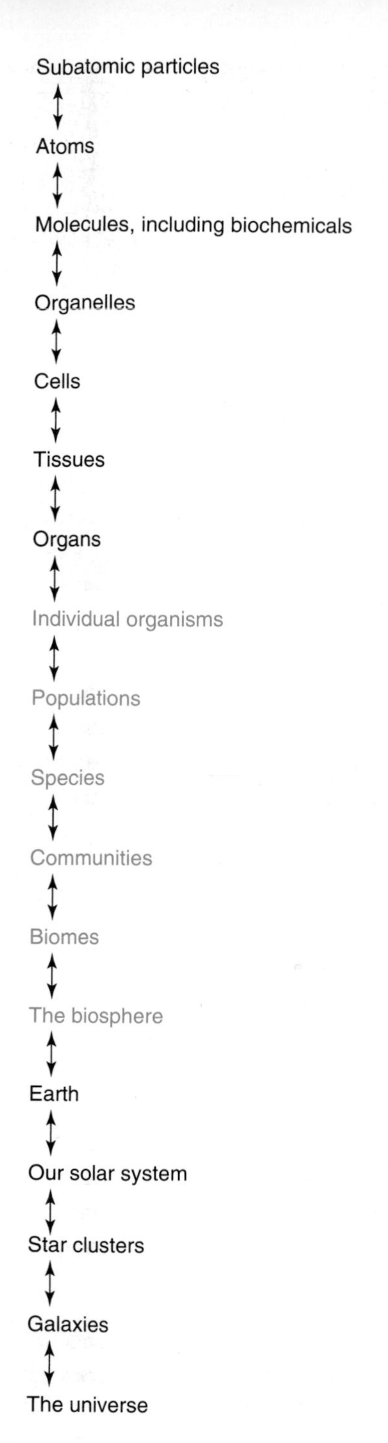

FIGURE 1.2
Hierarchical Organization of the Universe. To study its extraordinary complexity, we can organize the universe in a hierarchical manner, which in this diagram proceeds from smaller at the top to larger at the bottom. Note, however, that all of the elements are intrinsically connected. The realm of ecology is shown in the green font.

Like any celestial body, Earth has unique characteristics. But what makes the planet especially astonishing is the fact that its environments have supported a spontaneous genesis and subsequent evolution of organisms. Life first appeared about 3.5 billion years ago, within only one billion years of the formation of the planet during the nativity of the solar system. We do not know how life first sparked from inanimate matter, although it is believed that genesis somehow occurred spontaneously, as a consequence of appropriate conditions of chemistry, temperature, solar radiation, pressure, and other critical factors.

The complexity of the universe is expressed at scales that range from the unimaginably vast, such as galaxies and the universe itself, to the infinitesimally minute, such as subatomic entities. The realm of life occupies intermediate levels of the hierarchy, ranging from biochemicals to the biosphere, but it is important to understand that these are intrinsically connected to all of the other levels. The realm of ecology encompasses the following levels:

- **individual organisms**—living entities that are genetically and physically discrete
- **populations**—individuals of the same species that co-occur in space and time
- **species**—individuals (and populations) that are capable of interbreeding and producing fertile offspring
- **communities**—populations of various species that occur together in the same space and time
- **ecoscapes**—mosaics of various kinds of community-level patches over large areas, known as **landscapes** in terrestrial environments and as **seascapes** in marine ones
- the **biosphere**—all space occupied by life on Earth

Individual organisms connect with lower levels of the hierarchy through their biochemistry and the physiology of their cells and organs. The biosphere connects with higher levels, and especially with the Sun, through the continuous input of solar radiation that sustains almost all ecological productivity and that influences other environmental qualities such as weather and climate.

Connections and Constraints

Much of the subject matter of ecology is about understanding connections—of interactions of organisms with other organisms and also with non-living environmental factors. The connections among organisms are diverse and web-like and involve contacts related to feeding, competition, and other behaviours. Interactions with abiotic factors are also complex, with diverse influences operating at the same time, although at different intensities. Connections are so important in ecology that environmental philosopher Barry Commoner (1971) formulated a "law" based on the following observation: "everything is connected to everything else."

Ecologists view the multifarious connections among the components of ecosystems in a holistic manner. This so-called **ecosystem approach** does not regard an ecological system as being a haphazard grouping of individuals, populations, communities, and environments—rather, these are all considered to be connected and interdependent, although in varying degrees. This is a necessary approach, because life and ecosystems have **emergent properties** that cannot be predicted from knowledge only of their parts and that exist only in systems that are operating as an integrated whole. Here are some examples of systems with emergent properties:

Bill Freedman

An individual organism is a living entity that is genetically and physically discrete. This photo shows several individual plants of the mountain cranberry, *Vaccinium vitis-idaea*, growing near Goose Bay, Labrador. Each red-coloured fruit has a diameter of about 8 mm.

Bill Freedman

An old-field community that is regenerating back to forest in Point Pelee National Park, southwestern Ontario. The pasture grasses and forbs are being replaced by shrubs and trees, such as gray dogwood (*Cornus racemosa*) and hackberry (*Celtis occidentalis*).

- A computer is a physical system with emergent properties—you could not predict its remarkable operating capabilities based only on knowledge of its elemental composition, or even with an inventory of its parts. A computer works properly only if its components are manufactured correctly and assembled well, the software is loaded, and it is operated by someone who understands how to use it.
- Organisms can exist only if the vital elements of their biochemistry, anatomy, and behaviour are intact. Moreover, environmental conditions must also be suitable if an organism is to survive and reproduce.
- A stand of forest consists of an assemblage of abiotic elements (rocks, water, gases) and diverse organic ones (species of trees and other plants, animals, microorganisms, and dead organic matter). From knowledge of only those components, it would be impossible to predict such wonderful emergent properties of a well-functioning forest as productivity, nutrient cycling, and feeding relationships.

Another ecological principle is that organisms are sustained by resources—the "goods and services" that are provided by ecosystems. All species have specific necessities, which they acquire from the particular habitats that they utilize. Plant species, for example, must have an adequate supply of sunlight, water, nutrients, such as carbon and nitrogen, and space. Other aspects of their environment must also be suitable, including the amount of disturbance and biotic influences, such as competition and herbivory. Likewise, animals must have sufficient access to appropriate plant or animal foods, and they have additional habitat needs that are particular for each species.

Commonly, however, vital resources are not sufficient to meet the biological demand, a situation that will constrain the growth, development, and reproduction of individual organisms, and therefore of populations, communities, and larger ecosystems. For example, a plant may experience an inadequate nutrient supply because it is growing in infertile soil, or light or moisture may be insufficient because of competition with nearby plants. Suboptimal access to vital resources results in physiological stress and a productivity that is less than the plant is genetically capable of achieving under optimal conditions. One result of this response to stress is that the plant may develop few or even no seeds during its lifetime. This is an important result because evolutionary success is related to an organism leaving progeny that carry its genetic lineage into future generations of its kind (see section 1.3 for an explanation of *fitness*).

Similarly, the productivity and development of an animal (including any human) may be limited by its environmental circumstances. An individual that must deal with stresses caused by a shortage of food or difficult relations with competitors, predators, or diseases may have little success in life.

The acme of ecological development occurs in regions in which environmental conditions are not excessively stressful to organisms. In terrestrial environments, old-growth tropical forest represents the highest level of ecosystem development because it sustains an enormous richness of biodiversity and other forms of complexity. This ecosystem develops in environments that provide an adequate supply of moisture and nutrients and are consistently warm, and in which severe disturbances caused by wildfire, windstorm, or disease are rare. The marine analogue is coral reefs, which support more species and biological complexity than any other oceanic ecosystem, again because they exist in an environment that is consistently well-supported by vital resources.

Other environments, however, are more stressful, and in those places ecological development may be limited to prairie, tundra, desert, or other ecosystems with relatively low levels of complexity and productivity.

Change is also a pervasive attribute of ecosystems. Some are particularly dynamic, regularly experiencing large changes in their species composition, biomass, and rates of productivity and nutrient cycling. This is the case of all ecosystems that occur in seasonally cold or dry climates, so that distinct growing seasons are followed by periods of dormancy during which there is little or no productivity. All Canadian ecosystems are like this, to varying degrees—a warm and productive growing season is followed by a cold and wintry dormant period. Animals survive the hard times of winter by feeding on plant biomass accumulated during the growing season, or they hibernate or migrate to a warmer clime.

Intense ecological change is also caused by **disturbances** by wildfires, windstorms, or biological factors, such as an acute pathogen. These cataclysms may kill the dominant organisms of an ecosystem, a severe damage that is followed by an extended period of recovery, referred to as **succession.** Some natural disturbances can affect millions of hectares, as occurs with extensive wildfires and irruptions of certain tree-killing insects, such as bark beetles and budworm moths. Because of their large scale and intensity, these are referred to as **stand-replacing disturbances**. Other disturbances are local, perhaps associated with the death of a large tree caused by a lightning strike—these **microdisturbances** produce gaps in an otherwise mature ecosystem, within which a recovery by **microsuccession** takes place.

Some ecosystems, however, are rarely disturbed and so they are relatively stable. Nevertheless, if they are closely monitored for a long time, they will also be found to be changing. At the very least, these and all ecosystems are influenced by changes in regional climate and by other long-term and pervasive dynamics, such as evolution.

Environmental stressors have always affected organisms and ecosystems. These days, however, ecosystems are not only influenced by "natural" stressors but also by **anthropogenic** ones (associated with human activities). Like any species, *Homo sapiens* affects the species with which it interacts and the ecosystems of which they are a component. But anthropogenic influences have intensified enormously in modern times, and throughout much of the world they are now a major influence on the productivity of species and on the structure and function of ecosystems.

People and their economy affect species and ecosystems in several key ways:

- by harvesting valuable biomass, such as trees and hunted animals
- by converting natural ecosystems into agricultural, urban, or industrial land-uses
- by introducing alien species that invade natural habitats and cause ecological damage
- by causing toxicity through pollution

These direct effects also engender a great variety of indirect ones. For example, the clear-cutting of trees from an area will devastate conditions for the diversity of plants and animals that need forested habitat, causing their abundance to decline on the affected site. At the same time, other species will be favoured by these changes. Moreover, timber harvesting indirectly affects functional properties of the ecosystem, such as productivity, streamflow, and erosion. These indirect ecological effects are important, and they are cumulative to the direct ones.

The population of our species in 2010 was about 6.8 billion individuals, and we are living in almost all habitable places on Earth. Directly or indirectly, more than half of the net terrestrial production of the planet is being diverted to the human economy (Vitousek et al., 1986). Moreover, over-consumption is rapidly depleting important natural resources, both renewable and non-renewable ones. The jeopardy to humans is that the resource mining cannot be sustained for very long. The risk to the natural world from the unprecedented and wanton influence of a single species (humans) is irreversible damage by the endangerment and extinction of species and of entire natural ecosystems. One of the great challenges of ecology is to provide timely advice that can help the human economy to transform itself into a sustainable enterprise that will support both itself and the natural world. We examine this subject in more detail in Chapters 15 and 17.

The Biosphere

The biosphere is the spatial envelope within which life exists, and Earth is the only place in the universe where this is known to occur. Moreover, the biosphere is the largest possible ecosystem, encompassing all life and its immediate environments. The biosphere extends from at least 3 km into the crust to as high as 41 km in the stratosphere—microorganisms have been recovered from both of those extreme environments (see Ecology in Depth 2.1). Of course, the

Bill Freedman

A stand-replacing disturbance affects a relatively large area and kills the dominant species. It is then followed by community-scale regeneration. This area of boreal forest dominated by black spruce (*Picea mariana*) in central Labrador was affected by wildfires several years previously. The linear unburnt areas are moist habitats along streams, while the larger tract of intact forest likely survived because of luck and wind direction.

biosphere is also intimately connected to influences from outside its boundaries, particularly by the continuous insolation that drives the photosynthesis that is the basis of almost all ecological productivity (Chapter 4).

The biosphere originated about 3.5 billion years ago, upon the genesis of life. The first life forms were bacteria-like organisms that fed on a soup of organic chemicals that had gradually accumulated in primordial aquatic environments. Those chemicals might have been synthesized during lightning-sparked reactions involving simple inorganic compounds, such as methane, ammonia, carbon dioxide, and water. The earliest bacteria were **heterotrophic** organisms that could survive only if they had access to organic matter as a source of nutrition.

The first **autotrophic** microorganisms, which feed themselves through biosynthesis, evolved about 3.1 billion years ago. They were probably **chemosynthetic** bacteria that could oxidize sulphide compounds and use some of the energy released to power a biosynthesis of sugars from carbon dioxide and water (Chapter 4). The evolution of chemosynthesis was an extremely important evolutionary outcome because it resulted in the production of much more organic matter than had the previous inorganic reactions.

The first **photosynthetic** organisms, possibly cyanobacteria (blue-green bacteria), evolved around 2.5 billion years ago. These were **phototrophs** (or **photoautotrophs**, meaning "light self-feeding") that used solar energy to biosynthesize sugars from CO_2 and H_2O, releasing O_2 as a metabolic by-product. The evolution of photosynthesis further amplified the ability of the biosphere to produce biomass and so to support the evolution of many kinds of heterotrophic organisms.

However, the discharge of large amounts of biogenic O_2 resulted in an enormous environmental change, because the atmosphere became transformed over several hundreds of millions of years from being essentially anaerobic (devoid of O_2) to having a concentration similar to the present value of 21 percent. This meant that the dominant chemical reactions in the environments of life were changed from being reducing in character (which result in an increase in the number of electrons) to those similar to the present, which are oxidizing (fewer electrons). The development of predominantly oxidizing conditions would have been catastrophic for most of the existing species and caused a mass extinction. The only survivors would have persisted in relatively uncommon anaerobic habitats, plus those few original species that were capable of tolerating oxygen. Those rare O_2-tolerant microbes then proliferated throughout the habitable parts of the planet and underwent an evolutionary radiation. Most species that are alive today are their descendants.

The abiotic components of the biosphere are exceedingly complex, and for the purposes of study it is helpful to divide them into three major environments—the atmosphere, hydrosphere, and lithosphere.

Atmosphere

The **atmosphere** is an envelope of gases, plus smaller amounts of suspended particulates and droplets, that surrounds the solid Earth, being retained by gravitational attraction. The major gases are nitrogen (N_2; 78.08 percent, by volume), oxygen (O_2; 20.95 percent), argon (Ar; 0.93 percent), carbon dioxide (CO_2; 0.039 percent), and neon (Ne; 0.002 percent). The water content is highly variable, but it averages about 1 percent (in the lower atmosphere). The density of the atmosphere decreases rapidly with increasing distance from the surface (sea level), with half of its mass occurring within 5.6 km of the surface, and three-quarters within 11 km. The atmosphere extends at least to 120 km, beyond which is the void of outer space. The two lower strata of the atmosphere, the troposphere and stratosphere, are most important to functioning of the biosphere.

TROPOSPHERE. The **troposphere** is the lowest layer, extending to 7 km at the poles and 17–20 km at the equator (its upper boundary, the tropopause, is rather seasonal and is also affected by severe weather). The troposphere is heated by sunlight, but this effect varies greatly with latitude, being greatest in the tropics. The uneven distribution of heat content becomes dispersed by vertical mixing and by lateral air flows or winds, sometimes manifest in the extremes of hurricanes and tornadoes. The jet stream is a particularly vigorous, meandering, ribbon-like, westerly (in the northern hemisphere) airflow that occurs near the tropopause. Because of the continuous turbulence within the troposphere, it is sometimes called the "weather atmosphere." In general, air temperature decreases with increasing altitude; between sea level and about 11 km the average lapse (or cooling) rate is about 6.5°C per 1000 m.

STRATOSPHERE. The **stratosphere** extends from the tropopause to about 50 km above the surface. Unlike in the troposphere, temperature generally increases with height. The stratosphere is essentially devoid of H_2O, and it contains a distinct "ozone layer" with a high O_3 concentration (2–8 parts per million [ppm], compared with about 0.08 ppm at the surface). The O_3 is produced by a complex of ultraviolet-driven photochemical reactions. The O_3 provides a crucial environmental service by absorbing much of the high-energy solar ultraviolet radiation and thereby preventing it from reaching the surface, where it would harm organisms by damaging crucial biochemicals, such as DNA and photosynthetic pigments.

Hydrosphere

The **hydrosphere** consists of water occurring in various compartments—on the surface of the planet, in rocks, and in the atmosphere. About 98.5 percent of global water is in the oceans. Almost all the rest is in glaciers (which cover about 10 percent of the planet's surface), although this has varied over geological time—at the peak of the most recent ice age, more than 12 thousand years ago, sea level was about 120 m lower than today because so much water was present in glacial ice. About 0.32 percent of global water is groundwater, occurring in cracks and other interstices in soil and rocks, while only 0.2 percent is in surface waters (lakes, rivers, and wetlands), and 0.1 percent in the atmosphere. The **hydrological cycle** (or **water cycle**) refers to movements of water among the various compartments (**Figure 1.3**). These fluxes are powered by the energy of absorbed solar radiation, plus gravitational potential for downward flows. A key aspect of the hydrological cycle is **evaporation** of water to the atmosphere from the oceans, inorganic surfaces on land, and vegetation (the latter is called **transpiration**; the combined effect is **evapotranspiration**). About 90 percent of water evaporated to the atmosphere is from the oceans, even though only 70 percent of Earth's surface is marine. The atmospheric water may be transported by winds over long distances, but eventually it cools and forms droplets or ice crystals, which if large enough will settle gravitationally from the atmosphere as **precipitation** (rain or snow). Some of the deposited water percolates through soil and may join longer-term stores of groundwater deep in the ground (known as aquifers), or erupt to the surface at springs that feed streams, rivers, lakes, and wetlands. Eventually, the freshwater is returned to the oceans by riverflow, and the cycle is completed.

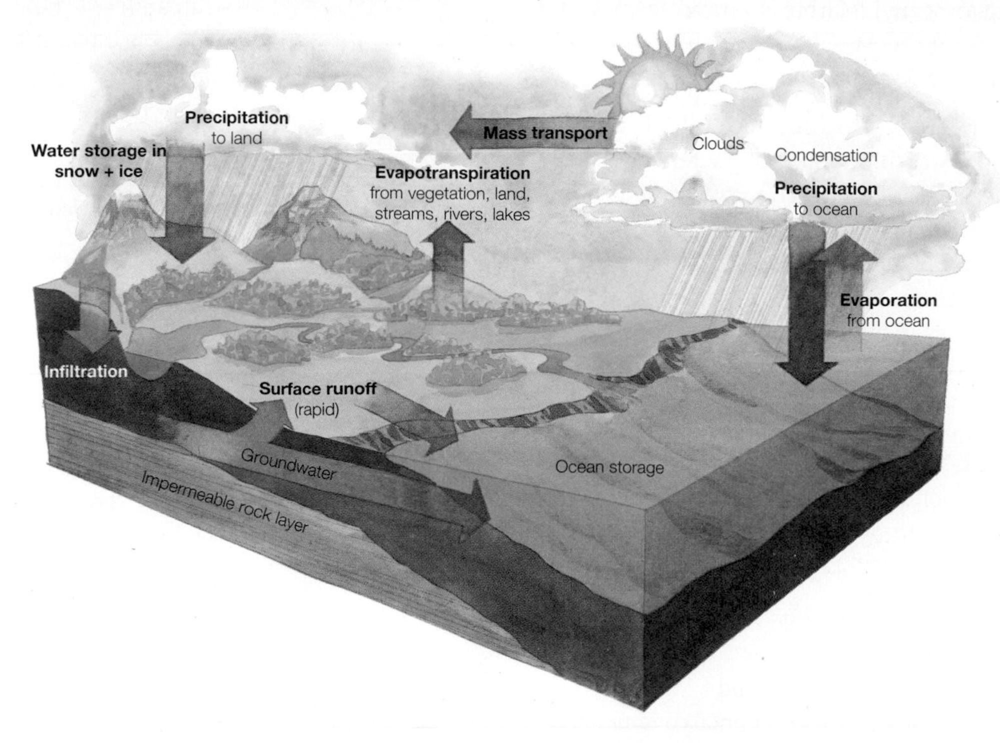

FIGURE 1.3

The Hydrological Cycle. The water cycle refers to quantities present in various compartments as well as movements occurring among those storage reservoirs. The absorbed energy of sunlight powers the evaporation of water and its transport by wind and oceanic currents, while all downward movement occurs in response to gradients of gravitational potential.

SOURCE: Modified from Draper/Reed. *Our Environment: A Canadian Perspective*, 4E.

Solid Earth

The solid Earth consists of several concentric layers. The innermost region is the **core**, with a diameter of 3500 km and mostly comprising molten metals, predominantly iron and nickel. The heat of the core is generated by the decay of unstable isotopes of uranium and other radioactive elements. The **mantle** occurs above the core and is about 2800 km thick and composed of less-dense minerals in a semi-liquid state known as magma, which contains large amounts of silicon, oxygen, magnesium, and other lighter elements. Magma from the upper mantle may erupt at the surface at volcanoes, and the lava that spews forth cools to form basaltic rock. The **lithosphere** is the top layer, averaging 80 km thick and comprising basaltic, granitic, and sedimentary rocks. The lithosphere consists of rocks in an uppermost region known as the **crust**, plus part of the upper mantle. Oceanic crust averages 10–15 km in thickness, while continental crust is 20–60 km thick. The mineralogy of the crust is highly complex, in contrast to the relatively uniform mantle and core. The most abundant crustal elements are oxygen (45 percent), silicon (27 percent), aluminum (8.0 percent), iron (5.8 percent), calcium (5.1 percent), magnesium (2.8 percent), sodium (2.3 percent), potassium (1.7 percent), titanium (0.86 percent), vanadium (0.17 percent), hydrogen (0.14 percent), phosphorus (0.10 percent), and carbon (0.032 percent). Rocks forming the crust are grouped into three types:

- *Igneous rocks* include basalt and granite, which form by the cooling of magma, with the mineral types largely depending on the speed of solidification. Basalt is a heavy, dark, fine-grained rock. It is the major constituent of oceanic crust, originating at deep-ocean spreading zones and abyssal volcanoes, and also at terrestrial volcanoes. Granitic rocks dominate the continental crust, and are relatively light in density and colour and are coarse-grained, with an evident crystalline structure. The mineral composition includes quartz and feldspar, with mica and hornblende often present.
- *Sedimentary rocks* include limestone, dolomite, shale, sandstone, and conglomerate. These are formed from rubble eroded from other rocks or from precipitated minerals, such as calcite ($CaCO_3$) and dolomite ($Ca, MgCO_3$), which become lithified (turned into stone) under immense pressure when buried deep in oceanic deposits. Sedimentary rocks usually overlie basalt or granite.
- *Metamorphic rocks* are formed from igneous or sedimentary rocks that were subjected to immense geological heat and pressure when they were carried deep into the lithosphere by crustal movements, such as those associated with mountain

building (orogeny). Marble is a metamorphic rock derived from limestone, while slate is developed from shale, and gneiss from granite.

The biosphere is also a complex mosaic of biotic environments, which support characteristic assemblages of species that develop collective structural and functional attributes. At the global scale, the most extensive kinds of natural ecosystems are referred to as **biomes** (Chapter 8). In the marine realm, the dominant biomes include the open ocean, at the surface and at all depths, as well as coastal ones, such as coral reefs, estuaries, upwellings of deep water, and continental shelves. Biomes of the terrestrial realm include forests, ranging from tropical to boreal, as well as grassland, tundra, and desert, plus various kinds of wetlands if water is abundant. These are all natural ecosystems whose distinctiveness is due to

- the particular species that have spontaneously assembled into communities;
- their biological interactions; and
- the prevailing abiotic environmental conditions.

Of course, the modern world also supports extensive anthropogenic ecosystems, which have their own distinctive environmental conditions and biodiversity. These include various agricultural ecosystems, as well as urbanized and industrial ones. Anthropogenic ecosystems are vital to the human economy, and they include the places where almost all of humanity lives. However, their biodiversity is generally degraded (alien species being notably abundant), as are the rates of system functioning (see Chapters 15 through 17).

1.2 The Science of Ecology

Context for Ecology

Ecology is highly **interdisciplinary**, meaning it incorporates and crosses the boundaries of many subject areas. Biology is central to ecology, but knowledge of chemistry, computer science, earth sciences (geology), geography, mathematics, meteorology, oceanography, physics, statistics, and other fields is also important (**Figure 1.4**).

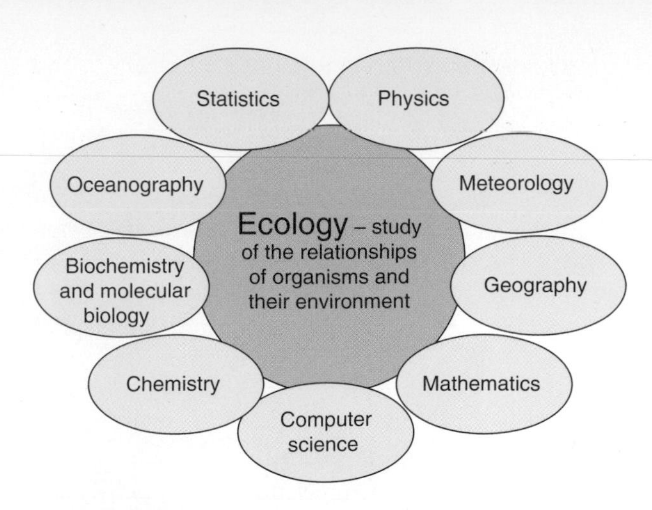

FIGURE 1.4
Ecology Is a Highly Interdisciplinary Field of Knowledge. The knowledge bases and methodologies of various kinds of science-related disciplines are relevant to the study of ecosystems.

In a general sense, studies by ecologists are intended to help understand the organization and functioning of the natural world—to determine environmental influences that result in observed patterns of

- species and their phylogenetic groupings, including their past and ongoing evolutionary change;
- the life-history and population-level attributes of species and of functional groups (the latter are clusters of species that are similar in their life history but are not necessarily closely related);
- the assembly of ecological communities;
- the patterns and dynamics of landscapes and seascapes;
- structural attributes of ecosystems, such as biodiversity at its various levels, and the storage of biomass and nutrients; and
- ecological functions, such as productivity and nutrient cycling.

However, the natural world is a notoriously complex system, and for this reason its past and present conditions are difficult to accurately describe, and its future ones even more so. This is vastly different from many aspects of the purely physical sciences, such as physics and chemistry. In those disciplines, it is often possible to make exacting measurements of conditions and to make accurate predictions of future ones. Here are a few simple examples:

- The trajectory and future location of an object moving through the vacuum of outer space can be predicted with exactness, as is evident from such celestial phenomena as the time it takes Earth to complete a revolution around the Sun (one year) and the return time of other orbiting bodies, such as Halley's comet (its next appearance will be in mid-2061).
- Even the trajectory and impact location of a projectile shot from a well-aimed artillery cannon can be predicted with confidence, with only minor variations caused by atmospheric conditions.
- Chemists can foretell the chemical and thermodynamic consequences of handling diverse substances in a laboratory—for instance, these are the consistent and inviolate properties of sodium chloride: 1 mole weighs 58.44 g (1 mole = 6.02×10^{23} atoms or molecules), the density is 2.16 g/cm^3, the melting point is 801°C, the boiling point is 1465°C,

solubility in water 35.9 g/100 mL (at 25°C), and when NaCl is dissolved into water, a small energy release (enthalpy of solution) of 5 kJ per mole occurs, which will slightly warm the solution.

- Physicists can predict the rate at which the intensity of radiation will diminish with increasing distance from a point source of its emission. For instance, although the Sun is an immense body, within a cosmic context, it is a point source of electromagnetic radiation, and its intensity can be calculated at various distances away—at the average distance of Earth from the Sun, the rate of energy input is 8.21 J/cm^2-min (this is known as the *solar constant*). At that intensity of insolation, it can be calculated that the average temperature of the surface of the planet would be about −33°C, as a consequence of the warming input of solar visible and near-infrared wavelengths and the cooling output from the planet of long-wave infrared. (However, because Earth has a greenhouse effect, the *actual* average surface temperature is about 15°C; see Chapter 4.)

In fact, some aspects of the physical and chemical world are so well-understood that universal "laws" have been formulated to explain them and to predict the future values of relevant variables. For instance, the first law of thermodynamics states that although energy can be transformed from one state to another, it cannot be created or destroyed, so its net quantity is constant (Chapter 4). The second law of thermodynamics states that energy transformations will occur spontaneously only if an increase occurs in the disorder (entropy) of the universe. Similarly, a number of universal physical constants exist—one is the speed of electromagnetic radiation (the speed of "light"), which is always 2.9979×10^8 m/sec, regardless of the velocity of the emitting body. Hard rules in geometry, such as the ratio of the circumference of a circle to its diameter, which always has a value of 3.14159, are also important. And for any right-angled triangle (with a 90° angle), the square of the longest side (the hypotenuse) is always equal to the sum of the squares of the other two.

It is rare, however, for ecologists to be able to make such accurate predictions about changes in the components or functions of ecosystems. This is why ecology has no true "laws," and why ecologists are sometimes alleged to have "physics envy." The awesome complexity of organisms and ecosystems, and the corresponding difficulties of biologists and ecologists in making accurate measurements and predictions, are due to three major circumstances:

- *Variations of the inorganic environment.* Some abiotic factors are exceedingly complicated and unpredictable, such as the systems that redistribute energy in the atmosphere—winds and storms. This is why weather forecasting is so commonly

Because of the large areas involved and other complexities, many ecological data are based on somewhat inaccurate and imprecise measurements of environmental or biological variables. How many semi-palmated sandpipers (*Calidris pusilla*) are there in this image of a migratory flock in the upper Bay of Fundy in New Brunswick? Note that there are many birds flying, but large numbers are also roosting densely on the ground.

inaccurate, as are predictions of future climatic conditions. The heat-distribution systems of the oceans—currents and upwellings—are also difficult to accurately measure or foretell. Seemingly capricious variations of the spatial and temporal values of these sorts of factors contribute to the complexity of biological and ecological responses.

- *Inherent biological complexity.* Biological systems are also unpredictable, in part because of genetic variations that result in differential responses to environmental conditions. The biological responses may involve aspects of biochemistry and physiology, anatomical development, productivity, fecundity, or behaviour. The genetic variations may be among individuals within a population, as well as among different species. Moreover, the genetic attributes of populations change over time (this is evolution), and species may become extinct if they cannot cope with environmental conditions.
- *Emergent properties.* As we previously noted, organisms and ecosystems have emergent properties that are difficult to predict. These synergetic qualities exist in an intact whole, but they cannot be predicted from knowledge only of the parts.

In addition, many ecological data are based on somewhat inaccurate and imprecise measurements of environmental or biological variables. Because those data are only approximations of the true values of natural phenomena, predictions based on them are subject to some degree of uncertainty. In the sense meant here,

- **accuracy** is the degree to which an observation or measurement reflects the true value of the subject, and
- **precision** is the degree of repeatability of those measurements.

Imagine the difficulty of estimating the number of trees or their biomass over a remote boreal landscape, or the number of caribou that are present there. Total direct counts cannot be made because the study area is so large, so sub-sampling procedures must be used. These methods have inherent inexactness, based on such factors as the size and number of the sampling plots—in general, however, a larger number of bigger samples will provide data that have better accuracy and precision. Of course, the numbers and sizes of plots are themselves partly determined by how much effort (funding) is available to conduct a study. Accuracy and precision are also relevant to environmental variables, such as determining the concentrations of nutrients or pollutants in samples of water, soil, or organisms, or in measuring climate-related factors. Imagine the difficulty of estimating the average carbon storage or surface temperature of a stand of old-growth forest in coastal British Columbia, or of mixedgrass prairie in Saskatchewan.

Problems associated with accuracy and precision are unavoidable aspects of doing ecological research in the real world. Ecologists cope with this circumstance in several ways:

1. They use the best sampling methodology and technology that their research budget can afford.
2. They do not report observations using excessive numbers of **significant figures**; because ecological-data are typically variable, they are usually reported with only 2–3 significant figures. This is most easily explained by examples: all of the following numbers have three significant figures: 444; 4.44; 0.00444; and 4.44×10^3.
3. The sampling variation is measured and reported using statistical parameters, such as the observed *range* of values about the calculated *average* (or *mean*) and the *standard deviation* (SD) or *standard error* (SE is the SD divided by the square root of the sample size). In an experiment, the statistical significance of the differences of the averages among treatments is analyzed using *t-tests* or *analysis of variance* if the data distribution is normal, or by chi-square or other non-parametric tests for non-normal data. Statistical and mathematical ecology are big subject areas and we cannot explore this fascinating arena in any detail here, but excellent textbooks are available that can be consulted for additional information and guidance.

Environmental and biological complexities can be daunting to ecologists even as they strive to understand them, but they do reflect a reality of the natural world. In essence, all work in ecology is intended to make progress in sorting out these hard-to-know attributes of ecosystems and hopefully to eventually discover their organizing principles.

Subject Areas of Ecology

Many ecologists work out of curiosity—their interest is to better understand the natural world. This "pure" science has intrinsic value, and it often results in knowledge that is of socioeconomic value. Other ecologists, however, are interested in "applied" research that is related to such important issues as

- finding improved ways of managing biological resources that are of economic importance, such as in agriculture, forestry, fisheries, and hunting;
- preventing or repairing ecological damage that has been caused by pollution, disturbances, and other causes of degradation;

- planning and management that is useful to the conservation of biodiversity-at-risk, including ways of conserving particular rare species, as well the establishing and stewarding of protected areas;
- managing ecological functions, such as productivity, hydrology, erosion, and nutrient cycling, including ways of managing greenhouse gases (such as promoting the fixation of carbon dioxide into the biomass of ecosystems).

Ecology is pursued mostly by specialists working within a number of smaller subject areas, although many of them overlap. Some of these fields have their own specialist journals and societies. Within this context, the major subject areas of ecology are the following:

- **Population ecology** is the study of the dynamics of the abundance of species, including environmental influences on those changes.
- **Community ecology** examines interactions occurring among populations of species within an ecological community.
- **Physiological ecology** involves study of the adaptive biochemistry and physiology of organisms in response to environmental conditions.
- **Behavioural ecology** examines the ways that behaviour adapts to changes in environmental conditions.
- **Ecosystem ecology (functional ecology)** studies the flows of energy and nutrients among organisms and the abiotic environment.
- **Systems ecology** uses a holistic approach to investigate the attributes of ecosystems.
- **Landscape ecology** examines the structural and functional attributes of ecosystems at large scales, including influences on the spatial and temporal dynamics of their communities.
- **Evolutionary ecology** is an overarching approach that provides context for much of ecology; the core theme is evolutionary aspects of adaptive ecological change, including interactions with selective forces.
- **Statistical ecology** involves the application of statistical methodologies to examining and explaining patterns and processes, while **mathematical ecology** involves the use of quantitative models.
- **Theoretical ecology** involves the identification of theories regarding the organization and functioning of ecosystems, and the use of rigorous methodologies to test their veracity; the field is particularly relevant to population ecology and biogeography.
- **Environmental ecology** is the study of ecological responses to stressors, usually with a focus on anthropogenic pollution and disturbance.
- **Paleoecology** deals with populations, communities, and ecosystems that existed in the distant past, while historical ecology examines more recent changes.
- **Applied ecology** is the integration of ecological knowledge with economic needs, such as finding improved ways to cultivate crops or to mitigate environmental damage.
- **Conservation ecology** is the application of ecological knowledge to the stewardship of biodiversity and protected areas.
- **Restoration ecology** involves the use of ecological knowledge and practices to repair environmental damage, such as by establishing vegetation on derelict land or by re-creating endangered natural ecosystems.

The subject areas of ecology can also be segregated according to the kinds of organisms that are being examined. In this sense, major subject areas are

- **animal ecology**, which is the study of the populations, ecophysiology, productivity, and behaviour of wild animals and their communities;
- **plant ecology**, which covers similar fields but with respect to plants and vegetation; and
- **microbial ecology**, which is again similar, but often the focus is on functional processes, such as decomposition and nutrient cycling.

A further way to segregate fields of study in ecology involves major kinds of habitats and environments:

- **Marine ecology** is the study of any aspects of ecology in the oceanic realm.
- **Forest ecology** investigates ecosystems that are dominated by trees, including non-treed successional stages that are recovering from a recent disturbance of a mature forest.
- **Freshwater ecology** is the study of lakes (limnology), ponds, rivers, streams, and wetlands.
- Arctic ecology, tropical ecology, desert ecology, and similar focal areas involve studies of those tagged natural environments.
- **Urban ecology** involves studying biodiversity and processes in urbanized habitats, with a focus on problems that can be mitigated by naturalization and the establishment of protected areas.

Ecologists

An **ecologist** is a specialist who studies some aspect of ecology. Ecologists are highly qualified scientists, meaning they have at least an undergraduate degree in science, although many also have graduate degrees, up to the Ph.D. Other than their university degree, however, not many ecologists are certified as being a specialist practitioner of ecology, in the way that doctors are licensed to practise medicine, engineers for engineering, and lawyers for law.

However, it *is* possible to become a certified ecologist. For example, the Ecological Society of America, a prestigious U.S. organization, will certify people at various professional levels of ecology, if asked to do so. Typically, however, this is only done by people working in the private

A CANADIAN ECOLOGIST 1.1

Chris Pielou: Mathematical Ecology and More

E. C. Pielou

Chris Pielou

E. C. (Chris) Pielou (b. 1924) earned her Ph.D. (and later the higher doctorate, D.Sc.) from the University of London (England). She began her career in Canada in 1963, as a research scientist in the federal Ministries of Forestry and Agriculture, before shifting to academia. She has been a professor at Queen's University (1968–1971), a Killam Professor at Dalhousie University (1974–1981), and an Alberta Oil Sands Environmental Research Professor working out of the University of Lethbridge (1981–1986). At various times she held visiting professorships at North Carolina State University, Yale University, and the University of Sydney, Australia.

Although "retired" since 1986, Pielou remains extraordinarily active, writing books at an impressive pace and serving on various scientific panels, among them the Clayoquot Sound Scientific Panel, which recommended better forestry practices for the forests around the Sound on the west coast of Vancouver Island, and the National Research Council (USA) study on the cumulative effects of oil and gas activities on Alaska's North Slope.

Pielou is best known for her research and books about the application of mathematics to ecological investigations, entailing the use of advanced probability theory. In fact, her explanations and demonstrations of those methodologies have been so significant that she is considered to be the originator of the field of mathematical ecology. This important contribution is recognized by the E. C. Pielou Award, given annually by the Statistical Ecology Section of the Ecological Society of America. Pielou's overall contribution to ecology has also been recognized by her receiving such awards as the Lawson Medal of the Canadian Botanical Association in 1984, an Eminent Ecologist Award from the Ecological Society of America, honorary membership of the British Ecological Society, foreign honorary membership of the American Academy of Arts and Science, and honorary doctorates from Dalhousie University and the University of British Columbia. Chris Pielou's extraordinary career and ideas have been inspirational to ecologists worldwide, perhaps more so because some of her greatest contributions occurred during a time when women were relatively uncommon among the practitioners of ecology.

Pielou has published many well-regarded papers in high-level ecological journals, and books about a wide diversity of topics in ecology and, most recently, popular natural history. Perhaps her most influential book is *Introduction to Mathematical Ecology* (1969), and its second edition *Mathematical Ecology* (1977), which essentially sparked the genesis of that field in that it inspired many ecologists to use and further develop techniques that she identified and advocated in it. Books by E. C. Pielou include the following:

Introduction to Mathematical Ecology. 1969. New York, NY: Wiley-Interscience.
Population and Community Ecology: Principles and Methods. 1974. New York, NY: Gordon and Breach.
Ecological Diversity. 1975. New York: Wiley.
Mathematical Ecology. 1977. New York, NY: Wiley.
Biogeography. 1979. New York: Wiley.
The Interpretation of Ecological Data: A Primer on Classification and Ordination. 1984. New York, NY: Wiley.
The World of Northern Evergreens. 1988. Ithaca, NY: Cornell University Press.
After the Ice Age: The Return of Life to Glaciated North America. 1992. Chicago, IL: University of Chicago Press.
A Naturalist's Guide to the Arctic. 1994. Chicago, IL: University of Chicago Press.
Fresh Water. 2000. Chicago, IL: University of Chicago Press.
The Energy of Nature. 2001. Chicago, IL: University of Chicago Press.

sector, such as in a consulting firm that provides services related to environmental planning or impact assessment. Interestingly, not many professors who are specialized to teach ecology are certified as being ecologists, including none of the people who wrote this textbook. Nevertheless, they are highly qualified practitioners.

An ecologist is not the same thing as an *environmental scientist*. The latter is a generalist who uses and applies any kind of science-related knowledge that is relevant to environmental issues. This might include atmospheric and water chemistry, climatic influences, and damage caused by pollution or disturbance to organisms and ecosystems. An ecologist is also not the same thing as an *environmentalist*, who is any person with a significant involvement with environmental issues, especially in advocacy, which means taking a strong public stance on issues. Nevertheless, many ecologists might refer to themselves as being environmental scientists, and most would also be concerned with environmental issues and so would consider themselves to be environmentalists. But the reverses are not necessarily true.

Ecologists work in all parts of the world, although most reside in relatively developed countries, such as Canada. Although the general methodologies and knowledge of ecology are universal in their scope, a great deal of local and ecoregional context is needed. In fact, it was in recognition of that ecoregional perspective that the authors undertook to prepare this introductory textbook about ecology within the context of the biodiversity and environments of Canada.

Many ecologists have productive careers as professors in universities and colleges, or as scientists in government agencies, in the private sector, or in non-governmental organizations (NGOs or environmental charities, such as Ducks Unlimited Canada, the Nature Conservancy of Canada, and the World Wildlife Fund). Some ecologists working in Canada have become well-known in their field of study—as researchers, authors, and advocates for science and for conserving the natural world. A selection of these people is highlighted in all chapters of this book, in the special boxes titled "A Canadian Ecologist."

The Scientific Method

In view of the exceeding complexity of the natural world—and especially those aspects that involve biology and ecology—it is necessary to adopt a rigorous scientific approach to investigations in those fields. But what is meant by a scientific approach?

Origins of Science

The word **science** originates from the Latin word *scientia*, which means "knowing" or "knowledge." The purview of science is to further a lofty goal of achieving knowledge—to use systematic and objective methodologies to better understand the natural world. This includes the discovery of general principles, which if understood can provide insight into factors that control the structure and function of nature and so would allow predictions to be made about the future. Science is also characterized by a rapidly growing body of knowledge that is based on empirical (observational), theoretical, and practical (applied) ideas and observations.

Thinking people have always wondered about "big questions," such as existence and the place of humans within the natural world. The initial ways of knowing about these problems involved belief (or faith-based) systems based on religion, morality, and aesthetics. Even today, many people choose faith-based understanding associated with religion as a preferred alternative to knowledge gained from scientific investigation. This is particularly the case of philosophical issues, such as the existence of God, discovering a meaning of life that goes beyond mere existence, the difference between right and wrong, and understanding the inherent value of art and other aesthetic expressions.

Nevertheless, science is the best system to use when investigating questions about past, present, and future conditions of the natural world. This includes the origin of life, its evolutionary change, the ecological context of humanity, and the characteristics and functioning of ecosystems. Of course, many people have answered these questions to their own satisfaction through the received wisdom of belief systems. Their faith-based interpretations may, however, be diametrically opposed to conclusions derived from rational scientific investigations, a circumstance that has resulted in controversy and conflict. This is an ongoing difficulty and context in our society—it involves disagreement between belief systems and science about important issues in biology, medicine, and the environment. While acknowledging this discordant fact, we must understand that science-based investigations are fundamental to the pursuit of knowledge in ecology.

The modern practice of science developed from a much-older endeavour known as natural philosophy. This was a way of learning used by classical Greeks and other ancients who were interested in rational enquiries into the meaning of natural phenomena and of existence itself. Of course, their old-time investigations were relatively unsophisticated in methodology, often involving only the application of logic. Modern science is considered to have begun with the methodical studies of several well-known practitioners of the 16th and 17th centuries, such as

- Nicolaus Copernicus (1473–1543), a Polish astronomer who originated a heliocentric theory of the solar system, in which planets orbit the Sun;
- Galileo Galilei (1564–1642), an Italian who worked in astronomy and the physics of objects in motion; and
- Isaac Newton (1642–1727), an Englishman who formulated laws about the motion of objects, including the role of gravity, as well as the nature of light, and who invented the mathematics of calculus.

Goals and Methods of Science

A higher goal of scientific enquiry is to formulate general principles about the workings of the universe (for example, see Chapter 4 for an explanation of the laws of thermodynamics that govern transformations of energy). However, many natural phenomena involve extremely complex systems that may never be fully understood in terms of physical laws. This is particularly true of much of the organization and functioning of organisms and ecosystems.

Scientists undertake systematic observations of natural phenomena and conduct experiments to try to determine their controlling influences. Scientific investigations may be pure or applied. Pure science is driven by curiosity—it is a search for knowledge without regard to its usefulness, including to human welfare. Applied science, in contrast, deals with questions that are economically important. Applied scientists might work to discovery new machines or other technologies, improved ways to manage natural resources, or methods to reduce pollution or to deal with other environmental problems.

Logic

Francis Bacon (1561–1626), an English philosopher, was a promoter of the emerging methodologies of rational scientific investigations. His greatest influence was as an advocate of the use of **inductive logic**, in which accumulations of evidence based on observations of nature and the results of experiments are used to reach conclusions about phenomena. Consider the following application of inductive logic, applied to an ecological question:

- *Observation 1:* Plants are observed to increase their biomass even though they do not feed on other organisms.
- *Observation 2:* If plants are kept in the dark, they do not grow larger; rather, they eventually die.
- *Observation 3:* If deprived of water, plants do not grow—they desiccate and perish.
- *Observation 4:* If deprived of nutrients, such as carbon dioxide, nitrate, phosphate, or potassium, plants do not grow, or they do so extremely slowly.
- *Inductive conclusion:* Plants are able to grow only if they have access to light, moisture, and nutrients.

Deductive logic is a different way of reasoning that involves making an assumption, or several of them, and then drawing logical conclusions. In such a case, the veracity of the assumptions determines the truth of subsequent inferences. Therefore, if assumptions are based on incorrect supernatural belief, or on false information, then any deduced conclusions are likely to be in error. Here is an example of the use of deductive logic, applied to an ecological question:

- *Assumption:* Sunlight captured by photosynthetic organisms is the foundation of ecological productivity, because that energy drives the biosynthesis of simple sugars from carbon dioxide and water (see Chapter 4).
- *Deduced conclusion:* Biological energy fixation cannot occur in a dark environment.

For a long time, this assumption and deduction were considered to be true. In 1892, however, Sergei Winogradsky (1856–1953), a Russian scientist, discovered that certain bacteria could link their autotrophic productivity to energy released during the oxidation of sulphide chemicals. This process, now known as chemosynthesis, occurs in environments where sulphide compounds become exposed to oxygen, for example, if coal mining exposes iron sulphide (FeS_2) to the atmosphere. This allows chemosynthetic *Thiobacillus* bacteria to grow while generating sulphate and acidity and sometimes causing a severe environmental problem known as acid-mine drainage.

In general, inductive logic plays a much stronger role in the conduct of science than deductive logic. However, conclusions based on either kind of logic depend on the accuracy of the data or presumed knowledge that is used. Deductive logic works well only if the original assumptions are correct, and inductive conclusions based on faulty data will be erroneous.

Facts, Hypotheses, and Experiments

A **fact** is an event or a thing that is true—it is known to have happened or to exist. Facts are confirmed as being genuine on the basis of evidence from experience and scientific investigations.

By comparison, a **hypothesis** is a proposed explanation of a phenomenon or its cause. Logic, inference, statistics, and mathematics may be used to formulate a hypothesis, usually as a statement that can be tested by experiments or other kinds of research. In fact, a hypothesis should always be designed in a way that allows it to be proven wrong. If a hypothesis cannot be refuted, then the methods of science cannot test its predictions. Here is an example of a faulty hypothesis of that sort: "Cats are so intelligent that they are able prevent humans from discovering their cleverness." A better hypothesis would be "cats are intelligent," because it can be examined in various ways, including by standard methodologies in ethology (the science of animal behaviour).

A **theory** is a bigger idea that relates to a unifying principle—one that explains a large body of knowledge, such as facts based on observational and experimental evidence and any laws that are based on them. Examples of celebrated theories in science are

- gravitation, which was first proposed by Isaac Newton (1642–1727);
- evolution by natural selection, published in 1858 by its co-discoverers, English naturalists Charles Darwin (1809–1882) and Alfred Russel Wallace (1823–1913); and
- relativity, originating with German–Swiss physicist Albert Einstein (1879–1955).

These well-established theories have been examined by a great deal of research and so they are supported by increasingly large bodies of scientific evidence. This does not mean, however, that future research will not refute them and by so doing prove them to be false. In fact, scientific research is commonly designed to test whether the predictions of a hypothesis or a larger theory can be disproved (or falsified).

In practice, the **scientific method** begins with a researcher identifying a question about a phenomenon—about some aspect of the organization or functioning of the natural world. Often, the question is developed from the "bottom" upward—using inductive logic and an existing body of knowledge (**Figure 1.5**). The question is interpreted in terms of existing theory, and hypotheses are formulated to test predictions of the theory. The hypotheses are then reformulated as **null hypotheses**, which seek to disprove the hypotheses. Research is then undertaken to test the null hypotheses. This research can involve controlled experiments, as well as careful observations of patterns in nature. If a null hypothesis is proven to be correct, then the original hypothesis is incorrect and is discarded. However, if research disproves a null hypothesis, it is still necessary to conduct further research that re-tests the original hypothesis by formulating additional null hypotheses. Eventually, if a large body of evidence accumulates that fails to falsify a hypothesis, it helps to substantiate the original theory.

Because null hypotheses seek to disprove rather than support a question, they are an efficient way to conduct research. Consider a case in which a hypothesis has been subjected to a great deal of research and is supported by numerous confirming experiments and observations. This circumstance may support a conditional acceptance of the hypothesis, but no amount of confirming evidence can "prove" it. In fact, as soon as a well-defined research question confirms a null hypothesis, the original hypothesis is disproved. This is why it is most efficient to do research that proceeds immediately to examine null hypotheses and why the scientific method seeks to disprove the predictions of hypotheses.

An **experiment** is an investigation that is designed to provide evidence that tests a hypothesis. A **manipulative experiment** involves modifications of one or more **variables** that are hypothesized to influence a natural phenomenon. The results of manipulated treatments are compared against a **control**, which was not modified and sets the baseline condition. For instance, tree seedlings growing in the understorey of a forest might be exposed to the following set of experimental manipulations:

- *Treatment 1:* The control, with no modification of environmental factors
- *Treatment 2:* Nitrogen fertilizer is added.
- *Treatment 3:* Phosphorus fertilizer is added.
- *Treatment 4:* Water is added.

If the seedlings grow better in response to any of the additions (compared with the control), then that factor would be judged to be limiting the productivity. On the other hand, if none of the treatments resulted in higher productivity than the control, the conclusion would be that some other environmental factor is limiting, perhaps inadequate light availability because of a shading overstory of tree foliage.

So-called **natural experiments** involve studying gradients in nature or other variations of environmental

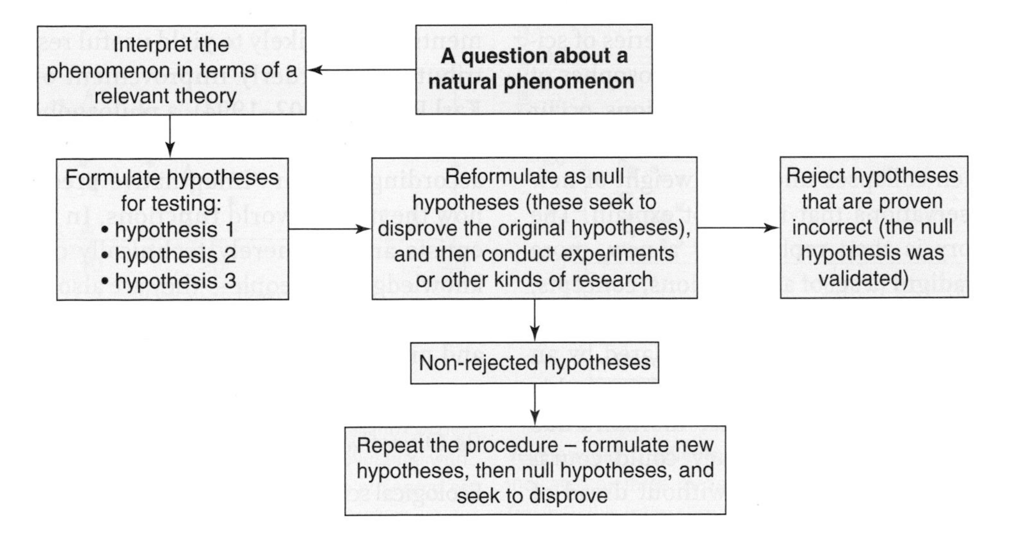

FIGURE 1.5
Diagrammatic Representation of the Scientific Method. The process is to formulate a question about the natural world, interpret it using the existing theory, then develop hypotheses, and re-formulate them as null hypotheses, which are tested by research. If a null hypothesis is found to be correct, then the original hypothesis must be rejected. However, if the null hypothesis is proven incorrect, the original hypothesis is not necessarily proven to be correct. Rather, it is subjected to additional examination, but again with the intent of disproving it.

economic considerations than to scientific ones. This is particularly the case if scientific uncertainty about an issue exists, which is often the case. Because of ongoing controversy about such concerns as global climate change, the endangerment and extinction of biodiversity, the diminishment of natural resources, and the importance of various kinds of pollution, decision makers are receiving scientific advice that is to some degree contrary or ambiguous. Moreover, decision makers often worry about short-term implications of their decisions on their chances for re-election or continued employment, or on the economic activity of their company or of society. They may view those considerations as being more important than the consequences of ecological and other kinds of environmental damage (see Chapter 17). This circumstance has a great influence on how seriously they consider advice offered by ecologists or other scientists.

It is obvious and intuitive that the knowledge of ecology is crucial to the development and implementation of a sustainable human economy. However, ecologists must work hard to ensure that their well-considered advice is having an appropriately serious influence on societal-level decisions that carry the risk of causing environmental damages. Ultimately, this goes beyond the conduct of excellent research—it also requires a deep engagement of some ecologists in consultative and advocacy activities. Ecologists and their knowledge are too important to remain coolly detached from important issues about which their advice is required and should be heeded.

VOCABULARY OF ECOLOGY

phenotypic plasticity, p. 25
photosynthetic, p. 11
phototroph (or photoautotroph), p. 11
physiological ecology, p. 17
plant ecology, p. 17
population, p. 8
population ecology, p. 17
precipitation, p. 12
precision, p. 16
predation, p. 5
renewable resource, p. 27
restoration ecology, p. 17
science, p. 19
scientific method, p. 21
scientific revolution, p. 22
significant figures, p. 16
species, p. 8
stand-replacing disturbance, p. 10
statistical ecology, p. 17
stratosphere, p. 12
structural attributes, p. 6
succession, p. 10
sustainable economy, p. 26
systems ecology, p. 17
theoretical ecology, p. 17
theory, p. 20
transpiration, p. 12
troposphere, p. 12
urban ecology, p. 17
variable, p. 21

QUESTIONS FOR REVIEW AND DISCUSSION

1. What is the subject matter of ecology? Explain the difference between curiosity-driven and applied work in ecology.
2. Make a list of important environmental factors, including abiotic and biotic ones. Explain how they influence the productivity of organisms and ecosystems.
3. Which levels of the hierarchical organization of the universe are most relevant to ecology? Provide a brief explanation of each of them, including how they are linked to levels above and below.
4. What is fitness, and how is it related to evolution by natural selection?
5. Why do ecologists have "physics envy"?
6. What is the scientific method? Explain a case in which that methodology is applied to investigating a question in ecological research.
7. Explain how the knowledge of ecology is important to the sustainability of the human economy.

HELPFUL WEBSITES

BRITISH ECOLOGICAL SOCIETY (BES)
http://www.britishecologicalsociety.org/
The BES is the professional organization for ecologists in the United Kingdom. Excellent educational resources are posted on its website.

CANADIAN SOCIETY FOR ECOLOGY AND EVOLUTION (CSEE)
http://www.ecoevo.ca/
The CSEE is the Canadian professional organization for ecologists. It exists to promote the study of ecology and evolution, to raise awareness with the public and decision makers, and to foster interactions among ecologists.

ECOLOGICAL SOCIETY OF AMERICA (ESA)
http://esa.org/
The ESA is a leading organization for ecologists in North America. It is a professional organization, and also posts excellent educational resources on its website. The ESA has a Canada Chapter (http://www.esa.org/canada/) devoted to the ecology of Canadian ecoregions.

ECOLOGY GLOBAL NETWORK
http://www.ecology.com/index.php
This website has information about ecology and environmental issues.

NATIONAL CENTER FOR SCIENCE EDUCATION
http://www.natcenscied.org/article.asp
The National Center for Science Education is an interest group whose mandate involves promoting the teaching of science and evolution.

PROJECT 2061, AMERICAN ASSOCIATION FOR THE ADVANCEMENT OF SCIENCE (AAAS)
http://www.project2061.org/default_flash.htm
The American Association for the Advancement of Science provides an overview of issues related to science literacy. Project 2061 is a long-term AAAS initiative to advance literacy in science, mathematics, and technology.

You'll find a rich array of additional resources for *Ecology* at www.ecology.nelson.com.

Clearly, differences of environmental factors, either abiotic or biotic, can act as agents of natural selection—evolution may occur in response to the conditions of relatively benign environments or to more stressful circumstances. Individuals whose phenotype renders them better adapted to coping with their environmental opportunities and challenges will have relatively high fitness compared with others in their population. In a sense, higher fitness can be interpreted as representing greater "success" in life, achieved by an individual reproducing prolifically, having progeny that themselves reproduce, and whose genotype has a disproportionately large influence on subsequent generations. Moreover, evolutionary ecologists believe that, in a general sense, individuals strive to maximize their fitness by optimizing the degree to which their genetic attributes will influence future generations of their species (Dawkins, 1976).

The effects of environmental influences are also relevant at ecological scales beyond that of individual organisms—such as those of populations, communities, and ecoscapes. The least difficult environments are distinguished by moisture, nutrients, temperature, and biotic interactions that are present at levels that are not unduly constraining to biological processes, while damage caused by disturbances, such as wildfire, windstorms, and disease, are rare. Relatively beneficial conditions such as these will allow for a high degree of ecosystem development, in the sense of relatively dense biodiversity (in terms of species per unit area), high structural complexity, and rapid productivity and nutrient cycling. On land, this acme is represented by tropical rainforest, and in the oceans by coral reefs.

On the other hand, difficult environmental conditions may only allow ecosystems with sparse biodiversity and productivity to develop. If the conditions are sufficiently inimical, no life or ecosystems are viable. As far as we know, such inhospitable conditions occur everywhere beyond the limits of Earth's biosphere, and even on this planet lifeless places are plentiful—occurring deep within the crust, on top of the highest mountains, in volcanic fumaroles, and in other utterly inhospitable places. Nevertheless, some forms of life occur in remarkably hostile conditions (see Ecology in Depth 2.1).

2.2 Environmental Stressors

Stressors are environmental factors that limit the performance of organisms, populations, communities, or larger ecoscapes. In the sense meant here, "performance" of an organism is related to such attributes as its productivity, behaviour, and reproductive fitness, relative to the genetic potential. To some degree, all

Bill Freedman

A tropical forest represents the acme of ecological development on land. This view of tropical rainforest is in Manu National Park, in Amazonian Peru.

ECOLOGY IN DEPTH 2.1

Extreme Environments

Abiotic environments are typical of virtually all the universe—save only for the relatively miniscule biosphere of Earth, the spatial bounds of which are defined by the presence of organisms. The outer limits of that biotic envelope, where life and ecosystems are barely viable, are referred to as **extreme environments**. Even on this habitable planet, however, extensive physical space is devoid of life—this extends from reaches deep in the crust to soaring tracts in the atmosphere and diverse places in between. The highest and lowest of these outermost places of life are

- *The stratosphere*—viable microorganisms have been recovered from atmospheric samples collected as high as 41 km, where ultraviolet radiation is intense and the temperature about −20°C (Wainwright et al., 2003).
- *In fissured geological formations in the crust*, as deep as 3 km (Golubic et al., 1981), in which endolithic ("within-rock") bacteria survive in a warm, high-pressure environment by oxidizing sulphides and sparse organic matter (see Chapter 4 for an explanation of chemosynthesis).

Extreme environments also occur in more intermediate places where conditions are intense because of geological or other circumstances:

- *Environments of severe acidity or alkalinity*, such as pHs less than 3 associated with the chemosynthetic oxidation of sulphide minerals by acidophilic ("acid-loving") *Thiobacillus* bacteria (see Chapter 4), and those with pH greater than 9 and supporting specialized alkaliphilic ("alkali-loving") microbes.
- *Hot environments* associated with geothermal heat, such as eruptions of searing water at geysers on land or at deep-sea vents, or in deep crustal places, in which thermophilic ("heat-loving") archaea microbes may survive even at temperatures exceeding 100°C.
- *Extremely dry habitats*, such as the most arid deserts, which may support only xerotolerant ("dry-tolerant") microbial crusts, such as that formed by *Microcoleus* cyanobacteria in salt desert (Campbell, 1979).
- *High-altitude habitats*, above the alpine tundra, in which extreme climatic and rocky conditions allow only a meagre productivity of lichens and bryophytes, a thin abundance of invertebrates, and constrained microbial activity.

Sometimes pollution can be intense enough to represent an extreme environment. For example, seams of bituminous shale (a low-grade coal) have spontaneously ignited and burned for centuries at the Smoking Hills, a remote place in the western Northwest Territories (see Ecology in Depth 2.2). This results in intense "natural pollution" of the nearby tundra with sulphur dioxide, which causes toxicity to plants and severe acidification, to the degree that the most intensely affected habitats are non-vegetated. This natural damage is similar to that caused by smelters that emit SO_2, such as the ones near Sudbury, Ontario (Freedman, 2010).

For that matter, many habitats constructed by people are extreme environments, including any expanses of concrete or asphalt, on which few organisms are able to survive. Often this does not have to be the case—many anthropogenic habitats could, in fact, be naturalized to some degree, for example, by allowing some vegetation to establish and grow. Increasingly, these benefits are being pursued through a naturalization approach to horticulture and also by the novel eco-technology of "green roofs," in which vegetation is grown on flat roof-tops instead of just covering them with asphalt or other abiotic surfaces. The improved ecological conditions provide habitat for biodiversity and also foster greater levels of environmental services, such as heat retention during the winter, cooling in summer, and carbon-storage benefits that are associated with well-developed vegetation.

organisms are affected by environmental stressors. They also affect ecosystems at larger scales, where performance might be indicated by the rates of such functions as decomposition, nutrient cycling, or productivity, compared with a less-stressed situation. Depending on the intensity of a stressor regime, the growth and fitness of individuals may be diminished or made impossible, and the development of ecosystems may be similarly constrained.

Environmental stressors that affect the structure and function of natural ecosystems are associated with such factors as

- inadequate or excessive regimes of temperature, moisture, nutrients, or physical space in which to grow;
- competition, predation, disease, and other biological interactions; and
- events of mass destruction (or **disturbance**), such as wildfires, windstorms, and lava flows.

In any particular circumstance, natural stressors may affect different species in dissimilar ways—typically, some members of a community will suffer damage from changes in a stressor regime, while others realize a benefit. Consider, for instance, the

A wildfire may be a stand-replacing disturbance, but it also creates opportunities for species of early stages of succession. This recent burn of conifer forest in Yukon is visually dominated by fireweed (*Epilobium angustifolium*), a perennial plant that may be abundant following a forest fire.

case of a wildfire that affects a mature stand of lodgepole pine (*Pinus contorta*) in the mountains of British Columbia or western Alberta. The trees may be killed by scorching or combustion, and the profound habitat changes are detrimental to local populations of most plant and animal species of the mature forest. However, the recently disturbed ecosystem provides other species with suitable habitat, such as the perennial herb fireweed (*Epilobium angustifolium*), and they will invade the site and be prominent during its post-fire succession. It might even be argued that, although the mature pines are killed by the disturbance, their large-scale metapopulation (a regional population) may benefit. This is because wildfire helps to prepare a seedbed that fosters the regeneration of cohorts of this pine species, which is necessary for its longer-term persistence on the landscape.

At any time and place, organisms are interacting with a complex regime of environmental stressors—this **exposure** can be intense and instantaneous, as in the case of a disturbance. Alternatively, it may accumulate over some period of time, as may occur with certain chemicals that increasingly biomagnify in long-lived organisms or in those at the top of a food web (persistent chlorinated hydrocarbons, such as DDT and PCBs, are well-known for doing this, as is methylmercury). In either case, if an exposure is intense enough to exceed a threshold of biological or ecological tolerance, it will cause a change to occur, called a **response**. This is the so-called **SER model** of stressor—exposure—response **(Figure 2.1).**

The idea of **tolerance** (or **resistance**) is important, because individual organisms, populations, communities, and ecoscapes all have a capability to function in a "healthy" manner within a range of intensities of environmental stressors—that is, without undergoing change that would be judged as representing damage. The tolerance of an increasing intensity of environmental stress can take various forms, some of which are illustrated in **Figure 2.2.** In model A there is little tolerance, and even a small increase in the intensity of a stressor results in a large ecological response. In model B, there is a direct proportionality between the stressor and the response. In model C there is some

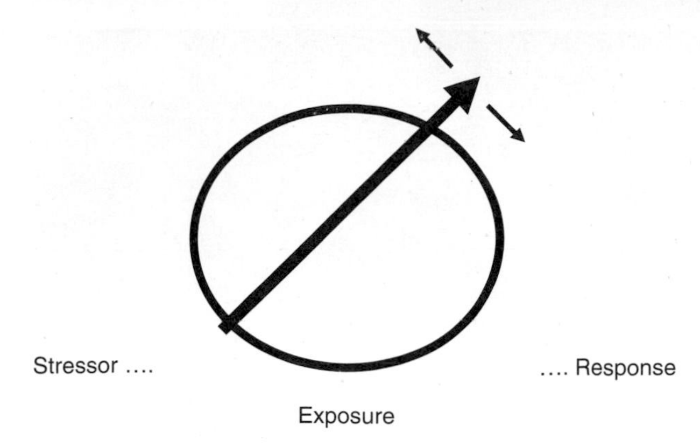

FIGURE 2.1

The SER Model. Exposure to environmental stressors may result in a biological or an ecological response. The symbol of a dial suggests that the intensity of exposure can vary, in a manner similar to a potentiometer—the volume knob of a radio, which can be turned to the left to diminish the level of sound, or to the right to intensify it. If the biological or ecological tolerance of intensified stress is exceeded, then a response will result.

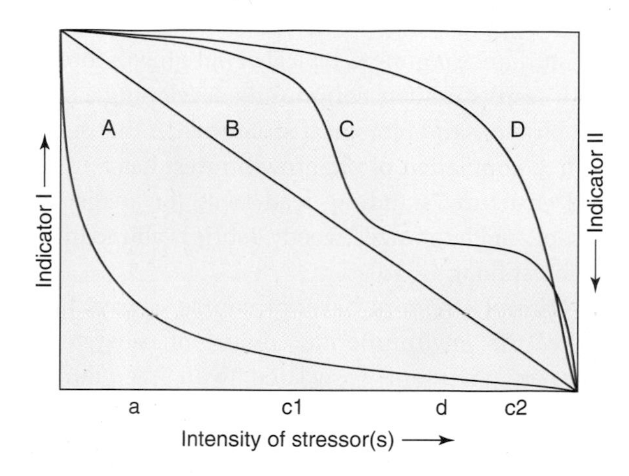

FIGURE 2.2

Stressors and Ecological Responses. The curves are hypothetical stress–response relationships, and they depict variations in the resistance to change brought about by an increase in environmental stress. The response variables may either decrease (Indicator 1) or increase (Indicator II) in value. A, B, C, and D represent relationships between increased stress and change in the indicator (and in ecological integrity): A is most valuable as an early-warning tool because it exhibits an initial rapid change, but this slows after a threshold (a) has been exceeded; B responds steadily and is a consistent measure throughout the range of the stressor; C exhibits a stepwise response with rapid change at one threshold (c1) followed by relative stability and then rapid response at another (c2); and D provides a late-warning signal because it shows a strong response only after a threshold of tolerance (d) is exceeded at a relatively advanced stage of ecological degradation. The shape of the response curves may differ substantially for increased and decreased stress because of resilience (hysteresis) in the stressor–response function.

SOURCES: Figure modified from Freedman (1995) and Lapaix et al. (2009).

resistance, but once it is overcome a small additional intensification of stress causes a large ecological change to occur, eventually levelling off at a new plateau of tolerance, which can in turn be overcome by a further increase in stress. In model D there is considerable tolerance, but if the intensity of stress is large enough, it too can be overcome and rapid ecological change will be caused.

Resilience is another important idea. It refers to the speed and degree to which an organism, population, community, or ecoscape can recover to its original condition following an event of disturbance or after some other stressor regime becomes lessened. An example of a system with a high degree of resilience is boreal forest dominated by jack pine (*Pinus banksiana*), which typically regenerates to similar stands following a wildfire. In contrast, the widespread collapse of the stocks of cod (*Gadus morhua*) in the northwestern Atlantic Ocean, caused by excessive fishing, has not been followed by a substantial recovery even though commercial harvesting has been greatly reduced since 1992 (see also Chapters 5 and 15). It appears that the degraded cod-dominated communities have been changed in some fundamental way, and this, in part, is preventing a full recovery of the stocks and ecosystem of this species.

An additional notion is that of **stability**, which refers to constancy over time. Stability may be due to resistance to environmental change as well as the degree of resilience after a perturbation.

Environmental stressors can exert their influence in various ways. They may have a **chronic** (or continuous) presence and exercise their influence over an extended time. For example, although nutrients in soil or water vary over space and time, they tend to have a relatively continuous influence on the productivity of local plants, as do many climate-related factors, such as temperature and moisture. Chronic environmental stressors have a great influence on ecological development, and if severe, they may restrict it to a relatively simple condition and low level of biodiversity, such as desert or tundra.

Other stressors involve a disturbance—a powerful but short-lived event of destruction. Examples include wildfire, severe windstorms, and irruptive biological agents, such as an infestation of defoliating insects or a disease epidemic (see Chapter 10). Some disturbances have an extensive effect in that they damage entire communities (these are stand-replacing disturbances) and sometimes even landscapes. For instance, millions of hectares of boreal forest are disturbed by wildfires in most years in remote regions of Canada, particularly in boreal and montane forests. Similarly, wide-ranging damage can be caused by irruptive insects, such as mountain pine beetle (*Dendroctonus ponderosae*), which causes extensive mortality in pine forest in British Columbia, and spruce budworm (*Choristoneura fumiferana*), which kills fir and spruce trees in eastern Canada. A particularly vast and persistent disturbance ended about 12 000 years ago, when

After glacial meltback, a new ecosystem develops by primary succession, which requires that organisms colonize the site after it is released from the ice cover. This is a view of a region still covered by glaciers on Ellesmere Island, Nunavut.

Bill Freedman

the continental-scale glaciers that had covered almost all of Canada in enormous ice-sheets up to several kilometres thick melted back. All of the ecosystems in Canada have developed since that most-recent glacial epoch, which ended 10 000–12 000 years ago.

Disturbances are followed by a period of community-level recovery over time, known as **succession.** It is typical that communities that occur during the earlier stages of succession will include species that are specifically adapted to environmental conditions of recently disturbed habitats. This includes a relatively low intensity of competition and a high availability of site resources. In fact, these relatively short-lived species may dominate the earlier years of the post-disturbance recovery. In forests, the successional recovery after a stand-replacing disturbance, such as a wildfire or clear-cut, often results in an even-aged cohort of trees dominating the mature community that eventually develops.

A **primary succession** occurs in situations where a disturbance was severe enough to destroy all organisms on the affected terrain. This obliterates the inherent ability to regenerate, so the site has to be invaded from surviving habitats elsewhere. Successions after deglaciation, lava flows, and severe wildfires are of this type. By comparison, **secondary succession** includes regeneration by organisms that survived the disturbance, as well as those that later invaded. Because secondary succession begins with an inherent regenerative capacity associated with the survivors, it is a much more rapid and vigorous process than primary succession.

In other cases, disturbance may be local in scale. For instance, the death of a large tree within an otherwise intact forest will create an area of local damage, referred to as a **microdisturbance**. This smaller-scale damage is followed by a **microsuccession** of vigorously growing plants that attempt to occupy the newly available gap in the forest canopy. This sort of disturbance regime is typical of old-growth forests, and it results in their community developing a complex physical and biological structure. In this sense, the tree population of old-growth forest has a multi-aged structure, standing dead trees (or snags) are present, and large-sized woody debris is abundant on the forest floor.

Natural stressors have, of course, always been part of the environmental context of ecosystems. However, stressors associated with the human economy are now having an increasingly important influence on the species and ecosystems of Earth. In fact, over vast areas **anthropogenic stressors** are now dominant over natural ones. In general, these influences of humans are having a damaging ecological effect, in the sense that they are

- diminishing the vital stocks of natural resources that are needed to sustain the human economy;
- decreasing the abundances of many species, and even of entire natural ecosystems, to the degree of endangerment and even extinction; and
- degrading essential environmental services, such as cleansing the air and water of pollutants, and storing carbon in biomass as an offset to emissions of greenhouse gases (such as carbon dioxide and methane; see Chapter 3).

Arguably, the aggregate influence of anthropogenic stressors is causing an environmental crisis, key components of which are risks to the sustainability of the human economy and severe damage caused to biodiversity.

For convenience, the diverse agents of environmental stress can be grouped into the following categories (Freedman, 2010):

ENVIRONMENTAL APPLICATIONS 2.2

Contamination, Pollution, and Biomagnification

All chemicals are potentially toxic—it is just a matter of how intense the dose is. This is because organisms have some degree of tolerance to certain exposures of any chemical, although this physiological resistance can be overwhelmed at higher doses. In fact, if the intensity of exposure is high enough, even water is poisonous if too much of it is drunk too quickly (the medical syndrome of hyponatremia refers to intoxication by water—it can be caused by an athlete re-hydrating too hastily during or after intense sweaty exercise, and in severe cases it is lethal).

Contamination refers to situations in which the concentration of a chemical is less than the biological tolerance. For instance, all of the naturally occurring metals are present in all parts of the environment, including organisms, if only in "an infinitesimal" concentration of a few parts per billion (1 ppb = 1 μg/kg). This fact can be easily demonstrated if the detection limits of the available analytical chemistry are low enough. This is also true of some chemicals that do not occur naturally but are synthesized and dispersed into the environment by human activities. Examples of this phenomenon are persistent chlorinated hydrocarbons (organochlorines), such as the insecticides DDT and dieldrin, the industrial chemicals known as PCBs, and the incidental compounds known as dioxins and furans. These chemicals now occur in a universal contamination—they are present in the fat of all organisms on Earth, but usually at concentrations that are not known to cause measurable toxicity. However, in the cases of both metals and organochlorines, higher exposures associated with industrial activities can result in the poisoning of organisms—when this is known to have happened, then the damaging exposures would be said to represent **pollution**.

Bioconcentration is another interesting phenomenon that is displayed by some chemicals. It refers to the tendency of certain substances to occur in larger concentrations in organisms than in their ambient, non-living environment. For this to happen, the solubility of a chemical must be higher in organisms than in their environment, particularly in water. For this reason, chemicals that bioconcentrate have a high solubility in fats (which are abundant in organisms but not in the abiotic environment) and a low solubility in water (which is generally abundant in the ambient environment). Among industrial chemicals of concern to wildlife toxicologists, the best examples of these sorts of substances are organochlorines and certain organo-metallic compounds, such as methylmercury. Moreover, if these chemicals are also persistent in organisms, meaning they are not easily excreted or metabolized to simpler compounds, then they will also **biomagnify** (or **food-web magnify**), meaning they occur in the highest residue levels in top predators (animals that feed at the top of the food web). The persistent organochlorines and methylmercury are well known for their tendency to biomagnify in wildlife and also in humans.

- *Climatic stress* is associated with temperature, solar radiation, wind, moisture, and combinations of these factors. They act as stressors if their ambient condition is excessive or insufficient, compared with the needs of organisms or of ecological functions. This could involve temperatures that are too hot or too cold, extremes of water availability, or other difficult conditions. Climatic stressors may exert themselves over all or part of the year, often in a seasonally predictable manner, or they may involve a rare but powerful event that causes great damage, such as disturbance by a hurricane, tornado, ice-storm, or an extreme amount of precipitation. Human-caused examples include discharges of warmed water into lakes, and anthropogenic global warming (Chapter 4).
- *Chemical stressors* involve environments in which substances occur in concentrations that are high enough to cause organisms to suffer from toxicity or some other physiological detriment. If enough organisms are affected, then larger-scale ecological change may occur. All chemicals are potentially toxic, but the frequently problematic ones include metals, such as mercury and lead; gases, such as ozone and sulphur dioxide; and pesticides. In general, organisms are tolerant of relatively low-level exposure to these substances, and chemicals may even accumulate in their bodies without causing discernible harm (see Ecology in Depth 2.2). In this regard, the mere presence of a potentially toxic chemical is referred to as contamination—for pollution to be caused, the agent must be shown to be causing a damaging biological or ecological response. Interestingly, an excessive supply of nutrients is also a stressor because it can distort productivity and other ecological functions, causing a problem known as eutrophication in aquatic ecosystems (see Environmental Applications 2.1). There are many anthropogenic emissions of chemical stressors into the environment, including large industrial sources, such as power plants and metal smelters, as well as personal ones, such as driving an automobile. There are also natural sources of pollution, such as volcanoes, and metallic deposits that occur close to the surface (see Ecology in Depth 2.2).

ENVIRONMENTAL APPLICATIONS 2.3

Endocrine Disruptors in Ecosystems

Hormones are biochemicals that are essential to the control systems of organisms—they are produced in specialized glands and are released in extremely small amounts to affect physiology or behaviour. All multicellular organisms produce hormones, and in animals they are usually transported in the blood. Hormones exert their effect by binding to specific receptors on their target cells, resulting in a signal that activates a particular biological response, such as a process in anatomical development, sexual behaviour, or metabolic functions related to diet.

The action of some hormones may be mimicked by other chemicals that resemble them structurally, and exposure to the imitators may result in adverse effects on the physiology of wild animals or people. When these chemical stressors occur in the environment they are referred to as hormonally active agents or as endocrine disruptors. A variety of chemicals may be active in this way, including:

- natural or synthetic hormones that have been used in birth-control pills or for other purposes, and that enter the environment with sewage
- phytoestrogens that are produced by certain plants, such as isoflavinoids found in soybean (*Gylcine max*) and red clover (*Trifolium arvense*)
- various anthropogenic chemicals, including DDT and related organochlorine insecticides, polychlorinated biphenyls (PCBs), bisphenol A, phthalates, nonophenol, and some other organic compounds.

There is much controversy about the effects of exposure of wild animals and people to these hormonally active agents, especially about the anthropogenic chemicals. However, field studies are beginning to show that damaging effects may occur. For example, Karen Kidd of the University of New Brunswick (Saint John) and colleagues (2007) added synthetic 17α-ethynylestradiol, an estrogen in birth-control pills, to a lake in the Experimental Lakes Area of northwestern Ontario. The estrogen was added in amounts that achieved lakewater concentrations that were comparable to that in urban sewage. The three-year treatment caused male fathead minnows (*Pimephales promelas*) to become feminized—they produced egg proteins, their own sperm atrophied, and some developed eggs in their gonads. These effects, plus effects on females, interfered with reproduction by the minnows, and their population soon collapsed in the treated lake because of a lack of recruitment. The minnows showed little recovery in the ensuring four years after the addition of estrogen was stopped, indicating a longer-term effect. Co-habiting fish that are longer-lived than the fathead minnow were not similarly affected, such as pearl dace (*Margariscus margarita*), white sucker (*Catostomus commersonii*), and lake trout (*Salvelinus namaycush*). However, Kidd et al. suggested that a longer-term study might observe reproductive disruption of those species as well.

- *Wildfire* is a disturbance that involves the combustion of much of the biomass of an ecosystem while damaging or killing organisms by exposure to scorching temperatures and poisonous gases, such as carbon monoxide and smoke. Wildfires in inaccessible regions are mostly naturally ignited by lightning, but those occurring near habitations are mostly lit by people.
- *Physical stress* is a disturbance that involves an intense exposure to kinetic energy, which damages habitats and ecosystems. Large and disruptive physical events include the blast of a volcanic eruption or the force of a tsunami (seismic sea wave). Anthropogenic examples include trampling and compaction by heavy machinery or by hikers, and the blast of explosions.
- *Biological stressors* are associated with interactions occurring among organisms. These may be caused directly by trophic interactions, in which one species feeds on another, as in herbivory, predation, parasitism, and disease. Alternatively, biological interactions may indirectly affect the intensity of physical or chemical stressors. For instance, limitations of nutrients, moisture, or space may be caused by *intraspecific competition* occurring among individuals of the same species, or by *interspecific competition* involving various species (Chapter 5). Biological stressors may be natural in origin, as when trees are damaged by native insects or an indigenous disease. They may also be anthropogenic, occurring when people harvest wild animals or trees as economic resources. Anthropogenic influences may also be indirect, as occurs when alien pathogens are introduced to previously non-exposed ecosystems. In fact, we may refer to "biological pollution" in cases where people have released **invasive aliens** beyond their natural range, resulting in ecological damage. Biological pollution might involve deliberate or accidental releases of non-native plants, animals, or diseases that damage natural ecosystems, as well as the release of pathogens through discharges of raw sewage.

ECOLOGY IN DEPTH 2.2

Natural Pollution at the Smoking Hills

The Smoking Hills are named after a natural phenomenon that occurs at a remote coastal location beside the Beaufort Sea near Cape Bathurst in the Northwest Territories. The region has a sedimentary geology, and seams of bituminous shale, a kind of low-grade coal, are present in the rocks. When the shale becomes exposed to atmospheric oxygen, as occurs when erosion causes slumps of the coastal cliffs to occur, sulphide minerals (such as iron sulphide, FeS_2) are oxidized by chemosynthetic *Thiobacillus* bacteria (see Chapter 4), which produce sulphate and heat as waste by-products. In certain insulated situations the heat may accumulate to the degree that there is a spontaneous ignition of the shale. The shale may then smoulder for years, releasing sulphur dioxide (SO_2) to the atmosphere, which is then blown inland by the prevailing winds as ground-level plumes. The SO_2 is toxic to plants, and further environmental damage is caused when dry deposition of the gas causes severe acidification to occur, resulting in pHs less than 3 in soil and water. At such low pHs, naturally occurring metals become water-soluble, which greatly adds to the toxicity of the environment. The Smoking Hills are likely an ancient phenomenon, at least thousands of years old, although the first historical reference to them was in 1826 by John Richardson, an early explorer. The case of the Smoking Hills represents "natural pollution" because neither the presence or ignition of the bituminous shale has anything to do with people.

The SO_2, severe acidity, and metal availability have caused intense ecological damage in the vicinity of the plumes. The ecological effects have been studied by Tom Hutchinson and colleagues from the University of Toronto. In the worst-affected places there is total devastation—no plants can survive and the land is barren. However, with increasing distance from the edge of the seacliffs, the plumes become progressively diluted by ambient air and the pollution becomes correspondingly less intense. The first vegetated community that is encountered supports only a few plants that are tolerant of the chemically stressful habitats—including a wormwood (*Artemesia tilesii*) and a polar-grass (*Arctagrostis latifolia*). These are both wide-ranging species, but their local populations are likely specifically adapted to tolerating the pollution. As one moves several kilometres further inland, the normal tundra vegetation is encountered, which supports a much richer community of more than 70 species. Aquatic habitats are also abundant at the Smoking Hills—ponds that are polluted by severe acidity and metals support only a few tolerant species, while the reference ponds have much more biodiversity and higher productivity.

As a natural phenomenon, the pollution and ecological damage at the Smoking Hills are of intrinsic interest to ecologists. However, they also provide some insight into the longer-term patterns of damage that might be expected from anthropogenic emissions of SO_2, for instance near large smelters, such as those at Sudbury, Ontario. These effects include severe acidification and toxic metals, a rapid decrease in the intensity of pollution with increasing distance from the source of emissions, severe damage caused to the biota of terrestrial and aquatic habitats, and the evolution of local ecotypes that are relatively tolerant of the toxic stressors.

Bill Freedman

Natural air pollution at the Smoking Hills, Northwest Territories. The sulphurous plumes are emitted by spontaneously ignited bituminous shale, and they damage the tundra by SO_2 toxicity, acidification, and solubilized metals.

2.3 Ecological Responses to Changes in Environmental Stress

An ecosystem that is disrupted by a disturbance typically suffers the mortality of some species, together with changes to its structural (e.g., species composition, biomass distribution) and functional properties (e.g., decomposition and nutrient cycling). A process of recovery through succession then begins, and if it proceeds for a long enough time, it will restore a mature ecosystem, perhaps one similar to that existing before the disturbance.

Chronic stressors, which influence ecosystems relatively continuously, include many climatic and chemical factors. Depending on their intensity, organisms may suffer a loss of productivity or acute effects, such as tissue damage, or, ultimately, death. At the community level, relatively vulnerable species will be reduced or eliminated if the intensity of stress increases markedly. Their niches may then be occupied by more-tolerant species of the original community, or by invaders that can exploit a stressful but weakly competitive habitat. Increased exposure to environmental stressors can also result in evolutionary change if individuals vary in their tolerance and those differences are genetically fixed. Under such conditions, natural selection may eventually result in increased tolerance at the population level.

Longer-term ecological change may result from a prolonged intensification of stress. This might occur, for example, if a metal smelter is constructed in a forested landscape, causing pollution by sulphur dioxide and metals. The toxic stressors may damage the tree-sized plants of the forest and eventually cause them to give way to shrub-sized and herbaceous vegetation. If the stress is severe enough the landscape may lose its plant cover entirely. Ecological damage of this sort has occurred around many smelters, such as those near Sudbury, Ontario (Freedman, 2010). Similar patterns of change have been caused by "natural" pollution by SO_2, such as at the Smoking Hills (see Ecology in Depth 2.2).

Because a smelter is a point-source of emissions (i.e., they are released from a discrete place), the intensity of pollution decreases in a more-or-less exponential pattern with increasing distance. As a consequence, the ecological responses will radiate outward from the source of pollution and may eventually become manifest as a spatial gradient of community change. Other spatial changes in stressors also result in corresponding patterns of ecological responses. For instance, a linear source (such as a highway) will establish an orthogonal (perpendicular) gradient that parallels the source. Road salt and vehicular tail-pipe emissions are distributed along roads in this way. A step-cline is a result of an immediate change at a boundary, for instance, between a lake and its surrounding terrestrial upland. Often, environmental gradients result in a transitional zone, known as an **ecotone**, between distinctive community types (see Chapter 13).

The intensity of environmental stress may also decrease over time and space. When this happens, the ecological responses are in many respects the reverse of those observed when stress intensifies (but not necessarily exactly so—resilience is the degree to which the succession recovers the characteristics of the original community). These changes represent a process of recovery after the relaxation of stress. In the case of the Sudbury smelters, the emissions of SO_2 and metals have decreased since the installation of pollution-control technology. This has resulted in decreased toxic stress in the surrounding environment, which allowed some ecological recovery to occur (Freedman, 2010).

As environmental stress intensifies, the following ecological responses are commonly observed:

- Depending on the sensitivity of species, there will be decreases of productivity, increased mortality, and reproductive failure.
- The community changes as sensitive species become replaced by more tolerant ones.
- Top predators and large-bodied species are lost from the system.

Gradients of toxic stress cause corresponding changes in the structure and function of affected ecosystems. In this case, emissions of SO_2 from a smelter near Sudbury, Ontario, have caused damage to vegetation by toxicity and acidification. The pollution and damage were most intense close to the source of emissions, and became rapidly less with increasing distances away, until non-affected (reference) conditions of mature mixed-species forest and clean lakes were reached.

Bill Freedman

A CANADIAN ECOLOGIST 2.1

Tom Hutchinson: An Environmental Ecologist

Tom Hutchinson

Tom Hutchinson

Tom Hutchinson is a plant ecologist, educated in England, whose research initially involved fundamental questions about the ability of certain plant species to occur over a range of sharply contrasting soil environments. However, soon after he immigrated to Canada to take up a faculty position at the University of Toronto, he became interested in the damaging effects that pollution has on vegetation near large smelters at Sudbury, Ontario. When he started this work in the late 1960s, few academic ecologists were studying anthropogenic damages in ecosystems—most were engaged in "curiosity-driven" research about natural environmental influences on organisms and ecosystems. In this sense, Tom was a leader in the emerging field of "environmental ecology"—research into the identification and mitigation of ecological problems that are caused by the human economy.

Hutchinson's conversion to applied work was sparked by a visit to Sudbury, where he was inspired by the sight of landscapes that had been devastated by decades of exposure to intense pollution emitted by local metal-processing industries. He recognized the possibility of doing research that would examine fundamental questions about the structure and function of the natural world, but in the context of exposure to steep gradients of toxic stressors. Tom engaged many enthusiastic students in studies of the patterns and causes of ecological damage in terrestrial and aquatic habitats near Sudbury, including the evolution of local plant populations, known as ecotypes, that had a genetically based tolerance of high concentrations of metals in their soil.

Subsequent to that work, Tom expanded his interests to a diversity of research areas relevant to environmental problems, including studies of pollution by metals and gases in various environmental contexts (smelters, recycling facilities, tailings disposal sites, urban areas), oil spills, forest decline of sugar maple, and climate change, including the potential effects of "nuclear winter" (a severe climatic deterioration that might follow a nuclear war).

In addition, to his research interests, Tom focused his teaching at the University of Toronto, and later at Trent University, on the subject area of environmental ecology and sustainability, thereby influencing the outlook and knowledge of thousands of students. Hutchinson's impressive career has helped to legitimize the research and teaching of academic ecologists who are interested in these sorts of applied subject areas, which are clearly important to the sustainable development of the Canadian and global economies.

- Species richness and species diversity are decreased.
- Community-level respiration exceeds production, so net production becomes negative and the amounts of biomass decrease.
- Nutrient capital is depleted by leaching and other losses.
- Rates of productivity, decomposition, and nutrient cycling are decreased.

If the intensified stress regime becomes stabilized at a high intensity, then the longer-term ecological change will reflect these responses. Compared with the original communities, the affected ecosystem will be simpler in structure and function, will sustain less biodiversity, will be dominated by relatively small and short-lived species, and will have low rates of productivity and slower decomposition and nutrient cycling. In the worst cases, no biota can survive.

In general, these changes would be interpreted as representing "damage," in the sense of impaired quality and natural condition of the ecosystem (or *ecological integrity*), and a degraded ability to supply the human economy with natural resources. Judgments of the quality of change are an important subject area in ecology. In general, however, changes are more likely to be considered as being damage if they are caused by an intensified stressor regime that has resulted from an anthropogenic influence, such as industrial activity. If the stressors are natural in origin, then the ecological change might not be viewed as being damage. These considerations are highly relevant to the intersection of ecology with environmental planning and impact assessment (Chapter 17), and are a key aspect of the applied relevance of the knowledge of ecologists.

VOCABULARY OF ECOLOGY

abiotic, p. 31
anthropogenic stressors, p. 38
bioconcentration, p. 39
biomagnify (food-web magnify), p. 39
biotic, p. 31
chronic, p. 37
contamination, p. 39
disturbance, p. 35
ecotone, p. 42
environmental factors, p. 31
eutrophication, p. 32
exposure, p. 36
extreme environments, p. 35
invasive aliens, p. 40
microdisturbance, p. 38
microsuccession, p. 38
natural stressors, p. 38
pollution, p. 39
primary succession, p. 38
principle of limiting factors, p. 32
resilience, p. 37
response, p. 36
secondary succession, p. 38
SER model, p. 36
stability, p. 37
stressors, p. 34
succession, p. 38
tolerance (or resistance), p. 36

QUESTIONS FOR REVIEW AND DISCUSSION

1. What are environmental factors? How do they affect the development of organisms and ecosystems?
2. What is the fundamental niche of a species, and what sets its boundaries? How do environmental factors influence the realized niche?
3. What, in the sense of evolutionary biology, is fitness? How do environmental factors affect fitness, and what is the intersection of this influence with the evolution of a population or species?
4. Explain the differences between the genotype and phenotype. How do environmental factors influence the expression of the phenotype?
5. What are environmental stressors? Describe the major types of stressors.
6. Explain the key differences in the ecological effects of a disturbance and a chronic stressor.
7. Compare the ecological effects of a stand-replacing disturbance and a microdisturbance.
8. What ecological changes are observed following a large and persistent increase in the intensity of environmental stress?

You'll find a rich array of additional resources for *Ecology* at www.ecology.nelson.com

CHAPTER 3

Ecological Energetics

BILL FREEDMAN, Department of Biology, Dalhousie University

LEARNING OBJECTIVES

After studying this chapter you should be able to

1. Define energy and describe the states in which it might exist.
2. Explain the laws of thermodynamics that govern the transformations of energy, including their ecological context.
3. Explain how the Earth is a flow-through system for solar energy.
4. Identify the major components of the energy budget of the Earth.
5. Explain the mechanism and importance of the Earth's natural greenhouse effect, and how it may be intensified by anthropogenic emissions of greenhouse gases.
6. Describe energy relationships within ecosystems, beginning with the fixation of solar energy by primary producers, through to the passage of that fixed energy to herbivores, carnivores, and decomposers.
7. Explain the differences in productivity and standing crop among the major kinds of terrestrial and aquatic ecosystems.
8. Explain why the trophic structure of ecological productivity is pyramid shaped, and why ecosystems cannot support many top predators.

The aurora borealis seen from Tobermory, ON. Photo by Bill Caulfeild-Browne

CHAPTER OUTLINE

3.1 Energy in Ecosystems

Ultimately, all physical processes occurring anywhere in the universe are driven by flows of energy. As far as we know, however, Earth is the only place in the universe where there is a biological fixation of energy, principally of solar radiation by photosynthetic organisms, and this phenomenon imparts the energetic basis for all life.

The field of **ecological energetics** involves study of the ways that solar energy becomes fixed by plants and other photosynthetic organisms and is then transferred to other species, including its accumulation as organic matter in ecosystems. Important aspects of ecological energetics are the amounts of energy and biomass that are stored and transferred among the various trophic (or feeding) levels of ecosystems, and how certain physical and biological principles influence those structural and functional characteristics.

A foundation of ecological energetics is the principle that organisms and ecosystems are open systems with respect to energy, rather than closed ones. This means that energy flows into them, becomes used in various ways, and is then discarded in a degraded form. A corollary of this principle is that organisms and ecosystems are not self-sustaining. Rather, they require an ongoing supply of energy from the Sun to continue to function and survive.

In almost all ecosystems, solar radiation supports the existence of both organisms and ecological productivity. **Autotrophs** (self-feeding organisms), such as plants and algae, absorb solar energy and use it to drive their fixation of carbon dioxide and water into simple sugars, generating oxygen as a waste. This process, known as **photosynthesis**, is summarized by the following equation:

$$\textit{Sunlight} + 6\ CO_2 + 6\ H_2O \rightarrow C_6H_{12}O_6 + 6\ O_2$$

The fixed energy content of the sugar produced by photosynthesis is the ultimate organic fuel for the vast complex of biochemical reactions by which autotrophs synthesize the enormous diversity of carbohydrates, proteins, fats, and other compounds that they need to grow and to reproduce. The biomass produced by autotrophs may then become food for **heterotrophs**—organisms such as animals, fungi, and most bacteria. These

Plants are autotrophs that absorb sunlight and use some of that energy to drive photosynthesis. Plants are coloured green because their chlorophyll absorbs blue and red wavelengths of light, but reflect most of the green. This is a low-growing coastal plant known as sea sandwort, *Honckenya peploides*, growing on a beach in Nunavik, an arctic region of northern Quebec.

organisms cannot accomplish the direct fixation of solar energy, and so they must subsist by feeding on the biomass of other organisms.

Initially in this chapter we examine energy as a physical entity—one that exists in various forms or states. We then look at two laws of physics that govern the transformations of energy among its alternative states, and how it flows through and is stored in physical systems, including Earth and its ecosystems. Finally, we examine and compare the energy fixation and accumulation of biomass in major kinds of ecosystems.

3.2 Fundamentals of Energy

Energy is defined as the capacity of a body or a system to perform work. In turn, **work** is defined as the consequence of a force that is applied over a distance. In this meaning, work is accomplished when solar radiation is absorbed and warms a dark pavement, when wind blows a leaf through the air, when trees are burned during a wildfire, when a bicycle is driven along a road, when a plant utilizes sunlight in photosynthesis, and when an animal metabolizes the absorbed energy of its food to run its vital physiology.

Energy may exist in numerous distinct states, which under suitable conditions can be converted into other ones. All of the examples noted in the previous paragraph involved changes of the state of energy: sunlight is electromagnetic energy, but if absorbed by an asphalt surface it becomes transformed into heat, a form of kinetic energy (these kinds of energy are explained below). During a forest fire, the potential energy of biomass is converted into heat and electromagnetic energy. And during photosynthesis, solar electromagnetic energy is absorbed by chlorophyll, a pigment in plant foliage, and used to join carbon dioxide and water to form a sugar that stores potential energy.

The standard measure of energy content is the joule (J), according to the Système Internationale d'Unités (SI), which is the international system by which scientific units are established. The definition of one joule is the amount of energy needed to accelerate 1 kg of mass at 1 metre per second per second (m/s^2) over a distance of 1 m. Another commonly reported energy unit is the calorie (cal or gram-calorie), which is equivalent to 4.18 joules and is defined as the energy needed to heat one gram of water from 15°C to 16°C. This is not, however, the same as the "Calorie" by which dieticians measure the energy content of foods, which is actually 1000 calories (10^3 cal = 1 kilocalorie or kcal = 1 Calorie).

States of Energy

The numerous states of energy can be assembled into three fundamental types: electromagnetic, kinetic, and potential.

Electromagnetic Energy

Electromagnetic energy (or electromagnetic radiation) is associated with fundamental entities known as photons, which display characteristics of both particles and waves. Photons move through space at an unvarying velocity of 3×10^{10} cm/s, known as the "speed of light." Electromagnetic energy occurs as an unbroken spectrum that extends from extremely long wavelengths to very short ones. However, the continuous wavelength ranges are arranged into discrete segments, which are known as radio, microwave, infrared, visible, ultraviolet, X-ray, and gamma **(Figure 3.1).** Visible radiation is the most familiar portion of the electromagnetic spectrum—it is perceived by the human eye as "light" and ranges from 0.4 to 0.7 micrometres (1 μm = 10^{-6} m). Shorter electromagnetic wavelengths are more "energetic" in that their higher frequency embeds a greater density of energy. Any object whose surface temperature exceeds –273°C or "absolute zero" (this is 0 degrees on the Kelvin scale and it is the coldest possible temperature) will radiate (or emit) electromagnetic energy. Moreover, the surface temperature of the object directly controls both the spectral quality and the rate of emission; hotter bodies—those with shorter, higher-frequency wavelengths—have much greater emission rates than cooler ones. The Sun, for instance, has a torrid surface temperature of about 5500°C, and its emitted radiation is mostly ultraviolet (0.2–0.38 μm), visible (0.38–0.75 μm), and near infrared (0.75–2 μm) (0.2–0.4 μm), visible (0.4–0.7 μm), and near infrared (0.7–2 μm) **(Figure 3.2).** In contrast, because Earth has a much cooler surface that averages about 15°C, it radiates much less energy and of lower frequencies (longer wavelengths) that peaks at about 10 μm in the longer-wave infrared part of the spectrum.

Kinetic Energy

Kinetic energy exists in two basic forms, both of which involve mass in motion, but at different scales of space:

1. **Thermal energy**, or sensible energy or "heat," is associated with the rate of vibration and rotation of atoms or molecules and of their internal components (such as electrons and the nucleus). This movement only occurs at temperatures above –273°C (0 K). At higher temperatures the rate of vibration increases rapidly, which accounts for increases in the amount of heat, or sensible energy.
2. **Mechanical energy** is associated with objects that are in motion, such as a planet moving through space, water flowing in a river, or a bison strolling across a prairie. In any such instance, the mass and velocity of the moving object determine the amount of mechanical kinetic energy that is present.

Potential Energy

Potential energy contains the capacity to perform work when it becomes transformed into kinetic or electromagnetic energy. Potential energy may exist in various states:

1. **Chemical energy** is stored in the bonds that link atoms within molecules. This kind of potential energy is released by various kinds of chemical reactions that lead to a release of kinetic or electromagnetic energy (if thermal energy is released,

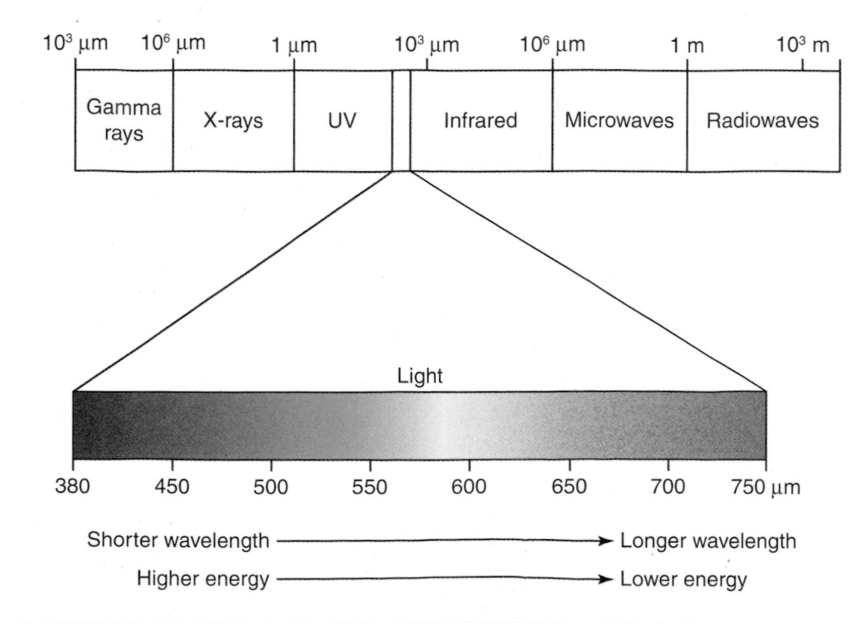

FIGURE 3.1

The Electromagnetic Spectrum. The spectrum is a continuum, but it is divided here into key sectors based on wavelength (or on its inverse, frequency). The spectrum is presented in units of millimicrons (also known as nanometres; 1 mμ = 1 nm = 10^{-9} m) on a logarithmic scale ($\log_{10}$). The visible component is expanded to show the wavelength ranges for the prismatic colours of the rainbow: red, orange, yellow, green, blue, and violet.

SOURCE: From Russell/Wolfe/Hertz/Starr. *Biology*, 1E. © 2010 Nelson Education Ltd. Reproduced by permission. www.cengage.com/permissions

the reaction is referred to as *exothermic*). Examples of these sorts of reactions include the following:

- If sodium chloride (NaCl) or other salts are dissolved into water, potential energy inherent in their ionic bonds is released, which generates heat that slightly warms the water.
- When iron sulphide (FeS_2) is oxidized, some of the potential energy inherent in its interatomic bonding is released; specialized bacteria known as *Thiobacillus* have the ability to tap the chemical potential of sulphides to support their productivity—this autotrophic process is known as *chemosynthesis* (examined later in the chapter).
- If organic compounds, such as hydrocarbons (molecules that contain only C and H atoms), are combusted in the presence of oxygen, the chemical potential of bonds among their atoms is released; for example, the combustion of diesel fuel in the engine of a truck releases its chemical potential, some of which is converted into the kinetic energy of moving pistons and ultimately to that of motion of the vehicle.
- When biochemicals produced by organisms are oxidized by metabolic processes, energy is provided to support all aspects of their physiology, growth, reproduction, and behaviour, along with some generation of heat; carbohydrates such as sugars and starches contain about 17 kJ of potential energy per gram; proteins, 21 kJ/g; and fats or lipids, 39 kJ/g.

2. *Gravitational energy* is a product of gravity, or the attractive forces that exist among all objects. Water that is situated at any height above sea level contains gravitational potential energy. If there is a path that allows for the water to flow to a lower altitude, the potential energy is converted into kinetic energy. Hydroelectric power plants are designed to convert some of the kinetic energy of flowing water into electricity.
3. *Compressed gases* store potential energy by virtue of their compacted situation, compared with the lower pressure of the ambient atmosphere. This potential energy can do work if the gases are permitted to expand—for example, within the piston chamber of an automobile engine.
4. *Electrical potential* exists when there are differences in the densities of electrons between areas. Electrons are negatively charged, subatomic particles. If a conducting material, such as a copper wire, connects two zones with higher and lower electron densities—and therefore different electrical potentials—electrons will flow down the gradient. When this happens, the electrical energy can be harnessed by various devices and machines that produce light, heat, or mechanical work. Voltage is a measure of the difference in electrical potential.
5. *Nuclear energy* is the densest kind of energy—it results from the enormously strong binding forces that exist within (rather than between) atoms. In essence, nuclear reactions convert matter into energy. Compared to all other energy-releasing processes, nuclear reactions release immense quantities of kinetic and electromagnetic energies per unit of fuel that is consumed. This may occur through two different kinds of nuclear reactions:
   - *Fission reactions* occur when certain isotopes of unstable (radioactive) atoms, such as the heavy metals uranium-235 and plutonium-239 (^{235}U and ^{239}Pu), are split to produce lighter elements plus an immense quantity of energy. The reactors of nuclear power plants utilize carefully controlled fission reactions to generate electricity. However, an uncontrolled fission reaction may result in a massive explosion, a fact that has been harnessed to manufacture devastating nuclear weapons.
   - *Fusion reactions* are another way of releasing nuclear potential energy. Nuclear fusion occurs when certain light elements, such as hydrogen, combine to form heavier atoms, in the process unleashing an immense amount of energy. So-called hydrogen bombs produce immense nuclear explosions based on hydrogen-fusion reactions. Natural fusion reactions fuelled by hydrogen occur in stars, resulting in the production of ginormous amounts of electromagnetic and kinetic energies, much of which is radiated into space.

3.3 Laws of Thermodynamics

Energy that exists in one state, such as electromagnetic, kinetic, or potential energy, can be transformed into other ones. These transformations may occur spontaneously, or various devices of human invention may enable them. However, all energy transformations obey certain constraints whatever the environmental circumstance. These constraints, or limiting conditions, are physical principles that are known as the laws of thermodynamics.

The **first law of thermodynamics** is expressed in this way: energy can be transformed among its various states, but it is never created or destroyed, and so the energy content of the universe stays constant. Because the energy content of the universe is conserved, in any particular system there is a zero-sum energetic balance among the inputs of energy, the amount stored within the system, and the outputs.

This concept can be illustrated by the case of an airplane, which consumes fuel, an energy input that

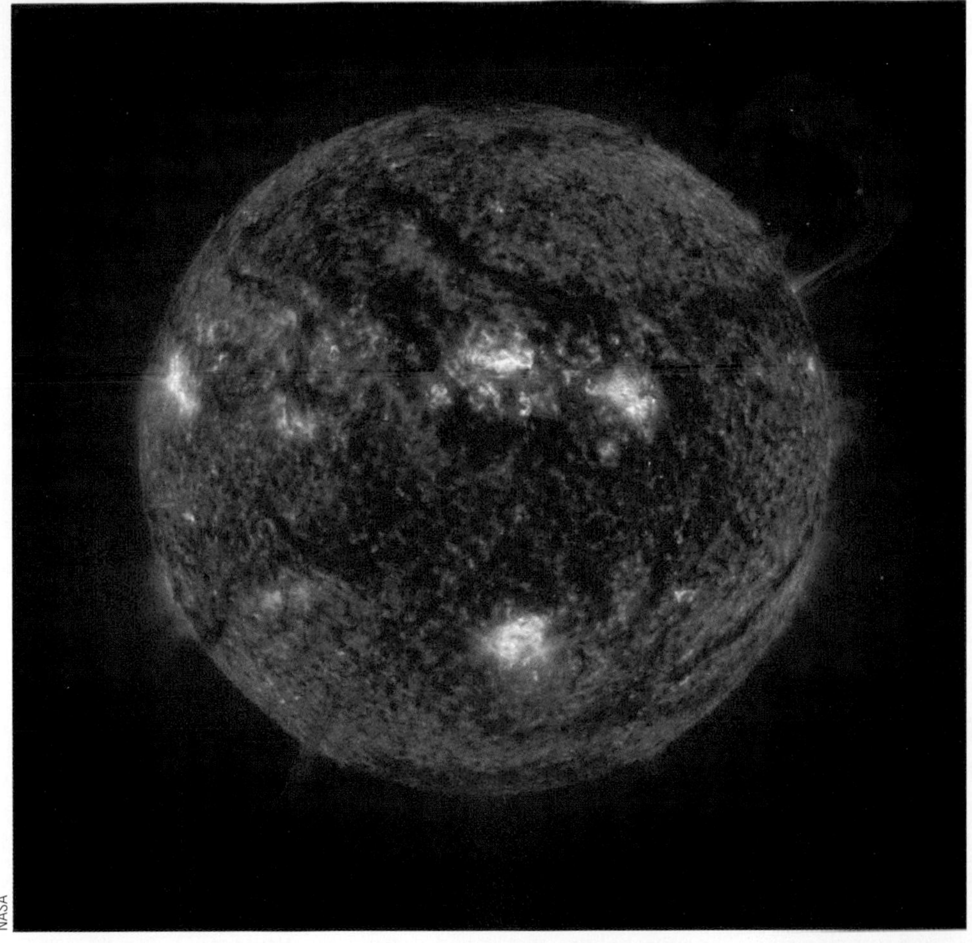

Energy from the Sun drives almost all ecological productivity on Earth. This is an image of the Sun taken on 14 September 1999, using an Extreme Ultraviolet Imaging Telescope. The huge handle-shaped prominence on the right-hand side of the image is an irruption of dense plasma suspended in the hot, thin corona of the Sun. The hottest areas on the surface of the Sun appear as whitish, while the darker reddish areas are somewhat cooler.

can be measured. The engines and other machinery convert the chemical potential of the fuel into other states, such as movement of the aircraft (kinetic energy), power for lights (electrical energy), friction with the atmosphere (thermal energy), and hot exhaust gases (thermal energy). Overall, however, the first law of thermodynamics dictates that, while these and many other energy transformations occur as an airplane flies through the atmosphere, an exact accounting of all the diverse reactions involving energy storage and outputs would show that the initial energetic content of the fuel was conserved.

An ecological example concerns the energy budget of Earth, which can be described as follows.

The planet receives an input of solar energy. Some of that incoming energy

- is reflected back to outer space;
- is absorbed by the atmosphere or by the surface of Earth, causing them to become warmer;
- serves to evaporate water or melt ice; and
- is absorbed by chlorophyll and used to drive photosynthesis.

However, there are energy outputs that balance the amounts that are absorbed:

- the increased heat contents of the atmosphere and surface are dissipated by a secondary re-radiation of infrared to outer space
- the potential energy of any accumulated biomass is eventually oxidized by the respiration of organisms or by wildfire.

Again, an accurate budgeting of these processes, plus any additional transformations, would find that although solar energy was converted into numerous other forms, the total amount of energy in or flowing through the system was conserved, or remained constant.

The **second law of thermodynamics** is explained as follows: *energy transformations can occur spontaneously only under conditions in which the entropy in the universe is increased*. Entropy is best described as a physical property that is linked to disorder, and it relates to the randomness and uncertainty of the distributions of matter and energy. Negative entropy involves a decrease in disorder (or an increase in order).

To understand the idea of entropy and the second law, think about a balloon. Experience tells us that the highly dispersed gases of the atmosphere would never spontaneously relocate to inflate a balloon. That would be an exceedingly improbable event that, in a physical sense, would represent a gain of negative entropy. However, if person blows forcefully into a balloon, it can be inflated. In that case, the local accumulation of negative entropy is made possible because energy has been put into the system to do the work of compressing gases. Once a balloon is inflated, it contains potential energy inherent in its compacted gases, and it may undergo a slow deflation, or a fast one if it is punctured and explodes. These decompression events can occur spontaneously because compressed gases in a balloon are in a highly ordered state, and they become much less so when they return to the atmosphere—this change represents an increase in entropy. The key lesson here is that increases in entropy can occur spontaneously but gains of negative entropy require an expenditure of energy through some kind of work.

Entropy is also increased when short-wave electromagnetic energy (such as sunlight) is absorbed by a surface, converted to thermal energy (increased temperature), and then dissipated by a re-radiation of longer-wave infrared. The solar radiation that continuously reaches Earth is composed primarily of visible and near-infrared wavelengths. The atmosphere and planetary surface absorb much of that radiation and convert it to an increasing thermal content, which is eventually dissipated to outer space by a spontaneous emission of long-wave infrared. The overall planetary function of absorption and re-radiation corresponds to an increase in entropy. This is because longer-wave radiation has somewhat less entropy than shorter-wave.

Another consequence of the second law is that energy transformations can never be totally efficient. In any technological application, this means that some of the initial energy content of a fuel must be converted into heat, which is a relatively low-grade form of energy, so that there is an increase of entropy. Therefore, in a power plant, only about 40 percent of the energy of a fuel, such as coal, can be converted into electricity, even if the best available technology is used. Similarly, the upper limit of the thermodynamic efficiency of an automobile is about 30 percent; this is calculated as the kinetic energy of a moving vehicle divided by the potential energy of its fuel. Plant metabolism also reveals thermodynamic inefficiency; even if plants have access to an optimal supply of water and nutrients in their environment, the process of photosynthesis does not capture a high percentage of the energy of the incoming solar radiation. In fact, natural ecosystems typically fix less than 1 percent of incident sunlight into biochemicals, although dense algal cultures in a laboratory may attain an efficiency of up to 6 percent.

It is interesting to ponder how the existence of life and ecosystems complements the universal, spontaneous increase in entropy as governed by the second law of thermodynamics. Initially, solar radiation (a diffuse form of energy) is absorbed during photosynthesis and used to drive the biological fixation of simple inorganic compounds—readily available and widely dispersed carbon dioxide and water in the environment—into simple sugars. That initial ecological productivity is followed by an astonishing complex of biochemical reactions in both photosynthetic and non-photosynthetic organisms. These utilize additional simple compounds (such as ammonium, nitrate, and phosphate) and ions (such as potassium, calcium, and magnesium) to synthesize an array of organic substances with a dense energy content and enormous diversity and complexity of molecular and physical structures. In this sense, organisms and ecosystems are built upon a foundation of local transformations of diffuse energy and mass into much denser and more highly organized structures that represent intense bio-concentrations of negative entropy.

However, these biological transformations do not contravene the second law of thermodynamics, which is inviolate. Because life and ecosystems are founded on an increase in negative entropy, they may seem to be paradoxical in a physical sense, but this ostensible contradiction can be logically resolved as follows:

> *Organisms and ecosystems represent local bio-concentrations of negative entropy, but this is thermodynamically feasible because of biological work that is made possible by harnessing some of the continuous input of solar radiation that is received by the biosphere. If this external energy subsidy were to somehow be terminated, all organisms and biomass would spontaneously disintegrate and release simple inorganic compounds and heat back into the environment. This would increase the entropy of the universe by a larger amount than that of the negative entropy that was gained by the original bio-fixation.*

Therefore, life and ecosystems can survive only if they receive incessant inputs of solar energy, which is used to perform the biological work that organizes their negative entropy. In this sense, we can consider the biosphere to represent a localized "island" of negative disorder, which is fuelled by the Sun.

Moreover, as far as we know, Earth is the only place in the vast universe where the negative entropy of life and ecosystems exists.

3.4 Energy Flows and Budgets

The Sun is the focal point of its solar system, accounting for almost all of its energy and mass. Earth is the third-closest of eight planets that revolve around that star. The Sun provides energy that heats the surface of Earth, promotes the circulation of its atmosphere and oceans, causes water to evaporate, and drives photosynthesis. In due course, all of the solar energy that Earth absorbs is dissipated back to outer space by an emission of long-wave infrared radiation. Because the inputs and outputs are in an essentially perfect balance, Earth is a **flow-through system** with respect to energy.

The input of energy to Earth is known as the **solar constant**. This insolation has a value of 8.21 J/cm²·min (1.96 cal/cm²·min), measured at the average distance from the Sun in Earth's elliptical orbit, and just beyond the atmosphere **(Figure 3.2)**. Visible radiation (ranging from about 380–750 µm in wavelength) and near-infrared (750–2500 µm) each account for about half of the incoming solar energy. Ultraviolet radiation accounts for less than 1 percent of the insolation, but it is biologically important because it can cause various injuries to organisms.

Earth has an **energy budget**, which describes how the input of sunlight is reflected, absorbed, temporarily stored in different ways, and then eventually re-radiated back to space **(Figure 3.3, p. 54)**. Important aspects of Earth's energy budget are examined below:

- *Reflection* refers to incoming sunlight that is not absorbed by either the atmosphere or surface of Earth. According to **Figure 3.3**, an average of 30 percent of the incoming solar radiation is reflected back to space. The reflectivity (or **albedo**) is affected by
  - *amounts of cloud cover and suspended atmospheric particulates*, both of which are highly reflective and are also extremely variable over time and space;
  - *character of the surface at a place or region*, with snow and ice being especially reflective and dark-coloured vegetation (such as boreal forest) or recently burnt areas being highly absorptive; and
  - *the angle of incidence* of the insolation (a lower angle means greater reflectivity); Canada occurs at relatively high latitudes, so the relative amount of reflection averages higher during the winter and lower in the summer, and also higher around dawn and dusk and lower at noon.
- *Absorption of certain wavelengths of solar radiation by atmospheric constituents*, such as certain gases and vapours, results in heating of their mass and causes differential thermal gradients to develop. The gradients become dissipated by winds (atmospheric mixing) and by the re-radiation of longer-wave infrared. The atmosphere absorbs about 25 percent of the incident solar radiation, with H_2O vapour and CO_2 gas being especially effective at doing this, particularly in the infrared part of the spectrum.
- *Absorption of solar radiation by the surface* accounts for about 45 percent of the solar energy received by Earth, but this varies greatly from place to place, depending on the local albedo. The absorptive surfaces include non-living ones such as water, rocks, and buildings, as well as living matter such as vegetation. Dark-coloured surfaces are especially effective at absorbing solar radiation.
- *Evaporation of water* occurs from both non-living surfaces, such as oceans, lakes, wetlands, and moist soil, and also from organisms. Evaporation occurring from all surfaces is called

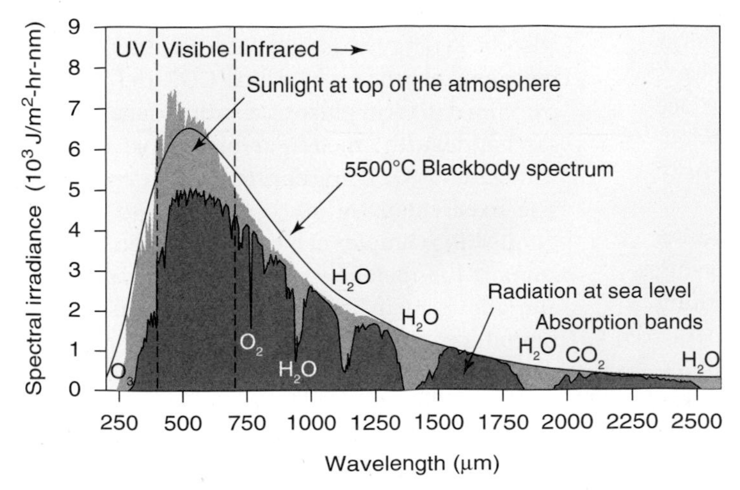

FIGURE 3.2
The Solar Spectrum. The solid line shows the radiative spectrum that would be exhibited by a theoretical black body with a surface temperature of 5500°C (similar to that of the Sun). The overlying coloured area is the similar quality of solar radiation as it is received at the outer limits of Earth's atmosphere. The jagged spectrum beneath is the average spectrum of sunlight that is received at Earth's surface, after the wavelength-specific reflection and absorption by atmospheric gases, particulates, and clouds.

SOURCE: Robert A. Rohde/Global Warming Art

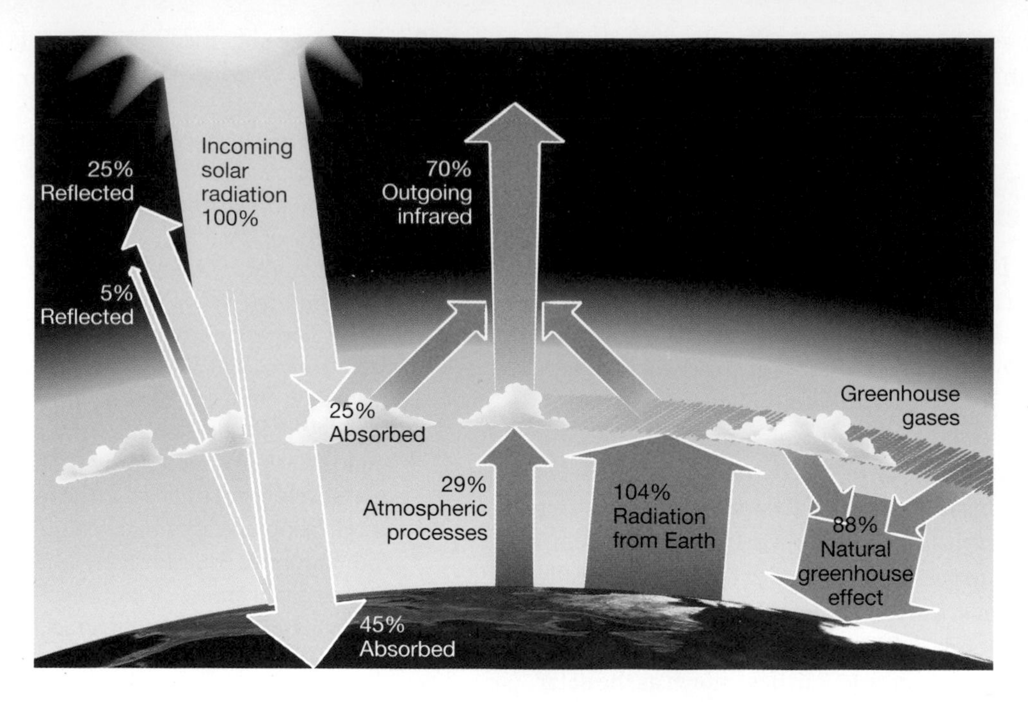

FIGURE 3.3

The Planetary Energy Budget. About 25 percent of the sunlight that reaches the outer limit of the atmosphere is reflected back to space by clouds and atmospheric particulates. An additional 5 percent is reflected away by the surface. The other 70 percent is absorbed and mostly heats the atmosphere and the surfaces of terrestrial and aquatic environments. The absorbed energy is eventually dissipated by a re-radiation of longer-wave infrared energy. Greenhouse gases in the atmosphere interfere with this re-radiation, and this phenomenon keeps the surface warmer than it would otherwise be. The numbers in the figure are "percentage of incoming solar radiation."

SOURCE: S.H. Schneider, "Climate Modeling," *Scientific American*, 256, 72–80 (figure on page 72) (May 1987). Reprinted by permission of Nature Publishing Group.

evapotranspiration, and that from organisms, principally from vegetation, is **transpiration**. The evaporation of water involves a change of state from a liquid to a gaseous form. This process absorbs energy, known as the latent heat (or enthalpy) of vapourization, which has a value of 2.26 kJ per g of H_2O at 100°C. However, it takes more energy to evaporate water that is at a cold temperature compared with a warm one. It also takes less energy to evaporate water at a higher altitude or at a lower barometric pressure (water boils at 100°C at sea level, but at 68°C at 8848 m on the summit of Mount Everest). Because the evaporation of water is endothermic (i.e., an energy input is needed to make it happen), this process helps to dissipate the heat content of the surface and so results in cooling. In contrast, the condensation of water is exothermic, so it releases heat; this happens when dew or frost occurs.

- *Melting of snow and ice* also absorbs energy, known as the latent heat (enthalpy) of fusion and having a value of 0.33 kJ/g at a temperature of 0°C. Melting helps to dissipate the heat of absorbed solar energy, as does any sub sequent increase in the temperature of the liquid water—for example, it takes about 4.19 J to raise the temperature of 1 g of water by 1°C (or 83.8 J to increase the temperature from 0°C to 20°C).
- *Wind and water currents* are large-scale phenomena by which the highly uneven distributions of heat content in the atmosphere and oceans become more evenly dispersed. In general, these processes involve convective flows of mass and thermal energy from lower-latitude regions, which are warmer because they have a much larger annual absorption of solar radiation, to cooler regions at higher latitudes.
- *Biological fixation* occurs when energy within the visible part of the solar spectrum, principally red and blue wavelengths, is absorbed by chlorophyll, a pigment that occurs in plants and algae. The absorbed energy is used to drive photosynthesis, a biochemical process by which CO2 and H2O are combined to form glucose, a simple sugar (monosaccharide) with a molecular formula of C6H12O6, with gaseous O2 being emitted as a waste product. The fixed energy of glucose is used to drive an astonishing complex of biochemical processes that support the metabolism of the plants and algae and allows them to accumulate biomass and to reproduce. The biomass of these autotrophs is then available to support animals and other heterotrophs, which are unable to directly utilize solar energy. Although biological fixation accounts for only a small fraction of the solar radiation absorbed by Earth's surface, averaging less than 1 percent

The evaporation of water from ecological surfaces is one way that the absorbed energy of sunlight becomes dissipated. Transpiration refers to the evaporation of water from plants, while evapotranspiration is from both vegetation and abiotic surfaces. This is a view of a forested swamp in Point Pelee National Park in southern Ontario.

overall, it is obviously crucial to the functioning of ecosystems.

Virtually all of the solar energy absorbed by Earth's surface is eventually re-radiated back to space, and so the planet as a whole represents a zero-sum flow-through system. This is also true of particular areas or places over longer periods of time, such as years and decades. However, during a day or between seasons, the net storage of thermal energy can significantly change. Seasonal changes may include conditions that are much warmer during the summer than in winter and are typical of temperate and higher latitudes, including all of Canada. Over an entire year, however, seasonal variations of energy absorption are evened out and dissipated by the re-radiation of long-wave infrared.

Another small exception involves a relatively tiny amount (at the planetary scale) of longer-term net storage of absorbed solar energy. Dead plant biomass may accumulate over long periods of time in bogs and other wetlands in which sub-surface oxygen is limited, so there is little decomposition. Initially, the organic matter accumulates as peat, at a rate of 20–100 cm per century in bogs. Over geologically long periods of time (millions of years), some of that peat may become deeply buried beneath layers of sediment and other materials, where chemical reactions occurring under conditions of high pressure, high temperature, and a lack of oxygen may form natural gas, petroleum, coal, and oil-sand. These fossil fuels represent a miniscule fraction of the solar energy that arrived to Earth, was fixed by autotrophs, and then accumulated at an exceedingly slow rate over geological time.

3.5 The Greenhouse Effect

Earth's energy budget has a crucial influence on environmental conditions on or near the surface of the planet. One of these influences is exerted by the so-called **greenhouse effect**, a natural phenomenon that exists because of the presence of certain gases in the atmosphere. These **greenhouse gases (GHGs)** absorb some of the long-wave infrared emitted by the surface of Earth as it cools itself of absorbed solar radiation. The GHGs become warmed by this process, and so they re-radiate even longer-wave infrared energy in all directions, including back to Earth's surface. The overall effect is to slow the radiative cooling of the surface, in a sense acting as a thermal blanket over the planet. Because of this greenhouse effect, Earth has an average surface temperature of about 15°C, or 33°C warmer than the –18°C that it would otherwise be.

Clearly, this natural greenhouse effect has a beneficial influence on environmental conditions on Earth. In the absence of this phenomenon, almost all water on the planet would be frozen. A primordial ice-covered planet would have been inhospitable to the genesis of life and to the subsequent evolution that has allowed myriad forms of life to diversify and flourish, including the species that survive today. Liquid water is necessary for almost all physiological functions, such as the action of enzymes, and it provides most of the mass of organisms. Abundant liquid water is also crucial to many ecological functions—it is a key feature of the matrix of ecosystems and is essential to certain mass-flows that are essential to nutrient cycling and for other reasons, as occur in rivers and oceanic currents.

The most important greenhouse gas is water vapour (H_2O), which is responsible for about 36 percent of the warming influence. Next in importance is carbon dioxide (CO_2), and then methane (CH_4), nitrous oxide (N_2O), ozone (O_3), carbon tetrachloride (CCl_4), and chlorofluorocarbons (CFCs). Of these various substances, CFCs are the most radiatively powerful, because on a per-molecule basis they are 4000 to 8000 times more effective at absorbing infrared than is CO_2 (this number is known as the *greenhouse warming potential*). By comparison, CCl_4 is 1400 times as strong as CO_2; N_2O, 310 times; CH_4, 20 times; and O_3, 17 times.

The above explanation of the greenhouse effect is not particularly controversial, and the following facts are widely acknowledged:

- Earth has a flow-through energy budget.
- The planet has a natural greenhouse effect caused by certain gases in the atmosphere.
- this phenomenon has been crucial in setting the environmental stage for biological genesis and evolution

TABLE 3.1 Increases in Concentration of Greenhouse Gases in the Atmosphere

	Greenhouse Gas Concentration	
	1750	2008
CO_2 (ppm)	280	385
CH_4 (ppm)	0.7	1.8
N_2O (ppm)	0.27	0.32
CFCs (ppb)	0.0	1.2

SOURCE: CDIAC (2009).

Two additional facts are that

- the concentrations of greenhouse gases, with the exception of water vapour, have been rapidly increasing during the past several centuries
- this important environmental change is occurring because of anthropogenic emissions

The concentration of CO_2 has increased from about 280 ppm in 1750 to 385 ppm in 2008 **(Table 3.1).** During the same period, CH_4 increased from 0.7 to 1.8 ppm, and changes have also occurred in other GHGs. The increases are coincident with the massive growth of both the human population and industrialization during the past several centuries.

The causes of the increases of CO_2 are particularly well understood. Principally, they are due to the combustion of fossil fuels, the clearing of forests, and to a much lesser degree, the manufacturing of cement. Recent increases of CO_2 concentration are shown in **Figure 3.4.** These increases have been observed at many places around the world in addition to Mauna Loa and Alert, and they represent one of the best-documented changes in global environmental chemistry caused by anthropogenic influences.

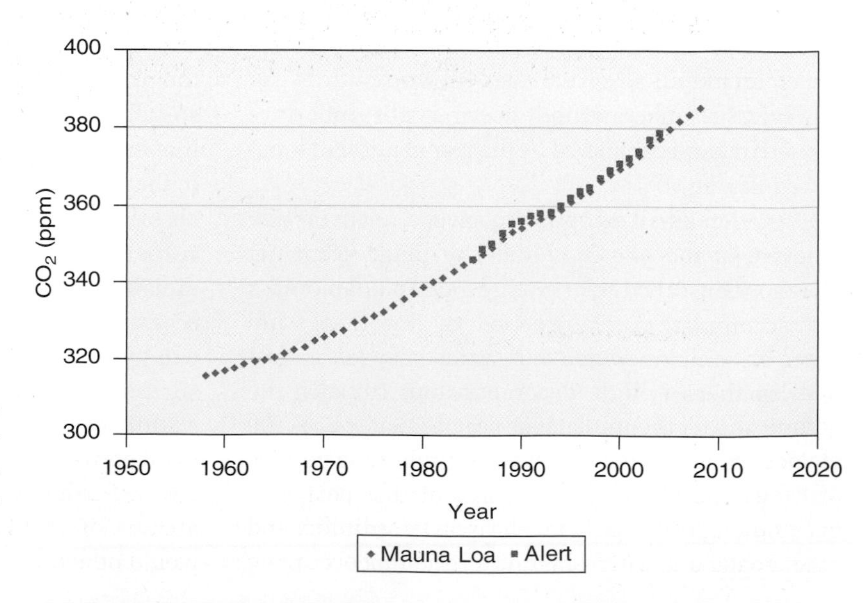

FIGURE 3.4

Recent Increases of CO_2 Concentration in the Atmosphere. The data are from environmental observatories located on Mauna Loa, Hawaii, and at Alert, Ellesmere Island, Nunavut.

SOURCE: Data from Keeling et al. (2009).

Bill Freedman

Since about 1850, one of the effects of a warming climate has been the widespread melting of glaciers. This glacier on Ellesmere Island is melting back by several metres each year, exposing new till substrates for colonization by tundra plants.

Although greenhouse gases help to maintain the temperature of Earth's atmosphere in a roughly equilibrium condition, their increasing concentrations may be intensifying the natural greenhouse effect. According to the Intergovernmental Panel on Climate Change (IPCC), an international organization under the auspices of the United Nations Environment Program, there is abundant evidence that the global climate has been warming for more than 100 years and that this important environmental change is being caused by anthropogenic emissions of GHGs (IPCC, 2007). The IPCC estimates that increased concentrations of CO_2 are responsible for about 60 percent of the anthropogenic warming, CH_4 for 15 percent, CFCs for 12 percent, O_3 for 8 percent, and N_2O for 5 percent.

Nevertheless, the fact and causes of anthropogenic global warming remain controversial. A strong majority of environmental scientists believes that global warming has been occurring for about 150 years and that it is being caused by anthropogenic emissions of GHGs. However, a minority of specialists believes that anthropogenic warming has not yet been proven.

To generate predictions about global warming, atmospheric scientists use supercomputers to run three-dimensional climatic models. The models are based on complex calculations that involve solar radiation inputs as well as their absorption in the atmosphere and at the surface, in various regions of the globe and at different times of year, plus the development of atmospheric thermal gradients and mixing by winds, along with other influences on temperature and additional climatic variables. Once the models can be demonstrated as being effective at predicting climatic conditions in the present and in the recent past (backcasting), they can be used to perform "virtual experiments." These involve re-parameterization to "modify" atmospheric conditions by increasing the strength of the greenhouse effect to see what changes might occur in future climates. Commonly examined scenarios include increases of atmospheric CO_2 concentrations by 50–100 percent or more (if recent rates of increase in atmospheric CO_2 were projected into the future, its concentration would double in about two centuries).

In general, these models predict that the average global surface temperature is likely to be 1°C–4°C warmer in 2050 than today. However, the warming will be most intense and occur more quickly in temperate and higher latitudes (including boreal and arctic regions) than in the tropics. It is probable that there will also be large changes in precipitation regimes, including the interior of continents becoming drier than they are today. Both alpine and high-latitude glaciers will melt back and in many places disappear, decreasing the flow in many rivers. If these and other predicted climatic changes occur, they will result in enormous challenges to vital economic activities, such as the practice of agriculture, while also causing massive ecological damage.

These sorts of forecasts of anthropogenic global warming and other elements of climate change, and of their economic and ecological consequences, are of course fraught with uncertainty. Climatic conditions, economies, and ecosystems are extraordinarily complex phenomena, and their responses to future

ECOLOGY IN DEPTH 3.1

Warming the Tundra

There is increasing evidence that anthropogenic increases in the concentrations of greenhouse gases in the atmosphere, particularly CO_2, are causing the global climate to become warmer. However, the warming will not be distributed evenly over the globe—it is predicted to be much more intense at higher latitudes, such as in the Arctic region. Signals of this climate change are already being observed, including glaciers that have been rapidly melting during the past century, a much longer ice-free season over vast regions of the Arctic Ocean, and the recent appearance of relatively southern birds in some places in the Arctic, such as American robins (*Turdus migratorius*).

Ecologists working in the Arctic believe that climatic warming is likely to have a number of effects on the vegetation of northern climes. These might include increased productivity and more prolific flowering due to a longer growing season, faster decomposition and nutrient cycling due to microbial activity being stimulated by warmer soil and an increased depth of the seasonally thawed active layer, and eventually the migration of boreal plants into presently tundra habitats. These predictions appear to be sensible, but they are conjectural, meaning they are based on an extrapolation of existing ideas and incomplete knowledge, rather than being derived from experimental work that is designed to test hypotheses about warming in the Arctic.

But there are ways of doing realistic experiments related to the effects of climate warming on Arctic vegetation. One method is remarkably low-tech—it involves enclosing small areas of natural tundra within open-topped frames covered with clear material (such as Plexiglas or greenhouse fibreglass sheeting) that passively warms the interior microclimate by reducing wind speeds, thereby slowing the dissipation of heat of absorbed solar radiation. Ecosystem processes such as plant growth and nutrient cycling are then compared with non-enclosed reference plots. Because the method is simple and inexpensive to use, it is feasible to examine various kinds of plant communities and to have good replication within all of them. This undemanding yet elegant experimental method was pioneered by Greg Henry of the University of British Columbia. Once he and others demonstrated that it is an effective way to do research on warming in the Arctic, it was adopted by ecologists in other northern countries. They established a collaborative network called the International Tundra Experiment (ITEX) to compare their results and develop predictions about the ecological effects of climate warming.

For instance, comparisons among 11 ITEX locations found that the open-top warming chambers raised the ground-level air temperature by 1°C–3°C, which stimulated the productivity and flowering of dwarf shrubs, grasses, and sedges (Arft et al., 1999). A general increase in the cover of shrub species in response to warming was found across the tundra biome (Walker et al., 2006). The experimental results suggest that increases in shrub abundance observed in many areas of the Arctic are a result of recent warming. However, the increased competition from these favoured plants may be decreasing the abundance of slower-growing species, such as lichens and bryophytes, resulting in an overall loss of species diversity. Studies of CO_2 flux at four ITEX locations found that the warming has caused a general increase in gross primary production (photosynthesis) and an increase in ecosystem-level respiration, with the greatest responses occurring in dry tundra communities (Oberbauer et al., 2007).

It is important to note, however, that the observed responses of tundra vegetation to warming were not always consistent among far-flung locations or among habitats that varied in soil moisture within particular study areas. This observation highlights the difficulty in making general predictions about the ecological responses to climate warming—ecosystems are just too complex in their structure and function, and in their reactions to changes in environmental conditions, to provide straightforward answers regarding these sorts of issues.

environmental change cannot always be predicted with accuracy. Nevertheless, there is an emerging consensus among environmental scientists that anthropogenic climate warming is already occurring and is likely to intensify in the near future. The consequences of this global change could be dire. As a result, there is a surge of popular and political support for actions to slow down the increase of greenhouse gases in the atmosphere, and to eventually reduce their concentrations.

Some of the proposed solutions to this environmental problem are ecological. One is to conserve existing forests and other ecosystems that store large amounts of biomass to prevent their organic carbon from ending up in the atmosphere as CO_2. Another tactic is intended to withdraw CO_2 that is already in the atmosphere, for example, by extensively planting trees on disused agricultural land to increase the amount of carbon stored in biomass (this is known as **afforestation**; see Ecology in Depth 3.2).

Anthropogenic climate change is an important issue—it has huge implications for the structure and sustainability of the human economy and for the viability of many wild species and natural ecosystems. Although the details of this issue are beyond the scope of this ecology textbook, it is important to know that recent climate warming appears to be forced by an intensification of the planet's natural greenhouse effect and that this influence is likely anthropogenic.

3.6 Energy Fixation in Ecosystems

The fixation of solar radiation by photosynthetic organisms, and the subsequent transfer of the organic energy of biomass through trophic systems, is another key subject area of ecological energetics. Ecologists classify organisms according to the manner in which they access energy.

Autotrophs

Autotrophs are organisms that have the capability of utilizing an external source of energy to drive their fixation of water and inorganic carbon (usually CO_2) into glucose, a simple sugar. The glucose is then used to power their other metabolic functions, such as synthesization of many different biochemicals, growth through an increase of biomass, and reproduction. Autotrophic organisms provide the biological foundation of ecological productivity, so they are referred to as being **primary producers.** There are two broad groups of autotrophs, which are distinguished by the source of energy they use to accomplish their initial biosynthesis of glucose:

- **Photoautotrophs** are the most abundant kinds of autotrophs and are responsible for almost all of the productivity of the biosphere. These organisms capture certain wavelengths of sunlight and use that energy to drive their photosynthesis. The most prominent groups of photoautotrophs are plants in terrestrial environments and algae and blue-green bacteria in aquatic ones. These organisms utilize certain pigments in their photosynthetic tissues, particularly chlorophyll, to capture visible electromagnetic radiation for use in photosynthesis. Because chlorophyll is a strong absorber within the red and blue ranges of visible light and is reflective to green, the photosynthetic tissues of these organisms appear to be green in colour.
- **Chemoautotrophs** are a less-prominent group of autotrophs. They are specialized bacteria that have the ability to harness energy from certain inorganic chemicals to power their **chemosynthesis** metabolism. One example is *Thiobacillus thiooxidans,* a bacterium with an extraordinary capability to oxidize sulphide minerals (such as iron sulphide, FeS_2) according to the following reaction:

  $$4\,FeS_2 + 15\,O_2 + 14\,H_2O \rightarrow 4\,Fe(OH)_3 + 16\,H^+ + 8\,SO_4^{2-}$$

  Because this reaction is exothermic, some of the released energy can be used to drive the biosynthesis of $CO_2 + H_2O$ to form glucose. As with photoautotrophs, that fixed energy is then available to fuel all other aspects of the metabolism of the bacteria.

The total amount of solar energy that is fixed by all of the autotrophs in an ecosystem is referred to as **gross primary production (GPP)**. Some of the GPP is used to support the **respiration (R)** of the primary producers, which is needed to maintain their essential metabolic health. Respiration involves an oxidation of biochemicals through metabolic reactions, and it requires O_2 and releases CO_2 and H_2O as wastes. In its simplest expression, R is the opposite of photosynthesis, as follows:

$$C_6H_{12}O_6 + 6\,O_2 \rightarrow 6\,H_2O + 6\,CO_2 + \text{energy to support metabolism}$$

Net primary production (NPP) is calculated as GPP minus R. In this sense, NPP is the amount of fixed energy that remains after autotrophs have used some

Almost all plants are autotrophs, using the pigment chlorophyll to capture sunlight that is used to power their photosynthesis. There are a few exceptions, however. The widespread boreal species pictured here is known as Indian-pipe or corpse-plant (*Monotropa uniflora*). It is a herbaceous perennial but lacks chlorophyll and so is non-photosynthetic. It gets its energy by parasitizing certain fungi that live in a mycorrhizal mutualism with trees. In effect, it uses some of the photosynthetic production of nearby trees but gets that energy from a fungal intermediary.

Bill Freedman

Herbivores are animals that feed on plants. These plains bison (*Bison bison*) are feeding on shortgrass prairie on the Old Man on His Back Ecological Preserve of the Nature Conservancy of Canada, near Eastend, Saskatchewan.

of their GPP to support their respiration, as follows: NPP = GPP – R. Often, NPP is measured as an accumulation of biomass (this is examined in more detail below).

Heterotrophs

Unlike autotrophs, heterotrophs do not have a capability to fix solar energy into biochemicals. Rather, they must feed on the biomass of other organisms and use that fixed energy to support their metabolism, growth, and reproduction. Several kinds of heterotrophs can be identified, depending on how they feed within an ecosystem:

- **Herbivores** (**primary consumers**) are animals that feed on the biomass of plants, familiar examples being locusts, sparrows, rabbits, and moose.
- **Carnivores** (**secondary consumers**) feed on other animals; they include preying mantis, spiders, salmon, eagles, coyotes, and orcas.
- **Omnivores** feed on the biomass of both plants and animals; examples are grizzly bears and humans.
- **Detritivores** (**decomposers** or **saprophytes**) eat dead organic matter; they include most kinds of bacteria and fungi, earthworms, and vultures.

Louise Murray/Getstock.com

Carnivores are heterotrophic animals that feed on other animals. These polar bears (*Ursus maritimus*) from southern Baffin Island, Nunavut, feed almost exclusively on marine mammals, especially ringed seals (*Phoca hispida*).

Ecological Productivity

Productivity is the rate at which energy is being fixed by an organism, a community, or a larger ecosystem. Productivity is usually standardized to time and area, and it may be reported in units of biomass, such as tonnes per hectare per year (t/ha·yr), or in units of energy, such as joules. Biomass data can be converted to energy using factors that vary among species, depending on the energy density of their tissues. For instance, one tonne of dry tree biomass is equivalent to 18–22 $\times 10^9$ J (GJ/t). Biomass is usually reported as dry weight, because the energy required to evaporate water prior to combustion is not part of the fixed-energy content of the material.

The various biomes vary greatly in their primary productivity **(Table 3.2)**. The rate of productivity is highest in ecosystems in which the environmental constraints on energy fixation are relatively low, particularly the availabilities of moisture, nutrients, and light. In general, tropical forest, marsh and swamp wetlands, coral reefs, and estuaries are the most productive ecosystems. The rates of productivity are much lower in ecosystems in which environmental factors are highly limiting. For example, the productivity of deserts is constrained by a lack of moisture, that of tundra by cold temperatures and a short growing season, and that of open oceans by sparse nutrients.

The **production** of an ecosystem is calculated as its productivity (usually on an annual basis) multiplied by the area being considered. Open oceans and tropical forests account for the largest amounts of global production **(Table 3.2)**. Open oceans have low productivity because they are relatively infertile, but their global production is enormous because their

TABLE 3.2 The Productivity of Major Biomes

Productivity is a rate function, so it is standardized by area and time. Global net production is the total amount of biomass that is annually produced by a biome. Biomass is the accumulated organic matter, on a per-hectare basis. The biomes are arranged in order of decreasing primary productivity.

Ecosystem	Net Primary Productivity (tC/ha·yr)	Area (10^6 km^2)	Global Net Production (10^9 tC/yr)	Biomass (tC/ha)
Terrestrial Biomes				
Wetlands	11.3	2.0	2.2	68
Tropical rain forest	9.0	17.0	15.3	200
Tropical seasonal forest	6.8	7.5	5.1	160
Temperate evergreen forest	5.9	5.0	2.9	160
Temperate deciduous forest	5.4	7.0	3.8	135
Savannah	3.2	15.0	4.7	18
Boreal forest	3.6	12.0	4.3	90
Open woodland	2.7	8.0	2.2	27
Cultivated land	2.9	14.0	4.1	5
Temperate grassland	2.3	9.0	2.0	7
Lake & stream	2.3	2.5	0.6	0.1
Tundra, arctic & alpine	0.65	8.0	0.5	3
Desert & semidesert scrub	0.32	18.0	0.6	3
Extreme desert	0.012	24.0	0.04	0.1
Marine Biomes				
Reefs	9.0	0.6	0.5	9
Estuary	8.1	1.4	1.1	4.5
Upwelling zones	2.3	0.4	0.1	0.1
Continental shelf	1.6	26.6	4.3	0.05
Open ocean	0.57	332.0	18.9	0.014
Global Summary				
Total Continental	3.2	149	48.3	55.5
Total Marine	0.7	361	24.9	0.05
Total World	1.4	510	73.2	16.3

SOURCE: Whittaker, R. H. and G. E. Likens. 1975. The biosphere and man. Pp. 305–328 in *Primary Productivity of the Biosphere*. (H. Lieth and R. H. Whittaker, eds.). Springer-Verlag, New York, NY. With kind permission of Springer Science+Business Media and the author.

total area is vast. Tropical forests cover a much smaller area of the globe, but their production is large because they have a relatively high productivity.

Biomass or **standing crop** refers to the weight of accumulated production of ecosystems rather than the rate at which it is occurring. Biomass is usually measured on a dry-weight basis, and it is standardized to area. Data on the typical biomass of major biomes are summarized in **Table 3.2.** Note that among terrestrial ecosystems, the largest biomass accumulations are in old-growth forests and other persistent ecosystems that are dominated by long-lived plants. For instance, temperate conifer forests growing in coastal humid climates of British Columbia typically have a tree biomass of 150–250 tC/ha, and they may exceed 500 tC/ha in old-growth stands (Smithwick et al., 2002; Freedman et al., 2009).

In contrast, the biomass is much smaller in younger ecosystems that are recovering from a disturbance, such as a forest affected by a recent wildfire or clear-cut. Biomass is also relatively low in ecosystems that are dominated by herbaceous plants that die back at the end of the growing season, as occurs in marshes and prairies.

Ecological studies may distinguish between the living biomass of plants or animals and that of litter and other dead materials, including the humified (partially decomposed) organic matter that occurs in soil. In some ecosystems, particularly older forests, much of the biomass occurs in the form of dead organic matter. For instance, a study of mature conifer forest in Nova Scotia found that 29 percent of the biomass occurred in the above-ground tree biomass, 10 percent in the roots, 8 percent in deadwood (standing dead trees, known as snags, plus large woody debris on the ground), 11 percent in the forest floor, and 42 percent in the soil (within the rooting depth of the trees) **(Figure 3.5).**

The occurrence of dead organic matter is consequential for various reasons, including the following ones:

- Well-humified organic matter in soil contributes to a fertility-related quality known as tilth, which affects beneficial attributes such as aeration, water-holding capacity, and nutrient-exchange capability.
- Much of the organic carbon stored in the ecosystem is in dead compartments, which must be taken into account when calculating the "carbon credits" inherent in the accumulating biomass (see Ecology in Depth 3.2).
- Many species require snags, woody debris, and associated cavities as critical habitat—among the many examples are woodpeckers, swallows, salamanders, and various fungi.

In some ecosystems, the dead organic matter may accumulate to amounts that greatly exceed the biomass of living organisms. This commonly occurs in bogs, which can have metres of peat that represent the accumulated remains of dead wetland vegetation over thousands of years of ecosystem development. Some bogs in Canada may have peat exceeding 10 m in depth. The typical carbon storage of northern peatlands is about 1400 tC/ha, increasing at 0.19 tC/ha.yr (Bridgham et al., 2006).

Ecologists may also study the ways that species allocate their biomass and productivity among various kinds of tissues, which for plants might include foliage, reproductive biomass such as flowers or fruits, wood, and roots. Differences in biomass allocation among species reflect adaptive variations of life-history strategies. Within a species, biomass allocation may also change profoundly with developmental stages, reflecting variations associated with age and reproductive status. Figure 3.6 compares the distribution of biomass between two species of trees—white spruce, a

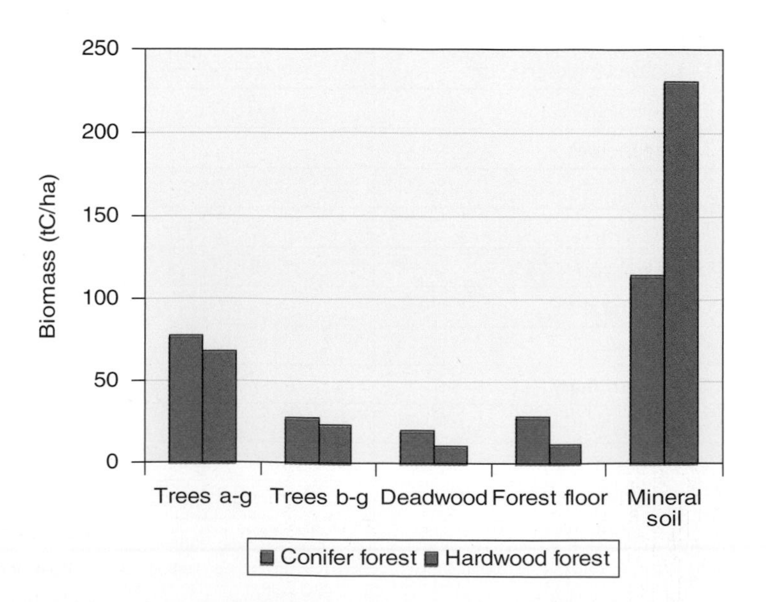

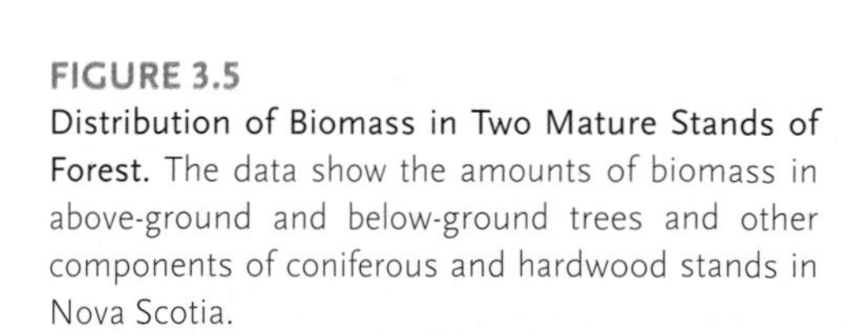
FIGURE 3.5
Distribution of Biomass in Two Mature Stands of Forest. The data show the amounts of biomass in above-ground and below-ground trees and other components of coniferous and hardwood stands in Nova Scotia.

SOURCE: Data from Freedman et al. (2009).

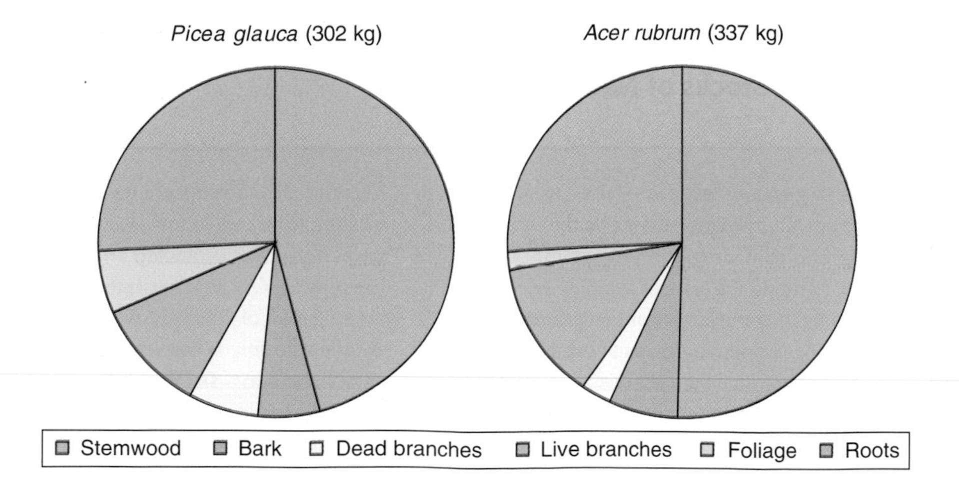

FIGURE 3.6
Distribution of Biomass among Major Tissues of a Coniferous and an Angiosperm Tree. The data are average dry weight, and percentage of total (in the pie sections), for mature white spruce (*Picea glauca*) and red maple (*Acer rubrum*) growing in Nova Scotia. Each diagram is the average of seven trees with stem diameters of 25–30 cm.

SOURCE: Data from Freedman et al. (1982).

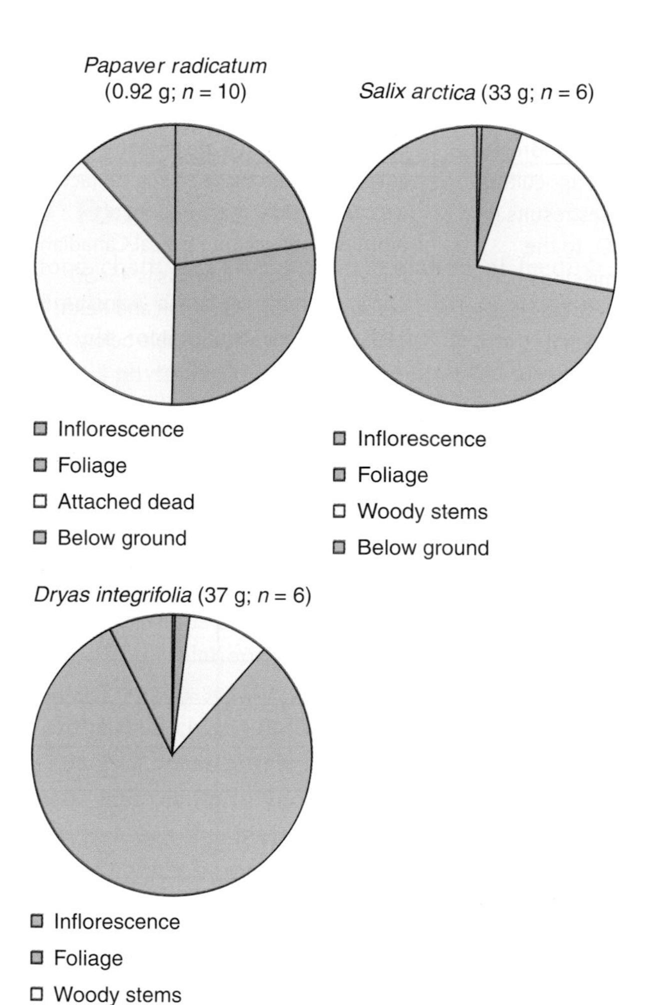

FIGURE 3.7
Distribution of Biomass among Major Tissues of a Selection of Tundra Plants. The data are for a perennial herbaceous plant, the Arctic poppy (*Papaver radicatum*); a dwarf shrub, Arctic willow (*Salix arctica*); and a cushion plant, mountain avens (*Dryas integrifolia*). All were studied on Ellesmere Island, Nunavut. The sample size (n) is indicated, as is the average dry weight of the whole plant.

SOURCE: Data from Maessen et al. (1983).

conifer (gymnosperm), and red maple, a hardwood (angiosperm). Key differences between these species include the relatively large foliar biomass of the conifer, because its evergreen leaves remain on the tree for more than five years while those of the maple are dropped each autumn, as well as the greater weight of branches in the spruce, including persistent dead ones.

Figure 3.7 extends this sort of comparison to smaller plants, in this case, species that grow in high-Arctic tundra. The Arctic poppy is a perennial herbaceous plant, meaning it is long-lived but dies back to the ground each year, with its roots being the perennating tissues. This species allocates a relatively large fraction of its biomass to flowering tissues and photosynthetic leaves and stems. In comparison, the Arctic willow is a dwarf shrub that grows no taller than about 5 cm, and it allocates most of its biomass to woody roots and above-ground stems, and relatively little to leaves or flowers. Lastly, the mountain avens is a long-lived cushion plant that allocates remarkably little of its biomass to living foliage or reproductive structures; rather, most of its biomass occurs as persistently attached dead foliage that provides a measure of relief from the severe microclimate while also helping the plant to retain its scarce reserves of nutrients.

A few studies have documented the productivity of the various trophic levels within ecosystems. For example, in an oak-pine forest on Long Island, the gross primary productivity was 48.1 megajoules per square metre per year ($MJ/m^2 \cdot yr$), equivalent to <0.1 percent of the solar radiation that was received (Odum, 1993). However, the net primary productivity (i.e., GPP – R) was 20.9 $MJ/m^2 \cdot yr$, because the vegetation used 27.2 $MJ/m^2 \cdot yr$ to support its respiration. The NPP mostly occurred as the accumulating biomass of trees. The various heterotrophic organisms used a further 12.6 $MJ/m^2 \cdot yr$, so the net ecosystem production was 8.4 $MJ/m^2 \cdot yr$.

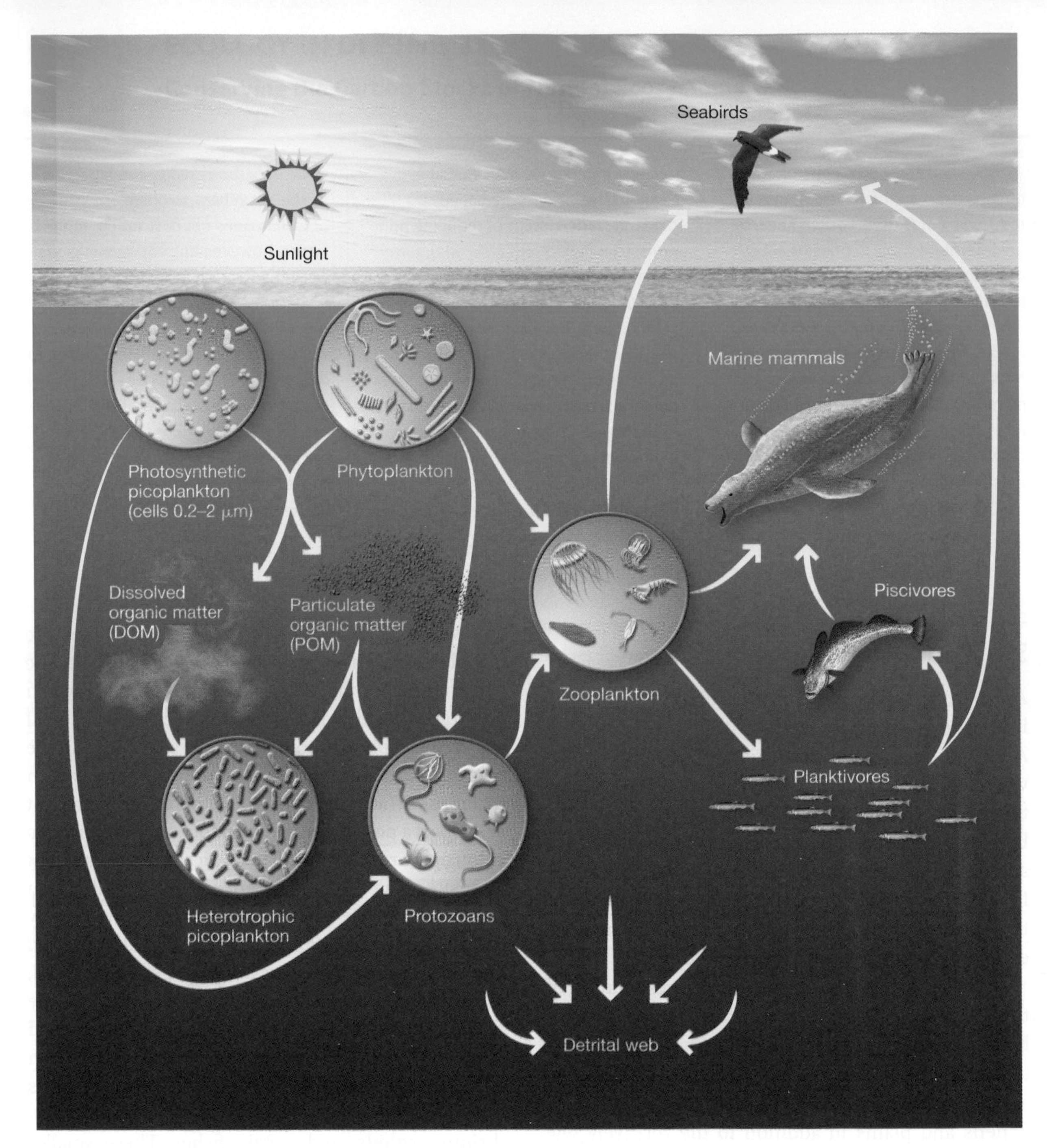

FIGURE 3.8
A Food Web. This diagram illustrates major components of the food web of coastal waters off Nova Scotia.

A portion of the marine euphotic food web is known as the microbial loop. Its basis is dead biomass, consisting of dissolved organic matter (DOM) and particulate organic matter (POM) that is small enough to remain suspended in the water column. The DOM and POM are fed upon by heterotrophic bacteria, which are eaten by single-celled flagellated protozoa, which are in turn fed upon by slightly larger ciliated protozoa. The latter are big enough to be filter-fed by zooplankton, and at that point the microbial loop intersects with the sunlight-fed part of the euphotic food web.

There is also a deep-water detrital food web, which is supported by biomass that sinks into the aphotic zone. This food web is based on dead organic matter, in both dissolved and particulate forms, as well as living organisms that die soon after they permanently descend to the aphotic zone. Some of the dead organic matter eventually reaches the oceanic sediment, where it is fed upon by an array of benthic animals, and is eventually mostly decomposed by a community of microorganisms. However, a small fraction of the organic matter of abyssal depths may eventually become buried, and

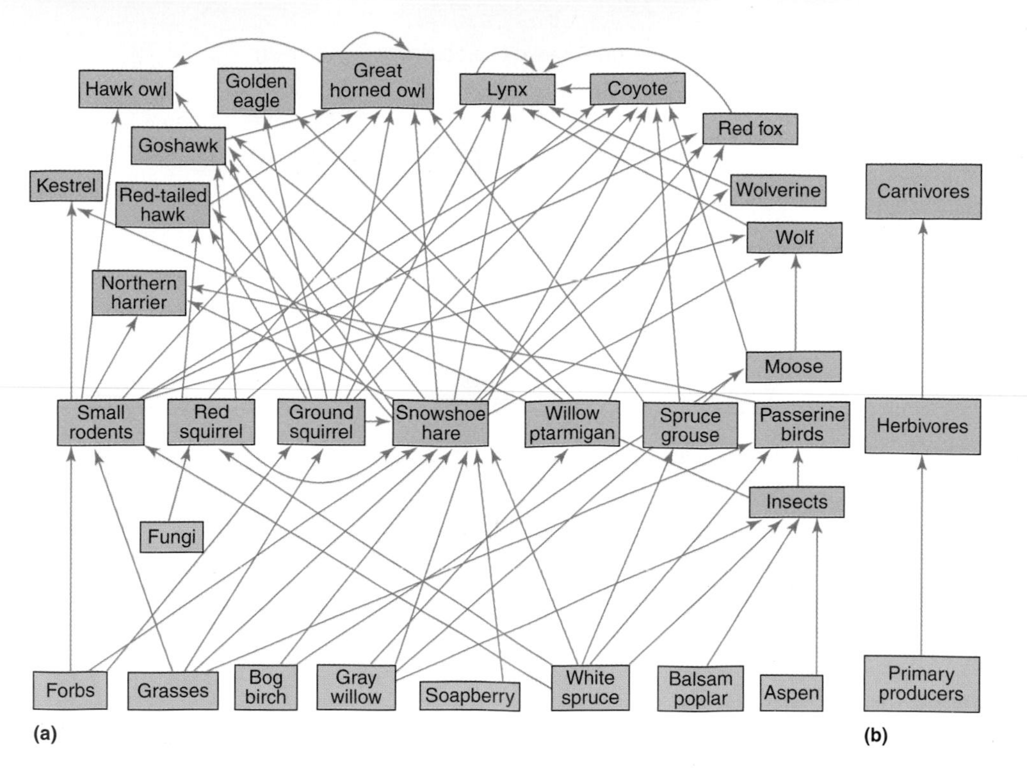

FIGURE 3.9

A Boreal-Forest Food Web in Yukon. This food web notes many of the species that are involved, and not just the functional groups, as in Figure 3.8.

SOURCE: Adapted from Krebs, C. J., Boutin, S., and R. Boonstra. 2001. *Ecosystem Dynamics of the Boreal Forest: The Kluane Project.* Oxford University Press, New York, NY. P. 21, Figure 2.8 "A simplified food web for the vertebrates of the Kluane Region." Adapted by permission of Oxford University Press, Inc.

over geological time it may become metamorphosed into a fossil fuel.

Another example of a food web is presented in **Figure 3.9**, this time for a boreal-forest community in the Kluane region of Yukon. This diagram is more complex than the one in **Figure 3.8**, because many of the key species in the ecosystem are identified, rather than just the functional energetic groups.

The second law of thermodynamics requires that entropy increases whenever there is a transfer of energy within a food web. This fact imposes a degree of inefficiency in the system. Although much of the energy content of a food is used for metabolism and to sustain growth, some of it becomes degraded into heat, which represents an increase in entropy. Essentially for this reason, when plant biomass is consumed by an herbivorous animal, only part of the energy content of the food can be absorbed and utilized to support metabolism and growth **(Figure 3.10).** A similar condition applies to other levels of food webs: a predator cannot absorb all of the energy content of its prey, the rest being excreted as feces, and not all of the

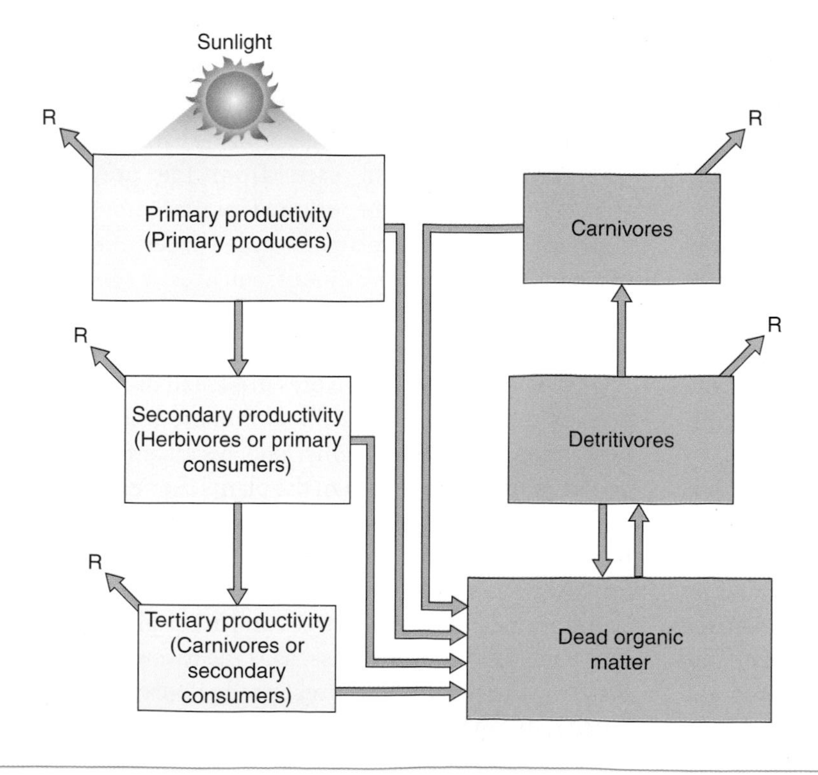

FIGURE 3.10

Model of Energy Transfer in Ecosystems. Because higher levels of a food web always have a smaller productivity than lower ones, the trophic structure of ecosystems is pyramid-shaped. This relationship is roughly indicated by the relative sizes of the boxes, although they are not drawn to a realistic scale. "R" indicates respiration.

assimilated energy can be converted into biomass; the remainder is eventually dissipated as heat.

Averaged over the biosphere, primary producers absorb about half of the sunlight that is available to them, and they then assimilate about 0.2 percent through GPP (the maximum is 6 percent; about half of the GPP is then used to support the autotrophic R; Odum and Barrett, 2005). Typically, herbivores assimilate about 10 percent of the energy content of their food, and carnivores as much as 20 percent (carnivores have a higher assimilation efficiency because they eat a higher-quality food—the flesh of animals, which is rich in protein, fat, and energy density). In a typical ecosystem, because of the stepwise and cumulative inefficiencies of energy transfer between trophic levels, only about 0.01 percent of the incoming sunlight ends up as gross production at the carnivore level.

The inefficiency of energy transfers within ecosystems means that autotrophs always have a greater productivity (on an annual basis) than herbivores that feed upon them. Similarly, the productivity of herbivores is always much greater than that of their predators. An inexact generalization is that each step of trophic level is accompanied by about a 90 percent difference of productivity; that of herbivores is 10 percent that of plants in their ecosystem, and carnivores are 10 percent of the herbivores. Ecological "pyramids" are graphical presentations of these productivity-related aspects of the **trophic structure** of ecosystems. The pyramids are arranged with plant productivity at the bottom, that of herbivores above, and carnivores at the apex. The area of each level is proportional to the annual amount of productivity (see **Figure 3.11**).

Although the distribution of productivity is pyramid-shaped, this is not necessarily the case of either the biomass of an ecosystem or the density of organisms. In the open ocean, for example, the primary producers are communities of picoplankton and phytoplankton, but their biomass may be similar to that of the small crustacean zooplankton that feed upon them. This occurs because, although the autotrophs are much more productive than the zooplankton on an annual basis, their cells are short-lived and so their biomass turns over relatively quickly. In contrast, individual zooplankters live much longer and may accumulate a standing crop that is comparable to that of the primary producers.

In fact, an inverted pyramid of biomass may occur in some ecosystems in which there is a seasonally larger biomass of herbivores than of plants. This may occur in temperate and tropical grasslands in which large animals are the dominant herbivores—they may maintain a larger biomass than the herbaceous vegetation, despite the greater productivity of the plants. This is especially the case during

(a) Pyramid of productivity (10^3 J/m^2-yr)

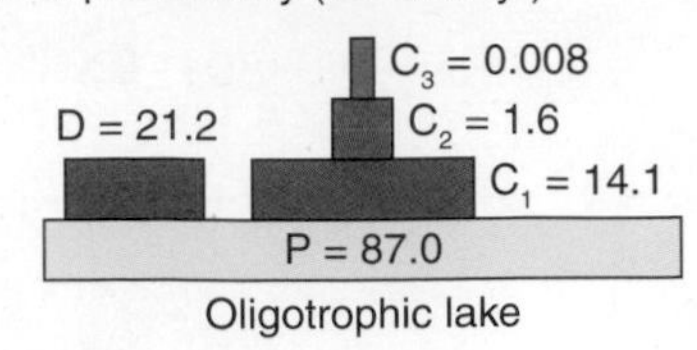

(b) Pyramids of density (10^3/ha)

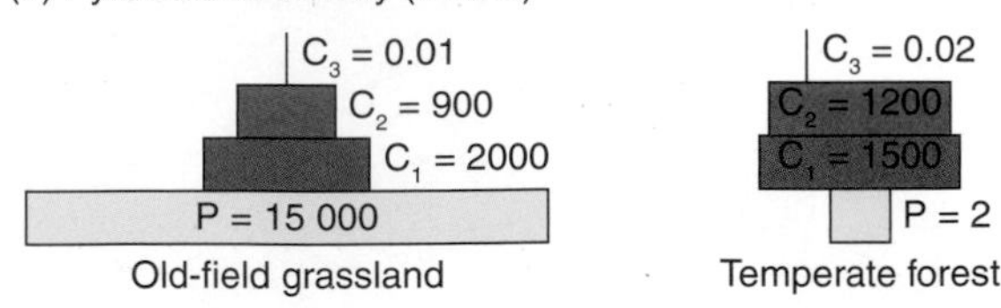

(c) Pyramids of biomass (g/m^3)

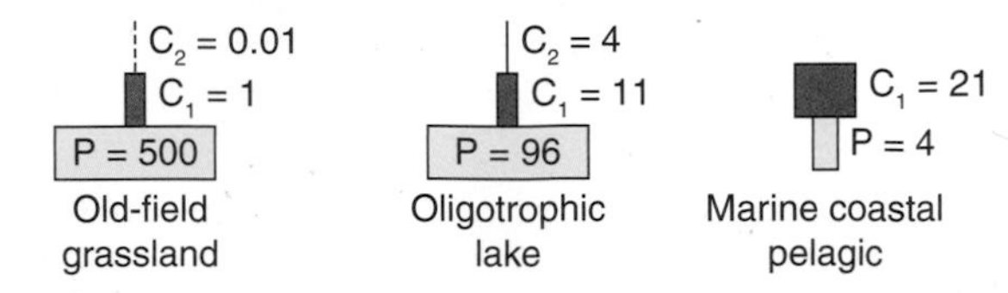

FIGURE 3.11

Ecological Pyramids. (a) A pyramid of productivity of an oligotrophic (unproductive) lake fed by groundwater in Florida; (b) pyramids of density of an old-field grassland in Michigan and temperate forest in Britain; (c) pyramids of biomass in an old-field grassland in Georgia, an oligotrophic lake in Wisconsin, and marine coastal pelagic waters in the English Channel. Symbols: P = primary producers, C_1 = primary consumers, C_2 = secondary consumers, C_3 = tertiary consumers, D = detritivores.

SOURCE: From Odum/Barrett. *Fundamentals of Ecology*, 5E. © 2005 Brooks/Cole, a part of Cengage Learning, Inc. Reproduced by permission.www.cengage.com/permissions

the non-growing season, when there is a sparse biomass of plants but large populations (and biomass) of big herbivores. In the prairies of Canada, for example, the plant biomass during winter is relatively small, consisting of the dormant below-ground perennating tissues of grasses and forbs plus their withered above-ground parts from the previous growing season. In the original prairie, however, there still might be a relatively large wintertime biomass of large grazing animals, such as bison and pronghorn antelope (today, the large grazers are more typically cows).

Of course, most herbivores are small animals—invertebrates are numerically dominant among the herbivores in all ecosystems, and because they are generally much smaller than the plants they eat, there can also be an inverted pyramid of population density. In most forests, for instance, insects are the most important herbivores and they maintain a much larger abundance than the trees and other plants that they feed upon. Nevertheless, as is the case of all ecosystems, the pyramid of forest productivity must be much narrower at the top than at the bottom.

A CANADIAN ECOLOGIST 3.1

Mike Apps: Carbon in Ecosystems

Mike Apps

Mike Apps was a research scientist (now retired) with the Canadian Forest Service (CFS) whose work focused on the relationships between boreal forest and the global carbon budget, and on the implications of management for emissions of greenhouse gases. Like most scientists, Apps' approach to his interests was through the diligent practice of research—he collaborated with many Canadian and international experts in the field of carbon cycling and published papers in specialized journals as well as research reports. He took particular interest in building relationships among boreal ecologists from North America, Europe, Russia, and China at a time when such international relationships were lacking.

Apps also played a lead role in the work of the Intergovernmental Panel on Climate Change (IPCC), an agency of the United Nations Environment Program. The IPCC is charged with leading a global effort to understand the causes and consequences of anthropogenic climate change. Apps and many other IPCC participants shared in the 2007 Nobel Peace Prize, which was co-awarded to the IPCC and former U.S. Vice-President Al Gore "for their efforts to build up and disseminate greater knowledge about man-made climate change, and to lay the foundations for the measures that are needed to counteract such change."

Among the key accomplishments of Apps and his co-researchers was the advancement of scientific understanding of the dynamics of biomass carbon in the terrestrial landscapes of Canada and other northern regions, particularly in forests. Critical to this work was the development of an improved understanding of the implications of forest management for biomass storage and productivity—including timber harvesting, plantation establishment, and the creation of protected areas. Canadian forests are important in these regards—about 400 million hectares, or half the land area of Canada, is forested—representing 10 percent of the global forest estate. Apps and his colleagues have shown that, while northern forests store enormous amounts of biomass carbon, they sometimes serve as a net sink (i.e., the amount of CO_2 fixation exceeds releases by respiration, decomposition, and disturbances) but at other times are a net source (CO_2 releases exceed fixation). The "source" years are related to times when wildfires are extensive or insect damage is severe, as is now occurring because of damage caused to western forests by the mountain pine beetle (*Dendroctonus ponderosae*). Apps and his colleagues have helped both scientists and policy makers to appreciate the role that natural disturbances play in the carbon budget of the boreal forest.

The ongoing work of Apps, Werner Kurz (also a CFS scientist), and other colleagues is now focused on improving our capability to model carbon storage and dynamics in forest ecosystems across Canada, including in tree biomass and the dead organic matter of litter and soil. Moreover, their simulation models can predict effects of management activities and environmental change. Their *National Forest Carbon Monitoring, Accounting and Reporting System* is an ongoing collaboration led by CFS that involves other agencies and many scientists (see http://carbon.cfs.nrcan.gc.ca/index_e.html). One of the key components of this system is the Carbon Budget Model of the Canadian Forest Sector (CBM-CFS3), which has become a widely used tool for research and by forest managers. The CBM-CFS3 helps us understand the climate-change and other environmental consequences of economic and stewardship choices that potentially affect immense tracts of the Canadian forest estate.

One consequence of the cumulative inefficiencies of energy transfers between trophic levels is that ecosystems cannot support a large productivity of top predators, such as mountain lions, timber wolves, orcas, or sharks. In general, high-level carnivores can be sustained only by ecosystems that are highly productive or very extensive. This is well illustrated by the savannas and grasslands of Africa, which may support numerous species of large-mammal predators: cheetahs, leopards, lions, hyenas, and wild dogs. The savannah is an extensive and—when there is no drought—a productive habitat that supports an abundance of top predators. In contrast, the tundra and boreal forest of northern Canada can support only one natural top predator, the wolf, because although these are vast habitats, they are not productive. Of course, during the past century, much of the area of African savannah and grassland has been settled and converted to agricultural land use. It is difficult for so many top-predator species to survive in a greatly diminished natural ecosystem.

Prior to their integration with the commercial economy, initially through the trapping and trading of wild-animal furs, the Arctic Inuit and the boreal-dwelling Indian peoples of Canada had a diet that was primarily carnivorous, so those cultures functioned as top predators in their ecosystem. As a consequence of feeding at a high level of their food web, these aboriginal peoples did not maintain large populations. In modern times, most people feed as omnivores and are participating in an increasingly globalized economy that harvests a wide range of foods derived from microbes, fungi, algae, plants, and invertebrate and vertebrate animals. Having access to such a wide array of foodstuffs is allowing humans to maintain an extremely large population—about 6.8 billion in 2010. However, with the rapid depletion of resources, it remains to be seen whether this global enterprise can be sustained for very long.

VOCABULARY OF ECOLOGY

albedo, p. 53
afforestation, p. 58
autotrophs, p. 47
biomass (standing crop), p. 62
carnivores (secondary consumers), p. 60
chemical energy, p. 49
chemosynthesis, p. 59
detritivores (decomposers or saprophytes), p. 60
ecological energetics, p. 47
chemoautotroph, p. 59
electromagnetic energy, p. 49
energy, p. 48
energy budget, p. 53
evapotranspiration, p. 54
first law of thermodynamics, p. 51
flow-through system, p. 53
food chain, p. 65
food web, p. 65
greenhouse effect, p. 55
greenhouse gases (GHGs), p. 55
gross primary production (GPP), p. 58
herbivores (primary consumers), p. 60
heterotrophs, p. 47
kinetic energy, p. 49
mechanical energy, p. 49
net primary production (NPP), p. 59
omnivores, p. 60
photoautotroph, p. 59
photosynthesis, p. 47
potential energy, p. 48
primary producers, p. 59
production, p. 61
productivity, p. 61
respiration (R), p. 59
second law of thermodynamics, p. 51
solar constant, p. 53
thermal energy, p. 49
top predator (top carnivore), p. 65
transpiration, p. 54
trophic structure, p. 68
work, p. 48

QUESTIONS FOR REVIEW AND DISCUSSION

1. What are the various states in which energy can exist? How can they be transformed from one to another?
2. What are the first and second laws of thermodynamics? Explain their implications for energy transformations and for life and ecosystems.
3. What is meant by an energy budget? Explain the major aspects of the energy budget of Earth.
4. What is meant by the greenhouse effect? Why does it exist? How might it be affected by anthropogenic influences?
5. Explain why tropical forests and coral reefs are considered to be the most highly developed ecosystems on Earth. What are the environmental circumstances that allow this to happen?
6. Describe a food web for a Canadian ecosystem with which you are familiar.
7. From an energetic perspective, why would it be more efficient for a person to feed as a vegetarian?

HELPFUL WEBSITES

ENTROPY ON THE WORLD WIDE WEB
http://www.math.uni-hamburg.de/home/gunesch/entropy.html
Learn more about entropy and its implications.

ENVIRONMENT CANADA CLIMATE CHANGE
http://www.ec.gc.ca/default.asp?lang=En&n=2967C31D-1
This is the key Government of Canada website related to climate change.

THERMODYNAMICS
http://en.wikipedia.org/wiki/Thermodynamics
This Wikipedia site and its links are a good reference for the principles and applications of thermodynamics.

You'll find a rich array of additional resources for *Ecology* at www.ecology.nelson.com.

FIGURE 4.3

Cyclic Annual Variation of the Concentration of Atmospheric CO_2. The data are for a high-arctic site at Alert, Nunavut, and a tropical one at Mauna Loa, Hawaii, from 2002 through 2004.

SOURCE: Data are from Keeling et al. (2009).

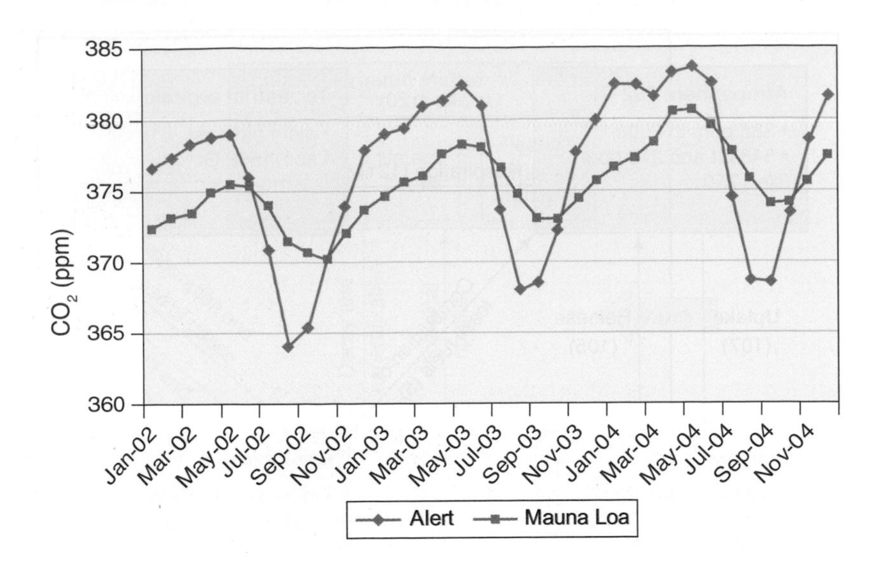

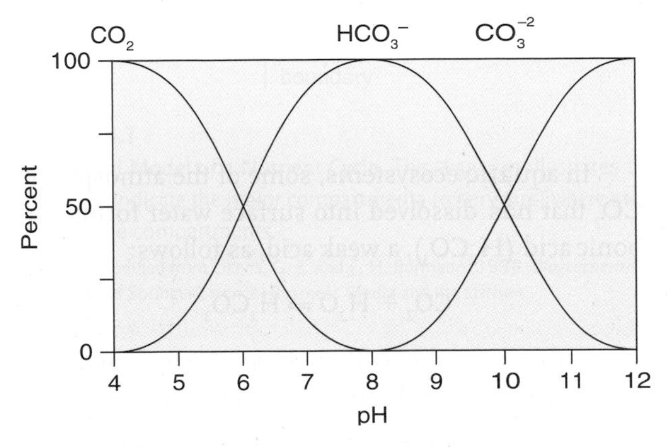

FIGURE 4.4

The Relationship among Carbon Dioxide, Bicarbonate, and Carbonate According to pH of the Solution. In alkaline solutions, CO_2 is the dominant form of inorganic carbon in water, while at circumneutral ones it is HCO_3^-, and in acidic ones it is CO_3^{-2}.

SOURCE: Modified from Wetzel. *Limnology*, 1E. © 1975 Brooks/Cole, a part of Cengage Learning, Inc. Reproduced by permission. www.cengage.com/permissions

organisms, including microbes that are responsible for most decomposition of dead organic matter (some is also oxidized by wildfires).

In aquatic or waterlogged environments, however, the process of decay may take place under **anaerobic** conditions (meaning O_2 is not available), and this results in both CH_4 and CO_2 being emitted. Because decomposition is much less efficient when occurring under anaerobic conditions than under aerobic ones (this is especially the case of lignin-containing tissues), dead plant biomass may accumulate in wetlands as peat, particularly in bogs. In fact, some bogs in Canada have accumulated peat depths exceeding 10 m since deglaciation occurred about 10 000 to 12 000 years ago. Over millions of years under certain geological conditions, peat and other kinds of buried organic matter may become slowly transformed into hydrocarbon-rich coal, petroleum, natural gas, or oil-sand. Geological circumstances that are suitable for these chemical changes involve deep burial beneath oceanic sediment, anaerobic conditions, and high pressure and temperature. In this sense, fossil fuels can be considered to be biogenic in origin. However, their rate of formation is exceedingly slow in comparison to the rate at which fossil fuels are being mined and used today, and this is why they are regarded as being non-renewable resources.

Anthropogenic influences have greatly affected the global cycling of carbon. This began in a small way in prehistoric times, when people engaged in a hunting lifestyle may have burned habitats to enhance their suitability for ungulates and other species that were desired as food. Initially, this would have had an insignificant influence on the carbon cycle, but it intensified when people began to engage in agricultural practices and forests and grasslands were cleared to grow crops for increasing human populations. In effect, these activities converted natural ecosystems that had accumulated large amounts of organic carbon in biomass, into other kinds of habitat that stored much less, with the difference being made up by a large emission of CO_2 to the atmosphere. About two centuries ago, with the beginning of the Industrial Revolution, the anthropogenic emissions of CO_2 greatly accelerated because fossil fuels started to become used as a source of energy. Further increases in releases associated with ecosystem conversions also occurred at about this time, as the rapidly growing human population necessitated further conversions of natural ecosystems into cultivated and urbanized ones. Today, only about half of Earth's original forest cover survives, the rest having been converted to agricultural, industrial, and urbanized uses. Large losses of native grasslands and savannas have also occurred, again with great consequences for ecological carbon storage (and also for biodiversity; see Chapter 12).

The global emission of CO_2 resulting from the combustion of fossil fuels is about 29.0×10^9 tonnes/year (in 2003), and there is an additional 6.3×10^9 t/yr from deforestation (the latter is the average from 1950 to 2000; WRI, 2010). Remarkably, the United States plus Canada are responsible for about 24.5 percent of the global emissions of CO_2 from the use of fossil fuels (the United States alone is 22.4 percent responsible), even though the two countries support only 5.1 percent of the world population **(Table 4.2)**. North America has such disproportionately large emissions because this wealthy region has a large and intensive economy, which like in other developed countries results in relatively high per-capita resource use, consumerism, and emissions of CO_2 and other pollutants (10–20 t CO_2/person·yr). Poorer, less-developed countries have a much smaller footprint on a per-capita basis (<2 t CO_2/person·yr), although those with large populations, such as China and India, still have huge national emissions.

TABLE 4.2 Anthropogenic Emissions of CO_2 to the Atmosphere

Data are emissions associated with the combustion of fossil fuels in 2003.

Country	Emissions of CO_2 per capita (t/person·yr)	National (10^6 t/yr)
DEVELOPED COUNTRIES		
Australia	17.1	338
Canada	17.0	537
Germany	10.2	845
Japan	9.8	1 247
Korea, South	9.8	463
United States	19.5	5 721
RAPIDLY DEVELOPING COUNTRIES		
Brazil	1.7	311
China	3.2	3 958
India	1.0	1 066
Indonesia	1.5	318
Mexico	3.7	382
LESS-DEVELOPED COUNTRIES		
Angola	0.5	7.8
Bangladesh	0.2	33.5
Cameroon	0.2	3.4
Congo	0.2	0.9
Haiti	0.2	1.6
Nepal	0.1	2.9
WORLD	**4.1**	**25 576**

SOURCE: Data from World Resources Institute (2010).

(Note, however, that a few countries with a resource-based economy that is highly dependent on the mining and processing of fossil fuels have even larger per-capita emissions of CO_2 than do Canada and other developed countries; examples are the United Arab Emirates (23.7 t CO_2/person·year), Kuwait (24.1 t CO_2/person·year), and Qatar (44.4 t CO_2/person·year)).

In any event, anthropogenic emissions have caused atmospheric CO_2 to increase in concentration from about 280 ppm in 1750 to 385 ppm in 2008 (the rate of increase during the past decade has been 1.6 ppm/yr). As a result of the increased concentrations of CO_2, the amount stored in the atmosphere is now about 782 gigatonnes (in 2008), which is considerably larger than the 568 Gt present in 1750 **(Figure 4.2)**. Atmospheric concentrations of CH_4 have also increased, from 0.7 ppm in 1750 to 1.8 ppm in 2008, largely because of emissions associated with fossil-fuel mining and increased populations of flatulent ruminant livestock. Because CO_2 and CH_4 are radiatively active gases, their increased concentrations in the atmosphere may be causing Earth's greenhouse effect to become more intensive, causing a warming of the global climate (Chapter 4).

4.4 The Nitrogen Cycle

The nitrogen cycle is distinguished by the fact that this element does not occur in significant amounts in rocks or minerals. Consequently, atmospheric gases and organic matter play key roles in the nitrogen cycle.

Most of the nitrogen on Earth occurs in the atmosphere as nitrogen gas (N_2; also known as dinitrogen), an inert compound that occurs at a concentration of 78 percent **(Figure 4.5)**. Additional atmospheric gases that occur in trace amounts (<1 ppm) are nitric oxide (NO), nitrogen dioxide (NO_2), nitrous oxide (N_2O), and ammonia (NH_3), as well as the particulates ammonium nitrate (NH_4NO_3) and ammonium sulphate ($(NH_4)_2SO_4$). In many places, these trace compounds are important air pollutants associated with emissions from combustion sources, such as vehicles, home furnaces, and power plants. Accumulations of livestock manure can also off-gas large amounts of ammonia.

Organic forms of nitrogen are ubiquitous in organisms and ecosystems, occurring in a wide variety of molecules. These range from proteins and nucleic acids in living organisms, to large and complex molecules of dead organic matter, including those known as humic substances. Important aspects of the nitrogen cycle involve transformations between inorganic and organic forms, their uptake by plants and other autotrophs, and the ways they are passed along

FIGURE 4.5
Model of the Global Nitrogen Cycle. The amounts of nitrogen stored in compartments are given in units of 10^6 tonnes (Mt or megatonnes), while fluxes are in 10^6 tN/yr.

SOURCES: Modified from Hutzinger (1982) and Freedman (2010).

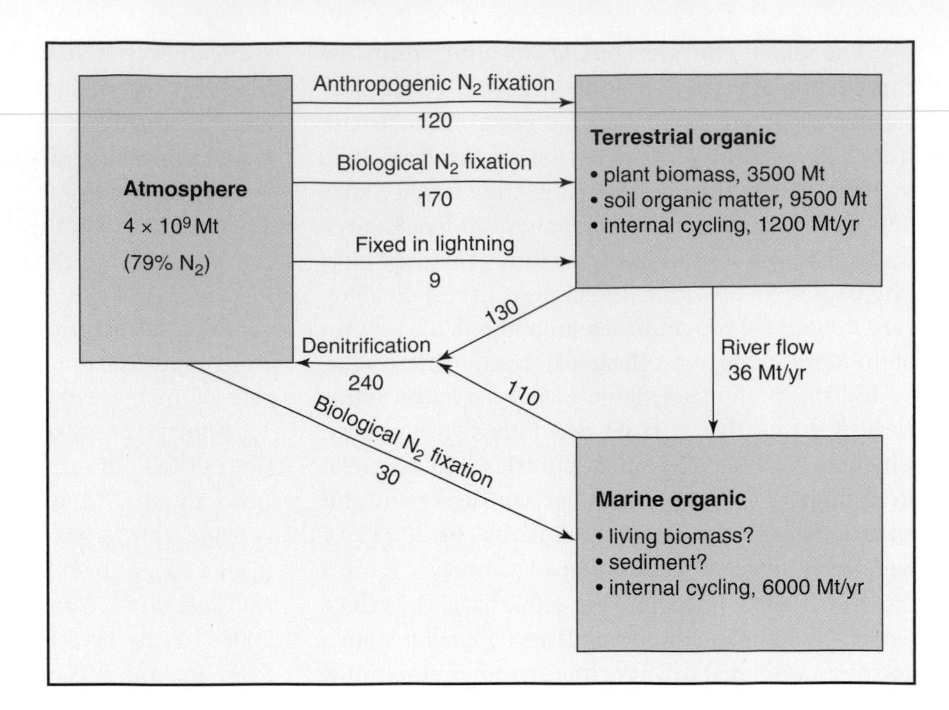

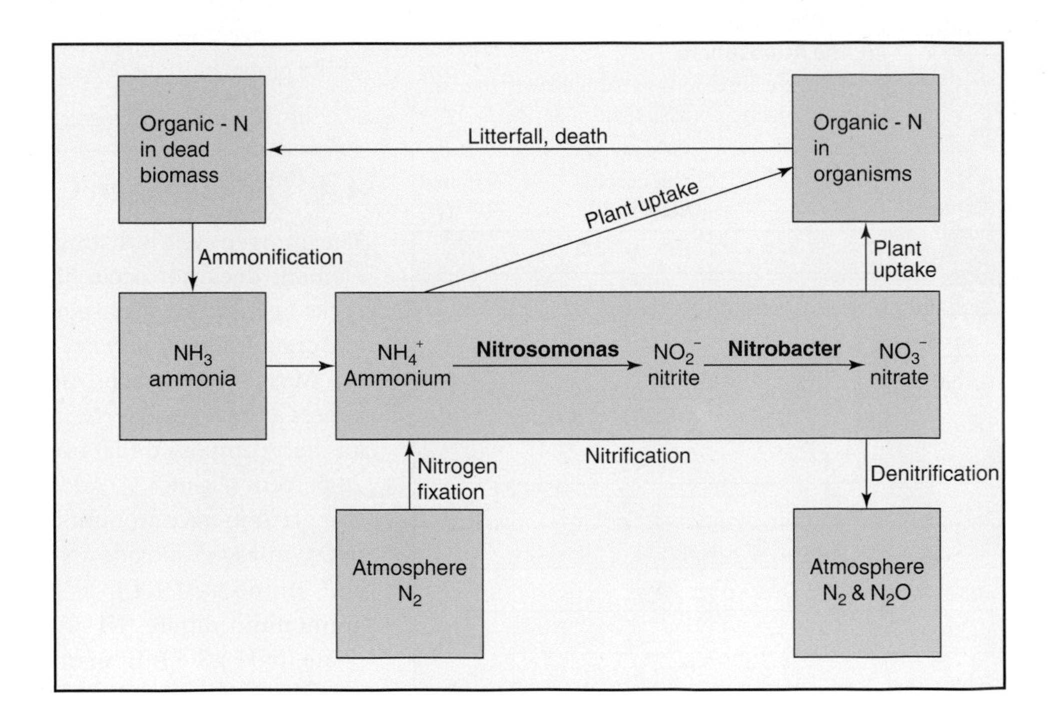

FIGURE 4.6
Key Transformations of Nitrogen Compounds Occurring within Ecosystems.

food webs (**Figure 4.6**). These transformations are examined below.

Nitrogen Fixation

Although N_2 gas is extremely abundant in the atmosphere, its two N atoms are joined by a triple bond, which is strong and renders the compound essentially inert. However, a few specialized microorganisms have evolved nitrogenase enzymes that are capable of cleaving the triple bond of N_2 to form ammonia gas (NH_3), in a process known as biological **nitrogen fixation**. The NH_3 acquires an H^+ to become an ammonium ion (NH_4^+), which is used by the N_2-fixing microbes in their nutrition. However, the "fixed" nitrogen of NH_4^+ may also become available to the many microbes and plants that are not able to fix N_2. In fact, essentially all of the nitrogen content of organisms and ecosystems is ultimately derived from the fixation of atmospheric nitrogen.

Although most nitrogen fixation is biological, some occurs by abiotic reactions. For example, during a lightning event, there is a brief but intense occurrence of extremely high temperature and pressure, which causes atmospheric N_2 to combine with O_2 to form NO gas. Some nitrogen fixation also occurs during the combustion of fossil fuels in machines, such as in the internal combustion engine of automobiles, where conditions of high temperature and pressure inside of pistons also promote the formation of NO gas from N_2 and O_2. Nitrogen fixation also occurs in the combustion chambers of power plants that are fired by coal, oil, or natural gas.

Bacteria in the family Rhizobiacae, collectively referred to as rhizobia, are well-known N_2 fixers that live in specialized nodules on the roots of plants in the legume family (Fabaceae), such as species of acacia (*Acacia*), bean (*Phaseolus*), clover (*Trifolium*), locust (*Robinia*), lupine (*Lupinus*), pea (*Pisum*), and vetch (*Vicia*). The leguminous plants synthesize a specialized pigment, known as leghemoglobin, which binds O_2 within the nodules and so provides an anaerobic microenvironment that is protective of the N_2-fixing nitrogenase of the rhizobia. The N_2-fixing reactions are rather "expensive" in an energetic sense, because 16 moles of ATP (adenosine triphosphate, an energy-transferring molecule in physiology) are required to produce 2 moles of ammonia from 1 mole of N_2 gas. This metabolic price is well paid, however, because the enhanced availability of the nutrient NH_3 allows the leguminous plants to increase their productivity. The rhizobia and their host species live in an obligate, mutually beneficial symbiosis (a mutualism), in which both partners receive a substantial benefit—the leguminous plant through increased access to ammonium as a nutrient, and the microbe through a protected anaerobic microhabitat in the root nodules.

Some non-leguminous plants also live in mutualisms with N_2-fixing microbes. Examples include species of alder (*Alnus*), myrtle (*Myrica*), and snowbush (*Ceanothus*). These shrubs have root nodules that provide microhabitat for *Frankia*, an N_2-fixing actinomycete. Many species of lichens can also fix nitrogen—they are a mutualism between a fungus and an N_2-fixing cyanobacterium (blue-green bacterium). In addition, many free-living species of bacteria and cyanobacteria can fix N_2 in anaerobic and aerobic habitats, both terrestrial and aquatic.

Of course, the use of synthetic nitrogen fertilizer has become an important aspect of intensive agricultural practices. The fertilizer is manufactured by an industrial fixation reaction known as the Haber process, in which N_2 is reacted with hydrogen (H_2, which is produced from methane) over an iron catalytic surface to yield ammonia.

Naturally occurring N_2 fixation amounts to about 170×10^6 t/yr, while anthropogenic fixation is 120×10^6 t/yr, of which 83 percent involves the manufacturing of fertilizer **(Figure 4.5)**.

Ammonification and Nitrification

The dead biomass of plant litter and deceased animals contains organic-N, but it is in molecular forms that plants and other autotrophs cannot directly use. However, microbial reactions associated with decomposition convert the organically bound nitrogen to inorganic compounds, which allows the biomass-N to be recycled for use by living organisms. The initial stage of this process is **ammonification**, in which the organic-N becomes oxidized to NH_3, which acquires an H^+ to form NH_4^+. A great diversity of free-living bacteria, fungi, and other microbes is involved in ammonification. The ammonium produced is available for uptake by plants as a nutrient, especially by those living in acidic habitats.

However, in non-acidic habitats, ammonium becomes oxidized to nitrate by the action of specialized bacteria in a two-stage process known as nitrification. The first step is the oxidation of NH_4^+ to NO_2^- (nitrite), which is done by bacteria in the genus *Nitrosomonas*. The NO_2^- is then almost immediately oxidized to NO_3^- by *Nitrobacter* bacteria. Both of these specialized bacteria are highly sensitive to acidic environments, so nitrification is much reduced at pHs lower than about 6. In general, plants growing in soil with pH higher than 6 prefer to use nitrate as their principal source of inorganic nitrogen, but at more acidic pHs ammonium is the major supply.

Denitrification

Many species of free-living bacteria are involved in the process of **denitrification**, in which nitrate is metabolically converted to gaseous N_2 or N_2O, which are released to the atmosphere. Denitrification requires anaerobic conditions and its rate is fastest when the nitrate concentration is high, as often occurs in agricultural soil that has been treated with nitrogen fertilizer. In a sense, denitrification is a reverse process to nitrogen fixation. At a global level, denitrification is occurring at a rate of about 240×10^6 t/yr, while nitrogen fixation from all sources is 299×10^6 t/yr **(Figure 4.5)**, suggesting that the amount of fixed nitrogen in ecosystems is increasing over time.

4.5 The Phosphorus Cycle

Most phosphorus occurs in rocks and minerals. Compared to the carbon and nitrogen cycles, that of phosphorus does not have a significant atmospheric phase.

A CANADIAN ECOLOGIST 4.1

Bob Jefferies: Nutrients and Geese in Subarctic Salt Marshes

R. L. Jefferies

Robert L. Jefferies (1936–2009) was not only one of the world's foremost Arctic scientists but also a leading global-change biologist who shared the 2007 Nobel Peace Prize.

Jefferies received his early training in ecology in England and at the University of California at Irvine, and then in 1974 took up a faculty position at the University of Toronto. Much of his research focused on nutrient cycling in salt marshes and the ways that the relative supplies of nitrogen and phosphorus, including the ratios of available nitrate and ammonium, influenced the species composition and productivity of those coastal habitats.

Jefferies' field research in Canada occurred mainly in the extensive salt marshes and tidal flats of the Hudson Bay lowlands, particularly in the vicinity of La Pérouse Bay near Churchill, Manitoba. There has been a long history of collaborative research at La Pérouse Bay, involving many ecologists, including Jefferies, Fred Cooke of Queen's University, Ken Abrahams of the Ontario Ministry of Natural Resources, Dawn Bazely of York University, and others. When Jefferies began in 1978, his research focused on interactions of grazing by snow geese (*Chen ceurulescens*) with nutrient cycling and salt-marsh productivity. Over the years, however, the geese increased enormously in abundance, and as their population exploded they over-grazed and severely damaged the local habitats they depended on for feeding. That seemingly pathological interaction between a native herbivore and its natural habitat became the adaptive focus of the fieldwork of Jefferies and his colleagues. His field research and knowledge of other aspects of the ecology of the geese led Jefferies and others to conclude that the animals were increasing in abundance largely because of improved habitat conditions in their wintering range in the southern United States, where they fed on residues of nutritious crops such as soybean, maize, and alfalfa, and because of decreased hunting there and during their southward migration. As a consequence, the geese were returning to the Hudson Bay lowlands in excellent condition for breeding, resulting in great reproductive success. This understanding of environmental influences across the life cycle of the snow goose led to important changes to wildlife management policies, including larger bag limits and relaxed seasonal restrictions on snow goose hunting.

Jefferies was also active in the broader environmental field. His advocacy contributed to the establishment of Wapusk National Park, which protects extensive tracts of the Hudson and James Bay lowlands. He was active in the scientific deliberations of the Intergovernmental Panel on Climate Change—work for which he and other scientists, as well as Al Gore, shared a Nobel Prize in 2007. And Jefferies was a dedicated teacher. He helped to develop the curriculum for the present course in introductory biology at the University of Toronto, the largest such class in Canada, and taught a section of lectures with great enthusiasm, even during his retirement.

Bob Jefferies' career is the epitome of what an academic ecologist can deliver to Canadian society. He taught with skill and passion, conducted research at the leading edge of his field, and was responsibly engaged in societal issues that intersected with his interests and knowledge.

Also in comparison to carbon and nitrogen, there are relatively small amounts of phosphorus cycling in ecosystems. This is a reason why the availability of phosphorus is often a limiting factor for productivity, especially in freshwater habitats. Phosphorus is also present in all organic matter—it is a constituent of many biochemicals, including the nucleic acids DNA and RNA, adenosine triphosphate (ATP), and certain lipids, and as a major component of bone (most of which is calcium phosphate).

The global phosphorus cycle resembles a large flow-through system in which P in terrestrial landscapes slowly moves into lakes and rivers, being carried in fine suspended materials or dissolved in water. In due course the aquatic phosphorus becomes delivered to the oceans. There, the phosphorus slowly deposits to sediment, which eventually becomes lithified into sedimentary rock. Over geological time, the P-rich minerals may become uplifted through orogeny (mountain-building processes). However, the geological return of phosphorus to terrestrial landscapes is an extremely slow process—it occurs on a scale that is beyond any meaningful ecological time frame.

There are also some biological means by which marine phosphorus (and nitrogen) is returned to local terrestrial landscapes, where it and nitrogen provide a nutrient-related subsidy to primary productivity. One involves the breeding migrations of Pacific salmon (species of *Oncorhynchus*), which spend most of their lives in the ocean, where they grow and accumulate marine phosphorus and other nutrients. The salmon then migrate up their birth river to breed in the headwaters, and die soon afterward. In essence, the journeys of the salmon result in a restoration of phosphorus to the upper reaches of navigable rivers and streams, where their dead bodies release it and other nutrients during decomposition. Moreover, when bears or bald eagles are predators of the migrating salmon, the nutrient content of the fish may be deposited in feces onto terrestrial parts of the watershed. For example, it has been estimated that primeval runs of salmon contributed about 0.36×10^6 kg/yr of phosphorus and 3×10^6 kg/yr of nitrogen to the Columbia River ecosystem (Gresh et al., 2000). However, because salmon stocks and migrating populations are now much smaller than in historical times in that river, the nutrient return has decreased by about 93 percent. Of course, when young salmon (known as smolts) migrate to the sea they also carry nutrients in their bodies, estimated in one study to be equivalent to 16 percent of the P that their parents bring from the oceans and 12 percent of the N (Moore and Schindler, 2004).

Another case involves certain fish-eating marine birds that nest in dense colonies on islands where the climate is extremely dry. Under these conditions, huge amounts of excrement rich in phosphorus can accumulate on the nesting islands. The most famous cases of this phenomenon occur on dry islands off the Pacific coast of Peru and Chile, where the abundant guano of the guanay cormorant (*Phalacrocorax bougainvillii*) and other piscivorous seabirds is mined for use as a P-rich fertilizer.

Phosphate (PO_4^{-3}) is the usual source of available phosphorus for uptake by plants. This ion typically occurs in extremely small concentrations in soil and water, but it is continually regenerated by several processes. One involves the slow dissolving of P-rich minerals in soil, such as phosphates of iron, calcium, and magnesium [$FePO_4$, $Ca_3(PO_4)_2$, and $Mg_3(PO_4)_2$]. The microbial decomposition of organic forms of phosphorus also generates phosphate as a product—this function is carried out by phosphatase enzymes, which may occur inside of microbial cells or extracellular in water. Soluble phosphate that is present in soil is rapidly absorbed by plant roots and microbes and used in their metabolism to synthesize P-containing biochemicals. Similarly, phosphate in surface waters such as ponds and lakes is quickly absorbed by phytoplankton.

At the global level, about 200×10^6 t/yr of phosphorus are absorbed by vegetation from soil (Freedman, 2010). In comparison, about 50×10^6 t of P/yr of fertilizer are manufactured, mostly from mined deposits of phosphate-rich rocks, but also from deposits of guano and by processing the bones of slaughtered livestock. Clearly, anthropogenic contributions have become an important component of the phosphorus cycle.

4.6 The Sulphur Cycle

Sulphur is present in many minerals and also in soil, surface waters, and the atmosphere. It is biologically important as a component of proteins and other biochemicals.

Gaseous sulphur dioxide (SO_2) is emitted by natural sources, such as volcanoes. There are also large anthropogenic sources, such as coal-fired power plants, metal smelters, and oil-fuelled home furnaces. Gaseous hydrogen sulphide (H_2S) is also present in the atmosphere. It is emitted by volcanoes and is also produced in the anaerobic sediment of wetlands. When SO_2 occurs in concentrations exceeding about 0.5 ppm, it causes toxicity to sensitive plants and lichens, and ecological damage results from that intensity of air pollution. In the atmosphere, SO_2 and H_2S become oxidized by photochemical reactions to sulphate (SO_4^{-2}), which may then become dissolved in suspended water droplets. The negative charges of the SO_4^{-2} (it is an anion) must be electrochemically balanced by positive charges of cations, such as calcium (Ca^{+2}), potassium (K^+), sodium (Na^+), and ammonium (NH_4^+). If these cations are not abundant enough to balance all of the negative charges of the sulphate that is present, then hydrogen ion (H^+) will go into solution to serve that function. This causes the solution to acidify—to become "acid rain," an important pollutant in some large regions. Atmospheric sulphate may also exist as tiny particulates, such as ammonium sulphate [$(NH_4)_2SO_4$] and ammonium nitrate (NH_4NO_3), which are the major constituents of urban haze, another kind of air pollution.

About 78 percent of the global emissions of SO_2 are from anthropogenic sources, mostly associated with the combustion of fossil fuels and the smelting of metal ores (Freedman, 2010). In contrast, 97 percent of the emissions of H_2S are natural, although there are some important industrial sources, such as sour-gas wells in Alberta that are rich in this gas.

Metal sulphides are the most abundant mineral forms of sulphur in rocks and soil. Iron sulphides (FeS_2, known as pyrite if present as cubic crystals) are especially abundant, but other metals such as copper and nickel also occur as sulphide compounds. Metal sulphides are chemically reduced substances. When they become exposed to the atmosphere, which is rich in oxygen (20.9 percent), specialized

ENVIRONMENTAL APPLICATIONS 4.1

Eutrophication: Pollution by Nutrients

Nutrients are essential to life but if their supply is excessive, the ecological responses may represent a degradation of ecological conditions. In such cases, the nutrients would be viewed as pollutants.

For instance, if agricultural fields are treated with too much nitrogen-containing fertilizer, such as ammonium nitrate (NH_4NO_3), the groundwater can build up large concentrations of nitrate (NO_3^-). This occurs because nitrate readily leaches downward through soil, as a consequence of its high solubility in water and its poor retention by ion-binding surfaces associated with clay and organic matter. The leaching of nitrate represents an inefficiency of agricultural fertilizer application, but if it occurs in a high concentration in groundwater it can also be a toxic hazard to people. This is particularly true in the case of infants, because their relatively acidic stomach environment fosters the transformation of nitrate to nitrite (NO_2^-). When it is absorbed into the blood, nitrite binds to hemoglobin to form methemoglobin. Because the affinity of nitrite for hemoglobin is stronger than that of oxygen, the oxygen-transporting capacity of an affected infant becomes tied up, resulting in physiological stress and even potential suffocation. Babies affected by drinking water with a high nitrate concentration often have a bluish hue, and so the toxic condition is called the "blue baby syndrome."

Eutrophication is another environmental problem that is caused by an excessive supply of nutrients. In this case, the nutrients cause the productivity of waterbodies to increase substantially. The most prominent symptom is a dense biomass of phytoplankton cells, known as an algal bloom. In shallow waters there may also be a large biomass of aquatic plants. In some cases, a moderate degree of eutrophication may be viewed as being favourable because it supports a higher productivity of fish and waterfowl. However, waterbodies that are highly eutrophic (referred to as hypertrophic) are severely degraded ecosystems because they have noxious blooms of blue-green bacteria and algae during the summer. The decomposition of their biomass results in anoxic conditions, which may kill fish and other aquatic animals and can result in the release of hydrogen sulphide (H_2S) and other smelly compounds. Severe eutrophication degrades the natural values of aquatic habitats; it may render them unable to support a fishery and unsuitable for use as drinking water or for recreation.

Some waterbodies are naturally eutrophic. This commonly occurs in parts of the Prairie provinces where many ponds and lakes are situated in watersheds with fertile soil. Often, however, "cultural eutrophication" is caused when large amounts of nutrients are dumped into lakes or rivers, usually with the sewage of livestock or people or as runoff from agricultural fields that were treated with fertilizer. Research done in Canada and elsewhere has shown that a high loading of phosphate is the primary cause of eutrophication in freshwater ecosystems, while nitrate is the usual culprit in marine waters (see Environmental Applications 2.1 on pp. 32–33). Once these controlling nutrients became identified, it was possible to prevent eutrophication by reducing the inputs of nitrogen and phosphorus into aquatic environments by, for example, properly treating sewage and by using agricultural fertilizer more judiciously.

Thiobacillus bacteria oxidize the sulphides and transform them into sulphate. The bacteria are autotrophic, in that they obtain energy to support their metabolism and growth by the oxidative reactions involving sulphides. Because sunlight is not involved in these autotrophic reactions, these primary producers are referred to as chemoautotrophs (and the reactions as chemosynthesis, as distinct from photosynthesis, which is coupled with the absorption of sunlight; see Chapter 3). *Thiobacillus thiooxidans* is a chemosynthetic bacterium that obtains energy by oxidizing sulphides; *T. ferrooxidans* is closely related but it utilizes energy liberated by the oxidation of Fe^{2+} to Fe^{3+}. Severe acidity is produced in situations where large amounts of sulphides are being oxidized, and this causes an important kind of environmental pollution known as acid-mine drainage.

Sulphur also occurs in organically bound forms in soil and water, which are mostly associated with dead organic matter. As a normal aspect of the process of decay, microbes oxidize the organic-S to sulphate, which is soluble in soil water and can be absorbed by plant roots for use as a nutrient. Plants can also absorb atmospheric SO_2 through their stomata for use as a nutrient, as long as the concentration of the gas is not so high as to cause toxicity.

4.7 Base Cations

Calcium, magnesium, potassium, and sodium are sometimes lumped together as **base cations** or **bases**; the name refers to the high alkalinity (basic conditions) that results when they are abundant. These elements are important physiologically, being needed by

NASA

Volcanoes are sources of emission of particulates, sulphur dioxide, and other materials to the atmosphere. This satellite view shows an eruption of the Cleveland Volcano in the Aleutian chain of islands in western Alaska. The image was taken on 23 May 2006.

all organisms to regulate various aspects of their physiology and for other purposes.

Alkalinity is an important attribute of soil and surface waters because of its role in resisting acidification, and it is closely associated with the amounts of calcium present in local soil and rocks. For instance, lakes, rivers, and streams with low alkalinity become acidified relatively easily if affected by "acid rain"—by acidifying substances deposited from the atmosphere, such as gaseous sulphur dioxide and oxides of nitrogen as well as rain and snow with high concentrations of hydrogen, sulphate, nitrate, and ammonium ions. This cause of acidification of surface waters is a problem over large regions where soils and bedrock are mostly granitic and quartzitic and therefore have sparse concentrations of calcium and magnesium. In Canada, the problem of acidification by atmospheric influences is most severe in a large area of south-central Ontario where the bedrock and soils are predominantly quartzitic (the geological region is Canadian Shield), but it also occurs elsewhere, such as in southern Quebec and parts of the Maritime provinces.

The principal reservoirs of Ca, Mg, and K are geological, because they are abundant in certain minerals and rocks. Na is abundant in seawater, typically occurring in a concentration of 10.6 g/L. These bases are also present in trace concentrations in the atmosphere, where they occur as minute suspended particulates or dissolved in precipitation. They also occur in trace concentrations in most surface waters, such as lakes and rivers. Because of their dilute concentrations of bases and other ions, these are known as "fresh" waters. In contrast, "salt" or "soda" lakes have extremely large dissolved concentrations of inorganic chemicals. Big Quill and Chaplin Lakes in Saskatchewan are the largest soda lakes in Canada; they have such high concentrations of sodium sulphate (Na_2SO_4) and other salts that they are mined for these useful minerals. While the Great Salt Lake in Utah can have a seasonal salt concentration of up to 27 percent, its ionic composition is close to that of seawater, being dominated by sodium and chloride ions and low in sulphate.

As we previously noted under the carbon cycle, some kinds of aquatic animals deposit hard protective shells of calcium carbonate ($CaCO_3$). These include mollusks, corals, barnacles, and foraminifera (a group of amoebic protists). This bio-mineral may accumulate in sediment and over geological time it can lithify into limestone rock. In this sense, limestone may be viewed as having a partially biogenic origin, in addition to being affected by millions of years of abiotic modification by exposure to intense geological pressure and high temperature. The bone tissue of vertebrate animals is also high in calcium, being composed mostly of a bio-mineral form of calcium phosphate [$Ca_3(PO_4)_2$] known as hydroxylapatite (typically composing about 70 percent of bone mass).

4.8 Soil as an Ecosystem

Soil consists of rocky fragments, other minerals, organic matter, moisture, gases, and organisms. Soil has great structural and biological complexity, and it covers most terrestrial landscapes. Soil provides a foundation for forest, prairie, tundra, and other terrestrial habitats, and is a vital component of those ecosystems. However, the soil may itself be studied as a discrete and dynamic ecosystem in the sense that it consists of a wide diversity of organisms plus the environmental conditions in which they live. Moreover, soil provides crucial environmental services, because it

- *stores much of the nutrient capital of its greater ecosystem*, while also providing water and soluble nutrients that are needed by growing plants, which absorb these materials through their roots, rhizomes, and mycorrhizae (a fungus-root symbiosis);
- *provides habitat* for the immense diversity of organisms that decompose dead organic matter and recycle its crucial nutrients; and
- *gives physical support* for rooted plants, even allowing trees taller than 100 m to stand against the pressing forces of gravity and wind.

Soils develop from **parent materials**, which are the particular surface rocks and minerals that have been freshly exposed for biological colonization and ecological development. In Canada, most parent materials are composed of inorganic debris associated with ancient glaciers. Other parent materials are derived from local bedrock that has been subjected to *in situ* (in place) fracturing by freeze-and-thaw cycles and the powerful actions of plant roots. The glacial deposits commonly occur as a complex mixture known as till, which contains stones and rocks of various mineralogies and sizes that were left behind when a glacier melted and dumped its load of rubble. Often, glacial parent materials were deposited after being transported by flowing melt-water, eventually being laid down as well-sorted (uniformly grained) sedimentary deposits in lakes. Some of those post-glacial lakes covered an immense area when melt-waters were abundant, but they later drained to provide flat expanses for colonization by terrestrial vegetation. Yet other parent materials are derived from finer-grained glacial materials that were picked up by strong winds at one place and then deposited elsewhere as a material known as loess.

The structure and composition of parent materials are affected by the sorts of depositional processes that laid them down. Having been directly deposited by local glacial melting, till is usually quite heterogenous in the size and mineralogy of its rocks and other minerals. These sorts of glacial deposits may be heaped into immense piles, such as drumlins (teardrop-shaped hills) and eskers (sinusoidal mounds deposited by a river running beneath a glacier), forming an undulating hill-and-valley landscape known as a moraine. In contrast, the terrain is flat and covered with a uniform and fine-grained substrate in places where the parent material was deposited in a post-glacial lake. Depending on the speed of water flow at the time of deposition, the material can range from clay to sand in texture. Loess is also relatively uniform and fine-grained, but it typically occurs where there is rolling terrain.

Words such as *sand* and *clay* have specific meaning in the jargon of soil science—they relate to the size ranges of particulates and fragments. Ordered from larger to smaller diameters, the soil fractions are as follows:

- Coarse gravel and rubble are larger than 20 mm.
- Gravel is 2 to 20 mm.
- Sand is 0.05 to 2 mm.
- Silt is 0.002 to 0.05 mm.
- Clay is smaller than 0.002 mm.

The particulate composition of a parent material greatly affects the properties of soils that eventually develop from it. For example, clay-dominated soils are poorly drained because water cannot easily penetrate through the substrate and so it may accumulate at the surface; root penetration is also difficult in a clayey soil. In contrast, soils dominated by sand or coarser materials will drain freely. Because they do not hold water or nutrients well, they are typically infertile and susceptible to drought. Soils are classified according to textural classes, based on the fractional composition of their particulate components, such as sand, silt, and clay-sized particles **(Figure 4.7)**.

Some of the less-desirable characteristics of soils dominated by either sand or clay can be partly mitigated by increasing the concentration of humified organic matter. Humus is derived from inputs of dead biomass in the form of plant litter, which is a source of organic nutrition for soil-dwelling animals, fungi, and bacteria that live in the soil. These saprophytes oxidize much of the plant debris into CO_2 and at the same time recycle inorganic nutrients such as ammonium. However, some of the dead organic material is resistant to decomposition, and it eventually forms **humus**, a complex material consisting of heavy organic molecules (meaning they have a large molecular-weight). Humus is a highly beneficial soil

Jerry Kobalenko/First Light

Glacial debris is a common parent material of soils in Canada. The tundra vegetation and its underlying soil have developed since they were released by the meltback of the glaciers, such as the one that looms in the background of the image. This scene is from Ellesmere Island, Nunavut.

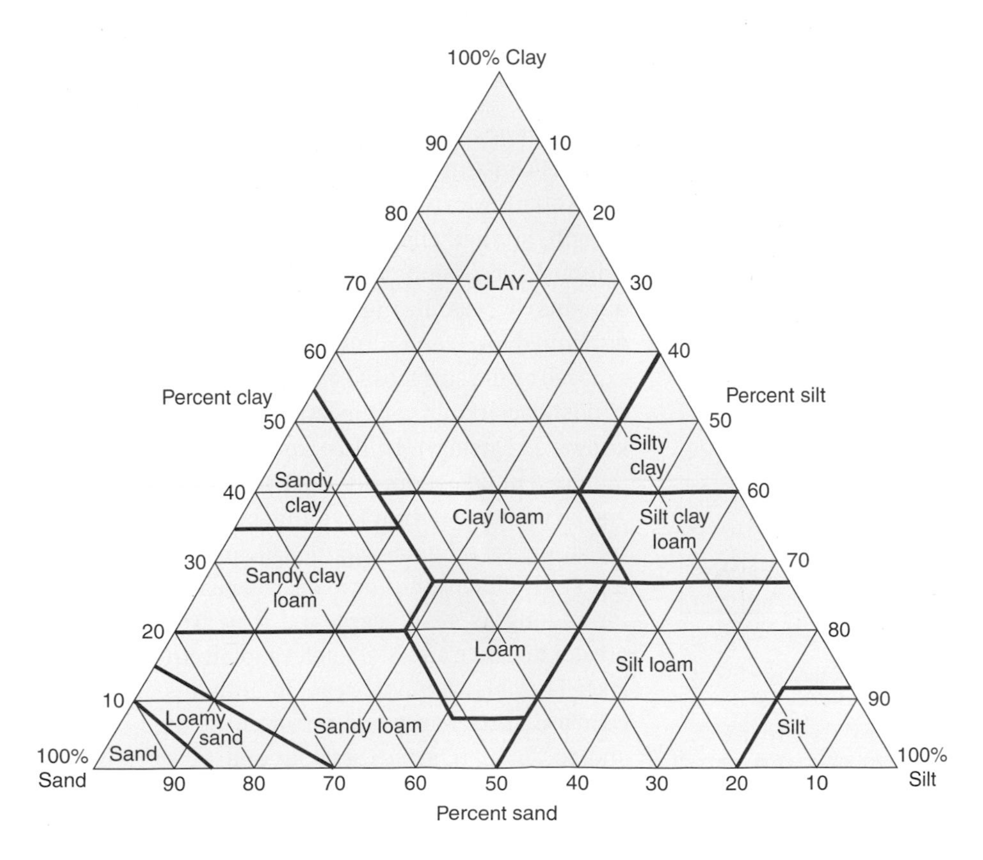

FIGURE 4.7

A Textural Classification of Soils. The fractional composition of clay, silt, and sand-sized particles is used to classify soils into 12 types.

SOURCE: Modified from USDA (2009).

component, because it contributes to a quality known as **tilth**. Soils with superior tilth have a relatively high capacity to retain moisture and nutrients, and they have an aggregated particle structure that allows easy root penetration and good aeration. This is the reason why humus in clay soils contributes to the formation of an aggregated structure and thereby improves aeration and drainage. In sandy soils, humus increases the capacity of the substrate to hold water and bind nutrients.

Initially, the original parent materials may have a rather uniform distribution of physical qualities at various depths below the surface. The subsequent development of soil proceeds under the influence of various environmental factors, particularly climatic and biological ones. For instance, as rainwater or snow meltwater percolates downward, it dissolves certain chemicals out of the parent material and carries them to deeper layers of the soil. This process is known as **leaching** and it changes the chemistry of both the surface and deeper soil horizons. Any nutrients that are leached beyond the rooting depth of plants can be considered to have left the "active" part of the terrestrial ecosystem. Biological influences are also crucial to soil development, particularly those that affect decomposition and the amount of humus present. Eventually, a pronounced vertical stratification of the soil, known as a profile, may develop. The **soil profile** of a forest consists of discrete layers known as horizons, which include the ones shown in the following table.

Horizon	Sub-Horizon	Description
LFH		This is the *forest floor*, an organic layer that sits upon the mineral soil and that consists of the following three layers:
	L	The *litter layer* contains fresh organic matter that is still identifiable as being the debris of particular kinds of plants.
	F	The *duff* or *fermentation layer* consists of partly decomposed organic matter, with litter fragments still evident.
	H	The *humus layer* contains well-decomposed (or humified) organic matter, with few identifiable fragments of the original litter.
A		The *A horizon* is a zone from which dissolved organic matter and ions of calcium, magnesium, potassium, iron, and aluminum are leached downward (this process is also known as eluviation).
	A_1	This upper part of the A horizon is transitional between the organic-rich zone above and the strongly leached one below; the A_1 has a high concentration of humified organic material mixed with an inorganic matrix.
	A_2 or A_e	This lower region of the A horizon is lighter coloured because it has little organic matter and most of the original iron and aluminum has been leached out (or eluviated) by acidic percolating water.
B		The *B horizon* is a zone where dissolved organic matter and ions precipitate out of solution (also known as illuviation); it has a darker colour associated with the deposition of organic matter, iron, aluminum, and clays that were leached from the A horizon.
C		The *C horizon* and deeper layers are composed of the original parent material and are not much influenced by soil-forming processes.
R		The *regolith* is solid rock that underlies the parent material.

Soil qualities may change profoundly during the ecological process of succession or community recovery following disturbance. This is particularly the case of primary succession, in which ecological development begins on a substrate that has not previously been vegetated, as is the case of freshly deglaciated terrain, after a lava flow, or following a severe wildfire that has consumed most of the previous forest floor.

Robert Morrison (1973) of the University of Toronto studied changes in soil properties during a primary succession near Grand Bend, Ontario. He did this by examining soil changes as vegetation developed on sand dunes that became gradually exposed as the surface of Lake Huron receded because of postglacial uplift of the landscape (a phenomenon known as isostasy). In this area, sand dunes close to the present lakeshore are relatively recently exposed and so their vegetation is young, being dominated by the dunegrass *Calamovilfa longifolia*. In contrast, in this study older dunes have been exposed above water for as long as 4800 years, and they are located at a greater distance and higher elevation from the present lake. They also support vegetation that is older, typically a mature hardwood forest dominated by black and red oaks (*Quercus serotina* and *Q. borealis*) and white and red pines (*Pinus strobus* and *P. resinosa*).

View of a pit dug in podzol (spodosol) soil in a stand of spruce-dominated boreal forest in Labrador. The golf tees show the places where soil horizons are changing.

The initial parent material that is exposed to the primary succession is a fine-grained sand with a pH of 6.9, almost devoid of organic matter (only 0.4 percent) and water-holding capacity (0.3 percent), and lacking in nutrients (soluble K of 5 ppm). As succession proceeds, there is a general accumulation of biomass in the ecosystem, including in the organic forest floor. The concentration of organic matter in the upper mineral soil reached an asymptote of 16 to 20 percent after 1000 years, and the accompanying improvement of tilth enhanced water-holding capacity to 5 to 10 percent and K to 100 ppm. At the same time, the soil became more acidic, reaching pH 5.5–5.9 under mature forest. The acidification was caused by the combined influences of the leaching of Ca^{2+} and other bases by percolating rainwater and the uptake of these nutrient cations by vegetation, which also reduces the amounts left in the soil. Furthermore, the uptake of cations such as Ca^{2+} was offset by the release of an equivalent amount of positive charges associated with H^+ to the soil, to maintain its electrochemical neutrality—this contributed to the soil acidification.

The types of soil that develop are also influenced by the kind of ecosystem that is present. Soil that has developed in a grassland ecosystem is different from that in temperate forest, and both of those vary from boreal forest, and so on. Soils are classified according to their key characteristics and the ecological circumstances that affected their development. The highest level in the classification is referred to as **soil order**. The most important of the soil orders found in Canada are the following:

- *Brunisol (brown forest soil)* forms under forests dominated by hardwood (angiosperm) trees that are growing in a temperate humid climate, usually developing from a parent material that is relatively high in calcium carbonate. Brunisol has a thin LFH layer, a dark-brown A horizon, and a lighter-coloured B horizon.
- *Podzol (spodosol)* develops under coniferous and mixedwood (conifer plus angiosperm) forests in a cool, humid, boreal climate. It has a thick, acidic LFH layer, a highly leached and light-coloured A_e horizon, and a reddish B horizon due to iron-oxide deposition.
- *Luvisol* develops under a range of forest types, ranging from coniferous to hardwood, and in temperate to boreal climates. It has a thin litter layer, a slightly acidic A_e horizon, and a B horizon that is lighter in colour, neutral in reaction, and rich in silicate clays.
- *Chernozem (black earth)* forms under a vegetation cover of tallgrass and mixedgrass prairie in a cool temperate climate with moderate availability of moisture. It is a fertile soil with a brown-black, organic-rich A horizon that is rich in calcium carbonate, while the B horizon is lighter-coloured.
- *Regosol* develops from a thin veneer of freshly deposited parent material, such as sand or silt and under various kinds of vegetation and climatic conditions. It is a young soil and therefore does not show much development.
- *Gleysol* develops in forests and other vegetation that are subjected to periodically flooded conditions in a cool temperate climate regime. The waterlogging results in anoxic conditions that promote the leaching of iron and manganese, which deposit lower down. Gleysols often have grey-red mottled bands present that are associated with oxygenated root channels.
- *Solonetz* forms in semi-desert and arid vegetation and climates, on sites with moderate drainage and saline conditions. It has a thin surface layer over a darker, alkaline horizon.
- *Organic soils (peat)* develop under cool and humid climatic conditions in bogs, fens, and other wetlands that have an anaerobic subsurface. The accumulated peat may be quite deep, even exceeding 10 m in places.

Soil is an important and diagnostic characteristic of terrestrial ecosystems. It has a great influence on

A CANADIAN ECOLOGIST 4.2

David Patriquin: A Champion of Organic Management

David Patriquin

David Patriquin

David Patriquin is a professor at Dalhousie University. His early career involved basic research into the physiology of nitrogen fixation, including work in natural ecosystems, such as salt marshes, as well as agricultural ones, such as crops of legumes and sugar cane. In addition to his academic research, however, Patriquin is concerned about the environmental consequences of intensively managed agricultural and horticultural systems, particularly their heavy reliance on synthetic fertilizer and pesticides. He worries about the damage these chemicals cause, such as the eutrophication of lakes, emissions of nitrous oxide (N_2O, a greenhouse gas), the poisoning of wild biota, and the potential risks to people exposed to pesticide residues in their food and in their general environment. Patriquin recognized that he could marry his academic work with his environmental concerns by engaging in research that examined organic management practices, while also integrating environmental issues into his teaching.

In organic agriculture, nitrogen fixation by legumes and the addition of composted organic waste are used instead of applying synthetic fertilizer to cultivated lands. As well as supplying nutrients, the inputs of organic matter improve the soil tilth, a beneficial property associated with high water-holding capacity, nutrient retention, oxygenation, and ease of root penetration. Weeds and pests are controlled by mechanical methods such as ploughing and hand-pulling, the enhancement of natural enemies, use of resistant varieties, and improved plant health. Patriquin's transition to applied research in organic agriculture was stimulated by practical questions that he received from farmers, such as "*How much of the land has to be in legumes to replace nitrogen fertilizer used by my cereal crops?*" His answer, after study of an organic farm, was: "*About 40 percent.*" The nitrogen is transferred from legumes to cereal crops by the use of rotations, and also by the return of livestock manure to the land. In addition to replacing synthetic fertilizer, Patriquin's studies demonstrated that organic sources of nitrogen help to reduce weed and insect pressure on crops, while avoiding soil acidification.

But Patriquin does not just do research—he also engages in outreach and advocacy to popularize ideas about organic practices. An initial success occurred in 1984, when he convinced his home university, Dalhousie, to stop using pesticides in its horticultural areas. He did this by using arguments about the health risks associated with pesticides, the cost savings of organic practices, and the notion that the "weeds" that are the targets of herbicide in this horticultural context are actually "wildflowers" to be appreciated. He also joined farmers in campaigns to stop roadside herbicide spraying and worked with environmental organizations to ban the cosmetic use of pesticides in horticulture. Along with many other advocates of organic practices in agriculture and horticulture, Patriquin has worked to foster a wider application of these ecologically softer methods by telling people how to use them, while also explaining their environmental and economic benefits.

the mineral nutrition and productivity of vegetation. For instance, acidic soils do not sustain the production of nitrate through bacterial nitrification; therefore, plants on those sites must be capable of using ammonium as their source of inorganic nitrogen. Sites that are permanently or periodically waterlogged will have anaerobic soil, which greatly affects many ecological processes, including decomposition and aspects of nutrient cycling. Soil quality also affects the agricultural crops that can be grown on sites that have been converted from their natural vegetation cover. Some of the highest-quality soils for both natural ecosystems and agroecosystems occur on alluvial sites. These typically occur in low reaches along rivers and in deltas, where flooding and associated silt deposition in the springtime provide abundant amounts of nutrients. Chernozems and brunisols are also generally fertile, but they may be excessively stony.

VOCABULARY OF ECOLOGY

ammonification, p. 83
anaerobic, p. 80
base cations (bases), p. 86
closed system, p. 76
compartments (reservoirs), p. 76
denitrification, p. 83
ecotype, p. 74
eutrophication, p. 86
humus, p. 88
inorganic nutrients, p. 73
leaching, p. 90
macronutrients, p. 73
micronutrients, p. 73
nitrification, p. 78
nitrogen fixation, p. 82
nutrients, p. 73
nutrient budget, p. 76
nutrient cycling, p. 76
organic chemicals (biochemicals), p. 75
parent material, p. 88
principle of limiting factors, p. 75
soil, p. 88
soil order, p. 91
soil profile, p. 90
tilth, p. 90
weathering (solubilization), p. 77

QUESTIONS FOR REVIEW AND DISCUSSION

1. What are the basic elements of a nutrient cycle, including the roles of key compartments and fluxes?
2. Compare key aspects of the cycles of carbon, nitrogen, phosphorus, and sulphur.
3. Choose a major nutrient (carbon, nitrogen, phosphorus, or sulphur) and explain how human influences are changing the rates of certain aspects of its cycling.
4. How do climatic and biological influences affect the formation of soil from parent material?
5. Choose a type of soil, and use information in the text and from other sources to prepare a detailed description of its physical and biological qualities, as well as the ecological circumstances that influence its development.
6. How do your daily activities intersect with key aspects of the carbon cycle? Are there ways that you could decrease the size of your carbon footprint—the amounts of carbon dioxide that are emitted to the atmosphere as a result of your personal activities, especially through your energy use that involves the combustion of fossil fuels?

HELPFUL WEBSITES

HUMAN ALTERATION OF THE GLOBAL NITROGEN CYCLE

http://www.esa.org/science_resources/issues/FileEnglish/issue1.pdf

The Ecological Society of America has issued this PDF document that explains how humans are affecting important aspects of the global nitrogen cycle.

NON-POINT POLLUTION OF SURFACE WATERS WITH PHOSPHORUS AND NITROGEN

http://www.esa.org/science_resources/issues/FileEnglish/issue3.pdf

This Ecological Society of America PDF document explains how pollution by nutrients affects aquatic ecosystems.

NUTRIENT POLLUTION OF COASTAL RIVERS, BAYS, AND SEAS

http://www.esa.org/science_resources/issues/FileEnglish/issue7.pdf

This PDF document from the Ecological Society of America explains how nutrients affect coastal waters.

THE HEALTH OF OUR SOILS: TOWARD SUSTAINABLE AGRICULTURE IN CANADA

http://www.agr.gc.ca/nlwis-snite/index_e.cfm?s1=pub&s2=hs_ss&page=intro

This Agriculture and Agri-Food Canada website explains how soil health is important to agriculture.

You'll find a rich array of additional resources for *Ecology* at www.ecology.nelson.com.

CHAPTER 5

Population Ecology

JEFFREY A. HUTCHINGS, Department of Biology, Dalhousie University

Atlantic puffins (*Fratercula arctica*) on Bird Island, NL. Photo by Bill Caulfeild-Browne

LEARNING OBJECTIVES

After studying this chapter you should be able to

1. Define population growth rate and explain how it is used to describe past, present, and predicted changes in the abundance of a species or a population.
2. Forecast changes in abundance given assumptions concerning the effects of density, age, and developmental stage on population growth rate.
3. Apply simple models for theoretical and applied purposes, such as predicting the recovery of depleted populations or the growth of newly established ones.
4. Understand how interactions with other species, such as competition and predation, can affect the growth rate and likelihood of persistence of populations or species.
5. Interpret graphs of population abundance trends, and understand how state-space graphs are used to predict outcomes of interspecific interactions.
6. Discuss why per capita population growth is of fundamental importance to population ecology, resource management, and conservation biology.

CHAPTER OUTLINE

5.1 Population Change

The abundance of any species waxes and wanes because of natural and anthropogenic influences. One of the most fundamental challenges in ecology lies in disentangling the various biotic and abiotic factors that affect the rates of change of populations. For example,

- plant species of early succession proliferate in areas that have been recently disturbed, perhaps by a forest fire or windstorm, while others that prefer older habitats decline in those same places;
- native herbivores will sometimes increase enormously (irrupt) in abundance, as occasionally happens with mountain pine beetle (*Dendroctonus ponderosae*) in western pine forest, spruce budworm (*Choristoneura fumiferana*) in fir-spruce forest, and green sea urchin (*Strongylocentrotus droebachiensis*) in Atlantic subtidal kelp habitats; and

- certain non-native species have increased enormously in abundance since their introduction to Canada, such as zebra mussel (*Dreissena polymorpha*) in the Great Lakes beginning in the late 1980s, the starling (*Sturnus vulgaris*) since the late 19th century, and the dandelion (*Taraxacum officinalis*) since the 17th century.

Long-term reductions in abundance can be particularly dramatic. Examples include the 80 to 90 percent declines that have been experienced by many over-harvested species, such as the Atlantic cod (*Gadus morhua*), American plaice (*Hippoglossoides platessoides*), and porbeagle shark (*Lamna nasus*) on the Atlantic coast; the bowhead whale (*Balaena mysticetus*) in the eastern Arctic; plains bison (*Bison bison bison*) in the prairies; and ginseng (*Panax quinquefolia*) in southern Quebec and Ontario. Other native species have experienced persistent declines because of the destruction of their habitat, such as the northern spotted owl (*Strix occidentalis caurina*) in southern British Columbia, or because of competition from invasive species, such as the eastern pond-mussel (*Ligumia nasuta*) in Ontario. Even climate change is a factor for certain species, such as the Peary caribou (*Rangifer tarandus pearyi*) on the islands of Nunavut.

In addition to increases or decreases in abundance caused by a disturbance or a slower change in environmental conditions, all populations fluctuate to some degree. Indeed, some may be cyclical, such as that of the snowshoe hare (*Lepus americanus*) and one of its major predators, the lynx (*Lynx canadensis*) (see **Figure 5.32**).

But before we can tease apart the factors that affect changes in the abundance of organisms, we need to model population growth. The greater the generality of the models that we construct, the more species to which they will apply. And the broader the applicability, the better the likelihood that we will identify general principles that underlie the diverse patterns of population change that are observed in natural and human-affected ecosystems.

5.2 Exponential Population Growth

A population can be defined as a group of conspecific individuals that inhabit a particular area. Members of a population have a greater probability of reproducing and of producing viable offspring among themselves than they do with conspecifics of other populations. Populations change in abundance for the following reasons:

- For a **closed population** that is isolated from other groups of the same species, such that no individuals move between them, changes in abundance are determined by the difference in the numbers of births (M) and deaths (D). In a closed population, the number of individuals, N, increases from one time unit (t) to the next ($t + 1$) when M exceeds D, and it decreases when D is greater than M. (An additional implicit assumption inherent to a closed population is that the spatial area it occupies remains constant.)
- For an **open population**, from which individuals are free to leave and into which others can immigrate from other groups, N is also influenced by the numbers of immigrants (I) and emigrants (E). In an open population, changes in population size between time units t and $t + 1$ can be described as

$$N_{t+1} = N_t + (M_t - D_t) + (I_t - E_t) \tag{5.1}$$

Peary caribou are found only in the Canadian Arctic and coastal northwestern Greenland. Having declined by 83 percent from 1961 to 2001, these endangered animals are threatened by increased amounts of snow and freezing rain associated with climate change, which limit their access to food.

Jerry Kobalenko/Photographer's Choice/Getty Images

The change in population size (ΔN) over a given change in time (Δt) describes a rate, measured in individuals per unit time, that can be described as

$$\Delta N/\Delta t = (N_{t+1} - N_t)/(t + 1 - t) \quad (5.2)$$

For simplicity, models of population growth often incorporate the assumption that there is no immigration or emigration, so that changes in N are a consequence only of the numbers of births and deaths. To a first approximation, this assumption is usually reasonable.

The time frame over which changes in abundance are measured can be either

- continuous, meaning that changes in population occur over extremely small intervals of time, also known as instantaneous change, or
- discrete and occurring at distinct intervals, such as once every year.

In general, however, neither continuous nor discrete intervals perfectly capture the time frames during which births and deaths actually take place and, thus, when they alter the abundance of a population. For example, although births might occur at a similar time within the year for species that breed during a particular season, such as the autumn for brook trout (*Salvelinus fontinalis*) or the early summer for white-throated sparrow (*Zonotrichia albicollis*), deaths do not necessarily follow such predictability in timing.

Density-Independent per Capita Growth Rate (r_{max})

Mathematically, it is often convenient to simplify population growth as a process that occurs continuously, because this allows us to adopt differential equations for the purposes of modelling. As noted above, Δt under this circumstance represents an infinitesimally short period of time, ∂t, meaning the rate of change in population size would be $\partial N / \partial t$. In continuous time, the number of births, M, will be the product of the population size N and the instantaneous birth rate, m (measured as births per individual per unit of time), such that

$$M = mN$$

or

$$m = M/N \quad (5.3)$$

Similarly, the number of deaths will be a function of population size and the instantaneous death rate, d, such that

$$D = dN$$

or

$$d = D/N \quad (5.4)$$

In a closed population, changes in abundance are equal to the difference in the number of births and deaths: $N = M - D$. Thus, in continuous time,

$$\partial N/\partial t = mN - dN$$

and

$$\partial N/\partial t = (m - d)N \quad (5.5)$$

The difference between the instantaneous rates of birth and death represents the **intrinsic rate of population growth** (r) in continuous time, such that $r = m - d$, also termed the Malthusian parameter (so named after the English minister Thomas Malthus, who argued in 1798 that the multiplicative growth of the human population would always outstrip the arithmetic rate of increase in food supply).

The intrinsic rate of increase is a per individual or **per capita rate of population growth**. An **exponential model of population growth** can thus be described by the equation

$$\partial N/\partial t = rN \quad (5.6)$$

Note also that

$$r = \partial N/N\partial t \quad (5.7)$$

in which r is measured as *individuals per individual per unit of time*. For an exponentially growing population, the per capita rate of increase does not change with either time or variations in the size of the population (although it does for populations that experience logistic growth, as is explained below). Rather, it remains constant at a value equal to the **maximum per capita rate of growth** for that population. Therefore, we will let the intrinsic rate of increase, which is equivalent to the maximum per capita rate of population growth, be r_{max}. For many situations, however, ecologists wish to estimate the **realized per capita rate of population growth** rather than the maximum rate of increase. For those situations, r will be used to represent the realized per capita rate of population growth.

Continuous-Time, Exponential Population Growth

The growth rate of a population that is increasing continuously and exponentially can be expressed by the following model:

$$\partial N/\partial t = r_{max} N \quad (5.8)$$

Often, equations can be more easily interpreted when they are plotted as a figure that shows abundance, N, plotted against time, t. If this is done for different values of r_{max}, various patterns of exponential population growth are seen. As the value of r_{max} increases, and because their growth is exponential, populations grow by increasingly larger amounts—$\Delta N/\Delta t$ increases over time. Compare, for example, the increases in N (from a starting point, N_0, of 10 individuals) exhibited by various species with hugely different r_{max} values, ranging from the deer mouse (*Peromyscus maniculatus*; r_{max}=15.9) to the extremely slow-growing shortfin mako shark (*Isurus oxyrinchus*; r_{max}=0.12) (**Figure 5.1**).

The curves plotted in **Figure 5.1** describe how population size increases over time. Under these circumstances of r_{max}, the number of individuals at any time t, or N_t, depends on two parameters (numbers that remain constant) and one variable (a number that can vary), such that N_t depends on the starting population size (N_0, a parameter), the intrinsic rate of increase (r_{max}, also a parameter), and time (t, a variable):

$$N_t = N_0 \exp(r_{max} t) \quad (5.9)$$

This basic equation is used to model exponential changes in abundance with changes in time. The phrase *exp*(r) means to exponentiate the bracketed term r. It can also be written as e^r (as will be done in this book), although *exp* can be more convenient when the bracketed terms contain superscripts or subscripts.

Using the rules of calculus, Equation 5.9 can be obtained by integrating Equation 5.8. For specific rates of growth, one can use Equation 5.9 to calculate the time required for a population to double, treble, and so on, over time. For example, the **doubling time** represents the time required for a population to increase from N_0 to $2N_0$. Following on from Equation 5.9,

$$2N_0 = N_0 \exp(r_{max} t_{double})$$

and, after dividing through by N_0,

$$2 = \exp(r_{max} t_{double})$$

Taking the natural logarithm of both sides of the equation yields the following expression:

$$\ln(2) = r_{max}\, t_{double}$$

which, following rearrangement, yields an equation for calculating the doubling time:

$$t_{double} = \ln(2)/r_{max} \quad (5.10)$$

Similarly, the trebling time for a population would be

$$t_{treble} = \ln(3)/r_{max} \quad (5.11)$$

As **Table 5.1** shows for the species in **Figure 5.1**, what might appear to be small changes in r_{max} can result in large differences in their doubling times.

TABLE 5.1 Estimated Population Doubling Times for Six Species of Vertebrate Animals

The doubling times are calculated using the equation $t_{double} = \ln(2)/r_{max}$.

Common Name	Binomial	r_{max}	Doubling Time (years)
Deer mouse	*Peromyscus maniculatus*	15.9	0.04 (~2 weeks)
Red fox	*Vulpes vulpes*	1.78	0.39 (~5 months)
Atlantic herring	*Clupea harengus*	1.08	0.64 (~8 months)
Northern pike	*Esox lucius*	0.60	1.16
Moose	*Alces alces*	0.27	2.57
Shortfin mako	*Isurus oxyrinchus*	0.12	5.78

SOURCE: Hutchings et al. (unpublished).

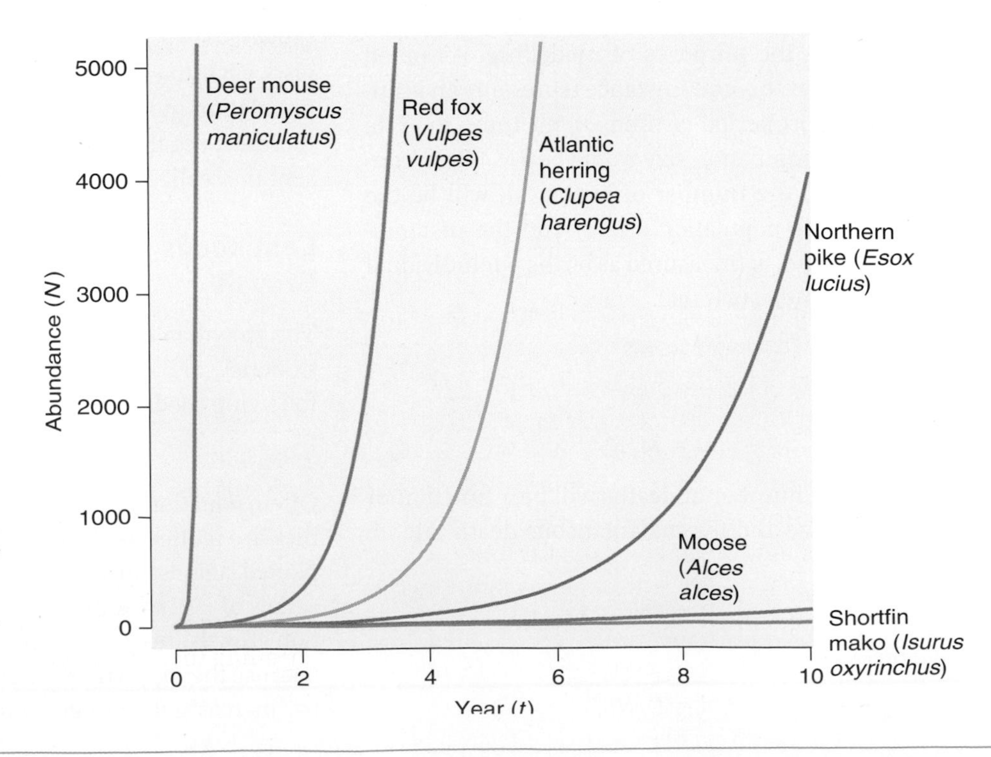

FIGURE 5.1
Exponential Growth Curves for Species That Are Increasing at Their Maximum Rate of per Capita Growth, r_{max}. In all cases, the starting abundance, N_0, is 10 individuals.

SOURCE: Estimates of r_{max} are from Hutchings et al. (2010).

ECOLOGY IN DEPTH 5.1

Linear versus Exponential Growth

Linear and exponential growth rates yield extremely different patterns of growth. Although the abundance of a population can be expected to increase steadily (in the density-independent case) with time, the rate at which it does so is extraordinarily faster under the exponential case. This can be illustrated by the case of repeatedly folding a piece of paper in half. The thickness of a single sheet is about 0.08 mm. After folding the sheet in half, the thickness doubles to 0.16 mm. Folding it in half a second, third, and fourth time yields a thickness of just more than 1 cm. Folding the piece of paper just another six times (10 in total) would yield a thickness of 82 cm. By the 24th fold, you would have attained a thickness of more than 1 km, and by the 35th, the bundle of paper would be thick enough to reach from Toronto to Calgary (roughly 2700 km). (Obviously, to have so many folds is physically impossible—in fact, even the thinnest paper can be folded only six or seven times.)

The thickness of the repeatedly folded paper increases to such an extraordinary degree because it was growing exponentially—by doubling in thickness every time step, it was increasing at a constant rate. By contrast, if the thickness had been increasing in a linear fashion, the depth of the paper after 35 time steps would have been considerably smaller. Linear growth refers to something that increases by the same amount at every time step. Recall that the initial increase in thickness of the paper when it was first folded was 0.08 mm. If the thickness of the paper had been growing linearly at that rate over 35 time steps, it would have attained a depth of only 2.9 mm.

In the simple example above, the exponential growth rate of the paper thickness was 100 percent per time step. But even if we were to take a considerably slower rate of increase, the difference between exponential and linear growth is still dramatic.

An excellent analogy of population growth rate is the compounded rate of interest that is received on a bank account or by financial instruments, such as a guaranteed interest certificate (GIC) or a Canada Savings Bond. In this sense, "compounded" means that the interest rate is applied to both the initial investment plus all of the accrued interest, so that their total increases exponentially over time. With an initial investment of $1000, and with interest accruing annually at a compounded rate of 5 percent, the value of the asset would double after only 13.8 years, and then again after another 13.8 years, and so on. However, if the interest was accruing in a linear fashion (5 percent of the original principal being added every year, as opposed to 5 percent of the accumulated amount), it would take 20 years to double the funds. After 50 years of compounded interest, the exponentially growing account would total $12 182, according to our continuous exponential population growth model (Equation 5.9). In contrast, a linearly growing account would have only $3500 in it after 50 years. Clearly, exponential growth is a powerful force in economics and also in population biology.

Discrete-Time, Exponential Population Growth

The continuous-time model of exponential population growth has the implicit assumption that births and deaths are occurring incessantly through time. In reality, this assumption is a reasonable approximation for relatively few organisms, mostly simple ones, such as bacteria and yeasts. Instead, most populations experience discrete pulses of births, especially those that breed in a particular season. Deaths may also be seasonal in some species, perhaps occurring during a difficult time of the year, such as the winter, although in many others, they tend to occur more continuously. Under these circumstances of discretely timed events, the number of individuals at a particular time $t + 1$ will be a function of the abundance at time t multiplied by a growth rate parameter λ, which is termed the finite rate of increase:

$$N_{t+1} = \lambda N_t \tag{5.12}$$

Therefore, the population at any time t will be equal to the abundance at time $t - 1$ multiplied by λ, meaning that

$$N_1 = \lambda N_0$$

and

$$N_2 = \lambda N_1 \qquad \text{or} \qquad N_2 = \lambda(\lambda N_0)$$

and

$$N_3 = \lambda N_2 \qquad \text{or} \qquad N_3 = \lambda[\lambda(\lambda N_0)]$$

In general, then, the abundance at any time t for a population growing exponentially at discrete time intervals can be calculated as

$$N_t = \lambda^t(N_0) \tag{5.13}$$

When the discrete time interval is infinitesimally brief, Equation 5.13 is equivalent to Equation 5.9, meaning that r is mathematically related to λ as

$$\lambda = e^r \tag{5.14}$$

or, taking the natural logarithm of both sides,

$$r = \ln(\lambda) \tag{5.15}$$

Therefore, a population is

- growing exponentially when $r > 0$ and $\lambda > 1$;
- declining exponentially when $r < 0$ and $\lambda < 1$; and
- unchanging in abundance when $r = 0$ and $\lambda = 1$.

Relevance of *r* to Evolutionary Ecology, Resource Management, and Conservation

Models of exponential population growth can, at times, seem overly simplistic to be of much practical utility. In actual practice, however, these models are extremely useful. Indeed, a strong argument can be made that the intrinsic rate of population growth, *r*, is one of the most unifying parameters in all of ecology. There are several reasons to support this assertion:

1. First, *r* can represent individual fitness, thereby reflecting the rate at which a particular genotype is increasing relative to others in the same population. Under this circumstance, *r* represents a genotypic rate of increase. In this sense, it is the average of all per capita genotypic rates of increase that yields a population-level per capita increase (either r_{max} or *r*). This provides a link between evolutionary change (individual fitness) and demographic change (per capita population growth rate).
2. Among populations having commercial value, the rate at which individuals can be sustainably harvested becomes larger if the per capita growth rate increases. In other words, all else being equal, the potentially sustainable **harvest rate** (i.e., the number of individuals removed from a population relative to the number available) is greater for populations with relatively high values of r_{max}. That is the reason why the stocks of Atlantic cod on Georges Bank, 175 km off southern Nova Scotia (with $r_{max} = 0.67$), can be harvested at a higher rate than those off northeastern Newfoundland (r_{max} ~0.09 to 0.26) (Myers et al., 1997; Hutchings, 1999).
3. Finally, *r* is of fundamental importance in the context of conservation biology. Because r_{max} describes the maximum per capita rate of population increase, which is also the growth rate at a relatively low level of abundance, this parameter informs us of the rate at which a depleted population might recover. All else being equal, populations for which r_{max} is relatively high will recover faster than those for which it is lower. Indeed, the exponential population growth model often provides an excellent representation of the temporal changes in population size when the initial abundance is low **(Figure 5.2).**

5.3 Logistic Population Growth

The exponential model of population growth is also termed the **density-independent model of population growth**, for the reason that per capita growth rate does not vary with population density, *N*. As we previously noted, this is for cases in which we are dealing with a closed population, meaning that (a) as *N* increases, individuals do not emigrate, and (b) the spatial area occupied by the population does not change. Under these circumstances, we can treat *N*, which represents

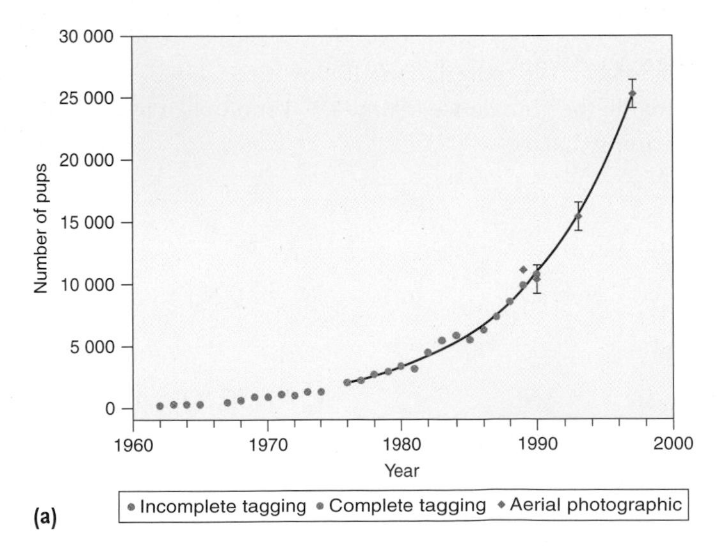

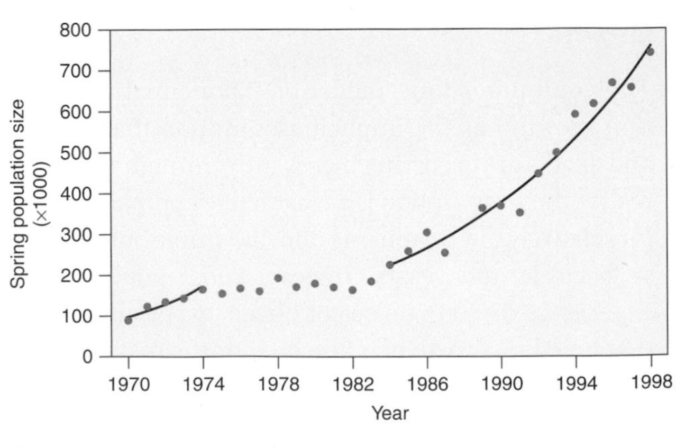

FIGURE 5.2
Empirical Examples of Exponential Population Growth in Canada. (a) The numbers of grey seal (*Halichoerus grypus*) pups on Sable Island, Nova Scotia; (b) greater snow goose (*Anser caerulescens atlanticus*) during the fall migration in southern Quebec.

SOURCES: (a) Bowen, W. D., J. McMillan, and R. Mohn. 2003. "Sustained exponential growth of grey seals at Sable Island, Nova Scotia," Oxford University Press, *ICES Journal of Marine Science*, 60: 1265–1274 (Figure 3, p. 1272). Reproduced by permission of Oxford University Press and the author. (b) Modified from Menu, S., G. Gauthier, and A. Reed. 2002. "Changes in survival rates and population dynamics of greater snow geese over a 30-year period: Implications for hunting regulations," *Journal of Applied Ecology*, 39: 91–102. Used with permission of Blackwell Publishing Ltd.

Bill Freedman

Grey seal (*Halichoerus grypus*) on Sable Island, Nova Scotia.

abundance, as being equivalent to density—to the numbers of individuals per unit of area.

In reality, however, there are limits to the growth of populations. As N increases, there is intensified competition for resources such as food and space. This has the effect of reducing the per capita rate of birth, m, and increasing that of death, d. Under the density-independent model, birth and death rates are assumed to be constant—neither m nor d changes as N increases or decreases. However, in the density-dependent case, birth and death rates are described as follows:

$$m = m_0 - aN \tag{5.16}$$

and

$$d = d_0 + cN \tag{5.17}$$

According to these equations, as the population increases, the per capita rates of birth and death decline and increase, respectively, at rates determined by the slopes a and c, in a linear manner with increases in N **(Figure 5.3).**

Density-Dependent per Capita Growth Rate (r)

In the presence of density dependence, per capita population growth is affected by changes in density. As mentioned earlier, it is frequently helpful to distinguish between two types of per capita growth. For populations growing exponentially, we previously let r_{max} be the maximum per capita rate of population growth. This is the highest rate at which a population is able to increase in abundance:

$$r_{max} = m_0 - d_0 \tag{5.18}$$

In practical terms, r_{max} is realized when the population abundance is extremely small relative to its **carrying capacity**, K—when N is about 0. Recall Equation 5.8, the exponential model for population growth:

$$\partial N/\partial t = r_{max} N$$

To incorporate an effect of increasing density (higher N) on population growth, the instantaneous rate of change in population size ($\partial N/\partial t$) can be reduced by an amount that is proportional to the unused portion of the carrying capacity. Given this condition and the fact that the per capita rate of increase will be highest when N is about 0, we now have

$$\partial N/\partial t = r_{max} N (1 - N/K) \tag{5.19}$$

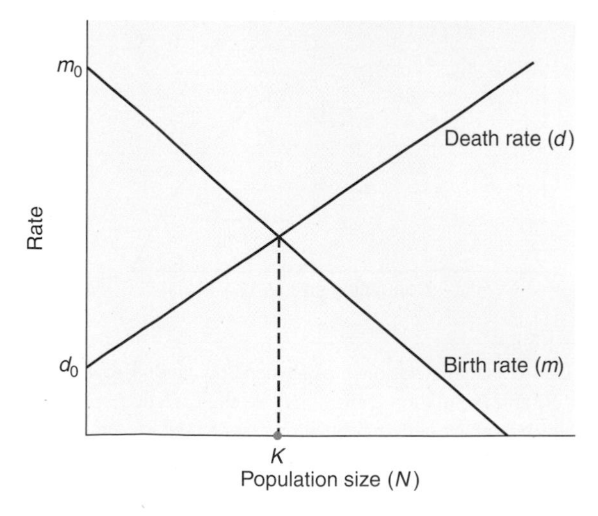

FIGURE 5.3
Linear Changes in per Capita Birth Rate (m) and Death Rate (d) with Changes in Density (N).

This equation describes a basic, continuous-time, **logistic model of population growth**. Note that under this case of density-dependent growth, the population growth rate, $\partial N/\partial t$, initially increases with increasing N before reaching a maximum value at $N/K = 0.5$, before declining again and eventually reaching 0 when $N = K$ **(Figure 5.4).**

Recall that the per capita rate of population growth ($\partial N/N\partial t$) for the exponential model is equal to the maximum per capita growth rate, i.e., r_{max}. However, in the logistic model the per capita rate of population growth changes with density. This can be shown by rearranging Equation 5.19 such that we now have

$$\partial N/N\partial t = r_{max} (1 - N/K) \tag{5.20}$$

Note that, unlike the exponential model, the per capita rate of population growth ($\partial N/N\partial t$) is no longer a constant value. This allows us to define r, the realized per capita rate of population growth, to distinguish it from r_{max}. For the logistic growth equation, the realized per capita rate of population increase is

$$r = r_{max} (1 - N/K) \tag{5.21}$$

This equation informs us that as population size N gets larger, the realized per capita growth rate, r, becomes smaller **(Figure 5.5).** John Fryxell and colleagues (1998) of the Universities of Guelph and Toronto studied wild populations of small terrestrial mammals in central Ontario and found good empirical evidence that their per capita growth rates decline linearly with population size **(Figure 5.6).** Although the logistic model implicitly assumes that r continues to increase as N declines **(Figure 5.5)**, there can be circumstances in which r begins to decline once N has fallen below a "threshold" population size. This phenomenon—termed the Allee effect in the ecological literature and depensation in the fisheries literature—is of concern from a conservation perspective because such declines in r would inhibit population or species recovery.

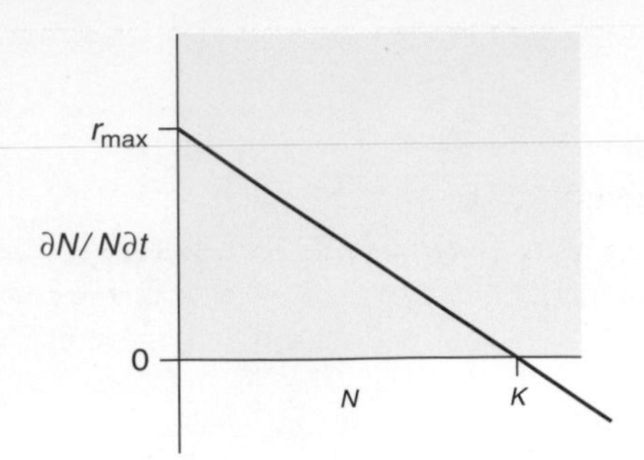

FIGURE 5.5
Realized per Capita Growth Rate $(1/N)(\partial N/\partial t)$ as a Function of Population Size (N) for the Logistic Population Growth Model. Realized per capita growth rate (r) declines with increases in population abundance, a reflection of the depressing influence that increased density has on r. Note that r is negative when N exceeds K.

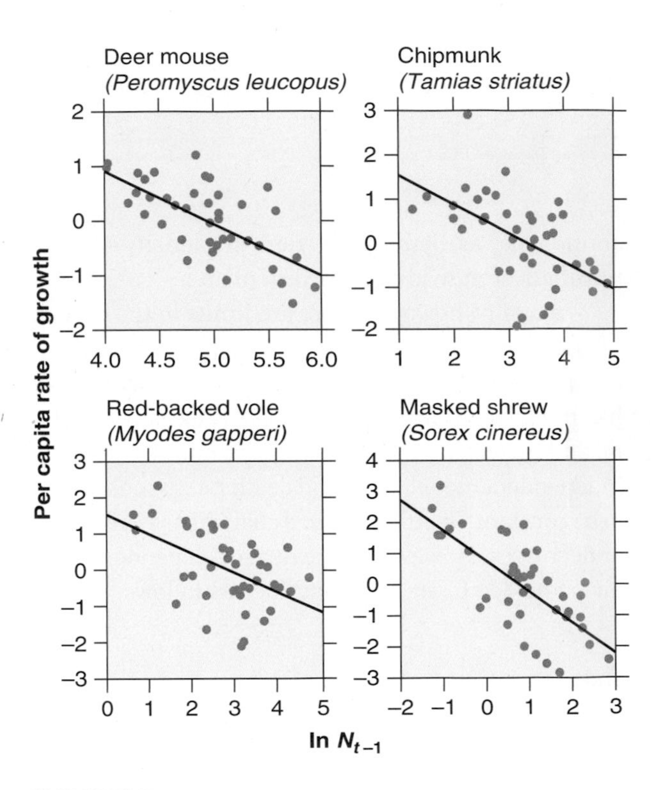

FIGURE 5.6
Linear Reductions in per Capita Population Growth Rate (r) with Increasing Density (N) for Four Small Mammals in Algonquin Provincial Park, Ontario.

SOURCE: Used with permission of the Ecological Society of America, from Fryxell, J. M., J. B. Falls, E. A. Falls, and R. J. Brooks. 1998. "Long-term dynamics of small-mammal populations in Ontario," *Ecology*, 79(1): 213–225; permission conveyed through Copyright Clearance Center, Inc.

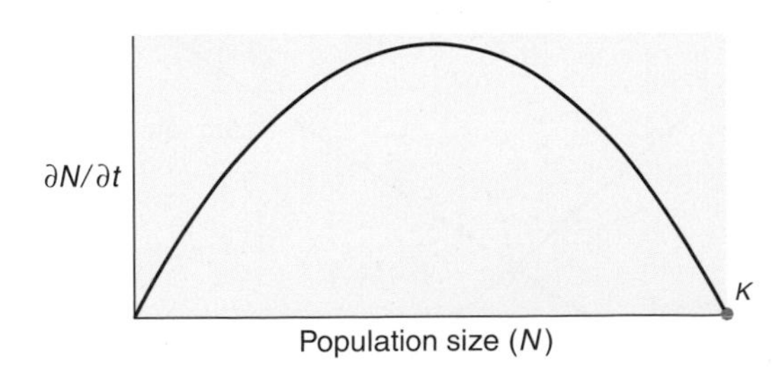

FIGURE 5.4
The Dome-Shaped Relationship between Population Growth Rate ($\partial N/\partial t$) and Population Density (N) for the Logistic Population Growth Model. Note that population growth rate, $\partial N/\partial t$, initially increases with increasing density before reaching a maximum value at $N/K = 0.5$, before declining again and eventually reaching 0 when the carrying capacity has been reached.

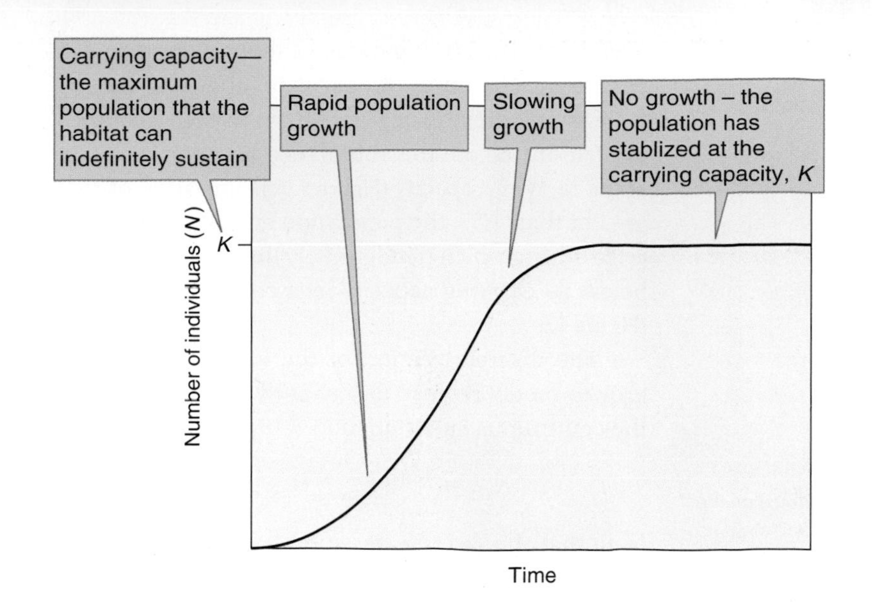

FIGURE 5.7

Population Growing in Accordance with a Logistic Population Growth Model. The sigmoidal or S-shaped curve is a characteristic feature of logistic growth. The growth rate of the population increases (as reflected by an escalating slope) until abundance reaches half of the carrying capacity (K), after which the growth rate declines (reflected by a declining and eventually flattening slope) until the abundance equals K.

As with the model of density-independent growth, Equation 5.19 can be integrated to produce an equation that describes changes in population growth with time:

$$N_t = \frac{K}{1 + [(K - N_0)/N_0] \exp(-r_{max} t)} \quad (5.22)$$

A plot of density-dependent growth versus time yields a graph in which N increases with t until N is equal to $0.5K$, after which the rate declines until $\partial N/\partial t = 0$ when $N = K$ **(Figure 5.7)**. This "S-shaped" pattern of population increase is variously termed a sigmoidal or logistic growth curve, and it can provide good fits to changes in abundance over time. One example is shown in **Figure 5.8** for growth of the numbers of breeding merlins (*Falco columbarius*) near Saskatoon, using data compiled by researchers at the University of Saskatchewan (Oliphant and Haug, 1985; Lieske, 1997).

Algonquin Provincial Park (established 1893), a wildlife sanctuary comprising 7630 square kilometres of coniferous and deciduous forests, rivers, and lakes, provides habitat for many of Canada's boreal fauna and flora.

Time Lags and Oscillations of Abundance

From a modelling perspective, it is useful to think of K as a point estimate, in the sense of representing a population that has reached its carrying capacity but is not fluctuating around it. However, the reality is different—in nature, populations may "hover" about their carrying capacity to varying degrees, sometimes exceeding it or falling below. One of the factors that can contribute to the overshooting and undershooting of K is a **time lag**. The logistic growth model presented in Equation 5.22 incorporates the implicit assumption that there is no time lag between changes in N and in $\partial N/\partial t$—that is, $\partial N/\partial t$ is assumed to be instantaneous.

In most populations, however, a temporal lag separates the time at which an increase in abundance occurs and that when negative effects of the increased density become manifested by decreases in per capita survival and/or birth rate. Consider, for example, a population of Arctic grayling (*Thymallus arcticus*) in a creek flowing into Great Slave Lake, Northwest Territories. Although those fish may spawn in the early summer (June) of year t, the consequences of an increase in density on per capita birth rate may not be

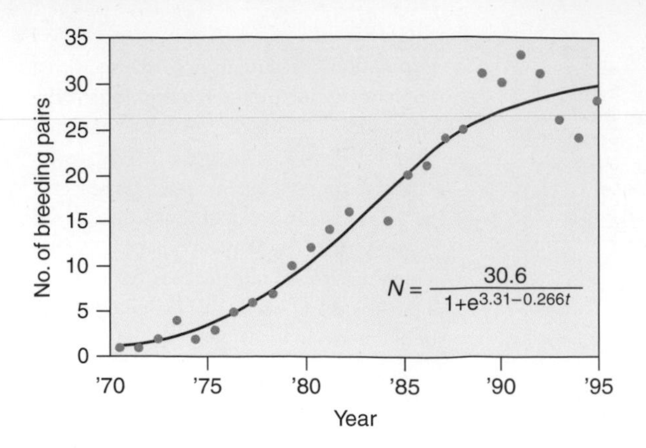

FIGURE 5.8
Logistic Population Growth of Merlins (*Falco columbarius*) on the South Saskatchewan River, Saskatchewan. From an initial abundance of fewer than five breeding pairs in the early 1970s, the number of merlins increased approximately six-fold until the early 1990s, when growth rate declined, which may mean that the population has reached its carrying capacity for this particular area.

SOURCE: Neal, D. 2004. *Introduction to Population Ecology.* Cambridge University Press, Cambridge, UK. Reprinted with the permission of Cambridge University Press.

realized until the offspring reach maturity and compete with one another for spawning sites. If the age at maturity is three years, then the density-dependent effects of an increase in N in year t will not be realized until year $t + 3$.

A time lag, τ, can be incorporated into the logistic growth model (Equation 5.19) as follows:

$$\partial N/\partial t = r_{max} N (1 - N_{t-\tau}/K) \quad (5.23)$$

Robert May examined the dynamics of population models in his 1976 book, *Theoretical Ecology: Principles and Applications*. He showed that the degree to which populations fluctuate about their carrying capacity, and the likelihood that they would ever stabilize at K, depends on the time lag and the **response time** of a population, which is defined as $1/r_{max}$ (populations with fast maximum per capita rates of growth have correspondingly short response times). May demonstrated that population growth can be predicted by the ratio of the time lag to the response time: $\tau(1/r_{max})^{-1}$, which simplifies to τr_{max}.

In essence, the higher the maximum rate of per capita population growth, or the longer the time lag, the more likely it will be that a population will overshoot and undershoot its carrying capacity. When τr_{max} is relatively small (between 0 and 0.37), the population grows to its carrying capacity and remains at that level of abundance **(Figure 5.9a)**. For our grayling example above (for which $\tau = 3$), r_{max} would have to be 0.12 or less for the population to grow to, and to not fluctuate about, its carrying capacity. For values of τr_{max} larger than 0.37 but less than 1.57, the growth dynamics are such that the population initially overshoots its carrying capacity, then undershoots it, and then continues to oscillate about K but by increasingly smaller degrees (this is termed a **damped oscillation**) before the abundance becomes constant at the carrying capacity **(Figure 5.9b)**. For values of τr_{max} greater than 1.57, the population enters a **stable limit cycle** during which it indefinitely fluctuates above and below its carrying capacity by a constant amplitude **(Figure 5.9c)**.

The discrete version of the logistic population growth model represents a slightly modified form of the continuous one (Equation 5.19):

$$N_{t+1} = N_t + r_{max} N_t(1 - N_t/K). \quad (5.24)$$

Note that the discrete version of the logistic model has an implicit lag τ of 1 time unit t (so that the

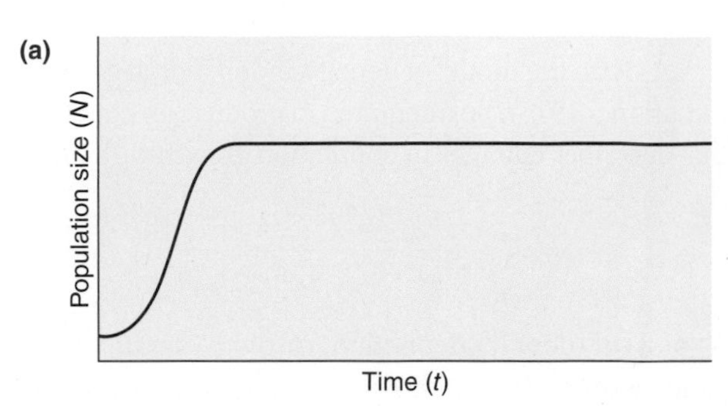

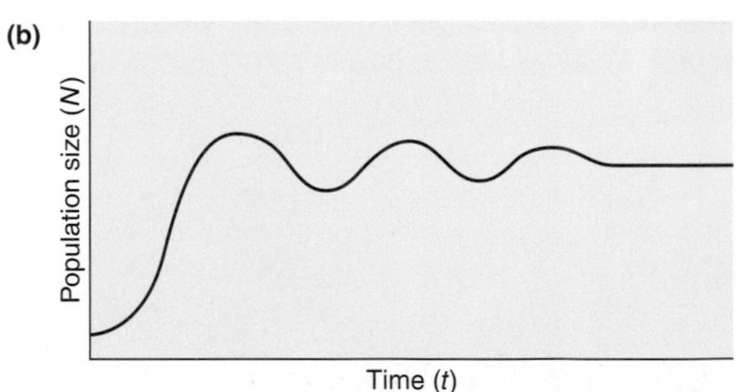

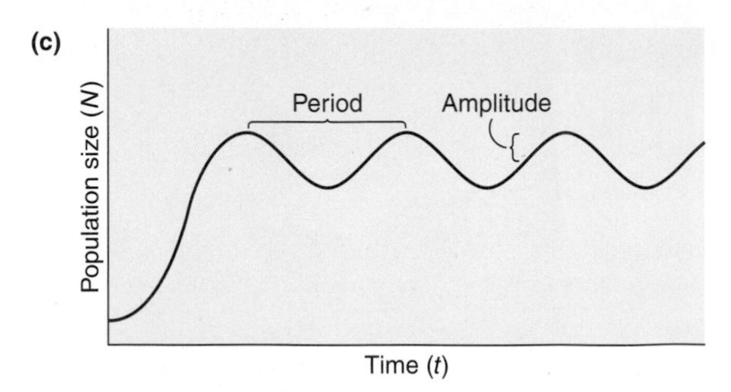

FIGURE 5.9
Examples of Continuous-Time, Logistic Population Growth Curves Having Different Time Lags. (a) A population for which the ratio of time lag to response time ($r\tau$) is small (0.00 to 0.37) grows in accordance with the classical logistic growth curve; (b) a population for which $r\tau$ is between >0.37 and <1.57 leads to damped oscillations whereby the abundance fluctuates with increasingly reduced amplitude about the carrying capacity; (c) large values of $r\tau$ (>1.57) lead to stable limit cycles in which populations continually oscillate about, but never persistently remain at, the carrying capacity.

effects of a change in density in year t are not manifested until year $t+1$). Thus, given that the dynamics in the presence of a time lag is reflected by τr_{max}, the degree to which a population stabilizes at its carrying capacity depends solely on r_{max} for the discrete model.

In a manner similar to that described for the continuous model, a population growing in accordance with the discrete version of the logistic model will reach its carrying capacity after experiencing a series of damped oscillations if r_{max} is less than 2 **(Figure 5.10a)**. If r_{max} ranges between 2.0 and 2.6, the population will continually oscillate above and below K in the form of either two- or four-point stable limit cycles (a four-point limit cycle is shown in **Figure 5.10b)**. If r_{max} is greater than 2.6, then **chaos** will ensue, which can be defined as a non-repeatable pattern **(Figure 5.10c)**.

Population biologists (such as May) were among the first scientists to appreciate the fact that simple deterministic equations (meaning the parameters are held constant and do not vary) can generate complex, chaotic patterns. Gotelli (2008) commented on this, but also cautioned that chaos should not be confused with **stochasticity**, which refers to patterns that are unpredictable. Chaotic patterns are, in fact, predictable and repeatable because they depend solely on the initial values of the parameters and variables in an equation. However, it should be noted that a maximum population growth rate of 2.6 (above which chaos results) is high indeed. If time t was measured in years, such a population would be increasing in abundance by more than 12 times per annum! This is why chaotic population dynamics, in the absence of strong regulatory factors such as predation (see below), are thought to be limited to the simplest organisms, such as viruses, bacteria, and some parasites.

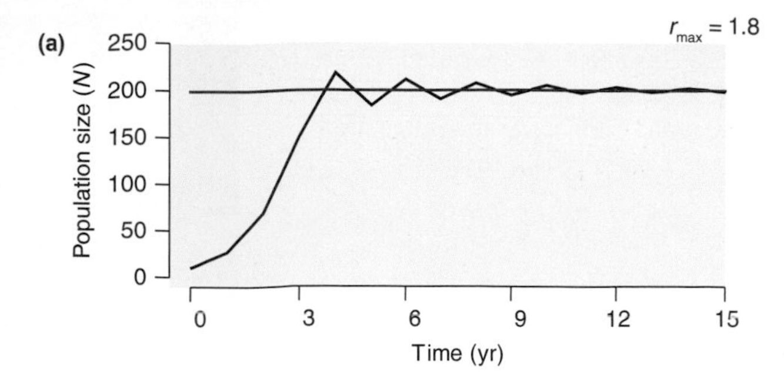

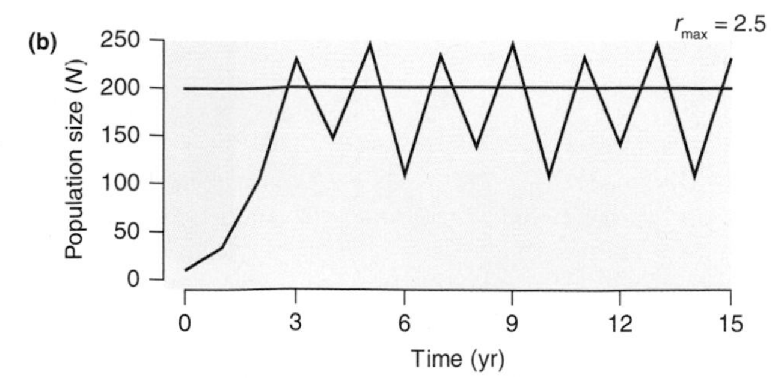

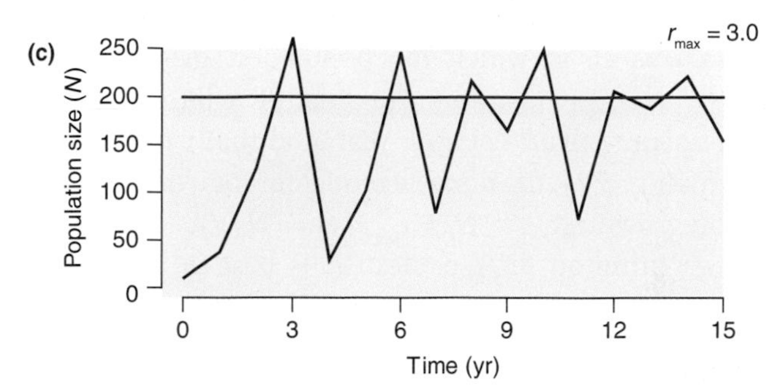

FIGURE 5.10
Examples of Discrete-Time, Logistic Population Growth Curves Having Different Values of r_{max}. (a) Populations for which r_{max} is less than 2 exhibit damped oscillations; (b) populations for which r_{max} is between 2 and 2.6 exhibit either 2- or 4-point stable limit cycles (the example illustrated here is a 4-point cycle); (c) populations for which r_{max} exceeds 2.6 exhibit chaos.

Population Growth Rate and Sustainable Rates of Harvesting

Predicting the effects of the harvesting of biological resources typically involves models based on the density-dependent population growth rate. Under many circumstances, a primary objective for resource managers is to identify a quota that will result in the largest, but sustainable, long-term harvest—this is known as the **maximum sustainable yield**, or **MSY**.

A primary responsibility of the managers of bio-resources is to maintain harvested populations at the abundance or biomass at which the MSY can be taken. In a fishery, this population target is termed B_{MSY}, meaning the biomass (often in terms of the total weight of individuals in a population) from which the maximum sustainable yield can be obtained. Indeed, in some jurisdictions, there are legal consequences for failing to attain this reference point or some percentage thereof. Under federal law in the United States, for example, the term "overfishing" is interpreted in terms of the capacity of a fishery to produce the MSY on a continuing basis. If an over-exploited fish stock falls below $0.5B_{MSY}$, by law a fishery rebuilding plan must be developed by the federal Secretary of Commerce. Such a legal requirement to rebuild overfished stocks does not exist in Canada, although comparable actions are often attempted.

The theoretical criteria for MSY originate directly from characteristics of the logistic growth model.

Pacific sardine (*Sardinops sagax*), fished in British Columbia's waters since 1917, has been subject to huge fluctuations in abundance and catch, driven primarily by fishing and environmental change.

Recall that, according to Equation 5.19, there is a population size N, or in the case of a fishery, a population biomass B, at which the population growth rate ($\partial N/\partial t$) is at a maximum. For illustrative purposes, let us assume that t equals 1 year, and that we can use Equation 5.24, the discrete model for logistic population growth: $N_{t+1} = N_t + r_{max}N_t(1 - N_t/K)$.

Within an MSY context, it is best to harvest a population when $(N_{t+1} - N_t)$ is at its maximum. According to the logistic growth model, this would occur at $0.5K$, although for many fisheries, it is estimated that maximum population growth rate might actually occur between $0.3K$ and $0.5K$ (Garcia et al., 1989). The maximum number of fish produced in a given year would correspond to the middle shaded area in **Figure 5.11.** During this year, $(N_{t+1} - N_t)$ would be at its maximum. The growth in population size $(N_{t+1} - N_t)$ is considered to be *surplus* from a fisheries perspective (but not from the perspective of the fish population) and therefore available to be harvested (this is the basis for *surplus yield models* in fisheries science).

If fishery managers could maintain a population at B_{MSY}, they would be able to produce the maximum yield that could be sustained over the long term. Today, however, many of the world's commercial fisheries have collapsed (Chapter 15), so that many fish populations are well below B_{MSY}. This means that the sustainable yields available to their respective fisheries are far smaller than what could be attained at or near B_{MSY} (Worm et al., 2009). Compare, for

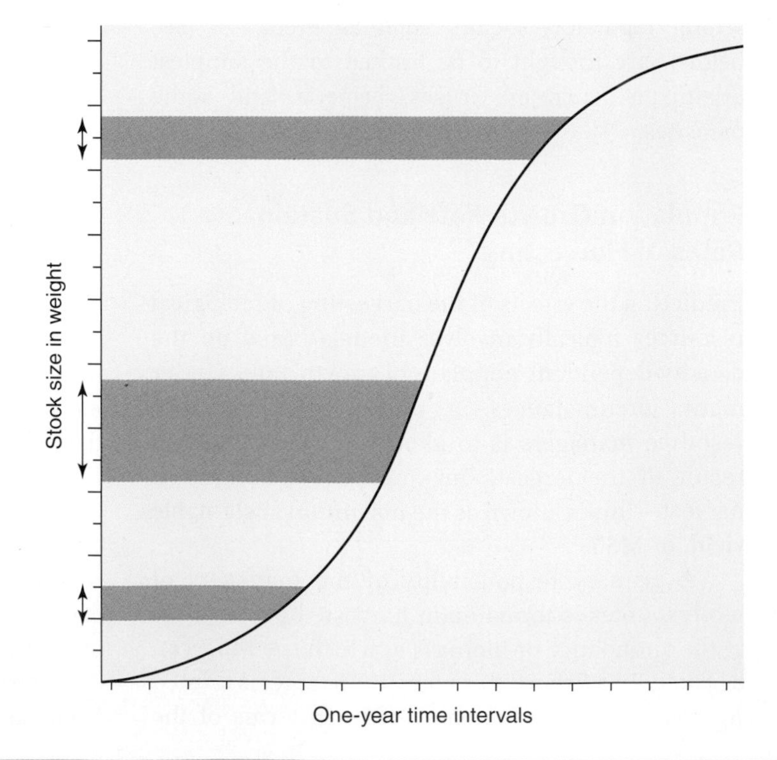

FIGURE 5.11
Logistic Growth of a Commercially Harvested Fish Population. This figure shows how the yearly increase in total fish biomass (B) changes with population size, being higher when B is near $K/2$, and smaller when B is small or large, relative to K. The highest "surplus population growth" (meaning surplus from a fisheries perspective, but not from that of a fish population) is represented by the shaded areas and represents the maximum sustainable yield. The biomass at which MSY is attained is termed B_{MSY}.

example, the yield that could theoretically be sustained at B_{MSY} (middle shaded area in **Figure 5.11**) with that corresponding to a population size considerably less than B_{MSY} (lowest shaded area).

5.4 Age- and Stage-Structured Population Growth

To this point, the models of population growth that we have considered have depended on birth and death rates and, for logistic growth, density (or abundance). For most organisms, however, the patterns of birth and survival vary with age. Body size and developmental stage might also affect birth and death rates, and models can be constructed to accommodate their influence. For the most part, we will consider age-specific effects, because of their generality and the fact that age is often positively correlated with size and life stage. Nonetheless, we will consider a simple stage-specific model and examine how it might be applied in a conservation context.

As will become evident later in this chapter, it is useful to distinguish *age* from *age class*, as follows:

```
Age:        0    1    2    3    4    5
            |----|----|----|----|----|
Age class:    1    2    3    4    5
```

A newborn individual is of age $x = 0$. It is in the first age class ($x = 1$) until it reaches the age of 1, at which time it enters the second year class. If the ages in a population range from 0 to k, the age classes range from 1 to k.

Age-Specific Schedules of Fecundity and Survival

Our objective initially will be to estimate the growth rate of an age-structured population that is experiencing exponential increase. Age will be denoted by x and will represent years. We will also assume that individuals begin to breed immediately upon the attainment of a given age, x. The age-specific birth rate, also referred to as **age-specific fecundity** or **fertility**, is denoted m_x. This represents the average number of offspring (e.g., seeds of a plant, eggs of a fish or turtle, newborns of a live-bearing mammal) that are born to a female at age x. Values of m_x need not be integers (whole numbers). For example, bighorn sheep (*Ovis canadensis*) females (ewes) in the mountains of western Canada have a litter size of one lamb (Bérubé et al., 1999), but not all of them breed every year. Therefore, the m_x value for bighorn sheep is calculated as 1 multiplied by the age-specific probabilities of breeding. For ewes aged 2–4 in Sheep River, Alberta, researchers at Université de Sherbrooke have estimated the corresponding values of m_x to be 0.36, 0.76, and 0.86, respectively (Loison et al., 1999).

The fecundity schedule of bighorn sheep is typical of species that experience **determinate growth**, which means that individuals stop growing after a certain age. Once maturity is attained, fecundity tends to be relatively constant from one age to the next, as typically occurs in birds and mammals. However, for organisms with **indeterminate growth** that continues throughout their lives, such as fish, reptiles, and perennial plants, the number of offspring produced

Bighorn sheep (*Ovis canadensis*) reside in alpine meadows and foothills near rocky cliffs in southern British Columbia and southwestern Alberta. Few animals are so well adapted to extremes of elevation and temperature.

tends to increase as age (and body mass) increases. Species whose individuals typically reproduce more than once in their lives are termed **iteroparous**, such as Atlantic salmon (*Salmo salar*), humans (*Homo sapiens*), and sugar maple (*Acer saccharum*). In contrast, individuals of **semelparous** species die after a single reproductive event, such as Pacific salmon (*Oncorhynchus* spp.), short-finned squid (*Illex illecebrosus*) off Atlantic Canada, and soapweed (*Yucca glauca*) in southern Alberta.

We can define **age-specific survival**, denoted as l_x, such that l_5 represents the probability of survival from birth until the beginning of the breeding season at 5 years of age (that is, at the beginning of age class 6). Schedules of age-specific survival typically follow one of three patterns **(Figure 5.12)**, as follows:

- **Type I survival**—This refers to species that exhibit relatively high survival during young and intermediate ages, after which survivorship declines steeply as the maximum longevity is approached (e.g., bighorn sheep [*Ovis canadensis*] and humans [*Homo sapiens*]; **Figure 5.13**)
- **Type II survival**—This is characteristic of the relatively few species that have a constant rate of mortality throughout their lives (e.g., some turtles and birds, such as the black-capped chickadee [*Poecile atricapilla*]).
- **Type III survival**—This refers to species in which mortality is exceedingly high in early life until individuals attain an age when their vulnerability to risks of death declines and they experience relatively high survival thereafter, as is the case of plants with wind-dispersed seeds, marine invertebrates, and fishes that broadcast their eggs in the water during spawning (e.g., Atlantic cod [*Gadus morhua*])

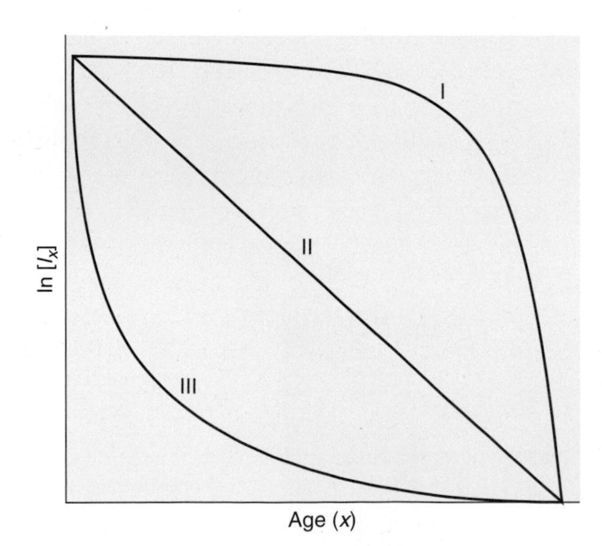

FIGURE 5.12
Three General Types of Survivorship Curves. The natural logarithms of age-specific survival (l_x) are plotted against age (x). The Type I curve reflects survival that is comparatively high in early life, but increasingly lower later on. The Type II curve reflects a relatively constant survival throughout life. The Type III curve reflects high mortality in early life, followed by decreasing mortality as individuals age.

Life Tables

The data required to estimate the exponential rate of growth in an age-structured population are often compiled in a **life table**. The core of a life table lies in its columns of data on age-specific survival and fecundity (or fertility). The survival data may be obtained in one of two ways:

1. The first involves an enumeration of the abundance of individuals at different ages, i.e., the estimation of N_x. Estimates of age-specific survival, l_x, based on such abundance data are most reliable when the relative numbers of individuals in each

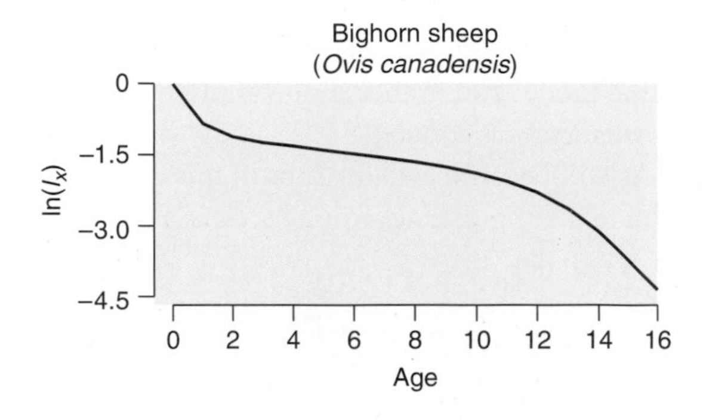

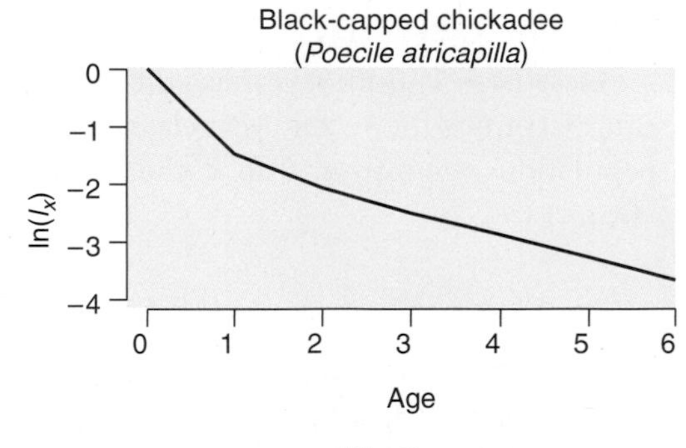

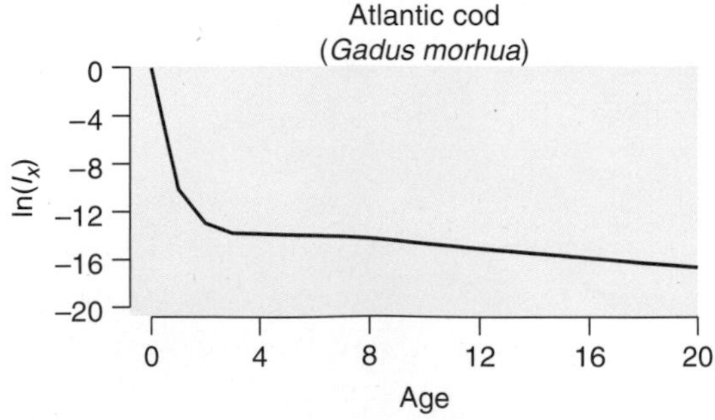

FIGURE 5.13
Examples of Type I, II, and II Survivorship Curves in Natural Populations. A Type I curve is shown for bighorn sheep (*Ovis canadensis*) in Alberta (Loison et al., 1999). A Type II curve corresponds well to data for black-capped chickadees (*Poecile atricapilla*) (Loery et al., 1987). Atlantic cod (*Gadus morhua*) survival data (Hutchings, 1999) provide a classical fit to a Type III curve. Age is in years.

SOURCES: Loison et al. (1999); Loery et al., (1987); Hutchings (1999).

The black-capped chickadee (*Poecile atricapilla*) ranges throughout all of Canada. It is a common inhabitant of deciduous and mixed forests and open woodlands.

Ron Rowan Photography/Shutterstock

age class are similar from one generation to the next. In such a case a population is said to have a **stable age distribution.**

2. For cases in which it is not practical to reliably estimate the age-specific abundance, annual survival (from one age, or year, to the next) can be approximated using a mark-recapture analysis. This involves marking a group of individuals of a given age x in one year, and then re-sampling the population one year later to determine the numbers that have survived.

Using these data, a life table can be assembled that describes the age-specific survival probabilities and fecundities that the average individual in a population can expect to experience from birth until death.

One means of obtaining these data is to monitor the fate of all of the individuals born at the same time, meaning they are all from the same **cohort.** The age-specific survival and fecundity schedules obtained from such a monitoring program comprise a **cohort life table.** Rather than following the fate of a single (or multiple) cohort(s), which can take several years, an alternative means of obtaining these data is to estimate them for all individuals in a population at a single point in time, thereby producing a **static life table.** One key assumption that is made when constructing a life table is that the data that are collected over the life span of a single cohort, or at a single point in time, are representative of age-specific schedules for other cohorts or time periods.

The black-capped chickadee is one of the most common birds in Canada, breeding in all provinces and territories except Nunavut. Despite its commonness, a life table for this bird has never been assembled for a particular population. However, one can be assembled using various sources of information. The first challenge is to estimate survival during the first year of life, a parameter that requires data on

- the number of eggs laid by an average female;
- the percentage that hatch (hatching survival);
- the percentage of hatchlings that fledge from the nest (nestling survival); and
- and the percentage of fledgings that survive to maturity at age 1 year.

Mahoney et al. (1997) studied black-capped chickadees in central Ontario and found that the clutch size averaged 6 eggs per female, of which 86 percent hatch. Half of the hatchlings are expected to be female (Ramsay et al., 2003). A nestling survival estimate of 74 percent is available from Albano (1992), although this is for an Illinois population of the closely related Carolina chickadee (*P. carolinensis*). Smith (1995) provides an estimate of over-summer survival of 1-year-old female black-capped chickadees of 65 percent, based on a 10-year-study, while Loery et al. (1987) estimated that 45 percent of fledged birds survived to the following year, based on a 26-year study. Based on these estimates of survival, we can calculate the probability of surviving to age 1, l_1, as $0.86 \times 0.74 \times 0.65 \times 0.45 = 0.19$. A life table for female black-capped chickadees is presented in **Table 5.2.**

Realized per Capita Growth Rate on a Generational Time Scale

There are two ways that a life table can be used to estimate the per capita growth of an age-structured population. The first parameter that can be estimated is the **net reproductive rate**, or R_0, the average number of offspring produced over the lifetime of an

TABLE 5.2	Life Table for a Population of Black-Capped Chickadees						
Age (x)	Annual Survival (s_x)	Abundance ($N_{x+1} = s_x N_x$)	Age-specific Survival ($l_x = N_x/N_0$)	Age-specific Fecundity (m_x)	$l_x m_x$	e^{-rx}	$l_x m_x e^{-rx}$
0	—	100	1	0	0	1	0
1	0.19	19	0.19	3	0.57	0.82	0.467
2	0.69	14	0.14	3	0.39	0.67	0.264
3	0.62	9	0.09	3	0.24	0.55	0.134
4	0.73	6	0.06	3	0.18	0.45	0.080
5	0.60	4	0.04	3	0.11	0.37	0.039
6	0.54	2	0.02	3	0.06	0.30	0.017

SOURCES: Loery et al. (1987); Albano (1992); Smith (1995); Mahoney et al. (1997).

individual. R_0 is related to age-specific schedules of survival and fecundity by the following equation:

$$R_0 = \Sigma\, l_x\, m_x \tag{5.25}$$

The net reproductive rate is defined as the number of offspring produced during the lifetime of an average individual, so it is a per-generational parameter. It is usual to consider only females when estimating the net reproductive rate, primarily because of the relative ease with which estimates of maternal fecundity can be obtained (the comparable paternal data are much more difficult to measure). In such cases, R_0 is defined as the average number of female offspring produced during the lifetime of a female.

If the lifetime production of offspring by a female (discounted in the life table by the probabilities of living to each age) is such that she is exactly able to replace herself, then $R_0 = 1$. For our chickadee population **(Table 5.2)**, $R_0 = 1.55$, which suggests that the population is growing exponentially at a rate of 1.55 females per female per generation. In general, if $R_0 > 1$, a net surplus of female offspring is being produced and the population increases exponentially over multiple generations. And if $R_0 < 1$, females are unable to produce enough females to replace themselves and the population declines exponentially.

Realized per Capita Growth Rate in Continuous Time

The net reproductive rate can be useful when evaluating how rapidly a population is changing in abundance. However, it is not particularly helpful when comparing per capita growth rates among populations of a species. This is because R_0 quantifies the rate of increase on a *per-generation* basis. If generation time differs among populations, then a comparison of R_0 will not be informative in comparing how their abundance is changing. To compare the growth rates of populations that differ in generation time (e.g., because they have different ages at maturity), we need to estimate the realized per capita rate of population growth (r). This is also true of comparisons among species.

To estimate the realized per capita rate of population growth in continuous time from R_0, we require a means of estimating the **generation time**, given that R_0 is a per-generation rate of increase. Generation time, G, can be defined as the mean age of reproductive individuals in a population:

$$G = \frac{\Sigma l_x m_x x}{\Sigma l_x m_x} \tag{5.26}$$

Therefore, for the chickadee example, $G = 3.68/1.55 = 2.37$ years. Once we have an estimate of the generation time, we can obtain an approximation of r.

Recall that, for an exponentially growing population,

$$N_t = N_0\, e^{rt}$$

Therefore, over the time frame of a single generation,

$$N_G = N_0\, e^{rG}$$

or, after rearrangement,

$$N_G/N_0 = e^{rG}$$

The left-hand side of the equation represents the number of individuals after one generation in relation to the abundance at the initial time zero, which yields an approximation of R_0. Thus,

$$R_0 \sim e^{rG} \tag{5.27}$$

Taking the natural logarithm of both sides of the equation and rearranging it to provide an expression of r yields

$$r \sim \ln(R_0)/G \tag{5.28}$$

For the chickadee population, $r = \ln(1.55)/2.37 = 0.438/2.37 = 0.18$. Therefore, to a first approximation, the estimate of per capita growth rate for the chickadee population is $r = 0.18$.

ECOLOGY IN DEPTH 5.2

Derivation of the Euler-Lotka Equation

The Euler-Lotka equation is of fundamental importance to studies of population dynamics, evolutionary ecology, conservation biology, and behavioural optimization. As such, it is worth understanding how this rather odd-looking equation is derived. In essence, the number of newborn individuals at any time t who are born to females of age x is

$$n_{newborn(t)} = n_{newborn(t-x)} \times l_x \times m_x$$

where

$n_{newborn(t)}$ is the number of newborn at time t

$n_{newborn(t-x)}$ is the number of newborn x time units ago

l_x is the probability of surviving to age x

m_x is the number of newborns produced by a female at age x

For several ages, ranging from age at maturity (α) to age at death (ω), we have

$$n_{newborn(t)} = \Sigma_{\alpha}^{\omega} n_{newborn(t-x)} l_x m_x \quad (1)$$

Now, we will assume that the population is growing exponentially. Recall that the model for exponential population growth is

$$N_t = N_0 e^{rt}$$

For our example, then, we have

$$n_{newborn(t)} = n_{newborn(t-x)} e^{rx}$$

Dividing both sides by e^{rx} yields

$$n_{newborn(t-x)} = n_{newborn(t)}/e^{rx}$$

or

$$n_{newborn(t-x)} = n_{newborn(t)} e^{-rx} \quad (2)$$

Substituting (2) into (1) yields

$$n_{newborn(t)} = \Sigma_{\alpha}^{\omega} n_{newborn(t)} e^{-rx} l_x m_x$$

Finally, dividing both sides by $n_{newborn(t)}$ yields the Euler-Lotka equation:

$$1 = \Sigma l_x m_x e^{-rx}$$

However, we can estimate r with greater accuracy by using the discrete-time version of the Euler-Lotka equation. This was named in part after Leonhard Euler, a Swiss mathematician (1707–1783) who, among other accomplishments, was the first to use the exponential function and logarithms in analytical proofs. Alfred Lotka (1880–1949) was a Ukrainian-born U.S. mathematician who was interested in questions related to population dynamics.

The discrete-time version of the Euler-Lotka equation is as follows:

$$1 = \Sigma l_x m_x e^{-rx} \quad (5.29)$$

The age-specific schedules of survival (l_x) and fecundity (m_x), and of course age (x), are known from the life table. The only unknown parameter is r, and it can be solved only by iteration, that is, by inserting various values of r into the Euler-Lotka equation to determine which one renders the right-hand side of Equation 5.29 closest to 1. For the chickadee population, we can begin by inserting the approximation of r (0.18) that was obtained by dividing $\ln(R_0)$ by G (Equation 5.28). If this is done, the right-hand side of Equation 5.29 is equal to 1.042, which is close to 1 but not by as much as it could be. Further iterations show that a value of $r = 0.20$ results in the right-hand side of Equation 5.29 being closest to 1 (to three decimal places). This indicates that while our approximation of r using data from the literature was not too bad, it was less than the exact value of r.

Recall that λ, the finite rate of increase, is a measure of the proportional change in population size from one time step (t) to the next, such that

$$N_{t+1} = \lambda N_t$$

If $\lambda = 1$, and if time is measured in years, then the population is not changing from one year t to the next ($t + 1$), so that the rate of increase is 0 percent. However, if $\lambda = 1.2$, the population is growing by an amount equal to its size at time t (N_t) plus 0.2 N_t, or by 20 percent per year. Similarly, if $\lambda = 1.5$, the population would be growing by 50 percent per annum.

Recall that λ is mathematically equivalent to e^r. This relationship becomes useful when translating values of r into rates that are meaningful and readily understood by most people. In general, the percentage increase in population size from one time step to the next is given by

$$(e^r - 1) \times 100 \text{ percent} \quad (5.30)$$

For our chickadee population, the exact value of r was 0.20. This is not a number that is readily interpretable by decision makers, such as conservation planners or politicians. However, if we use Equation 5.30, we can inform these people that the chickadee population is growing at a rate equal to

$$(e^{0.20} - 1) \times 100 \text{ percent}$$

or

$$(1.22 - 1) \times 100 \text{ percent} = 22 \text{ percent}$$

Given that our time step was one generation to the next, and that generation time is 2.37 years, we can inform decision makers that the chickadees are estimated to be increasing at a rate of 22 percent roughly every 2½ years. The doubling time would be $\ln(2)/0.20 = 3.5$ years.

Forecasting Changes in Abundance in an Age-Structured Population

Thus far, we have identified models than can be used to forecast, or predict, total population abundances over some defined period of time (e.g., Equations 5.9 and 5.22). However, for an age-structured population, rather than simply keeping track of total abundance, we want to know the numbers of individuals in various age classes through time. To do so, we will return to the age classes that were defined earlier.

Let the number of individuals at time t in age class x be designated as $n_X(t)$. A column vector will be used to represent the number of individuals in each of several age classes at time t, such that

$$\mathbf{n}(t) = \begin{matrix} n_1(t) \\ n_2(t) \\ n_3(t) \\ n_4(t) \\ \cdots\cdots \\ n_K(t) \end{matrix} \quad (5.31)$$

Following Caswell (1989), we will assume in the model that all individuals give birth immediately upon entering a new age class, and that the size of the population is enumerated immediately after the young are born.

Now it is necessary to think about how the number of individuals in a particular age class at the present time (t) will affect the numbers of both newborns and individuals in the next age class one time step into the future ($t+1$). For example, the number of newborns (n_1) at time $t+1$ will depend on the fecundity of individuals in age classes $X = 2$ to k. We define the fecundity (number of offspring of both sexes) of individuals in age class X to be

$$F_X = m_x\, P_X(t) \quad (5.32)$$

The number of newborns (n_1) at time $t+1$ will depend on the fecundity contributions from all age classes, such that

$$n_1(t+1) = \Sigma\, F_X\, n_X(t) \quad (5.33)$$

We can now turn to changes in the abundance of each age class. The number of individuals in age class $K+1$ at time $t+1$ will depend on those in age class K at time t, and the probability of them surviving from K to $K+1$. Let the probability of surviving age class K to age class $K+1$ be

$$P_X = l_x / l_{x-1} \quad (5.34)$$

The number of individuals in the 4th age class is simply those in the 3rd, multiplied by the probability of surviving through that age class, or

$$n_4(t+1) = n_3\, P_3(t)$$

In general, then,

$$n_{X+1}(t+1) = n_X\, P_X(t) \quad (5.35)$$

Thus, for a population having six age classes (such as our chickadee example), we can specify the equations that will forecast changes in the abundance of age classes from one year to the next, as follows:

$$n_1(t+1) = F_1\, n_1(t) + F_2\, n_2(t) + F_3\, n_3(t) + F_4\, n_4(t) + F_5\, n_5(t) + F_6\, n_6(t)$$

$$n_2(t+1) = P_1\, n_1(t)$$

$$n_3(t+1) = P_2\, n_2(t)$$

$$n_4(t+1) = P_3\, n_3(t)$$

$$n_5(t+1) = P_4\, n_4(t)$$

$$n_6(t+1) = P_5\, n_5(t)$$

The growth of an age-structured population is best represented by multiplying the column vector of age-class abundances (Equation 5.31) by a **transition matrix**, i.e., rows and columns of parameters that describe how the age-class abundances change from one time step to the next. This is termed a **Leslie matrix**, developed by and named after the population biologist P. H. Leslie (1945).

The Leslie matrix describes a $k \times k$ square matrix, where k represents the number of age classes in the population of interest. The first row of the matrix represents the fecundities of each of the age classes—the number of newborns produced per individual in each age class. The rows, positioned in a sub-diagonal pattern, identify the age-class survivorship values. The Leslie matrix has the following general form:

$$A = \begin{matrix} F1 & F2 & F3 & \ldots & Fk-1 & Fk \\ P1 & 0 & 0 & \ldots & 0 & 0 \\ 0 & P2 & 0 & \ldots & 0 & 0 \\ 0 & 0 & P3 & \ldots & Pk & 0 \end{matrix} \quad (5.36)$$

When this transition matrix is multiplied by its population vector, it yields the population vector for the next time step, such that

$$n(t+1) = A \times n(t) \quad (5.37)$$

Recall that when multiplying a column vector (e.g., $n(t)$) by a matrix that is composed of k columns (C) and k rows (R), one applies the following rules:

R1 of $n(t+1)$	= R1 of $n(t)$ × C1:R1 of matrix	+ R2 of $n(t)$× C2:R1 of matrix	+.......	+ R*k* of $n(t)$× C*k*:R1 of matrix
R2 of $n(t+1)$	= R1 of $n(t)$× C1:R2 of matrix	+ R2 of $n(t)$× C2:R2 of matrix	+.......	+ R*k* of $n(t)$× C*k*:R2 of matrix
...				
R*k* of $n(t+1)$	= R1 of $n(t)$× C1:R*k* of matrix	+ R2 of $n(t)$× C2:R*k* of matrix	+.......	+ R*k* of $n(t)$× C*k*:R*k* of matrix

To illustrate this, we will apply this transition matrix to the chickadee population considered earlier **(Table 5.3)**. The transition matrix for the chickadees is thus

$$A = \begin{matrix} 1.14 & 4.20 & 3.84 & 4.02 & 4.02 & 3.00 \\ 0.19 & 0 & 0 & 0 & 0 & 0 \\ 0 & 0.70 & 0 & 0 & 0 & 0 \\ 0 & 0 & 0.64 & 0 & 0 & 0 \\ 0 & 0 & 0 & 0.67 & 0 & 0 \\ 0 & 0 & 0 & 0 & 0.67 & 0 \end{matrix}$$

By way of example, let us assume that a tract of land has been set aside for conservation purposes, and that during the course of routine monitoring, we have noted the presence of 20 chickadees that we know are 2 years old (they had been banded as fledglings two years previously). The question we would like to explore is how fast the chickadee population is likely to grow in the protected area.

Our initial population vector would be

$$n(t) = \begin{matrix} 0 \\ 20 \\ 0 \\ 0 \\ 0 \\ 0 \end{matrix}$$

TABLE 5.3 **Age-Class Survival Probabilities and Fecundities for Use in Leslie Matrix Calculations to Forecast Changes in a Population of Black-Capped Chickadees**

Age (x)	Age Class (x)	l_x	m_x	$P_x = l_x / l_{x-1}$	$F_x = m_x P_x$
0		1	0		
1	1	0.19	6	0.19	1.14
2	2	0.14	6	0.70	4.20
3	3	0.09	6	0.64	3.84
4	4	0.06	6	0.67	4.02
5	5	0.04	6	0.67	4.02
6	6	0.02	6	0.50	3.00

SOURCE: Hutchings et al. (unpublished).

The numbers of individuals in each age class at time $t + 1$ would be

$$\begin{aligned} n_1(t+1) &= F_1 n_1(t) + F_2 n_2(t) + F_3 n_3(t) + F_4 n_4(t) \\ &\quad + F_5 n_5(t) + F_6 n_6(t) \\ &= (1.14 \times 0) + (4.20 \times 20) + (3.84 \times 0) \\ &\quad + (4.02 \times 0) + (4.02 \times 0) + (3.00 \times 0) \\ &= 84 \end{aligned}$$

$$n_2(t+1) = P_1 n_1(t) = 0.20 \times 0 = 0$$

$$n_3(t+1) = P_2 n_2(t) = 0.70 \times 20 = 14$$

$$n_4(t+1) = P_3 n_3(t) = 0.64 \times 0 = 0$$

$$n_5(t+1) = P_4 n_4(t) = 0.67 \times 0 = 0$$

$$n_6(t+1) = P_5 n_5(t) = 0.67 \times 0 = 0$$

Based on Equation 5.37, the population at various times in the future can be expressed as

$$n(1) = \begin{matrix} 84 \\ 0 \\ 14 \\ 0 \\ 0 \\ 0 \end{matrix} \quad n(5) = \begin{matrix} 903 \\ 95 \\ 36 \\ 13 \\ 5 \\ 0 \end{matrix} \quad n(10) = \begin{matrix} 17\,886 \\ 1\,870 \\ 720 \\ 254 \\ 93 \\ 35 \end{matrix}$$

The exponential growth in each of the age classes is illustrated in **Figure 5.14.** The figure also shows that the total number of adult chickadees is increasing exponentially from the initial number of 20 to a total of 2972 after 10 years. As the population is growing, it is achieving a stable age distribution, which means that

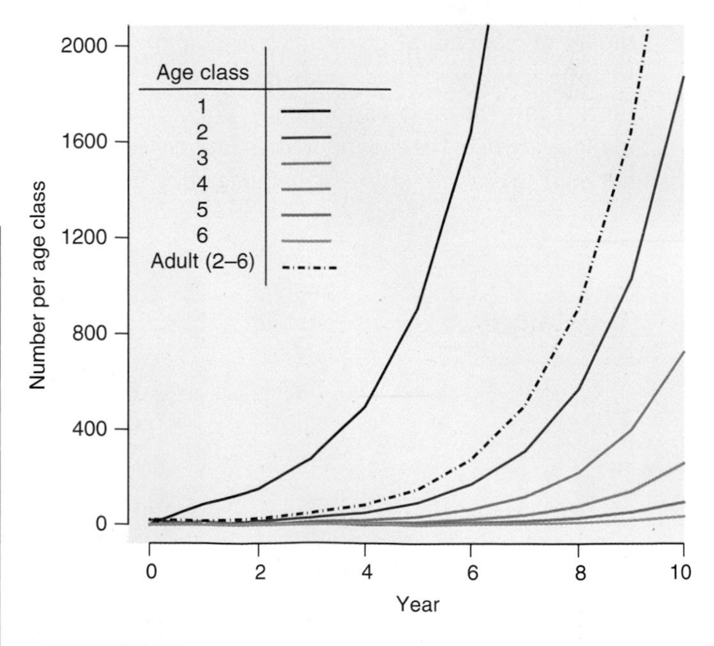

FIGURE 5.14
Projected Increases in an Age-Structured Population of Black-Capped Chickadee (*Poecile atricapilla*). Abundance is modelled separately for several age classes and for adults. The data source is Table 5.3.

the relative numbers of individuals in each age class does not change with time. For example, the ratio of (n_2/n_1) for the chickadees is 0.105 from $t = 5$ onwards.

Recall that our model does not incorporate an effect of increasing density on survival and/or fecundity—this is reflected in the fact that the population is growing exponentially. Once the total abundance reaches a level at which density begins to affect survival or fecundity (or that of age classes most sensitive to density), the growth rate begins to slow until the population reaches its carrying capacity. At that point the population will have a **stationary age distribution**, meaning that neither the relative nor absolute numbers of individuals in each age class changes over time.

Forecasting Changes in Abundance in a Stage-Structured Population

Although it is common to utilize age-structured models of population growth, individuals can also be collated on the basis of their size (size-based model) or life/developmental stage (stage-based model). Stage-based models are commonly used for species that have a complex life cycle, such as insects (stages of egg, larva, pupa, adult), plants (seed, vegetative, flowering), and amphibians (egg, larva, post-metamorphic juvenile, adult).

The key difference between an age-based model and a stage-based one is that, in the latter, individuals can either remain in a given stage from one time unit to the next with probability P, or they can move on to the next stage with probability G.

To illustrate the application of a stage-based model of population growth, we can apply one to Atlantic salmon (*Salmo salar*) that breed in rivers flowing into the inner Bay of Fundy. These small populations are listed as endangered in Canada under the national *Species at Risk Act*, because they breed in only a few rivers, having been widely extirpated from others in the region.

Imagine that fishery managers were to stock one of these rivers with 10 000 fertilized eggs (roughly the production of 4–5 female salmon). Although we might use an age-based model to model the growth of the population, a stage-based one can be more convenient **(Table 5.4)**. The salmon will be partitioned into five stages: (1) egg; (2) parr; (3) smolt; (4) virgin adult; and (5) previous spawner. We can forecast how the population might be expected to grow after this single stocking event. (In this example we can justifiably ignore intraspecific density-dependent effects, because the population is so small.) The transition matrix for a stage-based population with k stages is

$$A = \begin{matrix} P1,1 & F2 & F3 & F4 & F5 \\ P1,2 & P2,2 & 0 & 0 & 0 \\ 0 & P2,3 & P3,3 & 0 & 0 \\ 0 & 0 & P3,4 & P4,4 & 0 \\ 0 & 0 & 0 & P4,5 & P5,5 \end{matrix} \qquad (5.38)$$

TABLE 5.4 Stage-Specific Estimates of Survival and Fecundity for a Generic Atlantic Salmon (*Salmo salar*) Population in Eastern Canada

Life Stage Description	Stage (x)	Stage Survival	$P_{x,x}$	$P_{x,x+1}$	F_x
Egg	1	0.10	0	0.10	0
Parr	2	0.40	0.10	0.30	0
Smolt	3	0.16	0	0.16	0
Virgin adult	4	0.10	0	0.10	2569
Previous spawner	5	0	1	–	4576

SOURCE: Hutchings and Jones (1998).

Atlantic salmon (*Salmo salar*) inhabit rivers throughout eastern Canada from Ungava Bay in the north to the U.S.–New Brunswick border in the south. Having declined throughout much of the southern part of its range because of anthropogenic causes, it is a species that expresses a range of behaviours, migrations, and life histories matched by few vertebrates.

Paul Nicklen/National Geographic Stock

The results of this model reveal a few interesting things from a conservation, or recovery, perspective **(Table 5.5)**. First, the stocking of recently hatched individuals, although a common action in salmon enhancement, does not quickly yield positive results. This is because of the relatively lengthy generation time of the fish (4–5 years). As a consequence, although the population is growing exponentially, there is a lag of about 4 years in this increase. This is evident if one compares, for example, the abundance of eggs in years 0, 4, 8, and 12, or the abundance of parr in years 1, 5, 9, and 13.

Another interesting observation is that, because of the generational time lag, there are many years in which the abundance of various life stages remains quite low (e.g., 0 and 3 virgin adults in years 10 and 14, respectively). Finally, on a cautionary note, because of these years of low abundance in some life stages, unpredictably poor environmental conditions or stochastic influences might reduce the number of individuals in a particular age class to 0, which would increase the recovery time of the population even further.

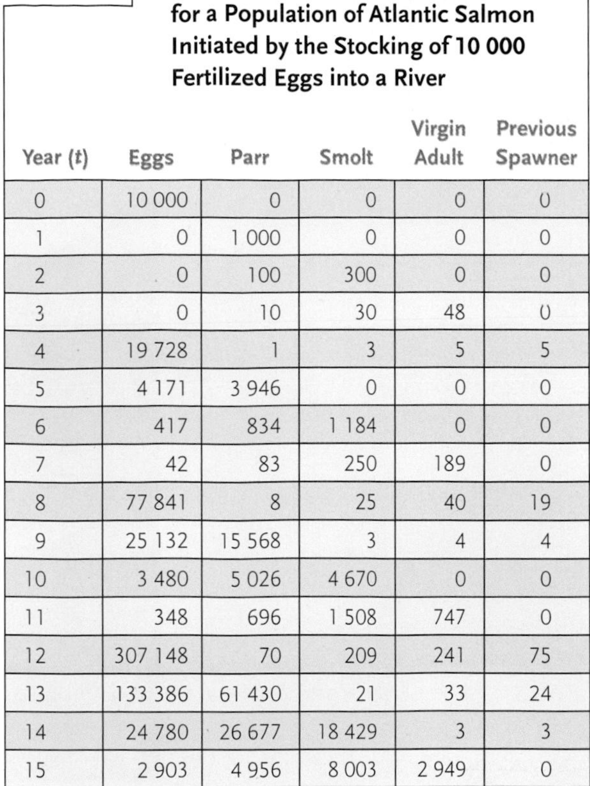

TABLE 5.5 Stage-Specific Abundance Projections for a Population of Atlantic Salmon Initiated by the Stocking of 10 000 Fertilized Eggs into a River

Year (t)	Eggs	Parr	Smolt	Virgin Adult	Previous Spawner
0	10 000	0	0	0	0
1	0	1 000	0	0	0
2	0	100	300	0	0
3	0	10	30	48	0
4	19 728	1	3	5	5
5	4 171	3 946	0	0	0
6	417	834	1 184	0	0
7	42	83	250	189	0
8	77 841	8	25	40	19
9	25 132	15 568	3	4	4
10	3 480	5 026	4 670	0	0
11	348	696	1 508	747	0
12	307 148	70	209	241	75
13	133 386	61 430	21	33	24
14	24 780	26 677	18 429	3	3
15	2 903	4 956	8 003	2 949	0

Application: The Collapse of Northern Atlantic Cod

Although discussion of parameters such as r can seem esoteric, the estimation of per capita population growth rates can have important socioeconomic and biological consequences.

For instance, when the fishery for northern cod off Newfoundland and Labrador collapsed in 1992, the federal Department of Fisheries and Oceans (DFO) imposed a moratorium on further harvesting, but predicted that the stocks would recover with sufficient vigour to allow the fishery to be reopened in 1994 (Parsons, 1993). This forecast was based on a set of analyses that predicted rapid increases in the abundance of spawning-age cod between 1992 and 1994 (the red lines in **Figure 5.15**). For the increases in cod predicted by DFO to be realized, the per capita growth (r) would need to have ranged between 0.80 to 1.10, corresponding to annual increases in spawner populations of 126 and 200 percent, respectively (Hutchings et al., 1997).

FIGURE 5.15

The Decline of Northern Atlantic Cod off Newfoundland and Labrador from 1962 to 2007. The solid black line shows the reduction in spawning stock biomass (total weight of cod aged 7 years and older) from 1962 to 1992. The red lines show the two increases predicted by the Department of Fisheries and Oceans in spawning stock biomass from 1992 to 1994. The orange dots show the catch rates (numbers per tow of a bottom trawl net) of cod aged 5 years and older from 1983 to 2007. By comparing the black line with the orange dots, we can see that the spawning stock biomass has not changed appreciably, and in fact has shown few substantive signs of recovery since the fishing moratorium was imposed in 1992. The DFO projections for recovery were much more optimistic than the reality turned out to be.

SOURCES: Brattey et al. (2008); Parsons (1993); http://www.fish.dal.ca

After being caught, Atlantic cod were brought to shore where mothers, wives, daughters, and sons helped remove each cod's head, spine, and guts before salting the fish and laying it out on wooden flakes to dry in the sun. This photo shows flakes, prior to 1898, at the Battery in the harbour of St. John's, Newfoundland.

Coll-137, 03.07.003. Archives and Special Collections, Queen Elizabeth II Library, Memorial University

We can use an age-structured model of population growth rate to examine whether DFO's predicted increases for northern cod were realistic in a population where, in the absence of fishing, reproductive maturity was attained at 6–7 years of age. As with the chickadee example **(Table 5.2)**, we first construct a life table for cod in the absence of fishing (the full analysis is in Hutchings, 1999). The estimates of age-specific survival and fecundity are provided in **Table 5.6.** Based on these data, we find R_0 to be 9.35 and the generation time to be 12.9 years. Using this information, we can approximate r to be $\ln(9.35)/12.9 = 0.174$ or, using the Euler-Lotka equation, $r = 0.195$. These estimates of r would correspond to annual rates of increase of 19–21 percent, which are much lower than the 126–200 percent required to realize the increase from 1992 to 1994 that was predicted by DFO. It is worth noting that these estimates of r are **deterministic**, meaning that age-specific rates of survival and fecundity are assumed to be fixed at constant values. However, if one allows l_x and m_x to vary in accordance with natural variability in survival and individual growth rate (which influences fecundity), then the stochastic estimate of r would be about 5 percent less than the deterministic estimate (Hutchings, 1999).

In actual fact, as of 2010, northern cod had not achieved a discernable recovery in abundance. This is

TABLE 5.6 Life Table for Northern Atlantic Cod (*Gadus morhua*) off Newfoundland and Labrador

Cod first mature at 7 years of age. Annual survival probabilities are about 0.82.

Age (x)	Age-specific Survival, l_x ($\times 10^{-7}$)	Age-specific Fecundity, m_x ($\times 10^{6}$)
3	0.0113	0
4	0.0103	0
5	0.0093	0
6	0.0085	0
7	0.0077	1.049
8	0.0063	1.275
9	0.0052	1.543
10	0.0042	1.817
11	0.0035	1.974
12	0.0028	2.425
13	0.0023	2.883
14	0.0019	3.438
15	0.0016	4.237
16	0.0013	4.676
17	0.0011	6.007
18	0.0009	7.391
19	0.0007	6.966
20	0.0006	7.499

SOURCE: Hutchings (1999).

partly because of excessive ongoing fishing pressure, as well as the relatively low per capita rate of growth of this cold-water fish.

Reproductive Value

Life tables provide information that allows for the estimation of a variety of metrics that are useful for assessing individual fitness and the evolution of life-history strategies. One such metric is **reproductive value** (Fisher, 1930; Williams, 1966). Reproductive value at age x represents the present and future production of offspring by an individual breeding at age x and living through its maximum possible life span (i.e., to age $x = \omega$), discounted by the probability of that individual surviving to that oldest potential age. The reproductive value can be calculated as

$$V_x = \sum_{t=x}^{\omega} \frac{l_t m_t}{l_x} \quad (5.39)$$

For Atlantic cod **(Figure 5.16)**, we find that the reproductive value is initially low, but increases to a maximum value near age 15 before declining again. The reproductive value of an individual tells us something about its importance for future population growth. For cod, the data indicate that the oldest individuals (14–15-year-olds) are most valuable to future population growth. This observation highlights the importance of keeping all anthropogenic causes of mortality as low as possible to maximize the likelihood that cod will live to these older ages. It is important to note, however, that this conclusion is most relevant to a population that is at a depleted level of abundance, relative to the carrying capacity of its ecosystem. At higher levels of abundance, and as a population recovery occurs, the strength of density-dependence on survival and fecundity increases, and the reproductive value of older individuals (relative to younger ones) becomes relatively less.

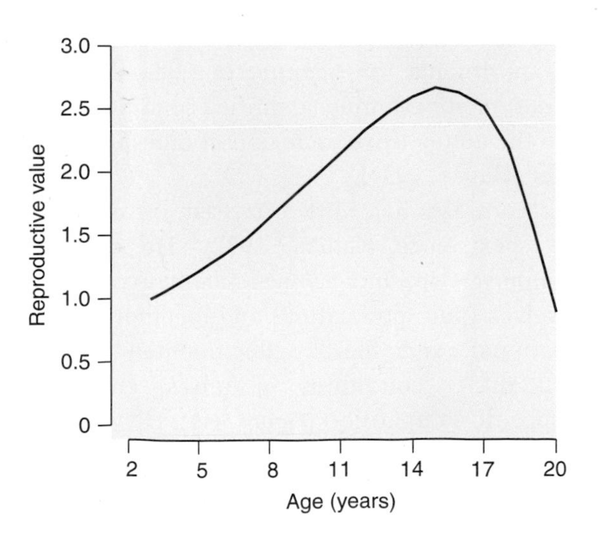

FIGURE 5.16
Reproductive Value of Northern Atlantic Cod. Reproductive value at age *x* represents the present and future production of offspring by an individual breeding at age *x* and living to its maximum possible life span, but discounted by the probability of that individual surviving to that longevity. For cod, the reproductive value between 10 and 15 years of age is 2–2.5 times that of fish at age 3. The data are scaled such that the reproductive value at age 3 is equal to 1.

SOURCE: Table 5.6 (p. 116 of this textbook).

5.5 Interspecific Competition

One of the premises underlying the concept of density-dependent growth is that there is a carrying capacity—an availability of resources that limits the size of a population that can be sustained. As a population increases in size, there is increased competition among individuals; this is **intraspecific competition.** The intensified competition is manifested by per capita reductions in birth rate and increases in death rate. These changes result in a reduction in the realized per capita growth rate as the population approaches the carrying capacity of its ecosystem.

Competition for a particular resource can also result from interactions among individuals of different species—this is **interspecific competition**. Both intra- and interspecific competition may be expressed by two primary means:

1. **Scramble** (or **exploitation**) **competition** involves a process whereby individuals reduce the access of others to a specific resource simply by consuming some of it. However, scramble competition does not involve direct or indirect actions taken by an individual to reduce access by others to a resource. An example is the browsing of shrubs and trees by moose (*Alces alces*), which reduces the food availability for other herbivores.
2. **Interference competition** involves action by an individual to reduce the access of others to a resource. Examples include the defence of a deer carcass by a grizzly bear (*Ursus arctos*) against other bears or from wolves (*Canis lupus*), and the protection of a breeding territory by songbirds. A plant example involves a chemical interference, known as allelopathy, such as the case of the black walnut (*Juglans nigra*). This species produces a chemical known as juglone, which is toxic to most plants and prevents them from growing beneath a walnut tree.

From a population-level perspective, interspecific competition can reduce the population growth rate in a manner somewhat analogous to that resulting from intraspecific competition. The degree to which one species reduces the population growth rate of another depends on the relative competitive abilities of the two.

The Lotka-Volterra Competition Model

The population dynamics associated with interspecific competition were explored by two mathematicians who were interested in biological problems, but worked independently of each other, although at about the same time: Alfred Lotka (1880–1949), an American, and Vito Volterra (1860–1940), an Italian (Lotka, 1925; Volterra, 1926). Lotka and Volterra developed first-order non-linear differential equations to explain how the growth rate of a population (or species) is affected by the presence of another, through competition, predation, or by being preyed upon (we will examine predator–prey interactions in the next section). Recall from Equation 5.19 that the logistic growth rate can be described by

$$\partial N/\partial t = r_{max} N\,(1 - N/K)$$

or, by rearrangement,

$$\partial N/\partial t = r_{max}\, N\,(K - N)/K$$

To avoid unnecessary subscripts, we will let r_{max} be represented by r in this section on interspecific competition, and also in the next one dealing with predator–prey relationships. Therefore, for two species 1 and 2, we would have

$$\partial N_1/\partial t = r_1\, N_1\, [(K_1 - N_1)/K_1] \tag{5.40}$$

and

$$\partial N_2/\partial t = r_2\, N_2\, [(K_2 - N_2)/K_1] \tag{5.41}$$

The right-hand side of these equations stipulates that the population growth rate ($\partial N/\partial t$) declines as the intensity of intraspecific competition increases, as reflected by increases in N. The effects of interspecific competition on population growth rate can also be incorporated. This is done by allowing $\partial N/\partial t$ to be reduced by an amount equal to the abundance of the competitor, multiplied by a constant that reflects its competitive ability. This constant is called a **competition coefficient**. Therefore, for our two species, we have

$$\partial N_1/\partial t = r_1\, N_1\, [(K_1 - N_1 - \alpha N_2)/K_1] \tag{5.42}$$

and

$$\partial N_2/\partial t = r_2\, N_2\, [(K_2 - N_2 - \beta N_1)/K_1] \tag{5.43}$$

The competition coefficients are α and β. They represent the *per capita* effect of a competing species on the growth rate of the species of interest. If, for example, $\alpha = 1$, then the addition of one individual of species 2 will have the same effect on the population growth rate of species 1 ($\partial N_1/\partial t$) as the addition of one of species 1. Another way of thinking about this is that when $\alpha = 1$, it means that species 1 and 2 are equally good competitors with each other. If $\alpha > 1$, an individual of species 2 is more effective as a competitor than is one of species 1. This can also be expressed as meaning that the *per capita effect of interspecific competition is greater than that of intraspecific competition*. If $\alpha < 1$, then the per capita effects of intraspecific competition exceed those resulting from interspecific competition. If $\alpha = 0$, there is no interspecific competition.

One way to visualize how the competition coefficients work is to consider the way that pieces move on a chessboard. Compare, for example, a pawn and a knight. After its initial two-square forward move, a pawn can move only one square at a time, whereas a knight covers three squares with every move. If each square on the board represents a unit of resource, then the knight might be said to have three times the resource-acquisition ability as a pawn. We might then reasonably assign it a competition coefficient of $\alpha = 3$. (Indeed, the argument could be made that the competition coefficient should be greater than 3, given that a pawn can only advance forward, while a knight is unlimited in its directional movement.)

Competition in the Laboratory

A classic set of competition experiments was undertaken by Georgii Gause (1910–1986), a Russian ecologist, to test hypotheses generated by the competition model of Lotka and Volterra. Using organisms that could be manipulated easily, such as protozoans and yeast, Gause examined patterns of population growth by species competing with each other under different levels of resource availability. His experiments on *Paramecium aurelia* and *P. caudatum*, for example, identified conditions that lead to the competitive exclusion of one species by another (Gause, 1934).

By contrast, his work on yeast focussed on stable coexistence (Gause, 1932). He cultured *Saccharomyces* sp. and *Schizosaccharomyces* sp. by themselves (pure population) and together (mixed populations), and thereby documented logistic growth under conditions of intraspecific and interspecific competition **(Figure 5.17)**. He was able to illustrate quantitatively how the carrying capacity for one species can be reduced by the presence of a competitor. He was also able to estimate competition coefficients (α, β) for each species.

After this initial set of experiments, Gause (1935) explored how the Lotka-Volterra models could be used to predict conditions that would result in the coexistence of two competing species, or to the exclusion of one by the other. He developed a series of analyses for this purpose that involved the plotting of species isoclines in state space.

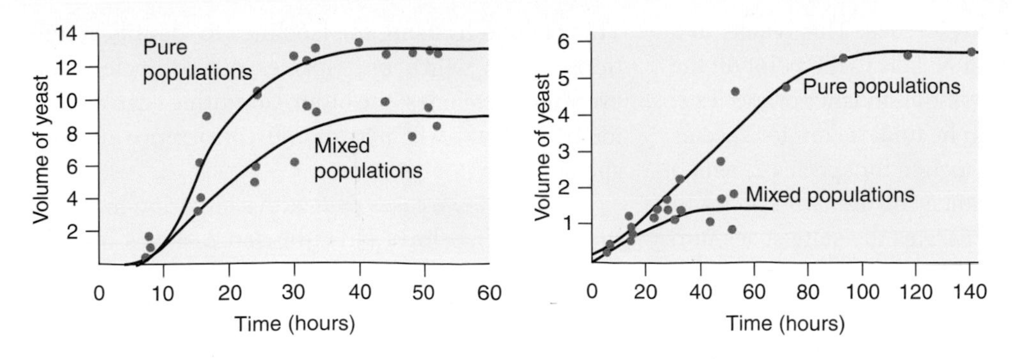

FIGURE 5.17
Population Growth of Two Species of Yeast (*Saccharomyces* sp. and *Schizosaccharomyces* sp.) When Each Is Cultured by Itself (Pure Population) and When Reared with the Competing Species (Mixed Population). Note that the data fit logistic growth curves and that the carrying capacities for each species are lower in the mixed populations than in the pure ones (after Gause, 1932).

SOURCE: After Gause (1932). Modified from Krebs, C. J. 2009. *Ecology: The Experimental Analysis of Distribution and Abundance.* © Benjamin-Cummings, San Francisco, CA, p. 188, Figures 12.9 and 12.10. Reprinted by permission of Pearson Education, Inc.

Equilibrium Conditions: Isoclines and State-Space Graphs

The dynamics of competitive interactions can be better understood if the **equilibrium conditions** for species 1 and 2 are identified, meaning those in which competing influences are in balance. These are the conditions at which $\partial N/\partial t = 0$. Setting Equations 5.42 and 5.43 to zero yields the following equations that specify the equilibrium population densities:

$$N_1 = K_1 - \alpha N_2 \quad (5.44)$$

$$N_2 = K_2 - \beta N_1 \quad (5.45)$$

As pioneered by Gause (1935), changes in the density of competing species and in factors that specify their equilibrium conditions are best examined with the aid of **state-space** graphs. These are bivariate plots in which the density of one species (N_1) is plotted against that of the other (N_2). **Figure 5.18** is a state-space graph that includes a single line having a negative slope. The line is Equation 5.44, the equation that specifies combinations of densities of species 1 and 2 at which the growth rate of species 1 ($\partial N_1/\partial t$) is 0. This line is called an **isocline** for species 1.

The position of the isocline in state space can be determined by setting the densities of species 1 and 2 in Equation 5.44 to zero, thus allowing the x- and y-intercepts of the isocline to be determined. Note that the slope of the isocline is equal to the competition coefficient, which is α in the case of species 1, while the x-intercept is K_1. At this equilibrium combination of densities, species 1 is at its carrying capacity (where $\partial N_1/\partial t = 0$) and species 2 is not present. At the other extreme of the isocline, the y-intercept specifies a situation in which the population is composed entirely of individuals of species 2, with its density equal to K_1/α.

The isocline separates the state-space graph into two areas. When the combined abundance of both species falls to the left of the isocline for species 1, it is less than that at which $\partial N_1/\partial t = 0$, i.e., less than when the carrying capacity of the ecosystem is "filled" by members of both species. In this region, the abundance of species 1 can be expected to increase, as indicated in **Figure 5.18** by horizontal arrows, reflecting an increase in N_1 and directed toward the isocline. In contrast, when the combined abundance of both species falls to the right of the isocline for species 1, the

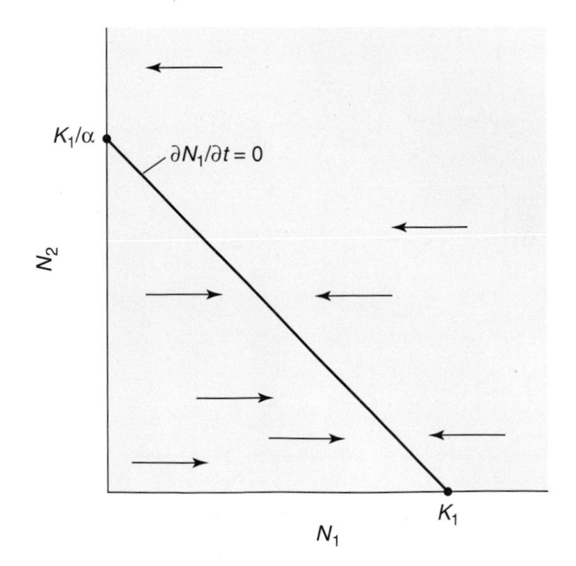

FIGURE 5.18
The Isocline for Species 1, as Articulated by the Lotka-Volterra Competition Model for Population Growth. The isocline specifies the combined abundances of species 1 and 2 at which the population growth rate of species 1 is zero, i.e., species 1 is at equilibrium ($\partial N_1/\partial t = 0$). When the combined abundance is to the right of the isocline, species 1 declines until its population matches its corresponding point on the isocline. If the joint abundance is to the left of the isocline, species 1 is expected to increase until its population matches its corresponding point on the isocline. In this figure, species 1 is the only one of the two competitors that will change its abundance in response to changes in the combined abundances.

carrying capacity has been exceeded. This results in a reduction in species 1 until N_1 falls to the point on the isocline that corresponds to the abundance of species 2.

The same exercise can be undertaken for species 2 **(Figure 5.19)**. Here, the isocline for species 2, which specifies the joint abundances of the two species at which $\partial N_2/\partial t = 0$, also separates the state space into two areas. At the extremes of the isocline, species 2 will neither increase or decrease when it is at its carrying capacity (y-intercept, at which $N_1 = 0$) and when the abundance of species 1 is equal to K_2/β (at which $N_2 = 0$). For joint species abundances that fall above the isocline, that of species 2 can be expected to decline (downward-facing arrows) because the carrying capacity of its environment has been exceeded. Similarly, when the combined abundances of species 1 and 2 fall below the isocline, the environment is capable of supporting a greater number of individuals of species 2, and N_2 can be expected to increase (upward arrows).

Competitive Exclusion and Stable Coexistence: Graphical Solutions

By plotting the iscolines of both species in the same state space, we can examine various outcomes of the Lotka-Volterra interspecific competition model. This is done by using the isoclines to identify conditions under which one species out-competes, and eventually excludes, the other. Conditions can also be identified that will permit the coexistence of both species.

The first two cases deal with a situation in which the species isoclines have the same slopes but different intercepts. Under this circumstance, one isocline will lie above the other in state space. As a general rule, the species with the higher-elevation isocline (greater y-intercept) will out-compete the other one and eventually exclude it from the habitat.

To illustrate this general rule, let us first consider the case in which the isocline for species 1 lies above that of species 2 **(Figure 5.20)**. When the combined abundances of the two species is in the lower-left corner of the state-space graph (green zone), both can be expected to increase because the abundance falls below *both* isoclines. We can depict this on the state-space graph as a joint vector that identifies the direction, or "movement," in the combined abundances of the competing species. (For the simplest case, in which $r_1 = r_2$, the joint vector would be at a 45° angle relative to the directional movements of the abundance of both species. If $r_1 > r_2$, the joint vector would increasingly flatten.) Once the combined abundances

K_2

$\partial N_2/\partial t = 0$

N_2

K_2/β

N_1

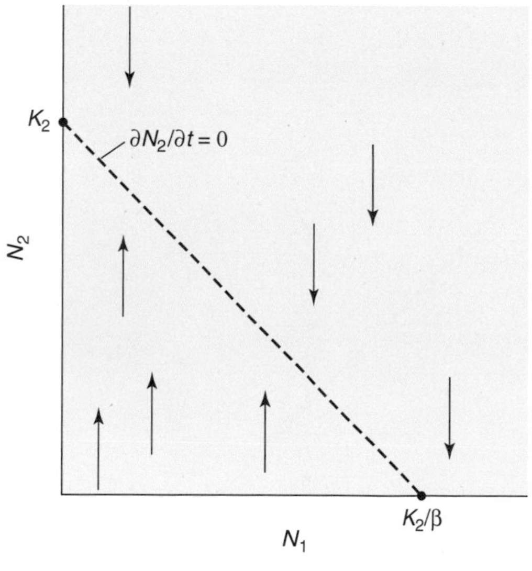

FIGURE 5.19
The Isocline for Species 2, as Articulated by the Lotka-Volterra Competition Model for Population Growth. The isocline specifies the combined abundances of species 1 and 2 at which the population growth rate of species 2 is zero, i.e., species 2 is at equilibrium ($\partial N_2/\partial t = 0$). When the combined abundance is above the isocline, species 2 declines until its population matches its corresponding point on the isocline. If the combined abundance is below the isocline, species 2 is expected to increase until its population matches its corresponding point on the isocline. In this figure, species 2 is the only one of the two competitors that will change its abundance in response to changes in the combined abundances.

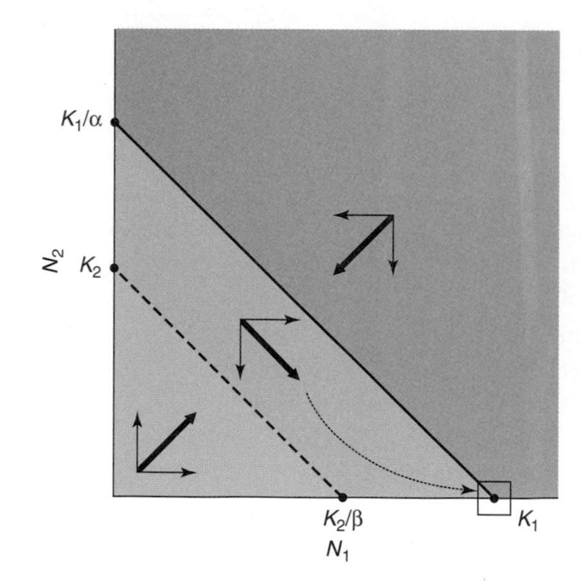

FIGURE 5.20
The Lotka-Volterra Competition Model Predicts the Exclusion of Species 2 by Its Competitor, Species 1. If the combined abundances are in the orange-coloured zone, both species will decline because their total population is above their isoclines. If the combined abundance is in the green zone, both competitors will increase because their total population is below their isoclines. In the blue zone, only species 1 can increase because the combined abundance is below its isocline but above that for species 2. The thick arrows are joint vectors that illustrate the direction in which the combined abundances will move in state space. Vertical thin arrows show the directional change in species 2 abundance, while horizontal thin arrows show that of species 1.

cross the species 2 isocline (blue zone), the combination of N_1 and N_2 would exceed the joint-abundance carrying capacity for species 2 (meaning that $\partial N_2/\partial t < 0$), and it would be predicted to decline (downward-facing vertical arrow in the blue area).

Although the combined abundances lie above the isocline for species 2, they still fall below the isocline for species 1. This means that species 1 is still able to increase in abundance (right-facing horizontal arrow in the blue zone). This combination of abundance trajectories—an increase in species 1 and a decrease in species 2—can lead to only one outcome: the **competitive exclusion** of species 2 ($N_2 = 0$), with species 1 filling of the carrying capacity of the environment at $N_1 = K_1$. Should the starting point of the combined abundance lie above the higher of the two isoclines (that for species 1) in the orange zone of the state-space graph, both species can be expected to decline in abundance. This will proceed until their combined abundance falls within the blue zone, at which, once again, species 2 will decline to zero and species 1 will increase until the carrying capacity is reached. Note that if the isocline for species 2 falls above that of species 1, then the outcome will be the competitive exclusion of species 1 and species 2 eventually attaining an abundance equal to its carrying capacity (i.e., $N_2 = K_2$) **(Figure 5.21)**.

The dynamics of interspecific interactions become more complicated when the competition coefficients α and β are not equal. This leads to isoclines that have unlike intercepts but also different slopes, a combination that results in the isoclines crossing in state space. One situation in which this can arise **(Figure 5.22)** occurs when the carrying capacity of each species, when filled with individuals of conspecifics K_1 and K_2, is greater than that of each when filled by members of the competing species, i.e., when K_1 is greater than $N_1 = K_2/\beta$, and when K_2 exceeds K_1/α.

When the joint abundance of the two species is in the green zone (below both isoclines), both can be expected to increase. When the joint abundance is in the orange zone (above both isoclines), both species can be expected to decrease. However, if the joint abundance falls in the left blue zone (above the isocline for species 1 but below that for species 2), the outcome will be the competitive exclusion of species 1 and the persistence of species 2. And if the joint abundance falls in the right blue zone (above the isocline for species 2 but below that for species 1), the outcome will be the competitive exclusion of species 2 and the persistence of species 1.

Isoclines having the characteristics just described will almost always lead to the competitive exclusion of one species, but there *is* an equilibrium, defined here as the point in state space at which both species can coexist (i.e., at which $\partial N_1/\partial t = 0$ and $\partial N_2/\partial t = 0$).

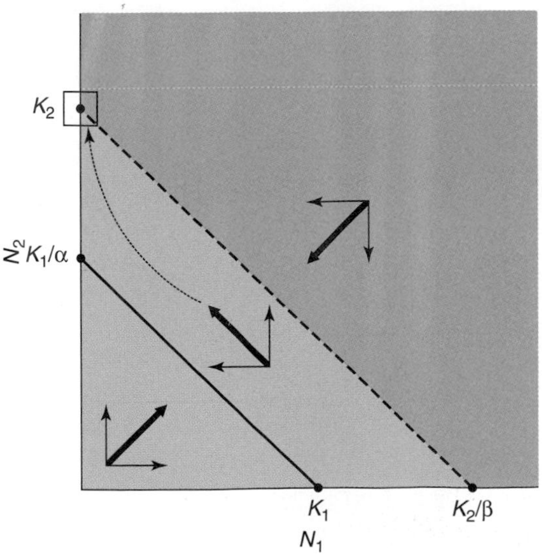

FIGURE 5.21

The Lotka-Volterra Competition Model Predicts the Exclusion of Species 1 by Its Competitor, Species 2. For the reasons explained in the caption to Figure 5.20, both species decline in the orange zone and increase in the green zone. In the blue zone, only species 2 can increase because the combined abundance of competitors is below its isocline but above that for species 1.

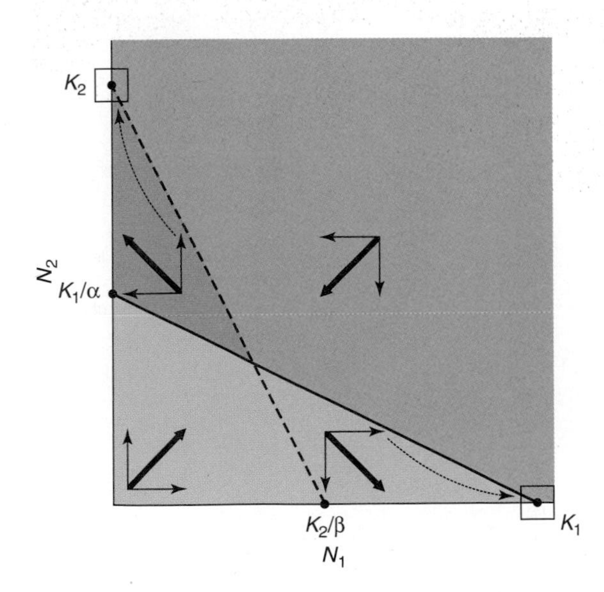

FIGURE 5.22

The Lotka-Volterra Competition Model Predicts Competitive Exclusion in an Unstable Equilibrium. For the reasons explained in the caption to Figure 5.20, both species decline in the orange zone and increase in the green zone. In the dark blue zone, only species 1 can increase because the combined abundance of competitors is below its isocline but above that for species 2. However, in the light blue zone, only species 2 can increase because the combined abundance of competitors is below its isocline but above that for species 1. The point of intersection of the two species isoclines represents a combined abundance at which both competitors are at equilibrium. However, the equilibrium is unstable because any divergence from this point of intersection will result in competitive exclusion of one species by the other.

This is represented by the joint species abundances at which the isoclines intersect. However, a change in either N_1 or N_2 from this equilibrium, resulting in a shift in the combined abundance from the isocline intersection point, will eventually result in the joint abundance falling within one of the two blue zones. This will lead to the competitive exclusion of one of the species by the other. This result means that the point of intersection of the two isoclines represents an **unstable equilibrium**. This is a state of equilibrium that can be upset if excessively displaced, so that it does not return to its original condition but instead moves to a new one.

If the crossing isoclines are shifted in state space, such that $K_1/\alpha > K_2$ and $K_2/\beta > K_2$, this will lead to conditions in which a **stable equilibrium** is achieved that will allow the persistent coexistence of both species **(Figure 5.23)**. As before, if the combined abundance of the two species falls within the green or orange zones, they will increase or decrease, respectively. However, if the combined abundance falls within either of the two blue zones, the joint abundance will move toward the intersection of the two isoclines—to the equilibrium joint abundance. That equilibrium is stable because, irrespective of the starting values of N_1 and N_2, the combined abundance will always move toward the joint equilibrium, leading to stable coexistence of the two species.

Competitive Exclusion and Stable Coexistence: Algebraic Solutions

The graphical solutions to the Lotka-Volterra equations are an extremely useful heuristic device for identifying conditions under which one species might exclude another from a particular ecosystem. Indeed, Robert MacArthur (1930–1972), one of the foremost ecologists of the 20th century (he was born and raised in Toronto but worked in the United States), used this approach to study the stable coexistence of wild organisms. His research involved the development and testing of hypotheses to explain how five species of warblers (*Dendroica* spp.), small insectivorous songbirds, are able to compete with one another yet coexist in a relatively homogeneous habitat of mature boreal forest **(Figure 5.23)**. Following the methods of a later study by MacArthur (1972), we can gain insight into the conditions that predict the persistence of species 1 and 2 by examining the algebraic solutions to the equations that he formulated.

We begin by assuming that if a species is able to increase in abundance under conditions that are less

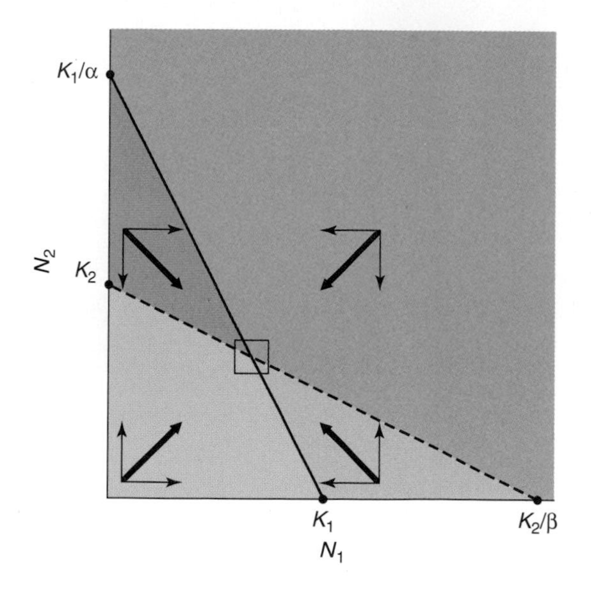

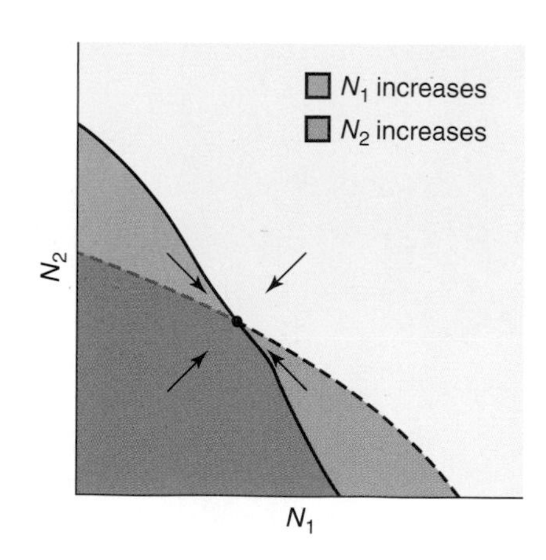

FIGURE 5.23

The Lotka-Volterra Competition Model Predicts Stable Coexistence of Both Competitors in a Stable Equilibrium. For the reasons explained in the caption to Figure 5.20, both species decline in the orange zone and increase in the green zone. In the dark blue zone, only species 2 can increase because the combined abundance of competitors is below its isocline but above that for species 1. In the light blue zone, only species 1 can increase because the combined abundance of competitors is below its isocline but above that for species 2. The point of intersection of the two species isoclines represents a combined abundance at which both competitors are at equilibrium. This equilibrium is stable because any divergence from this point of intersection will result in a return of the combined abundances to the point of intersection of the species isoclines. The diagram on the right is Figure 1 from MacArthur (1958).

SOURCE: Figure on right modified with permission of the Ecological Society of America, from MacArthur, R. H. 1958. "Population ecology of some warblers of northeastern coniferous forests," *Ecology*, 39(4): 599–619; permission conveyed through Copyright Clearance Center, Inc. (Figure from p. 600).

Stubblefield Photography/Shutterstock

Stubblefield Photography/Shutterstock

Jim Zipp/Photoresearchers/First Light

The Black-Throated Green, Blackburnian, and Bay-Breasted warblers often share the same breeding habitat in coniferous forests. They are three of the five species of warblers studied by Robert MacArthur in his classic 1958 study in community ecology.

favourable to its needs, then it is likely to persist there. These conditions can reasonably be presumed to exist for species 1 when its per capita growth rate ($\partial N_1/N\partial t$) is positive, even when it is at an exceedingly low level of abundance (approximated by zero), and when its competitor, species 2, is close to its carrying capacity ($N_2 \sim K_2$).

By rearranging Equation 5.42 to have per capita growth rate on the left side, and then substituting 0 for N_1 and K_2 for N_2, we obtain the following:

$$\partial N_1/\partial t \times 1/N_1 = r_1\,[(K_1 - 0 - \alpha K_2)/K_1] \tag{5.46}$$

For per capita growth to always be positive, the following must hold true (given that r_1 is always positive):

$$K_1 - \alpha K_2/K_1 > 0 \tag{5.47}$$

which means that

$$K_1/K_2 > \alpha \tag{5.48}$$

This inequality stipulates the condition that species 1 can persist only if its carrying capacity (relative to that of species 2) is greater than the competitive effect of species 2 on species 1. Expressed another way, if species 1 is to persist in the face of stiff competition (large α), then its carrying capacity must be relatively large. We can follow the same logic, and an analogous set of substitutions into Equation 5.43 to show that species 2 will persist when

$$K_2/K_1 > \beta \tag{5.49}$$

We can use the inequalities specified by Equations 5.48 and 5.49 to identify conditions under which coexistence at a stable equilibrium can exist. For both species to coexist,

$$K_1/K_2 > \alpha \text{ and } K_2/K_1 > \beta \text{ or } K_1/K_2 < 1/\beta$$

Placing these inequalities into a single expression that specifies the conditions for stable coexistence yields

$$\alpha < K_1/K_2 < 1/\beta \tag{5.50}$$

This expression allows us to address a question of fundamental importance to ecology: How similar can competitors be and still coexist?

Recall that if competitors are interchangeable in their respective effects on the population growth rate of each other, then the competition coefficients would be equal to unity: $\alpha = \beta = 1$. Therefore, if competitors are dissimilar in terms of their competitive abilities, the competition coefficients would be less than one. Let us set $\alpha = \beta = 0.05$. Substituting these values into Equation 5.50 we get

$$0.05 < K_1/K_2 < 20$$

This tells us that if competitors are highly dissimilar, the range in ratios of their respective carrying capacities that would support stable coexistence is extremely large. By contrast, if the competitors are extremely similar, such that $\alpha = \beta = 0.95$, then the conditions for stable coexistence would be

$$0.95 < K_1/K_2 < 1.05$$

This informs us that coexistence of similar competitors is possible only over an extremely narrow range of carrying capacities.

Character Displacement

Our exploration of algebraic constraints implicit to the Lotka-Volterra competition model tells us that the greater the similarity in resource use by potential competitors, the lower the likelihood that they will be able to coexist and the greater the probability that one of them will not persist (Gause, 1934). This necessity of divergence for the stable coexistence of competitors is reflected in the concept of **character displacement**, or a divergence in the phenotypic attributes of similar species as a result of competition occurring when they co-occur in a place or habitat. This idea was first championed by the British ornithologist David Lack (1910–1973) in his research on Darwin's finches (*Geospiza* spp.), which breed on the Galápagos Islands (Lack, 1947). Since then, the role of competition in phenotypic and genotypic divergence of close relatives sharing habitats has been explored in a wide variety of species. Dolph Schluter, an evolutionary biologist at the University of British Columbia, defines character displacement as the general process of phenotypic change induced or maintained by resource competition (Schluter, 2000). The process is one during which a character changes from being represented by a single, unimodal, phenotypic distribution for a species (or a feeding morph) in **allopatric** populations (which occupy geographically separate ranges) to being represented by a bimodal or even multi-modal phenotypic distribution in **sympatry** (within a shared range; see **Figure 5.24**).

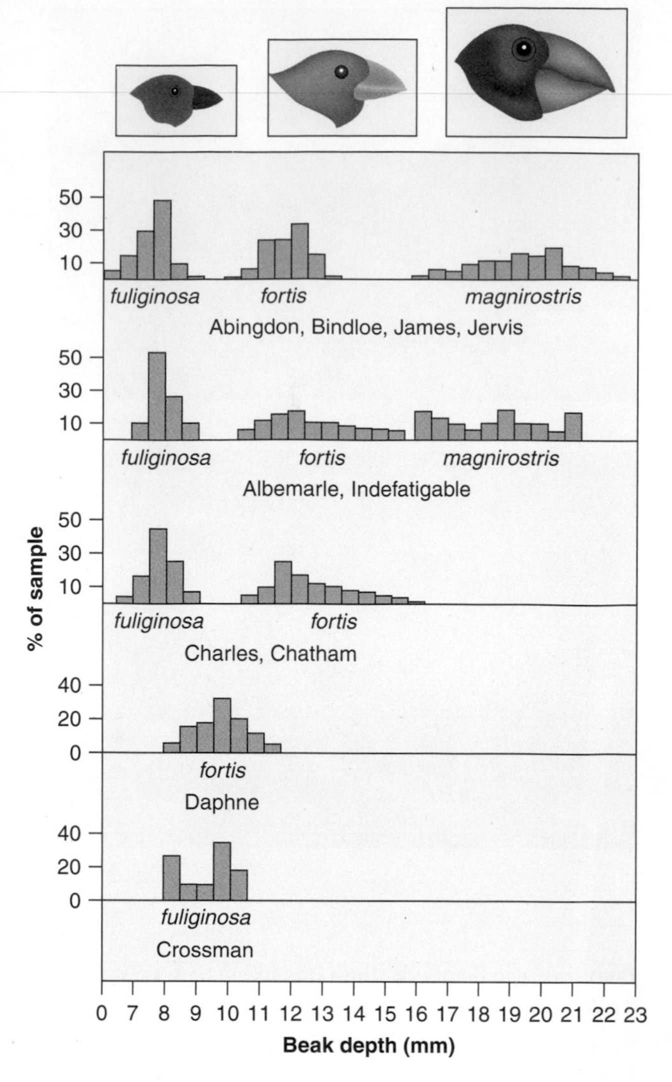

FIGURE 5.24
Character Displacement in Darwin's Finches on the Galápagos Islands. The histograms show the phenotypic distributions of beak depth for three species of finches that either compete for seeds on the same island (top three sets of histograms) or exist in allopatry (bottom two sets of histograms). Note two things: (1) the beak depths of *Geospiza fuliginosa*, *G. fortis*, and *G. magnirostris* do not overlap; (2) there is a divergence in the beak-depth distributions of *G. fuliginosa* and *G. fortis* when they occur sympatrically on Charles and Chatham Islands, but not when allopatric on Crossman and Daphne Islands.

SOURCE: Krebs, C. J. 2009. *Ecology: The Experimental Analysis of Distribution and Abundance*. © Benjamin-Cummings, San Francisco, CA, p. 202, Figure 12.23. Reprinted by permission of Pearson Education, Inc.

Schluter and colleagues have provided several examples of character displacement in fish populations, most notably those of the three-spined stickleback (*Gasterosteus aculeatus*), in which comparisons were made between competing feeding types of differing morphology. The key difference is in the lengths of their gill rakers, which are structures attached to the gills that help to prevent small invertebrates from escaping past the opercular opening and then out of the fish, when these foods are swallowed from the mouth cavity to the gut—the longer the rakers, the smaller the size of food items that are retained. In British Columbia lakes containing two morphs of sticklebacks, for example, the benthic morph (bottom-feeding benthivore) generally has shorter gill rakers than the limnetic morph (open-water feeding planktivore) with which it co-occurs (Schluter and McPhail, 1992; **Figure 5.25**).

Character displacement has been studied in Darwin's finches and in stickleback fishes. The Small Ground Finch (*Geospiza fuliginosa*) is one of four species of ground finch on the Galápagos that have bills of the "crushing" variety that are used to feed on seeds. The Threespine Stickleback (*Gasterosteus aculeatus*) exists as different feeding morphs within some lakes in British Columbia.

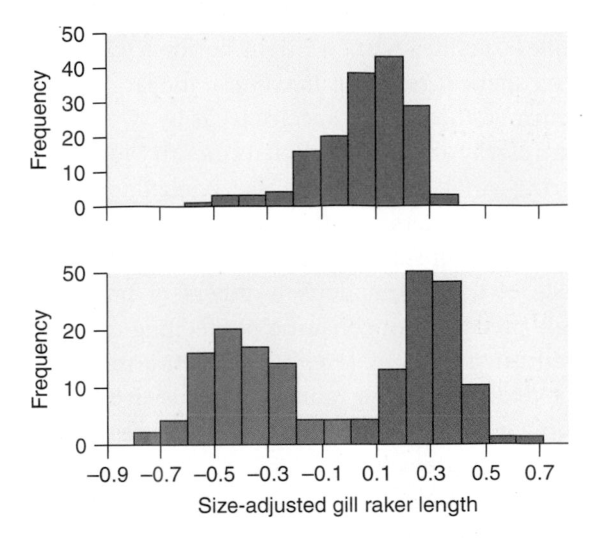

FIGURE 5.25
Frequency Distributions of Size-Adjusted Gill Raker Length in Coastal British Columbia Lakes with One or Two Trophic (Feeding) Morphs of Three-Spined Stickleback (*Gasterosteus aculeatus*). The upper panel represent data for sticklebacks inhabiting Cranby Lake, which supports only one feeding morph. The lower panel shows data for the benthic morph (green) and the limnetic morph (orange), which coexist in Paxton Lake.

SOURCE: Schluter, D., and J. D. McPhail. 1992. "Ecological character displacement and speciation in sticklebacks," *American Naturalist*, 140: 85–108, p. 91, Figure 3.

5.6 Predator–Prey Interactions

Thus far, we have considered the effects of density (intraspecific competition), age and life stage, and interspecific competition on the rate at which a population can change in abundance over time. These factors can all be identified as being ecological (e.g., competition, density) or biological (e.g., age) in nature. Although we have not dealt explicitly with physical environmental factors, such as temperature, light, or humidity, we have been incorporating their effects implicitly whenever we considered the carrying capacity. Predation is an additional major ecological factor that affects population growth. As an aside, we are referring to interspecific predation, in which the predator and the prey are different. Intraspecific predation, or cannibalism, is also somewhat common, occurring, for instance, in at least 10 percent of fish families (Smith and Reay, 1991) and being an important factor affecting population growth in some of them (e.g., Claessen et al., 2000). However, cannibalism is not considered to be a general determinant of population growth for most species of animals.

Influence of Predator–Prey Interactions on Population Growth

Predation affects the population growth rates of both predator and prey. For a predator, the consumption of prey can increase the predator's birth rate and/or reduce mortality, both of which may help to increase population growth. C. S. (Buzz) Holling (1959), a Canadian ecologist working at the time for the federal Department of Forestry in Ontario, doing research on the population dynamics of injurious insects, described four reactions of predators to changes in the density of their prey:

1. The **numerical response** is an increase of the abundance of predators in response to their consumption of prey.
2. The **functional response** describes the ways that the consumption of prey increases with its density.
3. The aggregative response refers to a spatial shift in the distribution of predators as they move into an area where their prey is abundant.
4. The developmental response is related to changes in the consumption of prey as a result of variations of the developmental state of a predator as it gets older.

In addition to models of interspecific competition, Lotka and Volterra developed models that describe the population dynamics of predator–prey interactions. They considered that the instantaneous population growth rate of a predator (P) will, to a first approximation, be a function (f) of the abundance of other members of its species and of their prey (p), such that

$$\partial P/\partial t = f(P, p)$$

As an additional simplification, it is assumed that the predator is a specialist that feeds only on a particular species of prey. In the absence of that prey, the predator will decline exponentially at a rate corresponding to its inherent death rate, d_p, such that

$$\partial P/\partial t = -d_p P \tag{5.51}$$

We can modify Equation 5.51 to describe the growth rate of the predator population when the prey is present, such that

$$\partial P/\partial t = \theta pP - d_p P \tag{5.52}$$

In Equation 5.52, θ is a measure of the **conversion efficiency** of a predator, i.e., the ability of the predator to convert the energy of its food into its growth plus investment in its offspring. The product of θp is directly related to the numerical response of a predator.

Similarly, we can assume that the population growth rate of the prey will be a function of its abundance plus that of its predator, as follows:

$$\partial p/\partial t = f(P, p)$$

In the absence of the predator, and to a first approximation, the prey (p) can be expected to increase in accordance with the exponential growth model (Equation 5.6), such that

$$\partial p/\partial t = rp \tag{5.53}$$

However, in the presence of a predator, a negative influence can be expected on the population growth rate of the prey because of the increased mortality it suffers, such that

$$\partial p/\partial t = rp - \phi Pp \tag{5.54}$$

In Equation 5.54, the constant ϕ is termed the **capture efficiency**, which is defined as the effect of a single predator on the per capita growth rate of its prey, i.e., $(\partial p/\partial t)(1/p)$.

It is important to understand two implicit, simplifying assumptions to Equation 5.54. The first is that predators and prey move randomly within their shared environment. This means that the movement of prey is not conditional on that of the predator, and vice-versa. The second assumption is that the reduction in $\partial p/\partial t$ that is attributable to predation is related to the likelihood that predators and prey will encounter one another. This encounter rate is related to the product of the abundances of the predators and prey (Pp). This makes sense, given that predators and their prey are moving randomly throughout their habitat, and is illustrated in the examples below.

Number of Predators:	P	1	1	3
Number of Prey:	p	1	2	2
Predators × Prey:	Pp	1	2	6

Therefore, the greater the probability of encounter between predators and prey (i.e., the larger the value of Pp), the greater the reduction in the population growth rate of the prey.

Turning back to the capture efficiency, the larger ϕ is, the more the prey population is negatively affected by the addition of a single predator. For example, consider what ϕ might be for a 12-metre basking shark (*Cetorhinus maximus*), the largest fish to occur in Canada. This species feeds by swimming forward slowly and steadily with its mouth wide open, capturing small prey known as zooplankton, and using its gill rakers to filter them from the water. A single basking shark might have a high value of ϕ because of the tremendous numbers of prey that a single predator can consume per feeding episode. By contrast, an osprey (*Pandion haliaetus*) might be expected to have a lower value of ϕ because it can capture only one fish at a time, and is not successful on every feeding attempt.

Functional Responses of Predators

The manner in which the consumption of prey increases with its density is called the functional response of a predator. Holling (1959), in a study of the effects of predation by small mammals on sawflies (hymenopteran insects in the suborder Symphyta that can damage certain trees), described several of these functional responses **(Figure 5.26)**.

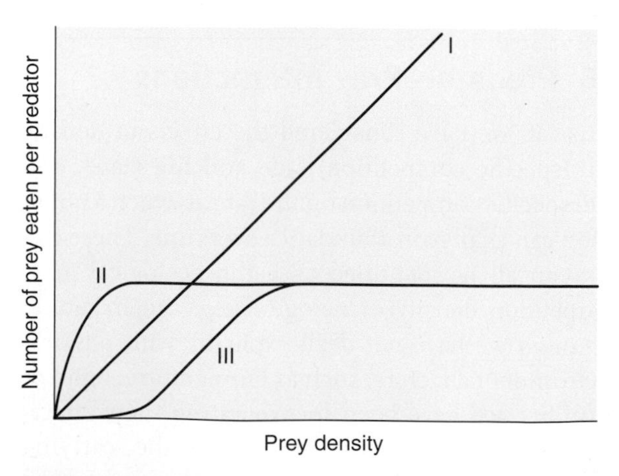

FIGURE 5.26
Functional Responses (Types I, II, and III) by Predators to Changes in the Density of Their Prey.

The Type I functional response describes a linear relationship between the prey density and the rate at which they are consumed by predators. This is the type of functional response that might be expected of predators that catch their prey using passive means, such as spiders that use a web to snare flies and other prey species. As the number of flies caught per unit area of web increases, the predatory spider can increase its feeding rate (number of flies consumed per unit of time). In a graph of prey density versus their rate of consumption by predators, the slope identifies the predation-related mortality rate of the prey. This allows us to interpret a Type I functional response as being one for which the proportion of the prey population consumed by the predators (the prey mortality rate) remains constant with changes in prey density **(Figure 5.27)**.

The Type II functional response identifies a relationship in which the slope of the functional response is highest near the origins of the x- and y-axes, and then declines gradually as the prey density steadily increases **(Figure 5.26)**. This is thought to typify many predator–prey relationships. This occurs because the searching time required to locate a prey individual declines as prey density increases. At high levels of prey density, there is less searching time, and the consumption rate by predators becomes limited by how long it takes to capture, subdue, and consume each food item—this is the handling time. The steadily declining slope that is characteristic of a Type II functional response means that the mortality rate of the prey is highest when their density is lowest **(Figure 5.27)**, but it declines with increases in abundance. As an example, imagine a group of harbour seals (*Phoca vitulina*) located just seaward of the mouth of a river from which migrating smolts of Atlantic salmon are departing en route to their feeding areas in the open ocean. When the production of smolts in the river is low, the proportion of the prey population that is consumed by the seals might be high. However, if the number of migrating smolts is higher, the consumption rate of each seal is no longer limited by the time required to locate a fish, but rather by the handling time. And at increasing levels of abundance of smolts, the proportion of the fish that is consumed by the predators will steadily decline, as is reflected by the negative linear function in **Figure 5.27.** Another example of a Type II functional response is the relationship between the densities of wolves (*Canis lupus*) and their prey of moose (*Alces alces*), as documented by François Messier of the University of Saskatchewan **(Figure 5.28)**.

The Type III functional response **(Figure 5.26)** has a shape that resembles the sigmoidal logistic growth curve that we examined earlier. An important mechanism by which a Type III functional response can arise is through prey-switching. This is reflected by the observation that the rate of feeding per predator increases slowly when prey are at a low density, and then occurs much more rapidly at intermediate levels of prey abundance. Within the context of prey abundance, the mortality attributable to predation is relatively low at low prey densities, and it reaches a maximum at an intermediate density, when the slope of the Type III functional response is at its greatest **(Figure 5.27)**.

Although the link might not be readily apparent, this functional response is part of the Equation 5.54 that describes how the growth rate of a prey population is affected by predation. Recall that Equation 5.54 stipulates that

$$\partial p/\partial t = rp - \phi Pp$$

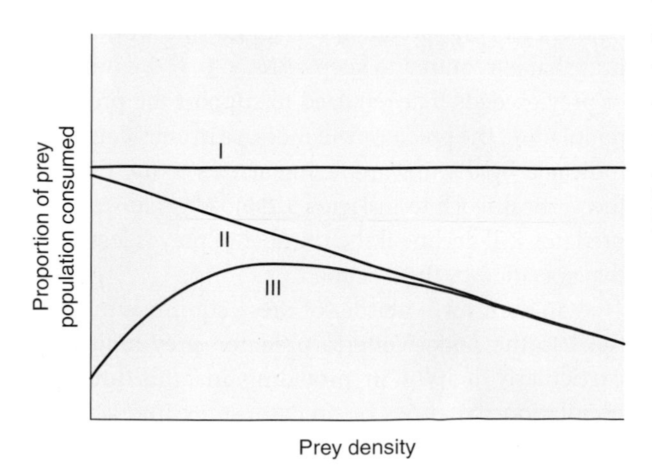

FIGURE 5.27
The Proportion of the Prey That Is Consumed by Predators at Different Levels of Prey Density, in Accordance with Functional Responses I, II, and III.

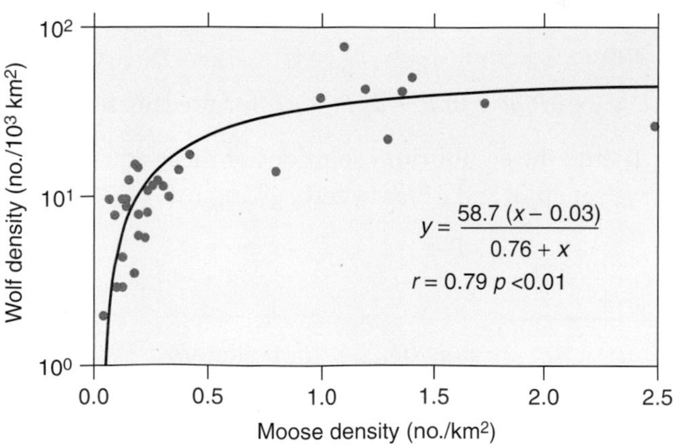

FIGURE 5.28
The Type II Functional Response of Wolf (*Canis lupis*) to Changes in the Density of Moose (*Alces alces*). Based on data from studies conducted in a broad region from southeastern Quebec west to Alaska.

SOURCE: Used with permission of the Ecological Society of America, from Messier, F. 1994. "Ungulate population models with predation: A case study with the North American moose," *Ecology*, 75(2): 478–488; permission conveyed through Copyright Clearance Center, Inc.

John Eastcott and Yva Momatiuk/National Geographic Stock

The predation of moose by wolves represents one of the classic predator–prey relationships between mammals in Canada's boreal forests.

where ϕ is the capture efficiency. This parameter has units of $p/(Pp)$, meaning the number of prey consumed per predator per prey. If we multiply ϕ by p, the product has the same units as the functional response, i.e., prey consumed per predator. Therefore, the functional response in Equation 5.55 is the product ϕp.

Population Dynamics of Predator–Prey Interactions

When examining the dynamics associated with interspecific competition, the population growth rates of both predators and prey are set to zero to determine the equilibrium solutions for their respective models—the abundances of predators and prey at which the population growth rates are nil.

Returning to the Lotka-Volterra population growth models for predators and prey, we have

$$\partial p/\partial t = rp - \phi Pp \qquad \text{for prey}$$

and

$$\partial P/\partial t = \theta pP - d_P P \qquad \text{for predators}$$

To find the equilibrium solutions of these equations, we set $\partial p/\partial t$ and $\partial P/\partial t$ to zero, giving us

$$P = r/\phi \qquad \text{for prey} \tag{5.55}$$

and

$$p = d_p/\theta \qquad \text{for predators} \tag{5.56}$$

Note that the equilibrium solution for the prey is specified in terms of the number of predators that is required to keep the prey population growth rate at zero. Similarly, the equilibrium solution for the predators is specified in terms of the number of prey required to maintain the predator population growth rate at zero.

The prey isocline (along which $\partial p/\partial t = 0$) is a horizontal line that separates the predator–prey state space into two regions **(Figure 5.29a)**. The number of predators required to keep the prey population at equilibrium is equal to r/ϕ. This ratio has a fairly straightforward biological interpretation—it means that at a higher per capita growth rate of the prey, and a lower capture efficiency of the predator, the greater the number of predators that is required to maintain the prey at equilibrium. An over-simplification of the Lotka-Volterra model that is associated with the horizontal isocline is that the number of predators required to maintain the prey at zero growth rate does not depend on the abundance of prey (we will revisit this issue later). If the number of predators falls above the prey isocline, the prey will decline; but if the number of predators falls below the isocline, the prey will increase **(Figure 5.29a)**.

The predator isocline is defined in terms of the numbers of prey that are required to maintain the predator at an abundance at which it is neither increasing nor decreasing. This is a vertical line in **Figure 5.29b** that intercepts the x-axis at d_p/θ, meaning that the greater the death rate of the predator, or the lower the conversion efficiency of the predator, the higher the number of prey that is required to keep $\partial P/\partial t = 0$. If the number of prey exceeds that required to support the predator population, the predator will increase in abundance (as indicated by the upward-facing arrows to the right of the vertical isocline in **Figure 5.29b**). Alternatively, the predator will decline if the number of prey is less than that specified by the isocline.

On their own, neither of these equilibrium solutions to the Lotka-Volterra predator–prey models is particularly helpful in providing insights into the population dynamics of predator–prey interactions. However, when we combine them into a single state-space graph, some interesting properties emerge from these simple models.

The isoclines divide the state space into four regions **(Figure 5.30)**. When the starting population

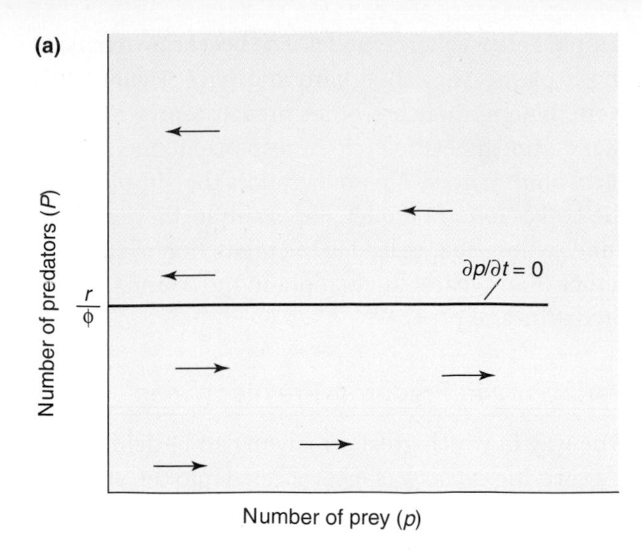

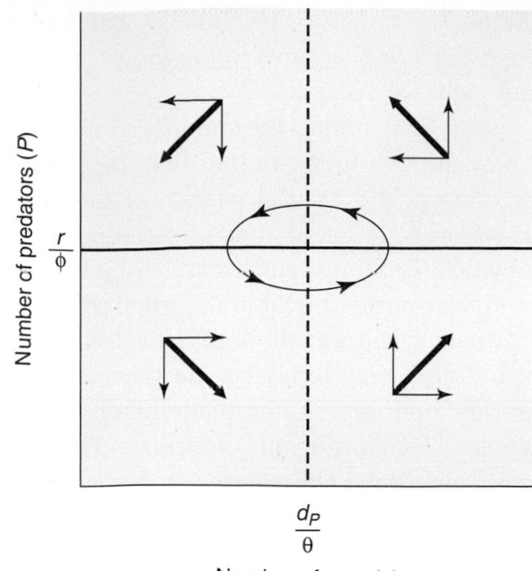

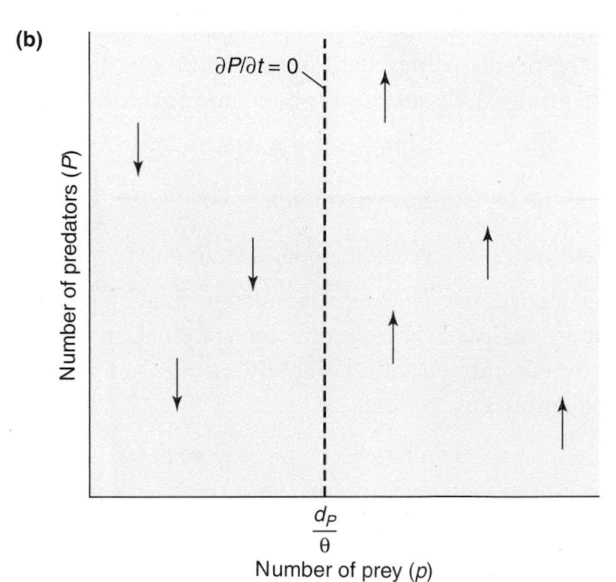

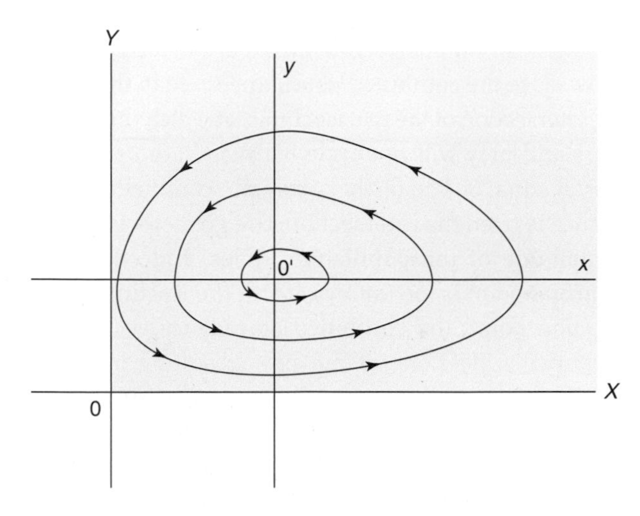

FIGURE 5.29
Prey and Predator Isoclines in State Space. (a) Directional changes in prey density, depending on whether the number of predators is above (prey decrease) or below (prey increase) the horizontal prey isocline (at which $\partial p/\partial t = 0$); (b) directional changes in predator density, depending on whether the number of prey is above (predators increase) or below (predators decline) the vertical predator isocline (at which $\partial P/\partial t = 0$).

FIGURE 5.30
Neutrally Stable Cyclical Population Dynamics of Predators and Prey Resulting from the Lotka-Volterra Predator–Prey Model. The right-hand panel shows the same state-space graph as it originally appeared in Lotka (1925). He used the state-space graph to display the cyclical dynamics that he predicted would be associated with a parasite infecting an insect **host**.

SOURCE: (image on right) Lotka, A. J. 1925. *Elements of Physical Biology.* Williams and Williams, Baltimore, MD.

sizes of predator and prey are in the upper-right quadrant, the number of predators is greater than that require to control the prey population, and so the number of prey can be expected to decline (for simplicity, we will use the word "control" when considering the number of predators that is required to keep $\partial p/\partial t = 0$; we will use the word "sustain" when identifying the number of prey required to keep $\partial P/\partial t = 0$). By contrast, an excessive number of prey is required to sustain the predator, meaning they will increase in the upper-right quadrant. The joint vector of predators and prey will move their combined abundance into the upper-left quadrant. Here, there are insufficient prey to sustain the predator (we are to the left of the vertical predator isocline), and there are more predators than are required to control the prey, meaning that both will decline.

Once the combined abundances fall below the horizontal prey isocline in the lower-left quadrant, the prey can increase because the number of predators is insufficient to control them. When the prey increase to a level of abundance greater than that required to sustain the predator (i.e., greater than d_p/θ), both predator and prey can increase (lower-right quadrant of the state space). The joint vector is now directed toward the upper right. And when the abundance of predators exceeds r/ϕ, the combined abundance of predators and prey will be, once again, in the upper-right quadrant. The combined abundances will then cycle through the four quadrants in the form of an ellipse on the state-space graph.

If we wish to project the abundance of predators and prey through time, we find that these elliptical trajectories yield a cyclical pattern of troughs and peaks **(Figure 5.31).** The abundance peaks of predators occur when the joint vector crosses from the upper-right to the upper-left quadrants, when the prey are approximately half-way through their decline. Similarly, the peak prey levels (at the transition of the lower-right and upper-right quadrants) occur when the predator is at its midpoint of increase. The troughs of prey and predator abundance occur when the joint abundances shift from the upper- to lower-left, and from the lower-left to lower-right quadrants, respectively. These patterns yield population cycles that are similar to those depicted in **Figure 5.31.**

The amplitudes of the cycles are determined by how close the combined abundances are to the point of intersection of the two isoclines, at which the predators and prey will not cycle because both $\partial p/\partial t$ and $\partial P/\partial t$ equal 0. The farther away the combined abundance is from the intersection, the greater will be the amplitude of the population cycles. Indeed, if the starting point is too far away from the isoclinal intersection point, the combined abundance vector will eventually meet one of the axes (resulting in either predator or prey abundance declining to zero), and the species will not cycle.

There are a number of real-world predator–prey systems that appear to fluctuate in abundance in cyclical patterns similar to those predicted by the simple Lotka-Volterra model. The best known may be those of the snowshoe hare and lynx **(Figure 5.32).** Nonetheless, there are other predator–prey systems that do not appear to cycle in response to their reciprocal abundances. This may reflect the simplicity of the Lotka-Volterra model. For example, there are isoclines whose shapes lead to the prediction of stability, rather than cyclical fluctuation, in the abundances of predators and prey.

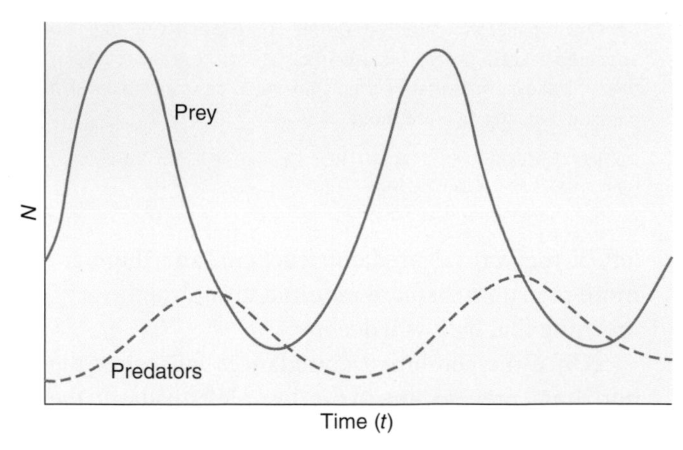

FIGURE 5.31
Cyclical Increases and Decreases in the Abundance of Predators and Prey through Time, as Predicted by the Lotka-Volterra Predation Model. Note the time lag in peak abundances of predators and prey. Given that the predators are tracking the increased abundance of their prey, their rise in abundance can be expected to follow that of the prey. The prey decline as their predators approach their peak abundance. Thereafter, the predators decline because of a lack of prey, and the cycles repeat themselves.

Variations in Predator–Prey Isoclines

One way in which greater realism can be achieved is if a carrying capacity is incorporated into the prey isocline (the Lotka-Volterra model includes the assumption that the abundance of predators is the only factor regulating prey density, rather than, for example, intraspecific competition occurring among the prey themselves). Recall the prey population growth model:

$$\partial p/\partial t = rp - \phi Pp$$

and the logistic growth model:

$$\partial N/\partial t = rN\,(1 - N/K)$$

To incorporate the negative effects that increasing prey density can have on their own population growth through intraspecific competition, we can modify Equation 5.54 to yield

$$\partial p/\partial t = rp\,(1 - p/K) - \phi Pp \tag{5.57}$$

To obtain the prey isocline, we again set $\partial p/\partial t = 0$, which yields

$$0 = rp\,(1 - p/K) - \phi Pp$$

or

$$0 = p\,[\,r(1 - p/K) - \phi P] \tag{5.58}$$

The case where $p = 0$ is not of interest, because we are trying to understand the dynamic interactions of *both* predators and prey. However, if we set the bracketed term on the right-hand side of the equation to zero, we have

$$0 = r\,(1 - p/K) - \phi P$$

which, following rearrangement, yields the prey isocline:

$$P = r/\phi - p(r/\phi K) \tag{5.59}$$

Notice that the form of this equation is analogous to that of a straight line with a negative slope, where the y-intercept is r/ϕ (after setting $p = 0$) and the x-intercept is K (after setting $P = 0$).

Plotted in state space, this new prey isocline, along with the unchanged vertical predator isocline, leads to a situation in which the combined abundances of predators and prey converge on a stable

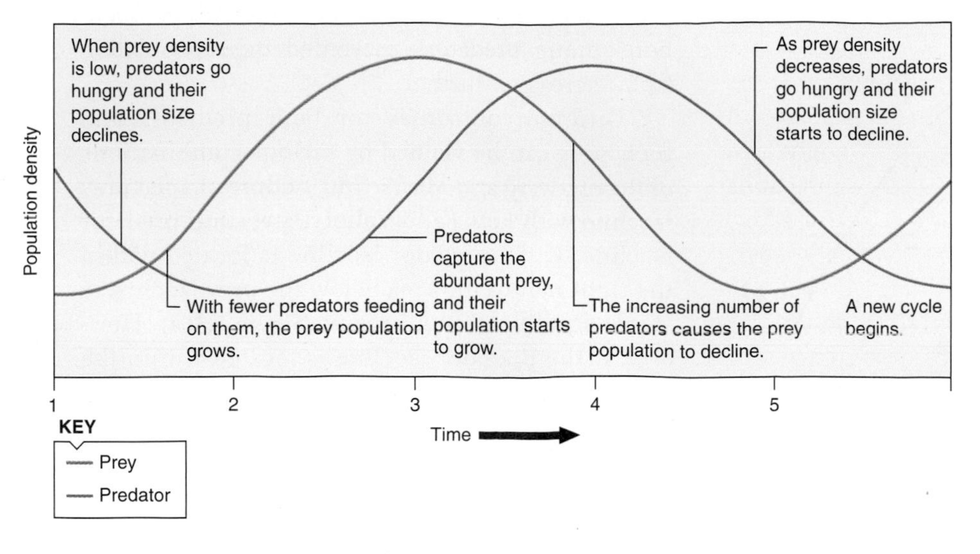

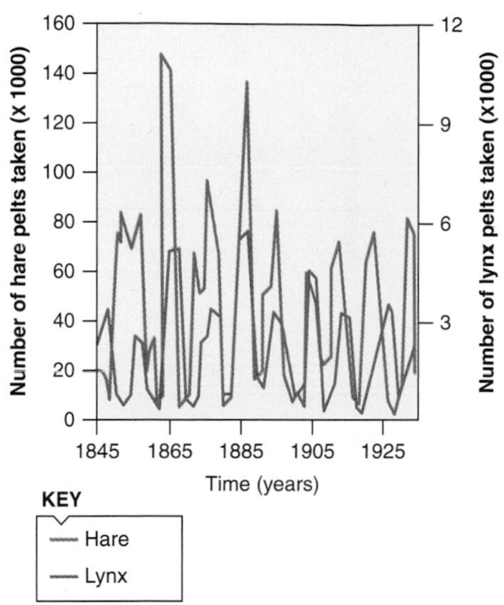

FIGURE 5.32

Cyclical Increases and Decreases in the Abundance of Lynx (*Lynx canadensis*) and Snowshoe Hare (*Lepus americanus*), Based on Pelt Records Maintained by the Hudson's Bay Company. The abundance of pelts is thought to be a good reflection of the abundance and possibly reflective of the predator–prey cycles predicted by the Lotka-Volterra model depicted in Fig. 5.31. The fit is particularly good from approximately 1910 to the early 1930s, with increases in hare (prey) abundance followed by increases in their predator (lynx) followed by reductions in prey and then reductions in the predator until the cycle begins anew.

SOURCE: Russell/Wolfe/Hertz/Starr. *Biology*, 1E. © 2010 Nelson Education Ltd. Reproduced by permission. www.cengage.com/permissions

equilibrium. This is represented by the intersection of the two isoclines **(Figure 5.33).** So, by incorporating additional factors (intraspecific competition and predator density) that can influence prey abundance, we reduce the probability that the predators and prey will cycle in response to one another's abundance.

Michael Rosenzweig and Robert MacArthur (1963) proposed an additional modification to the isoclines that can render them more realistic—they argued that the prey isocline should be dome-shaped **(Figure 5.34).** They reasoned that relatively few predators would be required to control the prey when they are at a low density, leading to a downward shape in the lower left part of the state space. They further suggested that if the prey are experiencing density-dependent growth, such that the relationship between $\partial p/\partial t$ and p is dome-shaped **(Figure 5.34)**, then the maximum number of predators required to control the population

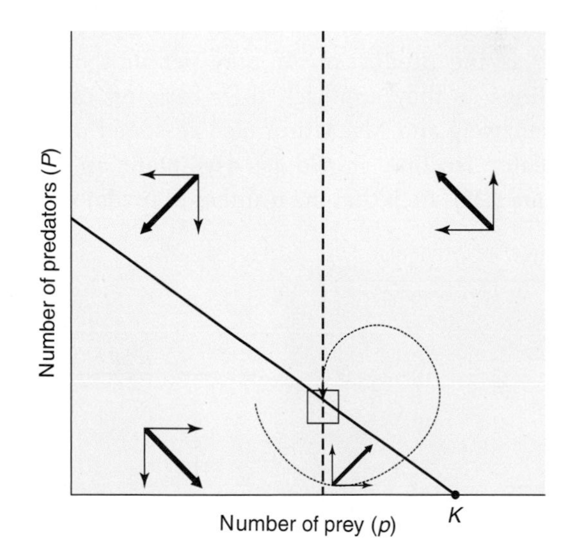

FIGURE 5.33

Predator–Prey Population Dynamics Associated with a Prey Isocline That Incorporates a Prey Carrying Capacity. The point of intersection of the two isoclines presents a stable equilibrium.

Predation of snowshoe hare by Canadian lynx provides the most widely cited empirical example of the cyclical population dynamics predicted by the Lotka-Volterra predator–prey model.

Tom Brakefield/Digital Vision/Jupiter Images

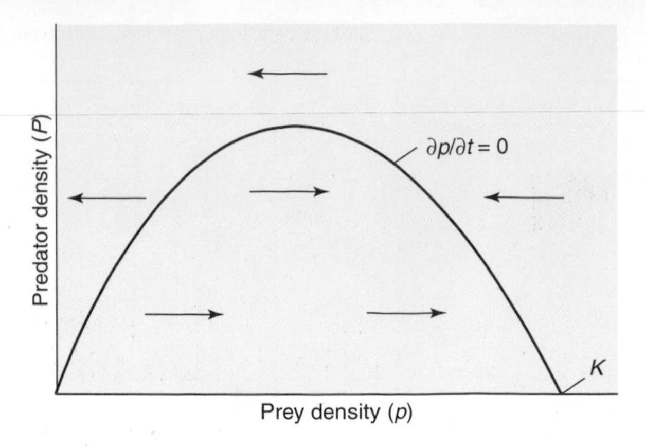

FIGURE 5.34
An Example of a Dome-Shaped Prey Isocline, Originally Envisaged by Rosenzweig and MacArthur (1963). Inside the dome, the prey is expected to increase because the number of predators is less than that required to control the prey population. Outside the dome, there are more predators than required to maintain the prey at an equilibrium, resulting in a decline in the abundance of their prey.

SOURCE: Neal, D. 2004. *Introduction to Population Ecology*. Cambridge University Press, Cambridge, UK. Reprinted with the permission of Cambridge University Press.

growth of the prey would occur at half of their carrying capacity. The necessary number of predators would decline thereafter with increasing prey densities, as the production of prey per unit of time declines as they approach their carrying capacity. Rosenzweig and MacArthur also reasoned that the predator isocline should be asymptotic in shape **(Figure 5.35)**, such that the number of predators that

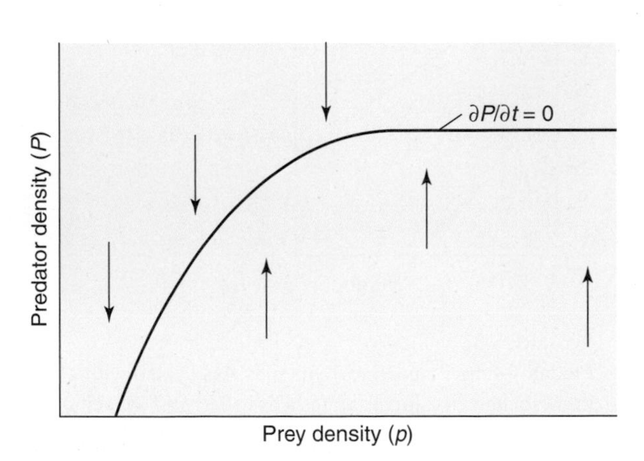

FIGURE 5.35
An Asymptotic Predator Isocline, following Rosenzweig and MacArthur (1963). Here, the number of predators that can be supported would increase with increasing prey density, until the effects of intraspecific competition prevented the population of predators from increasing further. Predator densities would increase in the state space below the isoclines, but decline in the state space above them.

SOURCE: Neal, D. 2004. *Introduction to Population Ecology*. Cambridge University Press, Cambridge, UK. Reprinted with the permission of Cambridge University Press.

could be supported would increase with increasing prey density until the effects of intraspecific competition among predators prevented their population from increasing further.

Different outcomes for both predators and their prey can be yielded by various combinations of Rosenzweig and MacArthur's dome-shaped prey isocline with Lotka and Volterra's vertical predator isocline. If the predator isocline is located within the right half of the area below the prey isocline, a stable equilibrium will result **(Figure 5.36a)**. However, if the predator isocline is located within the left half, the prey are predicted to become extirpated **(Figure 5.36b)**. And if the predator isocline perfectly divides the area under the prey isocline, predators and prey will cycle in accordance with the original prediction made by the Lotka-Volterra model **(Figure 5.36c)**.

Altered Predator–Prey Interactions Resulting from Overfishing

Many commercially exploited populations of marine fish have been reduced to historically unprecedented low levels of abundance. These ecological and economic catastrophes have raised concerns that the resultant changes in predator–prey interactions may slow, or even prevent, the recovery of the depleted populations. One potential example is provided by predator–prey relationships among species of fish in the southern Gulf of St. Lawrence. Atlantic cod in this region, which had the largest cod stock in the world in the mid-1980s, have declined to such low levels that Swain and Chouinard (2008) of the Department of Fisheries and Oceans have predicted they could become effectively extirpated from the southern Gulf of St. Lawrence by 2050.

One of the factors that is hypothesized to be retarding the recovery of cod in the southern Gulf of St. Lawrence is the increase in abundance of other fishes, such as mackerel (*Scomber scombrus*) and herring (*Clupea harengus*), which are smaller species that cod formerly preyed heavily upon. In recent years, however, the decline in cod may have resulted in a release of herring and mackerel from cod predation. However, these smaller fishes prey heavily upon the eggs and larvae of cod. This may be causing a reduction in the rate of offspring production by cod, which may be compromising the recovery potential of this once-abundant predator and the economically important fishery that is dependent on its stocks (Swain and Sinclair 2000).

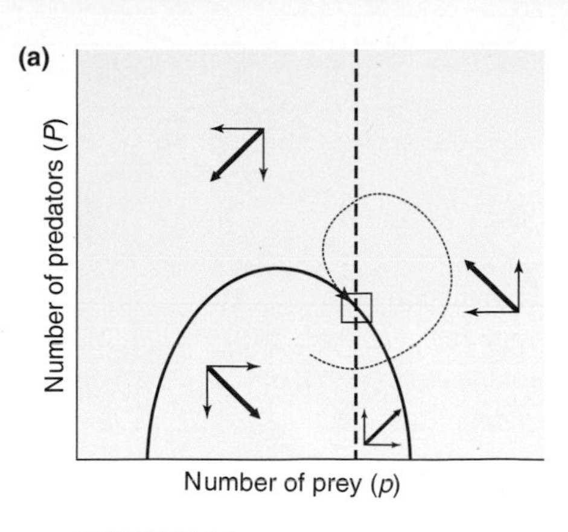

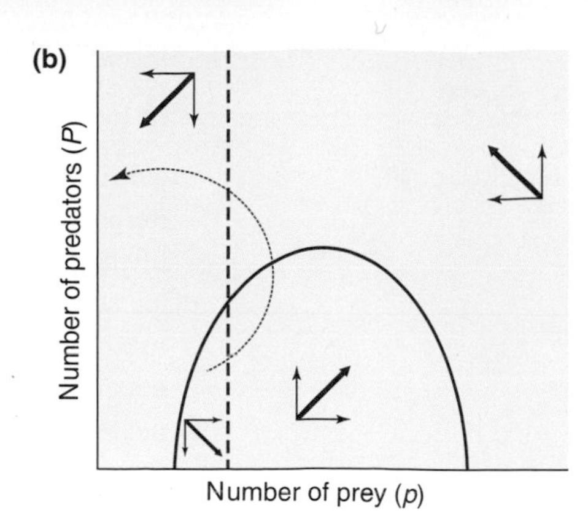

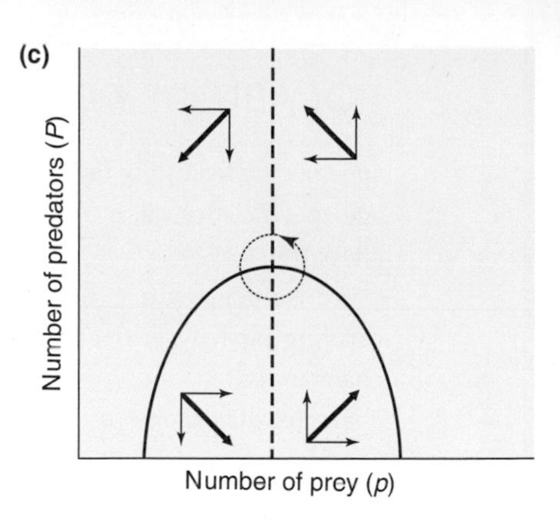

FIGURE 5.36

Predator–Prey Dynamics Associated with Dome-Shaped Prey Isoclines Depend on the Location of the Vertical Predator Isoclines. (a) The predator isocline is to the right of the hump in the prey isocline (suggestive of a relatively inefficient predator), resulting in stable coexistence between predator and prey; (b) the predator isocline is to the left of the hump in the prey isocline (suggestive of a relatively efficient predator), resulting in extinction of the prey and eventual starvation of the predator; (c) if the predator isocline intersects the prey isocline at a right angle, the predators and prey are predicted to exhibit stable cycles characteristic of the traditional Lotka-Volterra predation model.

A CANADIAN ECOLOGIST 5.1

Charles Krebs: An Ecologist's Population Ecologist

Charles Krebs

Charles Krebs

Charles (Charley) J. Krebs has had a large influence on the development of the science of ecology. Born in St. Louis, Missouri, he undertook his postgraduate degrees at the University of British Columbia (UBC). Since 1970, following six years at the Indiana University, Charley Krebs has been a member of the faculty of the Department of Zoology of UBC, where he is now Professor Emeritus.

The title of Krebs' first scientific publication, in the journal *Arctic* in 1961, carried several harbingers of his future research endeavours: "Population dynamics of the Mackenzie Delta reindeer herd, 1938–1958." The recurrent themes of population ecology in his work, notably cyclical dynamics, as well as Arctic research, mammals, and long-term studies, are all reflected there. More than 240 scientific publications later, Krebs and his colleagues are still working on the population dynamics of snowshoe hare, mice, voles, and their predators at Kluane Lake in southwestern Yukon (where he has been doing research since 1973), and of lemmings at several sites in arctic Canada including Herschel Island off the north Yukon coast (begun in 1987). In addition to his work in northern Canada, Krebs has undertaken studies of the dynamics of terrestrial mammals in Australia and in the United States.

Among the most prominent contributions of Krebs to ecology and teaching are his books (seven titles), which include two widely used textbooks: *Ecology: The Experimental Analysis of Distribution and Abundance* (6th edition, 2009) and *Ecological Methodology* (2nd edition, 1999). Moreover, he has effectively communicated the results and implications of ecology and ecological research to many elements of society, both in Canada and globally. This includes helping to foster educational programs in developing nations (he has taught ecology and pest management in China and in the Philippines) as well as participating on international expert panels in the developed world, such as the Cooperative Research Centre for Vertebrate Biocontrol in Australia.

Krebs' research achievements have been recognized by several notable awards, such as a Fellowship in the Royal Society of Canada (1979), the Fry Medal (1994) of the Canadian Society of Zoologists, and the inaugural President's Award from the Canadian Society for Ecology and Evolution (2009). Internationally, recognition has come in the form of an Eminent Ecologist Award from the Ecological Society of America (2002), the C. Hart Merriam Award from the American Society of Mammalogists (1994), an honorary doctorate from the University of Lund (1988), the President's Medal from the University of Helsinki (1986), and fellowships in the Norwegian and Australian Academies of Science.

VOCABULARY OF ECOLOGY

age-specific fecundity (age-specific fertility), p. 107
age-specific survival, p. 108
allopatric, p. 124
capture efficiency, p. 126
carrying capacity, p. 101
chaos, p. 105
character displacement, p. 124
closed population, p. 96
cohort, p. 109
cohort life table, p. 109
competition coefficient, p. 118
competitive exclusion, p. 121
conversion efficiency, p. 126
damped oscillation, p. 104
density-independent model of population growth, p. 100
determinate growth, p. 107
deterministic, p. 116
doubling time, p. 98
equilibrium condition, p. 119
exponential model of population growth, p. 97
functional response, p. 126
generation time, p. 110
harvest rate, p. 100
host, p. 129
indeterminate growth, p. 107
interference competition, p. 117
interspecific competition, p. 117
intraspecific competition, p. 117
intrinsic rate of population growth, p. 97
isocline, p. 119
iteroparous, p. 108
life table, p. 108
logistic model of population growth, p. 102
maximum per capita rate of growth, p. 97
maximum sustainable yield (MSY), p. 105
net reproductive rate, p. 109
numerical response, p. 126
open population, p. 96
per capita rate of population growth, p. 97
realized per capita rate of population growth, p. 97
reproductive value, p. 117
response time, p. 104
scramble (or exploitation) competition, p. 117
semelparous, p. 108
stable age distribution, p. 109
stable equilibrium, p. 122
stable limit cycle, p. 104
state-space, p. 119
static life table, p. 109
stationary age distribution, p. 114
stochasticity, p. 105
sympatry, p. 124
time lag, p. 103
transition matrix (Leslie matrix), p. 112
Type-I survival, p. 108
Type-II survival, p. 108
Type-III survival, p. 108
unstable equilibrium, p. 122

QUESTIONS FOR REVIEW AND DISCUSSION

1. It is anticipated that Canada's human population will attain an abundance of 34 million in 2010. At current rates of natural birth and immigration, it has been estimated that the population will double in 78 years. Calculate r for the Canadian human population. What will Canada's population size be in 2050?
2. Regarding population growth, which of the following statements is *not* true?
   (a) Birth (plus immigration) and death (plus emigration) rates must be equal for population size to remain constant over time.
   (b) Net recruitment is highest at intermediate densities when populations experience density-dependent growth.
   (c) $(K–N)/K$ represents the proportion of habitat or resources that remains available.
   (d) A time lag may cause a population to temporarily overshoot K and to oscillate above and below K.
   (e) Carrying capacity increases as population size decreases.
3. Using the following hypothetical life table for a population of cedar waxwings (*Bombycilla cedrorum*), answer the following questions:

Age (x)	Age-specific Survival (l_x)	Age-specific Fecundity (m_x)
0	1	0
1	0.167	2
2	0.083	3
3	0.048	3
4	0.016	4
5	0	–

   (a) This population will:
      (i) eventually become extinct.
      (ii) oscillate about its carrying capacity.
      (iii) increase exponentially.

(iv) experience logistic population growth.

(v) remain constant in abundance over time.

(b) What is the average number of offspring produced by each female in her lifetime? What is the generation time for this population?

(c) If the survival of waxwings from birth to age 1 were to increase by 50 percent, would this affect the long-term prognosis of the population?

4. In 2007, basking sharks (*Cetorhinus maximus*) off the Pacific coast of Canada were assessed as endangered by the Committee on the Status of Endangered Wildlife in Canada (COSEWIC). These are the largest fish in Canadian waters, and tens to hundreds of individuals were once observed in the bays and inlets of coastal British Columbia. However, only six have been observed since 1996. The species declined primarily because of a "pest eradication" program undertaken by Canada's Department of Fisheries and Oceans from 1954 to 1971. A large blade fitted to a DFO patrol vessel was used to kill basking sharks because their tendency to feed near the surface would cause them to become entangled in salmon gill nets, resulting in lost economic opportunities for commercial salmon fishermen. In comparison, basking sharks in eastern Canadian waters are thought to number between 5000 and 10 000 individuals. Assuming exponential growth by the species on the West Coast and an estimated $r_{max} = 0.03$ individuals per individual per year, how many years would it take for basking sharks to reach a presumably sustainable population abundance of 7500 individuals from an initial abundance of 100 individuals?

5. Two species of rodents that compete with one another in their native distribution have invaded a previously unoccupied patch of habitat. The carrying capacity of species 1 is 5000 individuals, whereas the carrying capacity for species 2 is three times that of species 1. The competition coefficients α and β are 0.5 and 2, respectively. Draw the state-space isoclines for these two species. If the initial population size of species 1 is ($N_1 = 4000$) and is double that of species 2, what is the predicted outcome of interspecific competition between these two species?

6. Canadian lynx and their primary prey, snowshoe hare, exhibit 9- to 11-year cyclical patterns in their abundance in Canada's boreal forests (see Figure 5.32b, p. 131). As discussed in this chapter, these cycles are often assumed to be directly linked to one another because the lynx is a specialist predator of snowshoe hare. However, on Anticosti Island at the mouth of the St. Lawrence River lynx are absent, yet the hare still exhibits cyclical patterns in abundance. Given the absence of lynx, what factors might be responsible for the regulation of snowshoe hare on Anticosti Island?

HELPFUL WEBSITES

POPULUS: SIMULATIONS OF POPULATION BIOLOGY

http://www.cbs.umn.edu/populus

Simulations of most of the models discussed in this chapter can be found at this website.

You'll find a rich array of additional resources for *Ecology* at www.ecology.nelson.com.

ECOLOGY IN DEPTH 6.1

Research Questions and Levels of Analysis in Behavioural Ecology

Scientific investigation proceeds by testing potential answers (hypotheses) to a question by using experiments, observations, and comparisons. In evolutionary studies, however, some of the potential answers are not alternatives. For example, answers to the question "Why do red-winged blackbirds (*Agelaius phoeniceus*) fly north in the springtime?" can be both

- ultimate, or related to fitness, such as "in order to breed successfully," and
- proximate, or mechanistic; for example, "because they are cued by increasing day-length to migrate."

Behavioural ecologists ask ultimate *why* questions, but proximate levels of analysis can sometimes inform the evolutionary answers. For example, consider the question "Why do crickets that are parasitized by hair worms jump into water?" Proximate evidence supports the hypothesis that the host cricket is manipulated by the hair worm to migrate to the aquatic breeding habitat of the parasite. Hair worm neurotransmitters are found in the brain of parasitized crickets, and they interfere with the normal behaviour of the hosts. Such chemicals are not predicted by an alternative ultimate hypothesis—that parasitized crickets seek water because they are ill, i.e., the cause is thirst alone (Biron et al., 2006).

have a short generation time that allows them to quickly evolve solutions to adaptive defences of their longer-lived hosts, which then must evolve new protections. Another example involves the mating preferences of females for ornamented males (such as male birds with showy plumage), which appears to have been a powerful force favouring the evolution of those male adaptations. This is despite the fact that sexual selection for ornamentation can be opposed by **viability selection** against ornaments when they reduce the likelihood of survival.

Adaptation, Selection, and Behaviour

Adaptive traits typically enhance reproduction or survival, but ultimately an increase in evolutionary fitness involves passing on the genes that underlie these traits. Within this context, behavioural ecologists strive to evaluate fitness by examining the relative **reproductive success** of individuals that differ in certain behavioural traits. This is a different approach from that used by population geneticists, who might examine fitness through the relative abundance of alternative alleles in subsequent generations. However, it is important to understand that variation in behaviour does not necessarily reflect genetic differences; the alternative behaviours may also be due to phenotypic plasticity. For example, there may be alternative ways of behaving that have differing consequences for fitness. Organisms are usually expected to opt for **optimal behaviour**, the one that maximizes fitness. A case in point concerns alternative ways of acquiring mates, which are conditional on the environmental conditions that have been experienced. For

A female redback spider (*Latrodectus hasselti*) looms over the partially eaten body of her tiny mate. The male is complicit in his own suicide. He somersaults into the female's jaws while copulating. Maydianne Andrade and her students at the University of Toronto (Scarborough) have examined the evolution of copulatory suicide.

ECOLOGY IN DEPTH 6.2

Genes and Individuals in Conflict

Usually, traits that increase the fitness of an individual organism and are passed along to offspring also increase gene fitness (gene replication). Occasionally, however, genes are "selfish" in the sense of enhancing their own replication (fitness) at the expense of decreasing the fitness of the individual. One such example is the case of the stalk-eyed fly (*Cyrtodiopsis dalmanni*), named for the bizarrely long eyestalks of males. This species has an outlaw allele on the X chromosome, which during meiosis in males inactivates Y-bearing sperm (Wilkinson et al., 1998a). Inactivation enhances the fitness of the outlaw gene because all of the fertilizing spermatozoa carry the X. Conversely, the fitness of the individual fly is decreased because there is diminished fertility of the ejaculate and a strong daughter bias in females that mate with these males. However, selection on individuals has produced suppressor alleles that in males disable the Y-inactivating outlaw genes. Because the suppressor genes are genetically linked to others that code for longer eyestalks, there is also sexual selection for "good genes" (see section 6.4) against outlaw alleles, because females prefer long-stalked males as mates.

In addition to the good-genes benefits of mating with long-stalked males, there is evidence that Fisherian runaway selection (section 6.4) may also play a role (Wilkinson et al., 1998b). Artificial selection experiments were set up to produce genetic lines of both long- and short-stalked males, and it was found that females preferred males with the stalk length that was characteristic of their own lineage. It appears, therefore, that female preference and male trait genes had coevolved.

example, male animals may increase mating success either by aggressively defending a female from rivals, or by sneaking in and surreptitiously mating. In such cases, much of the genetic variation can underlie not the alternative behaviours, but rather the plasticity of the potential behaviours. In this sense, the ability to exhibit a plastic response is itself an adaptation that is typically evolving in response to an unpredictable environment.

When behavioural ecologists examine fitness, they ask "why" questions about the traits of interest (Ecology in Depth 6.1). Behavioural traits that would seem to decrease fitness are particularly challenging. For example, why do male redback spiders (*Latrodectus hasselti*) copulate and then somersault into the lethal jaws of their cannibalistic mate? Why does the use of a barbed stinger in defence of the hive by a worker honeybee (*Apis mellifera*) invariably result in fatal self-evisceration? And why do crickets (*Nemobius sylvestris*) that are parasitized by a hair worm (*Paragordius tricuspidatus*) jump into a pool of water, where they die? As we will examine later on in more detail, fitness-enhancing behaviour explains all three of these examples. The point being made here is that although the answers to ultimate *why* questions of this sort may be difficult to fathom, they do reveal specific links between interesting behaviours and enhanced fitness.

A focus on the fitness of individuals rather than on populations or species began with G. C. Williams' book *Adaptation and Natural Selection* (1966), and was furthered by Richard Dawkins in *The Selfish Gene* (1976) (for additional discussion of the conceptual tension between selection on genes and individuals, see Ecology in Depth 6.2). Dawkins made an obvious but perceptive argument: each and every ancestor of all living organisms must have matured to adulthood, mated, and produced at least one offspring. However, most of the contemporary conspecifics of the ancestors did not achieve this fitness because, for example, they were felled by a pathogen while young, failed to find a mate, or provided inadequate parental care. An evolutionary consequence of this ancestral filtering mechanism—*natural selection*—is that organisms have inherited many successful (or adaptive) traits. As a consequence, animals are expected to choose the best mates and habitat, to make appropriate choices of food, and to avoid natural enemies. Occasionally, however, they will show adaptations that are more difficult to interpret, such as those that seem to decrease immediate survival but that enhance their reproductive success, or subversive tactics that decrease the fitness of other individuals, such as hosts in the case of parasites, and in certain situations, even mating partners.

6.2 Foraging

All animals need to eat, and many investigations have focused on how food choices and intake are optimized to increase fitness. Foraging strategies have been shown to be optimal in many ways, including how food items and patches are chosen and handled. A simple prediction is that animals will consume every edible item that they encounter. In many situations, however, it pays to be selective when foraging. For example, when items or patches of food differ in quality, fitness may be increased by focusing the foraging effort on targets of higher quality.

Preferences for items of higher quality are expected to occur whenever effort is expended to find or process food. This might be relevant if there is a cost of travelling between patches of food, or if an animal needs to manipulate items before consuming them, or if it must return to a particular location with the food, e.g. to feed nestlings. In a classic study, Krebs et al. (1977) studied great tits (*Parus major*; a relative of chickadees) that fly to a perch to eat captured prey items. In a laboratory experiment, birds were presented with a choice of two prey items that differed in quality (two lengths of mealworm, a kind of beetle larva) and that passed by on a conveyer belt. At low prey densities, the food types were eaten in the ratio of their relative availability. However, at high prey densities the birds made choices and were much more likely to focus on the longer, more profitable mealworms. This is the result that is predicted by an optimality model of predator choices.

A field study of foragers that prefer higher-quality food patches was conducted by Ralph Cartar (2004) of the University of Calgary. He decreased the quality of patches by stressing plants to diminish the amount of nectar available in their flowers to forging bumblebees (*Bombus* species). He examined two hypotheses to explain the preference of bees for the patch types: (1) local experience, in which bees stay longer when receiving more nectar in a particular patch, and (2) remembering the locations of high-quality patches. The hypotheses were examined by studying the foraging times and habits of individually marked bees. Both of the hypotheses received support, with evidence for the memory one coming from bees that were observed to pass by lower-quality plants and to return frequently and spend a disproportionate amount of time in those providing higher nectar rewards. Cartar concluded that memory of the location of the higher-quality plants indicates sophisticated cognitive processing in the bumblebees, especially considering the hundreds to thousands of individual plants that might be visited in a single foraging trip.

Foraging while Threatened by Enemies

Animals that are actively foraging might be exposed to an increased risk of predation or parasitism. This prediction has been supported in many studies, particularly in aquatic environments in which chemical cues of predators may occur in the water and be detected by their potential prey. Brad Anholt, now of the University of Victoria, and his colleagues (2000) videotaped the activity of tadpoles of four species of frogs under experimental conditions in which they modified both the availability of food and the density of predators (predaceous larvae of the dragonfly *Anax junius*). They found that increases in either food or predator density resulted in all tadpole species reducing their activity time and swimming speed, thereby lowering their risk of being eaten.

Aquatic insect larvae also decrease their activity when in the presence of predators. Macchiusi and Baker (1992) of the University of Toronto studied the aquatic tube-dwelling larvae of a midge (*Chironomus tentans*). The larvae must leave their refuge to feed, but they reduced the time spent outside their tube when predatory sunfish (*Lepomis gibbosus*) were present. The presence of fish had a direct impact on midge fitness because of their reduced food intake; the number of larvae that moulted to the next instar was reduced in the fish treatment.

Trade-offs have also been noted between foraging and risks of parasitism. Hutchings et al. (2002) studied lambs of wild sheep (*Ovis aries*) that were grazing in areas in which experimental differences had been created in the risk of suffering parasitism. Lambs that foraged in habitats that were well-fertilized with sheep manure had a food intake that was 1.5 times greater, but they were also exposed to more than five times the abundance of a helminth parasite that had come from the dung. Some of the lambs were treated with an anti-parasite medicine partway through the experiment, and their foraging was compared to a control group. At first, all of the lambs rejected the high-parasite/high-quality forage. Although lambs of both groups eventually began to graze on this conflicted food, the treated lambs grazed on it more often; these healthy, parasite-free lambs could apparently afford risking greater contact with the parasites.

A simple system for examining feeding choices versus risk of mortality was pointed out by Robert Anderson and Bernard Roitberg (1999) of Simon Fraser University. They used two types of mathematical models to examine the persistence of mosquitoes when they were feeding on blood, in a situation where greater feeding time increased both their egg production and the risk of death from being swatted by the host. Their models predicted that feeding would be more persistent when the death risk was low to moderate, or when the chance of getting a meal of blood was relatively high.

6.3 Natural Enemies and Adaptive Behaviour

Animals may face trade-offs among behaviours that are involved in reducing various kinds of risks. For instance, Baker and Smith (1997) of the University of Toronto examined larval dragonflies (*Ishnura verticalis*) that were faced with a conflict between removing parasitic mites and remaining still when predatory fish were nearby. When fish presence and the number of mites were both experimentally varied, the only significant effect was that there were more anti-parasite movements by the dragonfly larvae exposed to a high density of mites. However, this behaviour had fitness consequences for the larvae because their anti-mite movements made them conspicuous and more likely to be eaten by fish. These results suggest that the costs of parasitism are so high that the dragonfly larvae will tolerate an increased risk of predation. Indeed, parasites and pathogens are in general expected to be a strong selective force on the biology of their hosts, in part because their generation times are typically short compared to those of their hosts.

Parasites can be particularly effective in stimulating their host to divert its resources to benefit the parasite and its reproduction. This can involve various levels of effect, from merely stealing food from the host to preventing its reproduction. **Kleptoparasites** include certain spiders that specialize in scavenging prey from the webs of other spiders, and magnificent frigatebirds (*Fregata magnificens*) that obtain food by harassing other seabirds until they disgorge a recent meal of fish.

Brood parasites also can exploit the provisions of their hosts but are more virulent because they usually remove or kill the offspring of their host. Examples include slave-making ants that raid the nests of other species to capture their eggs or larvae for recruitment into their worker force, and certain wasps and flies whose larvae kill those of host solitary-wasps and bees. Another example is the brown-headed cowbird (*Molothrus ater*), which lays its eggs in the nests of many different kinds of songbirds, which raise the cowbird chicks while their own young usually die. Perhaps the best-studied example of the impact of brood parasites on host adaptations is that of the Eurasian cuckoo (*Cuculus canorus*), which swallows an egg of a host bird and then lays one of its own in the nest. The host birds are typically highly discriminating in evicting cuckoo eggs that are not excellent matches to the specific colour and pattern of their own eggs. The consequences of overlooking a cuckoo egg are dire—a newly hatched cuckoo chick pushes all eggs out of the nest and is then raised by the host parents.

Coevolution between cuckoos and their hosts is revealed by this syndrome of egg mimicry. It has resulted in a number of cuckoo races, each of which is specialized in laying eggs that mimic those of a particular host species. Clearly, host discrimination against poorly matched eggs is a powerful selective force that maintains differences in the eggs of cuckoo host-races. Remarkably, the host-races maintain the adaptive genetic differences that underlie egg patterns despite the fact that the races appear to freely interbreed. The mystery of this complex adaptation was solved by Lisle Gibbs et al. (2000) of McMaster University, who demonstrated that the races are restricted to female lineages; there are race-specific markers in maternally inherited mitochondrial DNA, a non-recombining genetic "surname," but not in nuclear DNA markers (microsatellites) that can come from either parent. However, the genes influencing egg type are probably not in the mitochondrial DNA, but instead are on the female-specific sex chromosome, which is also inherited from mother to daughter. Unlike many animals, in birds, the female and not the male is the heterogametic sex.

Certain invertebrate parasites are also extremely proficient at channelling the resources of their host into their own fitness. In a bizarre example, the parasitic larva of the wasp *Hymenoepimecis* modifies the normal web-spinning habits of its host orb-web spider *Plesiometra argyra* so that it spins a protective cocoon that encloses the wasp's pupa (Eberhard, 2000). This occurs just before the spider is killed and eaten by the larva. Some invertebrate parasites have a complex life history that involves them passing through several host species or habitats. In such cases, the parasite may adaptively manipulate host behaviour to ensure that its life cycle is completed. For example, orthopterans that are parasitized by a hair worm are stimulated to leave their woodland habitat and jump into water, where they die but also deliver the parasite to the habitat of its free-living adult stage.

Considerable research has focused on fitness-decreasing changes in the behaviour and structure of intermediate hosts. Consider the nematode *Myrmeconema neotropicum*, which completes its life cycle in a fruit-eating bird of tropical forests. The ant *Cephalotes atratus* is the intermediate host, and its normally black-coloured abdomen is manipulated by the nematode to become berry-red. Parasitized ants also elevate their abdomen to a conspicuous position, which further increases the likelihood that it will be detected and eaten by a frugivorous bird, which is the final host.

The manipulation of host behaviour is particularly common in various species of spiny-headed worms (Acanthocephala) that parasitize crustaceans

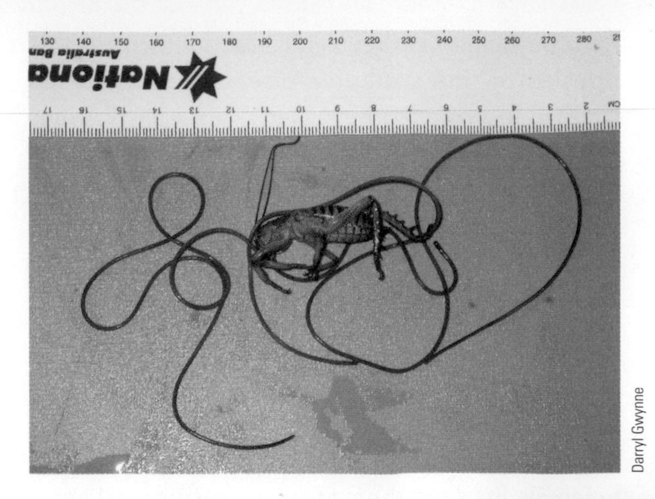

Darryl Gwynne

Stephen P. Yanoviak

Parasites that manipulate their hosts. Top: An orthopteran insect (tree weta: family Anostostomatidae) with two hair worms that emerged when it was placed in a pool of water. Right: An ant *Cephalotes atratus*, whose abdomen resembles the colour of a ripe berry when parasitized by the nematode *Myrmeconema neotropicum*.

as their intermediate host and vertebrates as the final one. Parasitized crustaceans are often modified in their colour and behaviour. Cézilly et al. (2000) experimented with two acanthocephalan species that manipulate an intermediate host, the amphipod *Gammarus pulex*, in different yet adaptive ways. Non-infected amphipods remain sheltered in poorly lit areas close to the river bed. However, infection by one of the acanthocephalan species causes amphipods to be attracted to open, well-lit areas where they are at greater risk of being eaten by the final fish host. In contrast, amphipods infected by the other acanthocephalan parasite move up in the water column, even when light conditions are experimentally controlled. Such behaviour places them near the water surface where their final hosts—ducks and other birds—are likely to be hunting.

When testing the proposition that a parasite is adaptively manipulating its host, it is important to rule out alternative hypotheses. For example, changes in host behaviour may simply be a symptom of parasite-induced illness, or a defensive reaction to parasitism. Moreover, modified behaviour must be shown to be a result of parasitism rather than the cause, i.e., a host behaving differently for some other reason may be more likely to become parasitized. Canadian Robert Poulin (2006) suggested that support for the adaptive manipulation hypothesis should include evidence that

- phenotypic alteration of the host is complex in character;
- there is an increased likelihood of encounter with the next stage in the parasite's life cycle; and
- and the parasite's fitness is increased.

All of these criteria are satisfied by experiments that examined the effects of a single-celled pathogen, the protozoan *Toxoplasma gondii*, on the behaviour of its intermediate rodent hosts. Berdoy et al. (2000) showed that rats (*Rattus norvegicus*) with toxoplasmosis are no longer repelled by the scent of their cat (*Felis domesticus*) predators, the final host of

Toxoplasma. Instead, the scent of cats becomes a fatal attraction for the infected rats. The attraction may be specific to cat odour because infected rats are not drawn to the scent of their own species or to that of rabbit (*Oryctolagus cuniculus*). Toxoplasmosis also occurs in humans. The effects are usually harmless in adults (but can be adverse for a developing fetus), but they include some intriguing evidence of personality changes.

6.4 Interacting with Sexual Competitors

Foraging and avoiding natural enemies are critical to survival, but for such adaptations to evolve they must be successfully passed along to offspring. Reproductive success is therefore key to fitness, and struggles among conspecifics to mate and reproduce are central areas of study in behavioural ecology.

Sexual selection is a general theory of selection in the context of mating, as elaborated by Charles Darwin (1871) in his book *The Descent of Man and Selection in Relation to Sex*. It most commonly involves selection on males to mate with many partners. In contrast, multiple matings can be less than optimal for the fitness of females. This sexual conflict over the mating rate that is optimal for fitness is central to understanding sex differences in the intensity of sexual selection.

Sexual selection results from competition for matings. In males this is about fertilizing more eggs, and it is reflected in a greater variation in the production of offspring (**reproductive skew**) among males than among females. Therefore, compared to females, males are usually adapted to maximizing their numbers of matings with different partners. Because copulation typically has costs for any females that re-mate, interactions between the sexes should reflect sexual differences in the mating rate. This is expected to result in selection for salesmanship among displaying males, and in sales discrimination and/or resistance to re-mating by females. It is the greater intensity of sexual selection on males that Darwin viewed as the evolutionary force that underlies structures such as ornaments and weapons, which are called **secondary sexual characters**. These characters are typically absent or not expressed to the same degree in females, resulting in sex differences or **sexual dimorphism**.

The nature of sexual selection varies greatly. Because sexually active males typically seek matings, there is **intrasexual selection**, or competition between members of the same sex. For males this can involve aggression between rivals or competition among gametes in rival stored ejaculates (**sperm competition**). These can result in the evolution of aggressive behaviour, risk-taking, weaponry such as antlers and tusks, and devices to remove or displace the sperm of rivals stored in the female's reproductive tract. In addition, **intersexual selection** (between the sexes) occurs when females discriminate among advertising males by mating only with certain individuals. This female choice has led to the evolution of ornamentation in males, which can include visual displays as well as acoustical and pheromonal signals. Female choice is adaptive when the costs of being choosy (e.g., of movements among potential partners) can be offset by the acquisition of a genetically superior mate or one that provides better resources, such as paternal care.

Both forms of sexual selection may interact with survival costs. In the classic Darwinian model, sexual selection on male ornaments may be opposed by viability selection. For example, the extent of ornamentation may be limited by natural selection due to increased risks of predation, as in the coloration patterns of male guppies (*Poecilia reticulata*). The threat of predation can also influence behaviour. For example, Clint Kelly and Jean-Guy Godin (2001) of Mount Allison University showed that agonistic interactions between male guppies were reduced in the presence of a predator, although attempts to court and copulate with females were not. Viability selection from predators or other sources may also influence female choice, as revealed by Godin and Briggs (1996), who showed that in the presence of a predator, female guppies from high-predation-risk environments took fewer risks by reducing their choosiness for colourful males.

An increased risk of predation can also mediate sexual selection via **sexual conflict**, especially over the number of matings. In this sense there are costs of re-mating, typically for females that have already been inseminated, either because of cumulative risks of predation or because copulation itself is costly. Examples of the latter are an increase in the added risk of infection by venereal disease and "toxic" ejaculates. In one example, male fruit flies (*Drosophila melanogaster*) ejaculate chastity-inducing chemicals that function in preventing the mate from copulating with rivals, but that also have a toxic side effect of reducing female fitness (Chapman et al., 1995). The outcome of sexual conflict over re-mating is either female rejection of males, or **convenience polyandry** in cases in which the costs of struggling with a male are sufficiently high that females will allow copulation.

Before discussing in more detail the various forms that sexual selection can take, we will address the central question of why males are typically more sexually competitive than females.

Two males of the Australian quacking frog *Crinia georgiana* have grasped a female. The sperm from the males can compete for fertilizations of her eggs, which are fertilized externally (Byrne and Roberts 2004).

Dale Roberts

Why Is Sexual Competition Greater in Males?

Darwin's theory of sexual selection concerns the evolutionary consequences of mechanisms such as female choice. But what about the causes of choosiness and other sexual differences such as ornaments and weapons? The factors that determine these differences stem from sexual differences in the underlying strategy of maximizing reproductive success.

As mentioned previously, in contrast to males, female success does not come from maximizing the number of matings. This is because, compared with males, females have a relatively large **parental investment** in each individual offspring, and this limits the number of young they can produce. This greater investment by females is due to the much larger material contribution of the egg to the fertilized zygote, compared with the sperm, and also in some species because of the maternal effort of time and energy in caring for offspring. This large maternal effort of females results in a low potential rate of reproduction, a greater time-out from mating, and thus fewer females available for mating (i.e., a negative female bias in the **operational sex ratio**). It is the limited number of females available for mating that induces reproductive competition among males.

This theory of sexual differences is testable because it predicts that the typical roles of the sexes in mating will reverse, with greater sexual selection on females, in cases in which males invest more than females in the offspring. Male investment can come from the delivery of goods and services that enhance the survival of his mate or her offspring. Examples include costly paternal care or beneficial substances given by the male to the female, which are eaten or absorbed from the ejaculate. These are known as mating or **nuptial gifts**, and they are commonly nutrients. For example, prey items are proferred by the males in certain species of birds, spiders, dance flies (dipterans in the family Empididae), and scorpionflies (Mecoptera). Some insects also offer nuptial gifts in a diverse menu of secretions from external glands or internal spermatophore-producing organs. Gifts may also be specialized chemicals that, when ejaculated into the female and translocated to her eggs, protect them from predation (such as pyrrolizidine alkaloids in certain moths, and cantharidin or Spanish fly in the beetle *Neopyrochroa flabellata*) (Gwynne, 1997).

The prediction of role reversal has been supported in species that show paternal care and nuptial gifts. For species with parental care, role reversal occurs when male investment decreases the male reproductive rate to below that of females (Clutton-Brock and Vincent, 1991). This occurs in certain birds in which males tend the nest and raise the young, such as jacanas (*Jacana*) and phalaropes (*Phalaropus*). In a well-studied system of nuptial feeding that involves species of katydids (or long-horned grasshoppers; family Tettigoniidae), not only do males feed their mates, but there is also plasticity in the mating roles. It is only when proteinaceous food is scarce that hungry females will compete to obtain nuptial meals

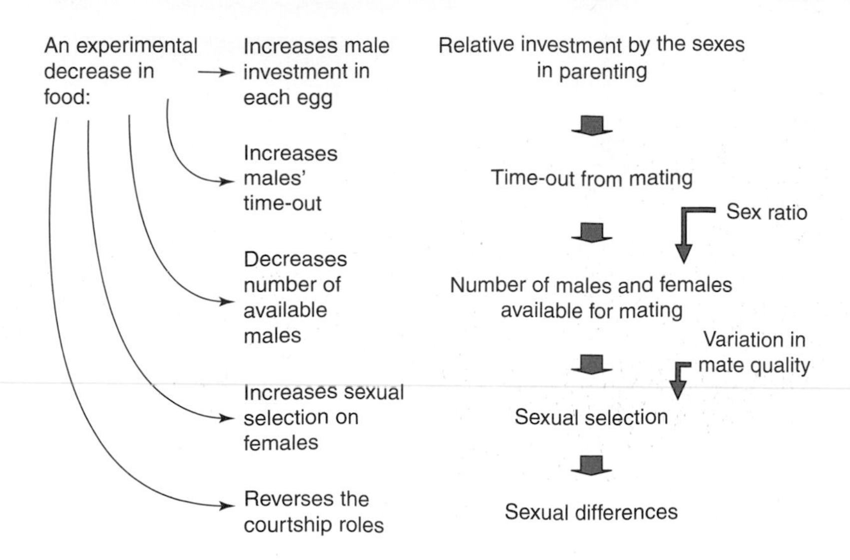

FIGURE 6.1
Nuptial Feeding in Katydids: A Test of Factors Controlling the Typical Sexual Differences. Factors hypothesized to control sexual selection and sexual differences (on the right) were examined in laboratory and field experiments (results on left) with katydids (Orthoptera: Tettigoniidae). A decrease in food availability resulted in an increase in paternal material in eggs as a result of male spermatophore (nuptial gift) nutrients (radiolabelled proteins) being eaten by the female (see photo below). This caused a reversal in the direction of sexual selection and sexual differences as hungry females competed for matings with the few males that were able to produce costly but nutritious spermatophores. Increased variation in mate quality can increase choosiness by the opposite sex, which in turn imposes sexual selection on the variable sex. A key factor is the number of sexually active males and females that are available (operational sex ratio), which can also be affected by large changes in the primary sex ratio—the ratio of all adult females to males. This factor has not been tested with katydids but there is an example of a butterfly in which male-killing *Wolbachia* bacteria changed the sex ratio, resulting in a reversal in the direction of sexual selection (females became sexually competitive; Jiggins et al., 2000).

SOURCE: Reprinted from Darryl T. Gwynne, *Katydids and Bush-crickets: Reproductive Behavior and Evolution of the Tettigoniidae.* Copyright © 2001 by Cornell University. Used by permission of the publisher, Cornell University Press.

Darryl Gwynne

Nuptial feeding katydid. Here a female Mormon cricket (*Anabrus simplex*) eats the large spermatophylax gift that was transferred during mating.

(Gwynne and Simmons, 1990). Manipulations of food availability in laboratory and field experiments have supported the theory that role reversal and sexual selection on females is caused by reversal in parental investment in offspring and a subsequent reversal in the operational sex ratio **(Figure 6.1)**.

Direct Competition between Rivals

Direct competition between males is one of the key mechanisms by which sexual selection occurs. This form of selection is responsible for the evolution of weapons and certain complex life histories. Male

Weapons used in fights between rival males have evolved in many animals, particularly certain insects and ungulates. In a study of caribou (*Rangifer tarandus caribou*), C. Barrette and D. Vandal of Laval University (1990) reported that males commonly spar with their antlers but there usually is little risk of injury. Fights for access to females will escalate, however, when antlers are similar in size, and this can lead to injury or death. Similarly, for males of a large orthopteran from New Zealand, the Wellington tree weta (*Hemideina crassidens*), Clint Kelly (2006a) of the University of Toronto showed that males use lengthy sword-like mandibles to fight for access to harems of females living in tree holes. Again, when males are evenly matched with respect to weapon size, combatants can receive fatal injuries, such as a crushed head.

weapons used in sexual combat include exaggerated tusks or horns that function in lifting and flipping rivals, as occurs in horned scarab beetles (of the family Scarabaeidae). It may also involve tests of rival strength, as are observed in antlered deer and horned rhinoceros. These structures may also function as signals of potential to win fights; for example, smaller-weaponed rivals often prudently withdraw and avoid combat-related injury.

Direct male–male competition and its link to the evolution of alternative life histories has been studied in bluegill sunfish (*Lepomis macrochirus*) at the Queen's University Biological Station (Gross and Charnov, 1980; Neff et al., 2003). Territorial males mature at about seven years old and defend a nest, whereas cuckolder males mature after only two years and parasitize the parental care provided by territorial ones. A cuckolder bluegill follows a sneaker tactic whereby it swims in quickly and ejaculates just as a female is spawning on the nest. At a slightly older age, cuckolder bluegills deceptively engage a breeding pair by mimicking the colour and behaviour of females. Territorial and sneaker males represent two different genetic and reproductive strategies. Similar alternative strategies have been well documented in Coho salmon (*Oncorhynchus kisutch*; see Chapter 8).

Three behavioural types that parallel those of the bluegill but that represent three genetic strategies were found by Schuster and Wade (1991) in their study of a sponge-inhabiting marine isopod crustacean (*Paracerceis sculpta*). Large dominant (or alpha) males fight other alphas to defend females living in protective cavities in sponges, while intermediate-sized (or beta) males are female-mimics that subversively obtain matings, and the smallest (or gamma) males use their diminutive size to avoid direct contact with alphas while sneaking matings. These behavioural and life-history differences are determined by three alleles, and genetic samples of natural populations of the isopod showed similar fitnesses for all of them.

If the fitness of one genetically based mate-locating strategy is consistently greater than that of others, then over evolutionary time, sexual selection is expected to eventually eliminate the alternatives. However, studies have found that differences in fitness are common among alternative mate-locating behaviours. This suggests the existence of mating systems in which alternatives are not genetic, but rather are conditional on environment circumstances (i.e., they represent a behavioural phenotypic plasticity). Consider the case of the beetle *Onthophagus acuminatus*, in which larger-bodied males use their cephalic horns to defend the nest entrance of their mate from rival males. In contrast, smaller, hornless males must "make the best of a bad situation" by using a lower-fitness tactic of sneaking matings by tunnelling into the side of the nest and breeding with the female there. Research has shown that neither body size nor mating tactic (horn state) is inherited (Emlen, 1997; Emlen et al., 2005). Instead, the amount and quality of feeding by the larva (which the female provisions with monkey dung) determines its size and thus whether the adult male will be large enough to develop a horn. Remarkably, the horned attribute of a male is conditional not only on its own body size, but also on a cue of the level of sexual competition that the larval male is likely to encounter as an adult; because dung quality is predictable, being high when fruit is a large part of the monkey diet, male beetles can vary their development adaptively. When the quality of dung eaten is high, male larvae of a certain body size are more likely to mature hornless because the high-quality food signals that the population-wide body size of rival males will on average be higher.

Mating Preferences

In addition to direct competition, Darwin proposed female choice as a mechanism that can impose sexual selection among males. There is now a wealth of evidence that females can choose among males, and that in some species they "shop" among a series of potential mates before mating with one of them. Given the effort required to make such a choice, what kinds of selection pressures caused female choice to evolve, and what are the benefits in terms of fitness?

One proposition is that females do not benefit. Instead, they are manipulated when they move toward male displays that most intensely stimulate the female senses. For example, Heather Proctor (1991) of the University of Alberta showed that a leg vibration display by male water mites (order Hydracarina) mimics the tremors of the locomotory appendages of their zooplankton prey, and this attracts females to the display.

However, other forms of female preference do have benefits. Direct benefits might enhance female survival, as occurs in arthropods that provide nuptial gifts of food. Female tree-crickets (*Oecanthus nigricornis*) prefer the lower-pitch songs of larger males, which provide bigger nuptial gifts in the form of secretions from their dorsal glands. Female scorpionflies (*Hylobittacus apicalis*) terminate copulation prematurely if the nuptial gift of a prey item from the male is too small, thus compromising the number of sperm he can transfer. Such males will live to mate again, but this is not the case with Australian redback spiders (*Latrodectus hasselti*). Maydianne Andrade (1996) of the University of Toronto has shown that the nuptial gift in this species represents an adaptive suicide—the meal is the body of the male, which he provides during copulation by somersaulting into the jaws of his mate. This is a compelling example of the importance of reproduction over individual survival in enhancing fitness.

Other examples of direct benefits arising from female choice are preferences for males that provide superior parental care, or more fertile ejaculates, or that are less infected by pathogens and parasites. A case in point concerns the barn swallow (*Hirundo rustica*), in which preferred males with longer tail-streamers also tend to have fewer blood-sucking mites than those with shorter tails (Moller, 1991).

Avoidance of parasites or pathogens is also an example of adaptive female choice for indirect benefits. This may be important when males provide no goods or services to the female or her brood, such as in lekking species in which males display together in areas (called **leks**) where females come to mate (this occurs in some insects, birds, and mammals). By preferring bright and vigorous male displays that are indicative of lower levels of parasitism, females may pass traits for resistance to their offspring. This is the hypothesis of Hamilton and Zuk (1982), and it is part of a larger argument that the display and vigour of a male are reliably connected, so that choosy females will have a greater chance of producing offspring that inherit the "good genes" of her preferred mate.

Elegant demonstrations of good-genes choice come from experiments that manipulated the external fertilization system of *Hyla* tree frogs (Welch et al., 1998). The hypothesis tested was that preferred males with a series of long calls in their song will sire better offspring. By comparing maternal half-siblings that were sired by males with long or short calls, offspring of long-call males were shown to perform better (e.g., grew faster) during larval and juvenile development. Experimental manipulation of the ejaculate of either of the different call-type males to fertilize the eggs of the same female ruled out an alternative hypothesis that effects on tadpole fitness are due to greater investment by females in the eggs fertilized by higher-quality males.

The question of how low-quality males are prevented from faking high-quality signals was addressed by Zahavi (1975). He argued that indicators of quality are kept honest by their high cost, so that the vigour of a male is demonstrated by the "handicaps" of exaggerated traits developed through sexual selection.

Anna Price

A male Trinidadian guppy (*Poecilia reticulata*), a species that has become a model system for research in sexual selection. Coloration differs among males, a variation that is related to both sexual and viability selection. More colourful males are preferred by females, possibly because they are of higher genetic quality, but they are also more vulnerable to predation (see text). Moreover, a hypothesis supported by Helen Rodd et al. (2002) of the University of Toronto is that the colourful spots mimic food, and so may be a form of sensory exploitation whereby males can attract females.

Godin and Dugatkin (1996) of Mount Allison University tested this by showing that certain male guppies, typically the most colourful ones, engage in high-risk behaviour when they leave their school to inspect a nearby predatory fish. They found that females preferred males that were experimentally manipulated to show boldness, i.e., by being positioned closest to a predator.

This and the other examples that we have looked at hypothesize that sexual selection—and thus evolutionary change in ornaments—is directional. This is because females consistently prefer males with the most intense displays or larger ornaments. Eventually, however, opposing natural selection for viability must limit further elaboration of the trait, for example, because highly ornamented males are more visible to predators. However, directional sexual selection is not the case when choosy females obtain good-genes benefits by mating with genetically compatible males, because the preferred mate for any particular female can differ. For example, females in many groups of animals (mammals, lizards, fish, and insects) prefer to mate with males that have dissimilar genetic loci in a series of genes known as the major histocompatibility complex (MHC). These genes are important for an effective immune system, particularly in individuals that are more heterozygous at these loci. Preferences for MHC-dissimilar mates is expected to increase heterozygosity in offspring. This may be the case in marsupial mice (*Antechinus agilis*) in which females prefer the scent of genetically dissimilar males (Parrott et al., 2007).

Once directional sexual selection by female choice for a particular trait is established in a population, females can in a sense "follow the fashion." This is because their preference for the trait is inherited and expressed by female descendents, while males inherit and express the attractive trait. This may result in genes for the separate traits becoming linked in a process of **runaway sexual selection**, as first described by the pioneering evolutionary biologist R. A. Fisher (1930). Thus, the male trait is no longer correlated with vigour or some other heritable fitness quality. Instead, female preference and the male trait co-evolve because they are genetically linked. With each ensuing generation of females preferring males with increasingly exaggerated traits, the sons express those traits and daughters show even stronger preference. An example may come from studies of stalk-eyed flies, a system that also exemplifies that several different mechanisms of choice of direct and indirect benefits may drive the evolution of secondary sexual characters in males (see Ecology in Depth 6.2, p. 139). One problem with the runaway model, however, is that costs of female choice mitigate against this form of selection.

The logic of runaway and other directional selection models of sexual selection raises another problem: Why does female choice for good genes persist? This question arises because the constancy of intersexual selection should erode the genetic variation underlying male ornamental traits. Often called the "lek paradox," this question was answered in the "genic capture" model outlined by Rowe and Houle (1996) of the University of Toronto. They pointed out that most male display traits appear to be costly, and so their degree of expression should be dependent on the condition of the male (e.g., the level of his energy reserves). Condition in turn is controlled by many physiological functions, and thus by many genes throughout the genome. Therefore, condition-dependent traits "capture," and over evolutionary time maintain, a large pool of genetic variation.

The Sexes in Conflict

Usually, there is a greater potential for males to increase fitness by multiple mating than for females. This results in sexual conflict, which can impose sexual selection on males for traits that function to overcome a mated female's attempts to reject unwanted matings. An example concerns water striders, insects in the family Gerridae. Locke Rowe of the University of Toronto and his colleagues have shown that male gerrids have clasping devices that function to grasp females during copulation, but also that females of certain species have co-evolved devices that serve to prevent the attempts of males to copulate with them. For one such species, *Gerris incognitus*, Arqvist and Rowe (1995) experimentally lengthened the female devices, which increased their ability to thwart unwanted grasping attempts by males.

In other insects, experimental manipulation of conditions that influence female and male re-mating has proven useful in revealing sexual conflict. In a burying beetle (*Nicrophorus defodiens*) studied in northern Ontario, a male and a female cooperate in burying a dead mouse and in caring for the brood of larvae that eat the carrion (Eggert and Sakaluk 1995). However, when a larger dead rodent such as a rat is buried, cooperation between the pair becomes disrupted by conflict over attempts by the male to attract additional mates to breed on the larger carrion resource. Mating with additional females would increases fitness of the male, but it could potentially decrease that of his first mate because of competition from the extra broods. Behavioural evidence of conflict is observed when a male beetle on rat carrion produces a calling pheromone to attract additional females. However, the pheromone also elicits his first mate to crawl over him, bite him, and thus prevent him from calling. Eggert and Sakaluk demonstrated this female coercion of monogamy by tethering the male's first female using dental floss. This freed the male to summon additional females and become polygamous.

Post-Copulatory Sexual Selection

Studies with *Nicrophorus* beetles are typical of those that examine male fitness by determining his ability to re-mate or by counting the number of matings. However, female *Nicrophorus* can also re-mate (between breeding bouts), and they can use stored sperm from previous matings to fertilize a portion of the brood with their current mate (House et al., 2007). Therefore, mating does not necessarily equate to fertilization success; there may be differential fertilization by the sperm of rivals stored within the female (Parker, 1970).

Our understanding of **post-copulatory sexual selection** has expanded greatly with the development of molecular markers that allow paternity to be estimated. Preston et al. (2001) studied such markers in an isolated population of wild Soay sheep (*Ovis aries*) living on an island off Scotland. They found that dominant males had the highest mating success throughout the rutting season. However, when "siring success" was examined during the last part of the season, the paternity of lower-status males equalled or slightly exceeded that of dominants. The reason was that frequent copulation by dominants had depleted their supplies of sperm.

Studies of the relative siring success of males have now been carried out on many species of birds. They have shown that most socially monogamous species, in which a male and female pair up and raise offspring, are not genetically monogamous because females almost always produce some offspring sired by non-partners. In the most extreme case, the superb fairy wren (*Malurus cyaneus*) of Australia, about 75 percent of all young and virtually all nests have extra-pair paternity (Double and Cockburn, 2000). Paternity in birds is thought to be controlled mainly by females, as was elegantly shown in a study of black-capped chickadees (*Poecile atricapilla*) by Mennill et al. (2002), working at the Queen's University Biological Station. Female chickadees were shown to eavesdrop on song contests, and they increased the extra-pair paternity of their offspring if their partner male was heard to "lose" the contest (which involved a playback of the song of a high-ranking male). Their study supported the eavesdropping hypothesis over one in which females responded to some sort of post-playback change in the behaviour of their partner.

When females mate multiple times, differences in paternity can be caused by sperm competition for fertilizations between the sperm of different males. Structures that function in sperm competition can flush out (e.g., some moths) or brush out (e.g., some dragonflies) the stored sperm of rivals. There are also sperm plugs (e.g., certain rodents and spiders) and chemical substances (some insects) that prevent insemination by rivals. These mechanisms and devices cause sperm competition among the males for fertilization of the ova. Biased paternity may also be a result of females manipulating the ejaculate of certain males, i.e., an intersexual selection by "cryptic" or post-copulatory female choice. For example, a male of the fly *Dryomyza anilis* courts the female during copulation by tapping his genitals on hers (Otronen, 1990). A higher tapping rate tends to increase the paternity of the male because it stimulates the female to favour his sperm.

Post-copulatory sexual selection is known to occur in many species. Female jungle fowl (*Gallus*

gallus), the wild progenitor of the chicken, may discriminate against certain males by expelling their sperm (Birkhead and Pizzari, 2002). There is even enticing evidence (from electron micrographs) of "sperm choice" by eggs. This involves a species of comb jelly (a marine invertebrate in the phylum Ctenophora) in which more than one sperm may penetrate an ovum, but the egg nucleus has been observed to move toward one sperm nucleus and away from another (Birkhead and Pizzari, 2002). Finally, sperm competition between copulating (and non-self fertilizing) hermaphrodite snails occurs when one individual attempts to inseminate the other, while limiting the amount of sperm its own female organs receive. In the brown garden snail (*Cantareus aspersus*), competition is mediated by 9-mm-long calcareous love darts that are used to stab copulatory partners. Chase and Blanchard (2006) of McGill University showed that if the stab area is near the partner's genital pore, mucus on the dart has a hormonal action on the recipient that results in a large increase in the number of sperm successfully transferred. The apparent cause is a reduction in the typically high level of sperm digestion in the genital tract of the recipient. Changes in paternity are likely a result of competition between the male functions of the two individuals. However, cryptic choice of sperm by an accurately stabbed partner is also possible.

6.5 Social Behaviour

In the 1970s, the young discipline of behavioural ecology was also known as sociobiology, which reflected a focus on studying interactions occurring within groups of conspecifics. Central to this work was the question of why, in some animals, individuals reduced their own reproduction while helping to increase that of others, leading to a large reproductive skew within the social group. This sort of helping behaviour is especially well developed in colonies of highly social insects. In fact, these colonies have been called "super-organisms" because they feature distinct reproductive and worker **castes** that in some respects parallel the separate germ and somatic cell lines within an individual organism. Unlike cells, however, individuals within most insect colonies are genetically different (see **Table 6.1**, p. 154, for exceptions), and this is reflected in conflict that can occur within a colony. Examples include a newly emerged queen honeybee using her unbarbed stinger to kill rival new queens, and in a few species of ants, bees, and wasps (order Hymenoptera) attempts made by female workers to produce sons. In Hymenoptera, males hatch from haploid parthenogenetic eggs, and so they can be produced by unmated females.

A key question is that, given the selfishness of natural selection on individuals, how did extreme helping behaviour evolve? Before addressing this question, we should first examine the reasons why animals live in groups in the first place, and then describe a form of helping behaviour that does not appear to reduce individual reproduction.

Advantages of Group Life

Given the universal costs of group life, which include increased competition for resources (and mates) and greater risk of infection by pathogens, there must be compensating fitness benefits to individuals. There are some physical advantages of grouping behaviour, such as thermoregulation in certain bats and maintaining hydration in terrestrial isopod crustaceans. Groups may also have greater success in foraging and hunting (e.g., pack hunting of large prey by wolves), and this may be a reason for the grouping and flocking behaviours of some birds and mammals. Another benefit is safety in numbers, which can occur when the risk of predation is reduced due to increased vigilance of groups or confusion of predators by an abundance of prey. There is also a dilution of predation risk in groups, in part because predators can become satiated. This has been shown for the periodical cicada (*Magicicada septendecim*), which may hold the record for the largest animal group; an emergence of adults in 2004 was estimated to be 10 trillion individuals (Lockwood, 2004). Where the density of cicadas was greatest within this enormous group of insects, the female reproductive fitness was higher. As predicted by the predator satiation hypothesis, the fitness increase correlated with a decrease in individual risk of capture as the density increased (Karban, 1982).

Predation pressure is thought to be the cause of tightly coordinated shoals of swimming fishes. However, one of the costs of group life may interfere with schooling ability: in rainbow trout (*Oncorhynchus mykiss*), vision may be impaired by eye-flukes (*Diplostomum spathaceum*), which may be more infectious in dense populations. Eye infections reduce the ability to form large schools, and they impair cohesion of those shoals when a threat of bird predation is present (Seppala et al., 2008).

In essence, swarms of insects and schools of fish are assemblages of individuals that are acting selfishly. For example, animals will typically attempt to move into the centre of their group to reduce the risk of predation. There are also social interactions that seem to be altruistic but in the long run are

ECOLOGY IN DEPTH 6.3

Methodology in Behavioural Ecology: Social Behaviour

Scientists formulate hypotheses and then test them using experiments or comparisons. In experiments, variables are controlled through manipulation, whereas with comparisons such variables can be statistically removed. For example, helping behaviour in Australian grey-crowned babblers (*Pomatostomus temporalis*) occurs when non-breeding mature birds in a social group help to feed the nestlings of a breeding pair. This **altruism**—enhancing another individual's reproductive success at a cost to one's own reproduction—can evolve through kin selection if the helpers are genetically close relatives of the breeders. This hypothesis predicts that helpers will increase the success of fledging young birds to which they are related. However, a simple positive correlation between these two variables might also be explained by a confounding variable, such as the higher-quality territory that may be held by a larger social group. Nevertheless, studies in which the number of helpers is experimentally reduced, as well as comparisons in which confounding variables are statistically controlled, both support the hypothesis that helpers increase fledging success (Brown et al., 1982; Blackmore et al., 2007).

The theory of kin selection also predicts that altruism will originate in species that have social systems in which the relatedness of altruist and recipient individuals is high. However, comparisons between species require phylogenetic controls in which the similarity due to common ancestry is removed statistically from the effects of adaptive evolution. Such comparisons can determine the number of independent origins of a trait, as well as correlations between traits and types of environment; the latter allows comparative tests of how environment influences the evolution of traits (see the books by Dan Brooks and Deborah McLennan (1991 and 2002) of the University of Toronto). Moreover, the variation in traits can be traced onto evolutionary trees to determine their ancestral states (see A Canadian Ecologist 6.1 and below for examples with kin selection and the evolution of castes in two groups of social insects).

actually selfish acts in terms of their consequences for fitness. One case involves vampire bats (*Desmodus rotundus*), which bite their host (such as a cow) and drink its blood as food. They need to feed at least every second night, but unsuccessful foragers may receive regurgitated blood from well-fed individuals in their colony. However, regurgitation turns out to be a type of reciprocal social exchange in that donors will be repaid if they in turn are unsuccessful on a night or two of seeking blood meals. One factor that selects for this **reciprocity** is that the relative value of an amount of blood received by a bat at risk of starvation is much higher than the same quantity donated by a well-fed animal. Other factors that select for the behaviour are frequent exchanges, so that donors are eventually paid, and a system whereby cheats are recognized and punished (Wilkinson, 1984).

Darryl Gwynne

A cluster of forest tent caterpillars (*Malacosoma disstria*) in southern Ontario. These insects cluster together as they move between temporary bivouacs and feeding locations. Emma Despland and Sarah Hamzah (2004) of Concordia University have shown that the presence of other caterpillars keeps individuals quiescent within the group and allows for efficient locomotion when groups move.

Why Do Some Organisms Help Others?

Extreme levels of reproductive skew occur when some organisms altruistically sacrifice their own reproduction to aid that of others. Cases are known in a diversity of species, including insects, crustaceans, mammals, birds, and even unicellular organisms. Species with both altruism and castes reflect an especially high level of social development and are referred to as being eusocial **(Table 6.1, page 154)**. **Eusociality** involves some phenotypes (castes) being specialized for

A large mound of the spinfex termite *Nasutitermes triodiae* in northwestern Australia. The mound contains a large colony of this eusocial insect.

reproduction, while others are altruists that reproduce far less or not at all, and instead provide work or defence for the colony, which ultimately increases the fitness of the reproductive caste.

Both genetic and ecological factors are important in the evolution of eusociality. The genetic ones were first highlighted in a group of highly social insects, the ants, and certain species of bees and wasps (order Hymenoptera). Eusociality has evolved independently many times in hymenopterans, and is typified by extreme acts of self-sacrifice, such as the suicidal use of a barbed sting by honeybee workers when defending their hive.

It was eusocial Hymenoptera that inspired William D. Hamilton (1936–2000), an evolutionary theorist, to seek to answer the question posed in the title of this section—Why do some organisms help others? He noted that individuals in a typical eusocial colony—a queen and her offspring—share many genes and so there could be selection for an altruism-coding gene through the reproduction of members of the reproductive caste. However, to compensate for cases in which an aided individual does not carry that gene, altruism to the reproductive individuals has to be large; for example, honeybee workers that join a squadron of suicidal defenders and thus prevent a predator from destroying their colony.

Hamilton developed a theory of **kin selection** that expands the concept of fitness beyond that of successful direct ancestry (see section 6.1). **Inclusive fitness** comprises both **direct fitness** via offspring and **indirect fitness** that comes from help given to close relatives (Hamilton, 1996). Thus, non-reproducing altruists are argued to benefit by increasing their indirect fitness. Hymenopterans are particularly relevant to kin selection and inclusive fitness because they are haplo-diploid: unfertilized eggs become haploid males and fertilized ones become diploid females. This system allows for female control over the sex ratio of offspring, but also has the effect of producing asymmetries in kin relatedness—a mother and daughter share one-half of their genes identical by descent, whereas on average this **coefficient of relationship** (Harpending, 2002) between two sisters averages three-quarters **(Figure 6.2).** Therefore, a worker obtains greater fitness returns on an investment that produces a sister than on one that generates a daughter.

Eusociality has also evolved in diplo-diploid animals, including termites (order Isoptera), at least two species of mole-rats (genera *Heterocephalus* and *Crytomys*), and some marine crustaceans **(Table 6.1).** In these cases, kin selection appears to be important because of high benefits to the recipients of altruism, but non-genetic factors also play a role (see discussion below). There is also an important role of kin selection in other altruistic vertebrates. In colonies of Belding's ground squirrel (*Spermophilus beldingi*), females produce risky alarm calls to alert nearby animals to predators. It turns out that these females are mothers

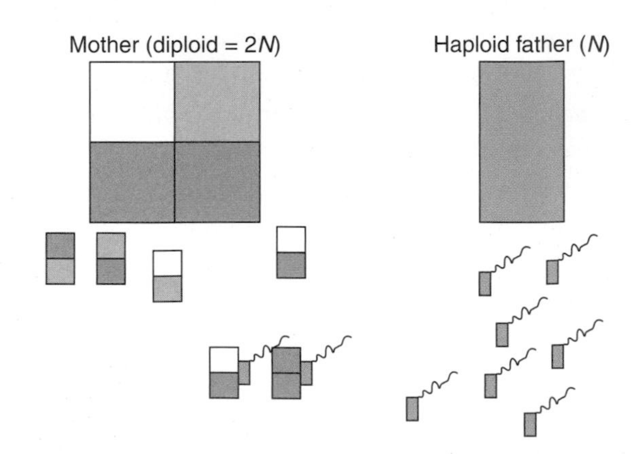

FIGURE 6.2

Asymmetry in the Relatedness of Haplo-Diploid Females to Their Sisters and Daughters. Gametes are represented by the small rectangles below the parents. Sperm from a haploid father contribute one-half of the genes, identical by descent, in two sisters. The diploid mother contributes another one-quarter of genes shared by her daughters. Therefore, on average, sisters are three-quarters related in terms of the genes they share.

protecting their own young and also alerting other close relatives to a risk of predation (Sherman, 1977).

Kin selection even explains altruism between presumed mating competitors: some male turkeys (*Meleagris gallopavo*) display in pairs, but only one of them gets to copulate (Krakauer, 2005). Partners turn out to be brothers, and the non-mating bird obtains higher inclusive fitness through his fraternal assistance than he would gain if attempting to obtain mates by displaying alone.

Finally, there is extreme altruism among some unicellular organisms, the best-studied example being the cellular slime-mould *Dictyostelium discoideum* (Kuzdzal-Fick et al., 2007; Strassmann and Queller, 2007). When solitary slime-mould amoebae are starved, those of identical and dissimilar genotypes will form a multicellular slug that differentiates into a stalk that lifts a fruiting body above the soil surface. The stalk cells are altruists because they die without reproducing. Some genotypes are able to gain favourable positions in the fruiting body, and they even show kin preferences by aggregating close to like genotypes.

The theory of kin selection along with haplodiploidy appeared to answer why eusociality has evolved so often in Hymenoptera. However, the explanatory power of this seemed to be weakened because, in many eusocial species, the three-quarters relationship to sisterly recipients of altruism is diluted. This occurs because queens (including in honeybees) mate more than once (so that half-sisters share only three-eighths of their genes), and as in some eusocial colonies, workers assist non-relatives because there are multiple queens. However, it is important to note that it is in the evolutionary *origin* of eusociality where kin selection is predicted to have been an important force. This contrasts to the subsequent *maintenance* of eusociality by natural selection, when other factors may be more important (as we examine below). Phylogenetic tests (see Ecology in Depth 6.3) by Hughes et al. (2008) have supported the hypothesis of close-relatedness when eusociality first originated in Hymenoptera. They showed that in all eight independent origins of eusociality in hymenopterans, both a single-mating queen (**monandry**) and a "single-queen" was the ancestral state in almost all of the origins (see A Canadian Ecologist 6.1, p. 155, for a case involving a different order of insects; see also **Figure 6.3** on p. 156).

Additional evolutionary pressures are important to the maintenance of eusociality, including manipulation by the queen of her offspring and/or sisters, either directly or via the worker force. Manipulation may include control of nutrition to affect the size of larvae, which determines their caste after metamorphosis. **Phylogenetic inertia** is also important, whereby a eusocial lineage has become so specialized with structural castes that workers have lost the ability to mate. This was supported in the phylogenetic analysis of Hughes et al., which showed that losses of reproductive ability in eusocial hymenopteran workers were associated with increases in multiple mating (**polyandry**) by queens and thus a reduction in the coefficient of relatedness. Once there is queen control and evolutionary loss of reproduction by specialized workers and other sterile castes, phylogenetic inertia may have allowed selection to promote queen polyandry. In honeybees and bumblebees, polyandry has been shown to strengthen the resistance of colonies to pathogens (Tarpy and Seely, 2006).

Kin selection is an *intrinsic* genetic factor that underlies the evolution of both altruism and eusociality. *Extrinsic* factors are ecological pressures that select for eusociality (Evans, 1977). Extrinsic factors account for the benefits to relatives (through inclusive fitness) that are necessary for kin selection to originate, in cases where relatedness to sisters is not higher than to offspring—as in the many eusocial species that are diplo-diploid (**Table 6.1**). One potential benefit in such cases is to remain and help to defend the natal nest (**philopatry**) where the fitness benefits are either indirect and/or direct if the nest is inherited by the helper when the original reproductives die. The latter was probably important in the origin of euociality in termites, a group of diplo-diploid insects; in the Termopsidae, a primitive family considered to have a biology similar to that of ancestral termites, there is high mortality of founding reproductives that start the nest, and workers retain the ability to reproduce if necessary (Thorne et al., 2003).

For some vertebrates, there are also direct reproductive benefits that eventually accrue to adults that assist in raising the progeny of other individuals. Such helping occurs in about 3 percent of bird species and also in a few mammals that show cooperative breeding (Alcock, 2009; see Ecology in Depth 6.3, p. 151). Although indirect benefits have been shown in most birds where helpers-at-the-nest raise siblings (Alcock, 2009), helpers in species such as the superb fairy wren (*Malurus cyaneus*) and the meerkat (*Suricata suricatta*) almost certainly obtain direct benefits because many of them are unrelated to the young that they raise (Clutton-Brock, 2002). Also unrelated are many of the females that cooperate in starting a nest in the primitively eusocial paper wasp *Polistes dominulus* (Queller et al., 2000). Only one female is the egg-laying queen, but high mortality among foundresses increases the probability that helper females may eventually inherit the nest to become queen (details in section 6.6).

Selection for the evolutionary origins of philopatry may lie in circumstances where there are high risks to dispersing and reproducing directly, such as in termites or mole-rats that live in tunnelled networks in wood or soil, or thrips (order Thysanoptera) living in plant galls **(Table 6.1).** These eusocial species are defenders of a "fortress" in the sense that all vital resources that need to be to protected are in the colony, so that workers tend to stay and forage within the nest (Queller and Strassmann, 2003).

In contrast, eusocial hymenopterans are "life-insurer, forager-defenders" that make forays away from the nest to obtain food for the colony (Queller and Strassmann, 2003). Foraging by the adults is hazardous, so the presence of multiple foundresses with the ability to reproduce or supply labour when needed ensures against the risk of loss of the reproductive queen and/or the nest. The latter was first shown by David Gibo (1978) of the University of Toronto in a pioneering experimental manipulation of predation and the numbers of foundresses on paper-wasp nests (*Polistes fuscatus*). Compared to a single foundress, when the intensity of predation by birds was high, multiple foundresses had an increased ability to re-establish the nest after its loss. Moreover, at higher levels of predation, the number of reproductives produced per foundress was relatively high (compared with lower predation), which supports a kin-selection model of the evolution of eusociality in this species.

6.6 Social Selection

Within social groups there are parallels between reproductive struggles over mates (typically occurring between males) and those for resources needed for breeding (usually between females). This observation suggested to West-Eberhard (1979) that Darwinian sexual selection might be expanded to a broader concept of **social selection.** Both sexual and social selection are screening processes that favour the most successful breeders, in a manner that parallels the artificial selection by humans of domesticated species and varieties.

TABLE 6.1 Eusocial Species with Reproductive and Non-Reproductive Castes

Workers feed the young, unless otherwise stated under extrinsic factors.

Species	Class (Order)	Sex-Determining System	Intrinsic Factors That Increase Relatedness	Extrinsic Factors	Weaponry for Nest Defence
Mole rats, *Heterocephalus glaber* and *Cryptomys damarensis*	Mammalia	Diplo-diploid	High levels of inbreeding	Fortress defenders of subterranean burrow system & need to cooperate in foraging	Teeth of non-reproductives (both sexes)
Marine snapping-shrimp, *Synalpheus* species (three evolutionary origins)	Crustacea	Diplo-diploid	None	Fortress defenders of a sponge that feed on organic matter within the sponge	Enlarged chelae
Termites (all species in the order Isoptera)	Insecta (Isoptera)	Diplo-diploid	Inbreeding	Fortress defenders of gallery systems within wood, their food source	Various elaborate modifications of soldiers (both sexes)
Certain aphids	Insecta (Homoptera)	Diplo-diploid	Clonal reproduction	Fortress defenders of a plant gall within which they feed; no nurturing workers	Piercing mouthparts and specialized legs
Certain thrips	Insecta (Thysanoptera)	Haplo-diploid	Inbreeding	Fortress defenders of a plant gall within which they feed; no nurturing workers	Enlarged forelegs of soldiers (both sexes)
Curculionid beetle, *Austroplatypus incompertus*	Insecta (Coleoptera)	Diplo-diploid	Unknown	Fortress defenders of gallery systems within wood; feed on fungi.	Not studied
Many Hymenoptera: Ants, bees, and wasps, with many independent evolutionary origins	Insecta (Hymenoptera)	Haplo-diploid	Haplo-diploidy	Forager-defenders that eat insects (ants; wasps), pollen (bees & a few wasps), and nectar	Sting of females

A CANADIAN ECOLOGIST 6.1

Bernard Crespi: Phylogeny and Evolution of Eusocial Thrips—Behavioural and Evolutionary Studies

Bernard Crespi

Bernard Crespi

Haplo-diploid theory is central to explaining the many independent cases of evolution of eusociality in the order Hymenoptera—the ants, bees, and wasps. Therefore, the discovery by Bernard Crespi of Simon Fraser University of eusociality in another group of haplo-diploid insects, the thrips (Thysanoptera), provides an important opportunity for a further examination of Hamiltonian theory. Somewhat ironically, the research of Crespi and his colleagues has shown that high coefficients of relationship and the evolutionary origins of castes (soldiers) in thrips is attributable more to high levels of inbreeding via brother–sister matings than to haplo-dipoidy. As a consequence, the hymenopteran asymmetry in sister–sister and sister–brother relatedness is less evident in eusocial thrips—in fact, there are both male and female soldier thrips.

Crespi has studied thrips as a model system for research in behavioural ecology and evolution, initially working on sexual selection and inter-male competition in solitary species and then describing their eusociality for the first time in gall-thrips from Australia (Crespi, 1992). He reported that some of the species of these comma-sized thrips, which are adapted to living and feeding inside of protective galls (formed from modified petioles) on *Acacia* shrubs, have evolved eusociality. This is revealed by the presence of soldiers within the gall, individuals that have enlarged spiked forelegs that are used to defend the colony from kleptoparasitic (food-stealing) intruders, typically other species of thrips. The soldiers are flightless, gall-bound individuals that reproduce little or not at all.

Subsequent research on these eusocial thrips includes the development of molecular phylogenies that were used to trace the evolution of coefficients of relatedness and inbreeding, two characters that are important to understanding kin selection (Chapman et al., 2000; Chapman, Perry, and Crespi, 2008). This allowed the first test of the hypothesis that high levels of relatedness between reproductives and altruists are necessary for kin selection to drive the *origin* of eusociality (see also the Hymenoptera example in section 6.5). When traced onto the thrips phylogeny, it was revealed that the ancestral population (for a single origin of eusociality) had a high relatedness level (78 percent) and that inbreeding was the main mechanism producing this (Figure 6.3). As is the case in eusocial Hymenoptera, relatedness values in thrips have evolved to be lower in more derived eusocial lineages.

Crespi's research interests in behavioural and evolutionary ecology have extended far beyond the behavioural ecology of thrips. His initial work in sexual and social evolution has now been extended to include molecular phylogenetic studies of other groups of animals, and the application of those evolutionary patterns to understanding life-history evolution, speciation, mating preferences, and reproductive isolation. Recently, he and his colleagues have been applying ideas about selection and evolution to diseases of humans, including the relationship of natural selection with cancer risk (Crespi and Summers, 2005) and the evolutionary-genetic bases of autism and schizophrenia (Crespi and Badcock, 2008).

In competition for both mating and breeding opportunities, high levels of reproductive skew have selected for elaborate displays between combatants, including sexual signals and ornaments—the gaudy and sex-specific traits that inspired Darwin to propose sexual selection. Social signals are parallels of these. For example, facial markings in the paper wasp (*Polistes dominulus*) communicate social status (body size) among females that are competing for status as the queen (the only reproductive individual) of the colony. Although there is little energetic cost in producing markings of high status, these marks are kept honest by direct competition. Low-ranked females that were altered with paint to signal higher status experienced a significant increase in aggressive mounting by non-painted, higher-ranked females (Tibbetts and Dale 2004). Being mounted imposes social costs in time and probably injury. Rank continues to be important even after the single reproductive female (the queen) has been determined. This is because the queen is often lost to predation, creating an opportunity for the next-ranking female to take over the egg-laying role in the colony.

Given that caste in most eusocial insects is dependent on the type and amount of nutrition received by the larva, queen and worker appear to represent condition-dependent alternative reproductive

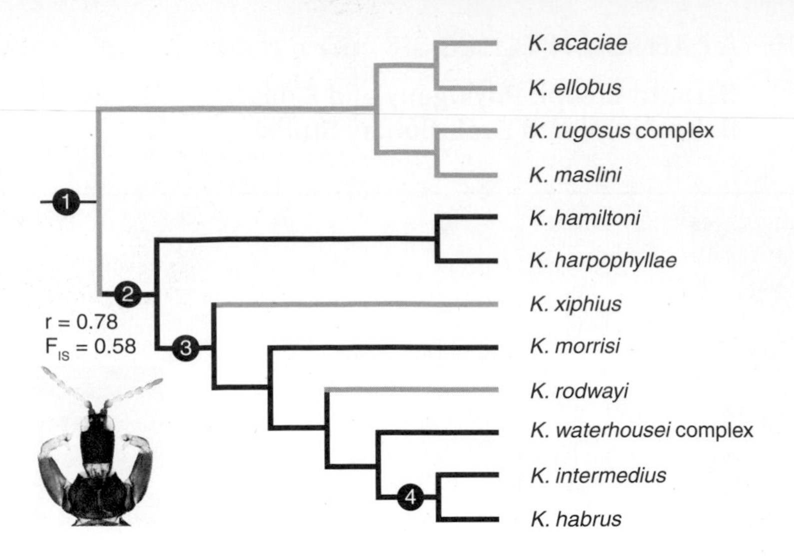

FIGURE 6.3

The Evolution of Eusociality in Australian Kladothrips. The origin and diversification of social life in these species of thrips involved both intrinsic and extrinsic factors. In the diagram, black branches represent eusocial species, those with soldiers, while grey ones are non-eusocial. The phylogeny shows a single origin of soldiers (point 2) and two losses of this caste (in *K. xiphius* and *K. rodwayi*). It is thought that foundresses of colonies in galls at point 1 on the phylogeny likely fought over access to the galls where social groups live, and this may have pre-adapted them to evolve a soldier caste. Tracing (optimizing) on the phylogeny values of the coefficients of relationship (r) and inbreeding coefficients (F_{IS}) for the different species gives high levels of both at the origin of soldiers (point 2). Character optimizing also revealed that founding females at this point had a decreased brood size and lived in smaller, more elongate galls that lasted longer on the host plant. Male founders were lost at points 3 and 4, and reproduction by soldiers was limited because they were more efficient members of the social group in their defensive role. The image at the lower left is a ventral view of the head and thorax of a soldier female, showing the enlarged foreleg weaponry.

SOURCE: Modified from Chapman, T. W., B. J. Crespi, and S. P. Perry, "The Evolutionary Ecology of Eusociality in Australian Gall Thrips: A 'Model Clades' Approach," pp. 57–82 in *Ecology of Social Evolution*. Eds. Judith Korb and Jörgen Heinze, Springer Verlag, Berlin. With kind permission of Springer Science+Business Media and the author. Photo by Laurence A. Mound, D.Sc.

behaviours that parallel the alternative mating strategies of male animals (section 6.4). In social insects, sterile workers appear to make the best of a bad situation by maximizing their kin-selected indirect fitness. In a related wasp, *Metapolybia aztecoides*, West-Eberhard (1979) even suggested a role of worker choice in the establishment of a new queen; workers appear to choose a new queen from displays among individuals that may function as tests of the quality of queen hopefuls.

Preference in the context of social competition also appears to underlie the evolution of ornamentation in yet another context: chicks of the American coot (*Fulica americana*) differ from related species in that they are brightly ornamented with red and orange coloration on their bill and dorsal plumage. Lyon et al. (1994) of the University of Calgary showed that parent coots preferentially feed the most ornamented chicks in their brood. Bright coloration may be an honest indicator of the phenotypic quality of offspring.

6.7 Plant Behaviour

It may seem strange to think about plants exhibiting behaviour, yet they do produce signals and respond to airborne chemicals produced by other plants. Importantly, plants can also respond to their social environments in adaptive ways (Karban, 2008).

For example, when attacked by an herbivore, some species of plants recruit aid by using volatile chemical signals that attract wasp parasitoids of the caterpillars eating their leaves (De Moraes et al., 1998). Other plants chemically attract nematode parasites that attack the beetle larvae that are consuming their roots (Rasmann et al., 2005). These plants may be quite sophisticated in using different chemical blends to target species that are specific natural enemies of the herbivore that is attacking them (De Moraes et al., 1998). This sort of evidence is important because it supports the hypothesis that the plants are actually signalling to their defenders, i.e., ruling out an alternative hypothesis that the defenders are simply attracted to a chemical by-product of herbivory, and that the plant receives benefits only as an incidental effect.

Some plants appear to monitor their environment for threats by eavesdropping on airborne chemicals produced by other species that are under attack by herbivores. Individuals of wild tobacco (*Nicotiana attenuata*) prime their chemical defences when they detect volatile "ouch" chemicals that are released by nearby sagebrush (*Artemesia tridentata*) plants whose leaves have been grazed by grasshoppers (Karban et al., 2003). The selfishness of individual selection rules out the possibility that the sagebrush plants are altruistically signalling the presence of grasshoppers to other plant species.

Evidence that plants can monitor their social environment comes from studies of two species of saltbrush (*Atriplex*). In these dioecious plants (in which individuals are either male or female), the time elapsed before pollen arrives to the stigma is used by females to assess the local sex ratio and thus to adaptively change the sex ratio of their offspring in response (Freeman et al., 2007).

6.8 Ecological and Conservation Consequences of Adaptive Behaviour

In their book *Behavioural Ecology* (1985), Sibly and Smith set out to understand how natural selection acting on individuals can also have effects on populations and ecological communities. Intriguing incidental effects on community structure have come to light, particularly from studies of the manipulation by parasites of their hosts (Lefèvre et al., 2009). Here are several examples:

- Two species of gammarid crustaceans are intermediate hosts for a bird-infecting trematode parasite, but only one of them is manipulated into suicidal behaviour that increases the probability that it will be eaten by a bird. However, non-infected individuals of the manipulated gammarid produce more offspring than those of the less-impacted species. Therefore, the adaptive strategy of the manipulative parasite may have an incidental effect of mediating the coexistence of the two gammarid species by depressing the fecundity of one of them.
- A trematode parasite of fish, the final host, manipulates its intermediate host, the mud snail (*Batillaria cumingi*), to move lower in the intertidal zone, which increases the likelihood of contact with fish. Furthermore, parasitic castration of the snail causes gigantism, which aids the parasite by diverting reproductive resources into the host's soma, and as a side effect, makes the snails more attractive to fish as food. The incidental effects of parasitic manipulation are changes in the use of habitat and resources that potentially reduce competition between parasitized and non-parasitized snails.
- When manipulated by a parasitic thorny-headed worm (phylum Acanthocephala), the freshwater isopod *Caecidotea communis* greatly decreases its consumption of leaf detritus. Because parasitism is greatest in the autumn when most leaf litter falls into streams, a likely side effect of parasitism is a reduction of energy flow through the food web.

Influences of adaptive behaviour on populations can be unexpected and profound. For example, models have revealed that if a **mating system** is **monogamous** (one male breeds with one female) there can be a decrease in population size because of a form of mate discrimination whereby the females that happen to be mated to unattractive males decrease their fecundity (Legendre et al., 1999). However, in most situations it is **polygyny** (one male breeds with several females) that results in high levels of sexual selection on males (resulting from monopolization of females by successful males), and thus appears to have negative effects on populations.

In one example involving intense sexual selection, models show that sexual conflict, such as that resulting in injury to females from re-mating (section 6.4), can reduce the average number of offspring produced by the females, and this "conflict load" can lead to an increased likelihood of population extinction. An empirical example involves sexual dichromatism (the sexes differ in colour), which correlates with intense sexual selection on males and is associated with higher mortality because colourful individuals attract predators and also experience higher levels of parasitism (Doherty et al., 2003). Comparative analyses of bird species showed that dichromatic ones had a 23 percent greater rate of population extinction than those where the sexes are similar in coloration.

This example indicates that the negative effects of sexual selection on populations can have consequences for species conservation. In fact, insights from the theory have been used in efforts to save endangered species. The kakapo (*Strigops habroptilus*) of New Zealand is the largest parrot in the world, and it had been reduced to only 61 individuals at the end of the 20th century. Of these, there were only 21 adult females. Despite high survivorship of this flightless bird on predator-free islands, a strong male bias in the sex ratio of offspring and a naturally low rate of reproduction led to grave predictions about the survival of the kakapo. It turned out, however, that the bias toward sons may have resulted from the high quality of supplemented food (fruits) that was being provided to increase reproductive success. This insight came from a hypothesis in behavioural ecology that predicted that in polygynous species, mothers in good condition should produce more sons that would themselves be of high condition and would consequently have a high mating success (Trivers and Willard, 1973). Therefore, the fitness of the mother would be enhanced by having more grandchildren (notwithstanding that kakapo sons are more costly to produce because they are larger than females). This prediction prompted conservation managers in 2002, a year of relatively high reproduction (kakapo lay eggs in anticipation of high fruit set by local trees), to provide supplemental food only *after* the eggs were laid. The outcome was successful in that not only did virtually all the females reproduce, but also the sex ratio of the nestlings was female-biased (Clout et al., 2002).

A male kakapo *Strigops habroptilus*. This nocturnal flightless parrot is a critically endangered species endemic to New Zealand. Research in behavioural ecology has provided insights into improved conservation actions to increase the reproduction and population status of this species.

Darryl Gwynne

6.9 Human Behaviour

Studies of human behaviour have been traditionally conducted by non-biologists, such as psychologists and sociologists, who do not deal with the adaptiveness of human behaviour. However, the rise of behavioural ecology in the 1970s led some psychologists and biologists to study **human behavioural ecology (HBE)**. Most of the research seeks to understand the fitness consequences of behaviour, often through naturalistic fieldwork involving both "traditional cultures" that have been little influenced by globalization, in addition to people living in urbanized and industrial societies. **Evolutionary psychology** is another approach to the evolution of human behaviour that investigates the cognitive structure of the mind as potentially adaptive. This field relies mainly on laboratory experiments and survey questionnaires to investigate potential mental adaptations, such as sex differences in criteria for selecting a mate (Hames, 2001).

Optimal foraging theory is a major research area of HBE, in which predictions may parallel those tested with other animals, such as the preferential use of high-quality food items when they are common, but a wider variety when they are rare (section 6.2). Such theory has been applied more broadly to include archaeological data, with the suggestion that early human cultures just prior to the emergence of agriculture had already begun to exploit wild plant foods such as grains and tubers (Borgerhoff Mulder, 2003). A more recent application involves software engineers using HBE theories to understand the ways that people can optimize their use of information-gathering tools, such as the World Wide Web (Winterhalder, 2000).

HBE studies have also applied life-history theory to tests of human behaviour. In one study, Margo Wilson and Martin Daly (1997) of McMaster University tested the hypothesis that poor economic opportunities and low life expectancy (from non-homicide factors) lead to an increase in risk-taking, including behaviours that could raise the possibility of suffering a homicide. Their work showed that much of the variation in homicide rates is highly and positively correlated with life expectancy when homicide mortality was statistically removed. As predicted, women with a low life expectancy reproduced at a younger age and had higher fertility.

Central to HBE studies of human mating is the **polygyny threshold model (PTM)**, originally applied to studies of birds, which predicts that women will pair with an already married man if he offers more resources than she can acquire from an unmarried male. Most human societies are polygynous, although as in birds (section 6.4), social monogamy in humans does not necessarily equate to genetic monogamy. In fact, extra-pair paternity is known to occur in most monogamous human societies. Moreover, the phenomenon of "serial monogamy," whereby men (typically of higher status) divorce and marry a series of women typically younger than them, is really a form of polygyny. However, there is only mixed support for the PTM model in humans. In some examples, the fertility of polygynously mated women actually declines, although it is possible that a female gains fitness through grandsons if her sons are polygynous. This model also assumes that women have the freedom to choose, which is not always the case in view of the fact that women in some societies may be coerced into marriage (Hames, 2001).

Rape as an extreme form of sexual coercion has been examined in HBE studies as an alternative mating tactic. (Please note that any evolutionary hypothesizing about human behaviour does not condone the traits being examined. HBE seeks to explain and understand human behaviour—it does not address how we ought to behave.) This led to a prediction by Starks and Blackie (2000) that an increase in serial monogamy, and thus the monopolization of fertile females, would lead to an increase in rape by males who are unable to obtain mates. Divorce rate was used as an index of serial monogamy, and showed a positive correlation with the frequency of rape (U.S. data from 1960 to 1995), which supported this rape hypothesis. However, the study overlooked an alternative hypothesis—that an increase in divorce rate is expected to have led (especially in the post-1960 era of relatively liberal socio-sexual behaviour) to an increase in the *opportunity* to rape, given the probable increase in the numbers of divorced women and men in potential pair-bonding habitats (such as bars and clubs). Importantly, other studies of this adaptive rape hypothesis have provided controls for the opportunity variable by comparing the incidence of rape with those of other forms of violent crime in age classes of women that are most likely to fall victim to rape. The study by Starks and Blackie exemplifies an often overlooked point in hypothesis testing—it is important to not only provide support against or for a hypothesis, but also to rule out alternatives.

6.10 Future Directions

A lack of robustness in hypothesis testing has been one of the criticisms of behavioural ecology—some researchers are accused of "adaptive storytelling"—of outlining hypotheses but not testing them. However, most papers in such leading journals as *Behavioral Ecology* and *Behavioral Ecology and Sociobiology* do contain rigorous empirical tests of hypotheses. Thus, the field continues to represent an exciting "synergy between evolution, ecology and behaviour" (Alonzo, 2008).

A more recent criticism is that behavioural ecologists rarely study the genetic mechanisms underlying models of adaptation. Although we learned that behavioural variation is not necessarily expected to map onto genetic variation (see section 6.1), in many models of adaptation—including adaptive phenotypic plasticity—there are assumptions about genetic mechanisms. Some models have explicit assumptions, such as in the association between genes for ornamentation and preference in runaway sexual selection (section 6.4). As a research direction, Owens (2006) urged behavioural ecologists to take advantage of model systems such as the fruit fly (*Drosophila melanogaster*) and house mouse (*Mus musculus*), in which genetic mechanisms are well known. These species are useful because replication of studies (rare in behavioural ecology; Kelly 2006b) is more feasible than in most behavioural-ecological research, and these model systems can guide research with other species. For example, as emphasized by Fitzpatrick et al. (2005) of the University of Toronto, *candidate genes* in very different animal systems (species) have been shown to underlie complex behaviours, such as foraging. These genes may therefore be useful in understanding general genetic mechanisms controlling adaptive behaviour.

While acknowledging the relevance of model systems and the need for genetic studies, it is also important to recognize that the strength of behavioural ecology—as in all sectors of ecology—is approached when the predictions of theory receive support from the study of a variety of complementary systems. Therefore, a consistently important direction for research is a type of replication in which models are tested with "novel systems," such as species about which we have little behavioural knowledge other than that they appear to have a life history that is appropriate for examining a particular hypothesis about behavioural adaptation.

VOCABULARY OF ECOLOGY

altruism, p. 151
behavioural ecology, p. 137
brood parasite, p. 141
caste, p. 150
coefficient of relationship, p. 152
coevolution, p. 141
convenience polyandry, p. 143
direct fitness, p. 152

CHAPTER 7

Physiological Ecology

RICHARD L. WALKER, Department of Biological Sciences, University of Calgary

River otters, Killarney, Ontario. Photo by Bill Caulfeild-Browne

LEARNING OBJECTIVES

After studying this chapter you should be able to

1. Compare ectothermy and endothermy, and also the responses of heterotherms and homeotherms to changes in ambient temperature, including the control system for thermoregulation in homeotherms, the strategies used by ecotherms to survive extreme cold, and the role of torpor and hibernation in energy conservation.
2. Compare the water-balance and ionic problems faced by marine animals with those faced by freshwater and terrestrial ones, and describe the various strategies used by these animals to cope with their environments.
3. Compare and contrast the means of gas exchange in water-breathing animals with that of air-breathing ones, including the role of respiratory pigments in blood gas transport, and how oxygen binding is affected by changes in blood carbon dioxide and acidity.
4. Describe the various types of blood acid–base disturbances and how they are corrected, including the effects of environmental acidification on the physiology of aquatic animals.

CHAPTER OUTLINE

7.1 Introduction to Physiological Ecology

Physiological ecology is the study of how organisms function in their environment. Physiologists are interested in the internal processes that are essential to survival, and how these biological functions are regulated. Major advances in the fields of physiology and biochemistry during the past century have led to fascinating discoveries about how organisms have adapted to occupy and exploit the astonishing variety of environmental niches on Earth—from the tops of the highest mountains to the depths of the oceans, and from the frigid poles to the tropics.

Much of what we know about physiology and biochemistry comes from research done under controlled conditions in the laboratory. However, much also comes from investigations done under conditions in the field, where organisms are interacting with the opportunities and difficulties of real-world environmental factors. It is a great challenge to integrate knowledge gained from laboratory and field studies to build a realistic understanding of the physiological adaptations of organisms—to comprehend how organisms survive and thrive in the natural world.

This chapter will focus on the physiological ecology of animals. It is divided into four major sections: (1) thermoregulation, (2) water, osmotic, and ionic balance, (3) gas exchange and transport, and (4) acid–base balance. Each section deals with similarities and differences among animals living in water or on land. These topics have been chosen for study because animals face major challenges in coping with such environmental factors as ambient temperature, salinity, oxygen availability, and the need to maintain an acid–base balance in bodily fluids. However, physiological ecology is a big field, and topics that we will not examine here are related to the nervous and endocrine systems and the cardiovascular and gastrointestinal systems. Although our scope is necessarily limited, our focus on the four chosen topics will allow us to view the core issues and methods used by physiological ecologists in their work.

7.2 Thermo-Biology

Introduction

Metabolism and all other physiological functions of life are sensitive to temperature. Despite this fact, animals are remarkably adept at occupying environments that are extreme in terms of temperature—some are adapted to life in the extreme heat of deserts, while others survive in the icy cold of polar regions. How do animals manage to survive under such extreme conditions? In this section we examine the fundaments of thermo-biology and the ways that animals have adapted to cope with the temperatures of their environment.

To begin, we need to understand several key concepts.

- *Heterotrophy*—All animals are **heterotrophs**, meaning they feed upon other organisms as sources of fixed energy and essential organic compounds needed to sustain life, such as proteins, fats, and carbohydrates.
- **Aerobic metabolism**—The consumption and digestion of organic foods occur primarily by **aerobic** metabolism. This means that oxygen (O_2) is involved in the biochemical reactions by which some of the energy of carbohydrates, fats, and proteins is converted into adenosine triphosphate (ATP; this is the principal molecule used to store and transfer energy in cells) via oxidative processes (glycolysis, Krebs cycle, and oxidative phosphorylation). Organelles known as mitochondria are the sites of aerobic metabolism, and the larger their number within the cells of a tissue, the greater is its **oxidative capacity** (this is the ability to use O_2; it is typically measured as mL O_2 per gram of tissue per minute).
- **Anaerobic metabolism**—During times when the O_2 supply is limited, either due to reduced availability in the environment or because demand within cells exceeds the local supply, animals may utilize **anaerobic** metabolism to maintain the necessary production of ATP. Anaerobic metabolism has a much lower efficiency in terms of conversion of the energy content of food into ATP, but it is crucial in maintaining necessary biological functions when the O_2 supply is limited.

Both aerobic and anaerobic metabolisms produce heat as a major waste product.

Metabolic Rate

The **metabolic rate** is most commonly measured as the rate of oxygen consumption, largely because this is a relatively easy measurement for physiologists to make. However, O_2 is consumed only during aerobic metabolism, so alternative measurements must be made for animals that have a substantial anaerobic capacity, such as the rate of heat production or the difference in the caloric contents of ingested food and excreted feces (these two measures are also relevant to aerobic metabolism). When comparing animals that differ in size and shape, it is important to standardize the measurement of metabolic rate, which is often done by expressing it per unit of body mass, such as O_2 consumed per kg·hour, also known as **mass-specific metabolism**. As a general rule, there is an inverse relationship between the mass-specific metabolic rate (O_2/kg·hr) and the body mass—the smaller the animal, the faster the metabolism. This is particularly apparent in small mammals, for reasons that will we examine later in this section.

Heat and Cold

As we examined in Chapter 4, heat is thermal kinetic energy, and cold is a lack of heat. Both are measured as temperature. When objects having different temperatures (including organisms) make contact, the colder one gains heat from the warmer, but according to the first law of thermodynamics, the total amount of energy is conserved.

Animals exchange heat with their environment by several transfer mechanisms, which integrate into a thermal energy budget **(Figure 7.1)**. The most important components of such a budget are the following:

- *Absorption* is the conversion of solar radiation into thermal energy, for instance by a lizard basking in the sun.
- *Radiation* involves the emission of electromagnetic energy by any body with a heat content; the Sun does this, as do all organisms, but at varying rates depending on their surface temperature.
- *Conduction* is heat transfer by the direct contact of masses differing in temperature—the warmer one loses heat to the cooler.

- *Convection* is heat transfer from an organism to cooler air passing over its warmer body surface.
- *Evaporation* is the dissipation of heat by the energy needed to convert water from a liquid state to a gaseous one; the specific heat of vaporization of water is 2.4 kJ/g (580 cal/g), so its evaporation from the body surface is an effective way for an animal (or plant) to cool itself.

Animals can variously heat or cool themselves by any or all these mechanisms—by relaxing in the shade or a breeze if it is hot, or by basking in the sun if it is cold, and by evaporating moisture from the body surface.

The Concept of Q_{10}

All biochemical reactions and physiological functions (such as muscle contraction and neurotransmission) are affected by temperature. In general, the warmer the temperature at which a reaction is occurring, the faster it will run, although the relationship is logarithmic **(Figure 7.2).** This relationship holds true for all biochemical reactions, at least within the range of temperatures that are suitable for the functioning of typical **enzymes** (proteins that catalyze biochemical reactions). Because the metabolic rate is a measure of the combined actions of all biochemical reactions in an organism, it also shows a logarithmic relationship with temperature, as do individual physiological functions such as heart rate and the velocity of nerve conduction. The relationship between temperature and the rate of a function is described by an equation known as the $\mathbf{Q_{10}}$:

$$Q_{10} = K_2(t+10°C)/K_1(t°C)$$

where: k_1 is a reaction velocity at temperature t and k_2 is the velocity at $t + 10°C$.

The usual range of the Q_{10} values for physiological functions and metabolic rate is 2 to 3 (no units; see **Table 7.1**). In essence, this means that we can anticipate a 2- to 3-fold increase in rate for a 10°C increase in ambient temperature (within a temperature range of 10°C–20°C). The value of Q_{10} varies depending on the temperature range because the relationship between metabolism and temperature is logarithmic. The Q_{10} values tend to be more than 3 at temperatures below 10°C, and less than 2 if above 20°C. However, the Q_{10} values may vary among physiological functions being examined, and also among species whose physiological adaptations reflect different climatic regimes.

TABLE 7.1 Q_{10} **Values for Crayfish Heart Rate and Potato Beetle Metabolic Rate (Oxygen Consumption,** VO_2**) at Various Temperatures**

Physiological Reaction	Temperature (°C)	Q_{10}
Crayfish heart rate	10	1.9
	15	1.6
	20	1.4
Potato beetle VO_2	10	2.4
	15	2.5
	20	2.1

SOURCE: Data from Withers , P. C. 1992. *Comparative Animal Physiology.* Saunders, Fort Worth, TX. (See Table 5-1 on p. 124.)

FIGURE 7.1
Mechanisms of Heat Exchange with the Environment. Endothermic animals like the wolf transmit heat to their environment via conduction, convection, and evaporation. They gain heat via radiation of thermal energy from the Sun.

ECOLOGY IN DEPTH 7.1

Scaling and Metabolism

Metabolic rate and body mass are directly related—as mass increases, so does the rate of oxygen consumption. However, the relationship is not linear: a 100 g animal does not have 10 times the metabolic rate of a 10 g one. In fact, the relationship between metabolic rate and body mass is logarithmic and is described by the following equation:

$$\log M = \log a \times b \log W$$

where

- M = the metabolic rate, measured as mL of O_2 consumed per gram of body mass
- W = the body mass (g)
- a = a parameter that is specific to each species
- b = a constant found for all species, including animals, plants, and micro-organisms

Remarkably, the value of b is 0.75 and is the same for all species. This equation, which is sometimes referred to as an allometric equation, is not restricted to metabolic rate. Almost all physiological phenomena, such as heart rate and ventilation rate, are also related to body mass as described by this relationship.

Mass-specific metabolic rate (mL O_2/unit time/unit mass) varies inversely with mass. This is true for all ectotherms and endotherms. In fact, on a per-gram basis, a shrew has about 100 times the metabolic rate of an elephant. At one time the higher mass-specific metabolic rate of smaller compared with larger mammals was explained on the basis of the surface area:volume ratio being larger for smaller animals (Rubner's surface law). This meant that smaller mammals have a greater rate of loss of heat energy, and so they need to maintain a higher metabolic rate to remain homeothermic (see **Figure 7.3**). However, this argument is weakened by the fact that ectotherms also show this relationship—smaller ones have a greater mass-specific metabolic rate. So why is mass-specific metabolic rate inversely related to mass? A number of alternative hypotheses have arisen, but none are adequate to explain the relationship in ectotherms. It is likely that multiple causes contribute to the phenomenon.

Ectothermy and Endothermy

Ectotherms are animals that have a relatively slow metabolic rate, so they rely on the external environment, rather than their internal metabolic one, as a source of heat. Many vertebrate animals, such as fish, amphibians, and reptiles, and almost all invertebrates, must warm themselves by basking in the Sun or by seeking other sources of environmental heat before they can comfortably move about. Ectotherms that live in cool or cold environments, such as all of the climatic regions of Canada, have evolved enzymes that function well at relatively low temperatures, thus allowing their metabolism, locomotion, nerves, and other vital physiological functions to operate and sustain life.

Other animals, such as birds and mammals, have the capacity to produce and retain enough heat from their own metabolism to keep their physiology and biochemical reactions running at a high rate. These animals are known as **endotherms**—organisms that produce their "heat from within." As we will see later, endotherms have evolved ways of conserving their metabolic heat though insulation and adaptive modifications of their circulatory system.

Heterothermy and Homeothermy

Animals also vary in terms of their ability to maintain a steady body temperature. **Homeotherms** are able to maintain a constant body-core temperature independent of the temperature of their environment. **Heterotherms** (or **poikilotherms**) cannot do this—their body temperature rises and falls with that of their environment.

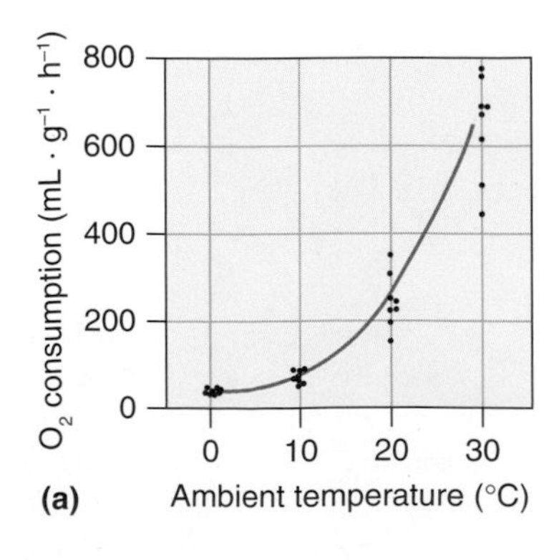

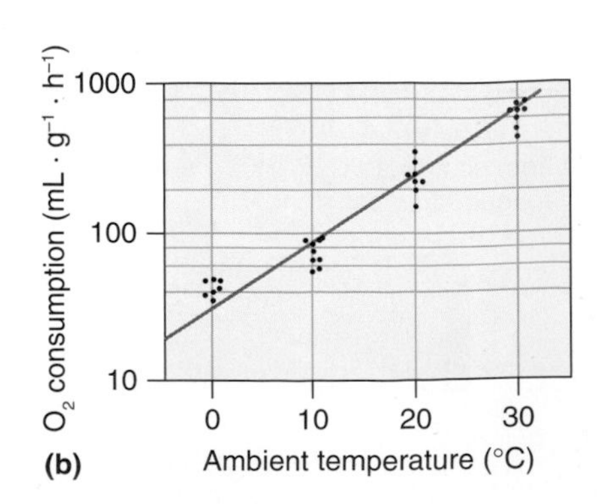

FIGURE 7.2
The Logarithmic Relationship of Physiological Reactions and Temperature. The oxygen consumption from tiger moth (*Arctia caja*) caterpillars was measured at four different temperatures. (a) shows the logarithmic increase in oxygen consumption with an increase in ambient temperature; (b) shows the relationship plotted as the log of oxygen consumption versus temperature.

SOURCE: Randall, D., W. Burggren and K. French. 2002. *Eckert Animal Physiology: Mechanisms and Adaptations*. 5th ed. W. H. Freeman and Co., New York, NY.

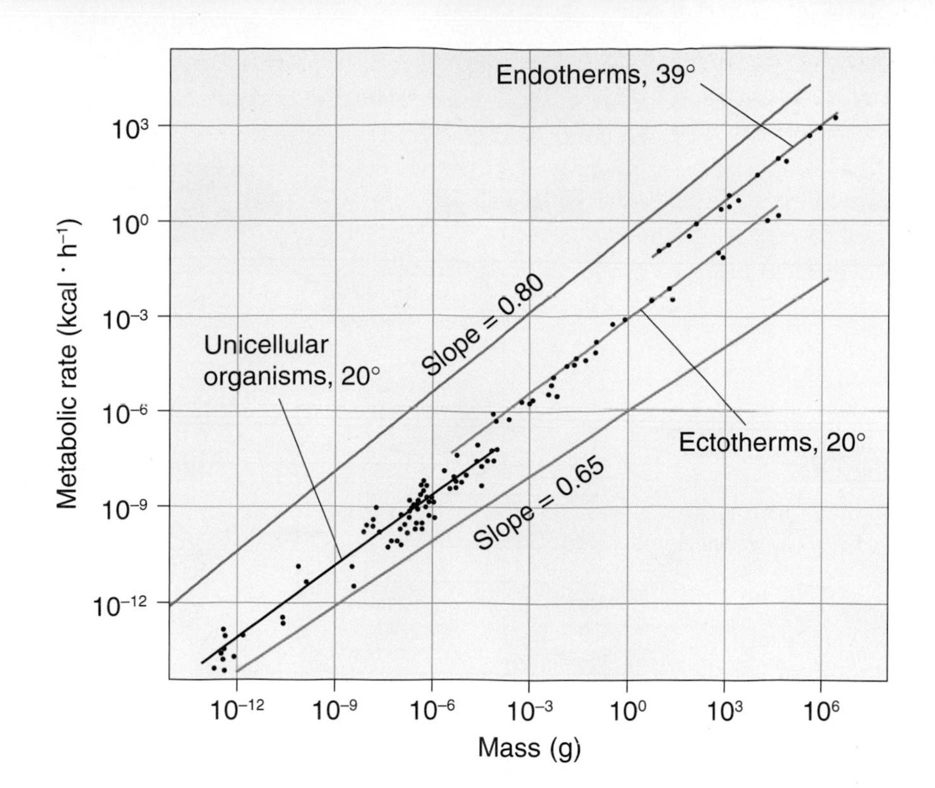

FIGURE 7.3
The Relationship between Body Mass and Metabolic Rate in a Variety of Animals. This plot shows a broad relationship between body mass and metabolic rate across a wide range of organisms, from microbes to large mammals. The three lines are closely parallel, and all of them have the same slope of 0.75.

SOURCE: Modified from Randall, D., W. Burggren and K. French. 2002. *Eckert Animal Physiology: Mechanisms and Adaptations*. 5th ed. W. H. Freeman and Co., New York, NY.

Generally speaking, endotherms are also homeothermic, as is the case of mammals and birds. However, there are cases of animals that are only "partial" endothermic homeotherms. For example, prior to flight on a cool day, bumblebees and large moths warm themselves by "shivering"—they rapidly contract and relax their flight muscles to generate body heat. Moreover, while flying they also generate metabolic heat, which maintains their body temperature above that of the ambient environment. **Figure 7.4** illustrates a range of organisms that are ectothermic homeotherms and endothermic heterotherms, as well as others that are ectothermic heterotherms and endothermic homeotherms.

Thermoregulation

The physiological functions that are involved in maintaining a relatively constant body temperature over a wide range of ambient temperatures are referred to as **thermoregulation**. If an animal is to thermoregulate for a sustained period of time, it must have a high oxidative capacity, thermal insulation, a closed circulatory system, and a nervous system that can respond to changes in body temperature. The emphasis in this section is on thermoregulation by metabolic functions—behavioural responses such as choosing to bask in the sun or cool in the shade are also means of thermoregulation, but we do not examine them here.

High Oxidative Capacity—How Does Metabolism Produce Heat?

About 75 percent of the energy released by the metabolism of glucose is released as heat, and only 25 percent generates molecules of ATP. Because endotherms (mammals and birds) have higher metabolic rates than ectotherms (reptiles, amphibians, fish, and invertebrates), they generate a lot more heat.

A number of small mammals, such as rodents and bats, utilize brown fat (or brown adipose tissue) as a key source of energy. Brown fat is a type of lipid that is stored in adipose cells found between the scapulas, and because it is rich in mitochondria it has a high oxidative capacity. However, the oxidation of brown fat does not produce ATP—all of its embedded energy is liberated as heat. How does this happen? In normal oxidative metabolism, protons are pumped into intermembrane spaces of the mitochondria during electron transport, and they then diffuse into the matrix inside of these organelles. This is coupled to the action of ATP synthase, and it thereby liberates energy needed to produce ATP. However, during times of increased demand for heat production, protons diffuse directly into the mitochondrial matrix through an alternative membrane protein called thermogenin (note that this occurs only in the mitochondria of brown fat cells). No ATP is synthesized in this process, and so all of the energy liberated is in the form of heat.

FIGURE 7.4
Examples of Ectothermy, Endothermy, Heterothermy, and Homeothermy. Animals occur in all four quadrants, and some species may move from one to another depending on the environmental conditions. MR, metabolic rate; T_a, ambient temperature; T_b, body temperature.

SOURCE: Willmer, P., G. Stone and I. Johnston. 2000. *Environmental Physiology of Animals*. Blackwell Science, Oxford, UK.

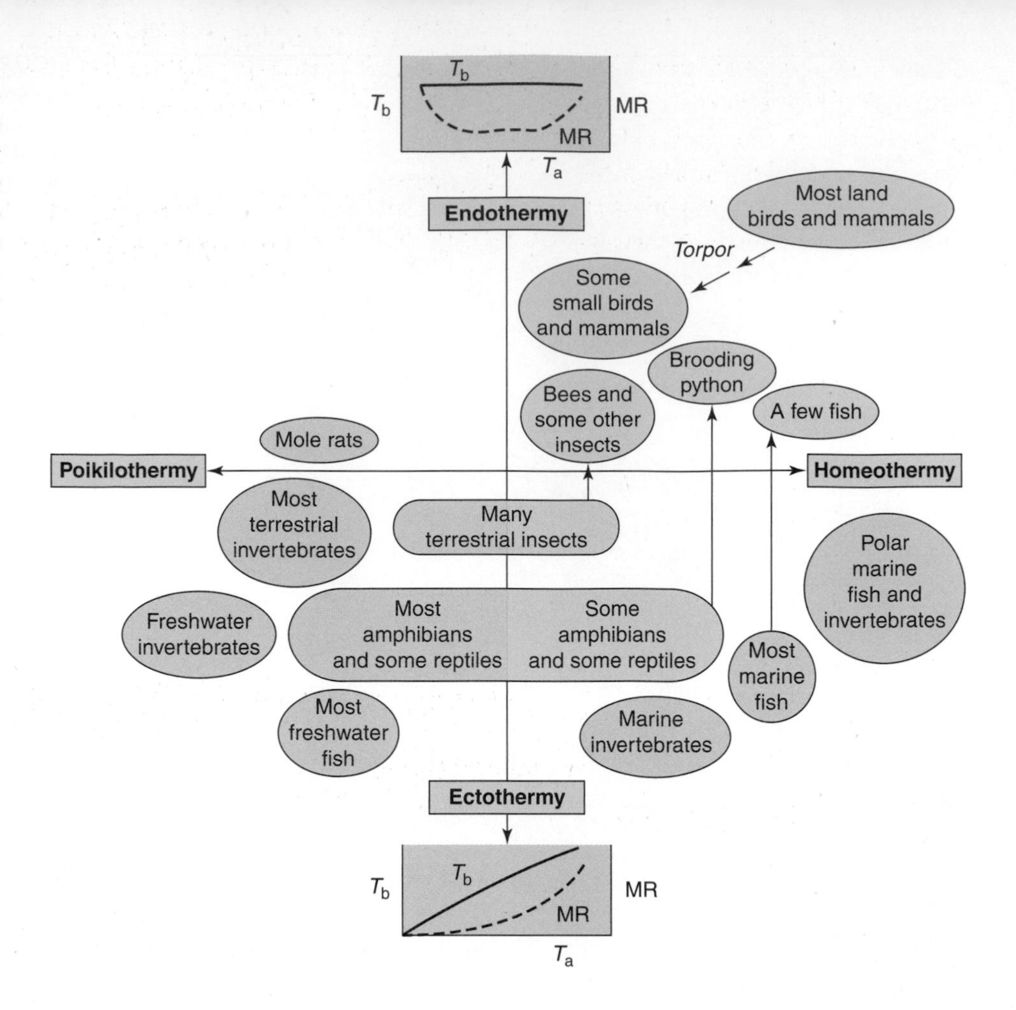

This source of heat is vital for small mammals, which have a high ratio of surface area to body mass and must generate a lot of heat to stay warm (for a similar reason, human infants also oxidize brown fat as a crucial source of heat). The oxidation of brown fat is also important to animals that enter daily or seasonal torpor or hibernation, during which the body temperature decreases. As much as 30 kJ/kg.min (500 W/kg) of heat production can result from the utilization of brown fat, which is about 10 times the thermal energy that is gained from the contraction of skeletal muscles during shivering.

Insulation—Keeping the Heat In

In addition to having a capacity for a high oxidative metabolism, effective thermoregulation also requires a means to conserve the metabolic heat (to limit its loss), which is accomplished by having a layer of insulation between the body core and the environment. Various tissues may be used for this purpose, including sub-dermal fat (just under the skin), as well as feathers in birds and hair in mammals **(Table 7.2)**. The hair and feathers work in much the same way as fibreglass insulation—the idea is to trap a layer of stagnant air among the fibres. Because air is not a good conductor of thermal energy, a trapped layer of air just above the skin reduces the rate of heat exchange with the environment. When they encounter cold air temperatures, most birds and mammals can "fluff up" their feathers or fur to trap additional air. This is accomplished by contracting muscles attached to the base of the feather or hair to cause it to

TABLE 7.2 **The Insulating Properties of Feathers, Fur, and Fat**

Material	Insulation (°C m^2 W^{-1})
Ice	2.9
Water	11
Dry soil	20
Fat	38
Pigeon feather (flat)	99
Sheep wool	102
Goose-down feathers	122
Husky dog fur	157
Lynx fur	170
Still air	270

SOURCE: Willmer, P., G. Stone and I. Johnston. 2000. *Environmental Physiology of Animals*. Blackwell Science, Oxford, UK.

"stand up," a process known as piloerection (in mammals) or ptiloerection (in birds).

Fat is also a good form of insulation, although not as effective as fur or feathers. A thick layer of subcutaneous fat is especially important in mammals that have little fur or hair covering their body, such as whales, seals, and humans. The thermal conductivity of the blubber of minke whales (*Balaenoptera acutorostrata*) is about 0.25 W/mK (watts per meter Kelvin), compared with 0.20 W/mK for human fat (Kvadsheim et al., 1998).

Regulation of Body Temperature—Control of Heat Production and Loss

Thermoregulation depends on the nervous system to monitor and react to changes in body temperature. This sensory function is an example of a **negative feedback system**. It involves the following elements **(Figure 7.5)**:

- a thermo-detector, which is composed of thermo-sensitive receptors;
- an optimal body temperature, known as the set point;
- an integrator that compares the actual body temperature to the desired one; and
- a set of outputs to the cardiovascular system, skeletal muscles, and endocrine system, which stimulate them to generate more or less heat to bring the temperature closer to the set point.

This physiological system works much like that of the thermostat and furnace in a home, which maintains the interior temperature within a comfortable range. The thermostat is set to a desired temperature, which is also a set point. A thermometer feeds information about the room temperature back to the thermostat. If the room temperature is cooler than the set point, the thermostat sends an electric signal to turn on the furnace, which runs until the room reaches the desired warmth.

In an animal, the corresponding function of a thermostat is played by temperature-control centres within the hypothalamus, a part of the brain. The set point, which is also set by the hypothalamus, is the desired body temperature. Thermoreceptors located on the body surface and within the core send information about the temperature of those regions to the hypothalamus. The hypothalamus integrates information about "temperature" relayed by the thermoreceptors, compares it with the desired set point, and makes compensating adjustments to key physiological functions, such as

- the activity of skeletal muscles, which can be stimulated by neural output from the hypothalamus via motor neurons;

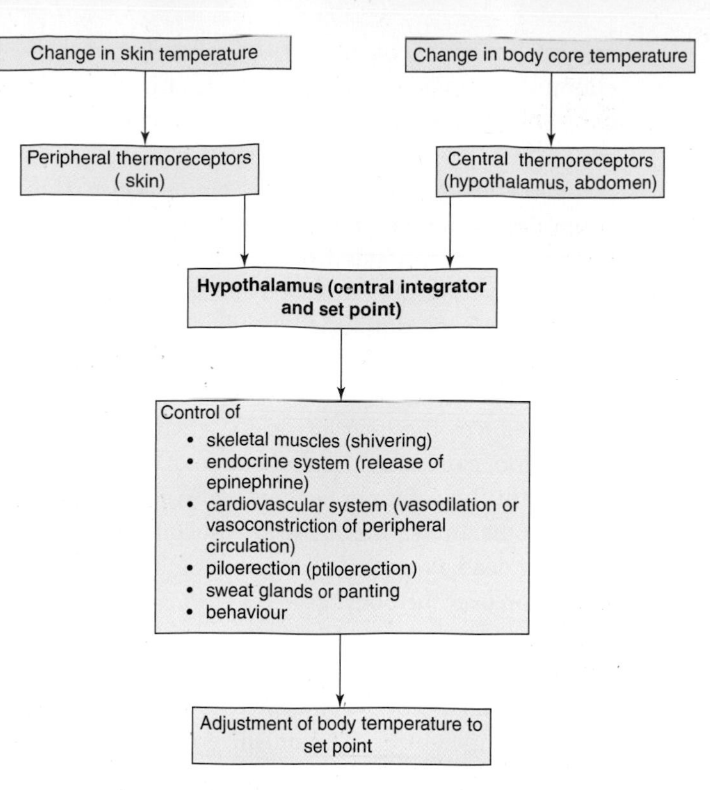

FIGURE 7.5
Negative Feedback Control of Body Temperature. Thermo-sensitive receptors detect changes in the body-surface or core temperature and relay this information to a central integrator (the hypothalamus), which compares it to the desired set point. Adjustments are made to the cardiovascular and endocrine systems, skeletal muscles, etc., to bring the body temperature closer to the set point.

SOURCE: Davenport , J. A. 1992. *Animal Life at Low Temperature.* Chapman and Hall, London. With kind permission of Springer Science+Business Media, and the author.

- adjustments of insulation by piloerection (or ptiloerection), also stimulated by output from the hypothalamus;
- circulation of the blood, for example, by vasodilation or vasoconstriction to adjust the blood supply to the skin;
- evaporative water loss by sweating or panting;
- the metabolic rate, which is influenced by release by the adrenal gland of the powerful, stress-related hormone epinephrine (or adrenaline), which stimulates metabolism; and
- behavioural functions, such as seeking a warmer or cooler environment

All of these adjustments help to adjust the skin and core temperatures closer to the set point.

Response to Cold

Physiological actions that are taken to correct a drop in the temperature of the body surface or core all involve the generation of metabolic heat or its conservation. One of the faster responses is shivering, which involves the rapid contraction and relaxation of skeletal muscles to generate metabolic heat in the body core. Shivering is not a process that can be consciously controlled—it is an automatic response to cold.

Vasoconstriction is another rapid response. It is controlled by the sympathetic nervous system, and is activated by commands from the hypothalamus in response to lowering of the body temperature. Vasoconstriction is accomplished by smooth muscle surrounding the arterioles that supply the skin, and it has the effect of slowing the flow of blood to the surface, which reduces the heat lost to the environment by convection, conduction, and radiation of infrared.

The fluffing of fur or feathers is also controlled by the hypothalamus, and helps to reduce heat loss by trapping dead air as an enhancement of the cover of insulation over the body.

The above three mechanisms are rapidly deployed when the body temperature drops below the set point. An additional mechanism is slower to have an impact on body temperature—it is **non-shivering thermogenesis**, which involves the endocrine system. It is stimulated by the release of the hormone epinephrine from the adrenal gland, which itself is activated by the hypothalamus via the sympathetic nervous system. The epinephrine is released into the circulation of the blood, and it stimulates metabolism mainly by increased lipolysis, which allows lipids (animal fats) to be used as an energy source. Non-shivering thermogenesis is prevalent in animals that have stores of brown fat, including young placental mammals. It is less prevalent in birds.

The behaviour of animals also changes in response to cooling. Individuals tend to seek out microhabitats where there is less opportunity to lose heat by convection, such as warm and windless places. They may also curl up to lessen the area of body surface that is exposed to cold air, thereby reducing heat loss by radiation and convection. Some mammals and a few birds may undergo torpor or hibernation during cold periods, including throughout the winter. **Torpor** is a relatively short-term condition of decreased activity—it is usually characterized by reduced metabolism, slower breathing, and often a lower body temperature. **Hibernation** lasts a longer time, and it involves similar physiological adjustments that are intended to maintain life during a period of prolonged cold temperatures, but at relatively low energy costs to the animal.

Response to Heat

A rise in body temperature above the set point results in the activation of various heat-loss mechanisms. One response is increased sweating and panting, which provide cooling by the evaporation of water—2427 joules (580 calories) of heat energy are dissipated per gram of water evaporated. The evaporation of water is an effective means of cooling if the humidity of the atmosphere is low, but not if it is high because under that condition, evaporation is constrained by the low diffusional gradient.

Another way for an animal to cool itself is by vasodilation to shunt more blood flow to the surface of the body, which increases heat loss by conduction and convection to the environment. In addition, fur and feathers may be flattened closer to the body to reduce their insulating effect. The amount of epinephrine in the blood circulation becomes less, which helps to reduce the metabolic rate so that less heat is generated. Muscular activity is also reduced, again to avoid the generation of metabolic heat.

There are also behavioural responses to heating of the body, such as moving to a cooler environment in a shaded place, burrowing underground, and orienting the body to lessen the surface area exposed to the sun.

Effect of Ambient Temperature on the Metabolic Rate of Endothermic Homeotherms

The metabolic rate of endothermic homeotherms (mammals and birds) varies inversely with the ambient temperature, at least within a certain range. This effect varies among species of endotherms depending on the body size, the amount of insulation, and the ratio of surface area to body volume. **Figure 7.6** is a typical plot of metabolic rate versus ambient temperature. Note that endothermic homeotherms maintain a constant body temperature over a wide range of ambient temperatures, the extremes of which are known the upper and lower incipient lethal limits. If the ambient temperature goes beyond those lethal limits, the animal will become either **hypothermic**, with a dangerously lowered body temperature, or **hyperthermic**, with an excessively elevated one. Animals in these extreme circumstances have exceeded their capacity to thermoregulate, and will soon die if they cannot find a more habitable thermal environment. Between the incipient lethal limits, however, the metabolic rate can be adjusted to thermoregulate by mechanisms described in the previous section.

Note the zone on **Figure 7.6** known as the **thermoneutral zone**, which defines a temperature range between the lethal limits where metabolism is at its lowest and independent of ambient temperature. Within this zone, body temperature is maintained by simply adjusting heat exchange with the environment by vasodilation and vasoconstriction and/or adjustments of the insulating properties of fur or feathers. These mechanisms are not energetically costly, so the metabolic rate is not significantly affected.

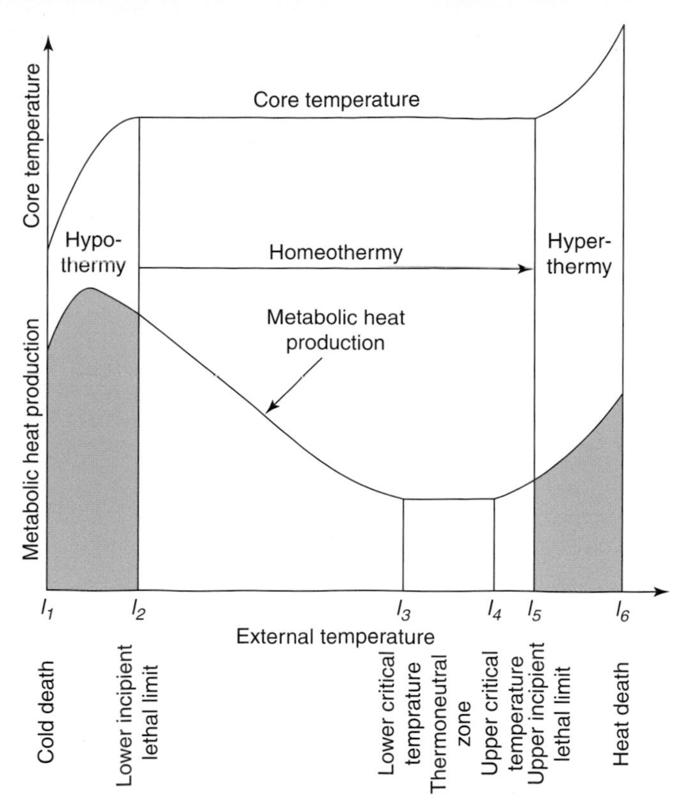

FIGURE 7.6
Body Core Temperature and Metabolic Heat Production as a Function of Ambient Temperature in a Typical Homeothermic Endotherm.

SOURCE: Modified from Hoar , W. S. 1960. *Comparative Biochemistry.* Vol. 1 (Florkin & Mason, eds.). Academic Press, New York.

The limits of the thermoneutral zone are referred to the upper and lower critical temperatures. It is notable that metabolism increases when ambient temperature rises above the upper critical temperature, and also below the lower one. The former change occurs because of increased energy demands for sweat production or panting to decrease body temperature, while the latter is for shivering and non-shivering thermogenesis to provide heat. In humans, for example, sweat production during sustained aerobic exercise, such as while running a marathon, can increase by 50-fold, from about 0.1 to 5 litres per day. Because sweating is an active process that involves the utilization of ATP, a large increase in sweat production will increase the metabolic rate.

The presence of surface insulation has a significant influence on the extent of the thermoneutral zone. As seen in **Figure 7.7,** increasing the amount of insulation extends the thermoneutral zone by lowering the lower critical temperature (LCT). Increased insulation also reduces the rate of increase of the metabolism in response to lowering of the ambient temperature. Both of these responses are due to a reduction in the loss of body heat by conductance to the environment. In a broader context, the effectiveness of insulation is evident when comparing the thermoneutral zones and changes in metabolic rate of tropical versus arctic mammals in response to temperatures below the lower critical temperature **(Figure 7.8).** The grey wolf (*Canis lupus*) has a wide latitudinal range in North America, extending from the northern tip of land on Ellesmere Island to as far south as Mexico (although it is now extirpated from the latter country). The southernmost animals are relatively lean and have a high ratio of surface area to body volume, and also a less-dense pelage, both of which facilitate cooling. In contrast, the northern animals have a lower ratio of surface to volume and much denser underfur to conserve their body heat.

The cold of winter can be a thermoregulatory challenge for endothermic homeotherms in much of Canada. The difficulty is particularly acute in the boreal and arctic zones, where ambient temperatures can fall below –40°C and wind chills close to –60°C. Having a thick layer of insulation is essential at these frigid temperatures. An additional adaptation is known as regional heterothermy, in which the temperature of the body core is maintained while that of the extremities may drop to nearly 0°C. Some mammals hibernate, such as the grizzly bear (*Ursus arctos*) and arctic ground squirrel (*Spermophilus parryii*), but others, such as the arctic fox (*Alopex lagopus*) and caribou (*Rangifer tarandus*), remain active and must have sufficient food or fat reserves to provide energy to maintain their body core temperature and other necessary functions.

Much of the mass of body appendages consists of bone, tendons, skin, and cartilage, none of which produce much heat because they have minimal metabolic rates. There is a small heat production if the muscles

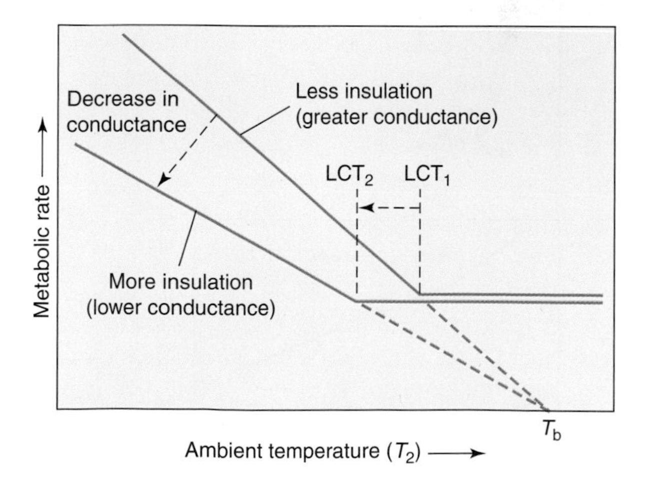

FIGURE 7.7
Surface insulation helps to reduce heat loss, decreases the lower critical temperature (LCT), and increases the breadth of the thermoneutral zone.

SOURCE: Randall , D., W. Burggren and K. French. 2002. *Eckert Animal Physiology: Mechanisms and Adaptations.* 5th ed. W. H. Freeman and Co., New York, NY.

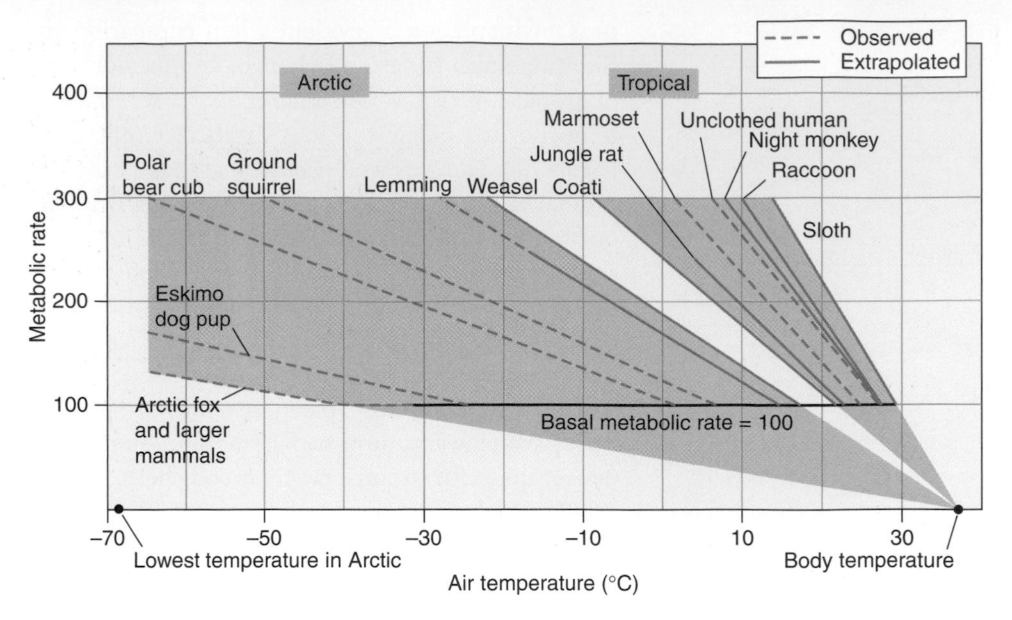

FIGURE 7.8

Range of the Thermoneutral Zones for Tropical and Arctic Mammals. Mammals living in a colder climate have a broader thermoneutral zone and a lower critical temperature.

SOURCE: Figure 7.9 from Scholander, P. F., et al. 1950. *Biological Bulletin* 99: 237–258. Reprinted with permission from the Marine Biological Laboratory, Woods Hole, MA.

are active, but the main source of warmth in appendages is from the flow of blood. However, not much blood flow is needed to maintain the most essential function—that of keeping tissues supplied with nutrients and oxygen. Therefore, restricting the blood flow to appendages is an effective adaptation that helps to prevent the loss of precious heat to the environment, as long as the extremities are not allowed to actually freeze. This is a common physiological trait of many endotherms that live in a cold climate. For example, the temperature of the foot pads of sled dogs may be only slightly above 0°C during the winter even if the ambient temperature is close to −50°C, which is enough to prevent frostbite.

Another adaptation that reduces heat loss in limbs is the presence of **counter-current heat exchanger**, a function that involves the major artery that supplies blood to the extremity, and the corresponding vein that drains back to the body **(Figure 7.9).** The artery supplying warm blood lies in close

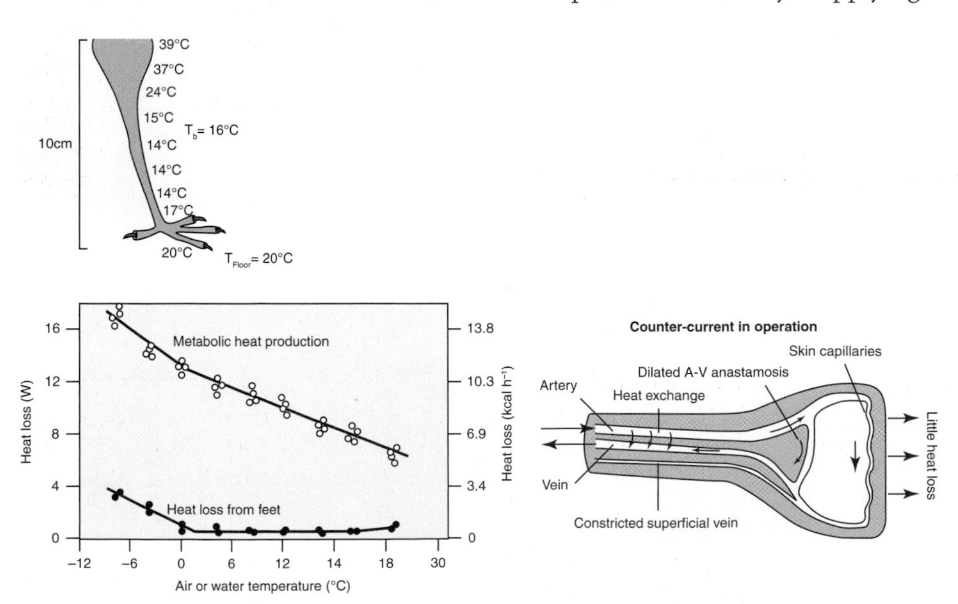

FIGURE 7.9

Counter-Current Heat Exchange. The artery and vein supplying the limb are in close proximity, so heat is exchanged between the two. As warm blood passes down the artery, heat is lost to the cooler venous blood returning from the distal end, thus reducing the amount of heat lost in the limb.

SOURCE: Graph from Kilgore, D. L. and K. Schmidt-Nielsen. 1975. "Heat loss from ducks' feet immersed in cold water," *The Condor*, 77: 475–478. (Page 477, Figure 3.) Drawings from Willmer, P., G. Stone and I. Johnston. 2000. *Environmental Physiology of Animals*. Blackwell Science, Oxford, UK.

ECOLOGY IN DEPTH 7.2

Torpor in Bats

The western long-eared bat (*Myotis evotis*) and big brown bat (*Eptesicus fuscus*) are examples of homeotherms that exhibit daily torpor. These bats are common along cliffs of the South Saskatchewan River in southeastern Alberta, where they have been studied by Robert Barclay and his students at the University of Calgary (Lausen and Barclay, 2003). The bats roost in cracks and crevices during the day and leave those refuges in the early evening for a night of foraging for flying insects, which they hunt by echolocation. When the bats return to the roost in the early morning, they allow their body temperature to drop close to that of ambient environment. Females of both species that are not pregnant or lactating use daily torpor more frequently than those that are reproductively active. However, the additional energy expenditure of non-torpor is offset by the enhanced ability of these females to bring their pregnancy to term, and to feed and raise their young during the short breeding season.

Big brown bat (*Eptesicus fuscus*).

proximity to the vein draining cooler blood, and the flow is in opposite directions in the two vessels, hence the term counter-current. As blood travels down the artery, heat moves from it to blood in the vein; this occurs because the arterial fluid is warmer than the venous all along the length of the limb. By the time the venous blood reaches the body at the upper end of the limb, there is only a slight difference in temperature from the arterial blood coming from the body core. At the other end (the distal one), the temperature of the arterial blood approaches that of the venous when the foot or hand is reached.

Torpor, Hibernation, and Estivation—Controlled Hypothermia

In an energetic sense, it is "costly" to maintain a constant core temperature. To conserve their energy, some animals allow their body temperature to decrease when they are sleeping and not behaviourally active. This function is known as hypothermy. Daily bouts of hypothermy are referred to as daily torpor, and they occur in many small mammals that live in temperate regions, such as rodents and bats (see Ecology in Depth 7.2) Alternatively, some homeotherms that live in boreal and arctic latitudes may undergo extended periods of hypothermy during the winter months, which is referred to as seasonal torpor or hibernation. Some animals even undergo prolonged periods of hypothemia during part of the summer, a phenomenon known as **estivation.** In all of these conditions—torpor, hibernation, and estivation—the body temperature is allowed to drop closer to that of the ambient environment. The process of entry into hypothermia is similar in both torpor and hibernation, and re-warming is also accomplished using the same mechanisms.

Hibernation is utilized by mammals from six different orders, including species of marmots, ground squirrels, mice, and bats. During the winter months in non-hibernating mammals, there is a steep thermal gradient between the body core and the ambient environment, which is energetically expensive to maintain. Rather than doing this, a hibernating mammal allows its body temperature to drop to just above freezing (about 5°C) for weeks on end, arousing only occasionally **(Figure 7.10).** The heart rate and ventilation frequency also drop dramatically. By the way, bears are not true hibernators because they do not undergo these dramatic changes in their physiology—in essence, they just enter a long and deep sleep during the winter.

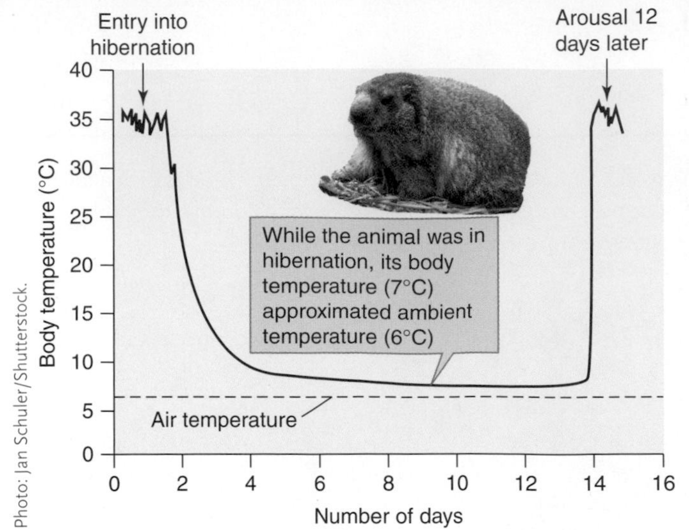

FIGURE 7.10

Effect of Hibernation on Body Temperature. Body temperature decreases with the onset of hibernation in the woodchuck (*Marmota monax*) and is maintained just above the ambient temperature.

SOURCE: Reprinted from Hill, R. W. 1975. "Daily torpor in *Peromyscus leucopus* on an adequate diet," *Comparative Biochemistry and Physiology—Part A: Physiology*, 51: 413–423, with permission from Elsevier.

Estivation is similar to hibernation in that homeotherms allow their body temperature and other physiological function to decrease substantially. Unlike hibernation, however, estivation occurs when the environment becomes exceedingly hot and dry. Estivation is beneficial in that reduced metabolism means less demand for oxygen, so there is reduced water loss associated with breathing. Estivation is relatively common among small mammals and a few birds of desert regions, as well as in many reptiles and amphibians.

In mammals the arousal from torpor or hibernation involves intense shivering and non-shivering thermogenesis utilizing stores of brown fat. The energetic cost of arousal is significant and is a factor in the overall cost–benefit equation of controlled hypothermia.

Endothermy and Homeothermy in Insects

Most insects are ectothermic heterotherms. However, there are a few exceptions that are endothermic during flight, owing to heat that is generated during vigorous muscle contractions. A few larger insects might also be considered to be homeothermic, in the sense that they can maintain their thorax temperature within a narrow range somewhat independent of that of the air. The homeothermic insects include species of sphinx moths (family Sphingidae), bumblebees (*Bombus* species) and the honeybee (*Apis mellifera*), all of which vigorously shiver their thoracic flight muscles in a "pre-flight warm-up" if their body is too cool to allow them to fly **(Figure 7.11)**.

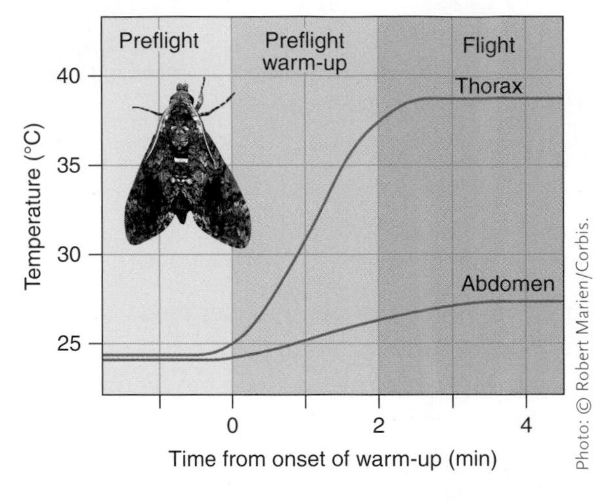

FIGURE 7.11

Pre-Flight Warm-Up in the Hawkmoth (*Manduca sexta*). Rapid contraction and relaxation ("shivering") of thoracic flight muscles helps to warm the animal to a high enough temperature to allow it to fly.

SOURCE: Heinrich , B., and G. A. Bartholomew. 1971. "An analysis of pre-flight warm-up in the sphinx moth *Manduca sexta*," *Journal of Experimental Biology*, 55: 233–239. http://jeb.biologists.org/cgi/content/abstract/55/1/223.

Tolerance to Extreme Cold

In regions with a seasonal climate that includes a cold winter, such as anywhere in Canada, many aquatic heterothermic animals burrow into mud at the bottom of ponds. This avoids freezing temperatures, because freshwater bodies deeper than 10–30 cm (depending on the local climate) do not freeze to the bottom. However, some heterothermic animals do have to cope with exposure to sub-freezing temperatures. One that has been well-studied is the wood frog (*Rana sylvatica*), a wide-ranging species in Canada that occurs in almost all forested areas, even in the boreal zone. This amphibian is remarkable for its ability to survive being frozen solid. The physiological mechanism that allows it to do this was discovered by Ken Storey and his collaborators at Carleton University (Storey and Storey, 1996). It involves ice being able to form in the extracellular fluids of tissues of the wood frog, but not in the intracellular fluids (i.e., within cells). If ice did form within cells, then their sharp crystals would pierce the membranes, which would rupture the cells and cause them to die.

Wood frogs and other animals that can tolerate freezing prepare for the cold of winter by producing anti-freeze compounds that enter the intracellular and extracellular fluids. These compounds are called **cryoprotectants**. Glucose is one such anti-freeze compound—it is produced in abundance from glycogen stores in the liver. A high concentration of glucose lowers the freezing point of aqueous fluids, which can prevent freezing from occurring (as in intracellular fluids) or at least slows the rate of freezing so that only small ice crystals form, which are less deadly to cellular membranes. When a wood frog first encounters extreme cold in its early-winter environment, slightly less than the freezing point of water at 0°C, there is a slow formation of ice in the extracellular fluids, which triggers the abundant release of glucose into the blood circulation. Some of this glucose becomes absorbed into cells, building to a high concentration that lowers the freezing point of the intracellular fluid. As more ice forms in the extracellular fluid, the unfrozen solution becomes increasingly more concentrated in solutes and thus, by the process of osmosis, draws water out from the cells. This causes the concentration of osmotically active chemicals in the intracellular fluid to increase to the degree where it does not freeze even in the slightly sub-zero temperatures that may occur in the benthic environment. From this point on, as much as 80 percent of the extracelluar fluid may freeze into ice, but the physical integrity of the cell is maintained because ice crystals do not form within the cells.

In the springtime, as temperatures slowly rise, the frozen wood frogs thaw. However, they do this from the inside outward, rather than the other way around. This occurs because the concentration of extracellular glucose is highest in vital internal organs, such as the heart and circulatory system, which have the lowest freezing point and so thaw first. In fact, wood frogs are the first amphibians, and among the first heterothermic animals, to emerge in the springtime.

Freeze-tolerance is actually quite widespread among animals that inhabit frigid environments. There are many examples of insects that overwinter by tolerating extremely cold temperatures, and then come to life in the spring to resume a new season of reproduction and growth (Danks et al., 1994; Danks, 2004—see Environmental Applications 7.1, p. 177). Most species use cryoprotectants of various kinds to protect their tissues, often low-molecular-weight compounds such as polyhydric alcohols (e.g., glycerol). However, some species **supercool**, meaning their body water remains unfrozen even in sub-zero temperatures because of the absence of seed crystals (or nuclei) around which ice crystals can form. Some arctic gall midges (tiny flies in the family Cecidomyiidae) may remain unfrozen even at temperatures as low as −62°C.

Similarly, many bony fish (teleosts) that live in polar waters, in which the temperature may be below zero much of the year, produce anti-freeze compounds (proteins and glycoproteins) or undergo supercooling, or both, to avoid freezing (see Ecology in Depth 7.3, p. 176). Polar marine fish living in shallow water typically rely on an accumulation of anti-freeze compounds to lower the freezing point of their body fluids, while deep-water ones utilize supercooling. As long as a supercooled fish does not encounter ice in its environment, it will remain unfrozen. However, as soon as ice is encountered, rapid freezing occurs and so does death. However, ice is rarely if ever encountered in deep polar water.

Adaptations of Ectotherms to Changes in Temperature

Most ectotherms are at the mercy of their environmental temperature, changes of which will directly affect their metabolism. Nevertheless, there are tactics that ectotherms can utilize to decrease the effects of changes in ambient temperature. These include certain behaviours, acclimatization, the production of specific enzymes suitable for particular temperature ranges, and changes to the properties of their cell membranes.

Behavioural Thermoregulation

Behavioural thermoregulation involves moving from a cooler environment to a warmer one, or vice versa. For example, reptiles and amphibians can raise their body temperature above that of the ambient environment by basking in the sun. Desert-dwelling reptiles are especially adept at behavioural thermoregulation, moving in and out of the sun, or flattening or raising

ECOLOGY IN DEPTH 7.3

The Convergent Evolution of Cryoprotectants in Fish: Similar Solutions to Similar Problems

The evolution of cryoprotectants in a number of different species of fish, insects, plants, and even bacteria appears to be a fairly recent event, perhaps in response to the ice ages that have sporadically occurred over the past 30 million years. This represents an example of convergent evolution, in which unrelated organisms living in similar environments have evolved similar traits or adaptations. One well-known case is the development of anti-freeze glycoproteins in Arctic cod (*Boreogadus saida*) and Antarctic toothfish (*Dissostichus mawsoni*) (Chen et al., 1997; Ewart et al. 1999). Both of these fish thrive in waters where the temperature is below the freezing point of oceanic saltwater (−1.9°C). Remarkably, although they are literally "poles apart" in terms of their biogeography and phylogeny (they are classified in different orders and superorders), the anti-freeze glycoproteins that they produce are almost identical in molecular structure. However, the genes that encode the sequences of amino acids for these glycoproteins have different origins and the codons within the genes are different. Furthermore, the molecular evidence for convergent evolution is supported by morphological, paleontological, and paleoclimatic evidence. Going far back in time, the two species appear to have diverged from a common ancestor at least 40 million years ago. This is well before the first cooling and glaciations of the Antarctic (10–14 million years ago) and Arctic regions (2.5 million years ago) that apparently led to the separate evolution of anti-freeze compounds in these fish.

their bodies off a substrate to maintain a comfortable body temperature. This does not mean that these animals are homeothermic, because they do not have the capacity to maintain a constant body temperature regardless of ambient conditions. However, on a sunny day they may be able to keep their temperature within a range that allows their muscles to contract rapidly, which is an advantage when trying to capture fast prey or when avoiding their own predators.

Some aquatic animals, such as lake trout (*Salvelinus namaycush*), will change their location to select cooler or warmer waters to maintain a comfortable body temperature. In most Canadian lakes, a warmer layer of water up to two metres deep (called the epilimnion) develops at the surface during the summer; it sits upon the cooler hypolimnion, and remains intact until the autumn, when the surface cools and the stratification is dispersed by strong winds.

There are constraints to behavioural thermoregulation. On cloudy or otherwise cool days, ectotherms may have difficulty finding warm places where they can raise their body temperature. Similarly, fish may not be able to find an ideal water temperature if their lake does not stratify during the summer.

Acclimatization

Acclimatization is a process of physiological adjustment that occurs in animals that are living in conditions outside of their comfort zone but within their physiological limits (the related term **acclimation** is used when only one environmental factor is involved). A familiar example involves people who live at high altitudes, more than about 3000 m above sea level, who have little difficulty exerting themselves in physical activity despite the relatively low atmospheric pressure and constrained oxygen supply to their blood and muscles. In contrast, people who are used to living closer to sea level may feel weak and dizzy at high altitudes, and they are vulnerable to a circulation-related sickness called pulmonary edema. This is the reason that mountain climbers typically spend some time acclimatizing to high-altitude conditions, before they ascend to even higher ones.

This is also the case with ectothermic animals that are acclimated to a particular ambient temperature. Many studies done with fish and aquatic invertebrates have demonstrated a remarkable ability to adjust to new habitats by acclimating their cellular biochemistry to allow normal physiological functioning. Much of the research on thermal acclimation has been done in the laboratory, where temperature,

ENVIRONMENTAL APPLICATIONS 7.1

The Mountain Pine Beetle and Anti-Freeze

Since its beginning in the late 1990s an infestation of the mountain pine beetle (*Dendroctonus ponderosae*) has devastated vast tracts of pine forest in the interior of British Columbia. When abundant, the larvae of this native beetle kill trees because their feeding tunnels in the cambium, a vital tissue located just under the bark, eventually become extensive enough to girdle the tree, meaning water can no longer be transported upward to the foliage or sugars downward to the roots. Other than cutting infested trees, there is little that forest managers can do to mitigate this natural disaster. As of 2008, about 14.5 million hectares of pine forest had been severely damaged, and the epidemic is still expanding. This forest damage has been devastating to the economically vital forest industry of central British Columbia.

The beetle thrives in the hot dry conditions of the summer in central British Columbia. The adults emerge from mid-July to late August. They fly seeking uninfested trees, where they mate and lay eggs under the bark, especially on lodgepole pine (*Pinus ponerosa*). After about two weeks, the eggs hatch and the larvae bore into the cambium, where they overwinter. During the late fall, the larvae produce anti-freeze compounds, mostly glycerol, which help them survive at temperatures as low as about –20°C during the winter months (Regniere and Bentz, 2007). However, if the ambient temperature falls to –35°C or lower for several days in a row, large numbers of the larvae are killed.

These kinds of deadly temperatures occurred routinely during most winters and they kept the populations of the mountain pine beetle in check. More recently, however, winter temperatures in the central interior of British Columbia have moderated—this may be a signal of a local consequence of global warming (see Chapter 3). Because beetle-killing temperatures have been uncommon, many larvae survive the winter to further the infestation.

In addition to warmer winters, the beetle irruption has likely been promoted by forest-management practices, especially the routine quenching of forest fires, a practice that promotes the extensive occurrence of mature pine forests—just the kind of menu that this pest favours.

Adult mountain pine beetle.

Aerial view of extensive attack by mountain pine beetle.

photoperiod, and other environmental factors can be controlled. Usually, investigations under these artificial conditions are measuring the ability of animals to acclimate to sudden changes in ambient temperature. For example, Dawson and Bartholomew (1956) did a classic series of experiments in which the western fence lizard (*Sceloporus occidentalis*) and side-blotched lizard (*Uta mearnsi*) were acclimated to either 16°C or 33°C **(Figure 7.12).** Following initial measurements of metabolic rate at the temperature of acclimation, the lizards were subjected to a rapid change in ambient temperature and the metabolic rate was measured again. This was repeated over a series of temperature changes—for example, lizards initially acclimated to 33°C experienced rapid changes to 28°C and then to 16°C. Likewise, animals acclimated to 16°C were rapidly exposed to 28°C and then 33°C. The lizards acclimated to 16°C had a significantly higher metabolic rate at all temperatures than did the animals acclimated to 33°C.

What is remarkable about this study is the fact that the *difference* in metabolic rates of the animals tested at their acclimation temperature was less than what was predicted by the sudden change in ambient temperature. In other words, something had occurred during acclimation that kept the metabolic rate of the two groups closer. Subsequent research by other investigators revealed that the acclimation of metabolic rate is attributable to changes in the activity of key enzymes that are involved in oxidative metabolism. Members of the same species acclimated to cooler temperatures have higher activity of these enzymes than do their counterparts acclimated to warmer conditions. This means that animals acclimated to cooler temperature are able to boost their metabolic rate, thus reducing the potentially negative effect of ambient temperature on their metabolism.

Isozymes

Isozymes are slightly different versions of a particular enzyme, and they may vary in their efficiency at different reaction temperatures. This is important because enzyme-substrate affinity is vital to the efficiency of biochemical reactions in the metabolism of organisms, and that relationship is affected by temperature. The relationship is indirect, in that enzyme-substrate affinity is lower at higher temperatures and higher at lower ones. Ideally, a biochemical reaction would be more efficient if the enzyme-substrate affinity did not change. However, during the acclimation process, animals have the remarkable ability to alter the enzyme-substrate affinity relationship by producing various isozymes (or isotypes) of key enzymes, each functioning optimally within a particular temperature range.

Peter Hochachka and George Somero of the University of British Columbia were among the first ecophysiologists to study the influence of isozymes in ectothermic animals. Their research on lactate dehydrogenase (LDH) showed that fish acclimatized to different ambient temperatures produced different isozymes of LDH. When they compared the enzyme-substrate affinities of the isozymes, it was apparent that they were similar when tested at their acclimation temperature **(Figure 7.13).** Therefore, the efficiency of

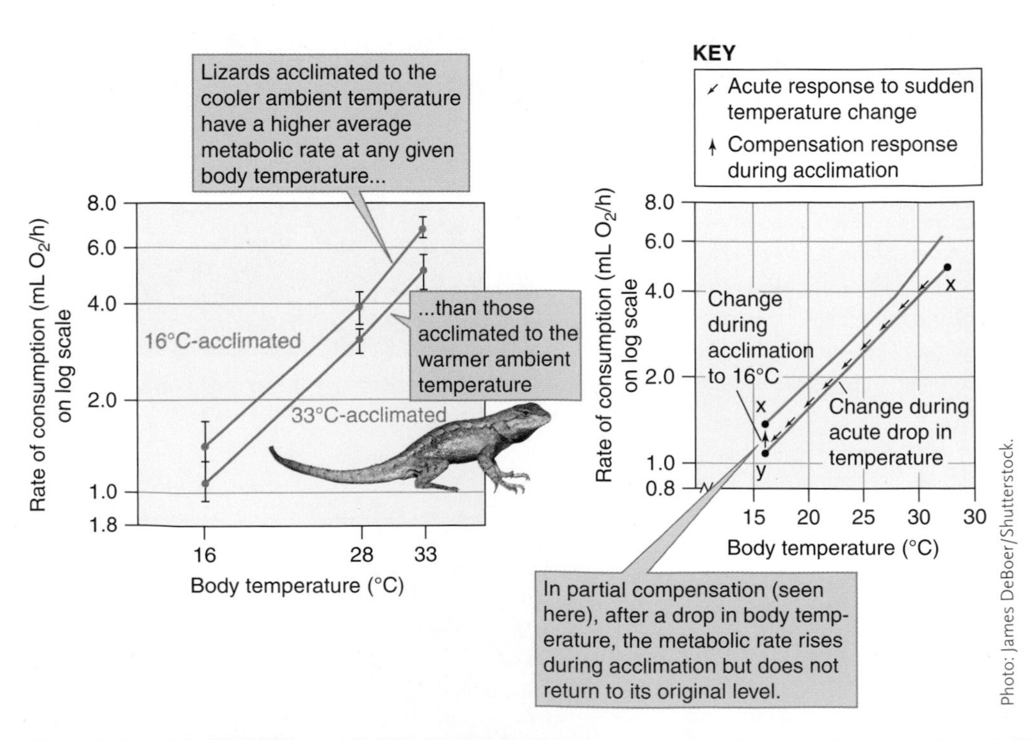

FIGURE 7.12
Effect of Acclimation Temperature on Metabolic Rate. Fence lizards (*Sceloporus occidentalis*) that were acclimated to 16°C had a higher metabolic rate than those acclimated to 33°C at all temperatures tested.

SOURCE: Dawson , W. R. and G. A. Bartholomew. 1956. "Relation of oxygen consumption to body weight, temperature, and temperature acclimation in lizards *Uta stansburia* and *Scelopwus occidentalis*" *Physiological Zoology*, 29: 40–51.

the biochemical reactions mediated by the LDH was maintained, reducing the effects of temperature on metabolic rate.

Properties of Cell Membranes Can Also Be Affected by Body Temperature

Cellular membranes are composed largely of phospholipids and cholesterol. Typically, when oils or other liquids containing lipids (fats) are subjected to cold, they solidify. When this occurs to the lipids in cell membranes, it changes their properties, which affects the viscosity (or fluidity) and flexibility of the membrane. This can be a physiological problem for ectotherms when they are exposed to changes in ambient temperature. However, membrane fluidity can be altered by changing the composition of the phospholipids found in cell membranes, particularly by adjusting their content of unsaturated fatty acids. In another study by Hochachka and Somero (1984), membrane fluidity was compared among fish species that were adapted to different temperatures. They found that the unsaturated fatty acid content of phospholipids is higher in membranes of animals that live in colder temperatures. Because of this adaptation, the membrane fluidity of the cells of cold-water fish is close to that of warm-water species. In fact, the similarities of membrane fluidity are as close as those of species of endotherms, such as mammals and birds. This effect is referred to as homeoviscous adaptation.

7.3 Water and Ion Balance

The Importance of Ions and Water to Life

Liquid water is essential for life. All animals must have a source of water to replace fluids lost due to evaporation, urination, and defecation. Animals obtain water by drinking, absorbing it by osmosis across their integument (body coating), or as a product of their oxidative metabolism (for example, when glucose is oxidized, carbon dioxide and water are by-products). Water typically composes 60–90 percent of the body mass of an animal, and it is compartmentalized

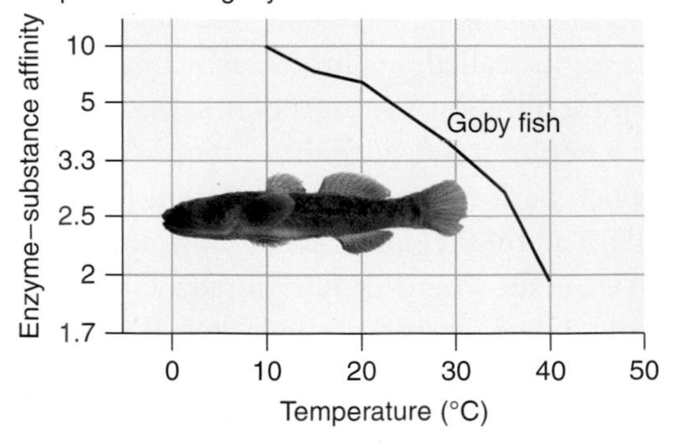

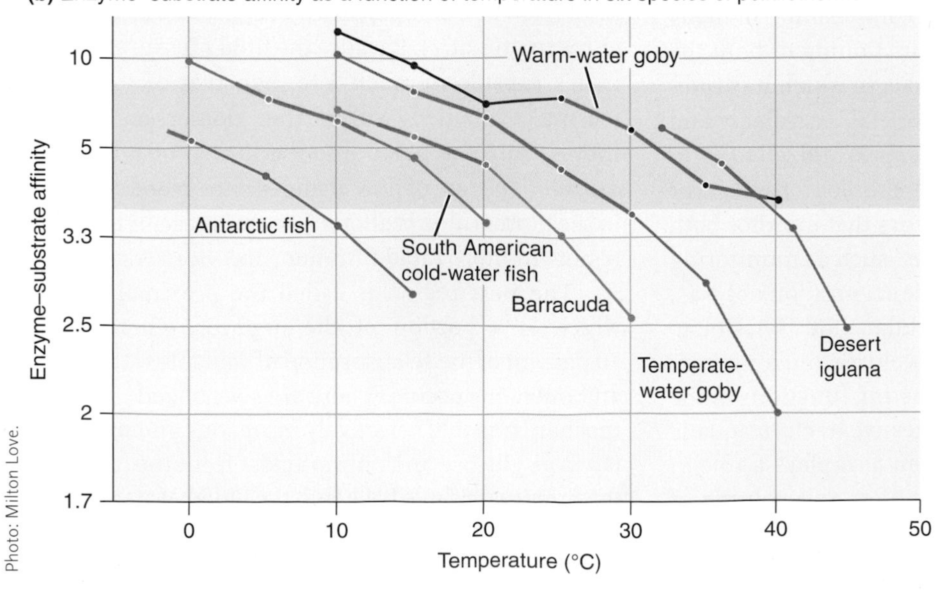

FIGURE 7.13
Lactate Dehydrogenase Enzyme-Substrate Affinity versus Acclimation Temperature in Fish. Note that the affinity for pyruvate (the substrate) is similar within the normal acclimated range of ambient temperature typical for each fish (shown in blue in part (b) below).

SOURCE: Hochachka , P. W. and G. N. Somero. 2002. *Biochemical Adaptation: Mechanism and Process in Physiological Evolution.* Oxford University Press, New York, NY. By permission of Oxford University Press, Inc.

into intracellular and extracellular fluids. In this section, we will examine the ways that animals regulate the water content of their bodies to prevent overhydration or dehydration. The intake of water must balance its loss; otherwise intracellular or extracellular volume might expand or contract excessively, either of which could be problematic.

Water enters cells via proteinaceous water channels known as aquaporins, which extend through the phospholipid bilayer of the cellular membrane. The net direction of water movement is determined by the concentration of solutes (mostly ions and proteins) dissolved in water on either side of the membrane. Because membranes are selectively permeable to some solutes but not others, an imbalance in the concentration of dissolved substances inside and outside of a cell may be corrected fairly quickly by simple diffusion across the membrane until an equilibrium is reached. However, because non-diffusible solutes, such as certain large proteins, cannot cross cell membranes, an imbalance in their concentration results in the movement of water molecules until the osmotic concentration (or osmolarity) of particles becomes equal on either side. Osmosis is the diffusion of water through a semi-permeable membrane along a gradient from a lower concentration of solutes (or low osmolarity of non-diffusible solutes) to a higher one; this is also known as the osmotic gradient.

Most cells cannot tolerate much change in their volume. Therefore, animals must limit the amount of difference in the solute concentrations between their extracellular and intracellular fluids to prevent large differences in osmotic concentration across cell membranes. This is done mostly by regulating two physiological variables: (1) the ionic composition of the extracellular fluid, and (2) the amount of water in the extracellular fluid.

Regulation of the ionic composition of body fluid is essential for proper functioning of both the nervous system (even in animals in which it is rudimentary) and muscles (skeletal, cardiac, and smooth). A variety of mechanisms is utilized to regulate the ionic composition of the body fluids. For example, mammals have sensors that monitor both the volume (via indirect means, such as monitoring vascular pressure) and ionic concentrations of Na^+, K^+, and Ca^{2+} in their extracellular fluid. Physiological adjustments that regulate volume and ionic concentration mostly involve adjusting functions of the renal organs (kidneys) and digestive tract. In aquatic animals, the respiratory system also plays a role in regulating the ionic concentration and volume of extracellular fluids.

Role of the Renal Organ

Most animals have a renal organ, also known as a kidney or excretory organ, that regulates ions and water in their extracellular fluids. The structure of the renal organ varies among animals, depending on their phylogenetic relatedness, but they all perform the same basic functions. These include filtration of the extracellular body fluids, re-absorption of essential ions and nutrients from the filtrate, secretion of non-filterable solutes into the filtrate, and excretion of excess ions, water, and nitrogenous wastes **(Figure 7.14)**.

The simplest forms of renal organs are tubiform structures, such as the metanephridia found in each segment of an earthworm, and the antennal glands of crustaceans. One end of the tube is porous to ions, water, various nutrients, and usually small peptides. However, large proteins such as albumens cannot move into the tube. Sometimes the filtrate is referred to as an ultrafiltrate because its concentration of proteins and other large solutes is so low. As the filtrate passes along the tube, water, ions, and nutrients (such as glucose) are re-absorbed back into the extracellular fluid, leaving behind excess water, ions, and nitrogenous waste products of metabolism, such as ammonia or urea. These "excess" materials are excreted into the environment.

The renal organs of vertebrate animals contain numerous units called nephrons, which are also responsible for filtration, re-absorption, secretion, and excretion. A nephron is divided into different regions, each of which performs a slightly different function **(Figure 7.15)**. The first region is called Bowman's capsule and it is the site where the ultrafiltrate of the extracellular fluid (blood plasma) accumulates. Bowman's capsule surrounds a capillary network called the glomerulus, from which filtration of fluid into Bowman's capsule occurs by **bulk flow** (this is the movement of fluid from one compartment to another due to differences in pressure). Because the fluid pressure in Bowman's capsule is much less than that of the blood plasma contained within the glomerulus, liquid moves from the blood into the lumen of Bowman's capsule. The rate of flow changes if the blood pressure in the glomerulus is altered—an increase in pressure results in more rapid filtration, and vice versa.

The next region is called the proximal tubule, which is a portion of the nephron where about 70 percent of the re-absorption of valuable water, ions, and nutrients occurs. There are specialized transport mechanisms that selectively move ions and nutrients (such as glucose and amino acids) from the lumen of the proximal tubule back into the blood; water follows the movements of these solutes by osmosis.

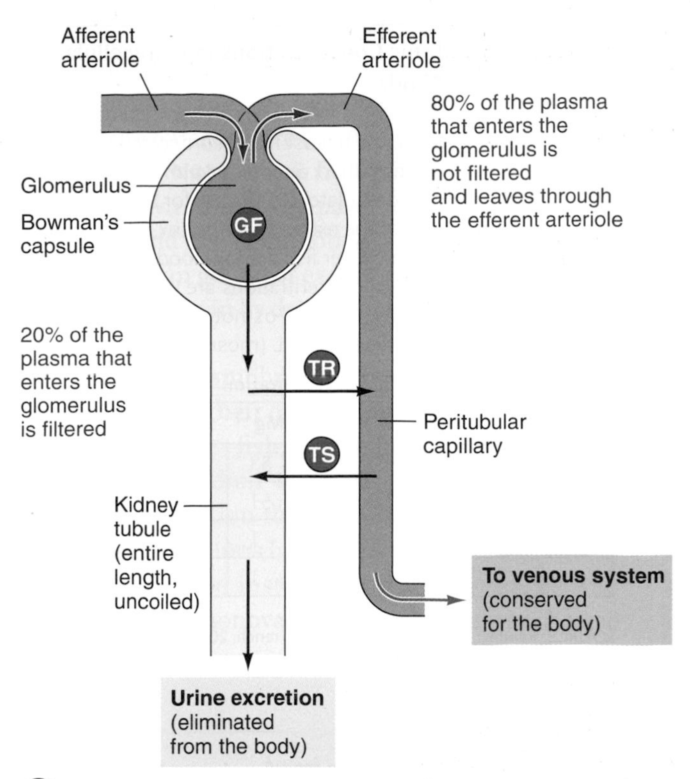

FIGURE 7.14

Filtration, Re-absorption, Secretion, and Excretion in a Kidney Tubule, or Nephron.

SOURCE: From Sherwood. *Human Physiology*, 1E. © 2010 Nelson Education Ltd. Reproduced by permission. www.cengage.com/permissions.

The loop of Henle is a U-shaped region of the nephron that connects the proximal tubule to the distal end. The length of the "loop" is variable, being short in cortical nephrons and long in juxtamedullary ones. However, the nephrons of some vertebrates, such as fish, reptiles, and amphibians, lack a loop; instead the proximal tubule is connected to the distal end by a short connecting length.

Juxtamedullary nephrons are an adaptation for more efficient re-absorption and conservation of water, and so their proportion is greater in mammals that live in desert habitats. Essentially, the loop re-absorbs more salt from the filtrate than it does water because of the impermeability of portions of the loop to water. The re-absorbed salt is concentrated in a portion of the kidney called the renal medulla, through which the loop travels. A more distal portion of the nephron, called the collecting duct, traverses the medulla and encounters the high salt concentration. The permeability of the collecting duct to water can be adjusted—therefore, if an animal needs to conserve water, its ducts become more permeable to water, which moves into the medulla by osmosis and eventually back into the blood plasma.

The rate of re-absorption can be regulated to compensate for changes in ionic composition and volume of the extracellular fluid. This involves increasing or decreasing the rate of re-absorption of selected ions and water. Both the endocrine system and nervous system are involved in the control of this regulation.

Life in Aquatic Environments

Aquatic environments present challenges to the maintenance of water balance and ionic composition of body fluids. If animals are to maintain ionic and osmotic concentrations in their extracellular fluids that are different from those of their aquatic environment, their regulatory biology must deal with the tendency for either an osmotic influx or efflux of water. Consequently, there must be physiological mechanisms to maintain the osmotic and ionic integrity of body fluids. However, some marine organisms actually conform to the osmotic concentration and ionic

TABLE 7.4 **Comparison of Blood Plasma of a Trout *(Salmo trutta)* and Its Freshwater Environment**

Ion concentrations are in mmol/L, and osmotic concentrations in mosm/L.

	Ionic Concentration					
	Na^+	K^+	Ca^{+2}	Mg^{+2}	$>Cl^-$	Osmolarity
Freshwater	0.4	0.1	0.8	0.2	0.2	0.5–10
Salmo	161	5.3	6.3	0.9	119	326

SOURCE: Hill, R. W., G. A. Wyse and M. Anderson. 2008. *Animal Physiology*. Sinauer Associates, Sunderland, MA. p. 682, Table 27.1.

Freshwater Environments

In contrast to seawater, life in freshwater is challenging because that matrix is very dilute in its ionic composition. This means that all freshwater animals are hyperosmotic and **hyperionic** to their environment **(Table 7.4)**. Because of this condition they tend to gain substantial amounts of water by osmosis and also tend to lose ions by diffusion. To maintain the osmotic and ionic gradients, freshwater animals must osmoregulate and ionoregulate their body fluids.

Excess water that seeps into the body fluids of freshwater teleosts by osmosis is excreted as a copious and dilute urine by the renal organ. The renal organ re-absorbs ions from the filtrate to conserve their extracellular concentrations. However, most ionoregulation occurs in the gills, which absorb ions from the aqueous environment (instead of pumping them out, as in marine teleosts). The gill cells that are responsible for ion uptake are similar to the chloride cells of marine teleosts, except the transporters are different. On the apical side of these cells, two kinds of transport proteins are involved in ionic exchange with the environment **(Figure 7.17)**. One transporter excretes HCO_3^- (bicarbonate) into the water in exchange for Cl^-. This involves HCO_3^- moving down a concentration gradient to the ambient water, and Cl^- into the cell against a gradient. The other transporter exchanges H^+ or NH_4^+ for Na^+. In this case, the H^+ or NH_4^+ move down a concentration gradient into the water, and Na^+ against a gradient into the cell. Once inside the cell, the Cl^- diffuses across the basolateral membrane into the extracellular fluid via a Cl^- channel. The Na^+ is actively transported out of the cell using energy liberated by Na^+/K^+ ATPase found in the basolateral membrane.

Freshwater crustaceans, such as crayfish, utilize similar tactics as teleosts to osmoregulate and ionoregulate. They excrete a dilute urine via an antennal gland, which re-absorbs ions from the filtrate of the extracellular fluid before releasing the excess as urine (similar to the renal organs of freshwater fish). The gills of crayfish are also efficient at extracting Na^+

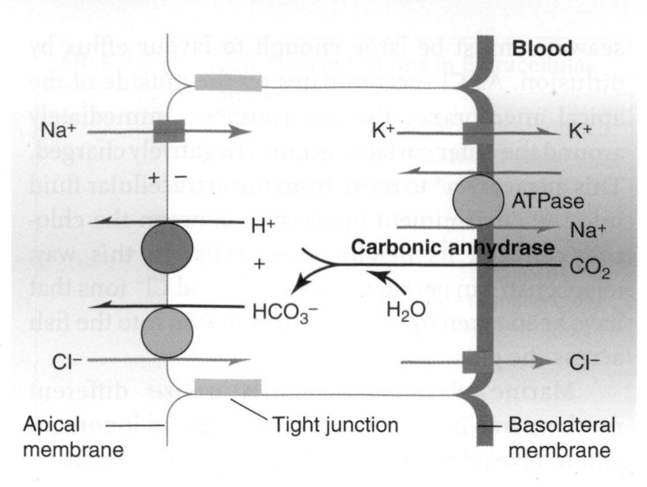

FIGURE 7.17

Transport Mechanisms for Ion Uptake in the Freshwater Teleost Gill. Na^+/K^+ ATPase in the basolateral membrane plays a key role in maintaining the gill epithelial cell Na^+ concentration low by actively transporting this ion into the blood plasma (hemolymph) in exchange for K^+. Intracellular K^+ eventually diffuses back into the hemolymph via a K^+ channel. Na^+ is exchanged for H^+ across the apical membrane and Cl^- is exchanged for HCO_3^-. The Cl^- moves across the basolateral membrane through a Cl^- channel.

SOURCE: Randall, D., W. Burggren and K. French. 2002. *Eckert Animal Physiology: Mechanisms and Adaptations*. 5th ed. W. H. Freeman and Co., New York, NY.

and Cl^- from the water in exchange for H^+ and HCO_3^-, respectively. Amphibians, such as frogs and salamanders, utilize transport mechanisms in the skin to ionoregulate. The transporters utilized are the same as those found in freshwater teleosts and crayfish.

Water and Ions in Terrestrial Environments

All terrestrial organisms have to deal with a basic problem: conserving water. The main ways that water is lost to the environment include excretion with the urine and feces and evaporation from the respiratory surfaces and integument (skin). Particularly in dry environments, the usual physiological strategy is to

1. reduce water loss by concentrating the urine and making the feces as dry as possible;
2. dehumidify the exhaled air during the ventilation cycle to reduce water loss, while hydrating the air during inhalation to keep the respiratory surface moist; and
3. make the integument impermeable to water.

Concentrating the Urine and Feces

The renal organs of terrestrial mammals and birds have the capacity to concentrate urine so that its osmotic concentration is higher than that of the extracellular fluid. In other words, more water is re-absorbed from the renal tubules than solutes. The ultrafiltrate that enters Bowman's capsule has a similar osmotic strength as the blood plasma, but due to re-absorption of water by the collecting tubules, the osmolarity of the urine is higher. The desert-dwelling kangaroo rat can do this particularly efficiently—the ionic concentration of its urine is as much as 16 times that of the blood plasma, thus conserving scarce body water (**Table 7.5**). The urine-concentrating ability is often referred to as the U:P ratio (urine to plasma ratio). Mammals that live in habitats where water is readily available have lower U:P ratios than those living where it is scarce.

The ability to concentrate urine is a function of the numbers of juxtamedullary nephrons (those with a long loop of Henle) and the length of their tubules. In desert-dwelling mammals, almost all of the nephrons are of this type, and they dip deep into the renal medulla. The renal medulla is also proportionally thicker than that of non-desert mammals.

The production of dry fecal pellets is also a way to conserve water in mammals. Most of the water re-absorption occurs in the large intestine or hind gut. **Table 7.6** shows the water content of the fecal materials of two ruminant mammals—the dromedary camel is adapted to dry habitats, and the cow is not.

Reducing Water Loss in Exhaled Air

Humans are not efficient at conserving water by trapping its vapour from air that we exhale to the atmosphere—this is why our breath is so "visible" as condensed vapour on a cold day. In contrast, some birds and mammals are very economical in conserving water vapour from their respiratory tract. As they inhale air, it passes through moist nasal passages and becomes warmed and humidified as it travels to the lungs. The nasal passages are cooled as moisture evaporates from their surface, and the warmed air is capable of absorbing more water vapour than the inhaled cooler air. By the time the inhaled air reaches the respiratory surface where gas exchange occurs, it is almost fully saturated with water vapour. When the stale air is exhaled, the reverse happens—the warm moist air travels outward over the cooler nasal passages, thus condensing vapour on their surface and conserving water by dehumidification. Animals that are exceptionally good at this function have narrow and convoluted nasal passages, which increases the surface area for efficient humidification and dehumidification of the air that they breathe. The desert-dwelling kangaroo rat (*Dipodomys* sp.) is a champion of water conservation by dehumidification of its exhaled air (**Figure 7.18**, p. 186). It can actually lower the temperature of its expired air below that of the ambient environment by condensing its load of water vapour—no other animal can do this to such a degree.

TABLE 7.5 Ability of Mammals to Concentrate Urine
A higher U:P ratio indicates a greater physiological efficiency at conserving water.

Animal	Maximum Urine Osmotic Concentration (mosm/L)	Urine:Plasma Ratio
Beaver (*Castor canadensis*)	520	1.7:1
Human (*Homo sapiens*)	1200	4:1
Rat (*Rattus norvegicus*)	2900	9:1
Vampire bat (*Desmodus rotundus*)	4650	14:1
Kangaroo rat (*Dipodomys* sp.)	5000	16:1

SOURCE: Willmer et al. (2000).

TABLE 7.6 Maximum U:P Ratio and Fecal Water Content in Two Ruminant Mammals
The fecal water content is in grams H_2O per kilogram feces.

	Maximum U:P Ratio	Fecal Water Content
Cow (*Bos primigenius*)	4	750
Dromedary (*Camelus dromedarius*)	8	440

SOURCE: Hill et al. (2008).

Reducing Water Loss across the Skin

The skin is another avenue of water gain or loss. Unless an animal lives in a very humid environment, it is in jeopardy of losing water by evaporation across its integument. Amphibians are especially vulnerable to water loss from their skin and this is why most species must have easy access to aquatic habitats to survive. However, toads (*Bufo* species) have a thicker skin and their epidermis is keratinized, which helps to prevent water loss through the skin. Terrestrial arthropods, such as insects, have a comparable solution—they secrete a water-conserving layer of wax over their exoskeleton (or cuticle, which is composed of chitin and protein).

Metabolic Water

Some desert-dwelling rodents have a remarkable ability to survive without drinking any water. Instead, they meet their needs by using water from their foods, plus that generated by oxidative metabolism. Even dry seeds yield so-called **metabolic water** when their biomass is oxidized. During metabolism in mitochondria, each atom of oxygen used in oxidative phosphorylation obtains two protons to form water at the end of the electron-transport chain. There is also some content of free water even in seemingly dry seeds, which can also contribute to the needs of desert animals.

All organisms have the capacity to make metabolic water, but desert mammals are highly efficient at retaining this vital substance. The kangaroo rat is

FIGURE 7.18

Temperature of Exhaled Air as a Function of That of Inhaled Air. The bold line ($T_e = T_a$) represents equality between the two temperatures. All birds and mammals, except for the kangaroo rat, are above the line of equality. Humans are well above the line and are not very efficient at trapping moisture from their expired air. T_e = exhaled air; T_a = inhaled air

SOURCE: Reprinted from Schmidt-Nielsen, K., F. R. Hainsworth and D. E. Murrish. 1970. "Countercurrent heat exchange in the respiratory passages. Effect on water and heat balance," *Respiration Physiology*, 9(2): 263–276, with permission from Elsevier.

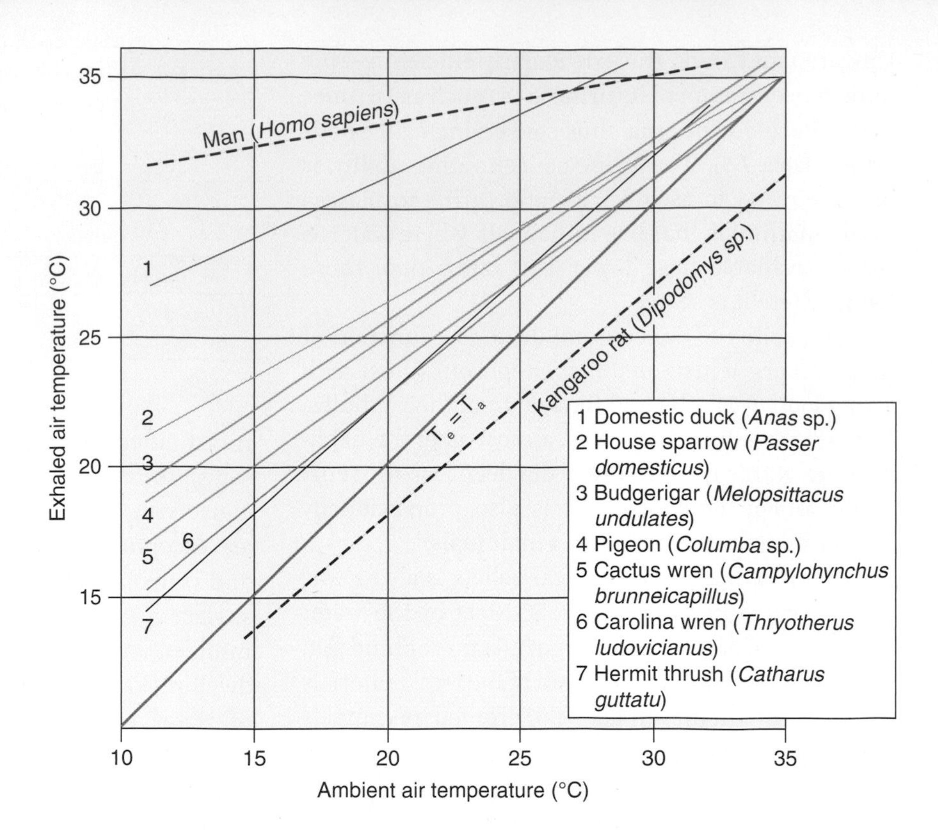

exceptionally competent in its water conservation, having a very low **obligatory water loss** to breathing, feces, and urine (see Ecology in Depth 7.4). Its fecal pellets are extremely dry, and its urine very concentrated in salts and nitrogenous wastes. This animal can survive without drinking.

Water Conservation in Insects

Insects are excellent at water conservation. Their waxy cuticle greatly reduces water loss across the integument, their respiratory system is efficient at preventing evaporation, and they produce highly concentrated excretions. Their fecal wastes are mixed with a product formed by their Malpighian tubules, which occur at the junction of the midgut and hindgut **(Figure 7.19).** The tubules are analogous to the nephron of vertebrates in that they process the extracellular fluid to remove waste products of metabolism. Ions (especially K^+) are pumped into the lumen of the tubules, and water and other solutes then follow. For example, Cl^- is drawn into the tubules by electrical attraction to K^+. The K^+-rich solution travels down the tubules and enters the hindgut, where Cl^- and K^+ (and Na^+) are absorbed back into the hemolymph (this extracellular fluid serves as a blood analogue in arthropods and many other invertebrates with an open circulatory system; there is no distinction between the interstitial fluid and blood, and the hemolymph fills the interior

Kangaroo rat (*Dipodomys merriami*).

© Buddy Mays/Alamy

ECOLOGY IN DEPTH 7.4

Water Balance in the Kangaroo Rat

The kangaroo rat (*Dipodomys merriami*) of the southwestern desert of the United States has been studied for its remarkable ability to conserve water (Schmidt-Nielsen and Schmidt-Nielsen, 1951). In their experiments, kangaroo rats were provided with a diet of barley seed but were not allowed to drink water. The experiments were conducted under a variety of relative humidities, ranging from 5 to 90 percent. These desert-adapted mammals remained healthy even at the lowest humidity.

Based on the amounts of carbohydrate, fat, and protein found in the grain, an estimate was obtained of the amount of "metabolic water" available to the kangaroo rats (this is water formed during the complete oxidation of the grain). The gross production of metabolic water from 1 g of barley was 0.54 g of H_2O (at 25°C and 33 percent relative humidity). In fact, as long as the ambient relative humidity was greater than 10 percent, kangaroo rats were capable of meeting all of their needs for water from a simple diet of barley seeds.

The total water loss by the kangaroo rats was 0.47 g per g of barley, equivalent to 86 percent of the water gained, as follows:

1. Ventilation = 0.33 g of H_2O per g of barley consumed (this number is based on the O_2 needed to oxidize the barley, and therefore the amount air passing in and out of the lung).
2. Urinary = 0.14 g of H_2O per g of barley (this is the water needed to excrete the urea produced as a nitrogenous waste).
3. Fecal = 0 g of H_2O.

Therefore, the net amount of water gained from the metabolism of 1 g of barley is 0.07 g (about 14 percent of the H_2O actually produced).

of the body and surrounds all cells). Water then follows into the hemolymph by osmosis, leaving behind a pasty, highly concentrated excretory product that is a combination of urine and feces.

Excreting Nitrogenous Waste

All animals metabolize proteins, and so they must deal with nitrogenous wastes that arise from deamination of amino acids (removal of the amino functional group), and from metabolism of nucleic acids. There are three common forms of nitrogenous waste: ammonia (NH_3), urea $(NH_2)_2CO$, and uric acid ($C_5H_4N_4O_3$).

Most animals that live in aquatic environments (except for elasmobranchs and marine mammals) excrete ammonia as their nitrogenous waste. The ammonia does not take much energy to produce, and it is excreted rapidly to prevent it from accumulating to toxic levels in body fluids. Animals that produce ammonia as the primary nitrogenous waste are referred to as **ammonotelic**.

However, terrestrial animals must conserve water, and so they tend to excrete nitrogenous waste in concentrated forms, but they cannot do this with ammonia because it is too toxic. Instead, they produce urea or uric acid, which are much less toxic, although there is a trade-off because these compounds are energetically costly to produce. Mammals and most terrestrial amphibians are **ureotelic**, meaning they

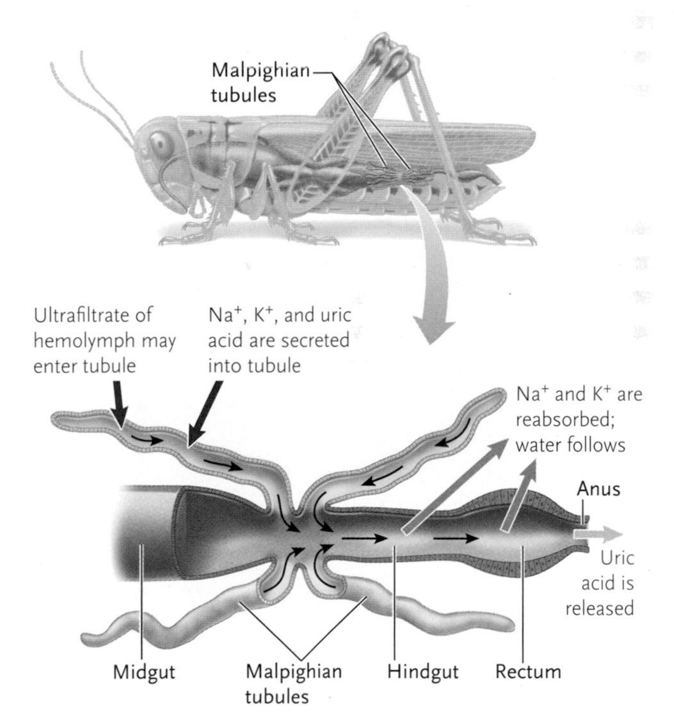

FIGURE 7.19
Function of the Malpighian Tubules of Insects. Ions (especially K^+) are pumped into the lumen of the Malpighian tubules, and water and other solutes follow. The K^+-rich solution then moves to the hindgut, where K^+ and Na^+ are transported back into the hemolymph. Water is then drawn into the hemolymph because of the osmotic gradient, leaving behind a pasty mixture of urine and feces that is highly concentrated in uric acid.

produce urea as a nitrogenous waste. Almost all birds and reptiles (except for some ureotelic turtles) produce uric acid as their nitrogenous waste, and thus are **uricotelic**. Most terrestrial invertebrates, including insects, are also uricotelic.

Unlike ureotelic animals that produce a liquid urine containing urea, uricotelic ones make a paste with a high concentration of uric acid, or they excrete a dry fecal pellet high in that substance. Normally in uricotelic animals, the product of the renal organ (Malpighian tubules in the case of insects) is mixed with fecal matter in the hindgut before being expelled through the cloaca (this is a shared passage for urine and feces). Water is re-absorbed in the hindgut and cloaca, causing the uric acid to precipitate as a fine crystal, and a paste or solid waste is excreted.

Animals that utilize either ureotelism or uricotelism have evolved a suite of enzymes to process their nitrogenous waste into either urea or uric acid. These enzymes, and the genetic information to produce them, are missing in ammonotelic animals. Recall that almost all aquatic animals are ammonotelic. Even though amphibians are semi-aquatic, they possess the genes necessary for urea enzyme production **(Figure 7.20)**. Frogs in the tadpole stage live in an aquatic environment and are ammontelic, but when they metamorphose into adults they start to produce urea, which is better suited to a terrestrial lifestyle. Thus, frogs possess the genetic capability for both ammonotelic and ureotelic physiology, with the stage of the life cycle determining which system is used.

7.4 Gas Exchange

Introduction

Animals must supply oxygen (O_2) to the mitochondria of their cells to support oxidative metabolism, and they must remove carbon dioxide (CO_2), a waste product of metabolism. All but the smallest animals have a circulatory system to transport these gases between their body tissues and a specialized surface where they are exchanged with the environment.

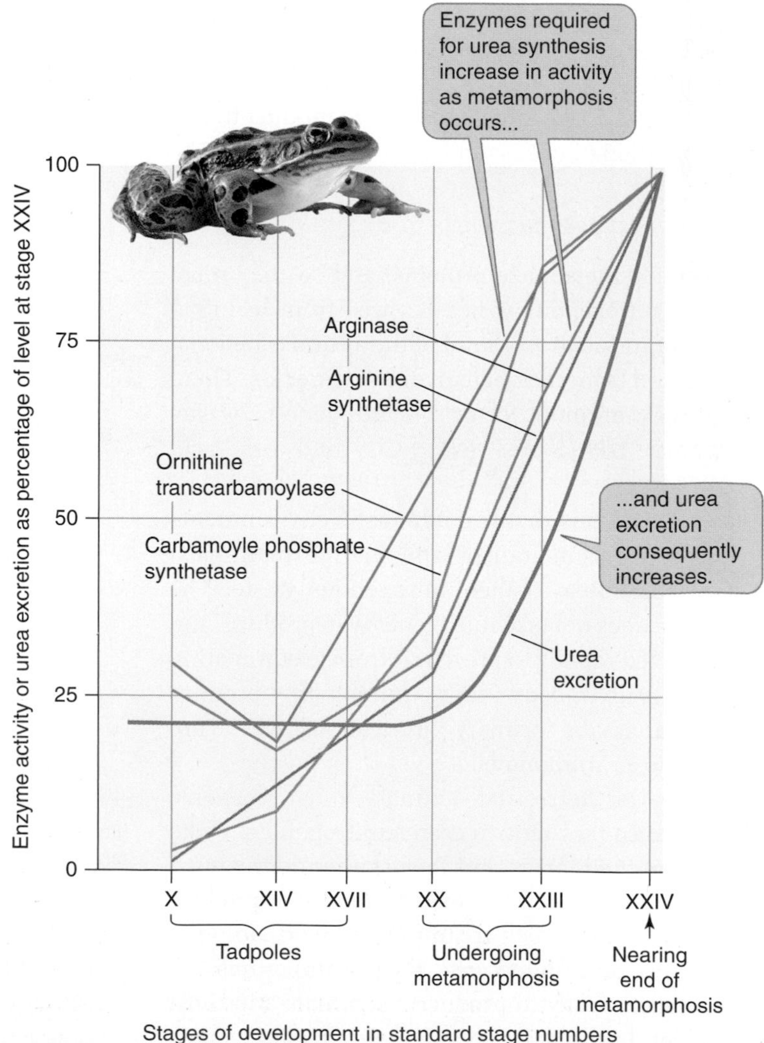

FIGURE 7.20
Conversion from Ammonotelism to Ureotelism in Frogs during Metamorphosis. There are several stages during the transition from the tadpole to the adult frog, identified by Roman numerals in the figure. Four liver enzymes that are essential to urea formation are produced during metamorphosis.

SOURCE: Adapted from Brown , G. W., W. R. Brown, and P. P. Cohen. 1959. "Comparative biochemistry of urea synthesis. II. Levels of urea cycle enzymes in metamorphosing *Rana catesbeiana* tadpoles," *Journal of Biological Chemistry*, 234: 1775–1780.

Alternatively, small animals such as insects have an extensive network of tracheae (tubes) that allows gases to penetrate deep into their body for exchange. In addition, most animals have a respiratory pigment in their circulating fluids that increases the capacity to transport O_2 and CO_2. In this section we will examine the different means of exchange and transport of O_2 and CO_2 in aquatic and terrestrial animals.

Role of the Circulatory System

There are two types of circulatory systems: open and closed. All vertebrate animals have a closed circulatory system, as do some invertebrates, such as annelid worms. Almost all other invertebrates have an open system.

A closed circulatory system is composed of a network of vessels that enclose an extracellular fluid that is referred to as blood. The walls of the vessels are a barrier between the blood and another kind of extracellular liquid that surrounds the cells, known as interstitial fluid. The vessels of a closed circulatory system take blood away from the heart and later return it to that pumping organ.

An open circulatory system also has vessels, but they are to a greater or lesser degree open to the body cavity (or hemocoel) and they carry a fluid called hemolymph. Some animals with an open system have a simple heart and a few vessels leading away from it that open to the hemocoel. Others have a complex set of vessels similar to what is found in animals with a closed circulatory system. Nevertheless, at some point within the system, the vessels are open and the circulating hemolymph mixes with similar fluids in the hemocoel.

Regardless of being open or closed, all circulatory systems have a heart or a series of them to pump fluid past the gas exchange surface, to tissues and organs of the body, and back to the pumping organ(s). The more primitive forms of heart are simple tubular structures that fill and contract to propel fluids around the body. At the other end of the scale, mammals and birds have a complex four-chambered heart, which is composed of two pumps working in parallel that force blood through separate pulmonary and systemic circuits.

Gas Fractions and Partial Pressures

To understand gas exchange, we must be familiar with the concept of **partial pressure** of a gas, which is proportional to its fractional concentration in the atmosphere. For example, about 21 percent of the atmospheric volume is O_2 and 79 percent is N_2 (this is for a dry atmosphere, or one without water vapour). At sea level, the atmospheric pressure is about 101.3 kiloPascals (this is the unit according to the Système Internationale; 101.3 kPa is equivalent to 1013 millibars and 760 mm of mercury). Therefore, the partial pressure of oxygen in the atmosphere is calculated as its fractional concentration multiplied by the atmospheric pressure, as follows:

- Fraction of O_2 in the atmosphere = 0.21 (or 21 percent).
- Barometric pressure at sea level = 101.3 kPa.
- Partial pressure of O_2 = 0.21 × 101.3 kPa = 21.3 kPa.
- Partial pressure of N_2 = 0.79 × 101.3 kPa = 80.0 kPa.
- Partial pressure of CO_2 = 0.00038 × 101.3 kPa = 0.0385 kPa.

In addition to these and other gases, the atmosphere contains some water vapour, which also exerts a partial pressure. If air at sea level is saturated with H_2O vapour, the partial pressure of O_2 would be some value less than 21.3 kPa (about 20.8 kPa at 20°C). Note that although atmospheric pressure decreases with increasing altitude (at a height of about 5500 m it is one-half that of sea level), the gas fractions remain constant—the concentration of O_2 is still 21 percent (dry air) at the summit of Mount Everest (8848 m). However, its partial pressure there is only 6.6 kPa (at a barometric pressure of 31.3 kPa).

As we will see, the partial pressure of oxygen or carbon dioxide on either side of a gas exchange surface determines the direction in which gas will diffuse. Gas always diffuses from an area of higher partial pressure to one where it is lower.

Animals That "Breathe" Water

Almost all animals of aquatic habitats "breathe" their environmental medium of water—meaning they pass this substance over their gas-exchange surface for the purpose of absorbing O_2 and releasing CO_2. All animals that do this face the same challenges:

1. Even water that is fully saturated with O_2 has a much smaller concentration than occurs in the atmosphere. Fresh water (at 15°C) that is saturated with O_2 contains 7.5 mL of O_2 per litre (this is also 0.00075 percent, or 7.5 parts per million [ppm]). In comparison, one litre of sea-level atmosphere contains about 210 mL of O_2 (21 percent).
2. The amount of O_2 that can dissolve in water decreases with increasing temperature (**Figure 7.21**, p. 190).
3. The amount of O_2 that can dissolve in water decreases with increasing salinity.
4. Water is more viscous than air, and so it takes much more energy for an animal to either move water over its gas exchange surface or to move that surface through the aquatic medium.

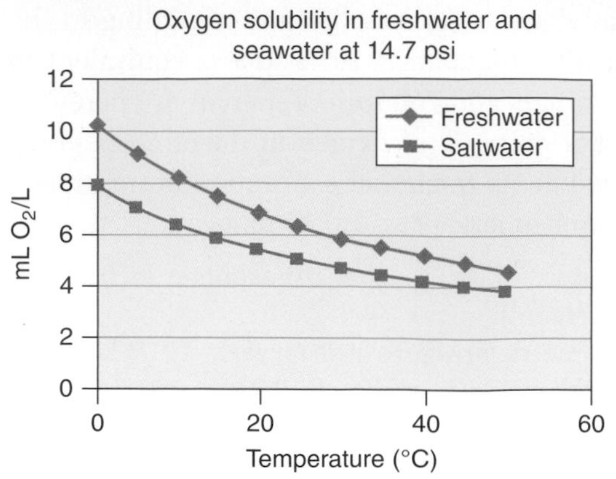

FIGURE 7.21

Oxygen Solubility in Freshwater and Seawater at Different Temperatures. (All data are for sea level, or 101 kPa.)

SOURCE: Data from http://www.engineeringtoolbox.com/oxygen-solubility-water-d_841.html.

5. Exposure of the gas exchange surface to water results in osmotic and ionic challenges if the body fluids are not isosmotic to the water.
6. If there is a thermal gradient between the body and the aqueous environment, heat is lost or gained across the gas-exchange surface.

Despite these challenges, aquatic animals have successfully employed water-breathing for hundreds of millions of years, in both marine and freshwater environments.

The gas exchange surface in aquatic animals is called a gill (except for marine reptiles and mammals, which have lungs). Gills are filamentous structures with a single layer of epithelial cells that form a barrier between the circulating body fluids and the environmental water. The gill filaments provide a very large surface area for gas exchange. Either water is drawn over the surface of the gill to ventilate the filaments, or the gill is moved through the water to achieve a more efficient gas exchange. Some vertebrate animals, such as certain salamanders, externalize their gills and rely mostly on water currents and diffusion for gas exchange. Others, such as teleost fishes, mollusks, and crustaceans, internalize the gills within a protective chamber. Although internalization requires a specialized mechanism to ventilate the gills by passing water over them, these vital organs are relatively protected from damage by contact with objects in the environment and also from predators.

Gill Ventilation

There are a variety of ways of ventilating internalized gills. Bivalve molluscs (**Figure 7.22b**) have a abundant cilia that cover the surface of their inhalant siphon, which by their constant beating cause a water current to pass over the gills. Cephalopod molluscs are much larger animals, and they utilize a pumping action of their inhalant siphon to draw water over their gills. Crustaceans have their gills enclosed in a chamber within the thorax, where a structure called a gill bailer (scaphognathite) beats to create a negative pressure that draws water over their gills (**Figure 7.22a**).

Teleost fish have their gills enclosed by a rigid operculum. Ventilation of their gills involves the coordinated action of pumping structures that provide both suction and pressure. At the start of a ventilatory cycle, the mouth opens, the floor of the buccal (mouth) cavity drops, and the operculum bulges slightly outward while maintaining a seal with the body wall, thus increasing the volume of the buccal and opercular

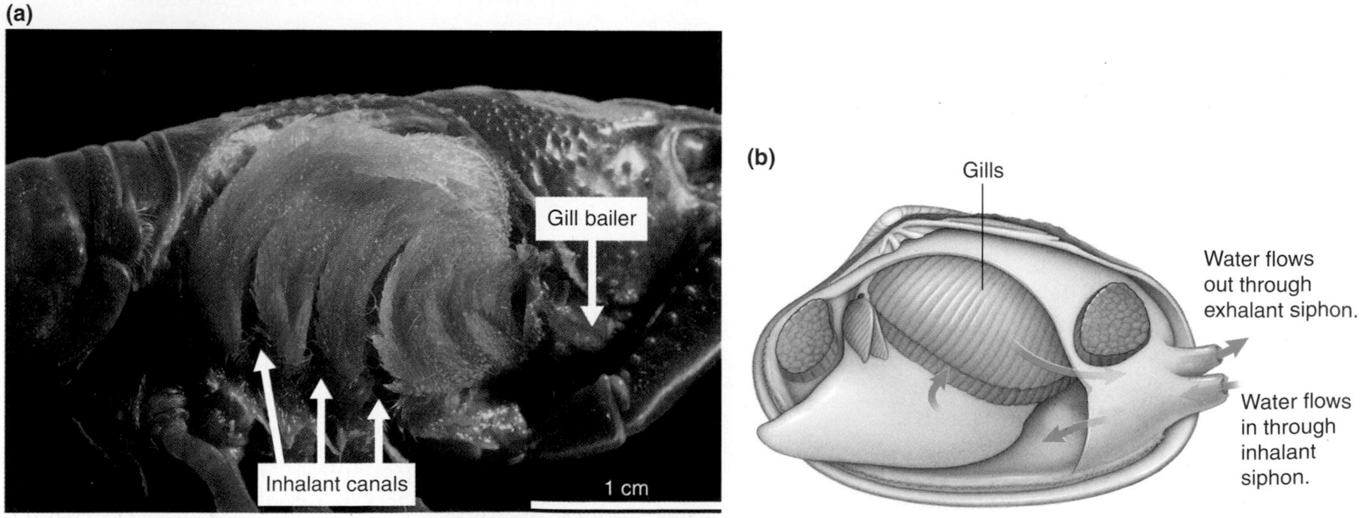

FIGURE 7.22

Ventilation of the Gills of Crayfish and Bivalve Molluscs. (a) Crayfish use a suction pump to draw water over their gills, while (b) bivalve molluscs use cilia to draw water into their inhalant siphon, then over the gills, and out the exhalant canal.

SOURCE: (a) John D. Cunningham/Visuals Unlimited, Inc. (b) From Russell/Wolfe/Hertz/Starr. *Biology*, 1E. © 2010 Nelson Education Ltd. Reproduced by permission. www.cengage.com/permissions.

cavities. This increase in volume lowers the pressure in these two areas and results in a flow of water into the mouth and over the gills by suction. Next, the mouth closes, the floor of the buccal cavity rises, and the operculum opens to allow water to be pushed over the surface of the gills, in essence working in the manner of a pressure pump. Note that the gills are ventilated during both the buccal expansion and contraction phases **(Figure 7.23).**

Gill Structure and Counter-Current Flow

Although gills come in different shapes and sizes, they all share the common function of acting as the interface between the circulating body fluids and the aquatic environment. The gills of teleost fish are composed of a series of five arches enclosed by the operculum on each side of the head (see **Figure 7.24, p. 192**). A series of filaments arises from each arch, like pages of a book, with each having plate-like structures called lamellae extending from both sides. The spaces between the lamellae are channels through which water is directed, either by the pumping action of the buccal cavity and operculum, or simply by swimming with the mouth open (this is known as ram ventilation).

The direction of the flow of water is from the leading edge of the lamellae to the trailing edge, while that of blood flow through the lamellae, is in the opposite way. This is known as **counter-current flow**, and it is important to the efficiency of gas exchange across the surface of the lamellae. Because of the counter-current flow, at any point along the lamellae the gradient of oxygen partial pressure between the blood and environmental water favours diffusion into the blood. This means that blood continuously picks up oxygen as it travels through the lamellae. If the blood and water

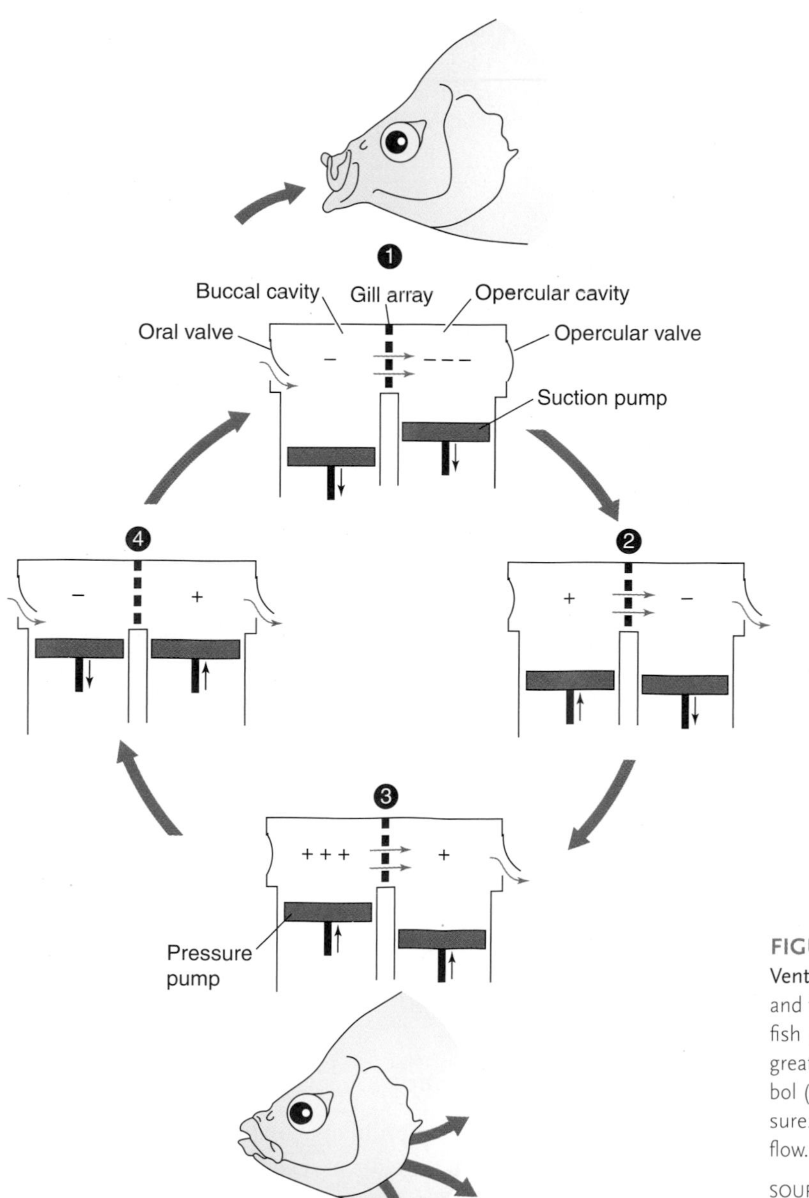

FIGURE 7.23
Ventilation of the Gill of a Teleost Fish. Both suction and force (thrusting) pumps are utilized to ventilate fish gills. The plus symbol (+) indicates a pressure greater than ambient pressure and the negative symbol (–) indicates a pressure less than ambient pressure. The blue arrows indicate the direction of water flow.

SOURCE: Hill , R. W., G. A. Wyse and M. Anderson. 2008. *Animal Physiology.* Sinauer Associates, Sunderland, MA. p. 556, Fig. 22.11.

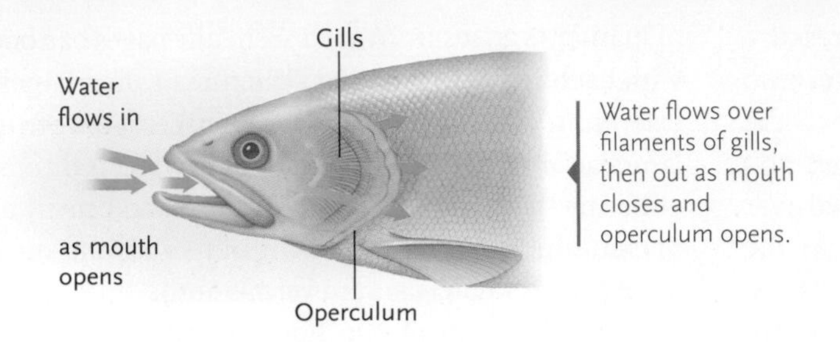

(a) The flow of water around the gill filaments

(b) Counter-current flow in fish gills, in which the blood and water move in opposite directions

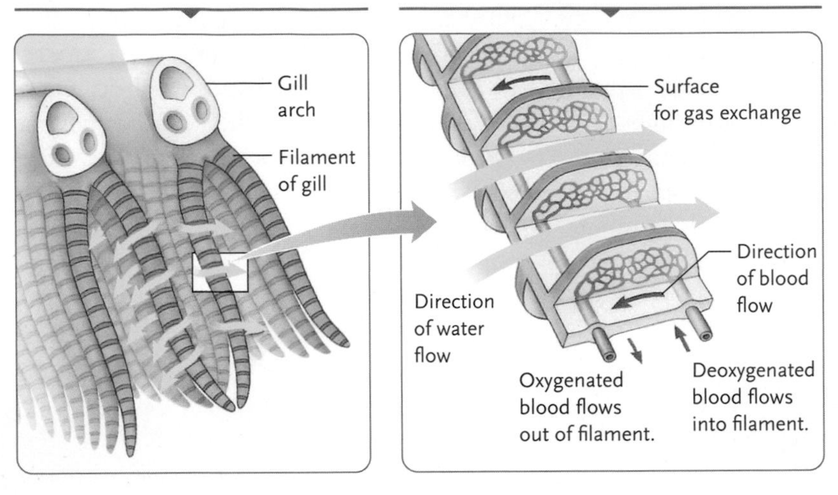

(c) In counter-current exchange, blood leaving the capillaries has the same O_2 content as fully oxygenated water entering the gills

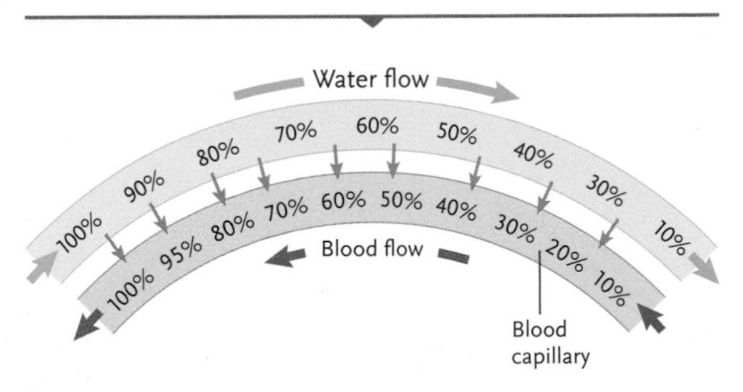

FIGURE 7.24

Structure of the Teleost Gill. The water flow by the secondary lamellae is counter (opposite) to the direction of that of blood through the lamellae. This provides for continual exchange of gases across the surface of the epithelium.

SOURCE: From Russell/Wolfe/Hertz/Starr. *Biology*, 1E. © 2010 Nelson Education Ltd. Reproduced by permission. www.cengage.com/permissions.

were flowing in the same direction, the blood would absorb oxygen only near the leading edge of the lamellae, and the diffusion gradient would quickly disappear prior to full oxygenation of the blood—this would be much less efficient than counter-current flow.

Animals That "Breathe" Air

All terrestrial animals are air-breathing, as are aquatic mammals and reptiles. Air is a much less dense medium than water, so less energy is expended to ventilate the gas-exchange surface, compared with pumping water over gills. Also, the concentration of oxygen in air (about 21 percent) is much greater than in water (typically 7 ppm in freshwater at 20°C). The key challenge faced by air breathers is the evaporation of water at their gas-exchange surface and possible desiccation of the body fluids. This effect is reduced by internalization of the gas-exchange surface and humidification of the air as it is inhaled.

The vast majority of vertebrate animals rely on "lungs" for the exchange of oxygen and elimination of carbon dioxide, although semi-terrestrial amphibians can also exchange gas across their skin. Terrestrial insects, the largest and most successful group of animals on the planet, rely on an internal tracheal system for gas exchange.

Vertebrate Lungs

The lungs of amphibians consist of a pair of simple air sacs that develop as extensions of the pharynx **(Figure 7.25).** The lungs are ventilated by forcing air into them by a pumping action of the buccal cavity. At the start of the ventilatory cycle, air is drawn in through the two nares (nostrils) as the buccal cavity is expanded by lowering its floor. During this time the opening to the lungs, called the glottis, is closed. Next, with the nares still open, the glottis opens and air from the previous inhalation is expelled along the roof of the buccal cavity and out the nares by elastic recoil of the lungs, in much the same way that air leaves a balloon. The nares then close and the floor of the buccal cavity is raised, forcing fresh air through the open glottis and into the lungs. Interestingly, the anatomical structure and function of the buccal cavity inhibits the mixing of fresh air in the ventral (lower) portion with stale air exhaled from the lungs as it passes along the dorsal aspect. The cycle then starts again as the nares are opened and the next charge of fresh air is drawn into the buccal cavity. This method of breathing is known as **positive-pressure ventilation** because air is forced into the lungs by the pumping action of the buccal floor.

Reptiles, mammals, and birds fill their lungs by **negative-pressure ventilation**. In this system, the lungs are contained within a thoracic cavity that expands by contraction of the diaphragm as well as muscles between the ribs **(Figure 7.26)**. Expansion of the thorax causes the lungs to expand, partly because of a liquid seal between their outer surface and the inside face of the thoracic cavity. As the lungs expand, their inner pressure falls below that of the atmosphere and this draws air in via the nostrils or the mouth, and through the airways (tubular passages) that connect to the lungs. During quiet breathing, exhalation occurs as the muscles of the thorax and diaphragm relax, thus allowing the thorax to recoil. This increases pressure in the lungs and forces air out the airways. However, during times of excitement or exercise, another set of thoracic muscles will contract to force larger volumes of air out of the lungs during exhalation.

A problem encountered by animals that have a relatively long airway is that not all of the air leaving the lungs during exhalation is expired to the environment. Some of it remains within the airway and becomes mixed with fresh air with the next inhalation. This reduces the amount of fresh air that gets down to the gas-exchange surface of the lungs, thus reducing the partial pressure of O_2 at that surface (and increasing that of CO_2). The volume of air that remains in the airways is referred to as the "dead space"—in humans, it represents about 25 percent of the volume inhaled with each breath. However, during times of activity when the volume inhaled is increased, the dead-space air is a smaller fraction.

The gas-exchange surface of the lungs of reptiles, birds, and mammals is much more complex than in amphibians. The inner lung surface of mammals is composed of abundant alveolar sacs at the end of a series of branched airways (terminal bronchioles). Each alveolar sac is divided into an aggregation of small alveoli, superficially resembling a cluster of grapes. Taken together, the alveoli have a very large surface area—in a human it would be comparable to a tennis court (75 m^2). Each alveolus receives its own blood supply, giving ample opportunity for gas exchange with the blood.

Birds are the champions of negative-pressure ventilation. Bird lungs are built differently than those of mammals or reptiles, and are composed of a series of air sacs at either end of the gas-exchange surface **(Figure 7.27)**. The gas-exchange surface of the lung is made up of a number of tubes called parabronchi, whose surrounding tissue is made of sponge-like material consisting of small "air capillaries" intermingled with blood vessels. Inhalation caused by expansion of the thorax results in enlargement of the air sacs. This causes fresh air to move along the airways into the posterior air sac, and air from the parabronchi is drawn into the anterior air sac. Upon exhalation,

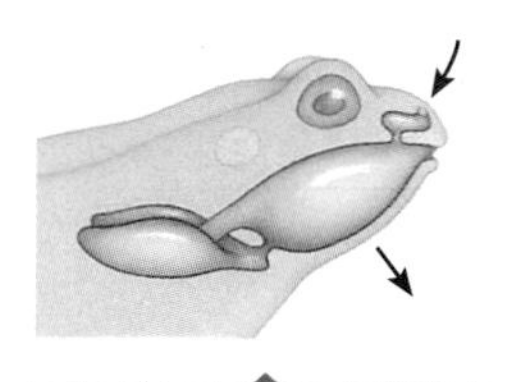

1 The frog lowers the floor of its mouth and inhales through its nostrils.

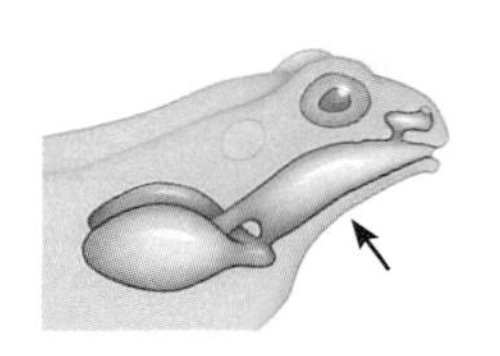

2 It closes its nostrils, opens the glottis, and elevates the floor of the mouth, forcing air into the lungs.

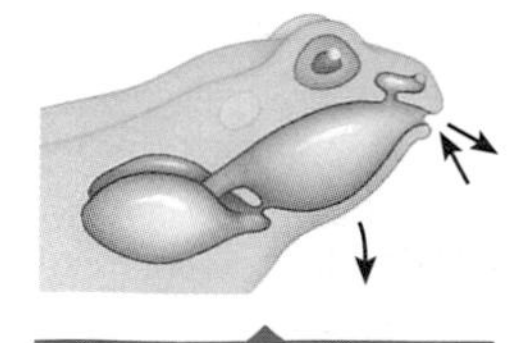

3 Rhythmic ventilation assists in gas exchange.

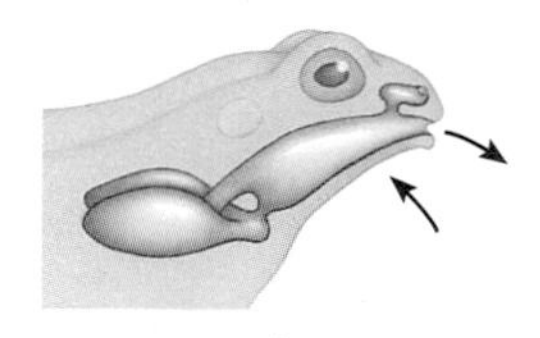

4 Air is forced out when muscles in the body wall above the lungs contract and the lungs recoil elastically.

FIGURE 7.25

Ventilation of the Frog Lung. Air is forced into the lungs by a buccal pump. This is known as positive-pressure ventilation because the lungs inflate due to the generation of a greater air pressure in the buccal cavity than in the lungs.

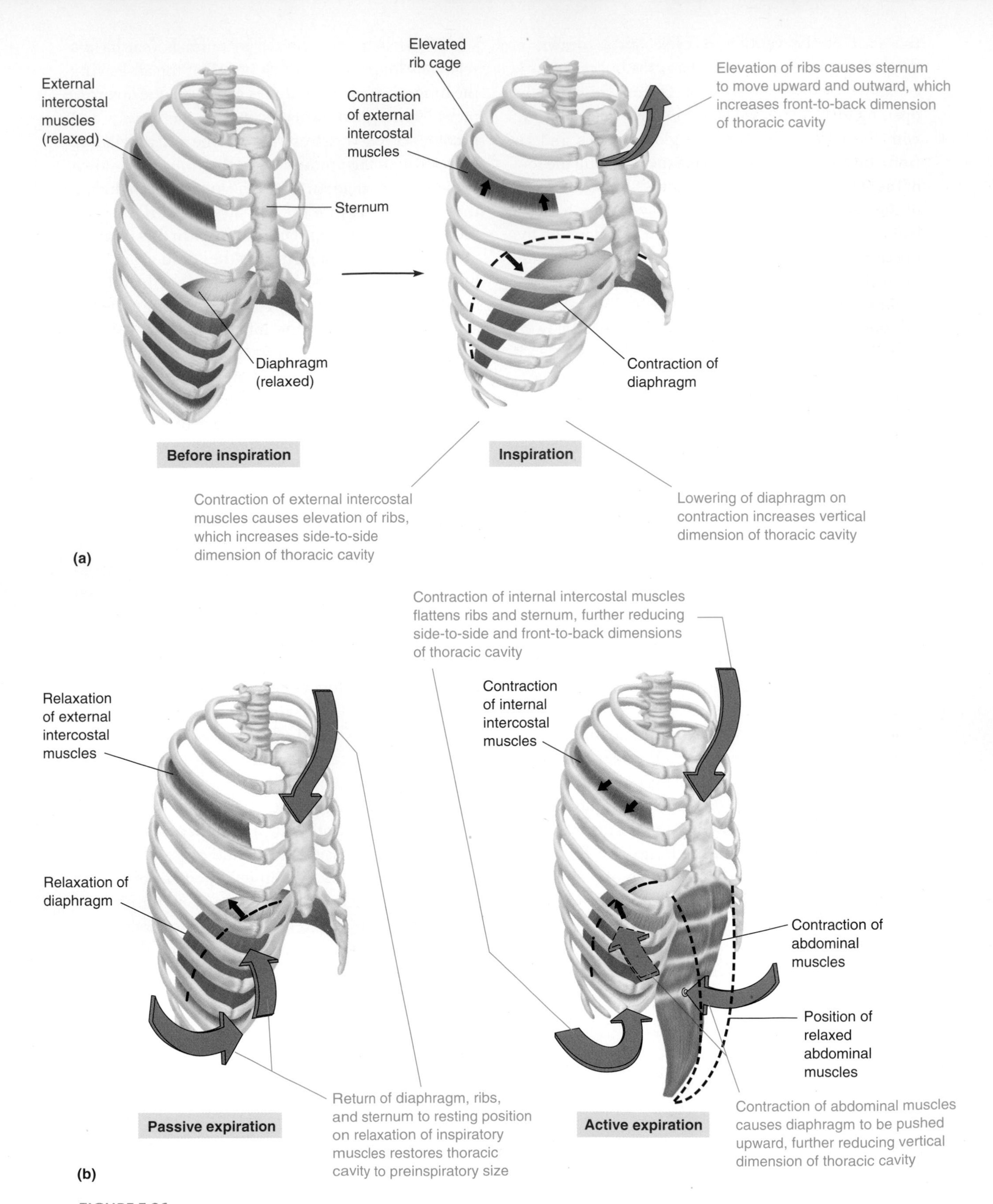

FIGURE 7.26

Mammalian Lung Structure Showing Inhalation and Exhalation. The lungs of mammals are filled by negative-pressure ventilation. (a) As the thorax and lungs expand during inhalation, the pressure in the lungs becomes less than that of the atmosphere, thus drawing air inward. (b) During exhalation the lungs recoil, thus increasing the intra-alveolar pressure and forcing air out of the lungs.

the air sacs are squeezed so that the fresh air from the posterior air sacs is forced into the parabronchi. At the same time, air from the previous breath, which is stored in the anterior air sacs, is squeezed out of the airways and into the atmosphere. This system results in a continual flow of fresh air over the parabronchi throughout the ventilatory cycle, and not just during inhalation as occurs in mammalian lungs.

Ventilation by Insects

Terrestrial insects do not have lungs or gills. Instead, they use a series of tubes called trachea to take oxygen deep within the muscles of their abdomen and thorax **(Figure 7.28)**. In fact, because of the small size of insects a circulatory system is not necessary to deliver oxygen to the tissues of the body. The openings to the trachea on the body surface are guarded by structures known as spiracles, which can open and close. The tracheae are branched and eventually give rise to thin-walled, blind-ended tubules known as tracheoles, where gas exchange occurs with the body tissues. No ventilatory muscles are associated with the tracheal system, and the movement of gases is simply by diffusion. Although this might seem to be an inefficient way to get oxygen to the working muscles, it works well with small animals like insects. However, the largest insects may increase their ventilation by contracting

(a) Lungs and air sacs of a bird

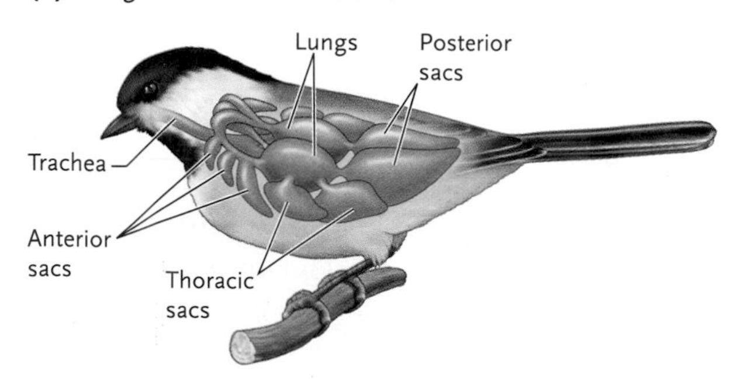

(b) Counter-current exchange

Cycle 1

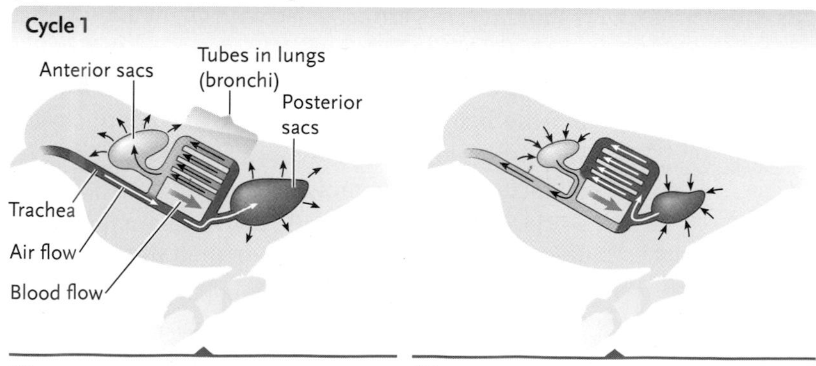

1 During the first inhalation, most of the oxygen flows directly to the posterior air sacs. The anterior air sacs also expand but do not receive any of the newly inhaled oxygen.

2 During the following exhalation, both anterior and posterior air sacs contract. Oxygen from the posterior sacs flows into the gas-exchanging tubes (bronchi) of the lungs.

Cycle 2

1 During the next inhalation, air from the lung (now deoxygenated) moves into the anterior air sacs.

2 In the second exhalation, air from anterior sacs is expelled to the outside through the trachea.

FIGURE 7.27
Anatomy of the Bird Lung and Air Sacs. Avian ventilation is extremely efficient in terms of gas exchange because fresh air is continually passing through the parabronchi of the lungs during both inspiration and expiration.

SOURCE: From Russell /Wolfe/Hertz/Starr. *Biology*, 1E.

and relaxing abdominal muscles, which indirectly pumps their tracheal system. Flight muscles also increase tracheal ventilation in flying insects.

Like all air breathers, terrestrial insects have the problem of loss of body water by evaporation, in this case via the openings to the tracheal system. To reduce this problem, insects open their spiracles only periodically to allow fresh air in; the build-up of CO_2 in the trachea and surrounding tissue fluids is a key stimulant for opening the spiracles.

Gas Transport: The Role of Respiratory Pigments

Animals that transport gases using a circulatory system have a **respiratory pigment** that allows more gas to be transported than can simply dissolve in the circulating fluid. Hemoglobin is the most common respiratory pigment, but there are also others: hemerythrin, hemocyanin, and chlorocruorin. All vertebrates and certain invertebrates utilize hemoglobin to increase the O_2-carrying capacity of their blood.

To illustrate the advantage of respiratory pigments, we can examine the O_2-carrying capacity of human blood, which carries about 3 mL O_2/L dissolved in the plasma, but up to 200 mL/L in association with its hemoglobin content. Therefore, 98.5 percent of the O_2 is carried bound to hemoglobin and only 1.5 percent is dissolved in plasma. Animals with a high metabolic rate are especially dependent on respiratory pigments to maintain the oxygenation of their hard-working muscles.

Hemoglobin is made up of four protein subunits called globulins (two alpha and two beta), each with a porphyrin ring containing iron. One O_2 molecule can bind to the iron in each porphyrin ring, and therefore each hemoglobin molecule can transport up to four molecules of O_2. However, the binding of one molecule of O_2 facilitates the binding of others, a phenomenon known as cooperativity, although usually fewer than four molecules of O_2 are bound at any time. The effect of partial pressure of O_2 (P_{O_2}) on the binding process and on the O_2-saturation of hemoglobin is illustrated by an oxygen binding curve (or O_2 dissociation curve; **Figure 7.29**). Note that at very low P_{O_2}, the curve is relatively slow-rising and less than 20 percent of the O_2-binding sites are occupied with O_2. At intermediate pressures there is a rapid increase in the rate of binding as cooperativity occurs between binding sites and the hemoglobin loads more and more oxygen. The curve slowly approaches saturation, giving it a characteristically sigmoidal shape.

How does this affect the delivery of oxygen to the tissues? The typical P_{O_2} of tissue fluid in mammals is 4.0–5.3 kPa (30–40 mm Hg), depending on the rate of

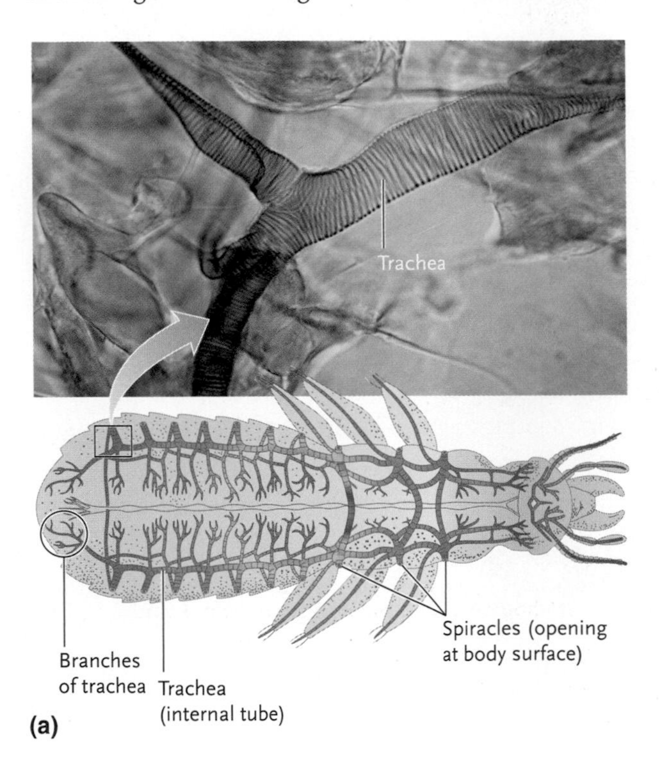

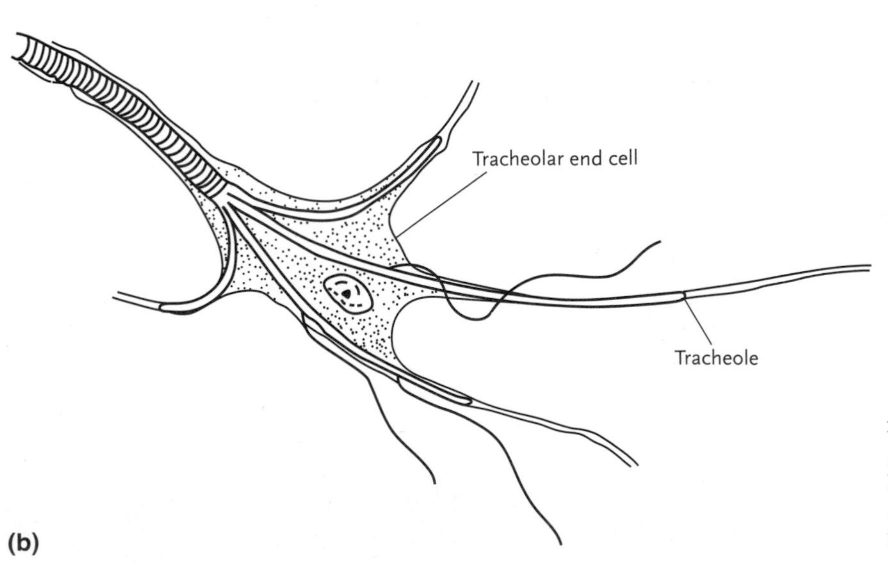

FIGURE 7.28
The Tracheal System of Insects. The entrance to each trachea is guarded by a valve-like spiracle, which opens to allow fresh air to diffuse inside. Each trachea extends deep into the tissues of the body, and because insects are small and have a limited demand for oxygen, there is no need for an active circulatory system.

SOURCE: From Russell /Wolfe/Hertz/ Starr. *Biology*, 1E. © 2010 Nelson Education Ltd. Reproduced by permission. www.cengage.com/permissions.

Photo: Ed Reschke.

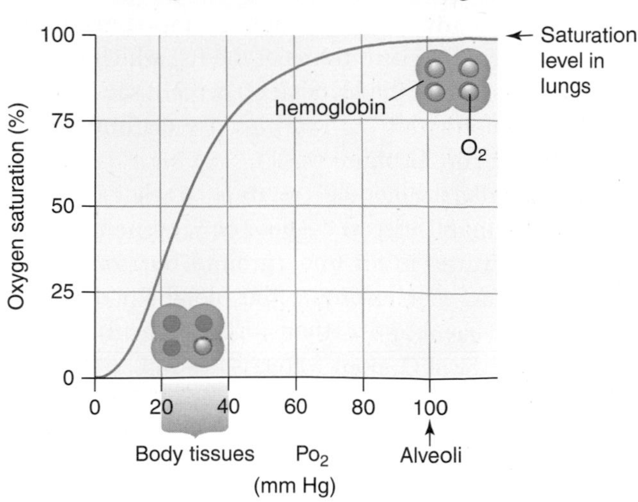

FIGURE 7.29

Oxygen Binding Curve. The curve has a similar shape for all animals that utilize a respiratory pigment, but the O_2-carrying capacity varies depending on the type of pigment used.

SOURCE: From Russell/Wolfe/Hertz/Starr. *Biology*, 1E. © 2010 Nelson Education Ltd. Reproduced by permission. www.cengage.com/permissions.

O_2 consumption by aerobic metabolism in the cells. The blood that leaves the gas-exchange surface has undergone O_2 loading and its hemoglobin is saturated with that vital gas. As the blood passes through the organs and various other tissues of the body, where the P_{O_2} is lower, the diffusion gradient favours the movement of O_2 off the hemoglobin and into the tissues. Looking again at the O_2-binding curve in **Figure 7.29**, it is apparent that 60–70 percent of the O_2 bound to hemoglobin will dissociate and move into the tissues.

The Bohr Effect and Root Effect

The strength of the affinity of hemoglobin for O_2 is affected by the pH and partial pressure of CO_2 (P_{CO_2}) of the blood. CO_2 occurs in a high concentration in tissues because of oxidative metabolism, and so it diffuses into the blood along a gradient of partial pressures. The high concentration of CO_2 affects the carbonic acid (H_2CO_3) equilibrium, so that acidity is generated, according to the following reaction:

$$CO_2 + H_2O \leftrightarrow H_2CO_3 \leftrightarrow H^+ + HCO_3^- \leftrightarrow 2H^+ + CO_3^{-2}$$

Essentially, the higher the concentration of CO_2 in the blood, the more acidic it becomes.

Normally in mammals, the P_{CO_2} of the oxygenated blood that is entering vessels that supply the tissues is about 5.3 kPa (40 mm Hg). However, the P_{CO_2} in the tissue itself is about 6.1 kPa (46 mm Hg), so CO_2 diffuses into the blood. The H^+ concentration of the tissue fluids is about 1.6 times that of the blood (pH = 7.2 for tissue fluid, or 6.3×10^{-8} M of H^+), but 7.4 for blood (3.9×10^{-8} M), and so H^+ diffuses into the blood. The increases in blood P_{CO_2} and H^+ reduce the affinity of hemoglobin for O_2, and this causes a rightward shift to occur in its binding curve, called the **Bohr effect** or **Bohr shift** **(Figure 7.30)**. As it turns out, the Bohr effect is advantageous to the unloading of oxygen from the blood to the tissues, increasing it by about 10 percent. At the level of the gas-exchange surface in the lungs or gills, there is a reversal of the Bohr effect as CO_2 diffuses out of the blood to the environmental matrix, where the P_{CO_2} is much lower (in animals with gills the CO_2 diffuses into the water, and for those with lungs it moves into the atmosphere of the alveoli). The H^+ concentration is also lowered as it combines with HCO_3^- in the blood to form water and CO_2, which then diffuses out of the blood.

Certain organophosphorus compounds lower the affinity of hemoglobin for oxygen, also resulting in a Bohr shift. Typically, these compounds are found in animals with red blood cells (or erythrocytes—these contain the hemoglobin) and are produced in response to low O_2 availability, such as might occur at high altitude or in O_2-poor water. The most common of these compounds are 2,3-diphosphoglycerate (2,3-DPG), adenosine triphosphate (ATP), and guanosine triphosphate (GTP). 2,3-DPG is commonly produced by mammalian red blood cells, and ATP and GTP are produced by other vertebrates, such as fish. Avian red blood cells also produce organophosphorus compounds, the most common one being inositol pentaphosphate (IPP). All of these compounds help to unload more O_2 at the tissue level, but they do not affect its absorption at the gas-exchange surface. Thus, they aid oxidative metabolism during times of sustained (chronic) oxygen deprivation.

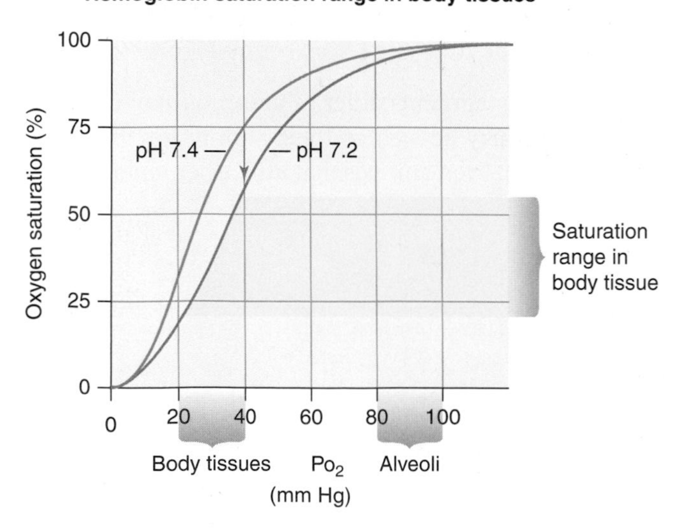

FIGURE 7.30

The Bohr Effect. An increase in the blood P_{CO_2} or a decrease in its pH causes a rightward shift of the curve.

SOURCE: From Russell/Wolfe/Hertz/Starr. *Biology*, 1E. © 2010 Nelson Education Ltd. Reproduced by permission. www.cengage.com/permissions.

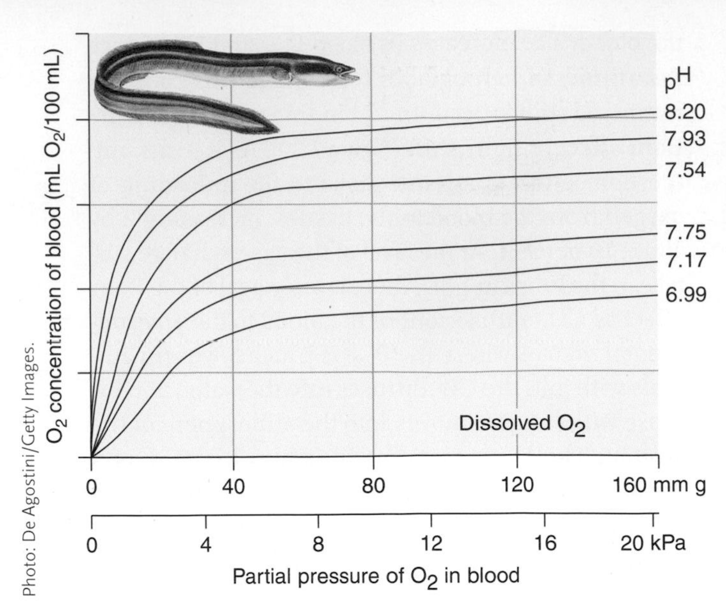

Photo: De Agostini/Getty Images.

FIGURE 7.31

The Root Effect. In some animals, such as teleost fish, an increase in blood P_{CO_2} or a reduction in its pH will result in a reduced oxygen content, even at full saturation of the respiratory pigment. These data are for the eel, *Anguilla vulgaris*.

SOURCE: Steen, J. B. 1963. "The physiology of the swimbladder in the eel *Anguilla vulgaris*," *Acta Physiologica Scandinavica*, 59: 221–241. Used by permission of Blackwell Publishing Ltd.

In some animals the accumulation of CO_2 and H^+ in the blood results in a phenomenon called the **Root effect (Figure 7.31).** It occurs commonly in teleost fish and serves to unload O_2 in the swim bladder and retina of the eye. Lactic acid (2-hydroxypropanoic acid, a carboxylic acid with the formula $C_3H_6O_3$) and/or CO_2 produced by these tissues results in a reduction in the maximum amount of O_2 that hemoglobin can carry at full saturation. As a result, oxygen diffuses from the hemoglobin into the swim bladder or retina, neither of which has an extensive blood supply.

Comparative Aspects of Respiratory Pigments

Respiratory pigments differ in the amount of oxygen they can carry as well as their affinity for that gas **(Figure 7.32).** Even animals that utilize hemoglobin do not necessarily show the same binding characteristics. The affinity characteristics of respiratory pigments are expressed in terms of the P_{50}, which is the partial pressure of the blood at 50 percent saturation of the pigment with O_2. The higher the affinity, the lower the P_{50} of the pigment.

Generally, the blood P_{50} tends to be relatively low in animals that live in an O_2-poor environment, such as low-O_2 water, in an underground burrow, or at high altitude. For example, the blood P_{50} of carp (*Cyprinus carpio*) and catfish (order Siluriformes), which can live in O_2-poor water, is lower than that of trout and salmon (Salmonidae) that cannot tolerate a low-O_2 environment. The blood of carp and catfish is able to load O_2 more readily than can that of trout at low P_{O_2}.

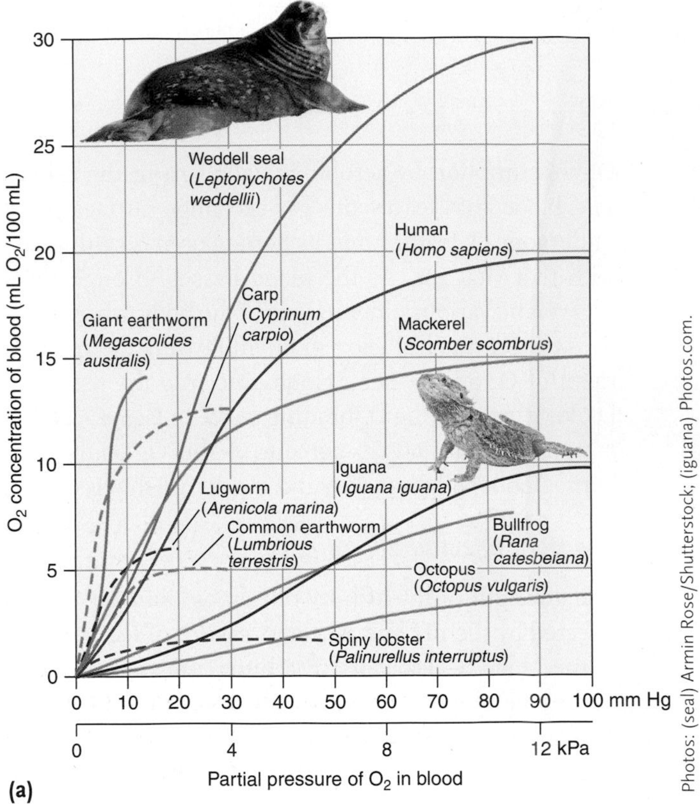

Photos: (seal) Armin Rose/Shutterstock; (iguana) Photos.com.

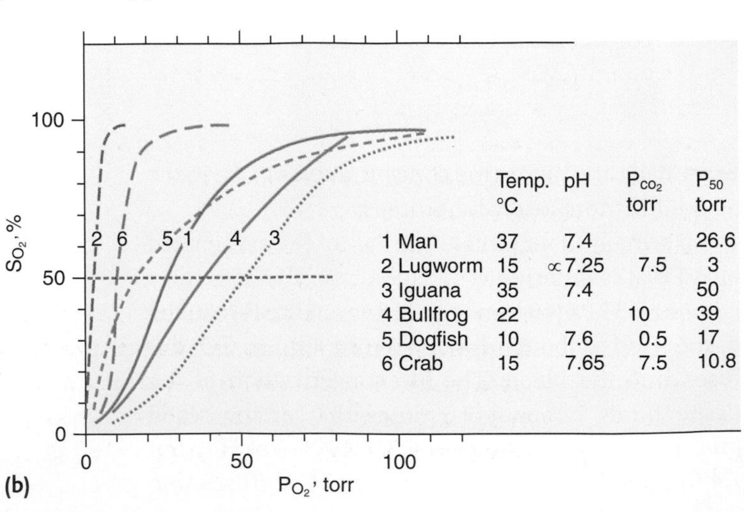

	Temp. °C	pH	P_{CO_2} torr	P_{50} torr
1 Man	37	7.4		26.6
2 Lugworm	15	∝7.25	7.5	3
3 Iguana	35	7.4		50
4 Bullfrog	22		10	39
5 Dogfish	10	7.6	0.5	17
6 Crab	15	7.65	7.5	10.8

FIGURE 7.32

Oxygen-Binding Curves of the Respiratory Pigments of Various Animals. The partial pressure of O_2 at 50 percent saturation (SO_2, %) is referred to as the P_{50} of the blood. The lower the P_{50} value, the greater the affinity for O_2.

SOURCES: (a) Hill, R. W., G. A. Wyse and M. Anderson. 2008. *Animal Physiology*. Sinauer Associates, Sunderland, MA. p. 592, Fig. 23-8. (b) Dejours, P. 1975. *Principles of Comparative Respiratory Physiology*. North Holland Publishing. Amsterdam.

Conversely, there is a trend among mammals for the O_2-affinity of the respiratory pigment to decrease with diminishing body mass, i.e., the blood P_{50} tends to be higher in smaller mammals regardless of environmental conditions. If the availability of O_2 is not a limiting factor for pigment saturation, then the advantage of higher blood P_{50} is a greater ease of unloading O_2 at the tissue level. Recall that smaller mammals have a larger mass-specific metabolism, which is required to maintain their body temperature. Therefore, the more efficient the unloading of O_2 is at the tissue level, the greater the ability to maintain a higher metabolic rate. In general, it is advantageous to have a lower blood P_{50} in environments where O_2 is limited, in order to saturate the respiratory pigment. In contrast, it is better to have a higher blood P_{50} in situations where O_2 is not limiting, because it helps to unload more O_2 at the tissue level.

Transport of Carbon Dioxide

Oxidative metabolism produces carbon dioxide and results in an increase in its partial pressure in cells. Because the P_{CO_2} of blood coming into organs is relatively low, it picks up this gas from the tissues **(Figure 7.33).** In animals that have red blood cells (all vertebrates and some invertebrates), the CO_2 enters the erythrocytes and some of it combines with hemoglobin to form **carbaminohemoglobin**. However, most CO_2 combines with water in the erythrocytes to form carbonic acid, some of which dissociates into HCO_3^- and H^+. The H^+ is buffered by hemoglobin (forming hydroxyhemoglobin) and the HCO_3^- is exchanged across the erythrocyte membrane for Cl^-, a phenomenon known as the **chloride ion shift**. At the gas-exchange surface, the process is reversed, with HCO_3^- moving from the blood plasma to the red blood cells in exchange for Cl^- and then recombining with H^+ in the erythrocytes to form H_2CO_3, CO_2, and water. The CO_2 then diffuses across the gas-exchange surface and into the environment.

Gas Transport and Exchange in Diving Mammals

Certain marine mammals can dive to great depths and stay submerged for long periods of time. The deepest dives are to astonishing depths: Cuvier's beaked whale (*Ziphius cavirostris*) has been recorded to 1885 m, elephant seal (*Mirounga angustirostris*) to 1640 m, and sperm whale (*Physeter catodon*) to 1200 m (Reynolds and Rommel, 1999; Whitehead, 2002; Tyack et al., 2006). The dive times may be as long as two hours.

During these astounding dives, the lungs are collapsed to prevent them from bursting under the enormous hydrostatic pressure. Of course, oxygen supplies are necessarily limited despite the demands for this gas by the muscles involved in swimming. The key

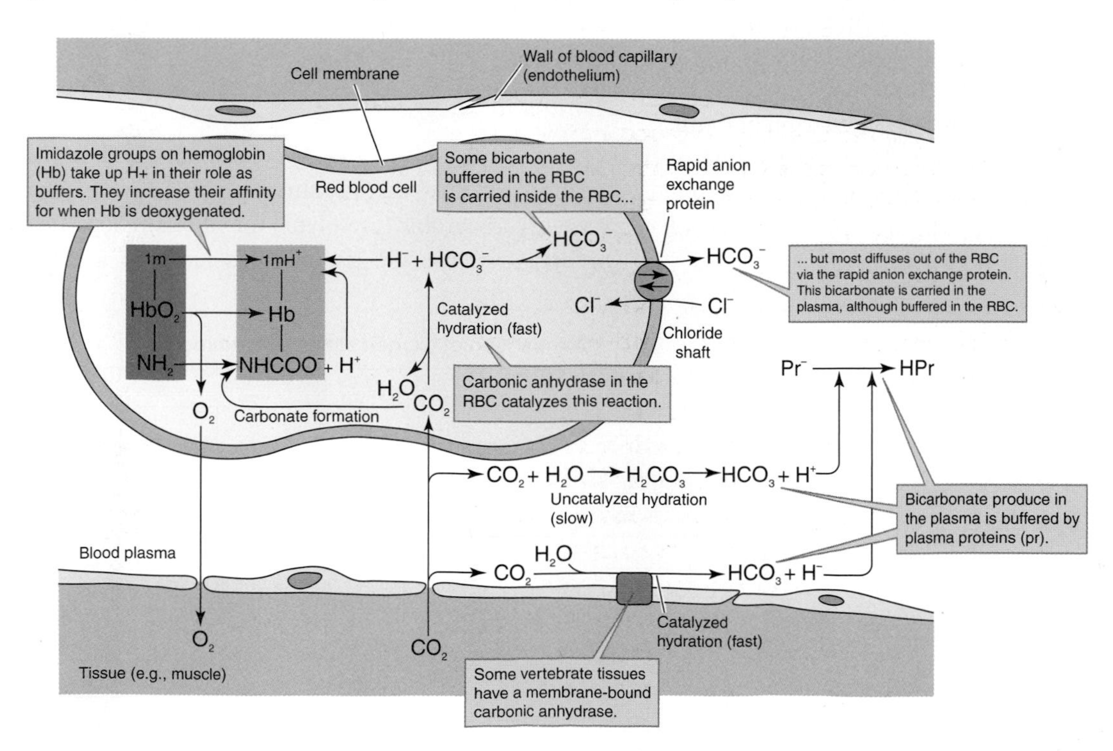

FIGURE 7.33

Carbon Dioxide Transport in the Blood. Animals that have red blood cells can carry CO_2 in the form of carbaminohemoglobin, as dissolved CO_2, or as HCO_3^- in the blood plasma. However, most of the CO_2 is carried as HCO_3^- in the plasma. The HCO_3^- is formed in the red blood cells and is exchanged for Cl^-, a phenomenon known as the chloride ion shift.

SOURCE: Hill, R. W., G. A. Wyse and M. Anderson. 2008. *Animal Physiology*. Sinauer Associates, Sunderland, MA. p. 606, Fig. 23-22.

physiological adjustments are: (1) supplying the brain and heart with enough O_2 to sustain aerobic metabolism; (2) reducing blood flow to areas of the body that are not as heavily reliant on O_2 as are the heart and brain; and (3) withstanding the enormous pressures that are encountered (1 additional atmosphere for every 10 m of depth).

Physiological Features of Diving Mammals

Marine mammals that can remain deeply submerged for a long time have unique physiological characteristics **(Figure 7.34).** First, their blood has a particularly large carrying capacity for oxygen. For example, the blood of the harbour seal (*Phoca vitulina*) at saturation can carry 26–29 mL of oxygen/100 mL (this is known as the volume % oxygen), while that of the sperm whale (*Physeter macrocephalus*) is 31 volume %, and the Weddell seal (*Leptonychotes weddellii*) 29–36 volume % (Hill et al., 2008). In comparison, human blood, and that of other terrestrial mammals living at altitudes below 3000 metres, typically carries 17–22 volume % O_2. The high volume % O_2 of deep-diving marine mammals is partly due to the higher concentration of hemoglobin and greater density of erythrocytes in their blood.

In addition, the blood volume of some deep-diving mammals (such as Weddell seal (*Leptonychotes weddellii*), elephant seal (*Mirounga* sp.), and sperm whale) is 2 to 3 times greater than that of non-diving mammals (200–250 mL/kg of body mass versus a more typical 60–110 mL/kg) (Butler and Jones, 1997; Kooyman and Ponganis, 1998). Considering both the high O_2-carrying capacity and the blood volume of deep-divers, the total maximum oxygen store is about 60–85 mL O_2/kg body weight, or 4–6 times that of terrestrial mammals (14–15 mL O_2/kg).

Skeletal muscle contains a respiratory pigment known as myoglobin, which serves as an O_2-storage compound that may be utilized during activities that require a sustained high consumption of O_2. The concentration of myoglobin in the muscle tissue of deep-diving mammals is 55–70 mg/g muscle (wet weight), compared with 4–9 mg/g in typical mammals. Therefore, deep-diving mammals have a far superior capacity to store oxygen in their muscles.

Other physiological adaptations that aid in deep and sustained diving include the following (Kooyman and Ponganis, 1998):

1. The lungs and thorax are collapsible, which prevents injury from high pressure while also decreasing buoyancy.
2. Blood is shunted away from non-utilized muscles and visceral organs (liver, kidney, spleen, stomach, and pancreas), while the brain and heart are provided with more circulation.
3. The heart rate is reduced to decrease the oxygen consumption (this is called diving bradycardia).
4. During a dive, the hematocrit may increase (this is the proportion of the blood volume that is composed of erythrocytes)—the Weddell seal has a hematocrit of 38 percent on the surface, but it may increase to 52 percent during a dive. Erythrocytes are added to the blood from the spleen over a 20-minute period (during a sequence of dives), and are removed during periods of prolonged rest.

Metabolism during Diving

Because oxygen is conserved for heart and brain function during diving (by shunting blood away from muscles), anaerobic (glycolytic) metabolism becomes important in muscle tissue. This leads to a large

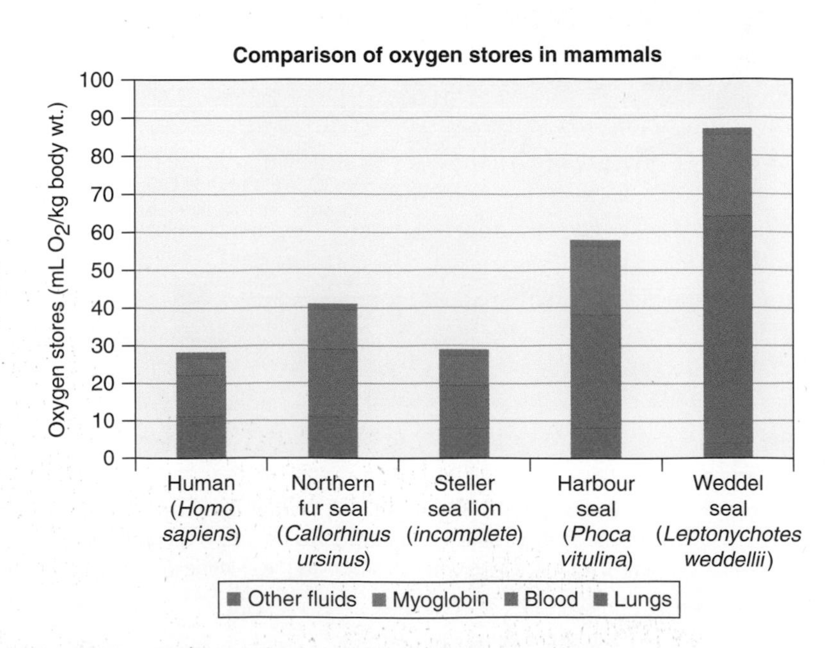

FIGURE 7.34

Comparison of Oxygen Stores in Mammals. Northern fur seal (*Callorhinus ursinus*) and Steller sea lion (*Eumetopias jubatus*) dive for relatively short periods of time, while harbour seal (*Phoca vitulina*) and Weddell seal (*Leptonychotes weddellii*) dive for longer times.

SOURCES: Modified from Lenfant, C., K. Johansen and J. D. Torrance. 1970. "Gas transport and oxygen storage capacity in some pinnipeds and the sea otter," *Respiration Physiology*, 9: 277–286; and Ponganis, P. J., G. L. Kooyman, and M. A. Castellini. 1993. "Determinants of the aerobic dive limit of Weddell seals: Analysis of diving metabolic rates, postdive end tidal PO_2's, and blood and muscle oxygen stores," *Physiological Zoology*, 66: 732–749.

accumulation of lactic acid and CO_2 in muscle tissue and blood, but deep-diving mammals can sustain this. For example, the lactate concentration may exceed 22 mmol/L of blood, about a 40-fold increase from that at rest. In comparison, during periods of intense physical activity in a human, such as sprinting, the muscle and blood may accumulate 15 mmol/L of lactate. When a deep-diver rests on the surface, the lactic acid is metabolized, but the longer the dive the more time it takes to remove the accumulated lactate. In fact, to avoid having to spend long periods on the surface trying to metabolize lactate, seals will choose to engage in shorter dive times so as to not exceed their "aerobic dive limit."

7.5 Acid–Base Balance

Introduction

The acid–base balance in an animal refers to its physiological ability to regulate the pH of intracellular and extracellular fluids within narrow limits close to neutrality (pH 7.0). There are several reasons for this tight regulation, including the sensitivity of enzymes to changes in pH and its effect on nerve and muscle function and on transport of oxygen by hemoglobin. The pH of body fluids is largely determined by the amount of dissolved CO_2 as well as the concentrations of non-volatile organic acids (such as lactic acid and keto acids). Carbonic acid, formed from the hydration of CO_2 (see the reaction on page 197), is considered a volatile acid because its concentration varies depending on the rate of CO_2 loss across the gas-exchange surface (lung or gill) as well as the rate of CO_2 production by metabolism. The greater the rate of ventilation of the gas-exchange surface, the more CO_2 is removed from the body and the lower the concentration of H_2CO_3 in body fluids. Organic acids are produced during metabolism and are considered non-volatile (or fixed) because they are not affected by gas exchange with the environment.

A lowering of the pH of body fluids to below the normal range is called an **acidosis,** and an increase is **alkalosis.** The normal range mostly depends on the temperature of the animal and its metabolic rate. Disruptions of the acid–base balance are classified according to the source of the excess acid or base. Those caused by the addition or removal of CO_2 in the blood are referred to as **respiratory disturbances** (or **disorders**). Those caused by the addition of fixed acids or bases to the blood are called **metabolic disturbances** (or **disorders**). The addition of a fixed acid results in a reduction in the blood HCO_3^- concentration, as the HCO_3^- neutralizes the H^+. Therefore, metabolic disturbances of the acid–base balance are sometimes characterized by changes in the blood HCO_3^- concentration by means other than changes in ventilation.

If the production of CO_2 exceeds the rate at which it is removed by ventilation, a **respiratory acidosis** is generated. Conversely, if the rate of ventilation is such that CO_2 removal exceeds its rate of production, a **respiratory alkalosis** results. A metabolic acidosis is generated when fixed acids are added to the blood, and a metabolic alkalosis is caused by the addition of a base (or alkali) to that fluid.

pH and Temperature

The pH of neutrality is defined as the pH of "pure" water, meaning distilled water that has not had contact with the atmosphere, so there is no dissolved CO_2 (if distilled water is in equilibrium with atmospheric CO_2 at 380 ppm, then the resulting carbonic acid equilibrium would generate a pH of about 5.65). Pure water at 25°C is neither acidic nor basic—it has a neutral pH of 7.00 because the concentration of H^+ is equal to that of OH^- (both have an identical concentration of 10^{-7} moles/L). However, the pH of neutrality varies slightly with temperature—the pH of neutrality rises at temperatures below 25°C and it falls above 25°C. Consequently, the pH of intracellular and extracellular fluids of animals is affected by their body temperature **(Figure 7.35).** Ectotherms living in cooler environments tend to have a higher blood pH than those at warmer temperatures.

Regardless of the temperature, the normal blood pH of animals is slightly more alkaline than the pH of neutrality—typically between 7.40 and 7.80 depending on whether the animal is air-breathing or water-breathing. A typical arterial blood pH of a rainbow trout at 15°C is 7.70, while that of an air-breathing mammal is 7.40 (body temperature 37°C). This is mainly due to the presence of **buffers** in the blood and intracellular fluid, i.e., chemicals that cause the pH to remain at a particular value.

Regulation of Acid–Base Status

There are three lines of physiological defence against changes in the acid–base status of an animal. They are (1) buffers; (2) regulation of ventilation of the gas-exchange surface; and (3) regulation of acid excretion and bicarbonate re-absorption by the renal organ.

Strong acids are readily buffered by proteins, such as hemoglobin, which occur in the intracellular or extracellular fluids, and by HCO_3^-, which combines with H^+ to form carbonic acid, a weak acid. These buffers do not necessarily prevent

FIGURE 7.35
Effect of Temperature on the pH of Water and Extracellular Fluid in a Variety of Animals. There is an inverse relationship between body temperature and the pH of extracellular fluids. Pure water shows a similar effect. Note that the extracellular fluid is slightly more alkaline than water at all temperatures.

SOURCE: Dejours, P. 1975. *Principles of Comparative Respiratory Physiology*. North Holland Publishing. Amsterdam.

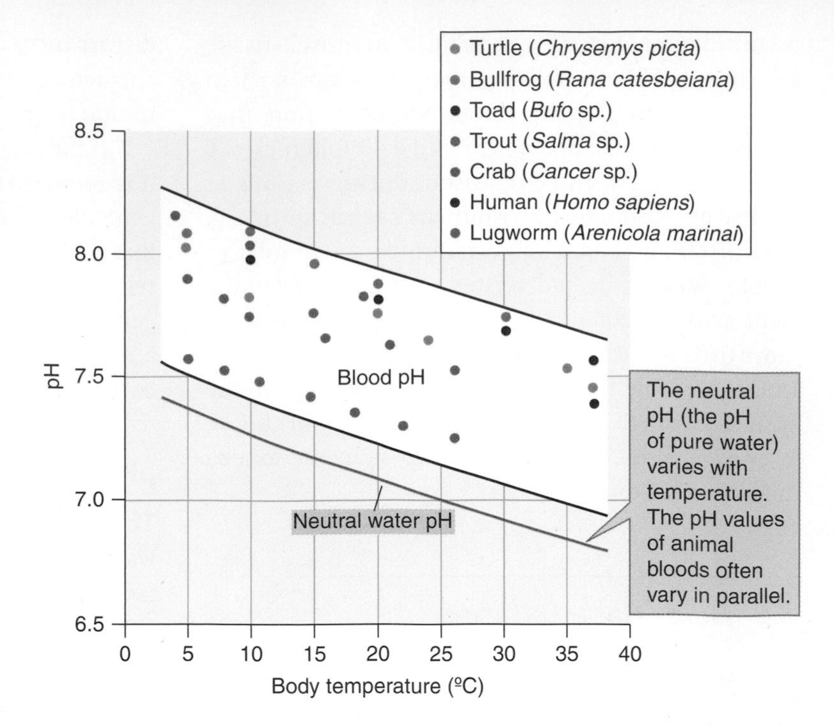

changes in blood pH, but they do reduce the amount of the change.

Alteration of the blood pH or P_{CO_2} can stimulate changes in ventilation of the gas-exchange surface. Chemoreceptors located in the cardiovascular system can detect changes in blood pH and P_{CO_2}. This information is relayed to the control centre in the brain for ventilation, resulting in an adjustment in its rate. Additionally, in mammals, the pH of the cerebral spinal fluid is sensitive to changes in blood P_{CO_2}. An increase in the P_{CO_2} of the blood results in diffusion of CO_2 into the spinal fluid, where it combines with water to form H^+ and HCO_3^-. Chemoreceptors in the brain detect the drop in pH and stimulate ventilation. The normal response to an acidosis, therefore, is an increase in ventilation, which lowers the blood P_{CO_2} and so drives the pH to a more alkaline condition. As we saw in the reaction on page 197, decreasing the CO_2 drives the reaction to the left, thereby reducing the H^+ concentration (and so raising the pH). Alkalosis is dealt with in the opposite way—as the pH rises or P_{CO_2} falls, ventilation is reduced, resulting in an accumulation of H^+ and lowering of the pH.

Although control of ventilation is a rapid way of correcting an acid–base disruption, it cannot always return the balance to normal. As well, if the ventilatory system is malfunctioning, it cannot correct an acid–base imbalance. However, the renal organ can also help to correct an acid–base disturbance, although the changes take place more slowly **(Figure 7.36).** The tubules of the renal organ can excrete acids and increase the rate of HCO_3^- reabsorption to compensate for an acidosis, or reduce the H^+ excretion and HCO_3^- reabsorption to compensate for an alkalosis.

Effects of Environmental Acidification

Large regions of Canada and extensive areas of other countries have suffered from an acidification of surface waters and sometimes also of soil. These environmental damages are often caused by the deposition of various acidifying substances from the atmosphere by the following mechanisms:

- acidic precipitation (acidic rain and snow);
- the dry deposition (or direct uptake) of gaseous sulphur dioxide (SO_2), which generates acidity when it becomes oxidized to sulphate (SO_4^{-2}) in the receiving ecosystem—because the SO_4^{-2} is electrochemically balanced by H^+, acidity is generated; and
- the dry deposition of gaseous oxides of nitrogen (NO_x, composed of NO and NO_2), which becomes oxidized to nitrate (NO_3^-), which is electrochemically balanced by H^+.

Surface waters (lakes, rivers, and streams) are vulnerable to acidification if they have a low concentration of calcium (Ca^{2+}; this ion is mostly derived from calcium carbonate, $CaCO_3$, in bedrock and soil of the watershed). The importance of the Ca^{2+} is in its relationship with alkalinity (HCO_3^-) in the water, because HCO_3^- is the key source of acid-neutralizing capacity (ANC) in fresh waters—if the concentration of calcium is high, so will be the alkalinity and ANC, and there is much greater resistance to becoming acidified.

Calcium is also important in protecting aquatic animals from acid-induced loss of ions from their body fluids. Species living in low-calcium water, therefore, are more susceptible to acid stress (low-Ca

A CANADIAN ECOLOGIST 7.1

Chris Wood: Studies of Fish Physiology

Chris Wood

Chris Wood of McMaster University is one of the world's foremost experts in the ecophysiology and toxicology of fish and aquatic invertebrates. Wood and his many students and colleagues have published hundreds of articles, mostly on the responses of aquatic animals to exposure to acidification, ammonia, and metals in their environment. He has conducted field studies around the world, including Africa, China, and Brazil, in addition to much of Canada. His research into the role of the gills and renal organs in ion and acid–base regulation has been recognized internationally as a major contribution to aquatic toxicology. In addition, Wood and his students were the first to identify cardiovascular collapse as the immediate cause of death in fish living in highly acidic waters. That finding has been highly important in understanding the global problem of acid rain, as well as its mitigation. Wood has also played a role in developing scientifically sound regulations and policies governing the release of metals to the environment. In 2001, Chris Wood was awarded a Canada Research Chair in Environment and Health, was elected to the Royal Society of Canada in 2003, and received the Romanowski Medal in Environmental Science of the Society in 2007.

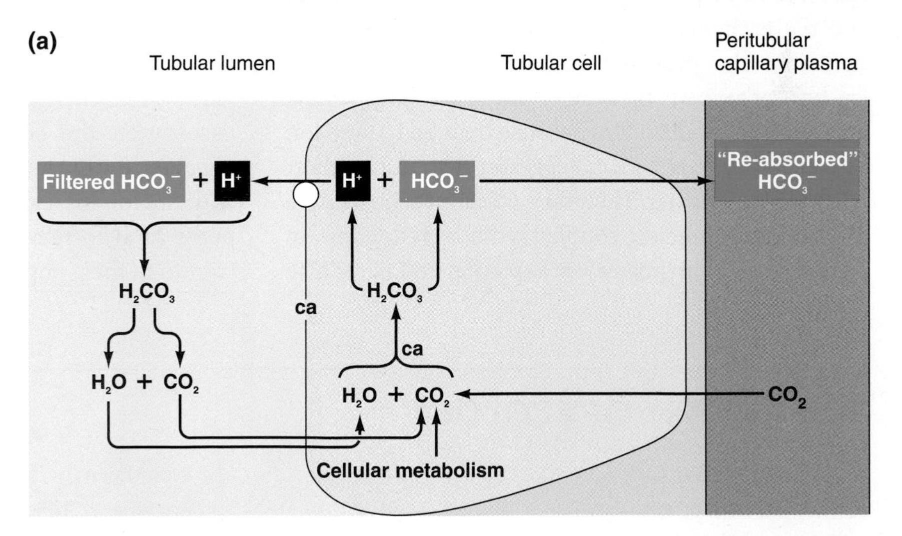

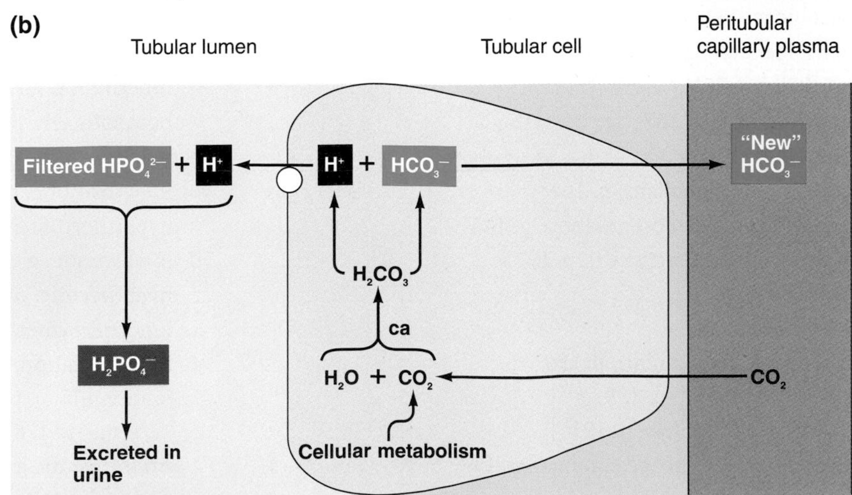

FIGURE 7.36

H^+ Excretion and HCO_3^- Re-absorption by Renal Tubules. Some of the H^+ secreted by the renal tubules is used in the re-absorption of HCO_3^-, and other secreted H^+ is trapped in the form of monobasic phosphate. In the process, a new molecule of HCO_3^- is added to the bloodstream.

SOURCE: From Sherwood. *Human Physiology*, 1E. © 2010 Nelson Education Ltd. Reproduced by permission. www.cengage.com/permissions.

is sometimes called "soft" water, while high-Ca is "hard" water). In addition, acidification of the water results in metals dissolving from minerals in soil and sediment, causing them to occur in high ionic concentrations in surface waters. In terms of causing toxicity to aquatic animals, the most important of the ionic metals is aluminum, occurring in the form of Al^{3+}. Chris Wood (McMaster University) and Gordon MacDonald (Guelph University) have studied the physiological effects of acidification on fish, and the following information is largely based on their research (Wood and McDonald, 1982; Wood and Rogano, 1986; Wood, 1989).

Strangely enough, acidification of soft water does not result in an acidosis in fish, but instead it causes a major loss of key cations across the gills, such as Na^+ and Cl^-. Conversely, in hard-water lakes, cation loss is not as large a problem, but aquatic animals may experience a metabolic acidosis. In either situation, the Na^+ loss occurs partly because of an inability to exchange Na^+ for H^+ across the gills. Normally, H^+ is moved into the environment in exchange for Na^+ uptake in a 1:1 ratio, but in acidified water the H^+ gradient is too great and the exchange is significantly reduced. As mentioned in the previous section on ionoregulation, freshwater animals face the problem of ion loss to the environment by diffusion because their body-fluid ion concentrations are so much greater than that of their environmental water. Therefore, continued ion leakage to the environment, coupled with a reduction in uptake, results in steady ion depletion and is a cause of death in fish in acidified soft waters (toxicity from Al^{3+} ions is also important).

Calcium seems to help protect the gills of fish and aquatic invertebrates against ion loss, and so many animals in hard waters can recover from acid exposure once the metabolic acidosis has been compensated. However, the low-Ca concentrations of soft water offer no such protection and upward of 30 percent ion loss is normally lethal to aquatic animals. The actual cause of death is likely due to circulatory failure. Dilution of the extracellular fluid because of the ion loss results in water movement into the intracellular fluid, which reduces the circulating blood volume and raises its viscosity. In addition, the erythrocytes tend to swell due to the movement of water into these cells from the blood plasma. The combination of increased blood viscosity and red blood cells swelling greatly increases stress on the heart, and that vital organ may fail.

The increased solubility of metals such as Al^{3+} at low pH (<5.5) adds to the problems faced by aquatic animals in soft-water conditions. Aluminum may accumulate on the surface of gills as a diffuse precipitate (or flocculate) of $Al(OH)_3$, which may cause an inflammatory response that thickens and distorts the lamellae and results in a mucous accumulation on the gill surface. This greatly reduces the ability to exchange gases with the environment, and results in both hypoxia (low O_2) and hypercapnia (high CO_2). Coupled with the ion losses, the hypoxia and hypercapnia may prove fatal to fish in acidified waters and can contribute to their populations becoming extirpated.

VOCABULARY OF ECOLOGY

acclimation, p. 176
acclimatization, p. 176
acidosis, p. 201
aerobic, p. 164
aerobic metabolism, p. 164
alkalosis, p. 201
ammonotelic, p. 187
anaerobic, p. 164
anaerobic metabolism, p. 164
behavioural thermoregulation, p. 175
Bohr effect (or Bohr shift), p. 197
buffer, p. 201
bulk flow, p. 180
carbaminohemoglobin, p. 199
chloride ion shift, p. 199
counter-current flow, p. 191
counter-current heat exchanger, p. 172
cryoprotectant, p. 175
ectotherm, p. 166
endotherm, p. 166
enzyme, p. 165
estivation, p. 173
heterotherm (or poikilotherm), p. 166
heterotroph, p. 164
hibernation (or seasonal torpor), p. 170
homeotherm, p. 166
hyperionic, p. 184
hyperosmotic, p. 183
hyperthermic, p. 170
hyposmotic, p. 183
hypothermic, p. 170
ionoconformer, p. 182
ionoregulation, p. 183
ionoregulator, p. 183
isozyme, p. 178
mass-specific metabolism, p. 164
metabolic disturbance (or metabolic disorder), p. 201
metabolic rate, p. 164

metabolic water, p. 185
negative feedback system, p. 169
negative-pressure ventilation, p. 193
non-shivering thermogenesis, p. 170
obligatory water loss, p. 186
osmoconformer, p. 182
osmoregulation, p. 183
osmoregulator, p. 183
oxidative capacity, p. 164
partial pressure, p. 189
positive-pressure ventilation, p. 193
Q_{10}, p. 165
respiratory acidosis, p. 201
respiratory alkalosis, p. 201
respiratory disturbance (or respiratory disorder), p. 201
respiratory pigment, p. 196
Root effect, p. 198
supercool, p. 175
thermoneutral zone, p. 170
thermoregulation, p. 167
torpor p. 170
ureotelic, p. 188
uricotelic, p. 188

QUESTIONS FOR REVIEW AND DISCUSSION

1. Explain why ectothermic animals tend to be heterothermic (or poikilothermic), and endotherms tend to be homeothermic. Can endotherms be heterothermic? Can ectotherms be homeothermic?
2. Describe the relationship between metabolism and environmental temperature in an endothermic homeotherm, such as a mammal or bird.
3. Describe a strategy used by some fish for coping with life in extremely cold water where temperatures can fall below the freezing point.
4. Explain the importance of insulation and metabolism in endothermic homeotherms.
5. What is the difference between torpor and hibernation? What is the advantage of daily torpor in small mammals like mice or bats?
6. Define the terms "osmoconform" and "osmoregulate."
7. Explain how marine teleost fish overcome the osmotic and ionic problems they face in their environment.
8. Explain why fish can produce ammonia but terrestrial animals must produce either urea or uric acid.
9. List the tactics used by terrestrial animals to overcome the water-balance problem.
10. Compare and contrast the advantages and disadvantages of being a water-breather versus an air-breather.
11. Explain the advantage of counter-current gas exchange in a fish gill.
12. Contrast positive-pressure and negative-pressure ventilation in air-breathing organisms.
13. Describe the gas-exchange system in insects. Why isn't a circulatory system necessary to transport gases in these animals?
14. Describe the Bohr effect and explain its advantage in terms of off-loading oxygen at the tissue level.
15. Explain how acidification of the environment can disrupt ionoregulation in soft-water acclimated fish.

HELPFUL WEBSITES

WOOD FROG FREEZING SURVIVAL

http://www.units.muohio.edu/cryolab/projects/woodfrogfreezing.htm

This site examines the astonishing phenomenon of frogs being able to freeze solid during the winter and then thaw in the springtime to breed.

ICE FISH

http://www.icefish.neu.edu/participants/marshall/

Visit this website to learn more about the ice fish.

ACID RAIN

http://www.epa.gov/acidrain/what/index.html

Learn more about acid rain and its consequences for aquatic biota.

You'll find a rich array of additional resources for *Ecology* at www.ecology.nelson.com

an innate or heritable component, but they will be conditional depending on age, developmental maturity, and experience. Actions taken may also be influenced by what other people are doing and by additional vagaries of environmental conditions.

In ecology, the life-history characteristics of a species can be distilled to a set of responses, influenced by natural selection, that affect the success of individuals through their fitness. Within this context, life-history theory provides an explanatory and predictive framework for understanding why organisms differ so extraordinarily in the means by which they propagate their genes to future generations (i.e., fitness). Here are some examples of those vast differences:

- *Age at Maturity*: Individuals of some species reproduce at a young age, which can be only minutes in some bacteria, a few days for many invertebrates, and several months for small mammals such as white-footed mouse (*Peromyscus leucopus*), while in others sexual maturity is delayed to a much later age, such as several decades in the humpback whale (*Megaptera novaeangliae*) and dogfish shark (*Squalus acanthias*).
- *Reproductive Events*: Some organisms may reproduce many times during their life, such as snapping turtle (*Chelydra serpentine*) and rockfishes (*Sebastes* spp.), whereas others do so only once and then die, such as Pacific salmon (*Oncorhnychus* spp.) and annual plants such as Indian tobacco (*Lobelia inflata*).
- *Size and Numbers of Offspring*: Some species have large numbers of small offspring, as occurs in swordfish (*Xiphius gladius*) that produce hundreds of millions of 1.7 mm eggs, while others have only a few but large offspring, as is the case of the great white shark (*Carcharodon carcharias*), which births only 2–14 pups at a time, each about 1.5 m long.
- *Parental Care*: Some parents invest a great deal of energy in caring for their young, such as female grey seals (*Halichoerus grypus*) that lose about 40 percent of their body mass during a 16–18-day lactation period as they transfer exceedingly rich milk (containing 60 percent fat) to their single pup. Other species provide no parental care at all, such as Atlantic cod (*Gadus morhua*) that release eggs and sperm directly into oceanic water, with the survival of the offspring depending entirely on environmental conditions.

A life history in ecology is often examined in terms of the expenditure of reproductive effort, which may be defined as the proportion of total energy that is devoted to reproduction (Hirshfield and Tinkle, 1975). There are physiological, anatomical, and behavioural aspects of reproductive effort, and depending on the species of animal, they might include gonad development, migration to breeding grounds, changes in feeding rate or preference, and energetic demands associated with competition for mates, nest construction, or parental care. In plants, reproductive effort is typically measured by the allocation of energy (often measured as biomass) to flowers or fruits.

Ecological studies of life history often examine changes in age-specific survival and fecundity of individuals and groups (such as a population) and how these traits have been influenced by factors based on genetics and environmental conditions. In fact, much of this chapter will examine *age-specific* schedules of survival and fecundity of certain animals. In other species, however, these data might be appropriately expressed as *developmental stage-specific* schedules, such as in insects (the stages may be egg, larva, pupa, adult), vascular plants (seed, seedling, pre-reproductive, flowering, fruiting), or mushrooms (spore, haploid hyphae, dikaryotic mycelium, and basidiocarp or mushroom).

The life history of an individual ultimately determines its fitness, as well as the persistence and growth rate of populations and the ability of commercially important species to sustain various levels of exploitation. The study of life histories is a vital field

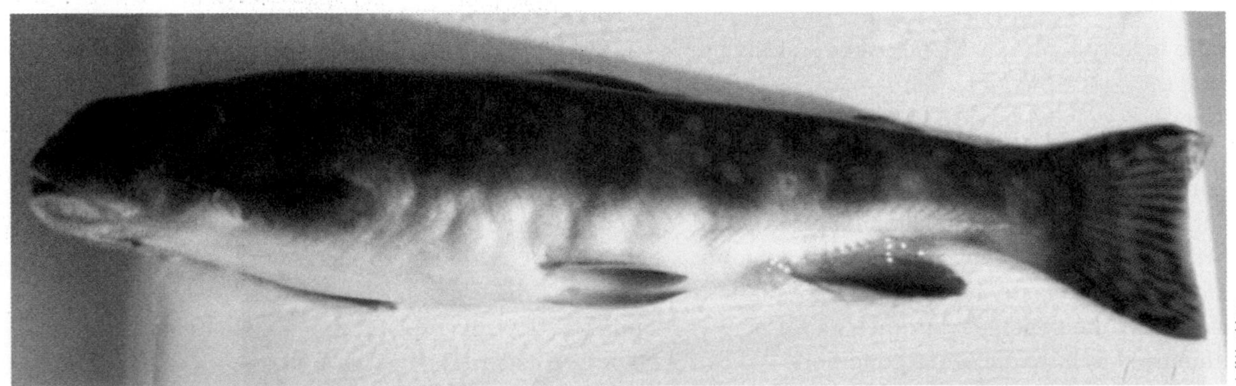

Jeff Hutchings

The eggs produced by this 12 cm long female brook trout (*Salvelinus fontinalis*) can actually be seen to be "bulging" along the ventral side of the fish. This is a visually striking example of high reproductive effort, in terms of the proportional allocation of body tissue to gonad development.

in ecology—it is at the core of research addressing evolutionary ecology, conservation of biodiversity, and the harvesting of bio-resources.

Life-History Traits

Life histories reflect the expression of traits that are closely related to fitness, including

- **age at maturity** and **size at maturity**, or the age and size at which an organism reproduces for the first time;
- **fecundity** or **fertility**, or the number of offspring produced by an individual in a single breeding season;
- offspring size, such as that of a seed, egg, embryo, or newborn; and
- **longevity (lifespan).**

The analytical link between life history and fitness can be expressed by the discrete-time version of the Euler-Lotka equation (examined in Chapter 5), in which the fitness of genotype i (r_i) can be calculated from

$$1 = \sum_{x=\alpha}^{x=\tau} l_x m_x \exp(-r_i x)$$

where l_x represents the probability of surviving from birth until age x, fecundity at age x is given by m_x, and age ranges from maturity (α) until death (τ).

The links between life-history traits and fitness are evident from close examination of the Euler-Lotka equation. For example, age at maturity (α) and longevity (τ) are explicitly denoted below and above the summation sign, respectively. Age-specific fecundity (m_x) is a function of the number and size of offspring that an individual produces. The influence of size at maturity on life history is less explicit. However, it becomes clear how the size at which an individual first reproduces (its size at maturity) can affect its age-specific schedules of survival and fecundity if we acknowledge that

1. the age-specific survival (l_x) of an individual often depends on its size, because larger individuals often have a higher likelihood of survival than smaller ones, and
2. fecundity (m) usually increases with body size, for instance, larger fish typically produce more eggs, and larger plants more seeds.

Parity (the number of breeding events in a lifetime) and individual growth rate are two additional traits that are commonly linked to life histories. As noted in Chapter 5, semelparous organisms reproduce once in their life and then die (semelparity), while iteroparous ones reproduce more than once (iteroparity). The link between life history and growth rate lies in the determination of an individual's body size at a given age. This connection is usually more relevant for organisms with indeterminate growth (meaning they increase in size, albeit at a declining rate, throughout their life, as occurs in most plants, fish, and amphibians) than for those that cease to grow following the attainment of maturity (determinate growth, as occurs in most insects, mammals, and birds).

Trait Variability

The variability of life histories is typically studied at three levels of biological organization: (1) among species; (2) among populations within a species; and (3) among individuals within a population.

As we previously noted, the diversity of expression of life-history traits among species is extraordinary. For example, the age at maturity can vary from minutes in bacteria to decades, such as 14 to >30 years in the white sturgeon (*Acipenser transmontanus*), an endangered fish of the Fraser River in British Columbia. Even within a single class of vertebrate animals, the age at maturity can range widely (**Figure 8.1**). The range of size at maturity is also huge, for instance varying over seven orders of magnitude in vertebrate animals. Among the smallest is the 6.2 mm male anglerfish (*Photocorynus spiniceps*), a sexually dimorphic deepsea fish whose much larger

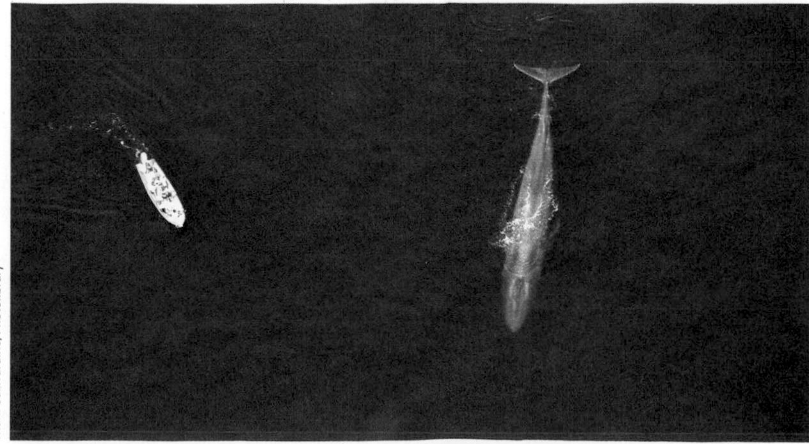

Mark Carwardine/Photolibrary

The blue whale (*Balaenoptera musculus*), the largest animal on Earth, matures at a length of 23 m or more and can attain sizes exceeding 33 m and 180 tonnes.

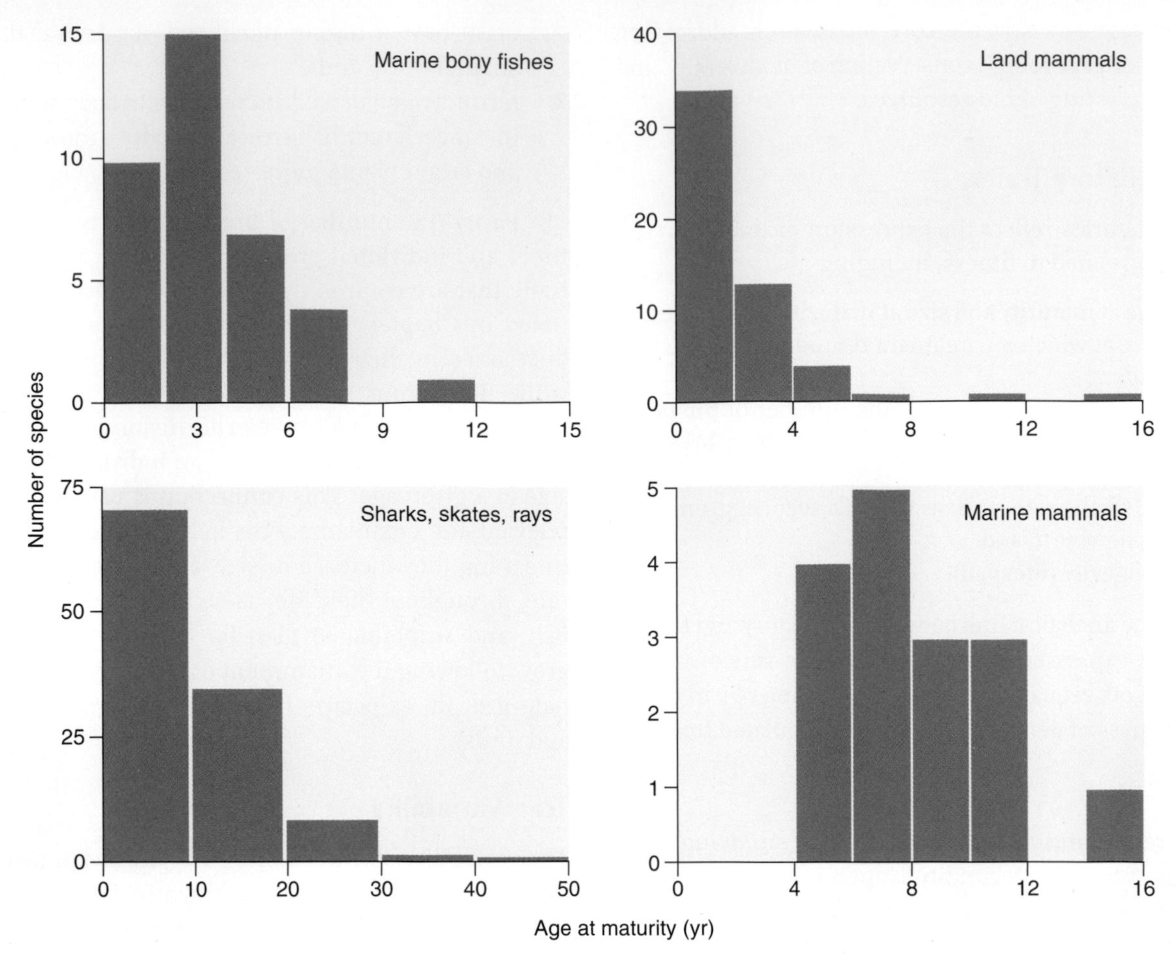

FIGURE 8.1
Distributions of Age at Maturity (years) for Various Kinds of Vertebrate Animals.

SOURCE: Hutchings et al. (2010).

females are about 5 cm long and serve as sexual hosts for the tiny parasitic males (Pietsch, 2005). At the larger end of the spectrum of size at maturity is the blue whale (*Balaenoptera musculus*), which matures at about 23 m or longer and grows as big as 33 m (Sears, 2002). The size of offspring can range from seeds and eggs less than 1 mm in diameter to individuals weighing several kilograms (a newborn blue whale weighs about 7 tonnes). In fact, seed size in plants varies by more than 10 orders of magnitude, with the smallest being orchid seeds weighing only 1 μg and the largest being those of the coco de mer (*Lodoicea maldivica*) of the Seychelles Islands, whose individual seeds weigh up to 18 kg (Westoby et al., 1992). The numbers of offspring per breeding episode can also vary enormously, by up to nine orders of magnitude, as is shown for three groups of vertebrates in **Figure 8.2.**

There can also be considerable variability of life-history traits within a species (Hutchings and Jones, 1998). Among populations of Atlantic salmon (*Salmo salar*), the age at maturity can range 10-fold, from only 1 year for males in the southern rivers of New Brunswick and Nova Scotia to as much as 10 years for females in Arctic Nunavik in northern Quebec. The size at maturity varies by more than 14-fold, from less than 7 cm for males in Newfoundland to more than 1 m among females in southern Norway. The number of eggs laid per female per breeding season ranges from tens to tens of thousands, while egg diameter ranges from 4.5 mm in Ouananiche Beck, a tributary of Bristol Cove River in southeastern Newfoundland, to 7.0 mm in the Restigouche River, northern New Brunswick.

Moreover, if environmental conditions are different enough, natural selection can result in surprisingly local differences in life-history traits. This has been illustrated by studies initiated in 1987 by Jeff Hutchings, then of Memorial University of Newfoundland, on populations of brook trout (*Salvelinus fontinalis*) separated by distances ranging from only a few hundred metres to 19 km on Cape Race in southeastern Newfoundland (e.g., Hutchings, 1991, 2006; Wilson et al., 2003; Purchase and Hutchings,

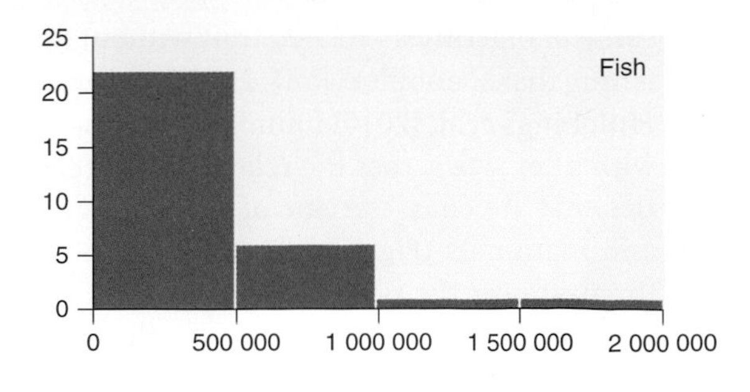

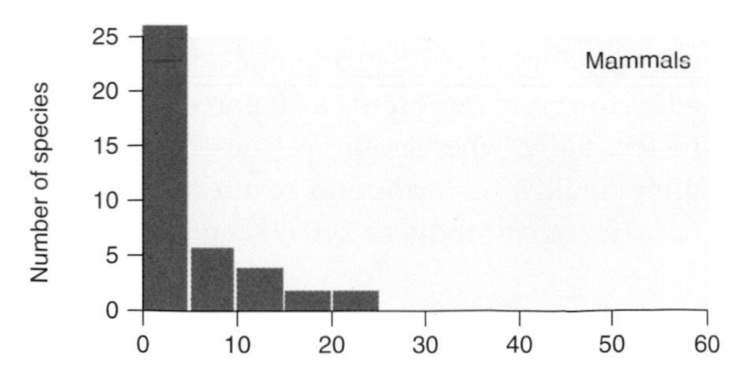

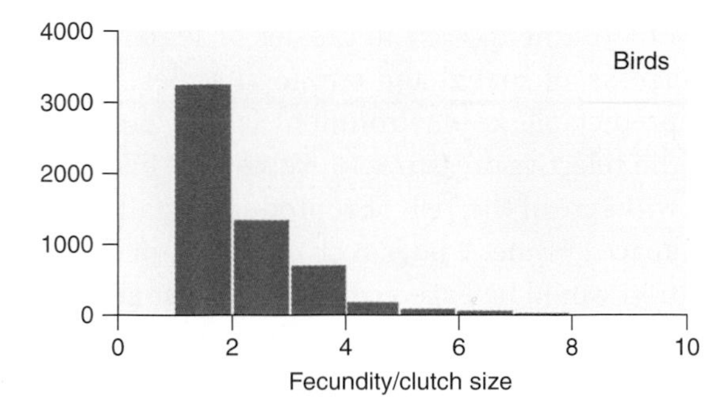

FIGURE 8.2

Numbers of Offspring per Breeding Episode. Distributions of fecundity, or clutch size, for marine teleost fish, terrestrial and marine mammals, and landbirds.

SOURCE: Fish and mammals are from Hutchings et al. (2010); Birds are redrawn from Jetz et al. (2008).

2008). The most divergent populations are in Freshwater River and Cripple Cove River, where the trout are unexploited, non-migratory, occur at a similar density, and are not affected by competition or predation from other species of fish. Despite these similarities, females in Freshwater River mature about one year earlier (at 3.1 years on average) than those in Cripple Cove River (4.2 years), and at a fivefold smaller weight (**Figure 8.3**). The smallest lengths at maturity—62 mm for males and 70 mm for females in Freshwater River—are the shortest recorded for this wide-ranging species. In addition, females in Freshwater River allocate about double the percentage of their body mass to gonadal tissue compared with those from Cripple Cove River, and they produce 30 percent more eggs for their size, each of which is almost double the volume (**Figure 8.3**). These differences in life-history traits between populations have been interpreted as representing adaptive responses to local environmental conditions, particularly in the food supply and quality of overwintering habitat, on age-specific survival, fecundity, and growth rate of the trout.

Linking Life-History Traits to Population Growth Rate

As mentioned above, the link between life history and individual fitness is made explicit in the Euler-Lotka equation. In that context, a population's per capita rate of increase, r, is simply a function of the average fitness of the various genotypes that occur within it, i.e., μ (r_i).

Two life-history traits in particular tend to be strongly associated with fitness and, by extension, with population growth rate. The first of these is age at maturity. Lamont Cole (1954), who modelled simulated data, was the first to demonstrate that, all else being equal, fitness (r) increases as age at maturity declines. This link between r and age at maturity provides one reason why populations characterized by a relatively young age at maturity tend to be more resistant to decline and are more resilient during recovery from a depletion, compared with those in which individuals mature at older ages (Reynolds et al., 2005).

Body size at maturity is a second important life-history correlate of individual fitness and population growth rate. Hutchings et al. (2010) performed an empirical study of how life-history traits can be correlated with one another and with maximum per capita population growth rate, r_{max}. They examined life-history data and estimates of r_{max} for 199 species (421 populations) of vertebrate animals (bony and cartilaginous fish and terrestrial and marine mammals). While age at maturity increased with body size among these animals (**Figure 8.4**), fecundity was positively associated with body size only in bony fish (**Figure 8.5**). They also examined which of age at maturity, maximum body size, or fecundity was the best predictor of maximum population growth rate (r_{max}). They found that body size had the strongest correlation, and that the association between size and r_{max} was similar among the groups examined (**Figure 8.6**). In contrast, there was no correlation between r_{max} and fecundity across seven orders of magnitude (ranging up to 5×10^8 eggs in swordfish) in bony fish (**Figure 8.7**).

It is not surprising to find that offspring production can be unrelated to r_{max} (as was first noted by Cole, 1954), given that (a) fecundity is only one of several traits that contribute to individual fitness (and thus to population growth rate) and (b) various trade-offs (reflected by negative associations among traits) often prevent selection from increasing the value of one fitness-related trait without diminishing that of another (Roff, 2002). Nonetheless, Hutchings et al. (2010) found that r_{max} increased with litter size across the relatively low fecundities that are characteristic of cartilaginous fish and mammals (**Figure 8.7**). This suggests that the narrower the range and the lower the absolute value of fecundity, the greater the potential influence on fitness of the addition of a single offspring. For example, in a mammal that typically produces two offspring, the addition of an additional one represents a 50 percent increase in fecundity, whereas there would be a negligible additive contribution to the fitness of a bony fish that produces 100 000 eggs.

Jeff Hutchings (top and bottom)

Cape Race is located on the southeastern tip of the island of Newfoundland. Brook trout (*Salvelinus fontinalis*) inhabit more than 10 small streams and rivers across a 19 km distance. Freshwater River (lower photo) is where the bulk of the trout life-history research on Cape Race has been undertaken.

Bet Hedging

Environments vary to greater or lesser degrees across all spatial and temporal scales. The less predictable an environment is, the greater are the selective pressures to evolve a life history that will spread the risk of reproductive failure over space or time. Under such circumstances, selection would be expected to act against genotypes whose life histories have them placing "all of their eggs in one basket." In other words, selection should act to reduce the variance in genotypic/individual fitness over generations, even if this would entail a "sacrifice" of the expected fitness within any one particular generation (Roff, 1992). Life histories such as these are referred to as **bet-hedging strategies**.

One common strategy that bet-hedging individuals can employ is the production of offspring

Freshwater River
Cripple Cove River
Mean size at maturity
93 mm
163 mm
Minimum size at maturity
70 mm
110 mm
Body size of 150 mm
Body weight composed of eggs
Fecundity (● = 5 eggs)
103
78
Egg size (diameter; volume)
5 mm
65 mm³
4 mm
33 mm³

FIGURE 8.3

Life Histories Can Vary Considerably across Small Geographic Scales. Brook trout (*Salvelinus fontinalis*) inhabiting rivers only 9 km apart on Cape Race, Newfoundland, differ in the expression of many life-history traits, including size at maturity, proportional allocation of body mass to gonads, fecundity, and egg size (the data on eggs are for 150 mm-long females, to control for body size).

SOURCES: Hutchings (1993, 1996). Illustration: Dorling Kindersley/Getty Images

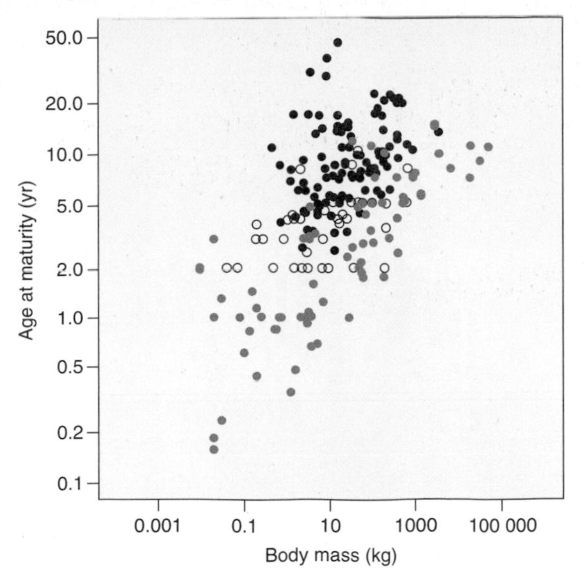

FIGURE 8.4

Age at Maturity with Respect to Body Size. At the species level, age at maturity increases with body size in vertebrates such as bony fish (open circles), cartilaginous fish (sharks, skates and rays; black circles), and terrestrial and marine mammals (orange circles).

SOURCE: Hutchings et al. (2010).

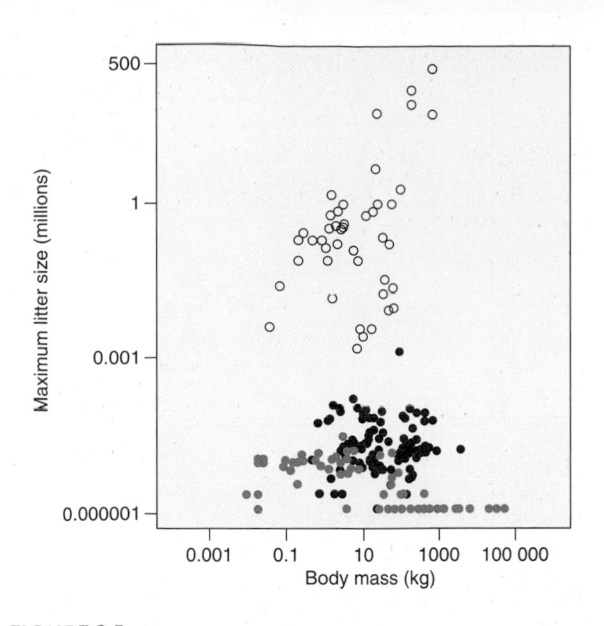

FIGURE 8.5

Fecundity with Respect to Body Size. At the species level, fecundity increases with body size in bony fish (open circles) but not in cartilaginous fish (black circles) or in mammals (orange circles).

SOURCE: Hutchings et al. (2010).

These Canadian vertebrate species vary tremendously in terms of life-history traits such as age at maturity and fecundity. Top row: Meadow voles (*Microtus pennsylvanicus*), found across Canada, mature at less than two months of age, whereas the endangered porbeagle (*Lamna nasus*) off eastern Canada matures at 8 (males) to 13 years (females). Bottom row: Every breeding season, British Columbia's Pacific halibut (*Hippoglossus stenolepis*) produces hundreds of thousands to several millions of eggs annually, whereas the humpback whale (*Megaptera novaeangliae*) bears a single calf every two to three years.

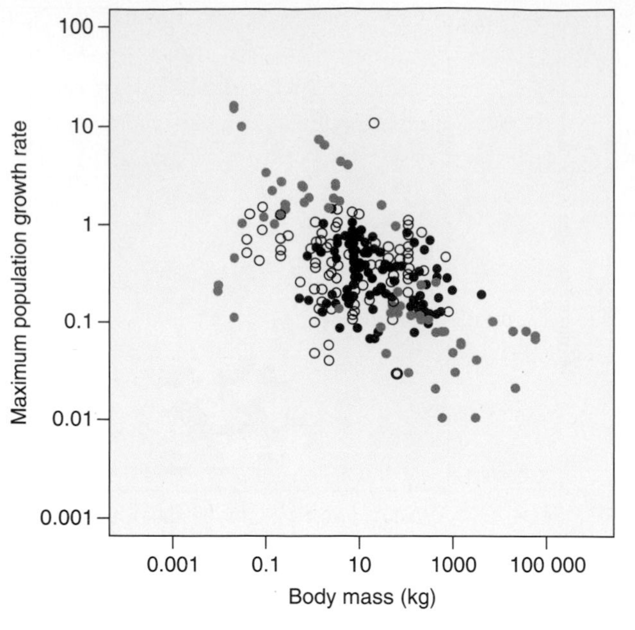

FIGURE 8.6

Maximum per Capita Rate of Population Growth (r_{max}) Declines as Body Size Increases in Vertebrates. This pattern of association does not differ among bony fish (open circles), cartilaginous fish (black circles), and mammals (orange circles).

SOURCE: Hutchings et al. (2010).

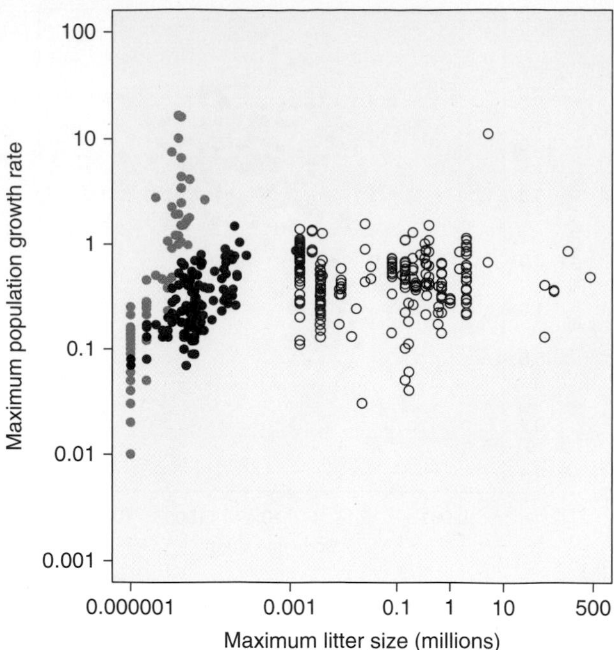

FIGURE 8.7

Divergent Associations between Population Growth Rate and Fecundity in Vertebrates. Maximum per capita rate of population growth (r_{max}) is not associated with fecundity in bony fish (open circles), but it does increase with litter size in cartilaginous fish (black circles) and in mammals (orange circles).

SOURCE: Hutchings et al. (2010).

that are phenotypically variable in traits that can affect survival in an unpredictable environment. In plants, for example, the size and timing of seed germination are traits that have been implicated as components of bet-hedging life histories. As summarized by Andrew Simons of Carleton University and Mark Johnston of Dalhousie University (2006), both of these traits affect fecundity and survival, and seed size influences the timing of germination. Within-plant variability in seed size has been interpreted as an adaptive response to variable environments (Capinera 1979). If some environmental conditions favour individuals that emerge from large seeds, while others favour those from small seeds, then the production of seeds of various sizes by an individual plant in a particular season may be favoured by natural selection. In bacteria, variability in the translucence of colonies produced by a single genotype is an analogue of seed-size variability in plants, as has been observed for *Pseudomonas fluorescens* by Beaumont et al. (2009) (**Figure 8.8**). In response to a selection regime in which the environment varied unpredictably from one generation to the next, they found that several populations of *P. fluorescens* evolved a bet-hedging strategy whereby populations stochastically switched their colony morphology, facilitating their persistence to the selection regime.

Even under controlled environmental conditions, the time of germination can vary considerably in plants, as was shown by Simons and Johnston (2006) for successive generations of the annual dicot *Lobelia*

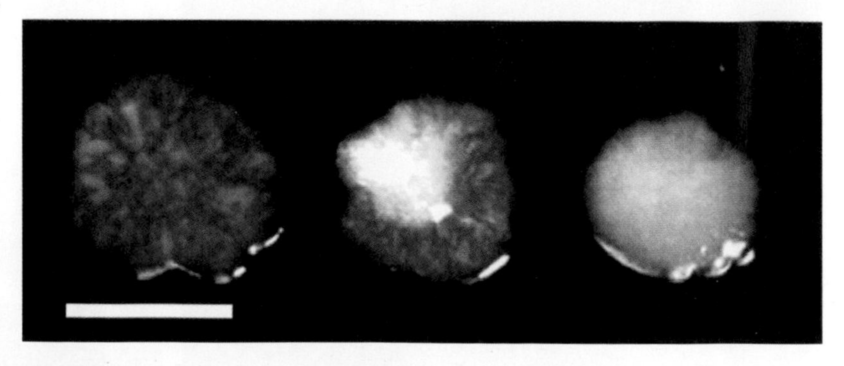

FIGURE 8.8

Pseudomonas fluorescens **Respond to Unpredictably Variable Environments by Evolving a Bet-Hedging Strategy That Produces Bacterial Colonies of Differing Morphology.** Translucent, sectored, and opaque colonies produced by a single bet-hedging genotype of the bacterium *P. fluorescens* (scale bar is 2 mm).

SOURCE: Beaumont et al. (2009), Figure 1(b).

inflata (**Figure 8.9**). Most interesting, however, is the observation that the variation in germination time can differ among genotypes within the same population (**Figure 8.10**). This suggests that natural selection can act on the *variance* in germination timing, rather than simply on the *mean* time, a finding that is consistent with the prediction that such diversification bet hedging can be an evolved strategy.

Bet hedgers can also spread their reproductive risks by reproducing multiple times throughout their lives, or within a single breeding season, and even numerous times within the same location (almost always with multiple mates, which spreads the risk even further). The Atlantic cod is an example of a species that bet hedges by spreading its reproductive risks. Presumably in response to the high temporal and spatial unpredictability of the environments in which cod larvae find themselves, natural selection has favoured the evolution of a life history in which females release their eggs in multiple batches (typically every four to seven days) during a breeding season. The longer the spawning period, the greater the likelihood that larvae will hatch at a time when the food availability is high (**Figure 8.11**), which lowers the chance of unusually poor reproductive success by a particular female. It is also instructive to note that larger individuals spawn over longer periods of time than smaller ones (Hutchings and Myers, 1993). In theory, this would mean that a population comprised of large spawners would have reduced temporal variability in offspring survival (this is termed "recruitment" in fisheries science) when compared to a population composed of small spawners.

Another way to think about bet-hedging life histories is to consider that the fitness associated with a particular genotype is best estimated as a geometric mean calculated across several generations (a geometric mean is the square root of the product of the values in a sample; it is used to determine the typical value or central tendency of a group of numbers). Use of the geometric mean makes explicit the fact that fitness is determined by a multiplicative

kpzfoto/Getstock.com

Indian tobacco (*Lobelia inflata*), a semelparous or monocarpic plant, is found in fields and thickets from Newfoundland to central Ontario. The seed germination of *Lobelia inflata* was studied by Simons and Johnston; see Figure 8.9.

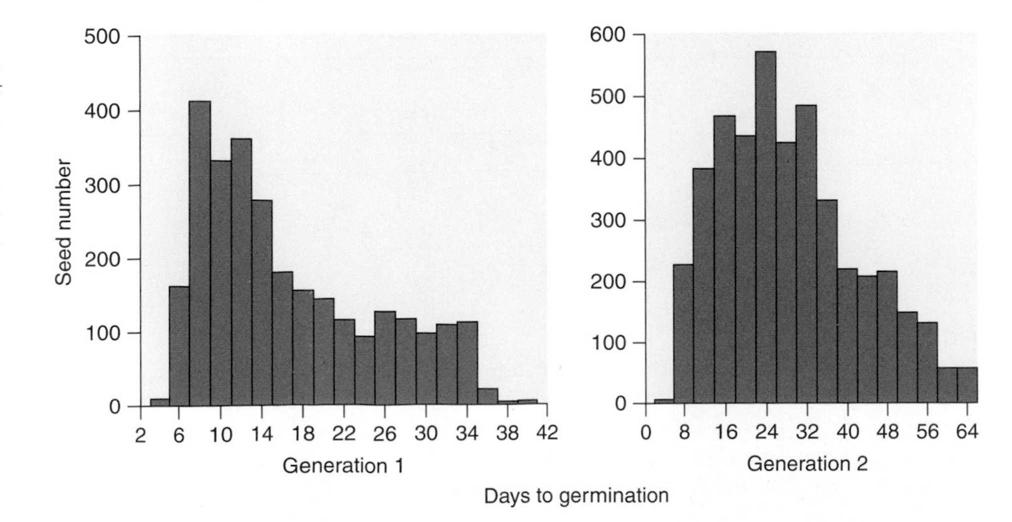

FIGURE 8.9
Bet Hedging in a Semelparous Plant. The timing of seed germination in *Lobelia inflata* can vary more than 10-fold from one generation to the next, even under controlled environmental conditions in a growth chamber.

SOURCE: Simons and Johnston (2006), Figure 2.

process: the total number of descendants left by an individual after n generations depends on the product of the number surviving to reproduce in each generation (Seger and Brockmann, 1987). Therefore, the geometric mean fitness of genotype i after n generations can be calculated as

$$(r_{i(1)}) \times (r_{i(2)}) \times (r_{i(3)}) \times (r_{i(4)}) \times \ldots \times (r_{i(n)})^{(1/n)}$$

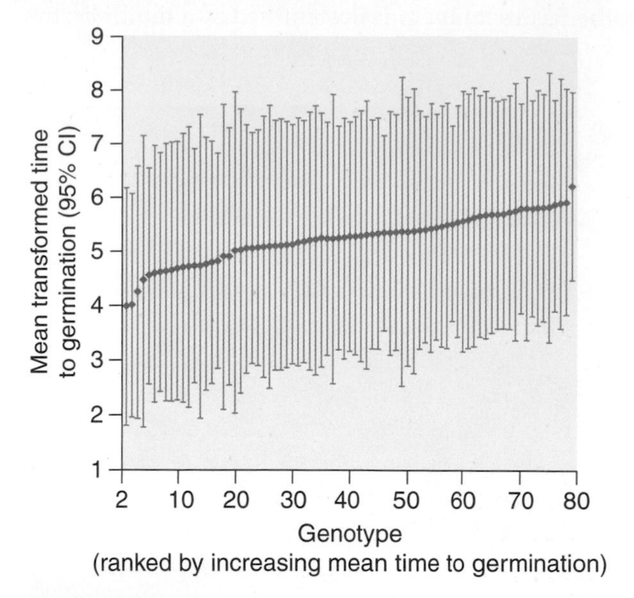

FIGURE 8.10

Germination Time Varies within and Among 79 Genotypes from a Single Population of *Lobelia inflata* under Controlled Environmental Conditions. Variation within genotypes (which are ranked in order of increasing mean time to germination; orange diamonds) is represented by the vertical bars (95 percent confidence intervals). Variation among genotypes is represented by the differences in the heights of the bars.

SOURCE: Simons and Johnston (2006), Figure 3(a).

An important thing to note in this formulation is that the geometric mean is strongly influenced by unusually low values. The more variable a set of values is, the lower the geometric mean, which underscores the tenet noted above and is best exemplified by bet-hedging life-history strategies—that natural selection should act to reduce the variance in fitness over generations.

8.2 Costs of Reproduction

Trade-Offs

The concept of a **trade-off** is fundamental to understanding the evolution of life histories and to predicting how organisms might respond to environmental change. A trade-off implies that an increase in the value of one life-history trait (and its potential importance in terms of influencing fitness) can be achieved only if there is a concomitant reduction in that of another one. In other words, it is not possible for an organism to maximize simultaneously all traits that are positively associated with fitness. A theoretical organism that can maximize all aspects of fitness

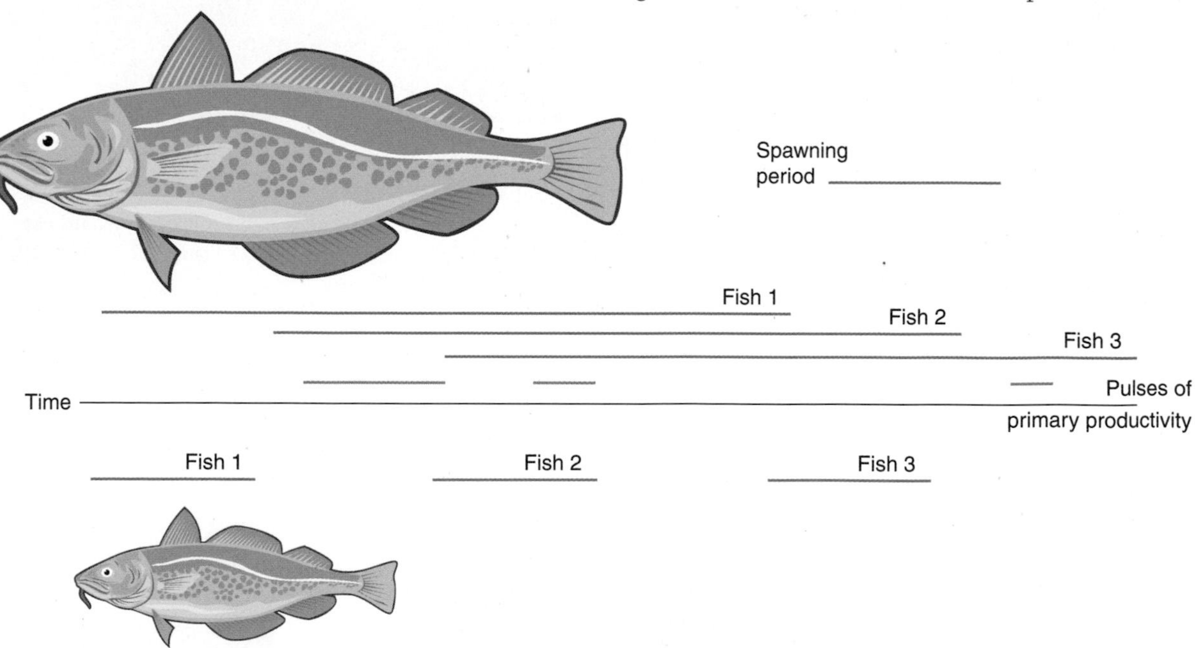

FIGURE 8.11

Atlantic Cod Exhibit a Bet Hedging Life-History Strategy by Producing Multiple Batches of Eggs throughout a Protracted Spawning Period. Large females spawn over longer periods of time (indicated by the three horizontal orange lines above the time axis) than small females (indicated by the three horizontal lines below the time axis). Because of longer spawning periods, the larvae produced by large cod are more likely to begin feeding in the presence of a pulse of food productivity (e.g., an algal bloom) than are those produced by small females. This is reflected by the general lack of overlap between temporal pulses of primary productivity (green lines) and the spawning periods of small females.

SOURCE: Side view of Atlantic cod (*Gadus morhua*). patrimonio designs limited/Shutterstock

concurrently can be termed a "Darwinian demon," and could exist only if its evolution was unconstrained. That is, in a life-history sense it might mature as early in life and at as large a size as possible, produce maximal numbers of maximally sized offspring, and suffer no consequences to its probability of surviving from one year to the next, and so would live to the maximum time span that is biologically possible for its species.

A trade-off, then, is a negative association or correlation between one trait and another, such as

- post-reproductive survival of an adult declining with increased reproductive effort;
- future individual growth rate declining with increased investment in the care of offspring; and
- the size of individual eggs produced by a female declining with increases in the number of eggs she produces.

It is important to realize that trade-offs may be purely phenotypic in origin. It is, for example, a negative phenotypic correlation that is quantified in experiments in which the numbers of eggs are manipulated (this is a method used to investigate the energetic costs associated with parental care) in order to explore how changes in clutch size might affect parental survival. Phenotypic correlations are not necessarily indicative of genetic correlations, but they can still be relevant from an evolutionary perspective if the traits involved are heritable.

Among species that have indeterminate growth, one widely acknowledged trade-off is the reduction in future growth that is caused by the diversion of energy from somatic biomass to the demands of reproduction—to behaviour, physiology, and reproductive tissues. This reduction of growth rate produces an associated decrease in future fecundity, because of the strong relationship that exists between seed/egg number per individual and plant/body size in most plants, fish, amphibians, and reptiles. This cost can be illustrated graphically, first by depicting possible growth trajectories that are associated with different ages at maturity, then by noting the body sizes associated with ages subsequent to maturity, and finally by estimating the fecundity associated with each of the resultant body sizes (**Figure 8.12**).

To determine whether a trade-off is genetic in origin, some metric of reproductive effort can be manipulated and the consequences measured for individuals of known genotype and degree of relatedness. Studies on genetically different individuals can be carried out using a "common-garden" experimental design, in which all experience the same environmental conditions so that non-genetic sources of trait variability are controlled.

An especially powerful way to detect negative genetic correlations between life-history traits is to perform a selection experiment. It might involve selection for increases in a trait, such as female reproductive gonadal volume (a product of egg number and egg size) and monitoring the correlated selection response in terms of post-reproductive survival. If positive directional selection in one trait is associated

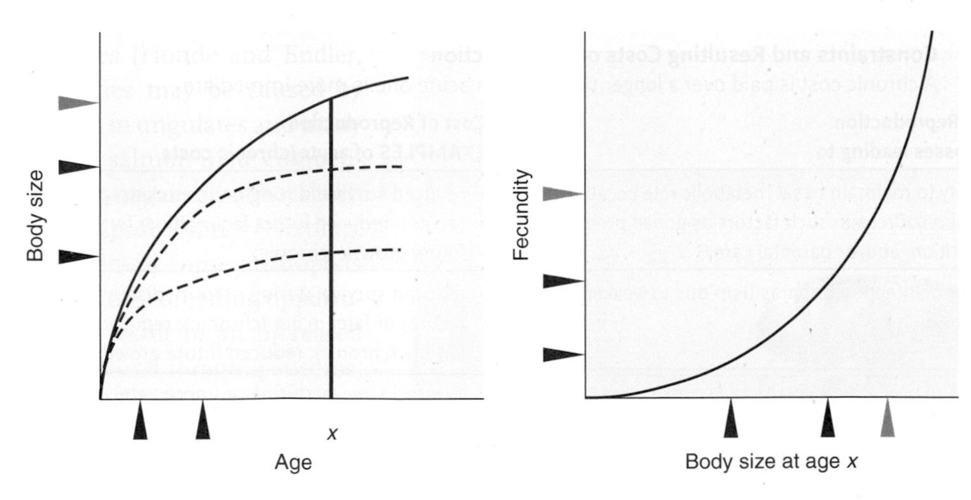

FIGURE 8.12

A Trade-Off between Age at Maturity and Future Fecundity, Mediated by Reductions in Growth Rate and Subsequent Sizes at Future Ages. In the absence of reproduction, the growth trajectory increases with age and would follow the uppermost (solid black) curve in the left panel. At ages at maturity indicated by the black and red triangles on the age axes, the associated growth trajectories (black- and red-dashed curves) would decline in both slope and asymptote because of the diversion of energy from somatic growth to tissues needed for reproduction (e.g., gonads). The body size at age *x* will differ under these three scenarios, as indicated by the green (no reproduction), black (reproduction), and red triangles (earlier reproduction) on the vertical axis of the left panel. The fecundity cost of reproduction can be illustrated in the right panel as the difference (decrease) in egg number at sizes at age *x* that are associated with the green and black triangles. The earlier age at maturity (red triangle) is associated with an even greater fecundity cost.

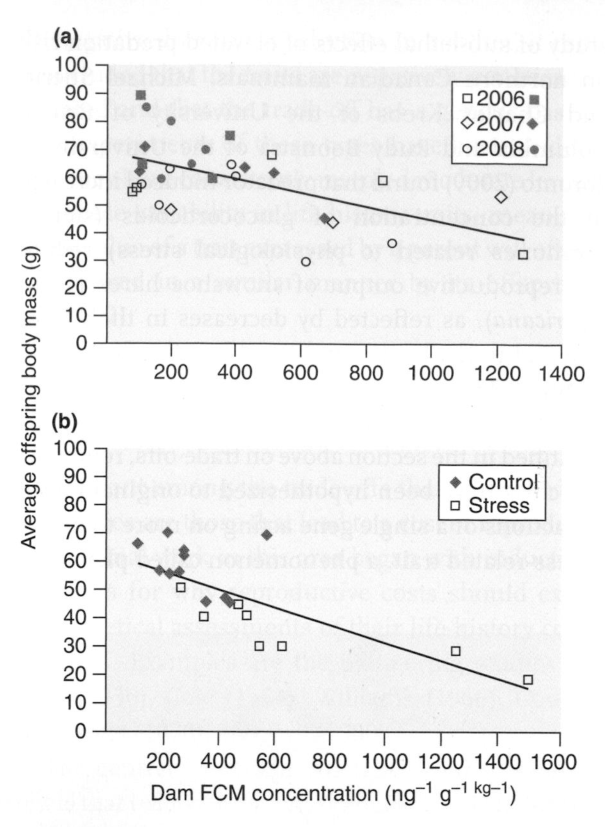

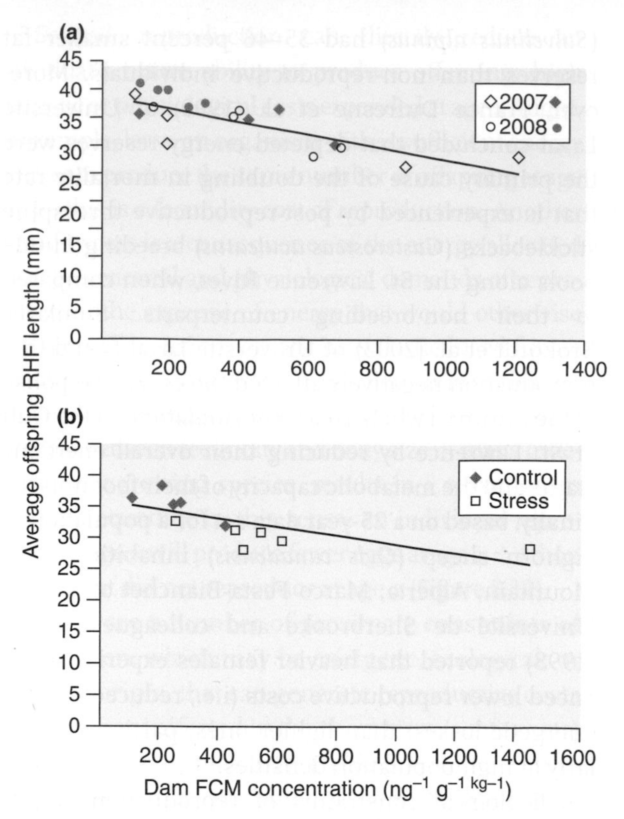

FIGURE 8.13

Physiological Stress Caused by Threat of Predation Can Generate Reproductive Costs. Elevated, predator-induced levels of faecal cortisol metabolite (FCM) in female snowshoe hares (*Lepus americanus*) is associated with reductions in offspring body mass (left panel) and offspring length, as reflected by the right hind foot (RHF) length (right panel).

SOURCE: Sheriff et al. (2009), Figures 4 (left panel) and 5 (right panel).

(a single gene influencing multiple phenotypic traits). As such, particular genes may have a positive influence on a trait in early life (e.g., fecundity) but a negative effect on another trait (e.g., survival) later on. This is known as **antagonistic pleiotropy**, and it was first proposed by Williams (1957) as a possible explanation for the evolution of aging, or senescence.

Finally, it is important to remember that to accurately quantify reproductive costs, you actually need to be able to estimate the future survival and/or growth of a specific individual at age $x + t$ depending on whether it had reproduced at age x or not. This is an important point that is not always reflected in life-history studies. Although you can get a sense of the magnitude of reproductive costs by comparing reproductive with non-reproductive individuals in the same population (and controlling for variables such as age and size), differences in *quality* between individuals (e.g., physiological condition, learning abilities, foraging behaviour) can, and often do, obscure the true magnitude of costs. For example, you might undertake a study and find that the average future survival of post-reproductive animals is the same as that of non-reproductive individuals of the same population. However, you cannot conclude from such a study that a survival cost of reproduction does not exist in this population. The post-reproductive individuals may have been in better physical condition prior to the breeding period, and better able to survive afterward, than non-reproductive individuals in poorer condition. To accurately quantify the reproductive costs experienced by a given individual, you need to be able to compare the future conditions (at age $x + t$) experienced by that individual (in terms of survival, fecundity/fertility, and/or growth) depending on whether it had reproduced in the past (at age x) or not. This is not an easy task to undertake, which is why the estimation of reproductive costs is very challenging, despite the logical basis for their existence.

8.3 Natural Selection on Life Histories

Life-History Evolution

A life history is based on the two most fundamental components of life, which are also the two most important metrics of fitness: survival and reproduction. If a genotype is to be successful in an evolutionary sense, it must contribute its genes to succeeding generations at the same rate as, or better than, other genotypes in its population. To do this it must survive to an age at which it can reproduce, and contribute to the production of offspring that themselves survive to reproduce and produce viable offspring, and so on.

The central premise of life-history theory is that natural selection favours genotypes whose age-specific schedules of survival (l_x) and fecundity (m_x) result in the highest per capita rate of increase (r), or fitness, relative to other genotypes in the population. This is a fundamental question about life, and the reason why the evolution of life histories is among the core areas of research in ecology. However, life-history research also has an integral role to play in the applied worlds of managing bio-resources and conserving biodiversity. This is because of the fundamental link that exists between individual life histories and the per capita rate of growth of populations. As we examined in Chapter 5, the per capita rate of increase is inextricably linked to the ability of a population to sustain various levels of exploitation, to recover after being reduced to a low abundance, and to persist in the face of introductions of non-native species with which it might interact as competitor, predator, or prey.

Life-history theory can also be used to predict how changes to abiotic and biotic environments might influence the fundamental "decisions" that genotypes face concerning reproduction. Consider, for example, the alteration or outright destruction of habitat that is critical for the persistence of a population or species. If such habitat change were to increase the mortality of adults, there are several questions that might arise:

- Would the increased mortality brought about by habitat change affect the average age at maturity, or the level of reproductive effort, in the population?
- If reproductive effort is affected, what are the potential consequences for survival, growth, and reproductive success?
- If changes in life-history traits are favoured by natural selection, what consequences might they have on per capita population growth rate, and thus on the likelihood of persistence of the population or species?

Age at Maturity and Reproductive Effort

Age at maturity reflects an evolutionary compromise between the benefits and costs to fitness of reproducing early or late in life. Benefits associated with early maturity, which results in a reduced generation time, include an increased probability of surviving to reproduce and a greater rate of gene input into the population. However, for many species, particularly those with indeterminate growth, early maturity can also result in reductions in fecundity/fertility and post-reproductive survival because of the smaller body size typically associated with earlier maturity. A major cost of delaying maturity is the increased risk that an individual will die before it actually gets a chance to reproduce. By contrast, the primary fitness advantage to delaying maturity (although not necessarily for those with determinant growth) is the larger initial body size attained by individuals when they first reproduce. In general, the larger an organism is, the greater are its chances of surviving to later years, the higher the number of offspring that can be produced (if female), the higher the probability of securing a mate and/or fertilizing eggs (if male), and the greater the ability to provide parental care.

Assuming that natural selection acts on age-specific expectations of producing future offspring (Fisher, 1930), the optimal age at which an individual matures can be predicted from the mean and variance of the probability of surviving through the juvenile and adult stages, i.e., of survival preceding and following the age at maturity, respectively. The life stages are as follows:

Birth--------------------Maturity------Senescence or Death
|----juvenile stage (j) ----| |----------adult stage (a)----------|

Under natural selection, reductions in the ratio of adult to juvenile survival (s_a/s_j), or increases in the variance in adult survival relative to that of juveniles [$\sigma^2(s_a)/\sigma^2(s_j)$], are predicted to favour younger age at maturity and increased reproductive effort (Cole, 1954; Gadgil and Bossert, 1970; Schaffer, 1974). These predictions make intuitive sense. As external mortality (i.e., that *not* associated with reproduction) at potentially reproductive ages increases, selection would be expected to favour those individuals (genotypes) that reproduce prior to those vulnerable ages, thereby increasing their probability of contributing genes to future generations. A similar argument can be made for environmental perturbations that increase the variance in survival at potentially reproductive ages, increased variance in survival being associated with increased uncertainty in an individual's persistence.

When considering the influence of survival on life-history evolution, it is vitally important that mortality attributable to external sources be distinguished from that caused by internal ones resulting from reproductive costs. External sources of mortality are those upon which natural selection will primarily act, potentially leading to changes in the expression of life-history traits of individuals. Internal sources of mortality are those resulting from "decisions" pertaining to reproduction, such as the amount of energetic resources to allocate to gonadal development or to parental care, and age and size at maturity. In other words, when thinking about how selection affects life history by acting on age-specific survival (l_x; and ultimately changes in r), it is the age-specific survival driven by external sources of mortality ($l_{x(ext)}$) that initiates or drives selection. But it is the age-specific survival, which incorporates both external and internal sources ($l_{x(ext + int)}$) that is included in life tables (Chapter 5) and in formulas such as the Euler-Lotka equation when we seek to estimate r.

The process of natural selection on age and reproductive effort at maturity can be illustrated in a graphical form. **Figure 8.14a** shows the age-specific survival schedule that is experienced by an individual in a particular environment (it is reminiscent of the Type III survival curve illustrated in Chapter 5). The ages encompassed by the juvenile (*j*) and adult (*a*) stages are shown. Predicated by this survivorship schedule (which we designate $l_{x(ext)}$ because it is driven by external factors in the environment), natural selection has favoured a particular age at maturity, α_{black} (indicated by the black triangle on the horizontal axis in **Figure 8.14b**), which in turn affects individual growth (for an indeterminately growing organism) by slowing the rate of increase in body size with increasing age (dashed line in **Figure 8.14b**) relative to what growth would have been if the individual had not matured at α_{black}. Because of the positive correlation that typically exists between body size and survival, the smaller size at age resulting from maturity (represented by **Figure 8.14b**) contributes to reduced survival post-maturity. This is depicted by the dashed line in **Figure 8.14c**, which identifies the age-specific schedule of survival resulting from both external sources and internal allocation decisions associated with reproduction, i.e., $l_{x(ext + int)}$. (Note that the solid line in **Figure 8.14c** is the same as the curve in **Figure 8.14a**; the cost of reproduction can be thought

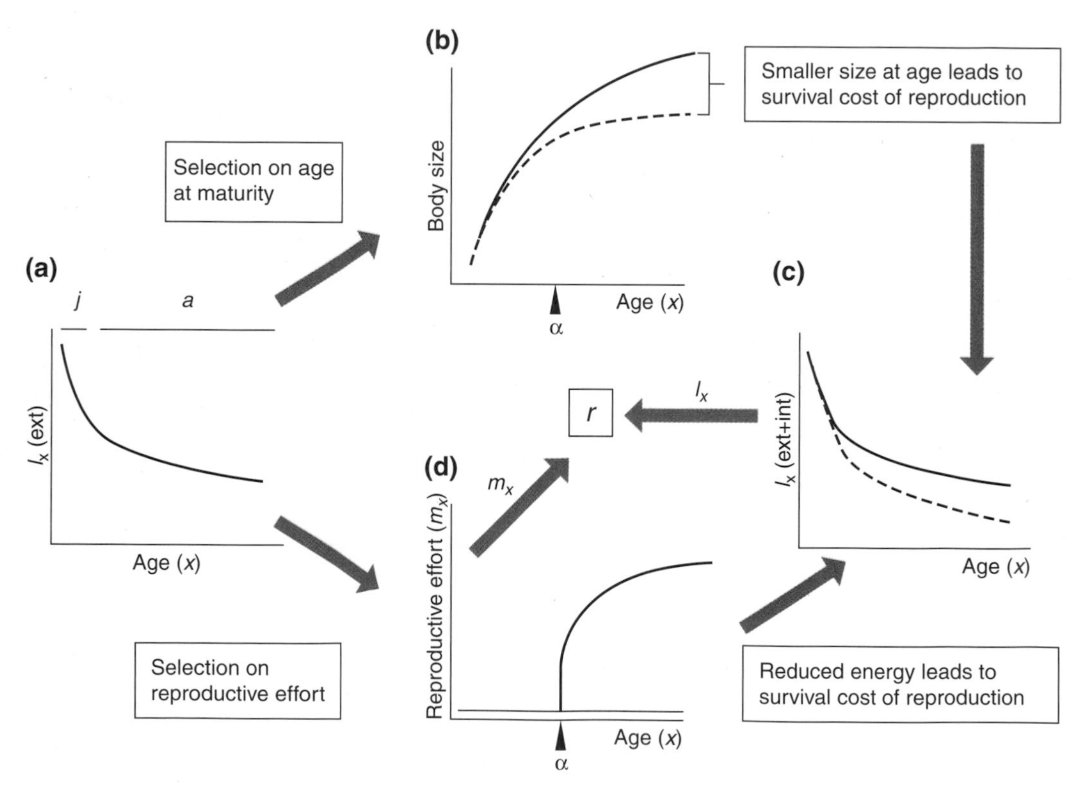

FIGURE 8.14
A Basic Framework for Illustrating How Age-Specific Schedules of Survival and Fecundity Determine the Fitness Associated with the Life History of an Indeterminately-Growing Organism. The pattern of survival due to external causes ($l_{x(ext)}$) experienced during the juvenile (*j*) and adult (*a*) stages (panel a) is a primary determinant of how selection acts on age at maturity (∝). Maturity results in a diversion of energy from somatic tissue (which increases body size) to gonadal tissue, resulting in a decline in the growth trajectory (panel b). The survival cost associated with reproduction leads to a downward shift in the curve that relates age-specific survival caused by both external and internal (reproductive decisions) sources of mortality ($l_{x(ext+int)}$) (panel c). The age at maturity also influences the amount of effort that is expended at reproduction, a pattern that can be represented by the number of eggs produced by a female (m_x) (panel d). The resulting fitness (represented by *r*) associated with the life history in question is, then, a consequence of both age-specific rates of survival and fecundity.

of as the *difference* in the survival functions in the absence (solid line) and presence (dashed line) of reproduction.)

The survivorship schedule given in **Figure 8.14a** will also favour, via natural selection, a particular reproductive effort at maturity (and pattern with subsequent ages). At α_{black}, the reproductive effort (represented in **Figure 8.14d** by m_x) will be higher (curved line) relative to what it would be in the absence of reproduction (essentially nil, as reflected by the horizontal solid line). Given that effort expended toward reproduction will necessitate the diversion of resources that might have enhanced survival in other ways, the reduced energy available to individuals after maturity can be expected to contribute to the survival cost of reproduction (**Figure 8.14c**). The resultant fitness associated with this life history is given by *r*, and it is a function of both l_x and m_x, as described by the Euler-Lotka equation.

Now, assume that some factor external to the organism results in increased mortality, which is realized primarily during the adult stage; this is reflected by the red survivorship function shown in **Figure 8.15a**. This change would result in a reduction in adult survival (s_a) relative to that experienced during the juvenile stage (s_j), leading to a decrease in the ratio of adult to juvenile survival (s_a/s_j). As illustrated in **Figure 8.15b**, life-history theory would predict that this would favour earlier maturity at α_{red} (represented by the red-coloured α) and a concomitant change in growth rate (red curve). The smaller sizes at subsequent ages would then result in further reductions in post-reproductive survival, resulting in lower values of $l_{x(ext + int)}$ (**Figure 8.15c**). Theory also predicts that the change in survivorship depicted in panel a would lead to increased reproductive effort at (and beyond) α_{red} (red line in **Figure 8.15d**) as well as increased survival costs. The new age-specific schedules of survival (red l_x) and fecundity (red m_x) can ultimately be expected to lead to a change in fitness, which is represented by the red-coloured *r*.

A long-term study of guppies inhabiting streams in Trinidad provides one of the best empirical tests in a wild population of the prediction that reductions in the ratio of adult to juvenile survival should favour earlier maturity and increased effort (Reznick et al. 1990).

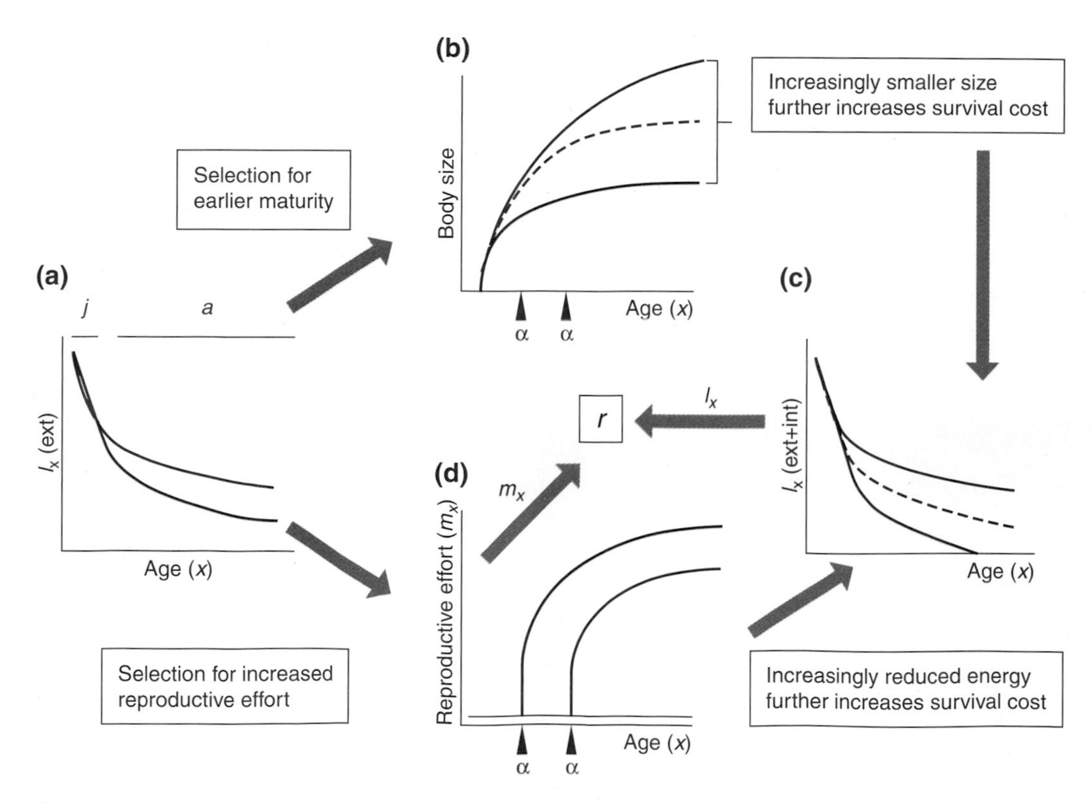

FIGURE 8.15

A Basic Framework for Illustrating How Reduced Adult Survival Can Select for Earlier Age and Increased Reproductive Effort at Maturity. Decreased age-specific survival, notably among adults, results in selection for earlier maturity and increased reproductive effort, both of which are associated with increased reproductive costs that ultimately have an impact on fitness. Compared to the original (black) survivorship schedule in panel a, the new age-specific schedule of survival (red) reflects a decline in the ratio of adult (*a*) to juvenile (*j*) survival which, in turn, is predicted to favour a reduction in age at maturity (red α, compared to the original age at maturity represented by the black α) (panel b). This reduction in α is associated with smaller size at maturity, which, in turn, leads to further reductions in age-specific survival (red curve) after reproduction (panel c). Higher reproductive costs, coupled with higher reproductive effort (panel d), will lead to a life-history induced change in fitness (*r*).

Guppies were transplanted from an area in which predation on adults was high, compared to that on juveniles, to another habitat where predation on adults was greatly reduced. This would have meant that the ratio of adult to juvenile survival (s_a/s_j) would have increased. After 30 to 60 generations following this shift in predator-induced mortality from adults to juveniles, guppies responded to the presumed increase in (s_a/s_j) by reducing their reproductive allotment (weight of eggs per unit of female body weight) and by increasing the age at maturity, exactly as theory would predict. In another study, Michael Fox and Allen Keast (1991) of Queen's University compared the life histories of pumpkinseed sunfish (*Lepomis macrochirus*) from five populations in eastern Ontario that experienced either high or low levels of overwinter mortality. They found that males and females that inhabited high adult-mortality environments matured earlier and allocated a greater proportion of their body tissue to their gonads than did populations in low adult-mortality habitats (**Figure 8.16**). Hutchings (1993), who estimated (s_a/s_j) directly for brook trout populations in southeastern Newfoundland, noted that reductions in the ratio of adult to juvenile survival were associated with earlier maturity and increased reproductive effort. Similarly, Wolfgang Jansen (1996) of the University of Alberta found a negative association between age at maturity and reproductive effort (the latter indicated by the proportion of gonadal tissue to total body weight, and by size-specific fecundity) for populations of yellow perch (*Perca flavescens*) in central Alberta.

Fish have also proven amenable to tests of predicted changes in life history that are associated with changes in the variance of adult survival relative to that of juveniles. Bill Leggett and Jim Carscadden (1978) of McGill University examined population differences in age at maturity among five populations of American shad (*Alosa sapidissima*) ranging from Florida to New Brunswick. In accordance with life-history theory, they found that males and females in the northern populations, for which they presumed juvenile mortality is more variable than in southern populations because of climatic influences, matured up to 11 percent and 14 percent older, respectively, than did southern ones. They also found that northern populations of shad produced fewer eggs per unit body size, and had a higher incidence of repeat spawning than southern ones, again because of presumed differences in variation in juvenile mortality. Similarly, Hutchings and Jones (1998) reported a negative correlation between variance in adult survival and age at maturity in anadromous Atlantic salmon.

Influence of Growth Rate on Life History

Growth rate is of major importance to life-history evolution, particularly in organisms that continue to grow after attaining maturity. This is because of the relationship of growth rate to the body size at any age, and the positive associations that can exist between body size and various metrics of fitness. Once the minimum body size has been attained at which reproduction can occur, the maturation strategy of an individual is predicted to depend on the consequences to its present and future survival and fecundity of reproducing at various ages.

A trade-off between present and future fecundity, caused by declines in growth rate once maturity has been attained, formed the basis of initial predictions of how growth rate might influence life history (Gadgil and Bossert, 1970; Bell, 1980). For example, Schaffer (1974) predicted that environments that allowed for increased growth during potentially reproductive ages should favour delayed maturity and increased reproductive effort. Hutchings (1993) introduced a theoretical framework similar to that of the ratio of adult to juvenile survival, and argued that studies of the effects of growth rate on life histories should partition the growth experienced during the juvenile stage from that experienced by adults (with effects of individual reproductive decisions excluded from the estimates). He predicted that increases in juvenile growth rate relative to that of adults should favour increases in reproductive effort and reductions in age at maturity. These predictions were subsequently borne out by empirical data

Mirage3/Dreamstime.com

The colourful pumpkinseed sunfish (*Lepomis gibbosus*) inhabits warm, still waters with abundant vegetation in southern and eastern Ontario and in southeastern Quebec. Its mortality rates were studied by Fox and Keast; see Figure 8.16.

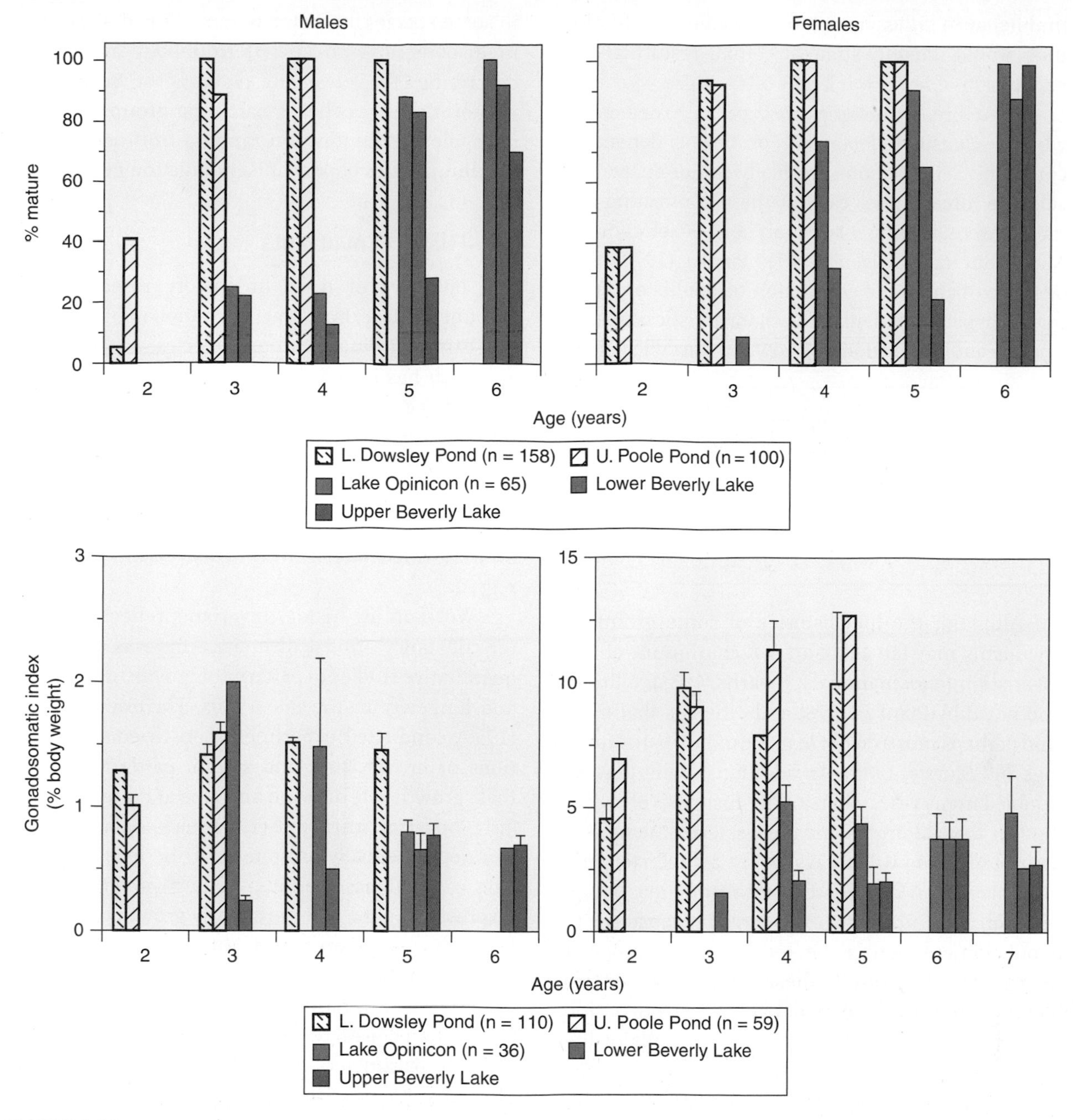

FIGURE 8.16

Population Differences in Life History Are Often Associated with Population Differences in Adult Mortality. Pumpkinseed sunfish (*Lepomis gibbosus*) from populations in which adult overwinter mortality is high (Lower Dowsley Pond, Upper Poole Pond) mature earlier in life (upper panel) and allocate greater reproductive effort (lower panel) than those from populations in which adult overwinter mortality is low.

SOURCE: Redrawn from Fox and Keast (1991).

on Newfoundland populations of brook trout, Ontario pumpkinseed sunfish (Fox, 1994), and Swedish brown trout (*Salmo trutta*; Näslund et al., 1998).

r- and *K*-Selection

It has long been assumed that life histories have evolved to form highly generalized patterns of co-adapted life-history traits, and that these should be broadly evident among various groups of organisms. In the 1960s, density was thought to be a key selective influence on life-history evolution (see Chapter 5). The idea is as follows. When density is low, and intraspecific competition is also low, organisms should be favoured to invest maximal amounts of energy and other resources into reproduction, and so to produce many small offspring, each of which should have a reasonable opportunity to survive within the low-competitive environment presumed to exist at low densities (Pianka, 1978). By contrast, in an environment with a high-density population, where competitive interactions are presumed to be intense, the optimal life-history strategy should be one in which resources are allocated to competition and body maintenance rather than to reproduction, a situation that would favour strategies that result in the production of fewer but larger offspring.

Therefore, life histories are expected to depend on whether density-independent or density-dependent competitive interactions are likely to dominate. The selective forces under each of these contrasting scenarios were termed *r*-selection and *K*-selection by MacArthur and Wilson (1967). Pianka (1970) then described patterns of covariation of life-history traits that he hypothesized might be characteristic of species under *r*- and *K*-selection, as shown in the table below.

Trait	*r*-selected	*K*-selected
Age at first reproduction	young	old
Size at first reproduction	small	large
Breeding events per lifetime	few	many
Number of offspring	many	few
Size of offspring	small	large

Although the life histories of some groups of organisms may fall along an *r*–*K* continuum of trait covariation (e.g., mammals; Stearns, 1983), a limitation noted by Pianka (1978) and others is that many (and perhaps most) do not (e.g., salmonid fish; Hutchings and Morris, 1985). An additional point that has troubled many researchers of life-history evolution is the fact that *all* organisms are *r*-selected, insofar as natural selection will always favour a life history that maximizes *r* in a particular environment. Natural selection does not act on the carrying capacity of a population, rendering the term "*K*-selection" confusing. However, despite these limitations, and perhaps driven by a human penchant for categorization, the terms *r*- and *K*-selection and the suites of life-history traits with which they are thought to be associated, are frequently used by ecologists.

An analogous and arguably similarly ambiguous set of terms is that of *fast* and *slow* life histories (Gaillard et al., 1989; Dobson and Oli, 2008). There is evidence within birds and mammals that species can be arranged along a continuum of life-history trait covariation that distinguishes species, as follows:

Trait	Fast	Slow
Fecundity	high	low
Life expectancy	short	long
Age at maturity	young	old

These are, however, essentially the same suites of traits that are characteristic of *r*- and *K*-selection, but they are given the new names of fast and slow life histories, respectively.

Rather than continuing to create new terms to describe patterns of life-history traits that are evident in some species but not in others, there may be merit in dispensing with such terminology and simply describing the observed patterns of covariation, whatever they may be for particular groups of organisms, along a continuum ranging from low to high maximum rates of per capita population growth, r_{max}.

Life-History Invariants

The objective of most life-history research is to account for the extraordinary variation in life histories that exists within and among species. An alternative approach has been to focus on constancy, or invariance, in the associations between various life-history traits that may reflect adaptive processes of a broad and universal nature across species. Charnov (1993) provides an overview of studies of such **life-history invariants** for a variety of species, and Beverton (1992) for fish, which have been particularly examined in this regard.

Work on life-history invariants reflects a search for constancy amidst diversity. This was evident in quantitative studies of patterns of growth, maturation, and longevity in the late 1950s. For example, Alm (1959) conducted experiments on Swedish populations of brown trout and sought patterns between their growth rate and age and size at maturity. Similarly, Beverton and Holt (1959) used data primarily from commercially exploited marine fish to investigate general associations among growth pattern (expressed by the von Bertalanffy growth coefficient, *k*, which is based on a model of growth as a function of age) and asymptotic length, L_∞; age (α) and length at maturity (L_α); natural mortality (*M*); and lifespan (proportional to M^{-1}). Life-history invariants, then, are ratios of parameters expressed in the same units of measure, so that their ratios are dimensionless. Among the most commonly examined life-history invariants are those between mortality and growth rate (M/k), and length at maturity and asymptotic length (L_α/L_∞).

The practical objective underlying much of the early search for life-history invariants was to identify generalizations that could then be used to estimate the natural mortality rate in commercially exploited fish. The value of natural mortality is a parameter that is fundamentally important to fisheries resource management models, but it can be extremely difficult to estimate. Daniel Pauly (1980), now of the University of British Columbia, analyzed 175 stocks of teleost (bony) fish and found that the invariant M/k was about 1.7. (Charnov (1993) later suggested a range of possible values of 1.6–2.1.) If an estimate is available of the von Bertalanffy growth coefficient, *k*, for a given population, which is a relatively easy metric to approximate, then the invariant $M/k = 1.7$ could be used to estimate the natural mortality for that population.

In addition to their practical utility, invariants have the potential to provide insight into life-history evolution. For example, the invariant M/k implies that fast-growing species experience higher natural mortality rates than slow-growing ones. Another invariant that appears to have some consistency among taxa is L_{α}/L_{∞}, which Jensen (1997) estimated to be 0.66 for fish, implying that maturity occurs at a length that is approximately two-thirds of the maximum.

Despite the study of life-history invariants for about five decades, our understanding and applications are still in an infancy. Much of the research undertaken to date has involved a search for pattern among combinations of life-history metrics. While this has been a useful approach, the greater challenge is to formulate and test hypotheses that would identify the processes responsible for the observed patterns. It must also be borne in mind that life-history invariants may be more evident in some species, such as fish and mammals (Charnov, 1993), than in others, such as birds (Bennett and Owens, 2002).

8.4 Offspring Size and Number

Theoretical Context

Why do some species produce large numbers of small offspring, while others produce only a few that are big? This is the central question that has driven ecologists to try to understand the observed variations that exist in what are referred to as offspring-size/offspring-number strategies. Among plants, the smallest seeds are produced by orchids, only 0.2–1.7 μm long and 1/5 as wide and weighing about 1 million per gram, and the largest by the coco de mer, up to 30 cm long and weighing up to 18 kg (Westoby et al., 1992). Among fish, the size of egg released by a female can range from those of the surfperch (*Cymatogaster aggregata*) of the Pacific coast, at only 0.3 mm diameter (Kamler, 1992), to the 14 mm eggs produced by tropical mouth-breeding catfish (Coates, 1988). Among mammals, the smallest newborns are those of the Etruscan shrew (*Suncus etruscus*), only 4–5 mm long, and the largest are the massive calves of the blue whale at up to 6.5 m and 7.3 tonnes (Whitehead and Mann, 2000).

Assuming that only a limited amount of resources can be allocated to the production of gonadal tissue, or

Jose B. Ruiz/NPL/Minden Pictures

The Etruscan shrew (*Suncus etruscus*), the smallest known mammal and bearing the smallest newborns (4–5 mm), is primarily confined to the Mediterranean lowlands from Portugal to the Middle East.

to seeds, eggs, or embryos, then the number of offspring produced by an individual female during a breeding event cannot increase unless the size of each one decreases. This apparent trade-off between offspring number and their size was first considered in detail by David Lack, a British ornithologist, in the late 1940s. In species of birds in which the young are fed by their parents at the nest (these are known as altricial birds), and for which food resources are limited, the number of young produced cannot increase without a reduction in the amount of nutrition provided to each offspring. Lack (1947) reasoned that the clutch size in these altricial birds was primarily influenced by the number of offspring that parents can feed and raise to the fledgling stage, at which time they become substantially independent of their parents.

The evolutionary implications of the trade-off between the number and size of offspring was considered by Gunnar Svärdson (1949), a Swedish fish biologist. He suggested that there must be an upper limit to fecundity, which depends on the influence of egg size on offspring survival and parental reproductive success. Otherwise, he argued, directional selection—or as he put it, a tendency to increase egg number every generation—would favour continually increasing numbers of eggs per female. Svärdson remarked that "From a theoretical point of view it is rather easy to conclude that there must be a selection pressure for decreasing egg numbers, but it is not so extremely evident how this selection works."

The theoretical underpinning of most research investigating the adaptive significance of variability in offspring size/number is a graphical model proposed by Smith and Fretwell (1974), who asked how a parent should distribute a fixed amount of resources to an indeterminate number of young. In their model, optimal offspring size is defined graphically by the point on the fitness function at which a straight line drawn from the origin (the dashed line in **Figure 8.17**) is tangential to the offspring survival curve (the solid curve). In other words, the optimum corresponds to the offspring size at which the instantaneous rate of gain in fitness per unit increase in offspring size is at its maximum. Smith and Fretwell's model has proven to be extremely influential, as evidenced by their 1974 paper being cited more than 1200 times in the scientific literature (*ISI Web of Knowledge*).

Optimal Egg Size

It has been argued that natural selection acts primarily on the size of offspring, and that their numbers are mainly a by-product of this selective process, given the trade-off described above. In a sense, this is what underlies the thesis of Smith and Fretwell (1974).

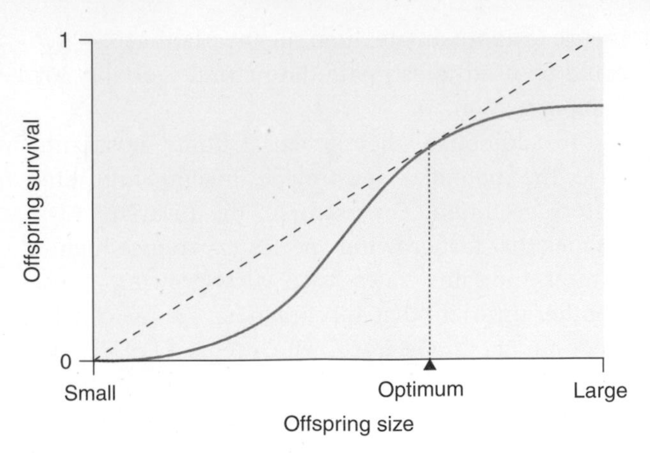

FIGURE 8.17
The Smith-Fretwell Model Relating Offspring Survival to Offspring Size. The optimal offspring size is defined by the point on the fitness function (curved solid line) at which a straight line drawn from the origin (the dashed line) is tangential to the fitness curve.

SOURCE: Modified from Smith and Fretwell (1974).

One might then be tempted to interpret population differences in offspring size as being a proxy for adaptive variation. But for selection to favour particular offspring sizes in different populations or environments, the relationship between their size and survival must also differ in those situations. This prerequisite for environment- or population-specific optima for offspring size can be illustrated in **Figure 8.18**.

Figure 8.18 illustrates the relationships between survival and offspring size given specific environments. Note that maternal fitness is approximated by the product of offspring survival and number (holding gonadal volume constant). Two basic functions are considered: (1) the size-dependent case, for which offspring survival varies continuously with egg size (**Figure 8.18a**), and (2) the size-independent case, for which survival above and below a narrow range of egg sizes is constant (**Figure 8.18b**). For the former, any factor that is expected to increase offspring survival across all egg sizes, such as food supply, is predicted to result in a reduction in optimal egg size (**Figure 8.18a**), thus favouring females that produce relatively numerous but smaller offspring (**Figure 8.18c**).

In contrast, if offspring survival is independent of their size, the optimal egg size is predicted to not be affected by changes in a factor that increases offspring survival (**Figure 8.18d**). The evolutionarily stable strategy of investment per off spring in these species would be to maximize the numbers of offspring, each of which approaches the physiological minimum size below which survival probability declines to zero. This may be the basis of the strategy employed by most wind-dispersing plants, most marine invertebrates, and fish that are broadcast spawners. These exhibit the classic life-history responses of organisms that provide

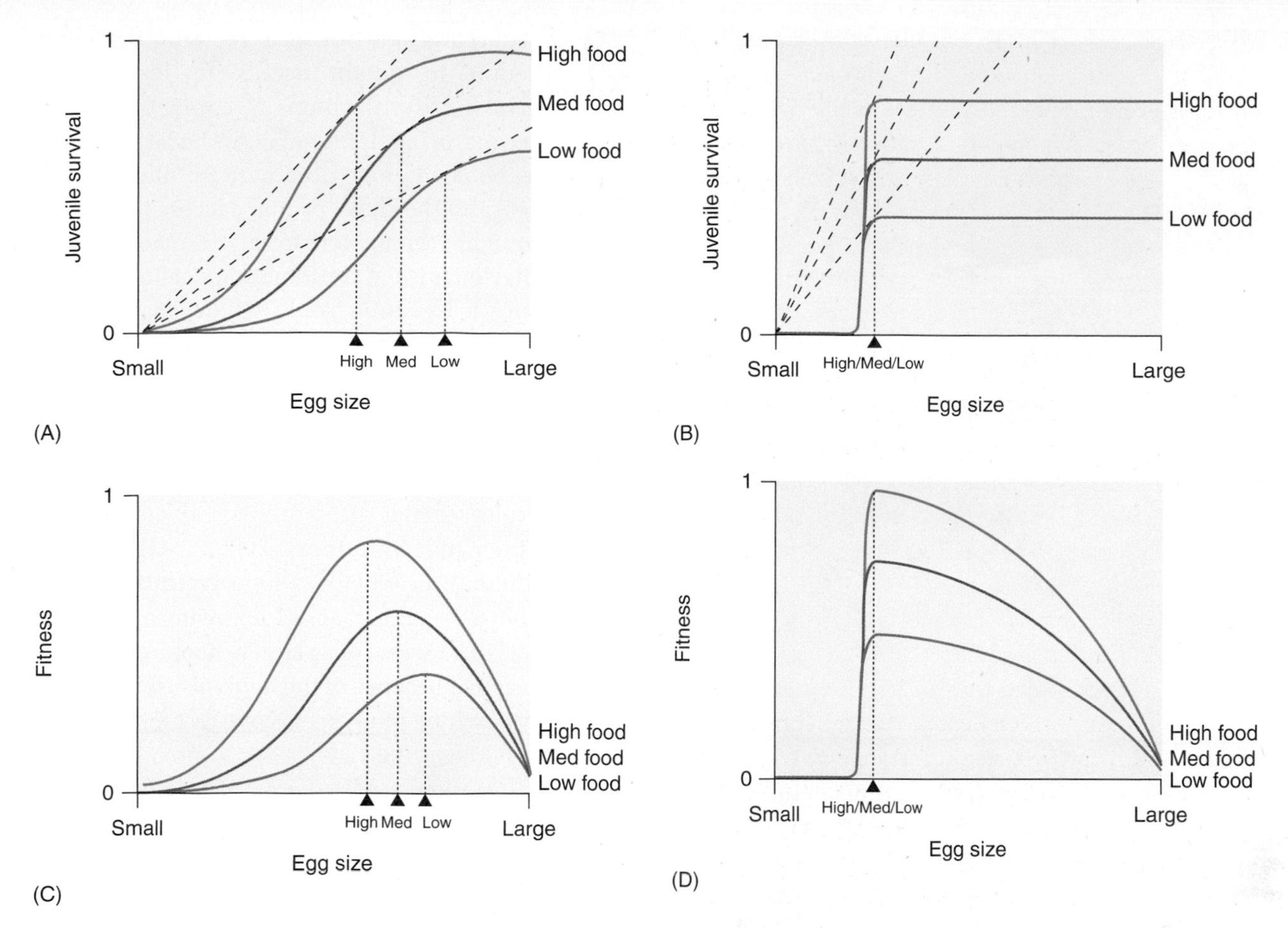

FIGURE 8.18

Functions Relating Juvenile Survival (A and B) and Maternal Fitness (C and D) to Egg Size. Solid triangles below each *x*-axis indicate optimal egg sizes. (A) Size-dependent survival case: optimum egg size declines with increased food abundance. (B) Size-independent survival case: optimum egg size does not vary with food abundance. (C) Size-dependent survival case: high-food and low-food environments favour the production of small and large eggs, respectively. (D) Size-independent case: the egg size at which parental fitness is maximized is independent of food abundance.

SOURCE: Hutchings (1997).

no parental care and disperse their offspring into the physical and biological vagaries of the environment.

The assumption that resources are allocated evenly among offspring is common to the Smith-Fretwell model (and many others). However, this pattern is not generally observed in nature. The size of eggs, for example, often varies considerably among females within the same population, and even within the gonad, or seed pod, of the same individual. Among-female variability (i.e., within a population) has been attributed in particular studies to such factors as habitat variation in parasitic trematodes (Poulin and Hamilton, 2000), female condition in common eiders (*Somateria mollissima*; Hanssen et al., 2002), and a host of variables in arthropods (e.g., female size, diet, oviposition host, density, temperature, predation risk; Fox and Czesak, 2000). Within particular females, variability in egg size has been attributed to age in arthropods (Fox and Czesak, 2000), pond type in *Hyla* spp. tree-frogs (temporary vs. permanent; Crump, 1981), male attractiveness in mallards (*Anas platyrhynchos*; Cunningham and Russell, 2000), and egg predation risk in shield bugs (Acanthosomatidae; Kudo, 2001).

Variability per se has been explained as an adaptation to unpredictable environments (Capinera, 1979). In cases where the environment changes little from year to year, natural selection might favour a relatively consistent offspring size, whereas a variable environment might favour the production of a range of offspring sizes (assuming, of course, that offspring survival varies with offspring size). Marten Koops of Dalhousie University and colleagues (2003) tested this prediction within and among female brook trout from 10 populations in Newfoundland. They found support for the hypothesis that females adjust the allocation of resources among eggs in response to unpredictable environmental conditions, as a way of offsetting the cost of imperfect information (**Figure 8.19**). However, they noted that care should be taken to not overly interpret the potential adaptive significance of egg size variability within clutches.

Marcelo Saavedra/Shutterstock

Individual female mallards (*Anas platyrhynchos*) lay larger eggs after copulating with preferred males and smaller eggs after copulating with less preferred males.

In summary, it should be evident that in order for natural selection to favour an increase in egg size, the resulting survival benefits to offspring must exceed the fitness costs to the parents of producing fewer eggs. Furthermore, the evolution of strategies for choosing offspring size, or their numbers, depends primarily upon the shape of the function that relates egg size to offspring survival.

8.5 Alternative Life Histories

Tactics and Strategies

Alternative life histories can be thought of as representing combinations of anatomical, physiological, and behavioural traits (polymorphisms) that are correlates of distinctive reproductive alternatives occurring within the same sex, in a single population, at a point in time. These reproductive polymorphisms are common in both invertebrate and vertebrate animals (Taborsky, 2001; Tomkins and Hazel, 2007). One frequent observation is to find that some males mature relatively early in life, usually at a comparatively small size, and that they attempt to obtain access to females by "sneaking" fertilizations in competition with later-maturing, larger males. The larger males are behaviourally dominant to the smaller ones, and they have primary access to females through various territorial or mate-defence behaviours (they are sometimes called "fighter males"). The dung beetle (*Onthophagus taurus*) is a widely studied example of alternative reproductive behaviours and associated dimorphisms. The larger males are armed with horns on their head, which help when they fight for access to females, whereas smaller hornless males attempt to sneak copulations (Hunt and Simmons, 2001). Male Pacific salmon (*Oncorhynchus* spp.) typically mature either as smaller "jacks," following a relatively short time at sea, or as larger "hooknose" males (so-called because of the hook-like shape of the jaws), which often spend one or more years at sea (Gross, 1985).

Another excellent example of a life-history polymorphism is that exhibited by male bluegill sunfish (**Figure 8.20**). Field research on bluegills has been undertaken in Lake Opinicon, Ontario, since the late 1970s to the present, as reflected by the work of Mart Gross (1979, 1982) of the University of Toronto and that carried out by Bryan Neff and Rosemary Knapp (2009) of the University of Western Ontario. In Lake Opinicon bluegills, "parental" males mature at about 7 years of age, construct nests, court and spawn with females, and eventually provide sole parental care for their developing young. However, smaller "cuckolder" males become sexually mature earlier in life at a smaller size, but do not construct nests or provide parental care. Cuckolders initially obtain some degree of reproductive success at two to three years of age as so-called "sneaker" males, which dart out from behind plants and woody debris into nests when a female is releasing her eggs while spawning with a territory-holding parental male. As the sneakers become older (four to five years) and larger, they become "satellite males" that obtain fertilizations by mimicking a female. By mimicking the colour and behaviour of a female, the satellite misleads a parental male, and manages to fertilize some of the clutch laid by a true female.

There are several means by which alternative maturation phenotypes can be maintained within populations. As with many characters, the origins of alternative phenotypes may be purely genetic, environmental, or a combination of these. From a semantic perspective, the genetic basis (or lack thereof) of alternative life histories is of some importance, as is reflected by a considerable literature on terminology in the field (e.g., Gross, 1996; Taborsky, 2001). The emerging consensus is that alternative life histories should be considered to be different "strategies" if the differences have an underlying genetic basis. However, if the differences are entirely a function of an individual's status (perhaps reflected by its condition or size) relative to that of others with whom it might compete for mates, then the differences are termed "tactics" (a strategy may comprise multiple tactics).

Environmentally Determined Tactics and "The Best of a Bad Job"

Within-population variation in reproductive strategies may not be under direct genetic control. Instead, they may reflect a range of mating behaviours and ages/sizes at maturity that are phenotypically plastic, and therefore a consequence of stochastic variability in environmental conditions. Under these circumstances, the existence of alternative life histories is usually predicated by a difference in dominance rank or status. For a variety of reasons (such as poor feeding opportunities or young age), individuals that are relatively small in size or poor in condition may be subordinate to others that are larger or healthier. It would be predicted that the fitness of individuals exhibiting such suboptimal maturation phenotypes, which may be fixed for a breeding season or for life, would be less than that of others. Rather than foregoing potential breeding opportunities, the subordinates may be making the "best of a bad situation."

For example, Julian Mainguy and colleagues (2008) of Université Laval studied a population of mountain goats (*Oreamnos americanus*) at Caw Ridge, Alberta, and found that subordinate males adopted an alternative mating tactic of "coursing" (i.e., disruption of a mating pair, often by pursuit of the female). They did this because of their inability to directly compete in jousts with dominant males. Another example involves male grey seals breeding on Sable Island, Nova Scotia, which exhibit two mating tactics. The primary one involves prolonged and vigorous defence of a harem of females. The alternative tactic, which results in a fertilization success three to four times less than the primary one, involves mating with females that have weaned their offspring and are leaving the colony (Lidgard et al., 2004). Male Atlantic cod also exhibit alternative tactics (Hutchings et al., 1999). The more successful tactic involves the release of sperm by a behaviourally dominant male during a ventral mount of a spawning female, whereas the subordinate behaviour by

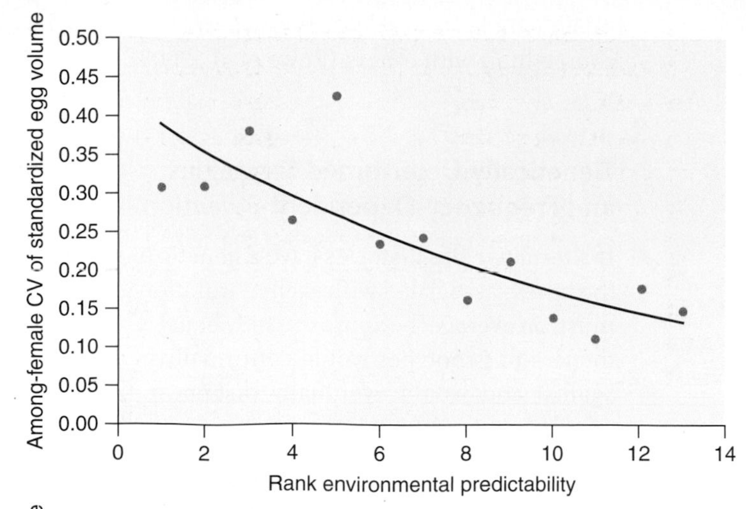

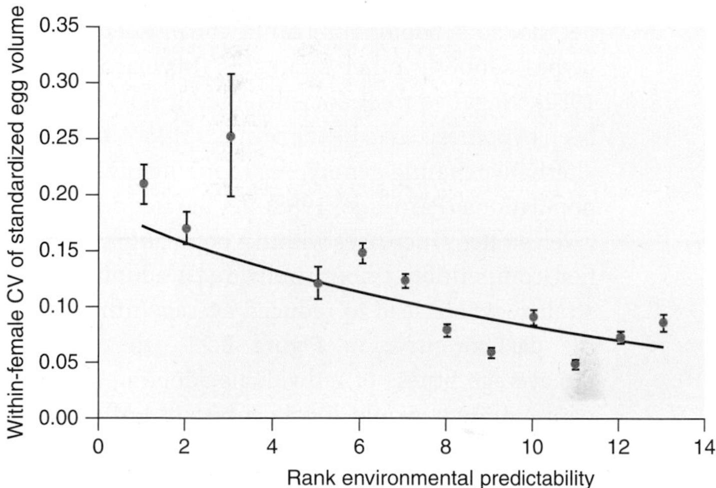

FIGURE 8.19

The Existence of Variable Egg Sizes within Females May Be Adaptive. As the year-to-year predictability in the environment declines, variability in egg size increases in Newfoundland brook trout (*Salvelinus fontinalis*), whether egg-size variation is measured among females (upper panel) or within females (lower panel). Each point represents a different population; error bars in the lower panel represent 1 standard error.

SOURCE: Koops et al. (2003).

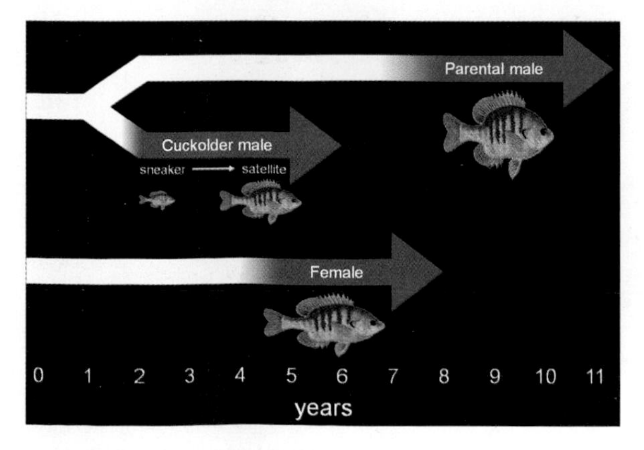

FIGURE 8.20

Male Bluegill Sunfish (*Lepomis macrochirus*) Have Two Alternative Life-History Strategies: Parental Male and Cuckholder Male. Cuckholder males exhibit two tactics as sneaker or satellite males. Females exhibit a single strategy. The blue portions of the errors represent sexual maturity.

SOURCE: Gross (1982).

satellite males is to release their sperm thereafter, in competition with others (Rowe et al., 2008).

Genetically Determined Strategies and Frequency-Dependent Selection

If alternative life histories have a genetic basis, then the fitness associated with each maturation genotype must, on average, be approximately equal. Otherwise the less-fit genotypes would continually be selected against and would eventually disappear from the population. Under such circumstances, the frequencies of the strategy-specific genotypes within populations are said to be evolutionarily stable—this is because such populations cannot be invaded by genotypes adopting other strategies (Maynard Smith, 1982). Negative frequency-dependent selection has been hypothesized to be the primary means by which alternative mating genotypes are maintained within populations (Partridge, 1988). As the frequency of a given strategy increases within a population, intensified competition among individuals adopting that strategy would lead to reduced average fitness (see the dashed curve in **Figure 8.21**). In contrast, the average fitness of individuals adopting an alternative strategy would increase because of reduced competition (solid curve in **Figure 8.21**). This would result in a shift in the incidence of strategies toward the less common of the two. In theory, the frequency of alternative strategies within a population would eventually achieve an equilibrium at which the average fitness of individuals adopting each strategy is equal (**Figure 8.21**).

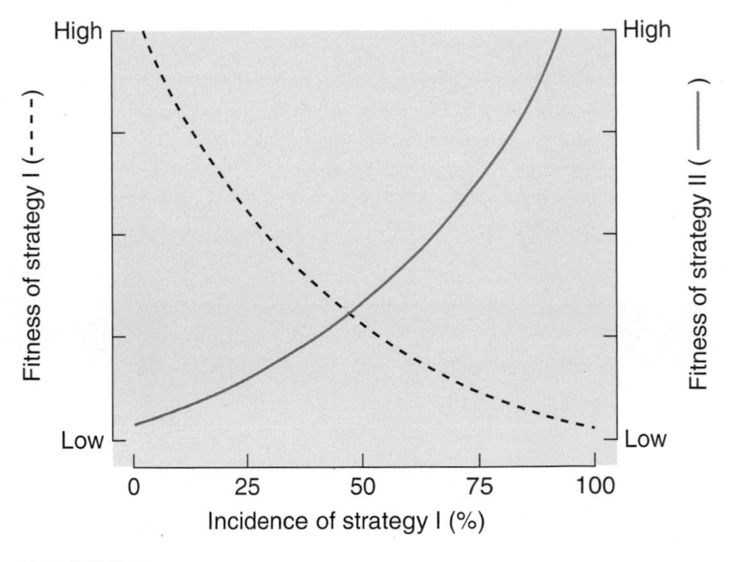

FIGURE 8.21
Alternative Life-History Strategies Can Be Maintained by Negative Frequency-Dependent Selection. When genes for strategy I (e.g., a small-male, sneaker strategy) are rare, competition among these individuals is comparatively weak and their average fitness (dashed curve) is relatively high. By contrast, competition among the common strategy II individuals (e.g., large-male, behaviourally dominant strategy) is comparatively strong and their average fitness (solid curve) is relatively low. As the genes for the rare strategy I increase in the population, the average fitness of individuals adopting this strategy declines, while that of the increasingly less frequent strategy II increases. The evolutionarily stable frequencies of the two strategies occur at the point of intersection of the two fitness functions, at which individuals adopting each strategy have, on average, the same fitness.

Evidence that alternative life histories can have a genetic basis has been forthcoming from studies of salmon in Canada. Dan Heath of the University of Windsor and colleagues (2002) estimated the heritability of jacking in Chinook salmon (*Oncoryhnchus tshawytscha*) to be quite high (h^2=0.62).

Threshold Traits: An Interaction Between Environment and Genotypes

Rather than being solely under genetic control (as the model in **Figure 8.21** implicitly assumes), alternative reproductive strategies can be maintained within populations through some form of adaptive phenotypic plasticity. To account for the influence of both environmental and genetic influences on age at maturity, the incidence of alternative life histories has been modelled as a threshold trait (Hazel et al., 1990; Hutchings and Myers, 1994). In the sense of quantitative genetics, threshold traits describe characters that are determined by alleles at multiple loci and that can be assigned to one of two or more distinct classes (Roff, 1996). However, although the threshold itself may be genetically determined, the likelihood that the threshold will be attained might be triggered by the environment. For example, individuals whose growth rate, body size, or condition (traits that are often heavily influenced by environmental conditions) exceeds a genetically determined threshold might adopt one maturation phenotype, while those whose state falls below the threshold would adopt the alternative one. The threshold-trait model incorporates the assumptions that (a) the threshold differs genetically among individuals within a population, (b) it is heritable, and (c) it differs genetically among populations (Shuster and Wade, 2003; Tomkins and Hazel, 2007).

Male Atlantic salmon can mature either as large anadromous males (>1 kg) that migrate to the ocean, or as small (10–150 g) parr that mature without such a migration. In some salmon populations in eastern Canada, more than 80 percent of the males mature as parr, whereas in others fewer than 5 percent of them do so (Myers et al., 1986). Jacinthe Piché and colleagues (2008) of Dalhousie University reported experimental support for genetic variability in maturation thresholds for male salmon. They interbred salmon from different Nova Scotian populations to determine whether the association between individual male

A CANADIAN ECOLOGIST 8.1

Derek Roff: Life Histories and Genetics—From Fish to Crickets

Derek Roff

Derek Roff

Derek Roff is a quantitative evolutionary geneticist who has had a profound influence on the study of life histories. After completing his B.Sc. at Sydney University, Australia, Roff moved to Canada where he undertook his Ph.D. at the University of British Columbia under the auspices of C. S. (Buzz) Holling (whose formulation of functional and numerical responses in predator–prey relationships were examined in Chapter 5). In 1978, two years after completing his Ph.D., Roff took up a position with the Department of Fisheries and Oceans in St. John's, Newfoundland, where he researched the life history and population dynamics of marine fish. He remained in Newfoundland until 1980, when he accepted a faculty position in the Biology Department at McGill University. After 21 years at McGill, he moved to the University of California at Riverside.

It was during his time at McGill that Roff completed four of his five books (to date), two of which have been particular landmarks in the study of life-history evolution: *The Evolution of Life Histories* (1992) and *Life History Evolution* (2002). His research on flatfish in Newfoundland led him to explore how correlations among age at maturity, individual growth, and mortality in fish might be a function of evolutionary changes in life-history trade-offs (Roff, 1984). He followed this work with an examination of how life-history models can be used to predict body size, based on the premise (underscored in the present chapter) that "survival and fecundity, two parameters at the core of Darwinian fitness, are both functions of body size" (Roff, 1986).

While at McGill, Roff began to articulate his research interests in the question of how life-history trade-offs might evolve. This collaborative research with Daphne Fairbairn (an evolutionary ecologist who spent 21 years at Concordia University in Montreal before moving to UC Riverside in 2001) focused particularly on the testing of hypotheses examining the evolution of trade-offs that exist between flight capability and reproductive traits; these exchanges are evident in many insects, notably the sand cricket, *Gryllus firmus*. Based on his ever-increasing research on the genetics of wing dimorphism in insects, Roff subsequently focused on the evolution of threshold traits (examined in the present chapter in the context of alternative reproductive strategies), whereby individuals whose trait exceeds a genetically determined "switch-point" develop into one morph, or life history, while individuals below the threshold develop into the alternative.

Swimming against the academic tide of increasing narrowness in research interests, Roff's intellectual breadth has made him one of few individuals who are fully cognizant and appreciative of life-history evolution, the trade-offs that constrain the expression of traits, the reproductive costs that affect fitness, and the underlying genetics that govern how natural selection moulds life histories given the ecological and evolutionary vagaries of existence. Derek Roff is a Fellow of the Royal Society of Canada and of the American Association for the Advancement of Science, and his sixth book, entitled *Modelling Evolution*, published in 2010.

growth rate and the incidence of parr maturity differed genetically between population crosses. Using a common-garden experimental protocol, they found that the growth rate at which the sneaker, small-male phenotype is expressed differed between pure- and mixed-population crosses (**Figure 8.22**). Maturation thresholds of hybrids were intermediate to those of pure crosses, which is consistent with the hypothesis that the life-history switch-points are heritable.

The genetic basis of these reproductive strategies of male Atlantic salmon was the subject of the first study of brain gene expression in wild vertebrates. Nadia Aubin-Horth et al. (2005a,b) of Université de Montréal compared the levels of gene expression of mature male parr with those of immatures of the same age that were destined to become anadromous males. They found that hundreds of genes varied in expression between the two male types, equivalent to about 15 percent of the portion of the genome that was examined. Among these genes, those related to cognition (learning and memory) and reproduction were up-regulated in sneaker males, while genes related to cellular growth were up-regulated in immature fighter males.

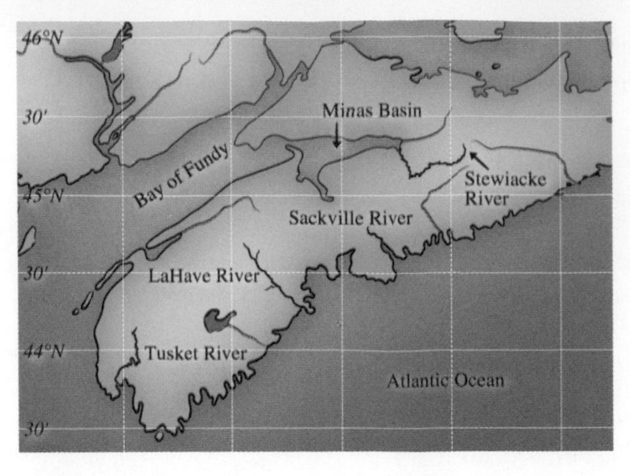

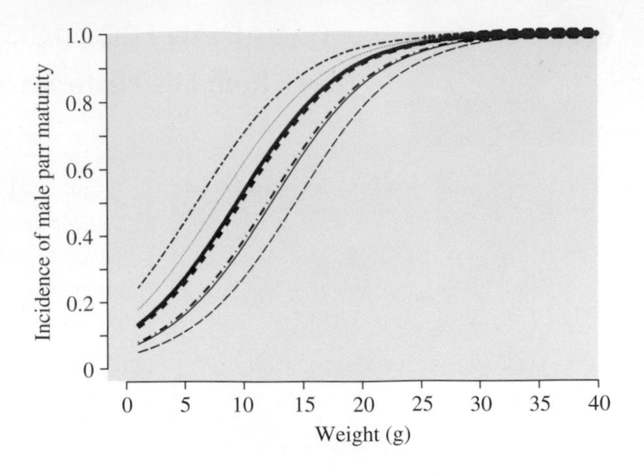

FIGURE 8.22

Genetic Variation in Threshold Norms of Reaction for Alternative Life Histories. Threshold norms of reaction between incidence of parr maturity and individual growth rate (body weight at seven months) in male Atlantic salmon (*Salmo salar*) populations from Nova Scotia. Left to right, the reaction norms are for the following population crosses: Tusket×Stewiacke; Sackville×Sackville; Stewiacke×Stewiacke; Stewiacke×LaHave; Sackville×LaHave; Tuset×LaHave; LaHave×LaHave.

SOURCE: Piché et al. (2008), Figure 2.

8.6 Harvest-Induced Evolution of Life History

Changes in Age and Size at Maturity Caused by Harvesting

Fisheries were once famously described by the Dutch fisheries ecologist Adriaan Rijnsdorp (1993) as uncontrolled experiments in evolution. His work was stimulated by the question of whether harvesting can produce evolutionary change in exploited populations by favouring some genotypes over others (Stokes et al., 1993). Evolution by natural selection involves pressures that select against individuals with "unfavourable" inherited traits, while those with more "favourable" ones survive and reproduce with greater success. As such, a commercial fishery, or any other kind of anthropogenic harvesting (for example, in forestry or big-game hunting), would seem to provide such a selective pressure.

In essence, fisheries usually target the largest and oldest individuals in a harvested population. They do so either

- directly, by using gear that preferentially catches larger, older individuals, or
- indirectly, by imposing higher mortalities across all sizes and ages, which reduces the likelihood of living to larger sizes and older ages.

Under these circumstances, individual fish that are genetically predisposed to mature at larger sizes and older ages are more likely to be caught before they can reproduce. Such harvesting pressures should theoretically favour earlier- and smaller-maturing genetic types. Interestingly, this consequence is reminiscent of other circumstances in which humans have unintentionally selected against that which they most desire, such as the evolution of pathogenic bacteria that are resistant to antibiotics.

The potential for fishing to cause evolutionary change in life-history traits is not appreciably different from that of other forms of predator-induced mortality—the key is the propensity of exploitation to result in differential rates of mortality among genotypes. Nevertheless, many fisheries scientists have been reluctant to acknowledge that fishing has the potential to elicit genetic change, or they are doubtful that such an effect would be harmful. The latter point is important because it raises questions as to whether human-induced evolution caused by exploitation is likely to significantly affect population attributes, such as the maximum sustainable yield, a population's resistance to natural environmental change, or the likelihood of recovery following depletion.

Fishing has long been associated with reductions in two key life-history traits: the age and size at maturity (Hutchings and Fraser, 2008). However, changes in these traits are not necessarily genetically based; they could also be caused by phenotypic plasticity in life-history responses to reductions in population density due to harvesting. As density decreases, competition for food and space is relaxed and this should lead to individuals growing at a faster rate. Fish generally respond to an increased growth rate by maturing earlier in life (Wootton,

TABLE 8.2 **Examples of Fish Species for Which Commercial or Recreational Fishing Has Been Hypothesized to Have Generated an Evolutionary Response in One or More Traits**

Species	Hypothesized Selection Response	Reference
Northern pike (*Esox lucius*)	Increased fecundity	Law (1979)
Lake whitefish (*Coregonus clupeaformis*)	Smaller body size; slower growth	Handford et al. (1977)
Atlantic salmon (*Salmo salar*)	Smaller size at maturity	Bielak and Power (1986); Consuegra et al. (2005); Quinn et al. (2006)
Pink salmon (*Oncorhynchus gorbuscha*)	Smaller size at maturity	Ricker (1981)
Chinook salmon (*O. tshawytscha*)	Smaller size at maturity	Ricker (1981)
Sockeye salmon (*O. nerka*)	Earlier run-timing	Quinn et al. (2007)
	Smaller girth	Hamon et al. (2000)
	Smaller size at maturity	Kendall et al. (2009)
European grayling (*Thymallus thymallus*)	Earlier age at maturity	Haugen (2000); Haugen and Vøllestad (2000)
Atlantic cod (*Gadus morhua*)	Earlier age at maturity	Hutchings (1999, 2005); Heino et al. (2002); Barot et al. (2004); Olsen et al. (2004, 2005)
	Smaller size at maturity	Barot et al. (2004); Hutchings (2005)
	Smaller body size	Law and Rowell (1993)
	Slower growth	Sinclair et al. (2002); Swain et al. (2007)
Smallmouth bass (*Micropterus dolomieui*)	Earlier age at maturity	Dunlop et al. (2005)
Orange roughy (*Hoplostethus atlanticus*)	Increased fecundity	Koslow et al. (1995)
European plaice (*Pleuronectes platessa*)	Earlier age at maturity	Rijnsdorp (1993); Grift et al. (2003)
	Increased reproductive investment	Rijnsdorp et al. (2005)
American plaice (*Hippoglossoides platessoides*)	Earlier age at maturity	Barot et al. (2005)

1998; Roff, 2002). Therefore, fishing could lead to earlier maturity solely as a consequence of density- or environmental-driven changes to individual growth rates. Alternatively, by selecting against individuals whose genes predispose them to breed at older ages and larger sizes, fishing might favour genotypes that mature at a relatively young age, or a small body size, or that grow at a slower rate.

Long-term changes in life-history traits have been interpreted as representing genetic responses to the size-selectivity of fishing gear in a number of fish (**Table 8.2**). Although it seems logical to hypothesize that harvesting can generate evolutionary change in exploited populations, it should also be acknowledged that there is no unequivocal empirical evidence of genetic change that has resulted from fishing.

There is, however, strong evidence of harvest-induced evolution in a terrestrial mammal. Male bighorn sheep in Alberta are sport-hunted for their impressive horns. The longer and more curved the horns, the more desirable they are to trophy hunters, some of whom will pay handsomely for the opportunity to fell a prized ram (one hunter reportedly paid over $1 million in 1998 and 1999 for special permits to hunt trophy rams in Alberta; Coltman et al. 2003). Not surprisingly, the largest horns are found on the biggest sheep. David Coltman of the University of Alberta and colleagues (2003) examined changes in horn size and body weight of bighorn sheep on Ram Mountain, Alberta, where trophy hunters had for several decades been targeting rams with large horns. Within that population, the body weight and horn size of rams declined significantly between 1975 and 2002 (**Figure 8.23**), and quantitative genetic analyses demonstrated that the reductions in those heritable traits represented an evolutionary response to hunting.

Consequences of Harvest-Induced Changes in Life History

Harvest-induced evolution shifts traits from their naturally selected optimal values. Within that context, it is unlikely that anthropogenic selection for earlier maturity would have positive consequences

ECOLOGY IN DEPTH 8.1

The Fallacy of Fecundity and Extinction Risk in Marine Fish

Unprecedented reductions in abundance of a variety of species have hastened efforts to identify factors related to the risks of extinction. Several life-history traits are potentially useful in this regard, as correlates of maximum per capita population growth rate (r_{max}, a proxy for extinction; see Chapter 5). The traits include large body size, slow individual growth, long life span, delayed age at maturity, and fecundity (e.g., Gaston and Blackburn, 1995; Reynolds et al., 2005).

Among the potential life-history correlates of r_{max}, arguably none has had a longer history of investigation than fecundity. Many have thought it obvious that fitness should increase with the numbers of offspring produced. Prominent among them are scientists who have studied marine fish in some capacity. Thomas Huxley (1825–1895), famously described as Charles Darwin's "bulldog" because of the tenacity with which he supported the theory of evolution by natural selection, proffered the following opinion about the sustainability of marine fisheries at the Great International Fisheries Exhibition in London in 1883:

". . . the cod fishery, the herring fishery, the pilchard fishery, the mackerel fishery, and probably all the great sea-fisheries, are inexhaustible; that is to say that nothing we do seriously affects the number of fish."

Obviously, in view of the many observations of depleted fish stocks in recent times, Huxley was wrong in this belief about limitless marine bioresources. However, his opinion was based partly on the knowledge that most marine fish of commercial importance produce vast numbers of eggs, a trait which he thought would prevent fishing from having any significant impact on their populations.

Remarkably, a similar argument is often heard today, albeit in a modified form. For example, the Food and Agricultural Organization of the United Nations argued that "greater potential fecundity tends to make aquatic species more resilient to depletion and results in a lower risk of extinction" (FAO 2002). The American Fisheries Society concurred with this view, identifying fecundity as a positive correlate of r_{max} (Musick et al., 2000) and a negative one of extinction risk.

However, to a life-history researcher this refrain is flawed because it obfuscates the importance of fecundity to reproductive fitness. This fallacy was, in a sense, recognized at the same Fisheries Exhibition of 1883 by the English biologist, Sir Ray Lankester (1847–1929), who argued, in effect, that the millions of young produced by marine fish are not superfluous. He posited that animal populations are in an equilibrium, such that "those that survive to maturity in the struggle for existence merely replace those which have gone before" (Smith, 1994).

If this is reworded using the terminology of today, it states that when an animal population is at or near equilibrium, for example, at its carrying capacity, natural selection will favour those individuals whose reproductive strategy allows them to produce enough offspring to replace themselves. However, phylogenetic constraints, coupled with the varying challenges that different environments pose to organisms, have conspired to produce a wide variety of reproductive strategies. For example, a porbeagle shark (*Lamna nasus*) produces only one to five large offspring every one to two years, for perhaps 10 to 15 years of reproductive activity; this is the porbeagle's strategy for replacement. In contrast, an Atlantic cod (*Gadus morhua*) produces several hundred thousand to a few million eggs every year for perhaps 5 to 10 years of reproductive activity; this is the cod's strategy for replacement. In an evolutionary sense, however, the two strategies are equivalent in terms of their result—replacement at equilibrium.

Mars Evis/Shutterstock

The size and weight of the horns of male bighorn sheep (*Ovis canadensis*) on Ram Mountain, Alberta, have declined as an evolutionary response to hunting; see Figure 8.23.

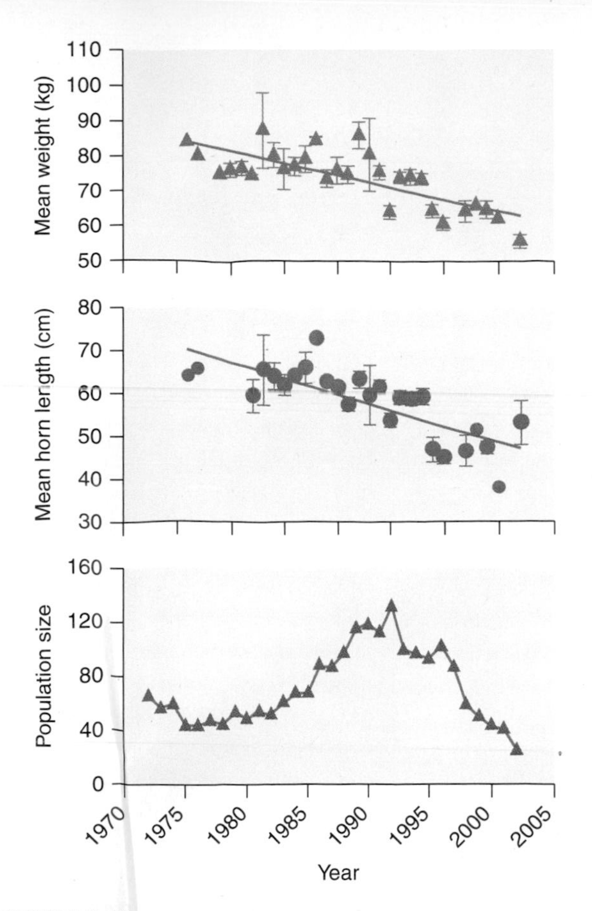

FIGURE 8.23
Evolutionary change in a terrestrial mammal caused by hunting. Reductions in horn length and body weight of male bighorn sheep (*Ovis canadensis*) on Ram Mountain, Alberta, caused by evolutionary responses to hunting pressure.

SOURCE: Coltman et al. (2003), Figure 2.

for an exploited population. Rather, it has the potential to reduce both individual fitness and the maximum per capita population growth rate. Changes such as these can be expected to lead to reduced harvests and diminished ability of exploited populations to recover from decline. Given the links between life-history traits and maximum population growth rate, it is surprising that relatively little research has examined the demographic consequences of harvest-induced changes in life history, including harvest-induced evolution.

The potential demographic consequences of life-history change have been examined in northern cod, a once commercially important marine species. Between the early 1960s and the early 1990s, northern cod declined by about 99 percent in the region between southeastern Labrador and the northern Grand Bank off Newfoundland (see Chapter 15). Between the mid-1950s and the early 1990s, the age at 50 percent maturity (i.e., the point at which half of the population is sexually mature) is estimated to have declined from 6.5–7.0 years to 5.0–5.5 years. It has been suggested that such reductions in the age at maturity of cod might be interpreted as a genetic response to intensive fishing (Olsen et al., 2004). Based on the empirically supported premise that the probability of surviving reproduction declines with reductions in age and size at maturity, Hutchings (2005) reported that a shift in age at maturity from six to four years for cod could potentially reduce the population growth rate by 25–30 percent, while doubling the likelihood of population decreases occurring in subsequent generations.

One prediction that is common to studies of harvest-induced evolution is that the genetic changes will be slow to reverse. An example of this may be provided by the work of Doug Swain and colleagues (2007) of the Department of Fisheries and Oceans on cod in the southern Gulf of St. Lawrence. They concluded that the observed decline in individual growth rate of cod can be attributed to fisheries-induced selection against individuals that are genetically predisposed to grow fast (more rapid growth leads to individuals more quickly achieving a size that is vulnerable to fishing, while also extending that period of exposure). An important observation is that slow growth has persisted in this over-exploited cod population, despite large reductions in fishing pressure and seemingly favourable environmental conditions for individual growth over the past two decades. The persistence of small sizes is consistent with the hypothesis that the strength of selection for rapid growth when fishing pressure is low is unlikely to be as large as that against fast growth when the harvesting intensity is high (Law, 2000).

There is a simple mitigation of the problem of harvest-induced life-history evolution—reduce the intensity of harvesting. There are good reasons to believe that management strategies that are designed to minimize deleterious evolutionary change are consistent with traditional objectives, such as the maximization of yield, establishment of mortality reference points, and minimization of the likelihood of population decline (Hutchings, 2009). As such, adherence to conventional management reference points may be sufficient to safeguard against undesirable evolutionary change in exploited populations.

ECOLOGY IN DEPTH 8.2

Extreme Alternative Life Histories

One of the more phenotypically extreme examples of an alternative life history in vertebrates is that of the Atlantic salmon (*Salmo salar*) (Jones, 1959; Myers, 1984; Myers et al., 1986; Fleming, 1996; Hutchings and Jones, 1998). Males can become sexually mature as **anadromous** males, which breed following a migration to the ocean, where they may spend one to three years before they return to their natal river at a weight of >1 kg and age of four to eight years. Alternatively, males may mature early as *parr*, and thereby reproduce at sizes that are two to three orders of magnitude smaller than anadromous males (only 10–150 g) and at a much younger age (only one to two years). Prior to spawning, mature parr compete physically among themselves for access to a female, fertilizing eggs in a stiff competition with one or more much larger anadromous males. As a group, the success that parr achieve in fertilizing eggs may vary between 15 percent and 60 percent; at the individual level, however, parr fertilization success tends to be low (usually less than 5 percent) and highly variable (the fertilization success of many parr is nil).

The adoption of either of the maturation phenotypes is associated with important life-history trade-offs. The fitness benefits gained by parr that mature at an earlier age include a greater likelihood of surviving to reproduce and an increased rate of gene input into the population, but these benefits are offset by reduced post-reproductive survival and reduced fertilization success. In contrast, the higher fertilization success of anadromous males is offset by the low probability of surviving the arduous migration to and from the ocean.

The expression of alternative reproductive strategies in Atlantic salmon depends on both the environment experienced by an individual and on that individual's genetic background; the fastest-growing males in a population tend to be those most likely to mature as parr and there is evidence that the male progeny of mature male parr are more likely to adopt that strategy than those fathered by anadromous males. To incorporate both the environmental and genetic determinants of alternative reproductive strategies in this species, parr maturation is modelled as a threshold trait such that adoption of either the parr or the anadromous strategy depends on whether an individual's growth rate in early life exceeds that specified by a genetically determined growth-rate threshold.

The existence of alternative strategies in salmon has implications from a management and a conservation perspective. The fact that more than 75 percent of the males in some populations mature as parr (Myers et al., 1986) means that, in some rivers, the number of male salmon returning from the ocean is very small because of the higher mortality experienced by males that mature as parr relative to those that do not. Fewer returning salmon translates into fewer angling opportunities for recreational fisheries. However, the existence of high numbers of mature male salmon parr may provide increased population resilience because of the high genetic variability that they can potentially contribute during spawning. Laura Weir of Dalhousie University (2008), for example, found that as many as 16 males—most of whom are parr—can contribute to the fertilization of a single female's egg batch in a tributary of the Miramichi River, New Brunswick. However, despite the ecological, management, socioeconomic, and conservation implications of alternative strategies in Atlantic salmon, there are no monitoring programs for mature male parr in Canada (although these do exist for Pacific salmon jacks in some British Columbia rivers).

VOCABULARY OF ECOLOGY

age at maturity, p. 209
anadromous, p. 238
antagonistic pleiotropy, p. 220
bet-hedging strategy, p. 212
constraints of reproduction, p. 218
cost of reproduction, p. 218
fecundity (fertility), p. 209
life history, p. 207
life-history invariants, p. 226
longevity (lifespan), p. 209
pleiotropy, p. 219
size at maturity, p. 209
trade-off, p. 216

QUESTIONS FOR REVIEW AND DISCUSSION

1. Age and size at maturity often differ between males and females in the same population. In birds and mammals, males usually mature at an older age, and larger size, than females. Natural selection may favour increased age in males because of the positive influence that larger size can have on male competitive attempts to secure a territory or to gain access to one or more females. In fish, however, it is usually the female that matures at an older age. Why might this be so?

2. The table below identifies a life table for a fish of moderate fecundity, such as a salmon. For each of four potential ages at maturity (2 through 5 years), the two right-hand columns indicate the age-specific schedules of survival (l_x) and fecundity (m_x) at each age x. (No individuals live beyond age 6 yrs.) Regarding age-specific survival, note that this value is the product of three factors: (a) the exploitation rate; (b) the survival cost of reproduction; and (c) annual survival probabilities from age x to age $x+1$. Regarding age-specific fecundity, these data include a fecundity cost of reproduction. (For example, note that the m_4 value for individuals maturing at age 4 (1600 eggs) is greater than the m_4 value for individuals maturing at age 2 (400 eggs).) The baseline table presented below represents a population that is not fished (exploitation rate = 0 at each age) and that does not experience a survival cost of reproduction. Using the Euler-Lotka equation to calculate the fitness (r), determine the optimal age at maturity for this unfished population for which survival reproductive costs are absent. (The optimal age at maturity is the one that yields the highest fitness.)

Age at Maturity (years)	Age (x)	(1—Exploitation Rate) (A)	(1—Survival Cost of Reproduction) (B)	Annual Survival (C)	Age-Specific Survival, l_x ($=l_{x-1}$*A* B*C)	Age-Specific Fecundity, m_x
2	0	1	1	1	1	0
	1	1	1	0.2	0.2	0
	2	1	1	0.1	0.02	100
	3	1	1	0.5	0.01	200
	4	1	1	0.5	0.005	400
	5	1	1	0.5	0.0025	800
	6	1	1	0.5	0.00125	1600
3	0	1	1	1	1	0
	1	1	1	0.2	0.2	0
	2	1	1	0.1	0.02	0
	3	1	1	0.5	0.01	400
	4	1	1	0.5	0.005	800
	5	1	1	0.5	0.0025	1600
	6	1	1	0.5	0.00125	3200
4	0	1	1	1	1	0
	1	1	1	0.2	0.2	0
	2	1	1	0.1	0.02	0
	3	1	1	0.5	0.01	0
	4	1	1	0.5	0.005	1600
	5	1	1	0.5	0.0025	3200
	6	1	1	0.5	0.00125	6400
5	0	1	1	1	1	0
	1	1	1	0.2	0.2	0
	2	1	1	0.1	0.02	0
	3	1	1	0.5	0.01	0
	4	1	1	0.5	0.005	0
	5	1	1	0.5	0.0025	6400
	6	1	1	0.5	0.00125	12800

3. The previous question required the determination of the optimal age at maturity for an unfished population for which survival reproductive costs were absent. To determine how a survival cost might influence this optimum, let the survival cost of reproduction (which can vary from 0 to 1) be 0.2. This can be interpreted as meaning that the probability of surviving from one age to the next *after maturity has been attained* is reduced by 80 percent (or [1–0.2]) in column 4 of the life table). How has the optimal age at maturity for this population changed once a survival cost of reproduction has been incorporated?

4. The previous question required the determination of the optimal age at maturity for an unfished population for which reproduction reduced annual survival probabilities by 80 percent. To determine how fishing mortality might influence this optimum, let the exploitation rate (which can vary from 0 to 1) be 0.4 for fish older than 2 years of age (meaning that 40 percent of the 3-, 4-, 5-, and 6-year-olds are removed annually by fishing). What is the optimal age at maturity for this population when it is subjected to a 40 percent exploitation rate?

HELPFUL WEBSITES

PARAMETER ESTIMATION FOR SOME LIFE HISTORY MODELS

http:// www.biology.ucr.edu/people/faculty/Roff.html

Computer codes in S-PLUS for calculating the parameters associated with threshold models, a simple logistic curve, and multiple variants of the von Bertalanffy growth curve are available at this site.

LIFE HISTORY EVOLUTION

http://academicearth.org/lectures/life-history-evolution

A lecture on life history evolution delivered by Stephen C. Stearns, Yale University.

You'll find a rich array of additional resources for *Ecology* at www.ecology.nelson.com.

CHAPTER 9

Community Ecology

ROY TURKINGTON, Department of Botany and, Biodiversity Research Centre, University of British Columbia

Mixedwood forest near Sault Ste. Marie, ON. Photo by Bill Caulfeild-Browne

LEARNING OBJECTIVES

After studying this chapter you should be able to

1. Distinguish between Clements' organismal concept of community organization and Gleason's individualistic concept, and explain the differences of equilibrium and non-equilibrium views of community organization.
2. Understand various levels of the functional organization of communities.
3. Explain different methods of describing the relative abundances of species in a community, such as the logarithmic series and the log-normal distribution.
4. Distinguish between an organism's fundamental niche and its realized niche.
5. Explain how various processes contribute to structuring natural communities, such as competition, facilitation, herbivory, predation, and disturbances, in addition to the effects of chance.
6. Describe circumstances under which a community may exist in more than one stable state.
7. Distinguish between dominant species and keystone species, and understand their impacts on a community.
8. Discuss the various models of community structure, such as top–down versus bottom–up regulation, trophic cascades, and those proposed by Connell and by Menge and Sutherland.

CHAPTER OUTLINE

9.1 The Nature of the Community

An ecological **community** is a group of organisms that live together at the same place and time and interact directly or indirectly. A community includes of all of the organisms present—plants, animals, fungi, and bacteria—and their interactions may involve competition for scarce resources (such as light, nutrients, food, or water), herbivory, predation, disease, or cooperative relations, referred to as **facilitation**.

But how do we define "a group of organisms"? Pioneers to North America would have had recognized the "forest community" in the east, which gave way abruptly to a vast "grassland community" that stretched to the Rocky Mountains. The vegetation of the Rockies provided yet another type of "forest community." But any hiker, trapper, or naturalist will be quick to point out that there are many different types of habitats within all of those regions. For example, if you were to travel eastward from coastal British Columbia, you would pass through a series of noticeably different vegetation zones (**Figure 9.1**) (Pojar and Meidinger, 1991; B.C. Ministry of Forests, 1996–1999):

- a low-elevation zone dominated by western hemlock (*Tsuga heterophylla*);
- a zone in the southern interior with open forests of Douglas-fir (*Pseudotsuga menziesii*) and interspersed dry grasslands;
- a cedar (*Thuja plicata*) and hemlock zone;
- a region dominated by ponderosa pine (*Pinus ponderosa*);
- and yet different types at higher elevation, such as forests dominated by Engelmann spruce (*Picea engelmanii*) and subalpine fir (*Abies lasiocarpa*); and
- above these there are alpine tundra and non-vegetated rockfields.

Moreover, all of these major biogeoclimatic zones are embedded with a variety of community types, including distinctive forests of various age and species composition, other terrestrial

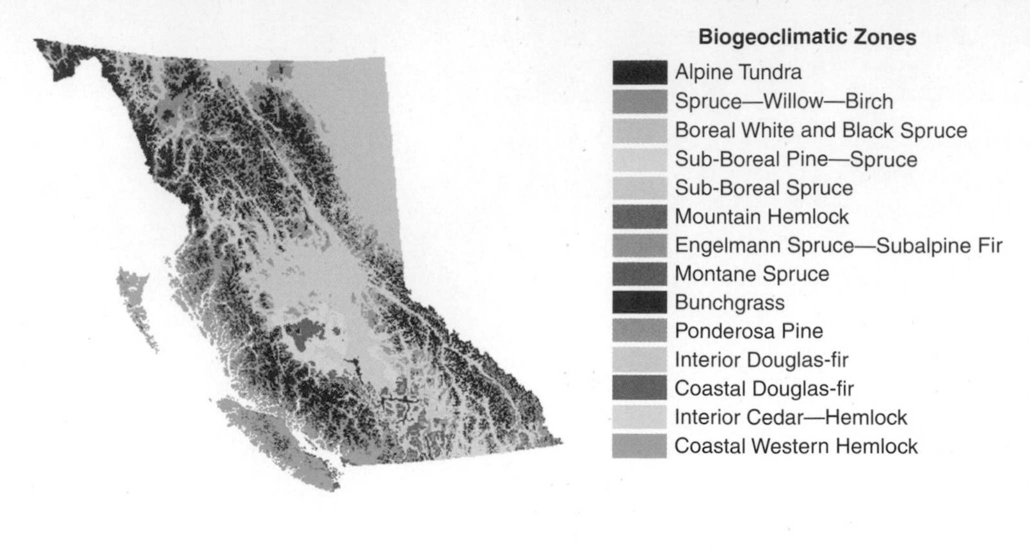

FIGURE 9.1
The Biogeoclimatic Zones of British Columbia. The distinctive geological and climatic environments of each zone results in the development of a characteristic vegetation type, mostly trees, after which the zone is named.

SOURCE: Ministry of Forests and Range. 2009. Biogeoclimatic Zones of British Columbia. http://www.for.gov.bc.ca/hfd/library/documents/treebook/biogeo/biogeo.htm.

communities, and various kinds of wetlands. The communities are identified on the basis of their dominant vegetation—as the plant composition changes, so too will the animals, fungi, bacteria, and functional groups such as pollinators and decomposers.

Community Organization

Discrete and Continuous Organization

As we travel across a landscape, there are occasions when one ecological community ends abruptly and is immediately replaced by a different one. It is more usual, however, for communities to gradually transition from one type to the next. In either case, rapid or gradual, the zone of transition is called an ecotone. The disparity of these changes reflects a fundamental difference of opinion about the nature of communities. The most extreme positions are represented by two American ecologists: Frederic Clements (1874–1945), who emphasized the nature of the community as a holistic entity (Clements, 1916, 1936), and Henry A. Gleason (1882–1975), who focused on the individualistic responses of species within a community (Gleason, 1926, 1939).

Clements, along with British ecologist Arthur G. Tansley (1871–1955, who was the first person to use the word "ecosystem" in a publication, in 1935), proposed the **organismal** (or **community unit**) **hypothesis** of the community. They argued that a community acts like a "superorganism"—a highly organized and closely integrated entity that is composed of mutually interdependent species that are to varying degrees co-adapted to one another (see the next section for more details about *symbioses*). Underlying this view is the assumption that the species comprising a community have overlapping habitat requirements, and therefore we would predict that fairly narrow boundaries would be observed between community types, with few species in common (**Figure 9.2a**). This view argues that groups of species interact in a cooperative manner toward some predictable end-point, including a stable and predictable culmination of succession, referred to as the climax (or **climax community**).

riekephotos/Shutterstock

The Coastal Western Hemlock zone occurs from sea level to mid-elevations (up to 900 m in British Columbia) mostly west of the coastal mountains, stretching from northern Oregon and Washington, along the entire BC coast and into Alaska. The zone covers much of Vancouver Island and Haida Gwaii (formerly the Queen Charlotte Islands).

In contrast, Gleason's **individualistic** (or **continuum**) **hypothesis** views the community as a coincidental assemblage of species that have similar environmental requirements. While the species of a community interact with each other, there is no predictable or repeatable end-point (**Figure 9.2b**). Indeed, each community is viewed as unique because it is the product of the specific environmental conditions that occur at any particular place and time. Because all species are distributed independently of others, they have overlapping distributions along physical environmental gradients, and so there is continuous variation in community composition, rather than the discrete boundaries of the Clementsian model.

Although many ecologists agreed with Gleason's arguments, the ideas of Clements had a stronger following at the time (about the 1920s through the 1940s). Indeed, it was not until the mid-1950s to 1960s that Robert Whittaker (1920–1980) seriously challenged the Clements' view of a community. Whittaker (1956, 1975) surveyed vegetation along elevational gradients in the Great Smoky Mountains of Tennessee, the Siskiyou Mountains of Oregon, and the Santa Catalina Mountains in Arizona. In all of those disparate places, he demonstrated that forest communities changed gradually in species composition and without sharp boundaries (**Figure 9.3**), and in so doing he showed that Gleason's view on boundaries was correct. Discrete boundaries do unquestionably occur in some cases, but they are related to underlying abrupt changes in environmental conditions, such as moisture or soil type.

Today, ecologists recognize that elements of both arguments are valid, but most hold to a view more similar to that of Gleason than of Clements. Nevertheless, like so many topics in ecology, wide variations of opinion are driven by differences in observations and analyses. An insufficiently critical interpretation of Gleason's arguments might lead us to believe that the distributions of species are determined solely by their individualistic tolerance to environmental factors, such as moisture, temperature, or light. However, species do interact and this inevitably forces us to consider the ways that competition and other biotic processes might influence the distribution of organisms. We will deal with this key topic in more detail in a later section, but for now we can imagine a situation in which competition between certain species may produce relatively discrete boundaries, so that we might observe some Clementsian-like ecotones embedded within an otherwise Gleason-like continuum (**Figure 9.4**). In addition, many communities are composed of several layers of species, for example, herbs, shrubs, and trees within a forest. If these layers act independently, it may be possible to observe continuous change in the composition of the herb layer, but discrete changes in the trees.

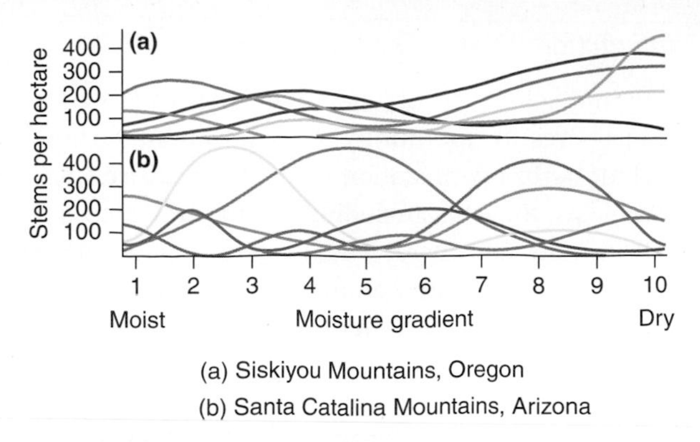

FIGURE 9.3
Whittaker's Distribution of Vegetation in Mountains in Oregon and Arizona. The distribution of tree species (each coloured line represents a tree species) is shown along a continuous gradient of environmental change (moisture) associated with increasing altitude.

SOURCE: Modified from Fig 4.2, p. 115 from COMMUNITIES AND ECOSYSTEMS, 2nd ed., by Robert H. Whittaker. Copyright © 1975 by Robert H. Whittaker. Reprinted by permission of Pearson Education, Inc.

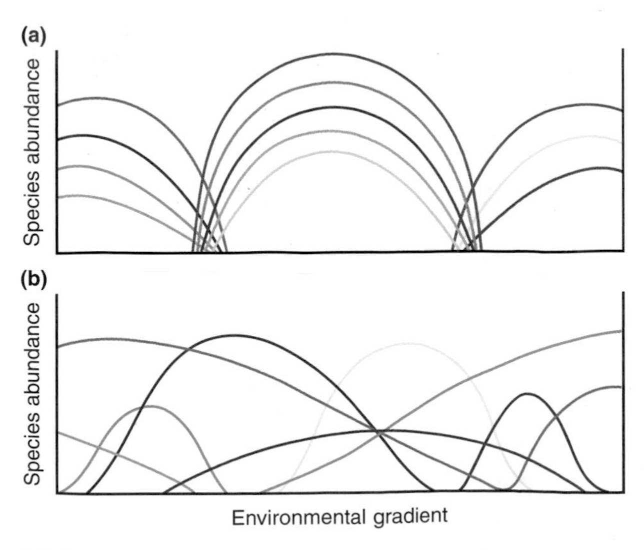

FIGURE 9.2
Comparison of Two Models of the Community. (a) Clements predicts discrete community types with sharp ecotones between them, while (b) Gleason suggests there is continuous variation.

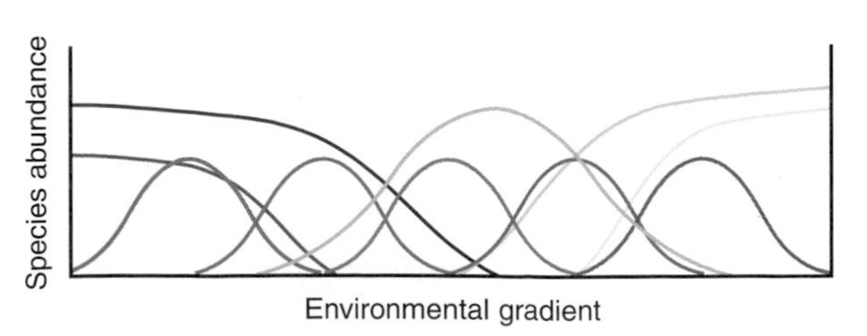

FIGURE 9.4
Combination of the Models of Clements and Gleason. Discrete, Clementsian boundaries may be embedded within an otherwise Gleason-like continuum.

Interactions among Species

The interactions occurring among species are a key subject area in community ecology. The interactions include herbivory, predation, competition, disease, and symbiosis, the latter including mutualism, commensalism, and parasitism. These interactions all influence the presence and abundance of species within communities, as shown in the following examples:

- **Herbivory:** Larvae of the spruce budworm (*Choristoneura fumiferana*) eat the foliage of fir and spruce trees, and they are always present in a low density in mature stands. Sometimes, however, environmental conditions promote a rapid proliferation of budworm, known as an irruption, and when this happens their voracious feeding can kill almost all mature fir and spruce trees in affected stands, as periodically occurs in eastern Canada. The destruction of the forest canopy results in many environmental effects, including a high availability of light for previously shaded understorey plants, which respond by growing vigorously. The resulting changes in vegetation affect the habitat of birds and other animals, and microorganisms and other detritivores are affected because large amounts of dead biomass of the killed trees are available to be decomposed. Similarly, when elk (*Cervus canadensis*) are abundant, their feeding can interfere with the regeneration of their favoured species of woody browse, such as aspen and willows, and this has an enormous impact on many of the other species in their community—including plants, herbivores, and carnivores.
- **Predation:** Some predators are sufficiently effective to significantly reduce the abundance of their prey, and in so doing they change the structure of their community. For example, during their breeding season most forest birds eat insects and other invertebrates, which are nutritious for both adults and their rapidly growing nestlings. Experimental studies have enclosed individual plants or small areas of vegetation in netting, which excludes avian predators but allows insects to freely move about. These studies have observed higher densities of invertebrates inside of the bird exclosures, but slower growth of plants because of defoliation suffered from herbivorous insects (Marquis and Whelan, 1994).
- **Competition:** Because the supply of environmental resources is generally less than the potential biological demand, organisms interfere with each other as they vie for scarce supplies. Plants typically compete for access to sunlight, nutrients, and water, while animals may contest for food, nesting sites, or mates. If there is great asymmetry in the competitive abilities of species, then the more competitive ones may reduce some of the others within the community, or in extreme cases, totally exclude some of them. On the other hand, if an effective competitor is removed, then previously suppressed species will increase in abundance. For instance, American chestnut (*Castanea dentata*) is a highly competitive tree that was once abundant and widespread in eastern hardwood forests, but it suffered a deadly blight from an introduced fungal pathogen (*Cryphonectria parasitica*) and was rapidly eliminated from essentially all of its original range. When this happened, various less-competitive species experienced a degree of ecological release and quickly filled in the gaps left by the dead chestnuts, assembling into "new" community types.
- **Disease:** Individuals that are healthy, meaning they have a relative absence of disease, are more competitive, productive, and fecund, and populations of such organisms may be prominent in their community. On the other hand, as we just noted above for the chestnut, populations that are affected by a virulent pathogen may be eliminated from their community, and other species will increase in abundance to fill any gaps that were created. An additional marine example involves the green sea urchin (*Strongylocentrotus droebachiensis*), which sometimes irrupts in abundances and severely overgrazes kelps in its intertidal habitat, creating so-called "lichen barrens" (Scheibling and Stephenson, 1984). However, unusually warm water induces a potent disease of the urchins, causing their population to collapse and allowing the kelp-dominated community to re-establish.
- **Symbiosis: Symbiosis** refers to intimate relationships among species, some of which are obligate so that the symbionts cannot live apart, but more commonly the association is flexible. Symbioses may affect the performance of species by improving their competitive ability and decreasing their vulnerability to predation, disease, or other stresses. There are several kinds of symbioses:
  - **Mutualism** is a relationship in which both of the partners benefit (wouldn't it be nice if all relationships were like this?). Lichens are a familiar example—these are an obligate association of a fungus and an alga or a blue-green bacterium. The fungus benefits from food provided by its photosynthetic symbiont, and the latter from improved access to nutrients and a relatively moist microhabitat. A mycorrhiza is another mutualism and is an intimate association between plant roots and soil fungi, with the plant having enhanced access to nutrients, especially phosphate, and the fungus receiving organic exudates from the roots. Many species of legumes (family Fabaceae) live in mutualisms with nitrogen-fixing bacteria (such as *Rhizobium japonicum* and *R. leguminosarum*),

which provide ammonia, an important nutrient, while benefiting from microhabitat provided in specialized root nodules. Another example involves single-celled algae known as Dinoflagellates that live within corals, where they receive protection and nutrients, while providing the cnidarians with products of photosynthesis. Pollination is another mutualism—the pollinator has access to nectar and pollen as food, and the plant is able to have its ova cross-fertilized with pollen from another individual. One last example involves the diverse community of microorganisms that lives in the gut of essentially all herbivorous vertebrate animals, and that secrete enzymes that help to digest cellulose and lignin so they can contribute to nutrition—deer, bison, and other ungulates have a fore-pouch of their stomach known as the rumen that provides specialized habitat for this beneficial community of microbes.

- **Parasitism** is a relationship in which one organism benefits but the other is harmed, an influence that may affect its competitive ability and thereby influence its relative abundance within its community.
- **Commensalism** is a relationship in which one organism benefits without harming the other. An example is the community of epiphytic lichens, mosses, and plants that often grows on trees. The epiphytes obviously benefit from this relationship, because they get to grow in a relatively sunny place high in the canopy, but the host trees are not affected to any significant degree.

Functional Organization

Communities are also organized in terms of the functional roles that species may play. We previously noted in Chapter 3 that species can be organized into *food webs*, in which functional relationships within a community are organized by feeding relationships. Within this context, communities can be studied in their entirety—including the various species that are *autotrophs, herbivores, carnivores*, or *detritivores* (**Figure 3.9**). Often, however, these are considered separately, as in the plant community, or the community associated with the detrital food web.

An additional way of looking at community organization is on the basis of similarities in the ways that species use resources. In this sense, species that use a similar resource base are referred to as a **guild**. For example, all of the seed-eating animals in a desert could be considered to be part of a guild, even though they are not necessarily taxonomically related. Likewise, birds, bats, and insects that feed on nectar and pollen can be grouped as a floral-visiting guild. Structurally similar groups of plants are also guilds, such as trees, shrubs, forbs (herbaceous dicotyledonous plants), graminoids (grass-like monocots), and epiphytes. Although most researchers use the terms *guild* and *functional group* more or less synonymously, these two concepts have different meanings. A guild primarily refers to the mechanisms of resource sharing by species whereas a **functional group** defines how a resource is processed by different species to provide a specific ecosystem service or function, for example, legumes, alders, and other plants that have the capacity to fix nitrogen.

At a grander life-history scale, Philip Grime (1977, 2002) has classified plants into three groups based on their life-history traits and their adaptedness to habitat conditions, particularly to disturbance and stress. According to Grime, disturbance involves the partial or total removal of vegetation and it can be mild or severe in intensity, and uncommon or frequent. Stress is any condition that reduces the rate of productivity, and it can be mild if moisture, nutrients, and light are

Steve Byland/Shutterstock

Birds, bats, and insects that feed on nectar and pollen can be grouped as a floral-visiting guild. This photo shows a ruby-throated hummingbird (*Archilochus colubris*).

freely available, or intense if any of them are deficient. Any environment can be characterized in terms of the influence of these two factors, resulting in four kinds of habitats:

- low stress, rare disturbance;
- low stress, frequent disturbance;
- intense stress, rare disturbance; and
- intense stress, frequent disturbance.

Because plants cannot cope with an environment that is both highly stressful and frequently disturbed, there are only three primary life-history strategies of plants, each of which is a guild:

- **Competitors** (C-type) dominate in habitats in which environmental stress is relatively benign and disturbance is rare, so that competition is the major agent of natural selection on plant evolution and on the organization of their communities. Competitive plants are effective at acquiring resources and in achieving a dominant position in their community. Typical adaptations are tall growth, a broad canopy, and a spreading root system, all of which occupy space and appropriate resources. Seedlings of competitive plants can usually establish beneath a closed canopy.
- **Ruderals** (R-type) are adapted to living in recently disturbed habitats with abundant resources, so that stress is not intense. Ruderals are typically short-lived and intolerant of competition and stress. They grow rapidly and produce large numbers of seeds that usually have an ability to widely disperse so that newly disturbed habitats can be colonized.
- **Stress-tolerators** (S-type) are adapted to difficult environments in terms of climate, moisture, and nutrient supply, but that are stable because they are infrequently disturbed. Stress-tolerant plants are typical of arctic, desert, and other severe environments, and they are generally short of stature, slow-growing, long-lived, and intolerant of competition.

Equilibrium versus Non-Equilibrium Organization

Much of the thinking in ecology, and many of the concepts and theories, have been structured within an **equilibrium** framework—in the context of a relative constancy of conditions. For instance:

- Many of the population models developed in Chapter 5 are based on an equilibrium view.
- The end-point of Clementsian succession is a stable community called the climax community.
- The theory of island biogeography of MacArthur and Wilson (1967) is an equilibrium model (Chapter 12).
- This is also true of David Tilman's (1985) resource-ratio hypothesis, which predicts that successional change proceeds toward an equilibrium condition that is determined by the nature of the limiting resources.

Of course, local environments vary over time and space, and they respond to changes in climate and many other factors. In addition, the populations of all organisms change in unpredictable ways. Because of these real-world variations we observe communities as being dynamic. As a consequence, much of our thinking about communities occurs within a **non-equilibrium** framework.

It is important to understand, however, that the distinction between equilibrium and non-equilibrium theories is only a matter of degree. Equilibrium theories are based on properties and processes that operate within a community at some point of stability, and they focus attention on how the system returns to that point after a disturbance. In contrast, non-equilibrium theories focus on the shift of a community away from any apparent equilibrium; the nature of the processes that cause the shift; and the time involved for the changes to occur. Expressed in simple terms, non-equilibrium theories focus on the shift away from any apparent equilibrium, and equilibrium theories focus on the return to an equilibrium.

Obviously, it is simplistic to think of a community revolving around an equilibrium point for more than a short period of time, but this does not negate the importance of equilibrium models. Disturbance and predation are the major non-equilibrium processes that we will consider in more detail later in this chapter. These processes can mediate the availability of resources and therefore have the potential to influence the outcome of species interactions, and thereby the structure of communities. Some of the issues raised in this paragraph will be clarified and expanded later on in this chapter, in the section on the intermediate disturbance hypothesis.

Centrifugal Organization

A general model of community organization, called **centrifugal organization**, was proposed by Paul Keddy (1990) of the University of Ottawa, building on earlier models by Rosenzweig and Abramsky (1986). Centrifugal organization is based on the notion of core and peripheral habitats—all species in a community have a shared preference for the core habitat, but each is also the best competitor in some habitat that is peripheral to the core (**Figure 9.5**). This means that the diversity of peripheral habitats will largely determine the richness of plant species in the community. Keddy has extended this model to more complex communities by proposing that environmental gradients may radiate outward from a central preferred habitat type. In particular, he presents evidence that communities of wetland plants are organized in this way, with a core habitat characterized by low disturbance and high productivity that supports taller species such as cattail (*Typha latifolia*), a

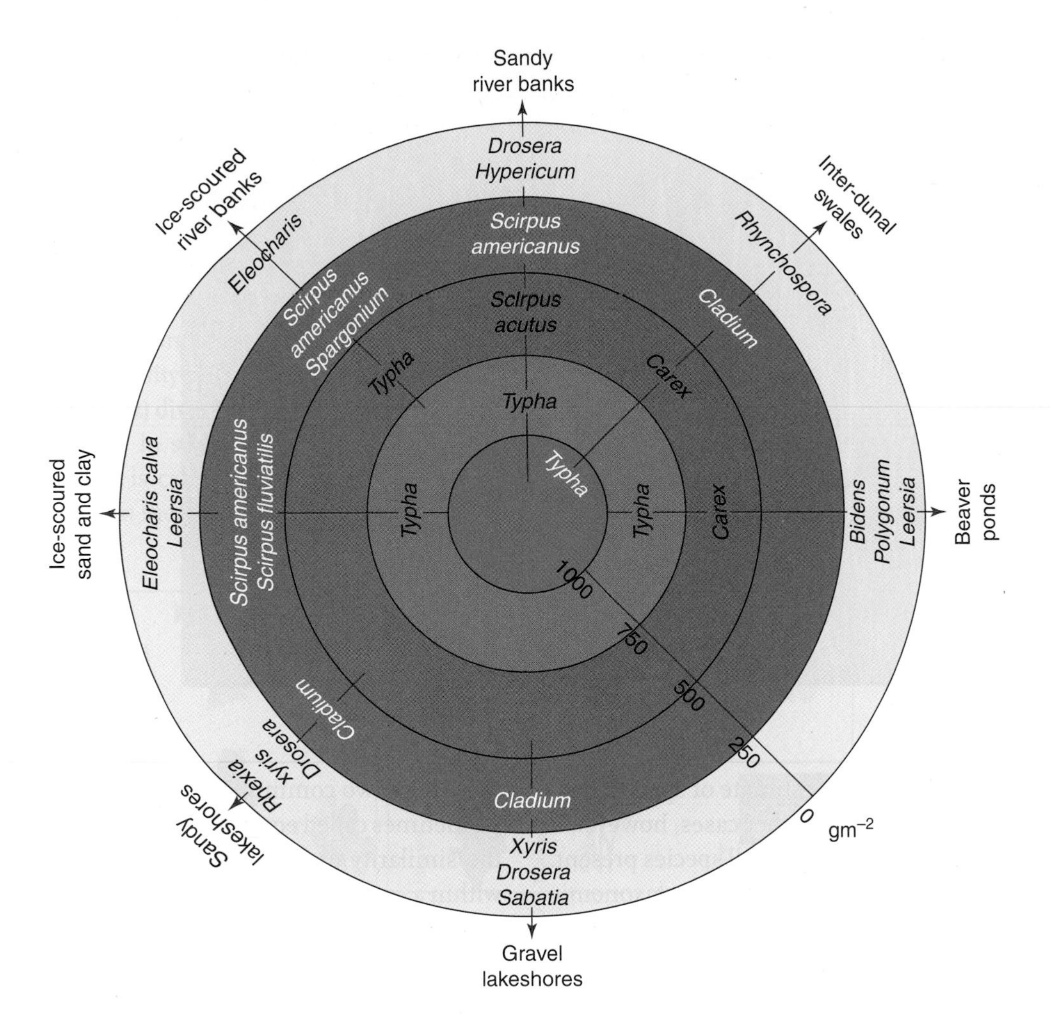

FIGURE 9.5

Centrifugal Organization of Communities. This model predicts that communities are organized along gradients of environmental factors that radiate outward from a core habitat, with species and communities sorting out according to their competitive abilities and tolerance of environmental stresses. Good competitors occur at the centre of the diagram, and inferior ones at the periphery.

SOURCE: Keddy, P. A. 1990. "Competitive hierarchies and centrifugal organization in plant communities," pp. 265–289. (Figure 5, p. 284). In *Perspectives on Plant Competition* (J. Grace and D. Tilman, eds.). Academic Press, New York, NY. Reprinted by permission of the author.

competitive species that can form a dense canopy (its life-history strategy is in the C-type group of Grime, described two sections previously). In other wetlands, a similar core area may be occupied by other C-type species having a similar morphology, such as the tall reed *Phragmites communis*, or the grass *Calamagrostis canadensis*. Radiating out from this core habitat are various environmental axes that are defined by levels of disturbance or nutrient availability; productivity and biomass of the vegetation decreases away from the centre and toward the periphery. Different groups of wetland species and community types occupy specific regions along these radiating axes, with competitively inferior species occurring in the most peripheral habitats.

Community Composition

Naturalists (and ecologists) have long been fascinated by the observation that species may be common or rare. Terms such as **diversity**, **species diversity**, and **biodiversity** all describe aspects of the richness and relative abundance of species in a community (Chapter 12). Of these various terms, biodiversity is the broadest concept, being relevant at a range of levels from

- the richness of alleles of a particular genetic locus;
- to the numbers of plant, animal, and microbial species in a community or region; and
- to the variety of communities on a landscape or geographic region.

Measuring these various aspects of biodiversity, and the factors affecting them, are important aspects of much of ecology and conservation biology. These are not simple tasks—although the notion of diversity is intuitively easy to understand, its elements are difficult to quantify.

One simple way to describe a community is to determine all of the species present—this is its **species richness**. In communities with a small area, and in those with few species, this may be a relatively

principle of competitive exclusion. However, the meticulously detailed observations of MacArthur showed that the various warblers foraged in and otherwise used different parts of the trees, and thus they do conform with the principle. For example, the Cape May warbler (*D. tigrina*) was observed almost exclusively near the tops of the trees. The distribution of the blackburnian warbler (*D. fusca*) overlapped with that of the Cape May but extended farther down the tree. Note that overlap in distribution does not necessarily lead to exclusion—in zones of overlap there may be competition, but if two species do not completely overlap they can coexist. The bay-breasted warbler (*D. castanea*) and black-throated green warbler (*D. virens*) concentrated on the middle branches, while the yellow-rumped warbler (*D. coronata*) spent most of its time in the lower parts of the trees and on the ground (**Figure 9.20**). MacArthur also documented that the nesting heights and breeding territories of the five birds varied, further differentiating their niches. This famous study demonstrated that although the five closely related birds lived in the same habitat and fed on similar foods, they were able to coexist by partitioning the resources.

Root and Shoot Competition

By this stage you may be thinking that competition is the primary structuring factor in communities, and that we have a good understanding of its effects. However, Welden and Slauson (1986) made an important distinction between the **intensity of competition** and the **importance of competition** in studies of plant communities. In the sense meant here, "intensity" is the degree to which competition for a limited resource reduces plant performance below the physiological maximum that is achievable in a given environment. "Importance" is the effect of competition relative to that of other environmental constraints.

Competition for light plays an obvious role in structuring plant communities, because larger plants can shade and competitively stress or exclude smaller ones; this is asymmetric competition based on size. In some communities, however, roots make up the majority of the plant biomass and most of the competition occurs below-ground. Again, we might expect that plants with a larger root system would have greater access to water and nutrients than those with a smaller one; this would be asymmetric competition based on root biomass.

Lamb and Cahill (2008) examined how competition influenced the structure of a rough-fescue (*Festuca campestris*) grassland community in Alberta. There was intense root competition, but it was seemingly unrelated to species richness or community composition, and only slightly related to a small decrease in species diversity. These results raise questions about the role of competition in structuring low-statured communities in which much of the biomass is below-ground, such as grassland, desert, and tundra. Root competition is intense in those habitats, but it may not be so important if it has few measurable consequences for the structure of the plant community (horizontal line on **Figure 9.21a**).

Lamb et al. (2009) further investigated this enigma using experimental "communities" that were planted with nine grassland plants growing under various levels of soil fertility. They measured root and shoot competition. Just as before, they found that increases in the intensity of root competition had no direct effect on species diversity. However, increasing the intensity of shoot competition did cause a reduction of diversity. They also found that an increased root-competition intensity resulted in higher shoot-competition intensity (**Figure 9.21**). Therefore, while root competition does not *directly* influence diversity in the plant community, it may affect shoot competition, which in turn influences community structure.

Facilitation

Earlier we emphasized the role of competition in structuring communities. However, plants in particular, may also interact in positive ways. This is referred to as **facilitation**, or a beneficial effect of one plant upon another, or enhancement of conditions for one species by the influence of another one. The role of facilitative interactions in plant communities was long neglected as a research area, but it has received considerable attention since the publications of Bertness and Callaway (1994), Callaway (1995), and, more recently, Brooker et al. (2008). They pointed out that facilitation occurs not only as one of the processes driving succession, but that it also influences plant success and community composition in stable, non-successional communities.

There has been a particular interest in positive, non-trophic interactions that occur between plants, and that are mediated through changes in the abiotic environment or through other organisms. Some researchers have described the classic "nurse-plant" effects in which rotting logs provide a substrate for the establishment of seedlings, such as those of hemlock trees (*Tsuga* species). Other well-recognized positive interactions include the improved attraction of pollinators by the simultaneous flowering of several species, the beneficial effects of nitrogen-fixing shrubs such as alders (*Alnus* species) on soil fertility, and the capacity for resource sharing through integrated networks of mycorrhizae (this is especially important for phosphorus nutrition).

One of the common themes is that facilitative effects among plants tend to be most important in severe environments, such as desert, arctic or alpine

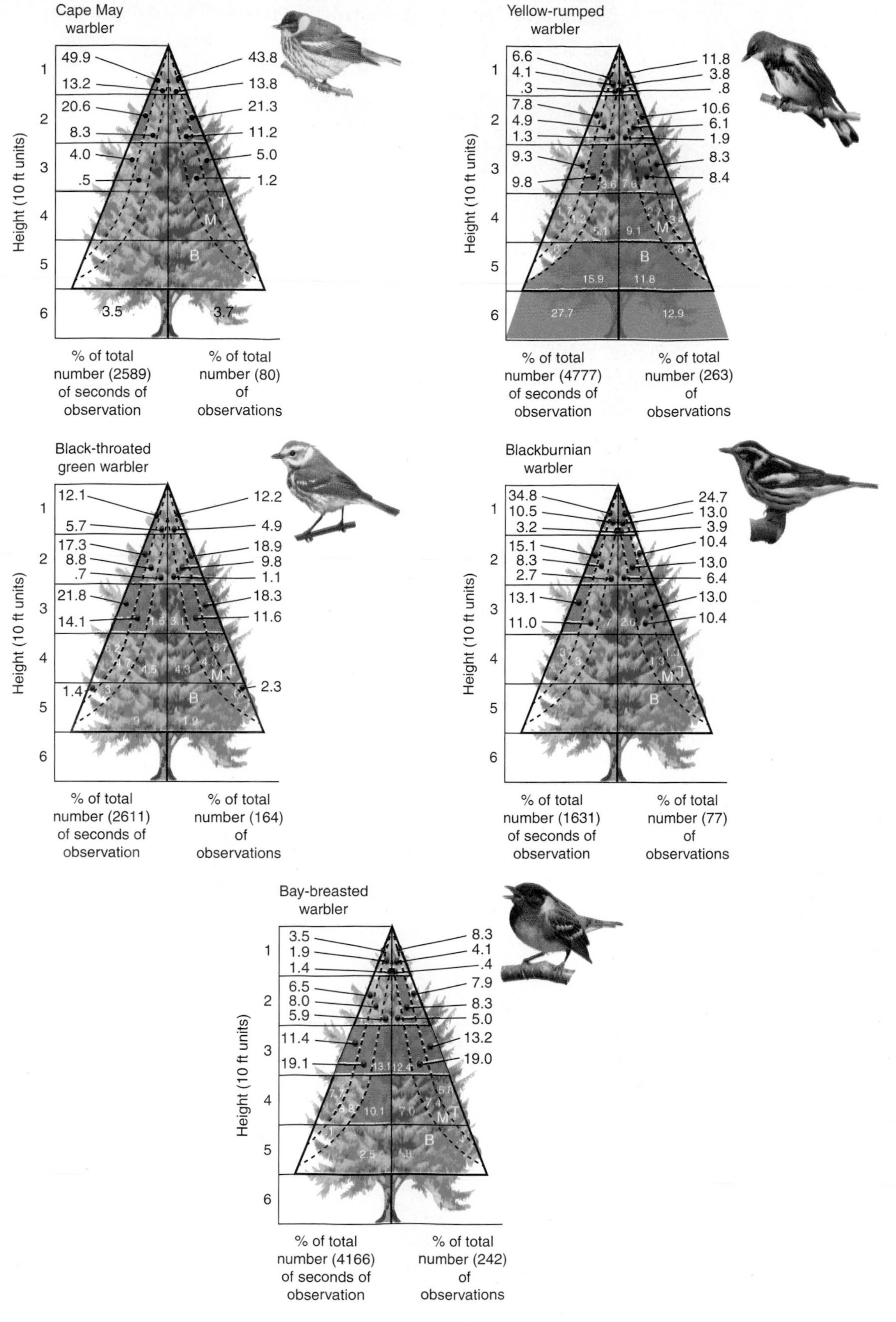

FIGURE 9.20

Niche Partitioning by Warblers in a Conifer Forest. The five species forage in different portions of the forest, and this allows them to coexist. The study area is in coastal Maine.

SOURCE: Used with permission of the Ecological Society of America, from "Population ecology of some warblers of northeastern coniferous forests," *Ecology*, 39(4): 599–619, MacArthur, R. H. © 1958. Permission conveyed through Copyright Clearance Center, Inc. Photos: Cape May warbler: Arthur Morris/Visuals Unlimited/Getty Images; yellow-rumped warbler: © Frank Leung/iStockphoto.com; black-throated green warbler: Stubblefield Photography/Shutterstock; Blackburnian warbler: Stubblefield Photography/Shutterstock; bay-breasted warbler: Jim Zipp/Photoresearchers/First Light

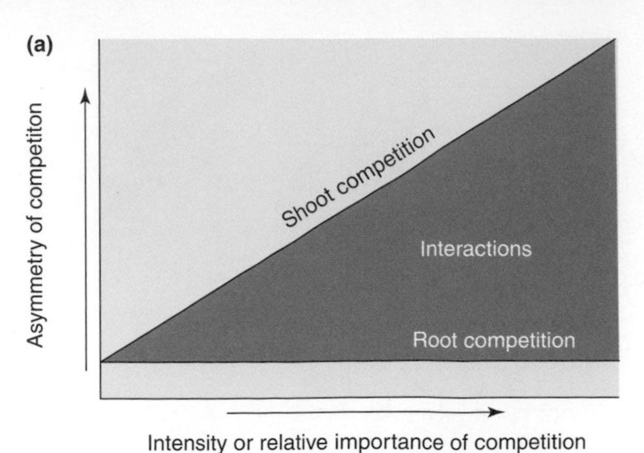

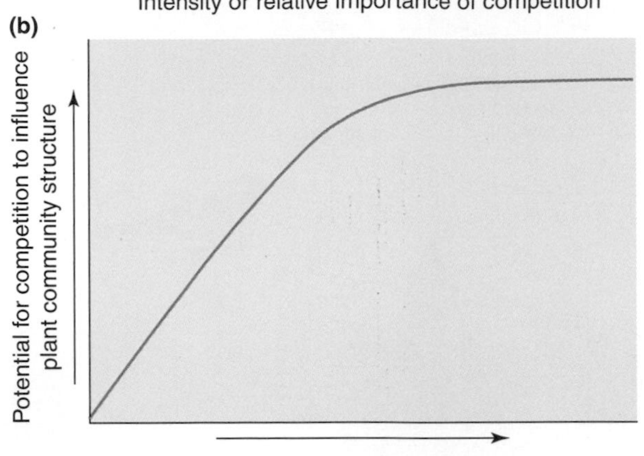

FIGURE 9.21

Conceptual Model of Root and Shoot Competition in a Fescue Grassland in Alberta. (a) An increase in the intensity of root competition has no influence on the overall asymmetry of plant competition (horizontal line), and therefore (b) the low asymmetry has little impact on plant community structure (bottom left portion of (b)). In contrast, as the intensity of shoot competition increases (a) it has a strong influence on the overall asymmetry of plant competition, and therefore (b) the higher asymmetry has a large impact on plant community structure.

SOURCE: Lamb, E. G., S. W. Kembel, and J. F. Cahill. 2009. "Shoot, but not root, competition reduces community diversity in experimental mesocosms," *Journal of Ecology*, 97: 155–163. Reprinted by permission of John Wiley and Sons, Inc.

Bill Freedman

An ecotonal transition between the boreal forest and alpine tundra near Postville, Labrador. This landscape is similar to that in which Cranston and Hermanutz did their research.

tundra, and salt marsh. They are also more likely to increase in prominence with increasing altitude, over a shift from warmer to colder environments, and from damper to arid conditions (Bruno et al., 2003). However, it should be remembered that plants may be simultaneously competing and facilitating. For example, plants that compete for nutrients may have simultaneous facilitative interactions through the provision of shelter or by protection from herbivory.

Brittany Cranston and Luise Hermanutz (2009) of Memorial University of Newfoundland have been investigating whether shrubs of dwarf birch (*Betula glandulosa*) might facilitate the recruitment of tree seedlings (black and white spruce, *Picea mariana* and *P. glauca*). Their study was conducted in an area of tree-line in the Mealy Mountains of Labrador, an ecotone where boreal forest is transitioning to alpine tundra. Compared with lower-altitude forest, the tundra experiences colder temperatures, stronger winds, and a shorter growing season. The hypothesized mechanisms of facilitation involve the birches serving as "nurse shrubs" that enhance the growth and survival of tree seedlings during the critical first growing seasons following germination. However, as the tree-line and alpine climate warms due to anthropogenic climate change (Chapter 3), the relationship between nurse shrubs and tree seedlings could shift from facilitation to competition, which might help the tree-line to advance into presently alpine habitats. In their fieldwork, Cranston and Hermanutz found that the germination and initial survival of spruce seedlings is higher beneath nurse shrubs than in the open tundra. Additional facilitation is associated with the calcium-rich leaf litter of the birch shrubs, which essentially double the content of that crucial nutrient in the surface organic mat. Calcium is important because it enhances tolerance to cold, drought, and shade in spruces. The observation that spruce seedlings have improved emergence and survival within the moderated microenvironment provided by birch shrubs suggests that this facilitative interaction could be a mechanism that could help the boreal forest to invade the tundra as the regional climate warms. As the boreal forest advances, there will be a corresponding decline in the vegetation of the alpine tundra. If the mountains are not high enough to allow tundra plant communities to persist in the region, there will be a decline in the biodiversity of plants and other organisms that are dependent on tundra habitats.

Jennie McLaren

Roy Turkington

The effect of herbivores and predators on plant communities can be devastating. (a) Snow geese on La Pérouse Bay in Manitoba (see text on pages 271–272), and (b) dead trees caused by spruce bark beetle in Kluane, Yukon.

Effects of Herbivory, Predation, and Disturbance on Community Structure

In addition to competition, other biological interactions such as herbivory and predation, as well as disturbances, have an influence on the structure and dynamics of communities. Consider these remarks by Charles Darwin (1859) in *On the Origin of Species*:

> *Seedlings, also, are destroyed in vast numbers by various enemies; for instance, on a piece of ground three feet long and two wide, dug and cleared, and where there could be no choking from other plants, I marked all the seedlings of our native weeds as they came up, and out of 357 no less than 295 were destroyed, chiefly by slugs and insects. If turf which has long been mown, and the case would be the same with turf closely browsed by quadrupeds, be let to grow, the more vigorous plants gradually kill the less vigorous, though fully grown plants; thus out of twenty species grown on a little plot of mown turf (three feet by four) nine species perished, from the other species being allowed to grow up freely.*

Introduction

A theme that we have developed in this chapter, and in other places in this book, is that biological interactions have effects on individuals and on populations, and thus on the structure of communities. Farmers have long made practical use of this sort of knowledge, for instance, by adjusting the numbers and species of grazing livestock, such as cattle, sheep, and goats, to manage the species composition and productivity of managed grasslands.

However, the effects of herbivores and predators are not always easy to separate from those of disturbances. For example, in his theory of three primary plant strategies, Grime (1977) defines a **disturbance** as "the total or partial removal of vegetation," which of course is what herbivores do when they are eating plant biomass. Some authors limit the use of the word disturbance to abiotic events that kill or damage organisms, such as wildfire, flooding, or crashing waves on a shore. But it may be argued that whatever the agent of damage, whether a biotic or abiotic one, a space is opened in a community that may be advantageous to certain species.

There are many cases in which the effects of herbivores or predators on community structure are the result of them causing a diminished abundance of competitively dominant species. In some cases, the resulting biological disturbance can be devastating, such as the damaging effects of overgrazing by abundant snow goose (*Chen caerulescens*) on the coastal marshes on La Pérouse Bay in northern Manitoba, or the mountain pine beetle (*Dendroctonus ponderosae*) in central British Columbia, or spruce budworm (*Choristoneura fumiferana*) in the Maritime provinces. These are all native herbivores, and they can cause stand-replacing disturbances when they are abundant and widespread (see also Chapter 10).

More commonly, however, herbivores cause less-severe disturbances that result in damage, but not of an intensity that is catastrophic to the entire community—these are microdisturbances. For example:

> *Grazing animals frequently sit, lie, scratch, and paw on the pasture, in addition to walking, running and jumping on it. (Spedding 1971, p. 114)*

And of course, herbivores also eat plants in that pasture, but they do so in a selective manner—they find some species to be tasty, and others to be unpalatable, or they may eat only certain plants that grow low to the ground, while leaving taller ones alone. Grazers, for example, feed on graminoids (mostly grasses and sedges) and forbs (herbaceous dicots), while browsers eat leaves and twigs of woody plants, granivores consume seeds and grains, and frugivores eat entire soft fruits. By feeding differentially on plants according to their distinct preferences, herbivores have a great influence on their communities.

We examine the topic of disturbances in more detail in Chapter 10. However, the various causes of disturbances, including anthropogenic ones, are nicely summed up by Townsend et al. (2000, p. 331):

> *Disturbances that open up gaps (patches) are common in all kinds of communities. In forests, they may be caused by high winds, lightning, earthquakes, elephants, lumberjacks, or simply death of a tree through disease or old age. Agents of disturbance in grassland include frost, burrowing animals, and teeth, feet, and dung of grazers. On rocky shores or coral reefs, gaps in algal or sessile animal communities can be formed as a result of severe wave action during hurricanes, tidal waves, battering by logs or moored boats, fins of careless scuba divers, or action of predators.*

Because the effects of predation can lead to so many different outcomes, we will focus on a few examples that highlight key ecological principles. Nevertheless, continue to remember that biological interactions and disturbances can have an enormous range of effects in ecological systems.

The Intermediate Disturbance Hypothesis

The great richness of species in tropical rain forests and coral reefs is legendary. Such observations force us to question how such high levels of diversity are maintained. Joseph Connell (1978) argued that in the absence of disturbances, these communities would progress toward lower levels of diversity—to communities dominated by the most competitive species. However, it appears that tropical forests and coral reefs are subject to disturbances frequently enough that this longer-term equilibrium may never be attained. This is a clear illustration of the difference between equilibrium and non-equilibrium models that we referred to earlier in this chapter. In tropical forests, trees or groups of them may be killed or damaged by windstorms, landslides, or lightning strikes, and corals by severe storms, freshwater incursions, sedimentation, or predators.

Connell's **intermediate disturbance hypothesis** suggests that the highest levels of diversity are maintained at intermediate scales of disturbance (**Figure 9.22**). If the frequency of disturbances is high, then diversity will be low because the times for establishment and regeneration are short and only those few species that are producing seed and are within dispersal range will colonize. If disturbances continue on a frequent basis the communities will consist of a repeating cycle of species that are capable of quickly reaching maturity. Alternatively, if the interval between disturbances increases, diversity will also increase. The additional time permits species that may have poorer dispersal or slower growth

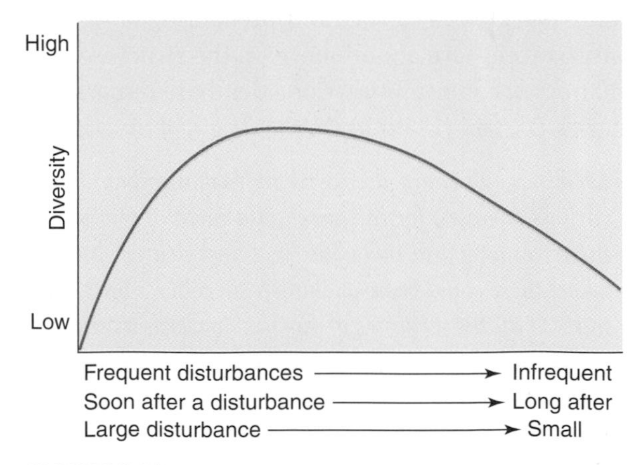

FIGURE 9.22

The Intermediate Disturbance Hypothesis. The highest levels of species diversity occur at an intermediate frequency of disturbance.

SOURCE: Connell, J. H. 1978. "Diversity in tropical rain forests and coral reefs," *Science*, 199: 1302–1310. Reprinted with permission from AAAS.

to invade, grow, and mature; these would have been excluded by more frequent disturbances. However, if the interval between major disturbances increases further, diversity will decline because the most competitive species will manage to exert their dominance over the system. At a certain frequency, disturbances will interrupt and prevent the process of competitive exclusion by damaging the most competitive species.

One of the first experimental tests of the intermediate disturbance hypothesis was carried out by Wayne Sousa (1979a,b), a graduate student of Connell. He classified intertidal boulders into groups of small, intermediate, or large, depending on the force of a wave that would be required to move them—smaller boulders are tumbled more frequently, and larger ones much less so, allowing more time for organisms to colonize. Sousa then monitored species richness on the various boulders on a monthly basis for two years. He found that the small boulders supported only barnacles and a green alga (*Ulva*), while intermediate-sized ones had a more diverse community, and the largest, infrequently moving boulders were covered with a single red alga, *Gigartina canaliculata* (**Figure 9.23**). These results support the intermediate disturbance hypothesis.

We will now consider an example in which the intensity of grazing by a herbivore is imposing the disturbance. This study by Zeevalking and Fresco (1977) examined the relationship between the intensity of grazing by rabbits (*Oryctolagus cuniculus*) and the species diversity of plants in coastal sand-dune vegetation in western Europe. The outcome is consistent with the intermediate disturbance hypothesis because plant species richness was highest under moderate grazing pressure (**Figure 9.24**). A similar pattern has been shown by studies of the burrowing activities of prairie dogs (*Cynomys* sp.) in shortgrass prairie (Whicker and Detling 1988). These colonial rodents cause major effects on community structure by their burrowing and grazing activities. Areas close to complexes of prairie-dog burrows are highly disturbed and are dominated by short-lived ruderal plants, while habitat farther away is less disturbed and is dominated by competitive plants. However, as in previous examples, in-between zones of moderate disturbance by the rodents have the highest levels of species diversity.

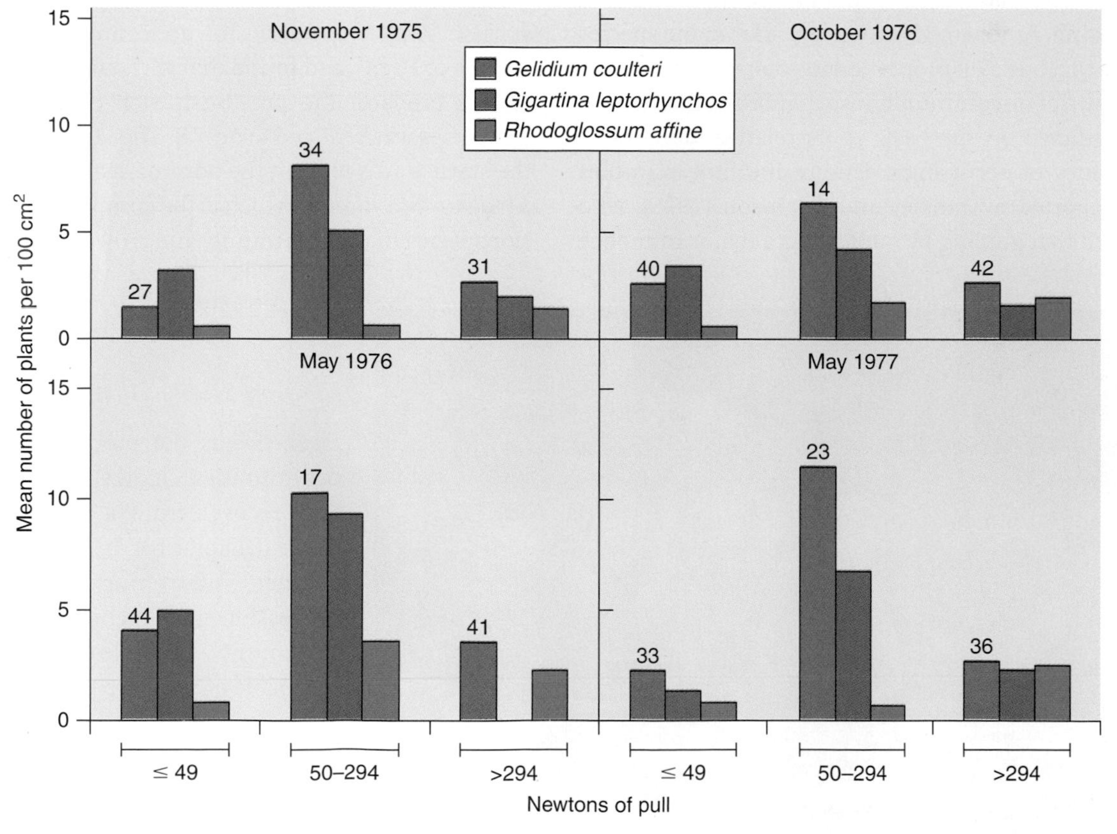

FIGURE 9.23

Illustration of the Intermediate Disturbance Hypothesis on Intertidal Boulders. Because of their smaller mass, small boulders are frequently moved and tumbled by wave action, which prevents many species from colonizing. The largest boulders provide a relatively stable environment, which becomes dominated by the most competitive species. The highest level of species diversity occurs in middle-sized boulders, on which species can colonize, but the most competitive ones do not have time to become strongly dominant.

SOURCE: Used with permission of the Ecological Society of America, from "Disturbance in marine intertidal boulder fields: the nonequilibrium maintenance of species diversity," *Ecology*, 60(6): 1225–1239, Sousa, W. P. © 1979. Permission conveyed through Copyright Clearance Center, Inc.

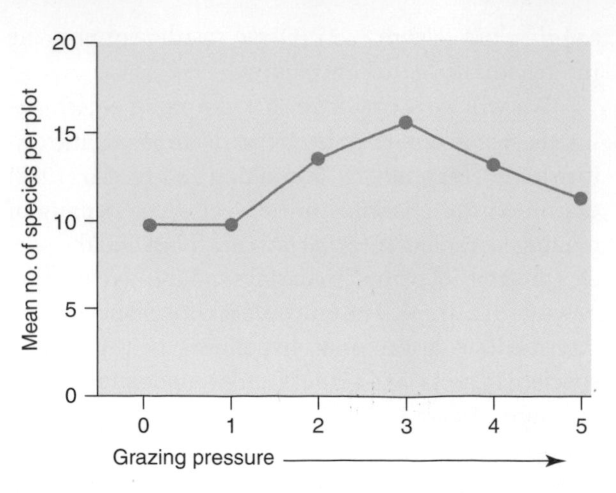

FIGURE 9.24

Another Illustration of the Intermediate Disturbance Hypothesis. In this case, an intermediate intensity of grazing by rabbits results in the highest level of species diversity in a coastal sand-dune plant community.

SOURCE: Begon, M., Harper, J. L. & C. R. Townsend. 1990. *Ecology* (2nd ed.). Blackwell.

Keystone Species

In architecture, a keystone is the piece that occurs at the top of a stone arch, and whose presence is the means that allows the structure to stand without collapsing. Analogously, in ecology a **keystone species** is one that has a disproportionately large effect on the structure of its community, much more so than would be predicted on the basis of its relative biomass or frequency of occurrence. One of the first examples was reported by Tansley and Adamson (1925), who showed that grazing by rabbits has a major influence on the species composition of grasslands in Britain. They did this by building small fenced plots that excluded rabbits, and within six years the initially species-rich community had degenerated to a taller one dominated by only a few species. At one of their study sites, a plot with rabbits had vegetation only 4–5 cm tall, dominated by short *Festuca ovina* and with 8000 plants/m^2 of 21 species. In contrast, a plot from which rabbits had been excluded for six years was also dominated by *Festuca ovina*, but it was 18–20 cm tall and the dense shade it cast limited the other vegetation to 320 plants/m^2 of 11 species. Eventually, the exclusion plots are colonized by woody species, which are otherwise eliminated by the rabbits (Hope-Simpson, 1940). Further evidence of the keystone action of rabbits is provided by a "natural experiment" that occurred in the mid-1950s, when a viral disease known as myxomatosis killed about 95 percent of those animals in the United Kingdom, and the resulting large-scale changes of vegetation were similar to those observed in the exclusion experiments.

Another famous demonstration of the effects of a keystone animal on community structure was done by Robert Paine (1966) in a rocky intertidal habitat in the Pacific northwest. He continually removed the starfish *Pisaster ochraceus* for up to three years from an area of 16 m^2, and found that without the influence of this predator the previously rich community of 15 species was reduced to only 8. The key influence of the starfish was to limit the dominance of the mussel *Mytilus californianus*, which is the competitively superior species in the community and crowded out others when the *Pisaster* was removed (**Figure 9.25**).

Fergus Spowart

A classic keystone species is the predatory starfish *Pisaster ochraceus*, which, when removed from rocky intertidal habitats in the Pacific northwest, results in a decline in the species richness of their community. Here, a conscientious researcher tests this effect by removing starfish from plots in Howe Sound, near Vancouver, British Columbia.

Multiple Stable States

Succession is the process by which communities change over time, as they recover from a major disturbance (Chapter 10). In the absence of another intervening disturbance, succession may achieve a climax community—a stable end-point that is capable of self-perpetuation under the prevailing environmental conditions. However, there is ongoing discussion among ecologists as to whether such a stable end-point is ever achieved, highlighting once again the difference between equilibrium and non-equilibrium views of how nature works.

Moreover, we can raise an intriguing question: If succession occurs

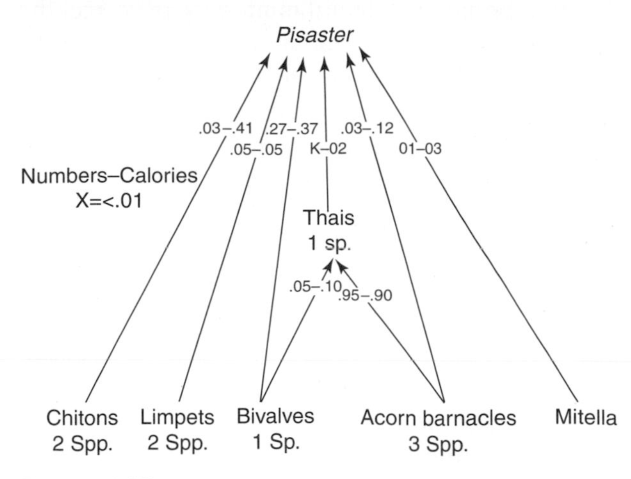

FIGURE 9.25

A Keystone Predator in a Rocky Intertidal Habitat. Predation by *Pisaster ochraceus* prevents the mussel *Mytilus californianus* from competitively excluding other species from the habitat.

SOURCE: Modified from Paine, R. T. 1966. "Food web complexity and species diversity," *American Naturalist*, 100: 65–75.

along a fairly predictable trajectory to an expected and stable end-point, are the initial stages of the process also predictable? Consider, for example, the case of an old field that was abandoned from agricultural use in the springtime—it would have different initial colonists than if it had been abandoned in the autumn. How different would the ensuing successions be in these two cases? Or, if after glacial meltback the exposed rock was colonized by various species of bryophytes, or alternatively the higher plant *Dryas integrifolia,* would the different initial colonists lead to varying successional trajectories and thus to dissimilar stable end-points? Or would there be a convergent and inevitable climax community that is determined by the prevailing environmental conditions, regardless of the initial colonists? The variable-climax view is one form of the concept of **multiple stable states** (or **alternative stable states**)—the occurrence of more than one possible stable community, even under similar environmental conditions.

There is yet another way of considering this concept of multiple stable states, if only two such communities are proposed (i.e., dual stable states). The question here revolves around the issue of whether an existing community can be perturbed to such a degree that it changes to an entirely different but stable community, and does not subsequently return to its initial state after the stressor has been relaxed. This principle is graphically illustrated in **Figure 9.26**, in which an initial community is represented by a ball located in a valley, one of many such basins across a landscape. If the ball is given a strong enough push, such as by a strong disturbance, then the inherent *resistance* of the community to substantial change can be overcome and it may move into a different valley, where it again stabilizes in an alternative state. An essential aspect of this model is that the ball is stable in either valley, and in the absence of a disturbance it does not spontaneously move between them. It is also understood that in either of the alternative stable states, the communities may be subjected to relatively minor intensities of disturbance or other stressors without being propelled out of the valley—in these cases, the community is *resilient* and returns to its original condition.

However, the existence of such alternative states is still being debated, largely because of disagreement among ecologists concerning the weight of evidence

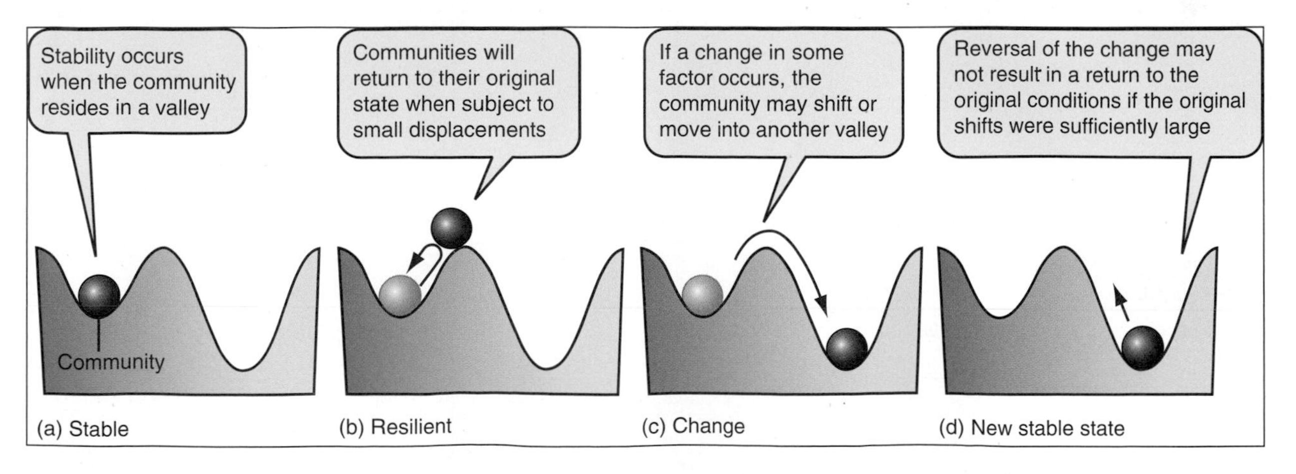

FIGURE 9.26

Multiple Stable States. In this diagrammatic model, the balls represent different kinds of communities, and the valleys are forces that retain them in a stable state. It takes a relatively large intensity of disturbance or another environmental stressor to overcome the inherent resistance of the community to substantial change in its structure and function. This resistance is illustrated by the force required to move a ball from one valley to another. If the applied force is not sufficient to move a ball out of its valley, then when the stressor is alleviated, the community will return to its original condition—this is a demonstration of resilience.

SOURCE: Modified from Beisner et al. (2003).

that is required to demonstrate their reality. To illustrate the difficulty we will review a classic study titled: "*Aleuts, sea otters, and alternate stable-state communities.*" Simenstad et al. (1978) investigated the contents of the middens (heaps of discarded shells, bones, and other garbage) of prehistoric Aleut settlements in the Aleutian Islands of Alaska, and suggested that these aboriginal peoples had disturbed their local ecosystem by over-harvesting sea otters (*Enhydra lutris*) in some areas, driving them close to extirpation. They also compared the flora and fauna of two subtidal habitats in the area, with and without otters, and demonstrated that predation by otters profoundly influences the organization of the communities (**Table 9.2**). The otters did this by greatly reducing the abundance of herbivorous sea urchins, limpets, and chitons, which then allowed an abundant community of macroalgae to flourish (known as a kelp "forest"), which attracted fishes typical of nearshore habitats. In contrast, habitats without otters supported large populations of the herbivorous invertebrates that overgraze the macroalgae, so that bare rocky substrate was abundant and there were few fish (and mostly pelagic ones).

Interestingly, the sea otter was almost rendered extinct by over-hunting for its dense and lustrous fur. In 1911, it was protected from further hunting and it has since made a population recovery in some regions, including on the west coast of Vancouver Island. During the period when the otters were scarce, the subtidal habitats were predominantly open rocky expanses maintained by the voracious feeding of abundant macroinvertebrate herbivores (such as urchins). But in areas where otters have recovered in abundance, their predation has reduced the herbivore populations, which has allowed macroalgae to again flourish. In other words, there are apparently two stable communities, with one or the other occurring depending on the presence of sea otters, which serve as a keystone predator in the ecosystem. However, these are not alternative stable states because the "apparent alternative state" persists only as long as there is hunting of sea otters. Once the hunting of otters was stopped, there was a slow but continual return to the former state. In the strict definition of an alternative stable state, there would be no recovery of the community after the hunting of otters was stopped.

Remarkably, this famous ecological case has developed a new wrinkle. In the early 1990s, local groups of killer whales (*Orcinus orca*) began to hunt sea otters in some areas (Estes et al., 1998). This caused the otters to rapidly decline in abundance, and where this happened there were increases in sea urchins and other herbivores, and the kelp forests were destroyed. It is thought that declines of fish stocks in the North Pacific, caused by commercial overfishing, have resulted in a decline in fur seals (*Callorhinus ursinus*) and sea lions (*Eumetopias jubatus*),

TABLE 9.2 Comparative Status of Nearshore Communities on Aleutian Islands with Sea Otters (Amchitka) and without Them (Shemya and Attu)

Species	Amchitka	Shemya and Attu
Sea otter (*Enhydra lutris*)	Abundant for several decades; population at time of the study >6000	None or sparse
Macroalgae	Abundant, principally four species of *Laminaria*, *Agarum cribosum*, *Rhodophyta*, and *Alaria fistulosa*	Rare and restricted to sublittoral fringe and patches
Sea urchins (*Strongylocentrotus polyacanthus*)	Rare; maximum size <32 mm; increasing size and density with depth	Dense; maximum size >100 mm; highest density and size in sublittoral fringe
Limpets (*Collisela pelta*)	Density 8/m^2 and maximum size 52 mm	Density 82–356/m^2 and maximum size 67 mm
Chitons (*Katharina tunicata* and *Cryptochiton stelleri*)	Rare; density <1/m^2	Common; density 32/m^2
Mussels (*Mytilis edulis* and *Modiolus* spp.)	Rare and small; density <4/m^2	Common and large; density 711/m^2
Barnacles (*Balanus glandula* and *B. cariosus*)	Rare and small; density <5/m^2	Common and large; density 1215/m^2; dominating upper littoral zone
Nearshore fishes	Abundant and diverse community; supported by algal detritus food web	Sparse fauna except for deepwater forms; associated with sparse deepwater patches of macroalgae
Harbour seal (*Phoca vitulina*)	Density 8/km of coastline; frequently observed in groups of >50 individuals	Density 2/km of coastline; seldom in groups of >10 individuals

SOURCE: Simenstad, C. A., J. A. Estes, and K. W. Kenyon. 1978. "Aleuts, sea otters, and alternate stable-state communities," *Science*, 200: 403–411. Reprinted with permission from AAAS.

(a)

Ian McAllister/All Canada Photos

Alternative stable states in subtidal habitats. The nearshore habitats may exist (a) as rocky urchin-dominated barrens, or (b) as lush kelp "forests," depending on the predatory relationships occurring among a complex of species, including humans. These photographs were taken on British Columbia shorelines.

(b)

Chris Cheadle/All Canada Photos

which are the usual food for killer whales in the region. As a consequence, the killer whales have turned to sea otters as an alternative food.

A demonstration of alternative stable states has emerged from the work of Bob Jefferies and his students at the University of Toronto. This research was done at La Pérouse Bay near Churchill, Manitoba, where vegetated areas of intertidal marshes are dominated by the grass *Puccinellia phryganodes* and the sedge *Carex subspathacea*. In 1976, there were about 3300 breeding pairs of snow geese in a 10 km^2 colony in the study area, but by 1997 the population had increased to 44 500 over 175 km^2 (Abraham et al., 2005). The enormous increase in geese has been attributed to less hunting during their autumn migration, the creation of wildlife refuges in the United States, and improved wintering habitat in the southern United States because of changes in agricultural practices that left grain in fields that the geese could eat. At La Pérouse Bay the intense foraging by increasing numbers of snow geese has severely altered plant communities and soil in intertidal and supratidal marshes. The damage begins when overgrazing of intertidal salt-marshes converts the preferred forage of *P. phryganodes* to a short "grazing lawn," and then to an unvegetated mudflat (refer back to upper panel on page 265). The unvegetated areas initially developed as isolated patches, which grew larger as the overgrazing continued, and then coalesced into expansive muddy barrens. As the intertidal vegetation deteriorated the geese moved to secondary feeding habitats in supratidal and brackish marshes, which were also converted to grazing lawns and then to mudflats.

McLaren and Jefferies (2004) investigated the ability of transplants of *P. phryganodes* to grow in bare soil and in intact grassy lawns. The transplants survived in the lawns, but not in the bare soil. Analyses of the soil found that the unvegetated areas had high salinity, low nitrogen, and were relatively compacted and dry, with the degradation being most acute in larger patches. It was these difficult soil conditions that prevented the transplants from surviving, and that interfere with revegetation of the damaged mudflats, along with continued grazing by the geese. Handa and Jefferies (2000) were able to mitigate the soil conditions by adding nutrients to increase fertility and peat to decrease the bulk density, and this allowed transplants

circumstances. For this reason, other models have been proposed that involve variations of the top–down and/or bottom–up hypotheses.

This is an important subject area, because understanding whether a community is primarily structured from the top–down or the bottom–up has key implications for conservation and wildlife management. This is important on larger landscapes, and also in protected areas, such as national parks. Moreover, the relative effects of these influences is being increasingly affected by anthropogenic stressors, such as

- the hunting of large carnivores, sometimes resulting in their eradication, which releases their prey from top–down control;
- excessive harvesting of herbivorous animals, whose choices during feeding exerts top–down influences on plant communities;
- nutrient loading to terrestrial and aquatic ecoscapes, which has a bottom–up influence by increasing primary productivity;
- pollution by toxic chemicals, such as pesticides and acidification, which has unpredictable ecological effects, depending on the relative sensitivities of species and trophic levels; and
- area-harvesting of ecosystems, such as by clear-cutting in forestry and trawling in a fishery, which has a large bottom–up effect by diminishing the food base of higher trophic levels.

In their aggregate, these anthropogenic influences are changing the relative strengths of top–down and bottom–up forces in ecosystems throughout much of Canada and worldwide.

Consider, for instance, the ecological consequences of hunters eradicating wolves (*Canis lupus*) from montane landscapes consisting of a mosaic of conifer and aspen forests and grasslands. Examples of such ecosystems include the Rocky Mountain parks of Canada (e.g., Banff and Jasper National Parks) and comparable ones in the United States (such as Yellowstone National Park). In the absence of predation by wolves, large ungulate herbivores such as elk (*Cervus canadensis*) become unusually abundant, and they overbrowse some of their preferred foods, such as shoots and seedlings of trembling aspen (*Populus tremuloides*) and willows (*Salix* species). These and other changes in vegetation caused by excessive populations of herbivores can result in habitat degradation, including an impairment of forest regeneration. Interestingly, when wolves were re-introduced to Yellowstone National Park, their influence on elk and other large herbivores resulted in a general improvement of the "health" of the ecosystem, including the first observations of aspen regeneration in many decades (Ripple et al., 2001). A comparable illustration from the boreal forest may involve lynx (*Lynx canadensis*) and snowshoe hare (*Lepus americana*). Imagine, for example, that excessive trapping for their fur depletes lynx, their reduced predation allows hare populations to increase, whose increased feeding may then decrease vegetation biomass and the abundance and species composition of the plant community (Krebs et al., 1995).

These kinds of serial changes in species abundances and distributions at lower trophic levels, occurring in response to changes at a higher level, are referred to as a trophic cascade (Carpenter et al., 1985; see also **Figure 9.35**).

In some boreal regions, the populations of woodland caribou (*Rangifer tarandus caribou*), a large ungulate herbivore, are declining. The cause appears to be a complex of factors, including excessive hunting, habitat damages by forestry and mining (particularly the loss of critical wintering habitat that is rich in lichen biomass), in some areas high predation by natural predators, and perhaps climate-related ecological changes (Bergerud, 1974; Bergerud et al., 2007). Because of a contracting range, declining abundance, and increasing population fragmentation, woodland caribou are now considered to be threatened over large areas of their range in Canada (COSEWIC, 2002). Wittmer et al. (2005) analyzed data for woodland caribou in British Columbia and suggested that they are declining as a consequence of increased predation, mostly by wolves. This was similar to a conclusion by Bergerud (1974), who hypothesized that caribou had declined due to wolf predation and over-hunting rather than from a shortage of their winter forage of lichens. To test these hypotheses, for 30 years, until 2003, Bergerud and his colleagues monitored caribou populations on islands in Lake Superior, where wolves were absent, and on

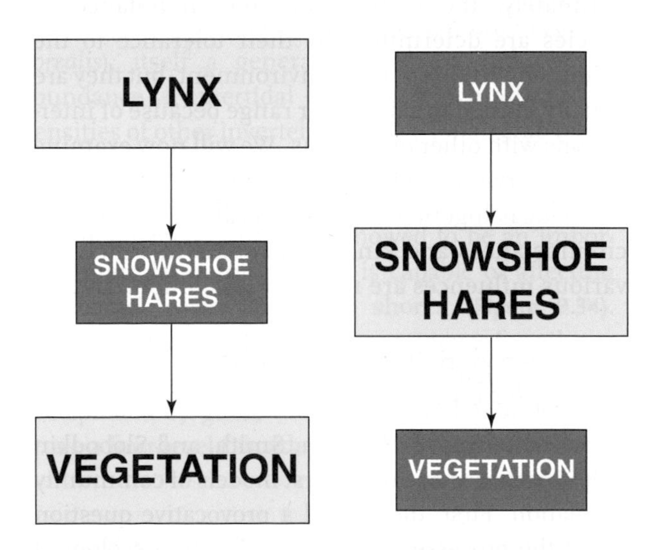

FIGURE 9.35

A Trophic Cascade. Hypothetically, if the abundance of lynx is high, they will reduce their prey, the snowshoe hare, to low levels, thereby reducing herbivory and consequently increasing vegetation.

the nearby mainland, which has wolves (Bergerud, 2007). The results concurred with the prediction that the caribou decline is being driven by predation rather than by a food shortage. These studies support the idea that ecosystems without predators are limited bottom–up by food, while those with predators are structured top–down by predation.

In one study area of the northern Serengeti that was monitored for more than 30 years, poaching removed the majority of mammalian carnivores, but in an adjacent area their populations remained intact (Sinclair et al., 2003). In the area with reduced predators, five smaller species of herbivores increased markedly in abundance, but not in the other area **(Figure 9.36)**. Once poaching stopped and the predators returned to the area, these herbivores declined in abundance. In contrast, the abundance of giraffe, one of the largest herbivores, did not increase in the area where predators had been removed, or change after the poaching stopped, apparently because they are too big to be hunted often by the local carnivores. It was concluded that in this savanna community with diverse herbivores, carnivores were imposing intense predation pressure in a manner related to choice of their prey according to body size. This and related factors resulted in top–down pressure that was somewhat focused on smaller prey species, and resource limitation (bottom–up influence) for larger ones. The researchers suggested that there is a threshold of prey body size of about 150 kg, above which the dominant influence on herbivores switches to bottom–up control.

It is a difficult task to test all of these predictions simultaneously in any one community. Ideally, an entire community or ecoscape would be studied as a whole, but in most terrestrial ecosystems this poses great challenges in terms of experimental design, statistical analysis, logistics, and funding. Nevertheless, there have been a few such ambitious attempts to study and understand an entire ecosystem. One is the Kluane Boreal Forest Ecosystem Project (KBFEP) in southern Yukon, led by ecologists from several Canadian universities (see Ecology in Depth 9.1, p. 284). Although the observations of this boreal ecosystem are best explained by a mixture of top–down and bottom–up influences, in other systems one or the other model may be predominant.

Sinclair et al. (2000) suggested that largely top–down effects may apply to aquatic ecosystems. Indirect effects are well known in freshwater and marine communities, and it is possible that they attenuate less rapidly than they usually do in many terrestrial ecosystems. In tropical savanna and temperate grassland, where herbivores dominate the large-animal community, there is likely to be (a) a top–down effect of herbivores on vegetation, (b) a bottom–up effect of herbivores on carnivores, and (c) a reciprocal effect of predators on herbivores. Both the Serengeti ecosystem and the Kluane Boreal Forest ecosystem demonstrate strong effects of predators on herbivores.

Connell's Model

Joseph Connell (1975) made another early attempt to provide a conceptual model of community structure under diverse influences. His emphasis was on marine subtidal and intertidal communities, but the principles may be applied to others dominated by sessile organisms, such as plants in terrestrial habitats **(Figure 9.37)**. Connell's model proposes that few species reach a high enough density to compete for resources. This is because of either harsh physical conditions or the loss of most of their recruits and juveniles to herbivores or predators. On occasion, however, the harsh conditions may be ameliorated, or the herbivores or predators reduced in abundance,

Data suggest that woodland caribou in British Columbia are declining as a consequence of increased predation, mostly by wolves.

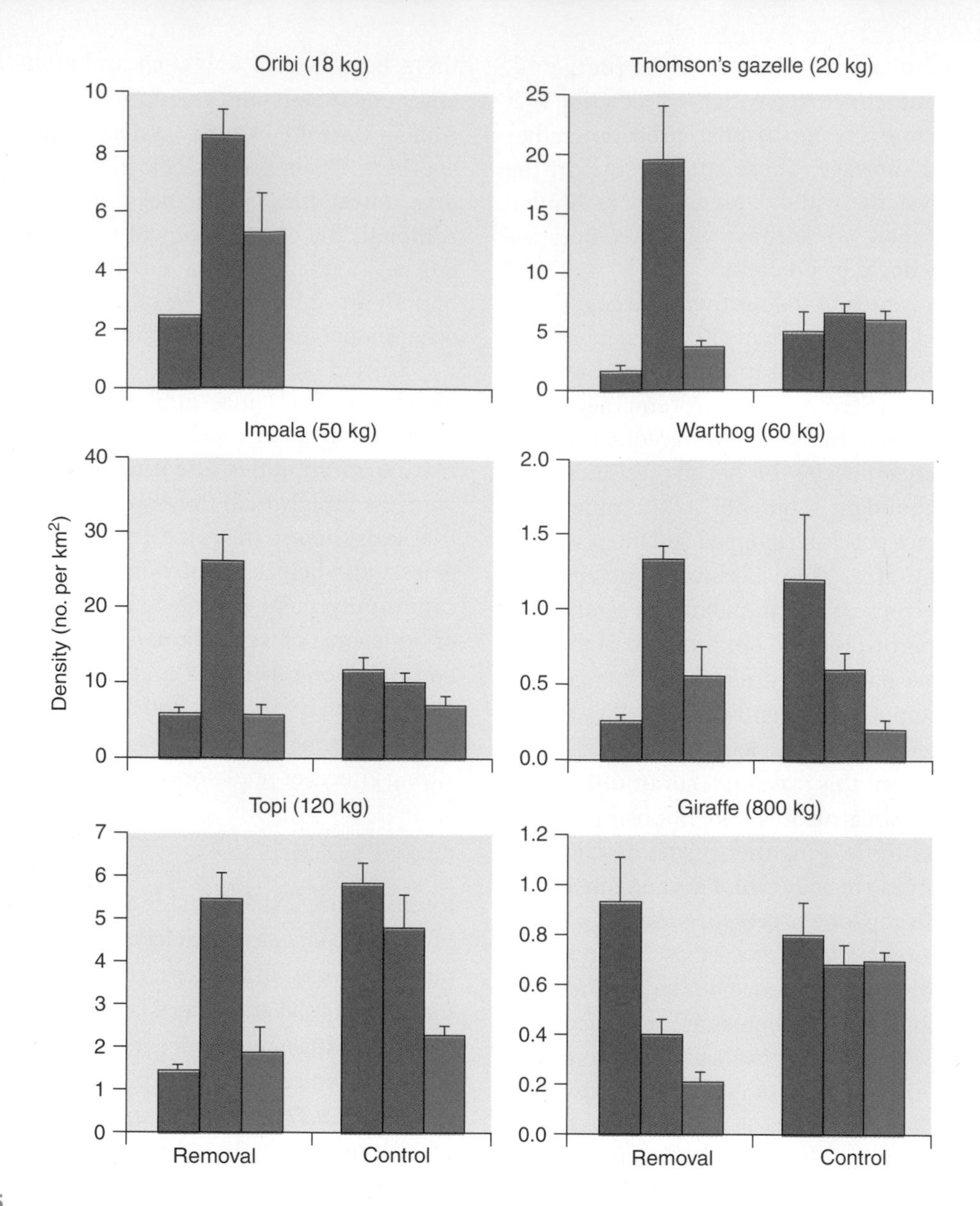

FIGURE 9.36

Top–Down and Bottom–Up Control of Herbivore Abundance in a Savanna Community. One study area in the northern Serengeti had a relatively small population of large predators because they were being poached, while in the adjacent Mara Reserve they had a normal abundance. The orange bars are for the period 1967–1980 prior to the reduction of predators; the brown bars are for 1981–1987 during which time predators were removed; the blue bars are for 1988–2001 when the predator removal stopped and their populations again increased. The prey species are (a) oribi (*Ourebia ourebi*; 18 kg); (b) Thomson's gazelle (*Eudorcas thomsoni*; 20 kg), (c) impala (*Aepyceros melampus*; 50 kg); (d) warthog (*Phacochoerus africanus*; 50 kg), (e) topi (*Damaliscus korrigum*; 120 kg); (f) giraffe (*Giraffa camelopardalis*; 800 kg).

SOURCE: Sinclair, A. R. E, S. A. R. Mduma, and J. S. Brashares. 2003. "Patterns of predation in a diverse predator–prey system," *Nature*, 425: 288–290. Reprinted by permission from Macmillan Publishers Ltd.

and when this happens the recruits may "escape" and achieve a large size class and successfully colonize open patches of habitat. Connell suggested that predation is more intense under relatively benign physical conditions, and that chance "escapes" are more likely in harsher ones, leaving competition as the dominant influence in intermediate physical conditions. His conceptual model was especially important because he was challenging the prevailing scientific viewpoint at the time—that competition was the principal influence on the structure of natural communities. However, when developing his model, Connell presented convincing evidence about the relative influences of physical factors, natural enemies (predators, herbivores, parasites, or pathogens), and competition as key mechanisms.

Menge and Sutherland's Model

An alternative model presented by Menge and Sutherland (1987) incorporated parts of the Hairston et al. (1960) model, and expanded the one by Connell (1975). They did this by adding a variable recruitment rate, and by applying it not only to the sessile organisms in a habitat, but also to the herbivore and

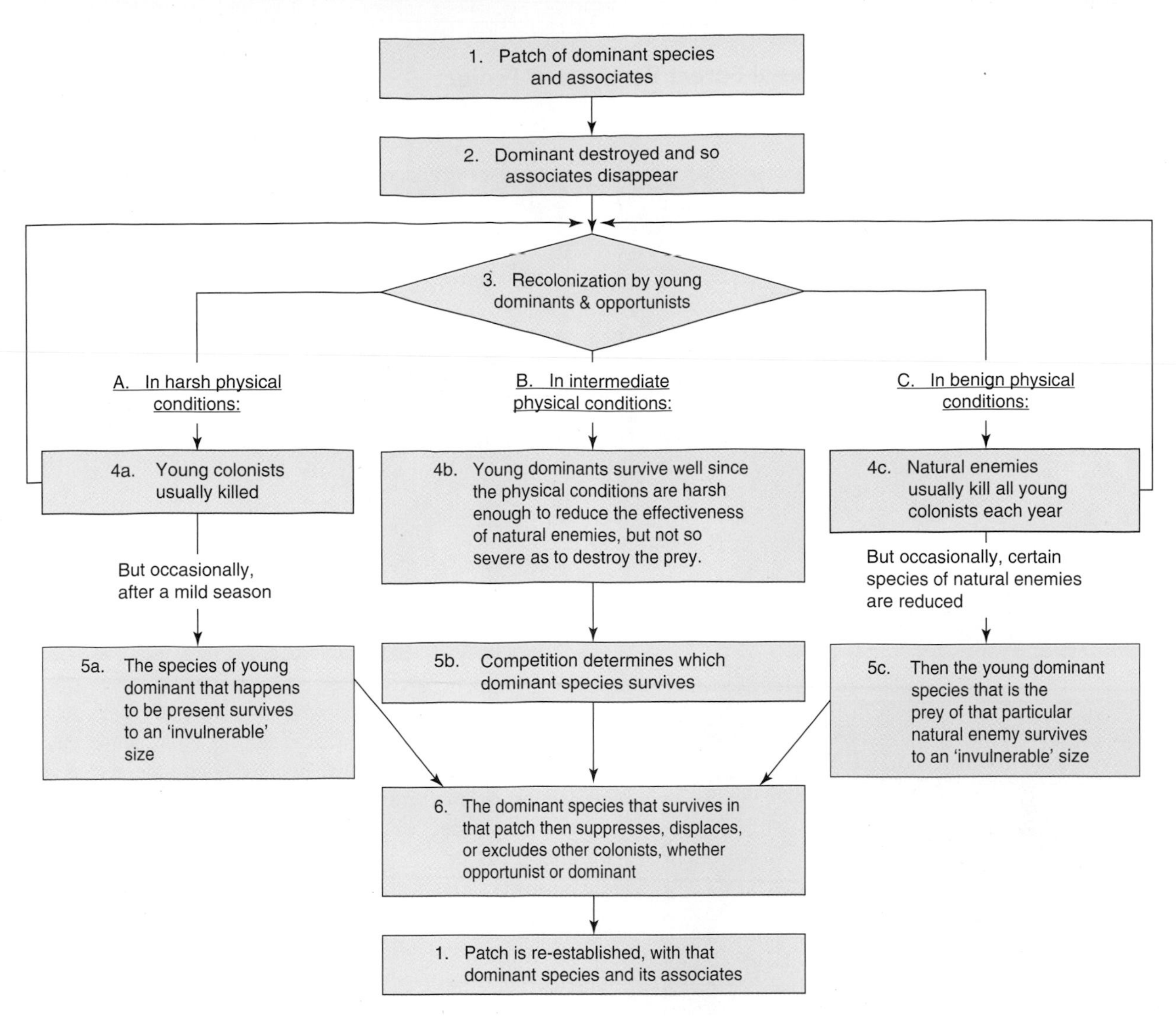

FIGURE 9.37

Connell's Conceptual Model of Influences on Community Structure. The model predicts the key influences that determine which "dominants" (sessile aquatic animals or terrestrial plants) will fill a gap in a community.

SOURCE: Reprinted by permission of the publisher from "Some Mechanisms Producing Structure in Natural Communities," by Joseph Connell in *Ecology and Evolution of Communities*, edited by Martin L. Cody and Jared M. Diamond, p. 478. Cambridge, MA: The Belknap Press of Harvard University Press. Copyright © 1975 by the President and Fellows of Harvard College.

carnivore components **(Figure 9.38)**. Their model suggests that the relative importance of physical environmental factors, competition, and herbivory and predation varies in a predictable way depending upon trophic level, amount of recruitment, and environmental conditions. Their model makes three predictions for communities that have high recruitment rates:

1. In a harsh environment, consumers will have little effect because they are rare, and plants are limited by the difficult conditions, so neither herbivory nor competition has much influence on the structure of the community.
2. In intermediate conditions, herbivores are more abundant but are still ineffective at regulating plant populations, which allows plants to attain high densities, leading to competition.
3. In benign environments, herbivores are numerous and are able to keep plant densities low enough to lessen or prevent competition among them, so that a reduction in the numbers of recruits reduces the influence of competition at any given stress level.

Among herbivores, and especially predators, low recruitment will slow their rate of population increase, meaning that competition will be less important even in benign conditions. In communities in harsh environments, the severe conditions will keep the density of consumers low regardless of recruitment rates.

SYNOPSIS

An ecological community is a group of organisms that live together at the same place and time and that interact directly or indirectly. A community includes

ECOLOGY IN DEPTH 9.1

The Kluane Boreal Forest Ecosystem Project

Jennie McLaren

Michael Sheriff

Michael Sheriff

Inhabitants of the Kluane Boreal Forest ecosystem include (clockwise from top left) lynx (*Lynx canadensis*), red squirrels (*Tamiasciurus hudsonicus*), and snowshoe hares (*Lepus americanus*).

The Kluane Boreal Forest Ecosystem Project (KBFEP) was an ambitious attempt to understand all of the links in an entire ecosystem—an area of boreal forest in southern Yukon (Krebs et al., 2001). The project was financed by the Natural Sciences and Engineering Research Council of Canada (NSERC), a federal agency that provides most funding for ecological research in Canada. The project and was carried out between 1986 and 1996, and was led by Charles Krebs, Tony Sinclair, and Stan Boutin. Overall it involved nine professors from three Canadian universities, 26 graduate students, and 93 summer students and technicians. The primary objective of the project was to address two questions:

1. What factors regulate the dynamics of species within the boreal forest around Kluane?
2. Are the species regulated from below (bottom–up control through primary productivity) or from above (top–down control through predators and herbivores), or by a combination of these mechanisms?

Manipulative field experiments were a key method used to explore these questions. Typically, a trophic level was systematically removed, or in some cases supplemented, and subsequent effects on the productivity, biomass, or activity of other levels were measured.

The main plants in the ecosystem are white spruce (*Picea glauca*), shrubs (mostly willow, *Salix*, and birch, *Betula*), and various grasses and herbaceous dicots. The dominant herbivores are snowshoe hare (*Lepus americanus*), which exhibits a 10-year population cycle, arctic ground squirrel (*Spermophilus parryii*), red squirrel (*Tamiasciurus hudsonicus*), and various species of voles (*Clethrionomys* and *Microtus*). The major carnivores are lynx (*Lynx canadensis*), coyote (*Canis latrans*), and various raptors, notably the great horned owl (*Bubo virginianus*).

The experimental manipulations included

- an aerial broadcast application of fertilizer to two areas of 100 ha;
- food supplementation for hares by the addition of commercial rabbit chow, year-round to satiation to two areas of 35 ha;
- reduction of carnivores from a 100 ha area using electrified wire fencing that was permeable to hares and squirrels; a central 10-ha portion of this area was covered with an overhead monofiliament screen to deter great horned owls;
- addition of commercial rabbit chow to a 35-ha area inside of a 100-ha carnivore exclusion (reduction) electrified fence;
- exclusion of hares from a 4-ha area;
- exclusion of hares and addition of fertilizer to a 4-ha area; and
- removal of vegetation from 50 plots, each of 1 m^2.

The direct effects of each manipulation produced strong top–down and bottom–up changes in biomass (Boutin et al., 1995; Krebs et al., 1995; Turkington et al., 1998; Sinclair et al., 2000). Fertilizer increased the growth rate of plants, but it increased the intensity of herbivory during the winter to an even greater degree so that biomass declined. Therefore, top–down effects outweighed bottom–up ones on the plant community in winter. In contrast, during the summer growing season, herbivory had virtually no effect on plant biomass, in comparison to the stimulation from fertilizer addition.

Top–down effects dominated bottom–up ones at the herbivore level. In fact, much of the vertebrate community is regulated by top–down influences. A number of the predator species act as a guild, and their populations were influenced by that of snowshoe hare, the major prey species. In addition, the dramatic population cycle of hares was tracked by that of lynx (*Lynx canadensis*).

No bottom–up influences of nutrients on vegetation were observed in populations of carnivores.

Overall, the experiments produced results that are consistent with two-way (reciprocal) interactions at each level. Indirect effects on species one or two levels removed from the experimental manipulation were either very weak or undetectable. Top–down effects were strong when direct but attenuated quickly. Bottom–up effects were less strong but persisted as indirect effects on herbivores.

This project has given us a detailed description of the food web of a boreal forest. Just as important, it provides a crucial database that will serve as a marvellous platform against which ecologists can compare their future research on questions related to, for example, global climate change.

Nils Stenseth (2002), an ecologist who reviewed the summary book about the Kluane Boreal Forest Ecosystem Project, stated the following:

> *This type of project is also exactly what is needed to enable ecologists to help politicians manage the biological diversity of the Earth when faced with a growing population, and the resulting increase in demand for resources. All such demands must ultimately be met from our natural resources. Research-funding agencies, and hence politicians, must realize that it is not enough to have had one Kluane project. We need many, so that we can compare the dynamics of ecosystems under different settings. Before the Kluane Project we had no role model—now we have one.*

all of the organisms present—plants, animals, fungi, and bacteria—and their interactions may involve competition for scarce resources (such as light, nutrients, food, or water), herbivory, predation, disease, or cooperative relations (referred to as facilitation). There are occasions when one community ends abruptly at a step-cline *ecotone* and is immediately replaced by a different one, but it is more usual for communities to gradually transition from one type to the next.

Communities may be organized in different ways:

- First, they may be organized in terms of the functional roles that their component species may play, such as autotrophs, herbivores, carnivores, or detritivores.
- Second, equilibrium models of community organization focus on the relative stability of the species composition, and resistance and resilience to disturbances. In contrast, non-equilibrium models posit that communities are not steady in composition, and never reach a stable condition because they are always recovering from disturbances.
- Third, centrifugal organization is based on the notion of core and peripheral habitats—all species in a community have a shared preference for the core habitat, but each is also the best competitor in some habitat that is peripheral to the core. This means that the diversity of peripheral habitats will largely determine the richness of plant species in the community.
- Species diversity has two components—the number of species in a community, called species richness, and their relative abundance, called evenness. Most communities have a few species that are extremely abundant (dominants), many that are moderately so, and a large number that are rare. A plot of the relative abundances of all species in a community often fits a logarithmic series, or with larger data sets, often a log-normal distribution. In some cases, as data sets get even larger, a zero-sum multinomial distribution better predicts the distribution of species abundances.

The niche of a species is defined by all of the environmental factors that limit its distribution, growth, and reproduction. The fundamental niche is the full range of environmental tolerances of a species, under circumstances in which it is free from interference from other species. In nature, however, species occupy a restricted range, referred to as the realized niche, which is constrained within the fundamental one by the influences of competitors, predators, diseases, and other factors.

The major factors contributing to community structure are physical conditions of the environment, competition, facilitation, herbivory and predation, disturbance, and chance:

- The physical conditions typically provide the limits of the distributions of species, and within these

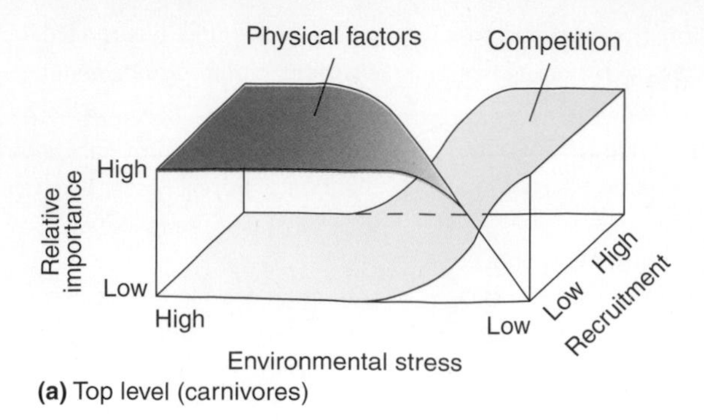

(a) Top level (carnivores)

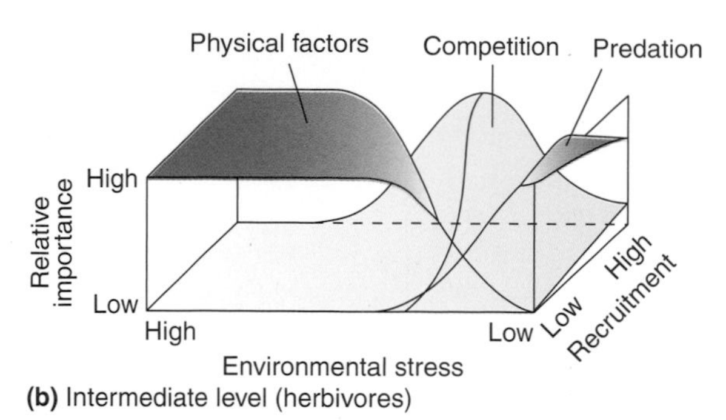

(b) Intermediate level (herbivores)

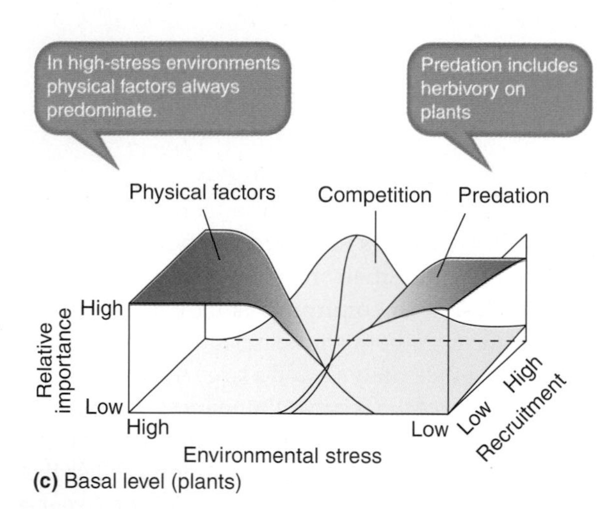

(c) Basal level (plants)

FIGURE 9.38

The Model of Menge and Sutherland. Three factors are viewed as driving community organization—competition among species, predation, and physical factors. The relative importance of the three influences varies with trophic level, overall harshness of the environment, and amount of recruitment into the population.

SOURCE: Modified from Menge, B. A. and J. P. Sutherland. 1987. "Community regulation: Variation in disturbance, competition, and predation in relation to environmental stress and recruitment," *American Naturalist*, 130: 730–757.

constraints biotic factors often determine their relative abundances.

- The influence of competition changes along environmental gradients. However, plants in particular may also interact in positive ways, an effect known as facilitation that typically involves an enhancement of conditions for one species by the influence of another one.
- Herbivores, predators, and disturbances often have similar effects on community composition. Intermediate levels of physical disturbance (e.g., windstorms) or of herbivory (grazing) typically promote higher diversity. In addition, a keystone species is one that has a disproportionately large effect on the structure of its community, as may be the case of certain herbivores on grasslands and of predators in intertidal zones.

If the effects of any of these factors, individually or combined, are strong enough, a community may be altered to such an extent that it will be pushed into an alternative stable state and will not recover to its original condition after the perturbation has been removed. Often, the factors that ultimately determine community structure are a complex interaction between many of these factors.

Ecologists have proposed a number of conceptual models in an attempt to tie all of these influences together, as follows:

- The so-called bottom–up model (or hypothesis) states that the abundance of a population is limited by nutrients or by the availability of food—communities are regulated by resource flows from below, and higher trophic levels have no regulating effect on the productivity or biomass of trophic levels below them.
- The top–down model states that the abundance of a population is limited by the consumers it supports—top predators are self-regulating, and they also regulate the herbivores upon which they feed, and plants are limited by their herbivores rather than by the availability of the resources that they need.
- Further, the models proposed by Connell and by Menge and Sutherland suggest that the relative importance of physical factors, competition, and herbivory and predation varies in a predictable way depending upon the trophic level, amount of recruitment, and environmental conditions. Their basic models predict that chance events are important in harsh environmental conditions, whereas in intermediate conditions, competition is the most important factor, and in benign environments, herbivory and predation are the most important factors influencing community structure.

Despite the considerable progress that has been made in understanding the factors that affect the distribution and abundance of organisms within ecological communities, ecologists have not yet achieved unanimity as to general models of the controlling influences. This does not represent any sort of failure among community ecologists—rather, it is a reflection of the importance and excitement of this field of study.

A CANADIAN ECOLOGIST 9.2

Roy Turkington: An Ecologist Who Is Curious

Elaine Simons

Roy Turkington

by Bill Freedman

Roy Turkington was born in Northern Ireland, and did his Ph.D. in Wales with the famous population ecologist, John Harper. Turkington then came to Canada, and has been a professor at the University of British Columbia since 1977. Like all ecologists, Turkington has an unbridled fascination with the natural world and its astonishing biological complexity. He is especially curious about how population-level processes, such as competition and herbivory, influence the organization and structure of ecosystems, particularly of plant communities, and this has provided a focus for his career as an ecologist doing fieldwork in Canada and around the world.

The methodological framework of Turkington's research, and that of the many graduate students and other colleagues who have worked with him, has been the pursuit of carefully designed field and laboratory experiments; this has resulted in more than 130 papers and book chapters. This work is intended to highlight the key environmental influences on the abundance and performance of plant species, usually within the context of their natural communities. Turkington and his students have done this sort of research in plant ecology in southern and central British Columbia, the Kluane region of southern Yukon, Africa, Britain, Israel, Iran, and China. This is a wide geographical reach, but fundamental research in ecology is relevant to any ecosystem, anywhere on the planet.

Almost of all of Turkington's research is driven by an uninhibited curiosity about how the natural world is organized, rather than by the necessities of fixing ecological problems wrought by humans and their economy. In other words, Turkington is engaged in **fundamental research**—an endeavour that is pursued with vigour and tenacity by many scientists who are deeply inquisitive about nature and its existence, and who are willing to devote their professional lives to improving our understanding of those great questions. Remarkably, many people hold the view that such curiosity-driven research is not as worthwhile as applied work—they cannot understand how non-applied work may be useful. In part, these critics are in error because they are unwilling to acknowledge the many cases in which insights gained from fundamental research have resulted in important applied advances in fields ranging from genetics to improved materials and energy sources to technology in general.

But this is not the most important reason why the critics of fundamental research are wrong-headed and even ignorant in their view of the role that fundamental science plays in our society. The purview of science is not merely to serve the human economy by discovering improved ways of harvesting resources, manufacturing and transporting commodities and products, and handling information. These are obviously important applications of scientific knowledge, but they are not its sole or even its primary rationale. Rather, science plays a special role in helping our society to understand how and why the natural world exists and functions, and in providing essential context for the position of humans within that grand realm. Fundamental research helps us to understand these big questions in ways that the narrow light-shafts of applied work cannot. This is the key reason why fundamental research is important, and why it should continue to be well supported in Canada.

VOCABULARY OF ECOLOGY

alpha (α) diversity, p. 251
alternative (or multiple) stable states, p. 269
asymmetric competition, p. 260
beta (β) diversity, p. 251
biodiversity, p. 249
bottom–up (or resource-control) hypothesis, p. 279
centrifugal organization, p. 248
climax community, p. 244
commensalism, p. 247
community, p. 243
competition, p. 246
competitive exclusion, p. 259
competitive release, p. 259
competitor, p. 248
cryptic herbivores, p. 273
disease, p. 246
disturbance, p. 265
diversity, p. 249
dominance-controlled community, p. 254
dominant species, p. 254
environmental gradient, p. 257
equilibrium, p. 248
evenness (equitability), p. 250
facilitation, p. 243
founder-controlled community, p. 254
functional group, p. 247
fundamental niche, p. 256
fundamental research, p. 287
gamma (γ) diversity, p. 251
guild, p. 247
herbivory, p. 246
importance of competition, p. 262
intensity of competition, p. 262
individualistic (or continuum) hypothesis, p. 245
intermediate disturbance hypothesis, p. 266
keystone species, p. 268
logarithmic series, p. 252
log-normal distribution, p. 252
multiple (or alternative) stable states, p. 269
mutualism, p. 245
neutral model, p. 253
niche, p. 256
non-equilibrium, p. 248
organismal hypothesis (or community unit hypothesis), p. 244
parasitism, p. 247
predation, p. 246
rank-abundance, p. 252
realized niche, p. 256
ruderal, p. 248
species diversity, p. 249
species richness, p. 249
stress-tolerator, p. 248
symbiosis, p. 246
top–down (or consumer-control) hypothesis, p. 279
trophic cascade, p. 278

QUESTIONS FOR REVIEW AND DISCUSSION

1. What is an ecological community? Provide examples of its structural characteristics, and of functional ones.
2. Consider the following argument: "The reason that the Atlantic coast of Canada supports so few species of intertidal barnacles, mussels, snails, and other sedentary or slow-moving herbivores compared to the Pacific coast is that predators (such as starfish) are rare on the Atlantic coast, thereby permitting only a few dominant herbivores to succeed." Describe an experiment that you would perform to test this idea about controlling factors in these intertidal communities.
3. Five grassland areas in the Negev Desert have been used by Bedouin herdsmen to graze their sheep and goats for nearly 90 years. Animal densities have been fairly consistent over that period. The table in the next column shows data that were collected recently in the grasslands.
   a. What ecological principle is illustrated by this data set?
   b. Why do areas with either low or high numbers of grazing animals have fewer plant species than those with intermediate levels of grazing?

Grasslands	Number of Animals/ha	Plant Species
1	2	7
2	8	22
3	15	36
4	22	43
5	30	18

4. Consider a case in which two species of birds coexist in a forest. They appear to overlap completely in all environmental factors related to resources (e.g., food, nest sites) and inorganic conditions (e.g., climatic factors) that you can measure. Do these species have the same niche?
5. It is sometimes claimed that species in one community are ecological "equivalents" of those in another community. For example, kangaroos of Australian grassland are sometimes likened to be equivalents of antelope in Africa or of bison in the original prairie of Canada. Does this imply that these large herbivores have the same niche?

6. Chance plays an important role in the success of dispersal. Isolated places like oceanic islands, or recently disturbed patches of land, are likely to be colonized mostly by such chance dispersal events. Does this mean that community structure in such places is determined *only* by chance? Explain your answer.
7. Two species of salamander are distributed in a broadly overlapping manner in hilly terrain. Three distributional zones are observed: one with only salamander A, one with both species, and another with only B. Outline a field experiment that you would use to determine if these species of salamander are competing with each other.
8. Explain the ecological principle that is illustrated by the studies that were described of sea otters in nearshore habitats of the Aleutian Islands.
9. In the Kluane Boreal Forest Ecosystem Project in southern Yukon, some plots in the understorey were treated with fertilizer for 20 years, while others were fenced to eliminate or reduce herbivores for 20 years, yet others received both fencing and fertilizer, and of course there was also a control treatment. In the table below, indicate what biomass responses you would predict to occur in the understorey plant community in the three treatment plots (the data are corrected for changes in the control plots), if they are (a) under strict bottom–up regulation, and (b) under strict top–down regulation. Note that the question is not asking about *both* bottom–up and top–down acting simultaneously. In plots where you predict a change in biomass, explain what might be happening to the species composition of those plots.

Treatment	Bottom–Up Predictions	Top–Down Predictions
Fertilized	Increase	No change
Fenced	No change	Increase
Fertilized & fenced	Increase	Increase

HELPFUL WEBSITES

THE NUTRIENT NETWORK (NUTNET)

http://nutnet.science.oregonstate.edu

NutNet is spearheaded by Eric Seabloom at Oregon State University. It is a global experiment that is investigating the effects of resources and consumption on ecosystem processes, and an ambitious attempt to unravel the complexities of top–down and bottom–up effects.

KLUANE BOREAL FOREST ECOSYSTEM PROJECT

http://www.aina.ucalgary.ca/scripts/minisa.dll/144/proe/klrsprok/se+kluane+boreal*?COMMANDSEARCH

This website contains the abstracts of 159 papers and theses related to the Kluane Boreal Forest Ecosystem Project in southern Yukon.

THE JENA EXPERIMENT

http://www.ufz.de/index.php?en=7000

The Jena Experiment is studying interactions between plant diversity and ecosystem processes, focusing on element cycling and trophic interactions. Artificial plant communities were established from a pool of 60 species from central European grasslands, with the main experiment carried out on 90 plots of 20 × 20 m, and plant species richness ranging from 1 to 60 species.

KONZA PRAIRIE LONG-TERM ECOLOGICAL RESEARCH (LTER)

http://www.konza.ksu.edu

The Konza Prairie, located in Kansas, is an ecological research and education program, focused on tallgrass prairie. The LTER program (Long-Term Ecological Research) began in 1982 with a focus on fire, grazing, and climatic variability as three key factors that affect grasslands worldwide. Current research addresses how changes in land use, climate change, nutrient enrichment, and biological invasions influence the sustainability and dynamics of grassland ecosystems.

CEDAR CREEK ECOSYSTEM SCIENCE RESERVE

http://www.cedarcreek.umn.edu/research

The Cedar Creek Ecosystem Science Reserve is a large research site in Minnesota with a diversity of natural habitats. Long-term studies were begun in 1982 and are focused on six major issues and questions that explore topics of fundamental scientific interest and of relevance to human-driven environmental change, including effects on ecosystem functioning of elevated nitrogen deposition, increased concentrations of atmospheric carbon dioxide, and of the loss of biodiversity.

THE PARK GRASS EXPERIMENT

http://www.rothamsted.bbsrc.ac.uk/resources/ClassicalExperiments.html

The Park Grass experiment at Rothamsted is one of the most important in the world in the area of biodiversity and ecology. This experiment started in 1856 on a field that had been in pasture for at least a century. Various combinations of inorganic fertilizers have been tested, and vegetation changes have been monitored for many years.

THE ARCTIC LONG TERM ECOLOGICAL RESEARCH (ARC LTER)

http://ecosystems.mbl.edu/ARC

The ARC LTER site is part of a network of sites established by the U.S. National Science Foundation to support long-term ecological research. The Toolik Field Station is located in the foothills region of the Brooks Range of Alaska.

You'll fi nd a rich array of additional resources for *Ecology* at www.ecology.nelson.com.

system to recover to its original condition. For instance, if a boreal stand of white spruce (*Picea glauca*) and its associated community in northern Saskatchewan were burned in a wildfire, and the site then recovered to a similar association through succession, the ecosystem would be judged to be resilient to this kind of disturbance. However, if that initial spruce-dominated community were clear-cut and the early succession became diverted to a persistent fen wetland dominated by a dense growth of blue-joint (*Calamagrostis canadensis*, a species of grass), then the ecosystem would not be as resilient in its longer-term dynamics and stability. This circumstance was demonstrated by field studies by Vic Liefers and others from the University of Alberta, who found that the blue-joint is highly competitive in post-clear-cutting succession, and that spruce seedlings cannot easily invade or be productive in that regenerating community (Liefers et al., 1993).

Resistance (sometimes known as **tolerance**) is different from resilience—it refers to the ability of an ecosystem to avoid a displacement from its present stage of ecological development as a result of either disturbance or another agent of intensified stress. For example, a lightning strike occurring during a prolonged rain event might not result in a wildfire: in such a circumstance an otherwise vulnerable forest might resist that potential disturbance. Similarly, a slope with a well-established forest might be better able to resist a devastating landslide, compared with a more-vulnerable lightly vegetated community.

Another example of resistance could involve a community with a high level of species richness, which might not change so much if one of its constituent species were to be devastated by a pathogen. Consider, for example, the case of the American chestnut (*Castanea dentata*) that was decimated by an introduced fungal blight (caused by *Cryphonectria parasitica*) in mixed-species hardwood forest in southern Ontario and elsewhere in eastern North America in the first third of the 20th century. However, its ecological community remained substantially intact because other species of trees survived and were able to occupy the space freed up by the dead chestnuts. This might be considered to represent an example of species redundancy in terms of the structural and functional characteristics of this mature temperate forest. However, this community-level interpretation of the effects of chestnut blight should not be viewed as somehow diminishing the importance of that devastating alien pathogen—it has, in fact, caused terrible damage to the population of American chestnut, a highly valued component of native biodiversity. Notwithstanding that context, the community of which the chestnut was formerly a prominent member has shown a high degree of resistance to suffering an ecological collapse initiated by the removal of one of its abundant members by a species-specific disease.

In any event, when resistance (or tolerance) is exceeded, an obvious result is large changes in communities and ecosystems (**Figure 10.1**). Once a disturbance event has ended, a period of ecological recovery begins, known as succession.

10.2 Causes and Consequences of Disturbance

Smaller-Scale Disturbances

At the lesser end of the spatial spectrum, **microdisturbances** occur at a small scale within an otherwise intact community. The disturbed area is a gap within which resources are relatively abundant and competition less severe. A **microsuccession** occurs within that gap as plants vie to take advantage of the opening and fill it with their biomass and propagules. The following are examples of microdisturbances:

- the death of a large tree within an old-growth forest in coastal British Columbia, occurring as a result of a lightning strike or a disease, but within a context of the surrounding forest remaining otherwise undamaged; the dynamics of the subsequent **gap-phase microsuccession** result in the development of the highly complex, multi-species, variously aged structure that is typical of trees in old-growth forest;
- a landslide in steep mountainous terrain in Yukon, which results in a locally disturbed patch

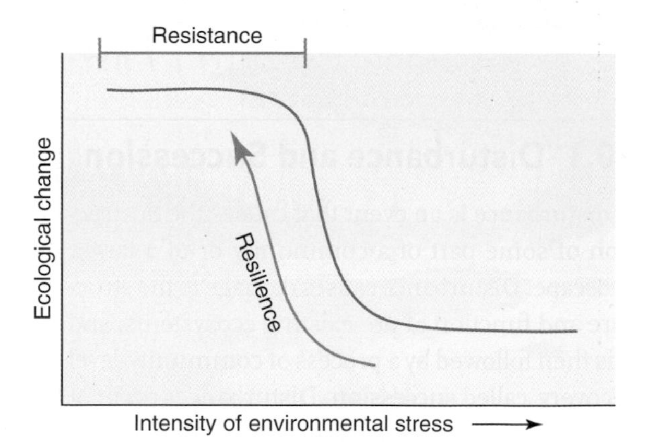

FIGURE 10.1

Resistance and Resilience. Communities have a certain ability to resist an intensification of environmental stressors, including those associated with disturbance, without undergoing a substantial change in their structure or function. Once this *resistance* (or *tolerance*) is overcome, however, large and rapid changes occur until a new ecological condition is established. Once the stressor relaxes or the disturbance event is finished, an ecological recovery by succession begins. If the succession regenerates a system that is similar to the original, then a high degree of *resilience* has been demonstrated. However, if the succession ends with a system that is markedly different from the original, the resilience is low.

within an otherwise intact expanse of older communities, and is followed by a successional recovery whose speed and plant composition vary depending on whether naked bedrock has been exposed as well as other terrain features;

- local diggings associated with a colony of black-tailed prairie dog (*Cynomys ludovicianus*) in otherwise unbroken mixedgrass prairie in southern Saskatchewan; the affected patches of loose dirt provide local refugia for early-successional (or ruderal) plant species that might not otherwise be part of the grassland community;
- the death of individual colonies of brain-coral (*Diploria labyrinthiformis*) or of other large coral species as a result of a disease or a warm-water bleaching event in the Caribbean Sea, which creates a gap in the community within which early-successional species occur and contribute to the recovery;
- linear disturbed features known as game trails, which are created within otherwise intact vegetation by the repeated passage of large animals, such as caribou (*Rangifer tarandus*) in arctic tundra and boreal forest of northern regions, and along which microhabitat for ruderal plants is maintained;
- ice-scoured patches that are caused when current-borne icebergs drift through shallow continental-shelf waters off Newfoundland and Labrador, where they occasionally scrape the bottom and form locally eroded areas that are initially devoid of life but then regenerate to develop communities typical of the substrate type.

Larger-Scale Disturbances

Toward the larger end of the spatial spectrum, **stand-replacing disturbances** affect entire communities. At the even grander scale of an ecoscape, the diverse community patches of various post-disturbance ages represent an ecological dynamic referred to as a **shifting mosaic** (see Chapter 13). These larger-scale disturbances are caused by various agents, which may be natural or anthropogenic in origin. Examples of natural disturbances include the following:

- *Wildfire* is a normal agent of disturbance of certain natural communities, including tallgrass prairie and various kinds of forest, particularly those that experience seasonal dryness and are dominated by conifers. Examples of fire-prone communities include boreal stands of black and white spruce (*Picea mariana* and *P. glauca*) and jack pine (*Pinus banksiana*), montane forests of ponderosa and lodgepole pine (*P. ponderosa* and *P. contorta*), and east-temperate stands of white and red pine (*P. strobus* and *P. resinosa*). The species found in these fire-prone communities are well-adapted to periodic wildfires and may even require this disturbance for their regeneration and persistence on the landscape. The area and configuration of a wildfire are highly contextual, being affected by site and community influences on vulnerability to burning, such as stand age, fuel loading, species composition, and site moisture, as well as weather conditions at the time of ignition, especially the wind speed and whether there has been a recent drought. Because of these variable influences, a wildfire may cover only a few or tens of thousands of hectares. Moreover, the boundaries of a wildfire are typically ragged and complex and there are many unburned "skips," often of moist or wet habitat. These variations contribute to the spatial complexity of both wildfires and the regenerating post-fire communities that exist on any fire-prone landscape. The average area burned in Canada every year is about 2.5 million ha, but in some years it may exceed 10 million ha (Freedman, 2010). There are about 8000 wildfires each year, of which 45 percent are ignited by lightning strikes. However, this natural cause of ignition is responsible for 81 percent of the

Bill Freedman

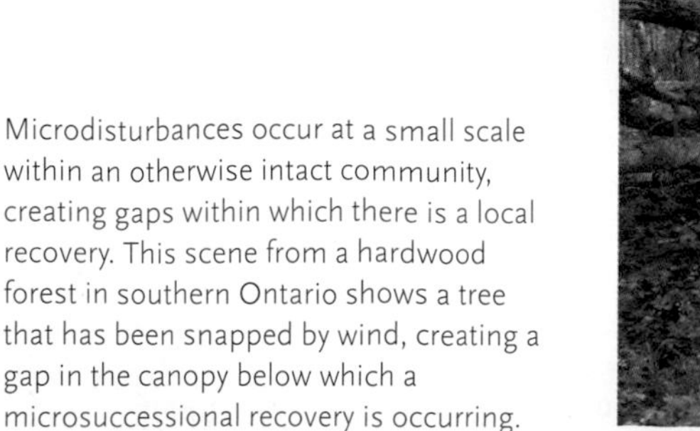

Microdisturbances occur at a small scale within an otherwise intact community, creating gaps within which there is a local recovery. This scene from a hardwood forest in southern Ontario shows a tree that has been snapped by wind, creating a gap in the canopy below which a microsuccessional recovery is occurring.

Stand-replacing disturbances occur at a larger scale, and are followed by a community-level successional recovery. (This fire took place in Yukon.)

burned area because it often occurs in remote regions where wildfires may not be quenched by fire-fighting. Fires started by people account for the other 55 percent of ignitions, but they mostly occur in developed regions and are usually extinguished relatively quickly.

- *Windstorms* are another disturbance that may operate at a large scale. Forests are particularly affected by this cause of disturbance, and stands are especially vulnerable if they occur in an exposed location, if the trees are large, and if a windstorm occurs when the soil is moist (which makes the roots more slippery within the ground). Wind-damaged trees may have their main stem or large branches broken, or they may be uprooted, which results in the development of a so-called pit-and-mound topography within a forest. Windstorms may occur as relatively small cyclonic phenomena that are embedded within thunderstorms and tropical storms, but they may also be massive events occurring during a rare hurricane-force gale (with wind speed >120 km/hr) that can blow down thousands of hectares of forest. One example is Hurricane Juan, which made landfall near Halifax in September 2003, and caused about 231 km^2 of stand-level forest damage (this is the sum of affected patches larger than 1 ha) along a broad swath, plus an additional 780 km^2 of windthrow at smaller scales (Bruce, 2009).
- *Biological agents* may also cause extensive damage to natural ecosystems, sometimes affecting millions of hectares. In terrestrial ecosystems, the damage is typically done to a dominant component of the plant community, such as an abundant species of tree in a specific kind of forest. The biological agent may be a defoliating or stem-boring insect that rapidly **irrupts** to an extremely high population level, or a microbial pathogen. In cases where only a particular species is damaged, we might think of such an event as being a **population-replacing disturbance** (as we earlier examined with respect to chestnut blight). This may cause serious ecological damage, but because much of the community survives it is not quite the same as a full community-replacing disturbance. In addition, the bio-disturbance "events" may be rather protracted, sometimes lasting for several years during which time there is a progressive accumulation of damage until the affected population or community is devastated; at this point the biological agent itself collapses in abundance. Some examples of extensive ecological damage caused by native species include the following (Freedman, 2010):
    - mountain pine beetle (*Dendroctonus ponderosae*), a devastating herbivore that is causing extensive damage to montane forests of lodgepole pine (*Pinus contorta*) in British Columbia (13.5-million ha were affected in 2009);
    - spruce budworm (*Choristoneura fumiferana*), an herbivore specializing on balsam fir (*Abies balsamea*) and white spruce (*Picea glauca*) in eastern Canada; about 60×10^6 ha were affected during an irruption that occurred between the early 1970s and early 1990s, causing extensive tree mortality;
    - the migratory grasshopper (*Melanoplus sanguinipes*) and other locusts, which periodically irrupt and cause damage to millions of hectares of agricultural cropland and pastures, especially in the prairie provinces, and to a much lesser degree, to native prairie;
    - the green sea urchin (*Strongylocentrotus droebachiensis*), which sometimes reaches a great abundance in coastal kelp "forests" dominated by *Laminaria* and *Agarum* off Nova Scotia—the urchin overgrazes these macroalgae and converts the ecosystem to a rocky "barren ground," which itself persists until a year with unusually warm water causes a bacterial disease to kill the urchins, after which their collapse allows the kelp to regenerate (Scheibling, 1986; Lauzon-Guay et al., 2009).

B ll Freedman

Biological agents may be causes of of disturbance. In this case, the pale-winged grey moth (*Iridopsis ephyraria*) has irrupted in Kejimkujik National Park, Nova Scotia, and its severe defoliation for several years has killed mature trees of eastern hemlock (*Tsuga canadensis*). Because only hemlock are affected by the moth, this might be considered a population-replacing disturbance.

Glaciation

The development of persistent sheets of ice over extensive terrestrial regions, or **glaciation**, may also be considered to represent a kind of disturbance. However, glaciation is a distinctive kind of disturbance in that it involves a highly protracted causal agent—the development of long-lasting sheets of glacial ice that smother, grind, and obliterate prior ecosystems on affected terrain, and that endure for centuries and even millennia, until an eventual melting of the glacier exposes the landscape and allows a successional recovery to occur.

The most recent continental-scale glaciation in North America was the Wisconsinan event (it has different names in other continents and regions). The last phase of that glaciation began about 30 000 years ago, reached a maximal extent 21 000 years ago, and then melted back due to climate warming and substantially ended 10 000 to 13 000 years ago, depending on the location. In fact, remnant glaciers still exist on Greenland and on several arctic islands in Canada, particularly on Baffin, Axel Heiberg, and Ellesmere Islands, and also at high altitudes in the Rockies and on other western mountains. Of course, the largest glaciers in the world are in Antarctica.

At the peak of the Wisconsinan ice age, glaciers covered virtually all of Canada, in some regions with ice as thick as several kilometres. In fact, so much of the water of Earth was tied up on land in glacial ice, that sea level was as much as 120 m lower that at present. This phenomenon resulted in extensive areas of the presently sub-oceanic continental shelf being exposed—during glacial times the "land" extended up to 100 km farther east off eastern Canada than it does today, onto what are now shallow marine waters.

When the continental glaciers eventually melted away, the freed-up terrestrial substrates became available for colonization by organisms that were capable of dispersing to these newly freed-up habitats. This resulted in an extended successional recovery on deglaciated landscapes. Virtually all of the terrestrial ecosystems of Canada have developed since the melting of those continental-scale glaciers. The only exceptions involve relatively small regions that were not glaciated, particularly in northwestern Canada, which were **refugia** from this disturbance. These non-glaciated areas of northern Yukon and adjacent coastal Northwest Territories supported plants and animals throughout the most recent glacial epoch, and today they are relatively rich in endemic species (see Chapters 12 and 16).

Anthropogenic Disturbances

A wide variety of disturbances is associated with human activities, and they are increasingly important causes of ecological damage. Sometimes the anthropogenic agents of disturbance have broad parallels to natural ones, but nevertheless they are novel to some degree and are affecting native species and natural communities in ways that have not previously been experienced.

- *Small-scale anthropogenic disturbances*. The selective harvesting of trees from a forest that is otherwise left intact is an example of an anthropogenic microdisturbance. This has obvious similarities to

A lithosere is a primary succession that occurs on a bare-rock surface. This kind of succession is common after deglaciation and other severe disturbances in northern Canada, especially in regions of Precambrian bedrock. Among the first colonists are lichens and mosses, whose accumulating organic matter makes it possible for plants to establish. This image shows various species of lichens growing on bare granite, and a bed of the moss *Rhacomitrium lanuginosum*, whose biomass provides a microhabitat in which several kinds of vascular plants are establishing. In essence, the moss facilitates the invasion of the site by the vascular plants. The location is near Deception Bay, in the Nunavik region of northern Quebec.

Bill Freedman

many of the plants that are typical of, and often dominant in, younger successional ecosystems (see also Chapter 9). Ruderal plants are relatively short-lived but fast-growing and are well-adapted to the environmental conditions of recently disturbed habitats, which include a relatively low intensity of competition and a high availability of site resources. Ruderals produce large numbers of seeds that have an ability to widely disperse so that other recently disturbed habitats can be colonized. Typically, ruderal species are prominent in the earlier years of a post-disturbance sere, along with plants of the original community that managed to survive the disturbance and then regenerate.

However, as time passes and succession progresses, vegetation becomes more abundant and so the intensity of competition increases markedly and resources become increasingly more limiting. This causes the early-successional and intolerant ruderal plants to become replaced by others that are more tolerant of these conditions—these are referred to as *competitors*. Competitors are roughly comparable to C-type species (Chapters 8 and 9)—they are effective at acquiring resources and in achieving a dominant position in their community. In plants, their typical adaptations include rapid tall growth, development of a broad and shading canopy, and a spreading root system, all of which help to occupy space and appropriate resources. Seedlings of competitive plants can usually establish beneath a closed canopy, while those of ruderals are intolerant of shaded conditions.

As noted above, however, ecological development may be constrained by an environmental regime that is stressful in terms of its climate, soil, nutrients, light availability, or frequency and intensity of disturbances. Under such conditions the climax community might be a grassland, tundra, desert, or hard-rock inter-tidal community. These types have a relatively sparse productivity and low level of ecological development, compared with what is possible under less stressful environmental conditions. On land, the kinds of plants that dominate these relatively difficult habitats are referred to as *stress-tolerators*. These species are adapted to habitats that are highly stressed but stable, in the sense that they are not often disturbed. Stress-tolerant plants are typical of arctic, alpine, desert, and other severe environments, and they are generally low-growing, unproductive, long-lived, and intolerant of competition.

Means of Regeneration

Regardless of the scale of a disturbance, it creates an ecological opportunity for organisms that can colonize or regenerate in a situation in which biological stresses associated with competition are at a relatively low intensity. The recovery may occur by the re-growth of individuals that survived the disturbance, or by the recruitment of "new" ones into the community.

We can illustrate the means of regeneration by examining the kinds of plants that participate in the recovery of a forest that has been disturbed by a wildfire, windstorm, or clear-cut. These disturbances kill or damage many of the plants that are present, and are then followed by a spontaneous regeneration involving a range of tactics:

- *Vegetative regeneration.* Individual plants that survive the disturbance and its aftermath conditions will proceed to re-grow. For example, burnt or cut trees and shrubs of certain species will re-sprout from their still-living roots or rhizomes. Species of ash, aspen, maple, and other "hardwoods" are proficient at this **vegetative regeneration**, and their vigorous sprouting contributes to the re-establishment of another forest. For instance, if a mature red maple (*Acer rubrum*) is cut, its living stump will issue as many as several hundred woody sprouts that are genetically identical (the group is known as a clone, and each stem is a **ramet**) and eventually self-thin to only one to three stems after several decades (Prager and Goldsmith, 1977). Lees (1981) excavated the below-ground parts of a red maple tree in New Brunswick and found that there were at least three stump-sprout generations of that individual plant.

- *Advanced regeneration.* This term refers to smaller individuals of tree species that are established in a mature forest. After a disturbance opens up the stand, the **advanced regeneration** is "released" from competitive stresses previously exerted by the mature trees, which allows them to grow more rapidly and be prominent in the next stand. For example, mature fir-spruce forest of the type that develops on the highlands of Cape Breton in Nova Scotia typically supports about 45 000 small individuals of balsam fir per hectare and more than 3000 of white spruce (MacLean, 1984). Most of these small plants will survive an infestation of spruce budworm, which preferentially kills the larger mature fir and spruce. The advanced regeneration then grows rapidly and helps to regenerate another forest that is similar in community structure to the original one.
- *New seedlings.* A major disturbance of a forest creates a mosaic of affected patches on the ground surface. The local damage ranges in intensity from areas where organic matter has been removed and the mineral soil exposed, to places where little harm has been caused. The removal of the overhead canopy and disruption of the forest floor result in conditions that favour the establishment of seedlings of various plant species. The seedlings may originate in three major ways:
    - Immigrants: Some of the seedlings will be invaders of the disturbed site, in that they originate with seeds that have undergone a long-distance dispersal. Typically, their parent plants are growing in some other place, but they produce large numbers of seeds that are highly vagile (they are widely dispersed) and well-adapted to colonizing suitable habitat elsewhere. For example, the fireweed (*Chamaenerion angustifolium*) produces tiny seeds with fluffy plumes that allow them to waft a long distance on the wind, in anticipation of finding a recent burn where they may germinate, establish, grow, and themselves reproduce. The seeds of many other plants, such as conifers and birches, are also small and wind-dispersed, although not over such long distances as those with plumed seeds. Other seeds are dispersed by animals, such as the shadbush or saskatoon (*Amerlanchier alnifolia*), whose seeds are embedded within a tasty fruit that is eaten by birds, are resistant to digestion, and so survive passage through the avian gut to eventually be eliminate somewhere else. Another animal-dispersed plant is the beggar-tick (*Bidens frondosa*), whose seeds stick to the fur of mammals and become dispersed in that way.
    - Local seeding: Any mature plants that survive the disturbance will produce seeds that may disperse locally and establish new seedlings. Although jack pine trees are usually killed by a wildfire, soon after the burn their seeds become locally dispersed from their serotinous cones. **Serotiny** is an adaptation of this and a few other pine species that involves the cones and their content of viable seeds being held persistently aloft on the branches for several years. The cone scales are sealed closed by a wax, which prevents their enclosed seeds from dispersing. However, if the serotinous cones are subjected to heat of more than 80°C, as can happen during a wildfire, the wax will melt, the scales gradually spread apart, and the seeds then scatter to produce seedlings that can participate in the regeneration of another stand of jack pines.
    - The seed bank: Most stands of forest have an enduring population of viable seeds in the forest floor that is referred to as a **seed bank**. When the dormant seeds are exposed to environmental cues associated with a disturbance, such as an increased availability of light (due to disruption of the forest canopy) or a high concentration of nitrate (from stimulation of nitrification; see Chapter 4), they are stimulated to germinate and so can participate in the regeneration. For instance, seeds of pin cherry (*Prunus pensylvanica*) and red raspberry (*Rubus idaeus*) can survive for more than a century in the forest floor, in patient (but non-sentient) anticipation of a disturbance that will stimulate them to germinate (Marks, 1974; Grignon, 1992). Many other species also have dormant seeds in the seed bank, but they are not necessarily as long-lived as those of pin cherry and red raspberry.

These various sources of natural regeneration help to quickly re-establish a new plant community on disturbed sites. As the vegetation develops through a relay of successional stages, the habitat becomes suitable for various species of animals that invade and take advantage of those opportunities.

Changes in Structural and Functional Properties during Succession

The structural and functional properties of communities and ecosystems change markedly during succession. The particulars of the changes vary greatly,

At a few places on central Ellesmere Island, Nunavut, glacial meltback is exposing dead vegetation that became covered by persistent snow and ice about 1450. Remarkably, the dead biomass is being released physically intact (but dead), as is the case of this dwarf shrub, arctic white heather (*Cassiope tetragona*). The living plant is the moss *Psilopilum cavifolium*, which is one of the earliest invaders in this primary succession.

Bill Freedman

Post-Glacial Succession at Glacier Bay

Another place where primary succession has been examined after deglaciation is at Glacier Bay, located in the vicinity of the border of southern Alaska and Yukon. This region has a cool-temperate climate, and the end-point of the succession is a high-biomass coniferous forest, as opposed to the dwarf-shrub tundra of Ellesmere Island. The glacier within Glacier Bay advanced a remarkably long distance during the Little Ice Age (more than 100 km) and achieved a thickness of up to 800 m (Crocker and Major, 1955; Reiners et al., 1971). The glacial front has also retreated quickly during the warming that began around 1850, and its known locations at certain times have been used to assemble a chronosequence of sites and communities of various post-release ages. Although there is a continuous variation of community change along the chronosequence, several broad types can be distinguished:

1. a pioneer stage that lasts for 5–20 years and is dominated by *Rhacomitrium* mosses and the vascular plants willow-herb (*Epilobium latifolium*), variegated horsetail (*Equisetum variegatum*), mountain-avens (*Dryas drummondii*), and arctic willow (*Salix arctica*);
2. alder-willow tall-shrub thicket that becomes dominant at 20–40 years, and whose most prominent species are willows (*S. alaxensis, S. barclayi*, and *S. sitchensis*) and green alder (*Alnus crispa*);
3. mature forest, which at 50–70 years is dominated by cottonwood (*Populus trichocarpa*) and then by Sitka spruce (*Picea sitchensis*)—these are eventually joined and out-competed by western hemlock (*Tsuga heterophylla*) and mountain hemlock (*T. mertensiana*); and
4. on well-drained sites on slopes, which are prevalent in the deglaciated terrain, old-growth conifer forest is the stable type of community, but on flatter sites where drainage is impeded, a process known as **paludification** may occur; this happens because the organic forest floor retains so much water that trees die from the waterlogging, so that a peat-rich, boggy wetland known as muskeg develops.

Crocker and Major (1955) studied soil development in the chronosequence at Glacier Bay. The initial post-glacial parent material was a fine till composed of a mixture of rocks derived from granite, gneiss, schist, and 7–10 percent carbonate minerals, with a pH of 8.0–8.4. As this substrate became leached by water and modified by the developing vegetation, its acidity increased progressively. The pH reached 5.0 after 70 years of succession, when a mature coniferous forest was developing. The acidity of the forest floor eventually stabilized at pH 4.4 in the oldest forest communities, and the underlying mineral soil at pH 4.6–4.8. The acidification was accompanied by a decrease of calcium in the mineral soil, from an initial concentration of 5–9 percent to less than 1 percent. The decrease of calcium was caused by its being leached by abundant rainfall to below the rooting depth of the trees, as well as its uptake by vegetation and storage in their biomass. Other changes in soil properties during succession included large accumulations of organic matter and nitrogen, due to the biological fixation of atmospheric CO_2 and N_2 into biomass. The fixation of nitrogen is carried out by a relay of species during the succession, beginning with lichens of the pioneer stage, then mountain-avens with N_2-fixing *Frankia* actinobacteria living in root nodules, and later at especially high rates by alder, which also has a *Frankia* mutualism.

Post-Glacial Succession Inferred from Palynology

Post-glacial succession has also been studied using the techniques of paleoecology (see Chapter 16). One of these methods is palynology, which involves the reconstruction of past communities through the study of fossil pollen grains and spores extracted from dated layers of lake sediment. If a sediment core that is long enough can be recovered, it is possible to gain insight about the kinds of vegetation that were in place in early post-glacial times, and then subsequently to the present.

Les Cwynar and colleagues from the University of New Brunswick have been doing this kind of research in various places in Canada and in other countries. One study involved cores taken from four ponds in central Yukon, in a region where the present vegetation is a shrubby tundra (Cwynar and Spear, 1991; **Figure 10.6** shows a pollen diagram from one of the ponds). The pollen record was interpreted as showing that 10 000–8000 years BP (before present) the site was a shrub-tundra with forested groves of balsam poplar (*Populus balsamifera*). White spruce (*Picea glauca*) colonized around 9400 BP, and its populations increased to form an open woodland that persisted until 6500 BP, when black spruce (*Picea mariana*) and green alder (*Alnus crispa*) became prominent. Until about 5000 BP there was an open boreal forest of a composition similar to that occurring today in the region, depending on site conditions and local climate: (a) stands dominated by white spruce in drier south-facing slopes and alluvial sites, and (b) balsam poplar and black spruce on colder, wetter, north-facing sites and bottoms of wide valleys. Then at 5000 BP the climate deteriorated and the forest began to revert to shrub tundra, comparable to that which is predominant on the landscape today. There are still groves of spruce present today, mostly of white spruce, but these are considered to be persistent relicts occurring in favourable sites with a warmer and drier microclimate. The overall conclusion of the study is that this region of northwestern Canada and adjacent Alaska experienced a relatively warm post-glacial growing-season climate from 10 000 BP to 5000–6000 BP, followed by a cooling that resulted in an extensive decline in tree populations and reversion to shrub-tundra vegetation.

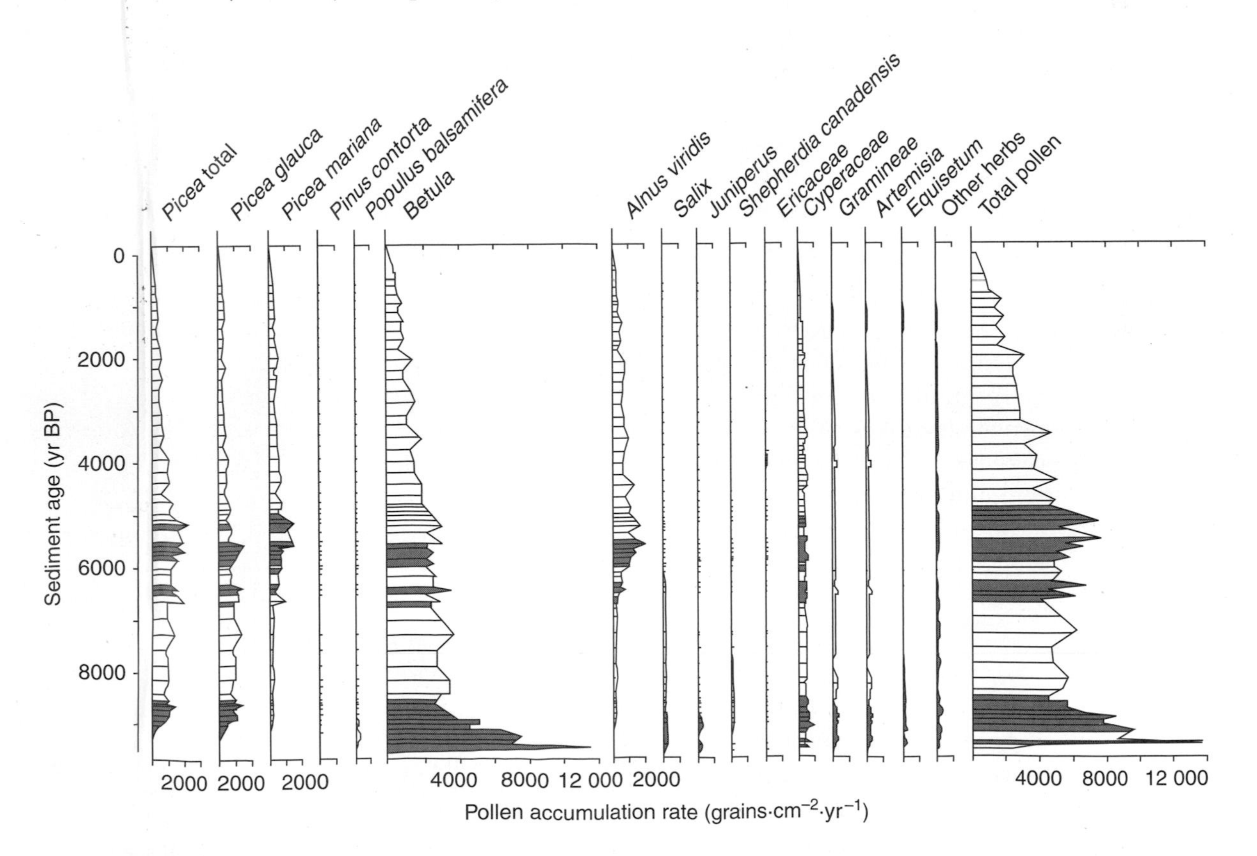

FIGURE 10.6

Pollen Diagram for Honeymoon Pond in Central Yukon. The vertical axis is years before present, and the individual graphs are the pollen accumulation rates for particular species or groups of them. See the text for an interpretation of changes in the absolute and relative rates of pollen deposition in terms of vegetational changes in the larger region.

SOURCE: Used with permission of the Ecological Society of America, from Cwynar, L.C. and R.W. Spear. 1991. "Reversion of forest to tundra in the central Yukon," *Ecology*, 72(1): 202–212; permission conveyed through Copyright Clearance Center, Inc.

Sand Dunes

Sand dunes at various places along the Great Lakes are slowly rising from extended submergence due to the phenomenon of isostasy. This is a geological process that is gradually elevating sandy lake-bottom sediment above the water, where it becomes a newly exposed substrate for terrestrial primary succession. In essence, isostasy is an elastic rebound of Earth's crust in response to release from the immense weight of several kilometres of overlying ice during the height of the continental glaciation, which was so heavy that it pressed the underlying bedrock hundreds of metres into the plastic mantle. When the glaciers retreated by melting, the bedrock was released from that colossal weight and it began to slowly uplift, and is still doing so in many regions. In certain places on the Great Lakes, where there is a gently sloping coastal terrain, isostasy has resulted in the occurrence of young dunes close to the lake, and progressively older ones farther inland. The age of the dunes can be estimated from their height above the present lake surface, coupled with knowledge of the rate of uplift of the terrain. This spatial progression of dunes of various ages, and the communities they support, can be studied as a chronosequence to reconstruct changes that occurred during succession. In fact, this was the basis of the early work of Cowles (1899) on succession on sand dunes along the shore of Lake Michigan.

A series of dunes at Grand Bend on southern Georgian Bay was also studied by Morrison and Yarranton (1973, 1974) of the University of Toronto. They divided the plant species of the sand-dune succession into two broad groups:

- *colonizing species* (type-I), which are important in stabilizing the sandy matrix and in accumulating organic matter and nutrients, and which are abundant in the initial communities, in which the intensity of competition is relatively low, and
- *persistent species* (type-II), which are prominent in the more stable communities of late-successional forest, in which competition is a major factor affecting the vegetation **(Figure 10.7)**

They divided the succession itself into three major periods:

1. A *colonizing stage* lasts about 1600 years and is dominated by type-I species. This stage begins on recently emerged sand, and initially involves a sparse cover of annual and biennial colonizing plants, such as sea rocket (*Cakile edentula*) and seaside spurge (*Euphorbia polygonifolia*). The succession rapidly progresses to a higher-biomass cover of the dune-grasses *Calamovilfa longifolia* and *Ammophila breviligulata* and various perennial forbs, such as wormwood *Artemisia biennis*. This community is replaced by a prairie-like community of more-competitive herbaceous plants, such as little bluestem (*Andropogon scoparius*), big bluestem (*A. gerardii*), indian-grass (*Sorghastrum nutans*), and dense blazing-star (*Liatris spicata*). The older communities within the colonizing stage are dominated by shrubs and trees that are relatively intolerant of competition, such as common juniper (*Juniperus communis*), eastern red-cedar (*J. virginiana*), and dwarf chinkapin oak (*Quercus prinoides*).
2. A *transitional phase* lasts from 1600 to 2900 years, during which type-II species of more intermediate tolerance become dominant, including a red-black oak hybrid (*Quercus velutina x rubra*), fragrant sumac (*Rhus aromatica*), and choke cherry (*Prunus virginiana*). The communities in this stage begin as small patches, which grow increasingly larger until they eventually coalesce, a dynamic successional process that is referred to as **nucleation**.
3. A *persistent climax-like stage* occurs from 2900 to >4800 years, which involves an extensive consolidation of a forest dominated by type-II species that are relatively tolerant of competition, growing within an environment characterized by periodic summer dryness, because the sand is so well-draining. The most prominent trees in the late-stage communities are red oak (*Quercus rubra*), black oak (*Q. velutina*),

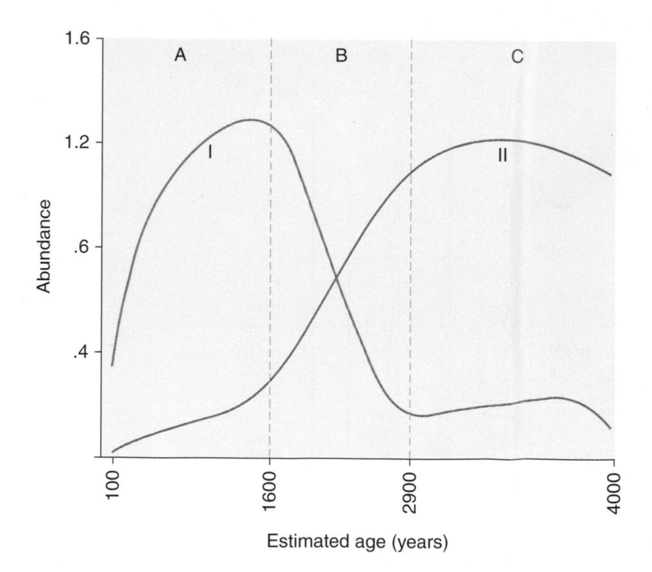

FIGURE 10.7
Diagrammatic Model of Plant Succession on Sand Dunes at Grand Bend, Ontario. The species are divided into two classes: (I) colonizing plants, which are important in stabilizing the substrate and are prominent in the initial communities, and (II) persistent plants, which occur in the more stable communities of late-successional forest. The primary succession is divided into three stages: (A) colonizing, (B) transitional, and (C) persistent.

SOURCE: Modified from: Morrison, R.G. and G.A. Yarranton. 1974. "Vegetational heterogeneity during a primary sand dune succession," *Canadian Journal of Botany*, 52: 397–410.

white oak (*Q. alba*), white pine (*Pinus strobus*), and red pine (*P. resinosa*).

Morrison and Yarranton also studied community-level changes in the vegetation, using summative indicators that are not related to the particular species that are present **(Figure 10.8)**. They found that species diversity (measured using the Shannon-Weiner index), evenness (a measure of how similarly abundant the various species are), and species richness (the number of species present in sampling plots) all increased rapidly during the early succession, and then became asymptotic (levelled off).

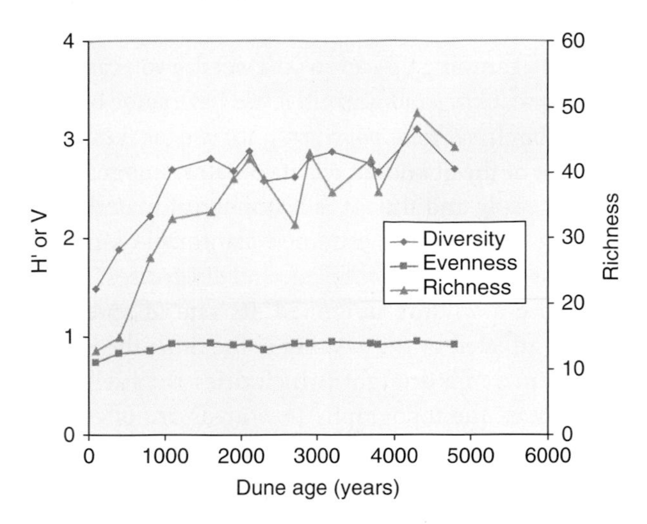

FIGURE 10.8

Changes in Community Indicators during Plant Succession on Sand Dunes at Grand Bend, Ontario. Species diversity, evenness, and richness all increase quickly in the early stages of succession, and then level off in the older communities.

SOURCE: Modified from: Morrison, R.G. and G.A. Yarranton. 1973. "Diversity, richness, and evenness during a primary sand dune succession at Grand Bend, Ontario," *Canadian Journal of Botany*, 51: 2401–2411. (Page 2404)

Ice-Scouring

During the winter, coastal areas of large lakes in much of Canada freeze over, and in cold regions, oceanic waters also do this. When the weather warms up in the springtime, the continuous layer of surface ice breaks up into large chunks that float about, being driven by the wind, currents, or tides, depending on the local circumstances. When the ice impacts a shoreline, it scours the rocks, sediment, and vegetation. The scraping may leave a bare surface that is devoid of ecological development, and so the ice-scouring can be viewed as initiating a local primary succession within a linear environment along the shoreline. These ice-scoured zones are readily apparent along the coast of any waterbodies that are affected in this manner. Along rivers and lakes, for example, the scour-zones are typically dominated by ruderal plants, with annuals prominent in the most heavily scraped places, and short-lived perennials in situations that are relatively protected, for example, on the lee side of large boulders.

On marine shores that are routinely affected by ice-scouring, the local habitats are dominated by annual seaweeds and R-type invertebrates. Bergeron and Bourget (1986) of Université Laval studied heavily ice-scoured shores of the northern Gulf of St. Lawrence. They found that the summer community of sessile organisms was sparse on exposed smooth-rock surfaces in the intertidal zone, but more abundant where there was structural heterogeneity in the form of crevices and cracks in the bedrock, which provide refugia from the ice-scouring. The seaweed *Fucus vesiculosus*, the mussel *Mytilus edulis*, and the barnacle *Semibalanus balanoides* were all much more abundant in crevices. Those organisms partitioned the refuge habitat, with

Bill Freedman

The initial stage of sand-dune succession is the establishment of grasses. They help to stabilize the substrate, causing additional sand to accumulate, and facilitate the invasion of other species of plants as the primary succession proceeds. This image shows sparse clumps of marram grass (*Ammophila breviligulata*), which is the primary invader of exposed sand on coastal beaches in eastern Canada. The image is from Sable Island, Nova Scotia.

Mytilus dominating the bottom of crevices and the other two taxa the zone above (but beneath the scoured areas). Macpherson et al. (2008) of St. Francis Xavier University studied the settlement of larvae of *S. balanoides* on ice-scoured intertidal habitat in the southern Gulf of St. Lawrence in Nova Scotia. They found extensive recruitment of larval barnacles throughout the area during the growing season, but survival and development to the adult stage was limited to microsites that were protected from ice-scouring.

Minchinton et al. (1997) of Dalhousie University studied a rare ice-scouring event on a rocky Atlantic shore of Nova Scotia. This is a region where sea ice does not form, but occasionally in the spring, ice from the St. Lawrence River and the Gulf of St. Lawrence is swept by the wind to the south, where it affects the normally ice-free coast. In this case, the ecologists had been studying intertidal habitats for another purpose prior to the ice-scouring event. However, when the disturbance obliterated the existing community of their study site they opportunistically switched their focus to examine its immediate effects and then the primary succession. Various ephemeral algae such as *Cladophora* and *Ulva lactuca* were the initial colonists and they dominated the ice-scoured habitats for the first growing season. They were soon replaced by perennial algae, such as *Fucus evanescens*, *F. vesiculosus*, *F. spiralis*, and *Chondrus crispus*. The mussels *Mytilus edulis* and *M. trossulus* originally covered more than half of the intertidal habitat, and they were devastated by the ice-scouring. The rate of recovery of the mussels was inversely related to height in the intertidal zone: in the low- and mid-zones, their cover was similar to the original after four years, but in the high-zone it had not recovered even after six post-scour years.

10.5 Secondary Succession

If a disturbance is not so severe that it wipes out all organisms from an affected area, then a measure of in situ regenerative capacity will survive. In such cases, the ecological recovery will involve a **secondary succession**, which includes regeneration by organisms that survived the disturbance, as well as by others that have invaded the disturbed area. Because secondary succession begins with an inherent capacity to regenerate that is associated with survivors, the recovery is more rapid and vigorous than primary succession.

Wildfire

Wildfires are uncontrolled burns, usually affecting natural areas or wilderness, although they may also impact areas close to rural or suburban habitation. Wildfires most commonly affect forests, but shrubby communities, grassland, and sometimes even peatlands may also be affected by this kind of disturbance. Wildfires are common disturbances in Canada, on average affecting about 2.5 million hectares annually, but more than 10 million ha in some years.

For a wildfire to occur there must be a source of ignition, plus an ecosystem with a large enough amount of combustible fuel to maintain the burn and allow it to spread. However, it is not just the amount of fuel that is important—its dryness is another critical factor, and in some cases its chemical composition. Some kinds of plant biomass contain a high concentration of combustible oils or resins, which will burn explosively if ignited. Here is a camping tip—even on a wet day you can start a fire for cooking and warmth if you have some bark of white birch (*Betula papyrifera*) to use as kindling; because of the abundant oils it contains, this material ignites easily and thus it is a wonderful material for starting a fire. Other extremely flammable kinds of biomass include conifer foliage and dry grasses.

Once a wildfire is ignited, its rate of spread is greatly affected by the weather at the time, the recent occurrence of a drought (which dries the fuel), and sometimes the topography (low areas are often wet and do not burn well). Key weather-related factors are the wind speed, relative humidity, and air temperature. However, the wind speed is particularly important, because strong winds can fan the flames and cause an uncontrollable conflagration to occur—one that cannot be quenched even by an army of firefighters using the best equipment. Wind-driven wildfires can easily jump natural firebreaks, such as wetlands and rivers, as well as constructed ones, such as roads and bulldozed gaps.

The largest wildfires typically occur during a windstorm, and they may cover tens of thousands of square kilometres. Some of the most devastating burns that have occurred in Canada include the following:

- Miramichi fire of 1825 in New Brunswick, which affected 12 000 km^2
- Saguenay fire of 1870 in Quebec; 3900 km^2
- Great Porcupine fire of 1911 in Ontario; 2000 km^2
- Great Matheson fire of 1916 in Ontario; 2000 km^2
- Great Temiskaming fire of 1922 in Ontario; 1700 km^2
- Mississagi-Chapleau fire of 1948 in Ontario; 2600 km^2
- Okanagan Mountain fire of 2003 in British Columbia; 2000 km^2

These particular wildfires are famous because they caused huge economic damage and sometimes a considerable loss of human life. Even larger wildfires occur in more remote regions of Canada, but they have not been "named" because they do not pose great risks to homes or businesses.

Many natural ecosystems are viewed as being fire-dependent, in the sense that this particular kind of disturbance is necessary for their periodic regeneration. Over the longer term, such ecosystems are engaged in a cyclic succession that involves repeated iterations of wildfire . . . successional recovery to a vulnerable condition . . . wildfire . . . recovery . . . and so on. Examples of fire-dependent ecosystems in Canada include forests dominated by pines, such as jack pine and lodgepole pine, as well as tallgrass prairie.

In some regions, management policies resulted in the extensive quenching of wildfires in these sorts of fire-prone ecosystems. This is particularly the case in certain regions of pine forests, with the result that landscapes have become increasingly vulnerable to severe fires. Consequently, recent management policies are more sympathetic to the role of fire in dependent ecosystems, and not all ignitions are quenched, unless there is an obvious risk to homes or other economic infrastructure. In some cases, deliberate burns are ignited, known as **prescribed fires**. This is done with the intent of reducing the risk of an uncontrollable conflagration, or to improve the habitat of rare species or endangered kinds of natural communities (such as tallgrass prairie and forest with Garry oak, *Quercus garryi*; see Chapter 14).

It is also possible for natural ecosystems to become degraded by wildfires if they occur too frequently. Usually this involves communities that have been penetrated by invasive alien plants whose biomass is extremely flammable, so that the fire rotation becomes shortened and a positive feedback loop is established that results in a degradation of the ecosystem. In North America, this has become a problem in chaparral and semi-desert in the western United States, particularly in regions affected by the cheatgrass (*Bromus tectorum*) (Brooks and Lusk, 2008). This annual grass accumulates a highly combustible biomass, and a result of it becoming dominant in a community is frequent and intense burns that favour the brome but not most native plants.

A wildfire generally causes severe damage to an affected community: biomass is combusted, many plants are killed by scorching, the forest floor may be partly consumed, erosion may be caused, some animals may die from heat or asphyxiation, and so on. Usually, however, the damage is not so severe that it precludes the affected ecosystem from still retaining a capacity for regeneration by surviving organisms, and by those invading from intact habitats elsewhere. Because of this characteristic ability to regenerate, the post-fire recovery is an example of a secondary succession. And because wildfire is such an important agent of disturbance of natural ecosystems in Canada, it has been widely studied, particularly in regions of boreal and montane forests.

Some of the key observations about wildfire in Canada are the following:

- *A shifting mosaic.* In regions where wildfire is the predominant agent of disturbance, the landscape becomes structured as a shifting mosaic composed of an assortment of stands in various stages of post-fire regeneration. The age-spectrum of the stands ranges from recently burnt to older-growth, the latter typically occurring in habitats that are low and moist, often in the vicinity of wetlands or bodies of water.
- *Within-stand heterogeneity.* When a stand burns, there are often local embedded "skips" where the damage is less or negligible. The skips tend to occur in microhabitats that are low and wet, but the intensity of the burn also has a great influence on this feature—a severe fire has fewer non-burnt areas than a less-severe one.
- *How much is burnt.* Wildfires vary in their intensity, and this greatly affects the amount of the pre-existing biomass that they consume. A ground-fire is a relatively light burn that mostly consumes low-growing vegetation and litter, and because it does not "ladder" into the foliated crown of the stand, many of the trees will survive the event. In contrast, a crown-fire is a much more intensive event that kills many trees, typically leaving many charred snags behind. However, the most severe wildfires may also consume much of the biomass of the dead trees, and even that of the forest floor, so that only an ashy mineral substrate is left and the recovery is by a primary succession.
- *Some plants survive—others do not.* Species of plants differ greatly in their ability to survive a wildfire, and this affects the means by which they regenerate afterward and contribute to the post-fire community. Among trees, for example, most conifer species are vulnerable to being killed by scorching, particularly by a crown fire in which the foliage is burnt; however, species with relatively thick bark, such as red pine, often survive ground fires that do not spread into their canopy. In contrast, the above-ground biomass of trembling aspen (*Populus tremuloides*) may be killed by a wildfire, but the underground rhizomes commonly survive and then regenerate prolifically by issuing large numbers of sprouts. Of course, species whose in situ population is killed by a wildfire must re-colonize the aftermath site to participate in the ensuing community, but they are generally well-adapted to doing this. In contrast, species that survive the disturbance are well-positioned to quickly regenerate afterward, and they are often prominent in the early years of succession.
- *Community change may be complex.* Successional changes in post-fire stands may be represented as a linear relay of species and community

replacements that eventually result in another fire-prone ecosystem. However, this is not necessarily the case, and local species mixes and environmental conditions may result in quite complex changes. Taylor et al. (1987) of the University of Toronto studied these sorts of patterns in a post-fire chronosequence of black-spruce stands up to 120 years old in northern Ontario **(Figure 10.9)**. The younger stands were dominated by reindeer-lichens (*Cladonia gracilis* and *C. rangiferina*), bryophytes, low-growing vascular plants, and a dense regeneration of spruce seedlings. As the canopy cover increased, the ground vegetation changed to stronger dominance by mosses, eventually resulting in a thick mat of feather-mosses such as *Pleurozium scheberi*, *Hylocomium splendens*, and *Ptilium crista-castrensis*. However, on sites that were relatively flat and low, the succession proceeded to a paludification stage that was dominated by peat-mosses (*Sphagnum* species), while under more mesic conditions there was greater prominence of alder (*Alnus rugosa*) and herbaceous plants.

- *Effects on animals.* Many animals suffer directly from a wildfire, particularly in the case of severe burns; they may be killed by heat, scorching, or toxic gases. However, larger animals that are relatively mobile can often flee from a less-intensive wildfire, assuming the burn is not moving so fast that it prevents their escape. In general, however, the indirect effects of a wildfire are more consequential for animals that are living in an affected habitat. By changing the species composition and physical structure of the plant community, a wildfire indirectly affects the kinds of animals that can use the regenerating habitat. For example, some larger animals, such as white-tailed deer (*Odocoileus virginiana*) and elk (*Cervus canadensis*), may receive a nutritional benefit from the abundant and nutritious forage of young woody shoots and herbaceous plants that occurs on regenerating burns, so long as there is also some nearby mature habitat that provides good cover for the animals at night and during the winter. In contrast, woodland caribou (*Rangifer tarandus*) need an extensive cover of older forest in their range, because this is where they obtain their essential winter food of lichens, and so they tend to become less abundant after a wildfire.
- *Pollution.* Wildfires are an important source of emission of pollutants to the atmosphere. The key air pollutants are
  - carbon dioxide (CO_2), an important greenhouse gas, from the combustion of biomass;
  - oxides of nitrogen (NO and NO_2, collectively known as NO_x), which are involved in the photochemical production of ozone as well as acid rain; and
  - and particulates in the form of ash and carbonized materials that are small enough to be wafted over great distances, where they may interfere with visibility and affect people by their odour and by respiratory irritation.

In addition, wildfires in hilly terrain may greatly increase the rate of erosion, and thereby damage aquatic ecosystems by increasing turbidity, siltation, and nutrient loading.

Wildfire also interacts with other natural agents of disturbance, such as windstorms, insect irruptions, and diseases. For example, the presence of large numbers of dead trees because of a recent infestation of insects or a windstorm can set the stage for a catastrophic wildfire if an ignition occurs. This is a present danger in

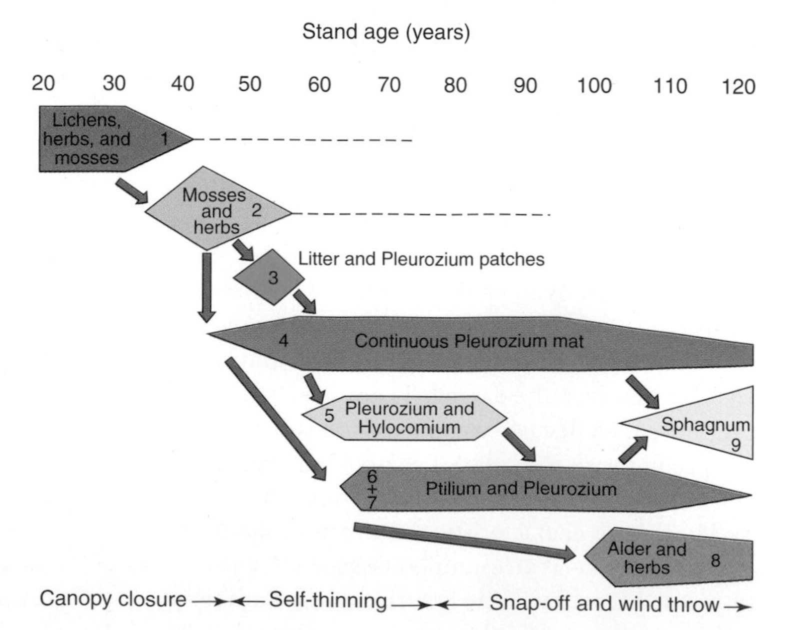

FIGURE 10.9
Changes in Communities of Ground Vegetation during Succession in Post-Fire Stands of Black Spruce in Northern Ontario. The younger stands are dominated by lichens, bryophytes, and low-growing vascular plants, but this changes to a stronger dominance by mosses, and depending on site conditions, may result in a wet community of peat mosses, or a more mesic one of alder and herbs.

SOURCE: Modified from: Taylor, S.J., T.J. Carleton, and P. Adams. 1987. "Understorey vegetation change in a Picea mariana chronosequence," *Vegetatio*, 73: 63–72; with kind permission from Springer Science and Business Media.

A CANADIAN ECOLOGIST 10.1

Yves Bergeron: Succession in the Eastern Boreal Forest

Yves Bergeron

Yves Bergeron of the Université du Québec à Montréal is a plant ecologist who is interested in basic research on the distribution and dynamics of boreal-forest ecosystems. His research on natural systems involves studies of species and communities in the field, supplemented by laboratory work in dendroecology. The basic approach is to examine the relationships among key environmental influences and the distributions and dynamics of species and communities, particularly disturbances in conjunction with abiotic factors such as climate, geomorphology, and soil. His work on natural disturbance regimes has included historical reconstructions of wildfires, windstorms, and insect irruptions.

However, Bergeron is also committed to seeing that his research on natural forest ecosystems results in improved management of forest resources. Within this realm his approach is to assess how the harvest and management of types of boreal-forest communities and landscapes can be undertaken in ways that emulate the effects of natural disturbances. Much of the fieldwork is done at a field-station in the vicinity of Lake Duparquet near Rouyn-Noranda. This well-equipped research facility is jointly run by the Université du Québec à Montréal and the Université du Québec en Abitibi-Temiscamingue, with support provided by federal and provincial governmental agencies and several industrial partners.

Bergeron and his colleagues are running a large and well-funded research program, and it can be judged as successful in several important ways:

- Large numbers of undergraduate and graduate students are being provided with excellent opportunities to engage in ecological research, with a focus of fieldwork in real-world situations.
- There is admirable output in terms of high-level publications in scientific journals and other reputable outlets—this is a clear demonstration of a contribution to the development of ecological science.
- There is an inherent commitment to integrating the outcomes of basic research in ecology with improved ways of managing one of Canada's most important renewable resources—forests and their biomass. This is a helpful contribution to the sustainable development of our country.

much of the interior of British Columbia, where millions of hectares of lodgepole-pine forest have been killed by the mountain pine beetle. Bergeron and Leduc (1999) of the Université du Québec à Montréal found that, in the absence of wildfire, conifer forest in northwestern Quebec became increasingly vulnerable to suffering intense mortality from an infestation of spruce budworm. This was due to the fact that balsam fir, the preferred food of the budworm, steadily increased in prominence the longer that a stand had not been affected by a wildfire.

Irruptive Animals and Diseases

Earlier in this chapter we learned that biological agents can irrupt in abundance and cause stand-replacing disturbances to occur, which are followed by a secondary succession. Examples of native invertebrates that can cause this sort of "natural" damage include the mountain pine beetle in montane pine forests in British Columbia, spruce budworm in fir-spruce forests in eastern Canada, and the green sea urchin in coastal kelp "forests" off Nova Scotia. Some introduced insects can also cause this intensity of damage to occur, including the emerald ash borer (*Agrilus planipennis*) in southern Ontario, as can certain introduced pathogens (usually fungi), such as the ones that cause chestnut blight (*Cryphonectria parasitica*), beech-bark disease (*Cryptococcus fagisuga*), and Dutch elm disease (*Ophiostoma ulmi*). Once these irruptions or diseases have caused their damage, the ecosystem regenerates by a secondary succession. In some cases the ecosystem is resilient and communities similar to the original ones regenerate, so that there is a longer-term stability to the cyclic phenomenon of biological disturbance and recovery. However, in the cases of alien pathogens, different communities eventually regenerate because the vulnerable native species have been eliminated from or greatly reduced in the affected ecosystem.

Numerous studies have been made of the effects of spruce budworm on affected conifer forest, and also of the subsequent recovery. The budworm is a native moth, and the preferred foods of its larvae are young cones and foliage of balsam fir, followed by those of white and then red spruce. The budworm is always present in a low density (referred to as an *endemic population level*) in mature forest within its range, but occasionally its populations increase rapidly in abundance, and when this occurs extensive damage may be caused to trees. It appears that periodic irruptions of eastern spruce budworm have long occurred in vulnerable boreal landscapes. J. R. Blais (1965) of the Canadian Forest Service studied the ring-width patterns of old host trees and established a budworm-outbreak chronology extending to the 18th century in Laurentide Park, Quebec. He found that budworm infestations had occurred at fairly regular intervals, and had begun in 1704, 1748, 1808, 1834, 1910, and 1947, plus one that was occurring at the time of his study, for a mean periodicity of about 35 years (see also **Figures 10.10** and **10.11**).

David MacLean (1984) of the University of New Brunswick found that spruce budworm causes a progressive tree mortality; about 4 percent of fir trees were dead after two years of heavy defoliation, 9 percent after four years, 22 percent after five years, 48 percent after eight years, 75 percent after ten years, and 95 percent after twelve years. Much of the mortality occurs after the budworm population has collapsed, as weakened trees succumb to environmental stresses that might otherwise be tolerated, particularly during the winter. Blais (1981) studied stands in the Ottawa Valley of Quebec in which a budworm outbreak had collapsed in 1975, at which time the mortality of balsam fir averaged 44 percent, but this increased to 91 percent after four additional years following the collapse of the irruption; during the same period, the mortality of spruce increased from 17 percent to 52 percent.

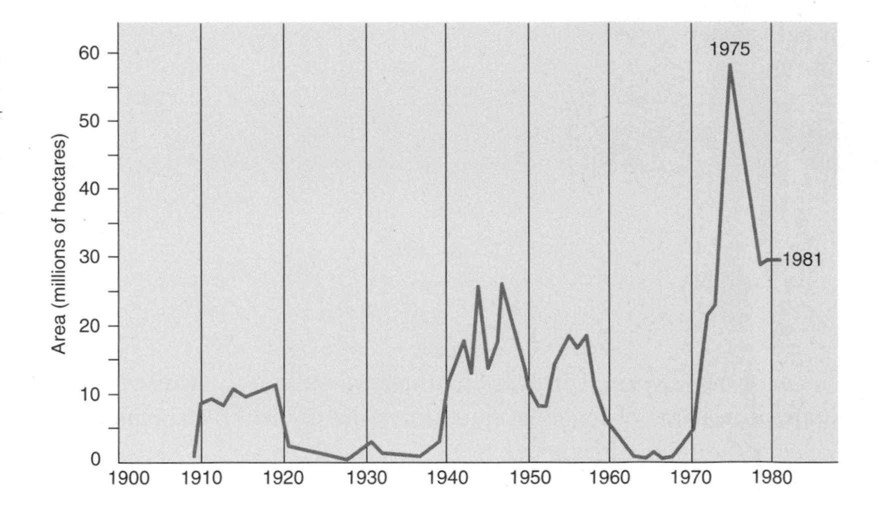

FIGURE 10.10

Area of Forest Affected by Spruce Budworm during the 20th Century. The data are for stands suffering moderate-to-severe levels of defoliation, and their pattern suggests that the irruptions became more extensive and prolonged over time. The most recent irruption collapsed in the early 1990s.

SOURCE: Modified from: Kettela, E. 1983. *A Cartographic History of Spruce Budworm Defoliation from 1967 to 1981 in Eastern North America.* Information Report DPC-X-14, Maritimes Forest Research Centre, Canadian Forestry Service, Fredericton, New Brunswick. Reprinted with permission of the Minister of Public Works and Government Services Canada, 2010.

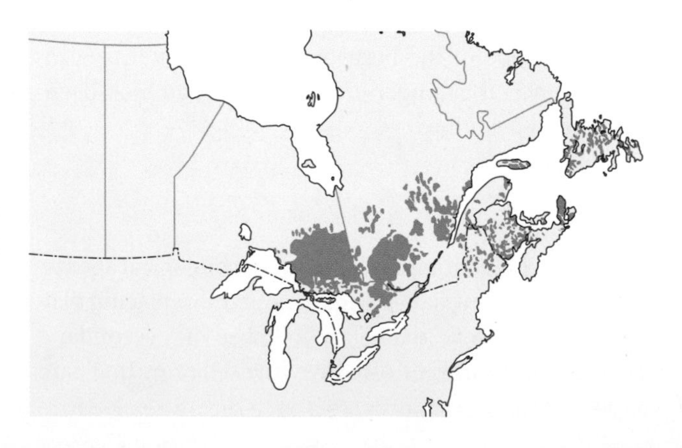

FIGURE 10.11

Regions Suffering Forest Damage Caused by the Most Recent Irruption of Spruce Budworm. The data are for stands suffering moderate-to-severe levels of defoliation.

SOURCE: Modified from: Kettela, E. 1983. *A Cartographic History of Spruce Budworm Defoliation from 1967 to 1981 in Eastern North America.* Information Report DPC-X-14, Maritimes Forest Research Centre, Canadian Forestry Service, Fredericton, New Brunswick. Reprinted with permission of the Minister of Public Works and Government Services Canada, 2010.

Bill Freedman

Spruce budworm (*Choristoneura fumiferana*) is a native moth that sometimes irrupts in abundance and damages mature forest dominated by balsam fir (*Abies balsamea*) and white spruce (*Picea glauca*). This image shows a fir-spruce forest on the highlands of Cape Breton Island, Nova Scotia, that was damaged by several years of intense defoliation by budworm during an irruption in the 1970s and 1980s. The surviving trees around the wetland are black spruce (*P. mariana*), which is relatively resistant to defoliation by the budworm.

Although mature fir and spruce trees are heavily defoliated and often killed by budworm, smaller individuals of these species are not much affected and they form an abundant advanced regeneration in the understorey of affected stands. For example, stands on the highlands of Cape Breton that were severely defoliated had an average density of 45 000 balsam fir per hectare and 3250 spruce/ha (MacLean, 1988). Most of these small individuals of tree species survived the budworm infestation, and then grew quickly in the aftermath succession to establish the next fir-spruce forest. Other low-growing plants of the ground vegetation also responded favourably to opening of the forest canopy by budworm-caused mortality, with large increases occurring in the abundances of shield fern (*Dryopteris carthusiana*), large-leaved goldenrod (*Solidago macrophylla*), wild sarsaparilla (*Aralia nudicaulis*), wood sorrel (*Oxalis montana*), and red raspberry (*Rubus strigosus*). Eventually, the secondary succession results in the development of another mature fir-spruce forest, which will again be vulnerable to supporting an irruption of budworm.

Overall, the dynamic budworm-conifer system can be viewed as a cyclic succession that has a longer-term ecological stability, and it has likely recurred on the landscape for thousands of years. Evidence supporting the hypothesis of longer-term stability includes (a) the presence of large areas of relatively even-aged forest dominated by balsam fir and white spruce; (b) the observed seral trajectory following stand-replacing disturbance by the budworm; and (c) paleoecological data showing that budworm outbreaks are ancient and periodic.

In contrast to this apparent longer-term ecological stability, the budworm causes economic instability by damaging a forest resource that is needed for the production of paper and lumber. In a sense, this native moth and the forest industry are in competition for a limited resource—fir-spruce forest. To try to manage the economic damages associated with budworm-caused resource depletion, tens of millions of hectares of conifer forest in eastern Canada were sprayed with various insecticides from the 1960s to 1993. A cumulative area of more than 118 million ha was treated with insecticide, including stands that were repeatedly sprayed in various years (Freedman, 2010; see also Chapter 15). The insecticide spraying was not intended to eradicate the budworm. Rather, the intent was to reduce its abundance enough that fir and spruce trees were not killed, and so would be available to be harvested by the forest industry.

Timber Harvesting

Timber harvesting is an important economic activity in Canada: in 2006, about 1 million hectares of forest were harvested, 91 percent by clear-cutting (Chapter 12). Tree seedlings were planted on 45 percent of the harvested area to establish plantations, and the rest regenerated naturally. As we previously noted in this chapter, the regeneration of plants after clear-cutting involves several mechanisms:

- growth by individual plants that survived the disturbance, including any advanced regeneration of smaller individuals of tree species;
- "new" plants that established as seedlings from the in situ seed bank or from seeds dispersed by surviving local plants;
- immigrants arriving as seeds that blew in or were transported by animals from elsewhere; and
- the natural regeneration may be augmented by foresters, who may plant seedlings of economically desired species of trees.

In some respects, natural regeneration after timber harvesting resembles the secondary succession that occurs following a wildfire in the comparable forest (see Environmental Applications 10.2). Of course, this is not exactly the case, particularly in situations where foresters have managed the post-harvest regeneration through some kind of silvicultural prescription (**silviculture** refers to management practices in forestry; Chapter 15). As just noted, this might involve the planting of conifer seedlings, but it can also include the use of herbicide to reduce the effects on crop trees of competition from "weeds," and mechanically thinning of an overly dense regeneration (usually achieved using motorized saws).

In Chapter 15 we examine information that is relevant to the recovery of forests after clear-cutting. For example, **Figure 15.6** shows the successional recovery of biomass after clear-cutting of hardwood forest, and **Table 15.4** examines some effects on birds. In this chapter, **Figure 10.4** provides a conceptual model of biomass recovery, while **Figure 10.5** examines patterns of change in selected indicators of biodiversity. Here, however, we examine studies of the effects of silvicultural management on the successional trajectory of plant communities after timber harvesting. We can do this by examining **Figure 10.12**, which shows data from a study in Nova Scotia of the effects of herbicide spraying in forestry. The research involved four experimental plots of about 5 hectares each that were sampled over a four-year period. The raw data are based on the amount of foliage cover of all plant species that were present in a grid of 32 permanently located quadrats of 1 m^2 per plot, which represents a huge database consisting of many species, treatment-plots, and years. This great complexity of information was mathematically reduced by the use of a multivariate analysis known as ordination. This method allows the plant "communities" occurring in the various plots and study years to be represented by relatively simple multivariate vectors, each of which reflects the mathematical influences of numerous variables, including the presence and relative abundances of all plant species in each of the plot-years. This analysis greatly reduces the complexity of the data to patterns that can be interpreted relatively easily.

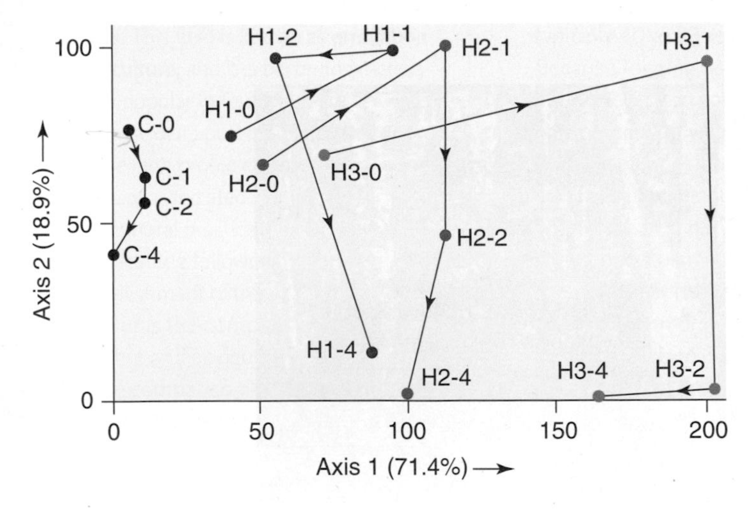

FIGURE 10.12

Effects of Silvicultural Herbicide Application on the Regeneration of Clear-Cuts in Nova Scotia. This study involved four experimental plots of about 5 hectares each. The original field data consisted of the cover of foliage (which is related to biomass) of all plant species present in a grid of 32 quadrats of 1 m^2 per plot. The mathematical analysis involved a multivariate technique called ordination, which develops single values (vectors) based on the data of all species at the time of sampling. The first axis represents the best multivariate fit to the initial variation of each dataset, and the second axis is the best fit to the residual data. All of the plots had their vegetation sampled in the first year of the study (C-0, H1-0, H2-0, H3-0). Three of the plots (H1, H2, H3) were then sprayed with the herbicide glyphosate to "release" small conifer seedlings from the effects of competition with other plants, while one (C) was left unsprayed as a control treatment. The vegetation of all of the plots was re-sampled in the first, second, and fourth post-spray years.

SOURCE: Modified from: Freedman, B., R. Morash, and D.S. MacKinnon. 1993. "Short-term changes in vegetation after the silvicultural spraying of glyphosate herbicide onto regenerating clearcuts in central Nova Scotia," *Canadian Journal of Forest Research*, 23(10): 2300–2311.

In this study of the effects of herbicide spraying, all of the plots had their vegetation sampled in the first year of the study. Then three of the plots received a silvicultural spray of the herbicide glyphosate to reduce the abundance of "weeds" that were competing with the economically desired conifer seedlings, while one plot was left unsprayed as a control. The analysis shows that, prior to the herbicide spraying, all four plots had similar plant communities (these are the plot-years C-0, H1-0, H2-0, and H3-0 in **Figure 10.12**). Over the subsequent four years of the study, the vegetation of the control plot did not change much, reflecting the normal course of secondary succession after clear-cutting (C-0, C-1, C-2, and C-4). In contrast, the herbicide-treated plots showed much larger changes in their vegetation. Initially, the herbicide resulted in large decreases in the amount of plant foliage, as well as changes in the relative abundances of species, but this was followed by a strong post-spray recovery (see also **Figure 10.13**). After four post-spray years, the herbicide-treated plots had almost the same plant cover as the control. None of the initial species of plants were lost from the plots treated with herbicide, although there were changes in their relative abundances that reflected differences in the plant communities.

Of course, there are also successional dynamics in animal communities after timber harvesting. In general, animals are not much affected by the direct effects of timber harvesting—they are not killed or injured by falling trees. Rather, their response is indirect and caused by the profound alterations of habitat conditions that are associated with changes in the species composition, abundance, and physical structure of plants. For example, when a stand of forest is

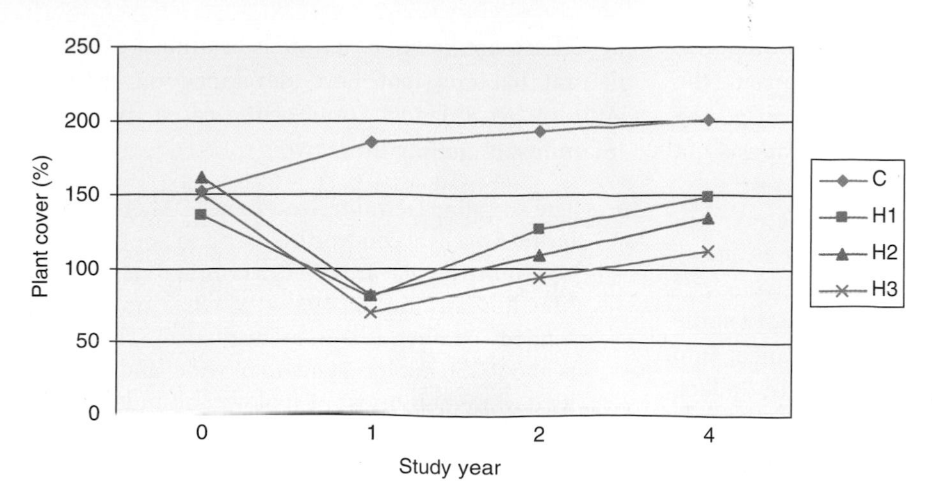

FIGURE 10.13

Changes in Plant Cover as a Result of Herbicide Treatment of Regenerating Clear-Cuts in Nova Scotia. The data show the initial plant cover in four communities (year 0), followed by the ensuing four years after being treated with the herbicide glyphosate (H1, H2, and H3), plus a non-sprayed control treatment (C). See text for further explanation.

SOURCE: Modified from: Freedman, B., R. Morash, and D.S. MacKinnon. 1993. "Short-term changes in vegetation after the silvicultural spraying of glyphosate herbicide onto regenerating clearcuts in central Nova Scotia," *Canadian Journal of Forest Research*, 23: 2300–2311. (Page 2303)

clear-cut, the bird community dependent on mature habitat becomes totally replaced by a different one that prefers younger vegetation. This effect is illustrated in **Table 15.4** (Chapter 15), which compares bird communities among stands of mature hardwood forest and recent clear-cuts. The forest and clear-cuts both supported rich avian communities, but the species of birds present in them were almost completely different (see also **Figure 10.5** in this chapter).

In contrast, herbicide spraying has much less of an effect on the breeding birds of treated clear-cuts. In a study of herbicide-treated sites in Nova Scotia, there were large initial changes in the vegetation, but the responses of birds were not as great **(Table 10.1)**. The abundance of birds decreased between the pre-spray and first post-spray years of the study, but this also occurred on the non-sprayed (or control) site, which suggests that it may have been caused by a factor unrelated to the herbicide treatment (such as weather). In the second year after spraying, the bird population on the sprayed plots remained similar to the first post-spray year, but on the unsprayed plot it increased to about the pre-spray value, possibly indicating a moderate effect of the herbicide treatment. The initially most abundant species were white-throated sparrow and common yellowthroat, which decreased on both the sprayed and reference plots in the second year after spraying and then recovered by the fourth post-spray year. On the reference plot, song sparrow and Lincoln's sparrow both declined because of habitat change during succession, whereas on the sprayed plots they were most abundant in the second and fourth years. Some new species colonized the reference plot as it matured, such as black-and-white

TABLE 10.1 Populations of Birds on Clear-Cuts Treated with Glyphosate Herbicide in Nova Scotia

The data are pairs of breeding birds per km^2, surveyed before the herbicide treatment (year 0) and then for four post-spray years. The data for sprayed plots are the average of four replicates; only abundant species are listed.

Species		Sprayed Plots				Control Plot			
	Year:	0	1	2	4	0	1	2	4
alder flycatcher (*Empidonax alnorum*)		36	7	17	63	20	40	41	102
American robin (*Turdus migratorius*)		14	21	30	31	10	10	20	10
red-eyed vireo (*Vireo olivaceous*)		0	0	0	4	0	10	31	41
magnolia warbler (*Dendroica magnolia*)		5	5	5	102	0	20	20	143
palm warbler (*Dendroica palmarum*)		0	4	18	53	0	10	51	31
mourning warbler (*Oporornis philadelphia*)		50	13	12	19	71	41	20	31
common yellowthroat (*Geothlypis trichas*)		151	140	90	136	122	112	122	163
white-throated sparrow (*Zonotrichia albicollis*)		203	118	89	155	143	71	93	163
dark-eyed junco (*Junco hyemalis*)		42	62	61	69	31	41	61	102
Lincoln's sparrow (*Melospiza lincolnii*)		23	20	41	44	20	+	+	0
song sparrow (*Melospiza melodia*)		43	28	60	86	41	20	10	10
American goldfinch (*Carduelis tristis*)		52	24	15	13	61	41	20	20
Total Birds		623	447	444	805	539	396	528	836

SOURCE: Data are from MacKinnon and Freedman (1993).

warbler, red-eyed vireo, ruby-throated hummingbird, and palm warbler. However, these did not invade the herbicided plots because that treatment caused the habitat to revert to a younger condition that was not suitable for these birds.

Abandoned Land

Often, natural ecosystems are converted into some sort of anthropogenic land use, for instance, into residential, industrial, or agricultural lands. In fact, these changes from natural land use to anthropogenic are the most important cause of damage to biodiversity today (Chapter 14). Sometimes, however, the converted lands become abandoned from their anthropogenic use, and this is followed by a period of ecological recovery. Typically, the recovery involves a primary succession, because the condition at abandonment is so devegetated that the sere must begin with an invasion of the site by local vagile organisms. Often, however, some organisms are initially present, such as horticultural plantings or weedy species, and in those cases the sere has qualities of a secondary succession. But in either case, the regenerating site becomes rapidly invaded by many ruderal species, which then dominate the early stages of the sere. Over time the site regenerates to a semi-natural condition, typically supporting a mixture of alien and native species. As further time passes, however, the relative prominence of the alien species may decrease and that of the native ones increases. As that happens the regenerating ecosystem becomes increasingly more "natural," and its ecological integrity improves (Chapter 17).

We have all encountered these sorts of places. In urban areas, disused lands are commonly regarded as being in a "derelict" condition—they may, for instance, be places where a building has been demolished, so the site is covered with rubble and garbage. Nevertheless, these open spaces do become invaded by various ruderal organisms, mostly by alien species, and depending on the regional climate and site conditions, they may eventually recover to a grassland or forested condition. In more rural places, there is a stronger likelihood that a post-abandonment succession will develop into a relatively natural community. For example, in eastern Canada, large areas of lower-quality farmland have been abandoned for agricultural purposes. This occurred because people were unable to earn a living on relatively small and hardscrabble farms, so they left them and migrated to cities and towns to find work. The abandoned cropland and pastures spontaneously underwent a so-called "old-field succession" that culminated in a cover of mature forest.

There are many other such examples of semi-natural habitats that have developed on disused anthropogenic lands. Some of the cases are rather infamous, including these two:

- The so-called Demilitarized Zone (DMZ) marks a buffer area between North Korea and South Korea, two countries that are still in a nominal state of war (the Korean War of 1950–1953 has not legally "ended"—rather, it is in an armistice). The DMZ is about 250 km long and 4 km wide, and prior to its designation, most of its lower-altitude terrain was in agricultural use. For the past half-century, however, the DMZ has functionally been a "protected area" because its boundaries are rigorously guarded against military incursions as well as most economic uses, including agriculture and hunting. Today, extensive tracts within the DMZ have developed into a natural condition and the area supports the best-conserved habitats on the Korean peninsula. The DMZ provides habitat for a wealth of native biodiversity, including many endangered species. It is hoped that even after a negotiated peace returns to the Korean peninsula, the present DMZ will continue to be managed as an officially designated protected area.
- In 1986, the worst-ever disaster involving a civilian nuclear-power facility occurred at Chernobyl, Ukraine. It was caused by an ill-planned technical experiment involving a test of the emergency cooling system, but that resulted in an uncontrolled fission reaction that caused a meltdown of the fissile material in one of the four reactors of the power plant. The immense heat generated by uncontrolled nuclear reactions quickly resulted in massive explosions of steam and chemicals (likely of hydrogen gas—it was not a nuclear explosion) and an intense graphite-fuelled fire (graphite was the moderator used to control the nuclear reactions during power generation). The explosions and fires released huge amounts of radioactive gases and dusts to the atmosphere, in plumes that dispersed widely so that contamination was detected as far away as western Europe and even beyond. However, by far the worst polluted areas were in Belarus, Russia, and Ukraine. More than 300 000 people were evacuated in those countries, and although most have since returned to their homes, there is still an Exclusion Zone (EZ) of about 2300 km^2 that remains badly polluted by radioactivity. Prior to the nuclear disaster, the EZ was mostly in urbanized and agricultural land uses, but since then much of the area has been steadily reverting to a more natural condition, and it now supports forested and wetland habitats that are otherwise uncommon in the greater region. Because of the toxic threat of radioactive pollution, hunting is prohibited in the EZ, so larger

animals are relatively abundant. In 1990, the Government of Ukraine designated the EZ as a wildlife sanctuary.

In addition to these cases, there are interesting Canadian examples of the regeneration of semi-natural habitats onto disused lands:

- The Outer Harbour East Headland, more popularly known as the Leslie Street Spit, is a constructed peninsula on the Toronto waterfront that extends into Lake Ontario, where its presence forms an outer protected harbour for the city. Its development began in the late 1950s and was mostly completed by the late 1980s. It proceeded as a two-stage process:
    1. the construction of a 5 km long spine into shallow coastal lake waters by the dumping of rocks, concrete, and other coarse fill obtained during the excavation of foundations for office towers and other buildings, plus inert construction waste, and
    2. the infilling of wide flat areas on the inner side of the spine by dumping a sand-silt material known as "dredgeate," which was obtained during the dredging of the commercially important inner harbour of the city.

    Because the dredgeate is a somewhat fertile material, when dumped on land it supported a vigorous ecological development, which in some areas has culminated in a bottomland forest dominated by cottonwood (*Populus deltoides*) and other terrestrial and wetland communities. The spit now supports an impressive amount of biodiversity, including at least 400 species of plants and more than 300 of birds, including 66 that breed there. In terms of conservation value, the most important of the breeding birds are common tern (*Sterna hirundo*), Caspian tern (*Hydroprogne caspia*), and black-crowned night heron (*Nycticorax nycticorax*), but the most abundant ones are as many as 100 000 pairs of ring-billed gull (*Larus delawarensis*) and 6 000 double-crested cormorant (*Phalacrocorax auritus*), herring gull (*L. argentatus*), and Canada goose (*Branta canadensis*). The site is now an urban park, and its most critical habitats have been set aside as protected areas for wildlife.
- At Copper Cliff near Sudbury, Ontario, a mining company has disposed of large amounts of a waste material known as tailings in low areas. Tailings are a silt-sized waste material that is left after mined ore has been crushed to a powder and its metallic content removed for processing. The tailings disposal areas are hundreds of hectares in area, and once they are filled up they are initially stabilized by planting a mixture of pasture species. They are then left alone to further revegetate spontaneously. Typically the revegetated tailings dumps have a central pond, which is surrounded by gradually sloping terrestrial vegetation. As vegetated habitat develops on the area, animals begin to invade. More than 90 species of birds occur on the reclaimed tailings dump and its pond at Copper Cliff, and some that breed there include savannah sparrow (*Passerculus sandwichensis*), killdeer (*Charadrius vociferus*), and mallard and black ducks (*Anas platyrhynchos* and *A. rubripes*).
- Shannon Tomlinson et al. (2008) of the University of Guelph examined spontaneous plant communities that had developed on 13 abandoned limestone quarries in southern Ontario, and compared them to those of alvars, a rare natural habitat. Alvars occur where limestone bedrock erupts at the surface, and because of its unusual soil chemistry (high pH and rich in calcium) and tendency to have pooled water in the spring but drought later in the growing

Bill Freedman

A view of semi-natural habitat on the Leslie Street Spit, located on the shore of Lake Ontario at Toronto. The trees are a naturally established stand of cottonwood (*Populus deltoides*), some of which have been damaged by the caustic excrement of colonial-nesting double-crested cormorants (*Phalacrocorax auritus*).

season, this habitat supports unusual communities and often many species-at-risk. Tomlinson et al. found that although the abandoned quarries supported many alien species, their communities also provided habitat for 24 native plants that are characteristic of alvar habitats, plus an additional five that occur only on alvars. They concluded that the development of alvar-like communities may be a reasonable goal of ecological restoration after limestone quarries are abandoned. If this were routinely done, there could be increased populations of some rare and endangered species. It is important to note, however, that these benefits may be offset by the destruction of natural alvars by the development of new quarries for their limestone rock—the alvars can never be fully restored from this kind of destructive use.

These examples show that land that is abandoned from anthropogenic uses can regenerate successionally to a semi-natural condition, to the degree that important ecological values are supported. This is a good thing. Nevertheless it is important to recognize that such developments do not represent adequate or even substantive offsets against the ecological damages that are caused by the reverse process—that of ongoing conversions of natural ecosystems into anthropogenic ones. The ecological damages caused by such losses of natural habitats are the leading cause of the ongoing biodiversity crisis, as we examine in Chapter 14.

VOCABULARY OF ECOLOGY

advanced regeneration, p. 305
aggradation phase, p. 306
chronosequence, p. 308
climatic climax, p. 299
climax, p. 299
conversion, p. 296
deglaciation, p. 310
devegetation, p.306
disclimax, p. 299
disturbance, p.291
ecotone, p. 299
edaphic climax, p. 299
emulation silviculture, p. 322
facilitation model, p. 302
gap-phase microdisturbance, p. 299
gap-phase microsuccession, p. 292
glaciation, p. 295
homogecene, p. 297
hydrosere, p. 301
inhibition model, p. 303
irrupt, p. 294
lithosere, p. 301
microdisturbance, p. 292
microsuccession, p. 292
monoclimax, p. 299
nucleation, p. 314
paludification, p. 312
polyclimax, p. 299
population-replacing disturbance, p. 296
prescribed fire, p. 317
primary succession, p. 309
psammosere, p. 301
ramet, p. 305
refugia, p. 295
re-organization phase, p. 306
resilience, p. 291
resistance (or tolerance), p. 292
return frequency (or rotation), p. 297
secondary succession, p. 316
seed bank, p. 305
seral stage, p. 298
sere, p. 298
serotiny, p. 305
shifting mosaic, p. 293
silviculture, p. 324
stand-replacing disturbance, p. 293
step-cline, p. 299
succession, p. 291
tolerance model, p. 303
vegetative regeneration, p. 304

QUESTIONS FOR REVIEW AND DISCUSSION

1. What is a stand-replacing disturbance? Provide two examples of their natural causes, and two that are anthropogenic.
2. Define resistance and resilience, and give examples of each. What factors result in decreasing levels of resistance and resilience in ecosystems?
3. What are the key differences between primary and secondary successions? Provide examples of each.
4. Why is wildfire such a common and extensive agent of disturbance in Canada? Is it a natural force, or an anthropogenic one? What factors should be considered when making a decision about whether to fight a forest fire?
5. What are key similarities and differences between wildfire and clear-cutting?
6. Find a plot of land that has been abandoned from an anthropogenic use in the area where you live, and describe how managed and/or spontaneous successional processes are restoring an improved habitat condition. Make a list of the most prominent species that are now present on the disused land, note whether they are native or alien, and comment on the implications for ecological integrity.

HELPFUL WEBSITES

FOREST ENCYCLOPEDIA NETWORK (DISTURBANCE AND SUCCESSION)

http://www.forestencyclopedia.net/p/p1448

This site provides information about forests, in both global and eastern U.S. contexts.

PHYSICAL GEOGRAPHY.NET (SUCCESSION)

http://www.physicalgeography.net/fundamentals/9i.html

This e-book is produced by Michael Pidwirny of the University of British Columbia, Okanagan Campus.

You'll find a rich array of additional resources for *Ecology* at www.ecology.nelson.com.

Second, ecological research is only doable if the complexity of the natural world is aggregated into units that can be studied—into clusters that reflect common attributes among species and their environmental circumstances. This is true of basic research in ecology, which is motivated by curiosity. It is also relevant to applied ecological work, which is driven by the need to develop practical solutions to problems, such as how to properly manage a forest or fishery, or to avoid or repair damages caused by pollution or disturbance.

Ecologists have developed classification schemes that allow them to investigate the natural world by dividing its complexity into reasonably discrete groups that represent distinct assemblies. In essence, ecologists have aggregated ecological variation into clusters that have a general similarity of structure and function. This is similar to how climatologists have grouped factors related to longer-term weather conditions into broad climatic zones, and have portrayed them on geographic maps that provide valuable information to engineers, architects, ecologists, and gardeners. The ecological clusters are referred to by various names, such as biomes and ecozones, and they are the topic of this chapter.

Biomes

At the global level, the largest kinds of ecosystem clusters are known as **biomes**. Each biome exists over an extensive geographic range, and it occurs anywhere in the world that the environmental conditions support its development. The morphological and physiological traits of the dominant organisms, or their **life form**, provide the defining characteristics of a biome. This means that the particular complement of species that is present is not the distinguishing feature—rather, it is their life form.

The primary characteristic of terrestrial biomes is their late-successional natural vegetation. The most influential environmental factors that affect the development of terrestrial biomes are the prevailing climatic conditions, with soil, bedrock, and other factors playing a lesser role. In marine biomes, the dominant animals are the distinguishing feature and physical oceanography and nutrient supply are the key environmental influences.

Although biomes are characterized by their existing qualities, they are refined products of the evolution of species and the spontaneous organization of their communities over long periods of time—even millions of years—under the prevailing environmental regimes. During those extended times, the biodiversity occurring within biomes changed and re-organized in response to the influences of evolution, extinction, and environmental variations. In Canada, for example, almost all biomes that exist today have spontaneously re-organized since the time of deglaciation some 10 000–12 000 years ago. Some of the original species of immediate post-glacial times are now extinct, such as the mastodon, mammoths, giant bison, sabre-toothed tiger, and other elements of a lost megafauna of the Pleistocene era (see Chapter 14).

The global distribution of the major terrestrial biomes is shown in **Figure 11.1**, and their range in North America is shown in **Figure 11.2.** The location and boundaries of the biomes are influenced by the distribution of environmental conditions that support the species that are their dominant life forms. The range of terrestrial biomes is mostly affected by soil moisture and the temperature

All situations are unique, but ecosystems may be similar enough to be grouped according to their commonalities of species and environmental conditions. In ecology, the largest such groupings are known as biomes. This landscape in southwestern Alberta is in the montane forest biome and also in the montane cordillera ecozone. Ecological communities that are visible include alpine tundra, open montane forest of lodgepole pine (*Pinus contorta*) at treeline, and lower-altitude closed montane forest.

Bill Freedman

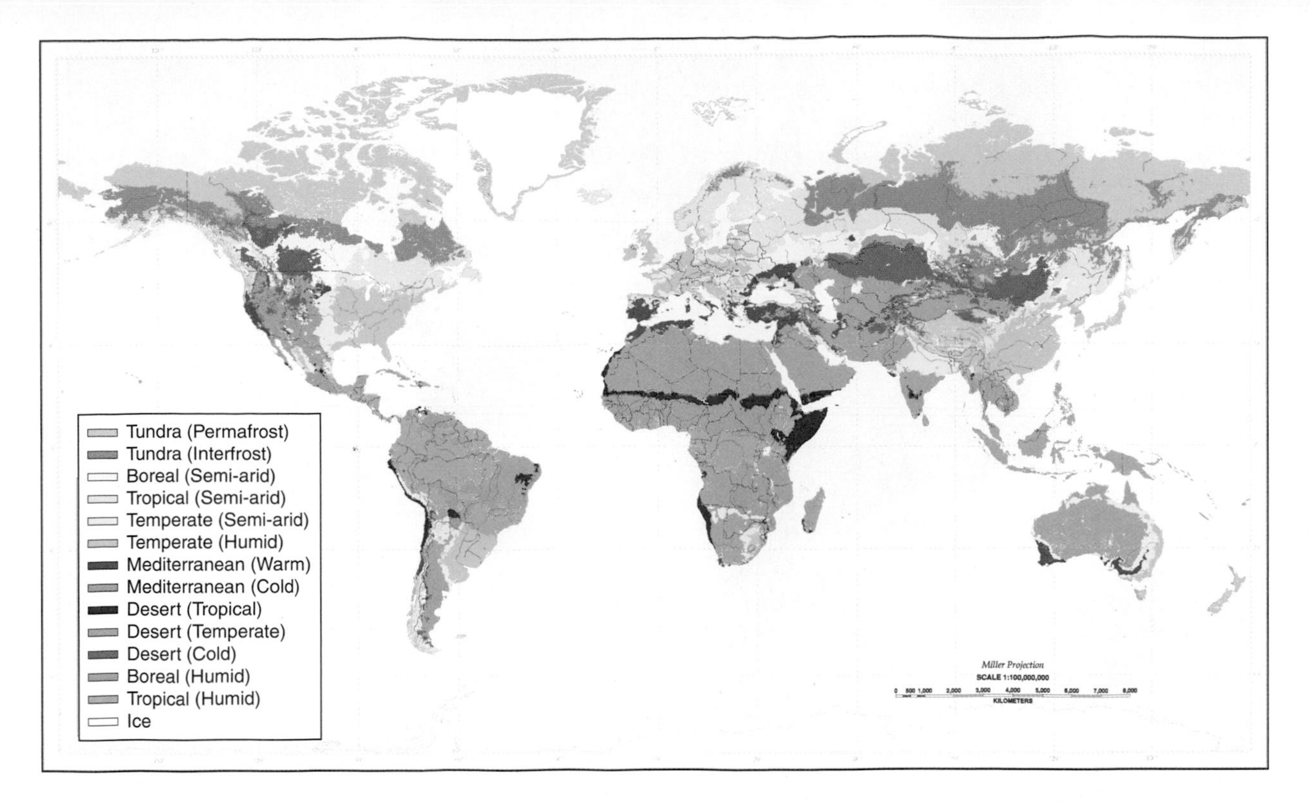

FIGURE 11.1

Global Distribution of the Terrestrial Biomes. Biomes are wide-ranging ecosystems that are similar in their structure and function and occur wherever environmental conditions are suitable for their development. Typically, however, the same biome on different continents is dominated by different species.

SOURCE: Modified from USDA. 2009. Major Biomes Map. United States Department of Agriculture, Natural Resources Conservation Service. Washington, DC. http://soils.usda.gov/use/worldsoils/mapindex/biomes.html

regime **(Figure 11.3)**. However, within a terrestrial biome, various distinct communities may occur; for example, an environmental gradient may be associated with moisture or elevation, which will affect the local habitats and the kinds of communities that are present. In a region of temperate forest, this can result in different communities of forest. If there is surface water there may also be various communities within streams, rivers, lakes, and wetlands such as swamps and marshes.

In the case of freshwater habitats, the local occurrence of surface water and the nutrient supply are key influences on the communities that develop. In the marine realm, open-water biomes are largely affected by water depth and its relation to the availability of light for autotrophs, as well as the distribution of upwellings of nutrient-rich deeper water to the surface. Benthic marine biomes are influenced by water currents and the physical characteristics of the substrate, and coastal ones by those factors along with the intensity of wave action.

Biomes, which are defined by their similarity of structure and classified by their dominant life forms, may develop in varying geographical regions and even on different continents if the right environmental conditions are available **(Figure 11.1)**. Nevertheless, different species may dominate in widely separated regions of the same biome. Although those dominant species may not be closely related in a phylogenetic sense, their life forms are convergent, which means they are similar in anatomy, physiology, and other key attributes. Their **convergent evolution** has occurred because although they inhabit widely spaced places, the environmental conditions are similar and so therefore are the regimes of natural selection. This results in parallel (or convergent) evolutionary responses of species occurring in far-flung reaches of a biome.

To illustrate the results of convergent evolution in a terrestrial context, we can examine the dominant life forms of the boreal forest that exists in northern tracts of Canada, Alaska, and Eurasia. This high-latitude biome is positioned south of the arctic tundra and north of the temperate forest and prairie grasslands. Its environment involves long and cold winters, short but warm summers, long days during

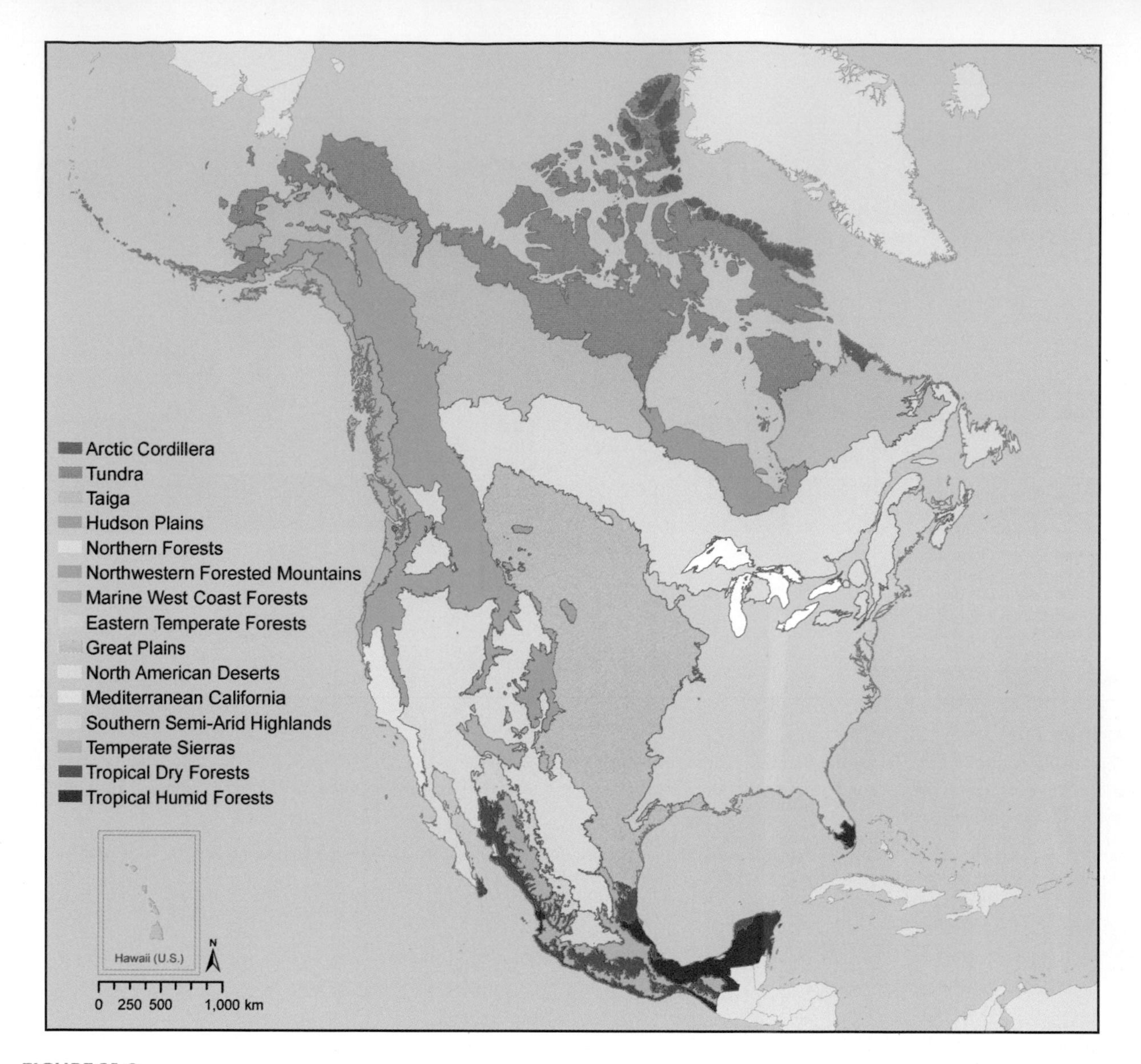

FIGURE 11.2

Distribution of the 15 Terrestrial Ecoregions (Level 1) Designated for North America. These are North American representatives of global biomes, such as tundra and boreal forest.

SOURCE: Commission for Environmental Cooperation. 1997. *Ecological Regions of North America: Toward a Common Perspective.*

the growing season, moist soil conditions, and a stand-replacing disturbance regime associated with wildfires, windstorms, and insect epidemics. Coniferous trees usually dominate the boreal forest, but the particular species of conifer differ among far-flung regions of the biome.

Most of the boreal forest of northern Canada is covered by stands of mature black spruce (*Picea mariana*). In some areas, however, balsam fir (*Abies balsamea*), jack pine (*Pinus banksiana*), tamarack (*Larix laricina*), or white spruce (*Picea glauca*) may be the prevailing species. In northern Eurasia, the boreal forest is dominated by other species of the same genera. In Scandinavia there are Norway spruce (*Picea abies*) and Scotch pine (*Pinus sylvestris*). Northern Russia has yet other species, such as *Abies sibirica*, *Larix sibirica*, *Picea obovata*, and *Pinus sibirica*. In the boreal regions of northern Japan, Korea, and far-eastern Russia, the boreal climate is relatively moderate because of the proximity of the Pacific Ocean, and these regions have yet other species of coniferous trees. Nevertheless, these various kinds of conifer-dominated boreal forests are similar ecosystems—their component species are convergent entities in an evolutionary and ecological sense.

Even though their ecosystems are structurally and functionally similar, biomes are not homogeneous across vast distances. Biomes are characterized by their

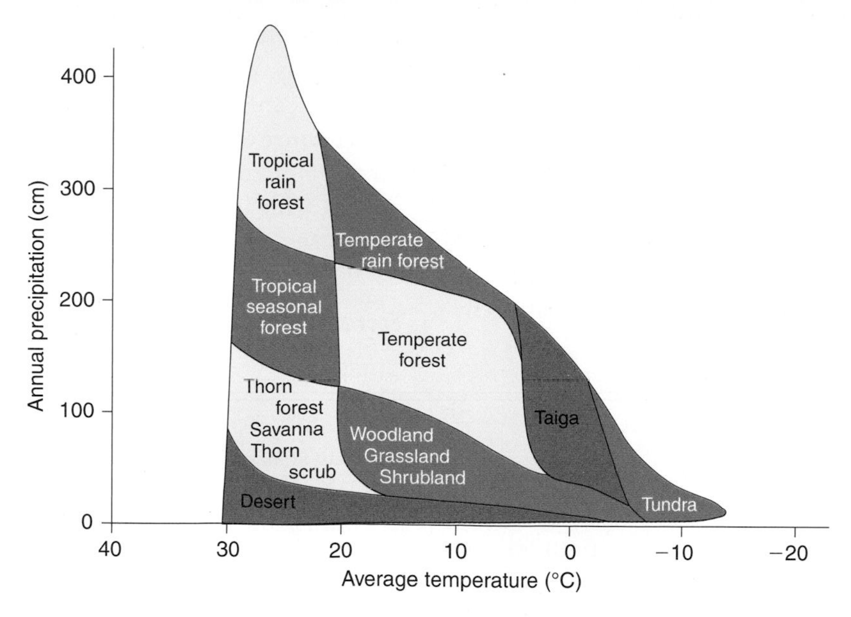

FIGURE 11.3
Average Temperature and Soil Moisture Are Key Factors Influencing the Distribution of Terrestrial Biomes.

SOURCE: Modified from Odum/Barrett. *Fundamentals of Ecology*, 5E. © 2005 Brooks/Cole, a part of Cengage Learning, Inc. Reproduced by permission. www.cengage.com/permissions

Bill Freedman

The boreal forest is characterized by its dominant life forms, which are conifer trees usually occurring in mature stands or in younger ones recovering from a stand-replacing disturbance such as wildfire. This is an aerial view of open boreal forest in Labrador in which black spruce (*Picea mariana*) and light-coloured reindeer lichens (*Cladina* species) are the dominant organisms. However, different species of conifers and lichens may be predominant in other regions of boreal forest.

most extensive mature communities, but they also contain other kinds of habitats. For instance, although coniferous trees dominate the boreal forest of Canada, there are also large areas of mature angiosperm (broad-leaved or hardwood) trees, such as trembling aspen (*Populus tremuloides*) and paper birch (*Betula papyrifera*). Moreover, persistently wet sites within the boreal forest will support communities typical of rivers and lakes, or wetlands such as fens and bogs.

Disturbances also affect the communities in a biome. They do this by killing the dominant organisms or otherwise disrupting the ecosystem. Natural disturbances such as wildfires, windstorms, and outbreaks of tree-killing pathogens may affect mature forests and kill most of the trees. Following such catastrophes, an ecological recovery occurs through succession, which initially results in new, younger communities that include many species that were not prominent in the original mature forest. The pervasive influence of natural disturbances means that boreal landscapes consist of a complex and dynamic mosaic of stands of various ages and stages of succession.

In addition, any biomes that support a large human population, and their economic activities, will have embedded within them habitats that are essentially anthropogenic in origin. In essence, the character of those habitats is most strongly determined by the ways they are managed or otherwise influenced by human activities. Such anthropogenic habitats include urban areas and lands that are used for agricultural or industrial purposes. Although they are embedded within the larger **natural biomes**, collectively they might be considered to represent **anthropogenic biomes** whose key attributes are determined by the kinds of human activities that occur within and help to define them.

11.2 The Major Biomes

The biomes mapped in Figures 11.1 and 11.2 are "natural" in the sense that their communities of plants, animals, and microorganisms have spontaneously organized under the influence of the prevailing environmental conditions.

In fact, however, anthropogenic influences have to some degree affected all of the biomes of modern times. For example, all living organisms, even those in the most remote places, now contain trace residues of organochlorine chemicals in their tissues (such as DDT, dieldrin, PCBs, dioxins, and furans). None of these chemicals has a natural origin: DDT and dieldrin were manufactured for use as insecticides, PCBs mainly as a dielectric fluid, and dioxins and furans were unintentionally synthesized during the production of other chemicals, or were inadvertently created in incinerators. These organochlorines have become widely dispersed in the environment, where they are persistent, almost insoluble in water, but highly soluble in fats (lipids). Within ecosystems, organochlorines preferentially sequester, or become isolated, in the tissues of organisms, because that is where much of the fat is. They also bio-magnify to especially high concentrations in the fatty tissues of top predators. Of course, there are additional reasons why ecologists might suggest that there are no longer any pristine habitats in the biosphere, including the pervasive influences of anthropogenic climate change (see Chapter 3).

Regardless of a widespread human influence, there remain extensive tracts of wild, self-organizing ecosystems dominated by species that are indigenous (i.e., native) to the local bioregion. These can be reasonably thought of as being "natural ecosystems," even if they are no longer absolutely pristine.

In the rest of this section, the distribution and characteristics of the major biomes of the world are examined. Note, however, that the emphasis is on the natural communities that dominate the various biomes. In actual fact, much of the original extent of some biomes has been extensively **converted** into anthropogenic ecosystems, such as agricultural and urban areas. We will also briefly examine the qualities of these anthropogenic habitats. An important consequence of widespread conversions is the endangerment of many natural communities and their species. This important conservation issue is examined in section 11.3 and in Chapter 14.

Terrestrial Biomes

Tundra

The tundra occurs in environments in which the growing season is cool and short and the winter is cold and long. It is a treeless biome dominated by plants of short stature. The arctic tundra exists in high-latitude regions, particularly far northern expanses of the Northern Hemisphere and the far south of the Southern Hemisphere. In comparison, alpine tundra may exist at any latitude, even at high elevations on tropical mountains, such as the equatorial island of New Guinea. However, alpine tundra occurs at lower elevations at higher latitudes, sometimes even merging with arctic tundra, as occurs near the coast of the Beaufort Sea in northern Yukon. Meteorologically, most tundra exists in a desert condition, in the sense that the amount of water input with rain and snow is less than 25 cm/year. However, because the cool climate of the tundra prevents moisture from evaporating at a high rate, and drainage is poor, the soil is usually moist during the growing season. The **permafrost**, or the persistently frozen subsoil, prevents water from draining downward. The **active layer** of soil that thaws seasonally is typically less than 50–70 cm deep. The soil itself, referred to as a regosol, is young and little-developed (Chapter 4). The plants that grow in tundra are short and small, and it is a relatively unproductive ecosystem with a small standing crop of biomass. In the polar desert and semi-desert of the most northerly tundra of the high-Arctic islands, the plants are diminutive but long-lived and grow no taller than 5–10 cm above the surface. In the mid-Arctic, where the climate is somewhat less severe and there is more moisture, the characteristic vegetation is low shrub-heath and graminoid (sedges, cottongrass, and grasses) meadows. In the Low Arctic, shrubs can grow up to 1–3 m tall in well-drained habitats, and in wetter places there are relatively productive meadows of graminoids.

Boreal Forest

The boreal forest is also known as taiga, a Siberian word for "little sticks." It is widespread in the Northern Hemisphere, especially in great northern expanses of Canada, Alaska, Russia, and Scandinavia. In these

The Canadian Press (Justin Nobel)

The arctic tundra is a northern biome dominated by plants of short stature. This is view of low-arctic tundra in coastal Nunavik, in northern Quebec. The dominant large herbivore in the region is migratory caribou (*Rangifer tarandus*).

regions the winter is cold and lengthy, the growing season is warm but brief (although the days are long during the summer), and the soil has abundant moisture. Most of the northernmost regions of boreal forest are underlain by permafrost, with a seasonally thawed active layer up to 1 m deep. The ground is subject to intense frost-heaving because of freeze–thaw action, and because the trees are shallow-rooted in the active layer, their trunks may lean in all directions, giving the name "drunken forest" to these boreal stands. The soils are mostly acidic podsols, and the dominant plants are coniferous trees, notably species of spruce, pine, and larch. However, some hardwood trees also occur, such as aspen, birch, and poplar. In most regions of boreal forest, natural disturbances periodically result in stand-replacing catastrophes, followed by successional recovery. The most frequent causes are lightning-ignited wildfires, severe windstorms, and irruptions of insects that kill trees after several years of infestation. Because of this disturbance regime, boreal landscapes are a dynamic mosaic consisting of forest communities of various ages of successional recovery.

Montane Forest

Montane forest exists below the tree-line that marks the beginning of alpine tundra in mountainous regions. In temperate latitudes, this biome is similar in structure to the boreal forest of higher latitudes and coniferous trees are also the dominant vegetation. The montane forest experiences a cold winter, but the growing season is relatively long and warm compared with the boreal zone. Climate-related influences are strongly affected by changes in altitude, and so montane forest at lower elevations are more productive and support larger and taller trees than do those higher up, and some sites may have large amounts of orographic precipitation. Near the tree-line the conifer trees may develop a distinctively stunted, gnarled, slow-growing form referred to as krummholtz (or "twisted-wood"; in Atlantic Canada, this growth form is called tuckamoor, and elsewhere it may be called elfin-wood). The montane forests of Canada occur in mountainous regions in the western provinces and territories. Montane forest is periodically disturbed by lightning-ignited wildfires, windstorms, and insect outbreaks, and so its landscape is a dynamic mosaic of stands of various ages.

Temperate Deciduous Forest

Temperate deciduous forest exists in regions where the winter is short and moderately cold and snowy, and the growing season is long, hot, and humid. In Canada, this biome occurs mostly in southern Ontario, southern Quebec, and parts of the Maritime provinces. The soils, known as a brunisol or brown forest soil, are relatively fertile. Temperate deciduous forest generally supports a diverse mixture of species of broadleaved trees, particularly in relatively southern regions, which in Canada are known as Carolinian forest. Deciduous trees and shrubs characterize this biome; their leaves are grown in the spring and summer and then senesce in the autumn, in some species turning brilliant colours of yellow, red, orange, or brown before they are shed. The colours are due to the oxidation of the green chlorophyll pigments during senescence, which destroys their dominant influence and unmasks other pigments that are present in the foliage, such as anthocyanins and carotenoids. The seasonal shedding of foliage is an adaptation to surviving the severe drought and other stresses that occur during the winter. Forest communities in this biome are variable in species composition, as they respond in complex ways to

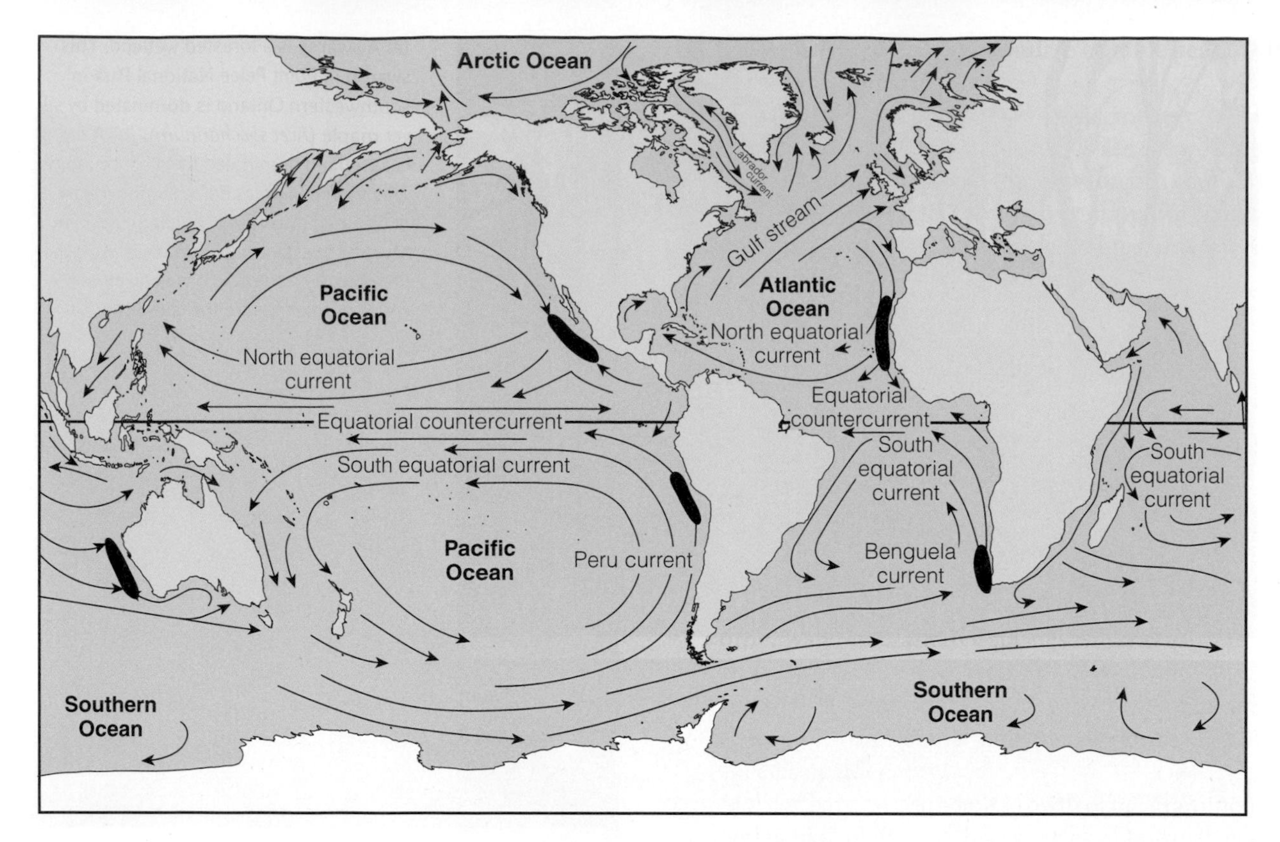

FIGURE 11.4

Major Oceanic Currents and Upwellings. The currents (shown by vectors) are driven by prevailing winds as well as by the Coriolis force that is associated with the direction of Earth's rotation. Upwellings (dark shading) are determined by deep currents and undersea topography and are naturally fertile regions that support high ecological productivity.

SOURCE: Modified from Odum/Barrett. *Fundamentals of Ecology*, 5E. © 2005 Brooks/Cole, a part of Cengage Learning, Inc. Reproduced by permission. www.cengage.com/permissions

as the Sargasso Sea, and another is the North Pacific gyre.

- *Seamounts* are uncommon oceanographic features that occur where oceanic mountains, usually volcanoes, rise from abyssal depths toward the surface, but do not necessarily emerge above it. In places where seamounts are physical obstructions to deepwater currents, they may cause local upwellings to occur. The resulting fertility of local surface waters may support a high rate of productivity, which, along with the complex physical structure of seamounts, results in them being rich "hot spots" of marine biodiversity.
- *Deep-sea hydrothermal vents* are rare places in geothermally active regions where seawater is heated by near-surface magma, establishing a convective current that is exhausted through vents on the sea bottom **(Figure 11.5)**. The hot water contains sulphide minerals that are oxidized by specialized chemosynthetic bacteria at the vents, supporting their primary productivity (Chapter 3). Hydrothermal vents are productive ecosystems that support unusual communities of specialized tube-worms, clams, crustaceans, and fish.

Continental-Shelf Waters

Oceanic waters above a continental shelf (an underwater projection of the emergent landmass), are relatively shallow, typically less than 100–200 m. In Canada, the most expansive continental-shelf waters are in the Arctic and Atlantic regions; for example, they extend offshore as far as 320 km from Newfoundland and 180 km from parts of Nova Scotia. British Columbia has narrower shelf waters, typically no more than 50 km beyond the landmass or major islands, such as Vancouver Island and Haida Gwaii (the Queen Charlotte Islands). Within the extensive biome in Atlantic Canada, shallow waters less than about 100 m deep are known as banks. These shallow coastal waters are relatively warm and fertile compared to the open ocean. The banks are more fertile because they receive nutrients from riverine

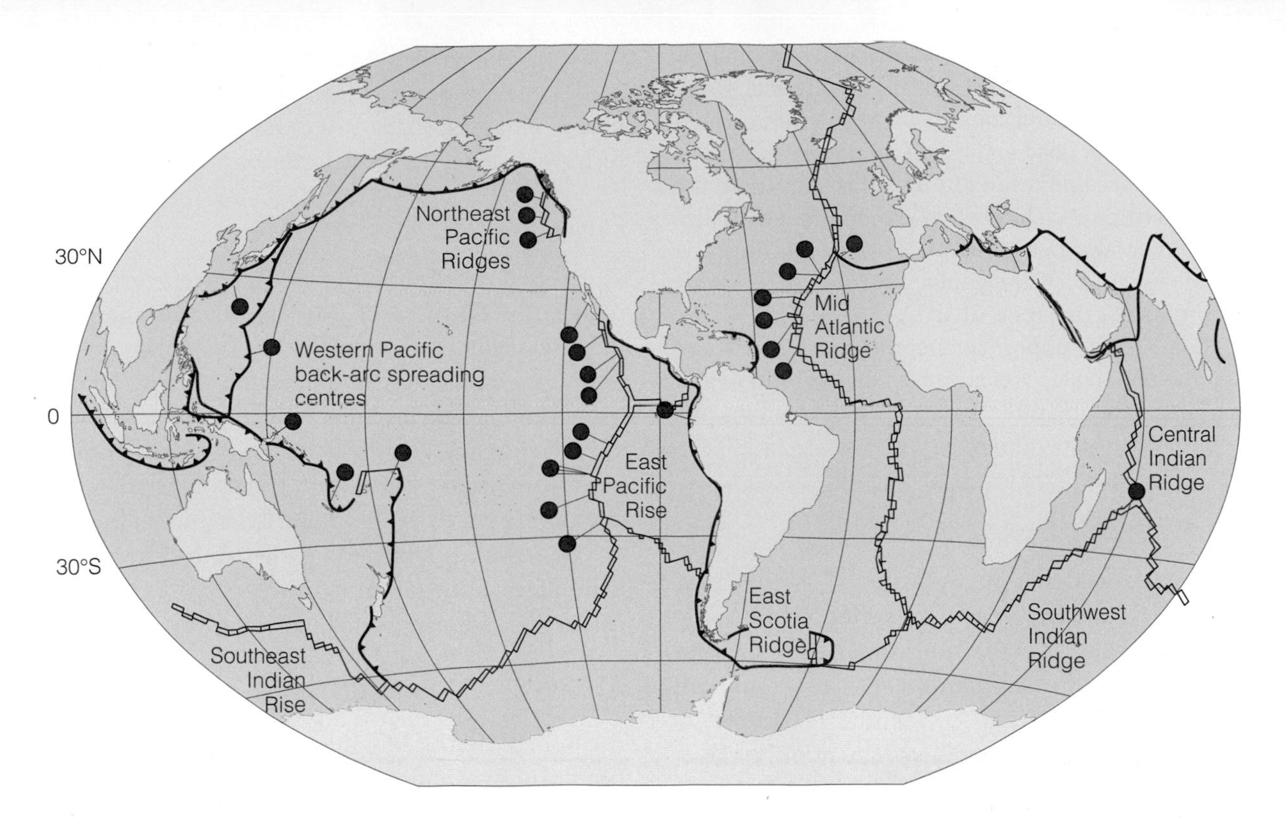

FIGURE 11.5
Locations of Major Deep-Sea Hydrothermal Vents. These uncommon features (red dots) are associated with places where magma occurring close to the surface heats seawater drawn into a hydrothermal system within the ocean floor that exhausts from the vent, supporting an unusual chemosynthetic ecosystem whose primary productivity is dependent on the oxidation of sulphide minerals rather than on sunlight. The jagged lines represent the edges of tectonic plates, where sea-floor spreading and subduction are occurring.

SOURCE: Modified from Odum/Barrett. *Fundamentals of Ecology*, 5E. © 2005 Brooks/Cole, a part of Cengage Learning, Inc. Reproduced by permission. www.cengage.com/permissions

inputs and from deeper oceanic waters that are lifted to the surface by turbulence during windstorms. An abundant nutrient supply allows coastal waters to be relatively productive and to support a much larger biomass of fish and other animals than occurs in the open ocean. In addition to their prevailing shallow pelagic areas, continental-shelf waters support spatially restricted ecosystems of note:

- *Seashores* are a complex of distinctive ecosystems that are an interface between the oceanic and terrestrial realms. Their specific character is influenced by local environmental factors, such as the characteristics of the bottom, the local strength of wave action, and the frequency of disturbances such as violent storms. In temperate regions, hard-rock and cobble bottoms support productive communities dominated by the biomass of large seaweeds (kelps). In areas with a softer bottom of silt or sand, the local communities are supported by inputs of organic detritus from elsewhere, plus the relatively small local productivity of a benthic film of microscopic algae. Invertebrates dominate these soft-bottom benthic communities, especially crustaceans, echinoderms, marine worms, and mollusks.
- *Estuaries* are semi-enclosed coastal ecosystems that are transitional between marine and freshwater habitats. They typically occur as a coastal embayment or semi-enclosed river mouth. An important characteristic of estuaries is their regular fluctuations of salinity due to the twice-daily tidal cycle, along with inflows of fresh water from the nearby land, usually from a river, and occasional storm-surges of saltwater intrusion. Because estuaries have a semi-enclosed geomorphology that retains much of the water-borne input of terrestrial nutrients, they are highly productive ecosystems. In the temperate and boreal climates of Canada, estuaries may support extensive mudflats, beds of eel-grass, and grass-dominated salt-marshes. In tropical regions, estuaries often sustain mangrove forest. The high productivity of estuaries nourishes many species of fish, including the juvenile stages of some economically important pelagic species, as well as abundant shellfish, crustaceans, and coastal birds and mammals.

- *Coral reefs* occur in tropical regions in shallow infertile water close to land. The physical structure of a coral reef consists of the calcium carbonate shells of dead and living corals and mollusks. Corals are cnidarian animals that dominate the reef structure. They live in a mutualism with unicellular algae, and because their symbiosis is efficient in absorbing nutrients they can be highly productive in spite of living in infertile water. Coral reefs support a veneer of many species of crustose algae, corals, other invertebrates, and fishes, making this the most biodiverse of marine ecosystems.

Anthropogenic Ecosystems

Immense areas that were formerly occupied by natural habitats have been converted into ecosystems that directly serve the human economy in various ways. Human-dominated ecosystems are anthropogenic, in the sense that their characteristics have developed as a consequence of environmental conditions that are heavily influenced by the activities of people. These ecosystems have a distinctive character that, like natural biomes, can be aggregated on the basis of broadly shared characteristics, even when they occur in far-flung reaches of the globe. In many cases their character is an intended result of management practices, such as occurs in agricultural and urbanized land-uses. However, other kinds of disturbances and pollution also indirectly affect the character of these ecosystems. Anthropogenic ecosystems are dominant wherever people live in dense populations, and also in rural areas where agriculture or resource-extraction industries are prominent, such as forestry and mining. The great diversity of types of anthropogenic ecosystems can be aggregated into three broad clusters: urban techno-ecosystems, rural techno-ecosystems, and agroecosystems.

Urban Techno-Ecosystems

The built environment characterizes urbanized regions: buildings, roads, parking lots, and other physical infrastructure occur wherever the human population is dense in towns and cities. Urban habitats support other species in addition to people, but most are aliens, that is, they are animals and plants that have been introduced from distant places. Most alien species cannot survive without the assistance of humans (for instance, in cultivated gardens), but some have naturalized and they now invade wild ecosystems, where they damage the habitat of native species.

Rural Techno-Ecosystems

Technological development includes an extensive rural infrastructure that consists of far-flung networks of highways, railroads, and electricity transmission lines, as well as more localized industrial facilities and towns that exist to harvest and process natural resources. These rural techno-ecosystems support a mixture of native and alien species that are tolerant of disturbances and other stressors that are associated with anthropogenic activities in rural habitats.

Agroecosystems

Agricultural ecosystems, or **agroecosystems**, are a vital part of the human economy because they are used to grow plants and animals for use as foods,

An agroecosystem is used to grow crops for use as food or for other purposes. This field of potatoes (*Solanum tuberosum*) is in Prince Edward Island.

Bill Freedman

medicines, materials, and energy. **Monocultures** are intensively managed agroecosystems, consisting of single-crop communities of alien plants or animals that are cultivated in agriculture, forestry, or aquaculture (see Chapter 15). The cultivation system is designed to enhance environmental conditions in ways that favour the productivity of the crop. Intensive management practices may include ploughing, fertilizer application, and the use of herbicide, insecticide, and other pesticides. Some less-intensively managed agroecosystems include so-called "organic" practices, which avoid the use of synthetic fertilizer and pesticides, and **polycultures**, in which mixtures of crops are grown in the same fields. The management of agroecosystems for grazing by livestock may include "tame pasture," in which native grassland has been converted to a mixture of alien grasses and legumes that provide good forage. Alternatively, native prairie may also be used for grazing by livestock, while at the same time maintaining much of the original biodiversity. Intensive management of livestock may also include rearing animals in dense conditions and feeding to satiation in feedlots and in indoor environments known as "factory-farms."

11.3 Ecozones and Ecological Regions

Ecozones are similar to biomes in that they are extensive regions that are distinguished and mapped largely on the basis of ecological similarities. What distinguishes ecozones, however, is that their categorization includes not only their dominant late-successional communities, but also their prominent species and their "enduring" attributes related to bedrock, soil types, climate, and topography. The kinds of human activities, and their environmental influences, are also a feature of ecozones. In a sense, ecozones integrate natural features and influences with human socioeconomic ones. The resulting classification and mapping is useful for the purposes of planning for conservation and other aspects of landuse. Within that context, ecozones are the largest elements into which the distinctive terrestrial and marine regions of Canada are classified (Ecological Stratification Working Group, 1995; Scott, 1995; Wiken et al., 1996; Wilkinson, 2008).

Ecozones are at the summit of a hierarchical classification of ecosystems of more local character. Canada has 15 terrestrial ecozones and five marine ones (**Figure 11.6** and **Tables 11.1** and **11.2**; a continental

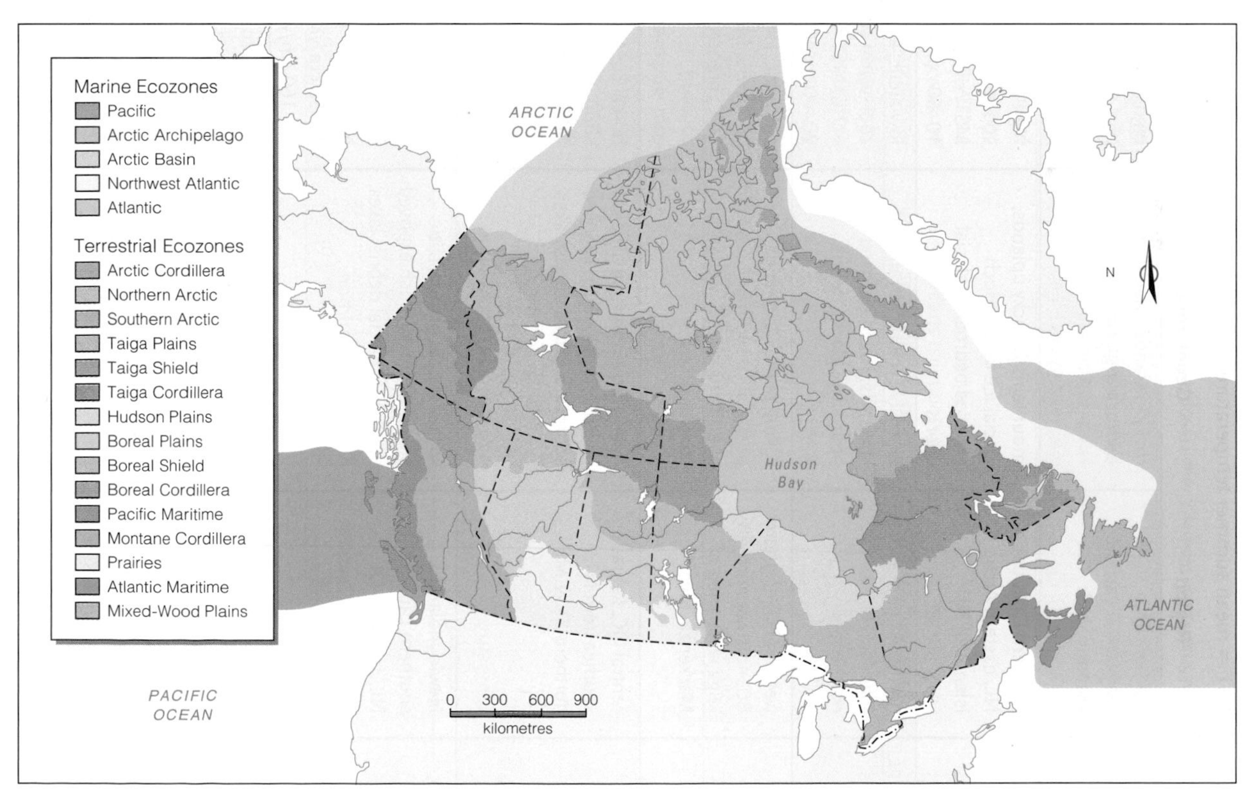

FIGURE 11.6
Distribution of the 15 Terrestrial and 5 Marine Ecozones of Canada.

SOURCE: *The State of Canada's Environment, 1996.* © Her Majesty the Queen in Right of Canada, Environment Canada, 1996. Reprinted with permission of the Minister of Public Works and Government Services Canada, 2010.

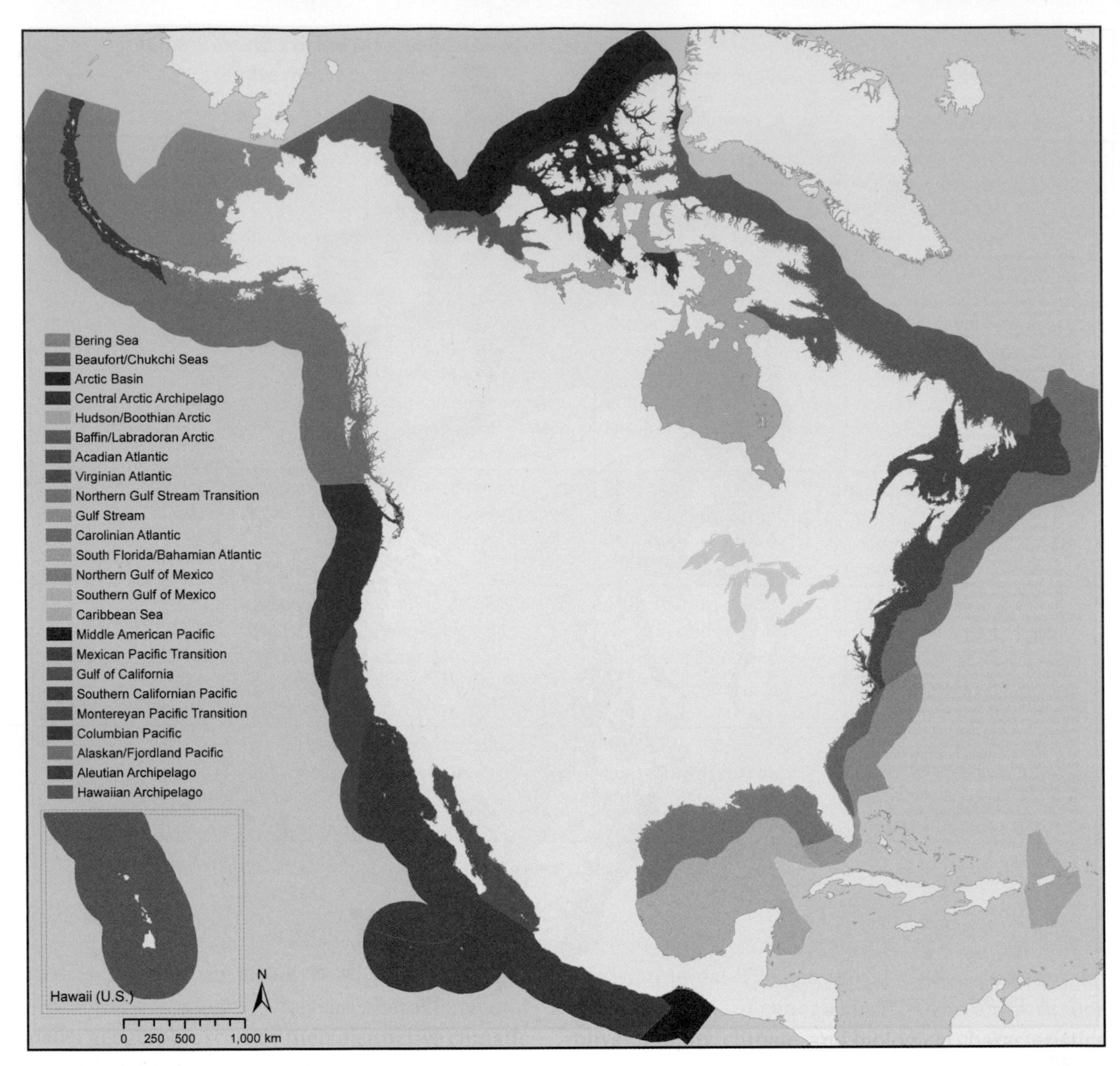

FIGURE 11.8

Distribution of the 24 Marine Ecological Regions (Level 2) Designated for North America. These are roughly comparable to the marine ecozones of Canada. The seaward boundaries of the marine ecoregions are inexact—they actually extend farther into the open ocean.

SOURCE: Wilkinson T., E. Wiken, J. Bezaury-Creel, T. Hourigan, T. Agardi, H. Herrmann, L. Janishevski, C. Madden, L. Morgan, M. Padilla. 2009. *Marine Ecoregions of North America*. Commission for Environmental Cooperation.

occurs throughout, with an active layer of up to 50 cm. The landscape is mostly exposed bedrock, rock fields, and glacial ice, and only a small area supports sparsely vegetated tundra. The most productive habitats occur in moist sites at lower elevation, and this is also where animal wildlife is more abundant. The ecozone is almost unpopulated, and there is little economic activity.

Southern Arctic

This is a remote low-arctic tundra of rolling hills and lowlands that ranges over northern Quebec, continental regions of Nunavut, much of the Northwest Territories, and northern Yukon. The climate is cold but less dry than in the High Arctic, with a long, cold winter and a short, cool summer. Permafrost is distributed throughout this ecozone, except below large lakes and rivers, and the active layer thaws up to 80 cm. Abundant glacial deposits include sinuous mounds of till, known as eskers, which were deposited by rivers of meltwater running beneath glaciers. Unusual surface features develop as a result of pressures exerted by formations of solid ice within the ground, including geometric-patterned ground caused by linear ice wedges, and ice-cored hills known as pingos that rise up to 50 m in height. This ecozone is also characterized by an abundance of lakes, ponds, rivers, streams, and wetlands. The region is well vegetated; most vegetation is less than 1 m tall, but in

Bill Freedman

The Northern Arctic ecozone is a remote region of high-arctic tundra. This artist is painting the Arctic landscape near Pangnirtung, on Baffin Island, Nunavut.

relatively protected habitats there may be shrubs up to several metres tall. This ecozone is sparsely populated, with little economic activity.

Taiga Plains

This is a remote region of undulating uplands and flats, encompassing the northern watershed of the Mackenzie River in the western Northwest Territories, Yukon, northern British Columbia, and northwestern Alberta. The winter is cold and long, but the growing season is moderately warm and improved by relatively long days. The distribution of permafrost is extensive but discontinuous. The amounts of precipitation are low, but the soil is usually moist because permafrost impedes drainage and the evaporation rate is low. There are widespread deposits of glacial debris and riverine outwash, and surface waters and wetlands are common features. The vegetation is primarily an open and slowly growing taiga, dominated by species of spruce, pine, and aspen. Most of the human population and economic activity occurs in the vicinity of the Mackenzie River.

Taiga Shield

This is a vast, remote region of open boreal forest growing on hard quartzitic bedrock and thin glacial soils of the Precambrian Shield of central Quebec, Labrador, southern Nunavut, the southeastern Northwest Territories, and northern Manitoba and Saskatchewan. The winter is extremely cold, but the growing season is moderately warm with long days. Permafrost is widespread, but not throughout. Deposits of glacial debris are prevalent and wetlands are abundant, mostly in impermeable basins in the rolling bedrock. The forest consists of open stands of short and unproductive conifer trees, mostly of spruce and pine. The ecozone is sparsely populated and supports little economic activity.

Boreal Shield

This is a vast ecozone that occurs on thin soil and hard quartzitic bedrock of more southern reaches of the Precambrian Shield. It extends through Newfoundland and Labrador, much of southern Quebec, most of northern Ontario, central Manitoba, and northern Saskatchewan. The climate is cold in the winter and warm in the summer. Glacial debris is widespread and waters and wetlands are common in perched basins. The dominant vegetation is a closed boreal forest dominated by conifers, particularly species of spruce, fir, and pine. Logging and mining are major economic activities in this ecozone.

Atlantic Maritime

This is an eastern ecozone that occurs throughout the Maritime provinces and in adjacent Gaspé and southeastern Quebec. The terrain is rolling and the bedrock is a complex mosaic of granites and sedimentary rocks. The ecozone has moderately abundant precipitation and is cold in winter and warm in summer, but the climate is more moderate closer to the Atlantic coast. Surface waters and wetlands are abundant and the temperate forest is made up of productive mixed-species communities of various coniferous and hardwood species. The ecozone is widely settled and supports diverse economic activities, including those associated with resource extraction, agriculture, manufacturing, and urbanization.

Mixedwood Plains

This ecozone is located in the valley of the St. Lawrence River and the postglacial floodplain of Lakes Erie and Ontario, in the most southerly regions of Ontario and Quebec. The terrain is gently rolling, bedrock is mostly limestone and other sedimentary rocks, and soils are relatively deep and fertile. The climate is continental temperate, with a cold winter and a hot summer. The natural forest is much richer in species than anywhere else in Canada, supporting species of hardwood trees of a relatively southern distribution. This is particularly the case in extreme southern Ontario, where the so-called Carolinian forest supports many species that are rare in Canada but widespread in the eastern United States. This is Canada's most densely populated and intensively used ecozone, where the main economic activities include agriculture, manufacturing, and urban-associated sectors.

Boreal Plains

This is a broad forested belt that extends from central Manitoba and Saskatchewan, across northern Alberta, to northeastern British Columbia. The hilly landscape consists of deposits of glacial moraine and flat areas with deep soil derived from post-glacial lake sediment. The climate is continental, with a cold winter and warm summer. Surface waters and wetlands are abundant. The forest consists mostly of conifer-dominated stands of spruce and pine, with aspen and poplar more abundant in southern regions. Forestry and fossil-fuel mining are major economic activities in this ecozone.

Prairies

This is a non-forested ecozone that covers southern regions of Alberta, Saskatchewan, and Manitoba. The landscape is a rolling moraine with flatter areas of fertile post-glacial lake sediment. The climate is continental, with a cold winter and hot summer, but soil moisture deficits often limit plant growth because of sparse precipitation and a hot windy summer that promotes evaporation. Lakes and ponds with fringing wetlands, known as potholes and sloughs, are common, especially in years with abundant precipitation. Three kinds of prairie are identified by the height and species composition of their vegetation, which is mostly species of grasses and forbs. Tallgrass prairie has plants 1–2 m tall, while mixedgrass prairie has medium and short grasses and forbs, and shortgrass prairie has species < 25 cm tall. Southernmost parts of the ecozone are drier and have areas of semi-desert habitat. Agriculture and fossil-fuel mining are major economic activities along with those associated with urbanization.

Taiga Cordillera

This is a mostly forested subarctic region of northern Yukon and parts of the adjacent Northwest Territories. It covers the northernmost region of the Rocky Mountains, so much of the terrain is steep, with wild rivers in deep valleys, and more gently sloping foothills at lower elevation. The climate is continental arctic and subarctic, with a long, cold winter and a short, cool summer with long days. Permafrost is extensively distributed. Surface waters are mostly rivers and streams, with ponds and lakes more frequent on the northern coastal plain and in lowlands of the Old Crow River. The landscape is a complex mosaic of vegetation that ranges from alpine tundra at high elevation, to low-arctic tundra on the coastal plain, to taiga forest of spruce and birch at lower elevations in the south. This is a remote ecozone, with few people and little economic activity.

Boreal Cordillera

This is a region of mountainous topography in southern Yukon and northern British Columbia. The ecozone has diverse terrain, with many steep slopes, deep and wide valleys, high plateaus, and sloping foothills and lowlands. The climate is continental boreal, with a long, cold winter and a warm summer. Surface waters are mostly streams and rivers, and northern regions have discontinuous permafrost. Local climatic conditions are greatly influenced by the inclination and aspect of the sloped terrain. In southern regions, south-facing slopes are relatively warm and dry and support grassland and open forest, while northerly exposures have boreal vegetation. Alpine tundra occurs at higher elevations. This is a sparsely populated ecozone, with forestry and mining the principal economic activities.

Pacific Maritime

This ecozone is situated in mountainous terrain of the islands and coastal mainland of British Columbia. The climate is moderated by proximity to the Pacific Ocean, and it is humid temperate, with a short, cool winter and a long, warm summer. However, altitude and aspect have a large influence on the local climate. Surface waters are mostly streams and rivers. A diverse mix of conifer species is the predominant vegetation of the extensive temperate rainforest. The wet climate favours the development of old-growth forest because wildfire is uncommon. Higher-altitude sites develop a boreal-like montane forest, or alpine tundra closer to the summit of mountains. Forestry and mining are the main economic activities in sparsely populated rural regions, but areas in the extreme south are urbanized.

Montane Cordillera

This is a mountainous ecozone of southern British Columbia and southwestern Alberta. The climate is temperate continental, with a cold winter and warm summer, but altitude and aspect greatly affect local conditions. Moisture is highly variable, ranging from dry valleys and plateaus in the rain shadow of mountains (this occurs where mountainous terrain has caused moist air masses originating over an ocean to rise in altitude and cool, so the water content condenses and precipitates out as abundant rain and snow, to the degree that when the mountains are traversed the moisture content is greatly depleted, resulting in a region of "rain shadow" with a drier climate), to wetter at higher elevations in southeastern areas with orographic precipitation (this is the seaward side of the mountains with abundant precipitation). Surface waters are mostly streams and rivers, with some large lakes occurring behind natural impoundments of rivers. The ecozone is dominated by coniferous forest, but community types vary according to the terrain and environmental conditions. Alpine tundra occurs at higher altitude, with coniferous montane forest below, and temperate stands in lower valleys. Some areas with relatively high rates of precipitation support inland temperate rainforest. This is a sparsely populated ecozone, with forestry the principal economic activity, except in the extreme south where there is agricultural and urbanized activity.

Bill Freedman

The Pacific Maritime ecozone sustains extensive tracts of temperate old-growth rainforest, although the ecosystem is greatly diminished because of logging. This is an old-growth tree of western red cedar (*Thuja plicata*) on Meares Island, near Tofino on western Vancouver Island.

Hudson Plains

This ecozone covers the extensive lowlands of post-glacial Hudson and James Bays, extending from northern Quebec and adjacent Ontario to northeastern Manitoba. The cold waters of Hudson and James Bays help to create a climate that is more subarctic than might be expected from the latitude, with a long, cold winter and a short, warm summer. Permafrost is discontinuous and there are abundant streams, rivers, ponds, lakes, and wetlands. Tidal flats develop extensive areas of salt marsh. Shrubby low-arctic tundra occurs near the coast, but the habitat changes inland to an open and short-treed taiga, and eventually to a closed-canopy boreal forest. This is a remote ecozone, with few people and little economic activity.

Marine Ecozones of Canada

Northwest Atlantic

This ecozone is located in the Gulf of St. Lawrence and the continental-shelf waters off western and northern Newfoundland, Quebec, Labrador, and Baffin Island. The hydrology of the St. Lawrence River has a powerful effect in the Gulf of St. Lawrence, and the southeast-flowing Labrador Current is a major influence elsewhere in the ecozone. The climate ranges from marine subarctic to boreal, with a cold winter and cool-to-warm summer. In winter the northern regions are covered by sea ice, which breaks up and melts completely in the springtime. Fish populations are abundant and widespread, as are seabirds and marine mammals. This ecozone supports commercial fishing and much shipping traffic, especially in the Gulf of St. Lawrence region.

Atlantic Marine

This ecozone covers continental-shelf waters off eastern Newfoundland and Nova Scotia, as well as the Bay of Fundy. Extensive regions shallower than about 150 m are known as banks, but there are also post-glacial riverine trenches and other deep habitats. The climate is marine temperate, with a cold winter and warm summer. Surface waters are particularly balmy in areas that are temporarily affected by eddies of the Gulf Stream, a warm-water current that flows from the Caribbean Sea toward northwestern Europe. Sea ice does not form during the winter, but icebergs carried by the Labrador Current regularly drift into the northern banks, and riverine pack ice may be imported from the Gulf of St. Lawrence in the springtime. Populations of fish are plentiful and widespread in both inshore waters and the offshore banks, and seabirds and marine mammals are abundant. This ecozone supports commercial fishing, fossil-fuel mining, and much shipping traffic.

Pacific

This ecozone occurs in waters off the islands and mainland of British Columbia. The climate is marine temperate, with a short cool winter, a long warm summer, and no sea ice. Shallow areas have extensive beds (or "forests") of giant kelp, while deeper regions have pelagic ecosystems. Species of Pacific salmon are prominent in the ecoregion—these fish spend their adult life at sea, but migrate up their birth river to spawn, after which they die. Some islands provide nesting habitat for large populations of marine birds. This ecozone supports commercial fishing and much shipping traffic.

Arctic Archipelago

This ecozone occurs in the waters of Hudson Bay and James Bay, the Beaufort Sea, and among the high-Arctic islands. The climate is marine arctic, with a long, cold winter and a short, cool summer. For most of the year the ocean surface is covered with ice up to several metres thick, and the ice-free summer is only 1–2 months long. Most of the primary productivity occurs during the ice-free season, but some takes place beneath the sea ice during the arctic springtime. In a few places, the bottom topography forces deep-water currents toward the surface, where the turbulence creates **polynya**—these are ice-free areas that provide critical habitat for marine birds and mammals. This is a remote ecozone, but southern regions support some commercial fishing and shipping.

Arctic Basin

This is a deep-water ecozone that is situated to the north and west of the high-Arctic islands. The climate is marine high-arctic, with a long and cold winter and a brief and cold summer. Sea ice has a continuous cover in the northernmost regions, and nearly so in the south. Large areas of sea ice break up during the summer into a drifting pack that moves in an immense counter-clockwise loop, rafting on a current known as the Arctic gyre that is roughly centred on the North Pole. This ecozone has a sparse marine productivity and it supports only small populations of fish and marine mammals. This is a remote ecozone, with no economic activity.

Bill Freedman

Within the Arctic Archipelago marine ecozone, polynyas are areas that are permanently ice-free or become open early in the summer. Because these open places support a high productivity of marine invertebrates and fish, they are critical habitat for polar bears, seals, cetaceans, and seabirds. This polynya exists on the east coast of central Ellesmere Island, Nunavut.

A CANADIAN ECOLOGIST 11.1

Stan Rowe: A Specialist in Biomes and a Scientist-Citizen

Dr. Rob Wright

Stan Rowe standing in a clear-cut of boreal forest.

Stan Rowe (1918–2004) was an ecologist, educated at the University of Manitoba and University of Nebraska, with a background in botany, forestry, and landscape ecology. He worked for 19 years as a research forester with the federal government, and then in 1967 became a professor at the University of Saskatchewan. There he worked with senior students and taught classes in plant ecology until his retirement in 1985. Much of the work of Rowe and his students involved studies of the distribution of the biomes and ecozones of Canada, including the effects of natural disturbances such as wildfire and windstorms on the dynamics of their communities. In 1959, Rowe wrote the first edition of the book *Forest Regions of Canada*, which has greatly influenced our knowledge of the distribution, biodiversity, and environmental factors affecting the natural regions of Canada. He also wrote a well-regarded paper with a more theoretical outlook, entitled "The Level-of-Integration Concept in Ecology." This paper explored the expansive unity of the ecological context, which ranges across all echelons of life, as well as the integrated environmental factors that allow and influence the existence of the biota.

In addition to his work on biomes and landscape ecology, Rowe was profoundly concerned about environmental issues and their intersection with conservation. His own ethics and worldview were ecocentric, meaning he regarded humans as being a component of ecosystems and as having an inherent responsibility to conduct their economy in a manner that does not threaten other species and natural habitats. Rowe showcased his love for species and the biosphere in the book *Home Place* (1990), a collection of essays that explored these themes and greatly influenced the rapidly developing conservation movement. A second book of essays, *Earth Alive*, was published posthumously in 2006. Rowe also gave many public addresses, particularly about the damaging effects of clear-cutting, the degradation of water resources, and the conservation of wilderness. He was also a key advisor to conservation NGOs, including the World Wildlife Fund (Canada). Rowe won numerous awards, including in 1994 the Harkin Conservation Award for his advocacy related to the conservation of parks and wilderness areas in Canada.

VOCABULARY OF ECOLOGY

active layer, p. 336
agroecosystem, p. 346
anthropogenic biome, p. 336
benthic zone, p. 341
biome, p. 332
convergent evolution, p. 333
conversion, p. 336
ecoregion (or ecological region), p. 350
ecozone, p. 347
endemics, p. 338
eutrophic, p. 341
lentic ecosystem, p. 341
life form, p. 332
littoral zone, p. 341
lotic ecosystem, p. 341
mesotrophic, p. 341
minerotrophic, p. 342
monoculture, p. 347
natural biome, p. 336
old-growth forest, p. 338
oligotrophic, p. 341
ombrotrophic, p. 342
pelagic zone, p. 341
permafrost, p. 336
polyculture, p. 347
polynya, p. 356
riparian, p. 342
turbidity, p. 341

QUESTIONS FOR REVIEW AND DISCUSSION

1. Describe the essential characteristics of five biomes that occur in Canada, and two tropical ones.
2. Identify an ecozone that occurs in your province or territory and describe its characteristics. What are the most important environmental influences on the species and ecological communities of the ecozone? How do you think these factors have changed during the past decade? Over the past century? How did the species and ecological communities respond?
3. Ecozones are characterized in part by their dominant native species, but they may also contain many alien ones. Why do the aliens not play more of a role in the description of ecozones? Does this somehow reflect the higher "value" that ecologists may place on native species?
4. You have been given the job of mapping and describing the kinds of ecological communities that occur in a park or some other kind of protected area (choose one that you are familiar with, perhaps close to where you live). What methods would you use to map the various terrestrial, wetland, and aquatic communities in the park, and to determine their characteristics?

HELPFUL WEBSITES

COMMISSION FOR ENVIRONMENTAL COOPERATION

http://www.cec.org

The CEC is an agency founded under the North American Free Trade Agreement. Under its auspices, Canada, Mexico, and the United States have cooperated to develop maps and descriptions of their shared ecozones.

MISSOURI BOTANICAL GARDEN

BIOMES OF THE WORLD

http://mbgnet.mobot.org/sets/index.htm

This well-designed site provides information about the major terrestrial biomes.

You'll find a rich array of additional resources for *Ecology* at www.ecology.nelson.com.

organisms (such as bacteria, fungi, and protists) that inhabit ecosystems that are not yet thoroughly explored, particularly the humid tropics.

Of the total number of species identified and assigned a name by taxonomists, about 35 percent occur in tropical habitats and 65 percent are in temperate and boreal climes (WRI, 2009). In contrast, an estimated 90 percent of the as yet undiscovered species live in tropical rainforests, in which the smaller biota is not yet well studied, particularly invertebrates and microorganisms. The largest part of this "hidden biodiversity" is likely to be undescribed small insects of tropical forests, particularly beetles (order Coleoptera). The evolutionary biologist J. B. S. Haldane (1892–1964) was once asked by a group of theologians to tell what he could infer of God's purpose and thinking, based on his knowledge of "His Creation" (meaning biodiversity as it was known in the 1950s). Haldane allegedly replied that God has "an inordinate fondness of beetles." In fact, more than 350 000 species of beetles have already been named, amounting to 37 percent of all insects and 20 percent of all named species. Moreover, entomologists have estimated that there are millions of additional species of beetles yet to be discovered.

The species richness of major groups of organisms in Canada is summarized in **Table 12.2.** Other than microorganisms, the numbers of species within these major groups are rather well known, a fact that reflects the relatively large numbers of biologists that have lived and worked in this country.

In comparison with many other countries, however, the ecosystems of Canada support a relatively low species richness **(Table 12.3).** Although Canada is the world's second-largest country (after Russia), it harbours many fewer species than the United States and enormously less than occurs in many tropical countries. The relatively low species richness of Canada is substantially due to almost all of its landmass being covered by glacial ice as recently as 10 000 to 12 000 years ago, so that present-day ecosystems have not had much time (on an ecological scale) to recover from this cataclysmic disturbance. Just as important, there has not been enough time for many endemic species to evolve in Canada—almost all of the species that occur in our country also have a broad distribution in other countries.

In contrast, regions where there have been longer periods of continuous ecological development generally support much higher levels of biodiversity. This is particularly true of low-latitude, tropical regions, but it is also the case of non-glaciated temperate regions, such as much of the southern United States. These trends are evident from consideration of data on the species richness of selected countries in **Table 12.3**. Note the especially rich biodiversity of Brazil, Mexico, and Peru in comparison to Canada. Those countries sustain a great variety of natural ecosystems and a

TABLE 12.2 Biodiversity of Canada

The estimated totals are based on the opinions of expert biologists about how many species may eventually be discovered.

Group	Identified	Estimated
Viruses	200	150 000
Bacteria	2 400	23 200
Fungi	11 310	16 500
Protozoans	1 000	2 000
Algae	5 303	7 300
Lichens	2 500	2 800
Bryophytes & liverworts	1 500	1 800
Vascular plants	4 153	4 400
Mollusks	1 500	1 635
Crustaceans	3 139	4 550
Arachnids	3 272	11 006
Insects	29 913	54 566
Fishes	1 100	1 600
Amphibians	42	44
Reptiles	42	42
Birds	430	430
Mammals	194	194
TOTAL	68 000	282 000

SOURCES: Environment Canada (1997), World Resources Institute (2009), IUCN (2009).

TABLE 12.3 Species Richness in Selected Countries

	Canada	USA	Mexico	Brazil	Peru
Vascular plants	4 153	19 473	26 071	56 215	17 144
Freshwater fish	128	1 101	674	471	166
Amphibians	42	285	358	695	361
Reptiles	42	360	837	651	354
Birds	430	888	1 026	1 712	1 781
Mammals	194	468	544	578	441
Country area (10^6 ha)	998.5	963.2	196.4	851.5	128.5

SOURCES: Data are from Environment Canada (1997) and World Resources Institute (2009).

huge richness of species in all groups of organisms, including numerous endemic species.

In fact, humid tropical forests support more species than any other habitats in the world. For this reason, ecologists consider the tropical rain forest to represent the pinnacle of ecosystem development. Unfortunately, the destruction of tropical rain forest is occurring at a rapid rate, mostly because the land is being converted to agricultural, industrial, and urbanized land uses (see Chapter 14). As a result of this irretrievable loss of tropical forests, many species have become extinct or endangered. This is the leading cause of the biodiversity crisis of the modern era. This crisis is less pronounced in Canada. Nevertheless, a number of indigenous species have become extinct or extirpated in Canada because of habitat destruction or excessive harvesting—and hundreds more are at risk of disappearing.

Estimates of the hidden biodiversity of Earth suggest that it may amount to several tens of millions of as yet unidentified species, compared to the 1.8 million that have already been named. One of the first researchers to arrive at this conclusion was the entomologist T. L. Erwin, whose research involved fogging small areas of tropical-forest canopy in South America with an insecticide. This method killed arboreal invertebrates, which fell as a "rain" of dead specimens that were collected in arrays of sampling devices on the ground. Erwin and his colleagues spent years to laboriously sort through and identify their many specimens, and as their work progressed they realized that many of the insects they had collected (especially small beetles) were new to science. Moreover, many of them were endemics, having a local geographic distribution and often restricted to only one kind of forest, or even to a particular species of tree. In a study of four kinds of Amazonian forest in Brazil, Erwin (1983) identified 24 000 beetles and found 1080 species among them; 83 percent of these species occurred only in a particular kind of forest, with 58–78 percent being endemics. In fact, the tree *Luehea seemannii* had more than 1100 species of beetles in its canopy, 14.5 percent of which were not found on other species of trees. Because this kind of work is difficult and expensive to undertake, there have not been many comparable studies. It is remarkable that so little is known of the "smaller-sized" biodiversity of Earth.

In comparison with tiny arthropods, the species richness is better known for larger organisms that inhabit tropical forest. This is particularly the case for vegetation, because plants are relatively easy to sample inside of plots (although specialized taxonomic knowledge is needed to identify the many species that occur in tropical communities). Consider the following data for primary lowland tropical forest in various regions (primary forest has not been logged or used for agriculture):

- 365 species of vascular plants occurred in a plot of only 0.1 ha in a lowland tropical forest in Ecuador (Gentry, 1986).
- 742 species of tree with diameter at breast height (DBH) greater than 10 cm occurred in a 3 ha plot of moist forest in Sarawak, Malaysia, with 50 percent occurring as single individuals (Primack and Hall, 1992).
- 240 tree species >10 cm DBH occurred in a 1 ha plot in lowland Kalimantan forest (Indonesian Borneo; MacKinnon et al., 1996).
- 83–113 tree species >10 cm DBH occurred among ten 1 ha plots of lowland forest in Cameroon (Comiskey et al., 2003).
- 90 tree species >20 cm DBH occurred in 0.8 ha of lowland forest in Papua New Guinea (Paijmans, 1970).
- 44–61 tree species >20 cm DBH (total of 112 species) occurred among five 1 ha plots of lowland forest on Barro Colorado Island, Panama (Thorington et al., 1982).
- More than 300 species of woody plants occurred in a 50 ha forest plot on Barro Colorado Island (Hubbell and Foster, 1983).
- 283 tree species occurred in a 1 ha plot in Amazonian Peru, with 63 percent represented by only one individual and 15 percent by two (Gentry, 1988).

However, it is important to recognized that not all tropical forests are so rich in species; in Sumatra and Borneo, for example, lowland stands dominated by ironwood (*Eusideroxylon zwageri*) are almost monospecific, with up to 96 percent of trees being that valuable species, occurring in all size and age categories (Whitten et al., 1987). Similarly, stands of coastal mangrove forest may have only a few species of tree present. As in all of ecology, we have to be careful about making broad generalizations, including about the rich biodiversity of all tropical forests.

In contrast, temperate forests in North America typically have only 9–12 or even fewer tree species in plots of comparable size to those noted above for rich tropical forest. The Great Smoky Mountains of the eastern United States have the richest temperate forests in the world. That region supports at least 131 species of native trees and 30–35 species in a typical stand (Stupka, 1964; Leigh, 1982), far fewer than in tropical forest. Boreal forests, which cover much of Canada, have only 1–4 species of trees present in a stand.

variation and species richness. However, throughout the world, natural communities and ecoscapes are being degraded and lost (Chapter 15).

The following are examples of such losses occurring in Canada (Freedman, 2010):

- Older forests in eastern Canada are becoming increasingly rare, for instance, less than 1 percent of the forest estate in Nova Scotia is now older than 100 years. Even in coastal British Columbia, where the humid climate is generally favourable to the development of old-growth forest (because wildfire is uncommon), this ecosystem is rapidly becoming less extensive. The rarest type is the dry coastal forest dominated by Douglas-fir (*Pseudotsuga menziesii*), of which only 2 percent of the original extent remains. Timber harvesting is primarily responsible for the depletion of old-growth forest and its subsequent conversion into a younger, second-growth forest. Near cities, urbanization is also an important cause of the loss of older forests.
- Only < 2 percent of the Carolinian forest of southern Ontario survives, because the rest was destroyed when its land-base was converted into agricultural and urbanized uses. Similarly, only 5 percent of the original extent of the Garry-oak (*Quercus garryi*) forest of southern Vancouver Island has avoided being converted into residential and urbanized land uses.
- During the past century, almost all the original tallgrass prairie in Canada was converted to agricultural use, so that only about 0.2 percent survives.
- Much of the original area of wetlands of southern Canada has been extensively destroyed or degraded by pollution, in-filling, and other disturbances.
- Natural fish populations have been widely decimated, including mixed-species communities in the Great Lakes, salmonid species (salmon and trout) in western Canada, and groundfish off the Atlantic Provinces.

These and other natural communities, landscapes, and seascapes of Canada are now endangered. They survive only in remnant patches rather than as integral parts of vast, robust, self-organizing, natural ecosystems. Furthermore, even the vestiges are at risk of being converted or suffering other damages from human use.

12.2 The Importance of Biodiversity

Biodiversity is important for many reasons, which range from the intrinsic value of unique and irreplaceable components of the natural world to the provision of ecological goods and services that are essential to the human economy. The following section describes the ways that biodiversity is important and valuable, and provide credence for its conservation.

Instrumental Value

Certain elements of biodiversity have **instrumental** or **utilitarian value** because they are useful to people and the economy as sources of food, medicine, materials, or energy. These necessary uses of biodiversity represent an inherent and vital connection between people and the rest of the biosphere. The instrumental values of various kinds of biodiversity include:

- *Food*: All foods that people consume are derived from biodiversity, being eaten directly or in some

Bill Freedman

Biodiversity is important to human welfare. These domestic cows (*Bos taurus*) on Prince Edward Island are being cultivated for their meat.

processed form. The foodstuffs are derived from edible biomass of various sorts:

- plant tissues or chemicals processed from them, such as grains, fruits, vegetables, tubers, sugars, and starches;
- animal products, such as the meat of cows, pigs, chickens, and fishes, or other foods such as milk and eggs;
- mushrooms and other fungal products; and
- microorganisms and their products, such as baking and brewing yeasts.

Most foodstuffs are derived from plants and livestock that are cultivated to provide commercial foods, but there is also considerable hunting of wild stocks of animals for the market economy or for subsistence, such as waterfowl, deer, and fish.

- *Medicine*: Prior to the 20th century, almost all medicines were derived from products of biodiversity (a few others were inorganic compounds of such elements as arsenic and mercury). Classical examples are acetylsalicylic acid (aspirin) derived from willows (*Salix* spp.), digitoxin from foxglove (*Digitalis purpurea*), alkaloids from the opium poppy (*Papaver somniferum*), and anti-microbial drugs from *Penicillium* and *Streptomyces* fungi. Although many newer medicines are based on synthetic active ingredients, most are still derived from biochemicals found in plants and other organisms. Between 1981 and 2006, 63 percent of 974 new, small-chemical entities that were examined as potential medicines were derived from natural compounds or inspired by them (the latter includes synthetic analogues of natural chemicals; Neuman and Cragg, 2007). For drugs used to treat microbial infections, cancer, hypertensivity, and inflammation, the figure is even higher, at 75 percent.
- *Materials*: Trees provide lumber that is used to construct buildings and homes, to manufacture furniture, and for many other purposes. Paper is another commercial product derived from tree biomass, as are methanol, turpentine, and plastic-like celluloid. Various plants supply fibres that are woven into textiles, including coconut (coir), cotton, flax, and hemp. Textiles are also woven from the wool of sheep, goats, and alpaca. Clothing is also made of furs and leather made from the skins of both livestock and wild animals.
- *Energy*: Biomass is a renewable source of energy that can be burned as a fuel for space heating, to provide industrial hot water, and to produce steam-driven electricity. Trees are the most commonly used source of biomass energy. In addition, oils derived from the seeds of certain plants (such as oilseed canola and oil-palm) can be used as a fuel in diesel engines, and starch and sugars can be fermented to produce ethanol or methanol, which can be used as fuels in internal-combustion engines and for other purposes.
- *Companionship*: Many animals are kept by people as pets, and in this capacity they provide important services as companions, sources of amusement, and even health benefits associated with walking and stress reduction. In Canada in 2007, there were about 7.9 million pet cats and 5.9 million dogs, living in about 70 percent of households (CAHI, 2008). In the United States in 2009, 62 percent of households owned a pet, and there were about 94 million pet cats, 78 million dogs, 16 million smaller mammals, 15 million birds, 14 million reptiles, and 183 million fishes (APPA, 2009). Total expenditures to acquire, feed, and otherwise care for pets were US$45.4 billion (comparable expenditures in Canada would be about one-tenth of that, based on relative human populations).

Remarkably, only a small proportion of known species has been examined for potential usefulness to humans; there is therefore a great wealth of undiscovered products of biodiversity that may prove to be valuable. Much field and laboratory research is being undertaken to find novel uses for the products of wild plants, animals, and microorganisms. This can be illustrated by the case of the rosy periwinkle (*Catharanthus roseus*), a small wildflower native to Madagascar (Myers, 1983; Miller and Tangley, 1991; this species is now endangered in the wild). The rosy periwinkle was long used in traditional medicine as a remedy for various diseases, and it caught the attention of health scientists when screening tests found that it is pharmacologically active in suppressing the growth of tumour cells. Further research showed that the active property is due to several alkaloid compounds that the periwinkle produces to deter herbivores. These chemicals, vincristine and vinblastine, are now extracted from periwinkles grown for the purpose and are used in chemotherapy to treat leukemia, lymphomas, and several other malignancies. Prior to the discovery of these drugs, children with leukemia had only a 5 percent likelihood of remission, but this was increased to 94 percent by treatment with periwinkle-based medicine; similarly, persons with Hodgkin's lymphoma had almost no chance of survival, but this was increased to 70 percent. A comparable example is taxol (paclitaxel) derived from various yews (*Taxus* species), which has been proven effective against lung, breast, and ovarian cancers. Wild stocks of two native species, the Pacific yew (*T. brevifolia*) and Canada yew (*T. canadensis*), are now being harvested to provide this medicine. These are only a few of many cases of recently discovered medicinal benefits that are provided by chemicals found in wild organisms,

Biodiversity can provide crucial sources of medicine. The foliage of Canada yew (*Taxus canadensis*) yields a chemical known as taxol that is effective in chemotherapy against several kinds of cancers.

AAltrendo/Getty Images

and there are many additional ones that have not yet been found. These sorts of future prospects are a good reason to prevent the extinction of elements of natural biodiversity.

In general, organisms or their populations are capable of regenerating after they or their products are harvested as sources of foods, medicines, materials, or energy. Because of this regeneration, biodiversity is a potentially renewable source of these natural goods. However, a sustainable system of harvesting and management is possible only if the harvest rate does not exceed the capacity of the stocks to regenerate (Chapter 15). Unfortunately, many biodiversity resources that are potentially renewable have been "mined" to such an extent that they have become depleted. This syndrome is known as **over-harvesting** or **over-exploitation**, and it is usually caused by an excessive harvesting rate and inadequate fostering of the regeneration, which results in biological resources becoming diminished in quantity and degraded in quality.

There are even cases of over-exploited species becoming **extinct** (no longer surviving anywhere) or locally **extirpated** (extinct in a place or region, but surviving elsewhere), so their unique resource values are no longer available to be used to benefit people. Examples of Canadian species that became extinct primarily because of commercial over-harvesting include the great auk (*Pinguinus impennis*), passenger pigeon (*Ectopistes migratorius*), Eskimo curlew (*Numenius borealis*), and sea mink (*Neovison macrodon*). Regional extirpations have been much more frequent in regions of Canada where the human economy is dominant, and include those of bison (*Bison bison*), cougar (*Puma concolor*), grizzly bear (*Ursus arctos*), timber wolf (*Canis lupus*), wolverine (*Gulo gulo*), and wild ginseng (*Panax quinquifolia*) over most of their original ranges.

Provision of Ecological Services

Ecological services are important both to the human economy and to the maintenance of wild biodiversity itself. Examples of ecological services include the following:

- *Nutrient cycling* refers to processes by which specific microorganisms or the broader microbial community act to transform non-available forms of nutrients into compounds that can be taken up by primary producers and used to generate new biomass. See Chapter 4 for an explanation of key processes, such as the decomposition of dead biomass, nitrogen fixation, and nitrification.
- *Biological productivity* is obviously important to the human economy, because it provides crucial sources of foods, materials, and energy. It is also vital to all other species, because it is the foundation of all ecosystems.
- *Clean-environment services (or waste-regulating services)* include the cleansing of soil, water, and air of pollutants, such as carbon dioxide, sulphur dioxide, and ozone, as well as the provision of atmospheric oxygen by photosynthesis, the control of erosion, and the hydrologic regulation of watersheds.
- *Stability of communities and larger ecosystems* is a notion that refers to constancy over time and that integrates both resistance to environmental change and the degree of resilience after a perturbation (Chapter 2). Stability is an over-arching quality, and it is relevant to all structural and functional attributes of ecosystems. Stability is

generally considered a desirable attribute of economically important ecosystems, because it allows for predictable harvests of natural resources.

The idea that ecosystems with greater levels of biodiversity are more stable began with the musings of Elton (1958) and MacArthur (1955) about community-level buffering and species redundancy in the face of biotic and inorganic perturbations. These ideas have been the subject of a great deal of theoretical and empirical research, some of which (including the modelling work of May, 1973) has resulted in contrary ideas, i.e., the suggestion that higher levels of diversity do not always result in greater stability. Although the subject area remains controversial and is not yet resolved (McCann, 2000), the notion of biodiversity promoting stability is a commonly expressed idea in support of the need for conservation actions. In actual fact, stability may be associated not only with the richness of biodiversity, but also with the kinds of species that are present and the particular roles they play within their communities.

Regardless of the controversy, it is clear that ecological services are crucial to maintaining the stability and integrity of natural ecosystems, including those managed to directly serve the human economy. Peter Raven, a well-known botanist and advocate of biodiversity conservation, once said: "In the aggregate, biodiversity keeps the planet habitable and ecosystems functional." However, despite their obvious importance, most people assume that vital ecological services are provided by biodiversity for "free" (at no cost). For this reason, society has not attributed an appropriate economic value to those ecological services. This is the case because few economists or leaders of society understand and appreciate the important role that ecological services play in sustaining the human economy and the natural world, and the vital role of biodiversity in providing those functions.

Some ecological services are dependent on the presence of specialized organisms, such as the nitrogen-fixing mutualism that involves *Rhizobium* bacteria living in root nodules of leguminous plants (Chapter 4). Another example is the top predators that help to regulate the abundance of organisms at lower trophic levels of their communities (Chapter 9). For instance, in 1995, wolves were re-introduced to Yellowstone National Park and its surrounding (or greater) ecosystem, a region where they had been extirpated for about a century (Hamlin and Cunningham, 2009). In the absence of wolves and other abundant predators (such as grizzly bear), an over-population of elk (*Cervus elaphus*) had developed and these herbivores were degrading their own food resource. In particular, they were preventing the regeneration of aspen and willows by their excessive feeding on shoots and saplings. The introduced wolves increased in abundance in the greater Yellowstone region, and in areas where they and other predators were relatively abundant, they reduced the elk population, which in turn allowed the woody species to regenerate and improved the overall health of the ecosystem.

In other cases, ecological services are driven by an entire community, such as the decomposition of dead organic matter, which in a terrestrial habitat is accomplished by all of the microbes, animals, and other members of the soil ecosystem. Landscape-level biodiversity is also relevant to functional ecology in, for example, modifying the flows and water quality of streams and rivers that drain a watershed.

Aesthetic Value

Aesthetic values are associated with sensory and emotional perceptions. Aesthetic values involve critical thought on cultural expressions (such as literature, art, music, and video) and also on aspects of the natural world, including judgments about sentiment and tastefulness. Perceptions of aesthetic values are conditioned by social influences, which may be associated with religion, group culture, and other collective ideals.

Aesthetic value is relevant to biodiversity in the sense that many people find certain elements to be charismatic and alluring, as is commonly the case of baby animals of all sorts, the species we keep as companions (pets), as well as iconic species such as the giant panda (*Ailuropoda melanoleuca*), polar bear (*Ursus maritimus*), orca (*Orcinus orca*), and harp seal (*Phoca groenlandica*). Many people also find certain kinds of natural ecosystems to be appealing and even to have a spiritual quality, such as old-growth forest with gigantic trees, free-flowing rivers, and other sorts of natural wilderness. Because so many people hold affectionate feelings about wild creatures and wild places, they are increasingly influencing politicians and other decision makers to conserve natural biodiversity.

Moreover, people in many countries believe that biodiversity and its aesthetics are important to their national cultural identify. In Canada, for example, images of biodiversity figure prominently on many of our symbols, starting with the flag (with a maple leaf) and extending to coinage, paper currency, and stamps, as well as different forms of artistic and literary expression. The native species and wild places of Canada are iconic in the minds of Canadians, and this indicates a great affection for those natural values.

J. E. H. MacDonald, *Algoma Bush, September*, 1920, McMichael Canadian Art Collection, Gift of Mr. R. A. Laidlaw, Object number 1966.15.3.

The iconic status of artists such as Emily Carr and the Group of Seven reflects the value Canadians attach to the natural landscape. This 1920 painting, *Algoma Bush, September*, is by Group of Seven artist J. E. H. MacDonald.

In some respects, aesthetic values of biodiversity can become instrumental values, if people are willing to pay money to have access to these appealing "resources." They may do this by spending time in wild places to directly experience biodiversity, and may travel long distances to do so. People may also engage biodiversity indirectly, by spending time and money to read about it, and by watching its coverage on television and other visual media. They may also donate funds to environmental charities whose focus is the conservation of biodiversity.

Intrinsic Value

Intrinsic value or **inherent value** is associated with unique, irreplaceable, and aesthetic qualities that are assigned to biodiversity and other components of the natural world. Intrinsic value exists "within itself" and "for its own sake," and it is different from utilitarian valuation because it is not based on what people need, either directly or indirectly.

Because biodiversity has intrinsic value, ethical questions arise concerning human actions that might threaten any of its levels: genetics, species, communities, and ecoscapes. Although humans can survive only by harvesting and using the products of biodiversity, do we have the right to degrade or exterminate its unique and irretrievable elements? Clearly, the modern human enterprise is physically empowered by our advanced sociocultural-technological systems to easily achieve this sort of destruction, and in fact this damage is now occurring widely in the form of extinctions of many species and the endangerment of certain natural communities. But is it the correct thing to do, in view of the losses of irreplaceable entities having their own intrinsic value? Is human existence itself degraded by extinctions and endangerment caused by our wanton practices? These are, of course, philosophical issues that cannot be resolved by the cool logic of natural science. However, truly enlightened people and societies would not facilitate irreparable damage caused to biodiversity. This is an ethic and opinion that many ecologists recognize.

Biodiversity Is Viewed as Important

Those who understand the issues about biodiversity believe that it is worthwhile and must be conserved. This broadly held public view is increasingly being shared by politicians and other decision makers, who are beginning to take coordinated actions to help conserve biodiversity within their arenas of responsibility.

At the international level, this fact is evidenced by the Convention on Biological Diversity (CBD). The

CBD was presented in 1992 at the "Earth Summit" in Rio de Janeiro, Brazil. Canada was the first industrialized country to sign on to the CBD at Rio and then to ratify it a few months later; as of 2009, the CBD was ratified by 191 countries. The vision of the CBD is to sustain life on Earth, and to promote this goal it has three broad objectives (CBD, 2009):

1. the conservation of biodiversity;
2. sustainable use of biological resources; and
3. fair and equitable sharing of benefits from the use of genetic resources.

As a signatory nation to the CBD, Canada is obliged to assess the adequacy of its efforts to conserve biodiversity, to use biological resources in a sustainable manner, and to identify and fill gaps in its relevant policies and actions. One obligation is to develop a national strategy for implementation of the CBD. This has led to the development of important policies and actions, including

- a Canadian biodiversity strategy to guide the implementation of the provisions of the CBD (Environment Canada, 1995);
- assessments of biodiversity and its conservation needs in Canada (Environment Canada, 1994; CESCC, 2006); and
- a national *Species at Risk Act* (2002) and comparable legislation in the provinces and territories.

These initiatives and others by environmental organizations in Canada (including non-governmental ones) are examined in more detail in Chapter 14.

For now, it is important to acknowledge that issues related to the conservation of biodiversity and the sustainable use of its products are now widely recognized as being important to society, and effective actions to achieve these goals are beginning to be undertaken. It is also important to note, however, that the global biodiversity crisis is proceeding apace, and much more must yet be done.

12.3 Measuring Biodiversity

Biodiversity is a broad and hierarchical concept, and ecologists need standard measures that are relevant at its various levels. These measures provide useful indicators that enable comparisons of biodiversity among different environmental situations, and that help to evaluate the outcomes of management actions that may be undertaken to conserve biodiversity. The following indicators are frequently used in ecological studies to measure and report on biodiversity. It should be noted, however, that ecologists do not all agree on which indicators are the best ones to use.

Genetic-Level Biodiversity

Genetic variability within populations, or among them, may be studied by examining various kinds of **markers**—a genetic element (allele, gene, DNA sequence, or chromosome feature) of an individual that can be detected by cytological, molecular, or phenotypic methods. Frequently reported indicators at the molecular level include heterozygosity and the number of different allele forms per gene in a population. Heterozygosity is the frequency of occurrence of heterozygotes (pairs of different alleles) for a particular gene. Genetic variation may be studied by a variety of methods, including the sequencing of genes or selected DNA sequences, or other analyses such as "DNA fingerprinting" that examine particularly variable regions of a genome.

An additional method involves studying the phenotypic variations that occur when organisms are grown under identical environmental conditions. Such experiments presume that any observed differences in morphology or biochemistry are due to genetic differences among individuals; this is because the common-environment research design (also known as a "common-garden" experiment) reduces the influence of phenotypic plasticity.

Differences in any of these indicators might be examined among populations occurring in different environmental regimes, along geographical or environmental gradients, or under varying management regimes.

Diversity of Species

Most ecological references to biodiversity allude to the numbers of species occurring within communities or in some geographic area, such as a park or other protected area, or even in a province or country.

In many studies, community-level biodiversity is considered separately for groups of organisms, either on a phylogenetic basis (such as bryophytes, vascular plants, arthropods, fishes, birds, or mammals) or as groups with a functional similarity (or guilds, such as ground vegetation, trees, epiphytes, or foraging or nesting guilds of birds). The particular choices of groups are usually made to suit the needs of the research project (for instance, there may be an interest in studying only birds).

Species Richness

Species richness is the simplest indicator. It is usually expressed as the number of species encountered after

A CANADIAN ECOLOGIST 12.1

John Macoun and Paul Hebert: Two Cataloguers of Canadian Biodiversity—The Old and the New

Topley Studio/Library and Archives Canada/PA-033784

John Macoun

Paul Hebert

Paul Hebert

The first people to seriously begin the cataloguing of the biodiversity of Canada were field naturalists. These were early biologists working in the 17th to early 20th centuries who were interested in the kinds of organisms that populated unexplored or otherwise poorly known regions. Some of them were brave and intrepid explorers of enormous tracts of Canadian wilderness, spending long uncomfortable months in wild places collecting specimens during the growing season, and then using the lingering winters to prepare, identify, and classify their many specimens. One of the best known of the early field-naturalists to work in Canada was John Macoun (1831–1920), the first Dominion Botanist of the Geological Survey of Canada. Macoun was a tireless and insightful biologist who worked all across our country, from coast to coast and also in the Arctic. He identified many new species and clarified the ranges of untold others, catalogued thousands of botanical specimens (these are deposited in the National Herbarium at the Canadian Museum of Nature in Ottawa), and wrote the epic tomes *Catalogue of Canadian Plants* (in seven parts, published between 1883 and 1902) and *Catalogue of Canadian Birds* (in three parts, 1900–1902; co-authored with James Macoun, his son).

The taxonomic work of Macoun and other earlier biologists largely involved working with the anatomical characteristics of specimens, often of whole organisms. Today their valuable amassed collections, together with those of many other collectors and taxonomists, fill voluminous shelves and drawers in museums and herbaria (plant collections), and these great compendia of Canadian biodiversity are still being added to. These repositories provide vital support to biologists working on biodiversity using the relatively traditional methodologies of classification, taxonomy, and phylogenetics of the 20th century, such as careful measurements of the bones of vertebrates or the exoskeleton of invertebrates, or of the floral and foliar organs of plants, followed by statistical and mathematical analyses to establish differences and relationships among groups of organisms.

The classical methods of systematic research still have great value, but they are being augmented by new developments involving advanced techniques in molecular biology. For instance, the identity and relatedness of species is being studied using such molecular techniques as the direct analysis of nucleotide sequences of nucleic acids, particularly DNA. Molecular biologists are also developing innovative methods for the identification of unknown specimens.

One of the leaders in this approach is Paul Hebert of the University of Guelph. Hebert has undertaken work on the molecular biology and evolutionary relationships of various groups of organisms, particularly insects. Perhaps more importantly, however, he is the champion of the International Barcode of Life Project, a global, collaborative initiative that involves the collection of biological specimens of diverse types from around the world, analysis of their DNA, and cataloguing of the data on high-capacity computer systems for easy retrieval and comparison with new specimens as they arrive. One goal of this program is to develop a practical facility that would allow ecologists to easily identify large numbers of specimens collected during fieldwork. Another goal is loftier—to analyze the large accumulated database in ways that will allow novel insights into the evolutionary relationships of biodiversity, ranging from those of closely related groups to others more distantly connected on the diverse tree of life.

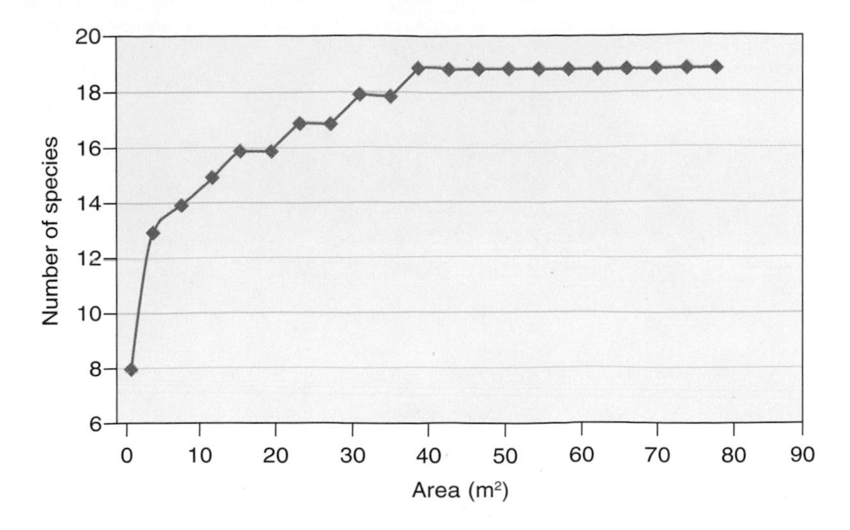

FIGURE 12.1
A Species-Area Curve. These data show that within a community, the observed species richness increases as the sampled area becomes larger, eventually reaching an asymptote where no new species are added. The data are for an alpine meadow community in Kluane National Park, Yukon.

SOURCE: Unpublished data of J. McLaren and R. Turkington.

a search of a community, or of some designated geographical area, such as a park. This is sometimes known as **alpha diversity**: the number of species within a community or in another delineated ecosystem. Occasionally, species richness within a community may be expressed as a density function, such as species/m^2 or species/ha. Of course, the sampling effort has an influence on the number of species that are detected—the larger the area searched, the longer the time spent doing so, and the number of observers all affect how many species are discovered. This effect is illustrated in **Figure 12.1,** which shows that increasing effort initially has a direct influence on the numbers of species detected, but this declines and eventually becomes asymptotic as the total species richness of a particular environment is being approached.

Species Diversity

Species diversity is a commonly reported indicator of biodiversity at the community level. This measure accommodates both the number of species present and their relative abundances (**evenness**). The latter may be estimated in various ways, such as the relative population size (the abundance of a particular species divided by the total abundance of all species) or the relative biomass. The Shannon-Weiner function is a commonly used index of species diversity:

$$H' = -\sum_{i=1}^{s} p_i \log_e p_i$$

where H' is the index of species diversity and p_i is an estimate of the probability that any individual encountered during a random search will be of a designated, *i*th species. As just noted, p_i is often estimated as relative abundance. The natural logarithm is usually used (ln or log*e*) in this calculation, and the value of H' is greatest if evenness is maximized—if all species have the same relative abundance.

Simpson's Index (D)

Simpson's index (D) is another indicator of diversity in communities. It estimates the probability that two randomly sampled individuals will be of the same species, and is calculated using the following equation:

$$D = 1 - \frac{\Sigma\, n(n-1)}{N(N-1)}$$

where n = the number of individuals of a particular species and N = the total individuals of all species. The value of D may range from 0 (no diversity) to 1 (high diversity). Simpson's index is related to **beta diversity**: the number of species that is unique to a community or to another defined ecosystem.

Comparison of the Indicators

Consider the following table that shows two theoretical communities, each composed of five species and 100 individuals.

	Abundance (number of individuals)	
Species	**Community A**	**Community B**
A	96	20
B	1	20
C	1	20
D	1	20
E	1	20
Species richness	5	5
Shannon-Weiner (H')	0.2	1.3
Simpson's (D)	0.079	0.808

Both communities have the same species richness, but their diversity as measured by the Shannon-Weiner and Simpson's functions are vastly different on the basis of the equitability of distribution of individuals among species. In general, these latter are better

Some alien species may be beautiful and useful in other ways, but communities in which they are abundant are viewed as having degraded ecological integrity. The dominant plant in this Ontario scene is purple loosestrife (*Lythrum salicaria*), an invasive weed that damages native plants by crowding them from shallow wetland habitats.

indicators because they accommodate differences among species in their rarity and commonness, whereas species richness does not do this.

Native and Alien

It is important to understand that none of the community-level indicators just presented take into account whether species are native or alien to the local biogeography. For habitats that have been penetrated by non-native species this is an important consideration, because the presence and/or dominance by aliens is considered to represent a degradation of ecological integrity (Chapter 17). For this reason, in spite of some of the ecological benefits that may be associated with higher levels of community-level biodiversity, conservation managers would not seek to maximize this objective if it were accomplished by adding alien species (see Chapter 14).

Richness of Communities

At the level of an ecoscape, biodiversity is related to the variety of distinct ecological communities, as well as the heterogeneity of their spatial distribution and dynamics over time. A landscape or seascape that is blanketed with a single community has little biodiversity at this level, compared with one that supports a rich and dynamic mosaic of types. This is related to **gamma diversity**, or the richness of different communities within a larger study region.

Indicators of biodiversity at the ecoscape level might be examined over a large area that has been designated for the purposes of management (such as a park), or for an ecological study (such as an ecozone or ecoregion; Chapter 11), or for a political purpose (such as a country or province). The indicators typically involve measures that parallel those used for communities:

- *Richness*: This involves the number of distinctive community types (patches) occurring within a large designated area.
- *Shannon-Weiner and Simpson's diversity*: These are computed from community richness and the relative area of the types, calculated using the same equations as noted above.
- *Other criteria*: These relate to the spatial complexity of ecoscapes and are discussed in Chapter 13, such as the shape, size, connectedness, age-class adjacency, and edge:area ratios of patches.

12.4 Summary and Prognosis

Biodiversity is the very fabric of life, comprising all of the variation of genes, organisms, and larger ecosystems. Ultimately, it represents the richness of all life in the biosphere—of the only place in the universe where life and ecosystems are known to exist. Biodiversity is a long-term result of the genesis of life on this planet, and of its evolutionary modification over time in response to environmental changes. Biodiversity has never been a static attribute of the biosphere. During most of the history of life, biodiversity has changed slowly through evolution and extinction. However, there have also been a few catastrophic events of mass extinction during which most of the existing biota was lost. In a few cases, mass extinctions are thought to have occurred in an instant of time, apparently caused by an extraordinary and cataclysmic impact on Earth by a meteorite, most recently the one that hit in the Yucatan region about 65 million years ago. Today, biodiversity is also in the midst of a mass extinction, but in this case it is being caused by habitat destruction and other damages caused by the human economy. We will examine this crisis of biodiversity extinction and endangerment in Chapter 14.

VOCABULARY OF ECOLOGY

aesthetic value, p. 375
alpha diversity, p. 379
beta diversity, p. 379
biodiversity (biological diversity), p. 361
clone, p. 363
ecoscape, p. 361
endemic, p. 365
endemic species, p. 364
evenness, p. 379
extinct, p. 374
extirpated, p. 374
gamma diversity, p. 380
genome, p. 363
instrumental value (utilitarian value), p. 372
intrinsic value (inherent value), p. 376
marker (genetic marker), p. 377
nutrient cycling, p. 374
over-harvesting (over-exploitation), p. 374
phenotypic plasticity, p. 363
population diversity, p. 366
species, p. 366
species diversity, p. 379
species richness, p. 366
stability, p. 374

QUESTIONS FOR REVIEW AND DISCUSSION

1. What is biodiversity? Explain how it exists at several hierarchical levels.
2. What is an endemic species? Why are they uncommon in Canada, compared with tropical places?
3. Why is biodiversity important? Provide examples of how it affects your own life.
4. Explain the notion of intrinsic value, and why it is relevant to biodiversity.
5. The data in the table below relate to the cover (an estimate of abundance, measured in percentage) of the plant species in two tundra communities on Baffin Island. For each community, calculate the species richness, Shannon-Weiner diversity, and Simpson's Index.

Species	Community 1	Community 2
Arctagrostis latifolia (a grass)	1	1
Carex bigelowii (a sedge)	2	0
Cassiope tetragona (arctic heather)	5	25
Dryas integrifolia (arctic avens)	40	25
Empretrum nigrum (black crowberry)	17	5
Pedicularis capitata (capitate lousewort)	3	0
Salix arctica (arctic willow)	25	10
Saxifraga tricuspidata (prickly saxifrage)	2	0
Saxifraga oppositifolia (purple saxifrage)	3	5
Silene acaule (moss phlox)	1	1

HELPFUL WEBSITES

BIODIVERSITY

http://www.enviroliteracy.org/subcategory.php/107.html

The Environmental Literacy Council, a U.S. organization, explains biodiversity and provides numerous links to other sources of information.

BIODIVERSITY IN CANADA: A SCIENCE ASSESSMENT FOR ENVIRONMENT CANADA

http://www.eman-rese.ca/eman/reports/publications/biodiv-sci-asses/intro.html

Discover what biodiversity is and its effects in Canada at this comprehensive website.

CANADIAN BIODIVERSITY INFORMATION NETWORK

http://www.cbin.ec.gc.ca/index.cfm?lang=e

This website of Environment Canada provides information about biodiversity issues in Canada, and links to many other useful websites.

CANADIAN BIODIVERSITY WEBSITE

http://canadianbiodiversity.mcgill.ca

This website, cooperatively developed by McGill University and Heritage Canada, hosts information about the biodiversity of Canada, as well as many helpful links.

CENTRE FOR MARINE DIVERSITY

http://www.marinebiodiversity.ca

The CMB is a cooperative organization with a focus on the marine biodiversity of Atlantic Canada.

ENCYCLOPEDIA OF LIFE

http://www.eol.org

The *Encyclopedia of Life* is an online collaboration that ultimately hopes to have Web-accessible pages of information for all of the named species on Earth.

TREE OF LIFE WEB PROJECT

http://tolweb.org/tree/phylogeny.html

This is an international collaborative project that provides links to more than 10 000 Web pages with information about species and higher groups of organisms. The data are linked together in the form of the tree of life that connects all organisms.

WORLD RESOURCES INSTITUTE

http://www.wri.org

The WRI is a leading source of credible information about a wide range of environmental and ecological topics, including biodiversity. For information about countries all around the world, check out its *EarthTrends* database at http://earthtrends.wri.org.

You'll find a rich array of additional resources for *Ecology* at www.ecology.nelson.com.

CHAPTER 13

Landscape Ecology

ROGER SUFFLING, Faculty of Environment, University of Waterloo

Mixedgrass prairie in the vicinity of Waterton National Park, AB. Photo by Bill Caulfeild-Browne

LEARNING OBJECTIVES

After studying this chapter you should be able to

1. Define landscape ecology and describe how it examines hierarchical scales in space and time.
2. Discuss how European and North American approaches to landscape ecology can contribute to applications in Canada in urban, rural, and wilderness settings.
3. Employ landscape elements (patch, corridor, and matrix) in your further studies.
4. Understand basic landscape metrics.
5. Understand how landscapes have changed historically and will do so in the future, using spatial and graphical approaches.
6. Describe landscape-scale functions (processes), with attention to the water cycle and disturbances.
7. Understand the importance of remote sensing, geographic information systems, and computer modelling as tools for working in landscape ecology.
8. Explain the importance of landscape ecology in pure ecology and in real-world applications.

CHAPTER OUTLINE

13.1 Introduction to Landscape Ecology

Landscape ecology may be defined as integrative, scale-related study of the structure, function, and changes of ecosystems. There are five core themes of landscape ecology (McGarigal, 2009b):

1. detecting and quantifying spatial **patterns** on large areas (spatially repeated landscape elements);
2. characterizing abiotic and biotic agents that influence the formation of patterns, including landforms, species and their interactions, and anthropogenic influences;
3. understanding the implications of pattern for populations, communities, and landscape-scale ecosystems;
4. characterizing and quantifying changes in pattern and process (such as disturbances and movements of materials) over space and time; and
5. managing landscapes and their dynamics to achieve conservation and economic objectives.

Definitions of **landscape** have varied greatly, but an organism-orientated approach allows us to conceptualize a landscape at any scale that is relevant to the problem at hand. In this sense, a landscape may be only a square metre in extent from the perspective of an insect, or tens of kilometres across for many large mammals. Therefore, a landscape is a heterogeneous area with repeated forms at any appropriate scale.

In this chapter we will examine landscapes in a scale context, so it is appropriate to clarify "large" and "small" scales. However, because the meaning of these terms is confused in ordinary parlance, ecologists use the term "**coarse scale**" to mean covering a relatively large area (typically in relatively little detail), and "**fine scale**" to denote its opposite.

Landscapes are exceedingly complex systems whose components interact in an intriguing, nonlinear, and sometimes unpredictable fashion (Holling, 1992). Aspects of the ecology of streams that support Pacific salmon in western Canada illustrate this principle. In this non-linear system, one could start in any of many places, such as where avalanches and debris flows cause trees to topple into streams. This increases the abundance of woody debris that provides nutrients and physical structure that are important to many species, including salmon (Nakamura et al., 2000). Moderate accumulations of woody materials often improve the salmon habitat, but if the debris presents a blockage, salmon cannot migrate upstream and potential breeding habitat becomes unavailable to them. In this sense, erosion and other local factors mediate the ability of salmon to spawn and of their young to survive. There are important cascading effects of these influences on nursery streams. For instance, juvenile salmon migrate to the ocean, where they feed and grow to adulthood. Oceanic salmon are food for orcas, seals, and other large predators, and are an important fishery for humans. When adult salmon migrate back to their natal rivers to spawn, they are a "conveyor belt" that takes concentrated packages of nutrients inland from the ocean, helping to sustain the productivity of streams (Schindler et al., 2003). Moreover, bears drag salmon carcasses into streamside forest, thereby enhancing the nutrient supply in the terrestrial part of the watershed (Quinn et al., 2009). Clearly, all parts of this system are interconnected, and ecological properties emerge in the landscape system that cannot easily be predicted from its component ecosystems.

Therefore, landscapes are hierarchically structured and scale-dependent. Depending on the ecological questions being examined, a landscape can be large and coarse-scale. This is illustrated in **Figure 13.1** for the farms, woodlots, and cities of southern Ontario where landscape mosaics cascade from coarse land-use scales right down to fine patterns of mosses among driveway pavers.

Note that it is also possible to have aquatic "landscapes." These may include seascapes and riverscapes, or an integration of these with terrestrial areas, as in watersheds. The term **ecoscape** is useful in this context—it refers to coarse-scale ("large-scale")

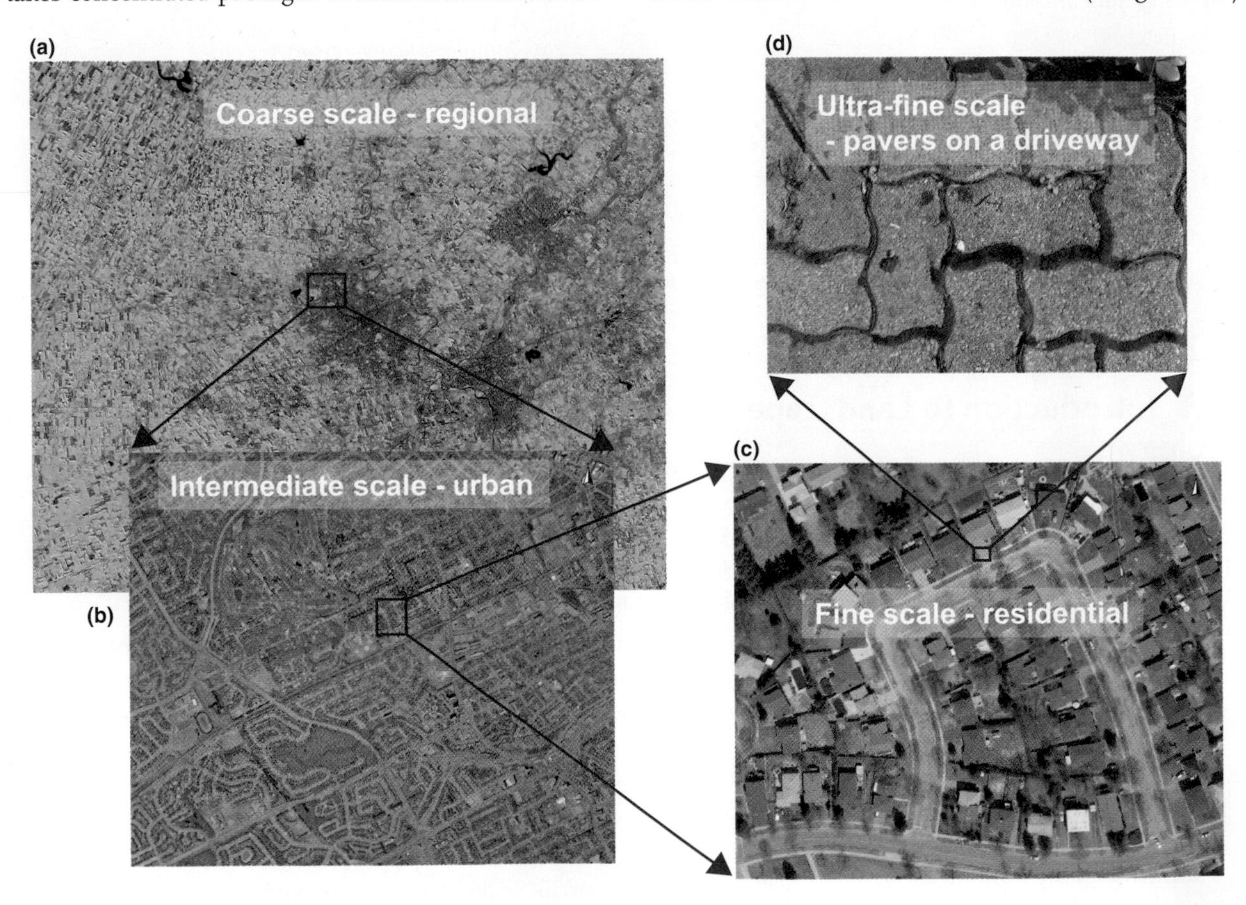

FIGURE 13.1

Much of Landscape Ecology Relates to Hierarchy and Spatial Scale. These images show hierarchical patterns in the southern Ontario region encompassing Guelph, Kitchener-Waterloo, and Cambridge. (a) At the coarsest scale, in a false colour image, a rectangular pattern has been created as a matrix of agricultural land (light green and pink), with isolated remnant woodlots (dark green) and growing city patches (purple and grey). (b) At intermediate scale, the suburban mosaic ecosystem is dictated artificially by a grid of streets. (c) At fine scale, the urban ecosystem pattern is influenced by lot lines and landscaping fashion. (d) At the ultra-fine scale, the moss micro-ecosystem is a network between the paving stones on a driveway.

SOURCE: Roger Suffing (top right); Landsat.org, Global Observatory for Ecosystem Services, Michigan State University (http://landsat.org) (top left); Geographic Information Systems (GIS), The City of Kitchener. http://www.kitchener.ca/maps/maps.html#Data (bottom left); Geographic Information Systems (GIS), The City of Kitchener. http://www.kitchener.ca/maps/maps.html#Data (bottom right).

patterns and ecological processes in both terrestrial and aquatic contexts.

The Importance of Landscape Ecology

Landscape ecology is an important way of understanding ecosystems, because it can allow for novel and useful insights into ecological problems. This can be illustrated by the work of Jens Roland (1993) of the University of Alberta, who investigated the ecology of tent caterpillars (*Malacosoma disstria*) in Ontario forests (**Figure 13.2**). This native moth periodically irrupts in huge numbers, and when this happens, aspen trees (*Populus tremuloides*) are defoliated at a regional scale, with important ecological and economic consequences. Rather surprisingly, Roland found that the abundance of the aspen host on the landscape had little influence on the persistence of the outbreak. He then hypothesized that regions in which the forest had become fragmented would have longer-lasting irruptions. Theoretical studies by others had already shown that if the mobility of pathogens and parasitoids is impaired more than that of the host, then outbreaks should be more persistent. Roland pursued this idea using techniques in landscape ecology. In his analysis, the amount of forest edge per km^2 of that habitat, an indicator of the degree of **fragmentation**, was the best predictor of the duration of outbreaks. Therefore, forest disturbances by wildfire, timber harvesting, and agriculture not only have large direct effects on this ecosystem, but fragmentation may mediate outbreaks through relationships among caterpillars and their parasitoids and pathogens. This is a typical example of how landscape ecology can improve our fundamental understanding of ecological science, as well as of land management.

(a) Forest tent caterpillar

(b) Defoliated aspen forest

(c) Forested (green) and non-forested land (white) in a single township

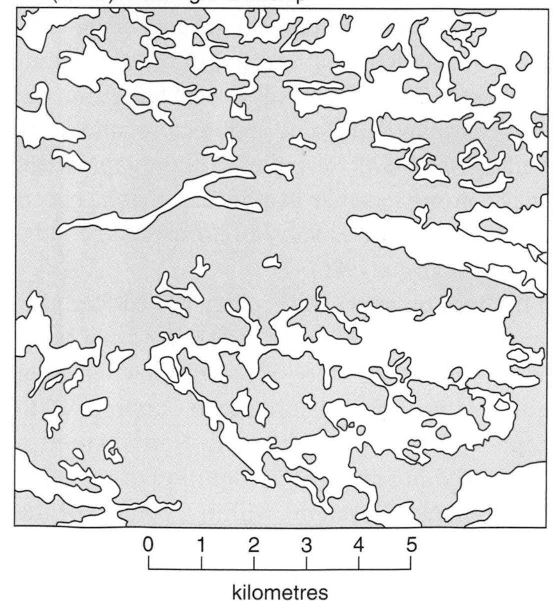

(d)

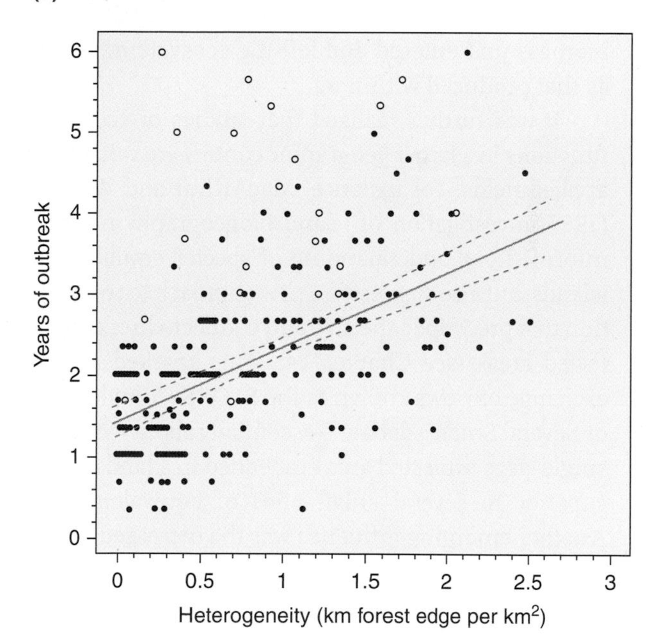

FIGURE 13.2

An Example of Landscape Ecological Research. Outbreaks of the tent caterpillar (*Malacosoma disstria*) (a) in forest of trembling aspen (*Populus tremuloides*) (b) last longer where there has been extensive land clearance and fragmentation of the surviving forest (c). Each dot on the graph (d) represents one township. Although there are more aspen trees in the disturbed townships, the effect is not related to the amount of aspen.

SOURCES: (a) Thérèse Arcand, Natural Resources Canada, Canadian Forestry Service http://imfc.cfl.scf.rncan.gc.ca/photo.asp?photo=021199&lang=en&pest=i&nomLatinFull=Malacosoma disstria&auteur=Hubner; (b) Doug Collicutt/Nature North Zine; (c) Roland, J. 1993. "Large-scale forest fragmentation increases the duration of tent caterpillar outbreak," *Oecologia*, 93: 25–30. Map 1C, p. 26. With kind permission from Springer Science and Business Media; (d) Roland, J. 1993. "Large-scale forest fragmentation increases the duration of tent caterpillar outbreak," *Oecologia*, 93: 25–30. Figure 2, page 27. With kind permission from Springer Science and Business Media.

Origins of Landscape Ecology

Early biogeographers tended to see the environment as integrating various influences—physical, biological, and human. In 1939 Carl Troll (1899–1975), a German professor, laid out an agenda and methodology for landscape ecology by unifying ecological and geographical studies that were based on aerial photography. Much of the subsequent work in Europe focused on the development of terminology and community classification and nomenclature, and on improving the design of "working" landscapes (where the human economy is the predominant land use). A more recent focus has emerged from concerns for rural landscapes that are rapidly losing the functional benefits of traditional land management, and the need to find innovative and adaptable paths to conserve nature on a densely settled continent.

In North America, landscape ecology emerged from a traditional focus on individual places—such as a marsh, lake, or stand of forest. This usually involved the study of populations of several to many species, or their communities, often as components of such processes as trophic dynamics. This classical approach, originally developed by Lindeman (1942), was extended by studies of influences that are extraneous to individual ecosystems. The latter is typified by H. T. Odum's (1957) work on the food web of a lake at Silver Springs, Florida, where he accounted for biomass that entered and left the ecosystem, as well as that produced within it.

It was further realized that studies of ecological functions in a larger geographic context are valuable in applied fields. For instance, MacArthur and Wilson's (1967) investigation of island biogeography not only informed our understanding of species equilibria on islands, but also suggested a new approach to conservation that prescribed the size and connectedness of protected areas (see Chapter 14). This sparked a lively exchange of views known as the SLOSS ("Single Large or Several Small") debate—essentially about whether a single large protected area embedded in a landscape is superior to several small ones of equivalent area. Another emerging influence was the increased understanding of ecology that accrues from studying entire ecosystems as opposed to single communities. This is exemplified by the famous whole-lake experiments in the Experimental Lakes Area in northwestern Ontario by David Schindler and colleagues from the Department of Fisheries and Oceans and various universities (Chapter 2). It is also seen in experiments manipulating the vegetation throughout whole-watersheds at Hubbard Brook, New Hampshire (Chapter 10).

At about the same time, ecologists were questioning the idea of succession as being a predictable dynamic that terminated in climax-type communities. Instead, succession was being viewed as a process contingent on the order of occurrence and relative severity of stochastic events, such as a wildfire or hurricane. This movement matured as the so-called **new ecology** that emphasized complexity over reductionism, change over stable states, and an ecological world that includes the human economy and activities (Botkin, 1990). In general, scientists were moving toward understanding ecology at coarser scales and in a more integrative context.

Also, beginning in the early 1970s, new technologies radically transformed landscape ecology, including access to satellite-based and airborne remote sensing. Later on, geographical information systems emerged that facilitated hierarchical, integrated, spatially referenced analyses of a spectrum of environmental and biological data.

These rapidly advancing influences led to an expansion and re-definition of landscape ecology, a field that had existed for several decades. In part, the transition in North America was marked by the appearance in 1987 of the first specialty journal, *Landscape Ecology*. The field as it is now practised can be characterized as being highly quantitative and computerized; based on a systems approach, including the development of models; and often oriented toward understanding and conserving the vital attributes of wilderness and natural areas. In North America, the field is mainly practised by ecologists and often taught in schools of natural-resource management and forestry. In contrast, landscape ecology in Europe is mostly conducted within the fields of geography, landscape architecture, and land-use planning (**Table 13.1**). Nevertheless, these approaches are slowly coming together in a process that has been catalyzed by *Landscape Ecology*, an influential book by Forman and Godron (1986).

At the root of landscape ecology is a concern for the management of a cluster of interrelated places. In Europe, an increasing cadre of practitioners is using the quantitative North American approach to landscape ecology. Meanwhile, in North America there is belated but growing recognition of the need to manage many ecosystems within a context of the human economy, as in the extensively modified forests of southern Ontario, Quebec, and the Maritime provinces (Schmitt and Suffling, 2006).

Canada is fortunate to have had practitioners of both schools, such as Pierre Dansereau of the University of Quebec at Montreal and the University of Michigan, and Robert Dorney of the University of Waterloo, with their emphasis on "ecoplanning," as well as Edward Johnson of the University of Calgary, who has a quantitative and wilderness focus. Moreover, conservation organizations such as the

TABLE 13.1 Comparison of the North American and European Schools of Landscape Ecology

Attribute	European School	North American School
Predominant Scale	fine	coarse
Quantification	mostly qualitative, but increasingly quantitative	quantitative, with more qualitative papers appearing
Landscape Focus	dominantly urban, rural context involves anthropogenic "working" ecosystems	wilderness and resource hinterland, but with more rural and urban studies recently appearing
Predominant Disciplinary Origin	geography, planning, landscape architecture	ecology, resource management, forestry, systems research
Predominant Methods	descriptive/design-based, increasing GIS emphasis	model-based, with increasing GIS emphasis
Predominant Applications	rural planning, biological conservation	biological conservation, forest management, with recently increasing interest in urbanized regions

Nature Conservancy of Canada and Parks Canada are widely applying the methods and tools of landscape ecology to the development of plans for the designation and management of parks and nature reserves, as well as for stewardship of greater systems of protected areas.

Landscape ecology is also spreading to other countries, and it is having an increasingly widespread influence on land management. Practitioners tend to develop a national focus for their work, such as the ecology of wildfire in Australia, of agricultural landscapes in the United Kingdom, and of large-scale disturbances and protected areas in Canada. Canadians have also emphasized the development of ecological land classification. Of course, some interests are transnational, such as the effects of logging in the humid old-growth forests of the west coasts of Canada and the United States, and planning for immense conservation projects such as the binational Yukon-to-Yellowstone initiative.

Landscape ecology is rapidly evolving as a lively and varied school of thought with practical applications to ecological sustainability. Increasingly, the practitioners are using a transdisciplinary vision that transcends the impediments of traditional disciplinary subject areas (such as biology and geography) and professions (e.g., agrology, forestry, planning) (**Figure 13.3**). We shall return to this theme later in the chapter.

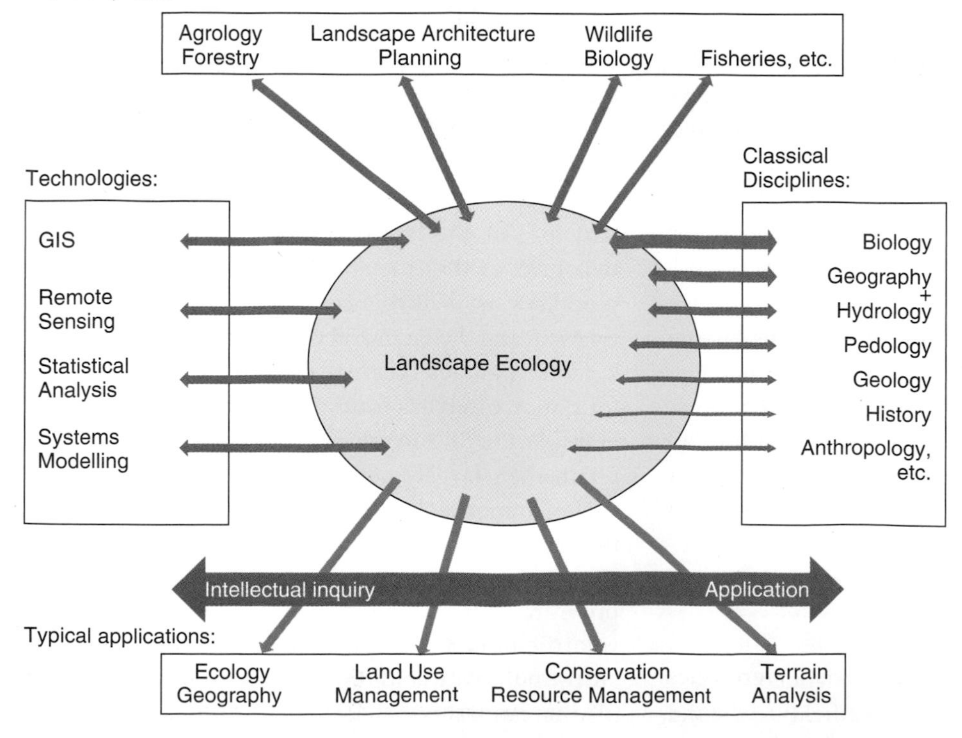

FIGURE 13.3
Professional Cultures. This conceptual model of landscape ecology shows the kinds of disciplinary and interdisciplinary fields that are engaged, the tools that are used, and the sorts of fundamental and applied investigations that are pursued.

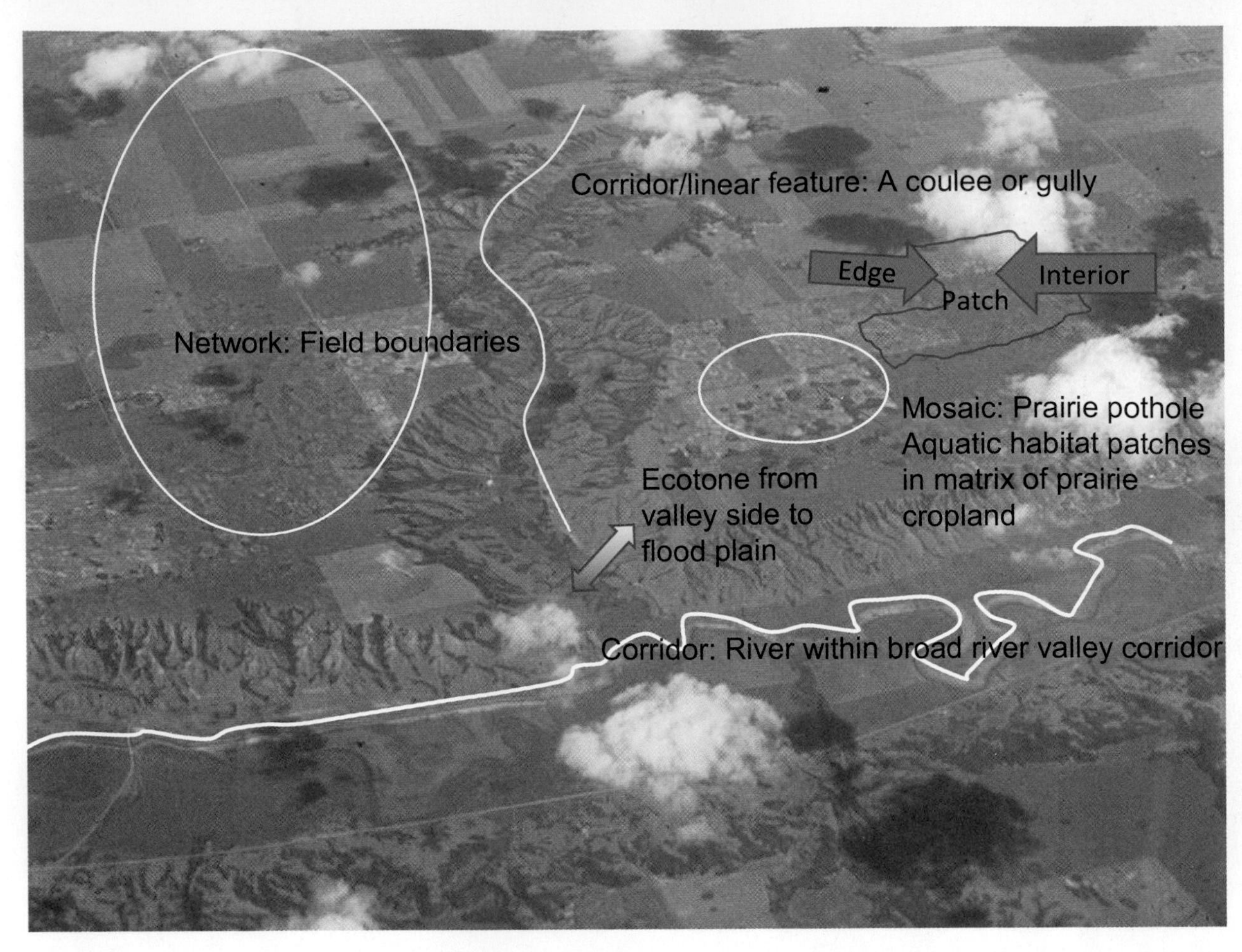

FIGURE 13.4

Landscape Elements: An Example from the Qu'Appelle Valley, Saskatchewan. The elements include mosaics, linear features, matrices, and patches, some occurring at various scales.

SOURCE: Roger Suffling.

13.2 Structure of Landscapes

Every landscape has **landscape structure**, in the sense of spatial elements that are generated by factors such as the underlying geology and geomorphology, as well as the disturbance history. Seemingly disordered landscape elements, such as patches of forest, prairie, wetlands, and water-courses, are all spatially interrelated. **Landscape elements** are the basis of describing the type, size, shape, number, and arrangement (configuration) of communities, and their use helps in the analysis of the distributions of energy and materials on a landscape (**Figure 13.4**). Such elements are usually classified as patches, corridors, and networks, all of which are examined in the following sections. These elements together form mosaics with their dominant matrices that are also described later.

Patches

A **patch** is a contiguous area of a single landcover class (such as a marsh, woodland, or wheatfield) or a stand of a particular community, and it is distinguished from its surroundings by discontinuities of environmental influences. Implicitly, the discontinuities influence the distribution and abundance of species and communities.

Patches can arise because of the underlying structure of the landscape, such as topography or moisture, or they may be created by such ecological processes as disturbances by wildfire, flooding, or clear-cutting. Forman and Godron (1986) defined five kinds of patches created by disturbances, but their formation often has multiple causes (**Figure 13.5**). For example, the St. Lawrence volcanic hills in **Figure 13.5e** retain their largely natural forest today because the rugged topography made the area unsuitable for the agricultural clearance that occurred on the surrounding sedimentary plain. However, even in pre-European settlement times, the forest of these volcanic hills must have differed from those of the surrounding lowlands and they may have constituted distinct landscape patches.

Roger Suffling

An Example of a Landscape Structure. This image is from Gros Morne National Park in Newfoundland. The boundary visible between the two communities is an inherent edge that is determined by a spatial change in geology and soil type. The lower community is influenced by serpentine minerals, which contain naturally occurring toxic nickel and cobalt and are highly deficient in the nutrients calcium, phosphorus, and nitrogen. This is also a wetter site. Plants growing in these soils are typically highly stressed and stunted in growth form, and they include species that are more usually found in arctic-alpine habitats. The higher community is a stand of mature boreal forest growing on a less-stressful site, and it is more typical of the region.

Patches have transitions where they abut other kinds of landcover units. Examples are a transition from forest to grassland, or where terrestrial vegetation meets a lake. Where the change is spatially abrupt it can be called an **edge**. Alternatively there is a gradual transition from one patch to another that exhibits characteristics of both types and is known as an **ecotone**. For instance, coastal salt marsh is an ecosystem type with distinct zonation—at the lower (seaward) edge is a community dominated by marine species, and at the upper margin by ones tolerant of a wide range of salinity because the higher terrain is only infrequently flooded by tides. Because species experience an ecotone differently, their individual reactions to these environmental transitions will vary. Some species, such as moose (*Alces alces*), take advantage of ecotones and edges by using resources from adjacent patches. The example in **Figure 13.6** shows a typology (classification) of edges.

Other scientific disciplines use different terms for ecotones, such as the **catena** of soil scientists, which is a gradation of conditions down a slope that has related changes in flora and fauna. Similarly, wetland ecologists refer to the transition from deeper to shallow water near a shore as a **littoral zone**, and from the river shoreline to terrestrial as a **riparian zone**.

Whether the spatial change in physical environment is gradual or sudden can control the development of either an abrupt edge or a gradual ecotone. For example, at relatively fine scales, a salt marsh can be studied as a number of distinct communities and patch types. At a coarser scale, salt marshes are a land–ocean ecotone whose width depends on the steepness of the coast. At an even coarser scale, the transition will be represented as an edge.

Patch shape is also an important consideration, because it affects the configuration and length of

Roger Suffling

The width of an ecotone may depend on the sharpness of an environmental gradient. On flat, sheltered coastal areas the gradual transition from land to sea allows the development of coastal salt marshes that flood and drain twice daily with the tides: a classic ecotone community. However, where the land rises steeply from the sea the transition will be spatially abrupt as on the far shore. This image shows coastal ecosystems on Cape Breton Island, Nova Scotia.

FIGURE 13.5

These Types Exemplify the Kinds of Patches Identified by Forman and Godron (1986) and Forman, (1995). (a) Spot patch. This disturbance patch is being created by a prescribed burn in boreal forest. (b) A regenerated patch. An aspen (*Populus tremuloides*) clone is spreading into grazing land in the Rocky Mountains, with more success to the right of the fence where there is less grazing pressure. (c) Remnant patches. Eucalypt groves among dairy pastures in Victoria, Australia. (d) An ephemeral patch/introduced patch. Corn and soy bean cropland on a karst hillside in Guangxi, China. (e) An environmental patch created by a sharp environmental discontinuity. In this case, three volcanic plugs in the St. Lawrence Valley of Quebec have retained their forest cover because the steep rugged terrain proved unsuitable for agricultural clearance in contrast to the surrounding field landscapes on sedimentary rock.

SOURCES: (a) Spot patch photo (fire): Terry Curran; (b) Charles E. Kay; (c) Roger Suffling; (d) Yuqing Huang; (e) Image Science and Analysis Laboratory, NASA-Johnson Space Center. "The Gateway to Astronaut Photography of Earth." <http://eol.jsc.nasa.gov/scripts/sseop/LargeImageAccess.pl?directory=EFS/highres/ISS014&filename= ISS014-E-19807.JPG&filesize=982258>

edges (**Figure 13.7**). A circular patch has the smallest ratio of edge to area and will have the largest interior for a given patch size. Conversely a patch with a highly irregular shape will have a large amount of edge in relation to its area. Patch shape is potentially influenced by both the inherent factors in the landscape as well as the history and nature of disturbance events and their aftermath.

A sufficiently large patch will have an **interior habitat** within which there are distinct environmental conditions and a separate community. The patch interior is surrounded by an ecotonal zone that is influenced by adjacent patches. Small patches may have only an ecotonal zone. Certain species may be primarily restricted to interiors or to patch ecotones (**Table 13.2**), For instance, ruderal plants are prominent in fragmented landscapes with abundant edge habitat, but are rare in extensively forested areas. This is also the case of some animals, such as the red-tailed hawk (*Buteo jamaicensis*), which in southern Ontario is found mainly in regions with highly fragmented forest occurring in small patches, and even in suburbs. In contrast, the red-shouldered hawk (*Buteo linearis*) requires a more extensively forested landscape with bigger patches having interior zones (Bosakowski and Smith, 1997).

Many people associate interiors and ecotonal zones with forested landscapes, but the concept is broader: any patch in any ecoscape type, including grassland and coral reefs, may also have ecotonal and interior zones.

Current terminology concerning *ecotone* and *edge* has become confusing because landscape ecologists are being influenced by conventions in their computer maps. They use a line to delineate a patch boundary,

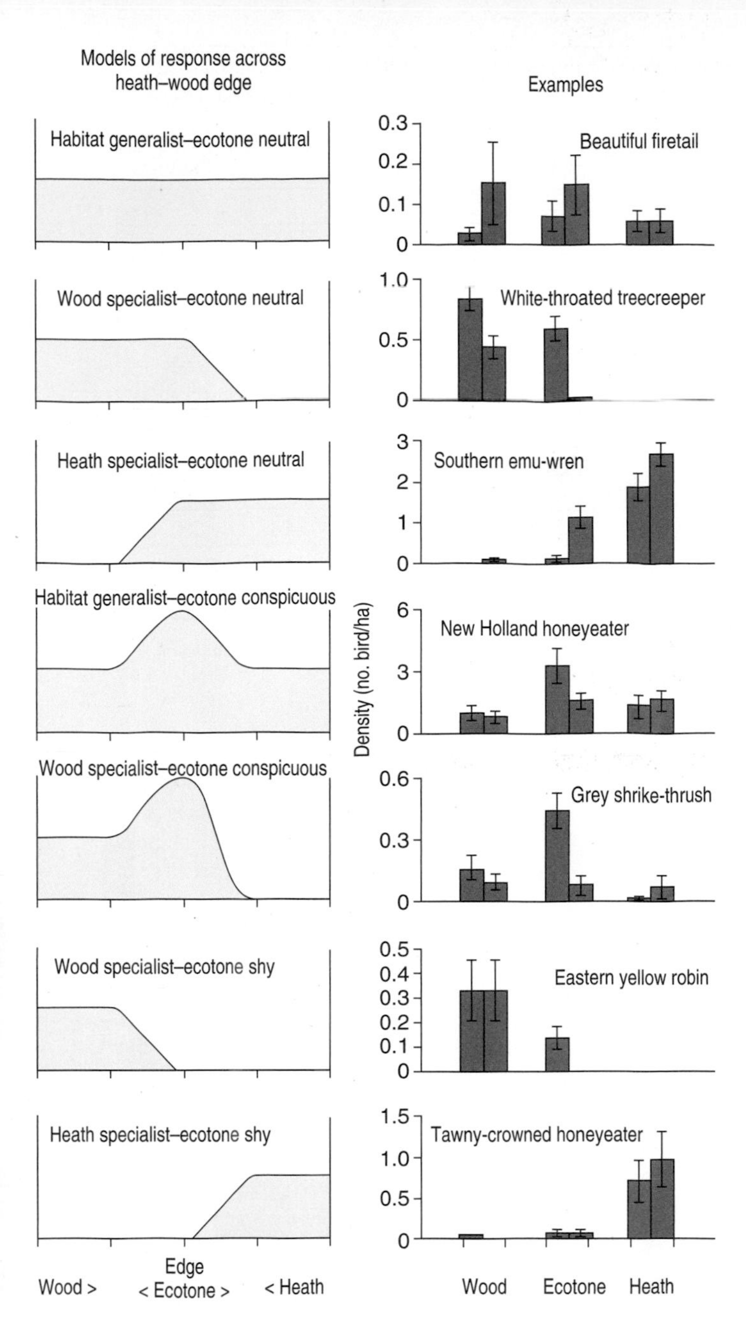

FIGURE 13.6

Various Species Experience an Ecotone Differently. In this Australian case different birds use the resources in the patches on either side of an ecotone in varying ways. The types identified here follow Odum's (1959) typology.

SOURCE: Used with permission of the Ecological Society of America, from Baker, J., K. French, and R.J. Whelan, 2002. "The edge effect and ecotonal species: Bird communities across a natural edge in southeastern Australia," *Ecology*, 83 (11): 3048–3059. Figure 7, p. 3054; permission conveyed through Copyright Clearance Center, Inc.

implying a distinct edge. This indicates that the ecotone is divided into two halves by a distinct edge, which is not often the case. For example, where patches abut each other they are often represented as having an ecotonal zone, so the sequence from one patch centre to the other is interior—ecotonal zone—patch boundary—ecotonal zone—interior. Moreover, various writers may use the terms *edge, edge zone, interior, patch boundary*, and *ecotone* in contradictory, ambiguous, and inconsistent ways.

Corridors

A **corridor** is a linear feature that differs from the matrix on either side. Corridors may be natural in origin, such as streams, rivers, and avalanche tracks through mountain forest. They may also be anthropogenic, such as rights-of-way for roads and transmission lines, seismic exploration lines, and shrubby or treed hedgerows between agricultural fields.

If the habitat present in a corridor is appropriate, it can provide a passage through which animals and plants can move between patches. This **connectivity** may allow a landscape with only limited areas of certain kinds of patches, such as older forest, to support extensive but viable **metapopulations** of various species. This is illustrated by a study by Bennett and colleagues (1994) of Carleton University, who found that chipmunks (*Tamias striata*) used shrubby fencerows to move between patches of forested habitat in a landscape dominated by agricultural fields **(Figure 13.8)**.

It is important to recognize that a corridor that facilitates the movement of one species between patches may not function well for others with different habitat needs. In fact, what is a corridor for one species may be a barrier to others—for example, a road may serve as a corridor to spread ruderal plants, but it can be a barrier for many animals. The quality of the habitat between patches in which a species lives is another important consideration—if this matrix is not so different from the primary habitat of a species, or if it can be crossed quickly, then it is **permeable** to movements even if it cannot be lived in on a long-term basis.

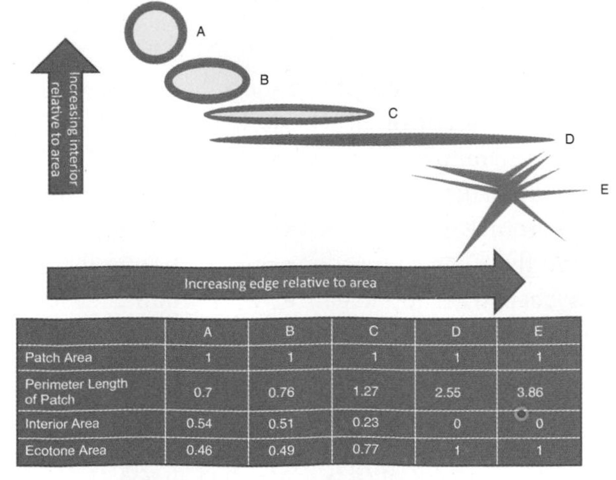

	A	B	C	D	E
Patch Area	1	1	1	1	1
Perimeter Length of Patch	0.7	0.76	1.27	2.55	3.86
Interior Area	0.54	0.51	0.23	0	0
Ecotone Area	0.46	0.49	0.77	1	1

FIGURE 13.7

The Influence of Patch Shape on Its Ecological Characteristics. Each of the hypothetical patches has the same area. Patch interiors are indicated by yellow, and edge/ecotones by blue. The effective width of the edge habitat is influenced by the requirements of species under study.

TABLE 13.2 The Incidence of Bat Species in the Edges and Interiors of Forest Patches in Illinois

The data are the numbers of each species captured at 41 sites in the Shawnee National Forest during 339 mist-net-nights of sampling.

Species	Edge	Interior	Total Captures
Northern long-eared bat *(Myotis septentrionalis)*	53	121	174
Red bat *(Lasiurus borealis)*	64	11	75
Eastern pipistrelle *(Pipistrellus subflavus)*	63	10	73
Big brown bat *(Eptesicus fuscus)*	25	6	31
Evening bat *(Nycticeius humeralis)*	17	3	20
Indiana bat *(Myotis sodalis)*	6	8	14
Little brown bat *(Myotis lucifugus)*	5	8	13
Southeastern bat *(Myotis austroriparius)*	10	0	10
Hoary bat *(Lasiurus cinereus)*	3	1	4
Silver-eared bat *(Lasionycteris noctivagans)*	3	0	3
TOTALS	**249**	**168**	**417**
Shannon-Wiener Diversity Index	1.84	1.09	1.71

SOURCE: Modified from Carroll, S.K., T.C. Carter, and D.A. Feldhammer. 2002. "Placement of nets for bats: Effects on perceived fauna," *Southeastern Naturalist*, 1: 193–198, Table 1.; permission conveyed through Copyright Clearance Center, Inc.

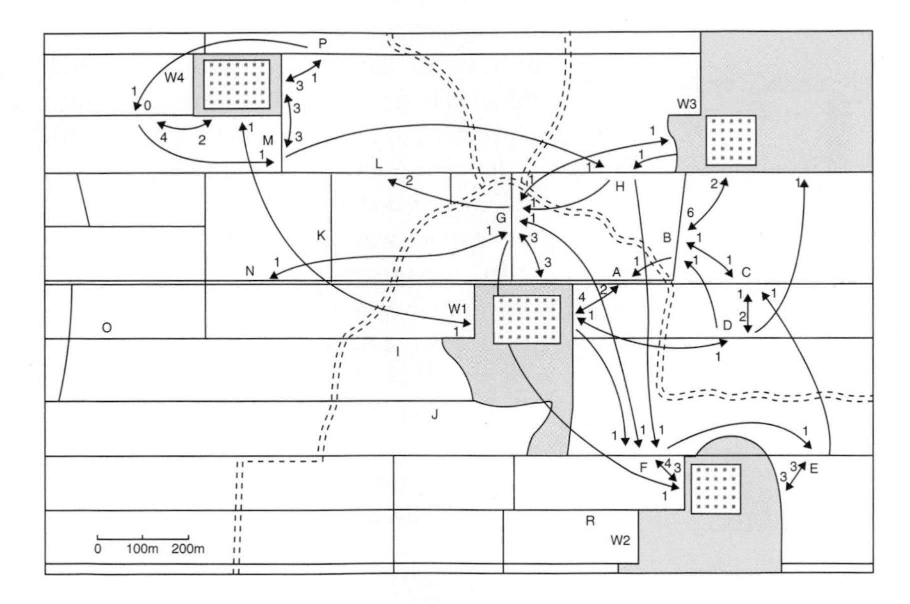

FIGURE 13.8

Inter-Patch Movements and Corridors. This map depicts the numbers and recorded movements of chipmunks (*Tamias striata*) between patches of woodland (W1–W4) in a largely agricultural landscape with fencerows (A–R). Most inter-patch movements involve animals travelling along shrubby fencerows at the margins of the open fields. Arrows indicate the direction of movement, but not the pathway. Fencerows are thin solid lines and streams are dashed lines.

SOURCE: Modified from: Bennett, A.F., K. Henein, and G. Merriam. 1994. "Corridor use and the elements of corridor quality–chipmunks and fencerows in a farmland mosaic," *Biological Conservation*, 68: 155–165. Figure 1, p. 159, with permission from Elsevier.

The functioning of corridors has been widely discussed on a theoretical basis, but empirical testing has been outpaced by the enthusiastic real-world implementation of corridors by planners, foresters, and resource managers. However, some studies have found that such connections can function well. This has been true, for instance, with wildlife "underpasses" and "overpasses" that have been constructed across the Trans-Canada Highway in Banff National Park. They are being routinely used by such animals as elk (*Cervus canadensis*), wolf (*Canis lupus*), and black bear (*Ursus americanus*) (Clevenger et al., 2002). However, in the absence of such evidence, one should not assume that a corridor provides a useful conservation function. A more conservative approach is to regard untested landscape corridors as being linear habitat features that may benefit some species.

Networks

A **network** is a series of interconnected linear elements, often surrounding patches of another type. A natural example of a landscape network is the net of aquatic connections that exist among lotic (streams and rivers) and lentic (ponds and lakes) waterbodies within a watershed. An anthropogenic example is the system of hedgerows that is often seen in agricultural regions.

Mosaic and Matrix

In most landscapes, the mix of elements forms a **mosaic**—a spatially integrated complex of patches, corridors, and networks that gives a landscape its ecological character. Two main groups of factors that affect the character of mosaics are (a) inherent

(a) A network of hedgerows in a cultural landscape in Worcestershire, United Kingdom.

Roger Suffling

(b) Ice-wedge polygons form a natural network in peatland of the Hudson Bay lowlands, Manitoba.

Reproduced with the permission of Natural Resources Canada 2010, courtesy of the Geological Survey of Canada (Photo 2001-120 by Lynda Dredge).

characteristics of the topography, geology, and climate, and (b) influences of more dynamic origin that are based on disturbance and succession. Of course, in most cases, a combination of these factors influences the characteristics of the mosaic.

The processes that generate and maintain mosaic patterns are a key area of study in landscape ecology. Mosaics can arise from underlying physiography and from ecological and other influences. For example, the numerous wetland complexes of the pothole prairie region were generated by melting blocks of glacial ice. The water that fills these depressions and allows wetlands to form is primarily maintained by snow-melt and rain, so fluctuations of weather regulate this system. However, the vitality of the pothole prairie ecosystem for breeding waterfowl is also tied to human activities. Farmers tend to plough farther into pothole depressions in dry years, thereby reducing marsh habitat, and the amount of cultivation pressure also depends on farm profitability. This in turn relates to commodity prices and global agricultural economics. Therefore, the pothole mosaic arises from inherent geological factors, and is also affected by dynamic influences that include climate, land use, and economic factors.

Ecological mosaics may be relatively fixed and enduring. This is the case of landscapes covered with old-growth forest, in which stand-replacing disturbances such as wildfire are uncommon. Some landscape mosaics are agricultural and thus are anthropogenic, such as those of the southern parts of prairie provinces, Quebec, and Ontario, in which there are persistent networks of roads and a mosaic of agricultural fields.

Landscapes whose pattern and functioning are strongly influenced by frequent disturbances may be in a dynamic equilibrium. One example is a

An aerial photo of prairie pothole ponds and lakes in Saskatchewan.

Two landscape mosaics. This mixed agricultural–forest landscape in eastern Ontario demonstrates two mosaics: (1) most of the area (left-hand) has deeper and relatively fertile soil and its matrix is mostly agricultural with isolated patches of forest; and (2) the south-eastern (lower right) has poorer-quality soil so its matrix is forest with islands of agricultural land use. Linear features such as roads, patch edges, and a boundary between the mosaic types are also visible. What are the implications of these sorts of landscapes for animals whose habitat requirement is forest, and for those that use open fields?

forestry-affected mosaic in which the patches are regenerating clear-cuts of various ages, and that are harvested again as soon as the trees grow big enough, depending on the growth rate, the harvest rotation might vary from only 20 years in the tropics to more than 80 years in boreal forest. The individual patches are changing through disturbance and subsequent ecosystem development, but the appearance of the whole mosaic may be relatively stable through time.

A mosaic usually consists of a predominant cover type, known as a **matrix** community, in which are embedded island-like patches of other kinds of ecosystems.

The characteristics of the matrix govern the coarse-scale distributions of organisms as they respond to variations of environmental conditions (**Figure 13.9**). There are critical thresholds at which a small change in the mosaic results in dramatic changes in the spatial distributions of species and communities. Communities also self-organize into mosaics during recovery after disturbance. For example, fire-dependent montane forests of lodgepole pine *(Pinus contorta)* in British Columbia and Alberta are naturally disturbed by mostly small, low-intensity, but frequent wildfires that create and perpetuate a fine-scale mosaic. However, routine fire suppression since European settlement has changed these conditions and created a de facto ecological experiment. The quenching of small burns has allowed forest stands to accumulate more biomass, which sets up the system for large, infrequent, intense wildfires and extensive pine-killing infestations by the mountain pine beetle *(Dendroctonus ponderosae)*. This change has created coarse-grained mosaics of large, uniform forest stands that represent a degradation of the natural ecological condition of the montane pine ecosystem

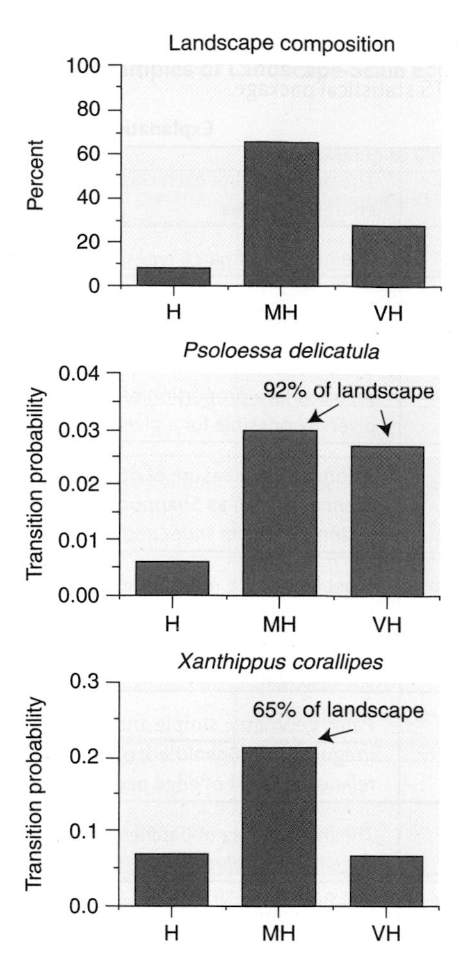

FIGURE 13.9

Change in the Dominant Matrix and Island Habitats Affects How Species Utilize a Landscape. In this case, two grasshopper species respond differently to variations in a microhabitat mosaic in shortgrass prairie in Colorado. The three mixtures of habitat types are H = homogeneous distribution of habitats; MH = moderately heterogeneous mixture; and VH = extremely heterogeneous. Heterogeneity is the degree to which the dominant shortgrass prairie matrix is interspersed by patches of other kinds of vegetation. The top diagram shows the composition of the landscape; the middle one shows the habitat use by the grasshopper *Psoloessa delicatula*; and the bottom one that of *Xanthippus corallipes*.

SOURCE: Modified with permission of the Ecological Society of America, from With, K.A. and T.O. Crist. 1995. "Critical thresholds in species responses to landscape structure," *Ecology*, 76 (8): 2446–2459, Fig. 10 Page 2455; permission conveyed through Copyright Clearance Center, Inc.

(Hessburg et al., 2005). These changes increase the risks to public safety and the forest-dependent economy from uncontrollable wildfires.

13.3 Measuring and Characterizing Landscapes

The size, shape, and separation of patches and corridors all affect the distributions of species and communities. Landscape ecologists need to characterize these attributes, and they use methods that range from subjective and pictorial to metrics (measurements used to characterize the landscape) that are objective, quantitative, and appropriate for statistical analyses. Both approaches are useful and have their place.

Landscape metrics are especially useful when testing hypotheses about the distribution and behaviour of species and communities. Commonly reported metrics that are available in the widely used FRAGSTATS statistical package are described in **Table 13.3.** They include measures that are compositional, such as the richness, evenness, and diversity of patches, and others that are related to spatial configuration, such as the density of patches and the complexity of their shapes.

In applied ecology, landscape metrics can be used to inform policy, land planning, and management activities, such as the development or application of regulations concerning non-developed buffers around wetlands and the configuration of clear-cuts. For instance, Fudge et al. (2007) from Dalhousie University related metrics of site and landscape conditions at places where white-tailed deer (*Odocoileus virginianus*), moose (*Alces alces*), and black bear (*Ursus americanus*) had been involved in vehicle collisions in Nova Scotia, and used that analysis as a platform to make recommendations for reducing the incidence of such lethal encounters.

Ecological Functions at the Scale of Landscape

Landscape-scale **ecological functions** (or processes) may be defined as flows of energy, materials, and species occurring among the patches or other spatial elements of landscapes (Forman and Godron, 1986). **Table 13.4** (p. 399) lists key ecological functions that operate in a landscape context, two of which we examine in detail in the following sections.

The Distribution of Water as a Landscape Function

The hydrological cycle operates at all scales, ranging from extremely local to biospheric. Its functional attributes in a terrestrial landscape include the extensive deposition of the water of rain and snow and its dissipation by evapotranspiration and by gravitational drainage to groundwater. Water may remain in a long-term underground reservoir known as an **aquifer**, or it may eventually emerge at a low point as a spring flowing into a pond, lake, or wetland, or into a stream or river for transport to the ocean. It is important to note, however, that the aquifer is the storage layer and not the stored water itself. The drainage of water through a landscape is determined by the physical structure of the terrain, including its topography, soil, and bedrock, but it is also considerably modified by organisms and their communities, especially by wetlands.

Terry Curran

An intense crown fire in northern Ontario. Fires of this kind in boreal forest usually kill most or all the trees and create new patches that regenerate to an even-aged forest.

On a particular landscape, communities are typically affected by only a few kinds of disturbances, and this has a major influence on ecological development. To illustrate this point we can examine the influence of wildfire on certain kinds of forests. The ecological effects of wildfire are complex, partly because these disturbances can vary greatly in their intensity (the rate of energy release per unit of burnt area):

- **Crown fires** burn the forest canopy, and in Canadian forests, generally kill the trees, so crown fires are a stand-replacing disturbance.
- **Surface fires** combust shrubs and ground vegetation but do not ladder into the canopy, so most trees survive the event.
- **Ground fires** are less common and are limited to burning the organic matter of the forest floor and soil.

Most wildfires in the boreal regions of Canada are crown fires that kill almost all of the mature trees so that new communities regenerate by secondary succession. However, forest communities vary greatly in their response to fire. For example, in the interior of British Columbia, open montane stands of lodgepole pine have a relatively small loading of shrubby fuel so that wildfires often do not reach the crown and most of the trees survive. However, in the same kind of forest, the long-term suppression of fire results in a high fuel loading, which sets the stage for an intense conflagration if an ignition occurs during windy and dry weather.

In Australia, even an intense crown fire in certain *Eucalyptus* forests may not be a stand-replacing disturbance, because the trees are adapted to and survive this kind of frequent disturbance. In contrast, even a low-intensity ground fire in wetland forest growing on peat may kill all trees by burning or steaming their roots. Therefore, it is useful to characterize the ecological effects of disturbances in terms of the severity of the damage that is caused (**Table 13.5**).

Petra Suffling

Even an intense fire may not be stand-replacing in some types of biome. These red tingle (*Eucalyptus jacksonii*) trees in western Australia live up to 400 years and are adapted to survive relatively frequent high-intensity crown fires. The circles show char from one or more previous non-lethal fires that reached high above the canopy.

Evan Seal Photography

A fire in the Burns Bog in the Fraser River delta, British Columbia. This ground fire cooks the tree roots. The intensity is low, but the severity is high and tree mortality complete. The relationship between fire intensity and severity is complex and depends on the frequency of burning, the weather, fuel loading, and the degree of adaptation of organisms.

TABLE 13.5 The Major Components of Natural Disturbance Regimes That Affect Forested Landscapes

Component of the Disturbance Regime	Definition	Example
Frequency (return interval)	Number of events caused by a given disturbance agent per unit of time at a given point in the landscape; return interval = 1/frequency	Wildfire events averaging every 75 years in boreal stands of black spruce (*Picea mariana*)
Rotation period	The time over which an area equal to that of the study area is disturbed; this component integrates the frequency and size of disturbance events	If 0.5 percent of a study are is burnt in an average year, then the rotation period is 200 years
Intensity	How much energy is released by a disturbance per unit area per unit time	Megajoules of energy released per hectare per minute during a wildfire, amount of snow released in an avalanche, or windspeed in a tornado
Severity	Effects of the disturbance on individual organisms, populations, communities, and landscapes	Numbers of trees that are killed per area by a wildfire event, area of avalanche track, area of tornado track
Patch size	The sizes of individual disturbed patches as well as their size-frequency on the landscape	In a particular region, the average wildfire might affect 1000 ha, and the modal size is 50 ha (this is the unit with the largest frequency of observations)
Residual structure or "legacy"	The complex of physical and biological materials that occurs after a disturbance event	Shapes of patches, density of surviving trees, density of snags, amount of large woody debris
Causal agent	The kinds of disturbance agents in a study region, as well as their frequency of occurrence	Wildfire, windstorm, flooding, avalanche, ice storm, insect irruptions
Relative influence of agents	How often each agent occurs and the magnitude of the impact relative to those of other agents	An average wildfire return interval of 75 years, annually affecting 0.5 percent of the study region, compared with windstorms return interval of 50 years affecting 0.2 percent of the area annually
Interactions, synergisms, and antagonisms among agents of disturbance	The ways that disturbance agents influence one another	An irruption of bark beetles or moths may kill many trees, resulting in a high loading of fuel that makes affected stands highly vulnerable to suffering a severe wildfire

SOURCE: Modified from: Pickett, S.T. and P.S. White. 1985. *The Ecology of Natural Disturbance and Patch Dynamics*. Academic Press, New York, NY; Suffling, R. and A. Perera. 2004. "Characterizing natural forest disturbance regimes," pp. 43–54 in: *Emulating Natural Forest Landscape Disturbances: Concepts and Applications*. (A. Perera, L.J. Buse, and M.G. Weber, eds.). Columbia University Press, New York, NY.

Change

Disturbance and its consequent succession are functions that bring about changes in landscapes, as do longer-term variations of climatic conditions. Change is another major theme, because landscapes are always in flux, as are their elements, such as patches. What happens at one place—in a particular abandoned pasture or a burn that is returning to forest—is often typical of a dominant change occurring on the greater landscape. Landscape change can be expressed in terms of **patch dynamics**, or the process of patch changes.

Change may be understood in terms of the function of landscape elements, which may, for example, become more or less permeable to the movements of organisms, water, or nutrients. Change may also be manifest through dynamics in the patch structure of a landscape—an overall pattern that is normally a **shifting mosaic**. Landscape functions are affected by net changes in the mosaic. For instance, Ludwig et al. (2005) described how vegetated patches in semi-arid Australian woodlands affect the broader landscape by absorbing runoff more efficiently than inter-patch areas without plants. Therefore, to understand the implications of the mosaic, it is often necessary to characterize what is happening in the various patch types, and to then extrapolate to the entire landscape.

Understanding Temporal Change: The Historical Landscape

Ecological change occurs at all time scales, including those longer than most research projects, ecological careers, and even human lives and collective memory. This makes longer-term **longitudinal studies** (or continuous studies) difficult to carry out and therefore rare. (One exception is the Broadbalk experiment in the United Kingdom, a managed field ecosystem that has been continuously studied since 1843; Rothamsted, 2009.) Because of the difficulty or impossibility of running continuous long-term studies in one place, ecologists have developed alternative methodologies, such as the chronosequence technique (Chapter 10) and those used in paleoecology, such as dendrochronology and analyses of pollen and diatoms in dated layers of lake sediment (Chapter 16).

Ecologists can also utilize certain historical information. For example, the Hudson's Bay Company kept remarkably detailed records of the numbers and kinds of furs and other commodities that were purchased by their trading posts in Canada from 1670 to the 1940s. Roger Suffling and colleagues of the University of Waterloo used those fur-trade data to track ecological change (Fritz et al., 1993). In the early 19th century at Osnaburgh House in northwestern Ontario, woodland caribou disappeared, as shown through financial accounts of skins and meat traded, as well as in letters. Caribou did not reappear for several decades. The disappearance corresponds with a multi-year outbreak of forest fires that was noted in reports and that can be verified by tracking the number of days on which smoke was observed in the weather record of the trading post. Suffling and Wilson (1994) have summarized numerous ways in which ecologists have used the records of the Hudson's Bay Company.

Similarly, early land surveyors recorded "witness trees" or they noted changes in vegetation along survey lines as these workers demarcated future roads and properties through the then-wilderness of Canada. When witness trees were used, a surveyor typically recorded its species and girth. The trees were selected on the basis of being the closest to a survey point, so they constitute a randomized and semi-quantitative sample of the kinds and sizes of trees in these historical forest communities. One example of a landscape reconstruction using survey data is presented in **Figure 13.10**, based on work by undergraduate students at the University of Waterloo. Another reconstruction was developed by Serge Lutz (1997) of the University of New Brunswick, who used early surveyor data to describe the character of the Acadian forest of the 19th century in a region of southern New Brunswick. Compared with the forests of today, the original ones were typical of older-growth forest, being dominated by large old trees of species that are relatively tolerant of competition, such as sugar maple (*Acer saccharum*), beech (*Fagus grandifolia*), red spruce (*Picea rubens*), and white pine (*Pinus strobus*). Old-growth forest is rare today in that region, and the forest is now typically dominated by younger, smaller, less shade-tolerant trees such as red maple (*Acer rubrum*), white birch (*Betula papyrifera*), white spruce (*Picea glauca*), and balsam fir (*Abies balsamea*).

Historical photographs, paintings, and drawings can also be useful for understanding how landscapes have changed. Jeanine Rhemtulla, Eric Higgs, and colleagues of the University of Victoria used this method with panoramic photographs created by a land surveyor in what is now Jasper National Park. It is evident that trees have been spreading into former grasslands in response to fire suppression. This is one source of historical information that has influenced decisions to use prescribed burns in this area to restore a more natural vegetation.

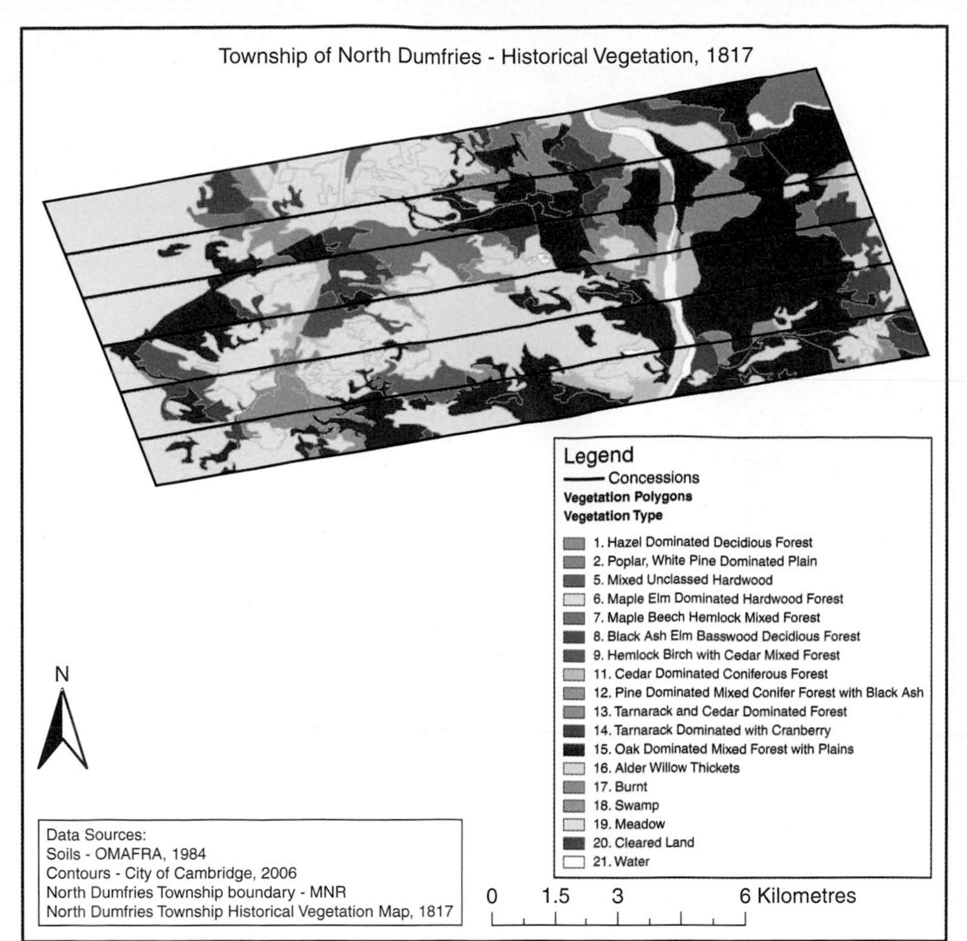

FIGURE 13.10

A Reconstruction of the Historical Vegetation of a Southern Ontario Township. This Reconstruction is Based on Land Survey Data in the 1817 Field Notes of a Land Surveyor. The kinds of vegetation are colour-coded. This study was done by groups of undergraduate students at the University of Waterloo in 2008 and 2009.

SOURCE: Students in EnvS 469, Landscape Ecology and Restoration, University of Waterloo 2008 and 2009.

Understanding Temporal Change: The Landscape Demographics Approach

Some landscape-scale stressors are diffuse in their spatial distribution, such as outbreaks of herbivorous insects, regional air pollution, and climate change. Others, however, are spatially well defined, such as flooding, wildfire, windstorms, and pollution near a point-source of emissions, such as a metal smelter. These differences in the spatial distributions of environmental influences have large effects on the patch dynamics of landscapes.

For instance, the natural disturbance regime in deciduous forests of southern Ontario, Quebec, and the Maritime provinces predominantly involves the deaths of individual old trees, which results in small-scale, gap-phase successional dynamics and the development of older-growth, uneven-aged, multi-species communities. In contrast, natural disturbances of boreal and montane forests of most of northern and western Canada mostly involve wider-scale, stand-replacing disturbances and the development of even-aged communities dominated by only a few species of trees.

The first comprehensive inventories of forest resources in Canada, such as those of the 1970s, were non-spatial, tabular summaries of data that were compiled to assess the amounts of timber available for harvesting. The tabular data were assembled manually from field cruises and air-photo information and were often expressed as a **stand age-class distribution** (**Figure 13.11**), which is a graph of the proportion of patches within each of the classes of stand age. These data can be analyzed to understand the influences of disturbances on the predominant ages of stands on a landscape.

Charles Van Wagner (1978) of the Canadian Forest Service developed landscape-scale models using these sorts of data. He demonstrated that a theoretical forest landscape will stabilize to a reverse J-shaped distribution of stand age-classes if it is affected by stand-replacing disturbances (for example, if wildfire is the controlling disturbance) at a uniform rate on a decadal scale, and with an equal chance of burning regardless of stand age (**Figure 13.11, A**). A simple interpretation of this model is that fires generate many patches of younger forest, but few of them live through subsequent fires to become old-growth forest. Theoretical age-class distributions, such as those developed from models, can be compared to what is actually observed on landscapes

(a)

M.P. Bridgland, 1915. Digital image copyright 2000, University of Alberta.

(b)

Copyright J.M. Rhemtulla and E.S. Higgs. University of Alberta

Repeat photographs can demonstrate landscape change. A 1915 surveyor's photograph in Jasper National Park, Alberta, (a) was re-taken in 1999 (b). Forest has spread into the original grasslands in response to fire suppression. Parks Canada is now using prescribed burns to restore the original ecosystem in this kind of habitat.

(**Figure 13.11, B**) to understand changes that may occur in the disturbance regime, whether in natural wildfires or windstorms, or caused by fire suppression or timber harvesting. Knowledge of the history of the unmanaged disturbance regime can be used to establish a relatively "natural" way of harvesting and managing bio-resources, as is done in emulation forestry (Chapter 15).

During the succession that follows stand-replacing disturbances, the standing crop of biomass increases rapidly in the younger forest but then tapers off asymptotically. This is due to competition intensifying as the stand develops, and because the maturing trees greatly increase their proportion of non-photosynthetic biomass, such as trunk, branches, and roots. If this late phase of succession is prolonged, the forest may develop into an old-growth condition, characterized by a gap-phase disturbance regime associated with the deaths of individual old trees. However, from the commercial perspective of a forester, it is considered economically undesirable to leave valuable trees to be destroyed by insects, wildfire, or wind. The preferable economic option is to harvest the stand soon after its growth begins to slow, which would maximize the longer-term production of harvestable biomass (**Figure 13.11, C**). While this kind of management provides economic benefits to the forest industry, it leads to a depletion of older-growth forest, a natural ecosystem that has become endangered in some regions of Canada.

A forested landscape in which the disturbance regime involves frequent and extensive stand-replacing disturbances will be dominated by patches in younger stages of successional development. In contrast, landscapes in which stand-replacing disturbances are rare will be mostly in a mature or old-growth condition. In both cases the landscape-scale diversity of patches will be relatively low. In comparison, landscapes with an intermediate disturbance regime will have a higher diversity of communities,

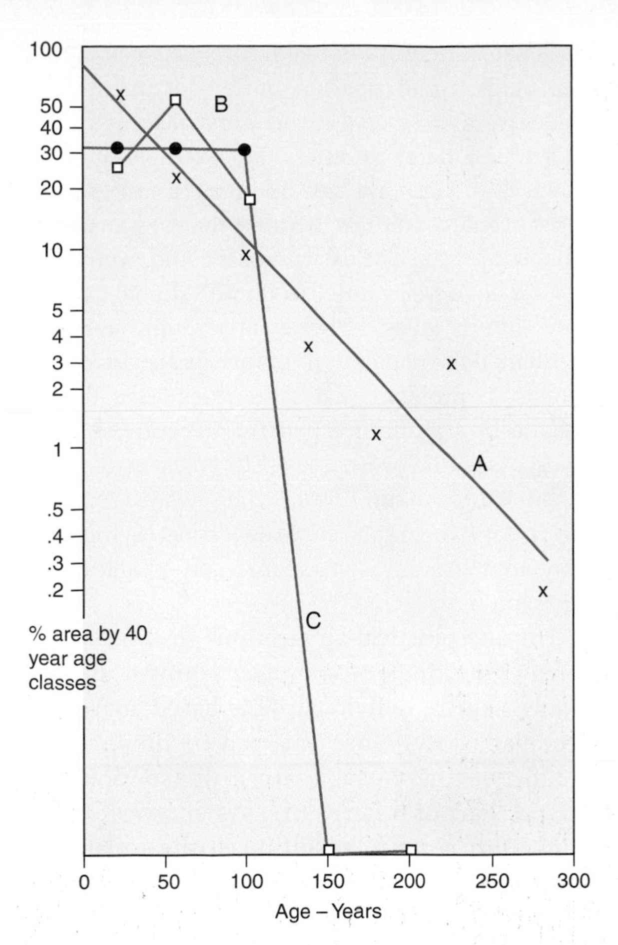

FIGURE 13.11

Stand Age-Class Distributions Indicate the Disturbance History and Successional State of Patches on a Landscape. (A) a stand-age class distribution of forest in the Boundary Waters Canoe Area in Minnesota; the theoretical negative exponential distribution is fitted by making adjustments for historical changes in the fire regime; note the logarithmic y-axis (after Van Wagner, 1978); (B) a stand-age class distribution from the boreal forest of northern Ontario; note that changes in fire occurrence over time obscure any theoretical distributions, such as the negative exponential or Weibull distributions (after Suffling and Molin, 1982); (C) the "ideal" stand age-class distribution based on commercial forestry tenets.

SOURCES: (A) after Van Wagner, 1978, p. 223; (B) after Suffling et al., 1982; (C) Roger Suffling.

ranging from young to old-growth. This mirrors, at the landscape scale, the predictions of the intermediate disturbance hypothesis for species diversity within communities (Chapter 9).

Therefore, non-spatial models can allow the disturbance regime of landscapes to be characterized This provides insight into the functioning of landscapes and also about their history and likely responses to changes in the disturbance regime, including the effects of anthropogenic interventions. However, there is an important disadvantage of this demographic approach to landscape ecology, at least when it is used in isolation—it cannot convey an understanding of the spatial ecology of the landscape.

Understanding Change: Spatial Approaches

Forman (1995) defined five major processes of landscape change, each with characteristic effects on the structural and functional attributes of patches (**Figure 13.12**). A value-neutral interpretation of landscape change is that as one patch type decreases, another will experience a compensating increase. However, for real-world practitioners of landscape ecology the context of their work is important—it may be profoundly different if their interest is the production of agricultural or forest biomass, compared with the conservation of biodiversity. For instance, a forester might view a particular change on a landscape as being beneficial to timber production, whereas a conservation-minded ecologist might consider the same change to represent damage to indigenous biodiversity (see Chapter 17 for further discussion of contextual interpretations of environmental and ecological change).

Permeability is a term used to connote the degree to which organisms can move between patches,

Spatial processes	Patch number	Average patch size	Total interior habitat	Connectivity across area	Total boundary length	Habitat	
						Loss	Isolation
Perforation	0	–	–	0	+	+	+
Dissection	+	–	–	–	+	+	+
Fragmentation	+	–	–	–	+	+	+
Shrinkage	0	–	–	0	–	+	+
Attrition	–	+	–	0	–	+	+

FIGURE 13.12

Major Processes of Landscape Transformation. The effects of each of the five processes on spatial attributes are indicated as: + = increase; – = decrease; and 0 = no change. In the block diagrams, orange and white indicate different community (or patch) types, and the paired comparisons show how they are affected by the process of transformation.

SOURCE: Modified from Forman, R.T.T. 1995. *Landscape Mosaics: The Ecology of Landscapes and Regions.* Cambridge University Press, Cambridge, UK. Page 407. Reprinted with the permission of Cambridge University Press.

whereas *connectivity* is concerned with the degree to which patches abut or are close to each other. It is often assumed that an interconnected and permeable landscape system is inherently desirable because it allows organisms to move among patches of suitable habitat. This allows a *metapopulation* to exist, or a group of spatially discrete sub-populations that are linked by dispersal, so there is gene flow among them. Permeability may allow genetic exchange to occur among populations, and may also permit the recolonization of local habitats from which a species has become extirpated (see **Figure 13.8**).

In contrast, *fragmentation* or habitat subdivision is usually regarded as an ecological damage—this is the process by which patches of a given type become increasingly separated and relegated to isolated fragments. But the issue is complex—connectivity is not necessarily a benign attribute of landscapes—for instance, it may also allow alien invasive species and diseases to spread.

Insularization is the process by which "islands" of habitat are produced, often through the fragmentation of once-extensive communities. Insularization is experienced differently by each species, depending on whether the matrix habitats are useful to them as places to live or are permeable for their dispersal. In this sense, a network of hedgerows between agricultural fields, or of riparian buffers of uncut forest beside rivers, may serve as corridors for some species, but act as barriers to others. For example, it is well known that highways can be barriers to the movements of many animals, because they are unsuitable as habitat, or are not easily crossed and even lethal. This has been well studied in Banff National Park and some other areas, where large highways have fragmented the populations of various species of large animals, a problem that authorities have tried to mitigate by installing expensive structures such as underpasses and overpasses (Clevenger et al., 2002). At the same time, however, highways represent corridors by which species of ruderal plants, including many that are invasive aliens, can penetrate the landscape.

For any practical applications in conservation ecology, the kinds of complexity hinted at above usually require individual, field-based analyses of particular ecosystems. This can be illustrated by a study of the Ausable River in southwestern Ontario. Part of this riverine system was diverted in the 19th century, resulting in the isolation of populations of various animals and plants in what is now Pinery Provincial Park (**Figure 13.13**).

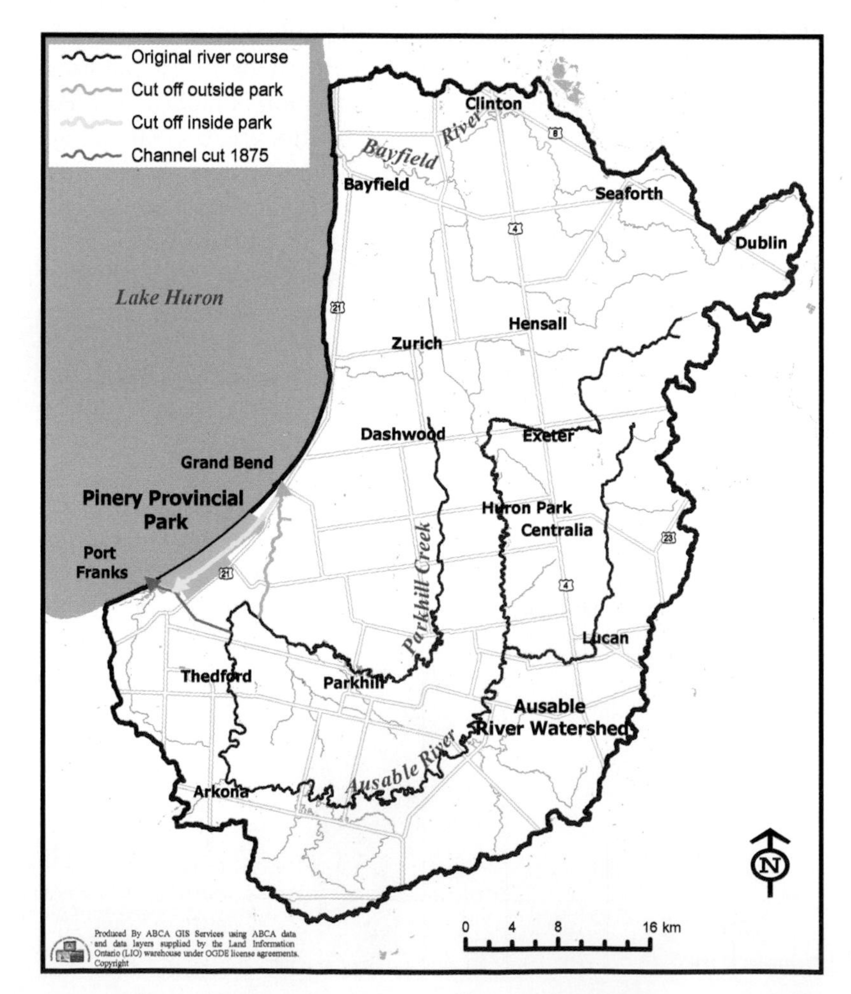

FIGURE 13.13

Insularization of Protected Areas is Generally a Problem, but Sometimes the Isolation of Habitats Can Produce Unexpected Results. The Ausable River in southern Ontario was greatly modified in the 19th century when a huge loop that flowed though coastal sand dunes of Lake Huron was cut off by an agricultural engineering project. The isolated Old Ausable Channel that is now in Pinery Provincial Park has remained biodiverse and mostly free of pollution. In contrast, the rest of the watershed has suffered numerous extirpations of fish and other organisms.

SOURCE: Modified from K. Killins, *A Management Plan for the Old Ausable Channel Watershed*, Maps 2–5 from pp. 6–9. Ausable Bayfield Conservation Authority.

Outside of the protected area, the river has become badly degraded by siltation and pollution associated with agriculture, so that today most of the aquatic species, and also many terrestrial ones, survive only in the park. In this case, isolation in the protected area helped to conserve a number of rare species, which otherwise might have become extirpated from the watershed. This is by no means a great conservation solution—it would have been much better if the agricultural activities had not damaged the river so badly. Nevertheless, at least some of the aquatic biota were able to survive in a protected area that was insulated from harm by fragmentation. This example illustrates how each case must be specifically evaluated, recognizing the complexity of real life, and not thoughtlessly applying a broad generalization about conservation, such as the "risks" of insularization.

Notwithstanding the above case, the insularization of protected areas is recognized as an increasingly important problem in Canada. This is especially true of southern regions, where protected areas are relatively small and embedded in a matrix dominated by agricultural, forestry, and other anthropogenic ecosystems that are hostile and impermeable to many native species and natural communities. A working group of ecologists from the University of New Brunswick, Parks Canada, and several other organizations was assembled to study the ecological implications of insularization in Fundy National Park, a protected area, and its surrounding region, which is largely used for forestry (Greater Fundy Ecosystem Project, 2009). A landscape analysis showed that the mature mixed-species forests of the park, which are representative of the dominant natural matrix in the region, were becoming rapidly insularized by the development of forestry plantations, which were being established right up to the park boundary. Research by the group made a number of findings relevant to insularization, such as the following:

- Landscape-dependent communities, such as older natural forest, appear to be at risk because the relatively small park (204 km^2) is not likely to be able to fully support the extensive stand-replacing disturbances associated with insect outbreaks and wildfire that are vital to its regeneration.
- Landscape-dependent species, such as black bear (*Ursus americanus*), are at risk because the park is too small to support a viable population in isolation from the surrounding area used for forestry, which does not provide habitats that are well suited to the species.
- The forestry plantations are a degraded habitat or non-habitat for many native species of birds, amphibians, and other wildlife; for instance, because there are few cavity trees and snags and not much large woody debris in the plantations, they cannot support populations of the many species that are dependent on these critical elements of habitat.
- The habitat conditions in the plantations, and the short time between successive clear-cut harvests (40 years), mean that many native plants cannot regenerate their populations after the timber harvesting, and so they can maintain only local populations inside the park.

Because of these and other effects of insularization, the Fundy working group recommended a number of mitigations that would improve habitat conditions in the "working" areas used for forestry, and so would enhance the ecological sustainability of the landscape of the **greater protected area** (the park and its surrounding landscape). The recommendations include the establishment of additional protected areas, including riparian buffers beside streams in which timber is not clear-cut, leaving uncut "islands" of natural forest within plantations, and not cutting known cavity trees. Some of these recommendations are being implemented by improved forest-management practices in the region, and their efficacy is also being tested.

Scale and Risk

Scale is a vital concern in landscape ecology. The term *fine scale* is used in reference to detailed observations made over a relatively small area, and *coarse scale* for less depth over a large area. Scale is relevant to observations in both space and time.

Scale in Space

Landscape ecologists regard landscapes as being "nested" or hierarchical in structure. Therefore, patterns can exist at various scales. In a forested landscape, for example, there may be patterns at the scale of tiny mosses and lichens growing on the forest floor, as well as larger patches that are related to distinctive tree communities, and yet others that are associated with networks of streams and rivers and their watersheds (see also **Figure 13.1**).

Pattern emerging at one scale may be influenced by other levels (Levin, 1992), representing an **emergent property**, or a complex pattern that arises from a multiplicity of relatively simple interactions. In this sense, Tanner (2006) found that the faunal composition within patches of seagrass depends on the surrounding matrix. Fauna in patches of *Posidonia* seagrass surrounded by unvegetated sand are different than in those surrounded by *Heterozostera*, another seagrass (which had more than double the abundance of amphipod crustaceans and polychaete worms). The results, which were confirmed by experimental manipulations, were not just due to a "spillover" effect between patches, but reflected an emergent property of the mosaic of habitat patches.

Organisms react to patterns in the landscape at different scales (Law and Dickman, 1998). For instance, Stephen Mayer, James Schaefer, and others (2009) at Trent University reported that woodland caribou (*Rangifer tarandus*) choose their winter forage from patches of lichens at one scale of pattern (within stands of forest), but select calving sites at another scale (they select isolated sites on lake islands and in treed bogs), and they avoid winter predation by using older forests at a third scale (they select large tracts of older forest).

Scale in Time

Temporal scales may be long or short, change may be continuous or abrupt, and the change may be recurring. Recurring change may be a predictable oscillation that is related to **exogenous** influences, meaning those that are external to the system, such as seasonal variations of weather. Alternatively, such variations may relate to **endogenous** population dynamics, such as periodic irruptions of caterpillars or grasshoppers, or fire-initiated forest succession to mature stands that are highly flammable and therefore vulnerable to another stand-replacing wildfire. These influences may cause **cyclic phenomena** to occur, resulting in regular and predictable changes on the landscape. For instance, the water levels of Lakes Michigan and Huron (two of the Great Lakes) both have long-term fluctuations but at different frequencies, with implications for the extent of coastal wetlands as well as large-scale processes such as erosion and flooding (Hanrahan et al., 2009).

However, much landscape change is apparently random through time (**stochastic change**). This is substantially the case with damage caused by events of severe weather, such as hurricanes, tornadoes, ice storms, and lightning strikes that ignite wildfires (although even these may be related to periodic phenomena, such as El Niño and other expressions of the southern oscillation). **Secular change** (in a consistent direction) also often occurs, either abruptly, as with a landslide into a lake, or gradually, as when basins slowly infill with silt and organic matter to eventually develop a wetland.

Woodland caribou select habitat at different scales depending on their immediate needs. In general, at a coarse scale, they seek out older forests of low productivity that have a low moose population and that are less attractive to predators like wolves. At a finer scale, female caribou select calving sites on islands in lakes, and in treed bogs, which are also relatively sheltered from predators. On any day, wintering caribou are seeking out areas in the forest (finer scale) that have lichen patches where they can feed.

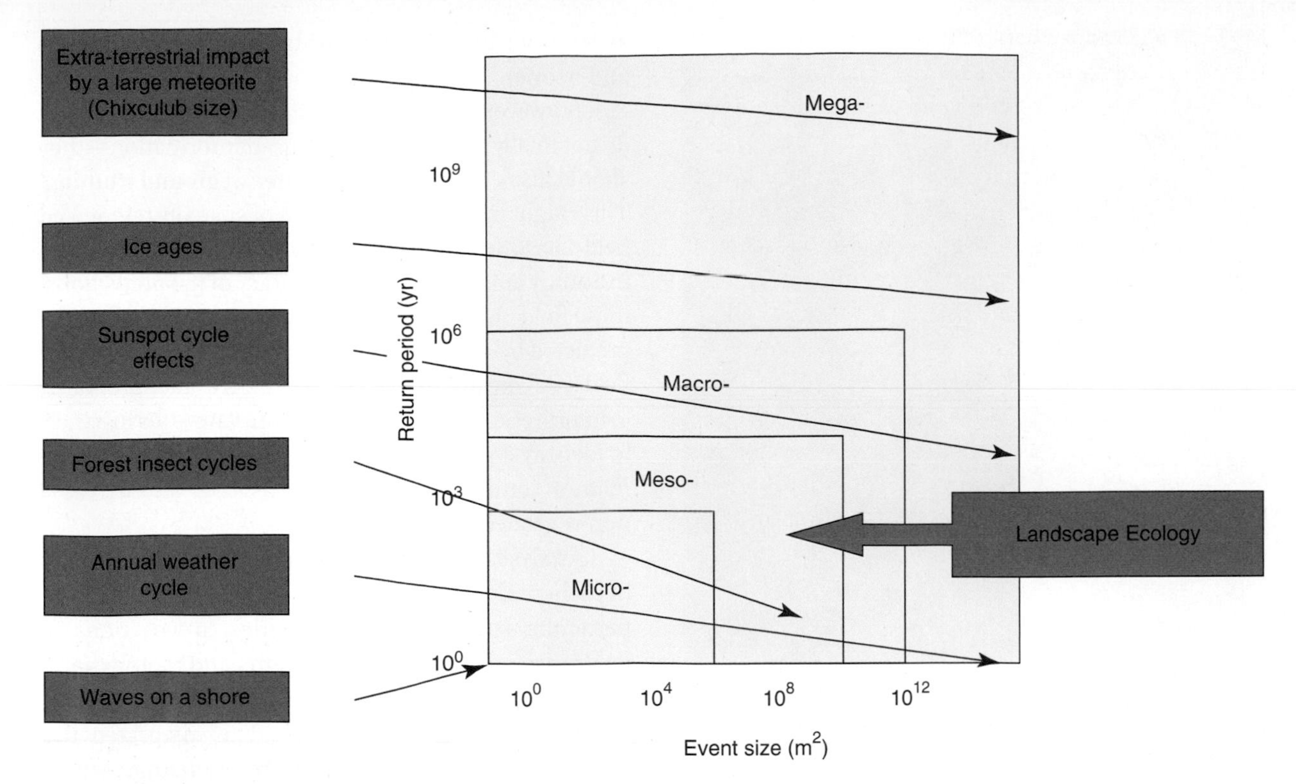

FIGURE 13.14

Scales in Time and Space. Some disturbance events occur in numerous places, in small increments, and frequently. Others are huge, infrequent, and intense. Landscape ecology tends to focus on mid-scale events.

SOURCE: Modified from Delcourt, H.R., P.A. Delcourt, and T. Webb. 1983. "Dynamic plant ecology: The spectrum of vegetational change in space and time," *Quaternary Science Review*, 1: 153–175.

However, cyclic, stochastic, and secular changes are often mixed and simultaneous, and this results in complex patterns of change on landscapes. For example, the incidence of Canadian forest fires generally shows elements of an annual cycle, being most frequent in late spring and early summer. However, there is great variation among years, depending on precipitation and drought, and all may be overlain by cyclic weather phenomena and pervasive climate change.

Integration of Scale in Time and Space

The model of Delcourt et al. (1983) is useful in explaining the process-related scales of time and space (**Figure 13.14**). In the diagram, time and space axes are plotted logarithmically, which allows us to examine huge ranges of space, from millimetres to thousands of kilometres, and also of time, from seconds to billions of years. In general, smaller spatial events are frequent but widespread, making them important in the aggregate. Other events are extremely rare in time but of huge intensity. Therefore, disturbances may range from waves impacting shores everywhere and always, to exceedingly rare meteorite impacts that may have resulted in at least one catastrophic mass extinction: the Chixculub event in Yucatan, Mexico, which occurred some 65 million years ago and which closed the Cretaceous Period.

13.4 Tools of Landscape Ecology

Landscape ecologists use an array of approaches and technologies in their work, including classical methods of field ecology, chemical and physical analyses done in laboratories, paleoecological methods, historical documentation, and simulation modelling. However, three technologies are especially crucial to the practice of landscape ecology: remote sensing, geographical information systems, and landscape simulation modelling.

Remote Sensing

As soon as aerial photography became readily available, it was routinely used by landscape ecologists. The first photographs were black and white, but they still provided amazing new perspectives for measuring and interpreting the structure and function of landscapes. Today, much more sophisticated, multispectral **remote sensing** allows ecologists to characterize landscapes in astonishing new ways (Pidwirny et al., 2009).

These technologies take advantage of the fact that Earth's surface reflects solar radiation in various wavelengths and intensities, depending on the local cover of inorganic surfaces and vegetation. In a typical project in landscape ecology, the terrain is depicted as

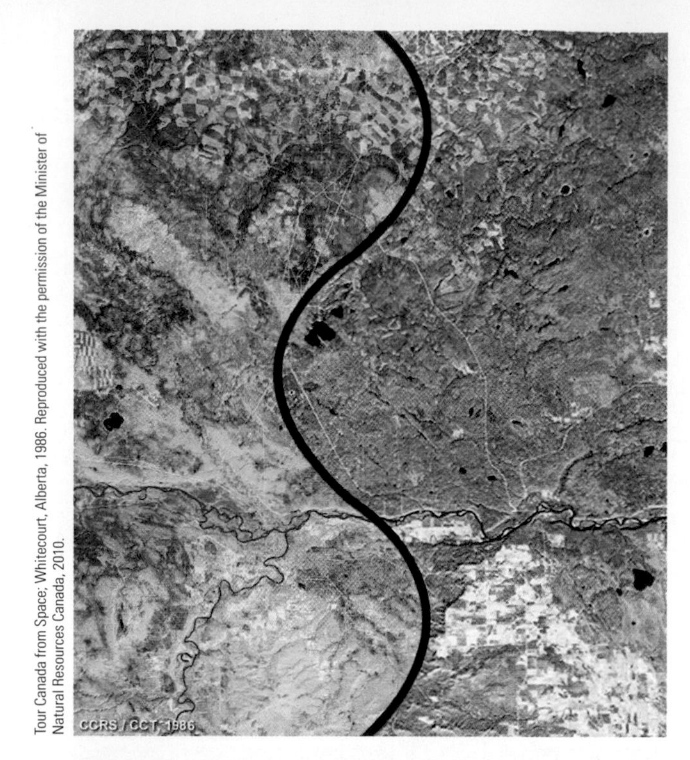

An area of foothills in the Rocky Mountains, northwest of Edmonton. Natural habitats and those created by human activity are both evident in these Landsat™ false-colour satellite images from August 1986 (left) and October 1986 (right). Patches of both coniferous and deciduous forest are evident. Wavebands 5, 4, and 3 (with near-infrared, red, and green sensitivities, respectively) are displayed as red, green, and blue, which in combination simulate green vegetation. The August image has an overall green appearance, but in October the deciduous trees have lost their foliage, resulting in more reflection in bands 3 and 5, which is displayed as a magenta colour (a mix of blue and red). The underlying geomorphology and drainage pattern are more obvious in the autumn. Another land cover type is wetlands found in low areas. The images also show an area affected by forest fires, logging, roads, and pipeline corridors for oil transportation. If you look closely, you will identify several cutover patterns, the result of changing logging practices.

a spatial array of pixels ("dots"), for which the reflected strengths of selected wavelengths are measured. These multi-spectral data allow the pixels to be classified into statistically identified groups, the distributions of which can be graphically displayed using assigned colours (a "false-colour image"). The groups tend to correspond with particular kinds of land cover or environmental factors of ecological interest, such as soil water content.

The multi-spectral classes that are identified may be statistically associated with ecological or other features of interest, which allows the mapping of abiotic factors such as soil moisture or water depth or turbidity, or biotic ones like particular species of plants or ecological communities. The health of vegetation can sometimes be assessed, by interpreting data that represent the spatial distribution of discoloured foliage (chlorophyll and other foliar pigments may be diminished by environmental stressors, such as drought and air pollutants like sulphur dioxide and ozone).

However, it is important that landscape ecologists do not totally rely on remote-sensed information—they should also engage in some degree of **ground truthing**. This might involve the collection of spatially referenced field data to develop a classification of plant communities in a study area. To verify the accuracy of the predictions, these field observations can be compared to the classes predicted by a parallel study using remote sensing. The field data can also be used to "train" computer programs to interpret spectral arrays in certain ways—for instance, to identify a particular spectral quality as representing mature conifer forest, another as bog, another as a non-vegetated surface, and so on.

Analyses can also be undertaken to test specific hypotheses, such as ones about the relationships of particular species or communities to variations of environmental factors. Ecosystems and their dynamics may also be modelled and the resulting predictions can be tested by field studies. The integrated use of ground-based studies, remote sensing, and a geographical information system may be used to develop models that can be used to elucidate the structure and function of a landscape.

Geographical Information Systems

A **geographical information system (GIS)** is a computer program that overlays digital maps or images of some part of the surface of Earth to reveal and create further information. Each mapped class is called a **layer**. For instance, layers of the distributions of rare species in an area might be combined in a new layer to show their collective locations—this analysis might identify a critical habitat that supports numerous species-at-risk and that would therefore be a good candidate for setting aside as a protected area. Similarly, maps of topography and the distributions of soil types could be used to develop a new layer that depicts basins underlain by clay, which are resistant to vertical drainage and therefore might be able to safely accommodate a landfill site. Moreover, if the composite layers of species-at-risk and landfill suitability are overlain, a further layer would be defined that shows where biodiversity is potentially at risk from proposals to develop landfills (**Figure 13.15**).

Angus Hills (1902–1979), a forest ecologist who spent his career at the University of Toronto and with the Ontario government, is credited with accelerating the use of overlays to better understand issues related to land-use planning and management. His applications were mostly in mapping land-capability classes for forestry and other uses (Hills, 1961), but the broader utility of the methodology was quickly

ENVIRONMENTAL APPLICATIONS 13.1

Putting It All Together: Landscape Ecology Helps Transdisciplinary Research

S. J. Thomas and C. W. Lindsay (2000) investigated local-scale variation in the transmission of malaria in children. They analyzed entomological and clinical data from villages in the Gambia, West Africa, finding that parasite prevalence correlated negatively with mosquito vector abundance and exposure to malaria parasites. Variation in bed net use did not explain this finding, so mosquito-breeding habitat was mapped using SPOT satellite imagery. Where mosquito exposure increased, so did parasite prevalence; but at higher levels of exposure, parasite prevalence actually declined. There were marked differences in exposure to malaria in different villages less than 2 km from mosquito breeding sites, suggesting that there are also large differences in immunity between residents of neighbouring settlements. This study used landscape ecology principles, GIS, epidemiology, clinical evaluations, remote sensing, statistical analysis, and entomology in a truly transdisciplinary approach.

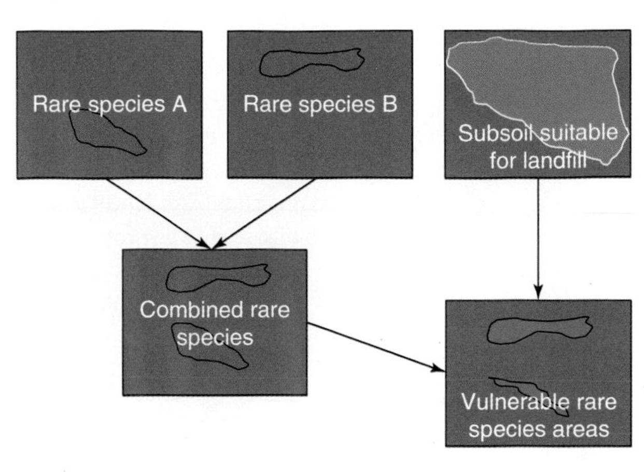

FIGURE 13.15

Using GIS to Develop New Information for Ecological Studies and to Guide Planning. When the layers concerning rare species and areas whose soils are safe for a landfill are overlain, spatial information is available to integrate land-use planning and biological conservation.

SOURCE: This figure (GIS material) is original to the chapter.

realized by ecologists and planners with other interests (as in Ian McHarg's influential 1969 book, *Design with Nature*). The overlaying of maps has now become fundamental to the practice of landscape ecology. Initially, such maps were drafted manually, and then with greatly improved ease and accuracy using computers. With increasingly powerful software and computers, and with ever-more abundant, inexpensive, and detailed remote-sensing images and data, opportunities to gather and manipulate information have hugely expanded in ecology. It has now become routine to do time-related, dynamic, and spatial modelling of landscapes and land-use changes. These methods are focal areas in landscape ecology, and also in landscape architecture, environmental and urban planning, and related fields.

Relational databases are a key to this analytical process. They are similar to spreadsheets, but allow each piece of data to be linked to others of relevance. For instance, when plotting the locations of all known locations of a species of plant on a landscape, one might also be able to specify which are growing beneath a forest canopy or in the open, which have been flooded (and when), and how old each one is. GIS analyses use relational databases to link tabular information and map layers, and this allows the map layers to be summarized and examined using statistical methods. Thus, the numbers of distinctive patches can be defined (e.g., all forest patches containing individuals of the plant that are older than the most recent flood), and their individual and collective areas can then be determined using FRAGSTATS or another statistical analysis software (see **Table 13.3**). However, some of the spatial terminology of GIS software and landscape ecology differs, practitioners must learn both of the lexicons.

An example of this approach is in Environmental Applications 13.1.

Modelling

Landscape ecologists use an array of models, which vary from conceptual to mathematical in their approach. However, the most characteristic models used in landscape ecology are ones that allow simulations to be run of structural and functional changes over large areas. Commonly used simulation models include FARSITE, LANDIS, and BFOLDS, which can be used to investigate theory and also to explore natural change or management scenarios for real landscapes. Many of the computer models use the same basic logic, albeit with variations, whereas others differ radically in their underlying assumptions.

Earlier simulation models were based on a grid of cells, and they were **deterministic**, meaning that a specific input gave a particular and reproducible output. These simple approaches have been supplanted by more complex and detailed models based on polygons that are integrated with GIS systems, especially ARCINFO. When using these models,

ENVIRONMENTAL APPLICATIONS 13.2

Landscape-Scale Planning by the Nature Conservancy of Canada

The methods and tools of landscape ecology are routinely used by conservation organizations in both government and the private sector to plan many of their large-scale activities. One such organization is the Nature Conservancy of Canada (NCC), an environmental charity that acquires important tracts of land and manages them as protected areas for native biodiversity. To guide its work and use its limited funding effectively, ecologists at NCC undertake landscape-scale planning exercises to identify areas and properties where its actions would make the greatest difference to conserving the biodiversity of Canada.

The first step in NCC's system planning is to undertake a conservation blueprint (or ecoregional assessment) of a particular ecoregion, which is a large-scale exercise that characterizes and maps the environmental conditions and communities that occur. As of 2010, NCC had completed 14 of those blueprints, covering much of southern Canada, where conservation risk is greatest and NCC does most of its work. An important aspect of a blueprint is that its boundaries are determined by the mapped distributions of the distinctive landforms, climate, and communities that define the ecoregion, rather than by political boundaries. This is illustrated in **Figure 13.16** for the Northern Appalachian–Acadian Ecoregion, which encompasses New Brunswick, Nova Scotia, Prince Edward Island, part of southeastern Quebec, and adjacent New England. A key purpose of a blueprint is to identify focal areas for potential conservation action. These are either large matrix blocks of representative habitat of high ecological integrity, or areas where there is important biodiversity-at-risk, either species or communities.

NCC then evaluates those focal areas for three broad attributes: (1) their biodiversity values and ecological integrity; (2) the degree of risk posed by anthropogenic stressors; and (3) whether there is opportunity to take conservation actions, such as acquiring strategic properties to set aside as protected areas. If all of the criteria are met, NCC may undertake the next stage in its planning process—the development of a Natural Area Conservation Plan (NACP) for an area where it intends to focus its conservation actions. An NACP identifies places that should be protected to conserve important biodiversity targets in the natural area—ultimately they involve the selection of individual

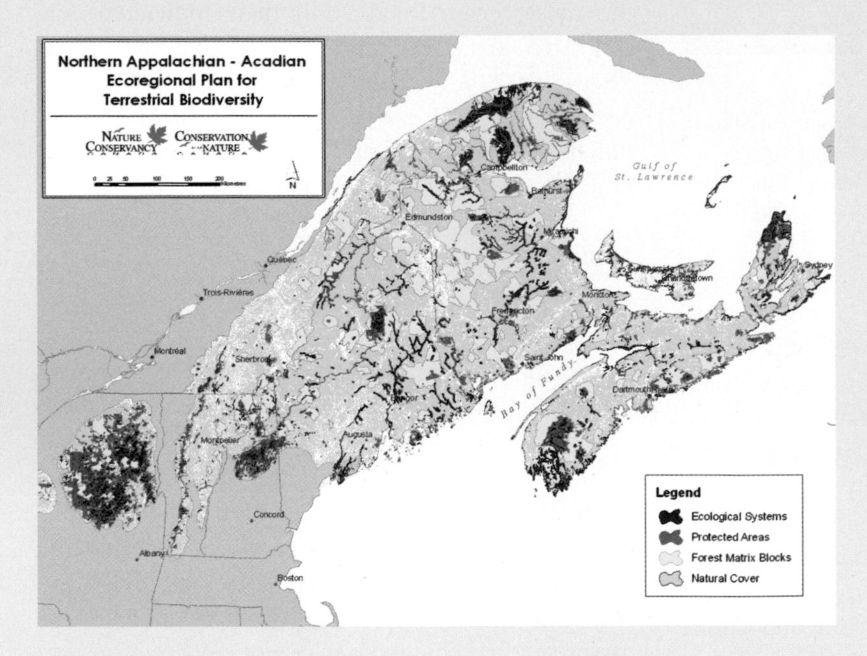

FIGURE 13.16

The Northern Appalachian–Acadian Ecoregion. The boundary of the ecoregion is based on the defining ranges of its landforms, climate, and ecological communities, rather than on political boundaries.

SOURCE: Map courtesy of the Nature Conservancy of Canada.

ecologists may run a scenario many times using randomly timed or spaced inputs that match a predetermined statistical pattern. Simulation "experiments" are done in this manner because neither the exact timing nor the locations of future disturbances are known. The methodology allows the most likely outcomes of scenarios and their statistical variation to be computed, a process known as **stochastic modelling**.

13.5 Who Uses Landscape Ecology?

Landscape ecology is a relatively young field that is distinguished by its spatial emphasis. In part, the vitality and utility of landscape ecology arises from its fusion of several disciplines and approaches in spatial analysis (see Environmental Applications 13.1). Many successful projects in landscape ecology could never

properties. The NACP also evaluates threats to the biodiversity in the natural area, proposes an action plan to conserve key properties, describes stewardship actions that must be undertaken once properties are secured, and outlines a budget for these integrated activities, including a viable business plan to raise the necessary funds. As of 2010, NCC had plans to develop and implement 94 NACPs across southern Canada.

An example of a mapped output is presented in **Figure 13.17** for Pelee Island, a vital area in NCC's Western Lake Erie Lake NACP. This natural area is in extreme southwestern Ontario, a region that supports a disproportionately large amount of Canadian biodiversity-at-risk. This is because (1) many native species and ecological communities reach the northern limits of their distribution in that region and (2) most of the landscape has been converted to economic uses, such as agriculture and urban areas, so that natural habitats are now rare. Within this context, Pelee Island provides extremely important habitat for endangered biodiversity. More than 30 federally designated species-at-risk occur, and there are 200 provincially rare species, along with rare communities, including stands of Carolinian forest dominated by southern plant species, and alvar habitat, where limestone pavement has been exposed by erosion and sustains unusual vegetation. The map shows the remaining natural habitats and the existing protected areas, and identifies the specific properties that must be acquired to complete a viable network of protected areas on Pelee Island.

In spite of the great importance of Pelee Island to endangered biodiversity, most of its area had already been converted into agricultural and residential land uses in the late 19th century. Moreover, some of the remaining privately owned natural habitats were also threatened. The tension between anthropogenic land uses, natural values, and legislation to protect endangered species led to intense and long-standing controversy and bad feelings between local proponents of economic "development" and more broadly based conservation interests. However, by engaging key stakeholders in the process of developing the NACP and vetting its recommendations, the Nature Conservancy of Canada was able to achieve wide consensual support for its proposed conservation actions. This has allowed NCC to move to secure the most important natural properties on Pelee Island and to manage them to foster their important biodiversity targets. This NACP and its implementation are an incipient "success story" of conservation in Canada.

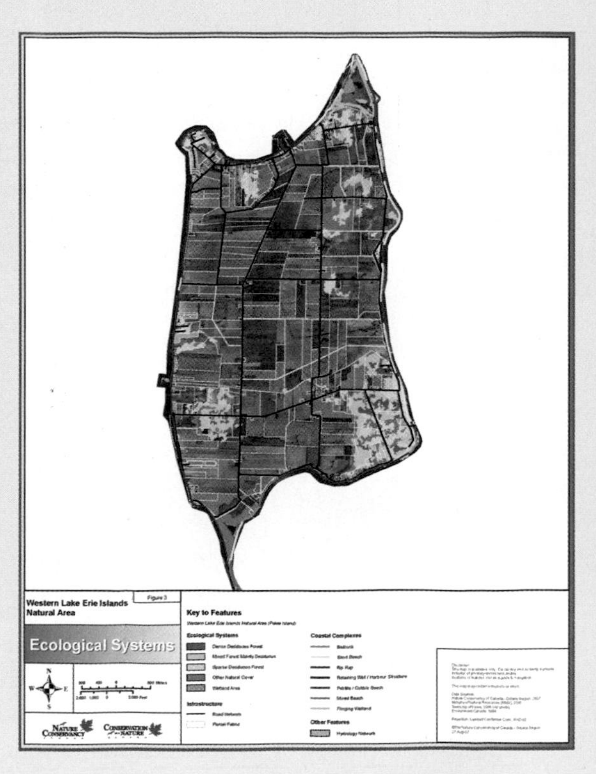

FIGURE 13.17
Conservation Plan for Pelee Island. The map shows all properties on the island and existing ecological systems that support habitat for species-at-risk and rare communities, such as alvar and stands of Carolinean forest.

SOURCE: Nature Conservatory of Canada (2009).

have been conceived and brought to fruition by individual researchers working in classical disciplines using a "silo" approach (which refers to working in a relatively narrow intellectual area without full regard to other relevant information and ideas). Rather, an interdisciplinary methodology was needed.

Most landscape ecologists work in developed countries such as Canada, but also increasingly in developing ones. The field is being applied in terrestrial and marine ecosystems, and from the tropics to the High Arctic. The methods of landscape ecology are used in fundamental research, with the intent of improving our understanding of factors that affect the structure and function of the natural world. However, most practitioners are working on applied ecological problems, in the contexts of agriculture,

A CANADIAN ECOLOGIST 13.1

Marie-Josée Fortin: A Landscape Ecologist

Marie-Josée Fortin

Marie-Josée Fortin

Marie-Josée Fortin studied biology at the University of Montréal. She then did graduate research on spatial statistics in ecology, working under the supervision of two well-known biostatisticians: Pierre Legendre of the University of Montreal and Robert Sokal of the State University of New York at Stony Brook. She went on to do postdoctoral research at Université Laval with Serge Payette on the spatial dynamics of forest fires in the boreal forest, a result of which was the development of improved tests for autocorrelation between ecological factors at landscape scale.

Fortin then taught at several Canadian universities (Sherbrooke, Simon Fraser, Montreal) and she now heads the Landscape Ecology Laboratory at the University of Toronto. Her group of postdoctoral fellows and students focuses on research on spatial ecology and the development and use of landscape and spatial statistics. Within that context, major research themes include the dynamics and modelling of ecosystem changes caused by wildfire and timber harvesting, and the effects of climate change on species, with a broader objective of conserving species and natural ecosystems.

One of Fortin's widely cited papers, prepared with Serge Payette and Isabel Gamache (Payette et al., 2001), is illustrative of her work and its application to global-change issues. The climate-sensitive forest-tundra transition extends across Canada from the limits of the continuous boreal forest in the south to the arctic tree line. This landscape has been compared metaphorically to a "Swiss cheese full of holes," reflecting its spatial qualities as a fire-prone forest with isolated treeless patches, grading northward to tundra with isolated patches of forest, and then to wholly treeless tundra. In the southern regions of that ecological gradient, the tundra-like "holes" occupy rocky hilltops with a relatively harsh microclimate, and the surrounding upland forest burns relatively easily. In their paper, Payette et al. (2001) showed how the proportions of upland tundra and forest varied over space, so that the continental-scale forest-tundra ecotone is actually a "constellation of treelines" (**Figure 13.18**). The various controlling factors on this latitudinally varying spatial mosaic include macroclimate, microclimate, site drainage, permafrost, and the capacity of wildfires to spread (which is greater in the more continuous forest of the south, and also where muskeg wetlands are less frequent). Payette et al. (2001) showed that the forest cover in the northern part of the transition can be up to several thousand years old, and does not regenerate well after a wildfire. This observation suggests that the tree line marks the northern limit of forest expansion during the warm Hypsothermal Period that occurred about 3000 years ago. Because the colonization of tundra patches by tree seedlings is sluggish, the reaction of

forestry, fisheries, conservation biology, protected-areas management, global change studies, environmental planning, and urban design. The applied studies are vital and necessary to guiding economic development along ecologically sustainable pathways. The approaches and tools of landscape ecology are extremely useful in those applications.

Given the above diversity of applications, landscape ecologists have a wide range of philosophies that raise intense debates (see Dessler and Parson, 2006). On one side are those who see landscape ecology as being driven by the classical approaches of hypothesis generation and objective testing through observation and experiment. Conversely, a minority sees the field as a manifestation of "post-normal science," and perceives science as a societal activity with its own culture, assumptions, and biases. They argue that landscape ecology, as a land management tool and as a response to the global ecological crisis, is inherently value-based and therefore, in a sense, political. This variety of philosophies is reflected in the wide range of places where landscape ecologists publish ideas and findings.

Achievements, Problems, and the Way Forward

Landscape ecology is contributing to advances in pure and theoretical ecology, but it is particularly successful in providing useful models and ideas for conservation biology and environmental planning. One example is the work of Lenore Fahrig of Carleton University on

the forest landscape to climatic warming in the region may also be slow.

Fortin and Mark Dale (University of Northern British Columbia) have written a book, *Spatial Analysis: A Guide for Ecologists* (2005), which is having a great influence on the approaches and methodologies used by ecologists to analyze spatial patterns on landscapes. Fortin has become widely recognized for her deep expertise in this field, and is frequently consulted by ecologists about ways to approach and analyze difficult problems using spatial statistical.

Source: World Resource Institute

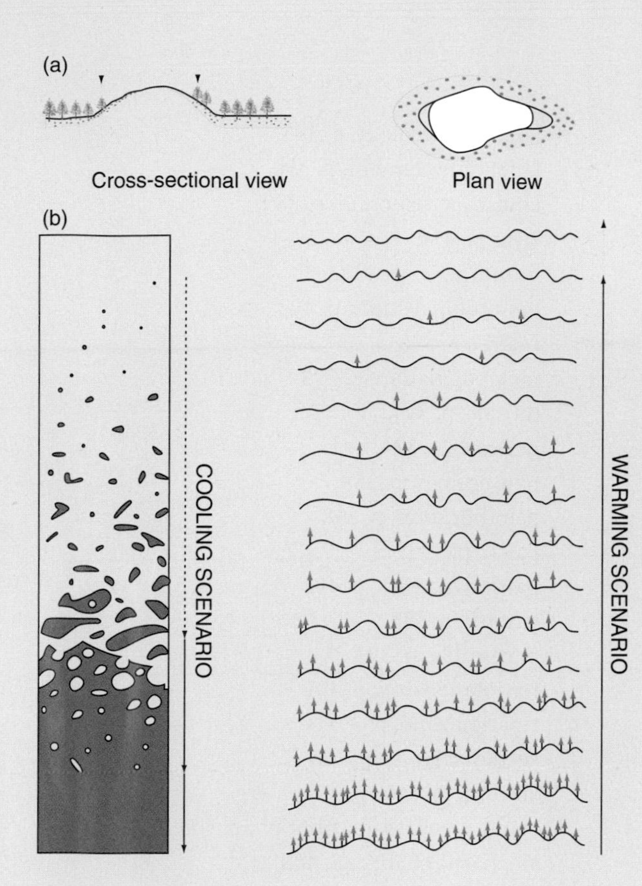

FIGURE 13.18

A Constellation of Treelines. Panel (a) shows cross-sectional (left) and overhead (right) views of a typical granitic hill supporting a fire-induced vegetation mosaic. A treeline exists at the junction of the forest with the treeless tundra-like vegetation on the hilltop (arrows). The overhead view shows the trees (dots) and subarctic treeline (solid line). Panel (b) shows overhead (left) and cross-sectional (right) views of the whole forest-tundra transition. The patchy distribution of tundra (white) increases in more northward regions. The cross sections show the distribution of forest from the continuous boreal forest limit, through the patchy subarctic treeline, to the continuous Arctic tundra.

SOURCE: Used with permission of the American Institute of Biological Sciences, from Payette, S., M.J. Fortin, and I. Gamache. 2001. "The subarctic forest-tundra: The structure of a biome in a changing climate," *BioScience*, 51(9): 709–718, fig. 3; permission conveyed through Copyright Clearance Center, Inc.

prescriptions for minimum viable areas for communities and populations of particular species (Fahrig, 2001). Landscape ecology has been empowered by its adoption of transdisciplinary approaches, and by the development of powerful technologies such as remote sensing, GIS, and modelling. Synthesis has been a great strength of this field, and it continues to rapidly develop and transform (Rapport, 1997).

However, the grand scale of inquiry in landscape ecology is unwieldy in space and time, and this has hampered experimental testing in real-world situations. Despite the lack of field testing, some of the concepts proposed by landscape ecologists are being enthusiastically adopted by foresters, landscape architects, and planners. Examples include the implementation of measures to establish corridors and to decrease fragmentation, without much prior field-testing of their efficacy. In such cases, it is essential that these conservation actions be studied after their implementation to see whether they are actually delivering their intended benefits. An example of this approach is a large-scale field experiment in Brazil to test the effects of Amazonian rain forest clearance. Blocks of uncleared forest ranging from a few to tens of thousands of hectares are being set aside from deforestation and being monitored for their surviving ecological values (Laurance, 2007).

As Turner (2005) has stressed, Integration of ecosystem and landscape ecology remains challenging but should enhance understanding of landscape function. Landscape ecology should continue to refine knowledge of when spatial heterogeneity is fundamentally important, rigorously test the generality of its concepts, and develop a more mechanistic understanding of the relationships between pattern and process.

Landscape ecology has largely progressed through the early stage of development, common to most disciplines, of defining the field and preparing a terminology. Its practitioners are now busy formulating ideas, but they have more good questions to examine than resources to evaluate them. This is an imbalance, but it is also a great opportunity. And it is an important one, because the approaches and methodologies of landscape ecology have emerged as some of the most powerful tools that ecology can offer to society as it strives to develop ecologically sustainable ways of developing the human economy.

VOCABULARY OF ECOLOGY

aquifer, p. 397
catena, p. 391
coarse scale, p. 385
connectivity, p. 393
corridor, p. 393
crown fire, p. 400
cyclic phenomenon, p. 408
deterministic, p. 411
ecological function (or ecological process), p. 397
ecoscape, p. 386
ecotone, p. 391
edge, p. 390
emergent property, p. 407
endogenous, p. 408
exogenous, p. 408
fine scale, p. 385
fragmentation, p. 387
geographical information system (GIS), p. 410
greater protected area, p. 407
ground fire, p. 400
ground truthing, p. 410
hydrology, p. 398
insularization, p. 406
interior habitat, p. 392
landscape, p. 385
landscape ecology, p. 385
landscape element, p. 390
landscape structure, p. 389
layer, p. 410
littoral zone, p. 391
longitudinal study, p. 402
matrix, p. 396
metapopulation, p. 393
mosaic, p. 394
network, p. 394
new ecology, p. 388
paludification, p. 398
patch, p. 390
patch dynamics, p. 402
pattern, p. 385
permeable, p. 393
remote sensing, p. 409
riparian zone, p. 391
secular change, p. 408
shifting mosaic, p. 402
stand age-class distribution, p. 403
stochastic change, p. 408
stochastic modelling, p. 412
surface fire, p. 400

QUESTIONS FOR REVIEW AND DISCUSSION

1. Describe a landscape that you can see from a local hill or tall building in terms of the structural elements described in the chapter. Alternatively, do this using a local air photo or remote-sensing imagery, such as from Google Earth. Speculate on how the elements of the landscape might interact in terms of biogeochemical cycling, drainage, the spatial distribution of disturbances, and the movements of plants and animals. Compare your observations with those of a classmate, and explain any differences in terms of your differing assumptions and knowledge of the system.
2. The geographer J. P. Jackson once wrote that "Landscape is history made visible." Using a landscape ecology approach, choose a favourite place (an area less than 100 m in diameter) in a landscape that you know well. It might be a home or cottage, a farm or woodlot, a place on a shore, or a park. Describe, in ecological terms, how this place affects the area around it, and how it has been affected by other parts of its landscape. How has the place changed over time, and why?
3. Examine the photographs on page 404, which show Henry House Flats in Jasper National Park. The photographs show how dramatically the landscape has changed, but can we assume that the 1915 situation was "natural"? What landscape-ecological or other approaches might help to answer this question? If we want to restore this system, what condition or date should be used as a reference benchmark, and why? Is it even possible to find an appropriate benchmark for the natural condition?
4. Using the information in Figure 13.12, summarize how landscapes' structure can change, and provide examples to fit each category from the region where you live. For instance, a forested landscape may be dissected by roads, railways, powerlines, and pipelines, or be disturbed by wildfire or clear-cutting. Explain which of these sorts of influences are most ecologically important in your landscape.
5. Using a simple spreadsheet, build a stand age-class distribution for a forested landscape with a constant rate of disturbance and with an equal chance of stand-replacing fire in each age class. Use age-classes of 20 years. Now imagine that a company wants to log the area, harvesting stands that are older than 80 years. Follow the graph through time to see how it changes. What are the conservation implications for a species that requires older forests, such as pileated woodpecker or woodland caribou? How might species of younger habitats fare, such as snowshoe hare and ruffed grouse?

HELPFUL WEBSITES

INTERNATIONAL ASSOCIATION FOR LANDSCAPE ECOLOGY
http://www.landscape-ecology.org
IALE provides an infrastructure as a worldwide organization of landscape ecologists, which serves as a discussion platform and stimulates interaction across the disciplines.

IALE LANDSCAPE ECOLOGY
http://www.landscape-ecology.org/links.htm#landscape_ecology
Links to other scientific and professional organizations, agencies, and international organizations.

LANDSCAPE ECOLOGY
http://forestlandscape.wisc.edu/landscapeEcology/
All early papers from *Landscape Ecology 1987–1997.*

LANDSCAPE ECOLOGY AND COMMUNITY KNOWLEDGE FOR CONSERVATION — A CANADIAN LANDSCAPE ECOLOGY SITE
http://www.lecol-ck.ca/index.php?pid=48
Collaborative research projects among federal, provincial, and territorial governments, universities, Aboriginal groups, industries, and communities.

U.S. ENVIRONMENTAL PROTECTION AGENCY
http://www.epa.gov/nerlesd1/land-sci/default.htm
Selected landscape ecology projects.

WORLD WILDLIFE FUND
http://www.worldwildlife.org/science/projects/cbr/item3384.html
Landscape ecology and conservation landscape design projects sponsored by the WWF.

You'll find a rich array of additional resources for *Ecology* at www.ecology.nelson.com.

not deplete their stocks and that benefit large numbers of people. Of course, this is possible only for renewable resources, which have the capability of regenerating after they are harvested. Renewable resources include all biological resources as well as various others that are associated with solar energy. These latter are the direct use of sunlight (for instance, as passive solar energy for heating), as well as indirect applications, such as electricity generated by flowing water (hydroelectricity), wind and tidal turbines, and photovoltaics. If potentially renewable resources are used wisely, meaning the rate at which they are harvested is less than that of regeneration, their stocks will not be diminished. This is the reason why a sustainable human economy must ultimately be based on renewable resources. Non-renewable ones like fossil fuels and metals also have a role to play, but one that is limited by the fact that their stocks are inexorably diminished by their use (see also Chapter 15).

These ideas about **resource conservation** are intuitive and well known. They were embraced by early leaders of the conservation movement in North America, such as George Perkins Marsh (1801–1882), Gifford Pinchot (1865–1946), and Theodore Roosevelt (1858–1919). These early conservationists were alarmed by their first-hand observations of the extensive destruction of forests, bison and other wild game, and other natural resources that was occurring so rampantly at the time, and they worked to bring a measure of control over that awful damage.

This kind of destruction was also occurring over much of southern Canada, and many Canadians were similarly apprehensive about that damage to natural resources. This led to the formation in 1909 of the Commission of Conservation, under the leadership of Wilfrid Laurier (1841–1919) and Clifford Sifton (1861–1929), with the aim of providing scientific advice about improved ways of using and managing the natural resources of Canada. James Harkin (1875–1955), who was the first commissioner of the new Dominion Parks Branch in 1911, was also highly influential, particularly in the early development of national parks. The initiatives of these and other Canadians who were deeply concerned about conservation issues as they were understood at the time resulted in a number of helpful governmental initiatives. They included the designation of the first large parks in the country (Banff National Park in 1885 and Algonquin Provincial Park in 1893) and legislative actions such as the *Migratory Birds Convention Act* of 1917, which controlled the previously wanton hunting of waterfowl and other birds.

The attitude of the early resource conservationists is encapsulated by a famous quote of Gifford Pinchot: "Conservation means the greatest good to the greatest number for the longest time." However, this sense of the word conservation—the wise use of natural resources to benefit people—is not the subject area of the present chapter. Rather, it is covered in Chapter 16, where we examine the application of ecological knowledge to the management of biological resources.

Conserving the Natural World

In the present chapter we explore the conservation of the **natural world**—a subject area also known as **biological conservation**. But what do we mean by the natural world? In the context of ecology, its major attribute is biodiversity, which we defined in Chapter 12 as the richness of biological variation, at scales ranging from genetics, to species within communities, and to the shifting mosaic of landscapes and seascapes. We also examined the reasons why biodiversity is important—it has intrinsic value, and is also vital to sustaining the human economy because it provides resources as well as ecological services.

Another aspect of the natural world that is relevant to biological conservation is that of **wilderness**. This term refers to wild and uninhabited tracts that are little used by modern industrial people, especially not for resource extraction or other intensive activities, although low-impact recreational activities may occur, such as hiking and subsistence hunting. Areas of wilderness usually have high levels of **ecological integrity**—they tend to be little affected by anthropogenic stressors and are characterized by native species, self-organized communities, and ecoscapes that are characteristic for the natural environmental regimes that are present (ecological integrity is examined in more detail in Chapter 17).

In the first section of this chapter we examine the dimensions of the modern biodiversity crisis, which is characterized by a spate of extinctions and endangerment of species and even of entire natural communities. This damage is being caused by anthropogenic influences, principally by the widespread destruction of natural habitats. Some of this ecological damage, such as extinctions, is not reversible. Nevertheless, many useful things can yet be done to mitigate the biodiversity crisis—if prudent actions are taken, it is still possible to avoid much destruction of biodiversity, and some of the damages already caused can be repaired. The following sections examine ways that ecological science can help society to resolve the biodiversity crisis. We will examine the aspects of ecological knowledge that are most crucial to understanding the causes and consequences of the biodiversity crisis, and to avoiding or repairing those damages so that all elements of biodiversity can continue to survive.

14.2 The Biodiversity Crisis

Natural Extinctions

The biodiversity crisis is a global phenomenon that involves high rates of extinction and endangerment of species, and even of entire natural communities. This destruction has been particularly acute for the past century or so, but today it is happening faster than ever, and it may further intensify in the near future. This modern biodiversity crisis is anthropogenic—it is being caused by economic activities that result in the destruction of natural ecosystems. This happens directly, as when natural forest is cleared and converted into an agricultural land use, and also indirectly, as when non-native species are introduced and become invasive of natural habitats. These stressors cause originally continuous and large populations of many vulnerable species to rapidly become smaller and fragmented, so they suffer from the deleterious effects of disturbances and inbreeding, and eventually become locally lost (extirpated) or globally extinct (**Figure 14.1**).

However, it is important to recognize that extinctions have always been an aspect of natural biological change, a fact that provides a context against which the anthropogenic biodiversity crisis can be compared. In fact, the great majority of species that have ever evolved and lived on Earth are now extinct—the only survivors are the relatively few that are presently extant (still living). The natural causes of extinction include extraordinarily rare and singular events, such as Earth being impacted by a meteorite. These have resulted in catastrophic damage of epic proportions, known as a **mass extinction**, which wiped out a large fraction of the species that existed at the time. But natural extinctions also occur at a pervasive, much slower rate, as species individually disappear because they cannot cope with longer-term changes in environmental conditions.

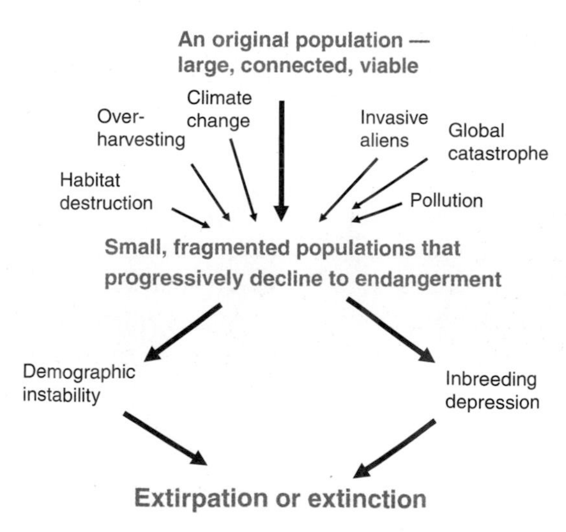

FIGURE 14.1

The Extinction Vortex. Extinction may be caused by natural or anthropogenic stressors, such as the destruction of natural habitats, climate change, excessive harvesting, and alien diseases. These stressors cause populations that are initially large and viable to become fragmented into increasingly smaller and isolated units that are vulnerable to the effects of inbreeding and population instability caused by disturbances and other environmental changes. These cumulative stressors may cause endangered populations to further decline, and may ultimately result in their extirpation or extinction. This accelerating spiral of endangerment is sometimes called the "extinction vortex".

SOURCE: See Gilpin and Soulé, 1986, for more information.

Events of natural mass extinction are used by geologists to mark the passage from one geological era to another. For example, as we noted in Chapter 1, the evolution of the first photosynthetic organisms about 2.5 billion years ago, likely cyanobacteria, resulted in an accumulation of oxygen in the atmosphere (O_2 is a by-product of photosynthesis). As the oxygen concentration increased, environmental conditions became progressively more toxic for almost all of the original (pre-photosynthesis) organisms, which must have suffered a mass extinction. However, the few surviving O_2-tolerant microbes then proliferated in habitable parts of the planet and underwent an **evolutionary radiation**. This is a likely scenario for what happened, but because the fossil record is extraordinarily difficult to interpret for such primeval changes in microbial biodiversity, there are few decipherable details.

More is known, however, about subsequent geological transitions that are marked by mass-extinction events. There have been about 10 of them, and they involved animals and other organisms that left more reliable fossil traces. Five of the transitions are particularly famous because of the large proportions of the existing biota that were lost (Raup and Seposki, 1982; Erwin, 1990; Bamback et al., 2004; Eldredge, 2005). The following are the greatest of the mass extinctions:

- *End of the Ordovician*: This event occurred about 440 million years ago (mya), likely caused by a sudden global cooling of unknown causation, and resulting in the loss of about 25 percent of marine families (each consisting of several to thousands of species).
- *End of the Devonian*: Occurred 370 mya, possibly caused by global climate change, with 19 percent of marine families being lost.
- *End of the Permian*: Occurred 245 mya, possibly because of global climate change somehow associated with plate tectonics, or perhaps by a meteorite impact, with 54 percent of families being lost, along with 84 percent of genera and 96 percent of species (this is the most intensive mass extinction in the geological record).
- *End of the Triassic*: Occurred 210 mya, of unknown causation, with 23 percent of families lost.

- *End of the Cretaceous*: Occurred 65 mya, likely caused by climatic deterioration resulting from a meteorite impact in the region of Yucatan, Mexico, which caused 17 percent of families, 57 percent of genera, and 76 percent of species to be lost across the phylogenetic spectrum, including the last of the dinosaurs, pterosaurs, and marine ammonites.

Each of the natural mass extinctions was followed by an evolutionary radiation and proliferation, as vacant niches became re-occupied by newly evolved species. The first of the radiations to be relatively well-documented occurred at the beginning of the Cambrian era about 542 mya, when there was a rapid proliferation of larger-bodied animals (Metazoa). This proliferation is best known from examination of fossil deposits located in Yoho National Park, British Columbia. A famous bed of stratified rocks known as the Burgess Shale (from about 505 mya, in the Middle Cambrian) has yielded 15–20 phyla of now-extinct metazoans, some of which are soft-bodied forms such as sponges (which rarely preserve well in the fossil record), as well as many kinds of arthropods with shells of chitin (a hard polysaccharide) (Conway Morris, 1998; Gould, 1998). Similar evolutionary radiations of surviving biodiversity occurred after all of the mass extinction events in the geological record. For example, following the end-of-Cretaceous mass extinction, which wiped out most of the large reptiles, there was a diverse radiation of birds and mammals.

Although almost all species that have ever existed became extinct as a result of natural forces, no biologist has ever directly observed a natural extinction of a full species—in other words, all observed extinctions during historical times have been anthropogenic. However, there have been a few observations of the natural extirpation of local populations of wide-ranging species on oceanic islands, or in isolated habitats on continents (Diamond, 1984). These events were stochastic—caused to a small population by an unpredictable catastrophe such as an event of severe weather. For instance, Ehrlich et al. (1972) had been studying an isolated, subalpine population of the butterfly *Glaucopsyche lygdamus* for several years in Colorado, when early one particular summer, a late snowstorm killed the flower primordia of the lupine (*Lupinus amplus*) that is the only food plant of the larvae of the butterfly. This weather-caused calamity resulted in the extirpation of the local population of the *Glaucopsyche*, although it recolonized the site several years later.

Small butterfly populations have also been observed to become extirpated in Canada, such as the Karner blue (*Lycaeides melissa samuelis*) and frosted elfin (*Incisalia irus*) studied in southern Ontario by Laurence Packer (1994) of York University. However, those losses were anthropogenic—the butterflies occurred only in savannah dominated by black oak (*Quercus velutina*) and containing their obligate food plant, another species of lupine (*Lupinus perennis*), but this rare natural habitat has mostly been destroyed and it now persists in only <1 percent of its original range in Canada.

Local extirpations of various species of birds were documented after the rising waters of Lake Gatun, created by flooding associated with the new Panama Canal in 1914, isolated Barro Colorado Island from previously continuous tropical lowland forest (Karr, 1982). Initially, the island supported at least 218 species of resident birds, but by 1981 at least 56 species or 26 percent of the

The last of the dinosaurs (order Dinosauria) became extinct in a mass-extinction event at the end of the Cretaceous period about 65 million years ago. This model of a *Troodon formosus*, a bird-like coelurosaurid dinosaur, is in the National Museum of Natural History in Ottawa. This smaller predator was about 1 m tall, weighed up to 45 kg, and lived in western North America between 75 and 65 million years ago. Its fossils have been found in southern Alberta.

Bill Freedman

avifauna were extirpated. However, 26 of the extirpated species inhabit younger, disturbed habitats, which disappeared from Barro Colorado Island as its forest underwent successional development. In addition, 8 aquatic birds disappeared because their prey of small fish was reduced by the introduction of a large, alien, piscivorous fish to the lake. The other 22 known extirpations were of birds that inhabit mature forest (the actual losses may have been up to 50–60 species, because the birds of this habitat were not completely documented in 1921). The reasons for their extirpations are not clear, especially in view of the fact that the area of mature forest considerably increased between 1921 and 1981 because of succession. Presumably, those mature-forest species became extirpated because of such factors as (1) changes in habitat quality; (2) inadequate areas of suitable habitat to support a long-term breeding population; and (3) stochastic extirpation events caused by occurrences of severe weather. Although the extirpated species are abundant and widespread in larger areas of continuous forest in the region, their limited dispersal ability has apparently prevented them from recolonizing Barro Colorado Island (i.e., they do not fly across long stretches of water).

And so, extinctions have always been a context for life and evolution. In rare cases they occurred as mass events, sometimes triggered by cataclysmic environmental changes associated with a meteorite strike or volcanic activity. These natural events of mass extinction were then followed by a biotic recovery through the evolutionary radiation of new species that took advantage of ecological opportunities that were presented by the vacant niches of extinct taxa. Moreover, even during the protracted intervening periods between mass-extinction catastrophes, there was a pervasive background of extinctions occurring at much slower rates, as species disappeared because they were unable to cope with moderate changes in their environmental circumstances. These natural extinctions provide an ecological context for the mass extinction that is presently ongoing, and that is being caused by anthropogenic influences.

Anthropogenic Extinctions and Endangerment

Of course, there is a sixth mass extinction of a scale comparable to the ones noted above, but this one is anthropogenic and ongoing, and will likely become even more intensive in the near future. This is the **modern biodiversity crisis**, sometimes referred to as the **Holocene biodiversity event**. Although this mass extinction began about 10 000 to 12 000 years ago, it has been rapidly intensifying since then into present times, and has been particularly accelerating during the past several centuries. This modern biodiversity crisis is mostly being caused by the activities and influences of people who are alive today.

The modern biodiversity crisis is characterized by the following elements:

- *A high rate of extinction.* Species are becoming rapidly extinct, at rates far higher than the natural background attrition. This is occurring in all biomes and ecosystems, but the damage is especially severe in tropical climes. Some biologists, such as E. O. Wilson, one of the best-known specialists in biodiversity, believe that about half of existing species will be lost within the next century.
- *Rapidly increasing numbers of species at risk.* Species are at conservation risk (at risk of becoming extinct) if their population is much smaller than it used to be, and/or their necessary habitat has become greatly reduced in area or quality (see section 14.3). The numbers of species that are endangered in this way are rapidly increasing in all countries, including Canada.
- *Endangerment of natural communities.* Some kinds of natural communities have been extensively destroyed, mostly by conversion to anthropogenic land uses. This great diminishment means that they may no longer be able to maintain their species mixture and functional qualities. In such cases, the affected communities are endangered in their entirety, as are their dependent species of plants, animals, and microorganisms.

The most important cause of the modern biodiversity crisis is the destruction of natural ecosystems. On land, this has primarily occurred through the conversion of natural ecosystems into various kinds of agricultural, urbanized, or industrial land uses whose habitats are unsuitable for supporting native species. This problem is acute everywhere, but particularly in countries with tropical forest, because those primary ecosystems support more biodiversity than any other kinds.

In the oceans, the destruction of natural ecosystems has primarily occurred through the over-harvesting of their commercially important species and collateral damages (such as by-catch; see Chapter 15). In the worst cases, species have been rendered extinct or endangered because they were excessively harvested as economic commodities or as wild game. This is the nastiest possible way to harvest a potentially renewable biological resource—so intensively that its populations collapse, even to the degree that extinction is caused. This is akin to the unsustainable mining of a non-renewable resource, such as metals or fossil fuels. Later in this chapter we will examine case material of these sorts of damages.

Another important cause of the biodiversity crisis is the introduction of **invasive aliens**. These are non-native species that become **naturalized** (are able to persist and regenerate in native habitats), and if they also become abundant they cause ecological changes that result in declines of native species. Invasive aliens include species of plants and animals, as well as introduced diseases that are devastating to certain indigenous species. Later in this section we will examine cases of invasive aliens that are causing important ecological damage in Canada.

Because various kinds of anthropogenic stressors have been affecting biodiversity in all parts of the world, the past several centuries have witnessed huge increases in the rate of extinction and in the numbers of species threatened with this catastrophe. Moreover, during this period the problem has become more and more intensified. It is more so now than it has ever been, and will likely become even more severe in the foreseeable future. This worsening situation is occurring because of the ongoing destruction and diminishment of natural ecosystems, particularly in the tropics, coupled with the cumulative effects of alien introductions and excessive harvesting of certain biological resources.

The Species Survival Commission (SSC) of the International Union for the Conservation of Nature and Natural Resources (IUCN) has the mandate to compile and analyze global data about species at risk. According to its database **(Table 14.1)**, there are 717 known cases of extinct animals (as of 2008) plus another 4309 that are threatened (this includes species that are critically endangered, endangered, or vulnerable; we examine these categories of risk in section 14.7). There are also 87 extinct plants and 8457 that are vulnerable.

These data should, however, be regarded as gross underestimates of the actual numbers of extinctions and of species at risk. In actual fact, numerous extinctions occurred prior to the affected species being "discovered" by biologists, especially in tropical regions and on remote islands. Even today there is little information about the conservation status of smaller organisms that occur in poorly explored ecosystems, such as tropical rain forest or large regions of the oceans. Because of this ignorance, there have undoubtedly been many thousands of "hidden" extinctions of species that were never documented by biologists. Therefore, although there is relatively good knowledge of extinct and vulnerable species for large and conspicuous animals, especially those of higher-latitude countries where most biologists live, such as Canada, we know little about the conservation status of other groups of organisms.

Prehistoric Extinctions

Although anthropogenic extinctions are occurring more rapidly today than ever before, they are not an exclusively modern phenomenon. At about the end of the Pleistocene era of continental-scale glaciation, around 10 000 to 12 000 years ago, there were advancing waves of synchronous extinctions of species of large animals (or megafauna, weighing more than 44 kg, or 100 pounds) in the Americas. The extinctions began in what is now Alaska, and then over about a millennium, progressed southward until even Patagonia in southern South America was affected. The timing of the extinctions coincided with the colonization of

TABLE 14.1 Global Data on Species at Risk

These data are compiled by the International Union for the Conservation of Nature and Natural Resources (IUCN).

Group of Organisms	Extinct	Critically Endangered	Endangered	Vulnerable
Mammals	76	188	448	505
Birds	134	190	361	671
Reptiles	21	86	134	203
Amphibians	38	475	755	675
Fish	90	266	240	640
Crustaceans	7	84	127	395
Insects	60	70	132	424
Molluscs	288	268	224	486
Other invertebrates	3	38	67	310
Total animals	717	1665	2488	4309
Bryophytes	3	23	32	28
Ferns	3	29	37	58
Conifers	0	66	95	162
Flowering plants	81	1457	2116	4354
Total plants	87	1575	2280	4602

SOURCE: International Union for the Conservation of Nature and Natural Resources (IUCN). 2008. The IUCN Red List of Threatened Species. IUCN, Gland, Switzerland. http://www.iucnredlist.org

previously uninhabited regions by the first peoples of the Americas, known as Paleoindians.

A compelling implication of the synchrony is that overhunting by Paleoindians caused or contributed to the extinctions of the large animals—they were unable to adapt to a sudden onslaught of anthropogenic predation. In essence, this is the "Pleistocene overkill" hypothesis that was first advanced by Paul Martin (1967, 2001).

Martin's idea is that when migrating peoples first discovered habitable new landmasses, they settled in and fed themselves largely by hunting big animals. He suggested that the colonizing Paleoindians were novel and effective predators, and many of their large-animal prey species were a naïve quarry that was unable to adapt to the new assault. This resulted in declining populations of many of the megafaunal species by attrition from hunting, likely over decades, until they eventually became extinct. Wandering Siberians colonized Alaska as early as 12 000 to 14 000 years ago, around the end of the Pleistocene glaciation. They did this by wandering eastward across a broad "land-bridge" up to 1600 km wide between Siberia and Alaska, This land-link existed because sea level was more than 120 m lower than today, owing to so much water being tied up in continental ice sheets. Those early immigrants increased in population and then spread as an expanding wave of human colonization through all of the Americas. As the stone-age peoples occupied new habitats, there was an accompanying extinction of vulnerable species of large-animal prey. About 73 percent of the large-bodied fauna became extinct in North America during this end-of-Pleistocene event, and 80 percent in South America.

In North America, the extinctions involved at least 35 genera and 56 species of large mammals (>44 kg), 21 species of smaller mammals, and several large birds (Martin, 1967, 1984; Diamond, 1982). Some of the notable losses were 10 species of horses (*Equus*), the giant ground sloth (*Gryptotherium listai*), a giant armadillo (*Holmesina septentrionalis*), four species of camels (Camelidae), two of bison (*Bison*), a native cow (*Bos*), the saiga antelope (*Saiga tatarica*; this species survives in Siberia, but it is critically endangered), the giant beaver (*Castoroides ohioensis*), and four species of the elephant family, including the mastodon (*Mammut americanum*) and woolly or tundra mammoth (*Mammuthus primigenius*). There were also extinctions of predators and scavengers of these big herbivores, including the sabre-toothed tiger (*Smilodon fatalis*), the American lion (*Panthera leo atrox*), two species of American cheetah (*Miracinonyx*), the giant short-faced bear (*Arctodus simus*), the dire wolf (*Canis dirus*), and the 25 kg scavenging raptor terratornis (*Terratornis merriami*). Many of these extinct, large animals are known as part of a fossil fauna in the Rancho la Brea tar pits in southern California. Today, the only extant representative of the large-animal fauna of those tar pits is the critically endangered California condor (*Gymnogyps californianus*).

The hypothesis of Martin is compelling and it has been built upon by others (e.g., Martin and Wright, 1967; Diamond, 1982; Pielou, 1991; Flannery, 2001; Baillie et al., 2004). Its strength rests with the apparent synchrony of the megafaunal extinctions and the arrival of human colonists, along with the discovery of some killing sites containing bones of large numbers of animals. However, not everyone believes that the overkill hypothesis is relevant to all of the large-animal extinctions to which it has been attributed. Some researchers believe that habitat changes caused by climatic shifts associated with glaciation and deglaciation were more important than hunting by stone-age humans in causing certain extinctions in parts of Siberia and northwestern North America (Shapiro et al., 2004).

Mass extinctions elsewhere have also been convincingly attributed to the colonization of new landmasses by prehistoric cultures. For instance, after New Guinea and Australia were colonized by Melanesian peoples 40 000 to 50 000 years ago, there were numerous extinctions of large marsupials, flightless birds, and tortoises (Diamond, 1982; Martin, 1984). In Australia, about 86 percent of the megafauna became extinct, likely because of overhunting in combination with land clearing by fire and perhaps the introduction of a lethal placental predator, the dingo (*Canis dingo*).

In New Zealand an extinction wave took place less than 1000 years ago (Diamond, 1984; Holdaway, 1989; McGlone, 1989; Holdaway and Jacomb, 2000). Within about only one century of the Polynesian colonization, 30 large bird species became extinct, with the losses progressing as a wave from the point of colonization on North Island to the southern tip of South Island. The losses included the 250 kg, 3 m tall giant moa (*Dinornis maximus*), 26 other big moas, a flightless goose (*Cnemiornis calcitrans*), a swan (*Cygnus sumnerensis*), a flightless giant coot (*Fulica chathamensis*), a pelican (*Pelecanus novaezealandiae*), an eagle (*Harpagornis moorei*), and larger species of lizards and frogs. Many of the moas had been herded into confined places, and the great bone deposits at those butchering sites were later mined by European colonists as a source of phosphate fertilizer.

The colonization of Madagascar about 1500 years ago resulted in a megafaunal extinction that involved four species of enormous elephant birds (Aepyornithidae; the largest was *Aepyornis maximus*, 3 m tall and weighing 400 kg), 14 species of the biggest lemurs (10 species of lemur are still extant), two giant tortoises, and various other big animals. Other well-known prehistoric mass extinctions occurred on Hawaii, New Caledonia, Fiji, and the West Indies. These are also believed to have been caused by some combination of overhunting, habitat changes associated with colonization, and introduced predators and diseases (Martin, 1984; Diamond, 1982; Steadman, 2006).

Vulnerability of Island Biota

In general, the species of isolated islands are much more vulnerable to extinction than those living in continental habitats. This is especially true of tropical islands, which often support small populations of endemic species. Moreover, because most endemic animals on islands had not been subjected to intense predation during their recent evolutionary history, they were poorly adapted to dealing with a sudden onslaught of anthropogenic predation after their habitat was colonized.

For example, many endemic birds of remote oceanic islands were flightless, relatively big, and did not fear novel predators, so they were easy to hunt and did not adapt well to the intense mortality. Moreover, endemic species of islands had often evolved without close competitors, so they were easily displaced by introduced species that exploited a similar niche. Finally, when people colonized oceanic islands, they typically changed much of the natural habitat by converting it to agricultural production, and this intensified the downward spiral of abundance of many endemic species. These sorts of ecological damages occurred when prehistoric aboriginal cultures colonized islands in the Pacific, Caribbean, and other oceanic regions, and it greatly intensified when Europeans moved in. The damage continues today as the indigenous biodiversity of islands is wracked by the destruction of natural habitats to develop the land for agriculture, tourism, and towns. At the same time, remnants of natural habitat are damaged by invasive aliens, and small lingering populations of native species are affected by introduced predators and diseases.

For instance, smaller Pacific islands supported long-isolated biotas that were highly vulnerable to extinction, and declined badly after the islands were colonized by prehistoric Polynesian cultures (Steadman, 2006). It is possible that most of the 800 or so Polynesian islands had several endemic species of rails (family Rallidae) plus other unique birds, possibly totalling thousands of species, most of which became extinct from overhunting, predation by introduced rats, and habitat changes. An excavation of bird bones from an archaeological site on the island of Ua Huka, in the Marquesas of the equatorial Pacific, revealed that 14 of the 16 original species of birds are now extinct or extirpated from the island, including 10 endemics.

In fact, most of the known extinctions of species since 1500 have occurred on islands (Baillie et al., 2004). A total of 88 percent of bird extinctions involved island endemics, as have 86 percent of reptiles, 68 percent of mollusks, 62 percent of mammals, and 54 percent of amphibians. These data are, however, only for the known extinctions—undoubtedly there have also been many unrecorded extinctions of these groups on both islands and in continental tropical regions where the original fauna was not well documented.

More Recent Extinctions

Clearly, humans have been causing extinctions for a long time. During the past century, however, the ability of the human economy to cause damage to biodiversity has increased enormously. In large part this is due to the enormous growth in our technological capability to destroy natural ecosystems and convert them into anthropogenic land uses. In the rest of this section we will briefly consider recent cases of extinction and endangerment and their causes. Then in following sections we will examine the role of ecology in helping to avoid those damages through the planning and implementation of conservation measures.

The first documented extinction during historical times was that of the dodo (*Raphus cucullatus*), a flightless, turkey-sized relative of pigeons (order Columbiformes) that was last seen alive in 1662 (Staub, 1996; IUCN, 2008). The dodo lived on Mauritius, an island in the Indian Ocean that was discovered by the Portuguese in 1507 and colonized by the Dutch in 1598. Sailors and colonists hunted the dodo and gathered its eggs as food, while clearing its lowland habitat for agricultural use and introducing cats, pigs, and monkeys that killed the birds or ate their eggs in ground-level nests. These stressors caused the dodo to rapidly decline and become extinct, and today not even a complete skeleton exists. The closely related solitaire (*Pezophaps solitaria*), another flightless bird from the nearby island of Rodrigues, also became extinct, around 1715, for similar reasons as the dodo.

Interestingly, it appears that the dodo may have co-evolved with an endemic tree, the tambalacoque (*Calvaria major*), to form a mutualistic relationship. The tambalacoque provided the dodo with an abundant and nutritious food of large seeds, while the tree benefited by the scarification of its hard-coated seeds by passage through the gut of dodos, which allowed them to germinate (Temple, 1977). The tambalacoque has become extremely rare in the wild, with only a few surviving mature trees, each older than three hundred years. The lack of young tambalacoques in the wild, even though the mature trees produce fertile fruit, may be due to their seeds no longer being scarified by passage through dodos. However, seeds that are eaten and passed through a domestic turkey (*Meleagris gallopavo*) will germinate afterward, and this may allow conservation biologists to increase the abundance of wild tambalacoque trees.

The extinction of the dodo was largely caused by excessive hunting as food, in combination with other stressors. Over-exploitation has also caused other extinctions, including several in North America. This kind of loss is particularly foolish, because it is caused by the irresponsible "mining" of a potentially renewable biological resource, so much so that it is wiped from the face of Earth. We will illustrate this point with two famous examples of grossly non-sustainable harvesting: the great auk and the passenger pigeon.

The great auk (*Pinguinus impennis*), a large seabird, was the first documented anthropogenic extinction of a species that occurred in North America (it had an amphi-Atlantic distribution, also occurring in European waters; Nettleship and Evans, 1985; Fuller, 2003). The great auk was the first bird to be named a penguin (or pennegoin) by early mariners and naturalists, but it was from the auk family (Alcidae) rather than the true penguins (Spheniscidae) of the southern hemisphere. The physical similarity of birds in these two families is due to their convergent evolution, occurring in response to comparable regimes of natural selection. The great auk was a flightless bird that ate small fish, nested on rocky islands that lacked mammalian predators, laid only a single egg, and likely bred only every several years. It was also extremely vulnerable to being hunted by people, because it was flightless and could be rounded up and killed in large numbers by clubbing. The species had long been eaten by aboriginals and European fishers, but it quickly declined in abundance when it became the target of a rapacious commercial hunt for its skin and feathers in the mid-1700s. The great auk was rendered extinct by 1852.

Funk Island off eastern Newfoundland supported the largest breeding colony of great auks in the northwestern Atlantic, and also the largest commercial harvest. This profitable but short-lived operation was described in 1785 (from Nettleship and Evans, 1985):

> *It has been customary of late years, for several crews of men to live all summer on that island, for the sole purpose of killing birds for the sake of their feathers,*

Natural History Museum/GetStock.com

The great auk (*Pinguinus impennis*) was a large, flightless seabird of the north Atlantic Ocean, and was the first documented anthropogenic extinction of a species that occurred in North America. This painting was made in 1839 by William Macgillvray of the University of Aberdeen, based on a specimen belonging to the great American artist, John James Audubon.

Bill Montevecchi, Memorial University

These bones of great auks were excavated by Bill Montevecchi of Memorial University on Funk Island off northeastern Newfoundland. They were used to assemble skeletal specimens of this extinct seabird.

the destruction of which they have made is incredible. If a stop is not soon put to that practice, the whole breed will be diminished to almost nothing, particularly the penguins.

The slaughter of great auks and other seabirds on Funk Island was so enormous that much of the soil that presently occurs there is formed from their composted bodies. Bill Montevecchi of Memorial University studies seabirds breeding on Funk Island, and has observed common puffins (*Fratercula arctica*) carrying auk bones out of the organic substrate as they dig their nesting burrows (Kirkham and Montevecchi, 1982). The great auk was extirpated on Funk Island by the early 1800s, and the last sighting anywhere was on the Grand Banks in 1852.

The passenger pigeon (*Ectopistes migratorius*) is another case of a species that was rendered extinct by relentless market hunting. The passenger pigeon may have been the most abundant terrestrial bird in the world, numbering some 3–5 billion individuals, or one-quarter of all birds in North America (Schorger, 1955; Eckert, 1965; Blockstein and Tordoff, 1985). It was a highly social animal that migrated in immense flocks, which were said to "blacken the sky." It was also a species that nested in large colonies, where up to a hundred nests might occur within an individual tree, and hundreds of millions in a colony. In 1810, Alexander Wilson, an American naturalist, estimated that a migrating flock was 0.6 km wide, 144 km long, and contained two billion pigeons. Its breeding range was the northeastern United States and southern Canada, including southern regions of the Maritimes, Quebec, Ontario, Manitoba, Saskatchewan, and possibly Alberta. Its breeding habitat was mature hardwood forest that produced abundant "mast" (nut-like seeds) of beech, chestnut, and oak (*Fagus grandifolia, Castanea dentata, Quercus rubra*, and other *Quercus* species), and it wintered in similarly mast-rich forests of the southeastern United States.

Mark Catesby was an English naturalist who travelled widely in eastern America in the early 1700s and published observations of the biota he observed. He wrote the following about an immense wintering roost of passenger pigeons (from Feduccia, 1985):

Of these [passenger pigeons] there came to winter in Virginia and Carolina, from the North, incredible numbers; insomuch that in some places where they roost, they often break down the limbs of oaks with their weight, and leave their dung some inches thick under the trees they roost on . . . they so effectively clear the woods of acorns and other mast, that the hogs that come after them . . . fare very poorly. In Virginia I have seen them fly in such continued trains three days successively, that there was not the least interval in losing sight of them, but that somewhere or other in the air they were to be seen continuing their flight south.

The irresistible abundance and communal habits of passenger pigeons combined to make it easy to harvest them in huge numbers, and they were subjected to a ravenous market hunt, mostly for meat to sell to the urban poor. The birds were killed in astonishing numbers by clubbing, shooting, and netting. According to Alexander Wilson in 1829 (Feduccia, 1985):

Wagon loads of them are poured into the market . . . and pigeons became the order of the day at dinner, breakfast, and supper, until the very name became sickening.

Some of the annual harvests were staggering in their quantity. In 1869, an estimated 1 billion pigeons were taken in Michigan alone. In 1874, netters took 700 000 pigeons over a 28-day period.

The relentless overhunting was an obvious cause of the precipitous decline of the passenger pigeon, but other stressors were also at work (Blockstein and Tordoff, 1985). They included the destruction of much of their breeding habitat by timber harvesting and clearing for agriculture. Also important was the precipitous decline of the American chestnut because of the ravages of chestnut blight (*Cryphonectria parasitica*), an alien fungal pathogen that virtually wiped out this once abundant and widespread mast-producing tree. Moreover, the pigeon was such a communal animal that once its abundance decreased below some level, perhaps still in the millions, there may have been insufficient social facilitation for the birds to breed successfully, particularly in view of the intense interference associated with the ongoing hunting. In any event, the last observed attempt at nesting was in 1894, and the last individual, a captive named Martha in the Cincinnati Zoo, died a solitary death in 1914. The hunting of this pigeon had been so intense that within only a few decades, the world's most abundant bird had been rendered extinct.

But commercial overhunting as food was not the only reason for causing species to become extinct. For instance, the Carolina parakeet (*Conuropsis carolinensis*) was exterminated because it was perceived to be an agricultural pest, owing to of damage it caused to crops when feeding in fruit orchards and grain fields. This native parrot was a common, brightly plumaged bird that foraged and roosted in social groups in mature hardwood forest in the southeastern United States. The Carolina parakeet was easy to eradicate because it lived in communal groups, and would assemble around a wounded colleague so that an entire flock could be wiped out by a hunter. The last

Bill Freedman

The destruction of tropical forest is the leading cause of extinction and endangerment. This is a view of moist tropical forest in Manu National Park, in lowland Amazonian Peru.

known individual died in the Cincinnati Zoo in 1918 (in the very cage that Martha had vacated in 1914).

Some other species were made extinct largely because most of their natural habitat was destroyed. An example of this is the ivory-billed woodpecker (*Campephilus principalis principalis*), which inhabited extensive mature hardwood forests and cypress swamps in the southeastern United States. Most of that habitat was heavily logged or converted to agriculture by the early 1900s, driving the ivory-billed woodpeckers into a rapid decline and eventually to likely extinction (notwithstanding claims of sightings in 2004–2005).

Tropical Deforestation and Extinctions

The selected cases of famous losses of species that we just examined are representative of the tragedy of extinction. The animals we considered were beautiful creatures that had evolved over millions of years, only to be removed from Earth in a few decades by avaricious humans. Those people valued their own immediate profit over the sustainability of their enterprise, and they paid no heed to the continued survival of the species they were harvesting. It would be nice to know that these sorts of appalling mistakes are only things of the past, but unfortunately, such is not the case. Extinctions are still being caused, and even at an accelerating rate. The worst of the damages are occurring in the biome that supports more of Earth's biodiversity than any other—primary tropical forest (**primary** or **frontier forest** occurs in large blocks of self-organizing ecosystems, often in an old-growth condition, and it sustains all of the appropriate species, including wide-ranging animals). These natural ecosystems are packed with a great richness of species, many of which are endemics, so when their habitat is destroyed they have no alternative refuges and become extinct. In the case of smaller species, the extinction typically happens before they have been "discovered" and named by biologists.

It is well known that the rate of deforestation in poorer countries has increased alarmingly during the present century, and particularly in the past several decades. As a group, less-developed countries lost 138 million hectares of forest cover between 1990 and 2005 **(Table 14.2)**. Most of the net deforestation involved the clearing of natural forest, followed by conversion of the land use to agriculture. The amount and rate of deforestation varies enormously among countries. China, for example, retains only 22 percent of its original forest cover, and only 2 percent of that is primary forest. However, its net forest cover has been increasing in recent years, by 2.2 percent annually and a net increase of 40 million ha between 1990 and 2005. This is because of a massive effort to establish tree plantations as timber-crops and to control soil erosion in hilly terrain.

However, most less-developed countries that support tropical forest are rapidly losing this natural ecosystem. Nigeria, for example, retains only 11 percent of its original forest cover and it is suffering an ongoing deforestation rate of 3.3 percent per year (**Table 14.2**; if maintained, a 3.3 percent rate of deforestation would decrease the remaining forest cover by half in only 21 years). Burundi is even worse—it has lost 96 percent of its original forest, is still deforesting at 5.5 percent per year, and could lose half of its remnant forest in only 13 years.

The situation is different in wealthier countries, where forest cover has recently been fairly stable—in fact, developed countries had a net gain of 13.5 million ha of forest between 2000 and 2005 **(Table 14.2)**. In North America, there was little net change (0.0 percent) in forest cover between 1990 and 2005, and 77 percent of the original forest area is still intact, although only 34 percent of the primary forest has survived. In Canada, 91 percent of the original forest cover remains, including 57 percent of the primary forest, and there

TABLE 14.2 Deforestation in Selected Countries

Original forest is the estimated cover about 8000 years ago. Frontier forest refers to extensive blocks of natural forest, dominated by native species and able to sustain large wide-ranging animals. Change in forest area is between 1990 and 2005, expressed in hectares and as annual percentage change.

Region or Country	Existing Forest Area as Percent of Original	Existing Frontier Forest as Percent of Original	Change in Forest Area (10^6 ha)	Change in Forest Area (percent/year)
WORLD	53.4	21.7	−125.3	−0.2
North America	77.3	34.1	4.4	0.0
South America	69.1	45.6	−59.3	−0.5
Central America	54.5	9.7	−9.4	−0.5
Europe	58.4	21.3	12.1	0.1
Sub-Saharan Africa			−66.9	−0.6
Less-developed countries			−138.2	−0.4
Bangladesh	7.9	3.8	−0.1	−0.3
Brazil	66.4	42.2	−42.3	−0.6
Burundi	3.5	0.0	−0.2	−5.2
Cambodia	65.1	7.3	−2.5	−2.0
China	21.6	1.8	40.1	2.2
Colombia	53.5	36.4	−0.7	−0.1
Cuba	28.8	0.0	0.6	2.2
Haiti	0.8	0.0	−0.1	−0.7
Honduras	51.6	16.4	−2.8	−3.1
India	20.5	1.3	3.8	0.0
Indonesia	64.6	28.5	−28.1	−2.0
Madagascar	13.1	0.0	−0.9	−0.3
Malaysia	63.8	14.5	−1.5	−0.7
Mexico	63.4	8.1	−4.7	−0.4
Nigeria	10.7	0.6	−6.2	−3.3
Peru	86.6	56.7	−1.4	−0.1
Venezuela	83.6	59.3	−4.4	−0.6
Developed countries			13.5	0.1
Canada	91.2	56.5	0.0	0.0
France	16.5	0.0	1.0	0.3
Germany	26.3	0.0	0.4	0.0
Japan	58.2	0.0	0.0	0.0
Russia	68.7	29.3	−0.2	0.0
United Kingdom	6.0	0.0	0.2	0.4
United States	60.2	6.3	4.4	0.1

SOURCE: World Resources Institute (WRI). 2010. EarthTrends database. http://earthtrends.wri.org/

has been no net deforestation in recent years. Of course, these national data hide a great deal of variation across Canada—there has been extensive deforestation in southern parts of our country, where most people live and most agriculture occurs.

Tropical deforestation is mostly caused when natural forests are cleared and the land is converted into an agricultural use. This may happen when landless people clear the forest to develop subsistence farms to support their family, or at a large industrial scale for commercial purposes. The conversion into subsistence agriculture often occurs rapidly if access to the forest interior is improved, such as when roads are constructed to extract timber or to explore for minerals. The social causes of the deforestation are complex and include the displacement of poor people by the commercialization and mechanization of agriculture, inequities of land ownership, and population growth. These factors in less-developed countries result in large numbers of poor citizens seeking arable land on which to grow food for subsistence and some cash income. Commonly, the deforestation results from a system of **shifting cultivation**, in which trees of the original forest are felled, the woody debris burned, and the land used to grow a mixture of crops for several years, by which time fertility declines and weeds become abundant. The land is then abandoned for several decades, and during this fallow period a secondary forest regenerates, while nearby patches of forest are cleared to provide land for cultivation. **Slash-and-burn** is a more intensive subsistence or commercial system that results in a longer-term conversion of the land to crop production. It also starts with cutting and burning the natural forest, but the land is then used continuously, without an extended fallow period during which a secondary forest regenerates.

Immense swaths of tropical forest are also being cleared to provide land for industrial-scale agriculture—for example, to develop oil-palm plantations, sugar cane fields, and cattle pastures. Tropical forests are also being damaged by commercial logging, flooding to develop hydroelectric reservoirs, and the harvesting of fuelwood. Wood is the predominant cooking fuel in many tropical countries, particularly for poorer people. The total fuelwood production in less-developed countries in 2006 was 1650×10^6 m^3, compared with 221×10^6 m^3 in developed countries, and it was 60 percent larger than in 1961 (WRI, 2010).

Because so many species live in tropical forest (see Chapter 12, **Table 12.3**), the rapid deforestation of this biome is catastrophic for biodiversity at both regional and global scales. This damage will further intensify into the future if the relentless pace of tropical deforestation continues.

Fortunately, awareness and concern about this important ecological problem are developing. As a result, governments are beginning to set aside large tracts of primary ecosystems as **protected areas** where intensive economic activity is not allowed, such as national parks, ecological reserves, and cultural reserves (the latter are primarily intended to benefit indigenous cultures, but they also help to protect natural heritage). The conservation needs of tropical countries are also stimulating a great deal of ecological research, much of it by ecologists from developed countries working in collaboration with local scientists. In 2006, there were 485×10^6 ha of protected areas in less-developed countries, compared with 315×10^6 ha in developed ones (WRI, 2010; these are IUCN class I–V, which receive a relatively high degree of protection). However, as we will examine in section 14.5, the effectiveness of this sort of protection varies greatly, depending on political stability, governmental priorities, and other issues.

Species Declines

Certain groups of animals have been recently suffering widespread and synchronous declines of species, with many becoming endangered or extinct. These groups include freshwater mollusks, large marine fish, amphibians, reptiles, predatory birds, migratory songbirds, primates, and wide-ranging carnivores. The causes of the declines are various. For the large marine fish, whose global biomass may have been reduced by 90 percent since pre-industrial times, the principal stressors are associated with excessive commercial harvesting (Myers and Worm, 2003; Lotze and Worm, 2009). For wide-ranging terrestrial carnivores it is a combination of hunting for sport and their body parts, and sometimes persecution by agricultural interests as "vermin" (Hummel and Pettigrew, 2002).

However, some other species declines are more complicated than non-sustainable mortality associated with hunting. For example, in various parts of the world many species of amphibians have been declining, and some have become extinct. Of the 6347 named amphibian species, about 43 percent are declining in abundance, 32 percent are threatened, 427 species are critically endangered, and as many as 122 have become extinct since 1980 (Stuart et al., 2004; McCallum, 2007). This is a greater intensity of threat and extinction than occurs in other groups of vertebrates. The reasons for the extreme vulnerability of amphibians are not known, but may be related to their complex life cycle and amphibious habitat needs. The amphibian declines have been especially acute in Australia, Central and South America, and the western United States. The first high-profile extinction involved the golden toad (*Bufo periglenes*) of Monteverde, Costa Rica, where it had been well studied, but suffered a precipitous decline in 1987 and has not been seen since. Various reasons have been suggested for the causes of the amphibian declines, including habitat destruction, pollution, and disease epidemics. Because of the rapidity of the declines, it seems likely that one or more virulent parasites or diseases may be important, such as the chytrid fungus (*Batrachochytrium dendrobatidis*) or the red-leg bacterium (*Aeromonas hydrophila*). In Canada, one of the worst affected species is the leopard frog (*Rana pipiens*) in the western provinces, where it was formerly abundant but is now rare.

Another widespread decline of the past several decades has affected populations of many species of migratory songbirds. Many of the affected species of the Americas are referred to as neotropical migrants—they breed in temperate and boreal forests at higher latitudes, such as Canada, and migrate to spend most of the year in tropical habitats. The songbird declines are probably due to some combination of deforestation in both their wintering ranges and in northern breeding areas, as well as damage to intervening habitats that are important during migration, and possibly effects of avian diseases (such as West Nile virus), nest predators and parasites, and pesticides and other toxic chemicals.

Four decades of data for Canadian landbird migrants are summarized in **Figure 14.2**. These data are compiled by the Canadian Wildlife Service as part of its program of avian population monitoring. The data are collected at a large number of monitoring stations across Canada, and when aggregated they provide a synoptic indicator of how terrestrial birds are doing population-wise. Overall, the trend is one of declines of abundance, including shorter-distance migrants as well as neotropical ones. In contrast, the populations of resident species that spend all of the year in Canada have been stable during the monitoring period. The shorter-distance migrants are 79 species of blackbirds, hawks, finches, sparrows, and others that typically winter in the United States. The neotropical migrants are 92 species of flycatchers, hummingbirds, swallows, swifts, thrushes, vireos, warblers, and others that winter in the Caribbean, Central America, and South America. The residents are 36 species of chickadees, grouse, nuthatches, owls, woodpeckers, and others that spend the entire year in Canadian habitats.

One species of neotropical migrant recently became extinct, likely because of the destruction of its

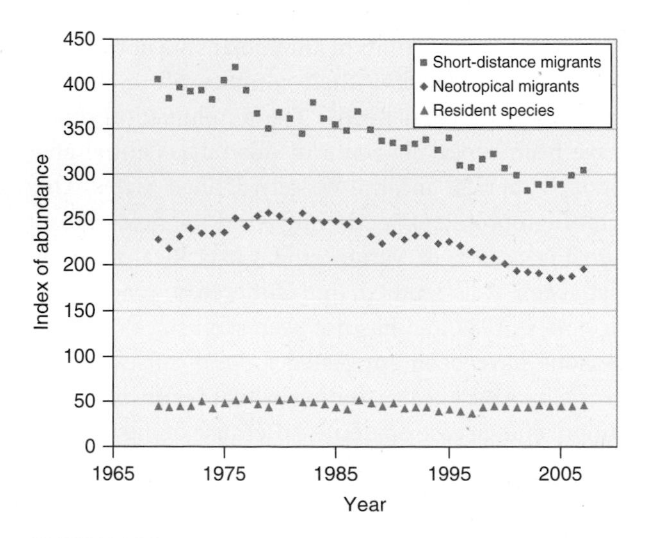

FIGURE 14.2
Changes in the Abundance of Landbirds in Canada. The abundance index is based on the analysis of a large number of surveys of breeding birds across Canada, carried out as part of an avian monitoring programme coordinated by the Canadian Wildlife Service.

SOURCE: Downes, C.M. and B.T. Collins, 2008. Canadian Bird Trends Web site, Version 2.2. Canadian Wildlife Service, Environment Canada, Gatineau, PQ. http://www.cws-scf.ec.gc.ca/mgbc/trends/index.cfm?lang=e&go=home.page&CFID=16644784&CFTOKEN=96168935

tropical wintering habitat. The Bachman's warbler (*Vermivora bachmanii*) bred in hardwood forest in the southeastern United States, where there is still appropriate habitat for it. However, this species has not been seen since the mid-1950s and it is likely extinct. Its loss was probably caused by the destruction of its wintering habitat of tropical forest on Cuba, which was converted to industrial sugarcane production.

One likely cause of declines of migratory birds is the reduction of certain breeding habitats in North America, due to the conversion of prairie and forests into agricultural and urban land uses, along with damage caused by forestry and other extractive industries. These factors have caused a large decrease to occur in the amount of high-quality natural habitat that the migratory birds need for breeding, while fragmenting much of the remainder into small "islands" (isolated patches on the landscape). The fragmentation is important because many birds are less successful when they attempt to breed in small patches of natural habitat. This is because small patches have larger ratios of edge to area, and nests closer to edges are more vulnerable to predation by crows, magpies, foxes, skunks, and other small carnivores.

Nests near forest **ecotones** (edges between discrete habitats types) are also more vulnerable to the brown-headed cowbird (*Molothrus ater*), a nest parasite (Freedman, 1995). This native blackbird lays its eggs in the nests of a wide range of other species, which raise the voracious cowbird chick, while their own young usually die. The cowbird has greatly expanded its range and abundance because formerly extensive tracts of forest have been converted into more open agricultural habitats. Many species of songbirds in the northern and eastern parts of the modern range of the cowbird are highly vulnerable to this parasite, likely because they have only recently come into contact with it and have not evolved an effective defence. Cowbirds are a threat to the survival of the Kirtland's warbler (*Dendroica kirtlandii*), an endangered species, 70 percent of whose nests may be parasitized, with each case resulting in reproductive failure. Similar rates of parasitism have been found for other species—in Illinois, a study found that 76 percent of 49 nests of neotropical migrants were parasitized by cowbirds. The cowbird problem is somewhat of an ethical dilemma, because killing large numbers of the native parasite is the best way to help songbirds that are threatened by its depredations.

Alien Species

Many species that occur in Canada are not indigenous to the country—they are **non-native** (or **alien**) species that have invaded. Many of the aliens occur in Canada because people deliberately introduced them, usually because they are cultivated as a crop, used in horticulture, kept as a pet, or for some other reason. Many other aliens invaded accidentally, such as rats that hitchhiked on ships, and plants whose seeds occurred in shipments of grain or soil (rocks and dirt were often carried as ballast by sailing ships from Europe; they would be dumped on land when the vessel arrived at a port).

Some non-native species penetrate into natural or managed ecosystems and cause damage to them—these are referred to as *invasive aliens* (Myers and Bazely, 2003). Some invasive species cause great damage to economically important ecosystems in agriculture, forestry, aquaculture, or horticulture, mostly by decreasing the productivity of crops. Others damage natural ecosystems by changing habitat conditions, displacing indigenous species, or by acting as pathogens that injure or kill natives. The ecological damage caused by invasive aliens is considered to be the second most important cause of damage to global biodiversity, after the outright destruction of natural habitats.

Invasive species are a global problem—they are causing damage in all countries and in almost all ecoregions. They are a serious problem in Canada, especially invasive plants—24 percent of our wild flora now consists of non-native species **(Table 14.3)**. In general, ecosystems that are most heavily impacted by alien plants are anthropogenic or semi-natural, such as horticultural and agricultural systems, including pastures of native prairie that are grazed by livestock. The penetration by aliens is least in wilder parts of Canada where the human footprint is lightest, such as in Nunavut, where only 1.5 percent of the flora is alien (CESCC, 2006). The numbers of alien animals are much smaller than for plants, although some of them are causing important ecological damage. In the following, we examine some of the worst alien invaders in Canada.

URBANIZED AREAS AND HORTICULTURE. Most of the animals that occur in Canadian cities and towns are aliens. The most prominent non-native birds are the rock dove (*Columba livea*), English sparrow (*Passer domesticus*), and starling (*Sturnus vulgaris*). These and other alien birds were deliberately introduced to North America by European immigrants who were homesick for familiar species of places where they had grown up. The most famous avian introductions were made by a late-Victorian group known as the American Acclimatization Society, led by Eugene Schieffelin, whose romantic notion was to ensure that all birds mentioned in any of the works of Shakespeare were breeding in the Americas (Mynott, 2009). Beginning in 1890 these foolish naturalists introduced at least 40 alien species to Central Park in New York, most of which did not manage to endure.

However, the three aliens noted above did survive and they are now among the most widespread and abundant birds in North America, particularly in urbanized and agricultural areas. In fact, the starling itself may number 200 million in North America, and is likely the most populous bird in the world. These alien birds cause important ecological damage by competing with native species for food and nesting sites (native cavity-nesting birds have particularly suffered from competition with starlings and house sparrows), and they may also cause health and aesthetic problems when they nest in buildings. Fortunately, attempted introductions

TABLE 14.3 Biodiversity Assessment of Major Groups of Organisms in Canada

Number at risk refers to taxa designated by COSEWIC (the Committee on the Status of Endangered Wildlife in Canada) as endangered or vulnerable. *May be at risk* refers to taxa not yet evaluated by COSEWIC, but that are considered likely to be at risk. *Sensitive* taxa are of special concern, and *secure* ones are thought to not be at risk. The category of *all species* is the sum of the ones listed plus some additional groups of arthropods. Note, however, that many species in some groups have not yet been assessed for their conservation status in Canada.

Group	Number of Species	Number of Aliens	Number at Risk	May Be at Risk	Sensitive	Secure
Mammals	218	11	21	10	26	139
Birds	653	11	30	10	41	357
Reptiles	47	2	15	1	11	12
Amphibians	46	0	9	0	7	30
Fish	1389	12	26	16	65	238
Odonates	209	0	1	27	27	145
Freshwater mussels	55	0	9	8	15	19
Vascular plants	5074	1216	118	545	458	2573
All species	7732	1254	220	622	655	3541

SOURCE: Canadian Endangered Species Conservation Council (CESCC), 2006. Wild Species: The General Status of Species in Canada. http://www.wildspecies.ca/wildspecies2005/

The Nature Conservancy of Canada (NCC) is a non-governmental organization (NGO) that acquires private property to establish protected areas in Canada. It is a national NGO, and hundreds of smaller land trusts also operate more locally in Canada. This protected area is on Brier Island, Nova Scotia.

Planning for Conservation

Ideally, the location, size, and dispersion of protected areas have been advised by a systematic process of **conservation planning.** The aim of conservation planning is to identify the most important places that should be set aside, within the context of a comprehensive network of protected areas. The **system plan** should capture those areas with the highest priority biodiversity values, while ensuring that all indigenous elements are conserved in the greater region, including in "working" areas. Key steps of conservation planning are the following (Margules and Pressey, 2000; NCC, 2010a):

- *Assemble data on biodiversity for the planning region.* The most important kinds of information involve the spatial distributions of natural communities, as well as the locations of rare habitats and species at risk. The data should be **geo-referenced** (the location is establishing according to latitude and longitude) so that the information can be recorded on maps using a computerized geographic information system (GIS).
- *Identify conservation goals.* The broader goal is to ensure that all indigenous biodiversity values are accommodated within the planning region. Usually the focus is on natural communities and native species of the ecological region—these are the biodiversity targets to be conserved at viable levels of abundance. An initial step is to determine which biodiversity targets must be accommodated in protected areas, as well as those that can be met in working areas.
- *Review existing protected areas.* If some protected areas are already established, then the biodiversity targets they support must be documented. A **gap analysis** is then done to identify the biodiversity targets that are not yet being conserved in protected areas.
- *Propose additional protected areas.* The results of the gap analysis are used to plan the locations of additional areas to be protected, to ensure that all targets are being met. The system should also have redundancy embedded, which will help to mitigate the potential effects of disturbances and other environmental changes. For example, if only one location is protected for a rare plant, the plant could become extinct if that location is disturbed by a wildfire or another catastrophe. Protecting several habitats helps to decrease this risk of irretrievable loss. An additional consideration is tenure of the land that is proposed for protection—whether the property is already owned by government (this is often referred to as public land or as Crown land) or by private interests, and if the latter, whether the owner is willing to sell or donate it to a conservation organization.
- *Implement conservation actions.* If a target property is owned by government, it can potentially be set aside as a protected area, assuming there are no irreconcilable conflicts with economic uses (such as permits to explore for or extract minerals, to harvest timber, or to graze livestock). If the property is privately owned, it can potentially be acquired for the purpose of establishing a protected area. This can be done by purchase or donation, either by a land-focused environmental charity such as the Nature Conservancy of Canada, or by a governmental agency.
- *Steward the natural values.* All protected areas must be managed appropriately to maintain the biodiversity and ecological values that they are intended to sustain. These ongoing actions are known as **stewardship**, and they are as essential to conservation success as is the act of designating protected areas. The intensity of stewardship can

vary enormously, from regular monitoring of the ecological condition of remote protected areas that are little affected by anthropogenic stressors, to more heroic measures such as restoring the depleted populations of endangered species or reconstructing rare ecological communities.

Conservation planning is undertaken by various agencies, with the ultimate goal of designing systems of protected areas that will be successful in conserving biodiversity. This goal may be relevant to various geographic scales—county, province, national, and global. In Canada, protected areas involve tracts that are controlled by governments (local, provincial, territorial, or federal), and also by aboriginal authorities and private interests. Ideally, the system of protected areas, in concert with conservation actions on "working" ecoscapes, would be capable of sustaining all native species and natural ecosystems over the longer term, including terrestrial, freshwater, and marine systems.

This is, of course, an ideal model—in fact, no country has yet designed and implemented a comprehensive system of protected areas that sustains all indigenous biodiversity. Moreover, many existing protected areas have important management problems because they are too small to meet their conservation objectives, or they are affected by various degrading environmental stressors (see the case studies of national parks in the "Stewardship of Protected Areas" section, pp. 453–454).

Design of Protected Areas

From the perspective of biodiversity, the conservation objectives are the most important considerations in the design of a protected area. If the intent is to protect the critical habitat of one or more species at risk, then a protected area must be designed to include sustainable tracts of those targeted communities. On the other hand, if the goal is to maintain representative tracts of certain kinds of ecosystems, such as old-growth forest, then a protected area must be designed to accommodate the ecological conditions that are essential to maintaining that type against the inexorable effects of disturbance, climate change, and other environmental influences. The latter consideration acknowledges that a particular stand of old-growth forest cannot be preserved forever—rather, ecoscape-scale protected areas are required to conserve the ecological dynamics that allow stands of old-growth forest to develop.

Some theoretical considerations are also relevant to the design of protected areas. There are always limited resources available to establish these sorts of reserves. Therefore, to use scarce resources efficiently, networks of protected areas should be designed to optimize their size, shape, and position on the ecoscape so that they can best deliver their intended function of conserving biodiversity. Two of the design-related recommendations of conservation biologists are not so controversial, because they will always increase the likelihood of achieving success when designating a system of protected areas:

1. *Number of protected areas*: The universal recommendation is to have many protected areas, given the various societal and economic constraints that may be operative in any context.
2. *Size of protected areas*: Protected areas should generally be as large as possible, especially if large-scale ecological functions are to be maintained within their boundaries.

However, other aspects of the design of protected areas are being actively debated by ecologists and conservation biologists, and the issues are not yet resolved. Much of the discussion of these controversial elements of design is related to the theory of island biogeography, which we examined in the previous section. Here are some of the prominent questions:

- *Size versus number*: To a substantial degree, there is a choice to be made between the size (area) and the number of protected areas. This being the case, is it preferable to have a large reserve, or a number of smaller ones of the same cumulative area **(Figure 14.5a)**? Conservation biologists identify this question with the acronym **SLOSS**, meaning single **l**arge **o**r **s**everal **s**mall. According to island biogeography, larger protected areas are a better choice because populations occurring in them are predicted to have a lower risk of extinction, compared with those in smaller reserves. However, separate protected areas also maintain discrete populations, which may provide a degree of helpful redundancy against a catastrophic loss of an endangered species in one of them.

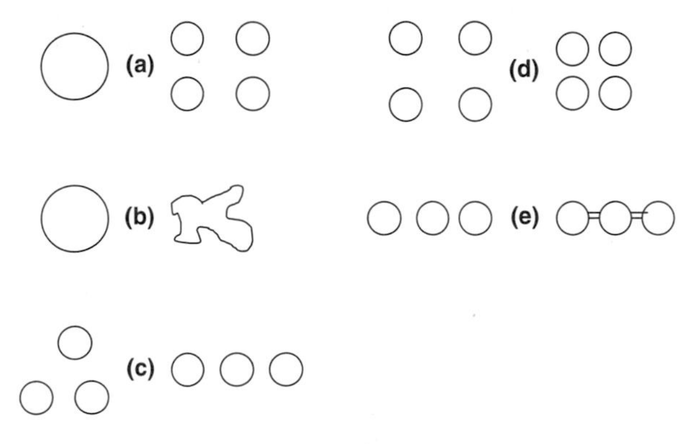

FIGURE 14.5
Conceptual Options for the Design of Protected Areas. In each paired comparison, the cumulative areas of each choice is assumed to be the same. See text for discussion of the benefits and risks of the paired choices.

SOURCE: Modified from Simberloff, D. 1988. The contribution of population and community ecology to conservation science. *Annual Reviews of Ecology and Systematics*, 19: 473–511.

Conservation of Nature and Natural Resources recognizes six categories of protected areas, which reflect the management intent of the reserve (IUCN, 2009):

- *Category Ia.* These are strictly protected **ecological reserves** that are set aside to conserve natural values, particularly biodiversity, and in which visitation is strictly limited and the only permitted activities are scientific monitoring and research.
- *Category Ib.* These are large **wilderness areas** that are managed to preserve their natural condition, with low levels of non-intensive, non-extractive visitation being permitted.
- *Category II.* These are co-managed for the conservation of natural ecosystems along with outdoor recreation and other compatible activities, as is typical of national parks and provincial parks.
- *Category III.* These are managed to conserve specific natural features, such as a prominent landform or other geological feature, or an ecological one such as a tract of old-growth forest. These protected areas are sometimes called *natural monuments* and they are usually relatively small and host a great deal of visitation.
- *Category IV.* These are **special management areas** for particular species or habitats, usually ones of economic importance, and are intended to achieve conservation through the protection and management of habitats; hunting, forestry, and some other extractive industries may be permitted.
- *Category V.* These are *protected landscapes and seascapes* that are co-managed to conserve those extensive regions together with their distinct cultural intersections with local peoples and their economic activities; these are sometimes referred to as *heritage areas*.
- *Category VI.* These *managed-resource protected areas* are intended to conserve natural values, but in the context of the sustainable use of natural resources using traditional (non-industrial) management systems.

Extent of Protected Areas

There has been rapid growth in the numbers and extent of protected areas throughout the world (**Figure 14.7**). There are now about 799 $\times$ 10^6 ha of IUCN categories I to V protected areas, and an additional 605 $\times$ 10^6 ha of IUCN VI (in 2006; **Table 14.4**). However, these protected areas vary greatly in the effectiveness of the conservation that they provide. This is especially true in less-developed countries, where the poaching (illegal harvesting) of animals and timber and other illicit activities may be rampant. This occurs because governmental priorities in developing countries do not necessarily focus on conserving biodiversity; rather it is typically directed to achieving political stability, alleviating poverty, and otherwise directly improving the human condition, or also often on corrupt ways of gaining personal wealth. However, even in wealthy countries like Canada it is common for there to be severe conflicts between the need to conserve biodiversity in protected areas, and that of economic activities in those same reserves or in other natural habitats, as we examine later in the section.

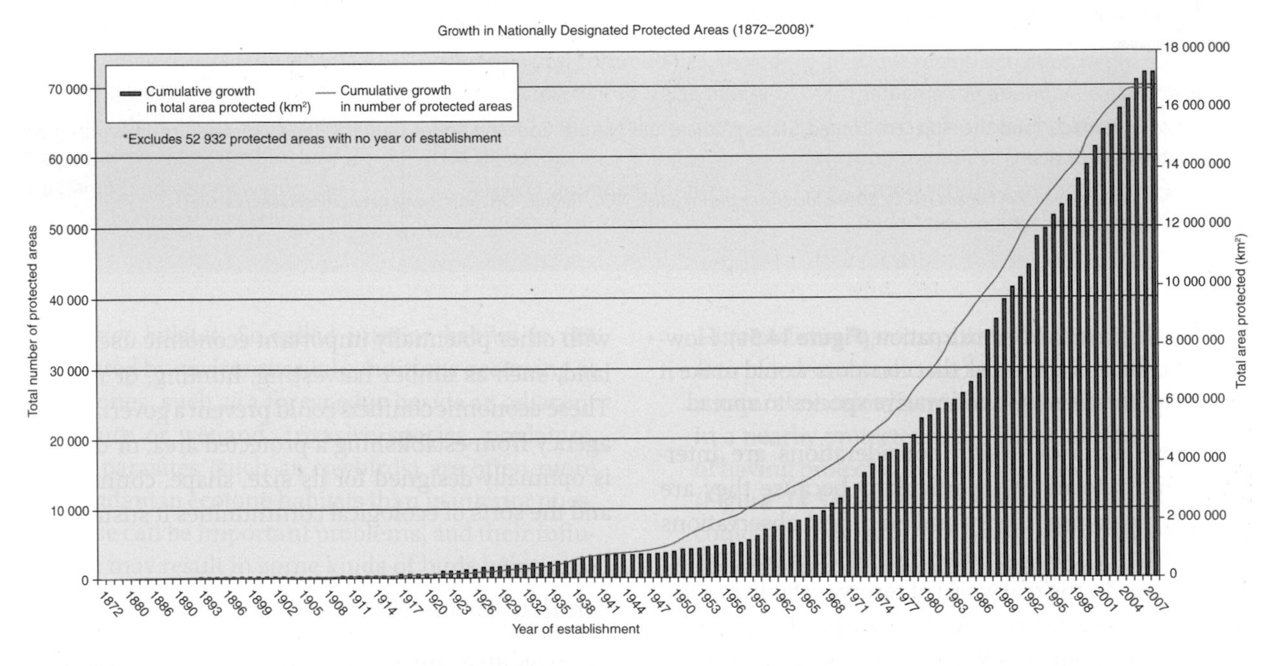

FIGURE 14.7

Growth in the Numbers and Extent of Protected Areas in the World. The database includes IUCN I–VI sites, but only those for which the year of designation is known (this excludes 43.7 $\times$ 10^3 sites).

SOURCE: United Nations Environment Programme–World Conservation Monitoring Centre (UNEP-WCMC), 2009. World Database on Protected Areas (WDPA). UNEP-WCMC, Cambridge, UK. http://www.unep-wcmc.org/wdpa/

TABLE 14.4 **Protected Areas**
The data are for IUCN categories I to V, and are current to 2006.

Region	Protected Areas IUCN Categories I to V (10^6 ha)	IUCN VI (10^6 ha)
WORLD	798.6	605.6
Developed countries	314.6	145.2
Developing countries	485.0	461.5
North America	109.9	75.4
Central America & Caribbean	6.4	16.1
South America	102.7	212.9
Europe	123.3	45.8
Asia	229.2	133.2
Middle East & North Africa	32.5	80.8
Oceania	57.5	26.2
Sub-Saharan Africa	137.1	117.2

SOURCE: World Resources Institute (WRI), 2010. EarthTrends database. http://earthtrends.wri.org/

TABLE 14.5 **Protected Areas in Canada**
The data are for IUCN categories I–VI protected areas, and are current to 2009. *Percent protected* refers to the part of the national area (terrestrial or marine) that has been given protected status.

All Protected Areas	
Total number	5,429
Total area (10^3 km^2)	849.9
percent protected	6.7
Terrestrial protected areas	
Total number	5,122
Total area (10^3 km^2)	820.8
percent protected	8.2
Marine protected areas	
Total number	563
Total area (10^3 km^2)	29.1
percent protected	1.1

SOURCE: United Nations Environment Programme–World Conservation Monitoring Centre (UNEP-WCMC), 2009. World Database on Protected Areas (WDPA). UNEP-WCMC, Cambridge, UK. http://www.unep-wcmc.org/wdpa/

In Canada, the largest kinds of protected areas are national parks, provincial parks, wilderness areas, and ecological reserves. According to data compiled by the World Conservation Monitoring Centre of the United Nations Environment Program, about 8.2 percent of the land area of Canada is now in protected status (IUCN classes I–VI), and 1.1 percent of the marine area (**Table 14.5**). Growth in the extent of protected areas in Canada is shown in **Figure 14.8**.

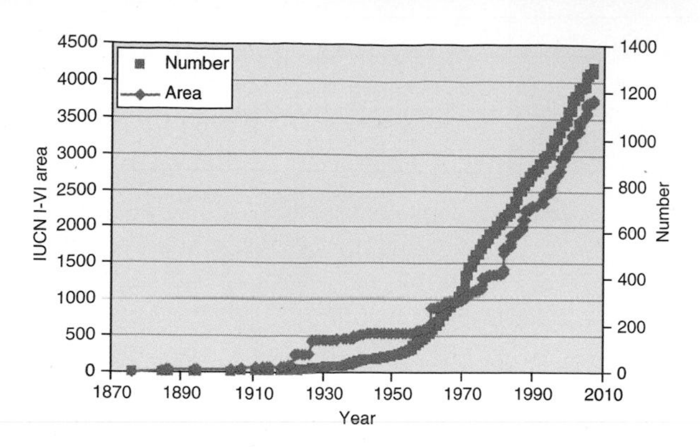

FIGURE 14.8
Growth in the Extent of Protected Areas in Canada. The database includes IUCN I–VI sites. Area is in 10^3 km^2.

SOURCE: Canadian Council on Ecological Areas (CCEA), 2009. Canadian Conservation Areas Database. CCEA, Natural Resources Canada and Environment Canada, Ottawa, ON.

Stewardship of Protected Areas

Protected areas will never be successful in meeting their conservation objectives if their boundaries are merely proclaimed to exist. It is also essential that the ecological values of reserves are monitored for change over time, and that appropriate management is undertaken when necessary. Collectively, those actions are referred to as stewardship.

For instance, if a species at risk is present in a protected area, its population and the condition of its habitat should be monitored, and if there are signs of degradation the causes should be identified and then mitigated, if possible. If the causes of a problem are not obvious, it may be necessary to undertake ecological research to determine what the stressors are and how to decrease their intensity.

A similar argument could be made for the stewardship of endangered communities in protected areas, such as tallgrass prairie or old-growth forest. The rare communities must be monitored, and if degrading changes are detected, research should be undertaken to understand their causes and consequences. It may then be necessary to actively manage the communities to maintain them in a healthy condition (see Environmental Applications 14.2).

In general, three broad types of anthropogenic stressors affect the biodiversity of protected areas:

1. *Internal stressors.* These originate with human activities occurring inside a protected area. Typically, they are associated with the influences of roads, hotels and other buildings, ski facilities, golf courses, lawns, trails, and other infrastructure connected to tourism and outdoor recreation.
2. *Stressors originating in the surrounding area.* Many protected areas are embedded within an ecoscape in which intensive economic activities are

ENVIRONMENTAL APPLICATIONS 14.2

Burn, Baby, Burn: The Use of Prescribed Burns in Conservation Management

Wildfire periodically affects certain kinds of natural communities, and species living in those habitats have evolved to be well adapted to that kind of disturbance. This is, for example, the case of jack pine (*Pinus banksiana*), a coniferous tree that is well adapted to regenerating after stand-replacing burns. Its mature cones are serotinous, meaning they are retained on the branches for a number of years, but their scales are sealed shut by a resin that has a melting point of about 50°C. It typically takes a wildfire to reach that temperature and if this occurs, the cones open and their ripe seeds scatter to regenerate the next post-fire stand of jack pine. There are many similar cases—for instance, the seeds of pin cherry (*Prunus pensylvanica*) are hard-coated and long-lived in the forest floor, where they may persist for more than 50 years. However, they are stimulated to germinate by exposure to high temperatures during a wildfire, allowing the species to be prominent in the post-fire succession (it is sometimes called "fire cherry"). One final example is the fireweed (*Chamaenerion angustifolium*), a perennial herbaceous plant whose rhizomes may survive a light wildfire, but most importantly, the species produces highly dispersible seeds that are well adapted to colonizing recent burns, where they can establish and dominate the ground vegetation for a decade or more.

Because many species and communities are adapted to wildfire, prescribed (or intentional) burns can be used as a tool to manage them in circumstances in which the natural fire regime is no longer operating well. This is generally relevant to conditions in which fires that are naturally ignited, usually by lightning, are routinely quenched to protect buildings or economically valuable forest. However, if practised over a long time this fire-fighting can lead to an extensive build-up of large amounts of fuel in the form of combustible biomass, which can set the stage for a dangerous conflagration. Such an occurrence happened in the vicinity of Kelowna, British Columbia, in August 2003, when an uncontrollable wildfire burned more than 250 km^2, some of it in residential areas, so that 239 homes were destroyed and 45 000 people were evacuated. That firestorm occurred during a lengthy drought and was wind-driven, but the forest ecosystem was highly vulnerable because it had not had a wildfire for many decades and so was "overmature" with high fuel loads. In those sorts of cases, prescribed burns can help to reduce dangerously large amounts of fuel, while also improving conditions for many species of plants and animals by opening up stands and enhancing regeneration.

Prescribed fire is also helpful in managing other kinds of ecological communities. Tallgrass prairie, for example, typically occurs in a climatic regime that is suitable for the development of habitats dominated by shrubs and even trees. However, the progression to later stages of successional development is set back by periodic wildfires, which keep the habitat open and suitable for the plants and animals that are characteristic of tallgrass prairie. Originally, the wildfires were naturally ignited by lightning strikes, and then the Plains Indians took over by regularly burning the prairie to improve the habitat for the hunting of deer and other species. However, during the past century it became common to quench wildfires, and that practice allowed shrubs and trees to invade and become prominent in conserved remnants of tallgrass prairie, which is an endangered community that survives to only about 0.2 percent of its original extent in North America. To properly steward tracts of tallgrass prairie, ecosystem managers typically use prescribed burns for two to three years in a row to rehabilitate shrub-invaded areas, and then every two to four years to maintain them in good condition. The burning is done in the early springtime, typically in mid-April, when woody plants are beginning to flush out and are relatively vulnerable to fire. The resulting decrease in shrub dominance, reduction in accumulated leaf litter, and blackened soil surface help to advance the growing season for prairie species, which benefit and flourish to a much greater degree than prior to the burn.

Of course, prescribed burns have to be carefully controlled. This is done in several ways, including

- training land stewards in the nuances of this land-management practice;
- burning only when the environmental conditions are suitable—during a drought or when it is excessively windy;
- ensuring there are fire breaks with low fuel loads; and
- having fire-fighting equipment on hand in case things start to get out of control.

Prescribed burns are now routinely used by conservation agencies across Canada and around the world in ecosystems where the practice is suitable. For instance, Parks Canada has become a routine practitioner, as have some provincial governments and the Nature Conservancy of Canada. This "burning solution" is an excellent case of the application of ecological knowledge to dealing with important management problems in biological conservation.

prominent, such as urbanization, agriculture, forestry, or mining. These anthropogenic land uses are incompatible with many of the natural values that protected areas are intended to conserve. Eventually, the protected area may become an ecological "island" of natural habitat, embedded within a "sea" of contrary habitats. Increasingly, the managers of protected areas view their responsibility to be one of engaging in partnerships with interested groups in the **"greater protected area"** to seek a sustainable balance between natural values and the regional human economy.

3. *Regional stressors*. Protected areas may also be affected by regional stressors, such as acid rain, ozone pollution, and climate change. Local anthropogenic stressors are cumulative upon the regional effects of these large-scale influences on ambient environmental conditions.

Management Activities

The kinds of management activities that must be undertaken in protected areas can vary enormously. In some cases it is necessary to have armed patrols to monitor and prevent the poaching of animals, timber, or medicinal plants. It may be necessary to take measures to prevent the use of unauthorized motor transport in protected areas, especially all-terrain vehicles (ATVs), which can damage the terrain and harass animal wildlife.

It may also be necessary to directly manage habitats to maintain them in good condition. For example, if natural disturbances are no longer functioning in a natural way, managers may have to simulate them to maintain certain kinds of ecological communities. For instance, some kinds of prairie must be periodically burned, or they will be degraded by incursions of shrubs (Environmental Applications 14.2). In the past, naturally ignited wildfires would have provided this function, but today prescribed burns may be necessary. Moreover, some kinds of prairie communities were once maintained in good condition by periodic grazing by herds of wild bison, but today this function may be played by domesticated cattle.

In other cases, rare species may have become extirpated from particular areas. If suitable habitat still exists, it may be possible to re-introduce the lost species, either using individuals taken from other places where they are still abundant, or stock that has been captive-reared for the purpose of releasing into the wild. This tactic of restoration ecology has been done many times in Canada; for example:

- Pine marten (*Martes americana*) have been re-introduced to temperate forest habitat in Fundy and Kejimkujik National Parks in eastern Canada.
- Swift foxes (*Vulpes velox*) and black-footed ferrets (*Musetla nigripes*) have been released to shortgrass prairie in Grasslands National Park in southern Saskatchewan.
- Vancouver Island marmots (*Marmota vancouverensis*) have been captive-bred and released to montane forest-tundra habitat on southern Vancouver Island.
- Sea otters (*Enydra lutris*) from the Aleutians were released to waters off western Vancouver Island.
- Captive-bred peregrine falcons (*Falco peregrinus*) have been released at coastal breeding cliffs in Fundy National Park in New Brunswick.
- Prairie bison (*Bison bison bison*) have been introduced by the Nature Conservancy of Canada to its shortgrass prairie reserve at Old Man on His Back in southwestern Saskatchewan.
- Trumpeter swans (*Cygnus buccinator*) have been captive-bred and released to wetlands in the Wye Marsh Wildlife Area in south-central Ontario.
- Burrowing owls (*Athene cunicularia*) have been released to dry grassland in southeastern British Columbia.

Bill Freedman

These prairie bison (*Bison bison bison*) were re-introduced to the Old Man on His Back Prairie Conservation Area in southwestern Saskatchewan, a protected area established by the Nature Conservancy of Canada (NCC). Grazing by the bison is an important aspect of the stewardship of the shortgrass prairie in this area.

- Ginseng (*Panax quinquefolia*) has been re-introduced to various temperate-forest habitats in eastern Canada.

In some cases, restoration ecologists have worked to re-create facsimiles of endangered communities on degraded lands. For instance, ecologists with the Nature Conservancy of Canada (NCC) are working to enlarge a stand of rare Carolinian forest at its Clear Creek Protected Area in southern Ontario by planting suitable trees and other vegetation onto surrounding disused cornfields. At a site in southeastern Manitoba, NCC is working to re-create endangered tallgrass prairie. And at its Cowichan Nature Reserve, NCC is expanding a rare stand of Garry oak forest by planting trees and other suitable vegetation onto an old pasture. These are examples of heroic and expensive projects of restoration ecology, but they are worthwhile because they significantly expand the areas of endangered ecosystems, while providing additional habitat for a suite of their dependent plants and animals.

Sometimes, stewardship activities in support of an endangered species result in highly integrated programs of ecological monitoring, research, and applied management. These may involve actions that occur in protected areas, in large regions around them, and sometimes far beyond. A well-known case involves the globally endangered whooping crane, which in 1941 numbered a perilously few 15 wild individuals, having been greatly diminished by excessive hunting and damage caused to its wintering and migratory habitats (BirdLife International, 2008a). Today, thanks to aggressive conservation measures in Canada and the United States, this rare crane numbers about 382 wild birds plus 145 in captivity (in 2007). The numbers of whooping cranes are monitored on their breeding grounds, which are mostly in peaty wetlands (a boreal habitat known as muskeg) in and near Wood Buffalo National Park in northern Alberta and the southern Northwest Territories. During their southward migration, these cranes use a number of wetlands as critical habitat, including Last Mountain Lake in Saskatchewan and Salt Plains National Wildlife Refuge in Oklahoma. The cranes winter at several places along the Texas Gulf Coast, particularly in the Aransas National Wildlife Refuge. Because of the importance of the breeding, migratory, and wintering habitats to these endangered birds, their locations have been a high priority for conservation, and most are now set aside in various kinds of protected areas.

Moreover, because so many species of cranes are endangered, a great deal of research has been done on their biology, and particularly on their breeding. This sort of work has also been done with whooping cranes, and the knowledge gained has been applied to programs of captive-breeding and release to the wild. This has allowed an additional breeding population to be established in the Necedah National Wildlife Refuge in Wisconsin. Remarkably, these cranes were trained to migrate to a wintering habitat in Florida by wildlife biologists in an ultra-light aircraft flying with them. Yet a third, non-migratory population has been established with captive-bred birds near Kissimmee, Florida. To prevent the captive-bred birds from imprinting on humans, the wildlife biologists who worked with them fed the chicks with crane-head puppets, and they utilized other fostering techniques that arose from research into the ethology (behaviour) of the species. These re-introductions are showing clear signs of success, although they are hampered by the inexperience of the young cranes in their first nesting attempts, and by occasional events of mortality caused by severe weather on the wintering grounds.

Of course, not all research in conservation biology produces results that are useful in the applied sense. For instance, studies showed that whooping cranes lay one to three eggs, but it is rare for more than one young to survive. Knowing this, an attempt was made to increase the numbers of whooping cranes by taking "surplus" eggs from their nests and fostering them with wild sandhill cranes (*Grus canadensis*), a much more abundant species. In a sense, this innovative experiment worked, because the sandhill cranes incubated the eggs and raised the chicks, which then migrated with their foster parents. However, when the fostered whooping cranes became reproductively mature they chose sandhill cranes as their potential mates, having been imprinted on their parents. This meant that the experiment was a practical failure, because the additional whooping cranes did not contribute to the breeding population of their endangered species.

Conflicts with Other Uses of Protected Areas

In addition to stewarding species and habitats in protected areas, it is sometimes necessary to manage the activities of large numbers of visitors, as well as other anthropogenic influences. This is particularly the case of parks that serve purposes in addition to the conservation of biodiversity, such as the provision of venues and infrastructure to support tourism and outdoor recreation. These uses of parks may be economically important, but they can challenge the parks' ability to conserve biodiversity. The degree to which this occurs depends on the kinds of activities that are allowed and the numbers of people engaging in them. For instance, national parks in southern Canada typically are well used by people and so they have embedded roads, campgrounds, interpretation facilities, and even resorts, golf courses, and other infrastructure to support tourism and recreation. In addition, the ability of protected areas to conserve biodiversity may be threatened by land-use activities in the areas around them. These external stressors may be associated with tourism, residential development, agriculture, forestry, mining, and hydroelectric facilities. In fact, all protected areas in southern regions of Canada are significantly affected in these ways—by anthropogenic stressors originating both within and beyond their borders. This problem is evident from consideration of the cases of several national parks (Freedman, 2010):

- *Banff National Park* (BNP) in southwestern Alberta was established in 1885, and it was the first national park in Canada (Page et al., 1996). It is also our most famous park because of its spectacular scenery, large animals that can be viewed easily, and superb infrastructure supporting tourism and outdoor recreation. These values attract visitors from across Canada and around the world—about 4 million people annually—generating more than $6 billion in economic activity. BNP covers a large area (6640 km^2) and so it is important in conserving natural ecological values of its region, a function that is further enhanced because it is bordered by other protected areas—Jasper, Yoho, and Kootenay National Parks and Peter Lougheed Provincial Park, which together cover 26 000 km^2. The initial purpose of BNP was to protect scenic viewscapes and hot springs, and to develop the area for the economic benefits of tourism, which was rapidly becoming fashionable and accessible because of the construction of the first trans-continental railroads. It was not until several decades later that the purpose of national parks in Canada shifted toward the protection of natural values. The development of BNP has featured the construction of several villages, hotels, skiing facilities, golf courses, part of the Trans-Canada Highway and other major roads, the Canadian Pacific railway, and various other built structures. Moreover, natural habitats of much of the surrounding area, particularly eastward toward Canmore and Calgary, have been extensively converted into urbanized, tourism-related, agricultural, forestry, and industrial land uses, and further changes are ongoing. The various facilities within the park, and its growing insularization by contrary land uses, severely threaten the conservation of some of its natural values. The economic developments in and around BNP are controversial, and were the subject of a federal task force led by Robert Page, an ecologist at the University of Calgary. That group was asked by Parks Canada to recommend changes to land use and other economic activities in the greater BNP region that would improve the sustainability of ecological, social, and economic values. The task force concluded that economic development in the greater BNP region was approaching or had exceeded what was sustainable, and that the ecological integrity of the national park was threatened. It made numerous recommendations for specific actions and policies to deal with the problems—in essence, that the pace and intensity of development be controlled, and in some cases reversed. Although Parks Canada accepted those recommendations, the situation today has not changed much and the ecological values of Banff National Park remain threatened by incompatible land uses and other anthropogenic stressors.
- *Point Pelee National Park* (PPNP) is a small park in southwestern Ontario, covering only 15.5 km^2. It was established in 1918 and contains rare Carolinian forest, wetlands, and many species at risk. PPNP is used intensively for recreation, including birdwatching, picnicking, and hiking. To support these activities, which are important to the local economy, much of the limited area of the park is converted to roads, pathways, parking lots, campgrounds, an information centre, lawns, and other infrastructure that compete with use of the same land to support native biodiversity. Moreover, although much of PPNP is bordered by Lake Erie, all of its landward boundaries are adjacent to agricultural fields and residential developments, so the park is an ecological "island" surrounded by incompatible terrain. As a result of these many stressors, PPNP is losing some of the natural features that it is intended to conserve. The park has lost 10 of its original 21 reptile species, and 6 of 11 amphibians. Some habitats are being degraded by invasive aliens, which are crowding out native plants—in fact, 37 percent of the vascular plants in PPNP are non-native.
- *Elk Island National Park* (EINP), located just east of Edmonton, was established in 1909 and covers 194 km^2. This park is almost rectangular in shape, is bounded by 2.2 m-high fences strong enough to contain bison, and is surrounded by mostly incompatible agricultural land uses. In effect EINP is an ecological "island" of natural fescue prairie, aspen parkland, and spruce boreal forest. The park is well known for its dense populations of large ungulates—elk, bison, deer, and moose, as well as timber wolf, coyote, bears, and abundant breeding and migratory birds. Of these, plains bison and wood bison were introduced to the park, as were beaver and trumpeter swans. In fact, some of the larger animals are excessively abundant, and population surpluses have been dealt with by shipping surplus animals elsewhere. This has recently included the sale of elk and bison to commercial interests, as well as the shipping of animals for re-introduction to other protected areas. For example, plains bison from EINP were used to re-establish the species in Grasslands National Park and Old Man on His Back Prairie Conservation Area, both in southern Saskatchewan, and even to re-introduce bison to the steppes of the Siberian region of Yakutia. Because EINP is relatively small,

its ungulates can be prevented from damaging their natural habitats only if park ecologists actively manage their populations within sustainable levels, and this requires an ongoing culling programme.

- *Fundy National Park* (FNP) in New Brunswick was established in 1948 and it supports 206 km^2 of mostly forested terrain. This park is a popular summer destination, and its supporting facilities include campgrounds, lawns, roads, trails, interpretive facilities, a golf course, and a heated salt-water swimming pool. FNP is roughly rectangular in shape, with one side bordering the Bay of Fundy, but along the other three sides, forestry is converting natural mixed-species forest into conifer plantations. In this sense, FNP is becoming insularized within a modified landscape that is hostile to some of its biodiversity values. There is concern that the park itself is not large enough to sustain viable populations of certain wide-ranging species, such as black bear, pine marten, and pileated woodpecker, or certain community types such as old-growth forest.

The national parks of Canada are commonly regarded as "jewels" in our system of protected areas. However, the cases we just briefly examined, and many others, involve formidable challenges to the ability of national parks to sustain native biodiversity. This is a typical context for the stewardship of protected areas—they are challenged by environmental stressors from contrary activities occurring inside of them, in their surrounding ecoscape, and in the greater region. Because of these various stressors, proper stewardship is an essential component of successful conservation in protected areas. Key elements of that stewardship are ecological monitoring, research, and applied conservation actions.

14.6 Roles of Governments and Other Organizations in Conservation

People who understand issues associated with biodiversity believe that it is worthwhile and should be conserved. This is a broadly held public view, and it is increasingly being shared by politicians and other decision makers in society, who are beginning to undertake coordinated actions to help conserve biodiversity within their areas of responsibility.

At the international level, this awareness is represented by the *Convention on Biological Diversity* (CBD), a treaty under the auspices of the United Nations Environment Program (UNEP). The CBD was presented in 1992 at the "Earth Summit" sponsored by UNEP in Rio de Janeiro, Brazil. Canada signed on to the CBD at Rio and ratified it a few months later (we were the first developed country to do this). The vision of the CBD is to sustain life on Earth, and there are three broad objectives (CBD, 2010):

- the conservation of biodiversity;
- sustainable use of biological resources; and
- equitable sharing of benefits from the use of genetic resources (such as newly discovered medicines derived from wild organisms).

As a signatory nation to the CBD, Canada is obliged to assess the adequacy of its national efforts to conserve biodiversity, to use biological resources in a sustainable manner, and to identify and fill gaps in its policies and actions. One requirement is to develop a national strategy for implementation of the CBD, and this led to the *Canadian Biodiversity Strategy* (Environment Canada, 1995). This document outlines three strategic elements:

- recognition of jurisdictional and legislative responsibilities;
- the need for cooperation among various governments and other organizations in the development and implementation of policies and actions; and
- a vision for the conservation of biodiversity within the context of sustainable development in Canada.

The Canadian Biodiversity Strategy has five goals:

- Conserve biodiversity and use biological resources in a sustainable manner.
- Improve our understanding of ecosystems and increase our capability for resource management.
- Promote an understanding by the public of the need to conserve biodiversity and use biological resources in a sustainable manner.
- Develop incentives and legislation toward these goals.
- Work internationally to promote these goals, and share benefits from the use of genetic resources.

The strategy also recognizes as guiding principles some of the qualities of biodiversity, ecology, and sustainable development that we have examined in this and other chapters:

- Biodiversity has instrumental, ecological, social-cultural, and intrinsic values.
- All life forms, including humans, are interconnected.
- Canadians depend on biodiversity and have an obligation to conserve it and use its products in a sustainable manner.
- Canadians should be encouraged to understand and appreciate the values of biodiversity and to participate in its conservation and that of biological resources.
- An ecological approach to resource management is key to conserving biodiversity and biological resources.

- Decisions about development must reflect a balance of ecological, economic, social, and cultural values.
- Biodiversity and biological resources can be effectively conserved in healthy ecosystems only where evolutionary forces are relevant and natural functions are able to operate.
- In some cases, intensive management practices (such as captive breeding and release) may be required to recover species at risk and other endangered biodiversity.
- Traditional ecological knowledge of indigenous and local communities is relevant.
- The conservation of biodiversity and of biological resources should be guided by the best available science, and be adaptive to the emergence of new knowledge.
- Successful conservation requires the sharing of knowledge and of costs and benefits among all levels of government and other organizations (the private sector, environmental charities, and universities).

Another federal response to Canada's responsibility to conserve biodiversity is the *Species at Risk Act* (SARA) of 2002, which has toughened the legal provisions in support of species that are designated as being at risk by COSEWIC. The provisions of SARA are especially strict with respect to species at risk and their habitat on lands falling within the jurisdiction of the federal government (in terms of ownership or regulatory responsibility). However, SARA is weaker outside of federal jurisdiction—for example, on lands controlled by provincial, territorial, aboriginal, municipal, or private entities. Although SARA has provisions that allow the federal government to intervene in such cases, it is not required to do so. However, the provinces and territories have also passed their own equivalents of SARA, and that also helps to protect biodiversity at risk within their jurisdictions.

Environmental non-governmental organizations (ENGOs; these are environmental charities or nonprofit organizations) also have an important role to play in the conservation of biodiversity. They do this in two broad ways:

1. **Advocacy** involves activities that are intended to influence decisions and outcomes that might affect people or the environment. With respect to biodiversity, advocacy might be used to influence governmental policies and legislation, the activities of private companies, and even educational curricula. Advocacy is commonly pursued in a public way, such as holding open meetings, staging demonstrations, and advertising in the mass media.
2. **Direct action** refers to activities that result in immediate benefits. In the context of biodiversity it involves the implementation of conservation measures, such as the establishment of protected areas to benefit species at risk or rare communities.

Examples of national advocacy ENGOs with a biodiversity mandate are the Canadian Parks and Wilderness Society, Greenpeace, Nature Canada, the Sierra Club (Canada), and the World Wildlife Fund (Canada). These ENGOs lobby governments and the private sector to implement effective biodiversity agendas, while also engaging in public campaigns and supporting research toward those ends. The Nature Conservancy of Canada and Ducks Unlimited Canada are ENGOs that engage in direct action to establish and steward protected areas, and they are joined in this work by hundreds of more local land trusts.

In aggregate, the activities of the various governmental and non-governmental organizations add up to a lot of conservation of the biodiversity of Canada. Nevertheless, much remains to be done. In fact, it is realistic to conclude that the condition of the biodiversity of Canada has recently been getting worse, rather than better. Each year, additional tracts of natural habitat are being destroyed and converted into anthropogenic land uses that are incompatible with native biodiversity, and the conservation status of many species at risk deteriorates. Even though Canada is a wealthy country, we do not yet have a national system plan for a comprehensive network of protected areas, and sufficient progress is not being made to set imperilled natural habitats aside from intensive economic development. Moreover, many of the existing protected areas are too small or insularized to successfully conserve their inherent biodiversity values over the longer term.

Clearly, there is no reason for complacency here—much has yet to be done. The most direct role for ecologists is in providing the scientific advice and oversight that society needs to move effectively forward with the conservation of biodiversity. Ecologists should also have a prominent influence on the advocacy and direct-action that are leading the charge to protect the biodiversity of Canada and of the world.

14.7 Some Good News

Because so many reports about biodiversity are dismal, the global situation has been characterized as a "crisis." It is important to recognize, however, that there are some good-news stories. They involve species that were taken to the brink of extinction, but thanks to effective conservation actions, their remnant populations and habitat were effectively protected and a substantial recovery occurred. Although these success stories are in a minority, in the sense that the numbers of endangered species are increasing much more rapidly, they are nevertheless instructive. We will end this chapter by examining some of the success stories, because they show us how effective and timely conservation actions can help to fix desperate situations. These lessons are worth learning, because in modified form they can allow us to achieve conservation success with other species whose survival is at risk. The only exception, of course, is that of extinction, which is not reversible.

Conservation Successes

Grey Seal and Some Other Pinnipeds

The grey seal (*Halichoerus grypus*) occurs in temperate Atlantic waters, and for many years it occurred only in an extremely small abundance in Canada because of excessive hunting in the past (Thompson and Harkonen, 2008; Freedman, 2010). It numbered only a few thousand animals in the 1950s, but because of protection from commercial hunting its abundance has grown rapidly and there are now more than 304 000 of them (in 2009). Another case is the northern fur seal (*Callorhinus ursinus*) of the north Pacific, which was hunted for its fur and by the early 20th century was depleted from an original several million to about 130 000 animals. In 1911 an international treaty was signed that regulated the hunting, and the population soon recovered to about 1 million. Since then, however, this seal population has again declined, although not to the point of endangerment. The recent drop may be due to a combination of factors, including commercial over-harvesting of its food fish, entanglement in fishing gear, and predation by orcas. One last example is that of the harp seal (*Phoca groenlandica*) in the northwest Atlantic, which is commercially hunted mostly for its fur. This hunt has been ongoing for about two centuries, and the abundance of harp seals in Canadian waters was taken to a relatively low population of about 1.7 million animals in the late 1980s from an original 5–6 million. Because the hunting has been regulated during the past several decades, the abundance of this seal has increased to about 5.5 million (in 2009). The commercial hunting continues today—the quota for 2009 was 300 000, most of which would be young seals only several weeks old. The commercial hunt for harp seals is one of the most controversial wildlife harvests in the world. Although opponents of the hunt claim that the seals are being over-exploited, this is not the case—they are one of the most populous large wild animals anywhere, and their abundance continues to grow despite the killing. Rather, the controversy is mostly about the ethics and aesthetics of the killing of the helpless babies of wild animals for commercial gain.

Grey Whale (Eschrichtius robustus) *and Other Great Whales*

Because the population of grey whales of the Pacific coast had been severely depleted by commercial over-hunting, (**Figure 14.9**), in 1949 the International Whaling Commission (IWC) banned further killing of the species. At that time there were only a few thousand grey whales, but the ban has allowed them to increase to about their original abundance of 26 000 (Reilly et al., 2008; IWC, 2009). However, populations of this species on both sides of the north Atlantic are extirpated, and another in the western Pacific numbers a critically endangered 120 animals.

Bill Freedman

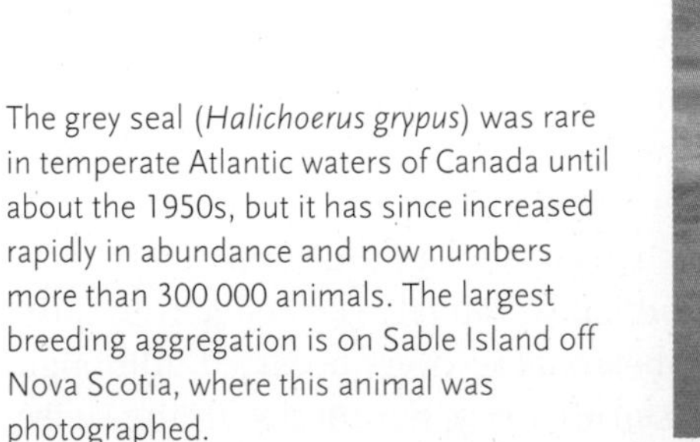

The grey seal (*Halichoerus grypus*) was rare in temperate Atlantic waters of Canada until about the 1950s, but it has since increased rapidly in abundance and now numbers more than 300 000 animals. The largest breeding aggregation is on Sable Island off Nova Scotia, where this animal was photographed.

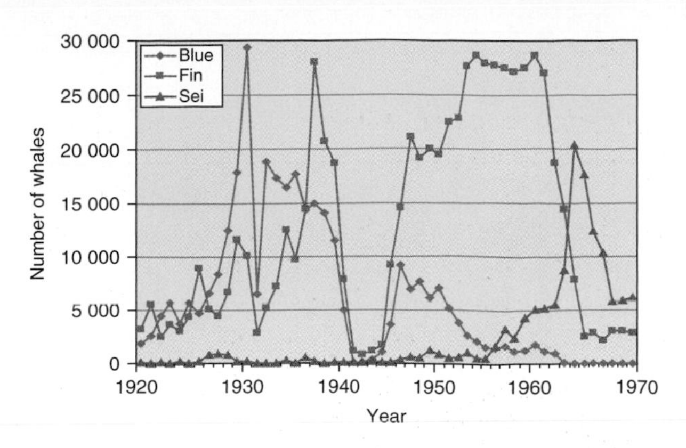

FIGURE 14.9
Numbers of Whales Killed in Antarctic Waters. The data show the rise and collapse of whaling for three species of baleen whales. Note the limited hunting during World War II, and the sequential collapses of the stocks of blue, then fin, and then sei whales.

SOURCE: Ellis, R. 1991. *Men and Whales*. Alfred A. Knopf, New York, NY.

Populations of all other large whales were also severely depleted by several centuries of commercial harvesting, and many species were endangered (**Figure 14.9**). Then in 1982, the IWC began a wide-scale moratorium, which was fully implemented in 1986, that greatly reduced the hunting (it was not eliminated because several countries are still engaged in limited harvesting, notably Japan and Norway). The reduced hunting has allowed most whales to increase slowly, although not yet to their original abundance. The sperm whale (*Physeter catodon*) now numbers about 1 million, compared with its pre-whaling abundance of 2 million (IWC, 2009; Freedman, 2010). The finback whale (*Balaenoptera physalus*) now numbers 163 000, compared with an initial 700 000. The blue whale (*B. musculus*) is now at about 3000, compared with an original 250 000. The humpback whale (*Megaptera novaeangliae*) is now 64 000, compared with an initial 100,000. The bowhead whale (*Balaena mysticetus*) is now at about 12 000 (these are still taken in an aboriginal hunt in northern Alaska, and a few also off Baffin Island). The right whale (*Balaena glacialis*) of the southern hemisphere now numbers about 7500 animals, but in the northwestern Atlantic they have shown little recovery and number only about 300 because of unsustainable mortality from entanglement in fishing gear and collisions with ships. The minke whale (*Balaenoptera acutorostrata*) numbers more than 1 million animals and it is the target of most ongoing whale hunting, although fin whales are also being taken. In 2008, Japanese whaling interests announced their intention to harvest 935 minke whales, 50 fin whales, and, for the first time since the IWC moratorium was enacted, 50 humpback whales in Antarctic waters. This is obviously a commercial harvest, but because biological and ecological data are collected it is profiled as "scientific" whaling. Because of intense international controversy, the decision to harvest humpback whales was later reversed.

American Bison

The original abundance of the American bison or buffalo (*Bison bison*) was more than 60 million, making it one of the most populous large wild land animals in the world (Freedman, 1995; Gates and Aune, 2008). An eastern subspecies (*B. b. pennsylvanicus*) inhabited forest openings, the plains bison (*B. b. bison*) occurred in the prairies, and the wood bison (*B. b. athabascae*) was in the southern boreal forest of western Canada. The plains bison was especially abundant and it once migrated in colossal herds, with densities of 25–38 animals/ha and moving over stupendous fronts—one was described as being 40 km × 80 km in extent, another as 320 km long, and another as advancing over a 160 km expanse. However, rapacious hunts caused the abundance of bison to precipitously decline. The eastern subspecies was extinct by the mid-19th century, and the plains bison perilously close to that end by the late 19th century. The plains bison were subjected to an insatiable market hunt for their hides, meat, and bones. Their extermination may also have been encouraged by governments of the time to foster agricultural development by disrupting the buffalo-dependent economy of the Plains Indians, and so making it easier to displace them with European colonists. In any event, the exceedingly non-sustainable hunting caused the bison to rapidly decline, so that by the late 19th century there were only a few hundred animals left in the prairies of Canada and the United States. Almost too late, several bison preserves were established and captive-breeding programs begun. There are now about 100 000 wild bison and another 250 000 that are ranched as livestock. The largest populations of wild plains bison are in national parks and other extensive tracts of public land, and on several private ranches. The wood bison are in and around Wood Buffalo National Park, plus a transplanted group in Elk Island National Park. Although some bison populations suffer from introduced diseases such as bovine tuberculosis and brucellosis, and from genetic damage from interbreeding with domestic cows, the species now appears to be secure. Of course, it will never recover to anywhere close to its original abundance, because almost all of its natural habitat has been converted to agricultural land uses.

Pronghorn Antelope (Antilocapra americana)

This endemic animal of the western plains may have originally numbered 35 million animals, but it was severely over-hunted during the 19th century and its

A CANADIAN ECOLOGIST 14.1

Dancing with Wolves

Doug Morris

The wolf (*Canis lupus*) is a large wild predator. People have always been fascinated by these animals, perhaps because, like humans for much of our evolutionary history, wolves and other wild carnivores are cunning and dangerous animals. Wolves are also the progenitor of all of the astonishingly diverse breeds of dog (*Canis lupus familiaris*), which humans first began to domesticate more than 15 000 years ago. Most people who keep dogs as pets love them as faithful and unquestioning friends, and perhaps this good feeling also transfers to a widespread admiration of wild wolves.

But not all people have good feelings about wolves—opinions about these predators are remarkably capricious, ranging from deep attraction to intense repulsion, sometimes in the same people, depending on circumstances. The reasons why some people fear and loathe wolves are complex, but typically involve some combination of anxiety about personal safety when these animals are around, and anger that these top predators kill and eat the same game animals that people hunt for food or as trophies (deer and other ungulates), or the perception that they kill too many livestock. Because of the resulting antipathy to wolves, plus the fact that their fur is valuable, they have been relentlessly persecuted over most of their natural range throughout the Northern Hemisphere—they are killed by trapping, shooting, and poisoning. This hunting, along with habitat degradation through conversions to anthropogenic land uses, has caused populations of wolves to decline over most of their historical range. Wolves are now widely extirpated, and they occur in robust populations only in extensively remote regions, such as the boreal forest and tundra of northern expanses of Canada, as well as montane forest in mountainous regions.

Many people are concerned about what is happening to the populations of wolves and other large predators. This includes some Canadian ecologists and wildlife biologists, who have transformed their apprehension of the future for large carnivores into a dedication of their professional lives to helping society find a sustainable accommodation with these wild animals. One of the first of these people was Farley Mowat, who studied biology at the University of Toronto and spent two field seasons in boreal Keewatin (this is now continental Nunavut) doing research on wildlife, including wolves. He wrote several popular accounts of his experiences, including the famous book *Never Cry Wolf* (1963). Although that book contains some apparently fictionalized accounts of the behaviour of wolves, it nevertheless played a powerful role in

population was reduced to fewer than 20 000 (Hoffman et al., 2008). Fortunately, strong conservation measures were implemented, and this species now numbers as many as 1 million and again sustains a sport hunt.

American Beaver (Castor canadensis)

This large rodent was the most sought-after furbearer in the early fur trade, a commercial enterprise that stimulated much of the exploration of the landmass of Canada and the central and western United States (Linzey et al., 2008). Beavers were excessively harvested everywhere, and they became extirpated from most of their original range by the first half of the 20th century. However, conservation measures since then, along with less demand for their fur, have resulted in beavers recovering their abundance over most of their range where habitats are still suitable. In fact, they are now considered to be a pest in some areas because their engineering works cause flooding.

Sea Otter (Enhydra lutris)

This furbearer of the Pacific coast was overhunted for its dense and lustrous fur during the 18th and 19th centuries (Doroff and Burdin, 2008). It became extirpated from almost all of its original range, and at its nadir may have numbered fewer than a thousand animals. A moratorium was placed on its hunting in 1911, and this allowed the population to increase to the degree that about two-thirds of its original range is now occupied. The recovery in Canada was assisted by a re-introduction to the west coast of Vancouver Island, but the Canadian population is small and designated by COSEWIC as special concern.

helping to demystify these animals, which had long been stereotypically portrayed as vicious killers.

Douglas Pimlott was another influential researcher of wolves, although in a more conventional context of ecology and wildlife biology than Farley Mowat. Pimlott worked with the governments of Newfoundland and then Ontario, and then landed a position as a professor at the University of Toronto. He and his students did ground-breaking research on the behaviour and community ecology of wolves, working in the vicinity of Algonquin Provincial Park in central Ontario. Their work contributed greatly to the knowledge that is necessary for the conservation of wolves, as well as to understanding their role as top predators in controlling the abundance of certain of their prey species. Pimlott was also a devoted and effective advocate for wolves—he helped to eliminate the wolf bounty in Ontario and provided a rational dissenting perspective to wolf-culling programs elsewhere. Pimlott also worked more widely in conservation issues related to northern Canada, and is a founder of the modern environmental movement in our country.

John and Mary Theberge of the University of Waterloo, students of Pimlott, continued to study the behaviour and community ecology of wolves around Algonquin Park. They were also advocates of the animals, which were being killed by trappers and hunters when they wandered outside of the protected area. Research by the Theberges suggested that the mortality was not sustainable, and that it was likely the Algonquin wolves would become both marginalized and hybridized by coyotes if the hunting was not stopped within a buffer zone around the park. Their advocacy on behalf of wolves created great difficulties for the Theberges, because they were resisting the policies of wildlife interests in the provincial government, who were key sponsors of their research, as well as powerful hunting and trapping constituencies. Fortunately, a "white knight" arrived to rescue their long-standing program of field research, in the form of support from the World Wildlife Fund (Canada). The WWF president, Monte Hummel, was also a former student of Pimlott and is himself a prominent campaigner on behalf of conservation of the natural world, including wild carnivores. The Theberges were able to continue their research and advocacy, eventually building up an impressive 40-year database and analysis of interactions of wolves and their prey (this includes the earlier studies led by Pimlott). Moreover, thanks to their research and advocacy, the provincial government enacted legislation to protect wolves in the area around Algonquin Park. This made Algonquin the first park in North America to have extended protection for a large carnivore beyond its boundaries. The Theberges have since retired from the University of Waterloo, but they remain engaged in wolf research and in advocacy for conservation, including for wolves, which are still being culled in parts of Canada to favour larger populations of ungulates for hunting by people. Meanwhile other ecologists have taken up the mantle of wolf research in the Algonquin region, including Brent Patterson of Trent University and the Ontario Ministry of Natural Resources.

Wild Turkey (Meleagris gallopavo)

This large landbird was extirpated from most of its original range by hunting and habitat loss, including southern regions of Manitoba, Ontario, Quebec, and New Brunswick (BirdLife International, 2008b). However, it has been widely re-introduced to many areas from which it was lost, including its former range in Canada and even beyond, to southern Saskatchewan, Alberta, and British Columbia. The wild turkey has now recovered to more than 7 million wild animals, enough to support sport hunting in many regions (of course, domestic varieties are abundant in agriculture; about 8 million were raised in Canada in 2006).

Wood Duck (Aix sponsa) *and Other Cavity Nesters*

This duck was over-hunted as food and for its beautiful feathers, and it also suffered extensive habitat loss from the drainage of wetlands and timber harvesting in swamps (BirdLife International, 2008c). The recovery of this bird has been aided by regulation of its hunting as well as the widespread provision of nesting boxes in wetlands. Its abundance is now about 3.5 million. The nest-box programs also benefit other depleted cavity-nesting ducks, such as the common goldeneye (*Bucephala clangula*) and hooded merganser (*Lophodytes cucullatus*). An unrelated program of providing terrestrial nest-boxes has helped to increase the diminished populations of eastern bluebird (*Sialia sialis*) and western bluebird (*S. exicana*).

Trumpeter Swan (Cygnus buccinator)

This largest native swan once bred extensively in western North America, but its populations were devastated by hunting for its meat and skin. However, this species was protected and has now recovered greatly in abundance, now numbering about 18 000 animals, including a re-introduced population in south-central Ontario (Moser, 2006; BirdLife International, 2008d).

Whooping Crane (Grus americana)

This tall crane was never abundant, and its initially small population was devastated by hunting for its meat and feathers, conversion of breeding habitat in prairie wetlands to agriculture, and damage to its wintering habitat along the Gulf of Mexico (BirdLife International, 2008a). The wild population plummeted to only 15 individuals (in 1941), but since then the whooping crane has been vigorously protected, and its major breeding habitat in Wood Buffalo National Park and the wintering range on the Gulf coast have been conserved. These measures, along with a program of captive breeding and release, have allowed the wild population to increase to about 382 individuals (in 2007; an additional 145 are in captivity). There is now cautious optimism for the survival of this species, although it remains endangered.

Peregrine Falcon (Falco peregrinus) *and Bald Eagle* (Hialiaeetus leucocephalus)

These predatory birds suffered large population declines over most of their range because of the ecotoxicological effects of organochlorine chemicals, particularly the insecticides DDT and dieldrin and the industrial substances polychlorinated biphenyls (PCBs) (BirdLife International, 2008e, f; Freedman, 2010). These chemicals caused toxicity to developing embryos and adults, which resulted in widespread reproductive failure in these and other species of birds. Almost all production and use of the organochlorines in North America was banned during the 1970s, and this has allowed the populations of affected species to recover. Because the eastern population of the peregrine falcon (*F. p. anatum*) had become critically endangered, its recovery was assisted by a program of captive breeding and release. The peregrine falcon now has a global population of more than 10 000 birds (it is one of the most widespread birds in the world), and the bald eagle more than 115 000 (it occurs only in North America).

Ongoing Challenges

These are some of the better known success stories of conservation in Canada and North America, and there are others from additional countries. There are useful lessons to be learned from all of these cases. However, it is important to recognize that, even while some damages to biodiversity are being repaired, many other losses are ongoing. It is a key responsibility and opportunity for ecologists to be deeply engaged in the scientific activities that are needed, in Canada and globally, to identify the ongoing problems of biodiversity and to recommend ways of avoiding or repairing those awful damages.

VOCABULARY OF ECOLOGY

advocacy, p. 455
behavioural ecology, p. 439
biological conservation, p. 420
coldspots of biodiversity, p. 442
conservation, p. 419
conservation planning, p. 444
data deficient, p. 437
direct action, p. 455
ecological economics, p. 439
ecological integrity, p. 420
ecological reserve, p. 448
ecotone, p. 432
endangered, p. 436
evolutionary radiation, p. 421
extinct, p. 436
extirpated, p. 436
flagship species, p. 441
functional ecology, p. 439
gap analysis, p. 444
geo-referenced, p. 444
greater protected area, p. 450
hotspots of biodiversity, p. 442
invasive alien, p. 423
island biogeography, p. 440
keystone species, p. 440
landscape ecology, p. 439
mass extinction, p. 421
minimum viable area (MVA), p. 439
minimum viable population (MVP), p. 439
modern biodiversity crisis (Holocene biodiversity event), p. 423
natural world, p. 420
naturalized, p. 424
non-native (alien), p. 432
permeability, p. 446
primary forest (frontier forest), p. 429
protected area, p. 431
rarity, p. 440
recovery strategy, p. 437
resource conservation, p. 420
shifting cultivation, p. 431
slash-and-burn, p. 431

SLOSS, p. 445
special concern (vulnerable), p. 437
special management area, p. 448
status report, p. 436
stewardship, p. 444
system plan, p. 444
taxon, p. 436
threatened, p. 436
umbrella species, p. 441
weed, p. 434
wilderness, p. 420
wilderness area, p. 448

QUESTIONS FOR REVIEW AND DISCUSSION

1. What are the several meanings of the word "conservation"?
2. What are "natural extinctions," and how do they provide context for the modern biodiversity crisis?
3. Explain the causes of the modern biodiversity crisis.
4. How do invasive aliens threaten the native biodiversity of Canada?
5. Explain the system used by COSEWIC (the Committee on the Status of Endangered Wildlife in Canada) to designate species at risk in Canada.
6. How is the theory of island biogeography relevant to conservation planning?
7. Choose a species listed by COSEWIC and prepare a report on key aspects of its biology, ecology, risk factors, and actions necessary for population recovery. You can get useful information from the COSEWIC website at http://www.cosewic.gc.ca, as well as other Web-based and library sources.
8. Explain the roles and responsibility of international, national, and regional organizations in the conservation of biodiversity. Include both governmental and non-governmental organizations.
9. Consider the following statement: "Conservation should be practised throughout working ecoscapes, but some large tracts must also be set aside as protected areas to ensure the survival of elements of biodiversity that are not compatible with economic activities." What, in the context of conservation biology, is meant by this statement?

HELPFUL WEBSITES

CANADIAN WILDLIFE SERVICE
http://www.cws-scf.ec.gc.ca
The CWS is an agency within Environment Canada that deals with migratory birds, nationally important habitat, and species at risk.

COMMITTEE ON THE STATUS OF ENDANGERED WILDLIFE IN CANADA (COSEWIC)
http://www.cosewic.gc.ca
COSEWIC is an arms-length agency that advises the Government of Canada about the status of species at risk. Their website provides a wealth of information about species at risk in Canada.

CONSERVATION INTERNATIONAL. *BIODIVERSITY HOTSPOTS*
http://www.conservation.org
Conservation International is committed to helping societies adopt a more sustainable approach to development—one that considers and values nature at every turn. Building upon a strong foundation of science, partnership, and field demonstration, CI empowers societies to responsibly and sustainably care for nature for the well-being of humanity.

ENVIRONMENT CANADA. *NATURE*
http://www.ec.gc.ca/default.asp?lang=En&n=9E3DC4EA-1
This website features pages on the biodiversity of Canada, representative and rare ecosystems, and related topics.

ENVIRONMENTAL LITERACY COUNCIL. *ECOSYSTEMS*
http://www.enviroliteracy.org/category.php/3.html
This site explains biodiversity and its conservation, and also provides many useful links to other information.

INTERNATIONAL UNION FOR CONSERVATION OF NATURE (IUCN). *IUCN RED LIST OF THREATENED SPECIES*
www.iucnredlist.org
The IUCN is a leading international conservation organization. This website provides information on a host of species at risk.

NATURE CONSERVANCY OF CANADA (NCC)
http://www.natureconservancy.ca/site/PageServer
The NCC is a non-advocacy conservation organization that does planning for protected areas, purchases private property to set them up, and then stewards them to foster their natural values. Learn about its mission and actions at this website.

WORLD RESOURCES INSTITUTE (WRI)
www.wri.org
The WRI provides a host of information relevant to biodiversity and its protection.

WORLD WILDLIFE FUND CANADA (WWF)
http://wwf.ca
The WWF is a leading environmental research and advocacy organization, with somewhat of a mission focus on conserving species and natural ecosystems. This website provides information about Canadian biodiversity at risk and how to conserve it.

You'll find a rich array of additional resources for *Ecology* at www.ecology.nelson.com.

NASA/Goddard Space Flight Center Scientific Visualization Studio

Images of Earth taken from space reinforce the metaphor of "spaceship Earth" as an isolated place whose resources are limited to those contained on the planet, with the key exception of sunlight. This March 2001 composite image was produced using data and images from several NASA satellites. Much of Canada is snow-covered.

enormously more complicated than those of any other species. There are several core aspects to the complex needs of humans for resources:

- On a per capita basis, people utilize resources far more intensively than do any other species.
- We harvest an astonishing diversity of natural resources from all accessible parts of the planet, exceedingly more so than any other species has ever done.
- The productivity of many of the resources we utilize becomes degraded in the process, so their stocks rapidly decline in amount and quality, a change that poses great risks for economic sustainability.
- We not only harvest raw foods, materials, and sources of energy from the environment and ecosystems—we also process them into manufactured goods, many of which are traded in an increasingly globalized economy, such as processed foods, machines, buildings, and so on.
- An inevitable consequence of the abundance of people, their lifestyles, and the industrial and commercial activities associated with the manufacturing and trading of goods is the release of large amounts of wastes and pollutants, so that the environment and ecosystems become degraded as a consequence.

The fact is that we individual humans, and our collective economy, are inherently dependent on the environment and ecosystems to provide us with sustenance. This reality means that questions about the long-term supply of resources are crucial to the sustainability of the human economy.

The science of ecology can be applied to dealing with vital problems related to the supply and quality of resources. This subject area is **resource ecology**—it deals with the linkages between ecological knowledge and the management of natural resources, and extends to framing the meaning and dimensions of economic sustainability. In this chapter we will examine the ways that ecological science informs the notion of **sustainable development**, which in essence refers to a human economy that can run forever because it is ultimately founded on the wise use of renewable resources. We will also consider the even loftier idea of development toward an **ecologically sustainable economy** (or **ecologically sustainable development**), which goes beyond mere resource sustainability to also include the maintenance of biodiversity and ecological services at viable and necessary levels. After we examine these themes, we will look at the role of applied ecology in advising the design of harvesting and management systems that are commonly used in agriculture, forestry, fisheries, and horticulture. We will finish by examining case material that illustrates severe problems that have arisen in many systems of resource harvesting and management, and how ecological knowledge can be used to prevent or mitigate those damages.

Economics and Ecology

Like ecology, **economics** is a highly interdisciplinary field. Its principal goal is to understand the complex ways that scarce **resources** (goods and services of different kinds) are allocated within an economy among various potential uses, many of which are in competition. If this can be understood, then it may be possible to control the ways that people and economic sectors consume resources and generate wastes, and in so doing to achieve increased profit and/or an improvement of society and its economy. Key premises of economics are that people will seek to enhance their wealth and lifestyle, and corporations to maximize their profit, while governments hope to advance both of those goals. Therefore the choices made by any of these entities will reveal how they value goods and services.

Key economic indicators are derived from the valuation of goods and services in an open marketplace—one in which resources and other commodities are freely traded. The valuation is routinely done in units of currency, such as dollars. In economics as it is usually practised (that is, **conventional economics**), valuation is assessed in a highly anthropocentric context, which reflects the perceived usefulness of goods or services to people. However, valuations are dynamic, in the sense that they change over time in ways that echo the supply of a good or service compared to the demand for it—if a resource is abundant, then its valuation will be relatively low, and if it is scarce it will be more expensive. Moreover, if a resource is limited or valuable then more effort and expense will be expended to increase its supply and to find less-costly substitutes. These conventional means of valuation perform relatively well when they are applied to goods and services that are directly needed by an economy, such as manufactured goods, physical infrastructure (e.g., buildings and roads), labour, expertise, and natural resources.

Conventional economics does not, however, perform so well when it is valuating goods and services for which there are no obvious or immediate markets. For instance, certain ecological services are vital to a healthy functioning of the biosphere—they include the fixation of carbon storage and release of oxygen by vegetation, cleansing the environment of pollutants released by the human economy, and the recycling of water through the hydrologic cycle. Conventional economists treat these sorts of useful ecosystem services as "externalities"—or benefits that are shared by society, but are not paid for, and so are not included in the valuation of a tract of ecosystem. From an ecological perspective, however, those services are clearly vital both to the human economy and also to biodiversity-at-large, and they should be properly valuated (see below).

It is also common to not valuate certain kinds of ecological damages, such as

- the extinction and endangerment of species and natural communities;
- damage caused by pollution to human health and to ecosystems, for example, by gaseous sulphur dioxide and ozone, by toxic metals, or by pesticides;
- the depletion of natural resources, which is not usually considered to be a "cost" of doing business, even though it threatens the sustainability of any dependent economic activity and is a grave risk to the livelihoods of future generations (these potential economic damages are known as "**opportunity costs**"); and
- socioeconomic inequalities, including poverty and the disenfranchisement and endangerment of indigenous peoples and other cultural groups.

These kinds of goods and services can be appropriately valuated only if society judges them to be important. If their value is acknowledged, then the cost of damage to them can be determined and used to adjust the calculation of "profit" associated with a threatening economic activity. For instance, when petroleum is mined, its remaining stocks in the environment are inexorably diminished, so there is less available to be used in the future. Because petroleum is such an important source of commercial energy and abundant substitutes are not yet fully available, huge opportunity costs are associated with its depletion. However, conventional economics has not yet provided an agreed-upon way of calculating those opportunity costs, and so the "price" of petroleum today mostly reflects the direct costs of mining it from the ground and transporting it to the places where it is refined into gasoline and other goods for consumers (in the special case of synthetic petroleum manufactured from oil sand, there are also direct costs of the upgrading process and other practices that are specific to that resource). However, this pricing system is inadequate because it irresponsibly passes the opportunity costs to future generations, without significant compensation being paid by the present one that is so rapidly using and depleting the petroleum resources of the world.

Similarly, a new housing development might cause damage to the scarce habitat of an endangered species. However, conventional economics does not take that damaging effect on biodiversity into account when determining the profit to be made from constructing and selling the new houses. Instead, the recourse is to rely on society to somehow prevent the ecological damage. Typically, this is done by regulating certain economic activities that carry a risk of harming the environment. However, if effective regulation is not in place, which is remarkably often the case, then there is no reckoning of the cost of the ecological damage. Rather, it is considered to be a "**free good**" that can be shared with society and the biosphere, but without significant costs that are borne by the perpetrator.

One additional example involves pollution and the ecological damages it causes. It might appear sensible that to calculate an accurate profit, the "cost" of those damages should be valuated and subtracted from the revenues gained from the economic activities that are causing the pollution to occur. In conventional economics, however, the deleterious activities may actually be regarded as being somehow "beneficial" because they contribute to economic growth by adding to the **gross domestic product** (or GDP; this is the total value of all goods and services produced within an economy in a year). One such example relates to the largest oil spill ever to occur in North American waters—caused by the grounding of the *Exxon Valdez* tanker in Alaska in 1989. That event caused enormous ecological damage by fouling marine habitats, killing several hundreds of thousands seabirds and numerous marine mammals, and so on. However, a great deal of money was spent on the clean-up of the spilled petroleum and to provide compensation to people who were temporarily displaced from the local fisheries, and that expenditure contributed to the GDP in that year (most economists and politicians believe it is beneficial to have a growing GDP). In total, that environmental disaster resulted in more than US$3 billion in economic activity (Freedman, 2010). In fact, however, costs associated with the clean-up and compensation of an environmental disaster should rightly be viewed as a depletion of natural capital and a contribution to the "natural debt," rather than a helpful contribution to the GDP.

However, there is increasing recognition that environmental damages associated with resource depletion, pollution, and endangerment of biodiversity are important, and that benefits can be realized if ways are found to valuate them. **Ecological economics** is a relatively new way of thinking about valuations related to environmental damage (Costanza, 1991; Daly, 1996; Tietenberg, 2002; Daly and Farley, 2003). This novel field emerged as a conceptual fusion of economics and ecology (both names share the Greek root *oikos*, meaning household). The distinction of ecological economics is that it seeks to examine and valuate the relationships of two kinds of systems—economies and ecosystems—in an objective and non-anthropocentric manner. It does this by using a variety of measures of scarcity and valuation to achieve a "full-cost" accounting of goods and services, such as

- the cost of repairing environmental damage that might be associated with an economic activity, such as the production of a commodity (e.g., paper, metals, or food);
- a comprehensive life-cycle assessment of the energy and material used to manufacture, transport, and eventually discard a product;
- surveys to determine how much money people would be willing to pay to ensure that an endangered species does not become extinct, or a natural community does not disappear;
- an evaluation of the costs of a project in restoration ecology that would produce an amount of comparable habitat to what is being destroyed by an economic activity, such as building a new subdivision; and
- the **ecological footprint** needed to support people living a certain lifestyle—this is the area of ecoscape that is needed to support the production of the energy and materials used by a person or an economy, and to treat any wastes.

Although the methodologies for making these sorts of valuations are controversial, they could potentially allow the marketplace to account for environmental

Bill Freedman

In conventional economics, pollution and other kinds of environmental damage are viewed as "free goods," whose costs are not borne by the perpetrator, but rather are shared with all of society and with the biosphere. In ecological economics, the costs of environmental damage would be valuated and debited from the profit of the enterprise that was causing the harm to occur. This photo shows a landscape severely degraded by air pollution in the vicinity of Sudbury, Ontario.

damage as a cost of doing business, and as an expense to be reckoned when calculating profit. As we just noted, there are many cases in which this has not been done, so that environmental damages were gratis—they were treated as free goods that did not detract from the profitability of an offending economic activity. There are many examples of these kinds of situations; they include ecological damage caused by pollution, clear-cutting, depletion of marine fisheries, urbanization, and other activities. If these damages were properly and sensibly valuated, they could be offset in cost–benefit analyses associated with rational economic decisions about whether to undertake activities that carry risks of causing important environmental problems.

By allowing a full-cost accounting to be made, ecological economics helps us to understand the true consequences of economic activities. This knowledge would encourage people, corporations, and society at large to make choices that are less damaging to ecology and the environment.

Growth, Development, and Sustainability

Although the two are often confounded, in the sense of ecological economics, growth and development are fundamentally different things. **Economic growth** merely refers to an economy that is increasing in size over time, in terms of such attributes as

- size of the human population;
- consumption of natural resources;
- manufacturing of goods;
- supply of money; and
- production of waste materials and pollution.

Two commonly reported indicators of the size of an economy are its human population and the gross domestic product. GDP is the total expenditures for goods and services produced within an economy. It may be calculated in various ways, but a relatively simple equation is: GDP = consumption + gross investment + government spending + exports − imports.

Figure 15.1a shows recent growth of population and GDP for so-called developing (poorer) and developed (richer) countries. During the 47-year time period of record (1960 to 2006), the human population of developed countries increased by 31 percent, compared with 270 percent in developing countries, whose proportion of the global population increased from 68 percent to 80 percent **(Table 15.1)**. Developing countries also had a more rapid growth of GDP, which overall increased by 10.5 times, compared

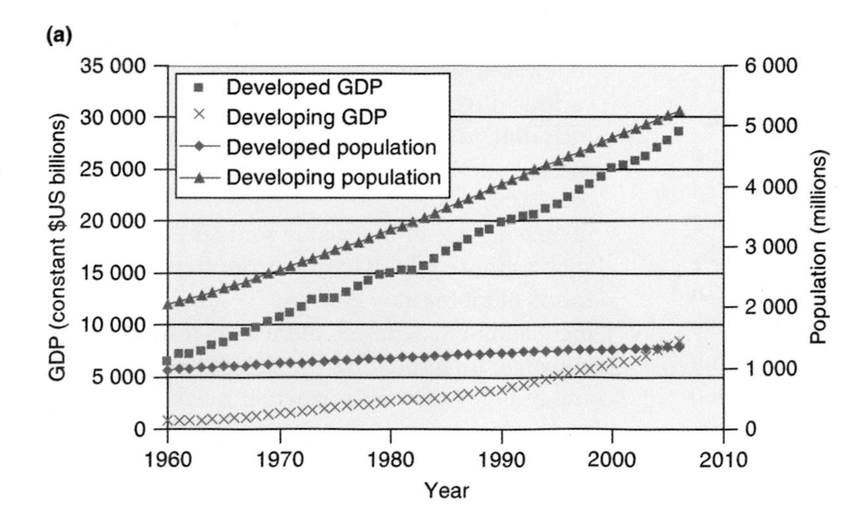

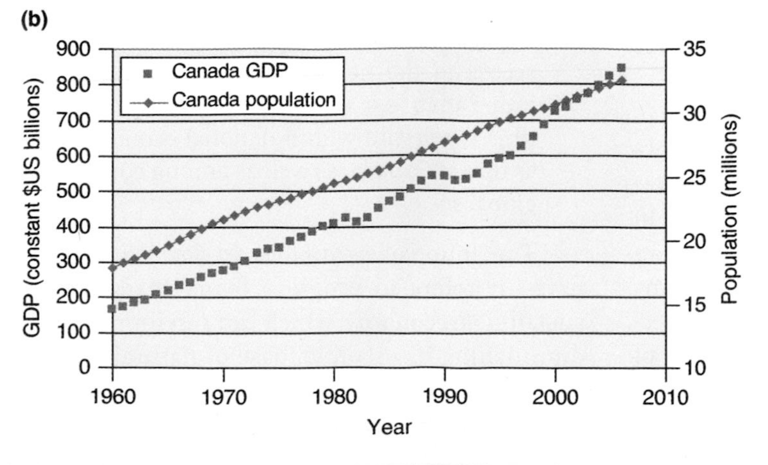

FIGURE 15.1

Economic Growth. The data show crude indicators of the growth of economies, separately for developed (relatively rich) and developing (poorer) countries. Population data are in millions, and gross domestic product (GDP) is in billions (10^9) of year-2000 U.S. dollars (10^9 2000 US$). For context, the global population in 2006 was 6.6 billion, and the global GDP was US$37.9 × 10^{12} (year 2000 US$). GDP is the total expenditures for all final goods and services produced within an economy.

SOURCE: World Resources Institute (WRI). 2010. EarthTrends database. http://earthtrends.wri.org.

TABLE 15.1 Economic Growth in Developed (Relatively Wealthy) and Developing (Less-Wealthy) Countries

The data show increases of both population and gross domestic product (GDP) over a 47-year period, as well as the percentage increase.

	Population (billions)			GDP (year-2000 US$ × 10^{12})		
	1960	2006	Increase	1960	2006	Increase
Developed	0.97	1.35	31%	6.5	28.7	442%
Developing	2.06	5.24	270%	0.80	8.41	1050%

SOURCE: World Resources Institute (WRI). 2010. EarthTrends database. http://earthtrends.wri.org.

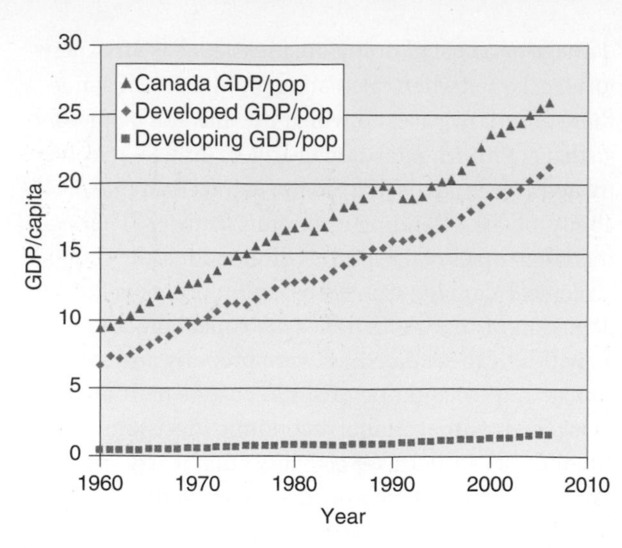

FIGURE 15.2

Per Capita GDP. The data show that, in absolute terms, relatively developed countries grew wealthier, on a per capita basis, much faster than did poorer (developing) countries during the study period. The data are in units of 10^3 year-2000 US$ per capita.

SOURCE: World Resources Institute (WRI). 2010. EarthTrends database. http://earthtrends.wri.org.

with 4.4 times in developed countries (note that because the GDP data are in constant dollars, the increases are not due to inflation). However, because the developing countries started from a much smaller base of GDP, their share of the global GDP increased from only 11 percent in 1960 to 23 percent in 2006. The data for Canada, by the way, are typical of developed countries **(Figure 15.1b)**, with the population growing by 1.8 times between 1960 and 2006, and GDP by 5 times.

It is well known that most politicians, economists, and businesspeople are enthusiastic advocates of continued economic growth. In general, they consider this growth to be a good way to increase the amount of wealth in society, and thereby to help citizens have a greater capacity to purchase goods and services, which itself is considered an indicator of prosperity. Of course, for this to occur, the rate of increase in the size of an economy, as indicated by the GDP, must exceed that of population growth. In **Figure 15.2** we can see that much of the recent economic growth in developing countries, representing an overall increase of GDP of 10.5-fold between 1960 and 2006, was offset by a rise of population of 2.5-fold. Consequently, the growth of per capita GDP was 4.1-fold. In contrast, the more moderate 4.4 times increase of GDP in developed countries was largely retained on a per capita basis (3.2 times) because of a slower increase of population.

Although most leaders of society are eager proponents of economic growth, there are important problems inherent in the phenomenon. They arise because economic growth is typically achieved by increases in population, the consumption (and depletion) of natural resources, the generation of wastes, and many resulting environmental damages. From the perspective of ecological economics, these indicators of growth are symptomatic of grave difficulties, rather than being desirable.

In marked contrast to such growth, the process of **economic development** implies an improving efficiency in the use of materials and energy in an economy. Indicators of development include the following:

- decreased use of non-renewable sources of energy in the economy, and their replacement by such renewable supplies as geothermal heat and the various direct and indirect forms of solar energy, including passive solar, hydroelectricity, wind, biomass, and photovoltaics (see the next section for details);
- increasing use of renewable sources of materials, such as those manufactured from trees and other forms of biomass;
- increasing efficiency of the use of resources, for instance, by improving the designs of machines and buildings to minimize their needs for energy and materials, by diligently recycling and reusing metals and other disused goods, and by less consumerism; and
- an improvement of social equity, so that progress is made to an economy in which all people have access to the necessities and amenities of life, rather than just a minority of wealthy individuals (this is relevant within national economies, such as that of Canada, as well as among countries on a global scale).

The notion of *sustainable development* is relevant here—it refers to progress being made toward a **sustainable economy**, which can run forever without diminishing its essential base of natural capital. In this sense, a sustainable economy does not use resources faster than the rate at which they are being produced by the natural world, and so does not compromise their availability to future generations. If this is to happen, a sustainable economy must be fundamentally based on the use of renewable resources, because they are capable of regenerating after they are harvested. Non-renewable resources cannot do this.

Nevertheless, according to ecological economics there is also a role for non-renewable resources in a sustainable economy. However, as their stocks become inevitably diminished by mining, they would be replaced by an equivalent amount of a renewable substitute. For instance, electricity can be produced by burning coal or gas, but eventually those non-renewable fuels will run out, and moreover, their combustion contributes to an accumulation of carbon dioxide, an important greenhouse gas, in the atmosphere. The connection of the use of coal or gas to sustainability might involve linking their depletion to an offset gained by increasing the amount of an equivalent renewable resource, such as forest biomass. In this sense, enough trees could be planted to provide an increase of biomass that would offset both (1) the depletion of non-renewable energy resources by the combustion of coal or gas (tree biomass can be used as a fuel, in a way comparable to coal and gas), and (2) the emissions of CO_2 to the atmosphere, because that gas is fixed by growing trees into their biomass.

It would take a lot of forest to do this. For example, a study in New Brunswick found that the CO_2 emissions from even a relatively small coal-fired power plant (200 MW capacity) would require the off-setting CO_2-fixation services of 0.72×10^3 ha of conifer plantations established on higher-quality land (Freedman et al., 1992). Alternatively, because of the slower rate of productivity, 1.9×10^3 ha of natural forest regeneration after clear-cutting would be required to offset the coal burning, or 4.7×10^3 ha of mature natural forest.

As we previously noted, it is abundantly clear that the human economy has been growing impressively during the past several centuries, and particularly in the last few decades **(Figure 15.1)**. However, any objective consideration of indicators related to the use and remaining stocks of natural resources must lead to the conclusion that not much of the economic growth has represented progress in terms of sustainable development. Obvious indicators of non-sustainability include the following:

- *Non-renewable sources of energy*, which consist of petroleum, gas, coal, oil sand, and nuclear power, account for 94 percent of the global production of primary energy (this refers to raw unprocessed fuels; the number for Canada is 74 percent, largely because our country is relatively well endowed with hydroelectric resources) (data for 2007; BP, 2010). Between 1983 and 2007, the global consumption of commercial energy increased by 66 percent (the increase was 49 percent in Canada). The heavy reliance on non-renewable sources of energy, all of which have relatively short **reserve lives** (this is calculated as the known recoverable reserves divided by the rate of mining), is an indication of non-sustainability.
- *Fossil fuels* are crucial resources that are used for commercial energy and as feedstock to manufacture asphalt and plastics and other synthetic materials. However, the non-renewable fossil resources all have relatively short reserve lives, suggesting there will be future scarcities of these economically vital materials. The global reserve life of petroleum is about 50 years (in 2007), and it is 60 years for natural gas, and 270 years for coal **(Table 15.2)**. During the 25-year period of 1983 to 2007, the global mining of petroleum increased by a factor of 42 percent, gas by 92 percent, and coal by 65 percent (in Canada, the increases were 102 percent, 158 percent, and 53 percent, respectively).
- *Metals* are used for many important purposes in the economy, including the manufacturing of tools, machines, furniture, and buildings. However, metals are non-renewable resources and their reserve lives are short, suggesting that the present rapid use threatens their future availability (although, unlike fossil fuels, the life span of metals in the economy can be extended by recycling disused products). The global reserve life of aluminum ore is about 133 years (in 2007), and it is 31 years for copper, 79 years for iron, 22 years for lead, 40 years for nickel, and 17 years for zinc **(Table 15.2)**. In the 25 years between 1983 and 2007, the global production of aluminum increased by 343 percent, copper by 94 percent, iron by 257 percent, nickel by 241 percent, and zinc by 68 percent (in Canada, the increases were 284 percent for aluminum and 211 percent for nickel; the other metals declined because some of the existing mines were exhausted and closed; **Table 15.2**).
- *Deforestation* is widespread and increasing. Only about 53 percent of the original forest cover of the world now survives, the rest having been converted to agricultural land-uses, and to a much lesser extent, to urbanized and industrial uses (91 percent of the original forest cover of Canada survives, although the amount is much less in southern Canada, where most agricultural production occurs and most people live; WRI, 2010).
- *Marine fisheries* are showing enormous strain, and many of the most important stocks are greatly depleted or have collapsed because of excessive

TABLE 15.2 Use of Fossil Fuels and Metals

The reserve life is calculated as the quantity of the resource that is considered to be economically recoverable divided by the amount mined per year; percent increase is the production in 2007 compared with 1987. Data for fossil fuels are for 2007, in tonnes of oil equivalent (toe; this standardization allows the data to be summed across the types of fuels). Data for metals are for 2007.

Fossil Fuels	Global Production (10^6 toe/yr)	Reserve Life (years)	Increase (percent)	Canada Production (10^6 toe/yr)	Reserve Life (years)	Increase (percent)
Petroleum						
conventional	3824	–		72.1	27.4	
+ oil sand	3905	49.5	42	153.4	188.4	102
Natural Gas	2654	60.1	92	165.3	8.9	158
Coal	3136	270	65	36.9	178	530
Metals	**(10^6 t/yr)**	**(years)**		**(10^6 t/yr)**	**(years)**	
Aluminum	47.5	133	343	3.1	–	284
Copper	15.6	31	94	0.585	15	−6
Iron	1900	79	257	33	52	−1
Lead	3.55	22	7	0.075	5.3	−70
Nickel	1.66	40	241	0.258	19	211
Zinc	10.5	17	68	0.68	7.4	−26

SOURCES: British Petroleum (2010), Freedman (2010), and U.S. Geological Survey (2010).

commercial fishing. This is particularly true of large, highly valued marine species; on average, over historical time scales, diadromous fish have declined by 96 percent (mostly migratory salmon), groundfish by 93 percent, reef fish by 89 percent, sharks by 87 percent, large pelagic fish by 76 percent (such as big tunas and billfishes), and sea turtles by 96 percent (Lotze and Worm, 2009). The global catch of marine fisheries strongly increased from about 14×10^6 t in 1950 to an asymptote of $68–73 \times 10^6$ t since the late 1980s (70×10^6 t in 2005; WRI, 2010). The Food and Agriculture Organization of the United Nations considers that about 28 percent of fish stocks are severely damaged, being over-exploited (19 percent), depleted (8 percent), or recovering from depletion (1 percent) (2007 data; FAO 2009).

- *Agricultural land* is being extensively degraded by inappropriate management practices. Wood et al. (2000) estimated that 85 percent of agricultural land has already been degraded by erosion, salinization, compaction, or other problems. They estimated that soil degradation since 1950 had reduced the potential global agricultural productivity by 13 percent. The damages are especially severe in poorer countries, which have less ability to mitigate the problems through improved management practices.

Clearly, the present human economy is characterized by crude economic growth, which is achieved by population increases and the rapid mining and use of both non-renewable and renewable resources. Although such growth can be maintained for some years, it is not sustainable over the longer term because of the integrated effects of resource depletion and environmental damage. Although it is seemingly heartening to know that many leading politicians, economists, and corporate spokespeople have openly avowed their support for the notion of sustainable development, they are mostly confusing it with "sustainable economic growth," which is an impossible phenomenon.

However, there is an important problem with the definition that we just examined of a sustainable economy—one that can run forever without diminishing its essential base of natural capital. From an ecological perspective, this definition is too anthropocentric in that it focuses on achieving a resource-neutral human economy. If that model were taken too far, the entire planet might become domesticated and converted to economic uses in the service of the human population. If that were to happen, grievous damage would be caused to the natural world. For this reason, it is useful to consider the notion of an *ecologically sustainable economy*. This idea incorporates conventional resource sustainability, and so it too is an economy that is based on the use of renewable resources in ways that do not compromise their future availability. At the same time, however, the human economy would accommodate the needs of biodiversity, so that all species and natural ecosystems would be maintained at viable levels of abundance. This goal would be achieved in two major ways: (1) by conserving, to the degree possible, habitats on ecoscapes that are working to provide resources for the human economy, while also (2) designating networks of protected areas to accommodate those species and natural ecosystems whose viability is not compatible with intensive economic use.

Capital and Natural Resources

An economy runs through the use of **capital**, such as the following kinds:

- **Natural capital** (or **natural resources**) refers to sources of materials and energy that are harvested from ecosystems and the broader environment. There are two fundamental types: **non-renewable resources**, which are always diminished by use, and **renewable resources**, which can regenerate after harvesting (these are examined in more detail below).
- **Manufactured capital** is created by human ingenuity, and it includes anything that is constructed from simpler resources, such as processed foods, textiles, lumber, and metals, as well as more complex goods made from these, such as machines and buildings.
- **Human capital** refers to the people who are participating in an economy, ranging from labourers performing relatively straightforward work, to highly trained professionals such as entertainers, engineers, medical practitioners, economists, and ecologists.
- **Intellectual capital** is the knowledge that resides within an economy—the know-how of organizing a complex society and doing all the things that are required to keep people fed, healthy, safe, and content, and also to maintain the environment in good condition. Intellectual capital resides in the minds of people, and also in books and other media, including computerized resources on the World Wide Web.

All of these kinds of capital are vital to the functioning of an economy. In this chapter on resource ecology, however, we will focus on the harvesting and management of natural resources, and particularly on the biological and ecological varieties. Natural capital is harvested from the environment, and it includes many potentially renewable resources that are reaped from ecosystems. It is because of that latter connection, coupled with ecological damages that are associated with the harvesting and management of natural resources, that a commonly stated truism of ecology is that "economic systems and ecological systems are inextricably linked."

Natural Resources

There are two kinds of natural resources: non-renewable and renewable:

NON-RENEWABLE RESOURCES. **Non-renewable resources** are present in a finite quantity on Earth, and they do not regenerate after they are mined from the environment. This means that their use always diminishes the amount available to be harvested in the future—this inescapable depletion is inherent in the meaning of the word "mining." The prime examples of non-renewable resources are metal ores and fossil fuels (coal, petroleum, oil sand, and natural gas). Of course, the known stocks of non-renewable resources can be increased by discoveries of additional exploitable quantities, and this helps to extend their calculated lifetimes (although the new findings do not change the physical amounts of the resources, which remain a finite quantity). In any event, the global stocks of non-renewable resources are being rapidly depleted. Although metal ores can be mined only once from the environment, it is possible to extend their use in the economy by recycling them after some initial use. This process is done very efficiently for the most valuable metals, such as platinum and gold, and much less so for those that are cheaper, such as iron and aluminum. In contrast, fossil fuels used as sources of energy cannot be recycled within an economy—they flow through the system. In a sense, their content of potential energy and fixed carbon can be recycled by ecological and geological processes that occur outside of the human economy, but these operate at exceedingly slow rates compared with the speed with which fossil fuels are now being mined and used.

RENEWABLE RESOURCES. **Renewable resources** are sources of food, materials, or energy that are capable of regenerating after they are harvested, so potentially their stocks can forever be available for use. Ultimately, a sustainable economy can be founded only on the prudent use of renewable resources. It must be remembered, however, that potentially renewable resources can be harvested too intensively (this is overharvesting) or inappropriately managed in other ways. If this happens their stocks become diminished, and in severe cases may even disappear. The use of potentially renewable resources in such a wanton manner rejects their sustainability and is comparable to the mining of a non-renewable resource. The most prominent examples of renewable resources are the diverse manifestations of sunlight, which include

- direct solar energy, which can be absorbed and used as heat (this is known as passive solar);
- wind, or movements of atmospheric mass that are driven by large-scale thermal gradients

Larry MacDougal/First Light

Non-renewable resources, such as fossil fuels and metals, are depleted as they are mined from the environment. This photo shows a large open-pit mine for oil sand near Fort McMurray in northern Alberta. The oil sand is mined and processed into synthetic petroleum.

created by regional differences in the absorption of solar energy;
- oceanic currents, which are flows of water that are solar-powered by thermal gradients in a manner similar to wind;
- hydroelectricity, which is generated by tapping into the gravitational kinetic energy of water flowing from higher to lower altitude (the water having previously been lifted by the solar-driven hydrological cycle);
- photovoltaics, in which sunlight is directly converted into electricity; and
- biomass in its various forms, which are initially based on the fixation of inorganic carbon and water into simple sugars through sunlight-powered photosynthesis; examples are
  - tree biomass that is harvested as a source of energy or to manufacture lumber or paper;
  - wild animals that are hunted as food or for materials (such as fur), including deer, seals, ducks, fish, lobster, and oysters;
  - wild plants that are gathered as food or medicine, such as blueberries, strawberries, and yew; and
  - agricultural crops, which are dependent on the fertility of soil and the ability of the environment to provide moisture.

A few additional renewable resources are not powered by solar energy. They include

- geothermal energy, which is produced by the heat of radioactive decay occurring in Earth's core, and
- tidal movements of water, which are driven by the gravitational attraction between Earth and its moon and can be harnessed to generate electricity.

It should be pointed out that, while many economic activities are dependent on the harvesting of natural resources, the actual benefits may vary considerably depending on what is done with the harvested commodities. The smallest local economic benefit is realized if a primary resource (the form in which it exists at the time of harvesting) is exported somewhere else to be processed into **value-added products** (this is the increased value of a product over that of the materials from which it was produced). For instance, if raw logs are retained in an area so that they can be used to manufacture such value-added products as sawn lumber, furniture, or guitars, the regional economic benefits associated with the harvested timber are much greater. In fact, by encouraging value-added operations that utilize the entire tree, a large regional economy might be maintained even while having smaller timber harvests.

Of the various kinds of resources noted above, biomass is most directly a product of ecosystems. Biomass resources are also the subject matter of the rest of this chapter. Biomass is harvested and used as the source of all of our food, much of our medicine and materials, and as a source of energy. Ecological knowledge is necessary to foster the productivity of **biological resources** (or **bio-resources**), to set appropriate harvest limits, and to mitigate damages that are inevitably caused by harvesting and management. Moreover, the harvesting of any of the non-biological resources noted above also carries the risk of causing many kinds of environmental damages, including to ecosystems and biodiversity.

Synopsis

Ultimately, the longer-term sustainability of the human enterprise will be limited by the ability of the biosphere to deliver resources and to assimilate anthropogenic wastes. Key non-renewable resources

Bill Freedman

Renewable resources can regenerate after they are harvested, and so they are the fundamental basis of a sustainable economy. Much of the flow of the Churchill River in Labrador is already used to generate hydroelectricity. This site, known as Muskrat Falls, is the proposed site of an additional dam and hydroelectric generating station. The riverflow is regenerated through the hydrologic cycle, which is ultimately powered by absorbed solar energy.

are already being rapidly depleted, and the limits of some potentially renewable ones have been reached or exceeded, resulting in declines or collapses of their stocks. These changes are well documented and they are forewarnings of a likely dire future for the human economy, unless it is transformed into a more sustainable enterprise.

However, such a transformation would not be easy to achieve. It would involve less intensive and more efficient use of resources by wealthier nations, while at the same time lifting the peoples of poorer countries to an acceptable standard of living. Some of the necessary changes would be extreme, and might not be popular among much of the public, or with politicians, government bureaucrats, and business and industrial interests. These shareholders might all experience a degree of short-term pain, likely over decades, to achieve the longer-term benefits of a sustainable economic system. The difficulties would be related to the abandonment of the paradigm of crude economic growth, less consumerism and diminished per capita use of natural resources, and a rapid stabilization and perhaps decrease of the human population. But the offsetting benefits would be enormous—a human economy that could sustain both present and future generations, as well as other species and natural ecosystems.

15.2 Harvesting and Managing Biological Resources

The discovery of improved ways of managing and harvesting biological resources is the main subject area of resource ecology. In the sense meant here, **management** involves actions that are undertaken to improve environmental conditions to enhance the productivity or quality of a biological resource, while **harvesting** refers to the gathering of wild biomass or the reaping of a cultivated crop.

Often, various activities associated with harvesting and management are undertaken in a coordinated manner—that is, as an **integrated system** (or an **integrated management system**) that is intended to increase the productivity and value of a biological resource. A key objective is to achieve resource sustainability—a level of harvesting that does not deplete the stocks of the bio-resource. Usually, there are also considerations intended to keep associated environmental impacts within acceptable limits, including the need to ensure that biodiversity and environmental services are not compromised to an intolerable degree (while recognizing that some damage to these and other ecological values is inevitable).

In many cases, it is wild and unmanaged biological resources that are being harvested. Examples include much of the timber that is harvested in Canada, as well as wild stocks of fish and other hunted animals, such as deer, rabbits, furbearers, and seals. In all of these cases, there is reliance on natural processes and self-organizing ecosystems to provide harvestable stocks of a bio-resource. In an economic sense, the biomass is provided by "free" ecological services that required no investment from the human economy.

Often, however, management actions may improve the quality of a biological resource, usually by increasing its productivity by enhancing recruitment, or by decreasing the natural mortality of economically desired species **(Figure 15.3)**. Improvements of the bio-resource might be reflected in larger stocks, faster productivity, or better quality in terms of the size or species composition of the harvested organisms. The improvements might be achieved by influencing the biology of target populations to increase their yield, for instance, by selective breeding, or by mitigating environmental constraints on their productivity.

ENVIRONMENTAL APPLICATIONS 15.1

Easter Island

gary yim/Shutterstock

Easter Island (Rapa Nui)

Easter Island, or Rapa Nui, is one of the most isolated places on Earth—a small (164 km^2) volcanic island in the southern Pacific Ocean (Ponting, 1991; Diamond, 2004). The time of its discovery by wandering Polynesians is not certain, but it was likely around 300–400 C.E. These colonizing people brought only chicken, sweet potato, and banana as useful crops, the warm-temperate climate of the island being unsuitable for their other foods, such as breadfruit and coconut. However, porpoises, fish, and other marine life were abundant in the near-shore waters, and the Polynesian colonists hunted them from boats made of local trees (particularly the now extinct endemic palm, *Paschalococos disperta*). By the 16th century, there was a flourishing economy on Easter Island, with a population of about 7000, and abundant food.

Life being relatively easy, the islanders had time to develop a cultural and religious activity that involved carving great blocks of volcanic stone into human-headed monoliths (moai), which were dragged to coastal places and erected on massive stone bases. Both the monoliths (weighing up to 75 t) and their similarly heavy bases were carved at an inland quarry, and then laboriously moved to coastal sites by rolling them on logs cut from the forest. Unfortunately, Easter Island quickly became deforested by the excessive cutting of trees for use as stone rollers, for timber to construct fishing boats and buildings, and as fuel. Once the vital forest resource disappeared, the core of the economy collapsed—most fishing became impossible because wooden boats were needed to safely pass through the oceanic surf, and it was difficult to cook food or heat homes because only shrubby and herbaceous biomass was available for use as fuel. The nuclear cultural activity of carving and erecting the great stone heads also ceased, because they could no longer be moved from the quarries.

Simply put, non-sustainable harvesting of trees caused a rapid collapse to occur in the economy of this prehistoric Polynesian society. Undoubtedly, the islanders were aware of their remote and precarious circumstances—they may even have considered the need to conserve the last of the trees, but cut them anyway. The resulting disintegration of their economy and culture was so massive that, when the first Europeans arrived in 1772, the indigenous people were living in squalid dwellings of reeds and in a few caves, were engaged in warfare among rival clans, were likely cannibals, and no longer remembered who had erected the coastal monoliths.

The case of Easter Island has become a well-used metaphor for Earth as a planetary "island." Earth also has limited stocks of non-renewable resources, which are depleted as they are used, as well as renewable ones, which can become ruined by excessive harvesting. If those planetary resources become exhausted, the global human economy must collapse, just like that of the Easter Islanders. Those prehistoric people had no alternative place rich in resources to which they could escape from their self-inflicted catastrophe. Similarly, there is no substitute for planet Earth.

Ultimately, the potential productivity of an organism is determined by its genome, which sets the upper limits of developmental and growth rates under optimal environmental conditions. It is rare, however, for that potential productivity to be realized, either in individual organisms, or their populations, or in multi-species communities. This is because of constraints that environmental conditions pose on recruitment, mortality, and productivity. In essence, management actions are intended to mitigate this reality by alleviating the intensity of environmental constraints, including biological ones. The management actions may result in higher rates of productivity of biological resources, resulting in larger harvests.

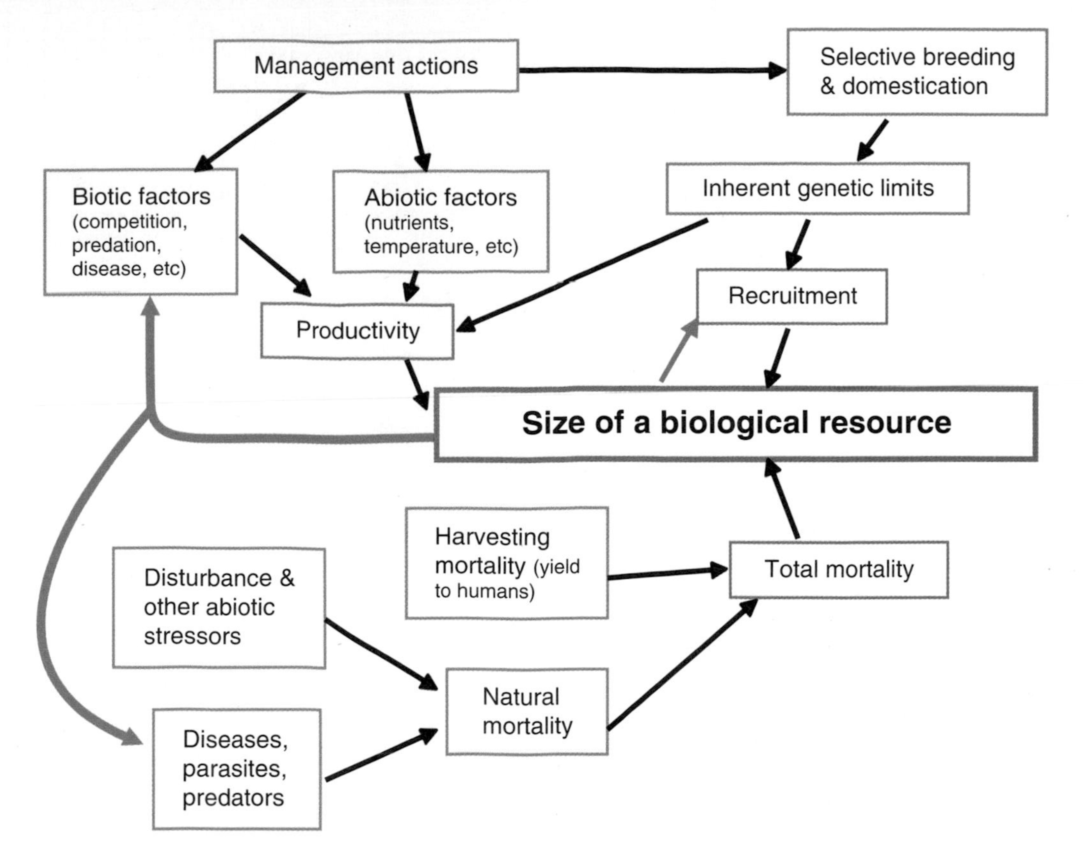

FIGURE 15.3

Conceptual Model of Constraints on the Productivity of a Biological Resource. The size of a biological resource is influenced by the rates of mortality, recruitment, and productivity. Management actions can mitigate biotic and abiotic environmental factors, as well as some genetic constraints on productivity and recruitment. The rate of harvesting affects the total mortality rate.

SOURCE: Modified from Begon, M., C. R. Townsend, and J. L. Harper. 2005. *Ecology: From Individuals to Ecosystems*, 3rd ed. Blackwell Publishing, Oxford, UK.

These benefits may, however, be somewhat offset by any environmental damages that are caused by the intensified management.

For any biological resource, there is a theoretical upper limit of harvesting that can be made without compromising the sustainability of the stocks. This ideal is known as the **maximum sustainable yield (MSY)**. If the MSY is exceeded, then the productivity of the resource becomes diminished and the size of its stocks decreases at a rate that is strongly influenced by the degree by which the overharvesting is exceeding the MSY. It should be understood, however, that the MSY is somewhat conditional—it is relatively large if environmental conditions are optimized for crop productivity, and smaller if they are highly constraining.

An ideal model of MSY, occurring at a constant rate of harvesting regardless of population size, is illustrated in **Figure 15.4**. The model shows that for any population size, a harvesting rate greater than the upper bounds of the curve would be non-sustainable, and if maintained would drive the population to extinction. In comparison, a harvesting rate smaller than MSY would force the population toward one of two equilibrium points. One of them is unstable because it forces the population to extinction, while the other is stable and sustainable because it is approached from two directions. Therefore, under conditions of a constant rate of harvesting there are several sustainable intensities of yield, the largest of which is the MSY.

Commercial interests that harvest biological resources generally maintain relatively fixed amounts of infrastructure, consisting of personnel and machinery for harvesting biomass (such as fishing boats using a particular technology, or comparable machines in forestry). Because large investments have been made in people and technology, there is a tendency for the harvesting effort to be relatively stable from year to year. Therefore, from the perspective of a resource manager, it may be more realistic to consider the effects of harvesting at a constant rate of effort, rather than at a constant yield (or amount). Because the size of a harvest depends on the interaction of both the effort and the size of the stock, a constant harvesting effort results in a variable yield (**Figure 15.5**). The constant-effort model predicts that there is an intensity of harvesting that will result in a MSY and a stable, equilibrium size of the stock being

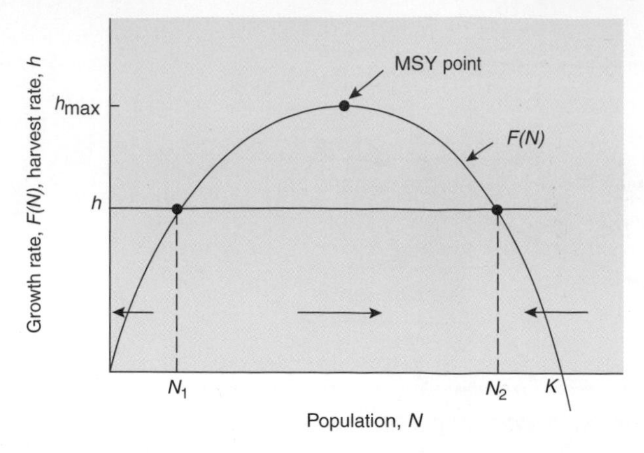

FIGURE 15.4

Maximum Sustainable Yield (MSY). This diagrammatic model of MSY is based on the productivity and harvesting of a single-species resource. The productivity of the stock under resource-constrained conditions is described by the logistic equation (Chapter 5). The logistic equation is an equilibrium model of continuous change, and it is relevant to populations in which births and deaths occur continuously, but there is limited environmental capacity to sustain the population. This MSY model describes the relationship between the growth rate of the population and the harvest rate ($F(N)$ and h, respectively; both on the vertical axis) with changes in the population size (N; horizontal axis). When the population is at carrying capacity (K), there is no net change in abundance, and no excess production (i.e., beyond what the carrying capacity can support) is available to be harvested. For obvious reasons, there is also no productivity to be harvested when the population size is zero. When the population is at the top of the curve, growth rates are maximal and MSY (h_{max}, occurring when $N = ½K$) can be achieved. Note that a fixed intensity of the harvest rate (h) can intersect the curve at two places, and so there are two population equilibria in the curve, N_1 and N_2. Harvesting from the population (at a constant rate, h) when it is smaller than N_1 will drive the resource to extinction (this is indicated by the arrow pointing to the left), and so represents over-exploitation. (Note also that at any particular population size, any effort of harvesting that is greater than the upper bound of the curve is also non-sustainable.) Harvesting (at h) when the population is larger than N_2 will drive the resource to N_2 and is a sustainable practice, although the yields are smaller than can potentially be achieved. Harvesting (at effort h) from a population that is larger than N_1 and smaller than N_2 will allow the population to grow toward N_2 and is also sustainable. The MSY occurs at the apex of the curve. Note that if the harvesting effort changes, so do the two population equilibria.

SOURCE: Modified from Clark, C.W. 1981. "Bioeconomics." Pp. 387–423 in *Theoretical Ecology: Principles and Applications*. Blackwell Scientific.

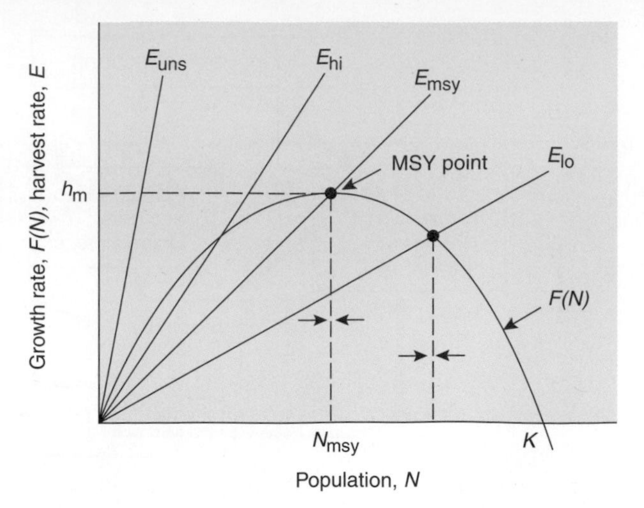

FIGURE 15.5

Maximum Sustainable Yield (MSY) under Constant Harvesting Effort. Because the harvesting effort is constant, the yield varies depending on the size of the exploited population. The population growth model, $F(N)$, is based on the logistic equation. In the model depicted here, a single, stable equilibrium point is associated with all levels of harvesting that intersect the curve. At an effort of E_{msy} the maximum sustainable yield (h_m) is being harvested, and this MSY is achieved at a population of N_{msy}. Harvesting at E_{msy} when the population is larger or smaller than N_{msy} will result in movement of the population toward N_{msy}, indicating that this is a stable equilibrium point. Harvesting at efforts of E_{hi} or E_{lo} also leads to stable equilibrium points, but these have smaller sustainable yields than are achieved by harvesting at E_{msy}. Harvesting at E_{uns} does not intersect the curve and represents an unsustainable effort that would drive the stock to extinction.

SOURCE: Modified from Clark, C.W. 1981. "Bioeconomics." Pp. 387–423 in *Theoretical Ecology: Principles and Applications*. Blackwell Scientific.

exploited. Within bounds set by the growth rate of the stock at various population sizes, there are also smaller levels of harvest that would be sustainable at other intensities of effort. However, greater intensities of harvest effort would not be sustainable, and would drive the stock to extinction.

There are also numerous, more sophisticated models of population growth that consider multi-species stocks, changes in harvesting effort, environmental dynamics, regulatory strategies, and other variables associated with demographics, environmental conditions, technology, and regulation. These models (often referred to as dynamic pool models) have been developed for use primarily in the management of fisheries, but they can also inform the ways that forests and hunted animals are managed. However, we will not examine these relatively advanced models, as they are beyond the scope of this book. Specialized textbooks in resource ecology and population ecology can be consulted for details.

For obvious reasons, the notion of MSY is intuitively attractive, and it has had great influence on the development of the theory and practice of fishery, wildlife, and forest management. MSYs are relatively easy to model in the ideal world of the logistic equation (Chapter 5), in which the environment and its carrying capacity are known and sometimes constant, and only one or a few species are growing without complex behaviour, such as social systems. In the real world, however, accurate MSYs are always difficult to determine. This is because environmental conditions are continually changing, sometimes in a dramatic manner, and there are corresponding adjustments by an interacting community of species.

For such reasons there is always uncertainty in the prediction of MSY and in understanding the degree to which it is limited by environmental factors. In essence, MSY is estimated using models of population growth, which can be modified (or parameterized) to account for the influence of environmental factors, including how they may be affected by both management activities and the harvesting rate. However, the models are always imperfect and so there is some degree of inaccuracy in their predictions. Because of uncertainty in predicting the MSY, it is always sensible to take a precautionary approach when setting the allowable harvest of a biological resource—it should be set low enough so that stocks are not put at risk. This approach takes a prudent longer-term view and is more likely to be sustainable, even if the harvest is not as large as might be physically possible. Unfortunately, such precautionary approaches are often not taken, as we will see later in this chapter when we examine case studies of resource degradation caused by excessive harvesting. In those cases the strategy was to maximize the short-term revenue flows and profits, rather than to ensure a resource-sustainable enterprise.

Another important problem with the implementation of the MSY concept is associated with the fact that the logistic equation is an "instantaneous" model in which the balance between mortality and density-dependent recruitment is continuously maintained. The introduction of time lags (or delays), especially those associated with reproduction, can greatly destabilize such models. This problem can be especially severe in species that take a long time to mature. Moreover, changes in population size in the real world may be influenced by complex social behaviour, interactions with other species, environmental change, disturbances, and other unpredictable variables.

As such, MSY is best viewed as a concept from which useful insights have been gathered about factors that influence the intrinsic rates of growth and mortality of simple populations and communities, including the effects of harvesting. Often, however, MSY models cannot be successfully applied to the management of real, biological resources.

In any event, managers do need to regulate or adjust the rates of mortality that are associated with harvesting. They typically do this by controlling the harvesting effort, which is an integrated function of the methods (e.g., types of fishing boats and their gear, or the weapons that hunters can use, such as bow or rifle) and intensity (e.g., the number of boats, or the number of hunting licences issued) of harvesting. In addition, management tactics may be applied in an attempt to increase the productivity and sizes of the stocks of bio-resources. In the remainder of this section we examine some factors that affect the renewability of biological resources, including harvesting and management options that can affect the productivity and MSY.

Regeneration

After a biological resource is harvested, it is potentially capable of recovering—this is the essence of its sustainability. The recovery may occur in various ways, including by the recruitment of new individuals into the population, as well as the regeneration of any that survived the harvest. **Natural regeneration** is the spontaneous recovery of a bio-resource after it has been harvested. It is the usual means of recovery following the harvesting of timber, fish, or deer and other terrestrial land animals, although in some cases certain management actions may be used to enhance the regeneration.

For example, after a timber harvest the trees may spontaneously regenerate in one or more of the following ways:

- **Vegetative regeneration**—Individuals of certain species will survive the cutting and then regenerate by sprouting from their stump, roots, or rhizomes. Species of ash, aspen, maple, and other angiosperm trees ("hardwoods") are good at doing this, and their hearty vegetative regeneration may quickly restore another forest.
- **Advanced regeneration**—This refers to smaller individuals of tree species that are established under a mature forest canopy. After timber harvesting opens up the stand they become ecologically "released" from competitive stresses that were previously exerted by the mature trees. When this happens the advanced regeneration grows rapidly and it can be prominent in the next stand.
- New seedlings—Timber harvesting opens up the forest canopy and creates a mosaic of microdisturbances of the forest floor, and these conditions are favourable to the establishment of seedlings of many species of trees and other plants.

In some kinds of forest, these means of natural regeneration can rather quickly re-establish a strong measure of biological functioning on sites affected by clear-cutting and other disturbances. For instance, after the clear-cutting of mature hardwood forest in Nova Scotia dominated by a mixture of hardwood species, the vigorous regeneration that occurred re-established a foliage biomass comparable to that of the original forest within only about five years **(Figure 15.6)**. This helped to quickly mitigate some of the environmental changes caused by the clear-cutting, such as warmed soil and disruption of the evaporation of water to the atmosphere (the rate of transpiration is strongly related to the amount of plant

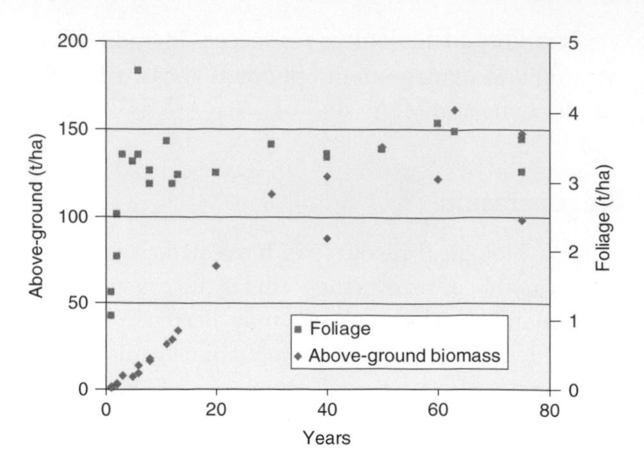

FIGURE 15.6

Rapid Regeneration of Biomass. The data show the recovery of the above-ground biomass and foliage after clear-cutting stands of hardwood forest dominated by species that are capable of vegetative regeneration, such as red maple (*Acer rubrum*), sugar maple (*A. saccharum*), yellow birch (*Betula alleghaniensis*), and white ash (*Fraxinus americana*). The data were assembled by studying a chronosequence (time-series) of stands of various ages after the clear-cutting of a mixed-species hardwood forest in Nova Scotia.

SOURCE: Crowell, M. and B. Freedman. 1994. "Vegetation development during a post-clearcutting chronosequence of hardwood forest in Nova Scotia, Canada," *Canadian Journal of Forest Research*, 24: 260–271.

foliage on a site). The rate of biomass accumulation was also rapid in this forest type. However, not all kinds of forests in Canada regenerate as rapidly as this one did.

In some cases, foresters might not consider the rate of natural regeneration to be fast enough, or the species mixture might be viewed as less desirable from the perspective of the forest industry. To deal with those perceived problems, foresters might use various management tactics to improve the rate and quality of the post-harvest recovery. Some of the options might include (a) using a prescribed burn or heavy machinery to scarify the ground surface, which breaks up the organic mat and exposes mineral soil that provides a better seedbed for the establishment of tree seedlings, or (b) planting seedlings of a preferred species, usually onto a scarified site and at a density intended to optimize the stand productivity.

Similarly, after a harvest is made of fish or deer from some area, reliance may be made on natural regeneration, or the recovery could be managed in some way. For instance, fishery managers may supplement the natural recruitment of wild salmon and trout by releasing large numbers of hatchery-raised fingerlings. This is an especially common practice for stocks that have been depleted by historical over-harvesting or by damage caused to the breeding habitat.

In some cases, the regeneration of depleted populations of deer may be fostered by allowing only adult males to be hunted. This takes advantage of the fact that the breeding system of deer is polygynous, with males mating with as many females as they can. In such a case, a population can suffer a relatively high mortality rate of male animals from hunting, as long as enough of them survive to impregnate all of the females. However, if the hunting disproportionately kills the largest, strongest, fastest-growing, and otherwise "most fit" male animals (as so-called "trophy hunting" does in some populations), this management tactic could potentially degrade the genetic quality of an exploited population.

Limitations on Productivity

Various environmental factors may act as stressors that reduce the productivity of a bio-resource. If these limitations can be alleviated to any degree, the MSY might be increased. The stressors may be abiotic or biological in origin, and they may be mitigated using various interventions. Sometimes an intensive management system is used, which involves a variety of tactics used in a coordinated manner. In general, however, intensive management is done only with relatively high-value crops, such as in agriculture, aquaculture, or plantation forestry. It is used much less often with wild bio-resources, such as hunted animals or in naturally regenerated forests.

The common sorts of environmental limitations and the associated management interventions include the following:

- **Abiotic stressors** include the limited availability of nutrients and moisture and extremes of climatic factors. Limitations of nutrients can be potentially mitigated by adding fertilizer or by incorporating nitrogen-fixing legumes into a crop rotation, while water stress may be alleviated by irrigation. The growing season for some high-value crops may be extended by cultivating them in greenhouses.
- **Interspecific competition** may occur between a crop and other species that are not viewed as being economically desirable. Non-crop plants are deemed to be "weeds," and in agriculture and forestry their influence may be reduced using a herbicide, or by mechanical methods such as tillage or the manual removal of offending plants.
- **Intraspecific competition** occurs within overly dense populations of a crop, and in such cases the density may be reduced by thinning. In agriculture and forestry this problem is managed primarily by planting at a density intended to achieve an appropriate density. Likewise, the density of livestock is usually managed to avoid the overgrazing of pastures. Sometimes, naturally regenerated populations of a crop species are excessively dense and they may be thinned to increase the overall productivity. For instance, overly dense populations of

saplings in forestry may be thinned to enhance the stand productivity.

- Disease may be a problem for some biological resources. Disease may be managed by manipulating habitat to make it less suitable to the pathogen. Some diseases of animals may be treated with veterinary medicines, such as antibiotics. Fungal diseases of plants may be treated using fungicide.
- Losses of crop production to non-human consumers are an issue for many bio-resources. Herbivorous animals may consume some crop production, sometimes killing the plants, and if the problem is severe it may be dealt with in various ways. In agriculture, sprays of insecticide are routinely used to reduce the depredations of herbivorous arthropods. In aquaculture involving Atlantic salmon (*Salmon salar*), the insecticide emamectin benzoate is used to treat infestations of the sea-louse parasite (*Caligus* species). In forestry, fencing and other mechanical guards may be used to reduce the effects of browsing by large and small mammals. Various crops as well as stored products may be protected from pest rodents using lethal traps and rodenticide.
- **Selective breeding** (or **cultural selection**) and **transgenic modification** are useful tactics that can reduce the vulnerability of crop varieties to any of the stressors noted above. Selective breeding has been used by agriculturalists for millennia to develop "improved" varieties of crop plants and livestock. This process has resulted in a number of domesticated plant crops that, compared with their wild progenitors, are relatively tolerant of many environmental stressors and more responsive to fertilizer addition and other mitigations. Transgenic modifications are a relatively recent application of bio-engineering, in which DNA coding for a trait that is beneficial in one species is incorporated into the genome of a different species, such as a crop plant, to realize an economically important benefit. (These are sometimes referred to as "**genetically modified organisms**" or **GMOs**, but that term is ambiguous because it could also logically apply to varieties that are affected by conventional selective breeding.) For instance, varieties of maize (*Zea mays*) have been genetically modified to include genes of *Bacillus thuringiensis* (*B.t.*). This is a soil bacterium that is toxic to many herbivorous insects, and its genes in maize confer a degree of resistance to pest insects. Another example is GMO varieties of soybean (*Glycine max*) and canola (*Brassica rapa*) that have been bioengineered to be tolerant of glyphosate, which allows that herbicide to be used to reduce the abundance of weeds in fields of the crop plants.
- Matching the crop with the regional and local environmental conditions is always an important consideration. This is particularly vital when choosing crops to grow in a larger region. It is the reason why plantations of black walnut (*Juglans nigra*) are not established in northern Ontario instead of black spruce (*Picea mariana*), and why peaches are not cultivated in northern Alberta, or barley in the Okanagan Valley of southern British Columbia. Growing conditions may also be important at a local scale, such as in low areas subjected to wet soil, in higher places where drought may be an issue, in soils that are excessively acidic or calcareous, and so on.

Natural Mortality

Deaths caused by predators, parasites, diseases, accidents, and disturbances are referred to as **natural mortality**. In addition, exploited stocks of biological resources are subjected to **anthropogenic mortality** by harvesting, which adds to that caused by natural agents. Any causes of mortality will affect the abundance of juvenile and adult organisms, and thereby the stocks of biological resources. Within this context, if natural causes of mortality can be reduced, larger harvests may be available to people. There are various ways of decreasing natural mortality, although it can never be eliminated. For example:

- Severe infestations of herbivorous insects may cause mortality to agricultural and forestry crops. Sometimes, the problem can be dealt with by modifying the habitat to make it less suitable to the pest, but often this does not work well enough and pesticides may be used. Sprays of insecticide are routinely used in agriculture to reduce irruptions of arthropods, especially those that can devastate a crop, such as the migratory grasshopper (*Melanoplus sanguinipes*) and other locusts. In forestry, tens of millions of hectares of conifer forest in eastern Canada were sprayed with insecticides from the 1960s to 1993 to reduce the abundance of spruce budworm (*Choristoneura fumiferana*), a devastating herbivore of balsam fir (*Abies balsamea*) and white spruce (*Picea glauca*) (a cumulative area exceeding 118×10^6 ha was sprayed, including stands that were repeatedly treated in various years; Freedman, 2010). Interestingly, a similarly destructive infestation of the mountain pine beetle (*Dendroctonus ponderosae*) in western forests of lodgepole pine (*Pinus contorta*) cannot be managed in this way, because insecticide cannot be delivered to the beetle larvae, which live beneath the bark of the trees. Instead, great swaths of mature pine forest are affected by the beetle (13.5×10^6 ha in 2009), resulting in most of the trees being killed, and much of the dead timber later being salvaged by clear-cutting.

- Sometimes, large carnivores are considered to be important predators of livestock or of wild ungulates hunted by people. If those losses to predators are considered unacceptable, the carnivores may be killed by shooting, trapping, or poisoning. Wolf (*Canis lupus*) culls usually occur in situations where relatively small populations of woodland caribou (*Rangifer tarandus*) or moose (*Alces alces*) are being affected. An alternative tactic has been used in Yukon to increase the population of the endangered Chisana herd of caribou. In that case, pregnant does were captured and released into a large fenced enclosure built within the range of that herd, where their calves were protected from predation by wolves or grizzly bear (*Ursus arctos*) and also provided with supplemental food. This management increased the first-year survival of calves from 13–15 percent under free-ranging conditions to 73 percent, and the supplemental recruitment is allowing the population to increase (Environment Yukon, 2007). In agricultural applications, access of predators to livestock may also be restricted using fences, or by guard animals such as dogs, donkeys, and llamas.

Keith Douglas/All Canada Photos

An irruption of the mountain pine beetle (*Dendroctonus ponderosae*) is causing severe damage to montane pine forests in British Columbia. This landscape in the Thompson River region of British Columbia contains extensively killed stands of pine.

Harvest-Related Mortality

The rate of harvesting should be managed to ensure that the total mortality (natural plus that from the harvest) does not exceed the MSY. The harvest-related mortality is influenced by three factors related to the effort: (1) the numbers of harvesting units that are deployed, (2) the technology being used, and (3) the time they spend harvesting. Any of these factors can potentially be regulated by resource managers to try to keep the harvest within a designated limit.

Various administrative and legal tools may be available to managers as they seek to regulate the harvesting effort. Relatively direct controls include

- limitation of the numbers of licences that are issued, which regulates the numbers of participants;
- regulation of the harvesting methods that are allowed;
- specification of quotas for each harvesting unit;
- limitation of the times during which harvesting can occur; and
- specification of the places where harvesting can take place.

A number of indirect mechanisms can also influence the harvesting rate, by affecting the operating costs:

- taxes or other levies to increase the cost of certain harvesting methods that might be damaging to the habitat, providing incentive to use methods that are less damaging;
- subsidies for less-damaging methods;
- fines for any aspect of non-compliance; and
- buy-outs of excess harvesting capacity (of licences or equipment).

The influence of technology on the harvesting rate can be illustrated in various ways. Clearly, a person wielding an axe can cut down trees and de-limb the logs, which can then be hauled to a roadside using oxen or horses trained for that job. However, a person with a chainsaw can fell and de-limb trees much faster, and a skidding machine can get logs to the roadside in larger numbers than a team of livestock can. And the latest logging equipment can do these tasks even more rapidly—these are machines with a single operator that can fell and de-limb trees, cut them to a desired length, and then carry them to the roadside. Because machines of this sort can perform these tasks so efficiently, people using axes and chainsaws and trained horses and oxen are now rarely employed in the logging industry. In this context, the "efficiency" is measured as tonnes of wood delivered to the landing per dollar of investment in the capacity to cut and haul this forest biomass. Moreover, the modern machines often work most profitably when used to clear-cut all of the timber from a stand, rather than by harvesting trees using environmentally softer methods, such as selection cutting (we will examine these harvesting systems later on in more detail). However, the greater environmental damages associated with clear-cutting compared with less-intensive harvesting systems are not fully costed when comparing the economic viability of the systems.

In a fishery, the simplest methods of harvesting involve people using hand-held equipment, such as jigs and rods. These methods are relatively well-targeted to the species that are the object of the fishery. The most intensive methods involve boats hauling large nets of various kinds, such as bag-like trawls or seines, or wall-like drift nets. These intensive technologies catch much more fish biomass per worker and per dollar of investment. However, depending on the stock being exploited, they may catch a much broader spectrum of species than is being commercially targeted. The non-targeted mortality is referred to as **by-catch**, and it represents a kind of collateral damage that may be discarded as non-economic "garbage." By-catch is particularly intense in shrimp trawling, which accounts for more than one-third of global marine by-catch, even though shrimp amount to only 2 percent of the commercial landings of marine animal biomass (Clucas, 1997). By-catch is also intense for some drift-net fisheries—these are gill-nets that float suspended in the water column, sometimes extending for tens of kilometres and representing a "wall-of-death" for creatures that swim into them, including dolphins and sea turtles (we examine this topic in more detail later in the chapter [pp. 511–512]).

Clearly, the choice of the harvesting method has a great influence on the species and sizes of organisms that are harvested, and this is an important consideration in resource management. In a fishery, for instance, the mesh size of the net has a direct effect on the sizes of animals that are captured. Well-regulated fisheries generally do not permit the capture of under-sized individuals, because they have a relatively low value on a per-weight basis than do larger animals, while also representing the future reproductive potential of the population. In forestry, all species and sizes are harvested in a clear-cut. However, alternative harvesting practices can be used that are more selective of species and sizes, and that can favour the regeneration of the most desirable tree species, while also having softer overall environmental impacts. The best of these practices is selection harvesting, which removes only some of the trees; when practised carefully, selection logging leaves the physical and ecological integrity of the managed forest substantially intact, even while timber is being harvested at intervals of one to several decades.

In some cases, managers have the power to issue licences that set a limit on the number of technological units that can participate in a harvest of a particular stock, in an attempt to ensure that an MSY is not exceeded. For example, the number of people allowed to hunt moose might be determined by a lottery, or a licence might be required to fish on a particular river. In a commercial harvest, a regulatory authority might also specify the kind of technology that may be used—such as the number of vessels using a particular kind of fishing gear.

The harvest-related mortality might also be managed by specifying the time that can be spent in the harvest. For example, waterfowl can be hunted only during the autumn, after they have bred and when their populations are relatively large. The only exceptions are for snow goose (*Chen caerulescens*) in some regions where they are abundant enough to be damaging their own habitat. Likewise, the hunting of deer is generally restricted to a period during the autumn, when their

Yves Marcoux/First Light

Fishing methods vary in their efficiency. Fishing with a rod and reel is not very efficient compared with the use of large ships deploying nets. However, recreational fishing provides much more value-added to the economy, on a per-fish basis, compared with commercial fishing.

populations are largest, the mating season is over, and the animals are well-fed in preparation for the winter. In coastal British Columbia and Alaska, the commercial fishery for pre-spawning herring (*Clupea pallasii*; their roe is a valuable product) is allowed to operate for only several hours or less on a few specified days, so as to help prevent over-fishing of the limited breeding stock.

Unsustainable Harvesting

There are many examples of biological resources that have been depleted by non-sustainable use. Such over-harvesting of a potentially renewable resource is comparable to the "mining" of a non-renewable one, such as a metal or fossil fuel. The first examples of this sort of resource destruction are prehistoric, and include the numerous extinctions that occurred on various oceanic islands after they were discovered by people, and likely also those of many large animals when the Americas were initially colonized (Chapter 14). More recently, several Canadian species were rendered extinct by commercial overharvesting, including the great auk (*Pinguinus impennis*), Labrador duck (*Camptorhynchus labradorium*), passenger pigeon (*Ectopistes migratorius*), deepwater cisco (*Coregonus johannae*), blue pike (*Stizostedion vitreum glaucum*), and Queen Charlotte Islands caribou (*Rangifer tarandus dawsoni*).

There is a much longer list of Canadian species that have become endangered as a result of overharvesting, including some that were initially superabundant, such as the plains bison (*Bison bison bison*), northern right whale (*Eubalaena glacialis*), Eskimo curlew (*Numenius borealis*), trumpeter swan (*Cygnus buccinator*), American ginseng (*Panax quinquefolium*), and many others. These species still survive, but in a small abundance that can no longer support commercial harvesting. In this sense, their hugely depleted stocks are referred to as being **commercially extinct**.

In some cases, entire communities of economic importance have been devastated by excessive harvesting or by the management system that has been applied (Chapter 14). Canadian examples include

- Carolinian forest of southern Ontario, of which <2 percent survives, the rest having been harvested or burned and the land converted into agricultural and urbanized land-uses;
- dry coastal Douglas-fir (*Pseudotsuga menziesii*) forest, of which 2 percent remains, the rest having been harvested and the terrain converted into anthropogenic uses;
- Garry oak (*Quercus garryi*) forest of southern Vancouver Island, of which <5 percent persists;
- old-growth forest communities in all parts of forested Canada; older forests are particularly scarce in the longer-settled eastern provinces, but they are increasingly being depleted even in coastal British Columbia, where the humid climate is especially favourable to their development; in some cases, the land is allowed to return to forest after old-growth stands are harvested for their timber, but the type never re-appears because the second-growth forest is harvested as soon as it becomes economically mature;
- tallgrass prairie of southeastern Manitoba and southwestern Ontario, of which only 1 percent of the original extent survives—this natural community was converted mostly into agricultural and urbanized land-uses;
- similarly, most of the mixedgrass and shortgrass prairie of western Canada has been converted into agricultural use, so that natural remnants are greatly depleted; and
- fish communities have also been widely decimated by overharvesting, including mixed-species ones in the Great Lakes, groundfish off the Atlantic provinces, and salmonids (salmon and trout) in western Canada.

In some cases, the badly depleted stocks of over-harvested species were rescued by effective conservation actions that allowed their populations to recover, sometimes to the degree that they regained their pre-exploitation abundance. Canadian examples that we noted in Chapter 14 include the grey seal (*Halichoerus grypus*), harp seal (*Phoca groenlandica*), grey whale (*Eschrichtius robustus*), humpback whale (*Megaptera novaeangliae*), sea otter (*Enhydra lutris*), white-tailed deer (*Odocoileus virginianus*), American beaver (*Castor canadensis*), wild turkey (*Meleagris gallopavo*), and various species of ducks and geese. Many other species, however, remain badly depleted, as was previously noted.

The over-exploitation of certain communities sometimes displayed a pattern of top–down degradation, which can be referred to as "**working-down**" the resource. Often, the original (or "virgin") community was dominated by large, old-growth individuals of particularly valuable species. These were selectively harvested in the initial phase of resource "development," which left smaller, younger individuals to dominate the post-harvest community. Because these are often relatively fast-growing compared with old-growth individuals, the net productivity of the secondary community was not necessarily diminished. However, subsequent harvests often used intensive methods that were less selective and intended to recover as much biomass as possible. If those harvests were made on a sustainable basis, the regeneration might recover the secondary community, but never the original old-growth one, because the harvest rotations were too short to allow that older condition to redevelop. On the other hand, if the harvests were non-sustainable, then the excessive harvesting mortality and inadequate recruitment would cause even the secondary communities to collapse in productivity and biomass.

In economic terms, this pattern of exploitation of mixed-species resources could be viewed as representing a series of harvests of commodities having increasingly smaller value (measured as value per individual, per weight, or per area harvested). First, the biggest individuals of the most desirable species were selectively harvested and quickly depleted. Then, smaller individuals of the most valuable species might be harvested, along with the largest ones of secondary species. The final stage typically involves an area-harvesting method that attempts to harvest all of the biomass for manufacturing into a bulk commodity.

This sequential process of working-down a biological resource can be illustrated by the commercial fishery of Lake Erie between 1880 and 2000. Initially, the fishery landed mainly high-value species, but they were over-fished and their stocks soon collapsed, although not all at the same time. Lake sturgeon (*Acipenser fulvescens*) and lake herring (*Coregonus artedii*) were the first to be extirpated from the lake **(Figure 15.7a)**, followed soon after by sauger (*Stizostedion canadense*) and blue pike (*Stizostedion vitreum glaucum*) (**Figure 15.7b**; the latter became globally extinct). Walleye (*Stizostedion vitreum vitreum*) and lake whitefish (*Coregonus clupeaformis*) have managed to survive, although in a variable abundance, partly depending on how well their harvest was managed **(Figure 15.7c)**. As the initially valuable species declined, they were replaced in the fishery by smaller species of lower commercial value, such as yellow perch (*Perca flavescens*), rainbow smelt (*Osmerus mordax*), sheepshead (*Aplodinotus grunniens*), and white bass (*Morone chrysops*) **(Figure 15.7d, e)**. Interestingly, the aggregate landings did not change much over the 120 years of record, although there was a substantial degradation of the quality of the fish being caught.

A broadly similar pattern of working-down occurred during the harvesting of the great temperate forests of eastern Canada following the European colonization. In Nova Scotia, for example, the original forest was an older mixed-species community that was dominated by immense individuals of white pine (*Pinus strobus*), red spruce (*Picea rubens*), eastern hemlock (*Tsuga canadensis*), yellow birch (*Betula alleghaniensis*), and several other species. The first commercial harvest was a selective one for the largest white pines, which were tall and straight and therefore highly prized for use as masts for the sailing ships of the time, particularly for naval vessels. The next harvest was also selective, but more intensive in that it removed the smaller pines and the larger red spruce, hemlock, and big hardwood trees, which were used to manufacture large-dimension lumber to construct buildings, wooden ships, and furniture. The secondary forest that regenerated was then harvested as soon as the trees were big enough to be sawn into lumber, so that the original old-growth condition was never re-attained. Late in the 19th century, a technology was developed to manufacture paper out of tree biomass, and this led to clear-cut harvesting of all trees for use as pulp, firewood, small-dimension lumber, and other uses for which relatively small and low-quality trees are suitable. Today, forests are still extensive in Nova Scotia and they continue to support a large forestry-based industry, but the harvesting almost entirely involves clear-cutting for the production of pulp, small lumber, and fuelwood. The harvest rotation is only 40–80 years, and there are virtually no stands older than 100 years.

Bill Freedman

Large, straight individuals of white pine (*Pinus strobus*) were an initial target of selective commercial timber harvesting in North America. When this primary resource was harvested, the working-down process then switched to lower-value species, and eventually led to area-harvesting methods such as clear-cutting. This white pine is growing in a region of Precambrian Shield in south-central Ontario.

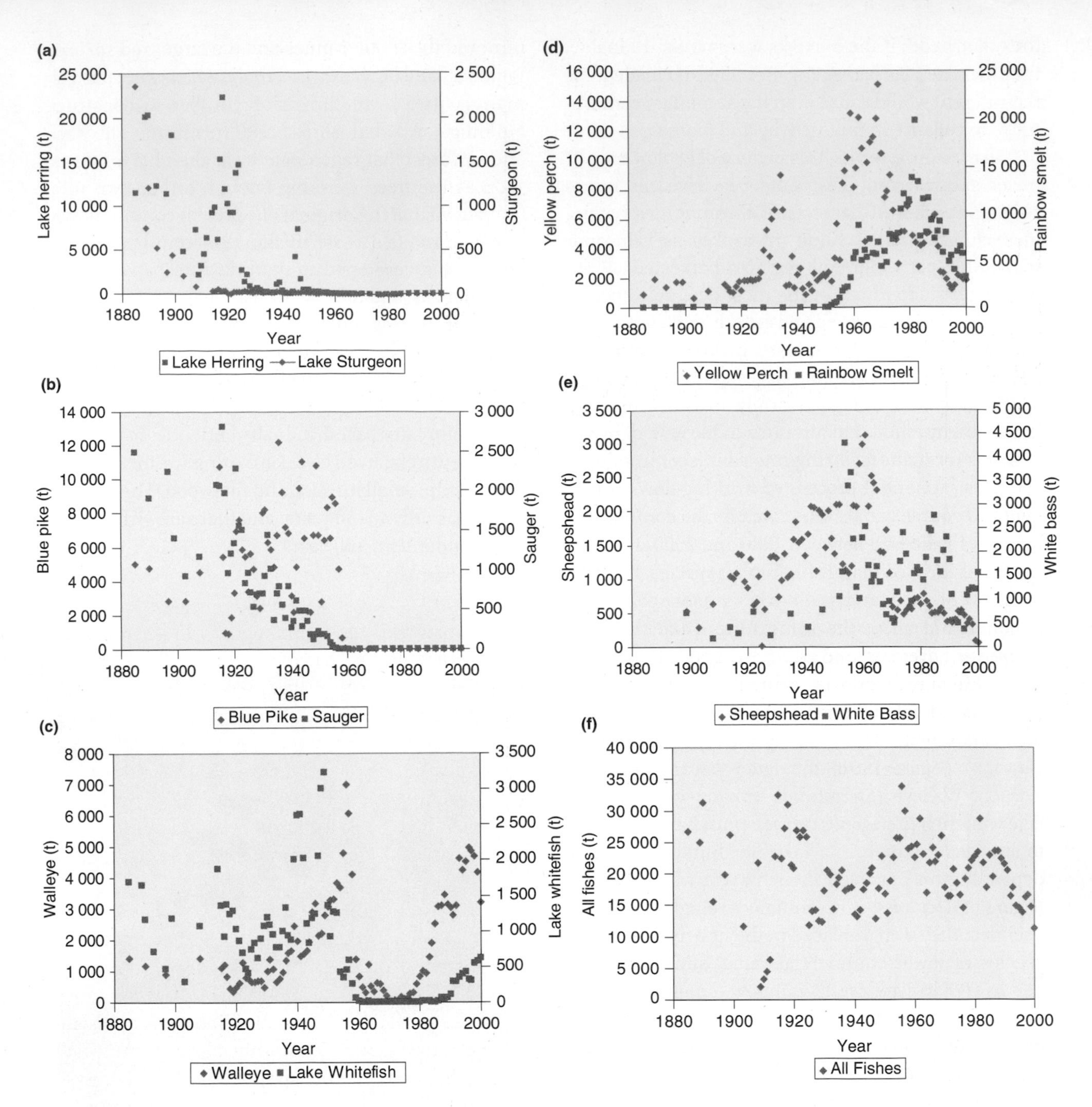

FIGURE 15.7

Historical Changes in the Fishery of Lake Erie. The data show changes in the commercial landings of lake herring (*Coregonus artedii*), lake sturgeon (*Acipenser fulvescens*), blue pike (*Stizostedion vitreum glaucum*), sauger (*Stizostedion canadense*), walleye (*Stizostedion vitreum vitreum*), lake whitefish (*Coregonus clupeaformis*), yellow perch (*Perca flavescens*), rainbow smelt (*Osmerus mordax*), sheepshead (*Aplodinotus grunniens*), white bass (*Morone chrysops*), and all fish.

SOURCE: Baldwin, N. A., R. W. Saalfeld, M. R. Dochoda, H. J. Buettner, and R. L. Eshenroder. 2002. *Commercial Fish Production in the Great Lakes 1867–2000*. Great Lakes Fishery Commission, Ann Arbor, MI. http://www.glfc.org/databases/commercial/commerc.php

Why Are Potentially Renewable Resources Overharvested?

An economy can function over the longer term only if it has sustained access to harvests of bio-resources, which are required as food, medicine, and energy, and to manufacture into various products. If this is the case, why is it that so many biological resources, all of which are potentially renewable, are depleted through overharvesting or other damages, such as conversion into other land-uses? Such mining of bio-resources can only be viewed as being a foolish and maladaptive behaviour, yet it has happened many times and continues to occur.

The seemingly self-destructive commercial activity of the mining of renewable resources can be rationalized in several ways. In the context of ecological economics, the reasons do not make much sense, but nevertheless they are the rationale for the wanton destruction of the biological resources that are needed by both present and future generations of people. The reasons are as follows:

1. *Humans are self-viewed as being legitimately empowered.* People have long held an anthropocentric ethic that presumes they have the right to take whatever they want from the natural world for the purposes of subsistence or other economic benefits. For many people, this ethic is based on the biblical story of creation, in which God is believed to have directed humans to "be fruitful, and multiply, and replenish the earth, and subdue it" and to "have dominion over the fish of the sea, and over the fowl of the air, and over the cattle, and over all the earth and over every creeping thing that creepeth upon the earth" (Genesis 1:28). Lynn White (1967) labelled this as the "**Judeo-Christian ethic**," although it is also held by other faiths, including Islam, whose beliefs include the account of anthropocentric empowerment as described in Genesis. Clearly, from an ecological perspective, this is an arrogant attitude, but it is typical of the world's dominant cultures and religions. This commanding world-view has had a profound influence on modern economic and technological ethics, and it serves to legitimize the mining of potentially renewable resources, as well as the collateral ecological damage that is often caused.
2. *Individuals and groups are self-interested.* Individual people, families, local societies, companies, and other self-identified groups are intrinsically self-interested. This attitude is responsible for many cases of irresponsible behaviour that may provide short-term benefits, even while damage is caused to other interests. In this context, the rapid depletion of both non-renewable and renewable resources, as well as the associated ecological damage, is often discounted as being unimportant. This is partly because the prevailing economic system treats both resources and environmental quality as being **common-property resources** (equity shared by all of society). Within such a context, self-interested individuals or groups that are causing damage are able to offload most of the consequences to the rest of society, and to the natural world. Garrett Hardin (1968) called this economic misadventure the "**tragedy of the commons.**" He explained it using the analogy of a publicly owned pasture (a commons) to which all local farmers had open access for grazing their livestock. Because each farmer is self-interested, they believed that they would benefit financially by grazing as many as possible of their own animals on the commonly owned pasture. However, because all of the farmers did this, the pasture became badly degraded by overgrazing. Hardin's conclusion was that "freedom in a commons brings ruin to all," and this has proven true in the foolish overharvesting of many renewable resources.
3. *Humans are socio-technologically empowered.* The defining attribute of modern *Homo sapiens* is our extraordinary and unprecedented ability to harvest natural resources, manufacture products, and increase our population and those of our mutualist species, while at the same time wreaking havoc on the natural world. In essence, these actions can occur because our species has achieved a high level of **socio-cultural evolution**. This is not biological evolution, which is characterized by changes in the collective genetic information embedded among the individual genomes of a population. Rather, socio-cultural evolution involves a progressive and adaptive improvement of the collective knowledge, means of social organization, and technological infrastructure in a society. For perhaps 99 percent of the history of *Homo sapiens,* all people were engaged in a hunting-and-gathering lifestyle, but then about 10 000 years ago the first inklings of agricultural practices were discovered and quickly became widespread (this is known as the Neolithic agricultural revolution). Since that time, there have been many additional and cumulative socio-cultural improvements, and all of them have contributed to the extraordinary empowerment of the present human population to exert its will over the biosphere. Today, if the right choices are made, people could implement a sustainable economy that would provide health and livelihoods for present and future generations, while also accommodating the needs of other species and natural ecosystems. Alternatively, choices might be made to continue overharvesting and degrading the natural capital of the planet, while causing a holocaust of biodiversity, or even to just blow everything up with a nuclear big bang. Any of these scenarios, plus others, is plausible, in view of the present state of socio-cultural evolution of our species.
4. *A cornucopian world-view.* Many people perceive nature and its resources to be boundless—unlimited in extent, quantity, and productivity. This is referred to as the "cornucopian" world-view (after the mythical "horn of plenty" that provides limitless food and other necessities). This view was relatively harmless when both the human population and our per capita use of resources were small. Today, however, it is clear that Earth has limited resources available for use

by the human economy, and most of them are already depleted or are being rapidly taken there by excessive use.

5. *A false economy.* As we noted earlier in this chapter, the reckoning of profit by conventional economics often fails to capture important damages that economic activities cause to the stocks and viability of natural resources, and also to biodiversity and ecological services. For instance, as we noted earlier, the more than US$3 billion spent to clean up and compensate the damage caused by the *Exxon Valdez* oil spill in 1989 should not be viewed as adding to the gross domestic product. Rather, it should be realistically and truthfully understood to be adding to the "natural debt," detracting from profit, and not contributing to sustainable economic development. Another aspect of a false economy is the commonly held perception that investments of money in some economic sectors will accumulate profit faster than the rate at which many bio-resources are growing. For instance, an older stand of forest might be accumulating biomass at a rate of only 3–5 percent per year, whereas money invested in stock-based equities might return 10 percent per year. If this were the case, then greater short-term profit might be made by liquidating a bio-resource (such as a stand of forest) and then investing the money earned in a faster growing sector of the economy. In fact, many regional and national economies have jump-started their economic growth by mining their "capital" of natural resources, including biological ones. Of course, this is an unrealistic financial system, because any sustainable economy ultimately depends on reliable flows of renewable resources.

The key lesson of ecological economics is that resource depletion and ecological damages detract from sustainable development. These damages are not free goods—in fact, they pose grave risks to future generations of humans and to the natural world more generally. These truths must become more widely acknowledged than they are at present. Once that is done, it will become possible to make great strides of progress toward the design and implementation of intelligent strategies for using natural resources and for sustaining biodiversity. In fact, that is what ecologically sustainable development is all about.

15.3 Resource Ecology in Practice

In this section, we will examine applications of the principles of resource ecology to the harvesting and management of a selection of biological resources that are important in the Canadian economy. This is a big subject area, so we cannot be exhaustive in the treatment. Rather, the intent is to provide an overview of key subject areas and their application, with particular emphasis on forestry and fisheries.

Forests and Forestry

Forests

A forest is any tree-dominated ecosystem. However, some trees grow rather quickly, and in such cases a forest may develop within only a few decades of a stand-replacing disturbance. Nevertheless, it might take centuries of development for the old-growth character of late-successional forest communities to become expressed. In general, forests have a complex physical structure, which is characterized by heterogeneity in both horizontal and vertical planes. The structural complexity involves the ways that biomass, especially of trees, is arranged within the community, as well as variations in the distributions of species. The occurrence of dead biomass may also be important, including large woody debris, such as standing dead trees (snags) and logs lying on the forest floor. Older forests store a higher density of living biomass-carbon (expressed per unit area) than any other kind of ecosystem. Moreover, forest communities sustain a relatively high density of biodiversity, which might be measured as the number of species occurring per hectare (of all organisms, including plants, animals, and microbes).

Forests cover about 402 million ha of Canada, or 41 percent of the terrestrial area of our country (CCFM, 2010). About 310 million ha are closed forest and 92 million ha are more open woodland and taiga. Forests are subjected to natural disturbances—in 2006, wildfires affected more than 3 million ha, and irruptions of tree-damaging insects about 20 million ha.

Forest Resources and Economy

Forests are also, of course, a source of valuable renewable resources. Tree biomass is the most important bio-resource that is harvested from forests. It is used as a feedstock to manufacture lumber or paper, and as a source of energy. Forest resources of secondary economic importance include hunted animals such as deer and fish, maple sugar and Christmas trees, as well as opportunities for outdoor recreation. Predictable flows of clean water are also a valuable resource that can be "harvested" from forested watersheds. In addition, forests provide notable ecological services that are not conventionally valuated, such as the storage of carbon, provision of oxygen, cleansing of the environment of pollutants, and control of erosion.

Bill Freedman

Forest resources are important to the national economy of Canada. In recent years, about 1 million hectares of mature forest have been harvested annually, about 90 percent by clear-cutting. This photo shows an area of clear-cut older montane forest on central Vancouver Island.

The forest resources of Canada are important to our national economy. In 2006, about 998 000 hectares of forest were harvested (91 percent of that area by clear-cutting) (CCFM, 2010). Tree seedlings were planted on 45 percent of the harvested area, and the rest regenerated naturally. The forest industry contributes about 3 percent of the GDP of Canada, or $78 billion (in 2007), including $23 billion to the balance of trade (this is the value of exports minus imports within the forest-products sector). About 294 000 Canadians are directly employed in the forest industries, plus another 453 000 in jobs that are indirect (CFS, 2010). Canada's harvest of wood for industrial use was 203×10^6 m^3 in 2006, accounting for 12 percent of the global total, and we are the world's leading exporter of forest products (US$29 billion in 2006), accounting for 14 percent of global exports (WRI, 2010).

Forest Harvesting and Management

Forestry is an applied aspect of ecological science that is concerned with the harvesting and management of trees and related forest resources. The focus is on the growing and nurturing of trees, also known as silviculture. However, foresters and forest ecologists are also concerned with wildlife of all descriptions on the forest estate, as well as protected areas, the management of aquatic resources, recreational opportunities, carbon storage, and related topics.

Forests may be harvested in various ways. By far the dominant system used in Canada is **clear-cutting** (91 percent of timber harvesting in 2006), in which all of the trees in an affected stand are harvested at the same time. Three other harvesting methods are variations of clear-cutting: (1) a shelterwood cut leaves 20–40 percent of the trees standing for several years to foster the establishment of tree seedlings (this method accounts for 3 percent of timber harvesting; once the seedlings are established the larger trees are harvested, completing the staged clear-cut); (2) a seed-tree cut (0.5 percent) leaves a few trees standing as a source of seeds for the regenerating cutover; and (3) a commercial thin (5 percent) removes some trees from a regenerating stand, with the intention of reducing competition and encouraging faster growth of those that are not harvested during a thinning operation.

Selection-cutting (or **uneven-aged management**) takes only some of the larger trees during a harvest (typically 20–40 percent, depending on the forest community), so that the physical and ecological integrity of the stand is left substantially intact. Selection-cutting accounts for about 5 percent of the area harvested in Canada. This non-clear-cutting method is particularly suited to the management of older-growth forest in humid climatic regions, which are rarely affected by natural stand-replacing disturbances. Clear-cutting is more appropriate to forest types that regenerate from periodic catastrophic disturbances, such as those caused by wildfire or epidemics of tree-killing insects. Of course, all methods of timber harvesting result in substantial ecological changes, but in general they are much less with selection-cutting than with clear-cutting.

The intensity of post-harvest management in forestry also varies greatly. The low-intensity end of the spectrum relies on *natural regeneration* to establish the next forest. As discussed earlier, this essentially depends on

- vegetative regeneration of tree species that can re-grow from cut stumps or rhizome systems;
- the growth of the advanced regeneration of small individuals of tree species that survive the timber harvest and then grow quickly because they are released from ecological stresses exerted by the previous overstorey; and

- new seedlings that establish either from a seed-bank in the original forest floor, or from seeds that blow in from elsewhere.

Natural regeneration can work well to establish a new forest after timber harvesting, although in areas that experience summer drought, enough trees may not re-grow, resulting in so-called "insufficiently regenerated" clear-cuts that may have to be planted with tree seedlings. Of course, natural regeneration requires no direct investment from the forest industry, because it relies on "free" ecological services to establish the post-harvest forest.

At the other end of the spectrum of management intensity are systems that are used to establish a **plantation** on a clear-cut site. In essence, a plantation is a "tree-farm," in which a crop of trees is sown and managed on a relatively short harvest rotation. A typical plantation may be established as follows:

- A clear-cut harvest is made of a natural stand of mixed-species forest.
- The clear-cut is site-prepared for planting using a prescribed burn of the logging debris, or by large machines that crush the logging slash and scarify (expose mineral soil) parts of the forest floor (site preparation was carried out on 273 000 ha in 2006; CCFM, 2010).
- The site is planted with tree seedlings at an optimal density (in 2006, 641 million seedlings, almost all conifers, were planted on 450 000 hectares).
- If the seedlings are subjected to intense competition from non-crop plants, they may be "released" by manual cutting of the "weeds," or more commonly by a herbicide treatment that damages the weeds but not the conifers (in 2006, 238 000 hectares received a release treatment, usually a spray of the herbicide glyphosate).
- If, at the sapling stage of plantation development, the regenerating trees are too dense, there may be a pre-commercial thin to reduce the intensity of competition (i.e., some of the saplings are cut, but no biomass is harvested).
- If the regeneration is too dense at the small-tree stage of development, there may be a commercial thin to reduce competition (the cut trees are large enough to be harvested).
- Once trees in the plantation are economically mature, it is harvested by a clear-cut and the entire process is repeated; depending on the species and intended use of the biomass, the harvest rotation may range from only 2–4 decades (for pulpwood) to as long as 80–100 years (for larger-dimension lumber).
- At any time during the process described above, attempts are made to quench any fires that might ignite in the plantation, and it may be necessary to use insecticide to protect the crop (and its financial investments) against insect infestations that might kill the trees.

Forest Productivity

The productivity and biomass accumulation of the natural forests of Canada vary enormously, depending on the climate, site conditions (especially fertility and moisture status), the species of trees in the community, and the age of the stand. **Figure 15.8** compares the rate of biomass accumulation among four typical kinds of forest. The two boreal types typically regenerate after a stand-replacing disturbance, such as a wildfire. The boreal aspen type regenerates by prolific sprouting from the surviving rhizomes of burnt or cut trees, while the spruce re-establishes by seedlings. According to the productivity models, the biomass accumulation of these two boreal types becomes asymptotic (levels off) at about 200 years of age, in large part because the growth rates of individual trees slow down, along with mortality of some individuals. The Acadian mixed-species forest occurs in a temperate

Plantations are anthropogenic forests that sustain a higher productivity of a tree crop than occurs in natural stands. Plantations are a result of the application of an agricultural model to forestry, but agroforestry requires more intensive investment and management practices than does reliance on natural regeneration. This 30-year-old spruce plantation is located in New Brunswick.

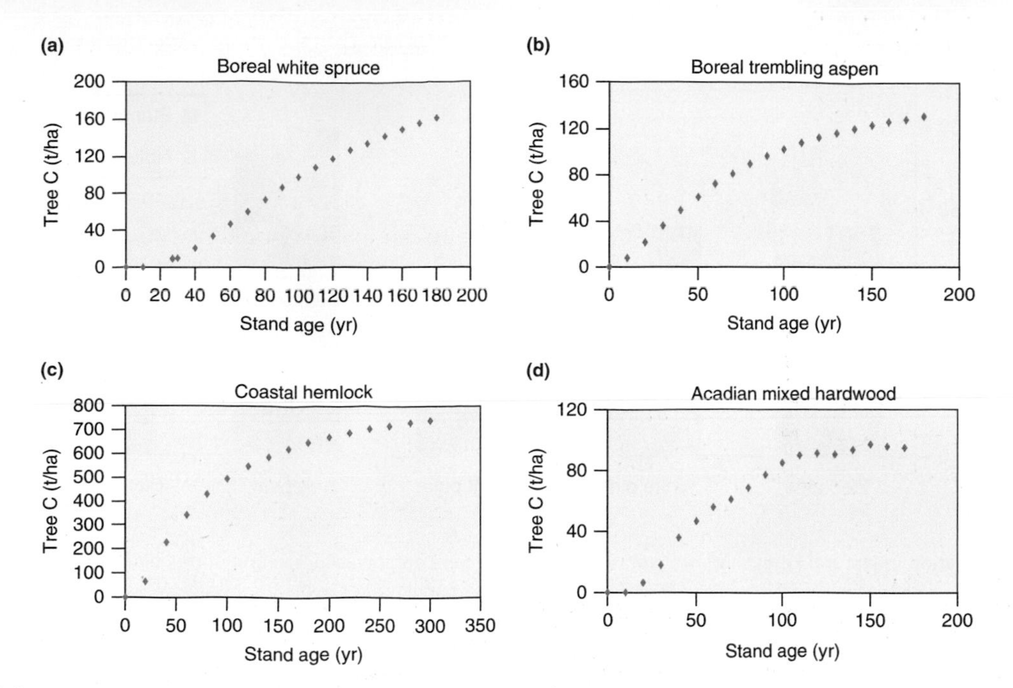

FIGURE 15.8

Biomass Accumulation in Four Kinds of Forest. The data show the patterns of accumulation of tree biomass with increasing stand age for four types of forest: (a) white spruce (*Picea glauca*) in the boreal region, (b) trembling aspen (*Populus tremuloides*) in the southern boreal, (c) western hemlock (*Tsuga heterophylla*) in the humid coastal zone of British Columbia, and (d) mixed-species tolerant hardwoods (*Acer saccharum*, *A. rubrum*, *Betula alleghaniensis*, *Fraxinus americana*) in New Brunswick. The biomass is measured in tonnes of carbon per hectare, and it refers to all living tissues of trees, both above- and below-ground. Note the changes in vertical scale for biomass. The data are predicted using stand-growth models, which are prepared for the major forest regions by governmental natural-resources agencies.

SOURCE: Data from Stinson and Freedman (2001).

climate region, but it grows on relatively infertile sites and its biomass accumulation becomes asymptotic at about 120 years. The coastal hemlock type grows in a humid climatic zone with a long growing season and with only rare catastrophic disturbances, so it can develop into an old-growth forest. This forest continues to accumulate tree biomass even after a stand age of 300 years, and the total amount of biomass is much larger than for any of the other types.

The effect of site quality is illustrated in **Figure 15.9.** Site quality is related to several local attributes, including the fertility of the soil and its depth, acidity, and moisture status. In the examples considered, which are both dominated by Douglas fir in British Columbia, higher-quality sites promote a faster growth of trees and a larger accumulation of stand biomass. However, trees growing in the humid coastal zone have a much longer and less-stressful growing season, and their productivity is much faster than occurs in the drier interior zone.

Trees growing in plantations are managed relatively intensively to promote a higher productivity. This effect is shown in **Figure 15.10** for several species of trees growing in Ontario. Remember, however, that the increased productivity of the plantations is gained as a result of investments of management, whereas the growth of natural forests does not require that expense.

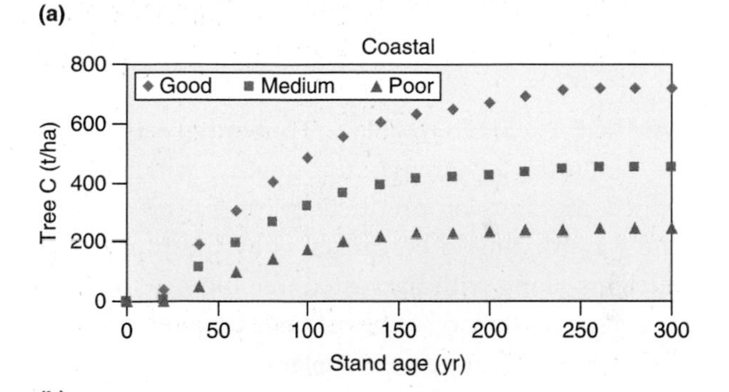

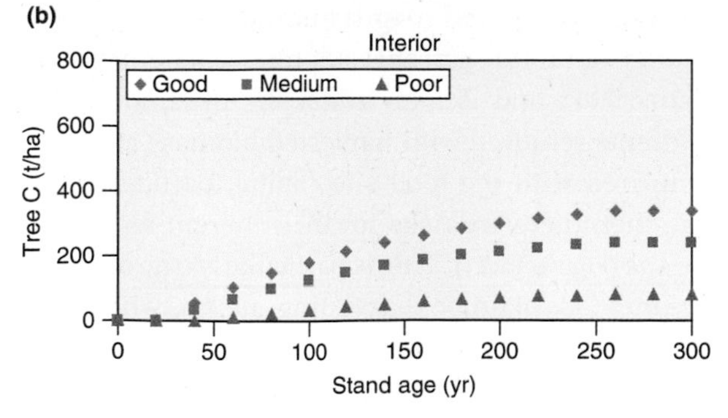

FIGURE 15.9

Biomass Accumulation in Douglas Fir Forests. The data compare the accumulation of tree biomass with increasing stand age for six stand types, all dominated by Douglas fir (*Pseudotsuga menziesii*) in British Columbia. The sites are classified as being of good, medium, or poor quality, and are in either the humid coastal zone or the drier interior.

SOURCE: Data from Freedman, B. and Keith, T. 1996. *Planting Trees for Carbon Credits. A Discussion of the Issues, Feasibility, and Environmental Benefits.* Tree Plan Canada, Ottawa, ON.

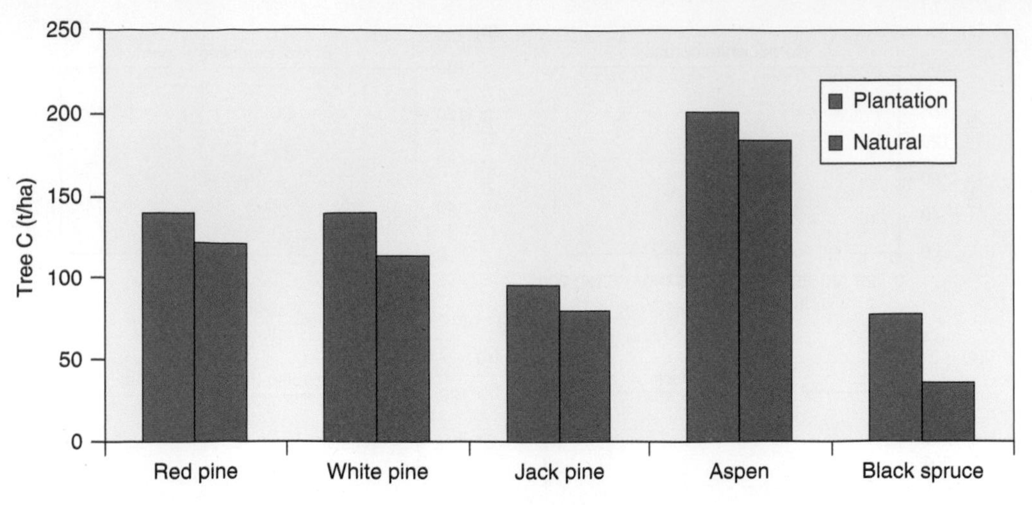

FIGURE 15.10

Biomass Accumulation in Natural Forest and in Plantations. The data compare the accumulation of tree biomass in natural forest and plantations of various species, all at stand ages of 80 years and on medium-quality sites in Ontario. Data are for red pine (*Pinus resinosa*), white pine (*P. strobus*), jack pine (*P. banksiana*), trembling aspen (*Populus tremuloides*), and black spruce (*Picea mariana*).

SOURCE: Data from Freedman, B. and Keith, T. 1996. *Planting Trees for Carbon Credits. A Discussion of the Issues, Feasibility, and Environmental Benefits.* Tree Plan Canada, Ottawa, ON.

Environmental Impacts

Many environmental damages are associated with the harvesting and management of timber and other forest resources. Because this is a large subject area, we cannot explore it in much depth. However, we can examine some of the key environmental effects of forestry that intersect with ecological values.

DAMAGE TO SITE QUALITY. Timber harvesting has the potential to damage site quality, which could reduce the rate of productivity of future forests. One way for this to be caused is by the removal of nutrients along with harvested tree biomass—about 1.5 percent of the dry weight of plant biomass consists of nitrogen, 1.0 percent potassium, 0.5 percent calcium, 0.2 percent magnesium, 0.2 percent phosphorus, and 0.1 percent sulphur (data for entire plants; Taiz and Zeiger, 2002). If the amounts of nutrients removed with harvested biomass are large compared with the total site capital, particularly in soil, then there are risks for the inherent fertility of the site **(Figure 15.11)**. This is particularly true of intensive methods of timber harvesting, such as whole-tree clear-cutting, which removes all of the above-ground tree biomass (including branches and foliage) and not just the stems as in a conventional clear-cut. If the purpose of a harvest is to recover as much biomass as possible, perhaps for use as bio-energy, then a whole-tree clear-cut typically yields 30–50 percent more biomass than would a stem-only harvest. However, the nutrient removal is increased by 100–200 percent, so the additional yield of biomass is gained at the ecological "expense" of much bigger losses of nutrients. For instance, Freedman et al. (1986) studied four stands of hardwood forest and four of conifers in Nova Scotia, and found that on average a whole-tree clear-cut would remove 50 percent more biomass than a stem-only harvest, while the increase for nitrogen was 170 percent, phosphorus 200 percent, potassium 160 percent, calcium 100 percent, and magnesium 120 percent (see also **Table 15.3**). Studies have been made of this issue in a number of places, and it has generally been found that site nutrient depletion is a potentially important consequence after several harvest rotations, particularly if whole-tree clear-cuts are made. The problem is likely to be especially acute for calcium removals in sites where the soil and bedrock are dominantly granite and related quartzitic rocks, which are relatively deficient in this substance. In addition to being a key nutrient for plants, calcium has a large influence on alkalinity, an attribute of soil and surface waters that helps to resist acidification (Chapter 5). Lakes and rivers that are vulnerable to becoming acidified by acid rain are deficient in alkalinity, and this sensitivity could potentially be made worse by calcium removals from their watershed with harvested forest biomass (Freedman et al., 1986; Jeziorski et al., 2008).

EROSION. Forestry operations can cause severe erosion, especially as a consequence of the clear-cutting of timber from steep slopes and the improper construction of woodland roads. Erosion associated with roads can usually be mitigated by installing properly sized culverts that allow streams to pass beneath the roadbed. Because of their extreme vulnerability to erosion, forests on steep slopes should not be harvested—they

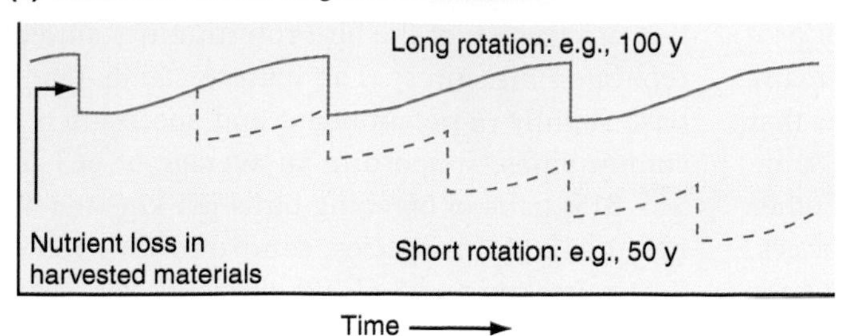

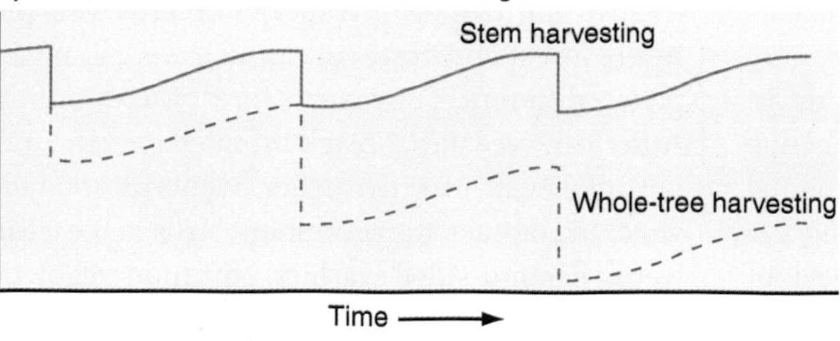

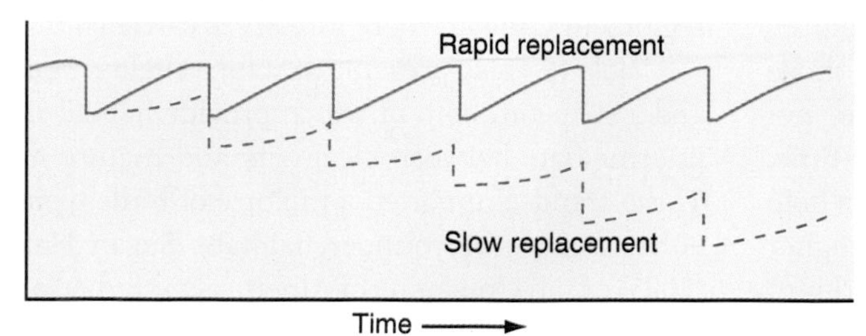

FIGURE 15.11

Conceptual Effects of Timber Harvesting on Site Fertility. Diagram (a) shows that a timber harvest removes a portion of the nutrient capital of a site, but that loss may be recovered during succession because of inputs with dustfall and precipitation from the atmosphere, as well as the weathering of soil minerals; however, if subsequent harvests are on too short a rotation, there will not be enough time for the nutrient losses to be fully replenished, so site fertility may become degraded; (b) comparison of a conventional (stem-only) clear-cut with a whole-tree harvest; the latter removes more nutrients because foliage and other rich tissues are also harvested; (c) this diagram suggests that an inherently fertile site (with rapid nutrient replacement by decomposition and other processes) can sustain a higher intensity of nutrient removals than a less-fertile one.

SOURCE: Modified from Figure 5.15, p. 119 from *Forest Ecology: A Foundation for Sustainable Management*, 2nd ed. by J. P. Kimmins. Copyright © 1997 by Prentice-Hall, Inc. Reprinted by permission of Pearson Education, Inc.

TABLE 15.3 **Biomass and Nutrient Removals by a Conventional and a Whole-Tree Clear-Cut**

The harvested stand in Nova Scotia was mature and dominated by red spruce (*Picea rubens*) and balsam fir (*Abies balsamea*). The tree stems and other above-ground biomass (branches and foliage) were weighed separately and sub-sampled to determine their water and nutrient contents. The percent increase is that of the whole-tree removals compared with the stem-only ones. The forest floor and upper mineral soil are key components of the longer-term site capital of nutrients, which may become diminished by repeated removals with harvested biomass.

Compartment	Biomass (t/ha)	N (kg/ha)	P (kg/ha)	K (kg/ha)	Ca (kg/ha)	Mg (kg/ha)
Trees above ground	153	239	35	133	337	37
Stems	118	120	18	76	219	20
Branches & foliage	35	119	17	57	118	17
Increase	30%	99%	94%	75%	54%	85%
Forest floor (8 cm)	45	900	62	110	290	32
Mineral soil (to 30 cm)	170	3860	1220	13 300	5460	1740

SOURCE: Data from Freedman, B., R. Morash, and A. J. Hanson. 1981. "Biomass and nutrient removals by conventional and whole tree clear-cutting of a red spruce balsam fir stand in central Nova Scotia," *Canadian Journal of Forest Research*, 11: 249–257.

should be left to provide their vital environmental service of keeping the soil in place. On more moderate slopes, the best mitigation against erosion involves leaving uncut strips of forest, known as **riparian buffers**, beside watercourses. However, when working in steep terrain, some amount of erosion is inevitable because of disturbances associated with timber harvesting. Severe erosion can strip away the soil, even to bedrock, which can make the local regeneration of a forest impossible. Eroded materials that reach watercourses eventually settle out in slow-moving reaches of streams and rivers, or in lakes. The gravelly spawning habitat of salmonid fish can be destroyed if there is excessive sedimentation of fine particles, which in-fill and smother the interstices of the rocky beds. Aquatic habitat is also damaged if excessive amounts of logging debris (known as slash) are deposited into streams, where it may block the movements of fish and other animals.

BIODIVERSITY. Timber harvesting represents a severe disturbance of a forest ecosystem, and it profoundly changes habitat conditions for the many species of animals, plants, and microorganisms that lived in the original mature community. At the same time, however, habitat is created for a variety of other species that prefer to inhabit recently disturbed places, including regenerating clear-cuts. The challenge for forestry operations is to ensure that species that are dependent on older habitats do not become endangered because of the diminishment of their habitat as a result of too much timber harvesting.

It is not enough to achieve this goal only in particular stands of habitat, because they will change over time in response to either natural environmental influences or to anthropogenic ones, including the harvesting of trees. Therefore, this broad goal of conserving biodiversity must be met at a larger spatial scale—that of landscape. For this to happen, it is important that not all stands of mature or older-growth forest are harvested—large tracts should be set aside as protected areas to accommodate those elements of biodiversity whose needs are not compatible with forestry operations. At the same time, certain modifications of harvesting practices can help to mitigate some effects on habitat, allowing higher levels of biodiversity to be supported in "working" areas. If these steps are taken in a planned and balanced manner at the landscape scale, then commercial forestry operations can be conducted, even while native biodiversity is sustained at a viable level of abundance. In fact, in a forestry context, this is the essence of the idea of ecological sustainability, which we have already examined several times.

The effects of forestry on biodiversity are too large a subject area to investigate in detail in a textbook like this one. There are two reasons for this: (1) there are many ways of harvesting timber and then of managing regenerating forests, and (2) the resulting ecological effects vary enormously depending on the kinds of species and communities that are being affected. Rather than examining this complexity in depth, we will draw out some ecological generalities by focusing only on timber harvesting, and especially clear-cutting, which is the dominant method used in Canada, and on effects on vertebrate animals, particularly birds.

In general, when a stand of forest is clear-cut, a community of birds that occurs in mature habitat becomes totally displaced by a different one that prefers younger vegetation. This effect is illustrated by a study by Bill Freedman and colleagues from Dalhousie University, who compared the avian species present in three mature stands of mixed-species hardwood forest and three recent clear-cuts (**Table 15.4**; this study involved several replicates of these treatments; try examining these data more closely to gain an appreciation of variation of the bird communities among the replicated measures). The mature stands tended to have slightly more abundant and species-rich avian communities, supporting an average of 663 (range 515–815) pairs of breeding birds per km^2 and a richness of 12 (9–16) species, compared with 588 (435–745) pairs/km^2 and 8 (7–10) species in the clear-cuts (none of the differences are statistically significant). However, these community-level indicators do not tell us anything about which species of birds were present in the forest and clear-cuts, which were almost completely different. The mature forest was dominated by American redstart, black-throated green warbler, hermit thrush, least flycatcher, ovenbird, and red-eyed vireo. In contrast, the prominent birds in the clear-cuts were chestnut-sided warbler, common yellowthroat, dark-eyed junco, song sparrow, and white-throated sparrow. All of the birds in this study are native species, which is typical of the avifaunal communities of regions in Canada where forestry is carried out.

Table 15.4 also presents data for a shelter-wood cut and a strip-cut, both of which provide habitat that is intermediate between clear-cuts and mature forest. These stands supported a mixture of birds typical of either mature or younger habitats. Susan Hannon (2005) of the University of Alberta also studied a wide range of harvest types, including stands in northern Alberta that had been selectively harvested, a method that leaves numerous trees standing and much of the physical integrity of the forest intact. This work also found that the relatively open-treed harvested stands supported a mixture of species typical of younger or older habitats. However, the important observation was also made that some birds that occur in older forest were not present in the selectively harvested stands. As such, Hannon's research suggests that selective cutting, a relatively "soft" method of timber harvesting, is an effective mitigation for some species of birds, but not for all of them. Because the latter species are dependent on older forest, they must be sustained on the landscape by ensuring that a network of protected areas is designated to accommodate their needs. Hannon identified a number of specialists of older forest, including brown creeper (*Certhia familiaris*), red-breasted nuthatch (*Sitta canadensis*), boreal chickadee (*Parus hudsonicus*), golden-crowned kinglet (*Regulus satrapa*), Swainson's thrush (*Catharus ustulatus*), black-throated green warbler (*Dendroica virens*), and bay-breasted warbler (*Dendroica castanea*). Hannon mostly studied songbirds, but some larger forest birds are also specialists that require old-growth forest, including the northern spotted owl (*Strix occidentalis caurina*) and marbled murrelet (*Brachyramphus marmoratus*) in British Columbia.

TABLE 15.4	**Birds in Various Forest Habitats**

The mature forest consists of mixed-species stands dominated by maples and birches in Nova Scotia. The harvested stands are 3–5 years old and are regenerating naturally. The clear-cuts had all trees removed, while about 40 percent of the trees were retained on the shelter-wood cut, and the strip-cut area had alternating 30 m-wide strips of mature forest and linear clear-cuts. There are three replicates of the mature forest and clear-cuts. The avian data are in pairs of breeding birds per km^2. Only abundant species are listed here.

Species	Mature Forest			Clear-Cuts			Shelter-wood	Strip-Cut
Common snipe (*Capella gallinago*)	0	0	0	10	15	0	0	0
Ruby-throated hummingbird (*Archilochus colubris*)	0	0	0	25	30	15	0	0
Least flycatcher (*Empidonax minimus*)	290	120	0	0	0	0	140	60
Hermit thrush (*Catharus guttatus*)	60	40	30	0	0	0	0	15
Veery (*Catharus fuscescens*)	50	10	0	25	0	0	0	15
Solitary vireo (*Vireo solitarius*)	60	30	0	0	0	0	0	15
Red-eyed vireo (*Vireo olivaceous*)	80	50	30	0	0	0	80	30
Black-and-white warbler (*Mniotilta varia*)	15	50	40	0	0	0	0	70
Northern parula (*Parula americana*)	15	30	40	0	0	0	0	10
Black-throated green warbler (*Dendroica virens*)	50	30	30	0	0	0	0	15
Chestnut-sided warbler (*Dendroica pensylvanica*)	0	0	0	100	40	190	110	50
Ovenbird (*Seiurus aurocapillus*)	150	120	200	0	0	0	0	60
Mourning warbler (*Oporornis philadelphia*)	0	0	0	0	0	90	80	20
Common yellowthroat (*Geothlypis trichas*)	0	0	0	25	300	130	80	0
American redstart (*Setophaga ruticilla*)	15	80	100	0	0	0	30	90
Rose-breasted grosbeak (*Pheucticus ludovicianus*)	15	10	0	0	0	0	0	0
Dark-eyed junco (*Junco hyemalis*)	15	20	15	50	70	30	0	25
White-throated sparrow (*Zonotrichia albicollis*)	0	20	0	90	190	100	30	0
Song sparrow (*Melospiza melodia*)	0	0	0	90	70	0	0	0
Total density	815	660	515	435	745	585	550	425
Species richness	12	16	9	10	8	7	7	13

SOURCE: Data from Freedman, B., R. Morash, and A. J. Hanson. 1981. "Biomass and nutrient removals by conventional and whole tree clear-cutting of a red spruce balsam fir stand in central Nova Scotia," *Canadian Journal of Forest Research,* 11: 249–257.

The marbled murrelet (*Brachyramphus marmoratus*) is at conservation risk throughout its range in western North America because of the loss of its breeding habitat of old-growth forest through timber harvesting. It is a critically endangered species in southern British Columbia.

Tim Zurowski/All Canada Photos

As clear-cuts regenerate, birds typical of mature forest begin to invade the community as soon as a suitable habitat develops for them during the process of succession. However, species do this at different times, so in stands of intermediate structure you find a mixture of bird species typical of both mature and younger habitats. This effect is apparent in a study of post–clear-cutting stands of black-spruce boreal forest in northern Ontario (Welsh and Fillman, 1980). The uncut forest was dominated by Tennessee warbler (*Vermivora peregrina*), yellow-rumped warbler (*Dendroica coronata*), least flycatcher (*Empidonax minimus*), Nashville warbler (*Vermivora ruficapilla*), Cape May warbler (*Dendroica tigrina*), and ruby-crowned kinglet (*Regulus calendula*). These species invaded regenerating clear-cuts as they matured, but at different times. The Tennessee and Nashville warblers did so first, breeding in stands only 5 years old, while least flycatcher, Cape May warbler, and ruby-crowned kinglet did so later, at 11 years. The clear-cuts examined in this study had embedded remnants of trees that had not been harvested, and this may have allowed some of the forest birds to re-invade relatively early. Interestingly, the highest levels of avian abundance and species richness occurred not in mature spruce forest, but in stands of an intermediate age following clear-cutting (17–19 years old). This was presumably because of a greater habitat complexity and better availability of invertebrate foods for breeding birds in the transitional stands. Similar observations have been made in other studies of post–clear-cutting recovery, such as one in eastern hardwood forest, where the richness of the avian community peaked at 20–40 years (Morgan and Freedman, 1986; see **Figure 10.5**). These observations are compatible with the intermediate disturbance hypothesis that we examined in Chapter 9.

The most intensively managed habitats in forestry are plantations, which in Canada are typically planted to a single conifer species and may then be subjected to herbicide spraying, thinning, and other silvicultural treatments. Plantations begin as clear-cuts, and when mature they support a cohort of trees of the same age, usually of the same species, that are regularly spaced in rows and have a dense canopy whose shade does not allow much vegetation to grow on the forest floor. As such, plantations have a relatively simple structure, in both the physical sense and in terms of their plant community. Nevertheless, some birds are able to breed abundantly in forestry plantations. This is illustrated in **Figure 15.12** for a series of conifer plantations of various ages in southern New Brunswick, plus stands of natural forest of the type that had been clear-cut and converted. These data show that the youngest plantations, aged less than 5 years, had a relatively low abundance and richness of breeding birds, but as the trees grew larger these community indicators increased. In fact, plantations aged 13–21 years maintained a higher abundance and species richness of birds than did the natural mixed-species forest in the area. The most abundant birds in the older plantations were yellow-bellied flycatcher (*Empidonax flavifrons*), magnolia warbler (*Dendroica magnolia*), yellow-rumped warbler (*Dendroica coronata*), palm warbler (*Dendroica palmarum*), common yellowthroat, and white-throated sparrow, most of which also occurred in the natural forest, but in lower abundance.

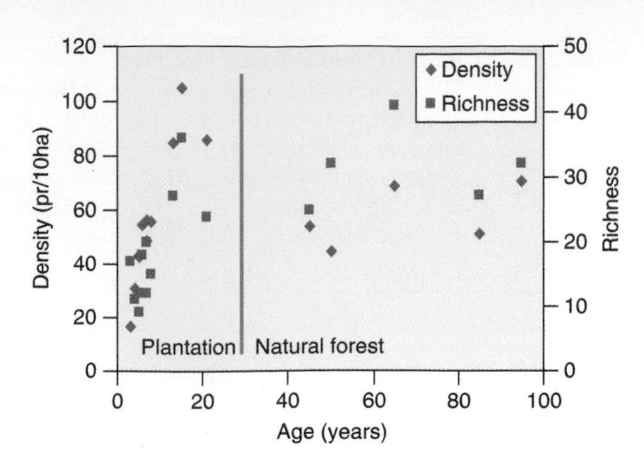

FIGURE 15.12

Bird Communities in Conifer Plantations and Natural Forest. The data are the densities of species of breeding birds, and the numbers of species present. Stands aged up to 21 years are spruce plantations, while those 45–95 years old are natural mixed-species forest. The study area is in southern New Brunswick.

SOURCE: Data from Johnson, G. A. M. and B. Freedman. 2002. "Breeding birds in forestry plantations and natural forest in the vicinity of Fundy National Park, New Brunswick," *Canadian Field-Naturalist*, 116: 475–487.

Although maturing plantations can support abundant avifauna, there is an important guild of birds that do not utilize them much as breeding habitat—these are species that require tree-cavities as a component of their habitat. Cavity-dependent species use these hollow features as places in which to nest, and also for roosting at night. The most prominent group of birds that do this is woodpeckers, of which 12 species breed in Canada, all of whom excavate cavities in heart-rotted trees, particularly in angiosperm trees such as aspen and maple. In addition, many other species are secondary users of cavities that woodpeckers have excavated but then abandoned, or they use naturally formed tree-hollows. Trees with cavities are regular components of the habitat in older natural forests, but they are typically rare in plantations. This is because the older trees or snags that have cavities are either harvested, or they are deemed to be "non-commercial" or hazardous and are knocked down while preparing the site for planting to conifer seedlings. **Figure 15.13** shows that conifer plantations studied in New Brunswick have almost no snags

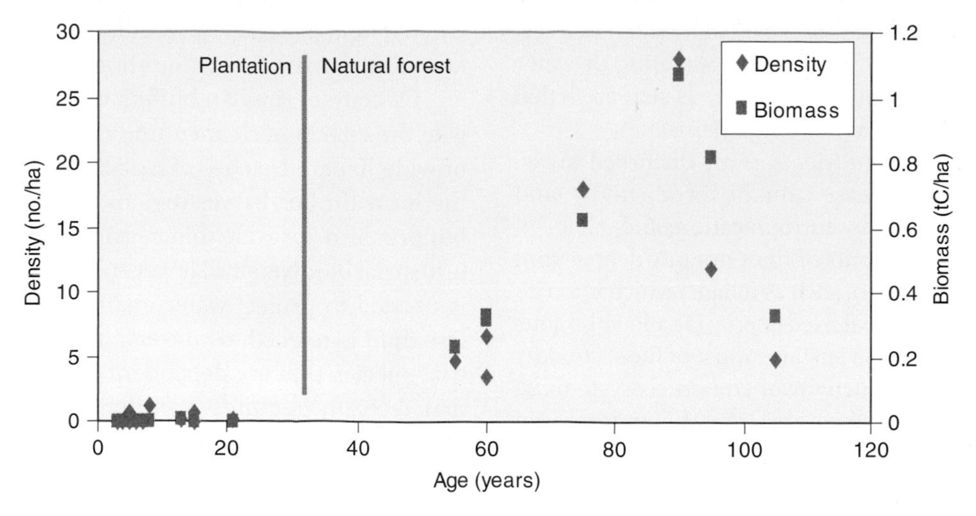

FIGURE 15.13

Snags in Conifer Plantations and Natural Forest. The data are the density and biomass of snags (standing dead trees). Stands aged up to 21 years are spruce plantations, while those older than 55 years are natural mixed-species forest. The study area is in southern New Brunswick.

SOURCE: data from Fleming, T. L. and B. Freedman. 1998. "Conversion of natural, mixed-species forests to conifer plantations: Implications for dead organic matter and carbon storage," *Ecoscience*, 5: 213–221.

(standing dead trees), which are important sources of cavity trees, whereas they are abundant in the natural forest, although to varying degrees among stands. In that region, stands with a higher abundance of snags had suffered damage from windstorms or insect infestations within the past decade or so.

The importance of cavities to some species of birds was shown by an experiment that involved placing artificial nest-boxes in a variety of plantations in New Brunswick (Woodley et al., 2006). In plantations, birds used the artificial cavities for nesting or roosting at a rate of 6.9/10 ha, compared with only 0.3/10 ha in the natural forest, where cavities were abundant. These data suggest that cavities are a limiting resource for a variety of species in plantations, and that is a reason why few of them breed in that kind of anthropogenic forest.

Because plantations are intended to be harvested by clear-cutting on a relatively short rotation, they will never develop cavity-trees and so will not be able to support species of birds that depend on cavities. However, to some degree this problem can be mitigated in simple ways, such as leaving existing cavity-trees standing during the clear-cut, and by embedding "islands" of uncut forest within harvested tracts for the purposes of supporting large trees that can eventually develop cavities. In Nova Scotia, for example, it is now required that at least 10 "typical" trees per hectare be left standing on harvested sites, arranged within no-harvest clumps with at least 30 trees in each, and at least 1 clump per 8 ha, located no more than 200 m apart, and within 20 m of a forested edge (NSDNR, 2009). These sorts of mitigations are being tried in various other jurisdictions, and they show promise in accommodating the needs of some cavity-dependent birds.

Another aspect of clear-cuts is that they create distinct edge habitat (ecotones) between forested and harvested areas. In agricultural and urbanized areas, edge habitats may be problematic for birds because they are places where their nests can suffer intense predation from foxes, skunks, crows, and other predators. Edges are also habitats with greater vulnerability to the brown-headed cowbird (*Molothrus ater*), a parasite that lays its eggs in the nests of other birds, whose own young usually die while the parents raise the cowbird chick. Hannon (2005) reported on a range of studies of reproductive success near edges in a forestry context, but found no consistent effect. This may be partly due to the fact that the study areas were relatively remote, so there were no predators such as the feral cats that are often found close to human settlements, and cowbirds were not abundant.

Forestry operations also affect aquatic habitats. Streams running through managed areas are at risk of being damaged in various ways, particularly by

- the **sedimentation** (deposition) of eroded fine materials, which can in-fill areas of gravelly substrate that are critical habitats used for spawning by salmonid fish;
- **turbidity**, or the suspension of eroded clay-sized materials, which can impede feeding by fish that are visual predators, and also interfere with their gill function;
- the deposition of excessive woody logging debris, which can block the movements of local fish and also prevent the long-distance migrations of anadromous species;

- the removal of shading provided by riparian trees, which can result in excessive warming of water during the summer, even to levels that are lethal to fish and other aquatic organisms;
- the leaching of nutrients from disturbed areas, which can increase aquatic productivity and degrade habitats by eutrophication; and
- a reduction of inputs of finer organic debris from riparian vegetation, such as foliage, which is a critical input of external fixed energy (as allochthonous dead biomass) that sustains most of the secondary and tertiary productivity of stream ecosystems in forested terrain (which are largely heterotrophic in their energetics).

Much of the erosion associated with forestry activities is caused by the improper construction of logging roads. This kind of damage is now routinely mitigated (although not entirely prevented) by provincial regulations that require the installation of properly sized culverts that allow streams to pass freely beneath roads. Additional measures that help to protect aquatic habitat include provisions against felling trees into streams, against depositing large amounts of logging debris in them, and against running logging machines along stream-courses. Another key measure that helps to mitigate damage to aquatic systems involves leaving riparian buffer strips of uncut forest beside waterbodies in logged areas.

The need for, and specifications of, riparian buffers are regulated by provincial and territorial governments, which have various names for these features, such as buffer zone, riparian reserve zone, and special management zone. As is often the case in Canada in contexts where provincial/territorial jurisdictions are involved, the guidelines and regulations for riparian buffers vary enormously (O'Carroll, 2004). The Northwest Territories is the only jurisdiction that has enacted mandatory no-logging reserve zones around all streams, lakes, and wetlands (with a width of at least 60 m; this and the following criteria are the minimum required widths). Manitoba requires a 100-m special management zone (SMZ) around these sorts of waterbodies, within which selective harvesting can be done, whereas British Columbia and Ontario have a 30-m SMZ requirement, and other provinces have even less stringent criteria. In Nova Scotia, the SMZ is 20 m on both sides of streams, and there must be an additional 1 m for each 2 percent increase in slope over 20 percent, to a maximum width of 60 m. New Brunswick requires a 15-m SMZ on both sides of small streams, but that doubles for stand types with a high risk of suffering wind damage after timber harvesting. Although the SMZ for Ontario is 30 m, it is 2000 m in certain streamside corridors in northwestern Ontario that are used by woodland caribou (*Rangifer tarandus*) during their migrations.

Of course, riparian buffers not only help to mitigate the effects of clear-cutting on streams, they also provide linear stretches of mature forest that survive the local timber harvesting. In this sense, riparian buffers also provide older conserved habitat for terrestrial biodiversity. However, the buffer width that is needed to protect water quality is typically much less than is needed to conserve the habitat of terrestrial species that are dependent on riparian forest—that typically requires a buffer of 100 m or more (Richardson, 2003; O'Carroll, 2004).

Emulating Natural Disturbances

The disturbance of mature forest by clear-cutting has some broad similarities to wildfire, but there are also key differences (McRae et al., 2001). Both are stand-replacing disturbances that kill the most prominent organisms in the community—the trees—after which a secondary succession begins. The initial stages of recovery of the community are dominated by ruderal plants, which are low-growing, early-successional species that are intolerant of competition. As biomass accumulates and site resources become limiting, the ruderals become replaced by more competitive species until eventually a community typical of mature and then old-growth forest is re-established. In general, changes in animal populations occur in response to alterations in the physical and vegetational attributes of their habitat, with some species preferring younger conditions, and others older ones.

The size and shape of a wildfire are highly situational, being affected by factors that influence the vulnerability of the forest community to burning (including its species composition, stand age, fuel loading, and site moisture) as well as the immediate weather conditions (especially the windspeed at the time of the burn, as well as the occurrence of a recent drought). Depending on these influences, a natural wildfire ignited by lightning may cover tens of thousands of hectares or only a few, while its boundaries are typically ragged and complex, and there will be many unburned "skips," often of relatively moist habitat. In contrast, clear-cuts are usually much smaller than areas burned by wildfire and are more uniformly arranged on the landscape, often occurring as a regular mosaic of rectangular blocks. Over a number of years, however, clear-cut areas may progress as a front of affected stands, as timber harvesting "eats away" at the original natural forest on the landscape (except for any areas that are deliberately set aside as protected). In regions where there are many smaller parcels of privately owned land, timber harvesting and other land-uses result in an especially complex mosaic of stands of varying character, but if larger blocks are being managed as a single unit, as is typical of Crown land and large private holdings, the stand types are usually larger and more uniform.

There are other important differences between wildfire and clear-cutting. One involves the presence of standing dead trees (snags) and large woody debris in the aftermath communities. These structural features, which are important as critical habitat for many animals, are abundant after most wildfires but not after clear-cuts (unless there are provisions to retain these key features). In addition, if a plantation is established after a clear-cut, the resulting forest will be highly uniform in its physical structure and community make-up, whereas regenerating burned areas are more complex in these and other ecological attributes.

Emulation forestry is a relatively new concept of modelling systems of timber harvesting and management to imitate the natural disturbance regime of a forest type, and to which its constituent species are presumably well adapted. For instance, the types of forest that develop after a stand-replacing disturbance, such as wildfire, might be viewed as being relatively compatible with clear-cutting. Forests of that type include boreal communities dominated by jack pine (*Pinus banksiana*), black spruce, or trembling aspen, as well as montane stands of ponderosa pine (*Pinus ponderosa*) or interior Douglas fir, and temperate forests of white pine or red pine (*Pinus resinosa*). These kinds of natural forest are periodically affected by stand-replacing wildfires, followed by regeneration by the establishment of a cohort of seedlings, which eventually develops an even-aged forest community similar in structure to the original. In these cases, the natural disturbance regime can be emulated to a degree by clear-cutting, followed by a light prescribed burn and establishment of a new cohort of trees by either seeding-in from nearby mature forest or by planting seedlings. The emulation would be further improved if a reasonable number of standing dead trees and tree-islands were left to imitate "skips" in a wildfire—these would also contribute to site regeneration by acting as a source of seeds.

In contrast, old-growth forests typically develop in a climatic regime that is consistently humid, so that stand-replacing disturbances are infrequent or rare. Instead, the disturbance regime involves the deaths of individual old trees, which create gaps in the canopy below which smaller trees compete to fill the vacated space. This gap-phase disturbance regime results in the development of a highly complex ecosystem in which wide ranges of sizes and ages of trees are represented, including some old ones, and usually various species are present. Old-growth forest also has large snags and abundant large-woody debris (dead logs) lying on the ground. If timber harvesting in this sort of ecosystem is to emulate the natural disturbance regime, then the best harvesting system to use would be selection harvesting every several decades. This would involve only some of the larger trees being taken during a particular harvest, so that the forest would always be physically intact and would retain the diversity of ages, sizes, and species that characterize old-growth forest. Therefore, clear-cutting is not an appropriate way to emulate the natural disturbance regime of old-growth forest, but selection harvesting can achieve that benefit.

The advantage of emulation forestry is that it can sustain most of the biodiversity and other ecological values of the forest type that is being harvested and managed, even while the human economy benefits from sustainable flows of timber and other economic products.

Marine Resources

In the sense meant here, marine resources are biological stocks that can be harvested as sources of food, chemicals, energy, or materials. They include the following:

- seaweeds (macroalgae) that are harvested from coastal waters and used as sources of industrial chemicals known as phycocolloids (alginate, agar, and carageenins), and as minor sources of food and medicine;
- invertebrates, particularly edible species of crustaceans and mollusks;
- fish, which are used as food for people, and also to produce feed for raising fish in aquaculture and livestock in agriculture;
- seabirds, which are a minor food crop in some places, although the greatest harvesting-related mortality is associated with their by-catch in commercial fisheries; and
- marine mammals, which are harvested for their meat, fur, and other products.

These marine resources are harvested from coastal waters throughout most of Canada, but especially in the boreal and temperate zones. Some countries also have high-seas fisheries. Canada has a marine coastline of about 265×10^3 km (16 percent of the global total), territorial marine waters of 2.7×10^6 km^2 (14 percent of global; territorial waters extend out 18.2 km from the coast), and it claims an additional exclusive economic zone (EEZ) of 3.0×10^6 km^2 (3 percent of global; the EEZ extends from 18.2 to 320 km), most of which is on continental shelf (WRI, 2010). An EEZ is designated to allow a country to manage its coastal resources and to prevent marine pollution.

TABLE 15.5 The Most Prominent Marine Bio-Resources in Canada

The data are commercial landings (in 10^3 t) of wet biomass in Pacific or Atlantic + northern waters in 2007.

Species	Atlantic	Pacific
Groundfish	109.4	120.5
Cod (*Gadus morhua*)	26.6	–
Haddock (*Melanogrammus aeglefinus*)	19.2	–
Redfish (*Sebastes* spp.)	9.2	19.1
Pacific halibut (*Hippoglossus stenolepis*)	–	6.8
Atlantic halibut (*Hippoglossus hippoglossus*)	2.0	–
Flatfishes (*Pleuronectes* spp.)	9.0	9.0
Turbot (*Reinhardtius hippoglossoides*)	13.7	–
Hake (*Merluccius* spp.)	15.2	66.7
Pelagics	263.2	36.9
Herring (*Clupea harengus*)	167.0	–
Pacific herring (*Clupea pallasii*)	–	10.6
Mackerel (*Scomber scombrus*)	52.0	–
Swordfish (*Xiphias gladius*)	1.3	–
Pacific salmon (*Oncorhynchus* spp.)	–	19.6
Capelin (*Mallotus villosus*)	37.4	–
Tuna (*Thunnus* spp.)	0.9	5.1
Shellfish	429.0	13.6
Clams and mussels (various species)	21.5	1.8
Scallop (*Placopecten magellanicus*)	65.1	–
Lobster (*Homarus americanus*)	43.5	–
Shrimp (*Pandalus borealis*)	186.0	–
Queen crab (*Chionoecetes opilio*)	20.3	–
Seaweed (various species of kelps)	11.5	–
TOTAL	815.9	171.0

SOURCE: Data from Department of Fisheries and Oceans (DFO). 2010. Statistical Services. Ottawa, ON. http://www.dfo-mpo.gc.ca/communic/statistics/main_e.htm

Robert A. Pawlowski, National Oceanic and Atmospheric Administration/Department of Commerce, NOAA's Fisheries Collection; 1994 assessment cruise; NOAA Image ID: fish0024http://www.photolib.noaa.gov/htmls/fish0024.htm

Commercial fishing technologies are highly efficient ways to catch marine fish. This load of fish was caught using a pelagic trawl.

Harvesting and Management

Most harvesting of marine biological resources in Canada involves the capture of wild animals—a sort of oceanic hunting. The Canadian capture fishery in 2007 had landings of 1.02×10^6 t and a value of $2.0 billion (Fisheries and Oceans Canada, 2010c). Of these totals, 0.82×10^6 t and $1.6 billion were in Atlantic and northern waters, and 0.17×10^6 t and $0.32 billion in the Pacific. Canada also has freshwater fisheries, with landings of 63×10^3 t and a value of $32 million. The most prominent species in the marine fisheries are summarized in **Table 15.5**.

A capture fishery relies on "free" ecological services to produce the biomass that is harvested. In essence, naturally produced stocks of biological resources are harvested, and then allowed to self-regenerate. Other than attempting to regulate the harvest within limits that should not exceed the productivity of the stock, or its MSY, there is almost no management of the regeneration of capture fisheries. However, even estimating an accurate MSY and then regulating the harvesting are not easy things to do, as we will see below when we examine case studies.

In addition, certain stocks of anadromous salmon may be managed in ways beyond just regulating the harvest. This is done by enhancing their recruitment in streams and rivers by the release of captive-reared fingerlings, or by managing the freshwater breeding habitat to mitigate the effects of land-based activities, such as those associated with forestry or urbanization.

In addition, the **aquaculture** industry is rapidly growing in Canada and other countries. Between 1950 and 2005, the global production of animal biomass in aquaculture increased by a factor of 79-fold, and in Canada by 57-fold (WRI, 2010). Aquaculture is essentially the "farming" of aquatic organisms, and it typically involves a number of intensive management practices integrated into a comprehensive system that is intended to maximize the productivity of the species being cultivated. At least this is the case in Canada and other wealthier countries—in developing nations, much of the aquaculture involves less-intensive practices, but it is undertaken over larger areas.

Atlantic salmon is the most commonly reared species in aquaculture in Canada. Its rearing typically involves the following practices:

- Adult fish are kept in captivity in a land-based hatchery facility; they are of a genetic lineage that is considered to have high survival and productivity under the prevailing environmental conditions in which the cultivation pens are located.
- Once a year, in the late autumn, the male fish are stripped of milt (sperm) and the females of ova; these are mixed to achieve fertilization and the eggs are incubated in the hatchery.
- The hatched fry are fed on a nutritionally superior artificial medium, which is modified to meet their changing dietary requirements as they grow.
- When the small fish are about 1–1.5 years old (about 15 cm long; at this stage they are called smolts), they are transferred to much larger rearing pens in saltwater, usually of a floating, 10–20 m deep, open-mesh, netted construction and located in a shallow, semi-sheltered, coastal embayment.
- The fish are kept at a dense level of stocking in the sea-pens and are fed to satiation with fish-meal and fish-oil obtained from marine fisheries (about one-third of the global marine fishery catch is manufactured into fish-meal and fish-oil products, much of it for use in finfish aquaculture); after 1.5 to 2.5 years they attain a harvest weight of 3 to 5 kg (but up to 10 kg).
- At any time during the process, medicine may be required to treat contagious diseases:
    - Antibiotics such as oxytetracycline are used to treat bacterial infections.
    - Insecticide and related pesticides are used to treat infestations of sea lice (*Caligus* species and *Lepeophtheirus salmonis*), which are crustacean ectoparasites.
    - Anti-foulants such as organotin and copper-based compounds may be used to keep the net-mesh clean so that the cages do not become excessively heavy with fouling biomass and to allow water to freely circulate through the pens.
- If wild carnivores, such as seals or sea lions, become pests as they try to eat the caged salmon, they may be shot as vermin (a licence is required to do this).

The use of this sort of intensive management system results in high rates of salmon production and an abundant and nutritious food for people. However, there are also important environmental impacts of aquacultural systems, which we examine later as a case study.

The most prominent species grown in aquaculture in Canada are Atlantic salmon (production in 2007 was 117×10^3 t, of which 61 percent was grown in British Columbia and the rest in Atlantic waters; Fisheries and Oceans Canada, 2010c), mussels (mostly *Mytilus edulis*; 23.7×10^3 t), and oysters (*Crassostrea virginica* on the Atlantic coast and *C. gigas* on the Pacific). The total value of the aquacultural crops was $846 million.

As we noted previously, management of the harvesting rate (or fishing mortality) is the major tool that is used to try to prevent the overharvesting of wild fisheries. Within this context, the first step toward determination of a sustainable level of harvesting is to apply the principles and practice of population ecology to estimate the biomass and productivity of the biological stock, as well as the natural rate of mortality. If these are known, then the biomass and productivity that remain after natural mortality is accounted for can be allocated to anthropogenic harvesting—this would be the maximum sustainable yield available to a typical capture fishery.

Conceptually, this is a simple process. However, fishery ecologists do not yet have a sufficient understanding of the biological and environmental factors that affect the productivity of the populations of most marine species of commercial importance. Because of this lack of knowledge, the available population models suffer from a degree of inaccuracy, and they may predict MSYs that are too large to be sustainable, or smaller than could be harvested without placing the stock at risk. A major part of the problem is the unpredictability of changes in environmental conditions, which can have major influences on recruitment into populations and on the growth rate of individuals. Because many important changes in key environmental variables are seemingly unpredictable (or stochastic), in the sense that we do not know what caused the changes to occur, they are therefore impossible to accurately model (other than in a probabilistic sense, which is not good enough for real-world setting of harvest quotas).

Moreover, it is extremely difficult to field-test the predictions of population-dynamic models that are used to assess the size and productivity of commercial stocks—this requires, for example, the need to estimate the numbers of fish in management zones. "Counting fish" is an extraordinarily difficult task—it is fraught with uncertainty and so the resulting estimates may be substantially inaccurate. We cannot discuss this subject area in much detail here, but the estimates of stock biomass and productivity are usually made using indirect methods and they involve various key assumptions, which typically require knowledge based on

- *the biology and life history of the exploited species,* including the age at first maturity (when spawning begins), the frequency of spawning, age-related fecundity (older animals often produce more offspring than younger ones), recruitment success (especially the survival of eggs and larvae) and growth rate under various environmental conditions, and natural rates and causes of juvenile and adult mortality.
- *the age structure of populations in particular years,* which must be known to predict the productivity of a stock; if the field-determined age-class structure is different from that used in a population-dynamic model to predict the size and productivity of a stock, then the assessment will be inaccurate;
- ***catch-per-unit effort* (CPUE), *and a presumed statistical relationship between CPUE and the stock biomass;*** of course, the kind of effort used to catch the fish must be adjusted for its efficiency—effort based on hand-lining for fish is extraordinarily different from net-based methods, such as trawls; and
- *assessment of the size and biomass of schools of fish using sonar-based technology,* which again is based on statistical relationships between sonar-estimated densities and the actual stock biomass.

Once fisheries ecologists have used these sorts of methods to predict a **total allowable catch (TAC)** from a biological stock, it is possible to recommend quotas. It must be understood, however, that these are only recommendations made by scientists. In actual fact, the setting of quotas is not simply based on the predictions of stock-assessment models—economic and social considerations are also important. In practice, these non-science influences often result in decisions to allow larger quotas than are recommended by fishery ecologists (while recognizing that the ecologists do not always agree among themselves). When this happens, it is usually because the decision maker, typically a non-science bureaucrat or a politician, has been influenced to do so by economic and political pressures that are brought to bear by commercial and labour-related interests.

In any event, once a TAC is recommended, the amount of harvesting mortality can be set, which is essentially done by the regulation of harvesting effort. This can be achieved by regulating the enterprise in a number of interacting ways:

- Only certain kinds of harvesting units may be permitted for use to harvest the marine resource, such as certain kinds or sizes of fishing boats and the sorts of gear they are allowed to deploy.
- The number of harvesting units may be regulated, usually by a licensing system.
- The amount of time that each unit can spend harvesting may be limited; this is usually done by setting a season, which may be long or short; in certain herring fisheries of western North America the harvesting time may be only several hours per year.
- A quota may be assigned to each harvesting unit, and once it is achieved, the harvesting must stop.
- There may also be restrictions on the sizes or organisms that can be harvested; in the Atlantic lobster fishery, for example, animals smaller than the regulated carapace length must be returned to the ocean, while for net fisheries the permissible mesh size sets a lower limit on the size of fish that are caught.

Of course, it is not enough to just have regulations—the catches must also be monitored and non-compliance punished in some meaningful way. Some of the tools that managers can use to do this include the following:

- the withdrawal of licences in cases of egregious non-compliance with regulations;
- fines for lesser cases of non-compliance; however, the fines must be consequential, otherwise they could just be absorbed by the enterprise as an affordable cost of doing business;
- providing subsidies for operators who voluntarily engage in less-damaging harvesting methods; the subsidies influence their profit by reducing their net operating costs; and
- if there is excessive harvesting capacity in the aggregate fishery, either in terms of equipment or licences, then the regulator might purchase and retire the excess capacity.

Potentially at least, the use of these various considerations and measures should result in predictable and sustainable harvests being made of marine biological resources. As is well known, however, this has often not been the case, and many potentially renewable harvests of marine bio-resources have been ruined by excessive harvesting. There is a remarkable litany of such cases of wanton damage, as summarized in recent books and scientific reviews (Busch, 1985; Ellis, 1991, 2003; Kurlansky, 1997; Jackson et al., 2001; Pauly et al., 2002; Myers and Worm, 2003; Hutchings and Reynolds, 2004; Clover, 2006; Worm et al., 2006; Roberts, 2007).

In the following sections, we will examine a number of case studies that are relevant to non-sustainable harvests of marine bio-resources in Canada. These cases are selected to illustrate important points about non-sustainability, as well as the environmental damages that are inherent in all cases of excessive harvesting or inappropriate management of marine biological resources.

The Bowhead Whale

The bowhead whale (*Balaena mysticetus*) has the most northern range of the large cetaceans, occurring in arctic and boreal waters of the northern hemisphere (Reilly et al., 2008). It is a filter-feeder, mostly of large planktonic crustaceans known as krill. Bowheads are often relatively abundant near the edges of sea-ice, but they also occur in open water during the brief arctic summer. They can achieve a remarkable longevity for a wild mammal of more than 100 years, and have a generation time of about 52 years.

The bowhead whale was hunted primarily for its fat, which was valuable as an oil-lamp fuel and for making smokeless candles, and also for its baleen. (Commonly referred to as "whalebone," baleen is actually a strong and flexible keratin-rich material found in the mouths of various kinds of whales; it is an adaptation for filtering small food items from immense gulps of seawater, and in the past had many uses in manufacturing.) The bowhead and more temperate right whale (*Eubalaena glacialis*) were the first large cetaceans to be hunted because they swim slowly, usually float when killed, and inhabit coastal waters.

The commercial hunting of bowhead whales began in the northeastern Atlantic around 1611, particularly around the Arctic island of Spitzbergen and in the Barents Sea to its south. The first hunting of bowheads in North America was by Basque seamen off Labrador in the 16th century. One of their key whaling stations was at Red Bay in Labrador, where they killed thousands of bowheads and right whales between about 1530 and 1600 as the animals migrated through the Strait of Belle Isle between Newfoundland and southern Labrador. The dead animals were towed to Red Bay, where the baleen was removed and the blubber flensed from the body and rendered into oil in large iron cauldrons known as try-pots. The pre-hunting populations of bowheads in the northern Atlantic Ocean were about 24 000 in the Spitsbergen-Barents Sea and 12 000 in the northwestern Atlantic, but after a number of decades of hunting they became quickly depleted by overharvesting.

In 1848, whalers discovered a "new" population of bowhead whales in waters of the northern Pacific Ocean, in a region encompassing the Bering, Chukchi, and Beaufort seas (the latter includes waters of northwestern Canada). The initial population of this Bering-Chukchi-Beaufort (BCB) stock was 10 000 to 20 000 animals. Relatively good data exist for the hunting of bowheads in the north Pacific, and they show a rapid increase in the harvest, followed by a collapse as the stocks were depleted (**Figure 15.14**). There were large variations in the annual harvest during the early years of the hunt, primarily because some years had severe sea-ice conditions—the sailing ships of the time were not effective at penetrating dense pack-ice. Over the period of time covered by **Figure 15.14**, a total of 20 735 bowheads were landed. However, the kill would have been considerably larger than this because some mortally wounded animals would not have been retrieved by the whalers, particularly in difficult sea-ice conditions.

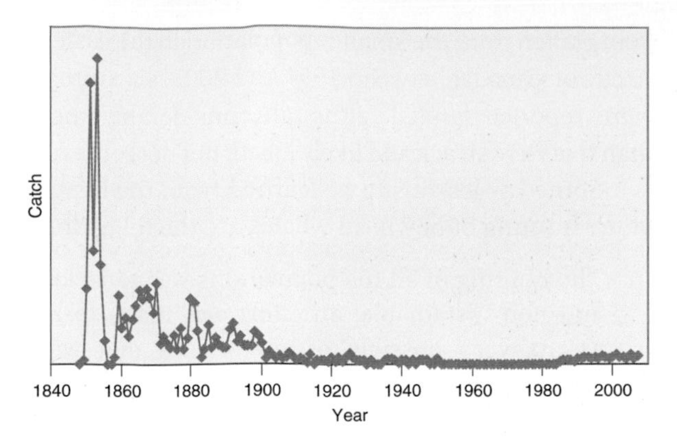

FIGURE 15.14
Annual Catch of Bowhead Whales in the Western Arctic. The data are the numbers of whales landed; the total annual kill is larger (but unknown) because many animals are struck but not landed.

SOURCES: Data from Cushing, D. H. 1988. *The Provident Sea*. Cambridge University Press, Cambridge, UK; International Whaling Commission (IWC). 2000. *Aboriginal Subsistence Whaling Catches Since 1985*. IWC, Cambridge, UK.

It is important to understand that throughout the history of bowhead hunting, and for that matter all whaling prior to about 1950, there was no ethic of conservation among the commercial whale hunters. They killed every animal that they could, regardless of species, rarity, or trend in population status. The inexorable intent was to convert whales into money and profit as quickly as possible. Sustainability was not much of a significant issue in the whaling industry, and certainly not an operational consideration.

The hunting of the BCB bowheads had essentially ceased by the 1930s, and in 1946 the newly created International Whaling Commission (IWC) banned further exploitation of these animals. This action has allowed the stocks to increase, and the present abundance is about 10 000 animals, similar to the pre-exploitation population of bowheads in the BCB region. Since 1985 the IWC has allowed aboriginal peoples in northern Alaska to engage in a "traditional" hunt of bowheads—between 2000 and 2007, an annual average of 56 whales was landed, and during 1985 through 2007 a total of 1082 animals (IWC, 2010). Even with this subsistence hunting, the population of bowheads in the BCB region is increasing at a rate of about 3.4 percent per year. Bowheads are also being taken from the smaller population in the eastern Arctic of Canada; between 1991 and 2007, six animals were reported landed, although considerably more than this were struck and likely killed, but not retrieved.

Some key lessons to be learned from the history of the hunting of bowhead whales are the following:

- The hunting of all the populations was rapacious and non-sustainable; an effort was made to kill as many as possible of any whales that were encountered.
- Consequently, as each "new" stock was discovered, it was rapidly overharvested and depleted to commercial extinction.
- Eventually the hunting stopped because of the combined influences of non-profitability and a ban by the IWC; these circumstances have allowed the surviving whales to rebuild their abundance.

Today, bowhead whales in the BCB region are considered to no longer be at risk (Reilly et al., 2008). The separate population in arctic waters of eastern Canada and Greenland is also increasing, and may no longer be at risk, while that of the northeastern Atlantic off Spitsbergen and in the Barents Sea is still greatly depleted.

Atlantic Cod

Atlantic cod (*Gadus morhua*) is an amphi-Atlantic species, meaning it occurs in temperate and boreal waters of the continental shelves of both North America and Europe. It has long been an important food fish in Europe, and when the first European mariners explored the coastal waters off what is now eastern Canada they were astonished by the immense numbers of cod that they encountered. In 1497, John Cabot wrote in his journal that the Grand Banks were so "swarming with fish [that they] could be taken not only with a net but in baskets let down [and weighted] with a stone." The largest cod stocks were on the Grand Banks off Newfoundland, a relatively shallow (25–110 m deep), productive marine ecosystem of about 250 000 km^2. However, cod were also abundant on banks off Labrador, Nova Scotia, and New England and in the Gulf of St. Lawrence.

Soon after these immense and productive fishing grounds were discovered, great fleets of vessels were sailing from Europe to harvest cod and other groundfish (species that feed on or near the bottom). In 1600, about 650 ships were fishing in the region, and in 1800 there were about 1600 vessels (Mowat, 1984; Hutchings and Myers, 1995). The typical landings during 1750–1800 were about 190 000 t per year, increasing to 400 000–460 000 t/yr during 1800–1900, and almost 1 million t/yr in 1899–1904 (Mowat, 1984; Cushing, 1988). During the earlier times, the fishers worked with hand-lines (a single hook-and-line that is hand-jigged), long-lines (lines with numerous baited hooks set between floating buoys), seines (bag-like nets), and near-shore traps (netted entrapments). Most of the individual fishers worked from a small dory (a wooden boat pointed at both ends), which on the banks would be launched from a mother ship, such as one of the illustrious schooners that were built in and sailed out of Nova Scotia and Newfoundland. These fishing methods are not particularly efficient, but the aggregate harvesting effort was large and so, therefore, were the catches. By the early 20th century, stocks of

Paul Nicklen/National Geographic Stock

Bowhead whales (*Balaena mysticetus*) were endangered by an intensive commercial hunt, but were protected and have since recovered much of their original abundance.

Simeon H. Parsons/Library and Archives Canada/PA-139025

(a)

The Rooms Provincial Archives, VA 21-18 / R. E. Holloway

(b)

The historical fishery for Atlantic cod (*Gadus morhua*) was much less intensive than modern industrial fishing, in terms of total harvest of fish biomass and damage caused to habitat, although it still depleted some inshore stocks. (a) Split cod drying on wooden flakes at Quidi Vidi, Newfoundland, around 1886. (b) Two large "mother cod" that were caught in a nearshore trap near Battle Harbour, Labrador, in 1903. The larger fish weighed 27 kg and was 1.6 m long.

cod in many near-shore waters were depleted, although those on the banks remained robust.

During the 20th century, however, more efficient technologies were developed and their use resulted in a major intensification of the cod fishery (and for that matter, of almost all commercial fisheries). Particularly important innovations were the change-over from wooden sailing vessels to increasingly powerful motorized ships, the invention of new netting technologies (especially monofilament gill nets and pelagic trawls), the use of sonar equipment to locate schools of fish, and the installation of on-ship methods to process and freeze fish, which allowed large vessels to remain at sea for an extended time. These hugely effective improvements resulted in much larger harvests of cod and other fish in the northwest Atlantic, particularly during the 1960s, when most of the fishery was an essentially unregulated enterprise that was open to all countries **(Figure 15.15)**. However, the immense catches were not sustainable, and the stocks plummeted.

The collapse of the cod stocks resulted in a crisis in the fishery-dependent economy of coastal regions of Atlantic Canada. In response to this socioeconomic and ecological calamity, in 1977 the Government of Canada proclaimed a 320 km-wide exclusive economic zone (EEZ). This allowed the Department of Fisheries and Oceans (DFO) to regulate the entire cod fishery and to allocate quotas. Those measures resulted in a moderate increase in landings, mostly by Canadian fishers, but the harvesting was still excessive and there was soon an even more ruinous collapse of the stocks **(Figure 15.15)**. In 1992, DFO declared a moratorium on commercial cod fishing, a ban that substantially remained in place in 2009 (there was a quota of 13 000 t in that year, plus a small food fishery by local people).

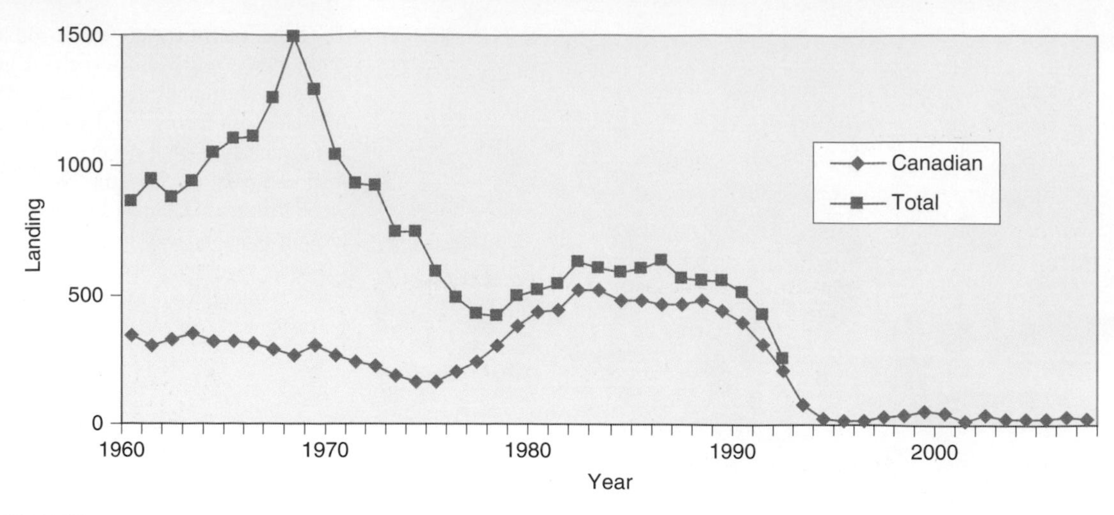

FIGURE 15.15

Commercial Landings of Cod in Atlantic Canada. In 1977, Canada declared a 320-km exclusive economic zone, resulting in higher catches by Canadian fishers. However, the stocks then collapsed further, and in 1992 a moratorium was placed on most cod fishing. There have been variable quotas and by-catch since then. Data are in 10^3 tonnes.

SOURCE: Data from Department of Fisheries and Oceans (DFO). 2010. Statistical Services. Ottawa, ON. http://www.dfo-mpo.gc.ca/communic/statistics/main_e.htm

It was initially hoped that reduced fishing pressure resulting from the 1992 moratorium would allow the cod stocks to recover, but this has not yet happened. The reasons for a lack of substantial recovery are not fully understood. However, they are probably due to some combination of the following factors:

- Only small populations of cod are old enough to spawn, relative to the carrying capacity of their habitat.
- Undue fishing pressure continues through recently permitted legal harvesting for recreational and commercial purposes, as well as by-catch in fisheries directed at other species.
- Excessive mortality from natural causes occurs, which may be caused by increased predation of eggs and larvae of cod by other fish, which are themselves no longer subjected to intense predation by cod. Predation by the increasingly larger populations of harp and grey seals, which feed on older cod, may also be important in some areas.

Hopefully, despite these factors, the cod stocks will eventually recover to the point where they could again be an abundant renewable resource.

At the time that the cod stocks collapsed in the late 1980s, there was controversy about the cause (Hutchings and Myers, 1995; Hutchings and Reynolds, 2004). Some fishery ecologists suggested that environmental factors, such as several years of unusually cold water in the southward-flowing Labrador current, could have been a factor. Others blamed the burgeoning populations of harp seals (*Phoca groenlandica*), which consume more than 1 million t of food per year, although mostly crustaceans and small fish such as Arctic cod (*Boreogadus saida*) and capelin (*Mallotus villosus*). However, it is now clear that it was overfishing that caused this resource calamity to occur—the stocks of cod were being harvested much faster than they could regenerate, particularly during the 1970s and 1980s, and this caused them to undergo a rapid and precipitous decline.

Several factors caused the non-sustainable harvesting to occur. One was the essentially unregulated fishery until 1977, when Canada proclaimed its 320-km EEZ (as did other coastal nations at that time). Another was the apparent use of inaccurate stock-assessment models to predict the MSY of the cod stocks—these over-estimated the fish biomass and resulted in the setting of quotas that were too large to be sustainable. Many people also thought that poorly regulated non-Canadian fishers were catching too many fish (even though Canadians landed 85 percent of the cod in the northwest Atlantic between 1977 and 1991, in a more-or-less regulated fishery). Finally, politicians and other decision makers were influenced by various socioeconomic interests (that is, by the concerns of fishers and their businesses) that were opposed to cutting the quotas to the degree the fishery scientists were recommending, which resulted in excessive harvests being allowed in the years immediately preceding the moratorium. All of these factors, and others, resulted in unsustainably intense harvesting of a potentially renewable resource. That over-exploitation has apparently ruined what was once one of the greatest marine fisheries in the world—that of cod in the northwestern Atlantic Ocean. Recovery of the cod stocks may yet be possible, but so far it has not occurred.

Pacific Salmon

Pacific salmon comprise a group of species of salmonid fish (family Salmonidae) in the genus *Oncorhynchus*. Most populations are **anadromous**, meaning they breed in freshwater but migrate to the sea where they spend most of their adult life **(Figure 15.16)**. Depending on the life history of the species, and sometimes on the particular geographic population, the down-river migration from freshwater to the ocean may be undertaken by recently hatched larvae, or by 1- to 2-year-old animals known as smolts. During their migration the larvae or smolts become physiologically tolerant of seawater, and they then spend one to several years in coastal or pelagic habitats. When they become sexually mature adults, they migrate as many as thousands of kilometres back to their natal stream to breed (often even to the same reach of the stream), navigating using smell and other environmental cues, and battling river currents, rapids, and waterfalls to reach an upstream gravel spawning bed (known as a redd). There the adults breed and in most species die soon afterward.

Migrating salmon are a crucial food for various other animal species, including bears and eagles, and they have long provided sustenance for indigenous peoples on the Pacific coast and on inland rivers. The migrating adults are also a "nutrient pump" that delivers phosphorus and nitrogen to up-river habitats, a function that enhances the overall productivity of their ecosystem (see Chapter 5).

Pacific salmon have complex life histories, which vary remarkably among the species and often also among geographic populations. There is a strong genetic component to the variation among populations, which has presumably arisen because of natural selection by the regimes of environmental conditions that have influenced their evolution. In general, the genetic differences are not sufficient to allow the discrete populations to be assigned a taxonomic designation, such as variety or subspecies. Nevertheless, the genetic differences are considered to be important in terms of management and conservation, and so the different populations are referred to as being **evolutionarily significant units** (or **ESU**s). Having noted this, a few of the ESUs are differentiated enough to have been named as varieties, such as the kokanee type of sockeye salmon.

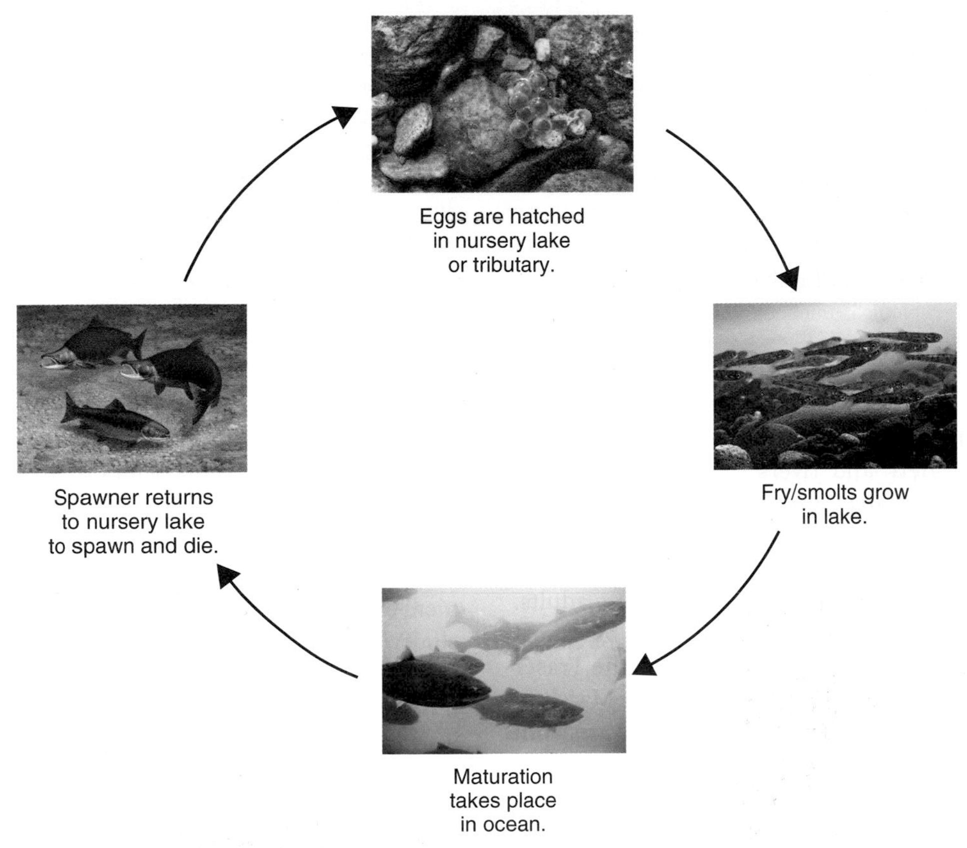

FIGURE 15.16
Life Cycle of Sockeye Salmon (*Oncorhynchus nerka*).

SOURCES: Clockwise from top: Photos.com; Sergey Gorshkov/Minden Pictures; Paul Edmondson/Photographer's Choice RF/Getty Images; Walter A. Weber/National Geographic Stock

Chris Cheadle/GetStock.com

Aquaculture is the rearing of fish under controlled conditions. This is an aerial view of an aquaculture facility for rearing Atlantic salmon (*Salmo salar*) in open-net sea-pens on Vancouver Island.

($364 million in British Columbia and $327 million in Atlantic Canada), compared with a wild salmon fishery of $31 million (DFO, 2010a,b).

Advocates of aquacultural systems point to the fact that they are highly productive of nutritious foodstuffs, which help to replace some of the collapsed yields of wild fisheries. Aquaculture also provides employment opportunities in coastal communities. While these benefits are real, aquaculture also causes some important ecological damages. Mostly for this reason, the establishment or expansion of aquaculture facilities may be bitterly resisted by various interest groups, including some local people (but not all of them), environmental organizations, First Nations, commercial and recreational fishers, and fishery scientists. The cultivation of fish in shallow-water netpens is particularly contentious; closed-tank facilities on land or in the ocean are less controversial.

The most important environmental issues associated with salmon aquaculture are the following:

- *Location*—Fish-farms are typically located in shallow protected embayments, which are also prime locations for some wild fisheries, residential properties, and recreational activities, resulting in conflicts with these alternative uses.
- *Benthic impacts*—If local tidal flushing is not vigorous, uneaten food and fish excrement will accumulate in large amounts beneath and in the vicinity of sea cages, resulting in severe ecological damage by smothering, deoxygenation, and eutrophication.
- *Chemical inputs*—Various toxic chemicals are used in salmon aquaculture, such as organotin and cupric compounds that are used as anti-foulants to keep net-meshes clean (allowing water to pass through and preventing the cages from becoming too heavy with attached biomass), pesticides used to treat infestations of parasitic copepods known as sea lice, and medicines used to treat bacterial infections.
- *Parasite transmission to wild fish*—It appears that sea lice (*Lepeophtheirus salmonis* and *Caligus clemensi*) infestations in penned salmon may be transmitted to wild fish that occur in the vicinity of aquaculture facilities, or that migrate past the cages; this can be debilitating or lethal to juvenile life-history stages, which because of their small size cannot tolerate many parasites. This stress has been attributed as the cause of a collapse of runs of pink salmon in the Broughton Archipelago (Morton et al., 2004; Krkošek et al., 2005).
- *Disease transmission to wild fish*—Penned Atlantic salmon are vulnerable to infectious salmon anemia, a lethal hemorrhagic disease caused by the virus *Isavirus*, which is directly transmitted fish-to-fish or by contact with contaminated netting or other equipment (Raynard et al., 2001; Cipriano, 2002). The only available treatment is to eradicate infected stock, which is an economic catastrophe to the grower. The virus can survive in seawater, so it is possible that it might spread to wild salmon in the vicinity of an aquaculture facility.
- *Escapes*—Penned salmon sometimes break out of damaged pens; when this happens on the Atlantic coast, the escapees may interbreed with endangered populations of wild salmon (such as those of the Bay of Fundy), potentially affecting the genetic integrity of those rare ESUs. When escapes occur on the Pacific Coast, there is a possibility of establishment of wild breeding populations, which would compete with indigenous Pacific salmon. In fact, observations of wild juvenile Atlantic salmon in various places confirms the occurrence

of feral breeding populations of that species in British Columbia (Volpe et al., 2000).

- *Feed*—Salmon are carnivores and must be provided with a high-quality feed, most of which is manufactured from meal and oil manufactured from wild-caught fish, although because of assimilation and food-web inefficiencies, most of the energy content of the feed does not end up in the biomass of the salmon. According to the World Wildlife Fund, fish caught to manufacture fishmeal and oil represent one-third of the global fish harvest.

These are all important issues, and only some of them are resolvable. As is the case of any economic activity, some degree of environmental damage is inevitably caused by salmon aquaculture. Nevertheless, it is clear that aquaculture is a viable enterprise and it will continue to be undertaken in environments where it is feasible. The key to sustainability rests in finding an appropriate balance between the benefits to the human economy that are realized through the production of a renewable resource and associated employment opportunities, and the damages caused to biodiversity and other components of the natural environment. Of course, this is true of any economic activity.

By-Catch

It is common that fishing effort that is directed to certain marine species also results in the inadvertent harvesting of other ones. This incidental take is referred to as by-catch, and it is usually lethal for the affected individuals. By-catch is also associated with lost or discarded fishing nets—so-called "ghost nets" that continue to kill marine biota until they eventually wash up on shore or sink irretrievably to the bottom.

Particularly intense by-catch occurs in shrimp trawling, in which it may account for as much as 95 percent of the harvested biomass, with an average of 85 percent (Clucas, 1997). Shrimping is responsible for more than one-third of the global by-catch, even though the commercial shrimp harvest is only 2 percent of the total landings of marine animal biomass. In various Canadian fisheries in the northwest Atlantic, an average of 10 percent of the total catch was discarded back to the ocean during a monitoring period in 1994 (Clucas, 1997; Fisheries and Oceans Canada, 2010c). The highest by-catch rates were 23 percent in the fishery for lobster, 21 percent in those for haddock and pollock, 20 percent for sea scallop, and 18 percent for cod and queen crab.

By-catch has been a huge issue for fisheries that use drift-nets—these are gill-nets that float suspended in the water column, sometimes extending for tens of kilometres and representing a "wall of death" for creatures that swim into them. Dolphins and sea turtles have been severely affected as by-catch in pelagic drift nets, and this is a key reason why that harvesting method was banned in international waters in 1992 (drift nets are still permitted in some coastal waters, but only in fisheries where the by-catch is relatively low).

By-catch is an important conservation risk for some marine species. For instance, the barndoor skate (*Dipturus laevis*) has declined precipitously and is now endangered in Canadian Atlantic waters because of excessive by-catch mortality in trawls directed at other species (Casey and Myers, 1998; Cheung et al., 2005). Each year, a number of northern right whales, a critically endangered species, become entangled in fishing gear on the Atlantic coast, as do other cetaceans. Large numbers of seabirds are also killed when they are snagged in fishing nets. For example, all of the 21 species of albatrosses (family Diomedeidae) are at conservation risk, and a leading cause of their declines is unsustainable mortality associated with the seabirds being caught in fishing nets or snagged on long-line hooks when they try to take the bait (there are additional important stressors for these seabirds, including alien mammalian predators that have been introduced to their nesting islands, declining stocks of their marine foods because of overfishing, and pollution).

Because by-catch is widely recognized as an important ecological problem, steps are being taken to mitigate some of the damages that are caused. For example, because of controversial mortality caused to the endangered Kemp's Ridley (*Lepidochelys kempii*) and other sea-turtles in U.S. waters, shrimp trawls are now required to incorporate turtle-exclusion devices (TEDs) that divert these animals from the rest of the catch, which is retained in the net. Similarly, by-catch of small cetaceans has been a major problem with tuna fisheries in Pacific waters, because these marine mammals often co-school with yellowfin tuna (*Thunnus albacares*) as they hunt similar foods—small baitfish. If a purse seine is set around such a co-school, the dolphins may drown when the net is closed and hauled in to harvest the tuna; particularly vulnerable species are the spotted dolphin (*Stenella attenuata*) and spinner dolphin (*S. lonqirostris*). This is now much less of a problem than in the past because methods have been developed to release the dolphins, and in some regions it has been made illegal to set purse seines on co-schooling tuna and dolphins. Other mitigations that can reduce by-catch include requiring net-mesh sizes that capture only larger fish, while allowing smaller ones to escape (although in a heavily laden net many of the smaller fishes may also be retained), and the use of various kinds of by-catch reduction devices (BRDs) that help to focus the harvesting on the target species. Many fisheries are also making greater commercial use of the by-catch, so that the inadvertently harvested biomass is not wasted.

The Marine Stewardship Council and other advocacy and research groups are working hard to require fishery managers to reduce the rates of by-catch. One of their most successful tools is the certification of seafoods as being harvested with low levels of by-catch. It must be recognized, however, that some degree of by-catch is inevitable. All enterprises that harvest resources from the natural world cause some degree of collateral environmental damage, and by-catch is one of the key impacts of industrial fishing.

15.4 Integrated Resource Management

As we have repeatedly stressed, all systems to harvest and manage renewable bio-resources cause environmental damages of varying kinds and to various degrees. In a general sense, the key damages include the following:

- *degradation of the primary resource* by overharvesting or inappropriate management, which diminishes the economic sustainability of the enterprise (timber, for example, is the primary resource in forestry; in fishing, it is fish);
- *damage caused to secondary resources*, which may be economically important in their own right and might also support commercial or subsistence harvesting (for instance, in a forested region, secondary resources might include hunted species such as deer and trout, as well as opportunities for outdoor recreation);
- *effects on ecological services*, such as carbon storage in the ecosystem, productivity in general, and the provision of reliable and clean flows of fresh water;
- *effects on biodiversity*, such as the endangerment of native species, or the excessive diminishment of natural communities; and
- *societal damages*, which can be various and are mostly borne by local people, including those whose culture and traditional livelihoods become disrupted when industrial resource-harvesting enterprises move into their area; in Canada, it is aboriginal peoples who are usually most strongly affected in this manner.

To varying degrees, these kinds of environmental damages can be prevented or at least mitigated by adopting a collaborative and broad-reaching approach known as **integrated resource management** (or **IRM**). In essence, IRM starts by identifying all of the key stakeholders and issues in an area that has been defined for the purpose of using this approach, including those associated with bio-resources. The partnership of stakeholders then collaborates to find ways to manage economic activities in a manner that is deemed acceptable by a consensus of the parties.

IRM approaches have been used in Canada in some landscapes in which forestry is the primary economic activity. In this context, foresters work with other interested parties to develop integrated management plans that accommodate the harvesting of timber from the landscape, while also sustaining other important forest values. Most typically, the IRM plan focuses on discovering ways that forestry can be conducted while still ensuring that the landscape continues to support a sizable abundance of hunted terrestrial animals such as deer, elk, and bears, and aquatic ones such as trout and salmon. In some cases there are also substantial efforts made to accommodate non-consumptive uses of the forest estate, such as outdoor recreation and ecotourism. Protected areas may also be accommodated in some IRM plans.

For this integrated system of management to work well, the partners must acknowledge that the forest industry is a legitimate player, and that it has a need to harvest trees from the landscape (as does society at large). At the same time, the forestry interests must understand that other views about use of the forest are also valid, and that they must be accommodated to a mutually acceptable degree. This may require the following sorts of accommodations:

- Less (or even no) clear-cutting is done; instead, timber is harvested using selective methods that have softer environmental impacts.
- Strict rules are required for road-building and timber harvesting to decrease their ecological effects, such as cavity-tree retention, leaving uncut groups of trees embedded in clear-cuts, maintaining riparian buffers, careful installation of culverts at stream crossings, and other sensible and helpful practices.
- Ecological surveys should be undertaken to identify critical habitats that should not be harvested, such as deer yards (these are important wintering habitats in regions that accumulate a deep snowpack), and ecological communities that support rare or endangered species.
- In some regions it is important to protect tracts of old-growth forest, and for this to be successful it is necessary to set aside protected areas that are large enough to conserve the ecological dynamics that allow this special ecosystem to develop—in essence, this means the protected area must be big enough to allow the natural disturbance regime to operate, but at a scale that will sustain a viable abundance of old-growth tracts.

- Local people should continue to have access to acceptable and dependable livelihoods, which might involve employment in forestry for some of them, but could also include traditional economic and subsistence activities such as hunting, fishing, trapping, and guiding.

It is not easy to balance all of these interests and needs in a way that is satisfactory to everyone, but if it can be done, there may be a lasting peace in the forest.

Typically, because of its size and influence, the forest industry is the most "powerful" interest in this sort of partnership. However, the activities of industrial forestry are increasingly being closely scrutinized by society because of the ecological and other environmental damages that it causes. This is resulting in closer regulation of forestry activities, as well as more-informed choices by consumers in favour of "greener" forest products. These emerging interests are economically powerful, and they are bringing the forest industry to the table as a partner in the development of working IRM partnerships. By cooperating in this way, the forest industry is attempting to come to grips with important controversies that are arising from its woodland and manufacturing operations.

The IRM model is also relevant to fisheries, agriculture, horticulture, and other systems that involve the harvesting of wild biomass or the cultivation of crops. In any of these cases, the key steps in a successful application of IRM are the identification of the interested parties, the discovery of their particular concerns, and the collaborative development of accommodations that would achieve a consensus about an appropriate IRM system to implement.

Clearly, society expects that the vast ecosystems of Canada will always deliver a wide range of goods and services. These include the large economic benefits that come from sustainable harvests of biomass as sources of food, materials, and energy, while also satisfying other economic and ecological needs. Even while bio-resources are used in these ways, the greater landscapes and seascapes are expected to always provide important ecological services, such as carbon storage and a clean environment, and to sustain native biodiversity at viable levels of abundance. In fact, the vision expressed in this paragraph is precisely that of ecological sustainability. The model is portable to the harvesting and management of any kind of bio-resource.

VOCABULARY OF ECOLOGY

abiotic stressor, p. 478
advanced regeneration, p. 477
anadromous, p. 505
anthropogenic mortality, p. 479
aquaculture, p. 498
biological resource (bio-resource), p. 472
by-catch, p. 481
capital, p. 471
catch-per-unit effort (CPUE), p. 500
clear-cutting, p. 487
commercially extinct (economically extinct), p. 482
common-property resource, p. 485
conventional economics, p. 465
disease, p. 479
ecological economics, p. 466
ecological footprint, p. 466
ecologically sustainable development, p. 464
ecologically sustainable economy, p. 464
economic development, p. 468
economic growth, p. 467
economics, p. 464
emulation forestry, p. 497
evolutionarily significant unit (ESU), p. 505
free good, p. 465
genetically modified organism (GMO), p. 479
gross domestic product (GDP), p. 466
harvesting, p. 473
human capital, p. 471
integrated resource management (IRM), p. 512
integrated system (integrated management system), p. 473
intellectual capital, p. 471
interspecific competition, p. 478
intraspecific competition, p. 478
Judeo-Christian ethic, p. 485
management, p. 473
manufactured capital, p. 471
maximum sustainable yield (MSY), p. 475
natural capital (natural resource), p. 471
natural mortality, p. 479
natural regeneration, p. 477
non-renewable resource (non-renewable capital), p. 471
opportunity cost, p. 465
overharvesting, p. 471
plantation, p. 488
renewable resource (renewable capital), p. 471
reserve life, p. 469
resource (capital), p. 464
resource ecology, p. 464
riparian buffer, p. 491
sedimentation, p. 495

and processes, as well as those of the watershed and even the landscape. The "words" of this historical "book" are represented by the physical, chemical, and biological indicators (proxy data) that are preserved in the sediment. Because this textbook is about ecology, we will focus on biological indicators. However it is important to remember that sediment also archives an extensive library of indicators that are physical (e.g., evidence of past erosion events) and chemical (e.g., records of contaminants such as mercury, lead, and other metals, as well as persistent organic pollutants such as DDT and PCBs). The task of the paleoecologist is to remove a core of this sediment profile, then to extract and quantify the proxy data, and finally to interpret the information in a meaningful and defendable manner.

Under ideal circumstances, the sediment record preserves a stratigraphic (layered) sequence that represents a depth-time profile. The deeper you go into the profile, the older is the sediment, until bedrock is reached, which marks the origin of the lake (in most regions of Canada this would indicate the time of the retreat of the last glaciation). Of course, problems are sometimes encountered. The sediment profile may have been mixed by physical processes such as currents, or by burrowing aquatic animals (referred to as bioturbation), thus blurring the record. The stratigraphic record is not, however, a complete "leap of faith" because paleoecologists often have independent ways to assess its integrity. For instance, the age of layers within a profile can be reliably dated using methods that are based on the rate of radioactive decay

FIGURE 16.3

Schematic of a Lake Gradually Filling with Sediment. Natural sedimentation is a cumulative process in a lake. It can yield time-dependent profiles that are important repositories of information about ecological and environmental changes that have occurred both in the lake and in its surrounding watershed and region. The paleolimnological record (i.e., from the sediment, which accumulates constantly) is composed of material from both allochthonous and autochthonous material (see the text for details).

(a)

Kathleen Rühland, Queen's University

(b)

Brian Cumming, Queen's University

Methods in paleolimnology. (a) Removing a short core of surface sediment from a lake; (b) a short sediment core. A core of this length would cover only the most recent two centuries or so of sediment accumulation for a typical Canadian lake. Longer cores, extending back to the end of the continental Ice Age, can be retrieved using different types of sediment corers.

of certain isotopes, such as carbon-14 (^{14}C or radiocarbon) and lead-210 (^{210}Pb).

The portfolio of biological indicators preserved in sediment is remarkably varied and surprisingly complete. Many indicators are preserved as morphological microfossils, meaning they are typically identified and enumerated using a microscope. These include the pollen grains of vascular plants, the siliceous cell walls of diatom algae and scales of chrysophyte algae, and the chitinous exoskeletal parts of invertebrates. In some cases, however, the only record of historical populations is in the biogeochemical record, such as fossil pigments that can be linked to specific groups, such as Cyanobacteria (blue-green algae).

Of course, recovering indicators in a sedimentary sequence is only the first part of the study. Continuing with the book analogy, we may now have recovered a series of words—the indicators, such as species of diatoms. But how can we interpret this information in a meaningful ecological context? To use this information we must understand the ecological optima and tolerances of the species that are encountered in the fossil record.

For example, if we were presented with information about the presence of a polar bear (*Ursus maritimus*) or a black bear (*U. americana*), we could deduce some meaningful information about the environments and ecosystems that these species represent. We would know that the polar bear is from an Arctic habitat, and because most of its diet is based on seals, it must be near an ocean or a large bay such as Hudson's Bay. In contrast, the presence of a black bear would lead us to think of temperate regions and a forested habitat. This example illustrates the principle of uniformitarianism—the present is a key to understanding the past, and vice versa.

The more indicators we have to work with, the more refined our ecological inferences can become. For this reason, much of paleoecology has been moving toward integrated or multi-proxy approaches, in which a suite of microbial, animal, and plant indicators, as well as chemical and physical ones, is gathered and interpreted together. Nevertheless, it is acknowledged that certain taxa will be better indicators than others. Returning to the ursine example, the polar bear is a carnivore that specializes in hunting seals, and so its niche is relatively narrow. In contrast, the black bear is omnivorous and it eats a wide range of plant and animal foods, depending on local habitat conditions. As a result, polar bears are a reliable indicator of changes in the abundance of their specific foods and environmental conditions necessary for hunting them (such as extensive and persistent sea ice), while black bears provide much more generalist inferences about their landscape-scale ecosystem. Similarly, knowledge of the presence of human beings might not be very informative about environmental conditions, because our species is such a generalist, capable of living in a wide variety of environments, from the equator to polar regions.

Figure 16.4 summarizes some of these relationships. If the abundance of most species is plotted relative to an environmental variable, such as lakewater pH or temperature for an aquatic organism, the

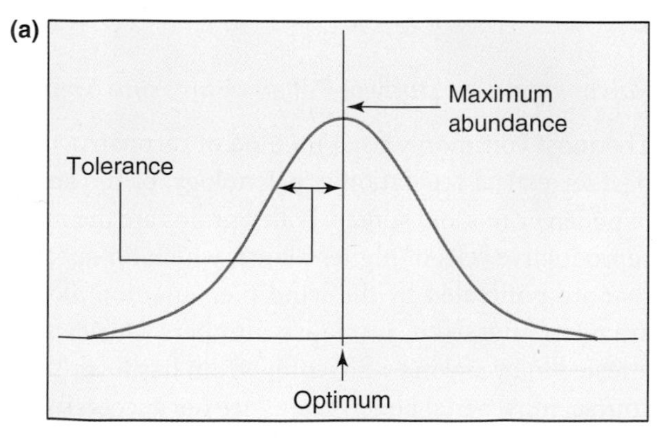

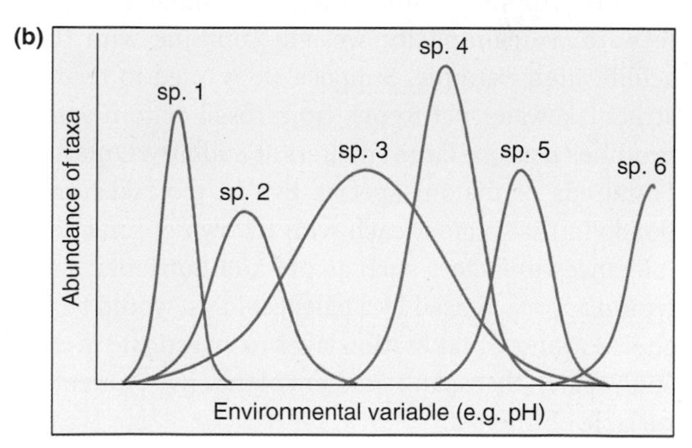

FIGURE 16.4

Conceptual Diagram of Environmental Optima and Tolerances. Species differ in their tolerances to environmental factors (such as temperature or pH), in individualistic ways that often approximate a bell curve (or unimodal or Gaussian distribution). Diagram (a) shows this for an individual species. Diagram (b) compares various species, showing that they have different optima and tolerances. For example, if the environmental variable of interest was lakewater pH (on the *x*-axis), then species-1 has its optimum in low-pH waters, while species-5 has its optimum in higher-pH habitats. Species-3, however, has a circumneutral optimum and a broader tolerance—it is more of a generalist with respect to pH. A paleoecologist can use these relationships to reconstruct past environmental conditions based on fossils of these organisms.

SOURCES: Diagram (a) modified from Jongman, R.H.G., C.J.F. ter Braak, and O.F.R. van Tongeren (eds.). 1995. *Data Analysis in Community and Landscape Ecology*. Cambridge University Press, (page 19). Cambridge, UK, and (b) modified from Smol, J.P. 2008. *Pollution of Lakes and Rivers: A Paleoenvironmental Perspective* (page 81), 2nd ed., Wiley-Blackwell Publishing, Oxford, UK.

relationship often approximates a bell curve (also known as a unimodal or Gaussian curve; **Figure 16.4a**). Most species would be particularly competitive at a certain pH level, and this would be its optimum pH within its community. However, the species would also be able to survive at pH levels higher and lower than its optimum, although only to degrees limited by physiological constraints. This is shown as the tolerance in the figure—a specialist has a relatively narrow tolerance whereas a generalist has a broader one **(Figure 16.4b)**. These are reasons why different species have varying optima and tolerances to environmental factors (in this case, pH), and this ecological information is critical for interpreting the paleoecological record. Once the environmental optima and tolerance of species are understood, they can be used in paleoecological reconstructions.

For some indicators, the characterization of ecological optima has been taken to a highly quantitative level. One of the examples presented later in this chapter will show how fossil algae in dated cores of lake sediment were used to determine how and which lakes had acidified due to acid rain, and to what degree. Although it should not be surprising that lakewater pH will affect algal species in different ways, one might ask how paleoecologists can use these relationships in ways that stand up to scientific and often political scrutiny. In essence, it is done by calibrating the historical data on the basis of the known relationships of species to present-day environmental conditions—an application of the principle of uniformitarianism.

The logic and approach behind developing surface–sediment calibration sets is quite straightforward. For simplicity, we will continue with the acidification example. Suppose we wanted to reconstruct lakewater pH trends from fossil diatom communities near the large smelters at Sudbury, Ontario. Hundreds of diatom species live in the lakes and ponds in that region, each with its own optima and tolerances to factors such as pH and nutrients. The typical approach used by a paleoecologist would be to choose a suite of calibration lakes to investigate in the study region that span a gradient of the environmental variable of interest.

In this example, let us assume that a suite of 80 calibration lakes has been chosen with present lakewater pH values ranging from 4.5 to 8.0. Other water-quality data, such as metal concentrations and nutrients, would also be gathered. Ideally, several years of monitoring data are available, so that inter-year variability can be assessed. These data would result in the first matrix of data: a listing of the 80 calibration lakes with their associated environmental data.

The next step would be to develop a second data matrix involving species of diatoms in the lakes. To do this, each calibration lake would be sampled for its uppermost sediments (typically the surface 1 cm or so, which contains the indicators that lived in that lake during the past two to three years). The sample would be taken near the centre of the lake, a location that integrates the entire waterbody and so provides the most representative place for sampling. Back in the laboratory, the diatom species would be identified and enumerated so that their relative abundance can be estimated (typically using percentage data) in all of the 80 calibration lakes.

Finally, using a variety of statistical approaches, the environmental optima and tolerances of the diatom species can be estimated (in this case with a focus on lakewater pH). This allows a quantitative transfer function to be developed for lakewater pH—this relates the percentage of various diatom species to the lakewater pH levels. The end result is that the paleoecologist now has a "paleo-pH meter" that allows past lakewater pH values to be inferred from the fossil diatom communities that are recovered from layers within sediment cores.

However, identifying and enumerating fossils and other indicators in sediment profiles is only part of the story. It is also necessary to develop a temporal chronology of the sedimentary profiles, so that changes of environmental and community factors can be put into a correct perspective of time. A variety of dating techniques is available, but the most commonly used methods are based on radioisotopes, such as carbon-14 dating for material ranging from about 500 to 40 000 years in age, and lead-210 dating for sediment less than about 150 years old.

Palynology: The Study of Pollen Grains and Spores

The most commonly used method of reconstructing past terrestrial vegetation is **palynology**, or the study of pollen grains and spores. Pollen grains are the male reproductive cells of higher plants, which for species that are pollinated by the wind (i.e., anemophilous) are often released in immense numbers (this can be attested to by anyone who suffers from hay fever!). Of course, most aerial pollen grains are not successful in fertilizing plant ova—most land on foliage, soil, or rocks, but many others land on the surface of lakes, where they sink to the bottom and become incorporated into the sediment, where they may remain well preserved for millennia. The pollen grain has a coat made of a highly resistant biopolymer called sporopollinin that resists degradation and remains well preserved in sediment. Mosses and fungi produce spores, which are also well preserved in sediment. Because plant species produce distinct pollen, their presence and relative abundances can be estimated by identifying and enumerating grains preserved in sediment profiles. This allows palynologists to develop insights into past changes in terrestrial vegetation, sometimes to the generic and species levels.

Pollen analyses have been used to track the re-vegetation and successional changes that occurred in Canadian landscapes following deglaciation. For instance, if a sediment core retrieved from an Ontario lake spans a temporal record dating back to the period of deglaciation (about 12 000 years ago), one could observe that the largely barren landscape left by the retreating ice sheets was soon colonized by northward-migrating plants.

This can be seen in **Figure 16.5**, which represents a simplified pollen diagram from a sediment core retrieved from van Nostrand Lake, located just north of Toronto (McAndrews, 1970). The diagram shows only the 11 most common pollen categories that were enumerated, and it divides the 12 000-year history of this lake into several major vegetation zones: spruce, jack pine, maple, and ragweed. The pollen grains that dominated the earliest "communities" were from spruce plus various sedges and grasses, which indicate that the pioneering vegetation consisted of open spruce-forest and tundra, similar to what now occurs in subarctic regions of northern Ontario. This vegetation indicates cooler conditions than presently occur in the vicinity of Toronto.

Then, between 10 500 and 9500 years ago, a pine-dominated boreal forest characterized the vegetation, suggesting a change to warmer and drier conditions. The succession continues to a third major zone, which represents a mixed deciduous–coniferous temperate

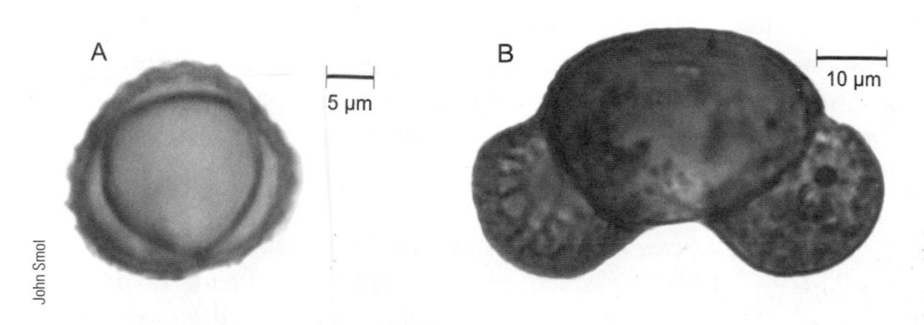

John Smol

Microscopic images of fossil pollen grains recovered from lake sediment. (A) pollen of *Ambrosia* (ragweed); a marked increase in this pollen in lake sediment cores from eastern Canada indicates the arrival of European settlers, as this taxon is especially competitive in culturally modified landscapes, such as open fields following deforestation; (B) *Pinus* (pine) pollen grain. Scale bars are shown to the right.

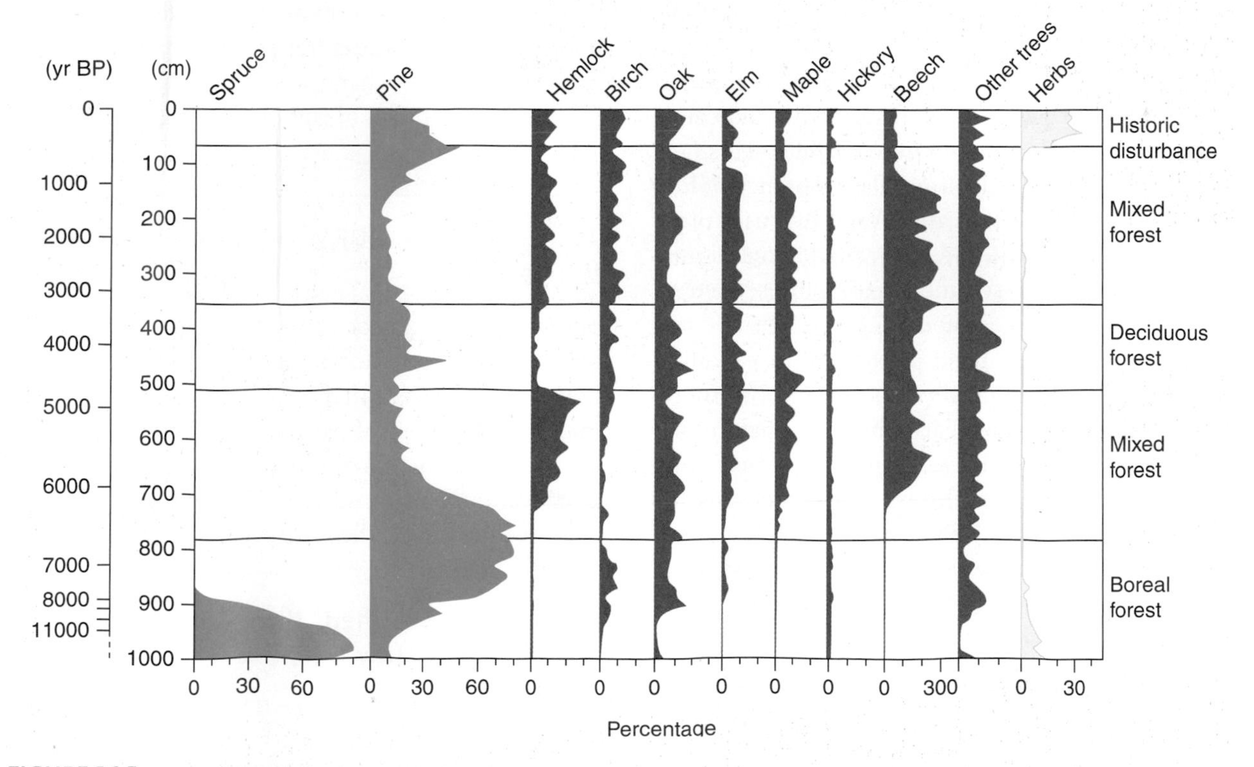

FIGURE 16.5

Pollen Diagram from van Nostrand Lake, Ontario. Recent times are at the top of the diagram, and older at the bottom. See text for further explanation.

SOURCE: McAndrews, J.H., North American Pollen Database: http://www.ncdc.noaa.gov/paleo/napd.html.

forest, with contributions from maple, birch, oak, elm and beech, as well as pine and hemlock that are especially common at the beginning and the end of this zone. This hardwood-dominated forest indicates warmer conditions than previously, and was prevalent about 5000 years ago—it is similar to the current forest of southern Ontario. There are other significant changes in the paleoflora, such as a decline in hemlock pollen about 4600 years ago, which may be linked to a pathogen that affected that species (similar to the decline in elm in many areas as a result of damage caused by the introduced Dutch-elm disease fungus during the 20th century; see Chapter 10).

The influence of European-style agriculture with its associated forest clearance is indicated near the surface of the core by the large increase in ragweed and other types of forbs and grasses. These are disturbance-related species common in agricultural and urbanized areas. In addition to pollen grains, there are larger identifiable plant fossils (often referred to as macrofossils because they can be seen with the naked eye), such as seeds, foliage, twigs, and other materials that can be retrieved from the sediment and used to validate the paleocommunities.

Aquatic Ecosystems: Reconstructing Changes in Lakes and Rivers

Pollen analyses provide important information on what was happening in the terrestrial part of the watershed, but what about the lake itself? To understand changes that have occurred in aquatic communities, we must examine autochthonous indicators that are preserved in sedimentary profiles. This field of research is called paleolimnology, a branch of **limnology** (the study of lakes and rivers) that uses proxy data based on physical, chemical, and biological indicators contained in sediment cores to reconstruct changes in aquatic ecosystems.

The most widely used proxy data in paleolimnology are based on the siliceous cell walls of microscopic diatom algae (Bacillariophyceae). Diatoms are a remarkably large and diverse group that may often dominate the species richness and sometimes the productivity of the algal flora, which itself is a major basal component of the food webs of ponds, lakes, rivers, and oceans. There are thousands of species of diatoms, each with its own optima and tolerances for environmental variables such as water pH, nutrient concentration, and climate-related factors. Importantly, the cell walls of diatoms (also known as frustules—they are composed of two overlapping siliceous valves, vaguely resembling a set of Petri dishes) are well preserved in sediment. Furthermore, the taxonomy of diatoms is based on the size, shape, and sculpturing of their glass frustules. Therefore, the parts of diatoms that preserve in sediments can be used to reconstruct both their past communities and historical environmental conditions. Other morphological remains, such as the siliceous cell-surface scales of some golden-brown algae (Chrysophyceae), have analogous characteristics to diatoms and can also be used in paleolimnological reconstructions.

Biomarkers of historical primary producers, such as algal fossils, are not the only indicators available to the paleolimnologist. Various invertebrate remains can also be recovered from sediment, such as the chitinous body parts of Cladocera, sometimes called water fleas, that include prominent genera such as *Daphnia* and *Bosmina*. Cladocerans are an important food-web link between primary producers such as phytoplankton (which they eat) and higher consumer levels such as larger invertebrates and fish. As such, understanding the long-term dynamics of cladocerans provides important information about the larger community.

Lakes and rivers also support a diverse array of aquatic insects, whose larval stages may be abundant in sediment. Midges (Chironomidae) are often the most abundant insect larvae in Canadian lakes, and their species may be identified by their hard, chitinous mouth parts, which preserve well in sediment. Particular midge species are reliable indicators of temperature, and so they have been useful in studies of paleoclimate. Species of midges also have different tolerances and optima of oxygen concentrations, and they have been used to track past changes in that important factor, particularly in studies of **eutrophication** (see below).

16.4 Paleoecology and Environmental Issues

The methods of paleocology have helped us to better understand some important environmental problems. In the sections that follow, we will examine case material of the use of paleolimnological methods to study important environmental issues in Canada: acidification, calcium declines in lakes, eutrophication, declines in Pacific salmon, and climate change.

Have Lakes Acidified? If So, When and by How Much?

The above questions have been widely asked in many parts of the world, including Canada, since the early 1970s. This is because of concern about the phenomenon of acidification caused by atmospheric deposition, which is indirectly caused by anthropogenic emissions of gaseous sulphur dioxide (SO_2) and

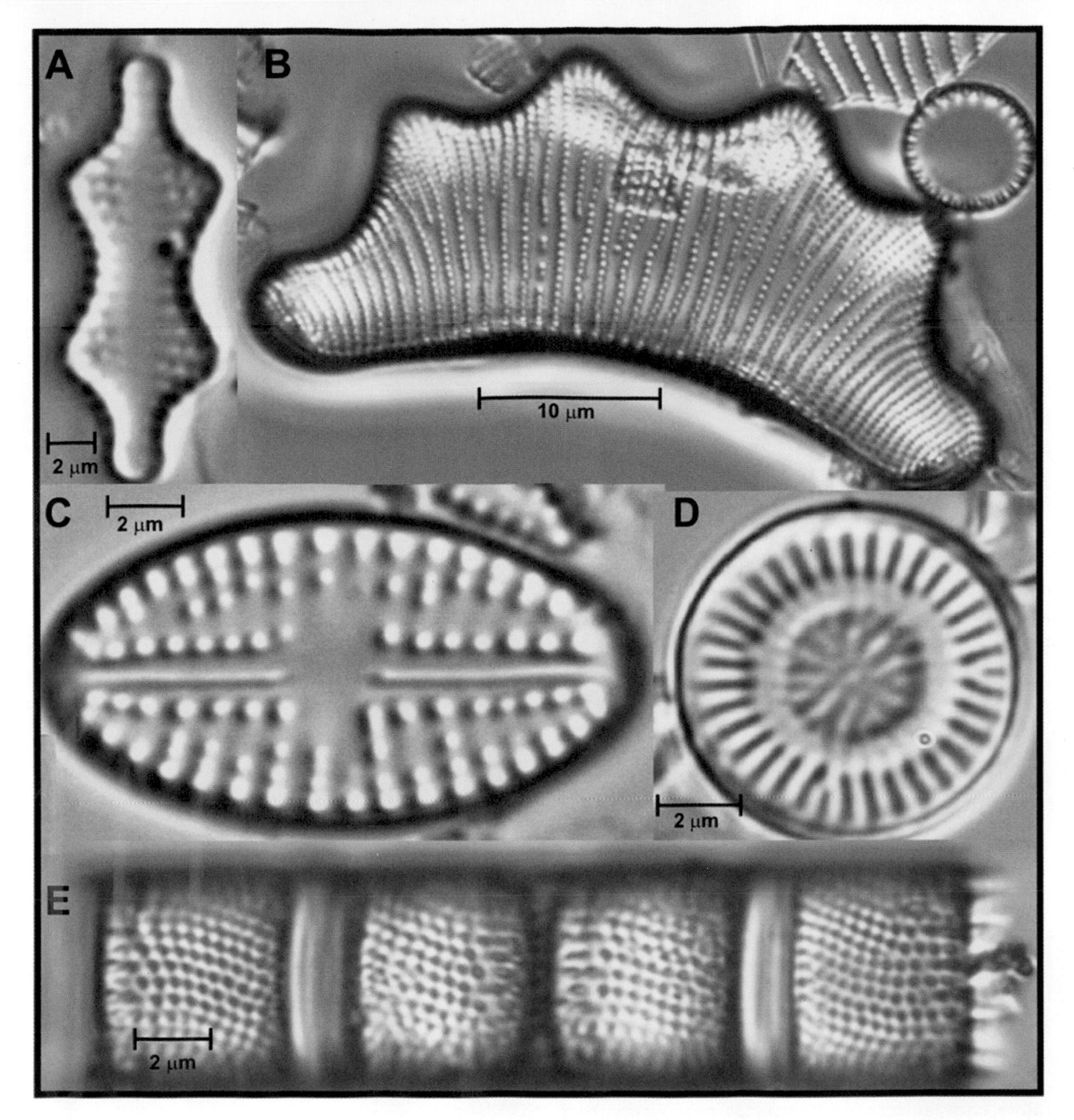

Light micrographs of fossil diatom valves recovered from lake sediment. (A) *Staurosira construens* var. *binodis*; (B) *Eunotia serra* var. *tetraodon*; (C) *Navicula farta*; (D) *Cyclotella pseudostelligera*; (E) *Aulacoseira subarctica*.

SOURCES: A, C, D, E: K. Rühland; B: A. Paul; both of Queen's University.

oxides of nitrogen (NO plus NO_2, which are collectively referred to as NO_x). These and other atmospheric substances can acidify aquatic and terrestrial habitats when they are deposited in the following ways:

- as "acid rain," or acidic rain and snow that are rich in dilute sulphuric acid (H_2SO_4) and nitric acid (HNO_3);
- by the direct (or dry) deposition of SO_2 and NO_x, which become oxidized in water or soil to sulphate (SO_4^{-2}) and nitrate (NO_3^-), respectively, which are acidic compounds;
- by the deposition of ammonium (NH_4^+) in precipitation and ammonia (NH_3) gas, which become oxidized to nitrate, generating acidity; and
- In addition to these atmospheric influences, some surface waters have been acidified by a phenomenon known as acid-mine drainage, which occurs when sulphide minerals (such as iron sulphide, FeS_2) become exposed to oxygen, causing them to acidify and generate sulphate (SO_4^{-2}), ionic iron (Fe^{2+}), plus acidity. Acid-mine drainage is often associated with coal mining, but it occurs whenever sulphide-bearing rocks become exposed to atmospheric oxygen.

The acidification of ecosystems is an important environmental problem because it causes toxicity and stress to many kinds of biota. In Canada, the problem is most severe near smelters (which emit SO_2 to the

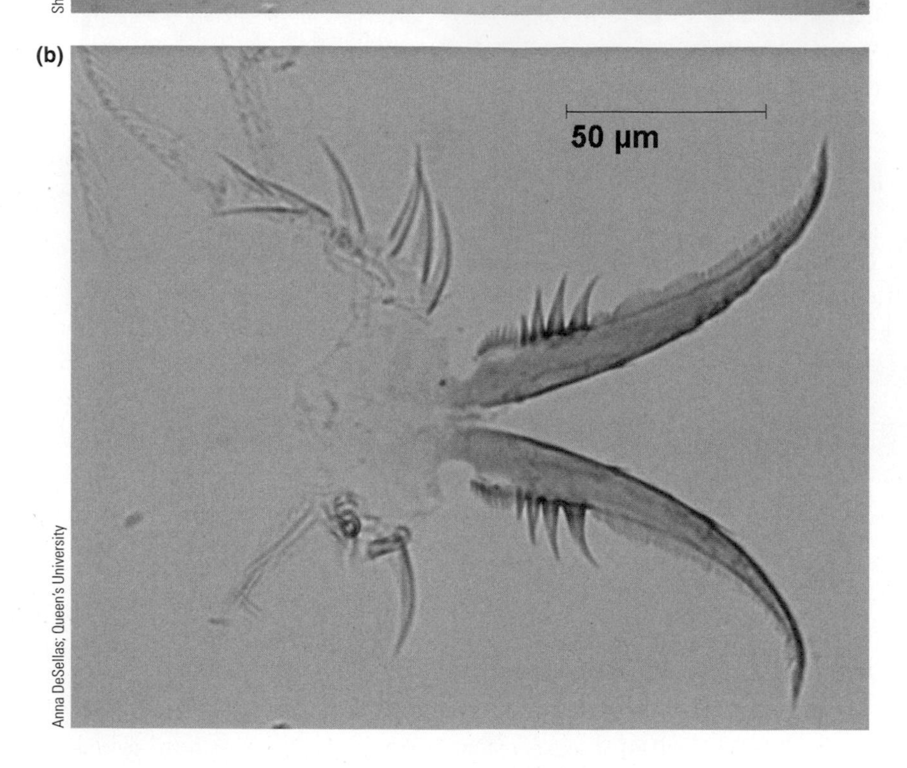

Cladocerans as paleo-indicators. (a) Micrograph of a living *Daphnia mendotae*, a common water-flea invertebrate in many lakes; (b) a post-abdominal claw from a calcium-rich daphniid fossil collected from lake sediment. These fossil body parts can be used to track long-term changes in invertebrate populations.

atmosphere) and also throughout much of the eastern provinces, where lakes are common on the Precambrian Shield—these waterbodies acidify easily because they naturally have low levels of alkalinity (HCO_3^-) and base cations such as calcium, which are key to neutralizing acid inputs. Interestingly, the most toxic aspect of acidification to some aquatic biota, and especially to fish, is caused by ions of aluminum (Al^{+3}) that become solubilized from watershed soils by acidity, rather than direct toxicity caused by hydrogen ions (H^+).

Although the phenomenon of acidifying deposition from the atmosphere is well understood, the issue and its mitigation have always been embroiled in both political and scientific debate. Certainly no one could deny that many lakes in parts of Ontario, Quebec, the Maritimes, and upstate New York are now acidic, but there have been vigorous and polarized discussions about the causes and history of the problem. While most environmental scientists believe that most lakes have acidified because of anthropogenic influences, others have suggested that they may be naturally acidic, or more affected by land-use activities than by atmospheric depositions. Because no one was measuring lakewater pH or aquatic communities in these lakes in the 1800s, before the time of marked anthropogenic influences, there were no suitable monitoring data to settle these divisive arguments. However, paleoecology has been able to provide some crucial information to settle the controversy, using biological indicators that are sensitive to ambient pH.

Many of the paleolimnological indicators mentioned previously, such as certain species of diatoms, chrysophytes, and invertebrates, can be closely linked to lakewater acidity levels. For example, among the diatoms, which have formed the mainstay of paleolimnological studies of acidification, calibration studies based on modern surface-sediment show that *Eunotia* species are abundant in acidic lakes, while most *Cyclotella* taxa are not and so are expected to decline as acidification progresses. And so, based on diatom community composition, paleolimnologists have constructed statistically robust transfer functions that allow the historical pH values of lakes to be reliably reconstructed, sometimes to within 0.2 pH units.

Figure 16.6 provides a summary of a case study of fossil chrysophyte algae from a sediment core taken from Baby Lake, located near the Coniston smelter at Sudbury, which operated between 1913 and 1972 and emitted large amounts of acidifying SO_2. The fossil-algal profile clearly tracks the acidification of that lake, as is shown by changes in four dominant chrysophytes in the ^{210}Pb-dated sediment core (Dixit et al., 1992). The three taxa on the left (shown in blue) are characteristic of circumneutral waters (around pH ~6–7), while the one on the right (shown in red) is abundant in acidic conditions.

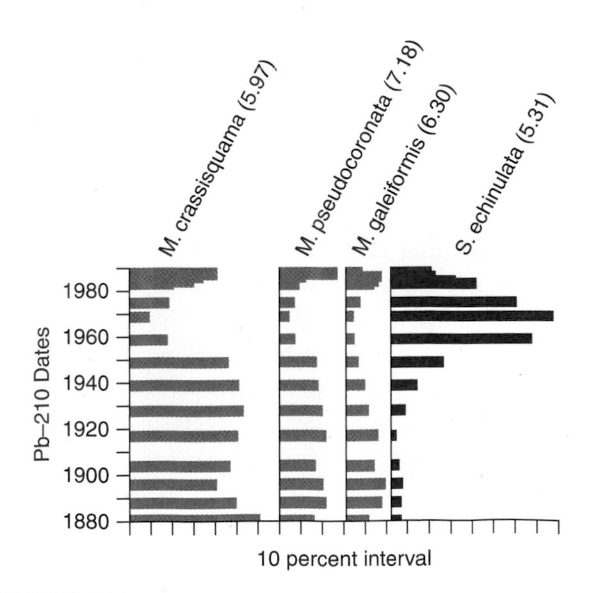

FIGURE 16.6

Simplified Diagram of the Baby Lake Fossil Algal Profile. Baby Lake is located near the Coniston smelter at Sudbury, Ontario, which stopped operating in 1972. The profile shows the acidification of this site, as well as a recovery following the closing of the smelter and other reductions in acidic deposition in the region. Only the four dominant chrysophyte species are shown, with their abundance weighted mean pH values shown in the brackets. The three taxa at the left (coloured in blue) are characteristic of circumneutral waters, while the taxon on the right (coloured in red) is more common in acid lakes.

SOURCE: Data from A. S. Dixit, S. S. Dixit, and J. P. Smol. 1992. "Algal microfossils provide high temporal resolution of environmental trends," *Water, Air, and Soil Pollution*, 62: 75–87. With kind permission from Springer Science and Business Media, and the authors.

There is an obvious change in the algal community beginning in the 1940s and continuing to the time when the smelter was closed in 1972. The algal-inferred pH (calculated using a transfer function developed from a calibration set of modern surface-sediment from lakes in the Sudbury region) indicates an acidification from an initial pH of about 6.5 to a low of pH 4.2 around 1975. Interestingly, after the smelter closed there was a striking recovery of pH, as indicated by the return of the circumneutral taxa to Baby Lake. This recent pattern closely matches the measured pH values for the lake (Dixit et al., 1992).

It is also important to know how fish populations have changed in acidified lakes, partly because they are economically important in recreational fisheries. While ecologists might know that many acidic lakes presently lack fish, they usually have little or no information about historical fish communities. Although fish scales and bones are sometimes preserved in sediment, they are too rare to allow for a detailed paleoecological assessment in most lake environments. Instead, indirect ways have been developed to track past fish populations.

One approach is to examine the remains of species of phantom-midges (*Chaoborus*), whose relatively big larvae are an important food of fish. There are five main species of *Chaoborus* in eastern North America, and of these *C. americanus* almost never co-exist with fish because it is such easy prey for them. Therefore, if remains of *C. americanus* are found in a historical sediment layer, that is an indicator that the lake was fishless at that time. For example, **Figure 16.7** shows the fossil

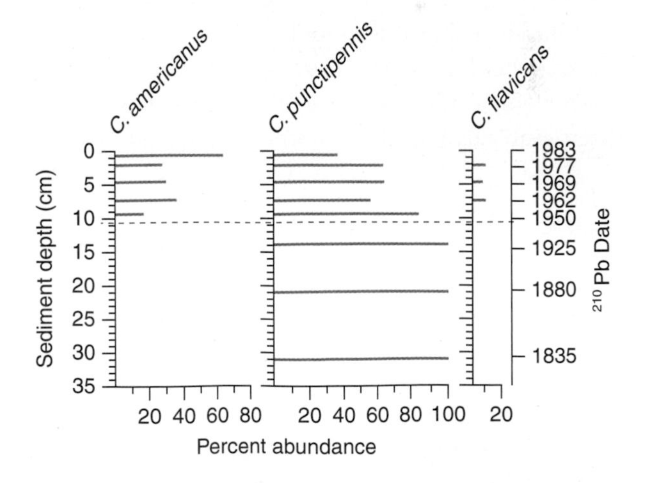

FIGURE 16.7

Changes in Phantom-Midge Fossils from a Dated Sediment Core from Swan Lake, Sudbury, Ontario. Because *Chaoborus americanus* cannot co-exist with fish, the profile indicates that Swan Lake became fishless in the 1940s, when acidifying deposition by SO became intense and the buffering capacity of the lake was exceeded.

SOURCE: A. J. Uutala, and J. P. Smol. 1996. "Paleolimnological reconstructions of long-term changes in fisheries status in Sudbury area lakes," *Canadian Journal of Fisheries and Aquatic Sciences*, 53: 174–180. © 2008 NRC Canada or its licensors. Reproduced with permission.

Chaoborus profiles for Swan Lake, a small lake in Sudbury for which both monitoring and paleolimnological data show there was a marked acidification because of deposition of SO_2 as a result of its proximity to local smelters. The lake is currently fishless, but the fossil *Chaoborus* analysis clearly indicates that it became fishless only in the 1940s, because that is when *C. americanus*, the phantom-midge that cannot co-exist with fish, began to thrive in this lake (Uutala and Smol, 1996).

Paleolimnological studies of the sort just described have been carried out in lake regions around the world, and they have been important in helping to sort out the issue of acidification caused by atmospheric deposition. These studies have provided evidence that acidification has occurred, that it is widespread, and its timing is coincident with large anthropogenic emissions of SO_2 and NO_x.

In addition, these approaches have been used to identify naturally acidic lakes. For example, work in Nova Scotia has shown that many of the lakes there are naturally acidic because of the influence of organic acids leaching from bogs and other sources (Ginn et al., 2007). However, not all of the Nova Scotian lakes are like this, and paleolimnological studies also identified some that are more recently acidified because of acid rain, such as several lakes in Kejimkujik National Park. Such data are important from a lake-management perspective, because knowing the pre-industrial conditions is critical to determining whether a restoration program may be justified. For example, if a lake is naturally acidic, it might not be considered as an appropriate candidate for a liming program to mitigate the effects of acid rain. Similarly, if a lake can be shown to be naturally fishless, it should not be stocked because its ecosystem supports communities that developed for millennia in the absence of fish, and so would be irretrievably damaged if fish were introduced.

Aquatic Osteoporosis: Calcium Declines in Lakes

The previous section illustrated how paleoecological techniques can be used to study one environmental problem. However, environmental stressors rarely occur in isolation—quite often, several anthropogenic influences occur simultaneously and they can synergistically interact to cause more serious damage to ecosystems. One such issue that has recently been identified is the problem of calcium declines in softwater lakes (these lakes naturally have relatively low concentrations of calcium and other ions). Lakes of this sort are common in regions of granitic bedrock, such on the Precambrian Shield.

We are familiar with medical problems of calcium deficiency in animals, such as bone disorders associated with osteoporosis in humans. However, calcium is essential for all life forms, although species differ in their requirements for this nutrient. One group of freshwater crustaceans with a high demand for calcium is the large *Daphnia* species, or water fleas, which need it to harden their chitinous exoskeleton. Both laboratory and field-based studies have shown that, if calcium availability declines beneath certain thresholds, large species of *Daphnia* such as *D. pulex* can no longer reproduce and they become extirpated.

But why would calcium levels decline in lakes? As with many environmental problems, there are several potential causes. The ultimate source of calcium in lakes is the local bedrock and soil in the watershed. In some areas, there is bedrock of limestone ($CaCO_3$) or dolomite ($Ca,MgCO_3$), and so there are ample supplies of calcium in soil and surface waters. In contrast, calcium-rich rocks and glacial debris are rare over almost all of the Precambrian Shield and other granitic regions. Nevertheless, for millennia even those Ca-depauperate regions had an adequate supply to satisfy the needs of dependent organisms, such as the large *Daphnia* species. More recently, however, the natural stocks of calcium have become depleted by anthropogenic influences, particularly acidic precipitation and logging.

One of the environmental impacts of acidification of soil is to accelerate the mobilization and leaching of base cations (such as calcium and magnesium) from soil and the watershed. In the early stages of acidification, this may result in calcium levels actually increasing in surface waters. However, if the catchment reservoir of calcium becomes depleted, its input to lakes declines and the lakewater concentrations may fall below the levels needed by organisms with high calcium requirements.

The problem of calcium depletion can be exacerbated by logging of a watershed. Trees need large amounts of calcium—it occurs in especially high concentrations in their foliage and bark (see **Table 15.3** in Chapter 15). Therefore, if trees are cut and removed, calcium is being removed from the watershed. Although new trees and other vegetation will re-grow in the logged area, they too need calcium, and will remove it from the soil. By combining the effects of acid rain and timber harvesting, we have an example of a multiple stressor—in this case, different stressors that have an additive effect on calcium declines.

But how widespread is the problem of calcium decline? We can survey a large number of lakes and show that their calcium concentrations are now low, but how do we know that this was not always the case? Once again, long-term monitoring data are lacking and so we must employ paleoecological approaches. By examining the long-term trends in paleo-indicators known to have a high calcium requirement (such as

Daphnia fossils; **Figure 16.8**), paleolimnologists have shown that calcium levels have been declining in many softwater lakes in Canada. This poses risks for species that have a high calcium requirement, such as *Daphnia* species, crayfish, snails, and bivalve mollusks.

In addition, the calcium supply is closely tied to the amount of alkalinity present in a lake—alkalinity is the key component of the acid-neutralizing capacity (ANC) of lakes with a circumneutral pH, and once the ANC becomes exhausted, a lake or river rapidly acidifies (see also Chapter 5).

Figure 16.8 shows one such paleolimnological application of this approach (Jeziorski et al., 2008) in Plastic Lake, Ontario. The pH of the lake has not changed much, but monitoring data clearly show that its calcium concentrations had declined since the 1970s. The decline in *Daphnia* zooplankton, which have a relatively high calcium requirement, closely tracks that chemical change.

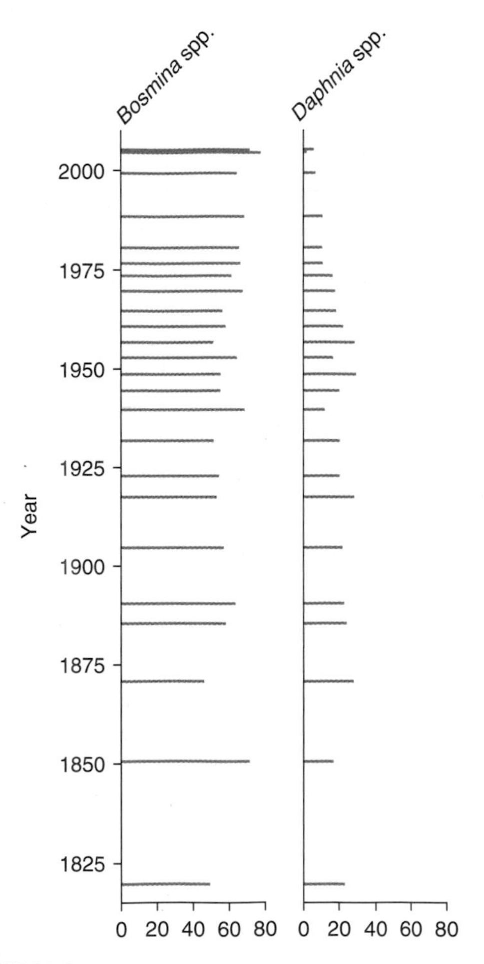

FIGURE 16.8

Changes in Two Dominant Zooplankton Fossils from Plastic Lake, Ontario, Since the early 1800s. *Daphnia* species have a higher calcium requirement than the smaller *Bosmina* zooplankters. Paleolimnological and monitoring data indicated that Plastic Lake has not yet acidified, but water-quality measurements dating back to the 1970s show that calcium levels have been steadily dropping. The decline in the *Daphnia* fossils closely matches that of lakewater calcium concentration.

SOURCE: A. Jeziorski, N.D. Yan, A.M. Paterson, A.M. DeSellas, M.A. Turner, D.S. Jeffries, W. Keller, R.C. Weeber, R.C. McNicol, M.E. Palmer, K. McIver, K. Arseneau, B.K. Ginn, B.F. Cumming, and J.P. Smol. 2008. "The widespread threat of calcium decline in fresh waters," *Science*, 322: 1374–1377, Figure 3 on page 1375.

Eutrophication of Lakes: The Problem of Over-Fertilization

One of the most common problems of freshwater ecosystems is caused by over-fertilization with nutrients, leading to excessive productivity or *eutrophication*. The productivity of most temperate lakes, such as those in Canada, is primarily limited by the supply of phosphorus (occurring as phosphate, PO_4^{-3}), with other nutrients such as nitrogen (usually as nitrate, NO_3^-) being of secondary importance. The most common anthropogenic sources of nutrient loading are run-off of agricultural and horticultural fertilizer and the dumping of sewage of livestock and people.

Phosphorus loading causes eutrophication by stimulating the growth of phytoplankton and larger aquatic plants (or macrophytes). To a certain point, increased primary productivity may seem desirable, but if excessive it causes serious ecological, aesthetic, and economic problems. Irruptions of algal biomass, known as blooms, can result in foul-tasting and smelly water that is unsuited for drinking or recreation. When the organic matter begins to decompose, it can sink to the bottom of the lake and deplete the oxygen supply, resulting in massive kills of fish and other animals.

Paleoecology has played a key role in studies dealing with the history of eutrophication in lakes. Various algal groups, such as diatoms, have been studied to develop transfer functions that allow past lakewater phosphorus concentrations to be inferred, using comparable approaches to those described for work on acidification.

In addition to helping us to better understand eutrophication, these ecological reconstructions have provided important insights into the resilience of freshwater ecosystems—the amount of stress they can tolerate before environmental problems become evident. For example, **Figure 16.9** is a summary of the major changes in diatom communities over the past three centuries, as evidenced by a dated sediment core from Gravenhurst Bay prior to and following sewage treatment (Little et al., 2000). By using a diatom transfer function developed from a surface sediment calibration set of Ontario lakes, the diatom-inferred (DI) total phosphorus (TP) concentrations were estimated (these are shown on the right of the diagram). These paleolimnological data clearly track the eutrophication of this bay, beginning in the latter part of the 19th century, as well as its recent recovery following sewage treatment and other mitigations to reduce nutrient inputs to the lake.

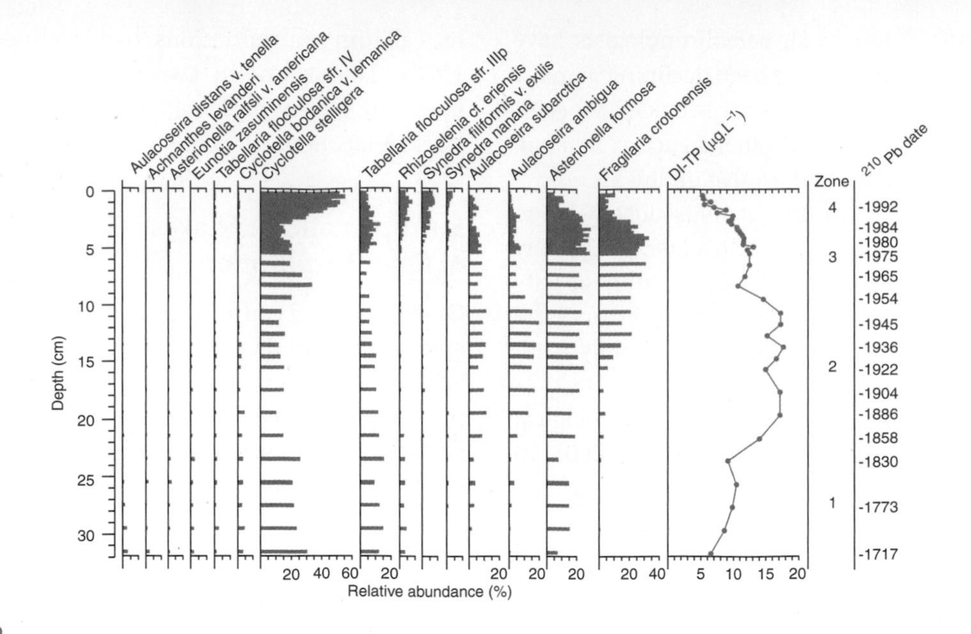

FIGURE 16.9

Summary Diagram of Major Changes in Diatom Community Composition That Show Changes in Eutrophication. The data cover the past three centuries and are inferred from a dated sediment core from Gravenhurst Bay, a small embayment of Lake Muskoka, Ontario. The data indicate diatom assemblages present before the period of cultural eutrophication (Zone 1), during the period of nutrient inputs by sewage and other sources (Zone 2), and recovery following mitigation efforts (Zones 3 and 4). The diatom-inferred total phosphorus (DI-TP) is shown to the right.

SOURCE: J. Little, R. Hall, R. Quinlan, and J. P. Smol. 2000. "Past trophic status and hypolimnetic anoxia during eutrophication and remediation of Gravenhurst Bay, Ontario: Comparison of diatoms, chironomids, and historical records," *Canadian Journal of Fisheries and Aquatic Sciences*, 57: 333–341. © 2008 NRC Canada or its licensors. Reproduced with permission.

However, increased nutrient loading has many other ecological repercussions, including declines in deepwater oxygen concentrations, which can have profound implications for other biota, such as deepwater fish. Algal indicators such as diatoms are not useful in reconstructing oxygen levels in deeper waters, but groups of benthic insect larvae, such as chironomids, do have varying tolerances to oxygen concentration. For instance, some species can tolerate anoxic conditions for extended periods of time. This includes some *Chironomus* species (also called blood worms, due to the hemoglobin in their hemolymph, which is used to bind oxygen under low-O_2 conditions). In contrast, genera such as *Heterotrissocladius* require much higher O_2 levels (Brodersen et al., 2004). Information like this, collected from many lakes, allows researchers to develop transfer functions that infer past changes in oxygen levels on the basis of fossil head capsules of chironomids that are found in dated layers of sediment. For example, using the Gravenhurst Bay example described above **(Figure 16.9)**, researchers found that, based on chironomid fossil assemblages, deepwater O_2 concentrations dropped rapidly with cultural eutrophication. However, unlike the recovery recorded in the diatom populations of surface waters, which tracked changes in nutrient concentrations, the deepwater O_2 concentrations have not yet recovered to their pre-eutrophication levels (Little et al., 2000).

Reconstructing Long-Term Trends in Pacific Salmon

Nutrient enrichment is usually associated with human activities, such as sewage dumping and agricultural run-off. However, there are also natural sources of nitrogen and phosphorus that may result in large fluctuations in nutrient concentrations in lakes and rivers. In this section we will explore how certain animals, such as migrating Pacific salmon (*Onchorhynchus* species), can act as **biovectors** that markedly increase the supply of nutrients to aquatic and terrestrial ecosystems. As we will see, paleoecologists have developed methods to reconstruct past changes of these organisms based on the nutrients they transport from the ocean to inland habitats. Such long-term reconstructions provide important clues about population fluctuations in economically important species, such as sockeye salmon (*Oncorhynchus nerka*).

As we saw in Chapter 15, collapsing fish stocks are a critically important problem. The usual causes are related to human influences, such as overfishing, habitat destruction, pollution, and perhaps climate change (which itself may now be mostly anthropogenic). However, as with other environmental issues discussed in this chapter, long-term monitoring data about fisheries rarely extend to pre-industrial times, and this hampers our ability to identify the root cause(s) of the declines. Lotze and Worm (2009) review the critical need for

Keith Douglas/First Light

Adult sockeye salmon can return in the millions back to their nursery lakes to spawn and die.

Irene Gregory-Eaves, McGill University

Carcasses of sockeye salmon (*Oncorhynchus nerka*) along the shore of O'Malley Creek, which drains into Karluk Lake, Alaska. After spawning, the adults die and their carcass-derived nutrients can significantly fertilize nursery lakes.

these types of data and some of the historical approaches that can be used to reconstruct past standing crops of large marine animals. To some degree, paleoecologists have been able to develop such a longer-term perspective for sockeye salmon, the commercially most important fish species on the Pacific coast.

Sockeye salmon are *anadromous*, meaning they spend part of their life in freshwater and the rest in the ocean (see also Chapter 15). They are also *semelparous*, meaning they reproduce once and then die. They usually breed in lakes (or sometimes in streams), and then their fry feed on invertebrates, typically for less than three years. They then leave the nursery lake and migrate along streams and rivers to the ocean, where they spend two to three years feeding and gaining more than 95 percent of their adult biomass. Then, following environmental cues that are not yet fully understood, adult sockeye salmon migrate back, with astonishing accuracy, to their nursery stream or lake, where they spawn and die. Thus, these west-coast breeding sites act as both nurseries and graveyards for sockeye salmon.

Of course, not all salmon survive these arduous journeys—many adult fish are intercepted by predators, such as bears, on their return migration. The bears and other predators, as well as scavengers, typically eat the salmon on land and defecate there also, so the migrating fish are a sort of "nutrient pump" of phosphorus and nitrogen from the ocean to inland habitats. Moreover, sockeye are semelparous, so any that do manage to spawn die soon afterward, and their carcasses provide a rich source of nutrients for their breeding stream or nursery lake. Therefore, declines in salmon populations have far-reaching ecological consequences—it is not only the human economy that suffers from collapses of the stocks of these or other over-harvested marine bio-resources.

Declining salmon populations are clearly a serious problem. But why are various stocks declining? The main candidates for blame are the following (see also Chapter 15):

- the blockage of migration routes by the construction of impassable hydroelectric dams;
- overfishing, particularly by the commercial fishery;
- destruction of breeding habitat by road-building and logging; and
- competition faced by wild-bred stocks from fish raised in hatcheries and then released to the wild (this may involve hatchery-raised sockeye and other Pacific salmon, as well as non-native Atlantic salmon (*Salmo salar*) that have escaped from aquaculture).

Oksana Perkins/Shutterstock

Many west coast animals, such as these grizzly bears (*Ursus arctos*), depend heavily on returning salmon runs for food. Once these marine-derived nutrients are recycled, they also fertilize the surrounding forests.

In addition to these formidable stressors, human-caused climate change, which appears to be affecting coastal oceanic habitats through warming, may be adding further complexity to the plight of sockeye and other Pacific salmon.

Fish fossils, such as bones and scales, are rare in lake sediment, but paleoecologists have developed other proxies that are used to reconstruct past abundances of sockeye salmon. These approaches take advantage of the anadromous and semelparous life history of this species, and the fact that most of the biomass of adults is accumulated in the ocean where they feed on plankton, small fish, and squid. Because salmon occupy a high position in the marine food web, they accumulate a relatively high proportion of a heavy nitrogen isotope, ^{15}N, in their body relative to the more abundant and lighter ^{14}N. This "heavier" nitrogen signal, which is expressed as a ratio of $^{15}N/^{14}N$ or its notation $\delta^{15}N$, is transported in the bodies of migrating salmon to their natal breeding habitat, where they spawn. The fish die soon afterward and release their heavier $\delta^{15}N$ signal into the nursery habitat, where it becomes incorporated into the sedimentary record of the lake. Paleolimnologists can then measure the isotope ratios in cores of dated lake sediment to obtain an indicator of the size of historical salmon returns.

The nitrogen isotope record is only one approach that paleolimnologists can use to track past sockeye salmon returns. Adult salmon are also a major source of marine-derived nitrogen and phosphorus, as well as other nutrients, to their breeding streams and nursery lakes. In fact, for some west-coast lakes, over 50 percent of the entire nutrient budget comes from decaying salmon carcasses (Finney et al., 2000). Given our previous discussion of using microscopic algae to track past nutrient levels, it should not be surprising that diatom species composition in dated sediment profiles can also be used to infer changes in marine-derived nutrients, and so to track historical salmon returns. When these data are taken together with the isotope data described above, a more reliable reconstruction of historical fish runs can be established. Such data have been used by paleoecologists to show the effects of fishing and dam construction on specific fish stocks, as well as longer-term changes unrelated to human activities (such as natural climatic changes, as reconstructed from tree-ring records).

For example, **Figure 16.10** summarizes some of the paleolimnological data spanning the last three centuries for Karluk Lake, a well-studied nursery lake for sockeye salmon on Kodiak Island, Alaska (Finney et al., 2000). This lake was of special interest to paleoecologists because there is a record of fish catches going back to the late 1800s, as well as escapement numbers (i.e., estimates of the numbers of sockeye salmon that reached the nursery lake) dating back to the early 1900s. Such longer-term data are critical for evaluating the reliability of paleoecological tools. As shown in **Figure 16.10**, the $\delta^{15}N$ in the dated lake sediments clearly drops once European-style commercial fishers began harvesting the salmon. This is confirmed by increases in diatom species that indicate lower nutrient concentrations, such as *Cyclotella pseudostelligera*, while those indicative of more fertile waters decline (such as *Stephanodiscus* species and *Fragilaria crotonensis*). These paleoecological data match the known catch and escapement data that are available for Karluk Lake.

At least as interesting, however, is the observation that the paleo-inferred numbers of returning sockeye salmon fluctuated markedly in the past, even before commercial fishing was a major concern. For example, there are decreases in sedimentary $\delta^{15}N$ in the early 1800s and the early 1700s, with associated changes in the species composition of diatoms that are indicating lowering nutrient concentrations (consistent with smaller inputs of marine-derived nutrients via migrating salmon). These observations indicate that

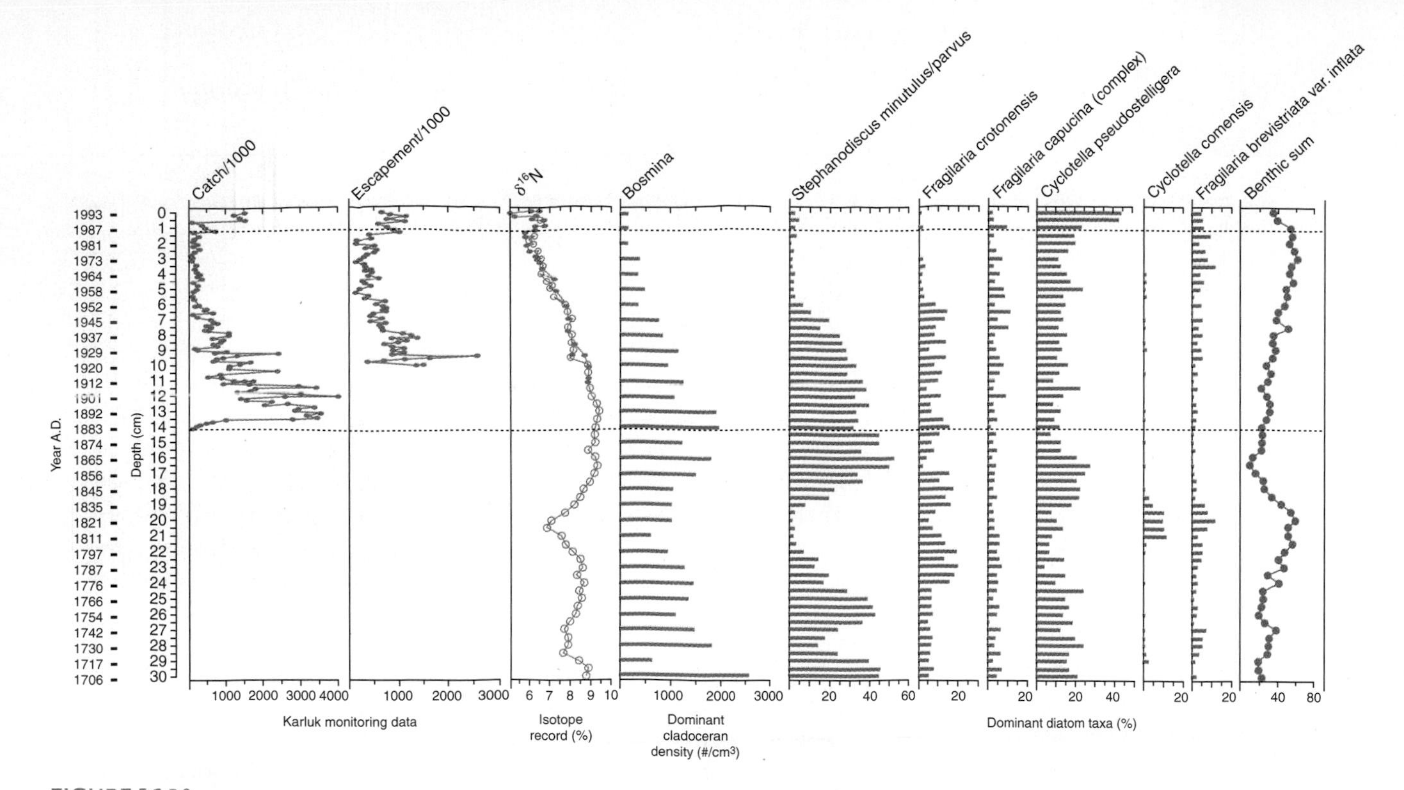

FIGURE 16.10

Historical and Paleolimnological Indicators of the Abundance of Sockeye Salmon in Karluk Lake, Alaska, over the Past Three Centuries. The routine collection of data on the commercial fishery began in 1882 and is shown to the left, as are escapement data since 1921 for migrating fish that reached the lake. The sediment-derived $\delta^{15}N$ data and relative abundances of certain prominent diatom species are also presented.

SOURCE: B. P. Finney, I. Gregory-Eaves, J. Sweetman, M. D. Douglas, and J. P. Smol. 2000. "Impacts of climatic change and fishing on Pacific salmon abundance over the past 300 years," *Science*, 290: 795–799, page 797, Figure 3.

salmon had previously declined markedly, even without interference by humans. Natural changes in climate were suspected as a cause of this, but since no long-term temperature data are available for this region, the researchers had to use the paleoclimatic record inferred from local tree-ring analyses. Those data showed that the periods of natural declines of sockeye salmon coincided with those of colder climate. These observations help us to better understand the environmental influences on salmon populations and the ecological consequences of their declines.

There are also many Canadian examples that detail how paleoecological techniques can be used to study nutrient dynamics in lakes, including the implications for eutrophication and related environmental problems. Ecology in Depth 16.2 provides an example that shows how these approaches can be linked to other scientific disciplines, such as archaeology.

Historical and Modern Climate Change

As described earlier in this chapter, climate varies according to a variety of natural cycles, and paleoecology has played a critical role in describing and studying those changes. Such research has provided important insights into the causes, nature, and magnitude of natural variability. However, as described more fully in Chapter 4, humans are undertaking large but unintentional "experiments" with the global climate system through a large and accelerating release of greenhouse gases to the atmosphere, particularly carbon dioxide from fossil-fuel combustion and deforestation. To place recent global warming into an appropriate context, data on longer-term changes are required.

Perhaps the best environmental time-series we have available are for temperature and other climate-related variables, such as precipitation. However, even these data are often too short and sparse to answer important questions. Given that Daniel G. Fahrenheit (1686–1735) and Anders Celsius (1701–1744) did not develop their temperature scales until the early 18th century, it should be no surprise that only a few reliable records date back even to the 1700s. And in Canada, only a few temperature data extend to the 19th century, and for most regions, there are simply none.

Fortunately for paleoecologists, however, climate often exerts an important influence on the distribution and abundances of species, including many whose parts are preserved in sedimentary profiles. By knowing the ecological optima of these organisms, including the

ECOLOGY IN DEPTH 16.2

Prehistoric Eutrophication: Blending Paleoecology with Archaeology

It is well known that environmental problems have become much worse in recent centuries because of the combined effects of human population growth and industrialization. One such problem is known as cultural eutrophication, or the fertilization of lakes and rivers by nutrients associated with agriculture and sewage. In Canada, eutrophication is usually associated with nutrient dumping by cites and large farms, but there are also a few cases in which it was caused by pre-Columbian aboriginal cultures, although at a much more local scale than typically occurs today. One example occurred in what may initially appear to be an unlikely place—it involved prehistoric whale hunters in the High Arctic.

The direct antecedents of the present-day Inuit were a group of whale-hunters, referred to by archaeologists as the Thule Inuit. Beginning about 1000 years ago, these aboriginal people migrated across the Arctic mainland coast and islands from Alaska to Greenland. They brought with them a whaling technology that was unprecedented in the North American Arctic, and their major prey was the bowhead whale (*Balaena mysticetus*), a huge mammal that can grow to 18.5 m and weigh as much as 80 tonnes. Several whaling crews of six to nine hunters each would chase a whale in umiaks (boats usually made of walrus skin) until one or more crews were within striking range for their harpoons, to which were attached sealskin floats to fatigue the animal and force it to surface. Once an exhausted whale surfaced, the death blows would be delivered using lances. The crews would then tow the carcass ashore where it would be butchered and the blubber, meat, and other products divided among the village.

The Thule Inuit were effective hunters and made efficient use of the whales they killed. The flesh, blubber, and skin were used for food, and the fat was also rendered for its oil to fuel stone lamps that provided heat and light for the long, dark winter. Some of the longer bones of whales were also used, particularly jaws and ribs, to form the frame of winter homes, which were then covered with skins, sod, and moss for insulation. It was in these small whale-bone huts that family units would survive the harsh winter. However, after about 1400–1600 C.E. Thule whaling declined, likely because of climatic deterioration. Some of the historically used areas were abandoned, and the remaining Inuit adopted a more diverse economy that focused on seals, fish, and caribou, as is also typical of their more recent descendants.

From an ecological perspective, the Thule archaeological sites provide important reference material for studying long-term effects of human influences in this extreme climate. When limnologists began to do water-quality surveys across the Arctic, they found that ponds receiving drainage from abandoned Thule sites typically had much higher nutrient concentrations than did other waterbodies, and the local vegetation was also more lush than the usual tundra. The causes of this enrichment and higher primary productivity were nutrients that were still leaching from bones and other discarded materials left by the Thule Inuit. Paleoecologists then asked: If we can still observe the effects of Thule whalers by higher nutrient concentrations and productivity in affected ponds, even though the habitations were abandoned centuries ago, then what were the characteristics of the high-Arctic ecosystems at the time?

One particular Thule winter settlement on Somerset Island, Nunavut, is of particular interest because of its large size (Savelle, 1997). Archaeologists have uncovered 11 whale-bone houses near a pond, which, with adjacent butchering areas, contain the remains of an estimated 230 bowhead whales, all dating from 1200 to 1600 C.E. There were also bones of several hundred ringed seals (*Phoca hispida*) and other animals. **Figure 16.11** summarizes some of the key paleoenvironmental data recorded in a sediment core from a pond that drained this abandoned Thule site (Douglas et al., 2004). Two types of proxy data are summarized in the diagram:

1. Similar to the salmon examples described earlier, nitrogen isotope data (i.e., $\delta^{15}N$) were measured in

John Smol

The whale-bone supports of a Thule Inuit over-wintering site, as reconstructed by the Canadian Museum of Civilization, at a site at Resolute Bay, Cornwallis Island, Nunavut. This structure would have been covered by animal skins, and then insulated with moss and sod.

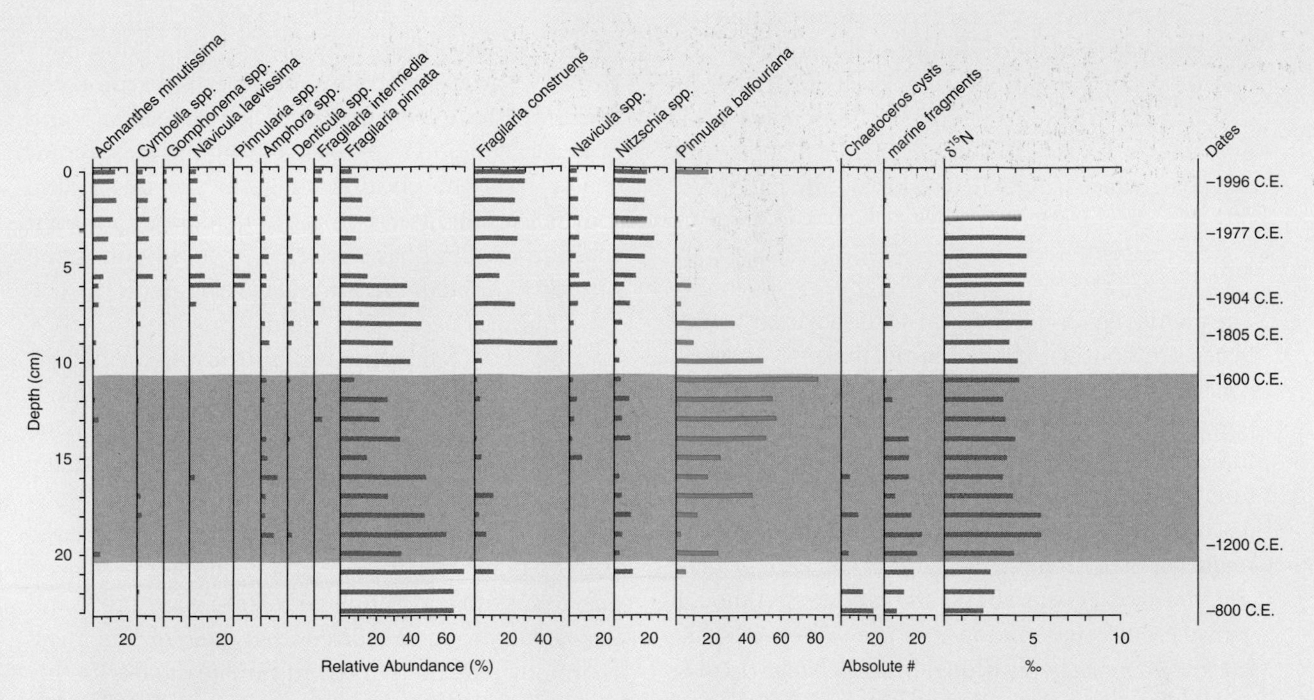

FIGURE 16.11

Diagram of Major Changes in Paleoenvironmental Indicators from a Sediment Profile of a Pond Draining a Thule Inuit Winter Settlement on Somerset Island, Nunavut. The increase in $\delta^{15}N$ at about 1200 C.E. marks the arrival of the Thule whalers, due to an increase in marine-derived nutrients from carcasses of marine mammals. The grey portion of the profile marks the period of inferred Thule occupation. The diatom community tracks the nutrient enrichment, particularly by an increase in the moss epiphyte *Pinnularia balfouriana*. After the site was abandoned around 1600 C.E. there was a partial return to pre-impact diatom assemblages. The diatom changes over the most recent century reflect warmer conditions.

SOURCE: M. S. V. Douglas, J. P. Smol, J. M. Savelle, and J. M. Blais. 2004. "Prehistoric Inuit whalers affected Arctic freshwater ecosystems," *Proceedings of the National Academy of Sciences*, 101: 1613–1617. Copyright 2004 National Academy of Sciences, U.S.A.

sediment, because if elevated it would confirm the presence of marine-derived nutrients from carcasses of marine mammals—their isotopic signature is higher than that in caribou, plants, and algae.

2. As an indicator of past changes in pond communities, the changes in diatom assemblages were recorded. Some marked changes are evident in the stratigraphy, which spans a period from about 800 C.E. to the present.

The first arrival of Thule whalers about 1200 C.E. is identified in the sediment profile by an increase in $\delta^{15}N$, as well as a striking change in the diatom community (**Figure 16.11**). The nutrient-poor, coldwater assemblage of small *Fragilaria* diatoms were partly replaced by *Pinnularia balfouriana*, a species that prefers higher nutrients and is especially common living on aquatic mosses (which are known to proliferate in Arctic ponds when nutrients are added). The Thule left the area about 1600 C.E., and the diatom assemblages began to return to pre-impact conditions, although there was not a full recovery (as also shown by the still-elevated $\delta^{15}N$ data). This is not surprising because even today the old whale bones and other debris are evident in the area. About a century ago there was another change in the diatom community, which is consistent with climate warming and longer growing seasons.

Comparable studies have been made of the ecological effects of other indigenous cultures in Canada. For example, Ekdahl et al. (2004) used paleolimnological approaches to examine the effects of agriculture and other activities of the Iroquoian culture at Crawford Lake in southern Ontario from about 1268 to 1486 C.E. The researchers documented how their sedentary agricultural economy resulted in increased nutrient input to the lake, higher primary productivity, and decreased oxygen in deep waters.

influences of climate-related factors, paleoecologists can reconstruct past climatic conditions. Some of the inferences are direct, meaning the data for certain species are linked to particular temperature conditions. In most cases, however, the species are related to environmental variables that are indirectly linked to climate. In this section we will explore two such applications: (1) reconstruction of the historical frequency of droughts in the prairie regions using the salinity optima of indicators, and (2) tracking changes in lake-ice cover in the Arctic.

Drought in the Prairies

The prairie regions of Canada and the adjacent United States are considered the "bread baskets" of North America, and are also major exporters of grain to other regions of the world. However, periodic droughts in these regions have had devastating effects on agriculture. To better understand this phenomenon and predict its consequences, we need to determine the historical frequency of drought, so that current conditions can be placed within a context of natural variations. Although it may seem counterintuitive to use waterbodies like lakes to track changes in drought, many changes in their ecology are linked to decreased precipitation and increased evaporation. These are often expressed together, as a ratio of precipitation to evaporation, or P:E.

Lakes with a closed basin (i.e., with no inlet or outlet streams) and small watershed are especially sensitive to changes in P:E **(Figure 16.12)**. The effects of drought on such lakes can be compared to leaving a pot of soup on a stove at low heat—if you return to your soup every 15 minutes or so, you will notice two things: (1) as some of the water in the soup evaporates, the height of liquid in the pot will decrease; and (2) if you taste the soup at intervals, you will notice it is getting saltier because water is evaporating and leaving the dissolved substances behind. Similar changes occur in a closed-basin lake when the P:E declines—the surface level drops, and salinity increases. Both of these changes in lake conditions are closely tracked by a variety of aquatic species that leave fossils in lake sediment. For example, certain diatoms are adapted to living in shallow water, while others occur in deeper, open-water conditions; species also vary in their tolerance of salinity. Therefore, we might expect a shift to shallow-water and salt-tolerant species as lake levels decrease and salinity increases.

Figure 16.13 shows one such paleolimnological study of a prairie lake (Laird et al., 1996). In this example, from Moon Lake (North Dakota), diatom taxa were identified and enumerated from a sediment core and lakewater salinity was reconstructed at decadal intervals going back about 2400 years (the research used transfer functions developed using methods similar to those described earlier for acid-rain studies, but instead of determining the pH optima for diatoms, they focused on salinity optima). Past events of high salinity indicate a decrease in P:E caused by drought, while lower salinity indicates wetter and/or cooler conditions. The persistent drought of the 1930s is clearly evident in the diagram—these are known as the "dust-bowl years." What is most striking, however, is that droughts over the past two millennia have been more intense and of longer duration than those during the most recent century. This observation suggests that this prairie region is naturally prone to droughts that are even more severe than have been experienced during the historical period of agricultural development.

This paleoecological study provides a sober warning about our perhaps optimistic view on the agricultural capability of this vital grain-growing region. It appears that when European settlers first arrived in the prairies, the region was experiencing an unusually "wet" climate, based on the data for Moon Lake. However, the salinity reconstruction suggests that for large periods in the past, this region would not have been able to sustain agriculture because of widespread and persistent droughts. Given that one of the most common predictions of recent climate models for this region is for an increased frequency of drought, this does not bode well for agriculture in the prairies.

Climatic Change in the Arctic

Polar regions are especially sensitive to the effects of climatic change due to a variety of positive feedback mechanisms, many of which are related to the surface albedo (or reflectivity). If you were to walk outside to a parking lot on a hot sunny day and approach two cars—one that is coloured white (i.e., high albedo) and one that is black (i.e., low albedo)—and put your hand on each, you would find that they differ markedly in surface temperature. The black car would be hotter because it has a lower albedo, and the white one cooler because it has reflected much of the incoming solar radiation rather than absorbing it. The Arctic, with its extensive areas of snow and ice, also has high albedo, and reflects much of the incoming solar radiation. However, with the climate warming, more and more of the light-coloured snow and ice melts on the land and over the water, thus decreasing the regional albedo. This results in more heating and more melting, and so on—a positive feedback system.

Because of its climate sensitivity, places like the Canadian Arctic are often considered to be the "miner's canaries" of the planet, in the sense that they are expected to respond earlier and to a greater degree to warming. Because about half of Canada's landmass is in the Arctic, it is important that we know how environmental change is affecting its ecosystems. Unfortunately, long-term monitoring records from polar

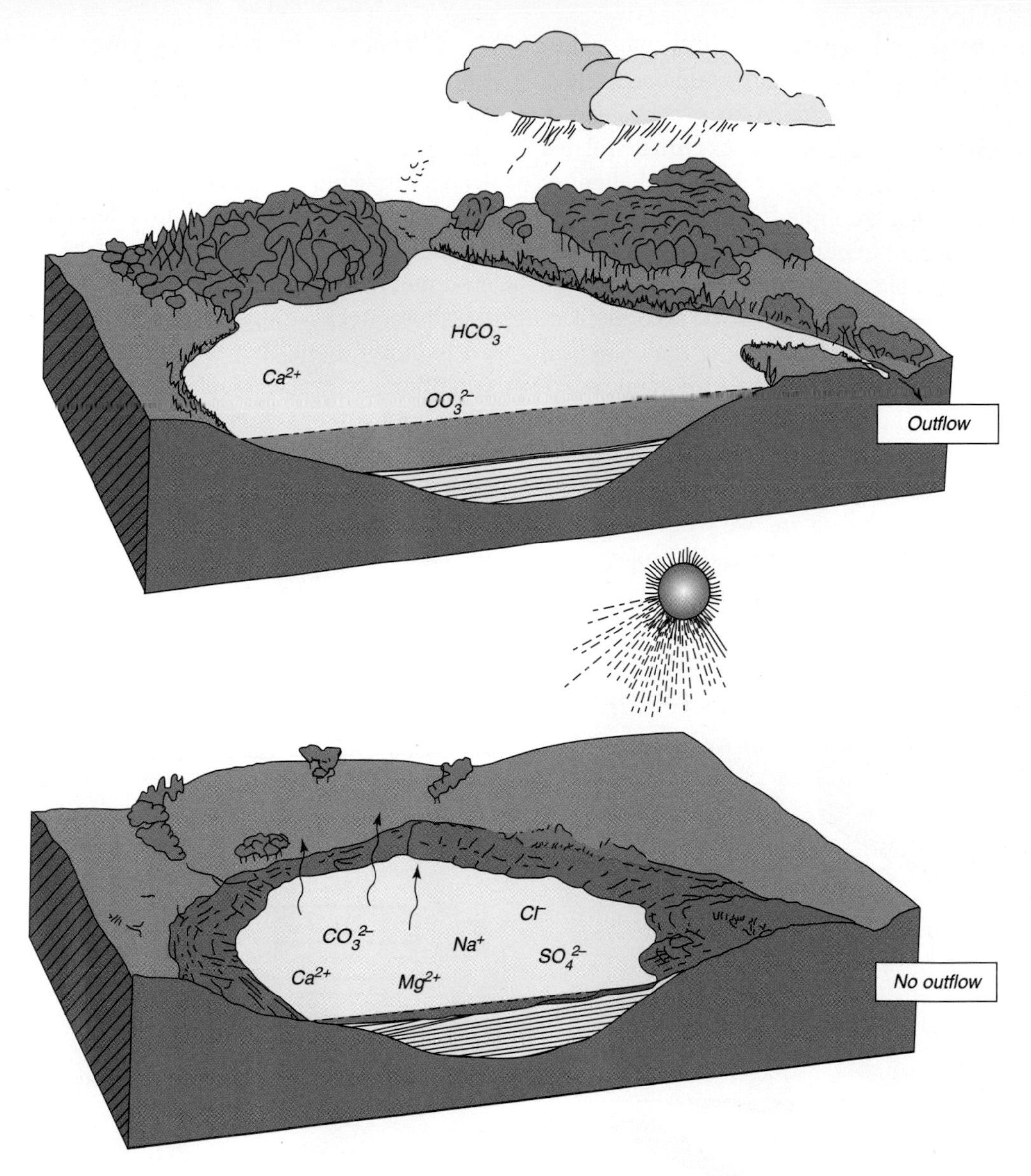

FIGURE 16.12

Changes in a Closed-Basin Lake with Shifts in Precipitation (P) and Evaporation (E). The upper diagram summarizes lake conditions during relatively wet periods, when P:E is relatively high, and as a result lake levels are high and salinity is low. The lower diagram shows the same lake under drought conditions, when P:E decreases so that the water level is lower and salinity higher. Species of diatoms and other aquatic organisms track these environmental changes, and their fossil remains can be used to reconstruct a chronology of historical changes that are due to periods of drought.

SOURCE: J. P. Smol, and B. F. Cumming, B. F. 2000. "Tracking long-term changes in climate using algal indicators in lake sediments," *Journal of Phycology*, 36: 986–1011, John Wiley and Sons.

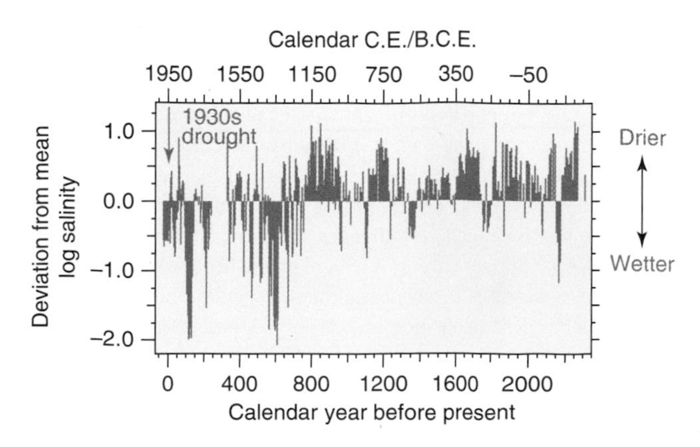

FIGURE 16.13

Reconstruction of Past Salinity of a Prairie Lake. The data are based on fossil diatoms recovered from a dated lake sediment core taken from Moon Lake, North Dakota. A diatom-based transfer function was used to reconstruct past lakewater salinity, based on the species composition of diatom assemblages preserved in the surface sediments from a variety of prairie lakes. The mean diatom-inferred salinity for the profile is shown as 0.0. Positive deviations from the mean salinity are shown in orange and indicate saltier conditions associated with drought. Negative deviations are in blue and they indicate wetter conditions. The 1930s drought is clearly discernable, but it is dwarfed by droughts that occurred in the past, such as the pronounced increases in diatom-inferred salinity around 800 years ago.

SOURCE: Data from K. R. Laird, S. C. Fritz, K. A. Maasch, and B. F. Cumming. 1996. "Greater drought intensity and frequency before AD 1200 in the Northern Great Plains," *USA Nature*, 384: 552–555.

regions are sparse, and so paleoecological approaches are critical for defining the trajectories and magnitudes of climate change in this region. A variety of paleoecological approaches are available to track climate-related variables in the Arctic, although there are challenges with all of them. For example, because most of the Arctic is well north of treeline, there is little potential to use dendrochronology, although some researchers have attempted to extract paleoclimatic records from the wood of low-growing arctic willow (*Salix arctica*) and a few other plant species. A more important source of paleoenvironmental data is from ice cores collected from glaciers on Greenland and several Arctic islands, as well as comparable studies in high-alpine areas. As useful as these ice-core data are, we will not discuss them in detail here because our theme is ecology, and not simply environmental reconstruction. Rather, we will again focus on lake sediment, because lakes and ponds are abundant in the Arctic, and they yield information on both environmental and biological changes.

Changes in ice and snow cover are often overriding factors affecting the limnological conditions of Arctic lakes. **Figure 16.14** illustrates three scenarios of changing ice conditions on a lake in the High Arctic. Under very cold conditions, a polar lake may be covered by ice and snow for all but a few weeks per year, and in fact some lakes have floating ice throughout the summer, with only a small moat of ice-free water near the shore. Because algae, mosses, and vascular plants are photosynthetic, they require light, and under these conditions only taxa adapted to shallow-water conditions and an ephemeral ice-free littoral zone will thrive. However, if the climate warms, more of the ice cover will melt, so there will be additional open-water habitat for photosynthetic organisms, and eventually the lake may become ice-free for an extended period during the summer. These changes will be reflected in the kinds of organisms that the lake can support.

Figure 16.14 illustrates climate-related changes in a relatively deep lake. However, shallow ponds, which

(a)

(b)

(c)

FIGURE 16.14

Effects of Climate-Related Changes in Ice and Snow Cover on Limnological Properties of Arctic and Alpine Lakes, and on Their Dominant Organisms. This schematic model shows changing ice and snow conditions on a polar lake during relatively cold (a), moderate (b), and warm (c) conditions. During colder years, a permanent raft of ice and snow may persist throughout the short summer (a), precluding the development of large populations of open-water phytoplankton and restricting much of the primary production to a shallow open-water moat along the shore. With warmer conditions, more of the lake becomes available for algal and plant growth.

SOURCE: J. P. Smol. 1988. "Paleoclimate proxy data from freshwater arctic diatoms." *Verhandlungen der Internationale Vereinigung von Limnologie*, 23: 837–844, Figure 2 on page 840.

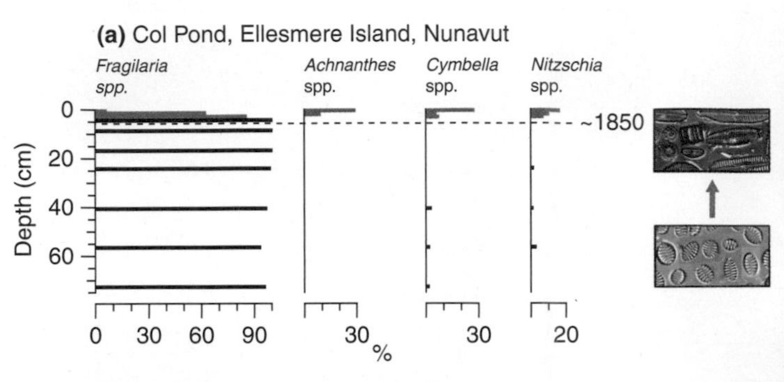

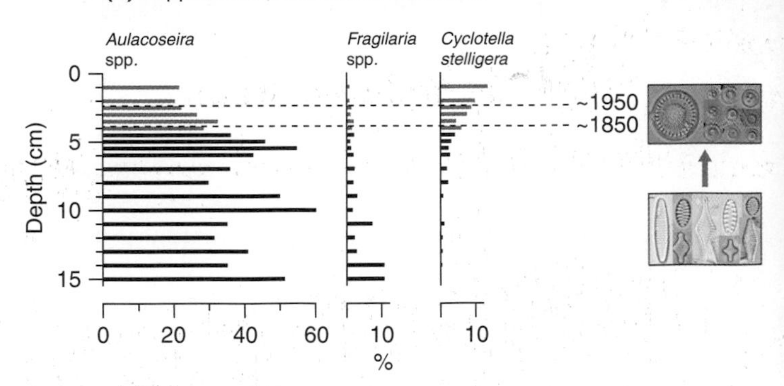

FIGURE 16.15

Climate-Related Changes in Diatoms in Two Waterbodies in the Arctic. (a) Changes in dominant species of diatoms in a sediment core representing the past few millennia in Col Pond (Ellesmere Island, NU). The figure highlights the marked changes occurring in post-1850 sediment, which indicate decreased ice cover and other climate-related effects; (b) changes in diatoms in a sediment core from deeper Slipper Lake, NWT, highlighting the marked increase in *Cyclotella* diatoms in recent sediment, which indicates decreased ice cover and possibly increased thermal stratification with recent warming. Approximate dates are shown to the right of the profiles.

SOURCE: Used with permission of Ecological Society of America, from J. P. Smol and M. S. V. Douglas. 2007. "From controversy to consensus: Making the case for recent climatic change in the Arctic using lake sediments," *Frontiers in Ecology and the Environment*, 5(9): 466–474; permission conveyed through Copyright Clearance Center, Inc.

A CANADIAN ECOLOGIST 16.1

Richard Harington: Ice-Age Fossil Hunter

Richard Harington

Dick Harington in 1971 with a skull of a steppe bison (*Bison priscus*) collected beside the Old Crow River, Yukon.

Richard (Dick) Harington is a paleoecologist in the Paleobiology Division of the Canadian Museum of Nature. However, he began his career working on present-day ecosystems, and from 1957 to 1965 he did Arctic research mainly with the Canadian Wildlife Service, studying muskox (*Ovibos moschatus*) and polar bear (*Ursus maritimus*) ecology. He then joined the museum and for the next four decades worked on ice-age vertebrates. He spent many summers collecting specimens in Yukon, the Northwest Territories, and Nunavut, and then working on the material at the museum throughout the winter. Collaborating with native peoples and other northerners, as well as many students, he collected more than 40 000 specimens, which today make up most of the national collection in the Museum of Nature.

Some of Harington's major work includes descriptions of the ice-age fauna of Yukon (2 million to 10 000 years ago), including woolly mammoth (*Mammuthus primigenius*), American lion (*Panthera leo spelaea*), scimitar cat (*Homotherium serum*), western camel (*Camelops hesternus*), giant beaver (*Castoroides ohioensis*), and extinct muskoxen (*Soergelia* sp., *Praeovibos* sp., *Bootherium bombifrons* and *Ovibos* sp.). He also documented evidence for the earliest humans in Canada. Working at an ancient beaver pond site on Ellesmere Island in the High Arctic, Harington and colleagues described a unique Arctic Pliocene (about 4 million years old) fauna, including a three-toed horse (like *Plesiohipparion* sp.), new kinds of fish (*Sander teneri*), deerlet (*Boreameryx braskerudi*), shrew (*Arctisorex polaris*), and badger (*Arctomeles sotnikovae*), as well as ancestors of the modern black bear (*Ursus abstrusus*) and wolverine (*Plesiogulo* sp.). Other research included fish and marine mammals of the Champlain Sea (12 000 to 10 000 years ago) in more southern regions of Quebec and Ontario.

The paleoecological perspectives that Harington and his colleagues have amassed provide a zoological and ecological history of environmental change in Canada. Although this kind of research was originally viewed as being esoteric and "basic research," it is now acknowledged as being very valuable to society in a broader sense. This is because of the insights paleoclimatic research provides for important environmental problems, such as climatic change.

are often the most frequent kind of standing water in the Arctic, are more sensitive bellwethers of climatic change. Even small changes in temperature will affect the ice-free period on shallow ponds, and hence the length of the growing season for primary producers. These changes are reflected in the composition of diatom communities and other indicators, which paleolimnologists can use to reconstruct trends in climate. Shallow ponds are also more greatly affected by changes in the P:E ratio, because of their small volume. **Figure 16.15a** shows changes in prominent diatom species in recent sediments of Col Pond, from Ellesmere Island in the High Arctic. The species shifts indicate a greater dominance of shallow-water diatoms of the littoral zone, indicating longer ice-free conditions in this shallow pond. For comparison, **Figure 16.15b** summarizes diatom changes in Slipper Lake, a much deeper lake farther to the south in the mainland Northwest Territories. This profile also indicates recent warming, but the species changes are expressed by variations of the open-water phytoplankton community rather than a littoral one. The marked increase in *Cyclotella* suggests longer ice-free conditions in the lake, and possibly an increased depth of thermal stratification.

These studies illustrate how ecological information preserved in lake and pond sediment samples can be used to track past changes in climate. There are additional approaches that can be used, such as tree-ring and pollen analysis, which we discussed earlier in this chapter. Furthermore, the chitinous mouth parts of chironomid larvae are frequently used as paleoclimatic indicators, with many Canadian examples (where this method was developed; Walker et al., 1991), and has been used extensively in regions such as the Maritimes to provide important climatic perspectives (e.g., Walker and Cwynar, 2006). Where possible, the most effective studies use an integrated approach—a variety of complementary indicators and techniques. Given the continuing debate and concerns related to climate change, and whether it is being caused by anthropogenic influences, paleoclimatic studies have an important role to play in these scientific, social, and political discussions.

16.5 Conclusions

We live in a constantly changing environment. Some of the changes are natural, but others are clearly linked to human activities. Without long-term monitoring data, we cannot place the environmental changes into an appropriate context. Advances in paleoecological approaches during the past several decades are helping to resolve this difficulty, and they are now being integrated into environmental and ecological assessments. The most reliable paleoecological assessments are based on multi-proxy approaches that use a variety of evidence to reach defendable conclusions.

This chapter has provided a sampling of approaches and applications used in paleoecology, although other sections of this book touch on relevant issues and methodologies (such as Chapter 14, which deals with the overkill hypothesis of megafaunal extinctions at the end of the Pleistocene, and Chapter 10, which examines the history of insect irruptions and post-glacial succession). Additional paleoenvironmental methods include the use of chemical approaches to track past contaminant levels (such as those of DDT and mercury) in sediment cores and museum specimens of birds. Novel molecular approaches are also being used, such as the sampling of ancient DNA. With the increasing prominence of environmental and ecological problems, there has never been a more pressing need for these types of data. We can expect to see continuing advances in paleoecology.

VOCABULARY OF ECOLOGY

allochthonous, p. 525
autochthonous, p. 525
biovector, p. 536
dendrochronology, p. 522
ecological amplitude, p. 522
eutrophication, p. 530
limnology, p. 530
paleoecology, p. 517
paleolimnology, p. 524
palynology, p. 528
principle of uniformitarianism, p. 518
proxy data, p. 517
refugium, p. 519
sclerochronology, p. 524

QUESTIONS FOR REVIEW AND DISCUSSION

1. Explain the principle of uniformitarianism, and discuss some of its limitations.
2. Provide examples of multiple stressors, and explain how climate warming might exacerbate some of these problems.
3. A major research area in paleoecology is the reconstruction of climate change using proxy data from lake sediment. Describe other environmental changes that were not covered in this chapter that you might be able to track using indicators extracted from lake sediment.

HELPFUL WEBSITES

CANADIAN MUSEUM OF NATURE
http://nature.ca/nature_e.cfm
Several research projects at the museum deal with paleoecological issues.

LABORATORY OF TREE-RING RESEARCH
http://www.ltrr.arizona.edu/treerings.html
A website sponsored by the University of Arizona dedicated to information about dendrochronology.

NOAA PALEOECLIMATOLOGY
http://www.ncdc.noaa.gov/paleo/paleo.html
This website summarizes many paleoenvironmental approaches and also provides links to wide range of images.

PAST GLOBAL CHANGES (PAGES)
http://www.pages-igbp.org/index.html
PAGES is an international effort to coordinate and promote past global change research.

You'll find a rich array of additional resources for *Ecology* at www.ecology.nelson.com.

CHAPTER 17

Ecology and Society

BILL FREEDMAN, Department of Biology, Dalhousie University

LEARNING OBJECTIVES

After studying this chapter you should be able to

1. Explain why the knowledge of ecology is defining the vision of sustainability and guiding the process of sustainable development.
2. Define ecological integrity and explain its key indicators.
3. Describe the importance of monitoring and research in understanding the causes and consequences of changes in environmental quality.
4. Explain the process of environmental impact assessment as it is practised in Canada.
5. Understand how ecologists play a vital role in advising and managing key aspects of sustainable development in Canada.

Big Tub Lighthouse at Tobermory, ON. Photo by Bill Caulfeild-Browne

CHAPTER OUTLINE

17.1 Ecology and Sustainability

Ecology is a vital scientific discipline. There are two reasons why this is true:

1. The knowledge of ecology is essential to understanding the existence and evolution of life, and the ways that organisms have spontaneously organized into ecosystems that exist at various hierarchical levels, the largest of which is the biosphere.
2. The wisdom of ecology is indispensable to guiding development of the human economy along an ecologically sustainable pathway—one that can forever provide people with a superior quality of life, while also sustaining the global biodiversity of all other species and natural ecosystems.

Ecologists seek to contribute to knowledge that is relevant to both of these kinds of values. They do this by engaging in fundamental and applied research.

Fundamental Research

Like many scientists, individual ecologists became interested in this profession because they have a deep and abiding interest in "big questions" about existence and life. They have a curiosity about the natural world—how it came to be present, and how it is organized and functions. These are primary, existential questions, and scientific work that is designed to investigate them is known as **fundamental research** (sometimes referred to as basic or curiosity-driven research). All ecologists have devoted their professional lives to improving our understanding of the natural world, and they typically pursue their work with energy and determination.

Because of the nature of the subject area, ecologists are interested in research that investigates the influence of environmental factors on the distribution and abundance of free-living organisms and their self-organizing communities and ecoscapes. This research is of great intrinsic worth because it helps us to understand the natural world, while also providing vital insight into the station and role of our own species. From this perspective, it is difficult to understand how some people might not view this sort of fundamental research, and the knowledge it provides, as being worthwhile.

Remarkably, however, many people do hold such a view—that curiosity-driven research is not as valuable as work that is directly intended to solve a practical problem (the latter is **applied research**, which we examine in the next section). Some of the people who feel this way are highly influential in society—they include many politicians, senior bureaucrats in government, businesspeople, and leaders in religion. The reasons for their attitude about fundamental research are varied and complex, but the most crucial one is a deeply held belief in the necessity of being engaged in practical work that directly contributes to solving real-world problems. It is also not helpful that many religious people hold faith-based opinions about creation and evolution that are in irresolvable opposition to those of biologists and most other scientists, and that are often the basis of hypotheses that they investigate in fundamental research.

The most important reason why critics of fundamental research are in error (outside of discussions about evolution) is that they do not understand or acknowledge the many cases in which insights gained from pure scientific work have indirectly resulted in important applied advances. This includes notable discoveries in fields ranging from genetics to medical biology to engineering and technology. There are legions of examples that demonstrate this fact, including several with Canadian storylines:

- the discovery in 1921 by Frederick Banting (1891–1941) and Charles Best (1899–1978) of the University of Toronto that insulin can be successfully used to treat diabetes, a disease that previously was almost incurable; the lives of millions of diabetics have been saved by this research, which originated with fundamental studies in animal physiology;
- the invention of the Java programming language in 1991 by James Gosling, a Canadian who created the original design of the system and implemented an enabling compiler and other technology; the work originated with theoretical approaches to computer science; and
- the discovery in the 1960s by David Schindler and colleagues in the federal Department of Fisheries and Oceans that phosphate is the usual limiting factor for the productivity of freshwaters; this allowed the problem of eutrophication of lakes and rivers to be tackled by removing phosphorus from detergent and by treating sewage to reduce its nutrient content before the effluent is discharged to the environment; the key research began as studies of nutrient cycling in oligotrophic lakes in northwestern Ontario.

Applied Research

However, it is important to understand that most ecologists today are not *only* fascinated by fundamental research—they are also interested in applied work, which contributes to the resolution of environmental problems that pose clear and present dangers to two vital goals: (1) the sustainability of the human economy, and (2) the continued viability of wild biodiversity, including natural ecosystems. Within this context, applied ecological research also involves extremely big questions—ones about the meaning and limits of sustainability.

Of course, ecological knowledge derived from research is also important at a finer level, for practical, day-to-day reasons that are related to the inherent needs of people for the necessities and amenities of life. These include the production and management of resources that are required as foods, materials, and energy, as well as for the ways that we design our urban and industrialized land-uses, and also for the aesthetics of pleasure and satisfaction. In this sense, the applied wisdom of ecology is vital to solving important problems related to the quality and sustainable use of natural resources—including bio-resources associated with agricultural production, forests, fisheries, and hunted wildlife. Of all the ways of knowing, ecology has the most to contribute to the vital societal objective of ecological sustainability (see pages 551–552).

Moreover, applied ecological knowledge is crucial to all plans or proposals that are intended to help conserve the biodiversity of Earth. This includes actions to implement networks of protected areas, and to appropriately steward them so their natural values do not become degraded over time. Applied ecological knowledge is also needed to develop management systems that will sustain more of native biodiversity on ecoscapes that are "working" to directly support the human economy—the places where we engage in agriculture, forestry, fisheries, and other kinds of resource management.

It is obvious that applied research in ecology is important and vital to sustainable development. But fundamental research also plays a key role in our society. The purview of science is not just to assist the human economy by discovering superior technologies related to materials, energy, and the handling of information. Science also plays a special role in improving our fundamental understanding of how

David Schindler

Applied ecological research is designed to understand the causes and consequences of problems related to bio-resources, pollution, biodiversity, and other issues that intersect with ecology, as well as ways to prevent or repair the damages. This is an aerial view of Lake 226 in the Experimental Lakes Area in northwestern Ontario. The hourglass-shaped lake was divided into two experimental basins by installing a heavy vinyl curtain in the narrows between them. The upper basin in the image was fertilized with nitrogen, phosphorus, and carbon, while the lower one received just nitrogen and carbon. Only the upper basin became eutrophic, as evidenced by its lighter colour, which is due to a mid-summer bloom of phytoplankton. This famous whole-lake experiment provided important evidence in support of the hypothesis that phosphorous is the key nutrient controlling eutrophication in oligotrophic freshwater ecosystems.

and why the natural world exists and functions, and in providing context for humans within that magnificent and unique realm. Curiosity-driven research in ecology helps us to understand those imperative questions, in ways that the more narrowly focused endeavours of applied work cannot do.

Ecology and Sustainability

In Chapter 15 we examined ideas about sustainable development, which refers to progress being made toward a human economy that can run forever because it is ultimately founded on the wise use of renewable resources. We also examined the even higher-altitude notion of ecologically sustainable development, which goes beyond resource sustainability for humans to include the vital need to maintain biodiversity and ecological services at viable abundances. Within this context of sustainability, the knowledge of ecology is vital to setting limits to growth of the human economy, and to finding accommodations for the genuine rights of coexistence of other species and natural ecosystems. Clearly, if the recommendations of ecologists and other environmental specialists are not heeded with respect to ecologically sustainable development, then the bitter alternative must be non-sustainability—which is not acceptable for many obvious reasons.

Arguably, the human enterprise is presently on a non-sustainability trajectory. Simply put, the evidence of this fact is the following (see Chapter 15 for details):

- *Population*—The human population is unprecedentedly large (about 6.8 billion in 2010), and it continues to increase (by 1.14 percent per year; WRI, 2010); the abundances of our mutualist species are also huge and growing (such as cows, pigs, chickens, potatoes, wheat, maize, and so on).
- *Resources*—The stocks of both non-renewable and renewable resources are being rapidly depleted; within only decades the human economy will become severely limited by the available supplies of fossil fuels and certain metals, and likely also by the amounts of water, high-quality agricultural land, stocks of wild fish, and timber.
- *Pollution*—Some kinds of pollution are causing widespread damage to bio-resources and to wild ecosystems (such as acid rain and ground-level ozone), while others may be affecting global climate (carbon dioxide and other greenhouse gases).
- *Damage to biodiversity*—Apart from risks to the human economy caused by growing populations, diminishing resources, and pollution, the biodiversity of Earth is increasing threatened by extinctions and endangerment that are caused by the destruction of natural ecosystems and damage by invasive aliens.

It is important to understand that these factors interact in a non-linear way to result in cumulative environmental and ecological damages. For example, a human population may be growing in size, and at the same time becoming more affluent, so that the per capita use of resources, generation of wastes, and destruction of natural ecosystems is also increasing. In such a case there is a multiplicative relationship among the factors. In a general sense, the collective effect of humans on the biosphere is a function of two factors: the size of the population and the per capita environmental impact. The population varies greatly among and within countries, as does the per capita

which are anthropogenic chemicals that were being used in refrigeration and other industrial and commercial applications. The CFCs are extremely stable in the troposphere and last a long time there, but they eventually wend their way to the stratosphere, where they break down under the influence of intense exposure to solar ultraviolet radiation. This releases ClO and other reactive compounds that deplete the otherwise high concentrations of O_3 that occur in the stratosphere. The O_3-depleting reactions are especially active during the winter, and that is when the O_3 holes are observed.

- *Research into the consequences:* It is well known that stratospheric O_3 provides a crucial environmental service by absorbing most of the incoming solar ultraviolet radiation, and thereby protecting organisms living on Earth's surface from the deleterious effects of exposure to this ionizing energy. Further research showed that stratospheric O_3 depletion could result in increases in skin cancers, including deadly melanoma, in humans and other animals, as well as increases in other diseases that are promoted by ultraviolet exposure. There could also be decreases in primary productivity in ecosystems due to the degradation of photosynthetic pigments and other biochemical effects on plants and phytoplankton.
- *Environmental action:* The global community, working under the auspices of the United Nations Environment Program, negotiated the *Montreal Protocol on Substances That Deplete the Ozone Layer* plus seven later revisions, which essentially banned or greatly reduced the further production and use of CFCs and other O_3-depleting substances. This environmental action was particularly effective because the manufacturing and use of CFCs were a discrete economic sector, and substitutes were available for the most important uses of those chemicals.

Of course, not all programs of monitoring and research have been as successful as the ones we just examined. Here are two examples that have not yet been adequately resolved: anthropogenic climate change and declines of migratory birds.

Anthropogenic Climate Change

- *Observations from monitoring:* Atmospheric chemists have documented large increases in the concentrations of certain greenhouse gases (GHGs) in the atmosphere, including CO_2, CH_4, O_3, CCl_4, and CFCs (**Figure 3.4**). These gases are radiatively active, in the sense that they absorb some of the long-wave infrared energy that is emitted from the surface of Earth as it cools itself of the heat of absorbed solar radiation. These gases, along with H_2O vapour, are responsible for the natural greenhouse effect, but it is possible that their increasing concentrations could be intensifying that phenomenon, resulting in anthropogenic global warming (Chapter 3).
- *Research into the causes:* Studies of the global emissions of GHGs have shown that their increasing concentrations in the atmosphere are being caused by anthropogenic releases, particularly those associated with the combustion of fossil fuels and deforestation.
- *Additional observations from monitoring:* Although the data are variable over space and time, during the past decades climatologists have observed various changes that indicate a warming of Earth's climate. These include a gradual but sporadic increase in the surface temperature, a decreasing extent or thickness of mountain and high-latitude glaciers, less sea-ice cover during the summer in the Arctic, and northward expansions of the ranges of certain species of animals.
- *Research into the causes:* A great deal of research is being undertaken into the likely causes of the global warming. The predominance of scientific opinion, as expressed by the Intergovernmental Panel on Climate Change (IPCC) of the United Nations Environment Program, is that an intensification of Earth's naturally occurring greenhouse effect is occurring because of increasing concentrations of GHGs. In effect, this is anthropogenic global warming. Note, however, that not all atmospheric scientists agree with this conclusion—some believe that the recent warming could be natural in origin.
- *Research into the consequences:* Much research is being done to understand the likely consequences of global warming. The economic effects might include catastrophic decreases in agricultural production and food security, an increase of certain contagious diseases, and an increase in severe weather events that could cause ruinous damage in urban and agricultural regions. The ecological effects could include awful damage caused to biodiversity.
- *Environmental action:* Spurred on by the increasingly assertive predictions of the IPCC, governments throughout the world are beginning to implement measures to decrease the emissions of greenhouse gases, especially of CO_2. However, the actions taken so far are relatively small and insufficient to make much of a difference. Even if fully implemented, they are only enough to slow down the rate of increase of GHGs in the atmosphere.

Declines of Migratory Birds

- *Observations from monitoring:* Large-scale declines are being observed in the populations of various species of so-called neotropical migratory birds. These are landbirds that breed in North America but migrate to spend the winter in Central and South America (see **Figure 17.5**).

- *Research into the causes:* Avian ecologists have undertaken many studies of the potential causes of the decline of neotropical migrants, but have not identified a single key factor. The most likely cause is the loss of wintering habitat because of deforestation in tropical countries. Other influences include habitat losses in the breeding range, increases of avian diseases such as West Nile virus, and effects of increased populations of nest parasites such as cowbirds.
- *Research into the consequences:* Research into the functional ecology of birds suggests that decreases in their populations could have important ecological ramifications, including an increase in the abundance of injurious insects, because most of the declining bird species are key predators of these and other invertebrates.
- *Environmental action:* Various governmental and non-governmental agencies are working to conserve the natural habitats that are needed to support the declining birds and other wildlife. However, their cumulative actions are not yet occurring at a large enough scale—natural habitats are being lost to deforestation and other damages much faster than others are being conserved, so the ecological damage continues to rapidly proceed.

Clearly, programs of monitoring and research are important to society because they provide crucial information and knowledge about the occurrence, causes, and consequences of environmental damage. This is necessary if effective programs are to be designed and implemented to prevent further degradations of environmental quality and ecological integrity, and to repair damages that have already been caused. These actions are necessary if society is to conduct its economy in a truly sustainable manner.

17.4 Ecological Change and Damage

The genesis of life on Earth occurred as early as 3.7 billion years ago, and before and since that momentous event, the biosphere has incessantly changed over time and space. Organisms have responded to those changes in environmental conditions, within limits set by their inherent genetics, phenotypic plasticity, and external biological influences such as competition, predation, and disease. Over longer time scales, populations and higher phylogenetic units (such as species, families, and orders) became modified by adaptive evolution, or they became extinct.

Environmental change is thought to have been relatively gradual during almost all of evolutionary history, involving slow variations of climate and other factors. The evolutionary responses by populations of organisms were also extremely slow—the extended periods of biological quiescence are sometimes referred to as **stasis**. The prolonged epochs of leisurely environmental change have, however, been punctuated by rare cataclysmic events. The biological responses to those catastrophes included widespread extinctions, followed by evolutionary radiation of the survivors as they took advantage of empty niches that had been made available.

The term **punctuated equilibrium** refers to the complex of these two kinds of environmental changes and the biological and ecological responses to them—an extended predominance of slow variations interspersed by rare but massive events of fast change (Eldredge and Gould, 1972). This theory is controversial, largely because it suggests that gradual evolutionary changes are much less important than those that are rapid. Nevertheless, it supports the notion that environmental change is universal and omnipresent, and that rare cataclysms are to be expected.

An example of an early catastrophe is the "poisoning" of the atmosphere by oxygen after the first photosynthetic organisms evolved and then proliferated, beginning about 2.5 billion years ago. This environmental change would have been disastrous for most of the existing species, which had an anaerobic metabolism. Nevertheless, it subsequently led to the rapid evolution, proliferation, and radiation of organisms that were tolerant of oxygen and even needed it to survive. Other examples of cataclysmic events are the awesome destruction caused by extraordinary strikes of large meteorites, such as the 10 km-wide one that apparently hit the Yucatan region about 65 million years ago and may have caused the mass extinction that marks the end of the Cretaceous era.

In any event, natural environmental change has always been pervasive, as have been the evolutionary and other responses by populations and ecosystems. In fact, many ecosystems are predictably dynamic, in that they experience recurrent changes in their component species, amounts of biomass, and functional properties such as productivity and nutrient cycling. This is true of all Canadian ecosystems, which occur in seasonal environments that are characterized by a warm growing season, followed by a wintry dormant period during which there is little or no plant productivity. Animals survive the hard times of winter in various ways: by migrating, hibernating, or feeding on plant biomass left from the previous growing season. Other natural ecological dynamics, such as disturbances by wildfires or windstorms, are less predictable, although over long periods of time they may have a regular frequency of occurrence (Chapter 10).

does not mean that environmental damage will not be caused by the development—some amount of harm is inevitable.

Because an EIA considers ecological and physical-chemical environmental consequences, as well as socioeconomic effects, its process is a highly multi- and interdisciplinary activity. **Multidisciplinary** means that various fields of study are engaged, including chemistry, ecology, economics, geography, geology, sociology, and others. **Interdisciplinary** means that a diversity of kinds of knowledge is used in an integrated manner, rather than in (or in addition to) a disconnected approach.

An EIA may be undertaken to examine various kinds of planned activities that might affect environmental quality. In Canada, they may include

- *an individual project,* such as a proposal to construct a power plant, dam, airport, school, or highway;
- *an integrated scheme,* such as a proposal to develop a pulp mill with its included plans for wood supply and forest management, an industrial park consisting of various enterprises and businesses, and other complex developments that involve numerous projects that are undertaken in a coordinated manner; and
- *governmental policies* that carry a risk of substantially affecting the environment, such as a strategy to increase the fossil-fuel, metal-mining, or agricultural sectors of the economy, or to increase the rate of immigration to a region or to the country as a whole.

Within this context, the spatial scale of an EIA can vary greatly. It can range from an examination of the risk to a small wetland posed by the proposed construction of a building nearby, to the examination of a complex megaproject to develop a large hydroelectric dam and reservoir in a region that is presently wilderness.

In Canada, environmental impact assessments for proposals that involve federal funding or jurisdiction are regulated under the *Canadian Environmental Assessment Act* (CEAA), which was enacted in 1992 (Department of Justice Canada, 1992). Provinces and territories also have legislated requirements for EIA, as do some local levels of government, such as municipalities and First Nations.

EIA is based on the premise that any proposed development, program, or policy carries inherent risks for the welfare of people, their economy, and for other species and ecosystems. For instance, an EIA of a proposed coal-fired generating station would have to study its emissions of chemicals to the atmosphere, such as sulphur dioxide, carbon dioxide, mercury vapour, and particulates. The predicted effects on local and regional air quality would have to be compared with levels that are known to already occur in the region (to assess the cumulative impacts), as well as those that are known to cause toxicity to sensitive biota. Of course, the predicted effects on air quality would also have to be compared with any environmental criteria that are regulated by governments. Construction of the power plant might also damage areas of natural habitat, and that ecological damage would have to be quantified and its importance evaluated before permission is given to start the project. Interestingly, under Canadian EIA law and practice, there would not be a need to study the plans to mine and transport coal to the power plant—that would be a separate proposal and EIA process.

Typically, the most stringent regulatory standards for pollutants apply to the maximum exposures that people can experience without a significant risk to their health. There are also criteria to protect wild species and ecosystems, but they are less exacting, meaning that higher exposures are tolerated. For example, the Canadian guideline for uranium in drinking water is 0.02 mg/L (Health Canada, 2008), but that for the protection of aquatic life is 40 mg/L for a short-term exposure (<1–4 days) and 5.5 mg/L for a long-term exposure (CCME, 2009). Note that the criteria for aquatic life accommodate the fact that, in terms of the cumulative dose received, a longer-term exposure to a low concentration may be as important as a shorter exposure to a higher concentration.

Any economic development is likely to affect a wide variety of species and communities. However, it is not possible to study all of the potential effects of such ecological values. Instead, EIAs are usually restricted to examining the likely effects on a carefully selected set of **valued ecosystem components** (or **VECs**). A VEC is considered to be important for one or more of these reasons:

- It is a bio-resource, such as a commercial forest, or a hunted stock of birds, mammals, or fish.
- It is a species or community that is at risk.
- It is of aesthetic importance, such as a prominent viewscape that local people or tourists like to visit.
- It is of cultural significance to an aboriginal community or other local people.

The initial phase of an EIA is known as a **screening**, and it is important because it helps to determine the level of assessment of a proposed development—whether a relatively minor review or a full assessment is necessary. Once this is decided by a regulatory authority, a **scoping exercise** is undertaken to identify the potentially important intersections of project-related activities and stressors with

Environmental impact assessments often focus on the examination of likely effects of a proposed development on a selected set of valued ecosystem components (or VECs). A VEC is considered important because it is a bio-resource, a species or community that is at risk, of aesthetic value, or of cultural significance to an aboriginal community or other local people. The Baird's sandpiper (*Calidris bairdii*, top) and the green heron (*Butorides virescens*, bottom) might be considered VECs because they are rare in parts of their range and are sought after for viewing by naturalists.

Bill Freedman (top and bottom)

VECs or human socioeconomic welfare. In essence, the scoping evaluates the intersections of the predicted spatial and temporal boundaries of stressors associated

- with the proposed development, and
- with those where VECs and humans occur.

If potential interactions are identified, the assessors must determine whether significant damage is likely to be caused.

If enough time and funding are available, it may be possible to conduct simulation modelling or field or laboratory research to investigate the potential interactions between project-related stressors and VECs. Often, however, this cannot be done because there is insufficient funding to do the work, or the EIA must be completed relatively quickly. If this is the case, then assessments of the likely environmental effects may be based on the expert opinions of ecologists and other professionals. Those opinions should be founded on careful and objective review of the best scientific information that is available. It must be understood, however, that even well-funded and properly designed and executed research may yield uncertain results. This is especially true of ecological damage that might be caused by exposure to a low intensity of project-related stressors.

Planning Options

If potentially important risks to human welfare or VECs are identified, a number of planning options must be considered. There are three broad choices:

- *Prevent or avoid:* One option is to avoid the predicted damage by ensuring that people or VECs do not suffer a significant exposure to damaging stressors related to the project. This can be done by modifying the characteristics of the development, or even by choosing to cancel the project if there is a severe conflict with human welfare or ecological values. Because prevention and avoidance may involve substantial costs, they may be viewed as a less-desirable option by proponents of a development. Cancelling a project is also

ENVIRONMENTAL APPLICATIONS 17.1

Cumulative Environmental Effects

Environmental impact assessment (EIA) is a planning activity that is used to identify and evaluate environmental problems that may be caused by a proposed economic activity. According to the *Canadian Environmental Assessment Act* (1995), this includes the need to evaluate **cumulative environmental impacts**, or those resulting from the effects of a proposed undertaking within some defined area, in addition to those caused by any past, existing, and imminent developments and activities. The concept of cumulative effects recognizes that the environmental effects of separate anthropogenic influences will combine and interact to cause changes that may be different from those occurring separately. In this context, it is prudent to consider all of the anthropogenic influences when examining the potential effects of a newly proposed project or activity.

Assessment of cumulative impacts requires knowledge of both the likely effects of a proposed development, as well as the existing ones of other anthropogenic activities in a study area, plus additional ones that are likely to occur. If all of this is known, then the incremental effects of a proposed undertaking can be estimated and evaluated for their relative importance. Cumulative effects can result from multiple pathways, and they may be manifested in physical, biological, and socioeconomic damages.

Examples of cumulative environmental effects that are primarily ecological and have occurred in Canada include the following:

- aggregate damage caused to populations of migratory salmon in the Fraser River watershed in British Columbia as a result of commercial fishing in the open Pacific or in the river itself, along with sport and subsistence fishing, plus degradation of freshwater habitat through such influences as the dumping of sewage, agricultural erosion and pesticides, warmer temperatures and woody debris in streams caused by forestry operations, risks of sea-louse infection from aquaculture in coastal waters, and warming oceanic waters caused by climate change;
- incremental losses of wetlands in the Prairie provinces caused by various agricultural practices, such as drainage, excessive fertilization with nutrients, toxicity caused by pesticides, and trampling by cattle, along with drying caused by periodic droughts whose frequency may become exacerbated by climate change;
- losses of biodiversity in southern Quebec and Ontario caused by deforestation to develop land for urbanized and agricultural uses, fragmentation by roads and transmission corridors, disturbances by forestry and mining, and various kinds of pollution;
- ecological degradation in a region of boreal forest in northern Alberta in which there are diverse anthropogenic stressors associated with timber harvesting, exploration and mining for oil and gas, oil-sand extraction and processing, and pipelines and roads to service all of those economic activities; and
- threats to the ecological integrity of Fundy National Park in New Brunswick that are associated with the development of internal infrastructure to support tourism, such as campgrounds, interpretation centres, roads and trails, and a golf course, along with economic activities in the surrounding area such as forestry and agriculture, as well as regional influences such as acid rain and climate change.

A requirement that environmental impacts be studied in a cumulative manner acknowledges the complexity of ecosystems and the fact that all aspects of their structure and function are affected by a diverse array of influences.

controversial, because substantial economic prospects may be forgone (this is known as an opportunity cost). Nevertheless, it is always prudent to identify and take as many precautions as possible before undertaking a development.

- *Mitigate:* Another option is to mitigate the predicted damages, or to repair or offset them to the degree that is possible. **Mitigation** is mainly relevant to damage that is caused to VECs and to low-level risks caused to people. For example, a wetland may be destroyed by a development, but the damage may be offset by creating or enhancing a comparable wetland somewhere else. Similarly, if the habitat of a rare species is threatened by a development, it may be possible to move the population that is at risk to another suitable place, or to create or enhance a habitat elsewhere, so that no net damage is caused. Mitigations are common response to conflicts between project-related stressors and VECs, but they are not perfect and there is often some degree of residual damage.
- *Accept the damages:* The third option is for decision makers to choose to allow a proposed project to cause some or all of the predicted damages to human welfare or VECs. This choice is often favoured by the proponents of projects, because of their belief that the socioeconomic benefits provided by a development would be greater than the cost of environmental damages that are predicted.

Inevitably, environmental impact assessments find that proposed developments carry some risks of causing damage. In almost all cases the development is allowed to move forward, but with important predicted damages being avoided or mitigated to a degree considered feasible, in both technological and economic terms. However, there will always be some damages that cannot be avoided or mitigated—these are environmental "costs" of a development.

Once the actual development of a project begins, it may be necessary to undertake compliance monitoring to ensure that regulatory criteria for pollution or health hazards are being met. If potential ecological damages were identified during the EIA, it may also be necessary to monitor those effects, although this is not always required. Ideally, the monitoring would be designed to test the predictions of the impact assessment, and to identify unanticipated "surprises" so they could be mitigated at some later time.

A properly designed monitoring program would begin prior to the implementation of a project, so that baseline conditions could be established. There should also be monitoring of nearby non-affected indicators, which provide a reference comparison to those affected by project-related stressors. The monitoring should continue for a long enough period to determine that important damage is not being caused by the development. If effects monitoring discovers that damage is occurring that was not predicted by the EIA, then the project operations might be changed to avoid or mitigate those unanticipated effects, or they might just be accepted as an ecological "cost" of development.

Examples of Impact Assessments

Environmental impact assessments are routinely conducted in all regions of Canada. They are required and scrutinized by various levels of government. The proponents of a project are usually a company or a governmental agency, and the EIA is typically undertaken by in-house professionals or by one or more private consulting firms (the latter would be viewed as having greater independence of the proponent than in-house staff). The proposed developments vary enormously in their scale, complexity, and potential environmental effects. The following case studies are brief examples of Canadian EIAs that had significant ecological dimensions.

Diamond Mines in the Northwest Territories

This proposal involved the construction of mines to extract diamonds from several columnar deposits, known as kimberlite pipes, located about 300 km northeast of Yellowknife. Because the kimberlite is softer than the surrounding granitic rocks, glaciers and other erosive forces have worn it away to form surface basins that support natural lakes. These waterbodies would be drained and thus destroyed—along with their aquatic biota—to develop open-pit mines. Ore would also be mined in deep underground shafts, and there would be large amounts of waste rock and tailings to be disposed of on land. In addition, huge amounts of gravel are needed to construct roads and ground-pads for buildings, and that aggregate would be obtained from local eskers, which are lengthy, sinuous features that provide critical denning habitat for grizzly bear, wolf, and other animals. Moreover, the mine and its network of roads are a potential hazard to large numbers of woodland caribou (*Rangifer tarandus*) that migrate through the region. Aboriginal peoples hunt in the region for country foods and for furs to sell, and these activities would be interfered with by the development. Finally, the region proposed for mining was a non-roaded wilderness, and conservation interests, led by the World Wildlife Fund, objected to the approval of the development unless a system of protected areas was established to ensure the landscape viability of both natural ecosystems and large carnivores, such as grizzly bear, wolf, and wolverine (*Gulo gulo*). The diamond mines passed their EIA and were allowed to proceed, subject to various restrictions, such as a ban on local hunting by mine employees, specified methods for the disposal of mining and tailings wastes, and actions to protect surface waters (other than the several lakes that must be destroyed to develop the mines and to dispose of waste tailings). A monitoring program was required to detect unanticipated damage to water or atmospheric quality, or to wildlife. At the same time the government of the Northwest Territories committed to setting aside protected areas in the larger region, although this has not yet been fully done. The mine opened in 1998.

Crude Oil on the Grand Banks

Large reservoirs of petroleum have been discovered on the Grand Banks, a region of continental shelf east of Newfoundland. A consortium of companies sought to develop this valuable resource by constructing the Hibernia project. This is an immense submersible platform located in 80 m-deep water to which petroleum is fed from a network of wells located on the seabed and eventually taken away by a fleet of tankers. The development is subjected to great risks associated with environmental hazards, such as hurricane-force winds and waves that sometimes affect the region and ginormous icebergs from the eastern Arctic that pass through in some years. The ecosystem of the Grand Banks is considered highly vulnerable to petroleum spills, as it supports a large fishery as well as important biodiversity, including abundant seabirds and marine mammals. Because the proposed Hibernia project included close monitoring of weather and icebergs, and rigorous systems to avoid icebergs and prevent spills of petroleum, it was considered by regulators to provide an acceptable degree of environmental safety and it passed through its impact assessment. It began producing petroleum in 1997.

Al-Pac Pulp Mill

This was a proposal to construct a mill to produce pulp in northern Alberta. The principal issues in the EIA were the potential effects on the Peace–Athabasca River system, including ecological damage that might be caused by the depletion of dissolved oxygen to decompose organic matter in effluent waters, and the contamination of fish with residues of persistent organochlorines, including dioxins and furans (these would have been produced in extremely small concentrations during the chlorine-bleaching process, but are known to biomagnify by thousands of times in aquatic food webs, endangering top predators and perhaps humans). Remarkably, the terms of reference of the EIA deliberately excluded the potential environmental effects of the wood-supply plan for the mill, which would be one of the largest in the world. The mill had access to about 55 000 km^2 of boreal mixed-wood forest in a region that at the time was a largely unroaded and pristine wilderness. About half of the area is capable of producing merchantable wood, and the management plan called for clear-cutting about 1 percent of the area annually on a 60–70 year rotation. In essence, the appointed federal–provincial EIA review panel was asked to consider the question: "Will the proposed mill harm the Athabasca River?" However, the panel had difficulty addressing that specific question, in part because there was so little baseline information about that particular riverine ecosystem. In view of the materials presented for its consideration, the panel recommended that the mill not be built, and that a series of ecological studies be undertaken to better document the baseline conditions of the Athabasca River before the proposal was reconsidered. The judgment of the panel was initially accepted by the Alberta premier at the time, Don Getty. Soon after, however, he declared the panel's judgment to be "flawed" and he hired a Finnish consulting firm to review its report; however, they supported the panel's findings. The government then declared the previous formal EIA process to have been only a preliminary "environmental review." The premier and his Minister of Environment, Ralph Klein, then appointed a technical panel of three governmental employees to address a modified technological system that the mill proponents claimed would produce no dioxins and furans. Although the novel technology had not yet been tested at a commercial scale, the technical panel agreed with its zero-organochlorine assertion. The premier then ordered that a permit be issued to allow the mill to be constructed, and the facility began production in 1993. This was done regardless of the intense public controversy about the potential effects of the mill on the Athabasca River, as well as the unconsidered ecological effects of converting an immense wood-supply area to timber production. At the same time, the provincial and federal governments co-funded an integrated research program known as the Northern River Basins Study, which was charged with documenting the ecology of the Athabasca River, even while the pulp mill was being constructed and operated. As it turned out, the new bleaching technology did result in immeasurable organochlorine production, and it has subsequently been adopted in many other pulp mills. Nevertheless, the interference by politicians in the EIA process, borne out of economic aspirations and political values, resulted in this being one of the most flawed environmental assessments ever undertaken for a large project in Canada.

Trans-Canada Highway Twinning in Banff National Park

This was a proposal to "twin" or double the capacity (from two to four lanes) of an existing 18 km stretch of the Trans-Canada Highway running through Banff National Park in southwestern Alberta (eventually, all 45 km of the highway in Banff were twinned). The larger highway would contribute to the fragmentation of populations of certain species of large animals, including ungulates such as elk (*Cervus canadensis*) and moose (*Alces alces*) and large carnivores such as black bear (*Ursus americanus*), grizzly bear, timber wolf, and coyote (*Canis latrans*). It would also increase their risks of suffering collisions with vehicles; such accidents are also a risk to people travelling on the highway. The proposed mitigations included the installation of 2.4 m-high fencing along both sides of the highway to prevent random crossings by large animals and to guide them to safe crossings, which were provided by the installation of 22 underpasses and 2 overpasses (these are for the entire 45 km of highway within Banff National Park). Although relatively little information was available at the time about the efficacy of the proposed mitigations to allow safe crossings, the twinning project passed through its EIA and construction began in 1995. Subsequent research has shown that the roadside fencing has reduced the numbers of collisions with large ungulates by about 96 percent, and both the underpasses and overpasses appear to be working well to provide safe passage for the target species.

Grande-Baleine Hydroelectric Complex

Rivers flowing into James and Hudson Bays from northwestern Quebec have enormous potential for the production of hydroelectricity, but to develop them for this purpose, dams must be constructed and huge reservoirs flooded. The Grande-Baleine proposal involved the construction of three generating stations with a capacity of 3212 MW. It would flood reservoirs about 1667 km^2 in area and would also affect the landscape by the construction of roads and high-voltage transmission lines. The most important environmental impacts were associated with the ecological effects of the creation of such immense reservoirs, which would destroy extensive terrestrial and wetland habitats, convert rivers into artificial lakes, and enormously affect the local aquatic biota, including that of nearby reaches of Hudson Bay. The movements of local herds of woodland caribou and fur-bearing mammals would also be affected. There were also cultural and socioeconomic consequences for aboriginal people living in the region. These and other potential effects were examined during the environmental impact assessment, including plans to avoid or mitigate damages to whatever extent was considered feasible. The proposal was highly controversial, largely because it was being resisted by the local Cree nation, which felt aggrieved by the environmental implications and lack of local benefits from previous hydro developments in the region. Ultimately, the proposed hydro development did not go forward, not because it would have failed its EIA, but because commitments to purchase the electricity in the northeastern United States were insufficient to support the business plan.

Eradication of Diseased Bison

Some of the bison (*Bison bison*) in the southern part of Wood Buffalo National Park and in its vicinity in northern Alberta and the southwestern NWT are infected with bovine tuberculosis and brucellosis. Because of this, Agriculture Canada proposed to slaughter as many of the bison as possible as a measure to prevent the spread of these infectious diseases to herds of cattle to the south of the region. The bison to be culled were hybrids of indigenous wood bison (*B. b. athabascae*) of the region and plains bison (*B. b. bison*) that had been introduced to the area in the 1920s. There was no intent to cull the populations of "pure" wood bison that roamed farther to the north. Nevertheless, the proposal engendered great controversy and it was opposed by conservationists and local aboriginal people. Although the proposal managed to successfully pass its impact assessment, it was then suspended by the Minister of the Environment, largely because of the powerful opposition it faced.

A Peat Mine in Nova Scotia

This was a relatively small proposal to mine peat as an industrial fuel from a bog. The major issue in the impact assessment was the fact that the bog intended for destruction was one of only a few places where the thread-leaved sundew (*Drosera filiformis*) occurred in Canada. This rare carnivorous plant is endangered in Canada and also in much of its range in the eastern United States. Because the proposed mine site supported the largest known population of the rare plant in Canada, the provincial Minister of Environment did not allow a mine to be developed at that location.

17.6 Ecology as a Career

A professional ecologist is a highly qualified scientist, typically with a master's degree (M.Sc.) or a doctorate (Ph.D.) in some aspect of ecology. However, some people with an undergraduate degree (B.Sc.) and considerable work experience also consider themselves to be ecologists. Nevertheless, it is important to understand that most ecologists are self-proclaimed to be of that profession—not many of them are actually certified as being a specialist practitioner of ecology.

However, since 1961 the Ecological Society of America, a U.S. organization, has offered a service by which ecologists can be certified at various professional levels—*associate ecologist*, *ecologist*, and *senior ecologist*. The certification is based on the kinds of classes that a person has taken toward college or university degrees, relevant work experience, publications or reports that have been written, and other pertinent information. Typically, this certification would be sought only by ecologists for whom it would represent a professional advantage, such as those employed in the private sector, including the environmental consulting industry. In fact, most highly qualified practitioners of ecology are not certified in this way, including most professors who teach the subject in universities and colleges in Canada.

In addition, some professional societies of specialists in the broader environmental field in Canada offer alternative certifications that ecologists might hold. They include those of registered professional biologist (R.P.Bio.), registered professional forester (R.P.For.), registered professional wetland scientist (R.P.Wetl.Sci.), and others.

Most ecologists live and work in relatively developed countries, such as Canada, but they can also be found in less-developed ones. In general, the global community of ecologists has developed a commonly used approach and toolkit of methodologies for use in their fieldwork, data analysis, and the preparation of reports, scientific papers, and books. In this sense, ecologists working in various parts of the world can easily understand the essentials of the issues and studies of their far-flung colleagues. The only real barrier to collective understanding and communications is differences in language rather than in scientific principles or approaches.

Nevertheless, much work in ecology has a local and ecoregional context, and therefore many practitioners have developed expertise at those levels, rather than at national or global ones.

The following is a list of the more frequent kinds of careers in which ecologists are engaged:

- a scientist working in a governmental agency whose mandate includes some aspect of ecology, such as biodiversity, bio-resources, or the broader environmental field, such as Canadian Forestry Service, Canadian Wildlife Service, Environment Canada, Natural Resources Canada, Parks Canada, or their provincial, territorial, or First-Nations equivalent;
- a scientist working in the private sector, either to provide in-house expertise for a company that is engaged in managing ecosystems or biodiversity, or working in a consulting firm that provides those services;
- a scientist working for an ENGO whose activity intersects with the conservation of biodiversity or other ecological values, such as the Canadian Parks and Wilderness Society (CPAWS), the Canadian Wildlife Federation (CWF), Ducks Unlimited Canada (DUC), Nature Canada, the Nature Conservancy of Canada (NCC), the Sierra Club of Canada, the World Wildlife Fund Canada

Bill Freedman (top and bottom)

Ecologists can work in various kinds of jobs, ranging from instructors at colleges and universities, to consultants in the private sector. These photos show ecologists doing fieldwork as part of an environmental impact assessment of a proposed hydroelectric development on the Churchill River in Labrador.

(WWF), or similar ENGOs working at provincial or international levels; and

- a professor or instructor working in a college or university who is involved in developing and teaching classes in ecology or related subjects, often while also running a research program and training senior students to do scientific investigations.

Most professional ecologists are engaged in applied work that is related to important issues or tasks, such as the following:

- the management of bio-resources of economic importance, such as those in forestry, fisheries, and hunting;
- environmental impact assessments of the potential ecological effects of proposed development activities;
- the management of ecological functions such as productivity, hydrology, erosion, nutrient cycling, and carbon-fixation and storage relevant to offsetting emissions of greenhouse gases;
- monitoring or mitigating ecological damage caused by pollution, disturbances, and other anthropogenic influences; and
- planning and stewardship to conserve biodiversity in protected areas, including tracts of representative ecosystems as well as the habitats of species at risk.

Many other ecologists, however, particularly those working in universities, are engaged in research that is undertaken for the inherent sake of curiosity—their interests help us to better understand the natural world. Their "pure" academic research has great intrinsic value, and this alone is sufficient to make it worthwhile, even while acknowledging that it may also sometimes result in knowledge that is important in an applied context.

17.7 Conclusions

Earth and its biosphere are the only place in the universe that is definitely known to sustain life and ecosystems. It is the purview of ecology, and of ecologists, to study this living system, and to understand environmental influences on the abundance and distribution of organisms and of higher levels of the ecological hierarchy, such as populations, communities, and ecoscapes.

Ecology is also a vital endeavour because of its central importance in defining the limits of an ecologically sustainable human enterprise. In essence, such an economy would be capable of running forever because it is founded on the prudent use of natural resources, especially renewable ones that are being used at rates that are lower than their productivity, while also conserving other species and natural ecosystems at sustainable levels of abundance and distribution.

VOCABULARY OF ECOLOGY

anthropocentric world-view, p. 566
applied research, p. 550
biocentric world-view, p. 566
composite indicator, p. 560
conservation data centre, p. 557
cumulative environmental impacts, p. 570
ecocentric world-view, p. 566
ecological integrity (EI), p. 554
ecosystem health, p. 554
environmental impact assessment (EIA), p. 567
environmental monitoring, p. 558
environmental non-governmental organization (ENGO), p. 557
environmental quality, p. 554
fundamental research, p. 549
indicator, p. 554
Indices of Biotic Integrity (IBI), p. 560
interdisciplinary, p. 568
IPAT (impact formula), p. 552
mitigation, p. 570
multidisciplinary, p. 568
multimetric indicator, p. 560
punctuated equilibrium, p. 565
reference condition, p. 561
research, p. 558
scoping exercise, p. 568
screening, p. 568
stasis, p. 565
valued ecosystem component (VEC), p. 568

QUESTIONS FOR REVIEW AND DISCUSSION

1. What are the key differences between fundamental and applied research in ecology? Explain why both of these kinds of research, and the knowledge they provide, are important.
2. What is ecological integrity, and how is it different from environmental quality? Consider a park or other protected area with which you are familiar. What are the most important challenges to its ecological integrity?
3. Explain the rationale and general process of environmental impact assessment, and when it must be done. Make sure that you explain the role of ecological studies in the process.
4. What factors must be considered when judging whether an ecological change should be viewed as representing "damage"?
5. Why is the knowledge of ecology important to sustainable development?

HELPFUL WEBSITES

BRITISH ECOLOGICAL SOCIETY (BES)

http://www.britishecologicalsociety.org

The BES is the professional organization for ecologists in the United Kingdom. Excellent educational resources are posted on its website.

CANADIAN ENVIRONMENTAL ASSESSMENT AGENCY (CEAA)

http://www.ceaa.gc.ca

The CEAA is the agency responsible for managing the process of environmental impact assessment of projects and policies related to the Government of Canada. This website provides information about its mandate as well as the conduct of EIAs.

CANADIAN SOCIETY FOR ECOLOGY AND EVOLUTION (CSEE)

http://www.ecoevo.ca

The CSEE is the Canadian professional organization for ecologists. It exists to promote the study of ecology and evolution, to raise awareness with the public and decision makers, and to foster interactions among ecologists.

ECOLOGICAL SOCIETY OF AMERICA (ESA)

http://esa.org

The ESA is a leading organization for ecologists in North America. It is a professional organization and also posts excellent educational resources on its website. The ESA has a Canadian chapter (http://www.esa.org/canada)

ECOLOGY GLOBAL NETWORK

http://www.ecology.com/index.php

This website has information about ecology and environmental issues.

PARKS CANADA

http://www.pc.gc.ca/eng/progs/np-pn/ie-ei.aspx

This website explains the concept of ecological integrity from the standpoint of Parks Canada and its mandate.

You'll find a rich array of additional resources for *Ecology* at www.ecology.nelson.com.

References

Chapter 1

Barnes, B. 1985. *About Science*. London, UK: Blackwell Ltd.

Begon, M., C. A. Townsend, and J. L. Harper. 2005. *Ecology: From Individuals to Ecosystems* (4th ed.). Oxford, UK: Wiley Blackwell.

Commoner, B. 1971. *The Closing Circle: Nature, Man and Technology*. New York: Alfred Knopf.

Cox, R. M. and T. C. Hutchinson. 1979. Metal co-tolerances in the grass *Deschampsia caespitosa*. *Nature* (London), 279, 231–233.

Freedman, B. 1995. *Environmental Ecology* (2nd ed.). San Diego, CA: Academic Press.

Freedman, B. 2010. *Environmental Science. A Canadian Perspective* (5th ed.). Toronto, ON: Pearson Education Canada.

Freedman, B. and T. C. Hutchinson. 1980a. Pollutant inputs from the atmosphere and accumulations in soils and vegetation near a nickel-copper smelter at Sudbury, Ontario, Canada. *Canadian Journal of Botany*, 58, 108–132.

Freedman, B. and T. C. Hutchinson. 1980b. Long-term effects of pollution near a nickel-copper smelter at Sudbury, Ontario, Canada, on surrounding forest communities. *Canadian Journal of Botany*, 58, 2123–2140.

Giere, R. N. 2005. *Understanding Scientific Reasoning* (5th ed.). New York: Wadsworth Publishing.

Kuhn, T. S. 1996. *The Structure of Scientific Revolutions* (3rd ed.). Chicago, IL: University of Chicago Press.

Lovelock, J. E. 2000. *Gaia: A New Look at Life on Earth*. New York: Oxford University Press.

Mayhew, P. J. 2006. *Discovering Evolutionary Ecology: Bringing Together Ecology and Evolution*. Oxford, UK: Oxford University Press.

Moore, J. A. 1999. *Science as a Way of Knowing*. Boston, MA: Harvard University Press.

Odum, E. P. 1997. *Ecology: A Bridge Between Science and Society*. New York: Sinauer Associates.

Odum, E. P. and G. W. Barrett. 2005. *Fundamentals of Ecology* (5th ed.). Belmont, CA: Thomson Brooks/Cole.

Pianka, E. R. 1999. *Evolutionary Ecology* (6th ed.). San Francisco, CA: Benjamin Cummings.

Popper, K. 1979. *Objective Knowledge: An Evolutionary Approach*. Oxford, UK: Clarendon Press.

Silver, B. L. 2000. *The Ascent of Science*. Oxford, UK: Oxford University Press.

Smith, L. E. 1991. *Gaia: The Growth of an Idea*. New York: St Martin's.

United States Geological Service (USGS). 2009. *Water Cycle*. Retrieved August 2009 from http://ga.water.usgs.gov/edu/watercycle.html.

Vitousek, P. M., P. R. Ehrlich, A. H. Ehrlich, and P. A. Matson. 1986. Human appropriation of the products of photosynthesis. *BioScience*, 36, 368–373.

Whitby, L. M. and T. C. Hutchinson. 1974. Heavy metal pollution in the Sudbury mining and smelting region of Canada. II. Soil toxicity tests. *Environmental Conservation*, 1, 191–200.

Chapter 2

Campbell, S. E. 1979. Soil stabilization by a prokaryotic desert crust: Implications for Precambrian land biota. *Origins of Life and Evolution of Biospheres*, 9, 335–348.

Dawkins, R. 1976. *The Selfish Gene*. New York, NY: Oxford University Press.

Freedman, B. 1995. *Environmental Ecology* (2nd ed.). San Diego, CA: Academic Press.

Freedman, B. 2010. *Environmental Science. A Canadian Perspective* (5th ed.). Toronto, ON: Pearson Education Canada.

Freedman, B., V. Zobens, and T. C. Hutchinson. 1990. Intense, natural pollution affects arctic tundra vegetation at the Smoking Hills, Canada. *Ecology*, 71, 492–503.

Golubic, S., E. I. Friedmann, and J. Schneider. 1981. The lithobiotic ecological niche, with special reference to microorganisms. *Journal of Sedimentary Research*, 51, 475–478.

Havas, M. and T. C. Hutchinson. 1983. The Smoking Hills: Natural acidification of an aquatic ecosystem. *Nature (London)*, 301, 23–27.

Kidd, K. A., P. J. Blanchfield, K. H. Mills, V. P. Palace, R. E. Evans, J. M. Lazorchak, and R. W. Flick. 2007. Collapse of a fish population after exposure to a synthetic estrogen. *Proceedings of the National Academy of Sciences USA*, 104, 8897–8901.

LaPaix, R., B. Freedman, and D. Patriquin. 2009. Ground vegetation as an indicator of ecological integrity. *Environmental Reviews* (in press).

Odum, E. P. Trends expected in stressed ecosystems. *BioScience*, 35, 419–422.

Schindler, D. W. 1987. Detecting ecosystem responses to anthropogenic stress. *Canadian Journal of Fisheries and Aquatic Science*, 44, 6–25.

Schindler, D. W. 1990. Experimental perturbations of whole lakes as tests of hypotheses concerning ecosystem structure and function. *Oikos*, 57, 25–41.

Schindler, D. W., R. E. Hecky, D. L. Findlay, M. P. Stainton, B. R. Parker, M. J. Paterson, K. G. Beaty, M. Lyng, and S. E. M. Kasian. 1990. Eutrophication of lakes cannot be controlled by reducing nitrogen input: Results of a 37-year whole-ecosystem experiment. *Proceedings of the National Academy of Science*, 105, 11254–11258.

Smith, W. H. Ecosystem pathology: A new perspective for phytopathology. *Forest Ecology and Management*, 9, 193–219.

Wainwright, M., N. C. Wickramasinghe, J. V. Narlikar, and P. Rajaratnam. 2003. Microoganisms cultured from stratospheric air samples obtained at 41 km. *FEMS Micorbiology Letters*, 218, 161–165.

Chapter 3

Arft, A. M., M. D. Walker, J. Gurevitch, M. Alatalo, S. Bret-Harte, M. Dale, M. Diemer, F. Gugerli, G. H. R. Henry, M. H. Jones, R. D. Hollister, I. S. Jonsdottir, K. Laine, E. Levesque, G. M. Marion, U. Molau, P. Mølgaard, U. Nordenhall, V. Raszhivin, C. H. Robinson, G. Starr, A. Stenstrom, M. Stenstrom, O. Totland, P. L. Turner, L. J. Walker, P. J. Webber, J. M. Welker, and P. A. Wookey. 1999. Responses of tundra plants to experimental warming;

Meta-analysis of the International Tundra Experiment. *Ecological Monographs*, 69, 491–511.
Botkin, D. B. and E. A. Keller. 2007. *Environmental Science: Earth as a Living Planet* (6th ed.). New York: Wiley & Sons.
Bridgham, S. D., J. P. Megonigal, J. K. Keller, N. B. Bliss and C. Trettin. 2006. The carbon balance of North American wetlands. *Wetlands*, 26, 889–916.
Carbon Dioxide Information Analysis Centre (CDIAC). 2009. *Trends. A Compendium of Data on Global Change.* Oak Ridge, TN: CDIAC. Retrieved August 2009 from: http://cdiac.esd.ornl.gov/trends/trends.htm.
Freedman, B. 2008. *Environmental Science. A Canadian Perspective* (4th ed.). Toronto: Pearson Education Canada.
Freedman, B., P. N. Duinker, R. Morash, and U. Prager. 1982. *Forest Biomass and Nutrient Studies in Central Nova Scotia.* Information Report M-X-134. Maritimes Forest Research Centre, Canadian Forestry Service. Fredericton, N. B.
Freedman, B. and T. Keith. 1995. *Planting Trees for Carbon Credits. A Discussion of the Issues, Feasibility, and Environmental Benefits.* Ottawa, ON: Tree Canada Foundation.
Freedman, B., G. Stinson, and P. Lacoul. 2009. Carbon credits and the conservation of natural areas. *Environmental Reviews* (submitted).
Gates, D. M. 1985. *Energy and Ecology.* New York: Sinauer.
Houghton, J. T. 2004. *Global Warming. The Complete Story* (3rd ed.). Cambridge, UK: Cambridge University Press.
IPCC (Intergovernmental Panel on Climate Change). 2007. *Climate Change 2007 Synthesis Report.* Oxford, UK: Oxford University Press.
Keeling, R. F., S. C. Piper, A. F. Bollenbacher, and J. S. Walker. 2009. Atmospheric CO_2 Records from Sites in the SIO Air Sampling Network. Oak Ridge National Laboratory, Carbon Dioxide Information Analysis Center, Oak Ridge, TN. http://cdiac.ornl.gov/trends/co2/sio-keel.html.
Krebs, C. J., Boutin, S., and R. Boonstra. 2001. *Ecosystem Dynamics of the Boreal Forest: The Kluane Project.* New York, NY: Oxford University Press.
Liu, P. I. 2005. *Introduction to Energy, Technology, and the Environment.* New York: ASME Press.
Maessen, O., B. Freedman, M. L. N. Nams, and J. Svoboda. 1983. Resource allocation in high arctic vascular plants of differing growth form. *Canadian Journal of Botany*, 61, 1680–1691.
Oberbauer, S. F., C. E. Tweedie, J. M. Welker, J. T. Fahnestock, G. H. R. Henry, P. J. Webber, R. D. Hollister, M. D. Walker, A. Kuchy, E. Elmore, and G. Starr. 2007. Tundra CO_2 Fluxes in Response to Experimental Warming Across Latitudinal and Moisture Gradients. *Ecological Monographs*, 77, 221–238.
Odum, E. P. 1983. *Basic Ecology.* New York: Saunders College Publishing.
Odum, E. P. and G. W. Barrett. 2005. *Fundamentals of Ecology* (5th ed.). New York, NY: Thomson Brooks/Cole.
Schneider, S. H. 1989. The changing climate. *Scientific American*, 261 (3), 70–79.
Smithwick, E. A. H., M. E. Harmon, S. M. Remillard, S. A. Acker, and J. F. Franklin. 2002. Potential upper bounds of carbon stores in forests of the Pacific Northwest. *Ecological Applications*, 12(5), 1303–1317.
Walker, M. D., C. H. Wahren, R. D. Hollister, G. H. R. Henry, L. E. Ahlquist, J. M. Alatalo, M. S. Bret-Harte, M. P. Calef, T. V. Callaghan, A. B. Carroll, H. E. Epstein, I. S. Jonsdottir, J.A. Klein, B. Magnusson, U. Molau, S. F. Oberbauer, S. P. Rewa, C. H. Robinson, G. R. Shaver, K. N. Suding, C. C. Thompson, A. Tolvanen, Ø. Totlandt, P. L. Turner, C. E. Tweedie, P. J. Webber, and P. A. Wookey. 2006. Plant community responses to experimental warming across the tundra biome. *Proceeding of the National Academy of Science*, 103, 1342–1346.
Whittaker, R. H. and G. E. Likens, 1975. The biosphere and man. In H. Lieth and R. H. Whittaker (Eds.), *Primary Productivity of the Biosphere.* (pp. 305–328). New York, NY: Springer-Verlag.
World Resources Institute. 2009. *Earth Trends. The Environmental Information Portal.* http://earthtrends.wri.org/.

Chapter 4

Adl, S. 2003. *The Ecology of Soil Decomposition.* Cambridge, MA: CABI Publishing.
Atlas, R. M. and R. Bartha. 1998. *Microbial Ecology. Fundamentals and Applications* (4th ed.). Menlo Park, CA: Benjamin Cummings.
Blasing, T. J. 1985. Background: Carbon cycle, climate, and vegetation responses. In *Characterization of Information Requirements for Studies of CO_2 Effects. Water Resources, Agriculture, Fisheries, Forests, and Human Health*, DOE/ER-0236. (pp. 9–22). Washington, DC: U. S. Department of Energy.
Brady, N. C. and R. R. Weil. 2003. *The Nature and Properties of Soils* (14th ed.). New York: Prentice Hall.
Cox, R. M. and T. C. Hutchinson. 1979. Metal co-tolerances in the grass *Deschampsia caespitosa. Nature*, 279, 231–233.
Foth, H. D. 1990. *Fundamentals of Soil Science.* New York: Wiley & Sons.
Freedman, B. 2010. *Environmental Science. A Canadian Perspective* (5th ed.). Don Mills, ON: Pearson Education Canada.
Gresh, T., J. Lichatowich, and P. Schoonmaker. 2000. An estimation of historic and current levels of salmon production in the Northeast Pacific ecosystem: Evidence of a nutrient deficit in the freshwater systems of the Pacific Northwest. *Fisheries*, 25, 15–21.
Hutzinger, O. (ed.). 1982. *The Handbook of Environmental Chemistry.* New York: Springer-Verlag.
Keeling, R. F., S. C. Piper, A. F. Bollenbacher, and J. S. Walker. 2009. Atmospheric CO_2 Records from Sites in the SIO Air Sampling Network. Oak Ridge, TN: Oak Ridge National Laboratory, Carbon Dioxide Information Analysis Center. http://cdiac.ornl.gov/trends/co2/sio-keel.html.
Likens, G. E. and F. H. Bormann. 1999. *Biogeochemistry of a Forested Ecosystem* (2nd ed.). New York: Springer Verlag.
Moore, J. W. and D. E. Schindler. 2004. Nutrient export from freshwater ecosystems by anadromous sockeye salmon (*Oncorhynchus nerka*). *Canadian Journal of Fisheries and Aquatic Science*, 61, 1582–1589.
Morrison, R. G. 1973. *Primary succession on sand dunes at Grand Bend, Ontario.* PhD Thesis, Department of Botany, University of Toronto, Toronto.

Plaster, E. J. 2002. *Soil Science and Management* (3rd ed.). Florence, KY: Delmar Thomson Learning.

Solomon, A. M., J. R. Trabolka, D. E. Reichle, and L. D. Voorhees. 1985. The global cycle of carbon. In: *Atmospheric Carbon Dioxide and the Global Carbon Cycle.* DOE/ER-0239. (pp. 1–12). Washington, DC: U. S. Department of Energy.

USDA. 2009. *Soil Science Glossary.* Washington, DC: United States Department of Agriculture, Natural Resources Conservation Service. http://soils.usda.gov/.

Wetzel, R. G. 1975. *Limnology*. Toronto, ON: Saunders.

World Resources Institute. 2010. *Earth Trends. The Environmental Information Portal.* Washington, DC: WRI. http://earthtrends.wri.org/.

Chapter 5

Albano, D. J. 1992. Nesting mortality of Carolina chickadees breeding in natural cavities. *The Condor*, 94, 371–382.

Bérubé, C. H., Festa-Bianchet, M., and J. T. Jorgenson. 1999. Individual differences, longevity, and reproductive senescence in bighorn ewes. *Ecology*, 80: 2555–2565.

Bowen, W. D., J. McMillan, and R. Mohn. 2003. Sustained exponential population growth of grey seals at Sable Island, Nova Scotia. *ICES Journal of Marine Science*, 60, 1265–1274.

Brattey, J., N. G. Cadigan, K. Dwyer, B. P. Healey, M. J. Morgan, E. F. Murphy, D. Maddock Parsons, and D. Power. 2008. Assessments of the cod (*Gadus morhua*) stock in NAFO Divisions 2J3KL (April 2007 and April 2008). *Canadian Science Advisory Secretariat Research Document* 2008/086, Ottawa, ON: Fisheries and Oceans Canada.

Caswell, H. 1989. *Matrix Population Models*. Sunderland, MA: Sinauer Associates.

Caughley, G. 1977. *Analysis of Vertebrate Populations.* New York: Wiley, New York.

Claessen, D., A. M. de Roos, and L. Persson. 2000. Dwarfs and giants: Cannibalism and competition in size-structured populations. *American Naturalist*, 155, 219–237.

Fisher, R. A. 1930. *The Genetical Theory of Natural Selection*. Oxford, UK: Clarendon Press.

Fryxell, J. M., J. B. Falls, E. A. Falls, and R. J. Brooks. 1998. Long-term dynamics of small-mammal populations in Ontario. *Ecology*, 79, 213–225.

Garcia, S., P. Sparre, and J. Csirke. 1989. Estimating surplus production and maximum sustainable yield from biomass data when catch and effort time series are not available. *Fisheries Research*, 8, 13–23.

Gause, G. F. 1932. Experimental studies on the struggle for existence. I. Mixed population of two species of yeast. *Journal of Experimental Biology*, 9, 389–402.

Gause, G. F. 1934. *The Struggle for Existence*. Baltimore, MD: Williams and Wilkins.

Gause, G. F. 1935. Vérifications expérimentales de la Théorie Mathématique de la Lutte Pour la Vie. Paris, France: Hermann.

Gotelli, N. J. 2008. *A Primer of Ecology* (4th ed.). Sunderland, MA: Sinauer.

Hayes, R. D. and A. S. Harestad. 2000. Wolf function response and regulation of moose in the Yukon. *Canadian Journal of Zoology*, 78, 60–66.

Holling, C. S. 1959. The components of predation as revealed by a study of small mammal predation of the European pine sawfly. *Canadian Entomologist*, 91, 293–320.

Hutchings, J. A. 1999. The influence of growth and survival costs of reproduction on Atlantic cod, *Gadus morhua*, population growth rate. *Canadian Journal of Fisheries and Aquatic Sciences*, 56, 1612–1623.

Hutchings, J. A. 2000. Collapse and recovery of marine fishes. *Nature*, 406, 882–885.

Hutchings, J. A., C. Walters, and R. L. Haedrich. 1997. Is scientific inquiry incompatible with government information control? *Canadian Journal of Fisheries and Aquatic Sciences*, 54, 1198–1210.

Hutchings, J. A. and M. E. B. Jones. 1998. Life history variation and growth rate thresholds for maturity in Atlantic salmon, *Salmo salar*. *Canadian Journal of Fisheries and Aquatic Sciences*, 55 (Supplement 1), 22–47.

Hutchings, J. A. and J. K. Baum. 2005. Measuring marine fish biodiversity: Temporal changes in abundance, life history and demography. *Philosophical Transactions of the Royal Society B*, 360, 315–338.

Hutchings, J. A., R. A. Myers, V. B. García, and L. O. Lucifora. 2010. Life history correlates of maximum population growth rate in vertebrates. *Submitted manuscript.*

Kingsland, S. E. 1985. *Modeling Nature.* Chicago, IL: University of Chicago Press.

Kranabetter, J. M., D. M. Durall, and W. H. MacKenzie. 2009. Diversity and species distribution of ectomycorrhizal fungi along productivity gradients of a southern boreal forest. *Mycorrhiza*, 19, 99–111.

Krebs, C. J. 2009. *Ecology: The Experimental Analysis of Distribution and Abundance.* San Francisco: Benjamin-Cummings.

Lack, D. 1947. *Darwin's Finches.* Cambridge, UK: Cambridge University Press.

Leslie, P. H. 1945. On the use of matrices in certain population mathematics. *Biometrika*, 35, 183–212.

Lieske, D. 1997. Population dynamics of urban merlins. M.Sc. Thesis, University of Saskatchewan.

Loery, G., K. H. Pollock, J. D. Nichols, and J. D. Hines. 1987. Age-specificity of black-capped chickadee survival rates: Analysis of capture-recapture data. *Ecology*, 64, 1038–1044.

Loison, A., M. Festa-Bianchet, J.-M. Gaillard, J. T. Jorgenson, and J.-M. Jullien. 1999. Age-specific survival in five populations of ungulates: Evidence of senescence. *Ecology*, 80, 2539–2554.

Lotka, A. J. 1925. *Elements of Physical Biology*. Baltimore, MD: Williams and Watkins.

MacArthur, R. H. 1958. Population ecology of some warblers of northeastern coniferous forests. *Ecology*, 39, 599–619.

MacArthur, R. H. 1972. *Geographical Ecology*. New York: Harper and Row.

MacArthur, R. H. and E. O. Wilson. 1967. *The Theory of Island Biogeography*. Princeton, NJ: Princeton University Press.

Mahoney, N., E. Nol, and T. C. Hutchinson. 1997. Food-chain chemistry, reproductive success, and foraging behaviour of songbirds in acidified maple forests of central Ontario. *Canadian Journal of Zoology*, 75, 509–517.

May, R. M. 1976. *Theoretical Ecology: Principles and Applications.* Philadelphia, PA: W. B. Saunders.

Menu, S., G. Gauthier, and A. Reed. 2002. Changes in survival rates and population dynamics of greater snow geese over a 30-year period: Implications for hunting regulations. *Journal of Applied Ecology*, 30, 91–102.

Messier, F. 1994. Ungulate population models with predation: A case study with the North American moose. *Ecology*, 75, 478–488.

Myers, R. A., G. Mertz, and P. S. Fowlow. 1997. Maximum population growth rates and recovery times for Atlantic cod, *Gadus morhua*. *Fishery Bulletin*, 95, 762–772.

Neal, D. 2004. *Introduction to Population Ecology*. Cambridge, UK: Cambridge University Press.

Oliphant, L. W., and E. Haug. 1985. Productivity, population density and rate of increase of an expanding Merlin population. *Raptor Research*, 19, 56–59.

Parsons, L. S. 1993. *Management of Marine Fisheries in Canada*. Ottawa, ON: NRC Press.

Ramsay, S. M., D. J. Mennill, K. A. Otter, L. M. Ratcliffe, and P. T. Boag. 2003. Sex allocation in black-capped chickadees *Poecile atricapilla*. *Journal of Avian Biology*, 34, 134–139.

Rosenzweig, M. L. and R. H. MacArthur. 1963. Graphical representation and stability conditions of predator–prey interactions. *American Naturalist*, 47, 209–223.

Russell, P. J., S. L. Wolfe., and P. E. Hertz. 2009. *Biology: Exploring the Diversity of Life*. Toronto: Nelson College Indigenous.

Schluter, D. 1996. Ecological speciation in postglacial fishes. *Philosophical Transactions of the Royal Society B*, 351, 807–814.

Schluter, D. 2000. *The Ecology of Adaptive Radiation*. Oxford, UK: Oxford University Press.

Schluter, D., and J. D. McPhail. 1992. Ecological character displacement and speciation in sticklebacks. *American Naturalist*, 140, 85–108.

Smith, C. and P. Reay. 1991. Cannibalism in teleost fishes. *Reviews in Fish Biology and Fisheries*, 1, 41–64.

Smith, S. M. 1995. Age-specific survival in breeding black-capped chickadees (*Parus atricapillus*). *The Auk*, 112, 840–846.

Swain, D. P. and A. F. Sinclair 2000. Pelagic fishes and the cod recruitment dilemma in the Northwest Atlantic. *Canadian Journal of Fisheries and Aquatic Sciences*, 57, 1321–1325.

Swain, D. P. and G. Chouinard. 2008. Predicted extirpation of the dominant demersal fish in a large marine ecosystem: Atlantic cod (*Gadus morhua*) in the southern Gulf of St. Lawrence. *Canadian Journal of Fisheries and Aquatic Sciences*, 65, 2315–2319.

Volterra, V. 1926. Fluctuations in the abundance of a species considered mathematically. *Nature*, 118, 558–560.

Williams, G. C. 1966. *Adaptation and Natural Selection*. Princeton, NJ: Princeton University Press.

Worm, B., R. Hilborn, J. K. Baum, T. A. Branch, J. S. Collie, C. Costello, M. J. Fogarty, E. A. Fulton, J. A. Hutchings, S. Jennings, O. P. Jensen, H. K. Lotze, P. M. Mace, T. R. McClanahan, C. Minto, S. R. Palumbi, A. M. Parma, D. Ricard, A. A. Rosenberg, R. Watson, and D. Zeller. 2009. Rebuilding Global Fisheries. *Science*, 325, 578–585.

Chapter 6

Alcock, J., 2009. *Animal Behavior* (9th ed.). Sunderland, MA: Sinauer Associates.

Alonzo, S. H., 2008. An inordinate fondess for behavioural ecology. *Trends in Ecology and Evolution*, 23, 600–601.

Anderson R. A. and B. D. Roitberg, 1999. Modeling trade-offs between mortality and fitness associated with persistent blood feeding by mosquitoes. *Ecology Letters*, 2, 98–105.

Andersson, M., 1994. *Sexual Selection*. Princeton, NJ: Princeton University Press.

Andersson, M. and Y. Iwasa, 1996. Sexual selection. *Trends in Ecology and Evolution*, 11, 53–58.

Andersson, M. and L. W. Simmons, 2006. Sexual selection and mate choice. *Trends in Ecology and Evolution*, 21, 296–302.

Andrade, M. C. B., 1996. Sexual selection for male sacrifice in the Australian redback spider. *Science*, 271, 70–72.

Anholt, B. R., E. Werner, and D. K. Skelly, 2000. Effect of food and predators on the activity of four larval ranid frogs. *Ecology*, 81, 3509–3521.

Arnqvist ,G. and L. Rowe, 1995. Sexual conflict and arms races between the sexes: a morphological adaptation for control of mating in a female insect. *Proceedings of the Royal Society of London* (B), 261, 123–127.

Arnqvist, G. and L. Rowe, 2005. *Sexual Conflict*. Princeton, NJ: Princeton University Press.

Baker R. L. and B. P. Smith, 1997. Conflict between antipredator and antiparasite behaviour in larval damselflies. *Oecologia*, 109, 622–628.

Barette, C. and D. Vandal, 1990. Sparring, relative antler size, and assessment in male caribou. *Behavioural Ecology and Sociobiology*, 26, 383–387.

Berdoy, M., J. P. Webster, and D. W. Macdonald, 2000. Fatal attraction in rats infected with *Toxoplasma gondii*. *Proceedings of the Royal Society of London (B)*, 267, 1591–1594.

Biron D. G., F. Ponton, L. Marche, N. Galeotti, L, Renault, E. Demey-Thomas, J. Poncet, S. P. Brown, P. Jouin, and F. Thomas, 2006. "Suicide" of crickets harbouring hairworms: A proteomics investigation. *Insect Molecular Biology*, 15, 731–742.

Birkhead, T. R. and A. P. Moller (eds.), 1998. *Sperm Competition and Sexual Selection*. San Diego, CA: Academic Press.

Birkhead, T. R. and T. Pizzari, 2002. Postcopulatory sexual selection. *Nature Reviews Genetics*, 3, 262–273.

Blackmore C. J. and R. Heinsohn, 2007. Reproductive success and helper effects in the cooperatively breeding grey-crowned babbler. *Journal of Zoology*, 273, 326–332.

Borgerhoff Mulder M., 2005. Human Behavioural Ecology. In *Encyclopedia of Life Sciences*. Chichester: John Wiley and Sons Ltd.

Brooks, D. R. and D. A. McLennan. 1991. *Phylogeny, Ecology, and Behavior: A Research Program in Comparative Biology*. Chicago, IL: University of Chicago Press.

Brooks, D. R., and D. A. McLennan. 2002. *The Nature of Diversity: An Evolutionary Voyage of Discovery*. Chicago, IL: University of Chicago Press.

Brown J. L., E. R. Brown, S. D. Brown, and D. D. Dow, 1982. Helpers: Effects of experimental removal on reproductive success. *Science*, 215, 421–422.

Byrne, P. G. and Roberts, J. D. 2004. Intrasexual selection and group spawning in quacking frogs (*Crinia georgiana*). *Behavioral Ecology*, 15, 872–882.

Cartar R. V. 2004. Resource tracking by bumble bees: Responses to plant-level differences in quality. *Ecology*, 85, 2764–2771.

Cézilly, F., A. Grégoire, and A. Bertin. 2000. Conflict between co-occurring manipulative parasites? An experimental study of the joint influence of two acanthocephalan parasites on the behaviour of *Gammarus pulex*. *Parasitology*, 120, 625–630.

Chapman T., L. F. Liddle, J. M. Kalb, M. F. Wolfner, and L. Partridge, 1995. Cost of mating in *Drosophila melanogaster* females is mediated by male accessory gland products. *Nature*, 373, 241–244.

Chapman, T. W., S. P. Perry, and B. J. Crespi. The Evolutionary Ecology of Eusociality in Australian Gall Thrips: A 'Model Clades' Approach. In J. Korb and J. Heinze (Eds.) *Ecology of Social Evolution*. (pp. 57–82). Berlin: Springer Verlag.

Chapman T. and B. J. Crespi, 2008. The evolutionary ecology of eusociality in Australian gall thrips: A "model clades" approach. In J. Korb and J. Heinze (Eds.), *Ecology of Social Evolution*. (pp. 57–82). Berlin, Germany: Springer Verlag.

Chapman T., B. J. Crespi., B. D. Kranz, and M. P. Schwarz, 2000. High relatedness and inbreeding at the origin of eusociality in gall-inducing thrips. *Proceedings of the National Academy of Sciences (USA)*, 97, 1648–650.

Chase, R. and K. C. Blanchard, 2006. The snail's love-dart delivers mucus to increase paternity. *Proceedings of the Royal Society B*, 273, 1471–1475.

Choe, J. C. and B. J. Crespi (eds.). 1997a. *The Evolution of Mating Systems in Insects and Arachnids*. Cambridge, UK: Cambridge University Press.

Choe, J. C. and B. J. Crespi (eds.). 1997b. *The Evolution of Social Behavior in Insects and Arachnids*. Cambridge, UK: Cambridge University Press.

Clout, M. N., G. P. Elliott, and B. C. Robertson. 2002. Effects of supplementary feeding on the offspring sex ratio of kakapo: A dilemma for the conservation of a polygynous parrot. *Biological Conservation*, 107, 13–18.

Clutton-Brock, T. H., 2002. Breeding together: Kin selection and mutualism in cooperative vertebrates. *Science*, 296, 69–72.

Clutton-Brock, T. H. and A. C. J. Vincent. 1991. Sexual selection and the potential reproductive rates of males and females. *Nature*, 351, 58–60.

Crespi, B. J., 1992. Eusociality in Australian gall thrips. *Nature*, 359, 724–726.

Crespi, B. J., 2001a. Altruism in the outback. *Natural History*, 110, 56–61.

Crespi, B. J. 2001b. The evolution of social behavior in microorganisms. *Trends in Ecology and Evolution*, 16, 178–183.

Crespi B. J. and C. Badcock. 2008. Psychosis and autism as diametrical disorders of the social brain. *Behavioral and Brain Sciences*, 31, 284–320.

Crespi, N. J., and K. Summers. 2005. The evolutionary biology of cancer. *Trends in Ecology and Evolution*, 20, 545–552.

Crozier, R. H., 2008. Advanced eusociality, kin selection and male haploidy. *Australian Journal of Entomology*, 47, 2–8.

Danchin, É., L-A. Giraldeau, and F. Cézilly, 2008. *Behavioural Ecology*. Oxford, UK: Oxford University Press.

Darwin, C. 1871., *The Descent of Man and Selection in Relation to Sex*. London, UK: John Murray.

Dawkins, R. 1976. *The Selfish Gene*. Oxford, UK: Oxford University Press.

De Moraes, C. M., W. J. Lewis, P. W. Paré, H. T. Alborn and J. H. Tumlinson. 1998. Herbivore-infested plants selectively attract parasitoids. *Nature*, 393, 570–573.

Despland, E. and S. Hamzah. 2004. Ontogenetic changes in social behaviour in the forest tent caterpillar, *Malacosoma disstria*. *Behavioral Ecology and Sociobiology*, 56, 177–184.

Doherty, P. F., G. Sorci, J. A. Royle, J. E. Hines, J. D. Nichols, and T. Boulinier. 2003. Sexual selection affects local extinction and turnover in bird communities. *Proceedings of the National Academy of Science*, 100, 5858–5862.

Double, M. and A. Cockburn, 2000. Pre-dawn infidelity: Females control extra-pair matings in superb fairy-wrens. *Proceedings of the Royal Society of London (B)*, 267, 465–470.

Eberhard. W. G. 1996. *Female Control: Sexual Selection by Cryptic Female Choice*. Princeton, NJ: Princeton University Press.

Eberhard W. G., 2000. Spider manipulation by a wasp larva. *Nature*, 406, 255–256.

Eggert A.-K. and S. K. Sakaluk, 1995. Female-coerced monogamy in burying beetles. *Behavioral Ecology and Sociobiology*, 37, 147–53.

Emlen D. J. 1997. Diet alters male horn allometry in the beetle *Onthophagus acuminatus* (Coleoptera, Scarabaeidae). *Proceedings of the Royal Society of Lond (B)*, 264, 567–574.

Emlen, D. J., J. Marangelo, B. Ball, and C. W. Cunningham. 2005. Diversity in the weapons of sexual selection: Horn evolution in the beetle genus *Onthophagus* (Coleoptera: Scarabaeidae). *Evolution*, 59, 1060–1084.

Evans H. E. 1977. Extrinsic versus intrinsic factors in the evolution of insect sociality. *BioScience*, 27, 613–617.

Fisher, R. A. 1930. *The Genetical Theory of Natural Selection*. Oxford, UK: Clarendon Press.

Fitzpatrick, M. J., Y. Ben-Shahar, H. M. Smid, L. E. M. Vet, G. E. Robinson, and M. B. Sokolowski. 2005. Candidate genes for behavioural ecology. *Trends in Ecology and Evolution*, 20, 96–104.

Freeman, D. C., E. D. McArthur , K. J. Miglial, M. J. Nilson and M. L. Brown. 2007. Sex and the lonely *Atriplex*. *Western North American Naturalist*, 67, 137–141.

Gibbs, H. L., M. D. Sorenson, K. Marchetti, M. D. Brooke, N. B. Davies, and H. Nakamura. 2000. Genetic evidence for female host-specific races of the common cuckoo. *Nature*, 407, 183–186.

Gibo, D. L. 1978. The selective advantage of foundress associations in *Polistes fuscatus* (Hymenoptera: Vespidae): A field study of the effects of predation on productivity. *Canadian Entomologist*, 110, 519–540.

Godin, J.-G. J. and S. E. Briggs, 1996. Female mate choice under predation risk in the guppy. *Animal Behavior*, 51, 117–130.

Godin, J.-G. J. and L. A. Dugatkin. 1996. Female mating preference for bold males in the guppy, *Poecilia reticulata*. *Proceedings of the National Academy of Science*, 93, 10262–10267.

Griffin, A. S. 2008. Naked mole-rat. *Current Biology*, 18, R844–R845.

Gross M. R. and E. L. Charnov. 1980. Alternative male life histories in bluegill sunfish. *Proceedings of the National Academy of Sciences (USA)*, 77, 6937–6940.

Gwynne, D. T. 1997. Glandular gifts. *Scientific American*, 277, 46–51.

Gwynne, D. T. 2009. Mating behavior. In V. Resh and R. Cardé (Eds.). *Encyclopedia of Insects* (2nd ed.). (pp. 604–609). New York: Academic Press.

Gwynne D. T., 2001., *Katydids and Bush-crickets: Reproductive Behavior and Evolution of the Tettigoniidae*. Ithaca, NY: Cornell University Press.

Gwynne, D. T. and L. W. Simmons, 1990. Experimental reversal of courtship roles in an insect. *Nature*, 346, 172–174.

Hames, R. 2001. Human Behavioral Ecology. In M. J. Smelser and P. B. Baltres, (Eds.), *International Encyclopedia of the Social and Behavioral Sciences* (pp. 6946–6951). London, UK: Elsevier.

Hamilton, W. D., 1996. *Narrow Roads of Gene Land, The Collected Papers of W. D. Hamilton, Volume 1, Evolution of Social Behaviour*. Oxford, UK: Oxford University Press.

Hamilton, W. D., and M. Zuk. 1982. Heritable true fitness and bright birds: A role for parasites? *Science*, 218, 384–387.

Harpending, H. 2002. Kinship and population subdivision. *Population and Environment*, 24, 141–147.

House C. M., J. Hunt, and A. J. Moore. 2007. Sperm competition, alternative mating tactics and context-dependent fertilization success in the burying beetle, *Nicrophorus vespilloides*. *Proceedings of the Royal Society of London (B)*, 274, 1309–1315.

Hughes, W. O. H., B. P. Oldroyd, M. Beekman, and F. L. W. Ratnieks. 2008. Ancestral monogamy shows kin selection is key to the evolution of eusociality. *Science*, 320, 1213–1216.

Hutchings, M. R., I. J. Gordon, I. Kyriazakis, E. Robertson, and F. Jackson. 2002. Grazing in heterogeneous environments: Infra- and supra-parasite distributions determine herbivore grazing decisions. *Oecologia*, 132, 453–460.

Jiggins, F. M., G. D. D. Hurst, and M. E. N. Majerus. 2000. Sex-ratio-distorting *Wolbachia* causes sex-role reversal in its butterfly host. *Proceedings of the Royal Society of London (B)*, 267, 69–73.

Karban, R. 1982. Increased reproductive success at high densities and predator satiation for periodical cicadas. *Ecology*, 63, 321–328.

Karban R., J. Maron, G. W. Felton, G. Ervin, and H. Eichenseer. 2003. Herbivore damage to sagebrush induces resistance in wild tobacco: Evidence for eavesdropping between plants. *Oiko*, 100, 325–332.

Karban, R. 2008. Plant behaviour and communication. *Ecology Letters*, 11, 727–739.

Kelly, C. D. and J.-G. J. Godin. 2001. Predation risk reduces male-male sexual competition in the Trinidadian guppy (*Poecilia reticulata*). *Behavioral Ecology and Sociobiology*, 51, 95–100.

Kelly, C. D., 2006a. Fighting for harems: assessment strategies during male-male contests in the sexually dimorphic Wellington tree weta. *Animal Behaviour*, 72, 727–736.

Kelly, C. D. 2006b. Replicating empirical research in behavioral ecology: How and why it should be done but rarely ever is. *Quarterly Review of Biology*, 81, 221–236.

Kilner, R. M., D. G. Noble, and N. B. Davies. 1999. Signals of need in parent-offspring communication and their exploitation by the common cuckoo. *Nature*, 397, 667–672.

Krakauer, A.H, 2005. Kin selection and cooperative courtship in wild turkeys. *Nature*, 434, 69–72.

Krebs, J. R., J. T. Erichsen, M. I. Webber and E. L. Charnov. 1977. Optimal prey selection by the great tit (*Parus major*). *Animal Behaviour*, 25, 30–38.

Krebs, J. R. and N. B. Davies. 1997. *An Introduction to Behavioural Ecology*. Oxford, UK: Blackwell Scientific.

Krebs, J. R. and N. B. Davies (Eds). 1997. *Behavioural Ecology: An Evolutionary Approach* (4th ed.). Oxford, UK: Blackwell Scientific.

Kuzdzal-Fick, J. J., K. R. Foster, D. C. Queller, and J. E. Strassmann. 2007. Exploiting new terrain: An advantage to sociality in the slime mold *Dictyostelium discoideum*. *Behavioral Ecology*, 18, 433–437.

Lefèvre, T., C. Lebarbenchon, M. Gauthier-Clerc, D. Misse, R. Poulin, and F. Thomas. 2009. The ecological significance of manipulative parasites. *Trends in Ecology and Evolution*, 24, 41–48.

Legendre, S., J. Clobert, A. P. Moller, and G. Sorci. 1999. Demographic stochasticity and social mating system in the process of extinction of small populations: The case of passerines introduced into New Zealand. *American Naturalist*, 153, 449–463.

Lockwood, J. 2004. The orgy in your backyard. *New York Times*, May 20, 2004.

Lyon, B. E., J. M. Eadie, and L. D. Hamilton. 1994. Parental choice selects for ornamental plumage in american coot chicks. *Nature*, 371, 240–243.

Macchiusi, F. and R. L. Baker. 1992. Effects of predators and food availability on activity and growth of *Chironomus tentans* (Chironomidae, Diptera). *Freshwater Biology*, 28, 207–216.

Mehdiabadi, N. J., C. N. Jack, T. T. Farnham, T. G. Platt, S. E. Kalla, G. Shaulsky, D. C. Queller, and J. E. Strassmann. 2006. Kin preference in a social microbe—Given the right circumstances, even an amoeba chooses to be altruistic towards its relatives. *Nature*, 442, 881–882.

Mennill, D. J., L. M. Ratcliffe, and P. T. Boag. 2002. Female eavesdropping on male song contests in songbirds. *Science*, 296, 873–873.

Moller A. P. 1991. Sexual selection in the monogamous barn swallow (*Hirundo rustica*) I. Determinants of tail ornament size. *Evolution*, 45, 1823–1836.

Moore, J. E. 2002. *Parasites and the Behavior of Animals*. Oxford, UK: Oxford University Press.

Mulder, R. A., P. O. Dunn, A. Cockburn, K. A. Lazenbycohen, and M. J. Howell. 1994. Helpers liberate female fairy-wrens from constraints on extra-pair mate choice. *Proceedings of the Royal Society of London (B)*, 255, 223–229.

Neff, B. D., P. Fu and M. R. Gross. 2003. Sperm investment and alternative mating tactics in bluegill sunfish (*Lepomis macrochirus*). *Behavioral Ecology*, 14, 634–641.

Owens, I. P. F. 2006. Where is behavioral ecology going? *Trends in Ecology and Evolution*, 21, 356–360.

Otronen M. 1990. Mating behavior and sperm competition in the fly, *Dryomyza anilis*. *Behavioral Ecology and Sociobiology*, 26, 349–356.

Parker G. A. 1970. Sperm competition and its evolutionary consequences in the insects. *Biological Reviews (Cambridge)*, 45, 525–567.

Parrott, M. L., S. J. Ward, and P. D. Temple-Smith. 2007. Olfactory cues, genetic relatedness and female mate choice in the agile antechinus (*Antechinus agilis*). *Behavioral Ecology and Sociobiology*, 61, 1075–1079.

Pizzari, T. 2004. Evolution: Sperm ejection near and far. *Current Biology*, 14, R511–R513.

Poulin, R. 2006. *Evolutionary Ecology of Parasites, 2nd ed.* Princeton, NJ: Princeton University Press.

Preston, B. T., I. R. Stevenson, J. M. Pemberton, and K. Wilson. 2001. Dominant rams lose out by sperm depletion. *Nature*, 409, 681–682.

Proctor, H. C. 1991. Courtship in the water mite *Neumania papillator*: Males capitalize on female adaptations for predation. *Animal Behavior*, 42, 589–598.

Queller D. C., F. Zacchi, R. Cervo, S. Turillazzi, M. T. Henshaw, L. A. Santorelli, and J. E. Strassmann. 2000. Unrelated helpers in a social insect. *Nature*, 405, 784–787.

Queller, D. C. and J. E. Strassmann. 2003. Eusociality. *Current Biology*, 13, R861–R863.

Rasmann, S., G. T. G. Köllner, J. Degenhardt, I. Hiltpold, S. Toepfer, U. Kuhlmann, J. Gershenzon and T. C. J. Turlings. 2005. Recruitment of entomo-pathogenic nematodes by insect-damaged maize roots. *Nature*, 434, 732–737.

Rodd, F. H., K. A. Hughes, G. F. Grether, and C. T. Baril. 2002. A possible non-sexual origin of mate preference: Are male guppies mimicking fruit? *Proceedings of the Royal Society of London (B)*, 269, 475–481.

Rowe, L., G. Arnqvist, A. Sih, and J. Krup. 1994. Sexual conflict and the evolutionary ecology of mating patterns—Water striders as a model system. *Trends in Ecology and Evolution*, 9, 289–293.

Rowe L. and D. Houle. 1996. The lek paradox and the capture of genetic variance by condition dependent traits. *Proceedings of the Royal Society of London (B)*, 263, 1415–1421.

Seppala, O., A. Karvonen, and E. T. Valtonen. 2008. Shoaling behaviour of fish under parasitism and predation risk. *Animal Behavior*, 75, 145–150.

Sherman, P. W. 1977. Nepotism and the evolution of alarm calls. *Science*, 197, 1246–1253.

Shuster, S. M. and M. J. Wade. 1991. Equal mating success among male reproductive strategies in a marine isopod. *Nature*, 350, 608–610.

Shuster, S. M. and M. J. Wade. 2003. *Mating Systems and Strategies.* Princeton, NJ: Princeton University Press.

Sibley, R. and R. Smith (eds.). 1985. *Behavioural Ecology: Ecological Consequences of Adaptive Behaviour.* Oxford, UK: Blackwell Scientific Publications.

Simmons, L. W. 2001. *Sperm Competition and its Evolutionary Consequences in the Insects.* Princeton, NJ: Princeton University Press.

Starks, P. T. and C. A. Blackie. 2000. The relationship between serial monogamy and rape in the United States (1960–1995). *Proceedings of the Royal Society of London (B)*, 267, 1259–1263.

Strassmann, J. E. and D. C. Queller. 2007. Altruism among amoebas. *Natural History*, 116, 24–29.

Tarpy, D. R. and T. D. Seeley. 2006. Lower disease infections in honeybee (*Apis mellifera*) colonies headed by polyandrous vs monandrous queens. *Naturwissenschaften*, 93, 195–199.

Thomas, F., J.-F. Guegan, and F. Renaud. (Eds.). 2007. *Ecology and Evolution of Parasitism*. Oxford, UK: Oxford University Press.

Thomas, F., A. Schmidt-Rhaesa, G. Martin, C. Manu, P. Durand, and F. Renaud. 2002. Do hair-worms (Nematomorpha) manipulate the water seeking behaviour of their terrestrial hosts? *Journal of Evolutionary Biology*, 15, 356–361.

Thorne, B. L., N. L. Breisch, and M. L. Muscedere. 2003. Evolution of eusociality and the soldier caste in termites: Influence of intraspecific competition and accelerated inheritance. *Proceedings of the National Academy of Science*, 100, 12808–12813.

Thornhill, R. 1980. Sexual selection in the black-tipped hangingfly. *Scientific American*, 242, 162–172.

Tibbetts, E. A. and J. Dale. 2004. A socially enforced signal of quality in a paper wasp. *Nature*, 432, 218–222.

Trivers, R. and D. Willard. 1973. Natural selection of parental ability to vary the sex ratio of offspring. *Science*, 179, 90–92.

Welch, A. M., R. D. Semlitsch, and H. C. Gerhardt. 1998. Call duration as an indicator of genetic quality in male gray tree frogs. *Science*, 280, 1928–1930.

West-Eberhard, M. J. 1979. Sexual selection, social competition, and evolution. *Proceedings of the American Philosophical Society*, 123, 222–234.

Wilkinson, G. S. 1984. Reciprocal food sharing in the vampire bat. *Nature*, 308, 181–184.

Wilkinson, G. S., D. C. Presgraves, and L. Crymes. 1998a. Male eye span in stalk-eyed flies indicates genetic quality by meiotic drive suppression. *Nature*, 391, 276–279.

Wilkinson, G. S., H. Kahler, and R. H. Baker. 1998b. Evolution of female mating preferences in stalk-eyed flies. *Behavioral Ecology*, 9, 525–533.

Williams, G. C. 1966. *Adaptation and Natural Selection*. Princeton, NJ: Princeton University Press.

Wilson, M. and M. Daly. 1997. Life expectancy, economic inequality, homicide, and reproductive timing in Chicago neighbourhoods. *British Medical Journal*, 314, 1271–1274.

Winterhalder, B., 2000. Analyzing adaptive strategies: Human behavioral ecology at twenty-five. *Evolutionary Anthropology: Issues, News, and Reviews*, 9, 51–72.

Yanoviak, S. P., M. Kaspari, R. Dudley, and G. Poinar. 2008. Parasite-induced fruit mimicry in a tropical canopy ant. *American Naturalist*, 171, 536–544.

Zahavi, A. 1975. Mate selection—A selection for a handicap. *Journal of Theoretical Biology*, 53, 205–214.

Chapter 7

Brown, G. W., W. R. Brown, and P. P. Cohen. 1959. Comparative biochemistry of urea synthesis. II. Levels of urea cycle enzymes in metamorphosing *Rana catesbeiana* tadpoles. *Journal of Biological Chemistry*, 234, 1775–1780.

Bryden, M. M. 1968. Growth and function of the subcutaneous fat of the elephant seal. *Nature*, 220, 597–599.

Butler, P. J. and D. R. Jones. 1997. Physiology of diving of birds and mammals. *Physiological Reviews*, 77, 837–899.

Chen, L., A. L. DeVries, and C. C. Cheng. 1997. Convergent evolution of antifreeze glycoproteins in Antarctic notothenioid fish and Arctic cod. *Proceedings of the National Academy of Science*, 94, 3817–3822.

Chruszcz, B. J. and R. M. R. Barclay. 2002. Thermoregulatory ecology of a solitary bat, *Myotis evotis*, roosting in rock crevices. *Functional Ecology*, 16, 18–26.

Danks, H. V. 2004. Seasonal adaptations in arctic insects. *Integrative and Comparative Biology*, 44, 85–94.

Danks H. V., O. Kukal, and R. A. Ring. 1994. Insect cold-hardiness: Insights from the Arctic. *Arctic* 47, 391–404.

Davenport, J. A. 1992. *Animal Life at Low Temperature.* London: Chapman and Hall.

Dawson, W. R. and Bartholomew, G. A. (1956). Relation of oxygen consumption to body weight, temperature, and temperature acclimation in lizards *Uta stansburia* and *Scelopwus occidentalis. Physiological Zoology*, 29, 40–51.

Degnan, K. J., K. J. Karnaky and J. A. Zadunaisky. 1977. Active chloride transport in the *in vitro* opercular skin of a teleost (*Fundulus heteroclitus*), a gill-like epithelium rich in chloride cells. *Journal of Physiology*, 271, 155–191.

Dejours, P. 1975. *Principles of Comparative Respiratory Physiology*. Amsterdam: North Holland Publishing.

Ewart, K. V., Q. Lin and C. L. Hew. 1999. Structure, function and evolution of antifreeze proteins. *Cellular and Molecular Life Sciences*, 55, 271–283.

Geiser, F. 2004. Metabolic rate and body temperature reduction during hibernation and daily torpor. *Annual Review of Physiology*, 66, 239–274.

Heinrich, B and G. A. Bartholomew. 1971. An analysis of pre-flight warm-up in the sphinx moth *Manduca sexta. Journal of Experimental Biology*, 55, 233–239.

Hill, R. W. 1975. Daily torpor in *Peromyscus leucopus* on an adequate diet. *Comparative Biochemistry and Physiology A*, 51, 413–423.

Hill, R. W., G. A. Wyse, and M. Anderson. 2008. *Animal Physiology*. Sunderland, MA: Sinauer Associates.

Hoar, W. S. 1983. *General and Comparative Physiology*. Englewood Heights, NJ: Prentice Hall.

Hochachka, P. W. and G. N. Somero. 1984. *Biochemical Adaptation*. Princeton, NJ: Princeton University Press.

Hochachka, P. W. and G. N. Somero. 2002. *Biochemical Adaptation: Mechanism and Process in Physiological Evolution*. New York: Oxford University Press.

Hohtola, E., H. Rintamaki, and R. Hissa. 1980. Shivering and piloerection as complementary cold defense responses in the pigeon during sleep and wakefulness. *Journal of Comparative Physiology*, 136, 77–81.

Jensen, F. B. 2004. Red blood cell pH, the Bohr effect, and other oxygenation-linked phenomena in blood O_2 and CO_2 transport. *Acta Physiologica Scandanavia*, 182, 215–227.

Jensen, F. B. and H. Malte. 1990. Acid-base and electrolyte regulation, and hemolymph gas transport in crayfish, *Astacus astacus*, exposed to soft, acid water with and without aluminum. *Journal of Comparative Physiology B*, 160, 483–490.

Kilgore, D. L. and K. Schmidt-Nielsen. 1975. Heat Loss from ducks' feet immersed in cold water. *The Condor*, 77, 475–478.

Kirschner, L. B. 1997. Extrarenal mechanisms in hydromineral and acid-base regulation of aquatic vertebrates. In W. H. Dantzler (Ed.), *Comparative Physiology, Volume 1* (pp. 577–622). Handbook of Physiology, Section 13, Bethesda, MD.

Kooyman, G. L. and P. J. Ponganis. 1998. The physiological basis of diving to depth: Birds and mammals. *Annual Review of Physiology*, 60, 19–32.

Kvadsheim, P. H., L. P. Folkow, and A. S. Blix. 1998. Thermal conductivity of minke whale blubber. *Journal of Thermal Biology*, 21, 123–128.

Lausen, C. L. and R. M. R. Barclay. 2003. Thermoregulation and roost selection by reproductive female big brown bats (*Eptesicus fuscus*) roosting in rock crevices. *Journal of Zoology, London*, 260, 235–244.

Lenfant, C, K. Johansen and J. D. Torrance. 1970. Gas transport and oxygen storage capacity in some pinnipeds and the sea otter. *Respiration Physiology*, 9, 277–286.

Michener, G. R. 1998. Sexual differences in reproductive effort of Richardson's ground squirrels. *Journal of Mammalogy*, 79, 1–19.

Ponganis, P. J., G. L. Kooyman, and M. A. Castellini. 1993. Determinants of the aerobic dive limit of Weddel seals: Analysis of diving metabolic rate, postdive end tidal PO_2's and blood and muscle oxygen stores. *Physiological Zoology* 66, 732–749.

Randall, D., W. Burggren and K. French. 2002. *Animal Physiology: Mechanisms and Adaptations* (5th ed.). New York, NY: W. H. Freeman and Co.

Regniere, J. and B. Bentz. 2007. Modeling cold tolerance in the mountain pine beetle, *Dendroctonus ponderosae. Journal of Insect Physiology*, 53, 559–572.

Reynolds, J. E. III, and S. A. Rommel (eds). 1999. Biology of Marine Mammals, Washington, DC: Smithsonian Institution Press.

Russell, P.J., S.L. Wolfe, P. E. Hertz, C. Starr, B. Fenton, H. J. Addy, D. Maxwell, T. E. Haffie. 2009. *Biology: Exploring the Diversity of Life* (1st Canadian Edition), Toronto: Nelson.

Sherwood, L. and R. Kell. 2010. *Human Physiology: From Cells to Systems* (1st Canadian Edition). Toronto: Nelson Education Ltd.

Schmidt-Nielsen, B. and K. Schmidt-Nielsen. 1951. A complete account of the water metabolism in kangaroo rats and an experimental verification. *Journal of Cellular and Comparative Physiology*, 38, 165–181.

Schmidt-Nielsen, K., F. R. Hainsworth and D. E. Murrish. 1970. Countercurrent heat exchange in the respiratory passages: Effect on water and heat balance. *Respiration Physiology*, 9, 263–276.

Schmidt-Nielsen, K. 1972. *How Animals Work*. Cambridge, UK: Cambridge University Press.

Schmidt-Nielsen, K. 1997. *Animal Physiology: Adaptation and Environment*. Cambridge, UK: Cambridge University Press.

Scholander, P. F., W. Flagg, V. Walters and L. Irving. 1953. Climatic adaptation in arctic and tropical poikilotherms. *Physiological Zoology*, 26, 67–92.

Scholander, P. F., R. Hock, V. Walters, F. Johnson, and L. Irving. 1950. Heat regulation in some arctic and tropical mammals and birds. *Biological Bulletin*, 99, 237–258.

Solick. D. I. and R. M. R. Barclay. 2007. Geographic variation in the use of torpor and roosting behaviour of female western long-eared bats. *Journal of Zoology*, 272, 358–366.

Steen, J. B. 1963. The physiology of the swimbladder in the eel *Anguilla vulgaris. Acta Physiologica Scandinavica*, 59, 221–241.

Storey, K. B. and J. M. Storey. 1996. Natural freezing survival in animals. *Annual Review of Ecology and Systematics*, 27, 365–386.

Tyack, P. L., M. Johnson, N. A. Soto, A. Sturlese, and P. T. Madsen. 2006. Extreme diving of beaked whales. *Journal of Experimental Biology*, 209, 4238–4253.

Wendelaar Bonga, S. E. and L. H. T. Dederen. 1986. Effects of acidified water on fish. *Endeavor*, 10, 198–202.

Whitehead, H. 2002. Sperm whale *Physeter macrocephalus*. In

W. Perrin, B. Würsig, and J. Thewissen, (Eds.) *Encyclopedia of Marine Mammals* (pp. 1165–1172). New York, NY: Academic Press.

Willmer, P., G. Stone and I. Johnston. 2000. *Environmental Physiology of Animals*. Oxford , UK: Blackwell Science.

Withers, P. C. 1992. *Comparative Animal Physiology*. Fort Worth, TX: Saunders.

Wood, C. M. 1989. The physiological problems of fish in acid waters. In R. Morris, D. Brown and J. Brown (Eds.). *Acid Toxicity and Aquatic Animals*, Society for Experimental Biology Seminar Series, No. 34 (pp. 125–152). Cambridge, UK: Cambridge University Press.

Wood, C. M., and McDonald, D. G. 1982. Physiological mechanisms of acid toxicity in fish. In R. E. Johnson (Ed.), *Acid Rain/Fisheries, Proceedings of an International Symposium on Acidic Precipitation and Fishery Impacts in North-eastern North America* (pp. 197–226). Bethesda, MD: American Fisheries Society.

Wood, C. M., and M. S. Rogano. 1986. Physiological responses to acid stress in crayfish (Orconectes): haemolymph ions, acid_base status, and exchanges with the environment. *Canadian Journal of Zoology*, 43, 1017–1026.

Chapter 8

Alm, G. 1959. Connection between maturity, size and age in fishes. *Report of the Institute of Freshwater Research, Drottningholm* 40, 5–145.

Arnqvist, G., and L. Rowe. 2005. *Sexual Conflict*. Princeton, NJ: Princeton University Press.

Aubin-Horth, N., C. R. Landry, B. H. Letcher, and H. A. Hofmann. 2005a. Alternative life histories shape brain gene expression profiles in males of the same population. *Proceedings of the Royal Society B*, 272, 1655–1662.

Aubin-Horth, N., B. H. Letcher, and H. A. Hofmann. 2005b. Interaction of rearing environment and reproductive tactic on gene expression profiles in Atlantic salmon. *Journal of Heredity*, 96, 261–278.

Barot, S., M. Heino, L. O'Brien, and U. Dieckmann. 2004. Long-term trend in the maturation reaction norm of two cod stocks. *Ecological Applications*, 14, 1257–1271.

Barot, S., M. Heino, M. J. Morgan, and U. Dieckmann. 2005. Maturation of Newfoundland American plaice (*Hippolossoides platessoides*): long-term trends in maturation reaction norms despite low fishing mortality? *ICES Journal of Marine Science*, 62, 56–64.

Beaumont, H. J. E., J. Gallie, C. Kjost, G. C. Ferguson, and P. B. Rainey. 2009. Experimental evolution of bet hedging. *Nature*, 462, 90–93.

Belk, M. C. 1995. Variation in growth and age at maturity in bluegill sunfish—genetic or environmental effects. *Journal of Fish Biology*, 47, 237–247.

Bell, G. 1980. The costs of reproduction and their consequences. *American Naturalist*, 116, 45–76.

Bennett, P. M., and I. P. F. Owens. 2002. *Evolutionary Ecology of Birds: Life Histories, Mating Systems and Extinction*. Oxford, UK: Oxford University Press.

Beverton, R. J. H. 1992. Patterns of reproductive strategy parameters in some marine teleost fishes. *Journal of Fish Biology*, 41 (Supplement B): 137–160.

Beverton, R. J. H., and S. J. Holt. 1959. A review of the lifespans and mortality rates of fish in nature, and their relation to growth and other physiological characteristics. *CIBA Foundation Coloquia on Ageing*, 54, 142–180.

Bielak, A. T., and G. Power. 1986. Changes in mean weight, sea-age composition, and catch-per-unit-effort of Atlantic (*Salmo salar*) angled in the Godbout River, Quebec, 1859–1983. *Canadian Journal of Fisheries and Aquatic Sciences*, 43, 281–287.

Brokordt, K. B., H. E. Guderley, M. Guay, C. F. Gaymer, and J. H. Himmelman. 2003. Sex differences in reproductive investment: Maternal care reduces escape response in the whelk, *Buccinum undatum*. *Journal of Experimental Marine Biology and Ecology*, 291, 161–180.

Capinera, J. L. 1979. Qualitative variation in plants and insects: effect of propagule size on ecological plasticity. *American Naturalist*, 117, 724–737.

Charnov, E. L. 1993. *Life History Invariants: Some Explorations of Symmetry in Evolutionary Ecology*. Oxford, UK: Oxford University Press.

Coates, D. 1988. Length-dependent changes in egg size and fecundity in females, and brooded embryo size in males, of fork-tailed catfishes (Pisces: Ariidae) from the Sepik River, Papua New Guinea, with some implications for stock assessments. *Journal of Fish Biology*, 33, 455–464.

Cole, L. C. 1954. The population consequences of life history phenomena. *Quarterly Review of Biology*, 29, 103–137.

Coltman, D. W., P. O'Donoghue, J. T. Jorgenson, J. T. Hogg, C. Strobeck, and M. Festa-Bianchet. 2003. Undesirable evolutionary consequences of trophy hunting. *Nature*, 426, 655–658.

Consuegra, S., C. G. De Leaniz, A. Serdio, and E. Verspoor. 2005. Selective exploitation of early running fish may induce genetic and phenotypic changes in Atlantic salmon. *Journal of Fish Biology*, 67 (Suppl. 1): 129–145.

Crump, M. L. 1981. Variation in propagule size as a function of environmental uncertainty for tree frogs. *American Naturalist*, 117, 724–737.

Cunningham, E. J. A. and A. F. Russell. 2000. Egg investment is influenced by male attractiveness in the mallard. *Nature*, 404, 74–77.

Dobson, F. S., and M. K. Oli. 2008. The life histories of orders of mammals: Fast and slow breeding. *Current Science*, 95, 862–865.

Dominey, W. J. 1980. Female mimicry in male bluegill sunfish—a genetic polymorphism? *Nature*, 284, 546–548.

Dufresne, F., G. J. FitzGerald, and S. Lachance. 1990. Age and size-related differences in reproductive success and reproductive costs in threespine stickleback (*Gasterosteus aculeatus*). *Behavioral Ecology*, 1, 140–147.

Dunlop, E. S., B. J. Shuter, and M. S. Ridgway. 2005. Isolating the influence of growth rate on maturation patterns in the smallmouth bass (*Micropterus dolomieui*). *Canadian Journal of Fisheries and Aquatic Sciences*, 62, 844–853.

Dutil, J.-D. 1986. Energetic constraints and spawning interval in the anadromous Arctic charr (*Salvelinus alpinus*). *Copeia*, 1986, 945–955.

FAO (Food and Agriculture Organization of the UN). 2002. Report of the second technical consultation on the suitability of the CITES criteria for listing commercially-exploited aquatic species. FAO Fisheries Report No. 667.

Festa-Bianchet, M. B., J.-M. Gaillard, and J. T. Jorgenson. 1998. Mass- and density-dependent reproductive success and reproductive costs in capital breeder. *American Naturalist*, 152, 367–379.

Fisher, R. A. 1930. *The Genetical Theory of Natural Selection*. Oxford, UK: Oxford University Press.

Fleming, I. A. 1996. Reproductive strategies of Atlantic salmon: Ecology and evolution. *Reviews in Fish Biology and Fisheries*, 6, 379–416.

Fox, C. W., and M. E. Czesak. 2000. Evolutionary ecology of progeny size in arthropods. *Annual Reviews in Entomology* 45, 341–369.

Fox, M. G. 1994. Growth, density, and interspecific influences on pumpkinseed sunfish life-histories. *Ecology*, 75, 1157–1171.

Fox, M. G., and A. Keast. 1991. Effect of overwinter mortality on reproductive life history characteristics of pumpkinseed (*Lepomis gibbosus*) populations. *Canadian Journal of Fisheries and Aquatic Sciences*, 48, 1791–1799.

Gadgil, M., and W. Bossert. 1970. Life historical consequences of natural selection. *American Naturalist*, 104, 1–24.

Gaillard, J.-M., D. Pontier, D. Allainé, J. D. Lebreton, J. Trouvilliez, and J. Clobert. 1989. An analysis of demographic tactics in birds and mammals. *Oikos*, 56, 59–76.

Gaston, K. J., and T. M. Blackburn. 1995. Mapping biodiversity using surrogates for species richness: macro-scales and New World birds. *Proceedings of the Royal Society B*, 262, 335–341.

Grift, R. E., A. D. Rijnsdorp, S. Barot, M. Heino, and U. Dieckmann. 2003. Fisheries-induced trends in reaction norms for maturation in North Sea plaice. *Marine Ecology Progress Series*, 257, 247–257.

Gross, M. R. 1979. Cuckoldry in sunfishes (*Lepomis*: Centrarchidae). *Canadian Journal of Zoology*, 57, 1507–1509.

Gross, M. R. 1982. Sneakers, satellites and parentals: polymorphic mating strategies in North American sunfishes. *Zeitschrift fur Tierpsychologie*, 60, 1–26.

Gross, M. R. 1985. Disruptive selection for alternative life histories in salmon, *Nature*, 313, 47–48.

Gross, M. R. 1996. Alternative reproductive strategies and tactics: diversity within sexes. *Trends in Ecology and Evolution*, 11, 92–98.

Hamon, T. R., C. J. Foote, R. Hilborn, and D. E. Rogers. 2000. Selection on morphology of spawning wild sockeye salmon by a gillnet fishery. *Transactions of the American Fisheries Society*, 129, 1300–1315.

Handford, P., G. Bell, and T. Reimchen. 1977. A gillnet fishery considered as an experiment in artificial selection. *Journal of the Fisheries Research Board of Canada*, 34, 954–961.

Hanssen, S. A., H. Engebretsen, and K. E. Erikstad. 2002. Incubation start and egg size in relation to body reserves in the common eider. *Behavioral Ecoogy and. Sociobiology* 52, 282–288.

Haugen, T. O. 2000. Growth and survival effects on maturation pattern in populations of grayling with recent common ancestors. *Oikos*, 90, 107–118.

Haugen, T. O., and L. A. Vøllestad. 2000. Population differences in early life-history traits in grayling. *Journal of Evolutionary Biology*, 13, 897–905.

Hazel, W. N., R. Smock, and M. D. Johnson. 1990. A polygenic model for the evolution of and maintenance of conditional strategies. *Proceedings of the Royal Society of London B*, 242, 181–187.

Heath, D. D., L. Rankin, C. A. Bryden, J. W. Heath, and J. M. Shrimpton. 2002. Heritability and Y-chromosome influence in the jack male life history of Chinook salmon (*Oncorhynchus tshawytscha*). *Heredity*, 89, 311–317.

Heino, M., U. Dieckmann, and O. R. Godo. 2002. Measuring probabilistic reaction norms for age and size at maturation. *Evolution*, 56, 669–678.

Hirshfield, M. F., and D. W. Tinkle. 1975. Natural selection and the evolution of reproductive effort. *Proceedings of the National Academy of Sciences of the U. S. A.*, 72, 2227–2231.

Houde, A. E., and J. A. Endler. 1990. Correlated evolution of female mating preferences and male patterns in the guppy, *Poecilia reticulata. Science*, 248, 1405–1408.

Hunt, J., and L. W. Simmons. 2001. Status-dependent selection in the dimorphic beetle *Onthophagus taurus. Proceedings of the Royal Society B*, 268, 2409–2414.

Hutchings, J. A. 1991. Fitness consequences of variation in egg size and food abundance in brook trout, *Salvelinus fontinalis. Evolution*, 45, 1162–1168.

Hutchings, J. A. 1993. Adaptive life histories effected by age-specific survival and growth rate. *Ecology*, 74, 673–684.

Hutchings, J. A. 1996. Adaptive phenotypic plasticity in brook trout, *Salvelinus fontinalis*, life histories. *Écoscience*, 3, 25–32.

Hutchings, J. A. 1999. The influence of growth and survival costs of reproduction on Atlantic cod, *Gadus morhua*, population growth rate. *Canadian Journal of Fisheries and Aquatic Sciences*, 56, 1612–1623.

Hutchings, J. A. 2005. Life history consequences of overexploitation to population recovery in Northwest Atlantic cod (*Gadus morhua*). *Canadian Journal of Fisheries and Aquatic Sciences*, 62, 824–832.

Hutchings, J. A. 2006. Survival consequences of sex-biased growth and the absence of a growth-mortality trade-off. *Functional Ecology*, 20, 347–353.

Hutchings, J. A. 2009. Avoidance of fisheries-induced evolution: management implications for catch selectivity and limit reference points. *Evolutionary Applications*, 2, 324–334.

Hutchigs, J. A., and D. W. Morris. 1985. The influence of phylogeny, size and behaviour on patterns of covariation in salmonid life histories. *Oikos*, 45, 118–124.

Hutchings, J. A., and R. A. Myers. 1993. Effect of age on the seasonality of maturation and spawning of Atlantic cod, *Gadus morhua*, in the Northwest Atlantic. *Canadian Journal of Fisheries and Aquatic Sciences*, 50, 2468–2474.

Hutchings, J. A., and R. A. Myers. 1994. The evolution of alternative mating strategies in variable environments. *Evolutionary Ecology*, 8, 256–268.

Hutchings, J. A., and M. E. B. Jones. 1998. Life history variation and growth rate thresholds for maturity in Atlantic salmon, *Salmo salar. Canadian Journal of Fisheries and Aquatic Sciences*, 55 (Suppl. 1): 22–47.

Hutchings, J. A., T. D. Bishop, and C. R. McGregor-Shaw. 1999. Spawning behaviour of Atlantic cod, *Gadus morhua*: Evidence of mate competition and mate choice in a broadcast spawner. *Canadian Journal of Fisheries and Aquatic Sciences*, 56, 97–104.

Hutchings, J. A., and D. J. Fraser. 2008. The nature of fisheries- and farming-induced evolution. *Molecular Ecology*, 17, 294–313.

Hutchings, J. A., R. A. Myers, V. B. Garcia, and L. O. Lucifora. 2010. Life history correlates of

extinction risk in vertebrates. Not yet published.
Jansen, W. A. 1996. Plasticity in maturity and fecundity of yellow perch, *Perca flavescens* (Mitchill): Comparisons of stunted and normal-growing populations. *Annales Zoologici Fennici*, 33, 403–415.
Jensen, A. L. 1997. Origin of the relation between K and L_{inf} and synthesis of relations among life history parameters. *Canadian Journal of Fisheries and Aquatic Sciences*, 54, 987–989.
Jetz, W., C. H. Sekercioglu, and K. Böhning-Gaese. 2008. The worldwide variation in avian clutch size across species and space. *PloS Biology*, 6, 2650–2657.
Jones, J. W. 1959. *The Salmon*. London, UK: Collins.
Kamler, E. 1992. *Early Life History of Fish: An Energetics Approach*. London, UK: Chapman & Hall.
Kendall, N. W., J. J. Hard, and T. P. Quinn. 2009. Quantifying six decades of fishery selection for size and age at maturity in sockeye salmon. *Evolutionary Applications*, 2, 523–536.
Koops, M. A., J. A. Hutchings, and B. K. Adams. 2003. Environmental predictability and the cost of imperfect information: Influences on offspring size variability. *Evolutionary Ecology Research*, 5, 29–42.
Koslow, J. A., J. Bell, P. Virtue, and D. C.Smith. 1995. Fecundity and its variability in orange roughy: Effects of population density, condition, egg size, and senescence. *Journal of Fish Biology*, 47, 1063–1080.
Kudo, S. 2001. Intraclutch egg-size variation in acanthosomatid bugs: adaptive allocation of maternal investment. *Oikos*, 92, 208–214.
Lack, D. 1947. The significance of clutch size. I. Intraspecific variations. *Ibis*, 89, 302–352.
Law, R. 1979. Optimal life histories under age-specific predation. *American Naturalist*, 114, 399–417.
Law, R. 2000. Fishing, selection, and phenotypic evolution. *ICES Journal of Marine Science*, 57, 659–668.
Law, R., and C. A. Rowell. 1993. Cohort-structured populations, selection responses, and exploitation of the North Sea cod. In T. K Stokes, J. M. McGlade, R. Law (Eds.), *The exploitation of evolving resources*. (pp. 155–174). Berlin: Springer-Verlag.
Leggett, W. C., and J. E. Carscadden. 1978. Latitudinal variation in reproductive characteristics of American shad (*Alosa sapidissima*): Evidence for population specific life history strategies in fish. *Journal of the Fisheries Research Board of Canada*, 35, 1469–1478.
Lidgard, D. C., D. J. Boness, W. D. Bowen, J. I. McMillan, and R. C. Fleischer. 2004. The rate of fertilization in male mating tactics of the polygynous grey seal. *Molecular Ecology*, 13, 3543–3548.
MacArthur, R. H., and E. O. Wilson. 1967. *The Theory of Island Biogeography*. Princeton, NJ: Princeton University Press.
Mainguy, J., S. D. Côté, E. Cardinal, and M. Houle. 2008. Mating tactics and mate choice in relation to age and social rank in male mountain goats. *Journal of Mammalogy*, 89, 626–635.
Maynard Smith, J. 1982. *Evolution and the Theory of Games*. Cambridge, UK: Cambridge University Press.
Musick, J. A., M. M. Harbin, S. A. Berkeley, G. H. Burgess, A. M. Eklund, L. Findley, R. G. Gilmore, J. T. Golden, D. S. Ha, G. R. Huntsman, J. C. McGovern, G. R. Sedberry, S. J. Parker, S. G. Poss, E. Sala, T. W. Schmidt, H. Weeks, and S. G. Wright. 2000. Marine, estuarine, and diadromous fish stocks at risk of extinction in North America (exclusive of Pacific salmonids). *Fisheries*, 25, 6–30.
Myers, R. A. 1984. Demographic consequences of precocious maturation of Atlantic salmon (*Salmo salar*). *Canadian Journal of Fisheries and Aquatic Sciences*, 41, 1349–1353.
Myers, R. A., J. A. Hutchings, and R. J. Gibson. 1986. Variation in male parr maturation within and among populations of Atlantic salmon, *Salmo salar*. *Canadian Journal of Fisheries and Aquatic Sciences*, 43, 1242–1248.
Näslund, I., E. Degerman, and F. Nordwall. 1998. Brown trout (*Salmo trutta*) habitat use and life history in Swedish streams: possible effects of biotic interactions. *Canadian Journal of Fisheries and Aquatic Sciences* 55, 1034–1042.
Neff, B. D., and R. Knapp. 2009. Paternity, parental behavior and circulating steroid hormone concentrations in nest-tending male bluegill. *Hormones and Behaviour*, 56, 239–245.
Olsen, E. M., M. Heino, G. R. Lilly, M. J. Morgan, J. Brattey, B. Ernande, and U. Dieckmann. 2004. Maturation trends indicative of rapid evolution preceded the collapse of northern cod. *Nature*, 428, 932–935.
Olsen, E. M., G. R. Lilly, M. Heino, M. J. Morgan, J. Brattey, and U. Dieckmann. 2005. Assessing changes in age and size at maturation in collapsing populations of Atlantic cod (*Gadus morhua*). *Canadian Journal of Fisheries and Aquatic Sciences*, 62, 811–823.
Partridge, L. 1988. The rare-male effect: What is its evolutionary significance? *Philosophical Transactions of the Royal Society B*, 319, 525–539.
Pauly, D. 1980. On the interrelationships between natural mortality, growth parameters, and mean environmental temperature in 175 fish stocks. *Journal du Conseil, Conseil International pour l'Exploration de la Mer*, 39, 175–192.
Pianka, E. R. 1970. On *r* and *K* selection. *American Naturalist*, 104, 592–597.
Pianka, E. R. 1978. *Evolutionary Ecology* (2nd ed.). New York: Harper & Row.
Piché, J., J. A Hutchings, and W. Blanchard. 2008. Genetic variation in threshold reaction norms for alternative reproductive tactics in male Atlantic salmon, *Salmo salar*. *Proceedings of the Royal Society B: Biological Sciences*, 275, 1571–1575.
Pietsch, T. W. 2005. Dimorphism, parasitism, and sex revisited: modes of reproduction among deep-sea ceratioid anglerfishes (Teleostei: Lophiiformes). *Ichthyological Research* 52: 207–236.
Poulin, R. and W. J. Hamilton. 2000. Egg size variation as a function of environmental variability in parasitic trematodes. *Canadian Journal of Zoology* 78, 564–569.
Purchase, C. F., and J. A. Hutchings. 2008. A temporally stable spatial pattern in the spawner density of a freshwater fish: evidence for an ideal dispotic distribution. *Canadian Journal of Fisheries and Aquatic Sciences*, 65, 382–388.
Quinn, T. P., P. McGinnity, and T. F. Cross. 2006. Long-term declines in body sizes and shifts in run-timing of Atlantic salmon in Ireland. *Journal of Fish Biology*, 68, 1713–1730.
Quinn, T. P., S. Hodson, L. Flynn, R. Hilborn, and D. E. Rogers. 2007. Directional selection by

fisheries and the timing of sockeye salmon (*Oncorhynchus nerka*) migrations. *Ecological Applications*, 17, 731–739.

Reynolds, J. D., N. K. Dulvy, N. B. Goodwin, and J.A. Hutchings. 2005. Biology of extinction risk in marine fishes. *Proceedings of the Royal Society B* 272, 2337–2344.

Reznick, D. N., H. Bryga, and J. A. Endler. 1990. Experimentally-induced life history evolution in a natural population. *Nature*, 346, 357–359.

Ricker, W. E. 1981. Changes in the average size and average age of Pacific salmon. *Canadian Journal of Fisheries and Aquatic Sciences*, 38, 1636–1656.

Rijnsdorp, A. D. 1993. Fisheries as a large-scale experiment on life-history evolution: Disentangling phenotypic and genetic effects in changes in maturation and reproduction of North Sea plaice, *Pleuronectes platessa* L. *Oecologia*, 96, 391–401.

Rijnsdorp, A. D., R. E. Grift, S. B. M. Kraak. 2005. Fisheries-induced adaptive change in reproductive investment in North Sea plaice (*Pleuronectes platessa*)? *Canadian Journal of Fisheries and Aquatic Sciences*, 62, 833–843.

Roff, D. A. 1984. The evolution of life history parameters in teleosts. *Canadian Journal of Fisheries and Aquatic Sciences*, 41, 989–1000.

Roff, D. A. 1986. Predicting body size with life-history models. *BioScience*, 36, 316–323.

Roff, D. A. 1992. *The Evolution of Life Histories*. New York: Chapman and Hall.

Roff, D. A. 1996. The evolution of threshold traits in animals. *Quarterly Review of Biology*, 71, 3–35.

Roff, D. A. 2002. *Life History Evolution*. Sunderland, MA: Sinauer.

Roff, D. A. 2010. *Modelling Evolution: An Introduction to Numerical Methods*. New York, NY: Oxford University Press.

Rowe, L. 1994. The cost of mating and mate choice in water striders. *Animal Behaviour*, 48, 1049–1056.

Rowe, S., J. A. Hutchings, J. E. Skjæraasen, and L. Bezanson. 2008. Morphological and behavioural correlates of reproductive success in Atlantic cod, *Gadus morhua*. *Marine Ecology Progress Series*, 354, 257–265.

Schaffer, W. M. 1974. Selection for optimal life histories: The effects of age structure. *Ecology*, 55, 291–303.

Sears, R. 2002. Blue Whale, *Balaenoptera musculus*. In W. F. Perrin, B. Wursig, and J. G. M. Thewissen (Eds). *Encyclopedia of Marine Mammals*. (pp. 112–116). San Diego, CA: Academic Press.

Seger, J., and H. J. Brockmann. 1987. What is bet-hedging? *Oxford Surveys in Evolutionary Biology*, 4, 182–211.

Sheriff, M. J., C. J. Krebs, and R. Boonstra. 2009. The sensitive hare: sublethal effects of predator stress on reproduction in snowshoe hares. *Journal of Animal Ecology*, 78, 1249–1258.

Shuster, S. M. and M. J. Wade. 2003. *Mating Systems and Strategies*. Princeton, NJ: Princeton University Press.

Simons, A. M., and M. O. Johnston. 2006. Environmental and genetic sources of diversification in the timing of seed germination: Implications for the evolution of bet hedging. *Evolution*, 60, 2280–2292.

Sinclair, A. F., D. P. Swain, and J. M. Hanson. 2002. Measuring changes in the direction and magnitude of size-selective mortality in a commercial fish population. *Canadian Journal of Fisheries and Aquatic Sciences*, 59, 361–371.

Smith, C. C., and S. D. Fretwell. 1974. The optimal balance between size and number of offspring. *American Naturalist*, 108, 499–506.

Smith, T. D. 1994. *Scaling Fisheries: The Science of Measuring the Effects of Fishing, 1855–1955*. Cambridge, UK: Cambridge University Press.

Stearns, S.C. 1983. The influence of size and phylogeny on patterns of covariation among life-history traits in the mammals. *Oikos* 41, 173–187.

Stokes, T. K., J. M. McGlade, and R. Law. 1993. *The Exploitation of Evolving Resources*. Berlin: Springer-Verlag.

Svärdson, G. 1949. Natural selection and egg number in fish. *Report of the Institute of Freshwater Research, Drottningholm*, 29, 115–122.

Swain, D. P., A. F. Sinclair, and J. M. Hanson. 2007. Evolutionary response to size-selective mortality in an exploited fish population. *Proceedings of the Royal Society B*, 274, 1015–1022.

Taborsky, M. 2001. The evolution of bourgeois, parasitic, and cooperative reproductive behaviors in fishes. *Journal of Heredity*, 92, 100–110.

Tomkins, J. L., and W. Hazel. 2007. The status of the conditional evolutionarily stable strategy. *Trends in Ecology and Evolution*, 22, 522–528.

Weir, L. K. 2008. Consequences of the intensity of male-male competition on the mating system of Atlantic salmon (*Salmo salar*). Ph.D. Thesis, Dalhousie University, Halifax, NS.

Westoby, M., E. Jurado, and M. Leishman. 1992. Comparative evolutionary ecology of seed size. *Trends in Ecology and Evolution*, 7, 368–372.

Whitehead, H., and J. Mann. 2000. Female reproductive strategies of cetaceans: Life histories and calf care. In J. Mann, R. C. Connor, P. L. Tyack, and H. Whitehead (Eds.). *Cetacean Societies: Field Studies of Dolphins and Whales* (pp. 219–246). Urbana IL: University of Chicago Press.

Williams, G. C. 1957. Pleiotropy, natural selection, and the evolution of senescence. *Evolution* 11, 398–411.

Williams, G. C. 1966. Natural selection, the cost of reproduction, and a refinement of Lack's principle. *American Naturalist*, 100, 687–690.

Wilson, A. J., J. A. Hutchings, and M. M. Ferguson. 2003. Selective and genetic constraints on the evolution of body size in a stream-dwelling salmonid fish. *Journal of Evolutionary Biology*, 16, 584–594.

Wootton, R. J. 1998. *Ecology of Teleost Fishes*. Dordrecht, Germany: Kluwer Academic Publishers.

Chapter 9

Abraham, K. F., R. L. Jefferies, and R. F. Rockwell. 2005. Goose-induced changes in vegetation and land cover between 1976 and 1997 in an arctic coastal marsh. *Arctic, Antarctic, and Alpine Research*, 37, 269–275.

Begon, M., C. R. Townsend, and J. L. Harper. 2006. *Ecology. From Individuals to Ecosystems* (4th ed.). Oxford, UK: Blackwell Science.

Beisner, B. E., D. T. Haydon, and K. Cuddington. 2003. Alternative stable states in ecology. *Frontiers in Ecology and the Environment* 1, 376–382.

Bergerud, A. T. 1974. Decline of caribou in North America following settlement. *Journal of Wildlife* Management 38, 757–770.

Bergerud, A. T., W. J. Dalton, H. Butler, L. Camps, and R. Ferguson. 2007. Woodland caribou persistence and extirpation in relic populations on Lake Superior. *Rangifer*, Special Issue 17, 57–78.

Bertness, M. D., and R. Callaway. 1994. Positive interactions in communities. *Trends in Ecology and Evolution*, 9, 191–193.

Boutin, S., C. J. Krebs, R. Boonstra, M. R. T. Dale, S. J. Hannon, K. Martin, A. R. E. Sinclair, J. N. M. Smith, R. Turkington, M. Blower, A. Byrom, F. I. Doyle, C. Doyle, D. Hik, L. Hofer, A. Hubbs, T. Karels, D. L. Murray, V. Nams, M. O'Donoghue, C. Rohner, and S. Schweiger. 1995. Population changes of the vertebrate community during a snowshoe hare cycle in Canada's boreal forest. *Oikos*, 74, 69–80.

British Columbia Ministry of Forests. 1996–1999. *The Biogeoclimatic Zones of British Columbia*. From http://www.for.gov.bc.ca/hfd/library/documents/treebook/biogeo/biogeo.htm.

Brooker, R. W., F. T. Maestre, R. M. Callaway, C. J. Lortie, L. A. Cavieres, G. Kunstler, P. Liancourt, K. Tielbörger, J. Travis, F. Anthelme, C. Armas, L. Coll, E. Corcket, S. Delzon, E. Forey, Z. Kikvidze, J. Olofsson, F. Pugnaire, C. I. Quiroz, P. Saccone, K. Schiffers, M. Seifan, B. Touzard, and R. Michalet. 2008. Facilitation in plant communities: The past, present, and the future. *Journal of Ecology*, 96, 18–34.

Brown, J. H., and D. W. Davidson. 1977. Competition between seed-eating rodents and ants in desert ecosystems. *Science*, 196, 880–882.

Brown, J. H., D. W. Davidson, and O. J. Reichman. 1979. An experimental study of competition between seed-eating desert rodents and ants. *American Zoologist*, 19, 1129–1143.

Brown, J. H., and E. J. Heske. 1990. Control of a desert-grassland transition by a keystone rodent guild. *Science*, 250, 1705–1707.

Bruno, J. F., J. J. Stachowicz, and M. D. Bertness. 2003. Inclusion of facilitation into ecological theory. *Trends in Ecology and Evolution*, 18, 119–125.

Callaway, R. M. 1995. Positive interactions among plants. *Botanical Review*, 61, 306–349.

Carpenter, S. R., J. F. Kitchell, and J. R. Hodgson. 1985. Cascading trophic indirections and lake productivity. *BioScience*, 35, 634–639.

Clements, F. E. 1916. *Plant Succession: An Analysis of the Development of Vegetation*. Publication No. 242, Washington, D. C.: Carnegie Institute.

Clements, F. E. 1936. Nature and structure of the climax. *Journal of Ecology*, 24, 252–284.

Connell, J. H. 1961a. The effects of competition, predation by *Thais lapillus* and other factors on natural populations of the barnacle, *Balanus balanoides*. *Ecological Monographs*, 31, 61–104.

Connell, J. H. 1961b. The influence of interspecific competition and other factors on the distribution of the barnacle, *Chthamalus stellatus*. *Ecology*, 42, 710–723.

Connell, J. H. 1975. Some mechanisms producing structure in natural communities: a model and evidence from field experiments. In M. L. Cody and J. M. Diamond, (Eds.) *Ecology and Evolution of Communities*. (pp. 460–490) Cambridge, MA: Belknap Press.

Connell, J. H. 1978. Diversity in tropical rain forests and coral reefs. *Science*, 199, 1302–1310.

COSEWIC. 2002. *Assessment and Update Status Report on the Woodland Caribou, Rangifer tarandus caribou, in Canada*. Ottawa: Committee on the Status of Endangered Wildlife in Canada.

Cranston, B., and L. Hermanutz. 2009. The stress gradient hypothesis: Facilitation at the forest-tundra transition zone in Labrador. Poster at INTECOL in Brisbane, Australia.

Darwin, C. 1859. *On the Origin of Species by Means of Natural Selection, or the Preservation of Favoured Races in the Struggle for Life* (1st ed.). London: John Murray.

Davidson, D. W. 1977a. Foraging ecology and community organization in desert seed-eating ants. *Ecology*, 58, 724–737.

Davidson, D. W. 1977b. Species diversity and community organization in desert seed-eating ants. *Ecology*, 58, 711–724.

Ellis, J. C., M. J. Shulman, M. Wood, J. D. Witman, and S. Lozyniak. 2007. Regulation of intertidal food webs by avian predators on New England rocky shores. *Ecology*, 88, 853–863.

Emery, N. C., P. J. Ewanchuk, and M. D. Bertness. 2001. Competition and salt marsh plant zonation: Stress tolerators may be dominant competitors. *Ecology*, 82, 2471–2485.

Estes, J., M. Tinker, T. Williams, D. Doak. 1998. Killer Whale Predation on Sea Otters Linking Oceanic and Nearshore Ecosystems. *Science*. New Series, Vol. 282 No. 5388, 473–476.

Gause, G. F. 1934. *The Struggle for Existence*. Baltimore, MD: Williams and Wilkins.

Gibbons, D. W., J. B. Reid, and R. A. Chapman. 1993. *The New Atlas of Breeding Birds in Britain and Ireland, 1988–1991*. London, UK: T. & A. D. Poyser.

Gleason, H. A. 1926. The individualistic concept of the plant association. *Torrey Botanical Club Bulletin*, 53, 7–26.

Gleason, H. A. 1939. The individualistic concept of the plant association. *American Midland Naturalist*, 21, 92–110.

Goheen, J. R., T. M. Palmer, F. Keesing, C. Riginos, and T. P. Young. 2010. Large herbivores facilitate savanna tree establishment via diverse and indirect pathways. *Journal of Animal Ecology*. In press.

Goheen, J. R., F. Keesing, B. F. Allan, D. Ogada and R. S. Ostfeld. 2004. Net effects of large mammals on *Acacia* seedling survival in an African savanna. *Ecology*, 85, 1555–1561.

Goldberg, D. E., R. Turkington, and L. Olsvig-Whittaker. 1995. Quantifying the community-level consequences of competition. *Folia Geobotanica and Phytotaxonomica*, 30, 231–242.

Goldberg, D. E., R. Turkington, L. Olsvig-Whittaker, and A. R. Dyer. 2001. Density-dependence in an annual plant community: Variation among life history stages. *Ecological Monographs*, 71, 423–446.

Grace, J. B. and R. G. Wetzel. 1981. Effects of size and growth rate on vegetative reproduction in *Typha*. *Oecologia*, 50, 158–161.

Grace, J. B. and R. G. Wetzel. 1982. Variations in growth and reproduction within populations of two rhizomatous plant species: *Typha latifolia* and *Typha angustifolia*. *Oecologia*, 53, 258–263.

Gregory, R. 1994. Species abundance patterns of British birds. *Proceedings of the Royal Society, London, Series B*, 257, 299–301.

Grime, J. P. (1977). Evidence for the existence of three primary strategies in plants and its relevance to ecological and evolutionary theory. *Am. Nat.* 111, 1169–1194.

Grime, J. P. 2002. *Plant Strategies and Vegetation Processes, and Ecosystem Properties* (2nd ed). Toronto, ON: John Wiley & Sons.

Hairston, N. G., F. E. Smith, and L. B. Slobodkin. 1960.

Community structure, population control, and competition. *American Naturalist*, 94, 421–425.

Handa, I. T. and R. L. Jefferies. 2000. Assisted revegetation trials in degraded salt-marshes of the Hudson Bay lowlands. Journal of Applied Ecology, 37, 944–958.

Hope-Simpson, J. F. 1940 Studies of the vegetation of the English chalk: vi. Late stages in succession leading to chalk grassland. *Journal of Ecology*, 28, 386–402.

Hubbell, S. P. 1979. Tree dispersion, abundance and diversity in a tropical dry forest. *Science* 203, 1299–1309.

Hubbell, S. P. 2001. *The Unified Neutral Theory of Biodiversity and Biogeography.* Princeton Monographs No. 32, Princeton, NJ: Princeton University Press.

Keddy, P. A. 1990. Competitive hierarchies and centrifugal organization in plant communities. In J. Grace and D. Tilman (Eds.), *Perspectives on Plant Competition.* (pp. 265–289). New York, NY: Academic Press.

Koplin, J. R., and R. S. Hoffmann. 1968. Habitat overlap and competitive exclusion in voles (*Microtus*). *American Midland Naturalist*, 80, 494–507.

Krebs, C. J., S. Boutin, S., and R. Boonstra. 2001. *Ecosystem Dynamics of the Boreal Forest: the Kluane Project.* New York: Oxford University Press.

Krebs, C. J., S. Boutin, R. Boonstra, A. R. A. Sinclair, J. N. M. Smith, M. R. T. Dale, K. Martin, and R. Turkington. 1995. Impact of food and predation on the snowshoe hare cycle. *Science*, 269, 1112–1115.

Lamb, E. G. and J. F. Cahill. 2008. When competition does not matter: Grassland diversity and community composition. American Naturalist, 171, 777–787.

Lamb, E. G., S. W. Kembel, and J. F. Cahill. 2009. Shoot, but not root, competition reduces community diversity in experimental mesocosms. *Journal of Ecology*, 97, 155–163.

Lubchenco, J. 1978. Plant species diversity in a marine intertidal community: Importance of herbivore food preferences and algal competitive abilities. *American Naturalist*, 112, 23–39.

MacArthur, R. H. 1958. Population ecology of some warblers of northeastern coniferous forests. *Ecology*, 39, 599–619.

MacArthur, R. H., and E. O. Wilson. 1967. *The Theory of Island Biogeography*. Monographs in Population Biology No. 1. Princeton, NJ: Princeton University Press.

MacDougall, A. S., and S. D. Wilson. 2007. Herbivory limits recruitment in an old-field seed addition experiment. *Ecology*, 88, 1105–1111.

Marquis, R. J., and C. J. Whelan. 1994. Insectivorous birds increase growth of white oak through consumption of leaf-chewing insects. *Ecology*, 75, 2007–2014.

McGill, B. J. 2003. A test of the unified neutral theory of biodiversity. Nature, 422, 881–885.

McLaren, J. R., and R. L. Jefferies. 2004. Initiation and maintenance of vegetation mosaics in an Arctic salt marsh. *Journal of Ecology*, 92, 648–660.

Menge, B. A., and J. P. Sutherland. 1987. Community regulation: Variation in disturbance, competition, and predation in relation to environmental stress and recruitment. *American Naturalist*, 130, 730–757.

Ministry of Forests and Range. 2009. *Biogeoclimatic Zones of British Columbia.* http://www.for.gov.bc.ca/hfd/library/documents/treebook/biogeo/biogeo.htm.

O., P. C., P. M. Kotanen, and K. F. Abraham. 2005. Survival and growth of the forage grass *Festuca rubra* in naturally and artificially devegetated sites in a sub-arctic coastal marsh. *Ecoscience*, 12, 279–285.

Paine, R. T. 1966. Food web complexity and species diversity. *American Naturalist*, 100, 65–75.

Pianka, E. R. 1994. *Evolutionary Ecology* (5th ed.). Harper Collins.

Pojar, J. and D. V. Meidinger. 1991. *Ecosystems of British Columbia.* B. C. Ministry of Forests, Forest Science Program, Special Report Series 6, from http://www.for.gov.bc.ca/hfd/pubs/Docs/Srs/Srs06.htm.

Rajaniemi, T. K., R. Turkington, and D. E. Goldberg. 2009. Population- and community-level consequences of regulation in an annual plant community under different resource levels. *Journal of Vegetation Science*, 20, 836–846.

Ripple, W. J., E. J. Larsen, R. A. Renkin, and D. W. Smith. 2001. Trophic cascades among wolves, elk and aspen on Yellowstone National Park's northern range. *Biological Conservation*, 102, 227–234.

Robertson, G. P., M. A. Huston, F. C. Evans, and J. M. Tiedje. 1988. Spatial variability in a successional plant community: Patterns of nitrogen availability. *Ecology*, 69, 1517–1524.

Rosenzweig, M. L., and Z. Abramsky. 1986. Centrifugal community organization. *Oikos*, 46, 339–348.

Sale, P. F., and W. A. Douglas. 1984. Temporal variability in the community structure of fish on coral patch reefs and the relation of community structure to reef structure. *Ecology*, 65, 409–422.

Scheibling, R. A., and R. L. Stephenson. 1984. Mass mortality of *Strongylocentrotus droebachiensis* off Nova Scotia, Canada. *Marine Biology*, 78, 153–164.

Sharam, G. J., A. R. E. Sinclair, and R. Turkington. 2009. Serengeti birds maintain forests by inhibiting seed predators. *Science*, 325, 51.

Shilo-Volin, H., A. Novoplansky, D. E. Goldberg, and R. Turkington. 2005. Density regulation in annual plant communities under different resource levels. *Oikos*, 108, 241–252.

Simenstad, C. A., J. A. Estes, and K. W. Kenyon. 1978. Aleuts, sea otters, and alternate stable-state communities. *Science*, 200, 403–411.

Sinclair, A. R. E., S. A. R. Mduma, and J. S. Brashares. 2003. Patterns of predation in a diverse predator-prey system. *Nature*, 425, 288–290.

Sinclair, A. R. E., C. J. Krebs, J. M. Fryxell, R. Turkington, S. Boutin, R. Boonstra, P. Lundberg, and L. Oksanen. 2000. Testing hypotheses of trophic level interactions using experimental perturbations of a boreal forest ecosystem. *Oikos*, 89, 313–328.

Sousa, W. P. 1979a. Disturbance in marine intertidal boulder fields: the nonequilibrium maintenance of species diversity. *Ecology*, 60, 1225–1239.

Sousa, W. P. 1979b. Experimental investigations of disturbance and ecological succession in a rocky intertidal algal community. *Ecological Monographs*, 49, 227–254.

Spedding, C. R. W. 1971. *Grassland Ecology*. Oxford, U.K.: Clarendon Press.

Stenseth, N. C. 2002. The story of an ecosystem: A ten-year study of a Canadian forest shows the way ahead for ecology. *Nature* 416, 679–680. (Book Review of Krebs et al. 2001).

Stoecker, R. E. 1972. Competitive relations between sympatric populations of voles (*Microtus montanus* and *M. pennsylvanicus*). *Journal of Animal Ecology*, 41, 311–319.

Tansley, A. G., and R. S. Adamson. 1925. Studies of the vegetation of the English chalk. III The chalk grasslands of the Hampshire-Sussex border. *Journal of Ecology*, 13, 177–223.

Tansley, A. G. 1917. On competition between *Galium saxatile* L. (*G. hercynicum* Weig.) and *Galium sylvestre* Poll. (*G. asperum* Schreb.) on different types of soil. *Journal of Ecology*, 5, 173–179.

Tilman, D. 1985. The resource ratio hypothesis of succession. *American Naturalist*, 125, 827–852.

Tilman, D. 1988. *Plant Strategies and the Dynamics and Structure of Plant Communities*. Princeton Monographs No. 26. Princeton, NJ: Princeton University Press.

Townsend, C. R., J. L. Harper, and M. Begon. 2000. *Essentials of Ecology*. Oxford: Blackwell Science.

Treberg, M. A. 2007. Community- and species-level consequences of competition in an unproductive environment: an experimental approach using boreal forest understory vegetation. Ph.D. Thesis, University of British Columbia.

Turkington, R., E. John, C. J. Krebs, M. Dale, V. O. Nams, R. Boonstra, S. Boutin, K. Martin, A. R. E. Sinclair, and J. N. M. Smith. 1998. The effects of NPK fertilization for nine years on the vegetation of the boreal forest in northwestern Canada. *Journal of Vegetation Science*, 9, 333–346.

Turkington, R., E. John, S. Watson, and P. Seccombe-Hett. 2002. The effects of fertilization and herbivory on the herbaceous vegetation of the boreal forest in northwestern Canada: A ten-year study. *Journal of Ecology*, 90, 325–227.

Welden, C. W., and W. L. Slauson. 1986. The intensity of competition versus its importance: an overlooked distinction and some implications. *Quarterly Review Biology* 61, 23–44.

Werner, P. A., and W. J. Platt. 1976. Ecological relationships of co-occurring goldenrods (*Solidago*: Compositae). *American Naturalist*, 110, 959–971.

Whicker, A. D., and J. K. Detling. 1988. Ecological consequences of prairie dog disturbances. *BioScience* 38, 778–785.

Whittaker, R. H. 1956. Vegetation of the Great Smokey Mountains. *Ecological Monographs*, 26, 1–80.

Whittaker, R. H. 1965. Dominance and diversity in land plant communities. *Science*, 147, 250–260.

Whittaker, R. H. 1975. *Communities and Ecosystems* (2nd ed.). New York, NY: Macmillan.

Williams, C. B. 1964. *Patterns in the Balance of Nature and Related Problems of Quantitative Biology*. London, U.K.: Academic Press.

Wittmer, H. U., A. R. E. Sinclair, and B. N. McLellan. 2005. The role of predation in the decline and extirpation of woodland caribou. *Oecologia*, 144, 257–267.

Zeevalking, H. J., and L. F. M. Fresco. 1977. Rabbit grazing and species diversity in a dune area. *Vegetatio* 35, 193–196.

Chapter 10

Bergeron P., and E. Bourget. 1986. Shore topography and spatial partitioning of crevice refuges by sessile epibenthos in an ice-disturbed environment. *Marine Ecology Progress Series*, 28, 129–145.

Bergeron, Y. and A. Leduc. 1999. Relationships between change in fire frequency and mortality due to spruce budworm outbreak in the southeastern Canadian boreal forest. *Journal of Vegetation Science*, 9, 492–500.

Bergsma, B. M., J. Svoboda, and B. Freedman. 1984. Entombed plant communities released by a retreating glacier at central Ellesmere Island, Canada. *Arctic*, 37, 49–52.

Blais, J. R. 1965. Spruce budworm outbreaks in the past three centuries in the Laurentide Park, Quebec. *Forest Science*, 11, 130–138.

Blais, J. R. 1981. Mortality of balsam fir and white spruce following a spruce budworm outbreak in the Ottawa River watershed in Quebec. *Canadian Journal of Forest Research*, 11, 620–629.

Bormann, F. H., and G. E. Likens. 1979. *Pattern and Process in a Forested Ecosystem*. New York: Springer-Verlag.

Brooks, M., and M. Lusk. 2008. *Fire Management and Invasive Plants: A Handbook*. United States Fish and Wildlife Service, Arlington, VA.

Bruce, J. 2009. *Identifying Forest Wind Throw in Nova Scotia due to Hurricane Juan using Landsat Satellite Imagery*. Nova Scotia Department of Natural Resources, Forestry Branch, Truro, NS. (manuscript).

Clements, F. E. 1916. *Plant Succession: An Analysis of the Development of Vegetation*. Publication No. 242, Washington DC: Carnegie Institute.

Clements, F. E. 1936. Nature and structure of the climax. *Journal of Ecology*, 24, 252–284.

Connell, J. H., and R. O. Slatyer. 1977. Mechanisms of succession in natural communities and their role in community stability and organization. *American Naturalist*, 111, 1119–1144.

Cowles, H. C. 1899. The ecological relations of the vegetation of the sand dunes of Lake Michigan. *Botanical Gazette*, 27, parts 2, 3, 4, 5.

Crocker, R. L., and J. Major. 1955. Soil development in relation to vegetation and surface age at Glacier Bay, Alaska. *Journal of Ecology*, 43, 427–448.

Crowell, M., and B. Freedman. 1994. Vegetation development during a post-clearcutting chronosequence of hardwood forest in Nova Scotia, Canada. *Canadian Journal of Forest Research*, 24, 260–271.

Cwynar, L. C., and R. W. Spear. 1991. Reversion of forest to tundra in the central Yukon. *Ecology*, 72, 202–212.

Damman, A. W. H. 1971. Effect of vegetation change on the fertility of a Newfoundland forest site. *Ecological Monographs*, 41, 253–270.

Freedman, B. 2010. *Environmental Science. A Canadian Perspective*. (5th ed.) Toronto: Pearson Education Canada.

Freedman, B., R. Morash, and D. S. MacKinnon. 1993. Short-term changes in vegetation after the silvicultural spraying of glyphosate herbicide onto regenerating clearcuts in central Nova Scotia. *Canadian Journal of Forest Research*, 23, 2300–2311.

Freedman, B., C. Stewart, and U. Prager. 1985. *Patterns of Water Chemistry of Four Drainage Basins in Central Nova Scotia*. Technical Report IWD-AR-WQB-85-93, Water Quality Branch, Inland Waters Directorate, Environment Canada, Moncton, NB.

Gleason, H. A. 1926. The individualistic concept of the plant association. *Torrey Botanical Club Bulletin*, 53, 7–26.

Gleason, H. A. 1939. The individualistic concept of the plant association. *American Midland Naturalist*, 21, 92–110.

Grignon, T. 1992. The Dynamics of *Rubus strigosus* (*Michx.*) in post-clearcut mixedwood and softwood forests of Nova Scotia. M.Sc. Thesis, Department of Biology, Dalhousie University, Halifax, N.S.

Grime, J. P. 2002. *Plant Strategies and Vegetation Processes, and Ecosystem Properties.* (2nd ed). Toronto: John Wiley & Sons.

Holling, C. S. 1973. Resilience and stability of ecological systems. *Annual Reviews in Ecology and Systematics*, 4, 1–23.

Jasinski, J. P. P. and Payette, S. 2005. The creation of alternative stable states in the southern boreal forest, Quebec, Canada. *Ecological Monographs*, 75, 561–583.

Jones, G. A. and G. H. R. Henry. 2003. Primary plant succession on recently deglaciated terrain in the Canadian High Arctic. *Journal of Biogeography*, 30, 277–296.

Kettela, E. 1983. *A Cartographic History of Spruce Budworm Defoliation from 1967 to 1981 in Eastern North America.* Information Report DPC-X-14, Maritimes Forest Research Centre, Canadian Forestry Service, Fredericton, New Brunswick.

Krause, H. H. 1982. Nitrate formation and movement before and after clear-cutting of a monitored watershed in central New Brunswick, Canada. *Canadian Journal of Forest Research*, 12, 922–930.

Lauzon-Guay, J.-S., R. E. Scheibling, and M. A. Barbeau. 2009. Modeling phase shifts in a rocky subtidal ecosystem. *Marine Ecology Progress Series* (in press).

Lees, J. C. 1981. *Three Generations of Red Maple Stump Sprouts.* M-X-119, Canadian Forestry Service, Maritimes, Fredericton, N. B.

Lewontin, R. C. 1969. The meaning of stability. In *Diversity and Stability in Ecological Systems* (pp. 13–24). Brookhaven Symposium in Biology, 22. Brookhaven, NJ.

Lieffers, V. J., S. E. Macdonald, and E. H. Hogg. 1993. Ecology of and control strategies for *Calamagrostis canadensis* in boreal forest sites. *Canadian Journal of Forest Research*, 23, 2070–2077.

Likens, G. E., F. H. Bormann, R. S. Pierce, and W. A. Reiners. 1978. Recovery of a deforested ecosystem. *Science*, 199, 492–496.

MacLean, D. A. 1984. Effects of spruce budworm outbreaks on the productivity and stability of balsam fir forests. *Forestry Chronicle*, 60, 273–279.

MacLean, D. A. 1988. Effects of spruce budworm outbreaks on vegetation, structure, and succession of balsam fir forests on Cape Breton Island, Canada. In M. J. A. Werger, P. J. M. van der Aart, H. J. During, and J. J. A. Verhoeven, (Eds.), *Plant Form and Vegetation Structure* (pp. 253–261). The Hague, The Netherlands: SPB Academic Publishers.

Macpherson, E. A., R. Scrosati, and P. Chareka. 2008. Barnacle recruitment on ice-scoured shores in eastern Canada. *Journal of the Marine Biological Association of the United Kingdom*, 88, 289–291.

Mallik, A. U. 1993. Ecology of a forest weed of Newfoundland: vegetative regeneration strategy of *Kalmia angustifolia*. *Canadian Journal of Botany*, 71, 161–166.

Marks, P. L. 1974. The role of pin cherry (*Prunus pensylvanica*) in the maintenance of stability in northern hardwood ecosystems. *Ecological Monographs*, 44, 73–88.

May, M. R. 1977. Thresholds and breakpoints in ecosystems with a multiplicity of stable states. *Nature*, 269, 471–477.

McRae, D. J., L. C. Duchesne, B. Freedman, T. J. Lynham, and S. Woodley. 2001. Differences between wildfire and clear-cutting and their implications in forest management. *Environmental Reviews*, 9, 223–260.

Minchinton, T. E., R. E. Scheibling, and H. L. Hunt. 1997. Recovery of an intertidal assemblage following a rare occurrence of scouring by sea ice in Nova Scotia, Canada. *Botanica Marina*, 40, 139–148.

Morgan, K. and B. Freedman. 1986. Breeding bird communities in a hardwood forest succession in Nova Scotia. *Canadian Field-Naturalist*, 100, 506–519.

Mori, A. S., T. Osono, M. Uchida, and H. Kanda. 2008. Changes in the structure and heterogeneity of vegetation and microsite environments with the chronosequence of primary succession on a glacier foreland in Ellesmere Island, high arctic Canada. *Ecological Research*, 23, 363–370.

Morrison, R. G. and G. A. Yarranton. 1973. Diversity, richness, and evenness during a primary sand dune succession at Grand Bend, Ontario. *Canadian Journal of Botany*, 51, 2401–2411.

Morrison, R. G. and G. A. Yarranton. 1974. Vegetational heterogeneity during a primary sand dune succession. *Canadian Journal of Botany*, 52, 397–410.

Prager, U. and F. B. Goldsmith. 1977. Stump sprout formation by red maple (*Acer rubrum*) in Nova Scotia. *Proceedings of the Nova Scotia Institute of Science*, 28, 93–99.

Reiners, W. A. , I. A. Worley, and D. B. Lawrence. 1971. Plant diversity in a chronosequence at Glacier Bay, Alaska. *Ecology* 52, 55–69.

Reynolds, J. W. 1977. *The Earthworms (Lumbricidae and Sparganophilidae) of Ontario.* Toronto: Life Sciences Miscellaneous Publications, Royal Ontario Museum.

Scheibling, R. 1986. Increased macroalgal abundance following mass mortalities of sea urchins (*Strongylocentrotus droebachiensis*) along the Atlantic coast of Nova Scotia. *Oecologia (Berlin)*, 68, 186–198.

Simenstad, C. A., J. A. Estes, and K. W. Kenyon. 1978. Aleuts, sea otters, and alternate stable-state communities. *Science*, 200, 403–410.

Svoboda, J. and B. Freedman. (eds). 1994. *Ecology of a Polar Oasis. Alexandra Fiord, Ellesmere Island, Canada.* Toronto: Captus Press.

Taylor, S. J., T. J. Carleton, and P. Adams. 1987. Understorey vegetation change in a *Picea mariana* chronosequence. *Vegetatio*, 73, 63–72.

Tomlinson, S., E. Matthes, P. J. Richardson, and D. W. Larson. 2008. The ecological equivalence of quarry floors to alvars. *Applied Vegetation Science*, 11, 73–82.

Chapter 11

Barbour, M. G. and W. D. Billings. 1988. *North American Terrestrial Vegetation.* New York: Cambridge University Press.

Bolen, E. G. 1998. *Ecology of North America.* New York: John Wiley & Sons.

Breckle, S. W. 2002. *Walter's Vegetation of the Earth. The Ecological Systems of the Geo-Sphere* (4th ed.). Berlin: Springer-Verlag.

Crabtree, P. (Ed.). 1970. *The Illustrated Natural History of Canada* (9 vol.). Toronto: NSL Natural Science of Canada.

Commission for Environmental Cooperation (CEC). 2009a.

Terrestrial Ecoregions, 2007. Retrieved October 2009, from the CEC website: http://www.cec.org/naatlas/maps/index.cfm?catId=7&mapId=15&varlan=English.

Commission for Environmental Cooperation (CEC). 2009b. *Marine Ecoregions, 2008*. Retrieved October 2009, from the CEC website: http://www.cec.org/naatlas/maps/index.cfm?catId=7&varlan=English.

Ecological Stratification Working Group. 1995. *A National Ecological Framework for Canada*. Ottawa: Environment Canada.

Freedman, B. 2010. *Environmental Science. A Canadian Perspective*. (5th ed.) Toronto: Pearson Education Canada.

National Wetlands Working Group. 1988. *Wetlands of Canada*. Ecological Land Classification Series, No. 24. Environment Canada, Ottawa, ON.

Odum, E. P. and G. W. Barrett. 2004. *Fundamentals of Ecology*. Florence, KY: Brooks.

Phillips, D. 1990. *The Climates of Canada*. Ottawa: Environment Canada.

Rowe, J. S. 1959. *Forest Regions of Canada*. Ottawa: Department of Northern Affairs and National Resources, Ottawa, ON.

Rowe, J. S. 1961. The level-of-integration concept in ecology. *Ecology*, 42, 420–427.

Rowe, J. S. 1990. *Home Place: Essays on Ecology*. Edmonton: NeWest Press.

Rowe, J. S. 2006. *Earth Alive: Essays on Ecology*. Edmonton: NeWest Press.

Schultz, J. 2004. *Ecozones of the World: The Ecological Divisions of the Geosphere* (2nd ed.). Berlin: Springer Verlag.

Scott, G. A. J. 1995. *Canada's Vegetation: A World Perspective*. Montreal: McGill-Queen's University Press.

Shelford, V. E. 1974. *The Ecology of North America*. Urbana, IL: University of Illinois Press.

USDA. 2009. *Major Biomes Map*. United States Department of Agriculture, Natural Resources Conservation Service. Retrieved October 2009, from the USDA website: http://soils.usda.gov/use/worldsoils/mapindex/biomes.html.

Walter, H. 1977. *Vegetation of the Earth*. New York: Springer.

Whittaker, R. H. 1975. *Communities and Ecosystems* (2nd ed.) New York: McMillan.

Wiken, E., D. Gauthier, I. Marshall, K. Lawton, and H. Hirvonen. 1996. *A Perspective on Canada's Ecosystems: An Overview of the Terrestrial and Marine Ecozones*. Occ. Pap. No. 14., Ottawa: Canadian Council on Ecological Areas.

Wilkinson, T., J. Bezaury-Creel, T. Hourigan, E. Wiken, C. Madden, M. Padilla, T. Agardy, H. Herrmann, L. Janishevski, and L. Morgan. 2007. *Marine Ecoregions of North America*. Montreal: Commission on Environmental Cooperation.

Woodward, S. L. 2003. *Biomes of the Earth: Terrestrial, Aquatic, and Human-Dominated*. Oxford, UK: Greenwood Press.

Chapter 12

American Pet Products Association. 2009. *Industry Statistics and Trends*. Retrieved October 2009 from: http://americanpetproducts.org/press_industrytrends.asp.

Canadian Animal Health Institute (CAHI). 2008. *Latest Pet Population Figures Released*. Guelph, ON: CAHI.

Canadian Endangered Species Conservation Council (CESCC). 2006. *Wild Species: The General Status of Species in Canada*. Retrieved October 2009: http://www.wildspecies.ca/wildspecies2005/index.cfm?lang=e.

Census of Marine Life (CoML). 2009. *Making Ocean Life Count*. CoML, University of Rhode Island, RI. Retrieved October 2009 from: http://www.coml.org/.

Centre for Applied Conservation Research. 2007. *Endemic Taxa of British Columbia*. Faculty of Forestry, University of British Columbia, Vancouver, BC. Retrieved October 2009, from: http://www.forestbiodiversityinbc.ca/manage_approach_species_endemic.asp.

Cheliak, W. M. and B. P. Dancik. 1982. Genic diversity of natural populations of a clone-forming tree *Populus tremuloides*. *Canadian Journal of Genetics & Cytology*, 24, 611–616.

Comiskey, J. A., T. C. H. Sunderland, and J. L. Sunderland-Groves (eds.). 2003. *Takamanda: The Biodiversity of a Tropical Forest*. Washington D.C.: Smithsonian Institution.

Convention on Biological Diversity (CBD). 2009. CBD Website. Retrieved October 2009 from: http://www.cbd.int/.

de March, B. G. E., L. D. Maiers, and M. K. Friesen. 2002. An overview of genetic relationships of Canadian and adjacent populations of belugas (*Delphinapterus leucas*) with emphasis on Baffin Bay and Canadian eastern Arctic populations. The North Atlantic Marine Mammal Commission (NAMMCO), *Scientific Publication*, 4, 17–38.

Eldredge, L. G. and N. L. Evenhuis. 2003. Hawaii's Biodiversity: A Detailed Assessment of the Numbers of Species in the Hawaiian Islands. Bishop Museum, Occasional Papers 76, 1–28. Honolulu, HI.

Elton, C. S. 1958. *The Ecology of Invasions by Plants and Animals*. Chicago, IL: University of Chicago Press.

Environment Canada. 1994. *Biodiversity in Canada: A Science Assessment for Environment Canada*. Biodiversity Assessment Team, Environment Canada. Retrieved October 2009 from: http://www.eman-rese.ca/eman/reports/publications/biodiv-sci-asses/intro.html.

Environment Canada. 1995. *Canadian Biodiversity Strategy, Canada's Response to the Convention on Biological Diversity*. Biodiversity Convention Office, Environment Canada. Retrieved October 2009 from http://www.cbin.ec.gc.ca/documents/national_reports/cbs_e.pdf.

Environment Canada. 1997. *The State of Canada's Environment*. State of the Environment Reporting Organization, Environment Canada, Ottawa, ON.

Erwin, T. L. 1983. Beetles and other insects of tropical forest canopies at Manaus, Brazil, sampled by insecticidal fogging. In S. L. Sutton, T. C. Whitmore, and A. C. Chadwick (Eds.) *Tropical Rain Forest: Ecology and Management* (pp. 59–75). Boston, MA: Blackwell.

Freedman, B. 2010. *Environmental Science. A Canadian Perspective* (5th ed.). Toronto: Pearson Education Canada.

Gaston, K. J. and J. I. Spicer. 2004. *Biodiversity: An Introduction* (2nd ed.). New York: Blackwell Publishing.

Gentry, A. H. 1986. Endemism in tropical vs. temperate plant communities. In M.E. Soule (Ed.) *Conservation Biology* (pp. 153–181.). Sunderland, MA: Sinauer Associates.

Gentry, A. H. 1988. Tree species of upper Amazonian forests. *Proceedings of the National Academy of Sciences*, 85, 156–159.

Goodman, S. M. and J. P. Benstead. 2004. *The Natural History of Madagascar.* Chicago: University of Chicago Press.

Groombridge, G. 1992. *Global Biodiversity.* London, U.K.: World Conservation Monitoring Center. Chapman & Hall.

Hamlin, K. L. and J. A. Cunningham. 2009. *Monitoring and Assessment of Wolf-Ungulate Interactions and Population Trends within the Greater Yellowstone Area, Southwestern Montana, and Montana Statewide.* Montana Department of Fish, Wildlife, and Parks, Wildlife Division, Helena, MT.

Heywood, V. H. (ed.). 1995. *Global Biodiversity Assessment.* Cambridge, U.K.: Cambridge University Press.

Holmes, R. T., T. W. Sherry, and F. W. Sturges. 1986. Bird community dynamics in a temperate deciduous forest: Long-term trends at Hubbard Brook. *Ecological Monographs*, 56, 201–220.

Hubbell, S. P. and R. B. Foster. 1983. Diversity of canopy trees in a neotropical forest and implications for conservation. In S. L. Sutton, T. C. Whitmore, and A. C. Chadwick (Eds.) *Tropical Rain Forest: Ecology and Management* (pp. 25–41). Boston: Blackwell Scientific Publishers.

Hughes, J. B., G. C. Daily, and P. R. Ehrlich. 1997. Population diversity: Its extent and extinction. *Science*, 278, 689–692.

International Union for the Conservation of Nature (IUCN). 2009. *2008 IUCN Red List Summary Statistics.* Retrieved in October 2009 from IUCN website: http://cms.iucn.org/about/work/programmes/species/red_list/2008_red_list_summary_statistics/.

Janzen, D. H. 1987. Insect diversity in a Costa Rican dry forest: why keep it, and how. *Biological Journal Linnaean Society*, 30, 343–356.

Leigh, E. G. 1982. Why are there so many kinds of tropical trees? In E. G. Leigh, A. S. Rand, and D. M. Windsor, (Eds.) *The Ecology of a Tropical Forest* (pp. 63–66). Washington, D.C.: Smithsonian Institution Press.

MacArthur, R. E. 1955. Fluctuations of animal populations and a measure of community stability. *Ecology*, 36, 533–36.

MacKinnon, K., G. Hatta, H. Halim, and A. Mangalik. 1996. *The Ecology of Kalimantan.* Singapore: Periplus Editions (HK) Ltd.

May, R. M. 1973. *Stability and Complexity in Model Ecosystems.* Princeton, NJ: Princeton University Press.

McCann, K. S. 2000. The diversity–stability debate. *Nature*, 405, 228–233.

Miller, K. and L. Tangley, L. 1991. *Trees of Life.* Boston, MA: Beacon Press.

Mitton, J. B. and M. C. Grant. 1996. Genetic variation and the natural history of quaking aspen. *BioScience*, 46, 25–31.

Mosquin, T., P. G. Whiting and D. E. McAllister, 1995. *Canada's Biodiversity: The Variety of Life, Its Status, Economic Benefits, Conservation Costs and Unmet Needs.* Canadian Centre for Biodiversity, Canadian Museum of Nature, Ottawa, Ontario.

Murray, B. W., S. Malik, and B. N. White. 1995. Sequence variation at the major histocompatibility complex locus DQB in beluga whales (*Delphinapterus leucas*). *Molecular Biology and Evolution*, 12, 582–593.

Myers, N. 1983. *A Wealth of Wild Species.* Boulder, CO: Westview Press.

Newman, D. and G. Cragg. 2007. Natural products as drugs over the past 25 years. *Journal of Natural Products*, 70, 461–477.

Paijmans, J. 1970. An analysis of four tropical rain forest sites in New Guinea. *Journal of Ecology*, 58, 77–101.

Patenaude, N. J., J. S. Quinn, P. Beland, M. Kingsley, and B. N. White. 1994. Genetic variation of the St. Lawrence beluga whale population assessed by DNA fingerprinting. *Molecular Ecology*, 3, 375–381.

Pimm, S. L., L. Dollar, and O. L. Bass. 2006. The genetic rescue of the Florida panther. *Animal Conservation*, 9, 115–122.

Primack, R. B. and P. Hall. 1992. Biodiversity and forest change in Malaysian Borneo. *BioScience*, 42, 829–837.

Staicer, C. 2001. *User's manual: Forest Bird Monitoring and Research Program at Kejimkujik National Park.* Research Report to Parks Canada, Atlantic Region. Department of Biology, Dalhousie University, Halifax, NS.

Stupka, A. 1964. Trees, Shrubs, and Woody Vines of Great Smoky Mountains National Park. Knoxville, TN: University of Tennessee Press.

Terborgh, J., S. K. Robinson, T. A. Parker, C. A. Muna, and N. Pierpont. 1990. Structure and organization of an Amazonian forest bird community. *Ecological Monographs*, 60, 312–238.

Thiollay, J.-M. 1992. Influence of selective logging on bird species diversity in a Guaianan rain forest. *Conservation Biology*, 6, 47–63.

Thorington, R. W., B. Tannenbaum, A. Tarak, and R. Rudran. 1982. Distribution of trees on Barro Colorado Island: A five hectare sample. In C. E. G. Leigh, A. S. Rand, and D. M. Windsor, (Eds.). *The Ecology of a Tropical Forest* (pp. 83–94). Washington, D.C.: Smithsonian Institution Press.

Vasseur, L., L. W. Aarssen, and D. D. Lefebvre. 1991. Allozymic and morphometric variation in *Lemna minor* (Lemnaceae). *Plant Systematics and Evolution*, 177, 139–148.

Vitousek, P. M. 1988. Diversity and biological invasions of oceanic islands. In E. O. Wilson (ed.). *Biodiversity* (pp. 181–189). Washington DC: National Academy Press.

Whitten, A. J., S. J. Damanik, J. Anwar, and N. Hisyam. 1987. *The Ecology of Sumatra.* Yogyokarta, Indonesia: Gadjah Mada University Press.

Wilson, E. O. (editor). 1988. *Biodiversity.* Washington, DC: National Academy Press.

World Conservation Monitoring Center (WCMC). 2009. *World Conservation Monitoring Center.* UNEP World Conservation Monitoring Centre, Cambridge, UK. Retrieved October 2009 from: http://www.unep-wcmc.org/.

World Resources Institute (WRI). 2009. *EarthTrends Environmental Information.* Retrieved October 2009 from: http://earthtrends.wri.org/.

Yeh, F. C., D. K. X. Chong, and R.-C. Yang. 1995. RAPD variation within and among natural populations of trembling aspen (*Populus tremuloides* Michx.) from Alberta. *Journal of Heredity*, 86, 454–460.

Chapter 13

Agee, J. K. 1998. Fire and pine ecosystems. In D. M. Richardson (Ed.), *Ecology and Biogeography of Pinus*. New York: Cambridge University Press.

Alftine, K. J. and G. P. Malanson. 2004. Directional positive feedback and pattern at an alpine tree line. *Journal of Vegetation Science*, 15, 3–12.

Baker, J., K. French, and R. J. Whelan. 2002. The edge effect and ecotonal species: Bird communities across a natural edge in southeastern Australia. *Ecology*, 83, 3048–3059.

Bennett, A. F., K. Henein, and G. Merriam. 1994. Corridor use and the elements of corridor quality—chipmunks and fencerows in a farmland mosaic. *Biological Conservation*, 68, 155–165.

Bosakowski, T. and D. G. Smith. 1997. Distribution and species richness of a forest raptor community in relation to urbanization. *Journal of Raptor Research*, 31, 26–33.

Botkin, D. 1990. Discordant Harmonies: A New Ecology for the Twenty-First Century. New York: Oxford University Press.

Carroll, S. K., T. C. Carter, and D. A. Feldhammer. 2002. Placement of nets for bats: Effects on perceived fauna. *Southeastern Naturalist*, 1, 193–198.

Clevenger, A. P., B. Chruszcz, K. Gunson, and J. Wierzchowski. 2002. *Roads and Wildlife in the Canadian Rocky Mountain Parks—Movements, Mortality and Mitigation*. Research Report prepared for Parks Canada, Banff, AB.

Delcourt, H. R., P. A. Delcourt, and T. Webb. 1983. Dynamic plant ecology: The spectrum of vegetational change in space and time. *Quaternary Science Review*, 1, 153–175.

Dessler, A. and E. A. Parson. 2006. *The Science and Politics of Global Climate Change: A Guide to the Debate*. Cambridge, United Kingdom: Cambridge University Press.

Dorney, R. S. and D. W. Hoffman. 1979. Development of landscape planning concepts and management strategies for an urbanizing agricultural region. *Landscape and Planning*, 6, 151–177.

Dunning, J. B., D. J. Stewart, B. J. Danielson, B. R. Noon, T. L. Root, R. H. Lamberson and E. E. Stevens. 1995. Spatially explicit population models—Current forms and future uses. *Ecological Applications*, 5, 3–11.

Fahrig, L. 1997. Relative effects of habitat loss and fragmentation on population extinction. *Journal of Wildlife Management*, 61, 603–610.

Fahrig, L. 2001. How much habitat is enough? *Biological Conservation*, 100, 65–74.

Fonseca, M. S. and S. S. Bell. 1998. Influence of physical setting on seagrass landscapes near Beaufort, North Carolina, USA. *Marine Ecology-Progress Series*, 171, 109–121.

Forman, R. T. T. 1995. *Landscape Mosaics: The Ecology of Landscapes and Regions*. Cambridge, UK: Cambridge University Press.

Forman, R. T. T. and M. Godron. 1986. *Landscape Ecology*. New York: John Wiley and Sons.

Fortin, M. J. and M. R. T. Dale. 2005. *Spatial Analysis: A Guide for Ecologists*. Cambridge, UK: Cambridge University Press.

Freedman, B. and T. C. Hutchinson. 1980. Long-term effects of smelter pollution at Sudbury, Ontario, on forest community composition. *Canadian Journal of Botany*, 58, 2123–2140.

Fries, C., M. Carlsson, B. Dahlin, T. Lämäs, and O. Sallnäs. 1998. A review of conceptual landscape planning models for multi-objective forestry in Sweden. *Canadian Journal of Forest Research*, 28, 167.

Fritz, R., R. Suffling, and A. K. Younger. 1993. Influence of fur trade, famine and forest fires on moose and caribou populations in northwestern Ontario from 1786–1911. *Environmental Management*, 17, 477–489.

Fudge, D., B. Freedman, M. Crowell, T. Nette, and V. Power. 2007. Road-kill of mammals in Nova Scotia. *Canadian Field-Naturalist*, 121, 265–273.

Greater Fundy Ecosystem Project. 2009. *About the Greater Fundy Ecosystem Project*. Retrieved September 2009 from: University of New Brunswick, Fredericton, NB. http://www.unbf.ca/forestry/centers/fundy/.

Hanrahan, J. L., S. V. Kravtsov, and P. J. Roebber. 2009. Quasi-periodic decadal cycles in levels of lakes Michigan and Huron. *Journal of Great Lakes Research*, 35, 30–35.

Hessburg, P. F, J. K. Agee, and J. F. Franklin. 2005. Dry forests and wildland fires of the inland Northwest USA: Contrasting the landscape ecology of the pre-settlement and modem eras. *Forest Ecology and Management*, 211, 117–139.

Hills, G. 1961. The ecological basis for natural resources management. In *The Ecological Basis for Land-use Planning*. (pp. 8–49). Research Branch, Ontario Department of Lands and Forests, Toronto, ON.

Holling, C. S. 1992. Cross-scale morphology, geometry, and dynamics of ecosystems. *Ecological Monographs*, 62, 447–502.

Killins, K. 2008. A Management Plan for the Old Ausable Channel Watershed. Retrieved January 12, 2009, from Ausable Bayfield Conservation Authority website: http://www.oldausablechannel.ca/OAC_MP_Final%20Draft_2008_small.pdf, http://www.oldausablechannel.ca/OAC%20Factsheet%20Fish%202%2007.pdf.

Laurence, W. F. 2007. Ecosystem decay of Amazonian forest fragments: Implications for conservation. In T. Tscharntke, C. Leuschner, M. Zeller, E. Guhardja, and A. Bidin, (Eds.). *The Stability of Tropical Rainforest Margins; Linking Ecological, Economic and Social Constraints of Land Use and Conservation*. (pp. 11–37). Berlin, Germany: Springer.

Law, B. S. and C. R. Dickman. 1998. The use of habitat mosaics by terrestrial vertebrate fauna: Implications for conservation and management. *Biodiversity and Conservation*, 7, 323–333.

Levin, S. A. 1992. The problem of pattern and scale in ecology. *Ecology*, 73, 1943–1967.

Lewis, P. 1964. Quality corridors for Wisconsin. *Landscape Architecture*, 54, 100–107.

Lima, S. L. and P. A. Zollner. 1996. Towards a behavioral ecology of ecological landscapes. *Trends in Ecology and Evolution*, 11, 131–135.

Lindeman, R. L. 1942. The trophic-dynamic aspect of ecology. *Ecology* 23, 399–418.

Ludwig, J. A., B. P. Wilcox, D. D. Breshears, D. J. Tongway, and A. C. Imeson. 2005. Vegetation patches and runoff-erosion as interacting ecohydrological processes in semiarid landscapes. *Ecology*, 86, 288–297.

Lutz, S. G. 1997. *Pre-European Settlement and Present Forest Composition in King's County, New Brunswick, Canada*. Master of

Forestry Thesis, University of New Brunswick, Fredericton, NB.

Mayer, S., J. A. Schaefer, D. C. Schneider, and S. P. Mahony. 2009. The spatial structure of habitat selection: A caribou's-eye-view. *Acta Oecologica-International Journal of Ecology*, 35, 253–260.

McArthur, R. H. and E. O. Wilson. 1967. *The Theory of Island Biogeography*. Princeton University Press, Princeton, NJ.

McGarigal, K. 2009a. *FRAGSTATS Spatial Pattern Analysis Program for Categorical Maps*. Landscape Ecology Program, University of Massachusetts, Amherst. Retrieved January 12, 2009 from: http://www.umass.edu/landeco/research/fragstats/fragstats.html.

McGarigal, K. 2009b. What is Landscape Ecology? Retrieved January 12, 2009 from: http://www.umass.edu/landeco/about/landeco.pdf.

McHarg, I. 1969. *Design with Nature*. Garden City, NY: Doubleday/Natural History Press.

Naiman, R. J., G. Pinay, C. A. Johnston, and J. Pastor. 1994. Beaver influences on the long-term biogeochemical characteristics of boreal forest drainage networks. *Ecology*, 75, 905–921.

Nakamura, F., F. J. Swanson, and S. M. Wondzell. 2000. Disturbance regimes of stream and riparian systems—A disturbance-cascade perspective. *Hydrological Processes*, 14, 2849–2860.

Odum, E. P. and H. T. Odum. 1959. *Fundamentals of Ecology* (2nd ed.). Philadelphia, PA: W. B. Saunders.

Odum, H. T. 1957. Trophic structure and productivity of Silver Springs, Florida. *Ecological Monographs*, 27, 55–112.

Parks Canada. 2009. *Fire Management*. Parks Canada, Ottawa. Retrieved October 2009 from: http://www.pc.gc.ca/eng/progs/np-pn/eco/eco5.aspx.

Payette, S., M. J. Fortin, and I. Gamache. 2001. The subarctic forest-tundra: The structure of a biome in a changing climate. *BioScience*, 51, 709–718.

Pickett, S. T. A., M. L. Cadenasso, and S. J. Meiners. 2009. Ever since Clements: From succession to vegetation dynamics and understanding to intervention. *Applied Vegetation Science*, 12, 9–21.

Pickett, S. T. A., M. L. Cadenasso, J. M. Grove, C. H. Nilon, R. V. Pouyat, and W. C. Zipperer. 2001. Urban ecological systems: Linking terrestrial ecological, physical, and socioeconomic components of metropolitan areas. *Annual Review of Ecology and Systematics*, 32, 127–157.

Pickett, S. T. and P. S. White. 1985. *The Ecology of Natural Disturbance and Patch Dynamics*. New York: Academic Press.

Pidwirny, M. et al. 2009. *Remote Sensing. The Encyclopedia of Earth*. Retrieved on January 12, 2010 from: http://www.eoearth.org/article/Remote_sensing.

Quinn, T. P., S. M. Carlson, S. M. Gende, and H. B. Rich. 2009. Transportation of Pacific salmon carcasses from streams to riparian forests by bears. *Canadian Journal of Zoology*, 87, 195–203.

Rapport, D. J. 1997. Transdisciplinarity: Transcending the disciplines. *Trends in Ecology and Evolution* 12, 289.

Rhemtulla, J. M., R. J. Hall, E. S. Higgs, and S. E. Macdonald. 2002. Eighty years of change: Vegetation in the montane ecoregion of Jasper National Park, Alberta, Canada. *Canadian Journal of Forest Research*, 32, 2010–2021.

Roland, J. 1993. Large-scale forest fragmentation increases the duration of tent caterpillar outbreak. *Oecologia*, 93, 25–30.

Rothamsted Research. 2009. *Broadbalk*. Rothamsted Research. Retrieved on January 12, 2010 from: http://www.rothamsted.bbsrc.ac.uk/resources/ClassicalExperiments.html#Broadbalk.

Schindler, D. E., M. D. Scheuerell, J. W. Moore, S. M. Gende, T. B. Francis, and W. J. Palen. 2003. Pacific salmon and the ecology of coastal ecosystems. *Frontiers in Ecology and the Environment*, 1, 31–37.

Schindler, D. W., R. E. Hecky, D. L. Findlay, M. P. Stainton, B. R. Parker, and M. J. Paterson. 2008. Eutrophication of lakes cannot be controlled by reducing nitrogen input: Results of a 37-year whole-ecosystem experiment. *Proceedings of the National Academy of Sciences (United States)*, 105, 11254–11258.

Schmitt, D. and R. Suffling. 2006. Managing eastern North American woodlands in a cultural context. *Landscape and Urban Planning*, 78, 457–464.

Simpson, E. H. 1949. Measurement of diversity. *Nature*, 163, 688.

Suffling, R. and A. Perera. 2004. Characterizing natural forest disturbance regimes. In A. Perera, L. J. Buse, and M. G. Weber (Eds.). *Emulating Natural Forest Landscape Disturbances: Concepts and Applications*. (pp. 43–54). New York: Columbia University Press.

Suffling, R. and C. Wilson. 1994. The use of Hudson's Bay Company records in climatic and ecological research, with particular reference to the Great Lakes Basin. In R. I. MacDonald (Ed.). *Great Lakes Archaeology and Paleoecology: Proceedings of a Symposium*. (pp. 295–319). Waterloo, ON: Quaternary Sciences Institute, University of Waterloo.

Suffling, R., B. Smith, and J. Dal Molin. 1982. Estimating past forest age distributions and disturbance rates in northwestern Ontario—A demographic approach. *Journal of Environmental Management*, 14, 45–56.

Tanner, J. E. 2006. Landscape ecology of interactions between seagrass and mobile epifauna: The matrix matters. *Estuarine Coastal and Shelf Science*, 68, 404–412.

Thomas, C. J. and S. W. Lindsay. 2000. Local-scale variation in malaria infection amongst rural Gambian children estimated by satellite remote sensing. *Transactions of the Royal Society of Tropical Medicine and Hygiene*, 94, 159–163.

Troll, C. 1939. Luftbildplan und ökologische Bodenforschung: Luftbildplan und ökologische Bodenforschung Ihr zweckmäßiger Einsatz für die wissenschaftliche Erforschung und praktische Erschließung wenig bekannter Länder (Aerial photography and ecological studies of the Earth). *Zeitschrift der Gesellschaft fur Erdkunde*, 241–298.

Turner M. G., R. H. Gardner, and R. V. O'Neill. 2001. *Landscape Ecology in Theory and Practice*. New York: Springer-Verlag.

Turner, M. G. 1989. Landscape ecology—The effect of pattern on process. *Annual Review of Ecology and Systematics*, 20, 171–197.

Turner, M. G. 2005. Landscape ecology: What is the state of the science? *Annual Review of Ecology Evolution and Systematics*, 36, 319–344.

Turner, M. G., W. H. Romme, R. H. Gardner, and W. W. Hargrove. 1997. Effects of fire size and pattern on early succession in Yellowstone National Park. *Ecological Monographs*, 67, 411–433.

Urban, D. L., R. V. O'Neill, and H. H. Shugart. 1987. Landscape ecology. *Bioscience*, 37, 119–127.

Van Wagner, C. E. 1978. Age-class distribution and the forest fire cycle. *Canadian Journal of Forest Research*, 8, 220–227.

Weaver, J. L., P. C. Paquet, and L. F. Ruggiero. 1996. Resilience and conservation of large carnivores in the Rocky Mountains. *Conservation Biology*, 10, 964–976.

With, K. A. and T. O. Crist. 1995. Critical thresholds in species responses to landscape structure. *Ecology*, 76, 2446–2459.

Chapter 14

Baillie, J. E. M., C. Hilton-Taylor, and S. N. Stuart (eds.). 2004. *A Global Species Assessment*. Cambridge, UK: IUCN—The World Conservation Union.

Bambach, R. K., A. H. Knoll, and S. C. Wang. 2004. Origination, extinction, and mass depletions of marine diversity. *Paleobiology*, 30, 522–542.

BirdLife International. 2008a. *Grus americana*. In: 2008 IUCN Red List of Threatened Species. www.iucnredlist.org.

BirdLife International 2008b. *Meleagris gallopavo*. In: 2008 IUCN Red List of Threatened Species. www.iucnredlist.org.

BirdLife International. 2008c. *Aix sponsa*. In: 2008 IUCN Red List of Threatened Species. www.iucnredlist.org.

BirdLife International. 2008d. *Cygnus buccinator*. In: 2008 IUCN Red List of Threatened Species. www.iucnredlist.org.

BirdLife International. 2008e. *Falco peregrinus*. In: 2008 IUCN Red List of Threatened Species. www.iucnredlist.org.

BirdLife International. 2008f. *Haliaeetus leucocephalus*. In: 2008 IUCN Red List of Threatened Species. www.iucnredlist.org.

Blockstein, D. E. and H. B. Tordoff. 1985. Gone forever. A contemporary look at the extinction of the passenger pigeon. *American Birds*, 39, 845–851.

Canadian Council on Ecological Areas (CCEA). 2009. *Canadian Conservation Areas Database*. Ottawa, ON: CCEA, Natural Resources Canada and Environment Canada.

Canadian Endangered Species Conservation Council (CESCC). 2006. *Wild Species: The General Status of Species in Canada*. Retrieved October 2009 from: http://www.wildspecies.ca/wildspecies2005/.

Committee on the Status of Endangered Wildlife in Canada (COSEWIC). 2008. *Canadian Wildlife Species at Risk. December, 2008*. COSEWIC, Ottawa, ON. Retrieved October 2009 from: http://www.cosewic.gc.ca/eng/scto/rpt/dsp_booklet_e.htm.

Committee on the Status of Endangered Wildlife in Canada (COSEWIC). 2010. *COSEWIC Website*. Retrieved January 2010 from the COSEWIC website: http://www.cosewic.gc.ca/.

Conservation International. 2009. Biodiversity Hotspots. Retrieved October 2009 from: http://www.biodiversityhotspots.org/xp/hotspots/Documents/cihotspotmap.pdf.

Convention on Biological Diversity (CBD). 2010. United Nations Environment Program, Secretariat of the Convention on Biological Diversity, Montreal, PQ. http://www.cbd.int/.

Conway Morris, S. 1998. *The Crucible of Cereation: The Burgess Shaleand the Rise of Animals*. Oxford, UK: Oxford University Press.

Costanza, R., R. d'Arge, R. de Groot, S. Farber, M. Grasso, B. Hannon, K. Limburg, S. Naeem, R. V. O'Neill, J. Paruelo, R. G. Raskin, P. Sutton, M. van den Belt. 1997. The value of the world's ecosystem services and natural capital. *Nature*, 387, 253–260.

Diamond, J. M. 1982. Man the exterminator. *Nature (London)*, 298, 787–789.

Diamond, J. M. 1984. "Natural" extinctions of isolated populations. In M. H. Nitecki (Ed.). *Extinctions*, (pp. 191–246). Chicago, IL: University of Chicago Press.

Doroff, A. and A. Burdin. 2008. *Enhydra lutris*. In: 2008 IUCN Red List of Threatened Species. www.iucnredlist.org.

Downes, C. M. and B. T. Collins. 2008. Canadian Bird Trends Website Version 2.2. Canadian Wildlife Service, Environment Canada, Gatineau, PQ. Retrieved October 1009 from: http://www.cws-scf.ec.gc.ca/mgbc/trends/index.cfm?lang=e&go=home.page&CFID=16644784&CFTOKEN=96168935.

Eaton, S. W. 1992. Wild Turkey (*Meleagris gallopavo*). In: The Birds of North America Online (A. Poole, ed.). Cornell Lab of Ornithology, Ithaca, NY. Retrieved October 2009 from: http://bna.birds.cornell.edu/bna/species/022/articles/introduction.

Eckert, A. W. 1965. *The Silent Sky: The Incredible Extinction of the Passenger Pigeon*. Dayton, OH: Landfall Press.

Ehrlich, P. R., D. E. Breedlove, P. F. Brussard, and M. A. Sharpe. 1972. Weather and the "regulation" of subalpine populations. *Ecology*, 53, 243–247.

Eldredge, N. 2005. The sixth extinction. *ActionBioscience*. Retrieved October 2009 from: http://www.actionbioscience.org/newfrontiers/eldredge2.html.

Ellis, R. 1991. *Men and Whales*. New York: Alfred A. Knopf.

Environment Canada. 1995. *Canadian Biodiversity Strategy. Canada's Response to the Convention on Biological Diversity*. Environment Canada, Hull, PQ. Retrieved October 2009 from: http://www.eman-rese.ca/eman/reports/publications/rt_biostrat/intro.html.

Environment Canada. 2010. *Recovery Strategies*. Retrieved January 2010 from the Environment Canada website: http://www.sararegistry.gc.ca.

Erwin, D. A. 1990. The end-Permian mass extinction. *Annual Reviews of Ecology and Systematics*, 21, 69–91.

Feduccia, A. 1985. *Catesby's Birds of Colonial America*. Chapel Hill, NC: University of North Carolina Press.

Flannery, T. 2001. *The Eternal Frontier: An Ecological History of North America and its Peoples*. New York: Atlantic Monthly Press.

Freedman, B. 1995. *Environmental Ecology. The Ecological Effects of Pollution and Disturbance*. San Diego, CA: Academic Press.

Freedman, B. 2010. *Environmental Science. A Canadian Perspective*. Toronto: Pearson Education Canada.

Freedman, B., S. Love, and B. O'Neil. 1996. Tree species, biomass, and carbon storage in stands of urban forest of varying character in Halifax, Nova Scotia, Canada. *Canadian Field-Naturalist*, 110, 675–682.

Fuller, E. 2003. *The Great Auk: The Extinction of the Original Penguin.* Piermont, NH: Bunker Hill Publishing.

Gates, C. and K. Aune. 2008. *Bison bison.* In: 2008 IUCN Red List of Threatened Species. www.iucnredlist.org.

Gilpin, M. E. and M. E. Soulé. 1986. Minimum Viable Populations: Processes of Species Extinction. In M. E. Soulé (Ed.). *Conservation Biology: The Science of Scarcity and Diversity.* (pp. 19–34). Sunderland, MA: Sinauer.

Groom, M. J., G. K. Meffe, and C. R. Carroll. 2006. *Principles of Conservation Biology (3rd ed.).* Sunderland, MA: Sinauer Associates.

Gould, S. J. 1989. *Wonderful Life: The Burgess Shale and the Nature of History.* New York: Norton.

Henson, B. L., K. E. Brodribb, and J. L. Riley. 2004. *Great Lakes Conservation Blueprint for Terrestrial Biodiversity.* Nature Conservancy of Canada, Toronto, ON. http://science.naturecons\ervancy.ca/resources/docs/Chap%201-%204%20Terr_Vol1_final_e-version.pdf.

Hoffmann, M., J. Byers, and J. Beckmann. 2008. *Antilocapra americana.* In: 2008 IUCN Red List of Threatened Species. www.iucnredlist.org.

Holdaway, R. N. 1989. New Zealand's pre-human avifauna and its vulnerability. *New Zealand Journal of Ecology,* 12 supplement: 11–25.

Holdaway, R. N. and C. Jacomb. 2000. Rapid extinction of the Moas (Aves: Dinornithiformes): Model, test, and implications. *Science,* 287, 2250–2254.

Hummel, M. and S. Pettigrew. 1991. *Wild Hunters: Predators in Peril.* Toronto: Key Porter Books.

Hummel, M. and S. Pettigrew. 2002. *Wild Hunters: Predators in Peril.* Toronto: Key Porter Books.

Hunter, M. L. 1996. *Fundamentals of Conservation Biology.* Cambridge, MA: Blackwell Science Inc.

International Union for the Conservation of Nature and Natural Resources (IUCN). 2008. *The IUCN Red List of Threatened Species.* IUCN, Gland, Switzerland. http://www.iucnredlist.org.

International Union for the Conservation of Nature and Natural Resources (IUCN). 2009. *IUCN Protected Areas Categories System.* WCPA Categories System for Protected Areas Task Force, IUCN, Gland, Switzerland. Retrieved October 2009 from: http://www.iucn.org/about/union/commissions/wcpa/wcpa_work/wcpa_strategic/wcpa_science/wcpa_categories/.

International Whaling Commission (IWC). 2000. *Whale Population Estimates.* Cambridge, UK. Retrieved October 2009 from: http://www.iwcoffice.org/conservation/estimate.htm#assessment.

Kareiva, P. and M. Marvier. 2003. Conserving biodiversity coldspots. *American Scientist,* 91, 344–351.

Karr, J. R. 1982. Avian extinction on Barro Colorado Island, Panama: A reassessment. *American Naturalist,* 119, 220–239.

Kirkham, I. R. and W. A. Montevecchi. 1982. The breeding birds of Funk Island: An historical perspective. *American Birds,* 36, 111–118.

Linzey, A. V., H. Hammerson, and S. Cannings. 2008. *Castor canadensis.* In: 2008 IUCN Red List of Threatened Species. www.iucnredlist.org.

Lotze, H. K. and B. Worm. 2009. Historical baselines for large marine animals. *TREE,* 24, 254–262.

MacArthur, R. H. and E. O. Wilson. 1967. *The Theory of Island Biogeography.* Princeton, NJ: Princeton University Press.

Margules, C. R. and R. L. Pressey. 2000. Systematic conservation planning. *Nature,* 405, 243–253.

Martin, P. S. 1967. Pleistocene overkill. *Natural History,* December, 32–38.

Martin, P. S. 1984. Catastrophic extinctions and late Pleistocene blitzkrieg: Two radiocarbon tests. In M. H. Nitecki (Ed.) *Extinctions* (pp. 153–189). Chicago, IL: University of Chicago Press.

Martin, P. S. and H. E. Wright, Jr. (Eds.). 1967. *Pleistocene Extinctions: The Search for a Cause.* New Haven, CT: Yale University Press.

Martin, P. S. 2001. Mammals, (late Quaternary), extinctions of. *Encyclopedia of Biodiversity,* 3, 825–839. San Diego, CA: Academic Press.

McCallum, M. L. 2007. Amphibian decline or extinction? Current declines dwarf background extinction rate. *Journal of Herpetology,* 41, 483–491.

McGlone, 1989. The Polynesian settlement of New Zealand in relation to environmental and biotic changes. *New Zealand Journal of Ecology,* 12 supplement: 115–164.

McNeil J. and W. J. Cody. 1978. Species-area relationships for vascular plants of some St. Lawrence River islands. *Canadian Field-Naturalist,* 92, 10–18.

Mills, L. S., M. E. Soule, and D. F. Doak. 1993. The keystone-species concept in ecology and conservation. *BioScience,* 43, 219–224.

Moser, T. J. 2006. The 2005 North American Trumpeter Swan Survey. U. S. Fish and Wildlife Service, Division of Migratory Bird Management, Denver, CO. http://library.fws.gov/Bird_Publications/trumpeterswan_survey05.pdf.

Mowat, F. 1963. *Never Cry Wolf.* Toronto: McClelland and Stewart.

Myers, J. H. and D. Bazely. 2003. *Ecology and Control of Introduced Species.* Cambridge, UK: Cambridge University Press.

Myers, N., R. A. Mittermeier, C. G. Mittermeier, G. A. B. da Fonseca, and J. Kent. 1999. Biodiversity hotspots for conservation priorities. *Nature,* 403, 853–858.

Myers, R. A. and B. Worm. 2003. Rapid worldwide depletion of predatory fish communities. *Nature,* 423, 280–283.

Mynott, J. 2009. *Birdscapes: Birds in Our Imagination and Experience.* Princeton, NJ: Princeton University Press.

Nature Conservancy of Canada (NCC). 2010a. *Identifying the Priorities.* Toronto: NCC. Retrieved January 2010 from: http://www.natureconservancy.ca/site/PageServer?pagename=ncc_work_science.

Nature Conservancy of Canada (NCC). 2010b. *Map of Ecoregions for Conservation Blueprints.* NCC, Toronto, ON. Retrieved October 2009 from: http://www.natureconservancy.ca/.

Nettleship, D. N. and P. G. H. Evans. 1985. Distribution and status of the Atlantic Alcidae. In D. N. Nettleship and T. R. Birkhead (Eds.). *The Atlantic Alcidae* (pp. 54–154). New York: Academic Press.

Packer, L. 1994. The extirpation of the Karner blue butterfly in Ontario. In *Karner Blue Butterfly: A Symbol of a Vanishing Landscape.* (pp. 143–151). Miscellaneous Publication 84, Minnesota Agricultural Experiment Station, St. Paul, MN.

Page, J. D., S. E. Bayley, D. J. Good, J. E. Green, and J. P. B. Ritchie. 1996. *Banff–Bow Valley: At the*

Crossroads. Summary Report. Report of the Banff–Bow Valley Task Force, Supply and Services Canada, Ottawa, ON.

Paine, R. T. 1969. A note on trophic complexity and community stability. *American Naturalist*, 103, 91–93.

Pielou, E. C. 1991. After the Ice Age: The Return of Life to Glaciated North America. Chicago, IL: University of Chicago Press.

Pimlott, D. H., J. A. Shannon, and G. B. Kolenosky. 1969. *The Ecology of the Timber Wolf in Algonquin Park*. Toronto: Ontario Department of Lands and Forests.

Power, M. E., D. Tilman, J. A. Estes, B. A. Menge, W. J. Bond, L. S. Mills, G. Daily, J. C. Castilla, J. Lubchenco, and R. T. Paine. 1996. Challenges in the quest for keystones. *Bioscience*, 46, 609–620.

Raup, D. and J. Sepkoski. 1982. Mass extinctions in the marine fossil record. *Science*, 215, 1501–1503.

Reilly, S. B., J. L. Bannister, P. B. Best, M. Brown, R. L. Brownell Jr., D. S. Butterworth, P. J. Clapham, J. Cooke, G. P. Donovan, J. Urbán, and A. N. Zerbini. 2008. *Eschrichtius robustus*. In: 2008 IUCN Red List of Threatened Species.www.iucnredlist.org.

Riley, J. L., S. E. Green, and K. E. Brodribb. 2007. *A Conservation Blueprint for Canada's Prairies and Parklands*. Nature Conservancy of Canada, Toronto, ON. http://science.natureconservancy.ca/resources/docs/PrairiesParklands_MainReport.pdf.

Roberge, J.-M. and P. Angelstam. 2004. Usefulness of the umbrella species concept as a conservation tool. *Conservation Biology*, 18, 76–85.

Schorger, A. W. 1955. *The Passenger Pigeon*. Madison, WI: University of Wisconsin Press.

Shaffer, M. L. 1981. Minimum population sizes for species conservation. *BioScience.*, 31, 131–134.

Shapiro, B., A. J. Drummond, A. R. Michael, C. Wilson, P. E. Matheus, A. V. Sher, O. G. Pybus, M. Thomas P. Gilbert, I. Barnes, J. Binladen, E. Willerslev, A. J. Hansen, G. F. Baryshnikov, J. A. Burns, S. Davydov, J. C. Driver, D. G. Froese, C. R. Harington, G. Keddie, P. Kosintsev, M. L. Kunz, L. D. Martin, R. O. Stephenson, J. Storer, R. Tedford, S. Zimov, and A. Cooper. 2004. Rise and Fall of the Beringian Steppe Bison. *Science*, 206, 1561–1565.

Simberloff, D. 1988. The contribution of population and community ecology to conservation science. *Annual Reviews of Ecology and Systematics*, 19, 473–511.

Soulé. M. E. 1986. What is conservation Biology? *BioScience*, 35, 727–734.

Soulé, M. E. and B. A. Wilcox. 1980. *Conservation Biology: An Evolutionary-Ecological Perspective*. Sunderland, MA: Sinauer Associatess.

Soulé, M. E. 1986. *Conservation Biology: The Science of Scarcity and Diversity*. Sunderland, MA: Sinauer Associates.

Staub, F. 1996. Dodo and Solitaires. Myth and Reality. *Proceedings of the Royal Society of Arts and Sciences of Mauritius*, 6, 89–122 http://www.potomitan.info/dodo/c32.php.

Steadman, D. W. 2006. Extinction and Biogeography of Tropical Pacific Birds. Chicago, IL: University of Chicago Press.

Stuart, S. N., J. S. Chanson, N. A. Cox, B. E. Young, A. S. L. Rodrigues, D. L. Fischman, and R. W. Waller. 2004. Status and trends of amphibian declines and extinctions worldwide. *Science*, 306, 1783–1786.

Temple, S. A. 1977. Plant-animal mutualism: Coevolution with dodo leads to near extinction of plant. *Science*, 197, 885–886.

Theberge, J. and M. Theberge. 1998. *Wolf Country: Eleven Years Tracking the Algonquin Wolves*. Toronto: McLelland and Stewart.

Theberge, J. and M. Theberge. 2004. *The Wolves of Algonquin Park: A 12 Year Ecological Study.* Department of Geography, Publication Series Number 56, University of Waterloo, Waterloo, ON.

Thompson, D. and T. Harkonen. 2008. *Halichoerus grypus*. In: 2008 IUCN Red List of Threatened Species. www.iucnredlist.org.

Traill, L. W., J. A. Bradshaw, B. W. Brook. 2007. Minimum viable population size: A meta-analysis of 30 years of published estimates. *Biological Conservation*, 139, 159–166.

Turner, K., L. Lefler, and B. Freedman. 2005. Plant communities of selected urbanized areas of Halifax, Nova Scotia, Canada. *Landscape and Urban Planning*, 71, 191–206.

United Nations Environment Programme—World Conservation Monitoring Centre (UNEP-WCMC). 2009. *World Database on Protected Areas (WDPA)*. Cambridge, UK: UNEP-WCMC. Retrieved October 2009 from: http://www.unep-wcmc.org/wdpa/.

U. S. Fish & Wildlife Service. 2010. *Whooping Crane (Grus americana)*. U. S. Fish & Wildlife Service, Bethesda, MD. Retrieved October 2009 from: http://ecos.fws.gov/speciesProfile/profile/speciesProfile.action?spcode=B003.

van Dyke, F. 2008. *Conservation Biology: Foundations, Concepts, Applications* (2nd ed.). New York: Springer Verlag.

World Resources Institute (WRI). 2010. EarthTrends database. http://earthtrends.wri.org/.

Chapter 15

Baldwin, N. A., R. W. Saalfeld, M. R. Dochoda, H. J. Buettner, and R. L. Eshenroder. 2002. *Commercial Fish Production in the Great Lakes 1867–2000*. Ann Arbor, MI: Great Lakes Fishery Commission. http://www.glfc.org/databases/commercial/commerc.php.

Begon, M., C. R. Townsend, and J. L. Harper. 2005. *Ecology: From Individuals to Ecosystems* (4th ed.). Oxford, UK: Blackwell Publishing.

British Petroleum (BP). 2010. *Statistical Review of World Energy, 2008*. Retrieved October 2009 from: http://www.bp.com/productlanding.do?categoryId=6929&contentId=7044622.

Busch, B. C. 1985. *The War Against the Seals. A History of the North American Seal Fishery*. Kingston, ON: McGill-Queen's University Press.

Canadian Council of Forest Ministers (CCFM). 2010. *National Forestry Database*. Ottawa, ON. Retrieved October 2009 from: http://nfdp.ccfm.org/index_e.php.

Canadian Forest Service (CFS). 2010. *Forest Industry in Canada*. Ottawa, ON. Retrieved October 2009 from: http://cfs.nrcan.gc.ca/index/forestindustryincanada.

Casey, J. M. and R. A. Myers. 1998. Near extinction of a widely distributed fish. *Science*, 281, 690–692.

Cheung, W. W. L., T. J. Pitcher, and D. Pauly. 2005 A fuzzy logic expert system to estimate intrinsic extinction vulnerabilities of marine fishes to fishing. *Biological Conservation*, 124, 97–111.

Cipriano, R. C. 2002. *Infectious Salmon Anemia Virus.* United States Geological Survey, National Fish Health Research Laboratory, Fish Disease Leaflet 85, Kearneysville, WV.

Clark, C. W. 1981. Bioeconomics. In *Theoretical Ecology: Principles and Applications.* (pp. 387–423). Sunderland, MA: Sinauer Associates.

Clover, C. 2006. *The End of the Line: How Overfishing Is Changing the World and What We Eat.* New York: The New Press.

Clucas, I. 1997. *A Study of the Options for Utilization of Bycatch and Discards from Marine Capture Fisheries.* FAO Fisheries Circular No. 928, Food and Agriculture Organization of the United Nations (FAO), Rome. http://www.fao.org/docrep/W6602E/w6602E00.HTM.

Costanza, R. 1991. *Ecological Economics: The Science and Management of Sustainability.* New York: Columbia University Press.

Crowell, M. and B. Freedman. 1994. Vegetation development during a post-clearcutting chronosequence of hardwood forest in Nova Scotia, Canada. *Canadian Journal of Forest Research,* 24, 260–271.

Cushing, D. H. 1988. *The Provident Sea.* Cambridge, UK: Cambridge University Press.

Daly, H. E. 1996. *Beyond Growth: The Economics of Sustainable Development.* Boston, MA: Beacon Press.

Daly, H. E. and J. Farley. 2003. *Ecological Economics: Principles and Applications.* Washington DC: Island Press.

Diamond, J. 2004. *Collapse: How Societies Choose to Fail or Success.* East Rutherford, NJ: Viking Press.

Ellis, R. 1991. *Men and Whales.* New York: Knopf.

Ellis, R. 2003. *The Empty Ocean.* Washington, DC: Island Press.

Environment Yukon. 2007. *Chisana Caribou Recovery Project.* Whitehorse, YT: Government of Yukon.

Fisheries and Oceans Canada (DFO). 2002. Pacific Salmon. Fisheries and Oceans Canada, Salmon Assessment Section, Science Branch, Pacific Biological Station, Nanaimo, BC. http://www.dfo-mpo.gc.ca/zone/underwater_sous-marin/salmon/salmon-saumon-eng.htm.

Fisheries and Oceans Canada (DFO). 2010a. *Aquaculture.* Statistical Services, DFO, Ottawa, ON. Retrieved October 2009 from: http://www.dfo-mpo.gc.ca/stats/aqua/aqua-prod-eng.htm.

Fisheries and Oceans Canada (DFO). 2010b. *Commercial Landings.* Statistical Services, DFO, Ottawa, ON. Retrieved October 2009 from: http://www.dfo-mpo.gc.ca/stats/commercial/land-debarq-eng.htm.

Fisheries and Oceans Canada (DFO). 2010c. *Statistical Services.* Ottawa, ON. Retrieved October 2009 from: http://www.dfo-mpo.gc.ca/communic/statistics/main_e.htm.

Fleming, T. L. and B. Freedman. 1998. Conversion of natural, mixed-species forests to conifer plantations: Implications for dead organic matter and carbon storage. *Ecoscience,* 5, 213–221.

Food and Agriculture Organization of the United Nations (FAO). 2009. *The State of World Fisheries and Aquaculture 2008.* FAO Fisheries and Aquaculture Department, Rome. Retrieved October 2009 from: http://www.fao.org/docrep/011/i0250e/i0250e00.htm.

Freedman, B. 2010. *Environmental Science. A Canadian Perspective* (5th ed.). Toronto: Pearson Education Canada.

Freedman, B., C. Beauchamp, I. A. McLaren, and S. I. Tingley. 1981. Effects of various forestry practices on populations of breeding birds in a hardwood forest in Nova Scotia. *Canadian Field-Naturalist,* 95, 307–311.

Freedman, B. and Keith, T. 1996. *Planting Trees for Carbon Credits. A Discussion of the Issues, Feasibility, and Environmental Benefits.* Tree Plan Canada, Ottawa, ON.

Freedman, B., P. N. Duinker, and R. Morash. 1986. Biomass and nutrients in Nova Scotian forests, and implications of intensive harvesting for future site productivity. *Forest Ecology and Management,* 15, 103–127.

Freedman, B., F. Meth, and C. Hickman. 1992. Temperate forest as a carbon-storage reservoir for carbon dioxide emitted from coal-fired generating stations. A case study for New Brunswick. *Forest Ecology and Management,* 55, 15–29.

Freedman, B., R. Morash, and A. J. Hanson. 1981. Biomass and nutrient removals by conventional and whole-tree clear-cutting of a red spruce—balsam fir stand in central Nova Scotia. *Canadian Journal of Forest Research,* 11, 249–257.

Hannon, S. 2005. *Effect of Stand versus Landscape Level Forest Structure on Species Abundance and Distribution.* Sustainable Forest Management Network, Edmonton, Alberta. Retrieved October 2009 from: http://www.sfmnetwork.ca/docs/e/SR_200405hannonseffe_en.pdf.

Hardin, G. 1968. The tragedy of the commons. *Science,* 162, 1243–1248.

Hutchings, J. A. and R. A. Myers. 1995. The biological collapse of Atlantic cod off Newfoundland and Labrador: An exploration of historical changes in exploitation, harvesting technology, and management. pp. 39–93 in: *The North Atlantic Fisheries: Successes, Failures, and Challenges.* Charlottetown, PE: Institute of Island Studies.

Hutchings, J. A. and J. D. Reynolds. 2004. Marine fish population collapses: Consequences for recovery and extinction risk. *BioScience,* 54, 297–309.

International Whaling Commission (IWC). 2000. *Aboriginal subsistence whaling catches since 1985.* IWC, Cambridge, UK. http://www.iwcoffice.org/conservation/table_aboriginal.htm.

Jackson, J. B. C., M. X. Kirby, W. H. Berger, K. A. Bjorndal, L. W. Botsford, B. J. Bourque, R. H. Bradbury, R. Cooke, J. Erlandson, J. A. Estes, T. P. Hughes, S. Kidwell, C. B. Lange, H. S. Lenihan, J. M. Pandolfi, C. H. Peterson, R. S. Steneck, M. J. Tegner, and R. R. Warner. 2001. Historical overfishing and the recent collapse of coastal ecosystems. *Science,* 293, 629–638.

Jeziorski, A., N. D. Yan, A. M. Paterson, A. M. DeSellas, M. A. Turner, D. S. Jeffries, B. Keller, R. C. Weeber, D. K. McNicol, M. E. Palmer, K. McIver, K. Arseneau, B. K. Ginn, B. F. Cumming, and J. P. Smol. 2008. The widespread threat of calcium decline in fresh waters. *Science,* 28, 1374–1377.

Johnson, G. A. M. and B. Freedman. 2002. Breeding birds in forestry plantations and natural forest in the vicinity of Fundy National Park, New Brunswick. *Canadian Field-Naturalist,* 116, 475–487.

Kimmins, J. P. 2003. *Forest Ecology. A Foundation for Sustainable*

Management (2nd ed.). Upper Saddle River, NJ: Prentice Hall.
Krkošek, M., M. A. Lewis, and J. P. Volpe. 2005. Transmission dynamics of parasitic sea lice from farm to wild salmon. *Proceedings of the Royal Society B: Biological Sciences*, 272, 689–696.
Kurlansky, M. 1997. *Cod: A Biography of the Fish That Changed the World*. New York: Walker.
Lotze, H. K. and B. Worm. 2009. Historical baselines for large marine animals. *Trends in Ecology and Evolution*, 24, 254–262.
McRae, D. J., L. C. Duchesne, B. Freedman, T. J. Lynham, and S. Woodley. 2001. Differences between wildfire and forest harvesting and their implications in forest management. *Environmental Reviews*, 9, 223–260.
Morgan, K. and B. Freedman. 1986. Breeding bird communities in a hardwood forest succession in Nova Scotia. *Canadian Field-Naturalist*, 100, 506–519.
Morton, A., R. Routledge, C. Peet, and A. Ladwig. 2004. Sea lice (*Lepeophtheirus salmonis*) infection rates on juvenile pink (*Oncorhynchus gorbuscha*) and chum (*Oncorhynchus keta*) salmon in the nearshore marine environment of British Columbia, Canada *Canadian Journal of Fisheries and Aquatic Sciences*, 61, 147–157.
Mowat, F. 1984. *Sea of Slaughter*. Toronto: McClelland-Stewart, Toronto.
Myers, R. A. and B. Worm. 2003. Rapid worldwide depletion of predatory fish communities. *Nature*, 423, 280–283.
Nova Scotia Department of Natural Resources (NSDNR). 2009. *Wildlife Habitat and Watercourses Protection Regulations*. NSDNR, Halifax, NS. Retrieved October 2009 from: http://www.gov.ns.ca/natr/wildlife/habitats/protection/.
O'Carroll, A. 2004. *Where Land and Waters Meet: An Assessment of Canada's Riparian Forest Management Standards*. (J. D. Gysbers, ed.). Global Forest Watch Canada, Edmonton, AB. Retrieved October 2009 from: http://www.globalforestwatch.ca/riparian/landandwaterslegal.pdf.
Pauly, D, V. Christensen, S. Guenette, T. J. Pitcher, U. R. Sumaila, C. J. Walters, R. Watson, and D. Zeller. 2002. Towards sustainability in world fisheries. *Nature*, 418, 689–695.
Ponting, C. 1991. *A Green History of the World*. Middlesex, UK: Penguin.
Raynard, R. S., A. G. Murray, and A. Gregory. 2001. Infectious salmon anaemia virus in wild fish from Scotland. *Diseases of Aquatic Organisms*, 46, 93–100.
Reilly, S. B., J. L. Bannister, P. B. Best, M. Brown, R. L. Brownell Jr., D. S. Butterworth, P. J. Clapham, J. Cooke, G. P. Donovan, J. Urbán, and A. N. Zerbini. 2008. *Balaena mysticetus*. In: IUCN. 2008. *2008 IUCN Red List of Threatened Species*. www.iucnredlist.org.
Richardson, J. S. 2003. Riparian management along headwater streams in coastal British Columbia. *Watershed Management Bulletin*, 7(3): 19–21.
Roberts, C. 2007. *Unnatural History of the Sea*. Washington, DC: Island Press.
Stinson, G. and B. Freedman. 2001. Potential for carbon sequestration in Canadian forests and agroecosystems. *Mitigation and Adaptation Strategies for Global Change* 6, 1–23.
Taiz, L. and E. Zeiger, 2002. *Plant Physiology* (2nd ed.). Sunderland, MA: Sinauer Associates.
Tietenberg, T. 2002. *Environmental and Natural Resource Economics* (6th ed.). Boston, MA: Addison Wesley, Boston.
United States Geological Service. 2008. *Mineral Commodity Summaries 2008*. Retrieved October 2009 from: http://minerals.er.usgs.gov/minerals/pubs/mcs/2007/mcs2007.pdf.
Volpe, J. P., E. B. Taylor, D. W. Rimmer, and B. W. Glickman. 2000. Evidence of natural reproduction of aquaculture escaped Atlantic salmon (*Salmo salar*) in a coastal British Columbia river. *Conservation Biology*, 14, 899–903.
Welsh, D. and Fillman, D. R. 1980. The impact of forest cutting on boreal bird populations. *American Birds*, 34, 84–94.
White, L. 1967. The historical roots of our ecological crisis. *Science*, 155, 1203–1207.
Wood, S., K. Sebastian, and S. Scherr. 2000. *Pilot Analysis of Global Ecosystems: Agroecosystems*. Washington, DC: International Food Policy Research Institute and World Resources Institute.
Woodley, S. J., G. Johnson, B. Freedman, and D. A. Kirk. 2006. Effects of timber harvesting and plantation development on cavity-nesting birds in New Brunswick. *Canadian Field-Naturalist*, 120, 298–306.
World Resources Institute (WRI). 2010. Retrieved October 2009 from EarthTrends database. http://earthtrends.wri.org/.
Worm, B., E. B. Barbier, N. Beaumont, J. E. Duffy, C. Folke, B. S. Halpern, J. B. C. Jackson, H. K. Lotze, F. Micheli, S. R. Palumbi, E. Sala, K. A. Selkoe, J. J. Stachowicz, and R. Watson. 2006. Impacts of biodiversity loss on ocean ecosystem services. *Science*, 314, 787–790.

Chapter 16

Basinger, J. F. 1991. The fossil forests if the Buchanan Lake Formation (early Tertiary), Axel Heiberg Island, Canadian Arctic Archipelago: Preliminary floristics and paleoclimate. In R. L. Christie and N. J. McMillan (Eds.), *Tertiary Fossil Forests of the Geodetic Hills, Axel Heiberg Island, Arctic Archipelago*. (pp. 39–65). Ottawa, ON: Geological Survey of Canada.
Blais, J. R. 1965. Spruce budworm outbreaks in the past three centuries in the Laurentide Park, Quebec. *Forest Science*, 11, 130–138.
Brodersen, K. P., O. Pedersen, C. Lindegaard, and K. Hamburger. 2004. Chironomids (Diptera) and oxy-regulatory capacity: An experimental approach to paleolimnological interpretation. *Limnology and Oceanography*, 49, 1549–1559.
Dawson, M. R. and Harington, C. R. (2007) *Boreameryx*, an unusual new artiodactyl (Mammalia) from the Pliocene of Arctic Canada and endemism in Arctic fossil mammals. *Canadian Journal of Earth Sciences*, 44, 585–592.
Dixit, A. S., Dixit, S. S. and Smol, J. P. (1992) Algal microfossils provide high temporal resolution of environmental trends. *Water, Air, and Soil Pollution*, 62, 75–87.
Douglas, M. S. V., J. P. Smol, J. M. Savelle, and J. M. Blais. 2004. Prehistoric Inuit whalers affected Arctic freshwater ecosystems. *Proceedings of the National Academy of Sciences*, 101, 1613–1617.

Dyke, A. S., A. Moore, and L. Robertson. 2003. *Deglaciation of North America*. Open File 1574, Geological Survey of Canada, Natural Resources Canada, Ottawa, ON. http://geopub.nrcan.gc.ca/moreinfo_e.php?id=214399.

Ekdahl, E. J., J. L. Teranses, T. P. Guilderson, C. A. Wittkop, C. F. Turton, J. H. McAndrews, and E. F. Stoermer. 2004. A prehistoric record of cultural eutrophication from Crawford lake, Ontario. *Geology*, 32, 745–748.

Finney, B. P., I. Gregory-Eaves, J. Sweetman, M. D. Douglas, and J. P. Smol. 2000. Impacts of climatic change and fishing on Pacific salmon abundance over the past 300 years. *Science*, 290, 795–799.

Ginn, B., B. F. Cumming, and J. P. Smol. 2007. Assessing pH changes since pre-industrial times in 51 low-alkalinity lakes in Nova Scotia, Canada. *Canadian Journal of Fisheries and Aquatic Science*, 64, 1043–1054.

Jahren, A. H. 2007. The Arctic forest of the Middle Eocene. *Annual Review of Earth and Planetary Sciences*, 35, 509–540.

Jeziorski, A., N. D. Yan, A. M. Paterson, A. M. DeSellas, M. A. Turner, D. S. Jeffries, W. Keller, R. C. Weeber, R. C. McNicol, M. E. Palmer, K. McIver, K. Arseneau, B. K. Ginn, B. F. Cumming, and J. P. Smol. 2008. The widespread threat of calcium decline in fresh waters. *Science*, 322, 1374–1377.

Jongman, R. H. G., C. J. F. ter Braak, and O. F. R. van Tongeren (eds.). 1995. *Data Analysis in Community and Landscape Ecology*. Cambridge, UK: Cambridge University Press.

Laird, K. R., S. C. Fritz, K. A. Maasch, and B. F. Cumming. 1996. Greater drought intensity and frequency before AD 1200 in the Northern Great Plains, USA. *Nature*, 384, 552–555.

Little, J., R. Hall, R., R. Quinlan, and J. P. Smol. 2000. Past trophic status and hypolimnetic anoxia during eutrophication and remediation of Gravenhurst Bay, Ontario: Comparison of diatoms, chironomids, and historical records. *Canadian Journal of Fisheries and Aquatic Sciences*, 57, 333–341.

Lotze, H. K. and B. Worm. 2009. Historical baselines for large marine mammals. *Trends in Ecology and the Environment*, 24, 254–262.

McAndrews, J. H. 1970. Fossil pollen and our changing landscape and climate. *Rotunda*, 3, 30–27.

Morneau, C. and S. Payette. 2000. Long-term fluctuations of a caribou population revealed by tree-ring data. *Canadian Journal of Zoology*, 78, 1784–1790.

National Oceanic and Oceanographic Administration (NOAA). 2008. Paleoclimatology Slides, National Climatic Data Center, NOAA, Washington, DC. Retrieved September 2009 from: http://www.ncdc.noaa.gov/paleo/slides/slideset/18/index.html.

Savelle, J. 1997. The role of architectural utility in the formation of archaeological whale bone assemblages. *Journal of Archeological Science*, 24, 869–885.

Smol, J. P. 1988. Paleoclimate proxy data from freshwater arctic diatoms. *Verhandlungen der Internationale Vereinigung von Limnologie*, 23, 837–844.

Smol, J. P. 2008. *Pollution of Lakes and Rivers: A Paleoenvironmental Perspective*, (2nd Ed.) Oxford, UK: Wiley-Blackwell Publishing.

Smol, J. P. and B. F. Cumming, B. F. 2000. Tracking long-term changes in climate using algal indicators in lake sediments. *Journal of Phycology*, 36, 986–1011.

Smol, J. P. and M. S. V. Douglas. 2007. From controversy to consensus: Making the case for recent climatic change in the Arctic using lake sediments. *Frontiers in Ecology and the Environment*, 5, 466–474.

St. George, S. 2009. Dendrohydrology and extreme floods along the Red River, Canada. In M. Stoffel, M. Bollschweiler, D. R. Butler, and B. H. Luckman (Eds.). *Tree-ring Reconstructions in Natural Hazards Research: A State-of-the-art*. Advances in Global Change Research Series, Springer (in press).

Tedford, H. and C. R. Harington. 2003. An Arctic mammal fauna from the Early Pliocene of North America. *Nature*, 425, 388–390.

Uutala, A. J. and J. P. Smol. 1996. Paleolimnological reconstructions of long-term changes in fisheries status in Sudbury area lakes. *Canadian Journal of Fisheries and Aquatic Sciences*, 53, 174–180.

Walker, I. R. and L. C. Cwynar. 2006. Midges and palaeotemperature reconstruction—the North American experience. *Quaternary Science Reviews*, 25, 1911–1925.

Walker, I. R., J. P. Smol, D. R. Engstrom and H. J. B. Birks. 1991. An assessment of Chironomidae as quantitative indicators of past climatic change. *Canadian Journal of Fisheries and Aquatic Sciences*, 48, 975–987.

Chapter 17

Blancher, P. 2003. *Importance of Canada's Boreal Forest to Landbirds*. Bird Studies Canada, Port Rowan, ON. http://www.bsc-eoc.org/library/borealbirdsreport.pdf.

Canadian Council of Ministers of Environment (CCME). 2009. *Scientific Criteria Document for Canadian Water Quality Guidelines for the Protection of Aquatic Life—Uranium*. CCME, Winnipeg, MB. http://www.ccme.ca/assets/pdf/u_fs_pub_consult_0.7_e.pdf.

Department of Justice Canada. 1992. *Canadian Environmental Assessment Act*. Government of Canada, Ottawa, ON. http://laws.justice.gc.ca/en/C-15.2/.

Didrickson, B. 2009. *Historic whooping crane numbers*. International Crane Foundation, Baraboo, WI. http://www.savingcranes.org/images/stories/pdf/species/whooper_table.pdf.

Eldredge, N. and S. J. Gould. 1972. Punctuated equilibria: An aternative to phyletic radiation. In T. J. M. Schopf (Ed.). *Models in Paleobiology*. (pp. 82–115). San Fransisco: Freeman Cooper.

Freedman, B. 1995. *Environmental Ecology. The Impacts of Pollution and Other Stresses on Ecosystem Structure and Function* (2nd ed.). San Diego, CA: Academic Press.

Freedman, B. 2010. *Environmental Science. A Canadian Perspective* (5th ed.). Toronto: Pearson Education Canada.

Gunton, T. I. 2005. *The Maple Leaf in the OECD. Comparing Progress Toward Sustainability*. School of Resource and Environmental Management, Simon Fraser University, and David Suzuki Foundation, Vancouver, BC.

Health Canada. 2008. *Guidelines for Drinking Water Quality*. Canada, Ottawa, ON. http://www.hc-sc.gc.ca/ewh-semt/pubs/water-eau/sum_guide-res_recom/revised-revisees-eng.php#tbl1.

Kane, D. D., S. I. Gordon, M. Munawar, M. N. Charlton, and D. A. Culver. 2006. A planktonic index of biotic integrity (P-IBI) for Lake Erie: A new technique for checking the pulse of Lake Erie. In M. Munawar and R. T. Heath (Eds.): *Checking the Pulse of Lake Erie*. Ecovision World Monograph Series. Aquatic Ecosystem Health and Management. Neiden, The Netherlands: Backhuys Publishers.

Karr, J. R. 1981. Assessment of biotic integrity using fish communities. *Fisheries*, 6, 21–27.

Karr, J. R. 2004. Beyond definitions: Maintaining biological integrity, diversity, and environmental health on national wildlife refuges. *Natural Resources Journal*, 44, 1067–1092.

LaPaix, R., B. Freedman and D. Patriquin. 2009. Ground vegetation as an indicator of ecological integrity. *Environmental Reviews*, 17, 249–265.

Odum, E. P. 1985. Trends expected in stressed ecosystems. *BioScience*, 35, 419–422.

Parks Canada. 2000a. Canada National Parks Act (2000). http://laws.justice.gc.ca/PDF/Statute/N/N-14.01.pdf.

Parks Canada. 2000b. *"Unimpaired for future generations"? Protecting Ecological Integrity with Canada's National Parks. Volume II. Setting a New Direction for Canada's National Parks*. Report of the Panel on the Ecological Integrity of Canada's National Parks, Parks Canada Agency, Ottawa, ON.

Reynoldson, T. B., D. M. Rosenberg, and V. H. Resh. 2001. Comparison of models predicting invertebrate assemblages for biomonitoring in the Fraser River catchment, British Columbia. *Canadian Journal of Fisheries and Aquatic Science*, 58, 1395–1410.

Ryckman, D. P., D. V. Weseloh, and C. A. Bishop. 2005. *Contaminants in Herring Gull Eggs from the Great Lakes: 25 Years of Monitoring Levels and Effects*. Ottawa: Environment Canada. Retrieved October 2009 from: http://www.on.ec.gc.ca/wildlife/factsheets/fs_herring_gulls-e.html.

Schindler, D. W. 1990. Experimental perturbations of whole lakes as tests of hypotheses concerning ecosystem structure and function. *Oikos*, 57, 25–41.

Steedman, R. J. 1988. Modification and assessment of an index of biotic integrity to quantify stream quality in southern Ontario. *Canadian Journal of Fisheries and Aquatic Sciences*, 45, 492–501.

Turner, K., L. Lefler, and B. Freedman. 2005. Plant communities of selected urbanized areas of Halifax, Nova Scotia, Canada. *Landscape and Urban Planning*, 71, 191–206.

World Resources Institute. 2010. *EarthTrends. The Environmental Information Portal.* Washington, DC: WRI. http://earthtrends.wri.org/.

anthropocentric world-view A world-view that places the needs and aspirations of people at the centre of moral consideration, and regards our species as being more important and worthwhile than other living entities. Compare with **biocentric world-view** and **ecocentric world-view**. p. 566

anthropogenic Associated with an influence of humans or their economy. p. 10

anthropogenic biome A biome whose characteristics are greatly influenced by stressors or management associated with humans. Compare with **natural biome**. p. 336

anthropogenic mortality Deaths caused by harvesting or some other human influence. Compare with **natural mortality**. p. 479

anthropogenic stressor A stressor associated with a human influence. p. 38

applied ecology The integration of ecological knowledge with economic needs, such as finding improved ways to cultivate crops or to mitigate environmental damage. p. 17

applied research Research that is directly intended to solve a practical problem. Compare with **fundamental research**. p. 550

aquaculture The cultivation of aquatic organisms using various management practices. p. 498

aquifer An underground bed or layer of earth, gravel, or porous stone that can store and yield water. p. 397

asymmetric competition A condition in which one species exploits a particular resource more efficiently than another, but both may persist in the community. p. 260

atmosphere The envelope of gases, plus smaller amounts of suspended particulates and droplets, that envelops Earth. p. 12

autochthonous Material that originates within a waterbody. Compare with **allochtonous**. p. 525

autotroph Refers to "self-feeding organisms," such as plants and algae that are able to utilize sunlight to drive the fixation of carbon dioxide and water into simple organic compounds. See also **heterotrohic**. p. 47

avalanche A mass of loose snow unexpectedly sliding down a slope in mountainous terrain. pp. 386, 393

base cation (or base) Refers to potassium, sodium, calcium, and/or magnesium. p. 86

base flow The part of stream flow that is sustained by groundwater, and is not attributable to direct runoff from rain or snowmelt. p. 398

basic research See **fundamental research**. p. 545

behaviour Adjustment of state in response to changes in the environment; the actions of organisms, including their conscious or unconscious, deliberate or involuntary reactions to other organisms, abiotic stimuli, and other circumstances. p. 137

behavioural ecology The study of behaviour and its associated structures and biological processes, with reference to their adaptive consequences. pp. 17, 137

behavioural thermoregulation The regulation of body temperature through changes in body position or movement to a different location. p. 175

benthic zone The bottom habitat of waterbodies and oceans, including the sediment and immediately overlying water. p. 341

beta (β) diversity The variety of organisms occurring in different habitats or in a region; sometimes called regional diversity. See also **alpha (α) diversity**, **diversity**, **species richness**, and **evenness**. p. 379

bet-hedging strategy A life history that reduces the variance in genotypic/individual fitness over generations, even if this would entail a "sacrifice" of the expected fitness within any particular generation, as an adaptive trait to deal with environmental change and unpredictability. p. 212

biocentric world-view A world-view that in addition to humans considers that individual organisms of other species have intrinsic value, and so they deserve to have moral standing; moreover, in the case of sentient animals there is a special obligation to avoid causing unnecessary suffering while in pursuit of a human interest. Compare with **anthropocentric world-view** and **ecocentric world-view**. p. 566

biochemicals Molecules of biosynthetic origin, including the many varieties of carbohydrates, proteins, and fats, and consisting primarily of carbon and hydrogen, but also containing smaller amounts of other elements (such as oxygen, nitrogen, and phosphorus). See also **organic chemicals**. p. 75

bioconcentration The tendency of certain substances to occur in larger concentrations in organisms than in their ambient, non-living environment. Compare with **biomagnification**. p. 39

biodiversity (biological diversity) The richness of biological variation, at all levels of biological organization; all of the populations (and genes), species, and communities in a particular area. pp. 249, 361

biogeochemistry The partitioning and cycling of elements and compounds (including nutrients) between living and non-living parts of an ecosystem. p. 78

biological conservation The conservation of the natural world, particularly biodiversity and the services it provides. p. 420

biological resource (bio-resource) Any biomass that is harvested as a source of food, material, or energy. p. 472

biomagnification The tendency for certain persistent chemicals to occur in their highest concentrations in top predators, such as organochlorines and methyl-mercury. Compare with **bioconcentration**. p. 39

biomagnify See **biomagnification**. p. 39

biomass The accumulated productivity of ecosystems; the mass of living matter in a given area or in a volume of water. p. 62

biome An ecosystem that exists over an extensive geographic range, occurring anywhere in the world that environmental conditions are suitable for its development. pp. 14, 332

biosphere All space occupied by life on Earth. p. 8

biotic An organic influence, meaning it is exerted by one or more organisms. Compare with **abiotic**. p. 31

biovector An organism that transports chemicals or other materials (e.g., nutrients and sometime pollutants) within or between ecosystems. p. 536

Bohr effect (or Bohr shift) A reduction in oxygen affinity of a respiratory pigment, i.e., a shift in the oxygen-binding curve as a result of an increase in acidity or carbon dioxide partial pressure in the blood or hemolymph. p. 197

boreal forest A northern forest of simple structure and low productivity; often dominated by conifer species. See also **taiga**. pp. 293, 336

bottom–up hypothesis (resource-control) A model based on the idea that community organization is determined by the effects of plants on herbivores, and of herbivores on carnivores, and the carnivores are self-regulating. Compare with **top–down hypothesis**. p. 279

brood parasite An individual that exploits the parental care of another individual other than its parents; may parasitize the parental care of the same or other species. p. 141

browser An animal that feeds upon leaves and twigs of woody plants. Compare with **grazer**. p. 266

buffer A chemical that causes the pH of a solution to remain at a particular value. p. 201

bulk flow Movement of fluid from one compartment to another as a result of differences in hydrostatic and colloid osmotic pressure. p. 180

by-catch Non-targeted mortality, usually used in reference to a fishery. p. 481

capital See **resource (capital)**. p. 471

capture efficiency The effect of a single predator on the per capita growth rate of its prey. p. 126

carbaminohemoglobin The compound formed when CO_2 combines with hemoglobin. p. 199

carnivore An animal that eats animal tissue. Compare with **herbivore** and **omnivore**. p. 60

carrying capacity The largest population size that a habitat can sustain without becoming degraded. p. 101

caste A biologically distinct group within a species of eusocial organism, such as a soldier or worker. See also **eusociality**. p. 150

catch-per-unit effort (CPUE) Standardization of the harvesting rate in terms of the effort being expended. p. 500

catena A related sequence of soil profile types created by changes from one drainage condition to another, usually down the side of a slope; these changes are usually transitional. p. 391

cations Positively charged ions, such as H^+, Na^+, NH_4^+, or Ca^{+2}. Compare with **anions**. p. 86

centrifugal organization A model of community organization in which the most competitive species occupies core habitat, while others become more prominent as one moves toward harsher conditions in peripheral habitats. p. 248

chaos Temporal variation that occurs with a non-repeatable pattern. Compare with **damped oscillation**, **stable limit cycle**, and **stochasticity**. p. 105

character displacement A divergence in the phenotypic attributes of similar species as a result of competition occurring when they co-occur in a place or habitat. p. 124

chemical energy Energy that is stored in bonds occurring among the atoms that comprise molecules. p. 49

chemoautotrophs Microorganisms that utilize potential energy of sulphides and certain other inorganic chemicals to drive their fixation of energy through chemosynthesis. Compare with **photoautotrophs**. p. 59

chemosynthesis Autotrophic productivity that utilizes energy released during the oxidation of sulphides and certain other inorganic chemicals to drive biosynthesis. Compare with **photosynthesis**. p. 59

chloride ion shift The movement of chloride ions across the red blood cell membrane in exchange for bicarbonate ions. p. 199

chronic A longer-term or continuous influence. p. 37

chronosequence A series of communities of various ages that have regenerated from a similar kind of disturbance, and are studied as a progression to infer patterns of ecological change occurring during a succession. p. 308

clear-cutting The harvesting of all trees in an affected stand at the same time. Compare with **selection-cutting**. p. 487

climatic climax According to the Clementsian view of succession, this is the "potential vegetation" of a site, which would be attained if succession were able to run its full course without an intervening disturbance that truncates the sere. See also **climax**. p. 299

climax (or climax community) A predictable end-point community of a succession in which a community has reached a steady state under a particular set of environmental conditions. pp. 244, 299

clone A group of genetically uniform organisms. p. 363

closed population One that is isolated from other groups of the same species, such that there is no movement of individuals between them. Compare with **open population**. p. 96

closed system A situation in which there is no gain in mass, energy, or information, and also no loss; see also **open system**. p. 76

coarse scale Relating to observing in relatively great detail over relatively small areas. Compare with **fine scale**. p. 385

coefficient of relationship (or coefficient of relatedness) Defined as two times the coefficient of kinship, which itself is the probability that alleles at any random locus chosen from two individuals are identical by descent. p. 152

coevolution The linked evolution of one or more biological attributes, including that of two or more species. p. 141

cohort A group of individuals that were born at about the same time. p. 109

cohort life table The age-specific survival and fecundity schedule of a cohort. See also **cohort** and **life table** and compare with **static life table**. p. 109

coldspots of biodiversity Regions with less-focused concentrations of biodiversity. Compare with **hotspots of biodiversity**. p. 442

commensalism A relationship in which one organism benefits without harming the other. p. 247

commercial extinction (economic extinction) Occurrence of a bio-resource in an abundance that has become too small to support commercial harvesting. p. 482

common-property resource Equity that is shared by a group or even all of society. See also **tragedy of the commons**. p. 485

community A group of organisms that live together in the same place and time and that interact directly or indirectly; a community consists of plants, animals, fungi, and bacteria. pp. 8, 243

community ecology Examines interactions occurring among populations of various species within an ecological community. p. 17

compartment A reservoir of mass in a nutrient cycle. p. 76

competition An interaction that occurs when two or more organisms require a common resource that is in short supply compared with the biological demand; it occurs when an organism uses more energy to obtain, or maintain, a unit of resource because of interference from other individuals, of the same or different species, than it would otherwise do. pp. 5, 246

competition coefficient A mathematical constant that reflects the competitive ability of a species. pp. 118, 259

competitive exclusion The great diminishment or extirpation of a species in a community because of the competitive dominance of another species. pp. 121, 259

competitive release The expansion of a species' distribution in the absence of a competitor. pp. 248, 259

competitor A species that is relatively effective at acquiring scarce resources, often to the detriment of less-competitive species. p. 248

composite indicator An artificial variable that integrates changes in a number of different metrics to broadly track changes in all of them. See also **multimetric indicator**. p. 560

connectivity The permeability of the landscape between patches, which is related to corridors, the matrix, and how closely adjacent the patches are; permeability will vary among species. See also **permeable**. p. 393

conservation (i) sustainable use of a renewable natural resource; or (ii) stewardship of the natural world. p. 419

conservation data centre An organization that collects data on the distribution and abundance of species-at-risk and of communities and other kinds of biophysical habitat types. p. 557

conservation ecology The application of ecological knowledge to the stewardship of biodiversity and protected areas. p. 17

conservation planning Planning that seeks to identify the most important places that should be set aside, within the context of a comprehensive system of protected areas. p. 444

constraints of reproduction Inherent limitations on reproduction (and on fitness), owing to costs associated with energetic, ecological, or genetic limitations. p. 218

consumer-control hypothesis See **top–down hypothesis**. p. 279

contamination The presence of a substance, but at a concentration or intensity that is too low to result in a measurable biological or ecological effect. p. 39

control A non-manipulated treatment in an experiment. p. 21

convenience polyandry Polyandry occurring when females re-mate to avoid costs of rejecting matings. p. 143

conventional economics Economics as it is usually practised, with valuation being assessed primarily in an anthropocentric context. Compare with **ecological economics**. p. 465

convergent evolution Evolution by different species, sometimes occurring in widely spaced places, but subjected to similar regimes of environmental conditions and natural selection, so that the evolutionary responses are parallel (or convergent). p. 333

conversion A change in character of an ecosystem from one type to another, often in reference to a change from a natural to an anthropogenic ecosystem. p. 296

conversion efficiency The rate at which a consumer converts the energy of its food into its growth plus investment in its offspring. p. 126

core The massive interior of Earth, consisting of molten metals. p. 13

corridor A linear feature that differs from the matrix on either side and that may provide connectivity between separated patches of habitat. p. 343

cost of reproduction Effort or resource allocation that is required to support reproduction. p. 218

counter-current flow A flow of fluids in opposite directions in tubules or vessels in close proximity. p. 191

counter-current heat exchange A heat conservation mechanism that occurs when an artery and vein are in close proximity, so heat is exchanged between the two, resulting in less loss to the environment. p. 172

crown fire Fires that burn the forest canopy, and in Canadian forests generally kill the trees, and so they are a stand-replacing disturbance. p. 500

crust The outermost layer of the solid sphere of Earth, and composed mostly of crystalline and sedimentary rocks. p. 13

cryoprotectant A compound that helps reduce the freezing point of water and prevents the formation of ice crystals in body fluids. p. 175

cryptic herbivore Small consumers, typically herbivores, that are not visually abundant in a community but have a major impact on community structure. p. 273

cumulative environmental impacts Environmental impacts resulting from the effects of a proposed undertaking within some defined area, on top of those caused by any past, existing, and imminent developments and activities. See also **environmental impact assessment**. p. 570

curiosity-driven research See **fundamental research**. p. 287

cyclic phenomena Regular and predictable temporal changes in the structure or function of a system. p. 408

damped oscillation Repetitive temporal variation about a central (average) value that becomes progressively less over time, and is eventually asymptotic with the mean as a point of equilibrium. Compare with **stable limit cycle** and **chaos**. p. 104

data deficient A COSEWIC designation that applies when the available information is not sufficient to resolve an assessment of conservation status of a species (or taxon). p. 437

debris flow A fast-moving mass of unconsolidated, water-saturated rocky debris that flows downslope, typically in a mountainous area. p. 386

decomposer See **detritivore**. p. 60

deductive logic Reasoning that involves making an initial assumption, or several of them, and then drawing conclusions. p. 20

deforestation The permanent conversion of a forest into a non-forested land use, for example, into agricultural production. Compare with **afforestation**. p. 469

deglaciation The meltback of glacial ice. p. 310

dendrochronology The branch of science that uses annual tree-ring couplets to reconstruct past environmental conditions. p. 522

denitrification Part of the nitrogen cycle, in which nitrate is converted by bacteria into either N_2 or N_2O, which are released to the atmosphere. p. 83

density-independent model of population growth An exponential model of population growth, in that the per capita growth rate does not vary with the density of the population. See also **exponential model of population growth**. p. 100

determinate growth Growth of individuals that ceases after a certain age. Compare with **indeterminate growth**. p. 107

deterministic (i) Refers to age-specific rates of survival and fecundity that are fixed at constant values. (ii) Relating to a specific input variable to a system, giving a specific and predictable output. Compare with **stochastic**. pp. 116, 411

detritivore Organisms that feed on dead organic matter. p. 60

detritus food chain (detritus food web) That component of a food chain or food web that includes dead organic matter and the organisms that feed on that biomass. p. 270

devegetation A severe disturbance that removes vegetation cover from an affected site, p. 306

direct action In the context of biodiversity, this refers to activities that result in immediate benefits, as occurs when protected areas are established to benefit species-at-risk or rare communities. p. 455

direct fitness Genes contributed by an individual to its population via its personal reproduction (its surviving offspring). Compare with **indirect fitness**. p. 152

disclimax A climax community that occurs in a situation with an unusual disturbance regime. See also **climax**. p. 299

disease A biological relationship that involves a pathogenic microorganism infecting a plant or animal, making the host ill or sometimes killing it; some other diseases may be caused by abiotic factors, such as toxic substances. pp. 5, 246, 291

disturbance A discrete event that disrupts a population or community and thereby changes substrates, resource availability, and the physical environment, and often provides opportunity for colonization by new individuals. pp. 10, 35, 265

diversity See **species diversity**. p. 249

dominance-controlled community A situation in which early colonizers of a recently disturbed habitat are dissimilar ecologically, and as the community matures it will become progressively more dominated by competitively superior species. See also **founder-control**. p. 254

dominant species A species having the highest abundance or biomass in a community, and thereby having a major influence on community structure. p. 254

doubling time The length of time required for an initial quantity to double in amount or size. p. 98

ecocentric world-view A world-view that includes the biocentric one but goes further by also affording inherent value to species and higher-order ecological levels, including natural communities and ecoscapes, as well as functional attributes such as clean-environment services and carbon storage. Compare with **anthropocentric world-view** and **biocentric world-view**. p. 566

ecological amplitude The limits of environmental conditions within which an organism (or species) can live and function. p. 522

ecological economics A conceptual fusion of economics and ecology, whose distinction is that it seeks to examine and valuate the relationships of economic systems and ecological systems in an objective and non-anthropocentric manner. Compare with **conventional economics**. pp. 439, 466

ecological energetics Study of the energy inputs, outputs, and transformations within ecosystems, including those involving biologically fixed energy. p. 47

ecological footprint The area of ecoscape that is needed to support the production of the energy and materials used by a person, city, or another economic unit. p. 466

ecological function (or ecological process) Flows and/or transformations of energy, materials, and species occurring among landscape elements. pp. 397, 466

ecological integrity (EI) An indicator related to environmental quality, but with a focus on changes in wild populations and natural ecosystems, rather than on humans and their economy; indicators of high levels of EI include dominance by native species, self-organized communities, and ecoscapes that are characteristic for the prevailing natural environmental regimes. See also **environmental quality** and **ecosystem health**. p. 554

ecological process See **ecological function**. p. 397

ecological region See **ecoregion**. p. 350

ecological reserve A protected area established to conserve natural values, particularly biodiversity, and in which visitation is strictly limited and the only permitted activities are scientific monitoring and research. p. 448

ecological system See **ecosystem**. p. 6

ecologically sustainable development An economy that is making progress toward ecological sustainability. See also **ecologically sustainable economy** and compare with **sustainable development**. pp. 26, 464

ecologically sustainable economy An economy that is resource-sustainable, and that also maintains biodiversity and ecological services at viable levels of abundance. Compare with **sustainable economy**. p. 464

ecologist A scientist who studies some aspect of ecology. p. 17

ecology The study of the relationships of organisms and their environment. p. 4

economic development Progress made in structuring an economy toward a greater use of renewable resources and other improvements. Compare with **sustainable** development and **economic growth**. p. 468

economic growth An economy that is increasing in size over time, in terms of its human population, consumption of resources, manufacturing of goods, supply of money, and generation of waste materials and pollution. Compare with **economic development** and **sustainable development**. p. 468

economics An interdisciplinary field whose principal goal is to understand the ways that scarce resources (goods and services of various kinds) are allocated among competing uses within an economy. p. 464

ecoregion (ecological region) Extensive regions of general similarity; terrestrial ecoregions are classified according to their physiography, climate, and biological characteristics, and marine ones by physiography, oceanography, and biological attributes. p. 350

ecoscape A heterogeneous terrestrial and/or aquatic area with repeated forms at any appropriate scale. See also **landscape** and **seascape**. pp. 8, 361

ecosystem (ecological system) A generalized term that cannot be precisely defined, but is a space in which organisms are interacting with environmental factors, and is delimited for the purposes of studying it. p. 6

ecosystem approach A holistic way of understanding an ecological systems, which considers all individuals, populations, communities, and environments to be intrinsically connected and interdependent, although in varying degrees. p. 8

ecosystem ecology (functional ecology) Examines the flows of energy and nutrients among organisms and the abiotic environment. p. 17

ecosystem health An indicator related to and not substantially different from ecological integrity, but with more of a focus on the functional attributes of ecosystems. See also **environmental quality** and **ecological integrity**. p. 554

ecotone An edge or zone of transition between discrete habitat types, such as between a forest and a wetland, or between neighbouring patches on a landscape. See also **edge**. pp. 42, 299, 391

ecotype A locally adapted population of a wide-ranging species. p. 74

ecozone Extensive ecological regions that are distinguished and mapped largely on the basis of their ecological similarities, particularly their dominant late-successional biota, the most prominent species, and their "enduring" environmental features related to bedrock, soil types, climate, and topography. p. 347

ectotherm An animal that relies on the environment as a heat source. p. 166

edaphic climax A climax community that is primarily determined by local soil conditions. See also **climax**. p. 299

edge (i) A linear place where a landscape patch abuts one or more other land-cover units. (ii) The collective occurrence of edges in a landscape. See also **ecotone**. p. 391

El Niño event Cyclic climatic disturbances rooted in surface warming of parts of the tropical Pacific Ocean, occurring every 3 to 7 years. p. 408

electromagnetic energy Energy associated with entities called photons, which have properties of both waves and particles and travel at an unvarying velocity known as the speed of light (3×10^8 m/s). p. 49

electromagnetic radiation See **electromagnetic energy**. p. 49

emergent property (i) An attribute of life or ecosystems that cannot be predicted from knowledge of the parts, and that exists only if the system is operating as an integrated whole. (ii) A complex pattern or phenomenon that arises from a multiplicity of relatively simple interactions or phenomena. p. 407

emulation forestry (emulation silviculture) Modelling timber-harvesting and management systems to imitate the natural disturbance regime of a forest type. pp. 322, 497

endangered A species that is at imminent risk of extinction or extirpation in all or an important portion of its range. p. 436

endemic A taxon (species or subspecies) with a local or restricted distribution. pp. 338, 364

endogenous Influences that are internal to the ecosystem being studied, especially ones that are biological in origin. Compare with **exogenous**. p. 408

endotherm An animal that obtains its body heat from its own metabolism. p. 166

energy A fundamental physical unit, simply defined as the capacity of a body or system to accomplish work. p. 48

energy budget A physical budget of a system that describes the rates of input and output of energy and any internal transformations among its states, including changes in stored amounts. p. 53

entropy A physical attribute related to the degree of randomness of the distributions of matter and energy. See also **second law of thermodynamics**. p. 51

environmental ecology Study of ecological responses to environmental stressors, with a focus on anthropogenic pollution and disturbance. p. 17

environmental factor (or influence) Influences that affect individual organisms, populations, communities, or ecoscapes (landscapes and seascapes), or functions such as productivity, decomposition, and nutrient cycling. pp. 5, 31

environmental gradient See **gradient**. p. 257

environmental impact assessment (EIA) A planning process that helps to identify and appraise environmental problems that are potentially involved with a proposed economic activity, and to find ways to avoid or mitigate them if possible. p. 567

environmental influence See **environmental factor**. p. 5

environmental monitoring Repeated measurements of variables related to either the abiotic (inorganic) environment or to the structure and functioning of ecosystems. p. 558

environmental non-governmental organization (ENGO) An environmental charity, such as the Nature Conservancy of Canada or the World Wildlife Fund. p. 557

environmental quality An indicator of the intensity of environmental stressors, particularly anthropogenic ones, as well as their effects on people, economic values, and other species and ecosystems. See also **ecological integrity** and **ecosystem health**. p. 420

enzyme A protein that catalyzes a biochemical reaction. p. 165

equilibrium A condition in which competing influences are in balance, resulting in a relative constancy of conditions. pp. 119, 248

equilibrium theories A view that communities are relatively constant in their species composition and resistance and resilience to changes in environmental stressors. See also **non-equilibrium theories**. p. 248

estivation A drop in metabolic rate and body temperature for two or more consecutive days during the summer months. p. 173

eusociality Social behaviour in which some individuals (usually in specific castes) are altruistic. p. 151

eutrophic Waterbodies that have a large nutrient supply and so are highly productive. Compare with **oligotrophic** and **mesotrophic**. p. 341

eutrophication An increase in the productivity of waterbodies, caused by an increase in the supply of nutrients. pp. 86, 530

evaporation The change of state of water from a liquid or solid to a gas. p. 12

evapotranspiration The evaporation of water from a landscape. See also **evaporation** and **transpiration**. pp. 12, 54

evenness A measure of how similarly abundant species are within a community; it is a measure of unpredictability—the higher the unpredictability, the higher the evenness. See also **species diversity** and **species richness**. pp. 379, 250

evolution (biological evolution) Change in the collective genetic information of a population or of higher-order groupings (such as species), occurring from generation to generation. p. 25

evolutionarily significant unit (ESU) A local population that is genetically distinct, but not sufficiently so to be assigned taxonomic rank. p. 505

evolutionary ecology An overarching theme that provides context for much of ecology; the core area is evolutionary aspects of adaptive ecological change, including interactions with selective forces. p. 17

evolutionary psychology Research that addresses the evolved cognitive mechanisms that underlie human behaviour. Compare with **human behavioural ecology**. p. 158

evolutionary radiation A proliferation of species (or of other taxa), often occurring relatively quickly, and in response to the opening up of new ecological space or by novel adaptive changes and opportunities. p. 421

exogenous Influences that are external to the system being studied. Compare with **endogenous**. p. 408

experiment An investigation that is designed to provide evidence relevant to testing a hypothesis. p. 21

exploitation competition See **scramble competition**. p. 117

exponential model of population growth A model that assumes that population is increasing at a constant rate. See also **density-independent model of population growth**. p. 97

exposure The intensity of an interaction of an organism or an ecosystem with an environmental stressor or a regime of stressors. p. 36

extinct A species (or taxon) that no longer exists anywhere in the world. pp. 374, 436

extirpated (extirpation) Refers to a species (or taxon) that formerly occurred in some region, but now only survives elsewhere; a local extinction. pp. 374, 436

extreme environment Habitat with severe environmental conditions, so that life is barely viable. p. 35

facilitation The positive effect of one species upon another, or the enhancement of the conditions for one species by the activities of another. p. 243

facilitation model A model of succession that suggests that early species in a sere are important in changing abiotic conditions in ways that enhance the environmental setting for species that invade later. Compare with **tolerance model** and **inhibition model**. p. 302

fact An event or thing that is true—it is known to have happened or to exist. p. 20

fecundity (fertility) The number of offspring produced by an individual in a single breeding season. p. 209

fine scale Relating to observing in relatively little detail over relatively large areas. Compare with **coarse scale**. p. 385

finite rate of increase The abundance at a particular time multiplied by a growth rate. p. 99

first law of thermodynamics A physical principle stating that energy may be transformed among its various states, but it is never created or destroyed, so that the energy content of the universe remains constant. See also **second law of thermodynamics**. p. 50

fitness The proportionate contribution that an individual's offspring make to the genetic make-up of subsequent generations. p. 25

flagship species Charismatic or otherwise "attractive" species that are used to profile the importance of conservation activities. p. 441

flow-through system See **open system**. p. 53

food chain A linear model of feeding relationships within a group of species. Compare with **food web**. p. 65

food web A representation of the feeding relationships of an ecosystem, including all of its food chains. Compare with **food chain**. p. 65

food-web magnification See **biomagnification**. p. 39

footprint See **ecological footprint**. p. 81

forb A broad-leaved, herbaceous, angiosperm plant. p. 254

forest ecology Investigation of ecosystems dominated by trees, including non-treed successional stages that are recovering from a disturbance of a mature forest. p. 17

founder-control A situation in which most of the early invaders to a gap are similar in their dispersal ability, tolerance to local conditions, growth rates, and competitive abilities, making such a community quite diverse and the composition of later seral stages primarily dependent upon the founder species. See also **dominance-controlled community**. p. 254

fragmentation The process whereby individual patches of a given type become increasingly separated in space through landscape change. p. 387

free good A value that exists, but in which there has been no significant investment of money. p. 465

freshwater ecology (limnology) The study of lakes, ponds, rivers, streams, and wetlands. p. 17

frontier forest See **primary forest**. p. 429

frugivore A fruit-eating animal. See also **granivore** and **insectivore**. p. 266

functional attribute Rate functions, such as productivity, nutrient flux, water flow, and other variables that are commonly reported as change of the amount per unit area and time. p. 7

functional ecology See **ecosystem ecology**. p. 17

functional group A group of species that perform essentially the same ecological function within a community. Compare with **guild**. p. 247

functional response Refers to the ways that a predator or herbivore varies its consumption of food according to the abundance of that resource. Compare with **numerical response**. p. 126

fundamental niche The complete range of conditions under which a species can establish, grow, and reproduce when it is free from interference from other species that might limit it in any way. Compare with **realized niche**. p. 256

fundamental research (basic research or curiosity-driven research) Research that is undertaken primarily to examine a question about the natural world or life—how it came to exist, is organized, and functions. Compare with **applied research**. p. 287

gamma diversity The richness of different communities within a larger study region, such as a landscape or seascape. pp. 251, 380

gap analysis In the context of conservation planning, this compares a list of biodiversity targets to those already captured in existing protected areas; the residuals are targets for the implementation of additional reserves. pp. 299, 444

gap-phase microdisturbance A small-scale disturbance that affects a small area within an otherwise intact community. p. 299

gap-phase microsuccession A small-scale succession that follows a microdisturbance occurring in an otherwise intact community. p. 292

generation time The average age of reproductive individuals in a population. p. 110

genetically modified organism (GMO) An organism whose genome has been modified by genetic engineering that has resulted in the incorporation of DNA of another species. See also **transgenic modification**. p. 479

genome The specific genetic information encoded within the DNA (deoxyribonucleic acid) of an organism; sometimes also used in reference to a population or species. pp. 24, 363

geographical information system (GIS) A computer program that overlays digital maps or images of some part of the surface of Earth to reveal and create further information. p. 410

geo-referenced Refers to a location being established using a coordinate system, such as latitude and longitude. p. 444

GIS See **geographical information system**. p. 295

glaciation An extensive expansion of glacial cover during a period of climatic cooling. p. 295

gradient Change in one or more environmental factors over space. pp. 5, 257

granivore A seed-eating animal. See also **frugivore** and **insectivore**. p. 288

grazer An animal that eats grasses and herbs; may also be applied to aquatic animals that feed on algae. Compare with **browser**. p. 266

greater protected area Refers to a protected plus a designated region of its surrounding terrain, which are co-managed as a single ecological system. pp. 407, 450

greenhouse effect A physical process by which infrared-absorbing (or "greenhouse") gases (such as H_2O and CO_2) in the atmosphere help to keep Earth warm. p. 55

greenhouse gas (GHG) A gas (such as water vapour or carbon dioxide) that absorbs infrared energy within the spectral range that Earth emits, and by doing so diminishes its ability to cool itself of the heat of absorbed solar radiation. p. 55

gross domestic product (GDP) The total value of all goods and services produced within an economy in a year. p. 466

gross primary production (GPP) The total fixation of solar energy by primary producers within an ecosystem. p. 59

ground fire A relatively uncommon type of fire that is limited to burning the organic matter of the forest floor and soil. p. 400

ground truthing The testing of a prediction by the examination of actual conditions in nature, such as when an air-photo prediction is tested by the examination of actual ecological conditions in the field. p. 410

group selection Evolutionary change that involves change in the genetic information of a population because of benefits realized by a group, regardless of effects on the fitness of the individuals involved. p. 26

guild All species in a community that use the same resource base in a similar way, e.g., all seed-eating animals, even though they may not be taxonomically related. Compare with **functional group**. p. 247

handling time The length of time required by a predator to capture, subdue, and consume each prey item. Compare with **searching time**. p. 127

harvest rate The number of individuals, or biomass, removed from a population relative to the number or amount that is available to be harvested. p. 100

harvesting The gathering of wild biomass or the reaping of a cultivated crop. p. 473

herbivore An animal that eats plants and plant tissues. Compare with **carnivore** and **omnivore**. p. 60

herbivory A biological relationship that involves animals eating the tissues of plants. pp. 5, 246

heterotherm (or poikilotherm) An animal that allows its body temperature to fluctuate with that of its environment. p. 166

heterotroph An organism that feeds on organic materials (any kind of biomass, living or dead) as a source of energy and nutrients; organisms that are not capable of fixing their own solar energy into biomass, such as animals, fungi, and most bacteria. See also **autotroph**. pp. 47, 164

heterotrophic Refers to organisms that can survive only if they have access to organic matter as a source of nutrition. Compare with **autotrophic**. p. 11

hibernation (or seasonal torpor) A drop in metabolic rate and body temperature for two or more consecutive days during the winter months. p. 170

holocene biodiversity event See **modern biodiversity crisis. p. 423**

homeotherm An animal that regulates its body temperature within a narrow range independent of that of its environment. p. 166

homogecene A colloquial term for the widespread introductions of many alien species throughout most of the inhabited regions of the world. p. 297

host An organism that supports a parasite. p. 130

hotspots of biodiversity Regions that, at a global scale, support a relatively high density of endemic species. Compare with **coldspots of biodiversity**. p. 442

human behavioural ecology (HBE) Study of the adaptive consequences of the behavioural qualities of humans. Compare with **evolutionary psychology**. p. 158

human capital The people who are participating in an economy, including their skill-sets. p. 471

humified The process of humification, by which organic matter is decomposed until only high-molecular weight molecules are left, referred to as humus. See also **humus**. p. 62

humus Amorphous, partially decomposed organic matter—an important and persistent component of soil that is important in tilth and fertility. p. 88

hydrological cycle (or water cycle) Refers to movements of water among its various compartments in the environment. p. 12

hydrology Study of the properties, distribution, and effects of water on the surface, in the soil and rocks, and in the atmosphere. p. 398

hydrosere A sere that begins with a lake, which gradually in-fills and develops into a wetland, and perhaps eventually into a forested habitat. p. 301

hydrosphere Consists of water occurring in various compartments—on the surface of the planet, in rocks, and in the atmosphere. p. 12

hyperionic Having an ionic pressure greater than that of another fluid. p. 184

hyperosmotic Having an osmotic pressure greater than that of another fluid. p. 183

hyperthermia A rise in body core temperature above normal. p. 170

hyposmotic Having an osmotic pressure less than that of another fluid. p. 182

hypothermia A drop in body core temperature below normal. p. 170

hypothesis A proposed explanation of a phenomenon or its cause. p. 20

importance of competition The effect of competition on a population or community, relative to other environmental factors. p. 262

inclusive fitness The sum of an individual's direct and indirect fitness. See also **direct fitness** and **indirect fitness**. p. 152

indeterminate growth Growth of individuals that continues throughout their life. Compare with **determinate growth**. p. 107

index of biotic integrity (IBI) A multimetric indicator in ecology that is based on metrics of species richness, relative abundances of functional groups, trophic structure, and sometimes the incidence of developmental abnormalities associated with pollution. p. 560

indicator A relatively simple measurement that is intended to represent complex aspects of something else, such as environmental quality or ecological integrity. p. 554

indirect fitness Fitness gained by an individual that helps non-descendant kin. Compare with **direct fitness** and see also **altruism**. p. 152

individual organism (individual) A living entity that is genetically and physically discrete. p. 8

individualistic (or continuum) hypothesis A view of community organization proposed by Henry Gleason that views the community as a coincidental assemblage of species that have similar environmental requirements; while they interact, there is no predictable or repeatable end-point of succession. Compare with **organismal hypothesis**. p. 245

inductive logic Reasoning in which conclusions about natural phenomena are based on the gathering of evidence based on experience and the results of experiments. p. 20

inhibition model A model of succession that suggests that early-establishing species resist invasions of later ones, so the latter can penetrate the community only when early ones die. Compare with **facilitation model** and **tolerance model**. p. 303

inorganic (abiotic or non-living) Refers to environmental influences that are non-biological in origin. p. 5

inorganic nutrient Chemicals that autotrophs need to support their biosynthesis and metabolism, including carbon, nitrogen, phosphorus, potassium, and others. p. 73

insectivore An insect-eating organism. Compare with **frugivore** and **granivore**. pp. 122, 272

instantaneous birth rate The rate of births at a particular time, measured in units of births per individual per unit of time. p. 97

instantaneous death rate The rate of deaths at a particular time, measured in units of deaths per individual per unit of time. p. 97

instrumental value (utilitarian value) Value that exists because something is useful to humans and their economy. p. 372

insularization The process of development of islands of habitat by removal of much of the connecting matrix. See also see **fragmentation**. p. 406

integrated resource management (IRM) A collaborative and broad-reaching approach that identifies all stakeholders and issues in an area that has been defined for the purpose of using this approach, then finds ways to manage economic activities in a manner that is deemed acceptable to a consensus of the parties. p. 512

integrated system (integrated management system) A system in which various activities associated with harvesting and management are undertaken in a coordinated manner, so as to increase the productivity and value of a biological resource. p. 473

intellectual capital The knowledge that resides within an economy and that is essential to organizing a complex society and doing all of the things that are required to keep people fed, healthy, safe, and content, and also keep the environment in good condition. p. 471

intensity of competition The degree to which competition for a limited resource reduces performance below the physiological maximum achievable in a given environment. p. 262

interdisciplinary Refers to knowledge that engages many subject areas in an integrated manner, as in ecology and environmental studies. pp. 14, 568

interference competition Involves action by an individual to reduce the access of others to a resource. p. 117

interior habitat Habitat within a patch or community that is distinct from that occurring in its ecotone or edge. p. 392

intermediate disturbance hypothesis A hypothesis that species diversity in communities is highest under conditions of an intermediate level of disturbance, rather than at lower or higher levels of disturbance. p. 266

intersexual selection Sexual selection within a sex, such as by direct competition. p. 143

interspecific competition Competition occurring among individuals of different species. Compare with **intraspecific competition**. p. 117

intrasexual selection Sexual selection occurring as a consequence of interactions between the sexes, such as mate choice. p. 143

intraspecific competition Competition occurring among individuals of a species. Compare with **interspecific competition**. p. 117

intrinsic rate of population growth The difference between the instantaneous rates of birth and death. p. 97

intrinsic value (inherent value) Value that is due to unique and irreplaceable qualities, that exists "for its own sake." p. 376

invasive alien Non-native organisms that can become abundant in natural habitats and cause ecological damage. pp. 40, 423

ionoconformer An animal that conforms to the ionic composition and concentration of its environment. p. 182

ionoregulation The process of maintaining a constant ionic concentration in a body fluid. p. 183

ionoregulator An animal that regulates the ionic composition and concentration of its body fluids. p. 183

IPAT A formula that allows the total environmental impact of a human population to be calculated, based on the multiplication of its size, affluence in terms of per capita consumption of resources, and technological development of the economy, in terms of environmental impact per unit of consumption. p. 552

irruption A rapid increase to an extremely high population level. p. 294

island biogeography An ecological theory that seeks to explain variations in the numbers of species found on oceanic islands based on their area, isolation, and related factors. p. 440

isocline A series of lines that have the same slope. p. 119

isostasy An elastic rebound of Earth's crust following its release by deglaciation from the immense weight of up to several kilometres of overlying ice during continental glaciation. pp. 90, 314

isozyme (or isotype or isoenzyme) Variations within the structure of a single enzyme. p. 178

iteroparous Refers to a species in which individuals are capable of reproducing more than once in their life. Compare with **semelparous**. p. 108

Judeo-Christian ethic An ethic that presumes that humans have the right to take whatever they want from the natural world for the purposes of subsistence or other economic benefits, based on a literal interpretation of the biblical myth of creation and Genesis 1:28. p. 485

karst A landscape where local ground has collapsed into subterranean cavities developed by the long-term dissolving of soluble minerals, such as limestone. p. 392

keystone species Species that have a disproportionately large influence on the ecological structure and functionality of their community. pp. 268, 440

kin selection Selection in the context of increasing indirect fitness. See also **indirect fitness**. p. 152

kinetic energy Energy that exists in two basic forms that involve mass in motion; thermal energy or heat, which involves atomic or molecular vibration, and mechanical energy, which involves mass in motion through space. p. 49

kleptoparasite An organism that steals food from another individual, typically of another species. p. 141

landscape A larger-scale, heterogenous integration of community-level patches in a terrestrial environment, with repeated forms at any appropriate scale. p. 385

landscape ecology Integrated, scale-related study of the structural and functional attributes and changes of ecosystems. pp. 17, 385

landscape element Patches, corridors, and networks that are the basis of landscape structure. p. 390

landscape structure A spatial pattern of elements that is dependent on influences of such factors as the underlying geology, topography, and disturbance history. p. 390

layer A mapped class of spatial data used in or produced by a geographical information system. See also **geographical information system**. p. 410

leaching A process that involves percolating water dissolving chemicals out of soil and carrying them to deeper layers. p. 90

lek An area, typically used from year to year (traditional), where males display and defend small territories but offer no direct goods or services to the female (such as parental care or nuptial gifts). p. 147

lentic ecosystem An aquatic ecosystem that occurs in a basin and whose hydrology does not include strong water flows, such as a lake or pond. Compare with **lotic ecosystem**. p. 341

Leslie matrix See **transition matrix**. p. 112

life form A grouping of organisms based on similarities of their dominant morphological and physiological traits, regardless of their evolutionary relatedness. p. 332

life history The attributes of the life cycle through which an organism passes (or more precisely, a genotype), with particular reference to strategies that influence its survival and reproduction. p. 207

life-history invariants The constancy, or invariance, in the associations between various life-history traits that may reflect adaptive processes of a broad and universal nature across species. p. 226

life table A data matrix with columns of data on age-specific survival and fecundity (or fertility). p. 108

limnology The study of inland waters, such as lakes and rivers. See also **freshwater ecology**. p. 530

lithosere A sere that begins on an exposed rocky surface. p. 301

lithosphere The surface layer of Earth's solid sphere, consisting of the crust and the upper mantle. p. 13

littoral zone A distinct shallow-water habitat that occurs along the shores of ponds and lakes. pp. 341, 391

logarithmic series A community in which a graph plotting the abundance of species is characterized by having a large number of rare species and few common ones. p. 252

logistic model of population growth A model that predicts an S-shaped or sigmoidal pattern of population increase, which starts slowly, increases, then slows and becomes asymptotic at the carrying capacity. p. 102

log-normal distribution A community in which a graph plotting the abundance of species in abundance classes is normally distributed when the *x* axis is plotted on a logarithmic scale rather than on an arithmetic one. p. 252

longevity (life span) The length of time that an organism lives. p. 209

longitudinal study A longer-term or continuous study of a particular place or experiment. p. 402

lotic ecosystem An aquatic ecosystem that is characterized by flowing water, such as a stream or river. Compare with **lentic ecosystem**. p. 341

macronutrient These are needed by plants in relatively large quantities, and include carbon (about 50% of dry biomass), oxygen (40%), hydrogen (6%), nitrogen and potassium (1–2%), and calcium, magnesium, phosphorus, and sulphur (0.1%–0.5%). Compare with **micronutrient**. p. 73

management Actions that are undertaken to improve environmental conditions so as to enhance the productivity or quality of a biological resource. p. 473

manipulative experiment An experiment that involves modifications of one or more variables that are hypothesized to influence natural phenomena. p. 21

mantle The region of Earth's solid sphere between the core and crust, and composed of minerals in a hot, plastic state known as magma. p. 13

manufactured capital Something created by human ingenuity and made from simpler resources, such as processed foods, textiles, lumber, metals, and more complex commodities such as machines and buildings. p. 471

marine ecology The study of any aspects of ecology in the oceanic realm. p. 17

marker (genetic marker) A genetic element (allele, locus, DNA sequence, or chromosome feature) of an individual that can be detected by cytological, molecular, or phenotypic methods. p. 377

mass extinction An event of catastrophic damage of epic proportions, which causes the extinction of a large fraction of species existing at the time. p. 421

mass-specific metabolism Metabolic rate expressed per unit of mass (for example: mL O_2 consumed/unit time/unit of mass). p. 164

mathematical ecology Involves the use of quantitative models; sometimes also includes **statistical ecology**. p. 17

mating system The number of different individuals with which each sex typically copulates. See also **monogamy**, **monandry**, **polygyny**, and **polyandry**. p. 157

matrix A predominant cover or community type on a landscape, in which are embedded island-like blocks (patches) of other kinds of ecosystem. p. 412

maximum per capita rate of growth (intrinsic rate of population growth) The highest per-individual rate of growth that a population can achieve, limited only by the biological attributes of a species. Compare with **realized per capita rate of population growth**. p. 97

maximum sustainable yield (MSY) A theoretical upper limit of harvesting of a biological resource that will result in the largest sustainable long-term yield. pp. 105, 126, 475

mechanical energy Energy associated with mass that is in motion through space. p. 49

mesotrophic Waterbodies that have a moderate nutrient supply and so have an intermediate level of productivity. Compare with **eutrophic** and **oligotrophic**. p. 341

metabolic disturbance (or metabolic disorder) Changes in acid-base status due to the addition or removal of organic acids or bases to the blood or hemolymph. p. 201

metabolic rate The rate at which an organism uses energy, which may be measured by oxygen consumption, excretion of carbon dioxide, heat production, or the difference in the caloric contents of ingested food and excreted feces. p. 164

metabolic water Water obtained from the reduction of oxygen at the end of the electron transport chain of metabolism. p. 185

metapopulation A regional population; spatially separated subpopulations that are linked by dispersal, leading to gene flow among them. p. 393

microbial ecology The study of the populations, ecophysiology, and productivity of microorganisms and their communities, often with a focus on functional processes such as decomposition and nutrient cycling. p. 17

microdisturbance Disturbance that is local in scale, such as the death of a large tree within an otherwise intact forest. Compare with **stand-replacing disturbance**. pp. 10, 38, 292

micronutrient These are needed by plants in relatively small quantities, 0.01% to several ppm, and include boron, chlorine, copper, iron, manganese, molybdenum, and zinc. Compare with **macronutrient**. p. 73

microsuccession Smaller-scale succession that follows a microdisturbance. pp. 10, 38, 272

minerotrophic Wetlands whose hydrology and nutrient supply are substantially derived from flows of groundwater. Compare with **ombrotrophic**. p. 342

minimum viable area (MVA) The least area of suitable habitat that would allow a population-at-risk to persist in the wild, or for an imperilled community type to survive. p. 439

minimum viable population (MVP) The least abundance that would allow a population to persist in the wild. p. 439

mitigation An action that helps to avoid or repair an ecological or other environmental damage. p. 576

modern biodiversity crisis (holocene biodiversity event) An ongoing mass extinction that is being caused by the activities and influences of modern people. p. 423

monandry A breeding system in which a female mates with one male. p. 153

monoclimax According to the Clementsian view of succession, this is the climax community that eventually develops, which is primarily influenced by climatic conditions. See also **climax**. p. 299

monoculture An agricultural ecosystem in which only a single crop is grown. Compare with **polyculture**. p. 347

monogamy A sexual or breeding pair that mates only with each other. p. 149

monogyny A mating system in which there is one mate. Compare with **polygyny** and **polyandry**. p. 157

mosaic A spatially integrated complex of patches, corridors, and networks that gives a landscape its ecological character. See also **shifting mosaic**. p. 394

MSY See **maximum sustainable yield**. p. 105

multidisciplinary Various fields of study are engaged, including chemistry, ecology, economics, geography, geology, sociology. Compare with **interdisciplinary**. p. 568

multimetric indicator A composite indicator that is developed using metrics whose data were transformed into a unitless score before being aggregated. See also **composite indicator**. p. 560

multiple stable states (or **alternative stable states**) The view that more than one type (state) of stable community may persist under similar abiotic and environmental conditions. p. 269

mutualism A mutually beneficial biological interaction. p. 246

natural biome A biome whose characteristics are not significantly influenced by stressors or management associated with humans. Compare with **anthropogenic biome**. p. 336

natural experiment Involves studying gradients in nature or other differences in environmental conditions and ecological change, and then developing explanations for the observed patterns using statistical analyses. p. 21

natural history The investigation of organisms in their wild habitats, also often extending to an interest in all natural phenomena, even astronomy; studies in natural history are relatively simple, with few or no quantitative data, and a rigorous scientific methodology is not used. p. 4

natural mortality Deaths caused by predators, parasites, diseases, accidents, or other disturbances. Compare with **anthropogenic mortality**. p. 479

natural regeneration The spontaneous recovery of a biological resource after it has been harvested. p. 477

natural resources (natural capital) Sources of materials and energy that are harvested from ecosystems and the broader environment. p. 471

natural selection An important cause of evolutionary change, in which organisms have an increased likelihood of leaving descendants (of having fitness) if their specific genetically based phenotypic attributes are better suited to coping with the constraints and opportunities presented by their environment, compared with other individuals in their population. p. 25

natural stressor A stressor that is not caused by a human influence. p. 38

natural world In the context of ecology, this refers to indigenous biodiversity and related values, such as self-organizing ecosystems, their environmental conditions, and the services that are provided. p. 420

naturalized An alien species that can persist and regenerate in native habitats. p. 424

negative feedback system A means of regulating a parameter by means of a detector, a set-point, an integrator, and various controlled outputs that keep the parameters within limits. p. 169

negative-pressure ventilation The filling of a lung as a result of air being drawn into it by suction. p. 193

net primary production (NPP) The difference between gross primary production and respiration. See also **gross primary production** and **respiration**. p. 59

net reproductive rate The average number of offspring produced over the lifetime of an individual. p. 109

network A series of interconnected linear elements on a landscape, often surrounding patches of another type. p. 394

neutral model A model proposed by Stephen Hubbell in which all individual organisms in a community are treated as essentially ecologically identical, i.e., all individuals of all species have the same parameters of ecological behaviour, such as birth rate and death rate; complex interactions such as competition are permitted among individuals, provided that they all follow the same rules. p. 253

new ecology An approach to ecology that emphasizes complexity over reductionism, change over stable states, and an ecological world that includes the human economy and activities. p. 388

niche (i) The ecological role of a species in a community; it describes all of the environmental factors that limit the distribution, growth, and reproduction of a species. (ii) The physical space occupied by an organism or species. See also **fundamental niche** and **realized niche**. p. 256

nitrification Part of the nitrogen cycle, in which bacteria oxidize ammonium to nitrate. p. 78

nitrogen fixation Part of the nitrogen cycle, in which the strong triple bond of N_2 gas is cleaved to form NH_3 or NO. p. 82

non-equilibrium theories A view that communities are not constant in species composition and never reach a stable condition because they are always responding to changes in environmental conditions or recovering from disturbances. Compare with **equilibrium theories**. p. 248

non-native (or alien) A species that is not part of the indigenous biota, having been introduced by humans. p. 432

non-renewable resource (non-renewable capital) A resource that is present in a fixed quantity and is diminished by use. pp. 27, 471

non-shivering thermogenesis An increase in heat production due to an increase in the metabolic rate. p. 170

nucleation A successional process in which communities begin as small patches that grow increasingly larger until they eventually coalesce. p. 314

null hypothesis A hypotheses that is formulated so that it can be disproved through research. p. 21

numerical response A response of the abundance of a predator or herbivore to a change in their consumption of food. Compare with **functional response**. p.126

nuptial gift A gift of food or other fitness-enhancing product, typically from the male, that is delivered orally or into the female's genital tract. p. 144

nutrient Substances needed for the healthy physiology and growth of organisms. p. 73

nutrient budget An estimate of the rates of input and output of nutrients for an ecosystem, and amounts and transfers among its compartments, such as plants, animals, dead organic matter, and soil. p. 76

nutrient cycling The movements, transformations, and recycling of nutrients in ecosystems. pp. 76, 374

obligatory water loss Water loss in feces, urine, and across cutaneous and gas exchange surfaces in animals. p. 186

old-growth forest Older stands of forest, which typically have a complex structure, with many species of trees present, of various sizes and ages, and supporting a large amount of biomass, including much dead organic matter. p. 338

oligotrophic Waterbodies that have a sparse nutrient supply and so are relatively unproductive. Compare with **eutrophic** and **mesotrophic**. p. 341

ombrotrophic A wetland whose hydrology and nutrient supply is cut off from flows of groundwater, so the only inputs are derived from precipitation and other atmospheric sources. Compare with **minerotrophic**. p. 342

omnivore An animal that feeds at more than one level of the food web. Compare with **herbivore** and **carnivore**. p. 60

open population One from which individuals are free to leave and into which others can immigrate from other populations. Compare with **closed population**. p. 96

open system A situation in which there is a gain in mass, energy, or information, and/or a loss. See also **closed system**. p. 47

operational sex ratio The ratio of females to males, of individuals that are available to mate. p. 144

opportunity cost The value of a foregone choice as a consequence of having made a decision to pursue some other option. p. 465

optimal behaviour Behaviour that maximizes fitness. p. 138

organic (biotic) Refers to environmental influences that are biological in origin, that are associated with influences of other organisms. p. 5

organic carbon Carbon stored in living and dead biomass. p. 80

organic chemicals Molecules ultimately of biosynthetic origin and consisting primarily of carbon and hydrogen, but also containing smaller amounts of other elements (such as oxygen, nitrogen, and phosphorus); organic chemicals include carbohydrates, proteins, and fats, as well as the molecules that comprise fossil fuels. See also **biochemicals**. p. 75

organismal (or community unit) hypothesis A view of community organization proposed by Frederic Clements that sees the community act like a superorganism, in that it is a highly organized and closely integrated entity composed of mutually interdependent species, and individual species are to some varying degree co-adapted to one another. Compare with **individualistic hypothesis**. p. 244

osmoconformer An animal that conforms to the osmotic concentration of its environment. p. 182

osmoregulation The process of maintaining a constant body fluid osmotic pressure. p. 183

osmoregulator An animal that regulates the osmotic concentration of its body fluids. p. 183

over-harvesting (over-exploitation) Harvesting a potentially renewable natural resource (such as a biological one) at a rate that exceeds its regeneration, so that the stocks become depleted in quantity and/or quality. pp. 374, 471

oxidative capacity The maximum scope of oxygen utilization in aerobic metabolism. p. 164

paleoecology The branch of ecology that deals with populations, communities, and ecosystems that existed in the past. p. 517

paleolimnology The branch of aquatic science that deals with reconstructing the histories of inland waters, such as lakes and rivers; paleolimnologists typically use the physical, chemical, and biological information preserved in sediment profiles to reconstruct past ecological and environmental conditions. p. 524

paludification A process in which the organic forest floor retains so much water that trees die from the waterlogging, so that a peat-rich, boggy wetland known as muskeg develops. pp. 312, 398

palynology The branch of science that deals with the study of pollen grains and spores. p. 528

paradigm A set of assumptions, concepts, practices, and values that constitutes an understanding of the natural world and is shared by an intellectual community. p. 22

parameter Numbers that remain constant in a mathematical equation. Compare with **variable**. p. 16

parasitism A biological relationship that involves one species of animal feeding on another, usually much larger one, but usually not killing it. pp. 5, 247

parasitoid An organism whose larva develops within the body of another organism, resulting in death of the host; the term is normally applied to animal parasites of animal hosts. p. 387

parent material Minerals and rocks from which soil is derived. p. 88

parental care Behaviour of a parent that is directed at offspring to increase their fitness. p. 208

parental investment Investment by a parent in the fitness of offspring, at a cost of not investing in future offspring. p. 144

partial pressure The pressure attributed to a specific gas found within an atmosphere; the product of the gas fraction and the atmospheric pressure. p. 189

patch A contiguous areal unit representing a single land-cover class, or a stand of a particular community that is distinguished from its surroundings by discontinuities of environmental influences. p. 390

patch dynamics Temporal change in the dynamics of communities or patches on a landscape. See also **patch**. p. 402

pathogen An organism that produces a disease. pp. 10, 530

pattern The spatially repeated occurrence of landscape elements. p. 385

patterned ground Distinct and often symmetrical geometric shapes formed by ground material in near-glacial environments. p. 352

peat A highly organic substrate of partially decomposed plant biomass, normally in wet areas such as bogs. p. 55

pelagic zone Deep open waters, with little influence of shorelines or shallow habitats. p. 341

per capita rate of population growth The intrinsic rate of population increase expressed on a per-individual basis. See also **intrinsic rate of population growth**. p. 97

permafrost Subsoil in cold regions that is frozen for at least three continuous years. See also **active layer**. p. 336

permeable In the context of conservation biology, this refers to habitat that is suitable for the movement of a species-of-interest; in landscape ecology it is the degree to which a matrix environment is suitable for organisms to use as they travel among patches of appropriate habitat on a landscape. See also **connectivity**. pp. 393, 446

phenotype The expression of the genetic potential of an individual. p. 25

phenotypic plasticity The variable expression of the genotype, occurring in response to vagaries of environmental conditions. pp. 25, 363

philopatry The property of an organism remaining in or returning to its natal area. p. 153

photoautotrophs (phototrophs) Green plants, algae, and certain bacteria that utilize sunlight to drive photosynthesis. See **phototroph**. Compare with **chemoautotrophs**. pp. 11, 59

photosynthesis Autotrophic productivity that uses visible electromagnetic energy (usually sunlight) to drive biosynthesis. Compare with **chemosynthesis**. p. 47

phylogenetic inertia The persistence of traits in a lineage due to the inheritance of those traits from ancestral species. p. 153

physiological ecology Involves study of the adaptive biochemistry and physiology of organisms in response to environmental conditions. p. 17

phytoplankton Microscopic algae that occur suspended in the water column. p. 301

plant ecology The study of the populations, ecophysiology, and productivity of wild plants and their communities. p. 17

plantation A tree-farm, in which a crop of trees is sown and managed. p. 488

pleiotropy A single gene influencing multiple phenotypic traits. p. 219

poikilotherm See **heterotherm**.

pollution The presence of a substance at a high enough concentration or intensity to result in a measurable biological or ecological damage. p. 39

polyandry A mating system in which the female mates with more than one male. Compare with **polygyny** and **monandry**. p. 153

polyclimax Multiple end-states of succession that are possible depending on variations of such key factors as topography, slope and exposure, the local regime of moisture and nutrients in soil, and the kinds of disturbances that affect the community. See also **climax**. p. 299

polyculture An agricultural ecosystem in which several crops are grown together. Compare with **monoculture**. p. 347

polygyny A mating system in which the male mates with more than one female. Compare with **monogamy** and **polyandry**. p. 157

polygyny threshold model (PTM) An explanation for polygyny in which females gain fitness by mating with a paired rather than unpaired male because the female gains access to resources controlled by the paired individual. See also **polygyny**. p. 158

polynya An ice-free area in a high-latitude ocean (arctic or antarctic) that provides critical habitat for marine birds and mammals. p. 356

population Individuals of the same species that are co-occurring in space and time. p. 8

population diversity Diversity that is related to the variation in genetic and phenotypic characters that exists among discrete populations of a species. p. 366

population dynamics Changes in the size and age composition of populations, as well as processes influencing those changes. p. 105

population ecology Study of the population dynamics of species, including environmental influences on those changes. p. 17

population-replacing disturbance A disturbance that affects only a particular species within a community. p. 294

positive-pressure ventilation The filling of a lung as a result of air being forced into it under pressure. p. 193

post-copulatory sexual selection Events occurring after fertilization in which the paternity of certain males is biased over that of others. See also **sperm competition**. p. 149

potential energy A stored ability to perform work, which can occur only if the potential energy becomes transformed into kinetic or electromagnetic energy. p. 49

precipitation Water settling gravitationally from the atmosphere as rain or snow. p. 12

precision The degree of repeatability of measurements. p. 16

predation A biological relationship that involves one species of animal killing and eating another kind. pp. 5, 246

prescribed fire A deliberate burn ignited with the intent of reducing the risk of an uncontrollable conflagration, or for a conservation purpose such as habitat improvement. p. 317

primary consumer See **herbivore**.

primary forest (frontier forest) Forest that occurs in large blocks of self-organizing ecosystems, often in an old-growth condition, and that sustains all of the appropriate species, including wide-ranging animals. p. 429

primary producer Autotrophic organisms, which form the biological foundation of ecological productivity. p. 59

primary succession A succession that occurs in situations where a disturbance was severe enough to destroy all organisms on the affected terrain, and so obliterated the inherent ability to regenerate, so that colonization is necessary. Compare with **secondary succession**. pp. 38, 309

principle of limiting factors An ecological theory that suggests that primary productivity is limited by whichever necessary metabolic requirement is present in the least supply relative to the demand. pp. 32, 75, 518

principle of uniformitarianism A theory that is most simply described as "the present is the key to the past," and that is the basis of most paleoecological research. p. 518

production The total productivity, usually calculated as the productivity multiplied by the area being considered. p. 61

productivity The rate at which energy is fixed in ecosystems, standardized to time and area. p. 61

protected area Tracts of natural habitat that are set aside from intensive economic use, such as parks, ecological reserves, and wilderness areas. p. 431

proxy data (i) Data indirectly measuring a cause-and-effect relationship between two or more variables, such as tree-ring counts as a predictor of tree age. (ii) Data obtained by scientists such as paleoecologists to reconstruct past ecological and environmental conditions, e.g., using fossil pollen to reconstruct past terrestrial vegetation and then using that information to reconstruct past climate. p. 517

psammosere A sere that begins on a sandy substrate. p. 301

punctuated equilibrium An extended predominance of slow variations interspersed by rare but massive events of fast change. p. 565

Q_{10} The rate of change in a reaction over a 10°C range of temperature. p. 165

radiatively active gas See **greenhouse gas**. p. 81

ramet A group of genetically identical "individuals" growing in a location, which have originated from a single ancestor by vegetative propagation (not by sexual reproduction). p. 305

rank abundance A graph of the relative abundance of each species in a community, ranked in the order of most abundant to the least. p. 252

rarity Related to a low likelihood of encountering a particular species, whether because of a low population density, or a species occurring only in small and isolated populations. p. 440

realized niche The observed resource use by a species in nature, in which the potential distribution is restricted by competition and other biotic interactions. Compare with **fundamental niche**. p. 256

realized per capita rate of population growth The per-individual rate of growth of a population. Compare with **maximum per capita rate of growth**. p. 97

reciprocity (or reciprocal altruism) Help that increases a recipient's direct fitness and that is paid back at a later time by the recipient to the donor. p. 151

recovery strategy All species listed by COSEWIC as endangered or threatened must have a recovery strategy developed that would promote an increase of the population to a more sustainable level. p. 437

reference condition The normal and natural conditions for a site or region, given the environmental circumstances, including the disturbance regime. p. 561

reforestation The regeneration of another forest after an original stand has had its trees harvested. Compare with **afforestation**. p. 58

refugium (plural, **refugia**) A place that has escaped regional ecological change and therefore provides a habitat where species may survive; often used in reference to glacial refugia. pp. 295, 519

remote sensing Measurements that are made from afar, often in reference to aerial photography or satellite images. p. 409

renewable resource (renewable capital) A resource that can regenerate after harvesting. pp. 27, 471

re-organization phase A stage of secondary succession that immediately follows a disturbance event, and during which there may be a further loss of biomass because of negative ecosystem-level net production (respiration exceeds productivity), and is then followed by an accumulation of biomass during the aggradation phase. See also **aggradation phase**. p. 306

reproductive skew Asymmetry in reproductive success within a sexually competing or social group. p. 143

reproductive success The number of progeny that an individual has during its lifetime. See also **fitness**. p. 138

reproductive value The average expected reproduction of individuals from their present age onward, given that they have survived to their present age. p. 117

research In ecology, it is a systematic activity undertaken in the laboratory or in the field, which may involve experiments or the investigation of patterns of co-variation of biotic and abiotic variables to investigate questions relevant to factors affecting the distribution and abundance of organisms, populations, communities, or ecoscapes. p. 558

reserve life This is calculated as the known recoverable reserves of a non-renewable resource divided by the rate of mining. p. 469

reservoir (i) A compartment of mass in a nutrient cycle. (ii) An artificial lake formed behind a dam. pp. 76, 431

resilience The speed and degree to which an organism, population, community, or ecoscape can recover to its original condition following an event of disturbance or after an intense stressor relaxes. pp. 37, 291

resistance (or tolerance) The ability of an organism or an ecological variable to function in a "healthy" manner within a range of intensities of environmental stressors, without undergoing change that would be judged as representing damage. p. 292

resource (capital) Goods and services of various kinds. Compare with **natural resources (natural capital)**, **manufactured capital**, **human capital**, and **intellectual capital**. p. 464

resource conservation The harvesting and management of renewable resources in ways that ensure that the harvest does not exceed the rate of renewal; may also refer to actions that help to prolong the lifetime of non-renewable resources. p. 420

resource-control hypothesis See **bottom–up hypothesis**. p. 279

resource ecology The branch of ecology that deals with linkages between ecological knowledge and the management of natural resources, including the meaning and dimensions of economic and ecological sustainability. p. 464

resource partitioning This occurs when different species in a community use limiting resources in different ways, i.e., they occupy different realized niches. p. 261

respiration (R) Fixed energy needed by organisms to support the physiology required to maintain a healthy condition. p. 59

respiratory acidosis An increase in the acidity (lowering of the pH) of the blood because of a high concentration of absorbed CO_2, which forms carbonic acid. Compare with **respiratory alkalosis**. p. 201

respiratory alkalosis A decrease in the acidity (raising of the pH) of the blood because of a low concentration of absorbed CO_2. Compare with **respiratory acidosis**. p. 201

respiratory disturbance (or respiratory disorder) Changes in acid-base status due to changes in the carbon dioxide partial pressure of the blood or hemolymph. p. 201

respiratory pigment A molecule that is capable of binding and transporting oxygen within the circulatory system. p. 196

response A biological or ecological change that has occurred as a result of an interaction with an environmental stressor or a regime of stressors. p. 36

response time The length of time required for a population to change in reaction to an altered environmental circumstance. p. 104

restoration ecology Use of ecological knowledge and practices to repair damaged habitats or ecosystems. p. 17

return frequency (or rotation) The length of time between successive disturbance events. p. 297

richness See **species richness**. p. 6

riparian (riparian zone) Related to river and stream banks; the transition zone between a stream and adjacent land, often but not always synonymous with flood plain. pp. 342, 391

riparian buffer (buffer zone, riparian reserve zone, special management zone) Uncut strips of forest left beside a lake or on both sides of a watercourse. p. 491

root effect A reduction in the amount of oxygen a respiratory pigment can carry at full saturation (i.e., oxygen-carrying capacity) as a result of an increase in acidity or carbon dioxide partial pressure in the blood or hemolymph. p. 198

rotation See **return frequency**. p. 297

ruderal A species that is adapted to recently disturbed habitats with abundant resources, so that stress and competition are not intense. p. 248

runaway sexual selection Sexual selection through female mating preferences for certain male traits where a positive feedback loop is created that favours males with the trait as well as females that prefer these males. p. 148

saprophyte See **detritivore**. p. 60

science The use of objective and systematic methodologies to better understand the character and dynamics of the natural world, including the discovery of general principles. p. 19

scientific method This begins with a researcher identifying a question about a natural phenomenon, then formulating hypotheses in the context of existing theory, then running experiments or doing other research to test null hypotheses in an attempt to falsify the original hypothesis. p. 21

scientific revolution This occurs when a well-established theory is rigorously tested and then collapses under the weight of new facts and observations that it cannot explain. p. 22

sclerochronology The use of calcified structures, such as fish otoliths, mollusk shells, and corals, to reconstruct environmental conditions. p. 524

scoping exercise A phase of an environmental impact assessment that is undertaken to identify the potentially important intersections of project-related activities and stressors with valued ecological components or human socioeconomic welfare. p. 568

scramble (or exploitation) competition Competition whereby individuals reduce the access of others to a resource by consuming some of it, but not involving direct or indirect actions to reduce access to the resource. p. 117

screening The initial phase of an environmental impact assessment that helps to determine the level of assessment of a proposed development—whether a relatively minor review or a full assessment is necessary. p. 568

searching time The length of time required by a predator to locate a prey individual. Compare with **handling time**. p. 127

seascape A larger-scale integration of various kinds of community-level patches in a marine environment. p. 8

seasonal torpor See **hibernation**. p. 170

second law of thermodynamics A physical principle stating that transformations of energy occur spontaneously only under conditions in which there is an increase in the entropy (or randomness) of the universe. See also **first law of thermodynamics** and **entropy**. p. 51

secondary consumer An animal that kills and feeds on herbivores. Compare with **carnivore**. p. 60

secondary sexual character Traits that distinguish the two sexes of a species, but that are not directly part of the gamete-producing or -receiving systems; they are derived by sexual selection. See also **sexual selection**. p. 143

secondary succession A succession that includes regeneration by organisms that survived a disturbance, as well as those that invaded. Compare with **primary succession**. pp. 38, 316

secular change Change in a consistent direction. p. 408

sedimentation The deposition of eroded fine materials from water as its velocity slows down. p. 495

seed bank An enduring population of viable seeds in the surface litter and soil. p. 305

selection See **natural selection**. p. 25

selection-cutting (uneven-aged management) Harvesting only some of the larger trees, so the physical and ecological integrity of the stand is left substantially intact. Compare with **clear-cutting**. p. 487

selection pressure The influence of natural (or sexual) selection on the phenotype. p. 137

selective breeding (cultural selection) The deliberate breeding of individuals that are viewed as having desirable traits; this is the principal means of the evolution of domesticated varieties and species. p. 479

semelparous Refers to a species in which individuals die after a single reproductive event. Compare with **iteroparous**. p. 108

SER model An acronym for stressor—exposure—response, used in reference to the relationship of environmental stressors and biological or ecological responses. p. 36

seral stage A community type occurring within a succession. See also **sere**. p. 298

sere A series of community types that make up a successional sequence. See also **seral stage**. p. 298

serotiny An adaptation of certain species of pines (*Pinus*) in which the cones and their viable seeds are held persistently aloft on branches for several years, to eventually be dispersed when a fire melts a wax that had sealed the scales together, allowing them to spread so the seeds can scatter and establish a regenerating cohort. p. 305

sexual conflict Conflict between the sexes over decisions that differentially affect their fitness, such as how much to invest in offspring and whether or not to mate. p. 143

sexual dimorphism Sex difference in structure or size. p. 143

sexual selection Selection in the context of competition to maximize the number of fertilizations or matings, or to maximize these with the best mates. p. 137

shifting cultivation A subsistence agricultural system practised in the tropics, in which trees of the original (primary) forest are felled, the woody debris burned, the land used to grow a mixture of crops for several years, by which time fertility declines and weeds become abundant, so the land is abandoned for a lengthy fallow period during which a secondary forest regenerates, while other primary forest is felled and cultivated. Compare with **slash-and-burn**. p. 431

shifting mosaic A landscape-scale model of succession that describes a diverse array of communities (patches) of various post-disturbance ages occurring over a large area. See also **mosaic**. pp. 293, 402

significant figures The number of digits used when reporting data from observations or calculations. p. 16

silviculture Refers to management practices in forestry, such as planting seedlings, thinning, and pesticide use. p. 324

size at maturity The size (weight, length, height) at which an organism reproduces for the first time (becomes sexually mature). Compare with **age at maturity**. p. 209

slash-and-burn A relatively intensive subsistence or commercial agricultural system practised in the tropics that results in a longer-term conversion of the land to crop production; it starts with cutting and burning the natural forest, but the land is then used continuously, without an extended fallow period during which a secondary forest regenerates. Compare with **shifting cultivation**. p. 431

SLOSS debate (single large or several small) A debate within the scientific community as to whether biodiversity is best protected by a single large protected area or several small ones of equivalent total area. p. 445

social selection Selection on individuals to reproduce within a group where there is competition to mate or to produce offspring. p. 154

sociocultural evolution A progressive and adaptive improvement of the knowledge, social organization, and technological infrastructure in a society. Compare with **evolution (biological evolution)**. p. 485

soil A complex matrix covering terrestrial landscapes and consisting of rocks, organic matter, moisture, gases, and organisms. p. 88

soil order The highest level in the classification of soil types. p. 91

soil profile The vertical stratification that soils develop, with horizons that are distinct in colour, chemistry, and texture. p. 90

solar constant The input of solar energy to Earth, measured at the average distance from the Sun and just beyond the atmosphere, and having a value of 8.21 J/ cm^2·min (1.96 cal/cm^2·min). p. 53

special concern (formerly referred to as **vulnerable**) A species (or taxon) that is at risk of becoming threatened because of small or declining numbers or occurrence in a limited range. p. 437

special management area A type of protected area that is managed to support particular species or habitats, usually ones of economic importance, and intended to achieve conservation through the protection and management of habitats; however, forestry, hunting, and some other extractive industries may be permitted. p. 448

species An aggregation of individuals (and populations) that are capable of interbreeding and producing fertile offspring. pp. 8, 366

species diversity An indicator of the number of species in a local area (α diversity) or region (β diversity), but also taking into account their relative abundances (or evenness). See also **alpha (α) diversity**, **species richness**, and **evenness**. pp. 379, 249

species richness The number of species in a community, or in a designated geographical area, such as a park. Compare with **species diversity** and **evenness**. pp. 249, 366

sperm competition Competition among the sperm of different males for fertilizations of the same female's eggs. p. 143

stability Refers to constancy over time, including resistance to environmental change and the degree of resilience after a perturbation. pp. 37, 374

stable age distribution A distribution in which the relative numbers of individuals in each age class are similar from one generation to the next. Compare with **stationary age distribution**. p. 109

stable equilibrium A state of equilibrium that returns to its original condition after it has been displaced. Compare with **unstable equilibrium**. p. 122

stable limit cycle Indefinite repetitive temporal variation about a central (average) value. Compare with **damped oscillation** and **chaos**. p. 104

stand An easily defined area, often of forest, that is relatively uniform in species composition or age and that can be studied or managed as a unit. p. 292

stand age-class distribution The proportion of patches (communities within a sere) within classes of stand age. p. 403

stand-replacing disturbance An extensive disturbance that damages entire communities and sometimes even a landscape. Compare with **microdisturbance**. pp. 10, 293

standing crop See **biomass**. p. 62

stasis An extended period of biological or ecological quiescence. p. 565

state space A configuration of discrete states that is used as a simple model. p. 119

static life table A life table based on the enumeration of all individuals in a population at a particular time. Compare with **cohort life table**. p. 109

stationary age distribution An age distribution in which neither the relative nor absolute numbers of individuals in each age class change over time. Compare with **stable age distribution**. p. 114

statistical ecology The application of statistical methodologies to examining and explaining patterns and processes. p. 17

status report In the context of the operations of COSEWIC, this is a report that is prepared for a candidate species-at-risk, based on an analysis of scientific information and traditional ecological knowledge relevant to Canada, but in a global context, and using a precautionary approach so as to be mindful of deficiencies of knowledge about key issues. p. 436

step-cline A zone of rapid change in environmental conditions. p. 299

stewardship All management activities that are needed to maintain protected areas, with particular attention to biodiversity and other ecological values. p. 444

stochastic Relating to a sequence of random variables. Compare with **deterministic**. p. 115

stochastic change Change that is apparently random. p. 408

stochastic modelling A modelling methodology of scenarios that allows the most likely outcomes and their statistical variation to be computed. p. 412

stochasticity Refers to patterns that are not predictable. Compare with **chaos**. p. 105

stratosphere The atmospheric layer above the troposphere, extending to about 51 km above the surface. p. 12

stressor Environmental factors that limit the performance of organisms, populations, communities, or larger ecoscapes. p. 34

stress-tolerator A species that is adapted to environments that are difficult in terms of climate, moisture, and nutrient supply, but that are stable because they are infrequently disturbed. p. 248

structural attribute Amounts, such as biomass, density, species richness, and other variables that are commonly reported in units of quantity per area. p. 6

succession The process of community-level recovery following a disturbance. p. 268

supercooling Cooling of a solution to below its freezing point but without freezing actually occurring. p. 175

surface fire Fires that combust shrubs and ground vegetation but do not ladder into the canopy, so most trees survive the event. p. 400

sustainable development Progress made in structuring an economy toward a greater use of renewable resources and other improvements, with the ultimate goal of having an economy that can potentially run forever. Compare with **economic development** and **economic growth**. p. 464

sustainable economy An economy that can run forever because it is fundamentally based on the prudent use of renewable resources. Compare with **ecologically sustainable economy**. pp. 26, 468

symbiosis Any close biological interaction occurring between species. p. 246

sympatric Refers to geographic areas where populations or species co-occur. Compare with **allopatric**. p. 124

system plan A plan for protected areas that captures areas that support the highest priority biodiversity values, while ensuring that all indigenous elements are conserved in the greater region. p. 444

systems ecology Uses a holistic approach to investigate the attributes of ecosystems. p. 17

taiga A boreal forest or region of boreal forest, usually with a relatively open stand structure. See also **boreal forest**. p. 336

taxon Any taxonomic unit, such as variety, subspecies, or species. p. 436

theoretical ecology The identification of theories regarding the organization and functioning of ecosystems, and then using rigorous methodologies to test their veracity; the field is particularly relevant to population ecology and biogeography. p. 17

theory A unifying principle that explains a body of knowledge—of facts based on observational and experimental evidence and any laws that are based on them. p. 20

thermal energy Also known as heat, and associated with the vibration of atoms or molecules. p. 49

thermoneutral zone A range of environmental temperature within which the metabolic rate of homeotherms is independent of changes in environmental temperature. p. 170

thermoregulation The ability to maintain the core temperature of the body within a narrow range. p. 167

threatened A species (or taxon) that is likely to become endangered unless factors affecting its risk are mitigated. p. 436

tilth A property of soil that relates to the capacity to retain moisture and nutrients and to have an aggregated particle structure that allows easy root penetration and good aeration. p. 90

time lag A delay in the realization of an anticipated event or result. p. 103

tolerance (or resistance) The ability of an organism or an ecological variable to function in a "healthy" manner within a range of intensities of environmental stressors, without undergoing change that would be judged as representing damage. pp. 36, 292

tolerance model A model of succession that suggests that a predictable sequence of species occurs in succession because they vary in their abilities to utilize the available resources, with early species being relatively intolerant of competition, and becoming replaced by others that are more tolerant of competitive interactions. Compare with **facilitation model** and **inhibition model**. p. 303

top–down hypothesis (consumer-control) A model of community organization based on the idea that carnivores affect the species composition and abundance of their herbivore prey, and that herbivores affect plants. Compare with **bottom–up hypothesis**. p. 279

top predator Predators that feed at the top of their food web, but that do not themselves have natural predators. p. 65

torpor (or daily torpor) Controlled reduction in metabolism and body temperature on a daily basis. p. 170

total allowable catch (TAC) The amount of harvesting of a biological resource that is being permitted, usually following the advice of scientists about the sustainable yield. Compare with **maximum sustainable yield**. p. 500

trade-off In the study of life histories, a trade-off implies that an increase in the value of one trait (and its potential importance in terms of influencing fitness) can be achieved only if there is a concomitant reduction in that of another one. p. 216

tragedy of the commons An environmental metaphor associated with the degradation of a common-property resource, in which individuals justify over-exploitation because they can share the degradation with many others. See also **common-property resource**. p. 485

transgenic modification An application of bioengineering, in which DNA of one species is incorporated into the genome of another one in order to realize an economic benefit. See also **genetically modified organism**. p. 479

transition matrix (Leslie matrix) Rows and columns of parameters (a matrix) that describe how age-class abundance changes from one time step to the next. p. 112

transpiration The evaporation of water from plants. Compare with **evapotranspiration**. pp. 12, 54

tree ring A visually distinct growth increment in the stems of woody plants, especially trees, that normally represents annual growth. p. 522

trophic cascade A model of community organization involving top–down control, such that a change in the rate of consumption at a higher trophic level results in a series of changes in species abundances that cascade down through lower trophic levels. p. 278

trophic chain See **food chain**. p. 65

trophic level A group of species in a food web that obtain their energy in similar ways, such as **primary producers**, **herbivores**, **carnivores**, or **detritivores**. p. 63

trophic structure The relative productivities and abundances of primary producers, herbivores, carnivores, and detritivores in an ecosystem, often represented using so-called trophic pyramids. p. 68

trophic web See **food web**. p. 65

troposphere The lower atmosphere, extending from the surface to 7 km at the poles and 17–20 km at the equator. p. 12

tundra A treeless ecosystem above the tree-line in high latitude (arctic and antarctic) regions or on mountains. p. 10

turbidity The load of suspended fine-sized particulates in water. pp. 341, 495

Type-I survival A survival schedule in which a species exhibits relatively high survival during young and intermediate ages, after which survivorship declines steeply as the maximum longevity is approached. Compare with **Type-II survival** and **Type-III survival**. p. 108

Type-II survival A survival schedule in which a species exhibits a constant rate of mortality throughout life. Compare with **Type-I survival** and **Type-III survival**. p. 108

Type-III survival A survival schedule in which a species exhibits exceedingly high mortality in early life, until individuals attain an age after which their vulnerability to risks of death declines and they have relatively high survival thereafter. Compare with **Type-I survival** and **Type-II survival**. p. 108

umbrella species Wide-ranging animals that utilize a large home range and are components of many communities; because of their extensive and complex habitat needs, any conservation actions that are effective at sustaining a viable population of them are also likely to achieve many other biodiversity benefits. p. 441

uniformitarianism See **principle of uniformitarianism**. p. 518

unstable equilibrium A state of equilibrium that can be upset if excessively displaced, so that it does not return to its original condition but instead moves to a new one. Compare with **stable equilibrium**. p. 122

urban ecology The study of biodiversity and ecological functions in urbanized habitats, with a focus on problems that can be mitigated by naturalization and the establishment of protected areas. p. 17

ureotelic An animal that produces urea as the primary nitrogenous waste product. p. 187

uricotelic An animal that produces uric acid as the primary nitrogenous waste product. p. 188

value-added product The increased value of a product over that of the materials from which it was produced. p. 472

valued ecosystem component (VEC) An ecological component that is considered important in an environmental impact assessment because it is a bio-resource, a species or community that is at risk, is of aesthetic importance, or is of cultural significance to an aboriginal community or other local people. p. 568

variable Numbers that change in a mathematical equation. Compare with **parameter**. p. 21

vegetative regeneration Regrowth of individuals of certain plant species that survive a disturbance and then regenerate by sprouting from the rhizomes or roots. pp. 304, 477

viability selection Natural selection that maximizes survival of the individual. p. 138

virulence Harm caused to a host by a pathogen or parasite. p. 141

vulnerable See **special concern**. p. 437

water cycle See **hydrological cycle**. p. 12

weathering Chemical reactions in which insoluble minerals in rocks and soil become available for biological uptake through chemical reactions that make them water-soluble. p. 77

weed A plant that is unwanted by people in some management-related context. p. 434

wilderness Wild and uninhabited tracts that are little used by people, especially not for resource extraction and other intensive activities. p. 420

wilderness area A type of protected area that is managed to preserve its natural condition, with low levels of non-intensive, non-extractive visitation being permitted. p. 448

work In the sense of physics, this is the consequence of a force that is applied over a distance. p. 48

working-down The sequential harvesting of a previously non-exploited multi-species biological resource; initially the best individuals are harvested, then secondary species, and eventually non-selective area-harvesting methods are used. p. 482

zooplankton Tiny invertebrates, mostly crustaceans, that occur in the water column. p. 65

Name Index

Species Index

This index consists of references to the scientific binomials of species mentioned in the text. For references to common names of species, please see the subject index.

Subject Index